# Management & Cost Accounting

# Management & Cost Accounting

**FIFTH EDITION**

## Colin Drury

Australia • Canada • Denmark • Japan • Mexico • New Zealand • Philippines
Puerto Rico • Singapore • South Africa • Spain • United Kingdom • United States

**Management & Cost Accounting: 5<sup>th</sup> Edition**

**Copyright © 2000 Colin Drury**

Business Press is a division of Thomson Learning. The Thomson Learning logo is a registered trademark used herein under licence.

For more information, contact Business Press, Berkshire House, 168 173 High Holborn, London, WC1V 7AA or visit us on the World Wide Web at: http://www.businesspress.co.uk

*British Library Cataloguing-in-Publication Data*
A catalogue record for this book is available from the British Library

**ISBN 1-86152-536-2**

**First edition published by Chapman & Hall 1983**
**Second edition published by Chapman & Hall 1988**
**Third edition published by Chapman & Hall 1992**
**Fourth edition published by International Thomson Business Press 1996**
**Fifth edition published by Thomson Learning 2000**

Typeset by Techset Composition Limited, Salisbury
Printed in Italy by Vincenzo Bona
Cover design by Design Deluxe, Bath
Text design by Design Deluxe, Bath

# Abbreviated contents

## Part Five: Cost Management and Strategic Management Accounting   887

## Part Six: The Application of Quantitative Methods to Management Accounting   951

## Notes   1067

## Bibliography   1073

## Appendices   1079

## Answers to self-assessment questions   1093

## Case study problems   1143

## Index   1189

# Contents

# Part Two
# Cost Accumulation for Inventory Valuation and Profit Measurement   43

## 3  Cost assignment   45

## 4  Accounting entries for a job costing system   97

## 5 Process costing   133

## 6 Joint and by-product costing   173

## 7 Income effects of alternative cost accumulation systems   201

# Part Three
# Information for Decision-making  233

## 8  Cost–volume–profit analysis  235

## 9  Measuring relevant costs and revenues for decision-making  279

## 14 Capital investment decisions: 2  493

# Part Four

# Information for Planning, Control and Performance Measurement  543

## 15 The budgeting process  545

## 16 Management control systems 593

## 17 Contingency theory and organizational and social aspects of management accounting 647

## 18 Standard costing and variance analysis 1 671

## 19 Standard costing and variance analysis 2: further aspects 729

# Part Five
# Cost Management and Strategic Management Accounting 887

## 22 Cost management 889

## 23 Strategic management accounting 923

# Part Six
# The Application of Quantitative Methods to Management Accounting   951

# Preface

The aim of the fifth edition of this book is to explain the principles involved in designing and evaluating management and cost accounting information systems. Management accounting systems accumulate, classify, summarize and report information that will assist employees within an organization in their decision-making, planning, control and performance measurement activities. A cost accounting system is concerned with accumulating costs for inventory valuation to meet external financial accounting and internal monthly or quarterly profit measurement requirements. As the title suggests, this book is concerned with both management and cost accounting but emphasis is placed on the former.

After many years of teaching management and cost accounting to various professional, undergraduate, postgraduate and post-experience courses I became convinced there was a need for a book with a more 'accessible' text. A large number of cost and management accounting text books have been published. Many of these books contain a detailed description of accounting techniques without any discussion of the principles involved in evaluating management and cost accounting systems. Such books often lack a conceptual framework, and ignore the considerable amount of research conducted in management accounting in the past three decades. At the other extreme some books focus entirely on a conceptual framework of management accounting with an emphasis on developing normative models of what ought to be. These books pay little attention to accounting techniques. My objective has been to produce a book which falls within these two extremes.

This book is intended primarily for undergraduate students who are pursuing a one or two year management accounting course, and for students who are preparing for the cost and management accounting examinations of the professional accountancy bodies at an intermediate or advanced professional level. It should also be of use to postgraduate and higher national diploma students who are studying cost and management accounting for the first time. An introductory course in financial accounting is not a prerequisite, although many students will have undertaken such a course.

## Structure and plan of the book

A major theme of this book is that different financial information is required for different purposes, but my experience indicates that this approach can confuse students. In one chapter of a typical book students are told that costs should be allocated to products including a fair share of overhead costs; in another chapter they are told that some of the allocated costs are irrelevant and should be disregarded. In yet another chapter they are told that costs should be related to people (responsibility centres) and not products, whereas elsewhere no mention is made of responsibility centres.

In writing this book I have devised a framework that is intended to overcome these difficulties. The framework is based on the principle that there are three ways of constructing accounting information. The first is cost accounting with its emphasis on producing product costs for allocating costs between cost of goods sold and inventories to meet external and internal financial accounting inventory valuation and profit measurement requirements. The second is the notion of decision relevant costs with the emphasis on providing information to help managers to make good decisions. The third is responsibility accounting and performance measurement which focuses on both financial and non-financial information, in particular the assignment of costs and revenues to responsibility centres.

This book is divided into six parts. The first part (Part One) consists of two chapters and provides an introduction to management and cost accounting and a framework for studying the remaining chapters. The following three parts reflect the three different ways of constructing accounting information. Part Two consists of five chapters and is entitled 'Cost Accumulation for Inventory Valuation and Profit Measurement'. This section focuses mainly on assigning costs to products to separate the costs incurred during a period between costs of goods sold and the closing inventory valuation for internal and external profit measurement. The extent to which product costs accumulated for inventory valuation and profit measurement should be adjusted for meeting decision-making, cost control and performance measurement requirements is also briefly considered. Part Three consists of seven chapters and is entitled 'Information for Decision-making'. Here the focus is on measuring and identifying those costs which are relevant for different types of decisions.

The title of Part Four is 'Information for Planning, Control and Performance Measurement'. It consists of seven chapters and concentrates on the process of translating goals and objectives into specific activities and the resources that are required, via the short-term (budgeting) and long-term *planning* processes, to achieve the goals and objectives. In addition, the management control systems that organizations use are described and the role that management accounting control systems play within the overall control process is examined. The emphasis here is on the accounting process as a means of providing information to help managers control the activities for which they are responsible. The organizational, social and political aspects of management accounting are included as separate chapters in this section. Performance measurement and evaluation within different segments of the organization is also examined.

Part Five consists of two chapters and is entitled 'Cost Management and Strategic Management Accounting'. The first chapter focuses on cost management and the second on strategic management accounting. The final part consists of three chapters and is entitled 'The Application of Quantitative Methods to Management Accounting'.

In devising a framework around the three methods of constructing financial information there is a risk that the student will not appreciate that the three categories use many common elements, that they overlap, and that they constitute a single overall management accounting system, rather than three independent systems. I have taken steps to minimize this risk in each section by emphasizing why financial information for one purpose should or should not be adjusted for another purpose. In short, each section of the book is not presented in isolation and an integrative approach has been taken.

When I wrote this book an important consideration was the extent to which the application of quantitative techniques should be integrated with the appropriate topics or considered separately. I have chosen to integrate quantitative techniques whenever they are an essential part of a chapter. For example, the use of probability statistics are essential to

Chapter 12 (Decision-making under conditions of risk and uncertainty) but my objective has been to confine them, where possible, to Part Five.

This approach allows for maximum flexibility. Lecturers wishing to integrate quantitative techniques with earlier chapters may do so but those who wish to concentrate on other matters will not be hampered by having to exclude the relevant quantitative portions of chapters.

# Major changes in the content of the fifth edition

During the late 1980s and the 1990s the theory and practice of management accounting have been subject to enormous changes. Many of these changes were described in the fourth edition of this book, published in 1996, but they were presented as emerging management accounting issues. They were also presented as separate topics, rather than being integrated with the existing theories, concepts and techniques. It was unclear at the time of writing the fourth edition whether the proposed changes would become part of mainstream management accounting. In the intervening years these changes have become firmly established in the literature and adopted by innovative companies around the world.

The major objective in writing the fifth edition has therefore been to integrate recent developments in management accounting with the established conventional wisdom of the subject. This objective created a need to thoroughly review the content of the fourth edition and, besides integrating recent developments, the opportunity was taken to rewrite and improve the presentation of much of the existing material. The end result has been the most extensive rewrite of the text since the book was first published. The feedback relating to the structure and content of previous editions, however, has been extremely favourable and therefore every attempt has been made to retain the existing structure, whilst incorporating the extensive changes that have been made to the content of the new edition.

The notable alterations are:

1. Chapter 28 (Past, current and future developments in management accounting) of the fourth edition has been deleted. As indicated above the current and future developments have been integrated with established conventional wisdom. Two new chapters (Chapters 22 and 23) have been added that incorporate and extend some of the material that has been deleted from Chapter 28 of the fourth edition.

   Chapter 22 is entitled 'Cost management' and examines the various approaches that fall within the area of cost management. These new approaches are compared with traditional management accounting control techniques and the text emphasizes how the new approaches, combined with traditional techniques, control and manage costs more effectively. Chapter 23 is titled 'Strategic management accounting'. Much has been written about strategic management accounting during the past decade but there is still no comprehensive framework as to what constitutes strategic management accounting. Chapter 23 examines the elements of strategic management accounting and describes the different contributions that have been made to its development. In addition, recent developments, such as the balanced scorecard approach, that seek to incorporate performance measurement within the strategic management process are described.

   Apart from cost management and strategic management accounting, the remaining future developments described in Chapter 28 of the fourth edition related to activity-based costing, throughput accounting, customer profitability analysis, the future role of standard costing and the integration of financial and non-financial measures. The issues relating to activity based costing have been incorporated into Chapter 10 (Activity-based costing). Throughput accounting has been included in Chapter 9 (Measuring relevant costs and revenues for decision-making), customer profitability analysis has been incorporated into Chapter 11 (Pricing decisions and profitability analysis) and the future role of standard costing is considered within the chapter on standard costing (Chapter 19). The integration of financial and non-financial measures is presented within a balanced scorecard framework in Chapter 23.

2. The two introductory chapters (Chapters 1 and 2) of the fourth edition have been merged. Some of the content has been deleted and new material has been added. The new chapter provides a more concise and relevant introduction to support the revised content of the fifth edition.

3. Extensive changes have been made to Chapter 3 (Cost and revenue classification). The content is now presented in Chapter 2 and re-titled 'An introduction to cost terms and concepts'.

4. Chapter 4 (Accounting for materials and labour) of the fourth edition has been deleted. Most of the content is concerned with clerical routines and is no longer essential to support the content of the fifth edition. The content of this chapter is covered in Chapter 3 of the author's successful *Costing: An Introduction*, the fourth edition of which is also published by Thomson Learning Business Press. The content of the deleted Chapter 4 is available on the website supporting this text (at http://www.businesspress.co.uk) if you wish to continue using it. The content relating to the pricing of material issues, however, is still considered to be relevant and has been incorporated within Chapter 4 of the fifth edition.

5. Chapter 5 (Accounting for overhead expenditure) has been rewritten and the content is presented in Chapter 4 of the fifth edition and retitled 'Cost assignment'. The new chapter emphasizes cost system design issues and explains why the optimal cost system is different for different organizations. The factors that determine the choice of an optimal cost system for an organization are also discussed. In the previous edition activity-based costing (ABC) was deferred to Chapter 11. It is now introduced in Chapter 3 so that traditional costing and activity-based cost assignment methods can be explained and compared.

6. Less extensive changes have been made to Chapters 6–10 of the fourth edition. These chapters are now Chapters 4–8 of the fifth edition. As indicated above the content relating to the materials recording procedure in the deleted chapter of the fourth edition has been incorporated into Chapter 4 of the fifth edition. The content of Chapter 5 (Process costing) remains similar to the corresponding chapter of the previous edition but substantial changes have been made to the presentation. The more complex material relating to losses in process and equivalent production has been transferred to the appendix of the chapter. This has resulted in a simplified and more concise presentation of the core material. The only notable change to Chapter 6 (Joint product and by-product costing) is that accounting for by-products has been rewritten and simplified. Chapter 7 has been re-titled 'Income effects of alternative costing systems'. The material relating to alternative denominator measures for overhead cost assignment from Chapter 5 of the fourth edition has been rewritten and incorporated into Chapter 7. New material relating to a mathematical model of profit functions for absorption and variable costing has also been included in Chapter 7. The only notable change in Chapter 8 (Cost–volume–profit–analysis) is the inclusion of new material relating to absorption costing cost–volume–profit analysis.

7. Chapter 11 (Special studies: Measuring relevant costs for decision-making) has been substantially rewritten. The content is presented in Chapter 9 which is now entitled 'Measuring relevant costs and revenues for decision-making'.

8. The chapter relating to activity-based-costing (Chapter 10) has also been extensively revised. The technical aspects are now covered in Chapter 3 thus enabling Chapter 10 to focus on the theoretical and conceptual aspects. A substantial amount of new material has been added including activity-based profitability analysis, pitfalls in using ABC information and ABC in service organizations.

9. Chapter 13 (Accounting information for pricing decisions) has been replaced by a new Chapter 11 entitled 'Pricing decisions and profitability analysis'. The new chapter is structured mainly around four areas – *price setting* firms facing *short-run* pricing decisions, *price setting* firms facing *long-run* pricing decisions, *price-taking* firms facing *short-run* product mix decisions and *price-taking* firms facing *long-run* product mix decisions. Profitability analysis is presented within the final two categories. As indicated above customer profitability analysis is also included within this chapter.

10. Less extensive changes have been made to Chapters 14–16 of the fourth edition. These chapters are now Chapters 12–14 of the fifth edition. The material on portfolio theory in Chapter 12 (Decision-making under conditions of risk and uncertainty) has been rewritten and simplified. In the two chapters relating to capital investment decisions (Chapters 13 and 14 ) major changes have been made to the text relating to the effect of performance measurement on capital investment decisions, taxation and investment decisions and the effect of inflation on capital investment appraisal.

11. Major structural changes have been made to Part Four (Information for Planning, Control and Performance Measurement) of the fourth edition. In the fourth edition the technical aspects of accounting control and performance measurement systems were presented prior to behavioural and social aspects. In the fifth edition the technical aspects are delayed so that it can be seen how they fit in within a broader picture of organizational control.

    Activity-based budgeting has been incorporated into Chapter 15 (The budgeting process). Chapter 16 (Management control systems) is a new chapter. To fully understand the role that management accounting control systems play in the control process, it is necessary to be aware of how they relate to the entire array of control mechanisms used by organizations. Chapter 16 describes the different types of controls that are used by companies. The elements of management accounting control systems are described within the context of the overall control process and the behavioural issues relating to accounting control systems are examined. To design effective management accounting control systems it is necessary to consider the circumstances in which they will be used. There is no universally best management accounting control system which can be applied to all organizations. The applicability of a management accounting control system is contingent on the circumstances faced by organizations. Chapter 17 includes new material that describes the contingency theory of management accounting. In addition, relevant content from Chapter 22 of the fourth edition relating to the role of management accounting within a social, organizational and political context has been incorporated into this chapter.

    Apart from the re-positioning of the chapters on standard costing and the introduction of new material relating to examining its future role, substantial changes have not been made to the content. Chapters 20 and 21 concentrate on the special problems of control and measuring the performance of divisions and other decentralized units within an organization. In the fifth edition these chapters have been integrated within Part Four. In the previous edition they were included within a separate section and not integrated to the same extent with the other chapters relating to planning, control and performance measurement. Both Chapters 20 and 21 have been extensively rewritten. Chapter 20 includes new material on Economic Value Added (EVA$^{(TM)}$), a new technique for measuring the performance of business units, and how the dysfunctional consequences of short-term financial measures can be minimized. The content of Chapter 21 (Transfer pricing in divisionalized companies) has also been reorganized and substantially re-written. The economic theory of transfer pricing has been relocated at the end of the chapter so that readers can grasp the principles without having to concentrate on complex economic theory. In addition, a case problem has been introduced that is used to illustrate the different methods of transfer pricing.

12. As indicated above Part Five includes two new chapters. Chapters 22 focuses on cost management and Chapter 23 on strategic management accounting.

13. Substantial changes have not been made to the final three chapters. Structural changes have been made to Chapters 24 (Cost estimation and cost behaviour) and 26 (The application of linear programming to management accounting). The more complex advanced material has been moved to the end of each chapter and some of the content of Chapter 24 has been rewritten. The objective has been to simplify the presentation and ensure that the content is more accessible for students who are not pursuing an advanced course in management accounting.

14. It will be apparent to adopters of the fourth edition that substantial changes have been made to the presentation of the material. In particular, the text is now presented in several colours and considerable improvements have been made to the exhibits, tables and diagrams in order to improve their explanatory effectiveness.

15. The fifth edition now includes case studies and a dedicated website.

# Case studies

The final section of this book includes 10 case studies. These cases generally cover the content of several chapters and contain questions to which there is no ideal answer. They are intended to encourage independent thought and initiative and to relate and apply your understanding of the content of this book in more uncertain situations. They are also intended to develop your critical thinking and analytical skills. The authors of the cases have provided teaching notes for lecturers and are included in the instructors' guide accompanying this book. Additional case studies and teaching notes are also available on the dedicated website.

# Highlighting of advanced reading sections

Feedback relating to previous editions has indicated that one of the major advantages of this book has been the comprehensive treatment of management accounting. Some readers, however, will not require a comprehensive treatment of all of the topics that are contained in the book. To meet the different requirements of the readers, the more advanced material that is not essential for those readers not requiring an in-depth knowledge of a particular topic has been highlighted. The start of each advanced reading section is marked with the symbol ⒜⒝ and a vertical red line is used to highlight the full section. If you do require an in-depth knowledge of a topic you may find it helpful initially to omit the advanced reading sections, or skim them, on your first reading. You should read them in detail only when you fully understand the content of the remaining parts of the chapter. The advanced reading sections are more appropriate for an advanced course and may normally be omitted if you are pursuing an introductory course.

## International focus

Previous editions of this book have presented the content within a UK setting. The book has now become an established text in many different countries throughout the world. Because of this, the fifth edition has adopted a more international focus and regulatory requirements and taxation aspects have not been restricted to a UK setting. A new feature is the presentation of boxed exhibits of surveys relating to management accounting in many different countries, particularly the European mainland. To simplify the presentation, however, the UK pound monetary unit has been used throughout the book. Most of the assessment material has incorporated questions set by the UK professional accountancy bodies. These questions are appropriate for world-wide use and users who are not familiar with the requirements of the UK professional accountancy bodies should note that many of the advanced level questions also contain the beneficial features described above for case study assignments.

## Recommended reading

A separate section is included at the end of most chapters providing advice on key articles or books which you are recommended to read if you wish to pursue topics and issues in more depth. Many of the references are the original work of writers who have played a major role in the development of management accounting. The contribution of such writers is often reflected in this book but there is frequently no substitute for the original work of the authors. The detailed references are presented in the Bibliography towards the end of the book.

## Assessment material

Throughout this book 1 have kept the illustrations simple. You can check your understanding of each chapter by answering the self-assessment questions. Answers to these questions are contained in a separate section at the end of this book. More complex questions are set at the end of each chapter to enable students to pursue certain topics in more depth. Each question is graded according to the level of difficulty. Questions graded 'Intermediate' are normally appropriate for a first year course whereas questions graded 'Advanced' are normally appropriate for a second year course or the final stages of the professional accountancy examinations.

This book is part of an integrated educational package. A *Students' Manual* provides suggested answers to the questions which are asterisked here in the main text and an *Instructors' Manual* provides answers to the remaining questions and teaching notes relating to the case studies. Students are strongly recommended to purchase the *Students' Manual*, which complements this book. It contains suggested answers to over 200 questions. Both the *Students' Manual* and the *Instructors' Manual* have been revised and extended. New answers have been added and the content of both manuals has been substantially revised.

In recognition of the increasing need for the integration of IT teaching into the curriculum, this book is accompanied by an on-line *Spreadsheet Applications Manual*, which has been written by Dr Alicia Gazely of Nottingham Business School. This explains basic spreadsheet techniques and then builds up ten spreadsheet models which illustrate, and allow students to explore, examples in the main text. The spreadsheets, guidance notes and on-line access are available to teachers on adoption. Further details of this package are given in the section covering the dedicated website below.

# Supplementary material

## Dedicated website

The dedicated website can be found at www.businesspress.co.uk. The lecturer section is password protected and the password is available free to lecturers who confirm their adoption of the fifth edition – lecturers should complete the registration form on the website to apply for their password, which will then be sent to them by e-mail.

The following range of material is available.

## For students and lecturers (open access)

### Extra case studies

Internationally focused case studies. (NB Teaching notes to accompany the cases are available in the password protected lecturer area of the site). Additional case studies will be added to the website during the life of the fifth edition.

### Testbank (compiled by Wayne Fiddler of Huddersfield University)

Interactive multiple choice questions to accompany each chapter. The student takes the test on-line to check their grasp of the key points in each chapter. Detailed feedback is provided for each question if the student chooses the wrong answer.

### Links to accounting and finance sites on the web

Including links to the main accounting firms, accounting magazines and journals and careers and job search pages.

### IEBM Definitions

Alphabetical list of accounting and finance definitions taken from the Pocket edition of the *International Encyclopedia of Business and Management*.

# For lecturers only (password protected)

## Instructors' manual

Available to download free from the site in PDF (Portable Document Format), the manual includes answers to the end of chapter questions included in the book and teaching notes to the case studies. (Please note: the instructors' manual is also available in print format, free to adopting lecturers, ISBN 1-86152-596-6.)

## New questions and answers

Extra exam-style questions with model answers to accompany each chapter.

## Teaching notes to the case studies

To accompany the extra case studies available in the student area of the website.

## Spreadsheet exercises (compiled and designed by Alicia Gazely of Nottingham Trent University)

Created in Excel to accompany the self-assessment exercises in the book, the exercises can be saved by the lecturer to their own directories and distributed to students as each topic is covered. Each exercise explains a basic spreadsheet technique which illustrates, and allows the student to explore examples in the main text.

## Overhead transparencies

Available to download free from the site in PDF. (Please note: the overhead transparencies are also available as hardcopy, free to adopting lecturers, see the next section for details.)

## PowerPoint (TM) slides

PowerPoint presentations to accompany each chapter.

# Printed supplementary materials

## For lecturers

Lecturers who adopt this text are provided with the following comprehensive package of additional materials to assist in the preparation and delivery of courses:
Students' Manual (ISBN 1-86152-537-0)*
Instructors' Manual (ISBN 1-86152-596-6)*
OHP Masters (ISBN 1-86152-597-4)*
Password access to additional teaching material on the website that is only available to lecturers who adopt the text, that is Spreadsheet applications, PowerPoint slides and other teaching material.

 *If you already have a copy of the text please order these individually. If you require the entire package, please use ISBN 1-86152-599-0) to order the comprehensive *Instructors' Pack for Management & Cost Accounting, fifth edition.*

To order additional material please contact the publisher on the Thomson Learning website: http:// www.businesspress.co.uk or telephone the Customer Services Department on 44 (0) 1264 342 932 (Fax to 44 (0) 1264 342 761).

### For students

A *Students' Manual* to help you work through the text is available from all good bookshops. Order it by quoting ISBN 1-86152-537-0)

# Alternative course sequences

Although conceived and developed as a unified whole, the book can be tailored to the individual requirements of a course, and so to the preferences of the individual reader. For a discussion of the alternative sequencing of the chapters see Guidelines to Using the Book in Chapter 1. The following are suggested programmes for various courses:

**A two-year management accounting course for undergraduates**
The content of all of the book should be relevant but if the aim is to exclude some of the technical aspects relating to cost accumulation for inventory valuation and profit measurement then Part One, Chapter 3 (Part Two) and Parts Three to Six are recommended.

**A one-year degree or post-experience course in management accounting**
Part One, Chapter 3 (Part Two), Part Three (the non-advanced reading sections within Chapters 8–13) and Part Four (non-advanced reading sections within Chapters 15, 16, 18, 20 and 21).

**Foundation/intermediate professional accountancy examinations with a major emphasis on cost accounting**
All of Parts One and Two, Chapters 8 and 9 of Part Three plus the non-advanced reading sections of Chapters 15, 16, 18 and 19 of Part Four.

**Professional accountancy examinations at the professional or advanced level**
Revision of prescribed reading for the foundation level plus the remaining chapters of the book.

# Acknowledgements

I am indebted to many individuals for their ideas and assistance in preparing this and previous editions of the book. In particular, I would like to thank the following who have provided material for inclusion in the text and the dedicated website or who have commented on this and earlier editions of the book:

Anthony Atkinson, University of Waterloo
Stan Brignall, Aston Business School
Jose Manuel de Matos Carvalho, ISCA de Coimbra, Portugal
Peter Clarke, University College Dublin
Jayne Ducker, Sheffield Hallam University
Ian G. Fisher, John Moores University
Lin Fitzgerald, Warwick Business School

Wayne Fiddler, University of Huddersfield
Richard Grey, University of Strathclyde
Alicia Gazely, Nottingham Trent University
Antony Head, Sheffield Hallam University
Mike Johnson, University of Dundee
Michel Lebas, Groupe HEC
Peter Nordgaard, Copenhagen Business School
Deryl Northcott, University of Manchester
David Owen, University of Sheffield
Dan Otzen, Copenhagen Business School
Rona O'Brien, Sheffield Hallam University
Graham Parker, Kingston University
John Perrin, University of Exeter
Tony Rayman, University of Bradford
James S. Reece, University of Michigan
Sue Richardson, University of Bradford Management Centre
Carsten Rohde, Copenhagen Business School
Robin Roslender, University of Stirling
John Shank, The Amos Tuck School of Business, Dartmouth College
Mike Tayles, University of Bradford
Richard M.S. Wilson, Loughborough University Business School

I am also indebted to Jennifer Pegg at Thomson Learning Business Press for her valuable publishing advice, support and assistance; and to all of the staff at Thomson Learning who have worked on the book; in particular, Fiona Freel and Jenny Clapham. My appreciation goes also to the Chartered Institute of Management Accountants, the Chartered Association of Certified Accountants, the Institute of Chartered Accountants in England and Wales, and the Association of Accounting Technicians for permission to reproduce examination questions. Questions from the Chartered Institute of Management Accountants' examinations are designated CIMA; questions from the Chartered Association of Certified Accountants are designated CACA or ACCA; questions from the Institute of Chartered Accountants in England and Wales are designated ICAEW; and questions from the Association of Accounting Technicians are designated AAT. The answers in the accompanying teachers' and students' guides to this book are my own and are in no way the approved solutions of the above professional bodies. Finally, and most importantly I would like to thank my wife, Bronwen, for converting the original manuscript of the earlier editions into final type-written form and for her continued help and support throughout the five editions of this book.

# Introduction to Management and Cost Accounting

The objective of this section is to provide an introduction to management and cost accounting. In Chapter 1 we define accounting and distinguish between financial, management and cost accounting. This is followed by an examination of the role of management accounting in providing information to managers for decision-making, planning, control and performance measurement. In addition, the important changes that are taking place in the business environment are considered. Progression through the book will reveal how these changes are influencing management accounting systems. In Chapter 2 the basic cost terms and concepts that are used in the management accounting literature are described.

# Introduction to Management and Cost Accounting

The objective of this section is to provide an introduction to management and cost accounting. In Chapter 1 we define accounting and distinguish between financial, management and cost accounting. This is followed by an examination of the role of management accounting in providing information to managers for decision-making, planning, control and performance measurement. In addition, the important changes that are taking place in the business environment, we examine throughout the book, will reveal how these changes are influencing management accounting systems. In Chapter 2 the basic cost terms and concepts that are used in the management accounting literature are described.

CHAPTER 1 INTRODUCTION TO MANAGEMENT ACCOUNTING
CHAPTER 2 AN INTRODUCTION TO COST TERMS AND CONCEPTS

# Introduction to management accounting

There are many definitions of accounting, but the one that captures the theme of this book is the definition formulated by the American Accounting Association. It describes accounting as

> the process of identifying, measuring and communicating economic information to permit informed judgements and decisions by users of the information.

In other words, accounting is concerned with providing both financial and non-financial information that will help decision-makers to make good decisions. An understanding of accounting therefore requires an understanding of the decision-making process and an awareness of the users of accounting information.

During the past decade many organizations in both the manufacturing and service sectors have faced dramatic changes in their business environment. Deregulation combined with extensive competition from overseas companies in domestic markets has resulted in a situation where most companies are now competing in a highly competitive global market. At the same time there has been a significant reduction in product life cycles arising from technological innovations and the need to meet increasingly discriminating customer demands. To compete successfully in today's highly competitive global environment companies are making customer satisfaction an overriding priority, adopting new management approaches, changing their manufacturing systems and investing in new technologies. These changes are having a significant influence on management accounting systems. Progression through the book will reveal how these changes are influencing management accounting systems, but first of all it is important that you have a good background knowledge of some of the important changes that are occurring in the business environment. This chapter aims to provide such knowledge.

The objective of this first chapter is to provide the background knowledge that will enable you to achieve a more meaningful insight into the issues and problems of management accounting

## Learning objectives

After studying this chapter, you should be able to:

- differentiate between management accounting, cost accounting and financial accounting;

- list and describe each of the seven factors involved in the decision-making, planning and control process;

- justify the view that, broadly, firms seek to maximize the present value of future net cash inflows;

- explain the factors that have influenced the changes in the competitive environment;

- outline the key success factors that directly affect customer satisfaction;

- describe the functions of a management accounting system.

that are discussed in the book. We begin by looking at the users of accounting information and identifying their requirements. This is followed by a description of the decision-making process and the changing business and manufacturing environment. Finally, the different functions of management accounting are described.

# The users of accounting information

Accounting is a language that communicates financial and non-financial information to people who have an interest in an organization – managers, shareholders and potential investors, employees, creditors and the government. Managers require information that will assist them in their decision-making and control activities; for example, information is needed on the estimated selling prices, costs, demand, competitive position and profitability of various products that are made by the organization. Shareholders require information on the value of their investment and the income that is derived from their shareholding. Employees require information on the ability of the firm to meet wage demands and avoid redundancies. Creditors and the providers of loan capital require information on a firm's ability to meets its financial obligations. Government agencies like the Central Statistical Office collect accounting information and require such information as the details of sales activity, profits, investments, stocks, dividends paid, the proportion of profits absorbed by taxation and so on. In addition, the tax authorities need information on the amount of profits that are subject to taxation. All this information is important for determining policies to manage a country's economy.

Accounting information is not confined to business organizations. Accounting information about individuals is also important and is used by other individuals; for example, credit will only be extended to an individual after the prospective borrower has furnished a reasonable accounting of his or her private financial affairs. Non-profit-making organizations such as churches, charitable organizations, clubs and government units such as local authorities, also require accounting information for decision-making, and for reporting the results of their activities. For example, a tennis club will require information on the cost of undertaking its various activities so that a decision can be made as to the amount of the annual subscription that it will charge to its members. Similarly, local authorities need information on the costs of undertaking specific activities so that decisions can be made as to which activities will be undertaken and the resources that must be raised to finance them.

The foregoing discussion has indicated that there are many users of accounting information who require information for decision-making. The objective of accounting is to provide sufficient information to meet the needs of the various users at the lowest possible cost. Obviously, the benefit derived from using an information system for decision-making must be greater than the cost of operating the system.

An examination of the various users of accounting information indicates that they can be divided into two categories:

1. internal parties within the organization;
2. external parties such as shareholders, creditors and regulatory agencies, outside the organization.

It is possible to distinguish between two branches of accounting, that reflect the internal and external users of accounting information. **Management accounting** is concerned with the provision of information to people within the organization to help them make better decisions and improve the efficiency and effectiveness of existing operations, whereas **financial accounting** is concerned with the provision of information to external parties outside the organization. This book concentrates on management accounting.

# Differences between management accounting and financial accounting

The major differences between these two branches of accounting are:

- *Legal requirements.* There is a statutory requirement for public limited companies to produce annual financial accounts regardless of whether or not management regards this information as useful. Management accounting, by contrast, is entirely optional and information should be produced only if it is considered that the benefits from the use of the information by management exceed the cost of collecting it.

- *Focus on individual parts or segments of the business.* Financial accounting reports describe the whole of the business whereas management accounting focuses on small parts of the organization, for example the cost and profitability of products, services, customers and activities. In addition, management accounting information measures the economic performance of decentralized operating units, such as divisions and departments.

- *Generally accepted accounting principles.* Financial accounting statements must be prepared to conform with the legal requirements and the generally accepted accounting principles established by the regulatory bodies such as the Financial Accounting Standards Board (FASB) in the USA and the Accounting Standards Board (ASB) in the UK. These requirements are essential to ensure the uniformity and consistency that is needed for external financial statements. Outside users need assurance that external statements are prepared in accordance with generally accepted accounting principles so that the inter-company and historical comparisons are possible. In contrast, management accountants are not required to adhere to generally accepted accounting principles when providing managerial information for internal purposes. Instead, the focus is on the serving management's needs and providing information that is useful to managers relating to their decision-making, planning and control functions.

- *Time dimension.* Financial accounting reports what has happened in the past in an organization, whereas management accounting is concerned with *future* information as well as past information. Decisions are concerned with *future* events and management therefore requires details of expected *future* costs and revenues.

- *Report frequency.* A detailed set of financial accounts is published annually and less detailed accounts are published semi-annually. Management requires information quickly if it is to act on it. Consequently management accounting reports on various activities may be prepared at daily, weekly or monthly intervals.

# The decision-making process

Because information produced by management accountants must be judged in the light of its ultimate effect on the outcome of decisions, a necessary precedent to an understanding of management accounting is an understanding of the *decision-making process*.

**FIGURE 1.1** *The decision-making, planning and control process.*

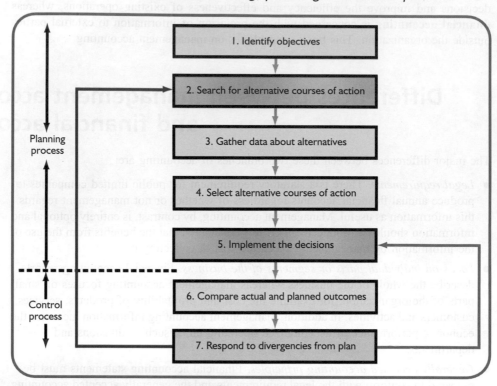

Figure 1.1 presents a diagram of a decision-making model. The first five stages represent the decision-making or the planning process. **Planning** involves making choices between alternatives and is primarily a decision-making activity. The final two stages represent the *control process*, which is the process of measuring and correcting actual performance to ensure that the alternatives that are chosen and the plans for implementing them are carried out. Let us now consider each of the elements of the decision-making and control process.

## IDENTIFYING OBJECTS

Before good decisions can be made there must be some guiding aim or direction that will enable the decision-makers to assess the desirability of favouring one course of action over another. Hence, the first stage in the decision-making process should be to specify the **goals** or **objectives of the organization**.

Considerable controversy exists as to what the objectives of firms are or should be. Economic theory normally assumes that firms seek to maximize profits for the owners of the firm (the ordinary shareholders in a limited company) or, more precisely, the maximization of shareholders' wealth. Various arguments have been used to support the profit maximization objective. There is the legal argument that the ordinary shareholders are the owners of the firm, which therefore should be run for their benefit by trustee managers. Another argument supporting the profit objective is that profit maximization leads to the maximization of overall economic welfare. That is, by doing the best for yourself, you are unconsciously doing the best for society. Moreover, it seems a reasonable belief that the interests of firms will be better served by a larger profit than by a smaller profit, so that maximization is at least a useful approximation.

Some writers (e.g. Simon, 1959) believe that businessmen are content to find a plan that provides satisfactory profits rather than to maximize profits. Because people have limited powers of understanding and can deal with only a limited amount of information at a time (Simon uses the term **bounded rationality** to describe these constraints), they tend to search for solutions only until the first acceptable solution is found. No further attempt is made to find an even better solution or to continue the search until the best solution is discovered. Such behaviour, where the search is terminated on finding a satisfactory, rather than optimal solution, is known as **satisficing**.

Cyert and March (1969) have argued that the firm is a coalition of various different groups – shareholders, employees, customers, suppliers and the government – each of whom must be paid a minimum to participate in the coalition. Any excess benefits after meeting these minimum constraints are seen as being the object of bargaining between the various groups. In addition, a firm is subject to constraints of a societal nature. Maintaining a clean environment, employing disabled workers and providing social and recreation facilities are all examples of social goals that a firm may pursue.

Clearly it is too simplistic to say that the only objective of a business firm is to maximize profits. Some managers seek to establish a power base and build an empire; another goal is security; the removal of uncertainty regarding the future may override the pure profit motive. Nevertheless, the view adopted in this book is that, broadly, firms seek to maximize the value of future net cash inflows (that is, future cash receipts less cash payments) or to be more precise the present value of future net cash inflows.[1] This is equivalent to maximizing shareholder value. (The concept of present value is explained in Chapter 13.) The reasons for choosing this objective are as follows:

1. It is unlikely that any other objective is as widely applicable in measuring the ability of the organization to survive in the future.

2. It is unlikely that maximizing the present value of future cash flows can be realized in practice, but by establishing the principles necessary to achieve this objective you will learn how to increase the present value of future cash flows.

3. It enables shareholders as a group in the bargaining coalition to know how much the pursuit of other goals is costing them by indicating the amount of cash distributed among the members of the coalition.

# THE SEARCH FOR ALTERNATIVE COURSES OF ACTION

The second stage in the decision-making model is a search for a range of possible courses of action (or **strategies**) that might enable the objectives to be achieved. If the management of a company concentrates entirely on its present product range and markets, and market shares and cash flows are allowed to decline, there is a danger that the company will be unable to generate sufficient cash flows to survive in the future. To maximize future cash flows, it is essential that management identifies potential opportunities and threats in its current environment and takes specific steps immediately so that the organization will not be taken by surprise by any developments which may occur in the future. In particular, the company should consider one or more of the following courses of action:

1. developing *new* products for sale in *existing* markets;
2. developing *new* products for *new* markets;
3. developing *new* markets for *existing* products.

The search for alternative courses of action involves the acquisition of information concerning future opportunities and environments; it is the most difficult and important stage of the decision-making process. Ideally, firms should consider all alternative courses of action, but, in practice they consider only a few alternatives, with the search process being localized initially. If this type of routine search activity fails to produce satisfactory solutions, the search will become more widespread (Cyert and March, 1969). We shall examine the search process in more detail in Chapter 15.

## GATHER DATA ABOUT ALTERNATIVES

When potential areas of activity are identified, management should assess the potential growth rate of the activities, the ability of the company to establish adequate market shares, and the cash flows for each alternative activity for various **states of nature**. Because decision problems exist in an uncertain environment, it is necessary to consider certain factors that are outside the decision-maker's control, which may occur for each alternative course of action. These uncontrollable factors are called states of nature. Some examples of possible states of nature are economic boom, high inflation, recession, the strength of competition and so on.

The course of action selected by a firm using the information presented above will commit its resources for a lengthy period of time, and how the overall place of the firm will be affected within its environment – that is, the products it makes, the markets it operates in and its ability to meet future changes. Such decisions dictate the firm's long-run possibilities and hence the type of decisions it can make in the future. These decisions are normally referred to as **long-run** or **strategic decisions**. Strategic decisions have a profound effect on the firm's future position, and it is therefore essential that adequate data are gathered about the firm's capabilities and the environment in which it operates. We shall discuss this topic in Chapters 13–15. Because of their importance, strategic decisions should be the concern of top management.

Besides strategic or long-term decisions, management must also make decisions that do not commit the firm's resources for a lengthy period of time. Such decisions are known as **short-term** or **operating decisions** and are normally the concern of lower-level managers. Short-term decisions are based on the environment of today, and the physical, human and financial resources presently available to the firm. These are, to a considerable extent, determined by the quality of the firm's long-term decisions. Examples of short-term decisions include the following.

1. What selling prices should be set for the firm's products?
2. How many units should be produced of each product?
3. What media shall we use for advertising the firm's products?
4. What level of service shall we offer customers in terms of the number of days required to deliver an order and the after-sales service?

Data must also be gathered for short-term decisions; for example, data on the selling prices of competitors' products, estimated demand at alternative selling prices, and predicted costs for different activity levels must be assembled for pricing and output decisions. When the data have been gathered, management must decide which courses of action to take.

## SELECT APPROPRIATE ALTERNATIVE COURSES OF ACTION

In practice, decision-making involves choosing between competing alternative courses of action and selecting the alternative that best satisfies the objectives of an organization. Assuming that our objective is to maximize future net cash inflows, the alternative selected should be based on a comparison of the differences between the cash flows. Consequently, an incremental analysis of the net cash benefits for each alternative should be applied. The alternatives are ranked in terms of net cash benefits, and those showing the greatest benefits are chosen subject to taking into account any qualitative factors. We shall discuss how incremental cash flows are measured for short-term and long-term decisions and the impact of qualitative factors in Chapters 8–14.

## IMPLEMENTATION OF THE DECISIONS

Once alternative courses of action have been selected, they should be implemented as part of the budgeting process. The **budget** is a financial plan for implementing the various decisions that management has made. The budgets for all of the various decisions are expressed in terms of cash inflows and outflows, and sales revenues and expenses. These budgets are merged together into a single unifying statement of the organization's expectations for future periods. This statement is known as a **master budget**. The master budget consists of a budgeted profit and loss account, cash flow statement and balance sheet. The budgeting process communicates to everyone in the organization the part that they are expected to play in implementing management's decisions. Chapter 15 focuses on the budgeting process.

## COMPARING ACTUAL AND PLANNED OUTCOMES AND RESPONDING TO DIVERGENCIES FROM PLAN

The final stages in the process outlined in Figure 1.1 of comparing actual and planned outcomes and responses to divergencies from plan represent the firm's control process. The managerial function of **control** consists of the measurement, reporting and subsequent correction of performance in an attempt to ensure that the firm's objectives and plans are achieved. In other words, the objective of the control process is to ensure that the work is done so as to fulfil the original intentions.

To monitor performance, the accountant produces **performance reports** and presents them to the appropriate managers who are responsible for implementing the various decisions. Performance reports consisting of a comparison of actual outcomes (actual costs and revenues) and planned outcomes (budgeted costs and revenues) should be issued at regular intervals. Performance reports provide **feedback** information by comparing planned and actual outcomes. Such reports should highlight those activities that do not conform to plans, so that managers can devote their scarce time to focusing on these items. This process represents the application of **management by exception**. Effective control requires that corrective action is taken so that actual outcomes conform to planned outcomes. Alternatively, the plans may require modification if the comparisons indicate that the plans are no longer attainable.

The process of taking corrective action so that actual outcomes conform to planning outcomes, or the modification of the plans if the comparisons indicate that actual outcomes do not conform to planned outcomes, is indicated by the arrowed lines in Figure 1.1 linking stages 7 and 5 and 7 and 2. These arrowed lines represent 'feedback loops'. They signify that the process is dynamic and stress the interdependencies between the various stages in the process. The feedback loop between stages 7 and 2 indicates that the plans should be regularly reviewed, and if they are no longer attainable then alternative courses of action must be considered for achieving the organization's objectives. The second loop stresses the corrective action taken so that actual outcomes conform to planned outcomes. Chapters 15–19 focus on the planning and control process.

# Changing competitive environment

Prior to the 1980s many organizations in Western countries operated in a protected competitive environment. Barriers of communication and geographical distance, and sometimes protected markets, limited the ability of overseas companies to compete in domestic markets. There was little incentive for firms to maximize efficiency and improve management practices, or to minimize costs, as cost increases could often be passed on to customers. During the 1980s, however, manufacturing organizations began to encounter severe competition from overseas competitors that offered high-quality products at low prices. By establishing global networks for acquiring raw materials and distributing goods overseas, competitors were able to gain access to domestic markets throughout the world. To be successful companies now have to compete not only against domestic competitors but also against the best companies in the world.

Excellence in manufacturing can provide a competitive weapon to compete in sophisticated world-wide markets. In order to compete effectively companies must be capable of manufacturing innovative products of high quality at a low cost, and also provide a first-class customer service. At the same time, they must have the flexibility to cope with short product life cycles, demands for greater product variety from more discriminating customers and increasing international competition. World-class manufacturing companies have responded to these competitive demands by replacing traditional production systems with new just-in-time production systems and investing in advanced manufacturing technologies (AMTs). The major features of these new systems and their implications for management accounting will be described throughout the book.

Virtually all types of service organization have also faced major changes in their competitive environment. Before the 1980s many service organizations, such as those operating in the airlines, utilities and financial service industries, were either government-owned monopolies or operated in a highly regulated, protected and non-competitive environment. These organizations were not subject to any great pressure to improve the quality and efficiency of their operations or to improve profitability by eliminating services or products that were making losses. Furthermore, more efficient competitors were often prevented from entering the markets in which the regulated companies operated. Prices were set to cover operating costs and provide a predetermined return on capital. Hence cost increases could often be absorbed by increasing the prices of the services. Little attention was therefore given to developing cost systems that accurately measured the costs and profitability of individual services.

Privatization of government-controlled companies and deregulation in the 1980s completely changed the competitive environment in which service companies operated. Pricing and competitive restrictions have been virtually eliminated. Deregulation, intensive competition and an expanding product range created the need for service organizations to focus on cost management and develop management accounting information systems that enabled them to understand their cost base and determine the sources of profitability for their products, customers and markets. Many service organizations have only recently turned their attention to management accounting.

# Changing product life cycles

A **product's life cycle** is the period of time from initial expenditure on research and development to the time at which support to customers is withdrawn. Intensive global competition and technological innovation combined with increasingly discrimating and sophisticated customer demands have resulted in a dramatic decline in product life cycles. To be successful companies must now speed up the rate at which they introduce new products to the market. Being later to the market than the competitors can have a dramatic effect on product profitability.

In many industries a large fraction of a product's life-cycle costs are determined by decisions made early in its life cycle. This has created a need for management accounting to place greater emphasis on providing information at the design stage because many of the costs are committed or locked in at this time. Therefore to compete successfully companies must be able to manage their costs effectively at the design stage, have the capability to adapt to new, different and changing customer requirements and reduce the time to market of new and modified products.

# Focus on customer satisfaction and new management approaches

In order to compete in today's competitive environment companies are having to become more 'customer-driven' and make customer satisfaction an overriding priority. Customers are demanding ever-improving levels of service in cost, quality, reliability, delivery, and the choice of innovative new products. Figure 1.2 illustrates this focus on customer satisfaction as the overriding priority. In order to provide customer satisfaction organizations must concentrate on those key success factors that directly affect it. Figure 1.2 identifies cost efficiency, quality, time and innovation as the key success factors. In addition to concentrating on these factors organizations are adopting new management approaches in their quest to achieve customer satisfaction. These new approaches are illustrated in Figure 1.2. They are continuous improvement, employee empowerment and total value-chain analysis. Let us now examine each of the items shown in Figure 1.2 in more detail.

Since customers will buy the product with the lowest price, all other things being equal, keeping costs low and being **cost efficient** provides an organization with a strong competitive advantage. Increased competition has also made decision errors due to poor cost information more probable and more costly. If the cost system results in distorted product costs being reported, then overcosted products will lead to higher bid prices and business lost to those competitors who are able to quote lower prices purely because their cost systems produce more accurate cost information.

These developments have made many companies aware of the need to improve their cost systems so that they can produce more accurate cost information to determine the cost of their products, pinpoint loss-making activities and analyse profits by products, sales outlets, customers and markets.

In addition to demanding low cost product customers are demanding high quality products and services. Most companies are responding to this by focusing on **total quality management** (TQM). The goal of TQM is customer satisfaction. TQM is a term used to describe a situation where *all* business functions are involved in a process of continuous quality improvement. TQM has broadened from its early concentration on the statistical monitoring of manufacturing processes, to a customer-oriented process of continuous

**FIGURE 1.2** *Focus on customer satisfaction.*

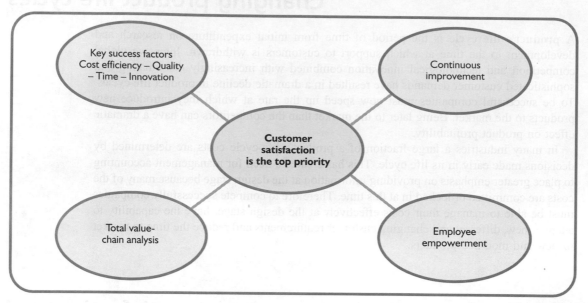

improvement that focuses on delivering products or services of consistently high quality in a timely fashion.

Most European and American companies had always considered quality an additional cost of manufacturing, but by the end of the 1980s they began to realize that quality saved money. The philosophy had been to emphasize production volume over quality; but this resulted in high levels of stocks at each production stage in order to protect against shortages caused by inferior quality at previous stages and excessive expenditure on inspection, rework, scrap and warranty repairs. Companies discovered that it was cheaper to produce the items correctly the first time rather than to waste resources making substandard items that had to be detected, reworked, scrapped or returned by customers. In other words, the emphasis in TQM is to design and build quality in rather than trying to inspect and repair it in. The emphasis on TQM has created fresh demands on the management accounting function to expand its role by becoming involved in measuring and evaluating the quality of products and services and the activities that produce them.

Organizations are also seeking to increase customer satisfaction by providing a speedier response to customer requests, ensuring 100% on-time delivery and reducing the time taken to develop and bring new products to market. For these reasons management accounting systems are starting to place more emphasis on **time-based measures**, which are now an important competitive variable. **Cycle time** is one measure that management accounting systems have begun to focus on. It is the length of time from start to completion of a product or service. It consists of the sum of processing time, move time, wait time and inspection time. Move time is the amount of time it takes to transfer the product during the production process from one location to another. Wait time is the amount of time that the product sits around waiting for processing, moving, inspecting, reworking or the amount of time it spends in finished goods stock waiting to be sold and despatched. Inspection time is the amount of time making sure that the product is defect free or the amount of time actually spent reworking the product to remedy identified defects in quality. Only processing time adds value to the product, and the remaining activities are **non-value added activities** in the sense that they can be reduced or eliminated without altering the product's service potential to the customer. Organizations are therefore focusing on minimizing cycle time by reducing the time spent on such activities. The management accounting system has an important role to play in this process by identifying and reporting on the time devoted to value added and non-value added activities.

The final key success factor shown in Figure 1.2 relates to **innovation**. To be successful companies must develop a steady stream of innovative new products and services and have the capability to adapt to changing customer requirements. It has already been stressed earlier in this chapter that being later to the market than competitors can have a dramatic effect on product profitability. Companies have therefore begun to incorporate performance measures that focus on flexibility and innovation into their management accounting systems. Flexibility relates to the responsiveness in meeting customer requirements. Flexibility measures include the total launch time for new products, the length of development cycles and the ability to change the production mix quickly. Innovation measures include an assessment of the key characteristics of new products relative to those of competitors, feedback on customer satisfaction with the new features and characteristics of newly introduced products, and the number of new products launched and their launch time.

You can see by referring to Figure 1.2 that organizations are attempting to achieve customer satisfaction by adopting a philosophy of **continuous improvement**. Traditionally, organizations have sought to study activities and establish standard operating procedures and materials requirements based on observing and establishing optimum input/output relationships. Operators were expected to follow the standard procedures and management accountants developed systems and measurements that compared actual results with predetermined standards. This process created a climate whereby the predetermined standards represented a target to be achieved and maintained rather than a policy of continuous improvement. In today's competitive environment performance against static historical standards is no longer appropriate. To compete successfully companies must adopt a philosophy of continuous improvement, an ongoing process that involves a continuous search to reduce costs, eliminate waste, and improve the quality and performance of activities that increase customer value or satisfaction.

**Benchmarking** is a technique that is increasingly being adopted as a mechanism for achieving continuous improvement. It is a continuous process of measuring a firm's products, services or activities against the other best performing organizations, either internal or external to the firm. The objective is to ascertain how the processes and activities can be improved. Ideally, benchmarking should involve an external focus on the latest developments, best practice and model examples that can be incorporated within various operations of business organizations. It therefore represents the ideal way of moving forward and achieving high competitive standards.

In their quest for the continuous improvement of organizational activities managers have found that they have had to rely more on the people closest to the operating processes and customers to develop new approaches to performing activities. This has led to employees being provided with relevant information to enable them to make continuous improvements to the output of processes. Allowing employees to take such actions without the authorization by superiors has come to be known as **employee empowerment**. It is argued that by empowering employees and giving them relevant information they will be able to respond faster to customers, increase process flexibility, reduce cycle time and improve morale. Management accounting is therefore moving from its traditional emphasis on providing information to managers to monitor the activities of employees to providing information to employees to empower them to focus on the continuous improvement of activities.

Increasing attention is now being given to **value-chain analysis** as a means of increasing customer satisfaction and managing costs more effectively. The value chain is illustrated in Figure 1.3. It is the linked set of value-creating activities all the way from

**FIGURE 1.3** *The value chain.*

basic raw material sources for component suppliers through to the ultimate end-use product or service delivered to the customer. Coordinating the individual parts of the value chain together to work as a team creates the conditions to improve customer satisfaction, particularly in terms of cost efficiency, quality and delivery. It is also appropriate to view the value chain from the customer's perspective, with each link being seen as the customer of the previous link. If each link in the value chain is designed to meet the needs of its customers, then end-customer satisfaction should ensue. Furthermore, by viewing each link in the value chain as a supplier–customer relationship, the opinions of the customers can be used to provide useful feedback information on assessing the quality of service provided by the supplier. Opportunities are thus identified for improving activities throughout the entire value chain.

Finally, there is one aspect of customer satisfaction that is not specified in Figure 1.2 – namely, **social responsibility** and **corporate ethics**. Customers are no longer satisfied if companies simply comply with the legal requirements of undertaking their activities. They expect company managers to be more proactive in terms of their social responsibility. Company stakeholders are now giving high priority to social responsibility, safety and environmental issues, besides corporate ethics. In response to these pressures many companies are now introducing a code of ethics as an essential part of their corporate culture. In addition, professional accounting organizations play an important role in promoting a high standard of ethical behaviour by their members. Both of the professional bodies representing management accountants in the UK (Chartered Institute of Management Accountants) and the USA (Institute of Management Accountants) have issued a code of ethical guidelines for their members.

# The impact of the changing environment of management accounting systems

All of the changes in the business environment that have been described in this chapter are having a significant influence on management accounting systems. Most organizations have faced changing cost structures with a growth in those costs which do not change directly with changes in output, and which are difficult to trace accurately to products or services. This change in cost structure has created a need for organizations to review their existing management accounting systems and consider implementing new systems that have emerged during the late 1980s and early 1990s.

In today's world-wide competitive environment we have noted that companies are competing in terms of product (or service) quality, delivery, reliability, after-sales service and customer satisfaction. Until recently management accounting systems have not reported on these variables, despite the fact that they represent key competitive variables.

Traditionally management accounting systems have focused mainly on reporting financial measures. However, in response to the changing environment management accounting systems have begun to place greater emphasis on collecting and reporting non-financial quantitative and qualitative information on those key variables that are necessary to compete effectively and which also support the strategies of an organization. There has been a shift from treating financial figures as the foundation of the management accounting system to treating them as part of a broader set of measures.

# Functions of management accounting

A cost and management accounting system should generate information to meet the following requirements. It should:

1. allocate costs between cost of goods sold and inventories for internal and external profit reporting;
2. provide relevant information to help managers make better decisions;
3. provide information for planning, control and performance measurement.

**Financial accounting** rules require that we match costs with revenues to calculate profit. Consequently any unsold finished goods stock or partly completed stock (work in progress) will *not* be included in the cost of goods sold, which is matched against sales revenue during a given period. In an organization that produces a wide range of different products it will be necessary, for stock (inventory) valuation purposes, to charge the costs to each individual product. The total value of the stocks of completed products and work in progress plus any unused raw materials forms the basis for determining the inventory valuation to be deducted from the current period's costs when calculating profit. This total is also the basis for determining the stock valuation for inclusion in the balance sheet. Costs are therefore traced to each individual job or product for financial accounting requirements in order to allocate the costs incurred during a period between cost of goods sold and inventories. This information is required for meeting external financial accounting requirements, but most organizations also produce *internal* profit reports at monthly intervals. Thus product costs are also required for periodic internal profit reporting. Many service organizations, however, do not carry any stocks and product costs are therefore not required by these organizations for valuing inventories.

The second requirement of a cost and management accounting system is to provide relevant financial information to managers to help them make better decisions. This involves both routine and non-routine reporting. Routine information is required relating to the profitability of various segments of the business such as products, services, customers and distribution channels in order to ensure that only profitable activities are undertaken. Information is also required for making resource allocation and product mix and discontinuation decisions. In some situations cost information extracted from the costing system also plays a crucial role in determining selling prices, particularly in markets where customized products and services are provided that do not have readily available market prices. Non-routine information is required for strategic decisions. These decisions are made at infrequent intervals and include decisions relating to the development and introduction of new products and services, investment in new plant and equipment and the negotiation of long-term contracts with customers and suppliers.

Accurate cost information is required in decision-making for distinguishing between profitable and unprofitable activities. If the cost system does not capture accurately enough the consumption of resources by products, the reported product (or service) costs will be distorted, and there is a danger that managers may drop profitable products or continue the production of unprofitable products. Where cost information is used to determine selling prices the undercosting of products can result in the acceptance of unprofitable business whereas overcosting can result in bids being rejected and the loss of profitable business.

Management accounting systems should also provide information for planning, control and performance measurement. Planning involves translating goals and objectives into the specific activities and resources that are required to achieve the goals and objectives. Companies develop both long-term and short-term plans and the management accounting function plays a critical role in this process. Short-term plans, in the form of the budgeting process, are prepared in more detail than the longer-term plans and are one of the mechanisms used by managers as a basis for control and performance evaluation. Control is the process of ensuring that the actual outcomes conform with the planned outcomes. The control process involves the setting of targets or standards (often derived from the budgeting process) against which actual results are measured. Performance is then measured and compared with the targets on a periodic basis. The management accountant's role is to provide managers with feedback information in the form of periodic reports, suitably analysed, to enable them to determine if operations are proceeding according to plan and identify those activities where corrective action is necessary. In particular, the management accounting function should provide economic feedback to managers to assist them in controlling costs and improving the efficiency and effectiveness of operations.

Periodic performance reports comparing actual and targeted outcomes rely heavily on financial measures (such as costs, revenues and profits) to report on managerial performance. These reports are used to evaluate managerial performance and therefore provide incentives for managers to try and ensure that favourable results are reported. In particular, managers are encouraged to achieve organizational goals by having rewards (or punishments) linked to their success (or failure) in achieving the targeted outcomes. The way in which managerial performance is measured and evaluated can have a profound effect on their rewards and behaviour. There is a danger, however, that the performance measurement system can cause serious behavioural problems and be harmful to motivation if accounting performance measures are used and interpreted without a sufficient consideration of the potential organizational behavioural problems. These issues will be considered in Chapters 16 and 17.

It is appropriate at this point to distinguish between cost accounting and management accounting. **Cost accounting** is concerned with cost accumulation for inventory valuation to meet the requirements of external reporting and internal profit measurement, whereas **management accounting** relates to the provision of appropriate information for decision-making, planning, control and performance evaluation. It is apparent from an examination of the literature that the distinction between cost accounting and management accounting is extremely vague with some writers referring to the decision-making aspects in terms of 'cost accounting' and other writers using the term 'management accounting'; the two terms are often used synonymously. In this book no attempt will be made to distinguish between these two terms.

You should now be aware from the above discussion that a management accounting system serves multiple purposes. The emphasis throughout the book is that costs must be assembled in different ways for different purposes. A firm can choose to have multiple accounting systems (i.e. a separate system for each purpose) or one basic accounting system and set of accounts that serve inventory valuation and profit measurement, decision-making and performance evaluation requirements. Most firms choose, on the basis of costs versus benefits criteria, to operate a single accounting system. A single database is maintained with costs appropriately coded and classified so that relevant cost information can be extracted to meet each of the above requirements. Where future cost information is required the database may be maintained at target (standard) costs, or if actual costs are recorded, they are adjusted for anticipated price changes. We shall examine in the next chapter how relevant cost information can be extracted from a single database and adjusted to meet different user requirements.

# Behavioural, organizational and social aspects of management accounting

The conventional wisdom of management accounting, as portrayed in most management accounting textbooks, is derived from neoclassical economic theory. It is assumed that decision-makers behave rationally and the role of management accounting is to aid rational economic decision-making. You will see in Chapter 17 that the assumption of rational economic behaviour described in the decision-making, planning and control process (see Figure 1.2) may not always reflect actual real-world behaviour. For example, objectives are often unclear and tasks are not well understood so that we do not know which course of action is likely to yield optimum results. In these circumstances management accounting information is also used for purposes other than rational decision-making.

Management accounting systems may be adopted ceremonially in order to convince the various interest groups of the legitimacy and rationality of organizational activities. Organizations without formal accounting systems are vulnerable to claims that they are negligent (Cooper *et al.*, 1981). Thus, managers can find value from management accounting systems for symbolic purposes even when the information has little or no relation to decision-making. Management accounting information is also used for political purposes because it is a key means of allocating scarce resources. Interested parties use accounting information to seek to promote their own vested interests to achive political power or a bargaining position. Other research studies have also shown that management accounting information may be used to justify actions that have already been taken on social or political grounds. In these circumstances the accounting information is used for legitimating/retrospective rationalizing purposes rather than as a decisional input. We shall discuss the different 'roles' or 'purposes' of management accounting in Chapter 17.

# Summary of the contents of this book

This book is divided into six parts. The first part (Part One) consists of two chapters and provides an introduction to management and cost accounting and a framework for studying the remaining chapters. Part Two consists of five chapters and is entitled 'Cost Accumulation for Inventory Valuation and Profit Measurement'. This section focuses mainly on assigning costs to products to separate costs incurred during a period between costs of goods sold and the closing inventory valuation. The extent to which product costs accumulated for inventory valuation and profit measurement should be adjusted for meeting decision-making, cost control and performance measurement requirements is also briefly considered. Part Three consists of seven chapters and is entitled 'Information for Decision-making'. Here the focus is on measuring and identifying those costs which are relevant for different types of decisions.

The title of Part Four is 'Information for Planning, Control and Performance Measurement'. It consists of seven chapters and concentrates on the process of translating goals and objectives into specific activities and the resources that are required, via the short-term (budgeting) and long-term planning processes, to achieve the goals and objectives. In addition, the management control systems that organizations use are described and the role that management accounting control systems play within the overall control process is examined. The emphasis here is on the accounting process as a means of providing information to help managers control the activities for which they are responsible. The organizational, social and political aspects of management accounting are included as separate chapters in this section. Performance measurement and evaluation within different segments of the organization is also examined.

Part Five consists of two chapters and is entitled 'Cost Management and Strategic Management Accounting.' The first chapter focuses on cost management and the second on strategic management accounting. The final part consists of three chapters and is entitled 'The Application of Quantitative Methods to Management Accounting'.

# Guidelines for using this book

If you are pursuing a course of management accounting, without cost accumulation for inventory valuation and profit measurement, Chapters 4–7 in Part Two can be omitted, since the rest of this book does not rely heavily on these chapters. Alternatively, you could delay your reading of Chapters 4–7 in Part Two until you have studied Parts Three and Four. Chapter 19 in Part Four is only appropriate if your curriculum requires a detailed knowledge of the technical aspects of variance analysis. If you wish to gain an insight into cost accumulation for inventory valuation and profit measurement but do not wish to study it in depth, you may prefer to read only Chapters 3 and 7 of Part Two. It is important that you read Chapter 3, which focuses on traditional methods of tracing overheads to cost objects prior to reading Chapter 10 on activity-based costing.

The chapters on the application of quantitative techniques to management accounting have been delayed until Part Six. An alternative approach would be to read Chapter 24 immediately after reading Chapter 8 on cost–volume–profit analysis. Chapter 25 is self-contained and may be assigned to follow any of the chapters in Part Four. Chapter 26 should be read only after you have studied Chapter 9.

A comprehensive treatment of all of the topics that are contained in this book will not be essential for all readers. To meet the different requirements of the readers, the more advanced material that is not essential for those readers not requiring an in-depth knowledge of a particular topic has been highlighted. The start of each advanced reading section is marked with the symbol **AR** and a vertical red line is used to highlight the full section. If you do require an in-depth knowledge of a topic you may find it helpful initially to omit the advanced reading sections, or skim them, on your first reading. You should read them in detail only when you fully understand the content of the remaining parts of the chapter. The advanced reading sections are more appropriate for an advanced course and may normally be omitted if you are pursuing an introductory course.

## Summary

Accounting is defined as the process of identifying, measuring and communicating financial and non-financial information to permit informed judgements and decisions by users of the information. We have distinguished between internal users (management accounting) and external users (financial accounting), and have considered a decision-making, planning and control model.

This chapter has also described some of the major changes in the business environment which organizations have faced over the past decade. Intensive competition from overseas companies has resulted in a situation where most companies are now having to operate in a highly competitive global market. Technical innovation and customer demands for a constant stream of innovative products have also resulted in a significant reduction in product life cycles. To compete successfully in today's highly competitive environment companies are finding that it is in their best interests to make customer satisfaction a top priority.

In order to provide customer satisfaction organizations must concentrate on four key success factors: cost efficiency, quality, time and innovation. Companies must manage their costs effectively if they are to become low cost suppliers and compete on the basis of selling price. Total quality management is a customer-oriented process that focuses on delivering products or services of consistent high quality in a timely fashion. Customers also value a prompt service and a speedy response to their request for products or services. Organizations have therefore begun to concentrate on time-based measures that focus on the length of time it takes to complete various activities. Finally, there is now an increasing awareness that a continuous flow of innovative products is essential to an organization's continued success. In addition to concentrating on key success factors organizations are adopting new management approaches such as continuous improvement and employee empowerment.

Conventional management accounting systems were designed for use in an environment which is very different from that of today. It is therefore important that, where necessary, management accounting systems are modified to meet the requirements of today's manufacturing and global competitive environment.

Finally, three different objectives of a management accounting system were described. They are:

1. to allocate costs between cost of goods sold and inventories for internal and external profit reporting;

2. to provide relevant information to help managers make better decisions;

3. to provide information for planning, operational control and performance measurement.

## Key Terms and Concepts

Each chapter includes a section like this. You should make sure that you understand each of the terms listed below before you proceed to the next chapter. Their meanings are explained on the page numbers indicated.

benchmarking (p. 13)
bounded rationality (p. 7)
budget (p. 9)
continuous improvement (p. 13)
control (p. 9)
corporate ethics (p. 14)
cost accounting (p. 16)
cost efficient (p. 11)
cycle time (p. 12)

employee empowerment (p. 13)
feedback (p. 9)
feedback loop (p. 9)
financial accounting (pp. 5, 15)
goals of the organization (p. 6)
innovation (p. 13)
long-run decisions (p. 8)
management accounting (pp. 4, 16)
management by exception (p. 9)
master budget (p. 9)
non-value added activities (p. 12)
objectives of the organization (p. 6)
operating decisions (p. 8)
performance reports (p. 9)

## Key Examination Points

Chapter 1 has provided an introduction to the scope of management accounting. It is unlikely that examination questions will be set that refer to the content of an introductory chapter. However, questions are sometimes set requiring you to outline how a costing system can assist the management of an organization. Note that the examiner may not distinguish between cost accounting and management accounting. Cost accounting is often used to

also embrace management accounting. Your discussion of a cost accounting system should therefore include a description (with illustrations) of how the system provides information for decision-making, planning and control. Make sure that you draw off your experience from the whole of a first-year course and not just this introductory chapter.

# An introduction to cost terms and concepts

In Chapter 1 it was pointed out that accounting systems measure costs which are used for profit measurement and inventory valuation, decision-making, performance measurement and controlling the behaviour of people. The term cost is a frequently used word that reflects a monetary measure of the resources sacrificed or forgone to achieve a specific objective, such as acquiring a good or service. However, the term must be defined more precisely before 'the cost' can be determined. You will find that the word *cost* is rarely used without a preceding adjective to specify the type of cost being considered.

To understand how accounting systems calculate costs and to communicate accounting information effectively to others requires a thorough understanding of what cost means. Unfortunately, the term has multiple meanings and different types of costs are used in different situations. Therefore a preceding term must be added to clarify the assumptions that underlie a cost measurement. A large terminology has emerged to indicate more clearly which cost meaning is being conveyed. Examples include variable cost, fixed cost, opportunity cost and sunk cost. The aim of this chapter is to provide you with an understanding of the basic cost terms and concepts that are used in the management accounting literature.

## Learning objectives

After studying this chapter, you should be able to:

- define and illustrate a cost object;
- explain the meaning of each of the key terms listed at the end of this chapter;
- describe the three purposes for which cost information is required;
- distinguish between job costing and process costing;
- explain why in the short term some costs and revenues are not relevant for decision-making.

## Cost objects

A **cost object** is any activity for which a separate measurement of costs is desired. In other words, if the users of accounting information want to know the cost of something, this something is called a cost object. Examples of cost objects include the cost of a product, the cost of rendering a service to a bank customer or hospital patient, the cost of operating a particular department or sales territory, or indeed anything for which one wants to measure the cost of resources used.

We shall see that the cost collection system typically accounts for costs in two broad stages:

1. It accumulates costs by classifying them into certain categories such as labour, materials and overhead costs (or by cost behaviour such as fixed and variable).

2. It then assigns these costs to cost objects.

In this chapter we shall focus on the following cost terms and concepts:

- direct and indirect costs;
- period and product costs;
- cost behaviour in relation to volume of activity;
- relevant and irrelevant costs;
- avoidable and unavoidable costs;
- sunk costs;
- opportunity costs;
- incremental and marginal costs.

# Direct and indirect costs

Costs that are assigned to cost objects can be divided into two categories: direct costs and indirect costs. **Direct costs** are those costs that can be specifically and exclusively identified with a particular cost object. In contrast, **indirect costs** cannot be identified specifically and exclusively with a given cost object. Let us assume that our cost object is a product, or to be more specific a particular type of desk that is manufactured by an organization. In this situation the wood that is used to manufacture the desk can be specifically and exclusively identified with a particular desk and can thus be classified as a direct cost. Similarly, the wages of operatives whose time can be traced to the specific desk are a direct cost. In contrast, the salaries of factory supervisors or the rent of the factory cannot be specifically and exclusively traced to a particular desk and these costs are therefore classified as indirect.

Sometimes, however, direct costs are treated as indirect because tracing costs directly to the cost object is not cost effective. For example, the nails used to manufacture a particular desk can be identified specifically with the desk, but, because the cost is likely to be insignificant, the expense of tracing such items does not justify the possible benefits from calculating more accurate product costs.

Direct costs can be accurately traced because they can be physically identified with a particular object whereas indirect costs cannot. An estimate must be made of resources consumed by cost objects for indirect costs. Therefore, the more direct costs that can be traced to a cost object, the more accurate is the cost assignment.

The distinction between direct and indirect costs also depends on the cost object. A cost can be treated as direct for one cost object but indirect in respect of another. If the cost object is the cost of using different distribution channels, then the rental of warehouses and the salaries of storekeepers will be regarded as direct for each distribution channel. Also consider a supervisor's salary in a maintenance department of a manufacturing company. If the cost object is the maintenance department, then the salary is a direct cost. However, if the cost object is the product, both the warehouse rental and the salaries of the storekeepers and the supervisor will be an indirect cost because these costs cannot be specifically identified with the product.

# CATEGORIES OF MANUFACTURING COSTS

In manufacturing organizations products are frequently the cost object. Traditionally, cost accounting systems in manufacturing organizations have reflected the need to assign costs to products to value stocks and measure profits based on imposed external financial accounting requirements. Traditional cost accounting systems accumulate product costs as follows:

| | |
|---|---|
| Direct materials | xxx |
| Direct labour | xxx |
| Prime cost | xxx |
| Manufacturing overhead | xxx |
| Total manufacturing cost | xxx |

**Direct materials** consist of all those materials that can be identified with a specific product. For example, wood that is used to manufacture a desk can easily be identified as part of the product, and can thus be classified as direct materials. Alternatively, materials used for the repair of a machine that is used for the manufacture of many different desks are classified as **indirect materials**. These items of materials cannot be identified with any one product, because they are used for the benefit of all products rather than for any one specific product. Note that indirect materials form part of the manufacturing overhead cost.

**Direct labor** consists of those labour costs that can be specifically traced to or identified with a particular product. Examples of direct labour costs include the wages of operatives who assemble parts into the finished product, or machine operatives engaged in the production process. By contrast, the salaries of factory supervisors or the wages paid to the staff in the stores department cannot be specifically identified with the product, and thus form part of the **indirect labour costs**. The wages of all employees who do not work on the product itself but who assist in the manufacturing operation are thus classified as part of the indirect labour costs. As with indirect materials, indirect labour is classified as part of the manufacturing overhead cost.

**Prime cost** refers to the direct costs of the product and consists of direct labour costs plus direct material costs plus any direct expenses. The cost of hiring a machine for producing a specific product is an example of a direct expense.

**Manufacturing overhead** consists of all manufacturing costs other than direct labour, direct materials and direct expenses. It therefore includes all indirect manufacturing labour and materials costs plus indirect manufacturing expenses. Examples of indirect manufacturing expenses in a multi-product company include rent of the factory and depreciation of machinery.

To ascertain the total manufacturing cost of a product, all that is required for the direct cost items is to record the amount of resources used on the appropriate documents. For example, the units of materials used in making a particular product are recorded on a stores requisition, and the hours of direct labour used are recorded on job cards. Having obtained the quantity of resources used for the direct items, it is necessary to ascertain the price paid for these resources. The total of the resources used multiplied by the price paid per unit of resources used provides us with the total of the direct costs or the prime cost for a product.

Manufacturing overheads cannot be directly traced to products. Instead they are assigned to products using **cost allocations**. A cost allocation is the process of estimating the cost of resources consumed by products that involves the use of surrogate, rather than direct measures. The process of assigning indirect costs (overheads) to cost objects will be explained in the next chapter.

# Period and product costs

External financial accounting rules in most countries require that for inventory valuation, only manufacturing costs should be included in the calculation of product costs (see United Kingdom Statement of Standard Accounting Practice (SSAP 9), published by the Accounting Standards Committee). Accountants therefore classify costs as product costs and period costs. **Product costs** are those costs that are identified with goods purchased or produced for resale. In a manufacturing organization they are costs that the accountant attaches to the product and that are included in the inventory valuation for finished goods, or for partly completed goods (work in progress), until they are sold; they are then recorded as expenses and matched against sales for calculating profit. **Period costs** are those costs that are not included in the inventory valuation and as a result are treated as expenses in the period in which they are incurred. *Hence no attempt is made to attach period costs to products for inventory valuation purposes.*

In a manufacturing organization all manufacturing costs are regarded as product costs and non-manufacturing costs are regarded as period costs.[1] Companies operating in the merchandising sector, such as retailing or wholesaling organizations, purchase goods for resale without changing their basic form. The cost of the goods purchased is regarded as a product cost and all other costs such as administration and selling and distribution expenses are considered to be period costs. The treatment of period and product costs for a manufacturing organization is illustrated in Figure 2.1. You will see that both product and period costs are eventually classified as expenses. The major difference is the point in time at which they are so classified.

Why are non-manufacturing costs treated as period costs and not included in the inventory valuation? There are two reasons. First, inventories are assets (unsold production) and assets represent resources that have been acquired that are expected to contribute to future revenue. Manufacturing costs incurred in making a product can be expected to generate future revenues to cover the cost of production. There is no guarantee, however, that non-manufacturing costs will generate future revenue, because they do not represent value added to any specific product. Therefore, they are not included in the inventory valuation. Second, many non-manufacturing costs (e.g. distribution costs) are not incurred when the product is being stored. Hence it is inappropriate to include such costs within the inventory valuation.

An illustration of the accounting treatment of period and product costs for income (profit) measurement purposes is presented in Example 2.1.

# Cost behaviour

A knowledge of how costs and revenues will vary with different levels of activity (or volume) is essential for decision-making. Activity or volume may be measured in terms of units of production or sales, hours worked, miles travelled, patients seen, students enrolled or any other appropriate measure of the activity of an organization. Examples of decisions that require information on how costs and revenues vary with different levels of activity include the following:

1. What should the planned level of activity be for the next year?
2. Should we reduce the selling price to sell more units?
3. Would it be wiser to pay our sales staff by a straight commission, a straight salary, or by some combination of the two?
4. How do the costs and revenues of a hospital change if one more patient is admitted for a seven-day stay?

**EXAMPLE 2.1**

The Flanders company produces 100 000 identical units of a product during period 1. The costs for the period are as follows:

|  | (£) | (£) |
|---|---|---|
| Manufacturing costs: | | |
| Direct labour | 400 000 | |
| Direct materials | 200 000 | |
| Manufacturing overheads | 200 000 | 800 000 |
| Non-manufacturing costs | | 300 000 |

During period 1, the company sold 50 000 units for £750 000, and the remaining 50 000 units were unsold at the end of the period. There was no opening stock at the start of the period. The profit and loss account for period 1 will be as follows:

|  | (£) | (£) |
|---|---|---|
| Sales (50 000) | | 750 000 |
| Manufacturing costs (*product costs*): | | |
| Direct labour | 400 000 | |
| Direct materials | 200 000 | |
| Manufacturing overheads | 200 000 | |
| | 800 000 | |
| Less closing stock (50% or 50 000 units) | 400 000 | |
| Cost of goods sold (50% or 50 000 units) | | 400 000 |
| Gross profit | | 350 000 |
| Less non-manufacturing costs (*period costs*) | | 300 000 |
| Net profit | | 50 000 |

Fifty per cent of the production was sold during the period and the remaining 50% was produced for inventories. Half of the product costs are therefore identified as an expense for the period and the remainder are included in the closing inventory valuation.[2] If we assume that the closing inventory is sold in the next accounting period, the remaining 50% of the product costs will become expenses in the next accounting period. However, all the period costs became an expense in this accounting period, because this is the period to which they relate. Note that only product costs form the basis for the calculation of cost of goods sold, and that period costs do not form part of this calculation.

5. How do the costs and revenues of a hotel change if a room and meals are provided for two guests for a seven-day stay?

For each of the above decisions management requires estimates of costs and revenues at different levels of activity for the alternative courses of action.

The terms 'variable', 'fixed', 'semi-variable' and 'semi-fixed' have been traditionally used in the management accounting literature to describe how a cost reacts to changes in

**FIGURE 2.1** *Treatment of period and product costs.*

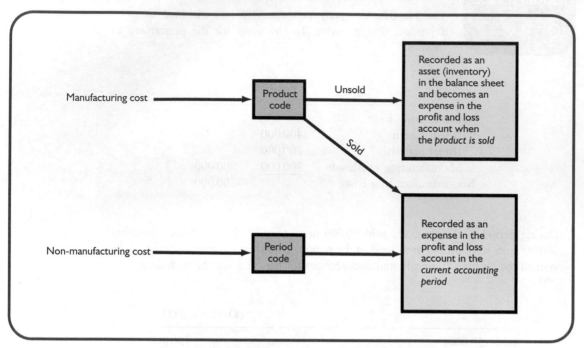

activity. Short-term **variable costs** vary in direct proportion to the volume of activity; that is, doubling the level of activity will double the total variable cost. Consequently, *total* variable costs are linear and *unit* variable cost is constant. Figure 2.2 illustrates a variable cost where the variable cost per unit of activity is £10. It is unlikely that variable cost per unit will be constant for all levels of activity. We shall discuss the reasons why accountants normally assume that variable costs are constant per unit of activity in Chapter 8. Examples of short-term variable manufacturing costs include piecework labour, direct materials and energy to operate the machines. These costs are assumed to fluctuate directly in proportion to operating activity within a certain range of activity. Examples of non-manufacturing variable costs include sales commissions, which fluctuate with sales value, and petrol, which fluctuates with the number of miles travelled.

**Fixed costs** remain constant over wide ranges of activity for a specified time period. Examples of fixed costs include depreciation of the factory building, supervisors' salaries and leasing charges for cars used by the salesforce. Figure 2.3 illustrates fixed costs.

You will see that the *total* fixed costs are constant for all levels of activity whereas *unit* fixed costs decrease proportionally with the level of activity. For example, if the total of the fixed costs is £5000 for a month the fixed costs per unit will be as follows:

| Units produced | Fixed cost per unit (£) |
|:---:|:---:|
| 1 | 5000 |
| 10 | 500 |
| 100 | 50 |
| 1000 | 5 |

Because unit fixed costs are not constant per unit they must be interpreted with caution. For decision-making, it is better to work with total fixed costs rather than unit costs.

**FIGURE 2.2**  *Variable costs: (a) total; (b) unit.*

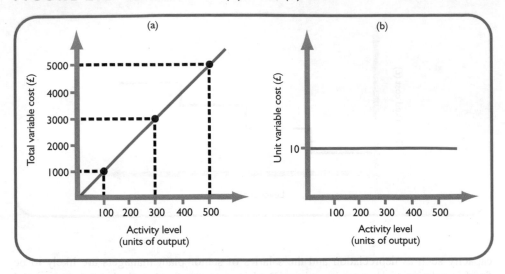

**FIGURE 2.3**  *Fixed costs: (a) total; (b) unit.*

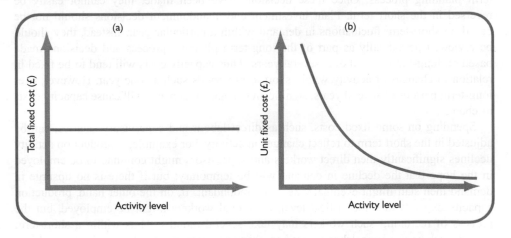

In practice it is unlikely that fixed costs will be constant over the full range of activity. They may increase in steps in the manner depicted in Figure 2.4. We shall discuss the justification for assuming that fixed costs are constant over a wide range of activity in Chapter 8.

The distinction between fixed and variable costs must be made relative to the time period under consideration. Over a sufficiently long time period of several years, virtually all costs are variable. During such a long period of time, contraction in demand will be accompanied by reductions in virtually all categories of costs. For example, senior managers can be released, machinery need not be replaced and even buildings and land can be sold. Similarly, large expansions in activity will eventually cause all categories of costs to increase.

Within shorter time periods, costs will be fixed or variable in relation to changes in activity. The shorter the time period, the greater the probability that a particular cost will be fixed. Consider a time period of one year. The costs of providing the firm's operating

**FIGURE 2.4** *Step fixed costs.*

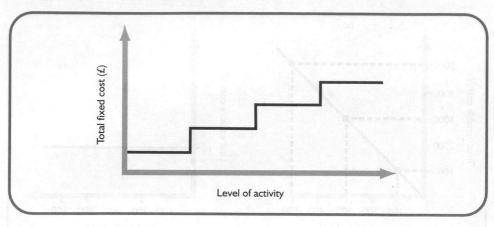

capacity such as depreciation and the salaries of senior plant managers are likely to be fixed in relation to changes in activity. Decisions on the firm's intended future potential level of operating capacity will determine the amount of capacity costs to be incurred. These decisions will have been made previously as part of the capital budgeting and long-term planning process. Once these decisions have been made, they cannot easily be reversed in the short term. Plant investment and abandonment decisions should not be based on short-term fluctuations in demand within a particular year. Instead, they should be reviewed periodically as part of the long-term planning process and decisions made based on long-run demand over several years. Thus capacity costs will tend to be fixed in relation to changes of activity within short-term periods such as one year. However, over long-term periods of several years, significant changes in demand will cause capacity costs to change.

Spending on some fixed costs, such as direct labour and supervisory salaries, can be adjusted in the short term to reflect changes in activity. For example, if production activity declines significantly then direct workers and supervisors might continue to be employed in the hope that the decline in demand will be temporary; but if there is no upsurge in demand then staff might eventually be made redundant. If, on the other hand, production capacity expands to some critical level, additional workers might be employed, but the process of recruiting such workers may take several months. Thus within a short-term period, such as one year, labour costs can change in response to changes in demand in a manner similar to that depicted in Figure 2.4. Costs that behave in this manner are described as **semi-fixed** or **step fixed costs**. The distinguishing feature of step fixed costs is that within a given time period they are fixed within specified activity levels, but they eventually increase or decrease by a constant amount at various critical activity levels as illustrated in Figure 2.4.

Our discussion so far has assumed a one-year time period. Consider a shorter time period such as one month and the circumstances outlined in the previous paragraph where it takes several months to respond to changes in activity and alter spending levels. Over very short-term periods such as one month, spending on direct labour and supervisory salaries will be fixed in relation to changes in activity.

You should now understand that over a given short-term period, such as one year, costs will be variable, fixed or semi-fixed. Over longer-term time periods of several years, all costs will tend to change in response to large changes in activity (or to changes in the range and variety of products or services marketed), and fixed costs will become semi-fixed and change in the manner depicted in Figure 2.4. Because fixed costs do not remain fixed in the long-term, some writers prefer to describe them as **long-term variable costs**, but we shall continue to use the term 'fixed costs' since this is the term most widely used in the literature.

Note, however, that in the short term, even though fixed costs are normally assumed to remain unchanged in response to changes in the level of activity, they may change in response to other factors. For example, if price levels increase then some fixed costs such as management salaries will increase.

Before concluding our discussion of cost behaviour in relation to volume of activity, we must consider **semi-variable costs**. These include both a fixed and a variable component. The cost of maintenance is a semi-variable cost consisting of planned maintenance that is undertaken whatever the level of activity, and a variable element that is directly related to the level of activity.

# Relevant and irrelevant costs and revenues

For decision-making, costs and revenues can be classified according to whether they are relevant to a particular decision. **Relevant costs and revenues** are those *future* costs and revenues that will be changed by a decision, whereas **irrelevant costs and revenues** are those that will not be affected by the decision. For example, if one is faced with a choice of making a journey by car or by public transport, the car tax and insurance costs are irrelevant, since they will remain the same whatever alternative is chosen. However, petrol costs for the car will differ depending on which alternative is chosen, and this cost will be relevant for decision-making.

Let us now consider a further illustration of the classification of relevant and irrelevant costs. Assume a company purchased raw materials a few years ago for £100 and that there appears to be no possibility of selling these materials or using them in future production apart from in connection with an enquiry from a former customer. This customer is prepared to purchase a product that will require the use of all these materials, but he is not prepared to play more than £250 per unit. The additional costs of converting these materials into the required product are £200. Should the company accept the order for £250? It appears that the cost of the order is £300, consisting of £100 material cost and £200 conversion cost, but this is incorrect because the £100 material cost will remain the same whether the order is accepted of rejected. The material cost is therefore irrelevant for the decision, but if the order is accepted the conversion costs will change by £200, and this conversion cost is a relevant cost. If we compare the revenue of £250 with the relevant cost for the order of £200, it means that the order should be accepted, assuming of course that no higher-priced orders can be obtained elsewhere. The following calculation shows that this is the correct decision.

|  | Do not accept order (£) | Accept order (£) |
|---|---|---|
| Materials | 100 | 100 |
| Conversion costs | — | 200 |
| Revenue | — | (250) |
| Net costs | 100 | 50 |

The net costs of the company are £50 less, or alternatively the company is £50 better off as a result of accepting the order. This agrees with the £50 advantage which was suggested by the relevant cost method.

In this illustration the sales revenue was relevant to the decision because future revenue changed depending on which alternative was selected; but sales revenue may also be irrelevant for decision-making. Consider a situation where a company can meet its sales demand by purchasing either machine A or machine B. The output of both machines is identical, but the operating costs and purchase costs of the machines are different. In this situation the sales revenue will remain unchanged irrespective of which machine is purchased (assuming of course that the quality of output is identical for both machines). Consequently, sales revenue is irrelevant for this decision; the relevant items are the operating costs and the cost of the machines. We have now established an important principle regarding the classification of cost and revenues for decision-making; namely, that in the short term not all costs and revenues are relevant for decision-making.

# Avoidable and unavoidable costs

Sometimes the terms **avoidable** and **unavoidable costs** are used instead of relevant and irrelevant cost. Avoidable costs are those costs that may be saved by not adopting a given alternative, whereas unavoidable costs cannot be saved. Therefore, only avoidable costs are relevant for decision-making purposes. Consider the example that we used to illustrate relevant and irrelevant costs. The material costs of £100 are unavoidable and irrelevant, but the conversion costs of £200 are avoidable and hence relevant. The decision rule is to accept those alternatives that generate revenues in excess of the avoidable costs.

# Sunk costs

These costs are the cost of resources already acquired where the total will be unaffected by the choice between various alternatives. They are costs that have been created by a decision made in the past and that cannot be changed by any decision that will be made in the future. The expenditure of £100 on materials that were no longer required, referred to in the preceding section, is an example of a **sunk cost**. Similarly, the written down values of assets previously purchased are sunk costs. For example, if a machine was purchased four years ago for £100 000 with an expected life of five years and nil scrap value then the written down value will be £20 000 if straight line depreciation is used. This written down value will have to be written off, no matter what possible alternative future action might be chosen. If the machine was scrapped, the £20 000 would be written off; if the machine was used for productive purposes, the £20 000 would still have to be written off. This cost cannot be changed by any future decision and is therefore classified as a sunk cost.

Sunk costs are irrelevant for decision-making, but they are distinguished from irrelevant costs because not all irrelevant costs are sunk costs. For example, a comparison of two alternative production methods may result in identical direct material expenditure for both alternatives, so the direct material cost is irrelevant because it will remain the same whichever alternative is chosen, but the material cost is not sunk cost since it will be incurred in the future.

# Opportunity costs

Some costs for decision-making cannot normally be collected within the accounting system. Costs that are collected within the accounting system are based on past payments or commitments to pay at some time in the future. Sometimes it is necessary for decision-making to impute costs that will not require cash outlays, and these imputed costs are called opportunity costs. An **opportunity cost** is a cost that measures the opportunity that is lost or sacrificed when the choice of one course of action requires that an alternative course of action be given up. Consider the information presented in Example 2.2.

It is important to note that opportunity costs only apply to the use of scarce resources. Where resources are not scarce, no sacrifice exists from using these resources. In Example 2.2 if machine X was operating at 80% of its potential capacity then the decision to accept the contract would not have resulted in reduced production of product A. Consequently, there would have been no loss of revenue, and the opportunity cost would be zero.

You should now be aware that opportunity costs are of vital importance for decision-making. If no alternative use of resources exist then the opportunity cost is zero, but if resources have an alternative use, and are scarce, then an opportunity cost does exist.

---

**EXAMPLE 2.2**

A company has an opportunity to obtain a contract for the production of a special component. This component will require 100 hours of processing on machine X. Machine X is working at full capacity on the production of product A, and the only way in which the contract can be fulfilled is by reducing the output of product A. This will mean a loss of revenue of £200. The contract will also result in *additional* variable costs of £1000.

If the company takes on the contract, it will sacrifice revenue of £200 from the lost output of product A. This represents an opportunity cost, and should be included as part of the cost when negotiating for the contract. The contract price should at least cover the additional costs of £1000 plus the £200 opportunity cost to ensure that the company will be better off in the short term by accepting the contract.

---

# Incremental and marginal costs

**Incremental** (also called **differential**) **costs** and revenues are the difference between costs and revenues for the corresponding items under each alternative being considered. For example, the incremental costs of increasing output from 1000 to 1100 units per week are the additional costs of producing an extra 100 units per week. Incremental costs may or may not include fixed costs. If fixed costs change as a result of a decision, the increase in costs represents an incremental cost. If fixed costs do not change as a result of a decision, the incremental costs will be zero.

Incremental costs and revenues are similar in principle to the economist's concept of **marginal cost** and **marginal revenue**. The main difference is that marginal cost/revenue represents the additional cost/revenue of one extra unit of output whereas incremental cost/revenue represents the additional cost/revenue resulting from a group of additional units of output. The economist normally represents the theoretical relationship between cost/revenue and output in terms of the marginal cost/revenue of single additional units of output. We shall see that the accountant is normally more interested in the incremental cost/revenue of increasing production and sales to whatever extent is contemplated, and this is most unlikely to be a single unit of output.

# Job costing and process costing systems

There are two basic types of systems that companies can adopt – job costing and process costing systems. **Job costing** relates to a costing system that is required in organizations where each unit or batch of output of a product or service is unique. This creates the need for the cost of each unit to be calculated separately. The term 'job' thus relates to each unique unit or batch of output. Job costing systems are used in industries that provide customized products or services. For example, accounting firms provide customized services to clients with each client requiring services that consume different quantities of resources. Engineering companies often make machines to meet individual customer specifications. The contracts undertaken by construction and civil engineering companies differ greatly for each customer. In all of these organizations costs must be traced to each individual customer's order.

In contrast, **process costing** relates to those situations where masses of identical units are produced and it is unnecessary to assign costs to individual units of output. Products are produced in the same manner and consume the same amount of direct costs and overheads. It is therefore unnecessary to assign costs to individual units of output. Instead, the average cost per unit of output is calculated by dividing the total costs assigned to a product or service for a period by the number of units of output for that period. Industries where process costing is widely used include chemical processing, oil refining, food processing and brewing.

In practice these two costing systems represent extreme ends of a continuum. The output of many organizations requires a combination of the elements of both job costing and process costing.

# Maintaining a cost database

In the previous chapter we noted that a cost and management accounting system should generate information to meet the following requirements:

1. to allocate costs between cost of goods sold and inventories for internal and external profit measurement and inventory valuation;
2. to provide relevant information to help managers make better decisions;
3. to provide information for planning, control and performance measurement.

A database should be maintained, with costs appropriately coded and classified, so that relevant cost information can be extracted to meet each of the above requirements.

A suitable coding system enables costs to be accumulated by the required cost objects (such as products or services, departments, responsibility centres, distribution channels, etc.) and also to be classified by appropriate categories. Typical cost classifications, within the database are by categories of expense (direct materials, direct labour and overheads) and by cost behaviour (fixed and variable). In practice, direct materials will be accumulated by each individual type of material, direct labour by different grades of labour and overhead costs by different categories of indirect expenses (e.g. rent, depreciation, supervision, etc.).

For *inventory valuation* the costs of all partly completed products (work in progress) and unsold finished products can be extracted from the database to ascertain the total cost assigned to inventories. The cost of goods sold that is deducted from sales revenues to compute the profit for the period can also be extracted by summing the manufacturing costs of all those products that have been sold during the period.

The allocation of costs to products is inappropriate for *cost control and performance measurement*, as the manufacture of the product may consist of several different operations, all of which are the responsibility of different individuals. To overcome this problem, costs and revenues must be traced to the individuals who are responsible for incurring them. This system is known as responsibility accounting.

Responsibility accounting is based on the recognition of individual areas of responsibility as specified in a firm's organization structure. These areas of responsibility are known as 'responsibility centres'; a responsibility centre may be defined as an organization unit for whose performance a manager is held responsible.

For *cost control and performance measurement* the accountant produces performance reports at regular intervals for each responsibility centre. The reports are generated by extracting from the database costs analysed by responsibility centres and categories of expenses. Actual costs for each item of expense listed on the performance report should be compared with budgeted costs so that those costs that do not conform to plan can be pinpointed and investigated.

Future costs, rather than past costs, are required for *decision-making*. Therefore costs extracted from the database should be adjusted for anticipated price changes. We have noted that classification of costs by cost behaviour is important for evaluating the financial impact of expansion or contraction decisions. Costs, however, are not classified as relevant or irrelevant within the database because relevance depends on the circumstances. Consider a situation where a company is negotiating a contract for the sale of one of its products with a customer in an overseas country which is not part of its normal market. If the company has temporary excess capacity and the contract is for 100 units for one month only, then the direct labour cost will remain the same irrespective of whether or not the contract is undertaken. The direct labour cost will therefore be irrelevant. Let us now assume that the contract is for 100 units per month for three years and the company has excess capacity. For long-term decisions direct labour will be a relevant cost because if the contract is not undertaken direct labour can be redeployed or made redundant. Undertaking the contract will result in additional direct labour costs.

The above example shows that the classification of costs as relevant or irrelevant depends on the circumstances. In one situation a cost may be relevant, but in another the same cost may not be relevant. Costs can only be classified as relevant or irrelevant when the circumstances have been identified relating to a particular decision.

Where a company sells many products or services their profitability should be monitored at regular intervals so that potentially unprofitable products can be highlighted for a more detailed study of their future viability. This information is extracted from the database with costs reported by categories of expenses and divided into their fixed and variable elements. In Chapter 9 we shall focus in more detail on product/segmented profitability analysis. Finally, you should note that when the activities of an organization consist of a series of common or repetitive operations, targets or standard product costs, rather than actual costs, may be recorded in the database. Standard costs are predetermined costs; they are target costs that should be incurred under efficient operating conditions. They should be reviewed and updated at periodic intervals. If product standard costs are recorded in the database there is no need continuously to trace costs to products and therefore a considerable amount of data processing time can be saved. Actual costs, however, will still be traced to responsibility centres for cost control and performance evaluation.

## Self-Assessment Questions

You should attempt to answer the question yourself before looking up the suggested answers, which appear on page 1093. If any part of your answer is incorrect, check back carefully to make sure you understand where you went wrong.

1. Classify each of the following as being usually fixed (F), variable (V), semi-fixed (SF) or semi-variable (SV):
   - (a) direct labour;
   - (b) depreciation on machinery;
   - (c) factory rental;
   - (d) supplies and other indirect materials;
   - (e) advertising;
   - (f) maintenance of machinery;
   - (g) factory manager's salary;
   - (h) supervisory personnel;
   - (i) royalty payments.

2. Which of the following costs are likely to be controllable by the head of the production department?
   - (a) price paid for materials;
   - (b) charge for floor space;
   - (c) raw materials used;
   - (d) electricity used for machinery;
   - (e) machinery depreciation;
   - (f) direct labour;
   - (g) insurance on machinery;
   - (h) share of cost of industrial relations department.

## Summary

The term cost has multiple meanings and different types of costs are used in different situations. Therefore a preceding term must be added to clarify the assumptions that underlie a cost measurement. A large terminology has emerged to indicate more clearly which cost meaning is being conveyed. This chapter has described the following basic cost terms that are used in the management accounting literature:

1. direct and indirect costs;
2. period and product costs;
3. cost behavior in relation to volume of activity;
4. relevant and irrelevant costs;
5. avoidable and unavoidable costs;
6. sunk costs;
7. opportunity costs;
8. incremental and marginal costs.

A cost and management accounting system should generate information to meet the following requirements:

1. to allocate costs between cost of goods sold and inventories for internal and external reporting;
2. to provide relevant information to help managers make better decisions;
3. to provide information for planning, control and performance measurement.

A database should be maintained with costs appropriately coded or classified, so that relevant cost information can be extracted to meet each of the above requirements.

## Key Terms and Concepts

avoidable cost (p. 30)
cost allocations (p. 23)
cost objects (p. 21)
differential cost (p. 31)
direct cost (p. 22)
direct labour (p. 23)
direct materials (p. 23)
fixed cost (p. 26)
incremental cost (p. 31)
indirect cost (p. 22)
indirect labour (p. 23)
indirect materials (p. 23)
irrelevant cost (p. 29)
job costing (p. 32)
long-term variable costs (p. 29)
manufacturing overhead (p. 23)

marginal cost/revenue (p. 31)
opportunity cost (p. 31)
period costs (p. 24)
prime cost (p. 23)
process costing (p. 32)
product costs (p. 24)
relevant cost (p. 29)
responsibility accounting (p. 33)
responsibility centre (p. 33)
semi-fixed costs (p. 28)
semi-variable costs (p. 29)
step fixed costs (p. 28)
sunk cost (p. 30)
unavoidable cost (p. 30)
variable cost (p. 26)

## Recommended Reading

This chapter has explained the meaning of the important terms that you will encounter when reading this book. For a more comprehensive description and detailed explanations of various cost terms you should refer to the Chartered Institute of Management Accountants' Official Terminology.

## Key Examination Points

First-year management accounting courses frequently require you to describe various cost terms or to explain that different costs are required for different purposes. It is therefore important that you understand all the cost terms that have been described in this chapter. In particular, you should be able to explain the context within which a cost term is normally used. For example, a cost such as wages paid to casual labourers will be classified as indirect for inventory valuation purposes but as a direct charge to a responsibility centre for cost control purposes. A common error is for students to produce a very short answer, but you must be prepared to expand your answer and to include the various situations within which the use of a cost term is appropriate. Always make sure that your answer includes illustrations of the cost terms.

## Questions

*Indicates that a suggested solution is to be found in the *Students' Manual*.

### 2.1* Intermediate

If actual output is lower than budgeted output, which of the following costs would you expect to be lower than the original budget?

A   Total variable costs
B   Total fixed costs
C   Variable costs per unit
D   Fixed costs per unit

*ACCA Foundation Paper 3*

### 2.2* Intermediate

The following data relate to two output levels of a department:

| | | |
|---|---|---|
| Machine hours | 17 000 | 18 500 |
| Overheads | £246 500 | £251 750 |

The variable overhead rate per hour is £3.50. The amount of fixed overheads is:

A   £5250
B   £59 500
C   £187 000
D   £246 500

*CIMA Stage 1*

## 2.3* Intermediate

Prime cost is:

A    all costs incurred in manufacturing a product;
B    the total of direct costs;
C    the material cost of a product;
D    the cost of operating a department.

*CIMA Stage 1*

## 2.4* Intermediate

A direct cost is a cost which:

A    is incurred as a direct consequence of a decision;
B    can be economically identified with the item being costed;
C    cannot be economically identified with the item being costed;
D    is immediately controllable;
E    is the responsibility of the board of directors

*CIMA Stage 2*

## 2.5* Intermediate

Which of the following would be classed as indirect labour?

A    assembly workers in a company manufacturing televisions;
B    a stores assistant in a factory store;
C    plasterers in a construction company;
D    an audit clerk in a firm of auditors.

*CIMA Stage 1 Cost Accounting*

## 2.6* Intermediate

Fixed costs are conventionally deemed to be:

A    constant per unit of output;
B    constant in total when production volume changes;
C    outside the control of management;
D    those unaffected by inflation.

*CIMA Stage 1 Cost Accounting*

## 2.7* Intermediate

Prepare a report for the Managing Director of your company explaining how costs may be classified by their behaviour, with particular reference to the effects both on total and on unit costs. Your report should

(i)    say why it is necessary to classify costs by their behaviour, and
(ii)   be illustrated by sketch graphs within the body of the report.          (15 marks)

*CIMA Stage 1 Accounting*

## 2.8* Intermediate

Describe three different methods of cost classification and explain the utility of each method.

(11 marks)

*ACCA Level 1 Costing*

## 2.9* Intermediate

Cost classifications used in costing include:

(i)    period costs
(ii)   product costs
(iii)  variable costs
(iv)   opportunity costs

Required:
Explain each of these classifications, with examples of the types of costs that may be included.

(17 marks)

*ACCA Level 1 Costing*

## 2.10* Intermediate

(a)    Describe the role of the cost accountant in a manufacturing organization.

(8 marks)

(b)    Explain whether you agree with each of the following statements:

(i)    'All direct costs are variable.'
(ii)   'Variable costs are controllable and fixed costs are not.'
(iii)  'Sunk costs are irrelevant when providing decision making information.'

(9 marks)
(Total 17 marks)

*ACCA Level 1 Costing*

## 2.11* Intermediate

'Cost may be classified in a variety of ways according to their nature and the information needs of management.' Explain and discuss this statement, illustrating with examples of the classifications required for different purposes.

(22 marks)

*ICSA Management Accounting*

## 2.12* Intermediate

It is commonly suggested that a management accounting system should be capable of supplying different measures of cost for different purposes. You are required to set out the main types of purpose for which cost information may be required in a business organization, and to discuss the alternative measures of cost which might be appropriate for each purpose.

*ICAEW Management Accounting*

## 2.13* Intermediate

*Opportunity cost* and *sunk cost* are among the concepts of cost commonly discussed.

You are required:
(i)   to define these terms precisely;
(4 marks)
(ii)  to suggest for each of them situations in which the concept might be applied;
(4 marks)
(iii) to assess briefly the significance of each of the concepts.
(4 marks)
*ICAEW P2 Management Accounting*

## 2.14* Intermediate

Distinguish between, and provide an illustration of:
(i)  'avoidable' and 'unavoidable' costs;
(ii) 'cost centres' and 'cost units'.
(8 marks)
*ACCA Foundation Paper 3*

## 2.15* Advanced

'The diverse uses of routinely recorded cost data give rise to a fundamental danger: information prepared for one purpose can be grossly misleading in another context' (from *Management Accounting: A Conceptual Approach*, by L.R. Amey and D.A. Egginton).

Required:
Discuss to what extent the above statement is valid and explain your conclusions.
(12 marks)
*ACCA P2 Management Accounting*

## 2.16* Advanced

(i)  Costs may be classified in a number of ways including classification by behaviour, by function, by expense type, by controllability and by relevance.
(ii) Management accounting should assist in EACH of the planning, control and decision making processes in an organisation.
Discuss the ways in which relationships between statements (i) and (ii) are relevant in the design of an effective management accounting system.
(15 marks)
*ACCA Paper 9 Information for Control and Decision Making*

## 2.17 Intermediate: Cost classification

For the relevant cost data in items (1)–(7), indicate which of the following is the best classification.

(a) sunk cost                  (f) semi-fixed cost
(b) incremental cost           (g) controllable cost
(c) variable cost              (h) non-controllable cost
(d) fixed cost                 (i) opportunity cost
(e) semi-variable cost

(1) A company is considering selling an old machine. The machine has a book value of £20 000. In evaluating the decision to sell the machine, the £20 000 is a ...
(2) As an alternative to the old machine, the company can rent a new one. It will cost £3000 a year. In analysing the cost–volume behaviour the rental is a ...
(3) To run the firm's machines, here are two alternative courses of action. One is to pay the operator a base salary plus a small amount per unit produced. This makes the total cost of the operators a ...
(4) As an alternative, the firm can pay the operators a flat salary. It would then use one machine when volume is low, two when it expands, and three during peak periods. This means that the total operator cost would now be a ...
(5) The machine mentioned in (1) could be sold for £8000. If the firm considers retaining and using it, the £8000 is a ...
(6) If the firm wishes to use the machine any longer, it must be repaired. For the decision to retain the machine, the repair cost is a ...
(7) The machine is charged to the foreman of each department at a rate of £3000 a year. In evaluating the foreman, the charge is a ...

## 2.18 Intermediate: Cost classification

A company manufactures and retails clothing. You are required to group the costs which are listed below and numbered (1)–(20) into the following classifications (each cost is intended to belong to only one classification):
(i)    direct materials
(ii)   direct labour
(iii)  direct expenses
(iv)   indirect production overhead
(v)    research and development costs
(vi)   selling and distribution costs
(vii)  administration costs
(viii) finance costs
(1) Lubricant for sewing machines
(2) Floppy disks for general office computer
(3) Maintenance contract for general office photocopying machine

(4) Telephone rental plus metered calls
(5) Interest on bank overdraft
(6) Performing Rights Society charge for music broadcast throughout the factory
(7) Market research undertaken prior to a new product launch
(8) Wages of security guards for factory
(9) Carriage on purchase of basic raw material
(10) Royalty payable on number of units of product XY produced
(11) Road fund licences for delivery vehicles
(12) Parcels sent to customers
(13) Cost of advertising products on television
(14) Audit fees
(15) Chief accountant's salary
(16) Wages of operatives in the cutting department
(17) Cost of painting advertising slogans on delivery vans
(18) Wages of storekeepers in materials store
(19) Wages of fork lift truck drivers who handle raw materials
(20) Developing a new product in the laboratory
(10 marks)
*CIMA Cost Accounting 1*

### 2.19* Intermediate

(a) 'Discretionary costs are troublesome because managers usually find it difficult to separate and quantify the results of their use in the business, as compared with variable and other fixed costs.'
You are required to discuss the above statement and include in your answer the meaning of discretionary costs, variable costs and fixed costs; give two illustrations of each of these three named costs.
(12 marks)
(b) A drug company has initiated a research project which is intended to develop a new product. Expenditures to date on this particular research total £500 000 but it is now estimated that a further £200 000 will need to be spent before the product can be marketed. Over the estimated life of the product the profit potential has a net present value of £350 000.
You are required to advise management whether they should continue or abandon the project. Support your conclusion with a numerate statement and state what kind of cost is the £500 000.
(5 marks)

(c) Opportunity costs and notional costs are not recognized by financial accounting systems but need to be considered in many decisions taken by management.
You are required to explain briefly the meanings of opportunity costs and notional costs; give two examples of each to illustrate the meanings you have attached to them.
(8 marks)
(Total 25 marks)
*CIMA Stage 2 Cost Accounting*

### 2.20* Intermediate: Cost behaviour

**Data** | **(£)**
---|---
Cost of motor car | 5500
Trade-in price after 2 years or 60 000 miles is expected to be | 1500
Maintenance – 6-monthly service costing | 60
Spares/replacement parts, per 1000 miles | 20
Vehicle licence, per annum | 80
Insurance, per annum | 150
Tyre replacements after 25 000 miles, four at £37.50 each |
Petrol, per gallon | 1.90
Average mileage from one gallon is 25 miles. |

(a) From the above data you are required:
(i) to prepare a schedule to be presented to management showing for the mileages of 5000, 10 000, 15 000 and 30 000 miles per annum:
(1) total variable cost
(2) total fixed cost
(3) total cost
(4) variable cost per mile (in pence to nearest penny)
(5) fixed cost per mile (in pence to nearest penny)
(6) total cost per mile (in pence to nearest penny)
If, in classifying the costs, you consider that some can be treated as either variable or fixed, state the assumption(s) on which your answer is based together with brief supporting reason(s).
(ii) on graph paper plot the information given in your answer to (i) above for

the costs listed against (1), (2), (3) and (6).

(iii) to read off from your graph(s) in (ii) and state the approximate total costs applicable to 18 000 miles and 25 000 miles and the total cost per mile at these two mileages.

(b) 'The more miles you travel, the cheaper it becomes.' Comment briefly on this statement.

(25 marks)
*CIMA Cost Accounting 1*

### 2.21 Intermediate: Analysis of costs by behaviour for decision-making

The Northshire Hospital Trust operates two types of specialist X-ray scanning machines, XR1 and XR50. Details for the next period are estimated as follows:

| Machine | XR1 | XR50 |
|---|---|---|
| Running hours | 1 100 | 2 000 |
| | (£) | (£) |
| Variable running costs (excluding plates) | 27 500 | 64 000 |
| Fixed costs | 20 000 | 97 500 |

A brain scan is normally carried out on machine type XR1: this task uses special X-ray plates costing £40 each and takes four hours of machine time. Because of the nature of the process, around 10% of the scans produce blurred and therefore useless results.

Required:

(a) Calculate the cost of a satisfactory brain scan on machine type XR1. (7 marks)

(b) Brain scans can also be done on machine type XR50 and would take only 1.8 hours per scan with a reduced reject rate of 6%. However, the cost of the X-ray plates would be £55 per scan.

Required:
Advise which type should be used, assuming sufficient capacity is available on both types of machine. (8 marks)

(Total marks 15)
*CIMA Stage 1 Cost Accounting*

### 2.22 Intermediate: Product cost calculation

From the information given below you are required to:

(a) prepare a standard cost sheet for one unit and enter on the standard cost sheet the costs to show sub-totals for:
   (i) prime cost
   (ii) variable production cost
   (iii) total production cost
   (iv) total cost

(b) calculate the selling price per unit allowing for a profit of 15% of the selling price.

The following data are given:

Budgeted output for the year    9800 units
Standard details for one unit:
Direct materials 40 square
   metres at £5.30 per square
   metre
Direct wages:
   Bonding department
      48 hours at £2.50 per
      hour
   Finishing department
      30 hours at £1.90 per
      hour
Budgeted costs and hours per annum:

| | (£) | (hours) |
|---|---|---|
| Variable overhead: | | |
| Bonding department | 375 000 | 500 000 |
| Finishing department | 150 000 | 300 000 |
| Fixed overhead: | | |
| Production | 392 000 | |
| Selling and distribution | 196 000 | |
| Administration | 98 000 | |

(15 marks)
*CIMA Cost Accounting 1*

### 2.23* Intermediate: Sunk and opportunity costs for decision-making

Mrs Johnston has taken out a lease on a shop for a down payment of £5000. Additionally, the rent under the lease amounts to £5000 per annum. If the lease is cancelled, the initial payment of £5000 is forfeit. Mrs Johnston plans to use the shop for the sale of clothing, and has estimated operations for the next twelve months as follows:

| | (£) | (£) |
|---|---|---|
| Sales | 115 000 | |
| *Less* Value-added tax (VAT) | 15 000 | |
| Sales Less VAT | | 100 000 |
| Cost of goods sold | 50 000 | |
| Wages and wage related costs | 12 000 | |
| Rent including the down payment | 10 000 | |
| Rates, heating, lighting and insurance | 13 000 | |
| Audit, legal and general expenses | 2 000 | |
| | | 87 000 |
| Net profit before tax | | 13 000 |

In the figures no provision has been made for the cost of Mrs Johnston but it is estimated that one half of her time will be devoted to the business. She is undecided whether to continue with her plans, because she knows that she can sublet the shop to a friend for a monthly rent of £550 if she does not use the shop herself.

You are required to:
(a) (i) explain and identify the 'sunk' and 'opportunity' costs in the situation depicted above;
    (ii) state what decision Mrs Johnston should make according to the information given, supporting your conclusion with a financial statement;

(11 marks)
(b) explain the meaning and use of 'notional' (or 'imputed') costs and quote *two* supporting examples.

(4 marks)
(Total 15 marks)
*CIMA Foundation Cost Accounting 1*

## 2.24* Intermediate: Relevant costs and cost behaviour
(a) Distinguish between 'opportunity cost' and 'out of pocket cost' giving a numerical example of each using your own figures to support your answer.

(6 marks)
(b) Jason travels to work by train to his 5-day week job. Instead of buying daily tickets he finds it cheaper to buy a quarterly season ticket which costs £188 for 13 weeks.
Debbie, an acquaintance, who also makes the same journey, suggests that they both travel in Jason's car and offers to give him £120 each quarter towards his car expenses. Except for weekend travelling and using it for local college attendance near his home on three evenings each week to study for his CIMA Stage 2, the car remains in Jason's garage.

Jason estimates that using his car for work would involve him, each quarter, in the following expenses:

| | (£) |
|---|---|
| Depreciation (proportion of annual figure) | 200 |
| Petrol and oil | 128 |
| Tyres and miscellaneous | 52 |

You are required to state whether Jason should accept Debbie's offer and to draft a statement to show clearly the monetary effect of your conclusion.

(5 marks)
(c) A company with a financial year 1 September to 31 August prepared a sales budget which resulted in the following cost structure:

| | | % of sales |
|---|---|---|
| Direct materials | | 32 |
| Direct wages | | 18 |
| Production overhead: | variable | 6 |
| | fixed | 24 |
| Administrative and selling costs: | variable | 3 |
| | fixed | 7 |
| Profit | | 10 |

After ten weeks, however, it became obvious that the sales budget was too optimistic and it has now been estimated that because of a reduction in sales volume, for the full year, sales will total £2 560 000 which is only 80% of the previously budgeted figure.

You are required to present a statement for management showing the amended sales and cost structure in £s and percentages, in a marginal costing format.

(4 marks)
(Total 15 marks)
*CIMA Stage 2 Cost Accounting*

# Cost Accumulation for Inventory Valuation and Profit Measurement

This section focuses mainly on assigning costs to products to separate costs incurred during a period between costs of goods sold and the closing inventory valuation. The extent to which product costs accumulated for inventory valuation and profit measurement should be adjusted for meeting decison-making, cost control and performance measurement requirements is also briefly considered.

Chapter 3 aims to provide you with an understanding of how costs are assigned to cost objects. In particular the chapter focuses on the assignment of indirect costs using traditional and activity-based systems. In Chapter 4 the emphasis is on the accounting entries necessary to record transactions within a job costing system. The issues relating to a cost accumulation procedure for a process costing system are described in Chapter 5. This is a system that is applicable to industries that produce many units of the same product during a particular period. In Chapter 6 the problems associated with calculating product costs in those industries that produce joint and by-products are discussed. The final chapter in this section is concerned with the alternative accounting methods of assigning fixed manufacturing overheads to products and their implications for profit measurement and inventory valuation.

# Cost assignment

In the previous chapter it was pointed out that companies need cost and management accounting systems to perform a number of different functions. In this chapter we are going to concentrate on two of these functions – they are (i) allocating costs between cost of goods sold and inventories for internal and external profit reporting and (ii) providing relevant decision-making information for distinguishing between profitable and unprofitable activities.

In order to perform the above functions a cost accumulation system is required that assigns costs to cost objects. The aim of this chapter is to provide you with an understanding of how costs are assigned to cost objects. You should have remembered from the previous chapter that a cost object is anything for which a separate measurement of cost is desired. Typical cost objects include products, services, customers and locations. In this chapter we shall either use the term cost object as a generic term or assume that products are the cost object. However, the same cost assignment principles can be applied to all cost objects.

We begin by explaining how the cost assignment process differs for direct and indirect costs.

## Learning objectives

After studying this chapter, you should be able to:

- distinguish between cause-and-effect and arbitrary cost allocations;
- explain why different cost information is required for different purposes;
- describe how cost systems differ in terms of their level of sophistication;
- understand the factors influencing the choice of optimal cost system;
- explain why departmental overhead rates should be used in preference to a single blanket overhead rate;
- construct an overhead analysis sheet and calculate cost centre allocation rates;
- distinguish between traditional and activity-based costing systems;
- justify why budgeted overhead rates should be used in preference to actual overhead rates;
- calculate and explain the accounting treatment of the under/over recovery of overheads;

- record inter-service department transfers using one of the methods described in Appendix 3.1.

# Assignment of direct and indirect costs

Costs that are assigned to cost objects can be divided into two categories – direct costs and indirect costs. Sometimes the term overheads is used instead of indirect costs. Direct costs can be accurately traced to cost objects because they can be specifically and exclusively traced to a particular cost object whereas indirect costs cannot. Where a cost can be directly assigned to a cost object the term cost tracing is used. In contrast, indirect costs cannot be traced directly to a cost object because they are usually common to several cost objects. Indirect costs are therefore assigned to cost objects using cost allocations.

A cost allocation is the process of assigning costs when a direct measure does not exist for the quantity of resources consumed by a particular cost object. Cost allocations involve the use of surrogate rather than direct measures. For example, consider an activity such as receiving incoming materials. Assuming that the cost of receiving materials is strongly influenced by the number of receipts then costs can be allocated to products (i.e. the cost object) based on the number of material receipts. The basis that is used to allocate costs to cost objects (i.e. the number of material receipts in our example) is called an allocation base or cost driver. If 20% of the total number of receipts for a period were required for a particular product then 20% of the total costs of receiving incoming materials would be allocated to that product. Assuming that the product was discontinued, and not replaced, we would expect action to be taken to reduce the resources required for receiving materials by 20%.

In the above illustration the allocation base is assumed to be a significant determinant of the cost of receiving incoming materials. Where allocation bases are significant determinants of the costs we shall describe them as cause-and-effect allocations. Where a cost allocation base is used that is not a significant determinant of its cost the term arbitrary allocation will be used. An example of an arbitrary allocation would be if direct labour hours were used as the allocation base to allocate the costs of materials receiving. If a labour intensive product required a large proportion of direct labour hours (say 30%) but few material receipts it would be allocated with a large proportion of the costs of material receiving. The allocation would be an inaccurate assignment of the resources consumed by the product. Furthermore, if the product were discontinued, and not replaced, the cost of the material receiving activity would not decline by 30% because the allocation base is not a significant determinant of the costs of the materials receiving activity. Arbitrary allocations are therefore likely to result in inaccurate allocations of indirect costs to cost objects.

Figure 3.1 provides a summary of the assignment process. You can see that direct costs are assigned to cost objects using cost tracing whereas indirect cost are assigned using cost allocations. For accurate assignment of indirect costs to cost objects cause-and-effect allocations should be used. Two types of systems can be used to assign indirect costs to cost objects. They are traditional costing systems and activity-based-costing (ABC) systems. Traditional costing systems were developed in the early 1900s and are still widely used today. They rely extensively on arbitrary cost allocations. ABC systems only emerged in the late 1980s. One of the major aims of ABC systems is to use only cause-and-effect cost allocations. Both cost systems adopt identical approaches to assigning direct costs to

**FIGURE 3.1**  *Cost allocations and cost tracing.*

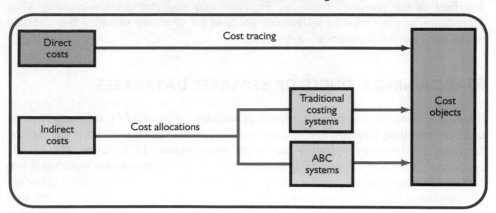

cost objects. We shall look at traditional and ABC systems in more detail later in the chapter.

# Different costs for different purposes

Manufacturing organizations assign costs to products for two purposes: first, for internal profit measurement and external financial accounting requirements in order to allocate the manufacturing costs incurred during a period between cost of goods sold and inventories; secondly, to provide useful information for managerial decision-making requirements. In order to meet financial accounting requirements, it may not be necessary to accurately trace costs to *individual* products. Consider a situation where a firm produces 1000 different products and the costs incurred during a period are £10 million. A well-designed product costing system should accurately analyse the £10 million costs incurred between cost of sales and inventories. Let us assume the true figures are £7 million and £3 million. Approximate but inaccurate *individual* product costs may provide a reasonable approximation of how much of the £10 million should be attributed to cost of sales and inventories. Some product costs may be overstated and others may be understated, but this would not matter for financial accounting purposes as long as the *total* of the individual product costs assigned to cost of sales and inventories was approximately £7 million and £3 million.

For decision-making purposes, however, more accurate product costs are required so that we can distinguish between profitable and unprofitable products. By more accurately measuring the resources consumed by products, or other cost objects, a firm can identify its sources of profits and losses. If the cost system does not capture sufficiently accurately the consumption of resources by products, the reported product costs will be distorted, and there is a danger that managers may drop profitable products or continue production of unprofitable products.

Besides different levels of accuracy, different cost information is required for different purposes. For meeting external financial accounting requirements, financial accounting regulations and legal requirements in most countries require that inventories should be valued at manufacturing cost. Therefore only manufacturing costs are assigned to products for meeting external financial accounting requirements. For decision-making non-manufacturing costs must be taken into account and assigned to products. Not all costs, however may be relevant for decision-making. For example, depreciation of plant and machinery will not be affected by a decision to discontinue a product. Such costs were described in the previous chapter as irrelevant and sunk for decision-making. Thus depreciation of plant must be assigned to products for inventory valuation but it should not be assigned for discontinuation decisions.

## MAINTAINING A SINGLE OR SEPARATE DATABASES

Because different costs and different levels of accuracy are required for different purposes some organizations maintain two separate costing systems, one for decision-making and the other for inventory valuation and profit measurement. In a survey of 187 UK companies Drury and Tayles (2000) reported that 9% of the companies maintained two cost accumulation systems, one for decision-making and the other for inventory valuation. The remaining 91% of organizations maintained a costing system on a single database from which appropriate cost information was extracted to provide the required information for both decision-making and inventory valuation. When a single database is maintained only costs that must be assigned for inventory valuation are extracted for meeting financial accounting requirements, whereas for decision-making only costs which are relevant for the decision are extracted. Inventory valuation is not an issue for many service organizations. They do not carry inventories and therefore a costing system is not required for meeting inventory valuation requirements.

Where a single database is maintained cost assignments cannot be at different levels of accuracy for different purposes. In the late 1980s, according to Johnson and Kaplan (1987), most organizations were relying on costing systems that had been designed primarily for meeting external financial accounting requirements. These systems were designed decades ago when information processing costs were high and precluded the use of more sophisticated methods of assigning indirect costs to products. Such systems are still widely used today. They rely extensively on arbitrary cost allocations which are sufficiently accurate for meeting external financial accounting requirements but not for meeting decision-making requirements. Johnson and Kaplan concluded that management accounting practices have followed and become subservient to meeting financial accounting requirements.

# Cost–benefit issues and cost systems design

These criticisms resulted in the emergence of ABC in the late 1980s. Surveys in many countries suggest that between 20 and 30% of the surveyed organizations have implemented ABC systems. The majority of organizations therefore continue to operate traditional systems. Both traditional and ABC systems vary in their level of sophistication but, as a general rule, traditional systems tend to be simplistic whereas ABC systems tend to be sophisticated. What determines the chosen level of sophistication of a costing system? The answer is that the choice should be made on costs versus benefits criteria. Simplistic systems are inexpensive to operate, but they are likely to result in inaccurate cost assignments and the reporting of inaccurate costs. Managers using cost information extracted from simplistic systems are more likely to make important mistakes arising from using inaccurate cost information. The end result may be a high cost of errors. Conversely, sophisticated systems are more expensive to operate but they minimize the cost of errors. However, the aim should not be to have the most accurate cost system. Improvements should be made in the level of sophistication of the costing system up to the point where the marginal cost of improvement equals the marginal benefit from the improvement.

**FIGURE 3.2** *Cost systems – varying levels of sophistication for cost assignment.*

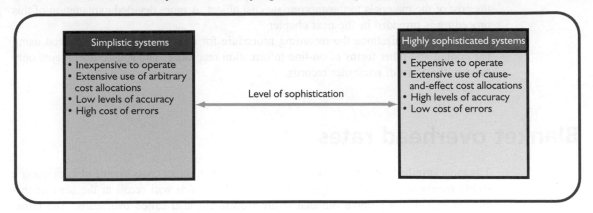

Figure 3.2 illustrates the above points with costing systems ranging from simplistic to sophisticated. Highly simplistic features are located on the extreme left. Common features of such systems are that they are inexpensive to operate, make extensive use of arbitrary allocations of indirect costs and normally result in low levels of accuracy and a high cost of errors. On the extreme right are highly sophisticated systems. These systems use only cause-and-effect allocations, are expensive to operate, have high levels of accuracy and minimize the cost of errors. Cost systems in most organizations are not located at either of these extreme points. Instead, they are located at different points within the range shown in Figure 3.2.

The optimal cost system is different for different organizations. For example, the optimal costing system will be located towards the extreme left for an organization whose indirect costs are a low percentage of total costs and which also has a fairly standardized product range, all consuming organizational resources in similar proportions. In these circumstances simplistic systems may not result in the reporting of inaccurate costs. In contrast, the optimal costing system for organizations with a high proportion of indirect costs, whose products consume organizational resources in different proportions, will be located towards the extreme right. More sophisticated costing systems are required to capture the diversity of consumption of organizational resources and accurately assign the high level of indirect costs to different cost objects.

# Assigning direct costs to objects

Both simplistic and sophisticated systems accurately assign direct costs to cost objects. Cost assignment merely involves the implementation of suitable clerical procedures to identify and record the resources consumed by cost objects. Consider direct labour. The time spent on providing a service to a specific customer, or manufacturing a specific product, is recorded on source documents, such as **time sheets** or **job cards**. Details of the customer's account number, job number or the product's code are also entered on these documents. The employee's hourly rate of pay is then entered so that the direct labour cost for the employee can be assigned to the appropriate cost object.

For direct materials the source document is a **materials requisition**. Details of the materials issued for manufacturing a product, or providing a specific service, are recorded on the materials requisition. The customer's account number, job number or product code is also entered and the items listed on the requisition are priced at their cost of acquisition.

The details on the material requisition thus represent the source information for assigning the cost of the materials to the appropriate cost object. A more detailed explanation of this procedure is provided in the next chapter.

In many organizations the recording procedure for direct costs is computerized using bar coding and other forms of on-line information recording. The source documents only exist in the form of computer records.

# Blanket overhead rates

The most simplistic traditional costing system assigns indirect costs to cost objects using a single overhead rate for the organization as a whole. You will recall at the start of this chapter that it was pointed out that indirect costs are also called overheads. The terms blanket overhead rate or plant-wide rate are used to describe a single overhead rate that is established for the organization as a whole. Let us assume that the total manufacturing overheads for the manufacturing plant of Arcadia are £900 000 and that the company has selected direct labour hours as the allocation base for assigning overheads to products. Assuming that the total number of direct labour hours are 60 000 for the period the blanket overhead rate for Arcadia is £15 per direct labour hour (£900 000/60 000 direct labour hours).

Assume also that Arcadia's factory has three separate production departments. The products made by the company require different operations and some products do not pass through all three departments. The following is an analysis of the £900 000 total manufacturing overheads and 60 000 direct labour hours by departments:

|  | Department A | Department B | Department C | Total |
| --- | --- | --- | --- | --- |
| Overheads | £200 000 | £600 000 | £100 000 | £900 000 |
| Direct labour hours | 20 000 | 20 000 | 20 000 | 60 000 |
| Overhead rate per direct labour hour | £10 | £30 | £5 | £15 |

Consider a situation where product Z requires 20 direct labour hours in department C but does not pass through departments A and B. If a blanket overhead rate is used then overheads of £300 (20 hours at £15 per hour) will be allocated to product Z. On the other hand, if a departmental overhead rate is used, only £100 would be allocated to product Z. Which method should be used? The logical answer must be to establish separate departmental overhead rates, since product Z only consumes overheads in department C. If the blanket overhead rate were applied, all the factory overhead rates would be averaged out and product Z would be indirectly allocated with some of the overheads of department B. This would not be satisfactory, since product Z does not consume any of the resources and this department incurs a large amount of the overhead expenditure.

We can conclude from the above example that a blanket overhead rate will generally result in the reporting of inaccurate product costs. A blanket overhead rate can only be justified when all products consume departmental overheads in approximately the same proportions. In the above illustration each department accounts for one-third of the total direct labour hours. If all products spend approximately one-third of their time in each department, a blanket overhead rate can be used. Consider a situation where product X spends one hour in each department and product Y spends five hours in each department. Overheads of £45 and £225 respectively would be allocated to products X and Y using either blanket rates (3 hours at £15 and 15 hours at £15) or separate departmental overhead rates. If a diverse product range is produced with products spending different proportions of time in each department, separate departmental overhead rates should be established.

However, significant usage of blanket overhead rates have been reported in surveys undertaken in many different countries. For example, the percentage usages vary from 20–30% in UK (Drury and Tayles, 1994), USA (Emore and Ness, 1991), Australian (Joye and Blayney, 1990; 1991) and Indian (Joshi, 1998) surveys. In contrast, in Scandinavia only 5% of the Finnish companies (Lukka and Granlund, 1996), one Norwegian company (Bjornenak, 1997b) and none of the Swedish companies sampled (Ask *et al.*, 1996) used a single plant-wide rate. Zero usage of plant-wide rates was also reported from a survey of Greek companies (Ballas and Venieris, 1996). In a more recent study of UK organizations Drury and Tayles (2000) reported that a blanket rate was used by 3% of surveyed organizations possibly suggesting a move towards more sophisticated costing systems.

# Cost centre overhead rates

In the previous example relating to Arcadia the advantages of using departmental overhead rates rather than a single blanket rate were illustrated. In some situations it is possible to go a stage further and establish separate overhead rates for smaller segments within an organization, such as groups of similar machines within the same department.

Consider our previous example relating to Arcadia. The overhead rate for Department B was £30 per direct labour hour derived from dividing £600 000 overheads assigned to department B by 20 000 direct labour hours. Let us assume that the overheads and direct labour hours for department B can be further analysed by production centres as follows:

|  | Production centre B1 | Production centre B2 | Production centre B3 | Total |
|---|---|---|---|---|
| Overheads | £80 000 | £400 000 | £120 000 | £600 000 |
| Direct labour hours | 2 000 | 8 000 | 10 000 | 20 000 |
| Overhead rate per direct labour hour | £40 | £50 | £12 | £30 |

A single overhead rate for the whole department will result in the inaccurate assignment of overheads when a department consists of a number of different production centres and products passing through the departments consume overheads of each production centre in different proportions. Consider a situation where a product requires 15 direct labour hours in production centre B3 and does not pass through any of the other two production centres within the department. If a departmental rate is used, overheads of £450 (15 direct labour hours at £30 per hour) will be allocated to the product whereas if a separate rate for the production centre is used, only £180 (15 hours at £12 per hour) will be allocated. In this illustration Arcadia should establish separate overhead rates for each production centre within department B. If a single rate for the whole department were applied, all of the overheads within the department would be averaged out and the product would be indirectly allocated with some of the overheads of the remaining production centres. We can therefore conclude that if a department consists of a number of different production centres, each with significant overhead costs, and products consume production centre overheads in different proportions, separate overhead rates should be established for each production centre within the department.

The terms **cost centres** or **cost pools** are used to describe a location to which overhead costs are initially assigned. The total costs accumulated in each cost centre are then assigned to cost objects using a separate allocation base for each cost centre. This process is illustrated in the next section. However, at this point you should note that frequently cost centres will consist of departments but they can also consist of smaller segments within departments.

# The two-stage allocation process

The two-stage allocation process can be used as a framework to summarize the different approaches we have looked at for Arcadia to assign overhead costs to products. The process applies to assigning costs to other cost objects, besides products, and is applicable to all organizations that assign indirect costs to cost objects. The framework applies to both traditional and ABC systems.

The framework is illustrated in Figure 3.3. You can see that in the first stage overheads are assigned to cost centres. In the second stage the costs accumulated in the cost centres are allocated to cost objects using selected allocation bases (you should remember from our discussion earlier that allocation bases are also called cost drivers). Traditional costing systems tend to use a small number of second stage allocation bases, typically direct labour hours or machine hours. In other words, traditional systems assume that direct labour or machine hours have a significant influence in the long term on the level of overhead expenditure. Other allocation bases used to a lesser extent by traditional systems are direct labour cost, direct materials cost and units of output. These methods are described and illustrated in Appendix 3.2 at the end of this chapter. Exhibit 3.1 (Section C) shows details of the extent to which different second stage allocation bases are used in different countries. You will see that direct labour and machine hours are the dominant methods.

Within the two-stage allocation process ABC systems differ from traditional systems by having a greater number of cost centres in the first stage and a greater number, and variety, of cost drivers or allocation bases in the second stage. Both systems will be described in more detail later in the chapter.

You will have noted from our discussion in the previous sections relating to Arcadia that increasing the number of cost centres resulted in a more accurate assignment of overheads to products. We started with a blanket overhead rate and omitted the first stage of the two-stage allocation process and noted that this process resulted in an inaccurate assignment of costs. Next we adopted the two-stage allocation process by establishing separate cost centre overhead rates (based on departments). This change resulted in a more accurate assignment of overheads to products. Finally, we noted that further improvements in the accuracy of cost assignments could be obtained by increasing the number of cost centres by establishing separate cost centres within a department.

How many cost centres should a firm establish? If only a small number of cost centres are established it is likely that activities within a cost centre will not be homogeneous and, if the consumption of the activities by products/services within the cost centres varies, activity resource consumption will not be accurately measured. Therefore, in most situations, increasing the number of cost centres increases the accuracy of measuring the indirect costs consumed by cost objects. The choice of the number of cost centres should be based on cost–benefit criteria using the principles described on pages 48–9. Exhibit 3.1 (Section A) shows the number of cost centres and second stage cost allocation bases reported by Drury *et al.* in a survey of 187 UK organizations. It can be seen that 35% of the organizations used less than 11 cost centres whereas 23% used more than 30 cost centres. In terms of the number of different second stage cost drivers/allocation bases 69% of the responding organizations used less than four.

**FIGURE 3.3** *An illustration of the two-stage allocation process for traditional and activity-based costing systems.*

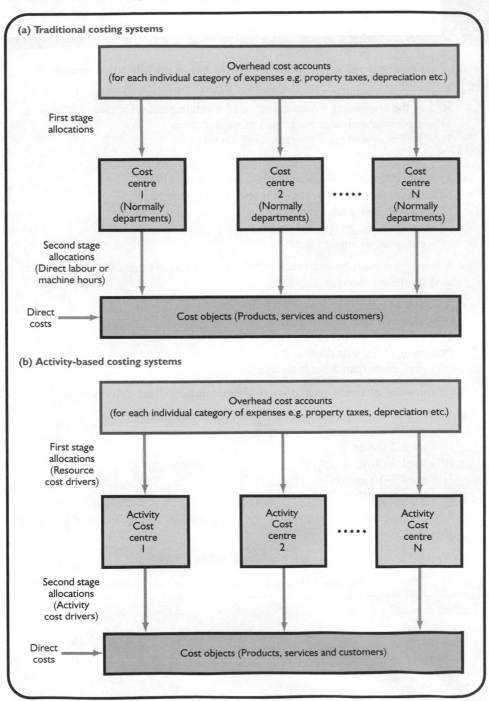

**EXHIBIT 3.1**

*Surveys of practice*

**(a) Cost centres used in the first stage of the two-stage allocation process**

- A survey of Australian organizations by Joye and Blayney (1990):
  36% of the responding organizations used a single plant-wide rate
  24% used overhead rates for groups of work centres
  31% used overhead rates for each work centre
  9% used overhead rates for each machine

- A survey of Swedish organizations by Ask and Ax (1992)[a]:
  70% indicated that cost centres consisted of departments
  32% consisted of work cells
  22% consisted of groups of machines
  15% consisted of single machines

- A Norwegian study by Bjornenak (1997b) reported an average of 38.3 cost centres used by the respondents

- A survey of UK organizations by Drury and Tayles (2000):
  14% used less than 6 cost centres
  21% used 6–10 cost centres
  29% used 11–20 cost centres
  36% used more than 20 cost centres

**(b) Number of different second stage allocation bases/cost drivers used**

- A survey of UK organizations by Drury and Tayles (2000):
  34% used 1 cost driver
  25% used 2 drivers
  10% used 3 drivers
  21% used 3–10 drivers
  10% used more than 10 drivers

- A Norwegian study by Bjornenak (1997a) reported an average usage of 1.79 cost drivers

**(c) Second stage cost allocation bases/cost drivers used[a]**

| | Norway[b] | Holland[c] | Ireland[d] | Australia[e] | Japan[e] | UK[f] | UK[f] |
|---|---|---|---|---|---|---|---|
| Direct labour hours/cost | 65% | 20% | 52% | 57% | 57% | 68% | 73% |
| Machine hours | 29 | 9 | 19 | 19 | 12 | 49 | 26 |
| Direct materials costs | 26 | 6 | 10 | 12 | 11 | 30 | 19 |
| Units of output | 40 | 30 | 28 | 20 | 16 | 42 | 31 |
| Prime cost | | | | 1 | 21 | | |
| Other | 23 | 35 | 9 | | | | |
| ABC cost drivers | | | | | | 9 | 7 |

A survey of Finnish companies by Lukka and Granlund (1996) reported that direct labour costs, direct labour hours, machine hours, materials use and production quantity were the most widely used allocation bases. Usage rates were not reported.

*Notes*

[a] The reported percentages exceed 100% because many companies used more than one type of cost centre or allocation base.

[b] Bjornenak (1997b).

[c] Boons *et al*. (1994).

[d] Clarke (1995).

[e] Blayney and Yokoyama (1991).

[f] Drury *et al*. (1993) – The first column relates to the responses for automated and the second to non-automated production centres.

# An illustration of the two-stage process for a traditional costing system

We shall now use Example 3.1 to provide a more detailed illustration of the two-stage allocation process for a traditional costing system. To keep the illustration manageable it is assumed that the company has only five cost centres – machine departments X and Y, an assembly department, materials handling and general factory support cost centres. The illustration focuses on manufacturing costs but we shall look at non-manufacturing costs later in the chapter. Applying the two-stage allocation process requires the following four steps:

1. assigning all manufacturing overheads to production and service cost centres;
2. reallocating the costs assigned to service cost centres to production cost centres;
3. computing separate overhead rates for each production cost centre;
4. assigning cost centre overheads to products or other chosen cost objects.

Steps 1 and 2 comprise stage one and steps 3 and 4 relate to the second stage of the two-stage allocation process. Let us now consider each of these steps in detail.

## STEP 1 – ASSIGNING ALL MANUFACTURING OVERHEADS TO PRODUCTION AND SERVICE COST CENTRES

Using the information given in Example 3.1 our initial objective is to assign all manufacturing overheads to production and service cost centres. To do this requires the preparation of an overhead analysis sheet. This document is shown in Exhibit 3.2. In many organizations it will consist only in computer form.

If you look at Example 3.1 you will see that the indirect labour and indirect material costs have been directly traced to cost centres. Although these items cannot be directly assigned to products they can be directly assigned to the cost centres. In other words, they are indirect costs when products are the cost objects and direct costs when cost centres are the cost object. Therefore they are traced directly to the cost centres shown in the overhead analysis sheet in Exhibit 3.2. The remaining costs shown in Example 3.1 cannot be traced directly to the cost centres and must be allocated to the cost centre using appropriate allocation bases. The term first stage allocation bases is used to describe allocations at this point. The following list summarizes commonly used first stage allocation bases:

**EXAMPLE 3.1**

The annual overhead costs for the Enterprise Company which has three production centres (two machine centres and one assembly centre) and two service centres (materials procurement and general factory support) are as follows:

|  | (£) | (£) |
|---|---|---|
| Indirect wages and supervision |  |  |
| Machine centres: X | 1 000 000 |  |
| Y | 1 000 000 |  |
| Assembly | 1 500 000 |  |
| Materials procurement | 1 100 000 |  |
| General factory support | 1 480 000 | 6 080 000 |
| Indirect materials |  |  |
| Machine centres: X | 500 000 |  |
| Y | 805 000 |  |
| Assembly | 105 000 |  |
| Materials procurement | 0 |  |
| General factory support | 10 000 | 1 420 000 |
| Lighting and heating | 500 000 |  |
| Property taxes | 1 000 000 |  |
| Insurance of machinery | 150 000 |  |
| Depreciation of machinery | 1 500 000 |  |
| Insurance of buildings | 250 000 |  |
| Salaries of works management | 800 000 | 4 200 000 |
|  |  | 11 700 000 |

The following information is also available:

| | Book value of machinery (£) | Area occupied (sq. metres) | Number of employees | Direct labour hours | Machine hours |
|---|---|---|---|---|---|
| Machine shop: X | 8 000 000 | 10 000 | 300 | 1 000 000 | 2 000 000 |
| Y | 5 000 000 | 5 000 | 200 | 1 000 000 | 1 000 000 |
| Assembly | 1 000 000 | 15 000 | 300 | 2 000 000 | |
| Stores | 500 000 | 15 000 | 100 | | |
| Maintenance | 500 000 | 5 000 | 100 | | |
| | 15 000 000 | 50 000 | 1000 | | |

Details of total materials issues (i.e. direct and indirect materials) to the production centres are as follows:

| | £ |
|---|---|
| Machine shop X | 4 000 000 |
| Machine shop Y | 3 000 000 |
| Assembly | 1 000 000 |
| | 8 000 000 |

To allocate the overheads listed above to the production and service centres we must prepare an overhead analysis sheet, as shown in Exhibit 3.2.

## EXHIBIT 3.2

*Overhead analysis sheet*

| Item of expenditure | Basis of allocation | Total (£) | Production centres | | | Service centres | |
|---|---|---|---|---|---|---|---|
| | | | Machine centre X (£) | Machine centre Y (£) | Assembly (£) | Materials procurement (£) | General factory support (£) |
| Indirect wage and supervision | Direct | 6 080 000 | 1 000 000 | 1 000 000 | 1 500 000 | 1 100 000 | 1 480 000 |
| Indirect materials | Direct | 1 420 000 | 500 000 | 805 000 | 105 000 | | 10 000 |
| Lighting and heating | Area | 500 000 | 100 000 | 50 000 | 150 000 | 150 000 | 50 000 |
| Property taxes | Area | 1 000 000 | 200 000 | 100 000 | 300 000 | 300 000 | 100 000 |
| Insurance of machinery | Book value of machinery | 150 000 | 80 000 | 50 000 | 10 000 | 5 000 | 5 000 |
| Depreciation of machinery | Book value of machinery | 1 500 000 | 800 000 | 500 000 | 100 000 | 50 000 | 50 000 |
| Insurance of buildings | Area | 250 000 | 50 000 | 25 000 | 75 000 | 75 000 | 25 000 |
| Salaries of works management | Number of employees | 800 000 | 240 000 | 160 000 | 240 000 | 80 000 | 80 000 |
| | (1) | 11 700 000 | 2 970 000 | 2 690 000 | 2 480 000 | 1 760 000 | 1 800 000 |
| Reallocation of service centre costs | | | | | | | |
| Materials procurement | Value of materials issued | — | 880 000 | 660 000 | 220 000 | 1 760 000 | |
| General factory support | Direct labour hours | — | 450 000 | 450 000 | 900 000 | | 1 800 000 |
| | (2) | 11 700 000 | 4 300 000 | 3 800 000 | 3 600 000 | — | — |
| Machine hours and direct labour hours | | | 2 000 000 | 1 000 000 | 2 000 000 | | |
| Machine hour overhead rate | | | £2.15 | £3.80 | | | |
| Direct labour hour overhead rate | | | | | £1.80 | | |

| Cost | Basis of allocation |
|---|---|
| Property taxes, lighting and heating | Area |
| Employee-related expenditure: works management, works canteen, payroll office | Number of employees |
| Depreciation and insurance of plant and machinery | Value of items of plant and machinery |

Applying the allocation bases to the data given in respect of the Enterprise Company in Example 3.1 it is assumed that property taxes, lighting and heating, and insurance of buildings are related to the total floor area of the buildings, and the benefit obtained by each cost centre can therefore be ascertained according to the proportion of floor area which it occupies. The total floor area of the factory shown in Example 3.1 is 50 000 square metres; machine centre X occupies 20% of this and machine centre Y a further 10%. Therefore, if you refer to the overhead analysis sheet in Exhibit 3.2 you will see that 20% of property taxes, lighting and heating and insurance of buildings are allocated to machine centre X, and 10% are allocated to machine centre Y.

The insurance premium paid and depreciation of machinery are generally regarded as being related to the book value of the machinery. Because the book value of machinery for machine centre X is 8/15 of the total book value and machine centre is 5/15 of the total book value then 8/15 and 5/15 of the insurance and depreciation of machinery is allocated to machine centres X and Y.

It is assumed that the amount of time that works management devotes to each cost centre is related to the number of employees in each centre; since 30% of the total employees are employed in machine centre X, 30% of the salaries of works management will be allocated to this centre.

If you now look at the overhead analysis sheet shown in Exhibit 3.2, you will see in the row labelled '(1)' that all manufacturing overheads for the Enterprise Company have been assigned to production and service cost centres.

## STEP 2 – REALLOCATING THE COSTS ASSIGNED TO SERVICE COST CENTRES TO PRODUCTION COST CENTRES

The next step is to reallocate the costs that have been assigned to service cost centres to production cost centres. Service departments (i.e. service cost centres) are those departments that exist to provide services of various kinds to other units within the organization. They are sometimes called support departments. The Enterprise Company has two service centres. They are materials procurement and general factory support which includes activities such as production scheduling and machine maintenance. These service centres render essential services that support the production process, but they do not deal directly with the products. Therefore it is not possible to allocate service centre costs to products passing through these centres. To assign costs to products traditional costing systems reallocate service centre costs to production centres that actually work on the product. The method that is chosen to allocate service centre costs to production centre should be related to the benefits that the production centres derive from the service rendered.

We shall assume that the value of materials issued provides a suitable approximation of the benefit that each of the production centres receives from materials procurement. Therefore 50% of the value of materials is issued to machine centre X, resulting in 50% of the total costs of materials procurement being allocated to this centre. If you refer to Exhibit 3.3 you will see that £880 000 (50% of material procurement costs of £1 760 000) has been reallocated to machine centre X. It is also assumed that direct labour hours provides an approximation of the benefits received by the production centres from general factory support resulting in the total costs for this centre being reallocated to the production centres proportionate to direct labour hours. Therefore since machine centre X consumes 25% of the direct labour hours £450 000 (25% of the total costs of £1 800 000 assigned to general factory support) has been reallocated to machine centre X. You will see in the row labelled '(2)' in Exhibit 3.2 that all manufacturing costs have now been assigned to the three production centres. This completes the first stage of the two-stage allocation process.

# STEP 3 – COMPUTING SEPARATE OVERHEAD RATES FOR EACH PRODUCTION COST CENTRE

The second stage of the two-stage process is to allocate overheads of each production centre to overheads passing through that centre. The most frequently used allocation bases used by traditional costing systems are based on the amount of time products spend in each production centre – for example direct labour hours, machine hours and direct wages. In respect of non-machine centres, direct labour hours is the most frequently used allocation base. This implies that the overheads incurred by a production centre are closely related to direct labour hours worked. In the case of machine centres a machine hour overhead rate is preferable since most of the overheads (e.g. depreciation) are likely to be more closely related to machine hours. We shall assume that the Enterprise Company uses a **machine hour rate** for the machine production centres and a **direct labour hour rate** for the assembly centre. The overhead rates are calculated by applying the following formula:

$$\frac{\text{cost centre overheads}}{\text{cost centre direct labour hours or machine hours}}$$

The calculations using the information given in Example 3.1 are as follows:

$$\text{Machine centre X} = \frac{£4\,300\,000}{2\,000\,000 \text{ machine hours}} = £2.15 \text{ per machine hour}$$

$$\text{Machine centre Y} = \frac{£3\,800\,000}{1\,000\,000 \text{ machine hours}} = £3.80 \text{ per machine hour}$$

$$\text{Assembly department} = \frac{£3\,600\,000}{2\,000\,000 \text{ direct labour hours}} = £1.80 \text{ per direct labour hour}$$

# STEP 4 – ASSIGNING COST CENTRE OVERHEADS TO PRODUCTS OR OTHER CHOSEN COST OBJECTS

The final step is to allocate the overheads to products passing through the production centres. Therefore if a product spends 10 hours in machine cost centre A overheads of £21.50 (10 × £2.15) will be allocated to the product. We shall compute the manufacturing costs of two products. Product A is a low sales volume product with direct costs of £100. It is manufactured in batches of 100 units and each unit requires 5 hours in machine centre A, 10 hours in machine centre B and 10 hours in the assembly centre. Product B is a high sales volume product thus enabling it to be manufactured in larger batches. It is manufactured in batches of 200 units and each unit requires 10 hours in machine centre A, 20 hours in machine centre B and 20 hours in the assembly centre. Direct costs of £200 have been assigned to product B. The calculations of the manufacturing costs assigned to the products are as follows:

| Product A | £ |
|---|---|
| Direct costs (100 units × £100) | 10 000 |
| Overhead allocations | |
|     Machine centre A (100 units × 5 machine hours × £2.15) | 1 075 |
|     Machine centre B (100 units × 10 machine hours × £3.80) | 3 800 |
|     Assembly (100 units × 10 direct labour hours × £1.80) | 1 800 |
| Total cost | 16 675 |
| Cost per unit (£16 675/100 units) = £166.75 | |

| **Product B** | **£** |
|---|---:|
| Direct costs (200 units × £200) | 40 000 |
| Overhead allocations | |
|    Machine centre A (200 units × 10 machine hours × £2.15) | 4 300 |
|    Machine centre B (200 units × 20 machine hours × £3.80) | 15 200 |
|    Assembly (200 units × 20 direct labour hours × £1.80) | 7 200 |
| Total cost | 66 700 |
| Cost per unit (£66 700/200 units) = £333.50 | |

The overhead allocation procedure is more complicated where service cost centres serve each other. In Example 3.1 it was assumed that materials procurement does not provide any services for general factory support and that general factory support does not provide any services for materials procurement. An understanding of situations where service cost centres do serve each other is not, however, necessary for a general understanding of the overhead procedure, and the problem of service centre reciprocal cost allocations is therefore dealt with in Appendix 3.1.

# An illustration of the two-stage process for an ABC system

**AR** Earlier in this chapter Figure 3.3 was used to contrast the general features of ABC systems with traditional costing systems. It was pointed out that ABC systems differ from traditional systems by having a greater number of cost centres in the first stage, and a greater number, and variety, of cost drivers/allocation bases in the second stage of the two-stage allocation process. We shall now look at ABC systems in more detail.

You will see from Figure 3.3 that another major distinguishing feature of ABC is that overheads are assigned to each major activity, rather than departments, which normally represent cost centres with traditional systems. Activities consist of the aggregation of many different tasks and are described by verbs associated with objects. Typical support activities include schedule production, set-up machines, move materials, purchase materials, inspect items, and process supplier records. When costs are accumulated by activities they are known as activity cost centres. Production process activities include machine products and assemble products. Thus within the production process, activity cost centres are often identical to the cost centres used by traditional cost systems.

A further distinguishing feature is that traditional systems normally assign service/support costs by reallocating their costs to production cost centres so that they are assigned to products within the production centre cost driver rates. In contrast, ABC systems tend to establish separate cost driver rates for support centres, and assign the cost of support activities directly to cost objects without any reallocation to production centres.

We shall now use Example 3.1 for the Enterprise Company to illustrate ABC in more detail. It is assumed that the activity cost centres for machining and assembling products are identical to the production cost centres used by the traditional costing system. We shall also assume that three activity cost centres have been established for each of the support functions. They are purchasing components, receiving components and disbursing materials for materials procurement and production scheduling, setting-up machines and a quality inspection of the completed products for general factory support. Both ABC and traditional systems use the same approach to assign costs to cost centres in the first stage of the two-stage allocation process. If you refer to column 2 in Exhibit 3.3 you will see that the costs assigned to the production activities have been extracted from row 1 in the overhead analysis sheet shown in Exhibit 3.2, which was used for the traditional costing system. In the overhead analysis sheet we only assigned costs with the traditional costing system to materials procurement and general factory support, and not to the activities within these processes. However, the costs for the activities within these processes would be derived adopting the same approach as that used in Exhibit 3.2, but to simplify the presentation the cost assignments to the materials procurement and general factory support activity cost centres are not shown.

Exhibit 3.3 shows the product cost calculations. The Enterprise Company has established nine activity cost centres and seven different second stage cost drivers. In practice most companies rely on a greater number of cost centres. Based on their observations of ABC systems Kaplan and Cooper (1998) suggest that relatively simple ABC systems having 30–50 activity cost centres and many cost drivers ought to report reasonably accurate costs.

You will see from Exhibit 3.3 that the cost drivers for the production activities are the same as those used for the traditional costing system. To emphasize the point that ABC systems use cause-and-effect second stage allocations the term cost driver tends to be used instead of allocation base. Cost drivers should be significant determinants of the cost of activities. For example, if the cost of processing purchase orders is determined by the number of purchase orders that each product generates, then the number of purchase orders would represent the cost driver for the cost of processing purchase orders. Other cost drivers used by the Enterprise Company are shown in column 3 of Exhibit 3.3. They are the number of receipts for receiving components, number of production runs for disbursing materials and scheduling production, number of set-up hours for setting up the machines and the number of first item inspections for quality inspection of a batch of completed products. You will see from column 5 in the first section of Exhibit 3.3 that cost driver rates are computed by dividing the activity centre cost by the quantity of the cost driver used.

Activity centre costs are assigned to products by multiplying the cost driver rate by the quantity of the cost driver used by products. These calculations are shown in the second section of Exhibit 3.3. You will see from the first section in Exhibit 3.3 that the costs assigned to the purchasing activity are £960 000 for processing 10 000 purchasing orders resulting in a cost driver rate of £96 per purchasing order. The second section shows that a batch of 100 units of product A, and 200 units of product B, each require one purchase order. Therefore purchase order costs of £96 are allocated to each batch. The same approach is used to allocate the costs of the remaining activities shown in Exhibit 3.3. You should now work through Exhibit 3.3 and study the product cost calculations.

The costs assigned to products using each costing system are as follows:

| | Traditional costing system £ | ABC system £ |
|---|---|---|
| Product A | 166.75 | 205.88 |
| Product B | 333.50301.03 | |

Compared with the ABC system the traditional system undercosts product A and overcosts product B. By reallocating the service centre costs to the production centres and allocating the costs to products on the basis of either machine hours or direct labour hours the traditional system incorrectly assumes that these allocation bases are the cause of the costs of the support functions. Compared with product A, product B consumes twice as many machine and direct labour hours. Therefore, relative to Product A, the traditional costing system allocates twice the amount of support costs to

**EXHIBIT 3.3**

*An illustration of cost assignment with an ABC system*

| (1) Activity | (2) Activity cost £ | (3) Activity cost driver | (4) Quantity of activity cost driver | (5) Activity cost driver rate (Col. 2 / Col. 4) |
|---|---|---|---|---|
| **Production activities:** | | | | |
| Machining: activity centre A | 2 970 000 | Number of machine hours | 2 000 000 machine hours | £1.485 per hour |
| Machining: activity centre B | 2 690 000 | Number of machine hours | 1 000 000 machine hours | £2.69 per hour |
| Assembly | 2 480 000 | Number of direct labour hours | 2 000 000 direct lab. hours | £1.24 per hour |
| | 8 140 000 | | | |
| **Materials procurement activities:** | | | | |
| Purchasing components | 960 000 | Number of purchase orders | 10 000 purchase orders | £96 per order |
| Receiving components | 600 000 | Number of material receipts | 5 000 receipts | £120 per receipt |
| Disburse materials | 200 000 | Number of production runs | 2 000 production runs | £100 per production run |
| | 1 760 000 | | | |
| **General factory support activities:** | | | | |
| Production scheduling | 1 000 000 | Number of production runs | 2 000 production runs | £500 per production run |
| Set-up machines | 600 000 | Number of set-up hours | 12 000 set-up hours | £50 per set-up hour |
| Quality inspection | 200 000 | Number of first item inspections | 1 000 inspections | £200 per inspection |
| | 1 800 000 | | | |
| Total cost of all manufacturing activities | 11 700 000 | | | |

**Computation of product costs**

| (1) Activity | (2) Activity cost driver rate | (3) Quantity of cost driver used by 100 units of product A | (4) Quantity of cost driver used by 200 units of product B | (5) Activity cost assigned to product A (Col. 2 × Col. 3) | (6) Activity cost assigned to product B (Col. 2 × Col. 4) |
|---|---|---|---|---|---|
| Machining: activity centre A | £1.485 per hour | 500 hours | 2 000 hours | 742.50 | 2 970.00 |
| Machining: activity centre B | £2.69 per hour | 1 000 hours | 4 000 hours | 2 690.00 | 10 760.00 |
| Assembly | £1.24 per hour | 1 000 hours | 4 000 hours | 1 240.00 | 4 960.00 |
| Purchasing components | £96 per order | 1 component | 1 component | 96.00 | 96.00 |
| Receiving components | £120 per receipt | 1 component | 1 component | 120.00 | 120.00 |
| Disburse materials | £100 per production run | 5 production runs[a] | 1 production run | 500.00 | 100.00 |
| Production scheduling | £500 per production run | 5 production runs[a] | 1 production run | 2 500.00 | 500.00 |
| Set-up machines | £50 per set-up hour | 50 set-up hours | 10 set-up hours | 2 500.00 | 500.00 |
| Quality inspection | £200 per inspection | 1 inspection | 1 inspection | 200.00 | 200.00 |
| Total overhead cost | | | | 10 588.50 | 20 206.00 |
| Units produced | | | | 100 units | 200 units |
| Overhead cost *per unit* | | | | £105.88 | £101.03 |
| Direct costs *per unit* | | | | 100.00 | 200.00 |
| Total cost *per unit* of output | | | | 205.88 | 301.03 |

*Note*
[a] Five production runs are required to machine several unique components before they can be assembled into a final product.

product B.

In contrast, ABC systems create separate cost centres for each major support activity and allocates costs to products using cost drivers that are the significant determinants of the cost of the activities. The ABC system recognizes that a batch of both products consume the same quantity of purchasing, receiving and inspection activities and, for these activities, allocates the same costs to both products. Because product B is manufactured in batches of 200 units, and product A in batches of 100 units, the cost per unit of output for product B is half the amount of Product A for these activities. Product A also has five unique components, whereas product B has only one, resulting in a batch of Product A requiring five production runs whereas a batch of Product B only requires one. Therefore, relative to product B, the ABC system assigns five times more costs to product A for the production scheduling and disbursement of materials activities (see columns 5 and 6 in the lower part of Exhibit 3.3). Because product A is a more complex product it requires relatively more support activity resources and the cost of this complexity is captured by the ABC system.

The unit costs derived from traditional and ABC systems must be used with care. For example, if a customer requested a batch of 400 units of product B the cost would not be twice the amount of a batch of 200 units. Assuming that for a batch of 400 units the number of purchase orders, material receipts, production runs, set-up hours and inspections remained the same as that required for a batch of 200 units the cost of the support activities would remain unchanged, but the direct costs would increase by a factor of two to reflect the fact that twice the amount of resources would be required.

●●●

# Extracting relevant costs for decision-making

The cost computations relating to the Enterprise Company for products A and B represent the costs that should be generated for meeting stock valuation and profit measurement requirements. For decision-making non-manufacturing costs should also be taken into account. In addition, some of the costs that have been assigned to the products may not be relevant for certain decisions. For example, if you look at the overhead analysis sheet in Exhibit 3.2 you will see that property taxes, depreciation of machinery and insurance of buildings and machinery have been assigned to cost centres, and thus included in the costs assigned to products, for both traditional and ABC systems. If these cost are unaffected by a decision to discontinue a product they should not be assigned to products when undertaking product discontinuation reviews. However, if cost information is used to determine selling prices such costs may need to be assigned to products to ensure that the selling price of a customer's order covers a fair share of all organizational costs. It is therefore necessary to ensure that the costs incorporated in the overhead analysis are suitably coded so that different overhead rates can be extracted for different combinations of costs. This will enable relevant cost information to be extracted from the database for meeting different requirements. For an illustration of this approach you should refer to the second self-assessment question and answer at the end of this chapter.

Our objective in this chapter has not been to focus on the cost information that should be extracted from the costing system for meeting decision-making requirements. Instead, it is to provide you with an understanding of how cost systems assign costs to cost objects. In Chapter 9 we shall concentrate on the cost information that should be extracted for decision-making. Also, only the basic principles of ABC have been introduced. A more theoretical approach to ABC will be presented in Chapter 10 with an emphasis being given to how cost information generated from an ABC system can be used for decision-making.

**EXAMPLE 3.2**

The fixed overheads for Euro are £24 000 000 per annum, and monthly production varies from 400 000 to 1 000 000 hours. The monthly overhead rate for fixed overhead will therefore fluctuate as follows:

| | | |
|---|---|---|
| Monthly overhead | £2 000 000 | £2 000 000 |
| Monthly production | 400 000 hours | 1 000 000 hours |
| Monthly overhead rate | £5 per hour | £2 per hour |

Overhead expenditure that is fixed in the short term remains constant each month, but monthly production fluctuates because of holiday periods and seasonal variations in demand. Consequently the overhead rate varies from £2 to £5 per hour. It would be unreasonable for a product worked on in one month to be allocated overheads at a rate of £5 per hour and an identical product worked on in another month allocated at a rate of only £2 per hour.

# Budgeted overhead rates

Our discussion in this chapter has assumed that the *actual* overheads for an accounting period have been allocated to the products. However, the calculation of overhead rates based on the *actual* overheads incurred during an accounting period causes a number of problems. First, the product cost calculations have to be delayed until the end of the accounting period, since the overhead rate calculations cannot be obtained before this date, but information on product costs is required quickly if it is to be used for monthly profit calculations and inventory valuations or as a basis for setting selling prices. Secondly, one may argue that the timing problem can be resolved by calculating actual overhead rates at more frequent intervals, say on a monthly basis, but the objection to this proposal is that a large amount of overhead expenditure is fixed in the short term whereas activity will vary from month to month, giving large fluctuations in the overhead rates. Consider Example 3.2.

Such fluctuating overhead rates are not representative of typical, normal production conditions. Management has committed itself to a specific level of fixed costs in the light of foreseeable needs for beyond one month. Thus, where production fluctuates, monthly overhead rates may be volatile. Furthermore, some costs such as repairs, maintenance and heating are not incurred evenly throughout the year. Therefore, if monthly overhead rates are used, these costs will not be allocated fairly to units of output. For example, heating costs would be charged only to winter production so that products produced in winter would be more expensive than those produced in summer.

An average, annualized rate based on the relationship of total annual overhead to total annual activity is more representative of typical relationships between total costs and volume than a monthly rate. What is required is a normal product cost based on average long-term production rather than an actual product cost, which is affected by month-to-month fluctuations in production volume. Taking these factors into consideration, it is preferable to establish a budgeted overhead rate based on annual estimated overhead expenditure and activity. Consequently the procedure outlined in the previous sections for calculating cost centre overhead rates for traditional and ABC systems should be based on *standard* activity levels and not *actual* activity levels. We shall consider how we might determine standard activity in Chapter 7. However, at this point you should note that most organizations use annual budgeted activity as a measure of standard activity.

**FIGURE 3.4** *Illustration of under-recovery of factory overheads.*

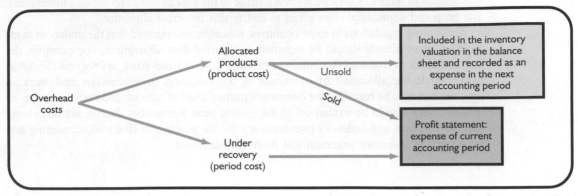

# Under- and over-recovery of overheads

The effect of calculating overhead rates based on budgeted annual overhead expenditure and activity is that it will be most unlikely that the overhead allocated to products manufactured during the period will be the same as the actual overhead incurred. Consider a situation where the estimated annual fixed overheads are £2 000 000 and the estimated annual activity is 1 000 000 direct labour hours. The estimated fixed overhead rate will be £2 per hour. Assume that actual overheads are £2 000 000 and are therefore identical with the estimate, but that actual activity is 900 000 direct labour hours instead of the estimated 1 000 000 hours. In this situation only £1 800 000 will be charged to production. This calculation is based on 900 000 direct labour hours at £2 per hour, giving an under-recovery of overheads of £200 000.

Consider an alternative situation where the actual overheads are £1 950 000 instead of the estimated £2 000 000, and actual activity is 1 000 000 direct labour hours, which is identical to the original estimate. In this situation 1 000 000 direct labour hours at £2 per hour will be charged to production giving an over-recovery of £50 000. This example illustrates that there will be an **under- or over-recovery of overheads** whenever actual activity or overhead expenditure is different from the budgeted overheads and activity used to estimate the budgeted overhead rate. This under- or over-recovery of fixed overheads is also called a **volume variance**.

The question now arises as to how the under- or over-recovery of overheads should be accounted for. We could go back and share the under- or over-recovery among all the products worked on during the year. In practice, this would not be worthwhile, and furthermore such historical information is probably of no future use to management. Another possibility would be to carry these costs forward to future accounting periods, but it can be argued that one should not adjust for a failure to recover past costs in future accounting periods as such a practice results in a distortion of performance figures.

The normal procedure is to treat any under- or over-recovery of overhead as a period cost. In other words, the under- or over-recovery of overhead should be written off against the profit and loss statement in the current accounting period. This procedure for an under recovery is illustrated in Figure 3.4.

Note that any under- or over-recovery of overhead is not allocated to products. Also note that the under-recovery is recorded as an expense of the current accounting period, and that none of this adjustment is included in the inventory valuation. There is a case for allocating any under- or over-recovery of overheads between cost of goods sold for the current period and closing inventories. This argument is based on the assumption that the under- or over-recovery is due to incorrect estimates of activity and overhead expenditure, which leads to incorrect allocations being made to the cost of sales and closing inventories. The proposed adjustment is an effort to rectify this incorrect allocation.

Accounting regulations in most countries, however, recommend that the under- or over-recovery of overheads should be regarded as a period cost adjustment. For example, the UK Statement of Standard Accounting Practice on Stocks and Work in Progress (SSAP 9) recommends the allocation of overheads in the valuation of inventories and work in progress needs to be based on the company's normal level of activity and that any under- or over-recovery should be written off in the current year. Remember that we are discussing here how to treat any under- or over-recovery for the purpose of financial accounting and its impact on inventory valuation and profit measurement.

# Maintaining the database at standard costs

Most organizations whose activities consist of a series of common or repetitive operations maintain their database at standard, rather than actual cost, for both traditional and ABC systems. Standard costs are pre-determined target costs that should be incurred under efficient operating conditions. For example, assume that the standard direct labour cost for performing a particular operation is £40 (consisting of 5 hours at £8 per hour) and the standard cost of a purchased component (say component Z) is £50. The direct costs for a product requiring only this operation and the purchased component Z would be recorded in the database at a standard cost of £90. Assuming that the product only passed through a single cost centre with a budgeted overhead rate of £20 per direct labour hour the overhead cost for the product would be recorded in the database at £100 standard cost (5 standard direct labour hours at £20 per hour). Instead of a product being recorded in the database at its standard *unit* cost the database may consist of the standard costs of a batch of output, such as normal batch sizes of say 100 or 200 units output of the product.

When a standard costing system is used the database is maintained at standard cost and actual output is costed at the standard cost. Actual costs are recorded, but not at the individual product level, and an adjustment is made at the end of the accounting period by recording as a period cost the difference between standard cost and actual cost for the actual output. This adjustment ensures that the standard costs are converted to actual costs in the profit statement for meeting external financial accounting reporting requirements.

It is not important at this point that you have a detailed understanding of a standard costing system. However, it is important that you are aware that a database may consist of standard costs rather than actual costs. We shall look at standard costing in detail in Chapters 18 and 19.

# Non-manufacturing overheads

In respect of financial accounting, only manufacturing costs are allocated to products. Non-manufacturing overheads are regarded as period costs and are disposed of in exactly the same way as the under- or over-recovery of manufacturing overheads outlined in Figure 3.4. For external reporting it is therefore unnecessary to allocate non-manufacturing overheads to products. However, for decision-making non-manufacturing costs should be assigned to products. For example, in many organizations it is not uncommon for selling prices to be based on estimates of total cost or even actual cost. Housing contractors and garages often charge for their services by adding a percentage profit margin to actual cost.

Some non-manufacturing costs may be a direct cost of the product. Delivery costs, salesmen's salaries and travelling expenses may be directly identifiable with the product, but it is likely that many non-manufacturing overheads cannot be allocated directly to specific products. On what basis should we allocate non-manufacturing overheads? The answer is that we should select an allocation base/cost driver that corresponds most closely to non-manufacturing overheads. The problem is that allocation bases that are widely used by traditional costing systems, such as direct labour hours, machine hours and direct labour cost are not necessarily those that are closely related to non-manufacturing overheads. Therefore traditional systems tend to use arbitrary, rather than cause-and-effect allocation bases, to allocate non-manufacturing overheads to products. The most widely used approach (see Exhibit 3.4) is to allocate non-manufacturing overheads on the ability of the products to bear such costs. This approach can be implemented by allocating non-manufacturing costs to products on the basis of their manufacturing costs. This procedure is illustrated in Example 3.3.

**EXHIBIT   3.4**

*Methods used by UK organizations to allocate non-manufacturing overheads to products*

|  | (%) |
|---|---|
| Allocation as a percentage of total manufacturing cost | 32 |
| Direct labour hours/cost methods | 25 |
| Percentage of total selling price | 12 |
| Non-manufacturing overheads not traced to products | 23 |
| Other method | 8 |
|  | 100 |

SOURCE: Drury *et al.* (1993).

**EXAMPLE   3.3**

The estimated non-manufacturing and manufacturing costs of a company for the year ending 31 December are £500 000 and £1 million respectively. The non-manufacturing overhead absorption rate is calculated as follows:

$$\frac{\text{estimated non-manufacturing overhead}}{\text{estimated manufacturing cost}}$$

In percentage terms each product will be allocated with non-manufacturing overheads at a rate of 50% of its total manufacturing cost.

Because of the arbitrary nature of the cost allocations, some organizations that use traditional costing systems as a basis for setting selling prices do not to allocate non-manufacturing overheads to products. Instead, they add a percentage profit margin to each product so that it provides a profit contribution and a contribution to non-manufacturing overheads. We shall consider in more detail how cost information can be used in determining selling prices in Chapter 11. Recent developments in ABC have provided a mechanism for more accurately assigning non-manufacturing overheads to products. These developments will be explained in Chapter 10 when ABC is examined in more depth.

## Self-Assessment Questions

You should attempt to answer these questions yourself before looking up the suggested answers, which appear on pages 1093–5. If any part of your answer is incorrect, check back carefully to make sure you understand where you went wrong.

1. Bookdon Public Limited Company manufactures three products in two production departments, a machine shop and a fitting section; it also has two service departments, a canteen and a machine maintenance section. Shown below are next year's budgeted production data and manufacturing costs for the company.

|  | Product X | Product Y | Product Z |
|---|---|---|---|
| Production | 4200 units | 6900 units | 1700 units |
| Prime cost: | | | |
| Direct materials | £11 per unit | £14 per unit | £17 per unit |
| Direct labour: | | | |
| Machine shop | £6 per unit | £4 per unit | £2 per unit |
| Fitting section | £12 per unit | £3 per unit | £21 per unit |
| Machine hours per unit | 6 hours per unit | 3 hours per unit | 4 hours per unit |

|  | Machine shop | Fitting section | Canteen | Machine maintenance section | Total |
|---|---|---|---|---|---|
| Budgeted overheads (£): | | | | | |
| Allocated overheads | 27 660 | 19 470 | 16 600 | 26 650 | 90 380 |
| Rent, rates, heat and light | | | | | 17 000 |
| Depreciation and insurance of equipment | | | | | 25 000 |
| Additional data: | | | | | |
| Gross book value of equipment (£) | 150 000 | 75 000 | 30 000 | 45 000 | |
| Number of employees | 18 | 14 | 4 | 4 | |
| Floor space occupied (square metres) | 3 600 | 1 400 | 1 000 | 800 | |

It has been estimated that approximately 70% of the machine maintenance section's costs are incurred servicing the machine shop and the remainder incurred servicing the fitting section.

Required:

(a) (i)  Calculate the following budgeted overhead absorption rates:
    A machine hour rate for the machine shop.
    A rate expressed as a percentage of direct wages for the fitting section.
    All workings and assumptions should be clearly shown. (12 marks)
   (ii) Calculate the budgeted manufacturing overhead cost per unit of product X. (2 marks)

(b) The production director of Bookdon PLC has suggested that 'as the actual overheads incurred and units produced are usually different from the budgeted and as a consequence profits of each month end are distorted by over/under absorbed overheads, it would be more accurate to calculate the actual overhead cost per unit each month end by dividing the total number of all units actually produced during the month into the actual overheads incurred.'

Critically examine the production director's suggestion. (8 marks)

(Total 22 marks)

*ACCA Level 1 Costing*

2. Shown below is next year's budget for the forming and finishing departments of Tooton Ltd. The departments manufacture three different types of component, which are incorporated into the output of the firm's finished products.

| | Component A | Component B | Component C |
|---|---|---|---|
| Production | 14 000 units | 10 000 units | 6000 units |
| Prime cost (£ per unit): | | | |
| Direct materials | | | |
| Forming dept | 8 | 7 | 9 |
| Direct labour | | | |
| Forming dept | 6 | 9 | 12 |
| Finish dept | 10 | 15 | 8 |
| | 24 | 31 | 29 |
| | | | |
| Manufacturing times (hours per unit): | | | |
| Machining | | | |
| Forming dept | 4 | 3 | 2 |
| Direct labour | | | |
| Forming dept | 2 | 3 | 4 |
| Finishing dept | 3 | 10 | 2 |

| | Forming department (£) | Finishing department (£) |
|---|---|---|
| Variable overheads | 200 900 | 115 500 |
| Fixed overheads | 401 800 | 231 000 |
| | £602 700 | £346 500 |
| | | |
| Machine time required and available | 98 000 hours | — |
| Labour hours required and available | 82 000 hours | 154 000 hours |

The forming department is mechanized and employs only one grade of labour, the finishing department employs several grades of labour with differing hourly rates of pay.

Required:

(a) Calculate suitable overhead absorption rates for the forming and finishing departments for next year and include a brief explanation for your choice of rates.

(6 marks)

(b) Another firm has offered to supply next year's budgeted quantities of the above components at the following prices:

> Component A   £30    Component B   £65    Component C   £60

Advise management whether it would be more economical to purchase any of the above components from the outside supplier. You must show your workings and, considering cost criteria only, clearly state any assumptions made or any aspects that may require further investigation. (8 marks)

(c) Critically consider the purpose of calculating production overheads absorption rates. (8 marks)

(Total 22 marks)

*ACCA Foundation Costing*

## Summary

The aim of this chapter has been to provide you with an understanding of how costs are assigned to cost objects. Direct costs can be accurately traced to cost objects whereas indirect costs cannot. Therefore indirect costs must be assigned using cost allocation bases. Allocation bases which are significant determinants of costs that are being allocated are described as cause-and-effect allocations whereas arbitrary allocations refer to allocation bases that are not the significant determinant of the costs. To accurately measure the cost of resources used by cost objects cause-and-effect allocations should be used.

Most organizations accumulate costs within a single database and different categories of costs are extracted for meeting different purposes. The sophistication and accuracy of costing systems vary and cost–benefit criteria should determine the optimal costing system for an organization. The range of the sophistication of costing systems varies from simplistic traditional to sophisticated ABC systems. Simplistic traditional systems make significant use of arbitrary cost allocations whereas ABC systems aim to use only cause-and-effect cost allocations.

Both systems use the two-stage allocation process. In the first stage overheads are assigned to cost centres, while the second stage allocates cost centre overheads to products. Some companies omit the first stage and use a blanket overhead rate, but it has been shown that this approach can only be justified where products spend approximately equal proportions of time in each production cost centre. The two-stage procedure involves the following steps:

1. the allocation of overheads to production and service centres or departments;

2. the apportionment of service department overhead to production departments;

3. the calculation of appropriate departmental overhead rates;

4. allocate overheads to products passing through each department.

These steps were illustrated with Example 3.1 for both traditional and ABC systems. The allocation bases that are most frequently used in the second stage by traditional costing systems are the direct labour hour method for non-machine departments and the machine hour rate for machine departments. Other methods of allocating overheads such as the direct wages percentage, units of output, direct materials and prime cost percentage methods are discussed in Appendix 3.2, but they can only be recommended in certain circumstances. The major distinguishing features of ABC compared with traditional systems, is that ABC systems assign costs to activity centres rather than departments. ABC systems thus tend to use a greater number of cost centres in the first stage of the allocation process. They also use a greater number, and variety, of second stage allocation bases. To emphasize the point that ABC systems aim to use only cause-and-effect allocation bases the term cost driver tends to be used instead of allocation base.

As the use of actual overhead rates causes a delay in the calculation of product costs, and the use of monthly overhead rates causes fluctuations in monthly overhead rates, it has been suggested that budgeted annual overhead rates should be used. However, the use of annual budgeted overhead rates gives an under or over-recovery of overhead whenever actual overhead expenditure or activity is different from budget. Any under- or over-recovery of overhead is generally regarded as a period cost adjustment and written off to the profit and loss account, although some writers argue that the under- over-recovery should be apportioned between the cost of sales and closing stocks.

For meeting financial accounting requirements non-manufacturing overheads are not assigned to products. Instead, they are treated as period costs.

For decision-making non-manufacturing costs must be considered but traditional costing systems allocate them using arbitrary allocations that result in the reporting of distorted product costs. Recent developments in ABC have provided a mechanism for more accurately assigning non-manufacturing overheads to products.

## Key Terms and Concepts

activities (p. 60)
activity-based-costing (ABC) (p. 46)
activity cost centre (p. 60)
allocation base (p. 46)
arbitrary allocation (p. 46)
blanket overhead rate (p. 50)
budgeted overhead rates (p. 64)
cause-and-effect allocations (p. 46)
cost allocation (p. 46)
cost centre (p. 51)
cost driver (p. 46)
cost pool (p. 51)
cost tracing (p. 46)
direct allocation method (p. 46, 76)
direct labour hour rate (p. 59)
direct materials percentage method (p. 79)
direct wages percentage method (p. 78)
first stage allocation bases (p. 55)

job cards (p. 49)
machine hour rate (p. 59)
materials requisition (p. 49)
overhead analysis sheet (p. 55)
overheads (p. 46)
plant-wide rate (p. 50)
prime cost percentage method (p. 79)
repeated distribution method (p. 73)
service departments (p. 58)
simultaneous equation method (p. 74)
specified order of closing method (p. 75)
standard costs (p. 66)
support departments (p. 58)
time sheets (p. 49)
traditional costing systems (p. 46)
under- or over-recovery of overheads (p. 65)
units of output method (p. 78)
volume variance (p. 65)

## Recommended Reading

If your course requires a detailed understanding of accounting for direct labour and materials you should refer to Chapter 3 of Drury (1998). Alternatively, you can look at this chapter on the website. For an explanation of how you can access the website you should refer to the preface. For a more detailed review of cost allocations for different

purposes see Ahmed and Scapens (1991). You should refer to Dhavale (1989) for a review of overhead allocations in an advanced automated environment. Detailed references for these readings are provided in the bibliography at the end of the book.

# Appendix 3.1: Inter-service department reallocations

Service departments provide services for other service departments as well as for production departments. For example, a personnel department provides services for other service departments such as the power generating plant, maintenance department and stores. The power generating department also provides heat and light for other service

EXAMPLE 3A.1

A company has three production departments and two service departments. The overhead analysis sheet provides the following totals of the overheads analysed to production and service departments:

|  |  | (£) |
|---|---|---|
| Production department | X | 48 000 |
|  | Y | 42 000 |
|  | Z | 30 000 |
| Service department | 1 | 14 040 |
|  | 2 | 18 000 |
|  |  | 152 040 |

The expenses of the service departments are apportioned as follows:

|  | Production departments | | | Service departments | |
|---|---|---|---|---|---|
|  | X | Y | Z | 1 | 2 |
| Service department 1 | 20% | 40% | 30% | — | 10% |
| Service department 2 | 40% | 20% | 20% | 20% | — |

departments, including the personnel department, and so on. When such interactions occur, the allocation process can become complicated. Difficulties arise because each service department begins to accumulate charges from other service departments from which it receives services, and these must be reallocated back to the user department. Once it has begun, this allocation and reallocation process can continue for a long time before a solution is found. The problem is illustrated in Example 3A.1. We shall use the example to illustrate four different methods of allocating the service department costs:

1. repeated distribution method;
2. simultaneous equation method;
3. specified order of closing method;
4. direct allocation method.

## REPEATED DISTRIBUTION METHOD

Where this method is adopted, the service department costs are repeatedly allocated in the specified percentages until the figures become too small to be significant. You can see from line 2 of Exhibit 3A.1 that the overheads of service department 1 are allocated according to the prescribed percentages. As a result, some of the overheads of service department 1 are transferred to service department 2. In line 3 the overheads of service department 2 are allocated, which means that service department 1 receives some further costs. The costs of service department 1 are again allocated, and service department 2 receives some further costs. This process continues until line 7, by which time the costs have become so small that any further detailed apportionments are unnecessary. As a result, the total overheads in line 8 of £152 040 are allocated to production departments only.

EXHIBIT 3A.1

*Repeated distribution method*

| Line | Production departments | | | Service departments | | Total |
|---|---|---|---|---|---|---|
| | X | Y | Z | 1 | 2 | |
| 1. Allocation as per overhead analysis | 48 000 | 42 000 | 30 000 | 14 040 | 18 000 | 152 040 |
| 2. Allocation of service department 1 | 2 808 (20%) | 5 616 (40%) | 4 212 (30%) | (14 040) | 1 404 (10%) <br> 19 404 | |
| 3. Allocation of service department 2 | 7 762 (40%) | 3 881 (20%) | 3 880 (20%) | 3 881 (20%) | (19 404) | |
| 4. Allocation of service department 1 | 776 (20%) | 1 552 (40%) | 1 165 (30%) | (3 881) | 388 (10%) | |
| 5. Allocation of service department 2 | 154 (40%) | 78 (20%) | 78 (20%) | 78 (20%) | (388) | |
| 6. Allocation of service department 1 | 16 (20%) | 31 (40%) | 23 (30%) | (78) | 8 (10%) | |
| 7. Allocation of service department 2 | 4 (40%) | 2 (20%) | 2 (20%) | — | (8) | |
| 8. Total overheads | 59 520 | 53 160 | 39 360 | — | — | 152 040 |

## SIMULTANEOUS EQUATION METHOD

When this method is used simultaneous equations are initially established as follows: Let

$$x = \text{total overhead of service department 1}$$
$$y = \text{total overhead of service department 2}$$

The total overhead transferred into service departments 1 and 2 can be expressed as

$$x = 14\,040 + 0.2y$$
$$y = 18\,000 + 0.1x$$

Rearranging the above equations:

$$x - 0.2y = 14\,040 \quad (1)$$
$$-0.1x + y = 18\,000 \quad (2)$$

We can now multiply equation (1) by 5 and equation (2) by 1, giving

$$5x - y = 70\,200$$
$$-0.1x + y = 18\,000$$

Adding the above equations together we have

$$4.9x = 88\,200$$

Therefore
$$x = 18\,000 \ (= 88\,200/4.9)$$

Substituting this value for x in equation (1), we have

$$18\,000 - 0.2y = 14\,040$$

Therefore
$$-0.2y = -3\,960$$

Therefore
$$y = 19\,800$$

We now apportion the values for $x$ and $y$ to the production departments in the agreed percentages.

| Line | X | Y | Z | Total |
|---|---|---|---|---|
| 1. Allocation as per overhead analysis | 48 000 | 42 000 | 30 000 | 120 000 |
| 2. Allocation of service department 1 | 3 600 (20%) | 7 200 (40%) | 5 400 (30%) | 16 200 |
| 3. Allocation of service department 2 | 7 920 (40%) | 3 960 (20%) | 3 960 (20%) | 15 840 |
| 4. | 59 520 | 53 160 | 39 360 | 152 040 |

You will see from line 2 that the value for X (service department 1) of £18 000 is allocated in the specified percentages. Similarly, in line 3 the value for Y (service department 2) of £19 800 is apportioned in the specified percentages. As a result the totals in line 4 are in agreement with the totals in line 8 of the repeated distribution method (Exhibit 3A.1).

## SPECIFIED ORDER OF CLOSING

If this method is used the service departments' overheads are allocated to the production departments in a certain order. The service department that does the largest proportion of work for other service departments is closed first; the service department that does the second largest proportion of work for other service departments is closed second; and so on. Return charges are not made to service departments whose costs have previously been allocated. Let us now apply this method to the information contained in Example 3A.1. The results are given in Exhibit 3A.2.

The costs of service department 2 are allocated first (line 2) because 20% of its work is related to service department 1, whereas only 10% of the work of service department 1 is related to service department 2. In line 3 we allocate the costs of service department 1, but the return charges are not made to department 2. This means that the proportions allocated have changed as 10% of the costs of service department 1 have not been allocated to service department 2. Therefore 20% out of a 90% total or 2/9 of the costs of service department 1 are allocated to department X.

EXHIBIT 3A.2

*Specified order of closing method*

You will see that the totals allocated in line 4 do not agree with the totals allocated under the repeated distribution or simultaneous equation methods. This is because the specified order of closing method sacrifices accuracy for

|  | | Production departments | | | Service departments | | |
| --- | --- | --- | --- | --- | --- | --- | --- |
| Line | | X | Y | Z | 1 | 2 | Total |
| 1. Allocation as per overhead analysis | | 48 000 | 42 000 | 30 000 | 14 040 | 18 000 | 152 040 |
| 2. Allocate service department 2 | | 7 200 (40%) | 3 600 (20%) | 3 600 (20%) | 3 600 (20%) | (18 000) | |
| 3. Allocate service department 1 | | 3 920 (2/9) | 7 840 (4/9) | 5 880 (3/9) | (17 640) | — | |
| 4. | | 59 120 | 53 440 | 39 480 | — | — | 152 040 |

clerical convenience. However, if this method provides a close approximation to an alternative accurate calculation then there are strong arguments for its use.

## DIRECT ALLOCATION METHOD

This method ignores inter-service department service reallocations. Therefore service department costs are reallocated only to production departments. This means that the proportions allocated have changed as 10% of the costs of service department 1 have not been allocated to service department 2. Therefore 20% out of a 90% total, or 2/9 of the costs of service department 1, are allocated to department X, 4/9 are allocated to department Y and 3/9 are allocated to department Z. Similarly the proportions allocated for service department 2 have changed with 4/8 (40% out of 80%) of the costs of service department 2 being allocated department X, 2/8 to department Y and 2/8 to department Z. The only justification for using the direct allocation method is its simplicity. The method is recommended when inter-service reallocations are relatively insignificant.

## USE OF MATHEMATICAL MODELS

In practice, the problems of service department allocations are likely to be far more complex than is apparent from the simple example illustrated here. For example, it is likely that more than two service departments will exist. However, it is possible to solve the allocation problem by using computer facilities based on mathematical models. For

EXHIBIT 3A.3

*Direct allocation method*

example, with the aid of computer facilities, matrix algebra can be easily applied to situations where many service departments exist. For a discussion of the application of the

| | Line | Production departments | | | Service departments | | Total |
|---|---|---|---|---|---|---|---|
| | | X | Y | Z | 1 | 2 | |
| 1. | Allocation as per overhead analysis | 48 000 | 42 000 | 30 000 | 14 040 | 18 000 | 152 040 |
| 2. | Allocate service department 1 | 3 120 (2/9) | 6 240 (4/9) | 4 680 (3/9) | (14 040) | | |
| 3. | Allocate service department 2 | 9 000 (4/8) | 4 500 (2/8) | 4 500 (2/8) | — | (18 000) | |
| 4 | | 60 120 | 52 740 | 39 180 | — | — | 152 040 |

matrix method to the reciprocal allocation of service department costs see Kaplan and Atkinson (1998). See also Elphick (1983) for a description of an approach that has been adopted by the ICI group.

# Appendix 3.2: Other allocation bases used by traditional systems

In the main body of this chapter it was pointed out that traditional costing systems tend to rely on using two second stage allocation bases – namely, direct labour hours and machine hours. Example 3.1 was used to illustrate the application of these allocation bases. With traditional systems it is generally assumed that overhead expenditure is related to output measured by either direct labour hours or machine hours required for a given volume. Products with a high direct labour or machine hour content are therefore assumed to consume a greater proportion of overheads. In addition, to direct labour and machine hours, the following allocation bases are also sometimes used by traditional costing systems:

1. **direct wages percentage method**;
2. **units of output method**;
3. **direct materials percentage method**;
4. **prime cost percentage method**.

Each of these methods is illustrated using the information given in Example 3A.2.

**EXAMPLE 3A.2**

The budgeted overheads for a department for the next accounting period are £200 000. In addition, the following information is available for the period:

| | |
|---|---|
| Estimated direct wages | £250 000 |
| Estimated direct materials | £100 000 |
| Estimated output | 10 000 units |

## DIRECT WAGES PERCENTAGE METHOD

The direct wages percentage overhead rate is calculated as follows:

$$\frac{\text{estimated departmental overheads} \times 100}{\text{estimated direct wages}}$$

Using information given in Example 3A.2,

$$\frac{£200\,000}{£250\,000} \times 100 = 80\% \text{ of direct wages}$$

If we assume that the direct wages cost for a product is £20 then overheads of £16 (80% × £20) will be allocated to the product.

The direct wages percentage method is suitable only where uniform wage rates apply within a cost centre or department. In such a situation this method will yield exactly the same results as the direct labour hour method. However, consider a situation where wage rates are not uniform. Products X and Y spend 20 hours in the same production department, but product X requires skilled labour and product Y requires unskilled labour, with direct wages costs respectively of £200 and £100. If we apply the direct wages percentage overhead rate of 80% we should allocate overheads of £160 to product X and £80 to product Y. If both products spend the same amount of time in the department, are such apportioned amounts fair? The answer would appear to be negative, and the direct wages percentage method should therefore only be recommended when similar wage rates are paid to direct employees in a production department.

## UNITS OF OUTPUT METHOD

If this method is used, the overhead rate is calculated as follows:

$$\frac{\text{estimated departmental overhead}}{\text{estimated output}}$$

Using the information given in Example 3A.2, this would give an overhead rate of £20 per unit produced. The units of output method is only suitable where all units produced within a department are identical. In other works, it is best suited to a process costing system, and it is not recommended for a job costing system where all jobs or products spend a different amount of time in each production department. If, for example, two of the units produced in Example 3A.2 required 100 hours and 2 hours respectively then they would both be allocated £20. Such an allocation would not be logical.

# DIRECT MATERIALS PERCENTAGE METHOD

The direct materials percentage overhead rate is calculated as follows:

$$\frac{\text{estimated departmental overhead}}{\text{estimated direct materials}}$$

Using the information given in Example 3A.2,

$$\frac{£200\,000}{£100\,000} = 200\% \text{ of direct materials}$$

If we assume that the direct material cost incurred by a product in the department is £50 then the product will be allocated with £100 for a share of the overheads of the department.

If the direct materials percentage overhead rate is used, the overheads allocated to products will bear little relationship to the amount of time that products spend in each department. Consequently, this method of recovery cannot normally be recommended, unless the majority of overheads incurred in a department are related to materials rather than time. In particular, the method is appropriate for allocating materials handling expenses to products. With this approach, a cost centre is created for material handling expenses and the expenses are allocated to products using a materials handling overhead rate (normally the direct materials percentage allocation method). Companies that use a materials handling overhead rate allocate the remaining factory overheads to products using one or more of the allocation bases described in this chapter.

# PRIME COST PERCENTAGE METHOD

The prime cost percentage overhead rate is calculated as follows:

$$\frac{\text{estimated departmental overheads}}{\text{estimated prime cost}} \times 100$$

Using the information given in Example 3A.2, you will see that the estimated prime cost is £350 000, which consists of direct wages of £250 000 plus direct materials of £100 000. The calculation of the overhead rate is

$$\frac{£200\,000}{£350\,000} \times 100 = 57.14\%$$

A product that incurs £100 prime cost in the department will be allocated £57.14 for the departmental overheads.

As prime cost consists of direct wages and direct materials, the disadvantages that apply to the direct materials and direct wages percentage methods also apply to the prime cost percentage method of overhead recovery. Consequently, the prime cost method is not recommended.

## *Key Examination Points*

A typical question will require you to analyse overheads by departments and calculate appropriate overhead allocation rates. These questions require a large number of calculations, and it is possible that you will make calculation errors. Do make sure that your answer is clearly presented, since marks tend to be allocated according to whether you have adopted the correct method. You are recommended to present your answer in a format similar to Exhibit 3.2. For a traditional costing system you should normally recommend a direct labour hour rate if a department is non-mechanized and a machine hour rate if machine hours are the dominant activity. You should only recommend the direct wages percentage method when the rates within a non-mechanized department are uniform.

Where a question requires you to present information for decision-making, do not include apportioned fixed overheads in the calculations. Remember the total manufacturing costs should be calculated for stock valuation, but incremental manufacturing costs should be calculated for decision-making purposes (see answer to Self-Assessment Question 2 and Question 3.31 for an illustration).

Finally, ensure that you can calculate under- or over-recoveries of overheads and deal with reciprocal cost allocations. Most questions on reciprocal cost allocations do not specify which allocation method should be adopted. You should therefore use either the simultaneous equation method or the repeated distribution method.

## Questions

*Indicates that a suggested solution is to be found in the *Students' Manual*.

### 3.1* Intermediate
A company uses a predetermined overhead recovery rate based on machine hours. Budgeted factory overhead for a year amounted to £720 000, but actual factory overhead incurred was £738 000. During the year, the company absorbed £714 000 of factory overhead on 119 000 actual machine hours.

What was the company's budgeted level of machine hours for the year?

A   116 098
B   119 000
C   120 000
D   123 000

*ACCA Foundation Paper 3*

### 3.2* Intermediate
A company absorbs overheads on machine hours which were budgeted at 11 250 with overheads of £258 750. Actual results were 10 980 hours with overheads of £254 692.

Overheads were:

A   under-absorbed by £2152
B   over-absorbed by £4058
C   under-absorbed by £4058
D   over-absorbed by £2152

*CIMA Stage 1*

### 3.3* Intermediate
The following data are to be used for sub-questions (i) and (ii) below:

| | |
|---|---|
| Budgeted labour hours | 8 500 |
| Budgeted overheads | £148 750 |
| Actual labour hours | 7 928 |
| Actual overheads | £146 200 |

(i)   Based on the data given above, what is the labour hour overhead absorption rate?

A   £17.50 per hour
B   £17.20 per hour
C   £18.44 per hour
D   £18.76 per hour

(ii)   Based on the data given above, what is the amount of overhead under/over-absorbed?

A   £2550 under-absorbed
B   £2529 over-absorbed
C   £2550 over-absorbed
D   £7460 under-absorbed

*CIMA Stage 1*

### 3.4* Intermediate
A firm makes special assemblies to customers' orders and uses job costing. The data for a period are:

| | Job no. AA10 (£) | Job no. BB15 (£) | Job no. CC20 (£) |
|---|---|---|---|
| Opening WIP | 26 800 | 42 790 | — |
| Material added in period | 17 275 | — | 18 500 |
| Labour for period | 14 500 | 3 500 | 24 600 |

The budgeted overheads for the period were £126 000.

(i) What overhead should be added to job number CC20 for the period?

A £24 600
B £65 157
C £72 761
D £126 000

(ii) Job no. BB15 was completed and delivered during the period and the firm wishes to earn $33\frac{1}{3}\%$ profit on sales.

What is the selling price of job number BB15?

A £69 435
B £75 521
C £84 963
D £138 870

(iii) What was the approximate value of closing work in progress at the end of the period?

A £58 575
B £101 675
C £147 965
D £217 323

*CIMA Stage 1*

## 3.5* Intermediate

A company absorbs overheads on machine hours. In a period, actual machine hours were 17 285, actual overheads were £496 500 and there was under-absorption of £12 520.
What was the budgeted level of overheads?

A £483 980
B £496 500
C £509 020
D It cannot be calculated from the information provided.

*CIMA Stage 1 Cost Accounting*

## 3.6 Intermediate

(a) Explain why predetermined overhead absorption rates are preferred to overhead absorption rates calculated from factual information after the end of a financial period.

(b) The production overhead absorption rates of factories X and Y are calculated using similar methods. However, the rate used by factory X is lower than that used by factory Y. Both factories produce the same type of product. You are required to discuss whether or not this can be taken to be a sign that factory X is more efficient than factory Y.

(20 marks)
*CIMA Cost Accounting 1*

## 3.7 Intermediate

Critically consider the purpose of calculating production overhead absorption rates.

## 3.8 Intermediate

(a) Specify and explain the factors to be considered in determining whether to utilize a single factory-wide recovery rate for all production overheads or a separate rate for each cost centre, production or service department.

(12 marks)

(b) Describe three methods of determining fixed overhead recovery rates and specify the circumstances under which each method is superior to the other methods mentioned.

(8 marks)
(Total 20 marks)
*ACCA P2 Management Accounting*

## 3.9 Intermediate: Overhead analysis, calculation of overhead rate and overhead charged to a unit of output

A company makes a range of products with total budgeted manufacturing overheads of £973 560 incurred in three production departments (A, B and C) and one service department.

Department A has 10 direct employees, who each work 37 hours per week.

Department B has five machines, each or which is operated for 24 hours per week.

Department C is expected to produce 148 000 units of final product in the budget period.

The company will operate for 48 weeks in the budget period.

Budgeted overheads incurred directly by each department are:

| | |
|---|---|
| Production department A | £261 745 |
| Production department B | £226 120 |
| Production department C | £93 890 |
| Service department | £53 305 |

The balance of budgeted overheads are apportioned to departments as follows:

| | |
|---|---|
| Production department A | 40% |
| Production department B | 35% |
| Production department C | 20% |
| Service department | 5% |

Service department overheads are apportioned equally to each production department.
You are required to:

(a) Calculate an appropriate predetermined overhead absorption rate in each production department. (9 marks)

(b) Calculate the manufacturing overhead cost per unit of finished product in a batch of 100 units which take 9 direct labour hours in department A and three machine hours in department B to produce. (3 marks)

(12 marks)

*ACCA Foundation Paper 3*

### 3.10 Intermediate: Overhead analysis sheet and calculation of overhead absorption rates

PTS Limited is a manufacturing company which uses three production departments to make its product. It has the following factory costs which are expected to be incurred in the year to 31 December:

| | | (£) |
|---|---|---|
| Direct wages | Machining | 234 980 |
| | Assembly | 345 900 |
| | Finishing | 134 525 |
| | | £ |
| Indirect wages and salaries | Machining | 120 354 |
| | Assembly | 238 970 |
| | Finishing | 89 700 |

| | £ |
|---|---|
| Factory rent | 12 685 500 |
| Business rates | 3 450 900 |
| Heat and lighting | 985 350 |
| Machinery power | 2 890 600 |
| Depreciation | 600 000 |
| Canteen subsidy | 256 000 |

Other information is available as follows:

| | Machining | Assembly | Finishing |
|---|---|---|---|
| Number of employees | 50 | 60 | 18 |
| Floor space occupied (m²) | 1 800 | 1 400 | 800 |
| Horse power of machinery | 13 000 | 500 | 6 500 |
| Value of machinery (£000) | 250 | 30 | 120 |
| Number of labour hours | 100 000 | 140 000 | 35 000 |
| Number of machine hours | 200 000 | 36 000 | 90 000 |

You are required

(a) to prepare the company's overhead analysis sheet for the year to 31 December; (9 marks)

(b) to calculate appropriate overhead absorption rates (to two decimal places) for each department. (6 marks)

(Total: 15 marks)

*CIMA Stage 1 Accounting*

### 3.11[*] Intermediate: Overhead analysis, calculation of overhead rates and a product cost

Knowing that you are studying for the CIMA qualification, a friend who manages a small business has sought your advice about how to produce quotations in response to the enquiries which her business receives. Her business is sheet metal fabrication – supplying ducting for dust extraction and airconditioning installations. She believes that she has lost orders recently through the use of a job cost estimating system which was introduced, on the advice of her auditors, seven years ago. You are invited to review this system.

Upon investigation, you find that a plant-wide percentage of 125% is added to prime costs in order to arrive at a selling price. The percentage added is intended to cover all overheads for the three production departments (Departments P, Q and R), all the selling, distribution and administration costs, and the profit.

You also discover that the selling, distribution and administration costs equate to roughly 20% of total production costs, and that to achieve the desired return on capital employed, a margin of 20% of sales value is necessary.

You recommend an analysis of overhead cost items be undertaken with the objective of determining a direct labour hour rate of overhead absorption for each of the three departments work passes through. (You think about activity-based costing but feel this would be too sophisticated and difficult to introduce at the present time.)

There are 50 direct workers in the business plus 5 indirect production people.

From the books, records and some measuring, you ascertain the following information which will enable you to compile an overhead analysis spreadsheet, and to determine overhead absorption rates per direct labour hour for departmental overhead purposes:

| Cost/expense | Annual amount | Basis for apportionment where allocation not given |
|---|---|---|
| | £ | |
| Repairs and maintenance | 62 000 | Technical assessment: P £42 000, Q £10 000, R £10 000 |
| Depreciation | 40 000 | Cost of plant and equipment |
| Consumable supplies | 9 000 | Direct labour hours |
| Wage-related costs | 87 000 | $12\frac{1}{2}$% of direct wages costs |
| Indirect labour | 90 000 | Direct labour hours |

| Canteen/rest/smoke room | 30 000 | Number of direct workers |
| Business rates and insurance | 26 000 | Floor area |

Other estimates/information

| | Department P | Department Q | Department R |
| --- | --- | --- | --- |
| Estimated direct labour hours | 50 000 | 30 000 | 20 000 |
| Direct wages costs | £386 000 | £210 000 | £100 000 |
| Number of direct workers | 25 | 15 | 10 |
| Floor area in square metres | 5 000 | 4 000 | 1 000 |
| Plant and equipment, at cost | £170 000 | £140 000 | £90 000 |

Required:
(a) Calculate the overhead absorption rates for each department, based on direct labour hours. (9 marks)
(b) Prepare a sample quotation for Job 976, utilizing information given in the question, your answer to (a) above, and the following additional information:

Estimated direct material
cost: £800
Estimated direct labour
hours: 30 in Department P
10 in Department Q
5 in Department R

(3 marks)
(c) Calculate what would have been quoted for Job 976 under the 'auditors' system' and comment on whether your friend's suspicions about lost business could be correct.

(3 marks)
(Total 15 marks)
*CIMA Stage 2 Cost Accounting*

## 3.12* Intermediate: Overhead analysis and calculation of product costs
A furniture-making business manufactures quality furniture to customers' orders. It has three production departments and two service departments. Budgeted overhead costs for the coming year are as follows:

| | Total (£) |
| --- | --- |
| Rent and Rates | 12 800 |
| Machine insurance | 6 000 |
| Telephone charges | 3 200 |

| | |
| --- | --- |
| Depreciation | 18 000 |
| Production Supervisor's salaries | 24 000 |
| Heating & Lighting | 6 400 |
| | 70 400 |

The three production departments – A, B and C, and the two service departments – X and Y, are housed in the new premises, the details of which, together with other statistics and information, are given below.

| | Departments | | | | |
| --- | --- | --- | --- | --- | --- |
| | A | B | C | X | Y |
| Floor area occupied (sq.metres) | 3000 | 1800 | 600 | 600 | 400 |
| Machine value (£000) | 24 | 10 | 8 | 4 | 2 |
| Direct labour hrs budgeted | 3200 | 1800 | 1000 | | |
| Labour rates per hour | £3.80 | £3.50 | £3.40 | £3.00 | £3.00 |
| Allocated Overheads: Specific to each department (£000) | 2.8 | 1.7 | 1.2 | 0.8 | 0.6 |
| Service Department X's costs apportioned | 50% | 25% | 25% | | |
| Service Department Y's costs apportioned | 20% | 30% | 50% | | |

Required:
(a) Prepare a statement showing the overhead cost budgeted for each department, showing the basis of apportionment used. Also calculate suitable overhead absorption rates. (9 marks)
(b) Two pieces of furniture are to be manufactured for customers. Direct costs are as follows:

| | Job 123 | Job 124 |
| --- | --- | --- |
| Direct Material | £154 | £108 |
| Direct Labour | 20 hours Dept A | 16 hours Dept A |
| | 12 hours Dept B | 10 hours Dept B |
| | 10 hours Dept C | 14 hours Dept C |

Calculate the total costs of each job.
(5 marks)
(c) If the firm quotes prices to customers that reflect a required profit of 25% on selling price, calculate the quoted selling price for each job. (2 marks)
(d) If material costs are a significant part of total costs in a manufacturing company, describe a system of material control that might be used in order to effectively control costs, paying particular attention to the stock control aspect. (9 marks)
(Total 25 marks)
*AAT Stage 3 Cost Accounting and Budgeting*

## 3.13 Intermediate: Overhead analysis sheet and calculation of overhead rates

Dunstan Ltd manufactures tents and sleeping bags in three separate production departments. The principal manufacturing processes consist of cutting material in the pattern cutting room, and sewing the material in either the tent or the sleeping bag departments. For the year to 31 July cost centre expenses and other relevant information are budgeted as follows:

| | Total (£) | Cutting room (£) | Tents (£) | Sleeping bags (£) | Raw material stores (£) | Canteen (£) | Maintenance (£) |
|---|---|---|---|---|---|---|---|
| Indirect wages | 147 200 | 6 400 | 19 500 | 20 100 | 41 200 | 15 000 | 45 000 |
| Consumable materials | 54 600 | 5 300 | 4 100 | 2 300 | – | 18 700 | 24 200 |
| Plant depreciation | 84 200 | 31 200 | 17 500 | 24 600 | 2 500 | 3 400 | 5 000 |
| Power | 31 700 | | | | | | |
| Heat and light | 13 800 | | | | | | |
| Rent and rates | 14 400 | | | | | | |
| Building insurance | 13 500 | | | | | | |
| Floor area (sq. ft) | 30 000 | 8 000 | 10 000 | 7 000 | 1 500 | 2 500 | 1 000 |
| Estimated power usage (%) | 100 | 17 | 38 | 32 | 3 | 8 | 2 |
| Direct labour (hours) | 112 000 | 7 000 | 48 000 | 57 000 | — | — | — |
| Machine usage (hours) | 87 000 | 2 000 | 40 000 | 45 000 | — | — | — |
| Value of raw material issues (%) | 100 | 62.5 | 12.5 | 12.5 | — | — | 12.5 |

Requirements:

(a) Prepare in columnar form a statement calculating the overhead absorption rates for each machine hour and each direct labour hour for each of the three production units. You should use bases of apportionment and absorption which you consider most appropriate, and the bases used should be clearly indicated in your statement. (16 marks)

(b) 'The use of pre-determined overhead absorption rates based on budgets is preferable to the use of absorption rates calculated from historical data available after the end of a financial period.'

Discuss this statement insofar as it relates to the financial management of a business.

(5 marks)
(Total 21 marks)
*ICAEW PI A/C Techniques*

## 3.14* Intermediate: Calculation of overhead rates and a product cost

DC Limited is an engineering company which uses job costing to attribute costs to individual products and services provided to its customers. It has commenced the preparation of its fixed production overhead cost budget for 2001 and has identified the following costs:

| | (£000) |
|---|---|
| Machining | 600 |
| Assembly | 250 |
| Finishing | 150 |
| Stores | 100 |
| Maintenance | 80 |
| | 1 180 |

The stores and maintenance departments are production service departments. An analysis of the services they provide indicates that their costs should be apportioned accordingly:

| | Machining | Assembly | Finishing | Stores | Maintenance |
|---|---|---|---|---|---|
| Stores | 40% | 30% | 20% | — | 10% |
| Maintenance | 55% | 20% | 20% | 5% | — |

The number of machine and labour hours budgeted for 2001 is:

| | Machining | Assembly | Finishing |
|---|---|---|---|
| Machine hours | 50 000 | 4 000 | 5 000 |
| Labour hours | 10 000 | 30 000 | 20 000 |

Requirements:

(a) Calculate appropriate overhead absorption rates for each production department for 2001. (9 marks)

(b) Prepare a quotation for job number XX34, which is to be commenced early in 2001, assuming that it has:

| | |
|---|---|
| Direct materials | costing £2400 |
| Direct labour | costing £1500 |

and requires:

| | machine hours | labour hours |
|---|---|---|
| Machining department | 45 | 10 |
| Assembly department | 5 | 15 |
| Finishing department | 4 | 12 |

and that profit is 20% of selling price.

(5 marks)

(c) Assume that in 2001 the actual fixed overhead cost of the assembly department totals £300 000 and that the actual machine hours were 4200 and actual labour hours were 30 700.

Prepare the fixed production overhead control account for the assembly department, showing clearly the causes of any over/under-absorption. (5 marks)

(d) Explain how activity based costing would be used in organisations like DC Limited.

(6 marks)

(Total marks 25)

*CIMA Stage 2 Operational Cost Accounting*

## 3.15* Intermediate: Job cost calculation

A printing and publishing company has been asked to provide an estimate for the production of 100 000 catalogues, of 64 pages (32 sheets of paper) each, for a potential customer.

Four operations are involved in the production process: photography, set-up, printing and binding.

Each page of the catalogue requires a separate photographic session. Each session costs £150.

Set-up would require a plate to be made for each page of the catalogue. Each plate requires 4 hours of labour at £7 per hour and £35 of materials. Overheads are absorbed on the basis of labour hours at an hourly rate of £9.50.

In printing, paper costs £12 per thousand sheets. Material losses are expected to be 2% of input. Other printing materials will cost £7 per 500 catalogues. 1000 catalogues are printed per hour of machine time. Labour and overhead costs incurred in printing are absorbed at a rate of £62 per machine hour.

Binding costs are recovered at a rate per machine hour. The rate is £43 per hour and 2500 catalogues are bound per hour of machine time.

A profit margin of 10% of selling price is required.

You are required to:

(a) determine the total amount that should be quoted for the catalogue job by the printing and publishing company. (11 marks)

(b) calculate the additional costs that would be charged to the job if the labour efficiency ratio achieved versus estimate in set-up is 90%.

(4 marks)

(Total 15 marks)

*ACCA Foundation Stage Paper 3*

## 3.16 Intermediate: Computation of three different overhead absorption rates and a cost-plus selling price

A manufacturing company has prepared the following budgeted information for the forthcoming year:

| | £ |
|---|---|
| Direct material | 800 000 |
| Direct labour | 200 000 |
| Direct expenses | 40 000 |
| Production overhead | 600 000 |
| Administrative overhead | 328 000 |
| Budgeted activity levels include: | |
| Budgeted production units | 600 000 |
| Machine hours | 50 000 |
| Labour hours | 40 000 |

It has recently spent heavily upon advanced technological machinery and reduced its workforce. As a consequence it is thinking about changing its basis for overhead absorption from a percentage of direct labour cost to either a machine hour or labour hour basis. The administrative overhead is to be absorbed as a percentage of factory cost.

Required:

(a) Prepare pre-determined overhead absorption rates for production overheads based upon the three different bases for absorption mentioned above. (6 marks)

(b) Outline the reasons for calculating a pre-determined overhead absorption rate.

(2 marks)

(c) Select the overhead absorption rate that you think the organization should use giving reasons for your decision. (3 marks)

(d) The company has been asked to price job AX,

this job requires the following:

| | |
|---|---|
| Direct material | £3788 |
| Direct labour | £1100 |
| Direct expenses | £422 |
| Machine hours | 120 |
| Labour hours | 220 |

Compute the price for this job using the absorption rate selected in (c) above, given that the company profit margin is equal to 10% of the price. (6 marks)

(e) The company previously paid its direct labour workers upon a time basis but is now contemplating moving over to an incentive scheme.

Required:

Draft a memo to the Chief Accountant outlining the general characteristics and advantages of employing a successful incentive scheme.

(8 marks)
(Total 25 marks)
*AAT Cost Accounting and Budgeting*

### 3.17* Intermediate: Various overhead absorption rates and under/over-recovery

The following data relate to a manufacturing department for a period:

| | Budget data (£) | Actual data (£) |
|---|---|---|
| Direct material cost | 100 000 | 150 000 |
| Direct labour cost | 250 000 | 275 000 |
| Production overhead | 250 000 | 350 000 |
| Direct labour hours | 50 000 hours | 55 000 hours |

Job ZX was one of the jobs worked on during the period. Direct material costing £7000 and direct labour (800 hours) costing £4000 were incurred.

Required:

(i) Calculate the production overhead absorption rate predetermined for the period based on:
  (a) percentage of direct material cost;
  (b) direct labour hours. (3 marks)
(ii) Calculate the production overhead cost to be charged to Job ZX based on the rates calculated in answer to (i) above. (2 marks)
(iii) Assume that the direct labour hour rate of absorption is used. Calculate the under or over absorption of production overheads for the period and state an appropriate treatment in the accounts. (4 marks)

(iv) Comment briefly on the relative merits of the two methods of overhead absorption used in (i) above. (6 marks)
(Total 15 marks)
*AAT Cost Accounting and Budgeting*

### 3.18 Intermediate: Calculation of overhead absorption rates and under/over-recovery of overheads

BEC Limited operates an absorption costing system. Its budget for the year ended 31 December shows that it expects its production overhead expenditure to be as follows:

| | Fixed £ | Variable £ |
|---|---|---|
| Machining department | 600 000 | 480 000 |
| Hand finishing department | 360 000 | 400 000 |

During the year it expects to make 200 000 units of its product. This is expected to take 80 000 machine hours in the machining department and 120 000 labour hours in the hand finishing department.

The costs and activity are expected to arise evenly throughout the year, and the budget has been used as the basis of calculating the company's absorption rates.

During March the monthly profit statement reported

(i) that the actual hours worked in each department were

| | |
|---|---|
| Machining | 6000 hours |
| Hand finishing | 9600 hours |

(ii) that the actual overhead costs incurred were

| | Fixed £ | Variable £ |
|---|---|---|
| Machining | 48 500 | 36 000 |
| Hand finishing | 33 600 | 33 500 |

(iii) that the actual production was 15 000 units.

Required:

(a) Calculate appropriate predetermined absorption rates for the year ended 31 December (4 marks)
(b) (i) Calculate the under/over absorption of overhead for each department of the

company for March; (4 marks)

(ii) Comment on the problems of using predetermined absorption rates based on the arbitrary apportionment of overhead costs, with regard to comparisons of actual/target performance; (4 marks)

(c) State the reasons why absorption costing is used by companies. (3 marks)

(Total 15 marks)

*CIMA Stage 1 Accounting*

### 3.19* Intermediate: Analysis of under/over-recovery of overheads and a discussion of blanket versus department overheads

(a) One of the factories in the XYZ Group of companies absorbs fixed production overheads into product cost using a predetermined machine hour rate.

In Year 1, machine hours budgeted were 132 500 and the absorption rate for fixed production overheads was £18.20 per machine hour. Overheads absorbed and incurred were £2 442 440 and £2 317 461 respectively.

In Year 2, machine hours were budgeted to be 5% higher than those actually worked in Year 1. Budgeted and actual fixed production overhead expenditure were £2 620 926 and £2 695 721 respectively, and actual machine hours were 139 260.

Required:

Analyse, in as much detail as possible, the under/over absorption of fixed production overhead occurring in Years 1 and 2, and the change in absorption rate between the two years. (15 marks)

(b) Contrast the use of

(i) blanket as opposed to departmental overhead absorption rates;

(ii) predetermined overhead absorption rates as opposed to rates calculated from actual activity and expenditure.

(10 marks)

(Total 25 marks)

*ACCA Cost and Management Accounting 1*

### 3.20 Intermediate: Various overhead absorption rates

AC Limited is a small company which undertakes a variety of jobs for its customers.

|  | Budgeted profit and loss statement for the year ending 31 December | |
|---|---:|---:|
|  | (£) | (£) |
| Sales |  | 750 000 |
| Cost: |  |  |
| Direct materials | 100 000 |  |
| Direct wages | 50 000 |  |
| Prime cost | 150 000 |  |
| Fixed production overhead | 300 000 |  |
| Production cost | 450 000 |  |
| Selling, distribution and administration cost | 160 000 |  |
|  |  | 610 000 |
| Profit |  | £140 000 |

Budgeted data:

| Labour hours for the year | 25 000 |
|---|---|
| Machine hours for the year | 15 000 |
| Number of jobs for the year | 300 |

An enquiry has been received, and the production department has produced estimates of the prime cost involved and of the hours required to complete job A57.

|  | (£) |
|---|---:|
| Direct materials | 250 |
| Direct wages | 200 |
| Prime cost | £450 |
| Labour hours required | 80 |
| Machine hours required | 50 |

You are required to:

(a) calculate by different methods *six* overhead absorption rates; (6 marks)

(b) comment briefly on the suitability of each method calculated in (a); (8 marks)

(c) calculate cost estimates for job A57 using in turn each of the six overhead absorption rates calculated in (a).

(6 marks)

(Total 20 marks)

*CIMA Foundation Cost Accounting 1*

### 3.21 Intermediate: Calculation of under/over recovery of overheads

A company produces several products which pass through the two production departments in its factory. These two departments are concerned with filling and sealing operations. There are two service departments, maintenance and canteen, in the factory.

Predetermined overhead absorption rates, based on direct labour hours, are established for the two production departments. The budgeted expenditure for these departments for the period just ended, including the apportionment of service department overheads, was £110 040 for filling, and £53 300 for sealing. Budgeted direct labour hours were 13 100 for filling and 10 250 for sealing.

Service department overheads are apportioned as follows:

| | | |
|---|---|---|
| Maintenance – Filling | | 70% |
| Maintenance – Sealing | | 27% |
| Maintenance – Canteen | | 3% |
| Canteen | – Filling | 60% |
| | – Sealing | 32% |
| | – Maintenance | 8% |

During the period just ended, actual overhead costs and activity were as follows:

| | (£) | Direct labour hours |
|---|---|---|
| Filling | 74 260 | 12 820 |
| Sealing | 38 115 | 10 075 |
| Maintenance | 25 050 | |
| Canteen | 24 375 | |

Required:
(a) Calculate the overheads absorbed in the period and the extent of the under/over absorption in each of the two production departments. (14 marks)
(b) State, and critically assess, the objectives of overhead apportionment and absorption.
(11 marks)
(Total 25 marks)
*ACCA Level 1 Cost and Management Accounting 1*

**3.22\* Intermediate: Calculation of fixed and variable overhead rates, normal activity level and under/over recovery of overheads**
(a) C Ltd is a manufacturing company. In one of the production departments in its main factory a machine hour rate is used for absorbing production overhead. This is established as a predetermined rate, based on normal activity.

The rate that will be used for the period which is just commencing is £15.00 per machine hour. Overhead expenditure anticipated, at a range of activity levels, is as follows:

| Activity level (machine hours) | (£) |
|---|---|
| 1500 | 25 650 |
| 1650 | 26 325 |
| 2000 | 27 900 |

Required:
Calculate:
(i) the variable overhead rate per machine hour;
(ii) the total budgeted fixed overhead;
(iii) the normal activity level of the department; and
(iv) the extent of over/under absorption if actual machine hours are 1700 and expenditure is as budgeted.

(10 marks)
(b) In another of its factories, C Ltd carries out jobs to customers' specifications. A particular job requires the following machine hours and direct labour hours in the two production departments:

| | Machining Department | Finishing Department |
|---|---|---|
| Direct labour hours | 25 | 28 |
| Machine hours | 46 | 8 |

Direct labour in both departments is paid at a basic rate of £4.00 per hour. 10% of the direct labour hours in the finishing department are overtime hours, paid at 125% of basic rate. Overtime premiums are charged to production overhead.

The job requires the manufacture of 189 components. Each component requires 1.1 kilos of prepared material. Loss on preparation is 10% of unprepared material, which costs £2.35 per kilo.

Overhead absorption rates are to be established from the following data:

| | Machining Department | Finishing Department |
|---|---|---|
| Production overhead | £35 280 | £12 480 |
| Direct labour hours | 3 500 | 7 800 |

| Machine hours | 11 200 | 2 100 |

Required:

(i) Calculate the overhead absorption rate for each department and justify the absorption method used.

(ii) Calculate the cost of the job. (15 marks)

(Total 25 marks)

*ACCA Level 1*

## 3.23 Intermediate: Under- and over-absorption of overheads and calculation of budgeted expenditure and activity

A large firm of solicitors uses a job costing system to identify costs with individual clients. Hours worked by professional staff are used as the basis for charging overhead costs to client services. A predetermined rate is used, derived from budgets drawn up at the beginning of each year commencing on 1 April.

In the year to 31 March 2000 the overheads of the solicitors' practice, which were absorbed at a rate of £7.50 per hour of professional staff, were over-absorbed by £4760. Actual overheads incurred were £742 600. Professional hours worked were 1360 over budget.

The solicitors' practice has decided to refine its overhead charging system by differentiating between the hours of senior and junior professional staff, respectively. A premium of 40% is to be applied to the hourly overhead rate for senior staff compared with junior staff.

Budgets for the year to 31 March 2001 are as follows:

| | |
|---|---|
| Senior professional staff hours | 21 600 |
| Junior professional staff hours | 79 300 |
| Practice overheads | £784 000 |

Required

(a) Calculate for the year ended 31 March 2000:
  (i) budgeted professional staff hours;
  (ii) budgeted overhead expenditure.
  (5 marks)

(b) Calculate, for the year ended 31 March 2001, the overhead absorption rates (to three decimal places of a £) to be applied to:
  (i) senior professional staff hours;
  (ii) junior professional staff hours.
  (4 marks)

(c) How is the change in method of charging overheads likely to improve the firm's job costing system? (3 marks)

(d) Explain briefly why overhead absorbed using predetermined rates may differ from actual overhead incurred for the same period.
(2 marks)

(Total 14 marks)

*ACCA Foundation Paper 3*

## 3.24* Intermediate: Reapportionment of service department overheads and a calculation of under/over-recovery of overheads

An organization has budgeted for the following production overheads for its production and service cost centres for the coming year:

| Cost centre | £ |
|---|---|
| Machining | 180 000 |
| Assembly | 160 000 |
| Paint shop | 130 000 |
| Engineering shop | 84 000 |
| Stores | 52 000 |
| Canteen | 75 000 |

The product passes through the machining, assembly and paint shop cost centres and the following data relates to the cost centres:

| | M/c | Ass | Paint shop | Eng shop | Stores |
|---|---|---|---|---|---|
| No. of employees | 81 | 51 | 39 | 30 | 24 |
| Eng Shop–service hrs | 18 000 | 12 000 | 10 000 | | |
| Stores (orders) | 180 | 135 | 90 | 45 | |

The following budgeted data relates to the production cost centres:

| | M/c | Assembly | Paint shop |
|---|---|---|---|
| M/c hours | 9 200 | 8 100 | 6 600 |
| Lab hours | 8 300 | 11 250 | 9 000 |
| Lab cost | £40 000 | £88 000 | £45 000 |

Required:

(a) Apportion the production overhead costs of the service cost centres to the production cost centres and determine predetermined overhead absorption rates for the 3 production cost centres on the following basis:
  Machining – Machine hours.
  Assembly – Labour hours.
  Paint shop – Labour costs. (11 marks)

(b) Actual results for the production cost centres were:

| | M/c | Assembly | Paint shop |
|---|---|---|---|
| M/c hours | 10 000 | 8 200 | 6 600 |
| Lab hours | 4 500 | 7 800 | 6 900 |
| Lab cost | £25 000 | £42 000 | £35 000 |
| Actual O/h | £290 000 | £167 000 | £155 000 |

Prepare a statement showing the under/over absorption per cost centre for the period under review.
(7 marks)

(c) Explain why overheads need to be absorbed upon pre-determined bases such as the above. Consider whether these bases for absorption are appropriate in the light of changing technology, suggesting any alternative basis that you consider appropriate.
(7 marks)
(Total 25 marks)
*AAT Cost Accounting and Budgeting*

## 3.25* Intermediate: Reapportionment of service department costs and a product cost calculation

Shown below is an extract from next year's budget for a company manufacturing three different products in three production departments:

| | Product A | Product B | Product C |
|---|---|---|---|
| Production (units) | 4000 | 3000 | 6000 |
| Direct material cost (£ per unit) | 7 | 4 | 9 |
| Direct labour requirements (hours per unit): | | | |
| Cutting department: | | | |
| Skilled operatives | 3 | 5 | 2 |
| Unskilled operatives | 6 | 1 | 3 |
| Machining department | $\frac{1}{2}$ | $\frac{1}{4}$ | $\frac{1}{3}$ |
| Pressing department | 2 | 3 | 4 |
| Machine hour requirements (hours per unit): | | | |
| Machining department | 2 | $1\frac{1}{2}$ | $2\frac{1}{2}$ |

The skilled operatives employed in the cutting department are paid £4 per hour and the unskilled operatives are paid £2.50 per hour. All the operatives in the machining and pressing departments are paid £3 per hour.

| | Production departments | | | Service departments | |
|---|---|---|---|---|---|
| | Cutting | Machining | Pressing | Engineering | Personnel |
| Budgeted total overheads (£) | 154 482 | 64 316 | 58 452 | 56 000 | 34 000 |
| Service | | | | | |

| | | | | | |
|---|---|---|---|---|---|
| department costs are incurred for the benefit of other departments as follows: | | | | | |
| Engineering services | 20% | 45% | 25% | — | 10% |
| Personnel services | 55% | 10% | 20% | 15% | — |

The company operates a full absorption costing system.

Required:
(a) Calculate, as equitably as possible, the total budgeted manufacturing cost of:
  (i) one completed unit of Product A, and
  (ii) one incomplete unit of Product B which has been processed by the cutting and machining departments but which has not yet been passed into the pressing department.
(15 marks)
(b) At the end of the first month of the year for which the above budget was prepared the production overhead control account for the machining department showed a credit balance. Explain the possible reasons for that credit balance.
(7 marks)
(Total 22 marks)
*ACCA Level 1 Costing*

## 3.26 Intermediate: Reapportionment of service department costs

JR Co. Ltd's budgeted overheads for the forthcoming period applicable to its production departments, are as follows:

| | (£000) |
|---|---|
| 1 | 870 |
| 2 | 690 |

The budgeted total costs for the forthcoming period for the service departments, are as follows:

| | (£000) |
|---|---|
| G | 160 |
| H | 82 |

The use made of each of the services has been estimated as follows.

| | Production department | | Service department | |
|---|---|---|---|---|
| | 1 | 2 | G | H |
| G(%) | 60 | 30 | — | 10 |

| H(%) | 50 | 30 | 20 | — |

**Required:**

Apportion the service department costs to production departments:

(i) using the step-wise ('elimination') method, starting with G;

(ii) using the reciprocal (simultaneous equation) method;

(iii) commenting briefly on your figures.

(8 marks)

(Total 20 marks)

*ACCA Paper 8 Managerial Finance*

## 3.27 Advanced: Reapportionment of service department costs and comments on apportionment and absorption calculation

The Isis Engineering Company operates a job order costing system which includes the use of predetermined overhead absorption rates. The company has two service cost centres and two production cost centres. The production cost centre overheads are charged to jobs via direct labour hour rates which are currently £3.10 per hour in production cost centre A and £11.00 per hour in production cost centre B. The calculations involved in determining these rates have excluded any consideration of the services that are provided by each service cost centre to the other.

The bases used to charge general factory overhead and service cost centre expenses to the production cost centres are as follows:

(i) general factory overhead is apportioned on the basis of the floor area used by each of the production and service cost centres,

(ii) the expenses of service cost centre 1 are charged out on the basis of the number of personnel in each production cost centre,

(iii) the expenses of service cost centre 2 are charged out on the basis of the usage of its services by each production cost centre.

The company's overhead absorption rates are revised annually prior to the beginning of each year, using an analysis of the outcome of the current year and the draft plans and forecasts for the forthcoming year. The revised rates for next year are to be based on the following data:

| | General factory overhead | Service cost centres | | Product cost centres | |
| --- | --- | --- | --- | --- | --- |
| | | 1 | 2 | A | B |
| Budgeted overhead for next year (before any reallocation) (£) | 210 000 | 93 800 | 38 600 | 182 800 | 124 800 |
| % of factory floor area | — | 5 | 10 | 15 | 70 |

| | General factory overhead | Service cost centres | | Product cost centres | |
| --- | --- | --- | --- | --- | --- |
| | | 1 | 2 | A | B |
| % of factory personnel | — | 10 | 18 | 63 | 9 |
| Estimated usage of services of service cost centre 2 in forthcoming year (hours) | — | 1 000 | — | 4 000 | 25 000 |
| Budgeted direct labour hours for next year (to be used to calculate next year's absorption rates) | — | — | — | 120 000 | 20 000 |
| Budgeted direct labour hours for current year (these figures were used in the calculation of this year's absorption rates) | — | — | — | 100 000 | 30 000 |

(a) Ignoring the question of reciprocal charges between the service cost centres, you are required to calculate the revised overhead absorption rates for the two production cost centres. Use the company's established procedures. (6 marks)

(b) Comment on the extent of the differences between the current overhead absorption rates and those you have calculated in your answer to (a). Set out the likely reasons for these differences. (4 marks)

(c) Each service cost centre provides services to the other. Recalculate next year's overhead absorption rates, recognizing the existence of such reciprocal services and assuming that they can be measured on the same bases as those used to allocate costs to the production cost centres. (6 marks)

(d) Assume that:

(i) General factory overhead is a fixed cost.

(ii) Service cost centre 1 is concerned with inspection and quality control, with its budgeted expenses (before any reallocations) being 10% fixed and 90% variable.

(iii) Service cost centre 2 is the company's plant maintenance section, with its budgeted expenses (before any reallocations) being 90% fixed and 10% variable.

(iv) Production cost centre A is labour-intensive, with its budgeted overhead (before any reallocation) being 90% fixed and 10% variable.

(v) Production cost centre B is highly mechanized, with its budgeted overhead (before any reallocations) being 20% fixed and 80% variable.

In the light of these assumptions, comment on the cost apportionment and absorption calculations made in parts (a) and (c) and suggest any improvements that you would consider appropriate.

(6 marks)
(Total 22 marks)
*ACCA Level 2 Management Accounting*

### 3.28* Advanced: Comparison of methods of reapportioning service department costs

Puerile Plastics Ltd consists of six departments: personnel and administration, maintenance, stores, moulding, extrusion and finishing. The accountant has collected data for the 12 months to 30 September relating to the six departments, which is given below.

The accountant wishes to use the data to derive the selling prices of the firm's products, based on their full costs. The selling price of each product will be equal to 250% of the product's full cost. The market for the products is supplied by five large companies, of which Puerile Plastics Ltd is one, and ten small companies. Puerile Plastics Ltd has approximately a 20% market share. The standard production quantities can be converted into standard equivalent units of output for each of the three production departments. The accountant is considering different ways of allocating the costs of the three service departments in order to obtain the full cost per standard equivalent unit, and hence the sales price of each product.

Required:

(a) Calculate the total cost for each of the three production departments using the direct method of allocation of the service depart-

ments' costs. (4 marks)

(b) Calculate the total cost of each of the three production departments using the step-down (sometimes called step or sequential) method of allocation of the service departments' costs. State any assumptions which you make.

(5 marks)

(c) *Formulate* the equations which will provide the total cost of each of the three production departments using the reciprocal or cross-allocation method of allocation of costs.

(4 marks)

(d) Compare and contrast the three methods of service cost allocation, using the results obtained in (a) and (b) above as examples.

(7 marks)

(e) Comment on the approach the accountant is considering for the derivation of the selling price of the products.

(5 marks)
(Total 25 marks)
*ICAEW P2 Management Accounting*

### 3.29* Advanced: Reapportionment of service department costs and a discussion of how fully allocated costs can be useful

Megalith Manufacturing divides its plant into two main production departments, Processing and Assembly. It also has three main service-providing

### Data relating to Question 3.28

| | Personnel and Administration | Maintenance | Stores | Moulding | Extrusion | Finishing | Total |
|---|---|---|---|---|---|---|---|
| Employees (number) | 20 | 4 | 3 | 25 | 16 | 10 | 78 |
| Proportion of total maintenance hours worked in each department (%) | 5 | 10 | 15 | 20 | 40 | 10 | 100 |
| Proportion of store's floorspace taken up by each department's materials (%) | — | 10 | – | 20 | 30 | 40 | 100 |
| Output levels (per thousand standard equivalent units) | — | – | – | 187 | 149 | 336 | |
| Direct costs (£000): | | | | | | | |
| Material | 36 | 23 | — | 330 | 170 | 20 | |
| Labour | 155 | 25 | 18.72 | 168.75 | 115.2 | 81 | |
| Variable overheads | – | — | — | 71.25 | 151.8 | 30 | |
| Fixed overheads | 15 | 15 | 17.28 | 449.3 | 371.7 | 67 | |

departments, Heat, Maintenance and Steam, which provide services to the production departments and to each other. The costs of providing these services are allocated to departments on the bases indicated below:

| | Total cost | Basis of allocation |
|---|---|---|
| Heat | £ 90 000 | Floor area |
| Maintenance | £ 300 000 | Hours worked |
| Steam | £ 240 000 | Units consumed |

During the last year, the services provided were:

| To | Heat | Mainten-ance | Steam | Processing | Assembly |
|---|---|---|---|---|---|
| From Heat (m²) | | 5 000 | 5 000 | 40 000 | 50 000 |
| Maintenance (hrs) | 3 000 | | 4 500 | 7 500 | 15 000 |
| Steam (units) | 192 000 | 48 000 | | 480 000 | 240 000 |

Requirements:
(a) Allocate the costs of service departments to production departments, using each of the following methods:
   (i)  direct                                 (3 marks)
   (ii) step-down                              (4 marks)
   (iii) reciprocal                            (6 marks)
(b) What is the main problem likely to be encountered in using the information generated by any of the above systems of allocation, given that a substantial proportion of the costs incurred in each service department are fixed for the year? How would you attempt to overcome this problem?          (5 marks)
(c) Given that cost allocation is an essentially arbitrary process, explain how total costs which include substantial amounts of allocated costs can be useful.        (7 marks)
                                            (Total 25 marks)
*ICAEW P2 Management Accounting*

### 3.30* Intermediate: Explanation of a product cost calculation

In order to identify the costs incurred in carrying out a range of work to customer specification in its factory, a company has a job costing system. This system identifies costs directly with a job where this is possible and reasonable. In addition, production overhead costs are absorbed into the cost of jobs at the end of each month, at an actual rate per

direct labour hour for each of the two production departments.

One of the jobs carried out in the factory during the month just ended was Job No. 123. The following information has been collected relating specifically to this job:

400 kilos of Material Y were issued from stores to Department A. 76 direct labour hours were worked in Department A at a basic wage of £4.50 per hour. 6 of these hours were classified as overtime at a premium of 50%.

300 kilos of Material Z were issued from stores to Department B. Department B returned 30 kilos of Material Z to the storeroom being excess to requirements for the job.

110 direct labour hours were worked in Department B at a basic wage of £4.00 per hour. 30 of these hours were classified as overtime at a premium of 40%. *All* overtime worked in Department B in the month is a result of the request of a customer for early completion of another job, which had been originally scheduled for completion in the month following.

Department B discovered defects in some of the work, which was returned to Department A for rectification. 3 labour hours were worked in Department A on rectification (these are additional to the 76 direct labour hours in Department A noted above). Such rectification is regarded as a normal part of the work carried out generally in the department.

Department B damaged 5 kilos of Material Z which then had to be disposed of. Such losses of material are not expected to occur.

| | Department A (£) | Department B (£) |
|---|---|---|
| Direct materials issued from stores* | 6500 | 13 730 |
| Direct materials returned to stores | 135 | 275 |
| Direct labour, at basic wage rate† | 9090 | 11 200 |
| Indirect labour, at basic wage rate | 2420 | 2 960 |
| Overtime premium | 450 | 120 |
| Lubricants and cleaning compounds | 520 | 680 |
| Maintenance | 720 | 510 |
| Other | 1200 | 2 150 |

Materials are priced at the end of each month on a weighted average basis. Relevant information of material stock movements during the month, for materials Y and Z, is as follows:

| | Material Y | Material Z |
|---|---|---|
| Opening stock | 1050 kilos | 6970 kilos |
| | (value £529.75) | (value £9946.50) |
| Purchases | 600 kilos at | 16 000 kilos at |
| | £0.50 per kilo | £1.46 per kilo |
| | 500 kilos at | |
| | £0.50 per kilo | |
| | 400 kilos at | |
| | £0.52 per kilo | |
| Issues from stores | 1430 kilos | 8100 kilos |
| Returns to stores | — | 30 kilos |

*This includes, in Department B, the scrapped Material Z. This was the only material scrapped in the month.

†All direct labour in Department A is paid a basic wage of £4.50 per hour, and in Department B £4.00 per hour. Department A direct labour includes a total of 20 hours spent on rectification work.

Required:
(a) Prepare a list of the costs that should be assigned to Job No. 123. Provide an explanation of your treatment of each item.

(17 marks)
(b) Discuss briefly how information concerning the cost of individual jobs can be used.

(5 marks)
(Total 22 marks)
*ACCA Level 1 Costing*

### 3.31 Advanced: Product cost calculation and costs for decision-making

Kaminsky Ltd manufactures belts and braces. The firm is organized into five departments. These are belt-making, braces-making, and three service departments (maintenance, warehousing, and administration).

Direct costs are accumulated for each department. Factory-wide indirect costs (which are fixed for all production levels within the present capacity limits) are apportioned to departments on the basis of the percentage of floorspace occupied. Service department costs are apportioned on the basis of estimated usage, measured as the percentage of the labour hours operated in the service department utilized by the user department.

Each service department also services at least one other service department.

Budgeted data for the forthcoming year are shown below:

| | Belts | Braces | Admin-istration dept | Main-tenance dept | Ware-housing | Company total |
|---|---|---|---|---|---|---|
| (1) Output and sales (units): | | | | | | |
| Output capacity | 150 000 | 60 000 | | | | |
| Output budgeted | 100 000 | 50 000 | | | | |
| Sales budgeted | 100 000 | 50 000 | | | | |
| (2) Direct variable costs (£000): | | | | | | |
| Materials | 120 | 130 | – | 20 | 30 | 300 |
| Labour | 80 | 70 | 50 | 80 | 20 | 300 |
| Total | 200 | 200 | 50 | 100 | 50 | 600 |
| (3) Factory-wide fixed indirect costs (£000) | | | | | | 1000 |
| (4) Floor-space (%) | 40 | 40 | 5 | 10 | 5 | 100 |
| (5) Usage of service department labour hours (%) | | | | | | |
| Administration | 40 | 40 | – | 10 | 10 | 100 |
| Warehousing | 50 | 25 | – | 25 | – | 100 |
| Maintenance | 30 | 30 | – | – | 40 | 100 |

(a) You are required to calculate the total cost per unit of belts and braces respectively, in accordance with the system operated by Kaminsky Ltd. (12 marks)
(b) In addition to the above data, it has been decided that the selling prices of the products are to be determined on a cost-plus basis, as the unit total cost plus 20%.

Two special orders have been received, outside the normal run of business, and not provided for in the budget.
They are as follows:
(i) an order for 1000 belts from Camfam, an international relief organization, offering to pay £5000 for them.
(ii) a contract to supply 2000 belts a week for 50 weeks to Mixon Spenders, a chainstore, at a price per belt of 'unit total cost plus 10%'.

You are required to set out the considerations which the management of Kaminsky Ltd should take into account in deciding whether to accept each of these orders, and to advise them as far as you are able on the basis of the information given. (8 marks)
(c) 'Normalized overhead rates largely eliminate from inventories, from cost of goods sold, and

from gross margin any unfavourable impact of having production out of balance with the long-run demand for a company's products.'

You are required to explain and comment upon the above statement.

(5 marks)

*ICAEW Management Accounting*

# Accounting entries for a job costing system

4

This chapter is concerned with the accounting entries necessary to record transactions within a job costing system. In Chapter 2 it was pointed out that job costing relates to a costing system that is required in organizations where each unit or batch of output of a product or service is unique. This creates the need for the cost of each unit to be calculated separately. The term 'job' thus relates to each unique unit or batch of output. In contrast, process costing relates to those situations where masses of identical units are produced and it is unnecessary to assign costs to individual units of output. Instead, the cost of a single unit of output can be obtained by merely dividing the total costs assigned to the cost object for a period by the units of output for that period. In practice these two costing systems represent extreme ends of a continuum. The output of many organizations requires a combination of the elements of both job costing and process costing. However, the accounting methods described in this chapter can be applied to all types of costing systems ranging from purely job to process, or a combination of both. In the next chapter we shall look at process costing in detail.

The accounting system on which we shall concentrate our attention is one in which the cost and financial accounts are combined in one set of accounts; this is known as an **integrated cost accounting system**. An alternative system, where the cost and financial accounts are maintained independently, is known as an **interlocking cost accounting system**. The integrated cost accounting system is generally considered to be preferable to the interlocking system, since the latter involves a duplication of accounting entries.

A knowledge of the materials recording procedure will enable you to have a better understanding of the accounting entries. Therefore we shall begin by looking at this procedure.

## Learning objectives

After studying this chapter, you should be able to:

- describe the materials recording procedure;
- distinguish between an integrated and interlocking accounting system;
- describe backflush costing;
- explain the distinguishing features of contract costing;
- prepare contract accounts and calculate attributable profit.

# Materials recording procedure

When goods are received they are inspected and details of the quantity of each type of goods received are listed on a goods received note. The goods received note is the source document for entering details of the items received in the receipts column of the appropriate stores ledger account. An illustration of a stores ledger account is provided in Exhibit 4.1. This document is merely a record of the quantity and value of each individual item of material stored by the organization. In most organizations this document will only consist in the form of a computer record.

The formal authorization for the issue of materials is a stores requisition. The type and quantity of materials issued are listed on the requisition. This document also contains details of the job number, product code or overhead account for which the materials are required. Exhibit 4.2 provides an illustration of a typical stores requisition. Each of the items listed on the materials requisition are priced from the information recorded in the receipts column of the appropriate stores ledger account. The information on the stores requisition is then recorded in the issues column of the appropriate stores ledger account and a balance of the quantity and value for each of the specific items of materials is calculated. The cost of each item of material listed on the stores requisition is assigned to the appropriate job number or overhead account. In practice this clerical process is likely to be computerized.

# Pricing the issues of materials

A difficulty that arises with material issues is the cost to associate with each issue. This is because the same type of material may have been purchased at several different prices. Actual cost can take on several different values, and some method of pricing material issues must be selected. Consider the situation presented in Example 4.1.

There are three alternative methods that you might consider for calculating the cost of materials issued to job Z which will impact on both the cost of sales and the inventory valuation that is incorporated in the April monthly profit statement and balance sheet. First, you can assume that the first item received was the first item to be issued, that is first in, first out (FIFO). In the example

**EXHIBIT 4.1**

*A stores ledger account*

| | | | | | | | | | | | |
|---|---|---|---|---|---|---|---|---|---|---|---|
| | | | | Stores ledger account | | | | | | | |
| Material: ......................... Code: ......................... | | | | | | | Maximum quantity: ......................... Minimum quantity: ......................... | | | | |

| | Receipts | | | | Issues | | | | Stock | | |
|---|---|---|---|---|---|---|---|---|---|---|---|
| Date | GRN no. | Quantity | Unit price (£) | Amount (£) | Stores req. no. | Quantity | Unit price (£) | Amount (£) | Quantity | Unit price (£) | Amount (£) |
| | | | | | | | | | | | |

EXHIBIT   4.2

A stores
requisition

the 5000 units issued to job Z would be priced at £1 and the
closing inventory would be valued at £6000 (5000 units at
£1.20 per unit).

| | | | | | | | |
|---|---|---|---|---|---|---|---|
| Stores requisition | | | | | No. | | |
| Material required for: | | | | | | | |
| (job or overhead account) | | | | | | | |
| Department: | | | | | | | |
| | | | | | Date: | | |
| [Quantity] | Description | Code no. | Weight | Rate | £ | [Notes] | |
| | | | | | | | |
| | | | | | | | |
| Foreman | | | | | | | |

EXAMPLE   4.1

On 5 March Nordic purchased 5000 units of materials at
£1 each. A further 5000 units were purchased on 30 March
at £1.20 each. During April 5000 units were issued to job
Z. No further issues were made during April and you are
now preparing the monthly accounts for April.

Secondly, you could assume that the last item to be received was the first item to be
issued, that is, **last in, first out (LIFO)**. Here a material cost of £6000 (5000 units at £1.20
per unit) would be recorded against the cost of job Z and the closing inventory would be
valued at £5000 (5000 units at £1 per unit).

Thirdly there may be a strong case for issuing the items at the average cost of the
materials in stock (i.e. £1.10 per unit). With an average cost system the job cost would be
recorded at £5500 and the closing inventory would also be valued at £5500. The following
is a summary of the three different materials pricing methods relating to Example 4.1:

| | Cost of sales (i.e. charge to job Z) (£) | Closing inventory (£) | Total costs (£) |
|---|---|---|---|
| First in first out (FIFO) | 5000 (5000 × £1) | 6000 (5000 × £1.20) | 11 000 |
| Last in, first out (LIFO) | 6000 (5000 × £1.20) | 5000 (5000 × £1) | 11 000 |
| Average cost | 5500 (5000 × £1.10) | 5500 (5000 × £1.10) | 11 000 |

FIFO appears to be the most logical method in the sense that it makes the same assumption
as the physical flow of materials through an organization; that is, it is assumed that items
received first will be issued first. During periods of inflation, the earliest materials that

have the lowest purchase price will be issued first. This assumption leads to a lower cost of sales calculation, and therefore a higher profit than would be obtained by using either of the other methods. Note also that the closing inventory will be at the latest and therefore higher prices. With the LIFO method the latest and higher prices are assigned to the cost of sales and therefore lower profits will be reported compared with using either FIFO or average cost. The value of the closing inventory will be at the earliest and therefore lower prices. Under the average cost method, the cost of sales and the closing inventory will fall somewhere between the values recorded for the FIFO and LIFO methods.

LIFO is not an acceptable method of pricing for taxation purposes in the UK, although this does not preclude its use provided that the accounts are adjusted for taxation purposes. The UK Statement of Standard Accounting Practice on Stocks and Work in Progress (SSAP 9), however, states that LIFO does not bear a reasonable relationship to actual costs obtained during the period, and implies that this method is inappropriate for external reporting. In view of these comments, the FIFO or the average cost method should be used for external financial accounting purposes. Instead of using FIFO or average cost for inventory valuation and profit measurement many organizations maintain their inventories at standard prices using a standard costing system. With a standard costing system the process of pricing material issues is considerably simplified. We shall look at standard costing in detail in Chapters 18 and 19.

The above discussion relates to pricing the issue of materials for internal and external profit measurement and inventory valuation. For decision-making the focus is on future costs, rather than the allocation of past costs, and therefore using different methods of pricing materials is not an issue.

# Control accounts

The recording system is based on a system of control accounts. A control account is a summary account, where entries are made from *totals* of transactions for a period. For example, the balance in the stores ledger control account will be supported by a voluminous file of stores ledger accounts, which will add up to agree with the total in the stores ledger control account. Assuming 1000 items of materials were received for a period that totalled £200 000, an entry of the total of £200 000 would be recorded on the debit (receipts side) of the stores ledger *control* account. This will be supported by 1000 separate entries in each of the individual stores ledger accounts. The total of all these *individual* entries will add up to £200 000. A system of control accounts enables one to check the accuracy of the various accounting entries, since the total of all the *individual* entries in the various stores ledger accounts should agree with the control account, which will have received the *totals* of the various transactions. The file of all the individual accounts (for example the individual stores ledger accounts) supporting the total control account is called the subsidiary ledger.

We shall now examine the accounting entries necessary to record the transaction outlined in Example 4.2. A manual system is described so that the accounting entries can be followed, but the normal practice is now for these accounts to be maintained on a computer. You will find a summary of the accounting entries set out in Exhibit 4.3, where each transaction is prefixed by the appropriate number to give a clearer understanding of the necessary entries relating to each transaction. In addition, the appropriate journal entry is shown for each transaction together with a supporting explanation.

**EXAMPLE 4.2**

The following are the transactions of AB Ltd for the month of April.

1. Raw materials of £182 000 were purchases on credit.
2. Raw materials of £2000 were returned to the supplier because of defects.
3. The total of stores requisitions for direct materials issued for the period was £165 000.
4. The total issues for indirect materials for the period was £10 000.
5. Gross wages of £185 000 were incurred during the period
   consisting of wages paid to employees                                    £105 000
   Tax deductions payable to the Government (i.e. Inland Revenue)             £60 000
   National Insurance contributions due                                      £20 000
6. All the amounts due in transaction 5 were settled by cash during the period.
7. The allocation of the gross wages for the period was as follows:
   Direct wages                                                             £145 000
   Indirect wages                                                            £40 000
8. The employer's contribution for National Insurance deductions was £25 000.
9. Indirect factory expenses of £41 000 were incurred during the period.
10. Depreciation of factory machinery was £30 000.
11. Overhead expenses allocated to jobs by means of overhead allocation rates was £140 000 for the period.
12. Non-manufacturing overhead incurred during the period was £40 000.
13. The cost of jobs completed and transferred to finished goods stock was £300 000.
14. The sales value of goods withdrawn from stock and delivered to customers was £400 000 for the period.
15. The cost of goods withdrawn from stock and delivered to customers was £240 000 for the period.

# Recording the purchase of raw materials

The entry to record the purchase of materials in transaction 1 is

> Dr Stores ledger control account          182 000
> Cr Creditors control account                        182 000

This accounting entry reflects the fact that the company has incurred a short-term liability to acquire a current asset consisting of raw material stock. Each purchase is also entered in the receipts column of an individual stores ledger account (a separate record is used for each item of materials purchases) for the quantity received, a unit price and amount. In addition, a separate credit entry is made in each individual creditor's account. Note that the entries in the control accounts form part of the system of double entry, whereas the separate entries in the individual accounts are detailed subsidiary records, which do not form part of the double entry system.

**EXHIBIT 4.3**

*Summary of accounting transactions for AB Ltd*

### Stores ledger control account

| | | | | |
|---|---|---:|---|---:|
| 1. | Creditors a/c | 182 000 | 2. Creditors a/c | 2 000 |
| | | | 3. Work in progress a/c | 165 000 |
| | | | 4. Factory overhead a/c | 10 000 |
| | | | Balance c/d | 5 000 |
| | | 182 000 | | 182 000 |
| | Balance b/d | 5 000 | | |

### Factory overhead control account

| | | | | |
|---|---|---:|---|---:|
| 4. | Stores ledger a/c | 10 000 | 11. Work in progress a/c | 140 000 |
| 7. | Wages control a/c | 40 000 | Balance – under recovery | |
| 8. | National Insurance | 25 000 | transferred to costing P&L a/c | 6 000 |
| | contributions a/c | | | |
| 9. | Expense creditors a/c | 41 000 | | |
| 10. | Provision for depreciation a/c | 30 000 | | |
| | | 146 000 | | 146 000 |

### Non-manufacturing overhead control account

| | | | | |
|---|---|---:|---|---:|
| 12. | Expense creditor a/c | 40 000 | Transferred to costing P&L a/c | 40 000 |

### Creditors account

| | | | | |
|---|---|---:|---|---:|
| 2. | Stores ledger a/c | 2 000 | 1. Stores ledger a/c | 182 000 |

### Wages accrued account

| | | | | |
|---|---|---:|---|---:|
| 6. | Cash/bank | 105 000 | 5. Wages control a/c | 105 000 |

### Tax payable account

| | | | | |
|---|---|---:|---|---:|
| 6. | Cash/bank | 60 000 | 5. Wages control a/c | 60 000 |

### National Insurance contributions account

| | | | | |
|---|---|---:|---|---:|
| 6. | Cash/bank | 20 000 | 5. Wage control a/c | 20 000 |
| 8. | Cash/bank | 25 000 | 8. Factory overhead a/c | 25 000 |
| | | 45 000 | | 45 000 |

### Expense creditors account

| | | | | |
|---|---|---:|---|---:|
| | | | 9. Factory overhead a/c | 41 000 |
| | | | 12. Non-manufacturing overhead | 40 000 |

### Work in progress control account

| | | | |
|---|---|---|---|
| 3. Stores ledger a/c | 165 000 | 13. Finished goods | |
| 7. Wages control a/c | 145 000 | stock a/c | 300 000 |
| 11. Factory overhead a/c | 140 000 | Balance c/d | 150 000 |
| | 450 000 | | 450 000 |
| Balanced b/ | 150 000 | | |

### Finished goods stock account

| | | | |
|---|---|---|---|
| 13. Work in progress a/c | 300 000 | 15. Cost of sales a/c | 240 000 |
| | | Balance c/d | 60 000 |
| | 300 000 | | 300 000 |
| Balance b/d | 60 000 | | |

### Cost of sales account

| | | | |
|---|---|---|---|
| 15. Finished goods stock a/c | 240 000 | Transferred to costing P&L a/c | 240 000 |

### Provision for depreciation account

| | | | |
|---|---|---|---|
| | | 10. Factory overhead | 30 000 |

### Wages control account

| | | | |
|---|---|---|---|
| 5. Wages accrued a/c | 105 000 | 7. Work in progress a/c | 145 000 |
| 5. Tax payable a/c | 60 000 | 7. Factory overhead a/c | 40 000 |
| 5. National Insurance a/c | 20 000 | | |
| | 185 000 | | 185 000 |

### Sales account

| | | | |
|---|---|---|---|
| Transferred to costing P&L | 400 000 | 14. Debtors | 400 000 |

### Debtors account

| | | | |
|---|---|---|---|
| 14. Sales a/c | 400 000 | | |

### Costing profit and loss account

| | | |
|---|---|---|
| Sales a/c | | 400 000 |
| Less cost of sales a/c | | 240 000 |
| Gross profit | | 160 000 |
| Less under recovery of factory overhead | 6 000 | |
| Non-manufacturing overhead | 40 000 | 46 000 |
| Net profit | | 114 000 |

The entry for transaction 2 for materials returned to suppliers is

| | | |
|---|---|---|
| Dr Creditors control account | 2000 | |
| Cr Stores ledger control account | | 2000 |

An entry for the returned materials is also made in the appropriate stores ledger records and in the individual creditors' accounts.

# Recording the issue of materials

The storekeeper issues materials from store in exchange for a duly authorized stores requisition. For direct materials the job number will be recorded on the stores requisition, while for indirect materials the overhead account number will be entered on the requisition. The issue of direct materials involves a transfer of the materials from stores to production. For transaction 3, material requisitions will have been summarized and the resulting totals will be recorded as follows:

| | | |
|---|---|---|
| Dr Work in progress account | 165 000 | |
| Cr Stores ledger control account | | 165 000 |

This accounting entry reflects the fact that raw material stock is being converted into work in progress (WIP) stock. In addition to the above entries in the control accounts, the individual jobs will be charged with the cost of the material issued so that job costs can be calculated. Each issue is also entered in the issues column on the appropriate stores ledger record.

The entry for transaction 4 for the issue of indirect materials is

| | | |
|---|---|---|
| Dr Factory overhead control account | 10 000 | |
| Cr Stores ledger control account | | 10 000 |

In addition to the entry in the factory overhead account, the cost of material issued will be entered in the individual overhead accounts. These separate overhead accounts will normally consist of individual indirect material accounts for each responsibility centre. Periodically, the totals of each responsibility centre account for indirect materials will be entered in performance reports for comparison with the budgeted indirect material cost.

After transactions 1–4 have been recorded, the stores ledger control account would look like this:

**Stores ledger control account**

| | | | | |
|---|---|---|---|---|
| 1. Creditors a/c | 182 000 | 2. Creditors a/c | | 2 000 |
| | | 3. Work in progress a/c | | 165 000 |
| | | 4. Factory overhead a/c | | 10 000 |
| | | Balance c/d | | 5 000 |
| | 182 000 | | | 182 000 |
| Balance b/d | 5 000 | | | |

# Accounting procedure for labour costs

Accounting for labour costs can be divided into the following two distinct phases:

1. Computations of the gross pay for each employee and calculation of payments to be made to employees, government, pension funds, etc. (**payroll accounting**).
2. Allocation of labour costs to jobs, overhead account and capital accounts (**labour cost accounting**).

An employee's gross pay is computed from information on the employee's personal record, and attendance or production records. For each employee a separate record is kept, showing the employee's employment history with the company, current rate of pay and authorized deductions such as National Insurance, pension plans, savings plans, union dues, and so on. The clock card contains details of attendance time; job cards provide details of bonuses due to employees; and if a piecework system is in operation, the piecework tickets will be analysed by employees and totalled to determine the gross wage. The gross wages are calculated from these documents, and an entry is then made in the payroll for each employee, showing the gross pay, tax deductions and other authorized deductions. The gross pay less the deductions gives the net pay, and this is the amount of cash paid to each employee.

The payroll gives details of the total amount of cash due to employees and the amounts due to the Government (i.e. Inland Revenue), Pension Funds and Savings Funds, etc. To keep the illustration simple at this stage, transaction 5 includes only deductions in respect of taxes and National Insurance. The accounting entries for transaction 5 are

| | |
|---|---|
| Dr Wages control account | |
| 185 000 | |
| Cr Tax payable account | 60 000 |
| Cr National Insurance contributions account | 20 000 |
| Cr Wages accrued account | 105 000 |

The credit entries in transaction 5 will be cleared by a payment of cash. The payment of wages will involve an immediate cash payment, but some slight delay may occur with the payment of tax and National Insurance since the final date for payment of these items is normally a few weeks after the payment of wages. The entries for the cash payments for these items (transaction 6) are

| | | |
|---|---|---|
| Dr Tax payable account | 60 000 | |
| Dr National Insurance contributions account | 20 000 | |
| Dr Wages accrued account | 105 000 | |
| Cr Cash/bank | | 185 000 |

Note that the credit entries for transaction 5 merely represent the recording of amounts due for future payments. The wages control account, however, represents the gross wages for the period, and it is the amount in this account that must be allocated to the job, overhead and capital accounts. Transaction 7 gives details of the allocation of the gross wages. The accounting entries are

| | | |
|---|---|---|
| Dr Work in progress control account | 145 000 | |
| Dr Factory overhead control account | 40 000 | |
| Cr Wages control account | | 185 000 |

In addition to the total entry in the work in progress control account, the labour cost will be charged to the individual job accounts. Similarly, the total entry in the factory overhead control account will be supported by an entry in each individual overhead account for the indirect labour cost incurred.

Transaction 8 represents the employer's contribution for National Insurance payments. The National Insurance deductions in transaction 5 represent the employees' contributions where the company acts merely as an agent, paying these contributions on behalf of the employee. The employer is also responsible for making a contribution in respect of each employee. To keep the accounting entries simple here, the employer's contributions will be charged to the factory overhead account. The accounting entry for transaction 8 is therefore:

| | | |
|---|---|---|
| Dr Factory overhead control account | 25 000 | |
| Cr National Insurance contributions account | | 25 000 |

The National Insurance contributions account will be closed with the following entry when the cash payment is made:

Dr National Insurance contributions account      25 000
     Cr Cash/bank      25 000

After recording these transactions, the wages control account would look like this:

**Wages control account**

| | | | |
|---|---|---|---|
| 5. Wages accrued a/c | 105 000 | 7. Work in progress a/c | 145 000 |
| 5. Tax payable a/c | 60 000 | 7. Factory overhead a/c | 40 000 |
| 5. National Insurance a/c | 20 000 | | |
| | 185 000 | | 185 000 |

# Accounting procedure for manufacturing overheads

Accounting for manufacturing overheads involves entering details of the actual amount of manufacturing overhead incurred on the debit side of the factory overhead control account. The total amount of overheads charged to production is recorded on the credit side of the factory overhead account. In the previous chapter we established that manufacturing overheads are charged to production using budgeted overhead rates. It is most unlikely, however, that the actual amount of overhead incurred, which is recorded on the debit side of the account, will be in agreement with the amount of overhead allocated to jobs, which is recorded on the credit side of the account. The difference represents the under- or over-recovery of factory overheads, which is transferred to the profit and loss account, in accordance with the requirements of the UK Statement of Standard Accounting Practice on Stocks and Work in Progress (SSAP 9).

Transaction 9 represents various indirect expenses that have been incurred and that will eventually have to be paid in cash, for example property taxes and lighting and heating. Transaction 10 includes other indirect expenses that do not involve a cash commitment. For simplicity it is assumed that depreciation of factory machinery is the only item that falls into this category. The accounting entries for transactions 9 and 10 are

Dr Factory overhead control account      71 000
     Cr Expense creditors control account      41 000
     Cr Provision of depreciation account      30 000

In addition, subsidiary entries, not forming part of the double entry system, will be made in individual overhead accounts. These accounts will be headed by the title of the cost centre followed by the object of expenditure. For example, it may be possible to assign indirect materials directly to specific cost centres, and separate records can then be kept of the indirect materials charge for each centre. It will not, however, be possible to allocate property taxes, lighting and heating directly to cost centres, and entries should be made in individual overhead accounts for these items. Such expenses could, if so requested by management, be apportioned to resonsibility cost centres according to, say, floor area, but note that they should be regarded as non-controllable by the cost centre managers.

Transaction 11 refers to the total overheads that have been charged to jobs using the estimated overhead absorption rates. The accounting entry in the control accounts for allocating overheads to jobs is

| | |
|---|---|
| Dr Work in progress control account | 140 000 |
| Cr Factory overhead control account | 140 000 |

In addition to this entry, the individual jobs are charged so that job costs can be calculated. When these entries have been made the factory overhead control account would look like this:

**Factory overhead control account**

| | | | |
|---|---|---|---|
| 4. Stores ledger control a/c | 10 000 | 11. Work in progress | |
| 7. Wages control a/c | 40 000 | control a/c | 140 000 |
| 8. Employer's National | | Balance – Under-recovery | |
| Insurance contributions a/c | 25 000 | of overhead transferred to | |
| | | costing profit and loss a/c | 6 000 |
| 9. Expense creditors a/c | 41 000 | | |
| 10. Provision for depreciation a/c | 30 000 | | |
| | 146 000 | | 146 000 |

The debit side of this account indicates that £146 000 overhead has been incurred, but examination of the credit side indicates that only £140 000 has been allocated to jobs via overhead allocation rates. The balance of £6000 represents an under-recovery of factory overhead, which is regarded as a period cost to be charged to the costing profit and loss account in the current accounting period. The reasons for this were explained in the previous chapter.

# Non-manufacturing overheads

You will have noted in the previous chapter that non-manufacturing overhead costs are regarded as period costs and not product costs, and non-manufacturing overheads are not therefore charged to the work in progress control account. The accounting entry for transaction 12 is

| | |
|---|---|
| Dr Non-manufacturing overheads account | 40 000 |
| Cr Expense creditors account | 40 000 |

At the end of the period the non-manufacturing overheads will be transferred to the profit and loss account as a period cost by means of the following accounting entry:

| | |
|---|---|
| Dr Profit and loss account | 40 000 |
| Cr Non-manufacturing overheads account | 40 000 |

In practice, separate control accounts are maintained for administrative, marketing and financial overheads, but, to simplify this example, all the non-manufacturing overheads are included in one control account. In addition, subsidiary records will be kept that analyse the total non-manufacturing overheads by individual accounts, for example office stationery account, sales person's travelling expenses account, etc.

Note that these accounts do not form part of the double entry system, but represent a detailed breakdown of the total entries included in the non-manufacturing overhead control account.

# Accounting procedures for jobs completed and products sold

When jobs have been completed, they are transferred from the factory floor to the finished goods store. The total of the job accounts for the completed jobs for the period is recorded as a transfer from the work in progress control account to the finished goods stock account. The accounting entry for transaction 13 is

| | | |
|---|---|---|
| Dr Finished goods stock account | 300 000 | |
| Cr Work in progress control account | | 300 000 |

When the goods are removed from the finished goods stock and delivered to the customers, the revenue is recognized. It is a fundamental principle of financial accounting that only costs associated with earning the revenue are included as expenses. The cost of those goods that have been delivered to customers must therefore be matched against the revenue due from delivery of the goods so that the gross profit can be calculated. Any goods that have not been delivered to customers will be included as part of the finished stock valuation. The accounting entries to reflect these transactions are:

Transaction 14

| | | |
|---|---|---|
| Dr Debtors control account | 400 000 | |
| Cr Sales account | | 400 000 |

Transaction 15

| | | |
|---|---|---|
| Dr Cost of sales account | 240 000 | |
| Cr Finished goods stock account | | 240 000 |

# Costing profit and loss account

At frequent intervals management may wish to ascertain the profit to date for the particular period. The accounting procedure outlined in this chapter provides a data base from which a costing profit and loss account may easily be prepared. The costing profit and loss account for AB Ltd based on the information given in Example 4.2 is set out in Exhibit 4.3 shown on page 103. As cost control procedures should exist at cost (responsibility) centre levels, management may find the final profit calculation sufficient when it is combined with a summary of the various performance reports. Alternatively, management may prefer the profit statement to be presented in a format similar to that which is necessary for external reporting. Such information can easily be extracted from the subsidiary records. For example, the factory and non-manufacturing overhead control accounts are supported by detailed individual accounts such as factory depreciation, factory lighting and heating, office salaries and so on. The items in the costing profit and loss account can therefore be easily replaced with those items normally presented in the financial accounts by extracting from the subsidiary records the appropriate information. The accounting procedure outlined in Exhibit 4.3, however, provides the data base for ascertaining the job costs and stock valuations that are essential to external reporting. In addition, information in the subsidiary records provides the data from which the accountant can extract relevant decision-making and control information to suit the needs of the various users of accounting information.

# Interlocking accounting

Interlocking accounting is a system where the cost and financial accounts are maintained independently of each other, and in the cost accounts no attempt is made to keep a separate record of the financial accounting transactions. Examples of financial accounting transactions include entries in the various creditors, debtors and capital accounts. To maintain the double entry records, an account must be maintained in the cost accounts to record the corresponding entry that, in an integrated accounting system, would normally be made in one of the financial accounts (creditors, debtors accounts, etc.). This account is called a cost control or general ledger adjustment account.

Using an interlocking accounting system to record the transactions listed in Example 4.2, the entries in the creditors, wages accrued, taxation payable, National Insurance contributions, expense creditors, provision for depreciation and debtors accounts would be replaced by the following entries in the cost control account:

## Cost control account

| | | | |
|---|---|---|---|
| 2. Stores ledger control a/c | 2 000 | 1. Stores ledger control a/c | 182 000 |
| 14. Sales a/c | 400 000 | 5. Wages control a/c | 185 000 |
| Balance c/d | 215 000 | 8. Factory overhead control a/c | 25 000 |
| | | 9. Expense creditors a/c | 41 000 |
| | | 12. Non-manufacturing overhead a/c | 40 000 |
| | | 10. Factory overhead a/c | 30 000 |
| | | Profit and loss a/c (profit for period) | 114 000 |
| | 617 000 | | 617 000 |
| | | Balance b/d | 215 000 |

The entries in the remaining accounts will be unchanged.

For a detailed answer to an interlocking accounts question you should refer to the solution to the self-assessment question at the end of this chapter. Sometimes examination questions are set that require you to reconcile the profit that has been calculated in the cost accounts with the profits calculated in the financial accounts. Most firms use an integrated accounting system, and hence there is no need to reconcile a separate set of cost and financial accounts. The reconciliation of cost and financial accounts is not therefore dealt with in this book. For an explanation of the reconciliation procedure you should refer to the solution to Question 4.11 that can be found in the *Students' Manual* that accompanies this book.

# Accounting entries for a JIT manufacturing sytem

During the last decade many organizations have adopted a just-in-time (JIT) manufacturing philosophy. The major features of a JIT philosophy will be explained in Chapter 22 but at this point it is appropriate to note that implementing a JIT philosophy is normally accompanied by a cellular production layout whereby each cell produces similar products. Consequently, a form of process costing environment emerges. There is also a high velocity of WIP movement throughout the cell, and so it is extremely difficult to trace actual costs to individual products. Adopting a JIT philosophy also results in a substantial reduction in inventories so that inventory valuation becomes less relevant. Therefore simplified accounting procedures can be adopted for allocating costs between cost of sales and inventories. This simplified procedure is known as **backflush costing**.

Both process costing and JIT techniques are covered in later chapters but you will find it easier at this point, if we compare the backflush costing system that has been advocated for a JIT production environment with the conventional job costing system that has been described in this chapter. Therefore in this section we shall move away from a job costing environment towards a process costing environment but we shall return to a special form of job costing in the next section.

Backflush costing aims to eliminate detailed accounting transactions. Rather than tracking the movement of materials through the production process, a backflush costing system focuses first on the output of the organization and then works backwards when allocating cost between costs of goods sold and inventories, with no separate accounting for WIP. In contrast, conventional product costing systems track costs in synchronization with the movement of the products from direct materials, through WIP to finished goods. We shall now use Example 4.3 to illustrate two variants of backflush costing. Trigger points determine when the entries are made in the accounting system.

Actual conversion costs are recorded as incurred, just the same as conventional recording systems. Conversion costs are then applied to products at various trigger points. It is assumed that any conversion costs not applied to products are carried forward and disposed of at the year end. The accounting entries are as follows:

## METHOD 1

Trigger point 1 – The purchase of raw materials and components
             2 – The manufacture of finished goods

|  | (£) | (£) |
|---|---|---|
| 1. Dr Raw material inventory account | 1 515 000 | |
| Cr Creditors | | 1 515 000 |
| 2. Dr Conversion costs | 1 010 000 | |
| Cr Expense creditors | | 1 010 000 |
| 3. Dr Finished goods inventory (100 000 × £25) | 2 500 000 | |
| Cr Raw material inventory (100 000 × £15) | | 1 500 000 |
| Cr Conversion costs (100 000 × £10) | | 1 000 000 |
| 4. Dr Cost of goods sold (98 000 × £25) | 2 450 000 | |
| Cr Finished goods inventory | | 2 450 000 |

The ledger accounts in respect of the above transactions are shown in Exhibit 4.4.

> **EXAMPLE 4.3**
>
> The transactions for the month of May for JIT plc are as follows:
>
> | | |
> |---|---|
> | Purchase of raw materials | £1 515 000 |
> | Conversion costs incurred during the period | £1 010 000 |
> | Finished goods manufactured during the period | 100 000 units |
> | Sales for the period | 98 000 units |
>
> There are no opening stocks of raw materials, WIP or finished goods. The standard and actual cost per unit of output is £25 (£15 materials and £10 conversion cost). The company uses an integrated cost accounting system.

## METHOD 2

This is the simplest variant of backflush costing. There is only one trigger point. We shall assume that the trigger point is the manufacture of a finished unit. Conversion costs are debited as the actual costs are incurred. The accounting entries are

| | (£) | (£) |
|---|---|---|
| 1. Dr Finished goods inventory (100 000 × £25) | 2 500 000 | |
|     Cr Creditors | | 1 500 000 |
|     Cr Conversion costs | | 1 000 000 |
| 2. Dr Cost of goods sold (98 000 × £25) | 2 450 000 | |
|     Cr Finished goods inventory | | 2 450 000 |

The end of month inventory balance is £50 000 finished goods. At the end of the period the £15 000 of raw materials purchased but not yet manufactured into finished goods will not have been recorded in the internal product costing system. It is therefore not included in the closing stock valuation.

You will see that the WIP account is eliminated with both the variants that are illustrated. If inventories are low, the vast majority of manufacturing costs will form part of cost of goods sold and will not be deferred in inventory. In this situation the volume of work involved in tracking costs through WIP, cost of goods sold and finished goods is unlikely to be justified. This considerably reduces the volume of transactions recorded in the internal accounting system. Note, however, that it may be necessary to track the progress of units on the production line, but there will be no attempt to trace costs to units progressing through the system.

The second variant is suitable only for JIT systems with minimum raw materials and WIP inventories. Note that both methods allocate identical amounts to the cost of goods sold for the period. The second method may yield significantly different inventory valuations from conventional product costing systems. It is therefore claimed that this method of backflush costing may not be acceptable for external financial reporting. However, if inventories are low or not subject to significant change from one accounting period to the next, operating income and inventory valuations derived from backflush costing will not be materially different from the results reported by the conventional

**EXHIBIT 4.4**

*Ledger accounts for a backflush costing system (Method 1)*

**Raw materials inventory**

| | |
|---|---|
| 1. Creditors £1 515 000 | 3. Finished goods £1 500 000 |

**Finished goods inventory**

| | |
|---|---|
| 3. Raw materials £1 500 000 | 4. COGS £2 450 000 |
| 3. Conversion costs £1 000 000 | |

**Conversion costs**

| | |
|---|---|
| 2. Creditors £1 010 000 | 3. Finished goods £1 000 000 |

**Cost of goods sold (COGS)**

| |
|---|
| 4. £2 450 000 |

The end of month inventory balances are

| | (£) |
|---|---|
| Raw materials | 15 000 |
| Finished goods | 50 000 |
| | 65 000 |

system. In these circumstances backflush costing is acceptable for external financial reporting.

# Contract costing

**Contract costing** is a system of job costing that is applied to relatively large cost units, which normally take a considerable length of time to complete. Building and construction work, civil engineering and shipbuilding are some examples of industries where large contract work is undertaken, and where contract costing is appropriate.

A contract account is maintained for each contract. All the direct costs of the contract are debited to the specific contract and overheads are apportioned in the manner prescribed in Chapter 3. The contract price is credited to the contract account, and each contract account therefore becomes a small profit and loss account.

Because of the considerable length of time that is taken to complete a contract, it is necessary to determine the profit to be attributed to each accounting period. Financial accounting normally recognizes revenue when the goods are delivered, but such an approach is inappropriate for long-term contracts, since profits on large contracts would not be reported until they were completed. The profit and loss account would not reflect a fair view of the profitability of the company during the year but would show only the results of contracts that had been completed before the year end. To overcome this problem, it is preferable to take credit for profit while contracts are in progress.

The UK Statement of Standard Accounting Practice on Stocks and Work in Progress (SSAP 9) provides the following guidance on the attributable profit to be taken up for a particular period:

> Where the business carries out long-term contracts and it is considered that their outcome can be assessed with reasonable certainty before their conclusion, the attributable profit should be calculated on a prudent basis and included in the accounts for the period under review. The profit taken up needs to reflect the proportion of the work carried out at the accounting date and to take into account any known inequalities of profitability in the various stages of a contract. The procedure to recognize profit is to include an appropriate proportion of total contract value as turnover in the profit and loss account as the contract activity progresses. The costs incurred in reaching that stage of completion are matched with this turnover, resulting in the reporting of results that can be attributed to the proportion of work completed.
>
> Where the outcome of long-term contracts cannot be assessed with reasonable certainty before the conclusion of the contract, no profit should be reflected in the profit and loss account in respect of those contracts although, in such circumstances, if no loss is expected it may be appropriate to show as turnover a proportion of the total contract value using a zero estimate of profit.
>
> If it is expected that there will be a loss on a contract as a whole, all of the loss should be recognized as soon as it is foreseen (in accordance with the prudence concept).

Let us now prepare some contract accounts and determine the attributable profit to be taken up for an accounting period. Consider Example 4.4.

Before we compile the accounts, some of the terms used in Example 4.4 require an explanation. A customer is likely to be required under the terms of the contract to make **progress payments** to the contractor throughout the course of the work. The amount of the payments will be based on the sales value of the work carried out, as assessed by the architect or surveyor in the **architect's certificate**. A certificate provides confirmation that work to a certain sales value has been completed, and that some payment to the contractor is now due. The amount of the progress payment will consist of:

1. the sales value of work carried out and certified by the architect; less
2. a retention; less
3. the payments made to date.

So if the architect's certificates assess the value of work carried out to be £300 000 and if the retention is 10%, and if £230 000 has already been paid in progress payments, the current payment will be

$$£300\,000 - £30\,000\,\text{retention} - £230\,000\,\text{previous payment} = £40\,000$$

There is frequently a contract clause which entitles the customer to withhold payment of **retention money** for a proportion of the value of work certified for a specified period after the end of the contract. During this period, the contractor must make good all contractual defects. When the defects have been satisfactorily completed the customer will release the retention money.

Let us now prepare the cost accounts from the information contained in Example 4.4 for contracts A, B and C:

**EXAMPLE 4.4**

A construction company is currently undertaking three separate contracts and information relating to these contracts for the previous year, together with other relevant data, are shown below:

| | Contract A (£000) | Contract B (£000) | Contract C (£000) |
|---|---|---|---|
| Contract price | 1760 | 1485 | 2420 |
| Balances b/fwd at beginning of year: | | | |
| Material on site | — | 20 | 30 |
| Written-down value of plant and machinery | — | 77 | 374 |
| Wages accrued | — | 5 | 10 |
| Transactions during previous year: | | | |
| Profit previously transferred to profit and loss a/c | — | — | 35 |
| Cost of work certified (cost of sales) | — | 418 | 814 |
| Transactions during current year: | | | |
| Materials delivered to sites | 88 | 220 | 396 |
| Wages paid | 45 | 100 | 220 |
| Salaries and other costs | 15 | 40 | 50 |
| Written-down value of plant issued to sites | 190 | 35 | — |
| Head office expenses apportioned during the year | 10 | 20 | 50 |
| Balances c/fwd at the end of year: | | | |
| Material on site | 20 | — | — |
| Written-down value of plant and machinery | 150 | 20 | 230 |
| Wages accrued | 5 | 10 | 15 |
| Value of work certified at end of year | 200 | 860 | 2100 |
| Cost of work not certified at end of year | — | — | 55 |

The agreed retention rate is 10% of the value of work certified by the contractee's architects. Contract C is scheduled for handing over to the contractee in the near future, and the site engineer estimates that the extra costs required to complete the contract, in addition to those tabulated above, will total £305 000. This amount includes an allowance for plant depreciation, construction services and for contingencies.

You are required to prepare a cost account for each of the three contracts and recommend how much profit or loss should be taken up for the year.

**Contract accounts**

| | A (£000) | B (£000) | C (£000) | | A (£000) | B (£000) | C (£000) |
|---|---|---|---|---|---|---|---|
| | | | | Wages accrued b/fwd | | 5 | 10 |
| Materials on site b/fwd | | 20 | 30 | Materials on site c/fwd | 20 | | |
| Plant on site b/fwd | | 77 | 374 | Plant on site c/fwd | 150 | 20 | 230 |
| Materials control a/c | 88 | 220 | 396 | Cost of work not certified c/fwd | | | 55 |

| | | | | | | | |
|---|---|---|---|---|---|---|---|
| Wages control a/c | 45 | 100 | 220 | Cost of sales – current | | | |
| Salaries | 15 | 40 | 50 | period (balance) | | | |
| Plant control a/c | 190 | 35 | | c/fwd | 183 | 497 | 840 |
| Apportionment of head office expenses | 10 | 20 | 50 | | | | |
| Wages accrued c/fwd | 5 | 10 | 15 | | | | |
| | 353 | 522 | 1135 | | 353 | 522 | 1135 |
| Cost of sales b/fwd | 183 | 497 | 840 | Attributable sales revenue (current period)[a] | 183 | 442 | 1122 |
| Profit taken this period | | | 282 | Loss taken | | 55 | |
| | 183 | 497 | 1122 | | 183 | 497 | 1122 |
| Cost of work not certified b/fwd | | | 55 | Wages accrued b/fwd | 5 | 10 | 15 |
| Materials on site b/fwd | 20 | | | | | | |
| Plant on site b/fwd | 150 | 20 | 230 | | | | |

[a] Profit taken plus cost of sales for the current period or cost of sales less loss to date.

You will see that the contract accounts are divided into three sections. The objective of the first section is to determine the costs that should be included in the cost of sales for the purposes of calculating the profit taken up for the period. The balance shown in the first section of the contract accounts represents the **cost of sales** (also known as **cost of work certified**) attributable to each of the contracts.

You should note that unexpired costs such as the cost of work not certified and the written-down balance of the plant at the end of the period are carried forward to the third section of the contract accounts. This section represents the unexpired costs of the current period which will become an expired cost in future periods. The third section of the account should therefore be regarded as a future cost section.

In the second section of the contract accounts the period cost of sales is compared with the sales revenue that is estimated to be attributable to the contracts. The sales revenues attributable to the contracts for each period are estimated by adding the attributable profit taken up for the current period to the cost of sales for the current period (or cost of sales less the loss where a contract is currently running at a loss). The profits/losses on the three contracts to date are calculated by deducting the cost of sales (consisting of the sum of the cost of sales for the current and previous peiods) from the value of work certified:

| | **(£000)** | |
|---|---|---|
| Contract A | 17 | (£200–£183) |
| Contract B | (55) | (£860–£915) |
| Contract C | 446 | (£2100–£1654) |

However, these profits/(losses) do not necessarily represent the profits/(losses) taken up on the contracts. According to SSAP 9, the concept of prudence should be applied when determining the profits/(losses) taken up on contracts. You are recommended to adopt the following guidelines:

1. If the contract is in its early stages, no profit should be taken. Profit should only be taken when the outcome of the contract can be assessed with reasonable certainty. You will see from Example 4.4 that the contract price for Contract A is £1 760 000, but the value of work certified is only £200 000. The contract is therefore approximately one-eighth complete, and it is unlikely that the outcome of the

contract can be foreseen with reasonable certainty. Despite the fact that the profit to date is £17 000, it is recommended that no profit be taken.

2. If a loss is incurred, the prudence concept should be applied, and the total loss should be recognized in the period in which it is incurred. Consequently, the loss of £55 000 on Contract B is recognized in the current accounting period. Where further additional future losses are anticipated, all of the loss should be recognized as soon as it is foreseen and added to the cost of sales. In addition, the foreseeable loss should be shown in the balance sheet under the heading 'Provision/accrual for foreseeable losses'.

3. If the contract is nearing completion, the size of the eventual profit should be foreseen with reasonable certainty, and there is less need to be excessively prudent in determining the amount of profit to be recorded in the profit and loss account. With regard to Contract C, the value of work certified is approximately 87% of the contract price, and the **anticipated profit** is calculated as follows:

|  | (£000) |
|---|---|
| Cost of work certified (cost of sales to date $= 814 + 840$) | 1654 |
| Cost of work not certified | 55 |
| Estimated costs to complete | 305 |
| Estimated cost of contract | 2014 |
| Contract price | 2420 |
| Anticipated profit | 406 |

The profit taken is calculated using the following formula:

$$\text{cash received to date } \frac{(0.90 \times £2100)}{\text{contract price } (£2420)}$$
$$\times \text{ estimated profit from the contract } (£406) \simeq £317\,000$$

You should note that other more prudent approaches are sometimes used to determine the profit earned to date. The profit for the current period consists of the profit to date (£317 000) less the profit of £35 000 previously transferred to the profit and loss account. The profit taken to the profit and loss account for the current period is therefore £282 000.

4. Where substantial costs have been incurred on a contract, and it is not nearing completion (say it is in the region of 35–85% complete), the following formula is often used to determine the attributable profit to date:

$$\text{profit taken} = 2/3 \times \text{notional profit} \times \frac{\text{cash received}}{\text{value of work certified}}$$

This formula is one of several approaches that can be used to apply the prudence concept. Estimates of anticipated profit are likely to be inaccurate when contracts are not near to completion. To overcome this problem, **notional profit** should be used instead of anticipated profit. Notional profit is the value of work certified to date less the cost of work certified (that is, cost of sales) to date less a provision for any anticipated unforeseen eventualities.

Note than for Contract C £35 000 profit was recognized in the previous period and cost of sales of £814 000 was recorded. Therefore attributable sales revenue of £849 000 (£814 000 + £35 000) would have been recorded in the contract account for the *previous* period. For Contract B, no profits were recognized in the *previous period* and attributable sales for the period will thus be identical to the cost of sales (£418 000). Contract A commenced in the current period and so no transactions will have been recorded in the previous period. The debit side of the debtors accounts will be as follows:

| | Contract A (£000) | Contract B (£000) | Contract C (£000) |
|---|---|---|---|
| Previous period – attributable sales | — | 418 | 849 |
| Current period – attributable sales | 183 | 442 | 1122 |
| Total to date | 183 | 860 | 1971 |

# Work in progress valuation and amounts recoverable on contracts

The UK Statement of Standard Accounting Practice on Stocks on Work in Progress (SSAP 9) requires that the proportion of the total contract value appropriate to the stage of completion reached at balance sheet date be recognized as sales revenue. The costs relating to that completed work are included in the cost of sales. Any further costs that are attributable to the contract but that have not been included in the cost of sales are included at cost in the balance sheet and separately disclosed as 'Long-term contract balances' under the balance sheet heading 'Stocks'.

The associated balance sheet item for the contract value that is recorded as sales is debtors. The debtors balance is calculated by deducting progress payments received on account from the amount recognized as sales. This balance is included as a separate item within debtors and described as 'Amounts recoverable on contracts'. The balance sheet entries for Example 4.4 are as follows:

| | Contract A (£000) | Contract B (£000) | Contract C (£000) | |
|---|---|---|---|---|
| **Stocks:** | | | | |
| Total costs incurred to date | 183 | 860 | 1709 | (814 + 840 + 55) |
| Included in cost of sales | 183 | 860 | 1654 | |
| Included in long-term contract balances | 0 | 0 | 55 | |
| **Debtors** | | | | |
| Cumulative sales turnover | 183 | 860 | 1971 | |
| Less cumulative progress payments | 180 | 774 | 1890 | |
| Amounts recoverable on contracts | 3 | 86 | 81 | |

For Contract B, the total costs incurred to date are £915 000 (£418 000 + £497 000) but £55 000 of these costs have been recognized as a loss in the current period, so that cumulative cost of sales to be matched against cumulative sales is £860 000 (£915 000 − £55 000). Note also that the cumulative progress payments are 90% of the value of work certified and that the loss on Contract B has been charged to the current period. Other balance sheet entries will include the following:

| | (£000) |
|---|---|
| Materials on site | 20 |
| Plant on site | 400 |
| Accruals | 30 |

commenced in the current period and so no transactions will have been recorded in the previous period. The debit side of the debtors accounts will be as follows:

| | Contract A (£000) | Contract B (£000) | Contract C (£000) |
|---|---|---|---|
| Previous period – attributable sales | | 418 | 840 |
| Current period – attributable sales | 1831 | 142 | 1137 |
| Total to date | | 560 | 1977 |

# Work in progress valuation and amounts recoverable on contracts

The UK Statement of Standard Accounting Practice on Stock and Work in Progress (SSAP 9) requires that the presentation of the total contract value appropriate to the stage of completion reached in the balance sheet date be recognized in the value of turnover. The costs relating to that contract work are included in the cost of sales. Any further costs that are attributable to the contract but have not been included in the cost of sales are included at cost in the balance sheet and separately disclosed as 'Long term contract balances' under the balance sheet heading 'Stocks'.

The associated balance sheet item for the contract value that is recorded as sales is debtors. The debtors balance is calculated by deducting progress payments received in account from the amount recognized in sales. This balance is included as a separate item within debtors and described as 'Amount recoverable on contracts'. The balance sheet entries for examples 1–3 are as follows:

| | Contract A (£000) | Contract B (£000) | Contract C (£000) |
|---|---|---|---|
| **Stocks** | | | |
| Total costs incurred to date | 145 | 860 | 1795 | (855 + 840 + 35) |
| Transferred to cost of sales | | 1831 | 560 | (855) |
| Stock in long term | | | | |
| **Debtors** | | | |
| Attributable sales turnover | 182 | 840 | A 1831 | |
| Less progress payments | | | | |
| on account | | | 197 | |
| Amounts recoverable on | | | | |
| contracts | | 51 | | |

For Contract C the total payment to date was £815 000 (£35 000 materials plus a further £35 000 of these costs have been recognized as a loss in the current period that cumulative recorded to date attributable profit is recognized. Note £915 000 progress payments also that the cumulative progress payments and note the stage of work reached at that the loss anticipated on the contract to be applied to the current period. Other balance sheet items are the following:

| | | |
|---|---|---|
| **Inventories the** | | |
| Stocks in file | 300 | |
| Accruals | 50 | |

## Self-Assessment Question

You should attempt to answer this question yourself before looking up the suggested answer, which appears on pages 1095–7. If any part of your answer is incorrect, check back carefully to make sure you understand where you went wrong.

CD Ltd, a company engaged in the manufacture of specialist marine engines, operates a historic job cost accounting system that is not integrated with the financial accounts.

At the beginning of May 2000 the opening balances in the cost ledger were as follows:

|  | (£) |
|---|---|
| Stores ledger control account | 85 400 |
| Work in progress control account | 167 350 |
| Finished goods control account | 49 250 |
| Cost ledger control account | 302 000 |

During the month, the following transactions took place:

|  | (£) |
|---|---|
| Materials: | |
| Purchases | 42 700 |
| Issues to production | 63 400 |
| to general maintenance | 1 450 |
| to construction of manufacturing equipment | 7 650 |
| Factory wages: | |
| Total gross wages paid | 124 000 |

£12 500 of the above gross wages were incurred on the construction of manufacturing equipment, £35 750 were indirect wages and the balance was direct.

Production overheads: the actual amount incurred, excluding items shown above, was £152 350; £30 000 was absorbed by the manufacturing equipment under construction and under absorbed overhead written off at the end of the month amounted to £7550.

Royalty payments: one of the engines produced is manufactured under licence. £2150 is the amount that will be paid to the inventor for the month's production of that particular engine.

Selling overheads: £22 000.

Sales: £410 000.

The company's gross profit margin is 25% on factory cost.

At the end of May stocks of work in progress had increased by £12 000. The manufacturing equipment under construction was completed within the month, and transferred out of the cost ledger at the end of the month.

Required:
Prepare the relevant control accounts, costing profit and loss account, and any other accounts you consider necessary to record the above transactions in the cost ledger for May 2000.                                      (22 marks)

*ACCA Foundation Costing*

## Summary

In this chapter we have examined the accounting entries necessary to record transactions within a job costing system. This was compared with a simplified backflush costing system that has been advocated when a JIT manufacturing philosophy has been adopted. Discussion has been concentrated on an integrated accounting system and the accounting transactions have been illustrated with a comprehensive example. A major feature of the system is the use of control accounts. A summary of the accounting entries, where all purchases and expenses are settled in cash, is shown diagrammatically in Figure 4.1 below. We have also examined a system of contract costing, which is the name given to a system of job costing that is applied to relatively large cost units, which normally take a considerable length of time to complete.

**FIGURE 4.1** *Flow of accounting entries in an integrated accounting system.*

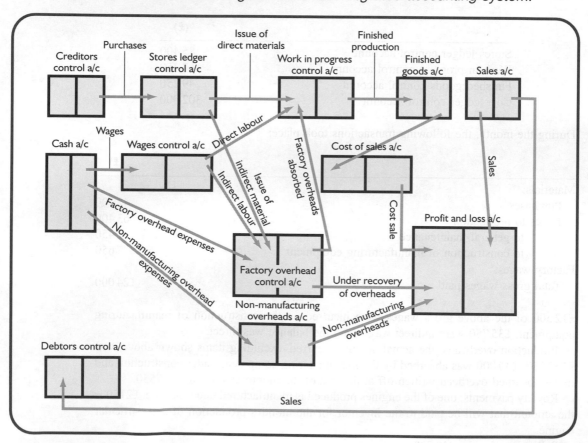

## Key Terms and Concepts

anticipated profit (p. 116)
architect's certificate (p. 113)
average cost (p. 99)
backflush costing (p. 110)
contract costing (p. 112)
control account (p. 100)
cost of sales (p. 115)
cost of work certified (p. 115)
first in, first out (FIFO) (p. 98)
goods received note (p. 98)

integrated cost accounting system (p. 97)
interlocking cost accounting system (pp. 97, 109)
labour cost accounting (p. 104)
last in, first out (LIFO) (p. 99)
notional profit (p. 116)
payroll accounting (p. 104)
progress payments (p. 113)
retention money (p. 113)
stores ledger account (p. 98)
stores requisition (p. 98)

## Recommended Reading

To illustrate the principles of stores pricing a simplistic situation was presented. For a more complex illustration you should refer to the Appendix to Chapter 3 in Drury (1998). Alternatively, you can look at this chapter on the website. For an explanation of how you can access the website you should refer to the preface of this book. For a more detailed explanation of backflush costing see Foster and Horngren (1988). You should refer to Dugdale (1989) for more information on contract costing.

## Key Examination Points

Examination questions require the preparation of accounts for both integrated and interlocking systems. You may also be required to reconcile the cost and financial accounts. For an illustration of the approach see the answer to Question 4.11, which can be found in the *Students' Manual* that accompanies this book. However, the reconciliation of cost and financial accounts is a topic that tends to be examined only on rare occasions.

Students often experience difficulty in recommending the amount of profit to be taken during a period for long-term contracts. Make sure you are familiar with the four recommendations listed on pp. 115–6 and that you can apply these recommendations to Questions 4.17–4.20.

## Questions

* Indicates that a suggested solution is to be found in the *Students' Manual*.

### 4.1* Intermediate
At the end of a period, in an integrated cost and financial accounting system, the accounting entries for £18 000 overheads under-absorbed would be

| | | |
|---|---|---|
| A | Debit work-in-progress control account | Credit overhead control account |
| B | Debit profit and loss account | Credit work-in-progress control account |
| C | Debit profit and loss account | Credit overhead control account |
| D | Debit overhead control account | Credit profit and loss account |

*CIMA Stage 1 Cost Accounting*

### 4.2* Intermediate
The profits shown in the financial accounts was £158 500 but the cost accounts showed a different figure. The following stock valuations were used:

| Stock valuations | Cost accounts | Financial accounts |
|---|---|---|
| | (£) | (£) |
| Opening stock | 35 260 | 41 735 |
| Closing stock | 68 490 | 57 336 |

What was the profit in the cost accounts?
A £163 179
B £140 871
C £176 129
D £153 821

*CIMA Stage 1*

### 4.3 Intermediate*
A construction company has the following data concerning one of its contracts:

| | |
|---|---|
| Contract price | £2 000 000 |
| Value certified | £1 300 000 |
| Cash received | £1 200 000 |
| Costs incurred | £1 050 000 |
| Cost of work certified | £1 000 000 |

The profit (to the nearest £1000) to be attributed to the contract is

A   £250 000
B   £277 000
C   £300 000
D   £950 000
E   £1 000 000

*CIMA Stage 2*

## 4.4* Intermediate: Stores Pricing

Z Ltd had the following transactions in one of its raw materials during April

| | | | |
|---|---|---|---|
| Opening stock | | 40 units | @£10 each |
| April 4 | Bought | 140 units | @£11 each |
| 10 | Used | 90 units | |
| 12 | Bought | 60 units | @£12 each |
| 13 | Used | 100 units | |
| 16 | Bought | 200 units | @£10 each |
| 21 | Used | 70 units | |
| 23 | Used | 80 units | |
| 26 | Bought | 50 units | @£12 each |
| 29 | Used | 60 units | |

You are required to:
(a) write up the stores ledger card using
  (i)  FIFO and
  (ii) LIFO
  methods of stock valuation;       (8 marks)
(b) state the cost of material used for each system during April;       (2 marks)
(c) describe the weighted-average method of valuing stocks and explain how the use of this method would affect the cost of materials used and the balance sheet of Z Ltd compared to FIFO and LIFO in times of consistently rising prices. (Do NOT restate the stores ledger card for the above transactions using this method.)       (5 marks)
        (Total 15 marks)
        *CIMA Stage 1 Accounting*

## 4.5* Intermediate: Stores pricing and preparation of the stores control account

A company operates an historic batch costing system, which is not integrated with the financial accounts, and uses the weighted average method of pricing raw material issues. A weighted average price (to three decimal places of a pound £) is calculated after each purchase of material.

Receipts and issues of Material X for a week were as follows:

| Receipts into stock | | | Issues to production | |
|---|---|---|---|---|
| Day | kg | £ | Day | kg |
| 1 | 1400 | 1092.00 | 2 | 1700 |
| 4 | 1630 | 1268.14 | 5 | 1250 |

At the beginning of the week, stock of material X was 3040 kg at a cost of £0.765 per kg. Of the issues of material on day 2, 60 kg were returned to stock on day 3. Of the receipts of material on day 1, 220 kg were returned to the supplier on day 4. Invoices for the material receipts during the week remained unpaid at the end of the week.

Required:
(a) Prepare a tabulation of the movement of stock during the week, showing the changes in the level of stock, its valuation per kilogram, and the total value of stock held.
(b) Record the week's transactions in the material X stock account in the cost ledger, indicating clearly in each case the account in which the corresponding entry should be posted.
        (9 marks)
        *ACCA Foundation Paper 3*

## 4.6* Intermediate: Integrated cost accounting

NB Limited operates an integrated accounting system. At the beginning of October, the following balances appeared in the trial balance:

| | (£000) | (£000) | (£000) |
|---|---|---|---|
| Freehold buildings | | 800 | |
| Plant and equipment, at cost | | 480 | |
| Provision for depreciation on plant and equipment | | | 100 |
| Stocks: | | | |
| Raw materials | | 400 | |
| Work in Process 1: | | | |
| direct materials | 71 | | |
| direct wages | 50 | | |
| production overhead | 125 | 246 | |
| Work in Process 2: | | | |
| direct materials | 127 | | |
| direct wages | 70 | | |
| production overhead | 105 | 302 | |
| Finished goods | | 60 | |
| Debtors | | 1120 | |
| Capital | | | 2200 |
| Profit retained | | | 220 |
| Creditors | | | 300 |
| Bank | | | 464 |
| Sales | | | 1200 |
| Cost of sales | | 888 | |
| Abnormal loss | | 9 | |
| Production overhead under/over absorbed | | | 21 |

| | |
|---|---|
| Administration overhead | 120 |
| Selling and distribution overhead | 80 |
| | 4505   4505 |

The transactions during the month of October were:

| | (£000) |
|---|---|
| Raw materials purchased on credit | 210 |
| Raw materials returned to suppliers | 10 |
| Raw materials issued to: | |
| Process 1 | 136 |
| Process 2 | 44 |
| Direct wages incurred: | |
| Process 1 | 84 |
| Process 2 | 130 |
| Direct wages paid | 200 |
| Production salaries paid | 170 |
| Production expenses paid | 250 |
| Received from debtors | 1140 |
| Paid to creditors | 330 |
| Administration overhead paid | 108 |
| Selling and distribution overhead paid | 84 |
| Sales, on credit | 1100 |
| Cost of goods sold | 844 |

| | Direct materials (£000) | Direct wages (£000) |
|---|---|---|
| Abnormal loss in: | | |
| Process 1 | 6 | 4 |
| Process 2 | 18 | 6 |
| Transfer from Process 1 to Process 2 | 154 | 94 |
| Transfer from Process 2 to finished goods | 558 | 140 |

Plant and equipment is depreciated at the rate of 20% per annum, using the straight-line basis. Production overhead is absorbed on the basis of direct wages cost.

You are required
(a) to ascertain and state the production overhead absorption rates used for Process 1 and for Process 2; (2 marks)
(b) to write up the ledger accounts; (25 marks)
(c) to explain the nature of abnormal losses and two possible reasons for their occurrence. (3 marks)
(Total 30 marks)
*CIMA Stage 2 Cost Accounting*

**4.7 Intermediate: Integrated cost accounting**
XY Limited commenced trading on 1 February with fully paid issued share capital of £500 000, Fixed Assets of £275 000 and Cash at Bank of £225 000. By the end of April, the following transactions had taken place:
1. Purchases on credit from suppliers amounted to £572 500 of which £525 000 was raw materials and £47 500 was for items classified as production overhead.
2. Wages incurred for all staff were £675 000, represented by cash paid £500 000 and wage deductions of £175 000 in respect of income tax etc.
3. Payments were made by cheque for the following overhead costs:

| | £ |
|---|---|
| Production | 20 000 |
| Selling | 40 000 |
| Administration | 25 000 |

4. Issues of raw materials were £180 000 to Department A, £192 500 to Department B and £65 000 for production overhead items.
5. Wages incurred were analysed to functions as follows:

| | £ |
|---|---|
| Work in progress – Department A | 300 000 |
| Work in progress – Department B | 260 000 |
| Production overhead | 42 500 |
| Selling overhead | 47 500 |
| Administration overhead | 25 000 |
| | 675 000 |

6. Production overhead absorbed in the period by Department A was £110 000 and by Department B £120 000.
7. The production facilities, when not in use, were patrolled by guards from a security firm and £26 000 was owing for this service. £39 000 was also owed to a firm of management consultants which advises on production procedures; invoices for these two services are to be entered into the accounts.

8. The cost of finished goods completed was

| | Department A £ | Department B £ |
|---|---|---|
| Direct labour | 290 000 | 255 000 |
| Direct materials | 175 000 | 185 000 |
| Production overhead | 105 000 | 115 000 |
| | 570 000 | 555 000 |

9. Sales on credit were £870 000 and the cost of those sales was £700 000.
10. Depreciation of productive plant and equipment was £15 000.
11. Cash received from debtors totalled £520 000.
12. Payments to creditors were £150 000.

You are required

(a) to open the ledger accounts at the commencement of the trading period;

(b) using integrated accounting, to record the transactions for the three months ended 30 April;

(c) to prepare, in vertical format, for presentation to management,
   (i) a profit statement for the period;
   (ii) the balance sheet at 30 April.

(20 marks)
*CIMA Stage 2 Cost Accounting*

**4.8 Intermediate: Interlocking accounts**
AZ Limited has separate cost and financial accounting systems interlocked by control accounts in the two ledgers. From the cost accounts, the following information was available for the period:

| | (£) |
|---|---|
| Cost of finished goods produced | 512 050 |
| Cost of goods sold | 493 460 |
| Direct materials issued | 197 750 |
| Direct wages | 85 480 |
| Production overheads (as per the financial accounts) | 208 220 |
| Direct material purchases | 216 590 |

In the cost accounts, additional depreciation of £12 500 per period is charged and production overheads are absorbed at 250% of wages.

The various account balances at the beginning of the period were:

| | (£) |
|---|---|
| Stores control | 54 250 |
| Work in progress control | 89 100 |
| Finished goods control | 42 075 |

Required:
(a) Prepare the following control accounts in the cost ledger, showing clearly the double entries between the accounts, and the closing balances:
   Stores control
   Work in progress control
   Finished goods control
   Production overhead control    (10 marks)
(b) Explain the meaning of the balance on the production overhead control account.

(2 marks)
(c) When separate ledgers are maintained, the differing treatment of certain items may cause variations to arise between costing and financial profits. Examples of such items include stock valuations, notional expenses, and non-costing items charged in the financial accounts. Briefly explain the above *three* examples and state why they may give rise to profit differences. (3 marks)
(Total 15 marks)
*CIMA Stage 1 Cost Accounting*

**4.9\* Intermediate: Interlocking cost accounts and reconciliation statement**
K Limited operates separate cost accounting and financial accounting systems. The following manufacturing and trading statement has been prepared from the financial accounts for the *quarter* ended 31 March:

| | (£) | (£) |
|---|---|---|
| Raw materials: | | |
| Opening stock | 48 800 | |
| Purchases | 108 000 | |
| | 156 800 | |
| Closing stock | 52 000 | |
| Raw materials consumed | | 104 800 |
| Direct wages | | 40 200 |
| Production overhead | | 60 900 |
| Production cost incurred | | 205 900 |
| Work in progress: | | |
| Opening stock | 64 000 | |
| Closing stock | 58 000 | 6 000 |

| | | |
|---|---|---|
| Cost of goods produced | | 211 900 |
| Sales | | 440 000 |
| Finishing goods: | | |
|    Opening stock | 120 000 | |
|    Cost of goods produced | 211 900 | |
| | 331 900 | |
|    Closing stock | 121 900 | |
| Cost of goods sold | | 210 000 |
| Gross profit | | 230 000 |

From the cost accounts, the following information has been extracted:

| Control account balances at 1st January | (£) |
|---|---|
| Raw material stores | 49 500 |
| Work in progress | 60 100 |
| Finished goods | 115 400 |

| Transactions for the quarter: | (£) |
|---|---|
| Raw materials issued | 104 800 |
| Cost of goods produced | 222 500 |
| Cost of goods sold | 212 100 |
| Loss of materials damaged by flood (insurance claim pending) | 2 400 |

A notional rent of £4000 *per month* has been charged in the cost accounts. Production overhead was absorbed at the rate of 185% of direct wages.

You are required to:
(a) prepare the following control accounts in the cost ledger:
    raw materials stores;
    work in process;
    finished goods;
    production overhead; (10 marks)
(b) prepare a statement reconciling the gross profits as per the cost accounts and the financial accounts; (11 marks)
(c) comment on the possible accounting treatment(s) of the under or over absorption of production overhead, assuming that the financial year of the company is 1 January to 31 December. (4 marks)
(Total 25 marks)
*CIMA Cost Accounting 1*

**4.10 Intermediate: Preparation of interlocking accounts from incomplete information**
(a) Describe briefly *three* major differences between:
   (i) financial accounting, and
   (ii) cost and management accounting.
(6 marks)
(b) Below are incomplete cost accounts for a period:

| Stores ledger control account (£000) | |
|---|---|
| Opening balance | 176.0 |
| Financial ledger control a/c | 224.2 |

| Production wages control account (£000) | |
|---|---|
| Financial ledger control a/c | 196.0 |

| Production overhead control account (£000) | |
|---|---|
| Financial ledger control a/c | 119.3 |

| Job ledger control account (£000) | |
|---|---|
| Opening balance | 114.9 |

The balances at the end of the period were:

| | (£000) |
|---|---|
| Stores ledger | 169.5 |
| Jobs ledger | 153.0 |

During the period 64 500 kilos of direct material were issued from stores at a weighted average price of £3.20 per kilo. The balance of materials issued from stores represented indirect materials.

75% of the production wages are classified as 'direct'. Average gross wages of direct workers was £5.00 per hour. Production overheads are absorbed at a predetermined rate of £6.50 per direct labour hour.

Required:
Complete the cost accounts for the period.
(8 marks)
(Total 14 marks)
*ACCA Foundation Paper 3*

## 4.11* Intermediate: Preparation of cost accounts from reconciliation statement

(a) The cost accountant and the financial accountant of C Limited had each completed their final accounts for the year. Shown below are the manufacturing, trading and profit and loss accounts, together with a statement reconciling the cost and financial profits. You are required to show the following accounts in the cost ledger:
   (i)   raw materials;
   (ii)  work in progress;
   (iii) finished goods;
   (iv)  profit and loss.

**Manufacturing, Trading and Profit and Loss Account for the year ended 31 December**

|  | £000 | £000 |  | £000 | £000 |
|---|---|---|---|---|---|
| Raw material |  |  | Trading account, |  |  |
|   Opening stock | 110 |  |   cost of goods |  |  |
|   Purchases | 640 |  |   manufactured |  | 1000 |
|  | 750 |  |  |  |  |
| Less: Returns | 20 |  |  |  |  |
|  | 730 |  |  |  |  |
| Closing stock | 130 | 600 |  |  |  |
| Direct wages |  |  |  |  |  |
|   Paid | 220 |  |  |  |  |
|   Accrued | 20 | 240 |  |  |  |
| Prime cost |  | 840 |  |  |  |
| Production expenses |  | 162 |  |  |  |
| Work in progress: |  |  |  |  |  |
|   Opening stock | 25 |  |  |  |  |
|   Closing stock | 27 | (2) |  |  |  |
|  |  | 1000 |  |  | 1000 |
| Finished goods: |  |  | Sales | 1530 |  |
|   Opening stock | 82 |  | Less: Returns | 30 |  |
|   Manufactured | 1000 |  |  |  | 1500 |
|  | 1082 |  |  |  |  |
| Closing stock | 72 |  |  |  |  |
|  |  | 1010 |  |  |  |
| Gross profit |  | 490 |  |  |  |
|  |  | 1500 |  |  | 1500 |
| Administration expenses |  | 200 | Gross Profit |  | 490 |
| Sales expenses |  | 70 | Discount received |  | 10 |
| Discount allowed |  | 20 |  |  |  |
| Debenture interest |  | 10 |  |  |  |
| Net profit |  | 200 |  |  |  |
|  |  | 500 |  |  | 500 |

[Reconciliation Statement]

|  | (£000) | (£000) | (£000) |
|---|---|---|---|
| Profit shown in the financial accounts |  |  | 200 |
| Items not shown in the cost accounts: |  |  |  |
|   Discount allowed |  | 20 |  |
|   Debenture interest |  | 10 |  |

|  |  |  |
|---|---|---|
| Sales expenses | 70 |  |
| Discount received | (10) | 90 |
|  |  | 290 |
| Difference in stock valuation: |  |  |
| Opening stock, raw materials | 7 |  |
| Opening stock, finished goods | 9 |  |
| Closing stock, raw materials | 15 |  |
|  |  | 31 |
| Closing stock, work in progress | (5) |  |
| Opening stock, work in progress | (3) |  |
| Closing stock, finished goods | (4) |  |
|  |  | (12) |
|  |  | 19 |
| Profit shown in the cost accounts |  | 309 |

*Notes:*
Production overhead is absorbed at a rate of $66\frac{2}{3}\%$ of wages.
Administration overhead is written off in the period in which it incurred.

(b) Discuss briefly the reasons for including in a cost accounting system notional interest on capital locked up in stock and its treatment in preparing a reconciliation of cost and financial profits. 
(25 marks)
*CIMA Cost Accounting 2*

## 4.12* Intermediate: Stores pricing and preparation of relevant ledger accounts

V Ltd operates interlocking financial and cost accounts. The following balances were in the cost ledger at the beginning of a month, the last month (Month 12) of the financial year:

|  | Dr | Cr |
|---|---|---|
| Raw material stock control a/c | £28 944 |  |
| Finished goods stock control a/c | £77 168 |  |
| Financial ledger control a/c |  | £106 112 |

There is no work in progress at the end of each month.

21 600 kilos of the single raw material were in stock at the beginning of Month 12. Purchases and issues during the month were as follows:

Purchases:
7th, 17 400 kilos at £1.35 per kilo
29th, 19 800 kilos at £1.35 per kilo
Issues:
1st, 7270 kilos
8th, 8120 kilos
15th, 8080 kilos
22nd, 9115 kilos

A weighted average price per kilo (to four decimal places of a £) is used to value issues of raw material to production. A new average price is determined after each material purchase, and issues are charged out in total to the nearest £.

Costs of labour and overhead incurred during Month 12 were £35 407. Production of the company's single product was 17 150 units.

Stocks of finished goods were:

Beginning of Month 12,      16 960 units.
End of Month 12,      17 080 units.

Transfers from finished goods stocks on sale of the product are made on a FIFO basis.

Required:
(a) Prepare the raw material stock control account, and the finished goods stock control account, for Month 12. (Show detailed workings to justify the summary entries made in the accounts.) (12 marks)
(b) Explain the purpose of the financial ledger control account. (4 marks)
(c) Prepare the raw material usage and the raw material purchases budgets for the year ahead (in kilos) using the following information where relevant:

Sales budget, 206 000 units.

Closing stock of finished goods at the end of the budget year should be sufficient to meet 20 days sales demand in the year following that, when sales are expected to be 10% higher in volume than in the budget year.

Closing stock of raw materials should be sufficient to produce 11 700 units.

(NB You should assume that production efficiency will be maintained at the same level, and that there are 250 working days in each year.) (9 marks)
(Total 25 marks)
*ACCA Level 1 Costing*

## 4.13* Intermediate: Labour cost accounting

(a) Describe briefly the purpose of the 'wages control account'. (3 marks)
(b) A manufacturing company has approximately 600 weekly paid direct and indirect production workers. It incurred the following costs and deductions relating to the payroll for the week ended 2 May:

|  | (£) | (£) |
|---|---|---|
| Gross wages |  | 180 460 |
| Deductions: |  |  |
| Employees' national insurance | 14 120 |  |
| Employees' pension fund contributions | 7 200 |  |
| Income tax (PAYE) | 27 800 |  |
| Court order retentions | 1 840 |  |
| Trade union subscriptions | 1 200 |  |
| Private health care contributions | 6 000 |  |
| Total deductions |  | 58 160 |
| Net wages paid |  | 122 300 |

The employer's national insurance contribution for the week was £18 770.

From the wages analysis the following information was extracted:

|  | Direct workers £ | Indirect workers £ |
|---|---|---|
| Paid for ordinary time | 77 460 | 38 400 |
| Overtime wages at normal hourly rates | 16 800 | 10 200 |
| Overtime premium (treat as overhead) | 5 600 | 3 400 |
| Shift premiums/ allowances | 8 500 | 4 500 |
| Capital work in progress expenditure* | — | 2 300* |
| Statutory sick pay | 5 700 | 3 300 |
| Paid for idle time | 4 300 | — |
|  | 118 360 | 62 100 |

*Work done by building maintenance workers concreting floor area for a warehouse extension.

You are required to show journal entries to indicate clearly how each item should be posted into the accounts
(i) from the payroll, and
(ii) from the Wages Control Account to other accounts, based on the wages analysis.

*Note:* Narrations for the journal entries are not required. (12 marks)

(Total 15 marks)

*CIMA Stage 2 Cost Accounting*

### 4.14 Intermediate: Labour cost accounting and recording of journal entries

(a) Identify the costs to a business arising from labour turnover. (5 marks)

(b) A company operates a factory which employed 40 direct workers throughout the four-week period just ended. Direct employees were paid at a basic rate of £4.00 per hour for a 38-hour week. Total hours of the direct workers in the four-week period were 6528. Overtime, which is paid at a premium of 35%, is worked in order to meet general production requirements. Employee deductions total 30% of gross wages. 188 hours of direct workers' time were registered as idle.

Required:

Prepare journal entries to account for the labour costs of direct workers for the period. (7 marks)

(Total 12 marks)

*ACCA Foundation Stage Paper 3*

### 4.15* Intermediate: Calculation as analysis of gross wages and preparation of wages and overhead control accounts

The finishing department in a factory has the following payroll data for the month just ended:

|  | Direct workers | Indirect workers |
|---|---|---|
| Total attendance time (including overtime) | 2640 hours | 940 hours |
| Productive time | 2515 hours | — |
| Non-productive time: |  |  |
|   Machine breakdown | 85 hours | — |
|   Waiting for work | 40 hours | — |
| Overtime | 180 hours | 75 hours |
| Basic hourly rate | £5.00 | £4.00 |
| Group bonuses | £2840 | £710 |
| Employers' National Insurance contributions | £1460 | £405 |

Overtime, which is paid at 140% of basic rate, is usually worked in order to meet the factory's general requirements. However, 40% of the overtime hours of both direct and indirect workers in the month were worked to meet the urgent request of a particular customer.

Required:

(a) Calculate the gross wages paid to direct workers and to indirect workers in the month. (4 marks)

(b) Using the above information, record the relevant entries for the month in the finishing department's wages control account and production overhead control account. (You should clearly indicate the account in which the corresponding entry would be made in the company's separate cost accounting system. Workings must be shown.) (10 marks)

(Total 14 marks)

*ACCA Foundation Paper 3*

### 4.16 Intermediate: Preparation of the wages control account plus an evaluation of the impact of a proposed piecework system

One of the production departments in A Ltd's factory employs 52 direct operatives and 9 indirect operatives. Basic hourly rates of pay are £4.80 and £3.90 respectively. Overtime, which is worked regularly to meet general production requirements, is paid at a premium of 30% over basic rate.

The following further information is provided for the period just ended:

**Hours worked:**

| Direct operatives: |  |
|---|---|
|   Total hours worked | 25 520 hours |
|   Overtime hours worked | 2 120 hours |
| Indirect operatives: |  |
|   Total hours worked | 4 430 hours |
|   Overtime hours worked | 380 hours |
| Production: |  |
| Product 1, 36 000 units in |  |
|   7200 hours |  |
| Product 2, 116 000 units in |  |
|   11 600 hours |  |
| Product 3, 52 800 units in |  |
|   4400 hours |  |
| Non-productive time: | 2 320 hours |
| Wages paid (net of tax and employees' National Insurance): |  |
|   Direct operatives | £97 955 |
|   Indirect operatives | £13 859 |

The senior management of A Ltd are considering the introduction of a piecework payment scheme into the factory. Following work study analysis, expected productivities and proposed piecework rates for the direct operatives, in the production department referred to above, have been determined as follows:

| | Productivity<br>(output per hour) | Piecework rate<br>(per unit) |
|---|---|---|
| Product 1 | 6 units | £1.00 |
| Product 2 | 12 units | £0.50 |
| Product 3 | 14.4 units | £0.40 |

Non-productive time is expected to remain at 10% of productive time, and would be paid at £3.50 per hour.

Required:
(a) Prepare the production department's wages control account for the period in A Ltd's integrated accounting system. (Ignore employers' National Insurance.)    (9 marks)
(b) Examine the effect of the proposed piecework payment scheme on direct labour and overhead costs.    (11 marks)
(Total 20 marks)
*ACCA Cost and Management Accounting 1*

## 4.17* Intermediate: Contract costing

HR Construction plc makes up its accounts to 31 March each year. The following details have been extracted in relation to two of its contracts:

| | Contract<br>A | Contract<br>B |
|---|---|---|
| Commencement date | 1 April 1999 | 1 December 1999 |
| Target completion date | 31 May 2000 | 30 June 2000 |
| Retention% | 4 | 3 |
| | £000 | £000 |
| Contract price | 2,000 | 550 |
| Materials sent to site | 700 | 150 |
| Materials returned to stores | 80 | 30 |
| Plant sent to site | 1,000 | 150 |
| Materials transferred | (40) | 40 |
| Materials on site 31 March 2000 | 75 | 15 |
| Plant hire charges | 200 | 30 |
| Labour cost incurred | 300 | 270 |
| Central overhead cost | 75 | 18 |
| Direct expenses incurred | 25 | 4 |
| Value certified | 1,500 | 500 |
| Cost of work not certified | 160 | 20 |
| Cash received from client | 1,440 | 460 |
| Estimated cost of completion | 135 | 110 |

Depreciation is charged on plant using the straight line method at the rate of 12% per annum.

Required:
(a) Prepare contract accounts, in columnar format, for EACH of the contracts A and B, showing clearly the amounts to be transferred to profit and loss in respect of each contract.    (20 marks)
(b) Show balance sheet extracts in respect of EACH contract for fixed assets, debtors and work in progress.    (4 marks)
(c) Distinguish between job, batch and contract costing.
Explain clearly the reasons why these methods are different.    (6 marks)
(Total 30 marks)
*CIMA Stage 2 Operational Cost Accounting*

## 4.18* Intermediate: Contract costing

A construction company is currently undertaking three separate contracts and information relating to these contracts for the previous year, together with other relevant data, is shown below.

| | Contract<br>MNO<br>(£000) | Contract<br>PQR<br>(£000) | Contract<br>STU<br>(£000) | Construction<br>services<br>dept<br>overhead<br>(£000s) |
|---|---|---|---|---|
| Contract price | 800 | 675 | 1100 | — |
| Balances brought forward at beginning of year: | | | | |
| Cost of work completed | — | 190 | 370 | — |
| Material on site | — | — | 25 | — |
| Written-down value of plant and machinery | — | 35 | 170 | 12 |
| Wages accrued | — | 2 | — | — |
| Profit previously transferred to profit/loss a/c | — | — | 15 | |
| Transactions during year: | | | | |
| Material delivered to site | 40 | 99 | 180 | — |
| Wages paid | 20 | 47 | 110 | 8 |
| Payments to subcontractors | — | — | 35 | — |
| Salaries and other costs | 6 | 20 | 25 | 21 |
| Written down value of plant: | | | | |
| issued to sites | 90 | 15 | — | — |
| transferred from sites | — | 8 | — | — |
| Balances carried forward at the end of year: | | | | |
| Material on site | 8 | — | — | — |
| Written-down value of plant and machinery | 70 | — | 110 | 5 |
| Wages accrued | — | 5 | — | — |
| Pre-payments to subcontractors | — | — | 15 | — |
| Value of work certified at end of year | 90 | 390 | 950 | — |
| Cost of work not certified at end of year | — | — | 26 | — |

The cost of operating the construction services department, which provides technical advice to each of the contracts, is apportioned over the contracts in proportion to wages incurred.

Contract STU is scheduled for handing over to the contractee in the near future and the site engineer estimates that the extra costs required to complete the contract in addition to those tabulated above, will total £138 000. This amount includes an allowance for plant depreciation, construction services and for contingencies.

Required:
(a) Construct a cost account for each of the three contracts for the previous year and show the cost of the work completed at the year end.

(9 marks)
(b) (i) Recommend how much profit or loss should be taken, for each contract, for the previous year. (7 marks)
    (ii) Explain the reasons for each of your recommendations in (b) (i) above.

(6 marks)
(Total 22 marks)
*ACCA Level 1 Costing*

### 4.19 Intermediate: Contract costing
Thornfield Ltd is a building contractor. During its financial year to 30 June 2000, it commenced three major contracts. Information relating to these contracts as at 30 June 2000 was as follows:

|  | Contract 1 | Contract 2 | Contract 3 |
|---|---|---|---|
| Date contract commenced | 1 July 1999 | 1 January 2000 | 1 April 2000 |
|  | (£) | (£) | (£) |
| Contract price | 210 000 | 215 000 | 190 000 |
| Expenditure to 30 June 2000: |  |  |  |
| Materials and subcontract work | 44 000 | 41 000 | 15 000 |
| Direct wages | 80 000 | 74 500 | 12 000 |
| General expenses | 3 000 | 1 800 | 700 |
| Position at 30 June 2000: |  |  |  |
| Materials on hand at cost | 3 000 | 3 000 | 1 500 |
| Accrued expenses | 700 | 600 | 600 |

| Value of work certified | 150 000 | 110 000 | 20 000 |
|---|---|---|---|
| Estimated cost of work completed but not certified | 4 000 | 6 000 | 9 000 |
| Plant and machinery allocated to contracts | 16 000 | 12 000 | 8 000 |

The plant and machinery allocated to the contracts was installed on the dates the contracts commenced. The plant and machinery is expected to have a working life of four years in the case of contracts 1 and 3 and three years in the case of contract 2, and is to be depreciated on a straight line basis assuming nil residual values.

Since the last certificate of work was certified on contract number 1, faulty work has been discovered which is expected to cost £10 000 to rectify. No rectification work has been commenced prior to 30 June 2000.

In addition to expending directly attributable to contracts, recoverable central overheads are estimated to amount to 2% of the cost of direct wages.

Thornfield Ltd has an accounting policy of taking two thirds of the profit attributable to the value of work certified on a contract, once the contract is one third completed. Anticipated losses on contracts are provided in full.

Progress claims equal to 80% of the value of work certified have been invoiced to customers.

You are required to:
(a) prepare contract accounts for each contract for the year to 30 June 2000, calculating any attributable profit or loss on each contract;

(12 marks)
(b) calculate the amount to be included in the balance sheet of Thornfield Ltd as on 30 June 2000 in respect of these contracts. (4 marks)
(Total 16 marks)
*ICAEW Accounting Techniques*

### 4.20 Intermediate: Contract costing
(a) PZ plc undertakes work to repair, maintain and construct roads. When a customer requests the company to do work PZ plc supplies a fixed price to the customer and allocates a works order number to the customer's request. This works order number is used as a reference number on material requisitions and timesheets to enable the costs of doing the work to be collected.

PZ plc's financial year ends on 30 April. At the end of April 2000 the data shown against four of PZ plc's works orders were:

| Works order number | 488 | 517 | 518 | 519 |
|---|---|---|---|---|
| Date started | 1/3/99 | 1/2/00 | 14/3/00 | 18/3/00 |
| Estimated completion date | 31/5/00 | 30/7/00 | 31/5/00 | 15/5/00 |
| | (£000) | (£000) | (£000) | (£000) |
| Direct labour costs | 105 | 10 | 5 | 2 |
| Direct material costs | 86 | 7 | 4 | 2 |
| Selling price | 450 | 135 | 18 | 9 |
| Estimated direct costs to complete orders: | | | | |
| Direct labour | 40 | 60 | 2 | 2 |
| Direct materials | 10 | 15 | 1 | 1 |
| Independent valuation of work done up to 30 April 2000 | 350 | 30 | 15 | 5 |

Overhead costs are allocated to works orders at the rate of 40% of direct labour costs.

It is company policy not to recognize profit on long-term contracts until they are at least 50% complete.

Required:
(i)  State, with reasons, whether they a works orders should be accounted using contract costing or job costing.
(4 mark:

(ii)  Based on your classification at (i) above, prepare a statement showing *clearly* the profit to be recognized and balance sheet work in progress valuation of *each* of the above works orders in respect of the financial year ended 30 April 2000.
(10 marks)

(iii)  Comment critically on the policy of attributing overhead costs to works orders on the basis of direct labour cost.
(6 marks)

(b)  Explain the main features of process costing. Describe what determines the choice between using process costing or specific order costing in a manufacturing organization.
(10 marks)
(Total 30 marks)
*CIMA Operational Cost Accounting Stage 2*

# Process costing

A process costing system is used in those industries where masses of similar products or services are produced. Products are produced in the same manner and consume the same amount of direct costs and overheads. It is therefore unnecessary to assign costs to individual units of output. Instead, the average cost per unit of output is calculated by dividing the total costs assigned to a product or service for a period by the number of units of output for that period. Industries where process costing is widely used include chemical processing, oil refining, food processing and brewing. In contrast, job costing relates to a costing system where each unit or batch of output is unique. This creates the need for the cost of each unit to be calculated separately.

Our objective in this chapter is to examine the cost accumulation procedure that is required for inventory valuation and profit measurement for a process costing system. We shall also discuss briefly at the end of the chapter how cost information should be accumulated and extracted for decision-making and cost control. We begin with a description of the flow of production and costs in a process costing environment. We shall then focus on the cost accumulation system. To provide a structured presentation three different scenarios will be presented. First, all output is fully complete. Second, ending work in progress exists, but no beginning work in progress, and some of the units started during the period are incomplete at the end of the period. Our third scenario is the existence of both beginning and ending work in progress of uncompleted units. Finally, we shall turn our attention to decision-making and cost control. One of the most complex areas in process costing is accounting for losses when units within the process are both fully and partially complete. Because some courses omit this topic it will be discussed in Appendix 5.1.

## Learning objectives

After studying this chapter you should be able to:

- distinguish between process and job costing;

- explain the accounting treatment for normal and abnormal losses;

- prepare process, normal loss, abnormal loss and abnormal gain accounts when there is no ending work in progress;

- compute the value of work in progress and completed production using the weighted average and first in, first out methods of valuing work in progress;

- differentiate between the different cost per unit calculations which are necessary for inventory valuation, decision-making and performance reporting for cost control;

- compute the value of normal and abnormal losses when there is ending work in progress.

# Flow of production and costs in a process costing system

The flow of production and costs in a process costing system is illustrated in Exhibit 5.1. The major differences between process and job costing are also highlighted. You will see that production moves from one process (or department) to the next until final completion occurs. Each production department performs some part of the total operation and transfers its completed production to the next department, where it becomes the input for further processing. The completed production of the last department is transferred to the finished goods inventory.

The cost accumulation procedure follows this production flow. Control accounts are established for each process (or department) and direct and indirect costs are assigned to each process. A process costing system is easier to operate than a job costing system because the detailed work of allocating costs to many individual cost units is unnecessary. Also, many of the costs that are indirect in a job costing system may be regarded as direct in a process costing system. For example, supervision and depreciation that is confined to one department would be treated as part of the direct costs of that department in a process costing system, since these costs are directly attributable to the cost object (i.e. the department or process). However, such costs are normally regarded as indirect in a job costing system because they are not directly attributable to a specific job.

**EXHIBIT 5.1**

*A comparison of job and process costing*

**Process costing**

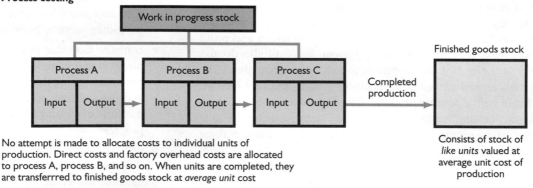

No attempt is made to allocate costs to individual units of production. Direct costs and factory overhead costs are allocated to process A, process B, and so on. When units are completed, they are transferred to finished goods stock at *average unit* cost

Consists of stock of *like units* valued at average unit cost of production

**Job costing**

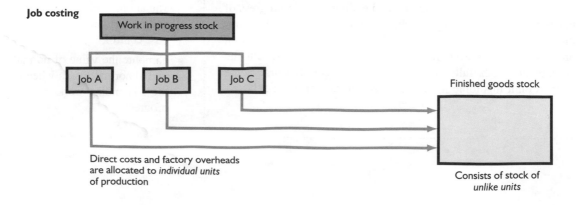

Direct costs and factory overheads are allocated to *individual units* of production

Consists of stock of *unlike units*

As production moves from process to process costs are transferred with it. For example, in Exhibit 5.1 the costs of process A would be transferred to process B; process B costs would then be added to this cost and the resulting total cost transferred to process C; process C costs would then added to this cost. Therefore the cost becomes cumulative as production proceeds and the addition of the costs from the last department's cost determines the total cost. The cost per unit of the completed product thus consists of the total cost accumulated in process C for the period divided by the output for that period.

# Process costing when all output is fully complete

Throughout this section it is assumed that all output within each process is fully complete. We shall examine the following situations:

1. no losses within a process;
2. normal losses with no scrap value;
3. abnormal losses with no scrap value;
4. normal losses with a scrap value;
5. abnormal losses with a scrap value;
6. abnormal gains with no scrap value;
7. abnormal gains with a scrap value.

You should now look at Example 5.1. The information shown in this example will be used to illustrate the accounting entries. To simplify the presentation it is assumed that the product is produced within a single process.

**EXAMPLE 5.1**

Dartmouth Company produces a liquid fertilizer within a single production process. During the month of May the input into the process was 12 000 litres at a cost of £120 000. There were no opening or closing inventories and all output was fully complete. We shall prepare the process account and calculate the cost per litre of output for the single process for each of the following seven cases:

| Case | Input (litres) | Output (litres) | Normal loss (litres) | Abnormal loss (litres) | Abnormal gain (litres) | Scrap value of spoilt output (£ per litre) |
|------|------|------|------|------|------|------|
| 1 | 12 000 | 12 000 | 0 | 0 | 0 | 0 |
| 2 | 12 000 | 10 000 | 2000 (1/6) | 0 | 0 | 0 |
| 3 | 12 000 | 9 000 | 2000 (1/6) | 1000 | 0 | 0 |
| 4 | 12 000 | 10 000 | 2000 (1/6) | 0 | 0 | 5 |
| 5 | 12 000 | 9 000 | 2000 (1/6) | 1000 | 0 | 5 |
| 6 | 12 000 | 11 000 | 2000 (1/6) | 0 | 1000 | 0 |
| 7 | 12 000 | 11 000 | 2000 (1/6) | 0 | 1000 | 5 |

## NO LOSSES WITHIN THE PROCESS

To calculate the cost per unit (i.e. litre) of output for case 1 in Example 5.1 we merely divide the total cost incurred for the period of £120 000 by the output for the period (12 000 litres). The cost per unit of output is £10. In practice the cost per unit is analysed by the different cost categories such as direct materials and **conversion cost** which consists of the sum of direct labour and overhead costs.

## NORMAL LOSSES IN PROCESS WITH NO SCRAP VALUE

Certain losses are inherent in the production process and cannot be eliminated. For example, liquids may evaporate, part of the cloth required to make a suit may be lost and losses occur in cutting wood to make furniture. These losses occur under efficient operating conditions and are unavoidable. They are referred to as **normal or uncontrollable losses**. Because they are an inherent part of the production process normal losses are absorbed by the good production. Where normal losses apply the cost per unit of output is calculated by dividing the costs incurred for a period by the *expected* output from the actual input for that period. Looking at case 2 in Example 5.1 you will see that the normal loss is one sixth of the input. Therefore for an input of 12 000 litres the *expected* output is 10 000 litres so that the cost per unit of output is £12 (£120 000/10 000 litres). Actual output is equal to expected output so there is neither an abnormal loss nor gain. Compared with case 1 the unit cost has increased by £2 per unit because the cost of the normal loss has been absorbed by the good production. Our objective is to calculate the cost of normal production under normal efficient operating conditions.

## ABNORMAL LOSSES IN PROCESS WITH NO SCRAP VALUE

In addition to losses that cannot be avoided, there are some losses that are not expected to occur under efficient operating conditions, for example the improper mixing of ingredients, the use of inferior materials and the incorrect cutting of cloth. These losses are not an inherent part of the production process, and are referred to as **abnormal or controllable losses**. Because they are not an inherent part of the production process and arise from inefficiencies they are not included in the process costs. Instead, they are removed from the appropriate process account and reported separately as an abnormal loss. The abnormal loss is treated as a period cost and written off in the profit statement at the end of the accounting period. This ensures that abnormal losses are not incorporated in any inventory valuations.

For case 3 in Example 5.1 the expected output is 10 000 litres but the actual output was 9000 litres, resulting in an abnormal loss of 1000 litres. Our objective is the same as that for normal losses. That is to calculate the cost per litre of the *expected* output (i.e. normal production), which is:

$$\frac{\text{input cost (£120 000)}}{\text{expected output (10 000 litres)}} = £12$$

Note that the unit cost is the same for an output of 10 000 or 9000 litres since our objective is to calculate the cost per unit of normal output. The distribution of the input costs is as follows:

| | (£) |
|---|---|
| Completed production transferred to the next process (or finished goods inventory) 9000 litres at £12 | 108 000 |
| Abnormal loss: 1000 litres at £12 | 12 000 |
| | 120 000 |

The abnormal loss is valued at the cost per unit of normal production. Abnormal losses can only be controlled in the future by establishing the cause of the abnormal loss and taking appropriate remedial action to ensure that it does not reoccur. The entries in the process account will look like this:

**[Process account]**

| | Litres | Unit cost (£) | (£) | | Litres | Unit cost (£) | (£) |
|---|---|---|---|---|---|---|---|
| Input cost | 12 000 | 10 | 120 000 | Normal loss | 2000 | — | — |
| | | | | Output to finished | | | |
| | | | | goods inventory | 9000 | 12 | 108 000 |
| | | | | Abnormal loss | 1000 | 12 | 12 000 |
| | | | 120 000 | | | | 120 000 |

Process accounts represent work in progress (WIP) accounts. For example, if a second process were required and the 9000 litres had remained from the first process at the end of the accounting period the £108 000 would have represented the work in progress valuation in the process. In our example all of the work in progress has been completed and transferred to the finished goods inventory. Input costs are debited to the process account and the output from the process is entered on the credit side.

You will see from the process account that no entry is made in the account for the normal loss (except for an entry made in the units column). The transfer to the finished goods inventory (or the next process) is at the cost of normal production. The abnormal loss is removed from the process costs and reported separately as a loss in the abnormal loss account. This draws the attention of management to those losses that may be controllable. At the end of the accounting period the abnormal loss account is written off in the profit statement as a period cost. The inventory valuation will not therefore include any abnormal expenses. The overall effect is that the abnormal losses are correctly allocated to the period in which they arise and are not carried forward as a future expense in the closing inventory valuation.

## NORMAL LOSSES IN PROCESS WITH A SCRAP VALUE

In case 4 actual output is equal to the expected output of 10 000 litres so there is neither an abnormal gain nor loss. All of the units lost represent a normal loss in process. However, the units lost now have a scrap value of £5 per litre. The sales value of the spoiled units should be offset against the costs of the appropriate process where the loss occurred. Therefore the sales value of the normal loss is credited to the process account and a corresponding debit entry will be made in the cash or accounts receivable (debtors) account. The calculation of the cost per unit of output is as follows:

$$\frac{\text{Input cost less scrap value of normal loss}}{\text{Expected output}} = \frac{£120\,000 - (2000 \times £5)}{10\,000\,\text{litres}} = £11$$

Compared with cases 3 and 4 the cost per unit has declined from £12 per litre to £11 per litre to reflect the fact that the normal spoilage has a scrap value which has been offset against the process costs.

The entries in the process account will look like this:

**[Process account]**

|  | Litres | Unit cost (£) | (£) |  | Litres | Unit cost (£) | (£) |
|---|---|---|---|---|---|---|---|
| Input cost | 12 000 | 10 | 120 000 | Normal loss | 2 000 | — | 10 000 |
|  |  |  |  | Output to finished goods inventory | 10 000 | 11 | 110 000 |
|  |  |  | 120 000 |  |  |  | 120 000 |

Note that the scrap value of the normal loss is credited against the normal loss entry in the process account.

## ABNORMAL LOSSES IN PROCESS WITH A SCRAP VALUE

In case 5 expected output is 10 000 litres for an input of 12 000 litres and actual output is 9000 litres resulting in a normal loss of 2000 litres and an abnormal loss of 1000 litres. The lost units have a scrap value of £5 per litre. Since our objective is to calculate the cost per unit for the expected (normal) output only the scrap value of the normal loss of 2000 litres should be deducted in ascertaining the cost per unit. Therefore the cost per unit calculation is the same as that for case 4 (i.e. £11). The sales value of the additional 1000 litres lost represents revenue of an abnormal nature and should not be used to reduce the process unit cost. This revenue is offset against the cost of the abnormal loss which is of interest to management. The net cost incurred in the process is £105 000 (£120 000 input cost less 3000 litres lost with a scrap value of £5 per litre), and the distribution of this cost is:

|  | (£) | (£) |
|---|---|---|
| Completed production transferred to the next process (or finished goods inventory) (9000 litres at £11 per litre) |  | 99 000 |
| Abnormal loss: |  |  |
| 1000 litres at £11 per litre | 11 000 |  |
| Less scrap value (1000 litres at £5) | 5 000 | 6 000 |
|  |  | 105 000 |

The entries in the process account will be as follows:

**[Process account]**

|  | Litres | Unit cost (£) | (£) |  | Litres | Unit cost (£) | (£) |
|---|---|---|---|---|---|---|---|
| Input cost | 12 000 | 10 | 120 000 | Normal loss | 2000 | — | 10 000 |
|  |  |  |  | Output to finished goods inventory | 9000 | 11 | 99 000 |
|  |  |  |  | Abnormal loss | 1000 | 11 | 11 000 |
|  |  |  | 120 000 |  |  |  | 120 000 |

The abnormal loss is valued at the cost per unit of normal production. Abnormal losses can only be controlled in the future by establishing the cause of the abnormal loss and taking appropriate remedial action to ensure that it does not reoccur. The entries in the process account will look like this:

**[Process account]**

|  | Litres | Unit cost (£) | (£) |  | Litres | Unit cost (£) | (£) |
|---|---|---|---|---|---|---|---|
| Input cost | 12 000 | 10 | 120 000 | Normal loss | 2000 | — | — |
|  |  |  |  | Output to finished |  |  |  |
|  |  |  |  | goods inventory | 9000 | 12 | 108 000 |
|  |  |  |  | Abnormal loss | 1000 | 12 | 12 000 |
|  |  |  | 120 000 |  |  |  | 120 000 |

Process accounts represent work in progress (WIP) accounts. For example, if a second process were required and the 9000 litres had remained from the first process at the end of the accounting period the £108 000 would have represented the work in progress valuation in the process. In our example all of the work in progress has been completed and transferred to the finished goods inventory. Input costs are debited to the process account and the output from the process is entered on the credit side.

You will see from the process account that no entry is made in the account for the normal loss (except for an entry made in the units column). The transfer to the finished goods inventory (or the next process) is at the cost of normal production. The abnormal loss is removed from the process costs and reported separately as a loss in the abnormal loss account. This draws the attention of management to those losses that may be controllable. At the end of the accounting period the abnormal loss account is written off in the profit statement as a period cost. The inventory valuation will not therefore include any abnormal expenses. The overall effect is that the abnormal losses are correctly allocated to the period in which they arise and are not carried forward as a future expense in the closing inventory valuation.

## NORMAL LOSSES IN PROCESS WITH A SCRAP VALUE

In case 4 actual output is equal to the expected output of 10 000 litres so there is neither an abnormal gain nor loss. All of the units lost represent a normal loss in process. However, the units lost now have a scrap value of £5 per litre. The sales value of the spoiled units should be offset against the costs of the appropriate process where the loss occurred. Therefore the sales value of the normal loss is credited to the process account and a corresponding debit entry will be made in the cash or accounts receivable (debtors) account. The calculation of the cost per unit of output is as follows:

$$\frac{\text{Input cost less scrap value of normal loss}}{\text{Expected output}} = \frac{£120\,000 - (2000 \times £5)}{10\,000 \text{ litres}} = £11$$

Compared with cases 3 and 4 the cost per unit has declined from £12 per litre to £11 per litre to reflect the fact that the normal spoilage has a scrap value which has been offset against the process costs.

The entries in the process account will look like this:

**[Process account]**

| | Litres | Unit cost (£) | (£) | | Litres | Unit cost (£) | (£) |
|---|---|---|---|---|---|---|---|
| Input cost | 12 000 | 10 | 120 000 | Normal loss | 2 000 | — | 10 000 |
| | | | | Output to finished goods inventory | 10 000 | 11 | 110 000 |
| | | | 120 000 | | | | 120 000 |

Note that the scrap value of the normal loss is credited against the normal loss entry in the process account.

## ABNORMAL LOSSES IN PROCESS WITH A SCRAP VALUE

In case 5 expected output is 10 000 litres for an input of 12 000 litres and actual output is 9000 litres resulting in a normal loss of 2000 litres and an abnormal loss of 1000 litres. The lost units have a scrap value of £5 per litre. Since our objective is to calculate the cost per unit for the expected (normal) output only the scrap value of the normal loss of 2000 litres should be deducted in ascertaining the cost per unit. Therefore the cost per unit calculation is the same as that for case 4 (i.e. £11). The sales value of the additional 1000 litres lost represents revenue of an abnormal nature and should not be used to reduce the process unit cost. This revenue is offset against the cost of the abnormal loss which is of interest to management. The net cost incurred in the process is £105 000 (£120 000 input cost less 3000 litres lost with a scrap value of £5 per litre), and the distribution of this cost is:

| | (£) | (£) |
|---|---|---|
| Completed production transferred to the next process (or finished goods inventory) (9000 litres at £11 per litre) | | 99 000 |
| Abnormal loss: | | |
| 1000 litres at £11 per litre | 11 000 | |
| Less scrap value (1000 litres at £5) | 5 000 | 6 000 |
| | | 105 000 |

The entries in the process account will be as follows:

**[Process account]**

| | Litres | Unit cost (£) | (£) | | Litres | Unit cost (£) | (£) |
|---|---|---|---|---|---|---|---|
| Input cost | 12 000 | 10 | 120 000 | Normal loss | 2000 | — | 10 000 |
| | | | | Output to finished goods inventory | 9000 | 11 | 99 000 |
| | | | | Abnormal loss | 1000 | 11 | 11 000 |
| | | | 120 000 | | | | 120 000 |

**[Abnormal loss account]**

| | (£) | | (£) |
|---|---|---|---|
| Process account | 11 000 | Cash sale for units scrapped | 5 000 |
| | | Balance transferred to profit statement | 6 000 |
| | 11 000 | | 11 000 |

## ABNORMAL GAINS WITH NO SCRAP VALUE

On occasions the actual loss in process may be less than expected, in which case an **abnormal gain** results. In case 6 the expected output is 10 000 litres for an input of 12 000 litres but the actual output is 11 000 litres resulting in an abnormal gain of 1000 litres. We are assuming for this case that the normal loss does not have a scrap value. As in the previous cases our objective is to calculate the cost per unit of expected (normal) output. The calculation of the cost per unit of normal output is the same as that for cases 2 and 3, which is:

$$\frac{\text{input cost } (£120\,000)}{\text{expected output } (10\,000\,\text{litres})} = £12$$

and the distribution of the input cost is as follows:

| | (£) |
|---|---|
| Completed production transferred to the next process (or finished goods inventory) 11 000 litres at £12 | 132 000 |
| Less: Abnormal gain: 1000 litres at £12 | 12 000 |
| | 120 000 |

The value of the gain is calculated in the same way as the abnormal loss and removed from the process account by debiting the account and crediting the abnormal gain account. The entries in the process account will be as follows:

**[Process account]**

| | Litres | Unit cost (£) | (£) | | Litres | Unit cost (£) | (£) |
|---|---|---|---|---|---|---|---|
| Input cost | 12 000 | 10 | 120 000 | Normal loss | 2 000 | — | — |
| Abnormal gain | 1 000 | 12 | 12 000 | Output to finished | | | |
| | | | | goods inventory | 11 000 | 12 | 132 000 |
| | | | 132 000 | | | | 132 000 |

You will see in the process account that 11 000 litres are passed to the next process at the cost per unit of *normal* output. The gain is credited to the abnormal gain account and transferred to the credit of the profit and loss statement at the end of the period. This procedure ensures that the inventory valuation is not understated by gains of an abnormal nature.

## ABNORMAL GAINS WITH A SCRAP VALUE

The only difference between cases 7 and 6 is that any losses have a scrap value of £5 per litre. As in the previous cases we start by calculating the cost per unit of normal output. For normal output our assumptions are the same as those for cases 4 and 5 (i.e. a normal loss of one sixth and a scrap value of £5 per litre) so the cost per unit of output is the same (i.e. £11 per litre). The calculation is as follows:

$$\frac{\text{Input cost less scrap value of normal loss}}{\text{Expected output}} = \frac{£120\,000 - (2000 \times £5)}{10\,000 \text{ litres}} = £11$$

The net cost incurred in the process is £115 000 (£120 000 input cost less 1000 litres spoilt with a sales value of £5 per litre), and the distribution of this cost is as follows:

|  |  | (£) |
| --- | --- | --- |
| Transferred to finished goods inventory | | |
| (11 000 litres at £11 per litre) | | 121 000 |
| Less abnormal gain (1000 litres at £11 per litre) | 11 000 | |
| lost sales of spoiled units (1000 litres at £5 per litre) | 5 000 | 6 000 |
| | | 115 000 |

Note that the cost per unit is based on the normal production cost per unit and is not affected by the fact that an abnormal gain occurred or that sales of the spoiled units with a sales value of £5000 did not materialize. Our objective is to produce a cost per unit based on normal operating efficiency.

The accounting entries are as follows:

**[Process account]**

| | Litres | Unit cost | | | Litres | Unit cost | |
| --- | --- | --- | --- | --- | --- | --- | --- |
| | | (£) | (£) | | | (£) | (£) |
| Input cost | 12 000 | 10 | 120 000 | Normal loss | 2 000 | — | 10 000 |
| Abnormal gain | 1 000 | 11 | 11 000 | Output to finished | | | |
| | | | | goods inventory | 11 000 | 11 | 121 000 |
| | | | 131 000 | | | | 131 000 |

**Abnormal gain account**

| | (£) | | (£) |
| --- | --- | --- | --- |
| Normal loss account | 5 000 | Process account | 11 000 |
| Profit and loss statement (Balance) | 6 000 | | |
| | 11 000 | | 11 000 |

**Income due from normal losses**

| | (£) | | (£) |
| --- | --- | --- | --- |
| Process account | 10 000 | Abnormal gain account | 5 000 |
| | | Cash from spoiled units | |
| | | (1000 litres at £5) | 5 000 |
| | 10 000 | | 10 000 |

You will see that the abnormal gain has been removed from the process account and that it is valued at the cost per unit of normal production. However, as 1000 litres were gained, there was a loss of sales revenue of £5000, and this lost revenue is offset against the abnormal gain. The net gain is therefore £6000, and this is the amount that should be credited to the profit statement.

The process account is credited with the expected sales revenue from the normal loss (2000 litres at £5), since the objective is to record in the process account normal net costs of production. Because the normal loss of 2000 litres does not occur, the company will not obtain the sales value of £10 000 from the expected lost output. This problem is resolved by making a corresponding debit entry in a normal loss account, which represents the amount due from the sale proceeds from the expected normal loss. The amount due (£10 000) is then reduced by £5000 to reflect the fact that only 1000 litres were lost. This is achieved by crediting the normal loss account (income due) and debiting the abnormal gain account with £5000, so that the balance of the normal loss account shows the actual amount of cash received for the income due from the spoiled units (i.e. £5000, which consists of 1000 litres at £5 per litre).

# Process costing with ending work in progress partially complete

So far we have assumed that all output within a process is fully complete. We shall now consider situations where output started during a period is partially complete at the end of the period. In other words, ending work in progress exists within a process. When some of the output started during a period is partially complete at the end of the period, unit costs cannot be computed by simply dividing the total costs for a period by the output for that period. For example, if 8000 units were started and completed during a period and another 2000 units were partly completed then these two items cannot be added together to ascertain their unit cost. We must convert the work in progress into finished equivalents (also referred to as **equivalent production**) so that the unit cost can be obtained.

To do this we must estimate the percentage degree of completion of the work in progress and multiply this by the number of units in progress at the end of the accounting period. If the 2000 partly completed units were 50% complete, we could express this as an equivalent production of 1000 fully completed units. This would then be added to the completed production of 8000 units to give a total equivalent production of 9000 units. The cost per unit would then be calculated in the normal way. For example, if the costs for the period were £180 000 then the cost per unit completed would be £20 (£180 000/9000 units) and the distribution of this cost would be as follows:

|  | (£) |
|---|---|
| Completed units transferred to the next process (8000 units at £20) | 160 000 |
| Work in progress (1000 equivalent units at £20) | 20 000 |
|  | 180 000 |

## ELEMENTS OF COSTS WITH DIFFERENT DEGREES OF COMPLETION

A complication that may arise concerning equivalent units is that in any given stock of work in progress not all of the elements that make up the total cost may have reached the same degree of completion. For example, materials may be added at the start of the process, and are thus fully complete, whereas labour and manufacturing overhead (i.e. the conversion costs) may be added uniformly throughout the process. Hence, the ending work in progress may consist of materials that are 100% complete and conversion costs that are only partially complete. Where this situation arises, separate equivalent production calculations must be made for each element of cost. The calculation of unit costs and the allocation of costs to work in progress and completed production when different elements of costs are subject to different degrees of completion will now be illustrated using the data given in Example 5.2.

**EXAMPLE 5.2**

The Fontenbleau Company manufactures a product that passes through two processes. The following information relates to the two processes:

|  | Process A | Process B |
|---|---|---|
| Opening work in progress | — | — |
| Units introduced into the process | 14 000 | 10 000 |
| Units completed and transferred to the next process or finished goods inventory | 10 000 | 9 000 |
| Closing work in progress | 4 000 | 1 000 |
| Costs of production transferred from process A[a] |  | £270 000 |
| Material costs added | £210 000 | £108 000 |
| Conversion costs | £144 000 | £171 000 |

Materials are added at the start of process A and at the end of process B and conversion costs are added uniformly throughout both processes. The closing work in progress is estimated to be 50% complete for both processes.

*Note*
[a] This information is derived from the preparation of process A accounts.

The following statement shows the calculation of the cost per unit for process A:

**[Calculation of cost per unit for process A]**

| Cost element | Total cost (£) | Completed units | WIP equivalent units | Total equivalent units | Cost per unit (£) |
|---|---|---|---|---|---|
| Materials | 210 000 | 10 000 | 4000 | 14 000 | 15.00 |
| Conversion cost | 144 000 | 10 000 | 2000 | 12 000 | 12.00 |
|  | 354 000 |  |  |  | 27.00 |

|  | (£) | (£) |
|---|---|---|
| Value of work in progress: |  |  |
| Materials (4000 units at £15) | 60 000 |  |
| Conversion cost (2000 units at £12) | 24 000 | 84 000 |
| Completed units (10 000) units at £27) |  | 270 000 |
|  |  | 354 000 |

The process account will look like this:

**Process A account**

| Materials | 210 000 | Completed units transferred to process B | 270 000 |
|---|---|---|---|
| Conversion cost | 144 000 | Closing WIP c/fwd | 84 000 |
|  | 354 000 |  | 354 000 |
| Opening WIP b/fwd | 84 000 |  |  |

You will see from the above statement that details are collected relating to the equivalent production for completed units and work in progress by materials and conversion costs. This information is required to calculate the cost per unit of equivalent production for each element of cost. The work in progress of 4000 units is considered to be fully complete regarding materials. As materials are issued at the start of the process any partly completed units in ending work in progress must be fully complete as far as materials are concerned. Therefore an entry of 4000 units is made in the work in progress equivalent units column in the above statement for materials. Regarding conversion cost, the 4000 units in progress are only 50% complete and therefore the entry in the work in progress column for this element of cost is 2000 units. To compute the value of work in progress, the unit costs are multiplied separately by the materials and conversion cost work in progress equivalent production figures. Only one calculation is required to ascertain the value of completed production. This is obtained by multiplying the total cost per unit of £27 by the completed production. Note that the cost of the output of £354 000 in the above statement is in agreement with the cost of input of £354 000.

## PREVIOUS PROCESS COST

As production moves through processing, the output of one process becomes the input of the next process. The next process will carry out additional conversion work, and may add further materials. It is important to distinguish between these different cost items; this is achieved by labelling the transferred cost from the previous process 'previous process cost'. Note that this element of cost will always be fully complete as far as closing work in progress is concerned. Let us now calculate the unit costs and the value of work in progress and completed production for process B. To do this we prepare a statement similar to the one we prepared for process A.

### Calculation of cost per unit for process B

| Cost element | Total cost (£) | Completed units | WIP equivalent units | Total equivalent units | Cost per unit (£) |
|---|---|---|---|---|---|
| Previous process cost | 270 000 | 9000 | 1000 | 10 000 | 27.00 |
| Materials | 108 000 | 9000 | — | 9 000 | 12.00 |
| Conversion cost | 171 000 | 9000 | 500 | 9 500 | 18.00 |
| | 549 000 | | | | 57.00 |

|  | (£) | (£) |
|---|---|---|
| Value of work in progress: | | |
| Previous process cost (1000 units at £27) | 27 000 | |
| Materials | — | |
| Conversion cost (500 units at £18) | 9 000 | 36 000 |
| Completed units (9000 units at £57) | | 513 000 |
| | | 549 000 ← |

**Process B account**

| | | | |
|---|---|---|---|
| Previous process cost | 270 000 | Completed production | |
| Materials | 108 000 | transferred to finished stock | 513 000 |
| Conversions cost | 171 000 | Closing work in progress c/fwd | 36 000 |
| | 549 000 | | 549 000 |
| Opening WIP b/fwd | 36 000 | | |

You will see that the previous process cost is treated as a separate process cost, and, since this element of cost will not be added to in process B, the closing work in progress must be fully complete as far as previous process cost is concerned. Note that, after the first process, materials may be issued at different stages of production. In process B materials are not issued until the end of the process, and the closing work in progress will not have reached this point; the equivalent production for the closing work in progress will therefore be zero for materials.

Normally, material costs are introduced at one stage in the process and not uniformly throughout the process. If the work in progress has passed the point at which the materials are added then the materials will be 100% complete. If this point has not been reached then the equivalent production for materials will be zero.

# Beginning and ending work in progress of uncompleted units

When opening stocks of work in progress exist, an assumption must be made regarding the allocation of this opening stock to the current accounting period to determine the unit cost for the period. Two alternative assumptions are possible. First, one may assume that opening work in progress is inextricably merged with the units introduced in the current period and can no longer be identified separately – the **weighted average method**. Secondly, one may assume that the opening work in progress is the first group of units to be processed and completed during the current month – the **first in, first out method**. Let us now compare these methods using the information contained in Example 5.3.

For more complex problems it is always a good idea to start by calculating the number of units completed during the period. The calculations are as follows:

| | Process X | Process Y |
|---|---|---|
| Opening work in progress | 6 000 | 2 000 |
| Units introduced during period | 16 000 | 18 000 |
| Total input for period | 22 000 | 20 000 |
| Less closing work in progress | 4 000 | 8 000 |
| Balance – completed production | 18 000 | 12 000 |

## WEIGHTED AVERAGE METHOD

The calculation of the unit cost for process X using the weighted average method is as follows:

## EXAMPLE 5.3

The Baltic Company has two processes, X and Y. Material is introduced at the start of process X, and additional material is added to process Y when the process is 70% complete. Conversion costs are applied uniformly throughout both processes. The completed units of process X are immediately transferred to process Y, and the completed production of process Y is transferred to finished goods stock. Data for the period include the following:

|  | Process X | Process Y |
|---|---|---|
| Opening work in progress | 6000 units 60% converted, consisting of materials £72 000 and conversion cost £45 900 | 2000 units 80% converted, consisting of previous process cost of £91 800, materials £12 000 and conversion costs £38 400 |
| Units started during the period | 16 000 units | 18 000 units |
| Closing work in progress | 4000 units 3/4 complete | 8000 units 1/2 complete |
| Material costs added during the period | £192 000 | £60 000 |
| Conversion costs added during the period | £225 000 | £259 200 |

### Process X – weighted average method

| Cost element | Opening WIP (£) | Current cost (£) | Total cost (£) | Completed units | WIP equiv. units | Total equiv. units | Cost per [unit] (£) |
|---|---|---|---|---|---|---|---|
| Materials | 72 000 | 192 000 | 264 000 | 18 000 | 4000 | 22 000 | 12.00 |
| Conversion cost | 45 900 | 225 000 | 270 900 | 18 000 | 3000 | 21 000 | 12.90 |
|  | 117 900 |  | 534 900 |  |  |  | 24.90 |

|  | (£) | (£) |
|---|---|---|
| Work in progress: |  |  |
| Materials (4000 units at £12) | 48 000 |  |
| Conversion (3000 units at £12.90) | 38 700 | 86 700 |
| Completed units (18 000 units at £24.90) |  | 448 200 |
|  |  | 534 900 |

### Process X account

| Opening work in progress |  | Completed production |  |
|---|---|---|---|
| b/fwd | 117 900 | transferred to process Y | 448 200 |
| Materials | 192 000 | Closing work in progress c/fwd | 86 700 |

|  |  |  |
|---|---|---|
| Conversion cost | 225 000 |  |
|  | 534 900 | 534 900 |
| Opening work in progress b/fwd | 86 700 |  |

You can see from the statement of unit cost calculations that the opening work in progress is assumed to be completed in the current period. The current period's costs will include the cost of finishing off the opening work in progress, and the cost of the work in progress will be included in the total cost figure. The completed units will include the 6000 units in progress that will have been completed during the period. The statement therefore includes all the costs of the opening work in progress and the resulting units, fully completed. In other words, we have assumed that the opening work in progress is intermingled with the production of the current period to form one homogeneous batch of production. The equivalent number of units for this batch of production is divided into the costs of the current period, plus the value of the opening work in progress, to calculate the cost per unit.

Let us now calculate the unit cost for process Y using the weighted average method. From the calculation of the unit costs you can see the previous process cost is fully complete as far as the closing work in progress is concerned. Note that materials are added when the process is 70% complete, but the closing work in progress is only 50% complete. At the stage in question no materials will have been added to the closing work in progress, and the equivalent production will be zero. As with process X, it is necessary to add the opening work in progress cost to the current cost. The equivalent production of opening work in progress is ignored since this is included as being fully complete in the completed units column. Note also that the completed production cost of process X is included in the current cost column for 'the previous process cost' in the unit cost calculation for process Y.

### Process Y – Weighted average method

| Cost element | Opening WIP value (£) | Current period cost (£) | Total cost (£) | Completed units | WIP equiv. units | Total equiv. units | Cost per unit (£) |
|---|---|---|---|---|---|---|---|
| Previous process cost | 91 800 | 448 200 | 540 000 | 12 000 | 8000 | 20 000 | 27.00 |
| Materials | 12 000 | 60 000 | 72 000 | 12 000 | — | 12 000 | 6.00 |
| Conversion cost | 38 400 | 259 200 | 297 600 | 12 000 | 4000 | 16 000 | 18.60 |
|  | 142 200 |  | 909 600 |  |  |  | 51.60 |

|  | (£) | (£) |
|---|---|---|
| Value of work in progress: |  |  |
| Previous process cost (8000 units at £27) | 216 000 |  |
| Materials | — |  |
| Conversion cost (4000 units at £18.60) | 74 400 | 290 400 |
| Completed units (12 000 units at £51.60) |  | 619 200 |
|  |  | 909 600 |

**Process Y account**

| | | | |
|---|---|---|---|
| Opening work in progress | 142 200 | Completed production | |
| Transferred from process X | 448 200 | transferred to finished stock | 619 200 |
| Materials | 60 000 | Closing work in progress c/fwd | 290 400 |
| Conversion cost | 259 200 | | |
| | 909 600 | | 909 600 |
| Opening work in progress b/fwd | 290 400 | | |

## FIRST IN FIRST OUT (FIFO) METHOD

The FIFO method of process costing assumes that the opening work in progress is the first group of units to be processed and completed during the current period. The opening work in progress is charged separately to completed production, and the cost per unit is based only on the *current period* costs and production for the current period. The closing work in progress is assumed to come from the new units started during the period. Let us now use Example 5.3 to illustrate the FIFO method for process X and Y.

### Process X – FIFO method

| Cost element | Current period costs (£) | Completed units less opening WIP equiv. units | Closing WIP equiv. units | Current total equiv. units | Cost per unit (£) |
|---|---|---|---|---|---|
| Materials | 192 000 | 12 000 (18 000 − 6000) | 4000 | 16 000 | 12.00 |
| Conversion cost | 225 000 | 14 400 (18 000 − 3600) | 3000 | 17 400 | 12.93 |
| | 417 000 | | | | 24.93 |

| | | (£) | (£) |
|---|---|---|---|
| Completed production: | | | |
| Opening WIP | | 117 900 | |
| Materials (12 000 units at £12) | | 144 000 | |
| Conversion cost (14 400 units at £12.93) | | 186 207 | 448 107 |
| Work in progress: | | | |
| Materials (4000 units at £12) | | 48 000 | |
| Conversion cost (3000 units at £12.93) | | 38 793 | 86 793 |
| | | | 534 900 |

From this calculation you can see that the average cost per unit is based on current period costs divided by the current total equivalent units for the period. The latter figure excludes the equivalent production for opening work in progress since this was performed in the previous period. Note that the closing work in progress is multiplied by the current period average cost per unit. The closing work in progress includes only the current costs and does not include any of the opening work in progress, which is carried forward from the previous period. The objective is to ensure that the opening work in progress is kept separate and is identified as part of the cost of the completed production. The opening work in progress of £117 900 is not therefore included in the unit cost calculations, but is added directly to the completed production.

Let us now calculate the units costs for process Y:

### Process Y – FIFO method

| Cost element | Current costs (£) | Completed units less opening WIP equiv. units | Closing WIP equiv. units | Current total equiv. units | Cost per unit (£) |
|---|---|---|---|---|---|
| Previous process cost | 448 107 | 10 000 (12 000 − 2000) | 8000 | 18 000 | 24.8948 |
| Materials | 60 000 | 10 000 (12 000 − 2000) | — | 10 000 | 6.0 |
| Conversion cost | 259 200 | 10 400 (12 000 − 1600) | 4000 | 14 400 | 18.0 |
| | 767 307 | | | | 48.8948 |

| | (£) | (£) |
|---|---|---|
| Cost of completed production: | | |
| Opening WIP | 142 200 | |
| Previous process cost (10 000 units at £24.8948) | 248 948 | |
| Materials (10 000 units at £6) | 60 000 | |
| Conversion cost (10 400 units at £18) | 187 200 | 638 348 |
| Cost of closing work in progress: | | |
| Previous process cost (8000 units at £24.8948) | 199 159 | |
| Materials | — | |
| Conversion cost (4000 units at £18) | 72 000 | 271 159 |
| | | 909 507 |

Note that in this calculation the *opening* work in progress is 80% completed, and that the materials are added when the process is 70% complete. Hence, they will be fully complete. Remember also that previous process cost is always 100% complete. Therefore in the third column of the above statement 2000 units opening work in progress is deducted for these two elements of cost from the 12 000 units of completed production. Conversion cost will be 80% complete so 1600 equivalent units are deducted from the completed production. Our objective in the third column is to extract the equivalent completed units that were derived from the units started during the current period. You should also note that the previous process cost of £448 107 represents the cost of completed production of process X, which has been transferred to process Y.

The closing work in progress valuations and the charges to completed production are fairly similar for both methods. The difference in the calculations between FIFO and the weighted average method is likely to be insignificant where the quantity of inventories and the input prices do not fluctuate significantly from month to month. Both methods are acceptable for product costing, but it appears that the FIFO method is not widely used in practice (Horngren, 1967).

# Partially completed output and losses in process

Earlier in this chapter we looked at how to deal with losses in process when all of the output in a process was fully complete. We also need to look at the treatment of losses when all of the output is not fully complete. When this situation occurs the computations can become complex. Accounting for losses when all of the output is not fully complete does not form part of the curriculum for many courses. However, most professional management accounting courses do require you to have a knowledge of this topic. Because of these different requirements this topic is dealt with in Appendix 5.1. You should therefore check the requirements of your curriculum to ascertain whether you can omit Appendix 5.1.

# Process costing for decision-making and control

The detailed calculations that we have made in this chapter are necessary for calculating profit and valuing stocks. For example, the process work in progress forms part of the balance sheet inventory valuations, and the transfers to succeeding processes become part of the work in progress of these processes or form part of the finished goods inventory. If the inventory is sold, these costs become part of the cost of goods sold for profit calculations. The calculations of unit costs, process work in progress valuations and the completed units valuation transferred to the next process are therefore necessary to determine the balance sheet inventory valuation and the cost of goods sold figure.

It is most unlikely that this same information will be appropriate for decision-making and cost control. In particular, process total unit costs will not be relevant for decision-making. What is required is an analysis of costs into their incremental and non-incremental elements for each process. A detailed discussion of those costs that are relevant for decision-making will be deferred to Chapter 9, but it is important that you should note at this point that the costs for decision-making purposes should be assembled in a different way.

## COST CONTROL

In respect of cost control, we must ensure that the actual costs that are included on a performance report are the costs incurred for the *current period only* and do not include any costs that have been carried forward from previous periods. This principle can be illustrated using the information given in Example 5.3 for process X.

The unit cost statement for product X, using the weighted average method, shown on page 145 was as follows:

| Cost element | Opening WIP value (£) | Current cost (£) | Total cost (£) | Completed units | WIP equiv. units | Total equiv. units | Cost per unit (£) |
|---|---|---|---|---|---|---|---|
| Materials | 72 000 | 192 000 | 264 000 | 18 000 | 4000 | 22 000 | 12.00 |
| Conversion cost | 45 900 | 225 000 | 270 900 | 18 000 | 3000 | 21 000 | 12.90 |

This statement is not appropriate for cost control, since it includes the value of work in progress brought forward from the previous period. Also, the total equivalent units includes the opening work in progress equivalent units partly processed in the previous period. The inclusion of previous period costs and production is appropriate for inventory valuation and profit measurement, since the objective is to match costs (irrespective of when they were incurred) with revenues, but it is not appropriate to include previous costs for cost control. The objective of cost control is to compare the actual costs of the *current* period with the budgeted cost for the equivalent units produced during the *current* period. We wish to measure a manager's performance for the current period and to avoid this measure being distorted by carrying forward costs that were incurred in the previous period. We must therefore calculate the equivalent units produced during the current period by deducting the equivalent units produced during the previous period from the total number of equivalent units. The calculation is as follows:

| | Total equivalent units | Opening WIP equiv. units | Equiv. units produced during period |
|---|---|---|---|
| Materials | 22 000 | 6000 | 16 000 |
| Conversion cost | 21 000 | 3600 (60% × 6000) | 17 400 |

Note that materials are introduced at the start of the process, and the 6000 units opening work in progress will have been fully completed in the previous period as far as materials are concerned. Assuming that the budgeted costs for the period are £11.40 for materials and £12 for conversion costs we can now present the following cost control performance report:

**Performance report**

| | Budgeted cost (£) | Current period actual cost (£) | Difference (£) |
|---|---|---|---|
| Materials | 182 400 (16 000 units at £11.40) | 192 000 | 9 600 adverse |
| Conversion cost | 208 800 (17 400 units at £12) | 225 000 | 16 200 adverse |

From this report you will see that we are comparing like with like; that is, both the budgeted costs and the actual costs refer to the equivalent units produced during the *current* period.

Note that information required for cost control must be analysed in far more detail than that presented in the performance report here. For example, the different types of materials and conversion costs must be listed and presented under separate headings for controllable and non-controllable expenses. The essential point to note, however, is that current period actual costs must be compared with the budgeted cost for the current period's production.

# Batch/operating costing

It is not always possible to classify cost accumulation systems into job costing and process costing systems. Where manufactured goods have some common characteristics and also some individual characteristics, the cost accumulation system may be a combination of both the job costing and process costing systems. For example, the production of footwear,

**EXHIBIT 5.2**

*A batch costing system*

clothing and furniture often involves the production of batches, which are variations of a single design and require a sequence of standardized operations. Let us consider a company that

| | Operations | | | | | |
|---|---|---|---|---|---|---|
| Product | 1 | 2 | 3 | 4 | 5 | Product cost |
| A | ✓ | ✓ | ✓ | | | A = cost of operations 1, 2, 3 |
| B | ✓ | | | ✓ | ✓ | B = cost of operations 1, 4, 5 |
| C | ✓ | ✓ | | ✓ | | C = cost of operations 1, 2, 4 |
| D | ✓ | | ✓ | | ✓ | D = cost of operations 1, 3, 5 |
| E | ✓ | ✓ | | | ✓ | E = cost of operations 1, 2, 5 |

makes kitchen units. Each unit may have the same basic frame, and require the same operation, but the remaining operations may differ: some frames may require sinks, others may require to be fitted with work tops; different types of doors may be fitted to each unit, some may be low-quality doors while others may be of a higher quality. The cost of a kitchen unit will therefore consist of the basic frame plus the conversion costs of the appropriate operations. The principles of the cost accumulation system are illustrated in Exhibit 5.2.

The cost of each product consists of the cost of operation 1 plus a combination of the conversion costs for operations 2–5. The cost per unit produced for a particular operation consists of the average unit cost of each batch produced for each operation. It may well be that some products may be subject to a final operation that is unique to the product. The production cost will then consist of the average cost of a combination of operations 1–5 plus the specific cost of the final unique operation. The cost of the final operation will be traced specifically to the product using a job costing system. The final product cost therefore consists of a combination of process costing techniques and job costing techniques. This system of costing is referred to as operation costing or batch costing.

# Surveys of practice

Little information is available on the extent to which process or job costing systems are used in practice. However, surveys of USA (Schwarzbach, 1985), Finnish (Lukka and Granlund, 1996) and Australian (Joye and Blayney, 1990) companies report the following usage rates:

| | USA % | Finland % | Australia % |
|---|---|---|---|
| Process costing | 36 | 32 | 63 |
| Job costing | 28 | 30 | 40 |
| No process or job costing | | 38 | |
| Process and Job combined | 10 | | |
| Operation costing | 18 | | |

Presumably the Australian survey adopted a wider definition of process and job costing resulting in the respondents choosing one of the two categories whereas the Finnish study may have adopted a narrower definition. This may account for the fact that 38% of the organizations indicated that they adopted neither purely job nor process costing systems. These companies are likely to combine elements of both job and process costing.

## Self-Assessment Questions

You should attempt to answer these questions yourself before looking up the suggested answers, which appear on pages 1097–1101. If any part of your answer is incorrect, check back carefully to make sure you understand where you went wrong.

1. 'No Friction' is an industrial lubricant, which is formed by subjecting certain crude chemicals to two successive processes. The output of process 1 is passed to process 2, where it is blended with other chemicals. The process costs for period 3 were as follows:

   Process 1
   Material: 3000 kg @ £0.25 per kg
   Labour: £120
   Process plant time: 12 hours @ £20 per hour

   Process 2
   Material: 2000 kg @ £0.40 per kg
   Labour: £84
   Process plant time: 20 hours @ £13.50 per hour

   General overhead for period 3 amounted to £357 and is absorbed into process costs on a process labour basis.
   The normal output of process 1 is 80% of input, while that of process 2 is 90% of input.
   Waste matter from process 1 is sold for £0.20 per kg, while that from process 2 is sold for £0.30 per kg.
   The output for period 3 was as follows:
   Process 1   2300 kg
   Process 2   4000 kg

   There was no stock or work in process at either the beginning or the end of the period, and it may be assumed that all available waste matter had been sold at the prices indicated.
   You are required to show how the foregoing data would be recorded in a system of cost accounts.

2. A concentrated liquid fertilizer is manufactured by passing chemicals through two consecutive processes. Stores record cards for the chemical ingredients used exclusively by the first process show the following data for May 2000:

   | | | |
   |---|---|---|
   | Opening stock | 4 000 litres | £10 800 |
   | Closing stock | 8 000 litres | £24 200 |
   | Receipts into store | 20 000 litres | £61 000 |

   Other process data for May is tabulated below:

   | | Process 1 | Process 2 |
   |---|---|---|
   | Direct labour | £4880 | £6000 |
   | Direct expenses | £4270 | — |
   | Overhead absorption rates | 250% of direct labour | 100% of direct labour |
   | Output | 8000 litres | 7500 litres |
   | Opening stock of work in process | — | — |
   | Closing stock of work in process | 5600 litres | — |
   | Normal yield | 85% of input | 90% of input |
   | Scrap value of loss | — | — |

153

In process 1 the closing stock of work in process has just passed through inspection, which is at the stage where materials and conversion costs are 100% and 75% completed respectively.

In process 2 inspection is the final operation.

Required:

(a) Prepare the relevant accounts to show the results of the processes for May 2000 and present a detailed working paper showing your calculations and any assumptions in arriving at the data shown in those accounts. (18 marks)

(b) If supplies of the required chemicals are severely restricted and all production can be sold immediately, briefly explain how you would calculate the total loss to the company if, at the beginning of June, 100 litres of the correct mix of chemicals were spilt on issue to process 1.

(4 marks)

(Total 22 marks)

*ACCA Foundation Costing*

## Summary

In this chapter we have examined the cost accumulation procedure necessary for a process costing system for inventory valuation and profit measurement. A process costing system is an average cost system that is appropriate for those industries where the units of final output are identical. The cost of an individual order for a single unit can be obtained by merely dividing the costs of production for the period by the units produced for that period. Examples of industries where a system of process costing is appropriate include chemical, cement, oil, paint and textile industries.

The accounting treatment for normal and abnormal losses has been explained and illustrated. Normal losses are inherent in the production process, and cannot be eliminated; their cost should be borne by the good production. Abnormal losses are avoidable, and the cost of these losses should not be assigned to products but reported separately as an abnormal loss and written off as a period cost in the profit and loss statement. Scrap sales (if any) that result from the losses should be allocated to the appropriate process account (for normal losses) and the abnormal loss account (for abnormal losses).

We have established that where stocks of work in progress are in existence, it is necessary in order to create homogeneous units of output to convert the work in progress into finished equivalent units of production. Since materials are normally introduced at the start or end of the process and conversion costs are added uniformly throughout the process, it is necessary to keep a separate record of these items of cost. When materials are added at the start of the process, the materials element of the WIP is 100% complete. Alternatively, if materials are added at the end of the process, they are zero complete. Costs transferred from previous processes are recorded separately for unit cost calculations, since they are always regarded as 100% complete.

We have discussed and examined two alternative methods of allocating the opening work in progress costs to production: the weighted average and the first in, first out methods. If the weighted average method is used, both the units and the value of the opening work in progress are merged with the current period and production to calculate the average cost per unit. Using the first in, first out method, the opening work in progress is assumed to be the first group of units to be processed and completed during the current month. The opening work in progress is therefore assigned separately to completed production and the cost per unit is based only on current costs and production for the period. The closing work in progress is assumed to come from the new units that have been started during the period.

Finally, we have briefly contrasted the differing ways in which cost information should be accumulated for decision-making and cost control. In respect of decision-making, we are interested in the additional future costs and revenue resulting from a decision, and only incremental costs may be relevant for short-term decisions. In respect of cost control, it is only current costs and production that should be included in performance reports, since we are interested in a manager's performance in the current period and wish to avoid distorting the report with costs carried forward from the previous period.

## Key Terms and Concepts

abnormal gain (p. 139)
abnormal losses (p. 136)
batch costing (p. 151)
conversion cost (p. 136)
equivalent production (p. 141)

first in, first out method (p. 144)
normal losses (p. 136)
operation costing (p. 151)
previous process cost (p. 143)
weighted average method (p. 144)

# Appendix 5.1: Losses in process and partially completed units

## NORMAL LOSSES

**AR** Earlier in this chapter, we established that normal losses should be considered as part of the cost of the good production. We need to know, however, at what stage in the process the loss occurs so that we can determine whether the whole loss should be allocated to completed production or whether some of the loss should also be allocated to the closing work in progress. If the loss occurs near the end of the process, or is discovered at the point of inspection, only the units which have reached the inspection point should be allocated with the cost of the loss. Alternatively, the loss could be assumed to occur at a specific point, earlier in the process.

Generally, it is assumed that normal losses take place at the stage of completion where inspection occurs. Where such an assumption is made, the normal loss will not be allocated to the closing work in progress, since the loss is related only to units that have reached the inspection point. Consider Example 5A.1.

To calculate the value of the normal loss, we prepare the normal unit cost statement, but with a separate column for the number of units lost:

| Element of cost | Total cost (£) | Completed units | Normal loss | WIP equiv. units | Total equiv. units | Cost per unit (£) |
|---|---|---|---|---|---|---|
| Materials | 5000 | 600 | 100 | 300 | 1000 | 5.0 |
| Conversion cost | 3400 | 600 | 100 | 150 | 850 | 4.0 |
| | 8400 | | | | | 9.0 |

|  |  | (£) | (£) |
|---|---|---|---|
| Value of work in progress: | | | |
| Materials (300 units at £5) | | 1500 | |
| Conversion cost (150 units at £4) | | 600 | 2100 |
| Completed units (600 units at £9) | | 5400 | |
| Normal loss (100 units at £9) | | 900 | 6300 |
| | | | 8400 |

**EXAMPLE 5A.1**

A department with no opening work in progress introduces 1000 units into the process; 600 are completed, 300 are half-completed and 100 units are lost (all normal). *Losses are detected upon completion.* Material costs are £5000 (all introduced at the start of the process) and conversion costs are £3400.

Note here that all of the cost of the normal loss is added to the completed production, since it is detected at the completion stage. The closing work in progress will not have reached this stage, and therefore does not bear any of the loss. The cost per unit completed after the allocation of the normal loss is £10.50 (£6300/600 units).

Some writers suggest that if the equivalent units computation for normal losses is ignored, the cost of the normal loss will be automatically apportioned to the good production. However, the results from adopting this short-cut are not as accurate. The calculations adopting this short-cut approach are as follows:

|  | Total cost (£) | Completed units | WIP equiv. units | Total equiv. units | Cost per unit (£) | WIP (£) |
|---|---|---|---|---|---|---|
| Materials | 5000 | 600 | 300 | 900 | 5.5555 | 1666.65 |
| Conversion cost | 3400 | 600 | 150 | 750 | 4.5333 | 680.00 |
|  |  |  |  |  | 10.0888 | 2346.65 |
|  |  |  | Completed units (600 × £10.0888) | | | 6053.35 |
|  |  |  |  |  |  | 8400.00 |

You can see that ignoring equivalent units for the normal loss decreased equivalent units and thus increases the cost per unit. The values of work in progress and completed production using each approach are as follows:

|  | Normal loss charged to good production (£) | Short-cut method (£) | Difference (£) |
|---|---|---|---|
| Work in progress | 2100 | 2347 | +247 |
| Completed units | 6300 | 6053 | −247 |

If the short-cut approach is used, the work in progress valuation includes £247 normal loss that is not attributable to these units because they have not reached the inspection point. The £247 should be charged only to completed units that have reached the inspection point. It is therefore recommended that the cost of the normal loss is calculated and charged only to those units that have reached the inspection point.

Let us now assume for Example 5A.1 that the loss is detected when the process has reached the 50% stage of completion. The revised cost per unit will be as follows:

| Element of cost | Total cost (£) | Completed units | Normal loss | WIP equiv. units | Total equiv. units | Cost per unit |
|---|---|---|---|---|---|---|
| Materials | 5000 | 600 | 100 | 300 | 1000 | 5.00 |
| Conversion cost | 3400 | 600 | 50 | 150 | 800 | 4.25 |
| | 8400 | | | | | 9.25 |

The 100 lost units will not be processed any further once the loss is detected at the 50% completion stage. Therefore 50 units equivalent production (100 units × 50%) is entered in the normal loss column for conversion cost equivalent production. Note that materials are introduced at the start of the process and are fully complete when the loss is detected. The cost of the normal loss is

|  | £ |
|---|---|
| Materials (100 × £5) | 500.00 |
| Conversion cost (50 × £4.25) | 212.50 |
| | 712.50 |

When losses are assumed to occur at a specific point in the production process, you should allocate the normal loss over all units that have reached this point. In our example the loss is detected at the 50% stage of completion, and the work in progress has reached this point. Therefore the loss should be allocated between completed production and work in progress. If the losses were detected at the 60% stage, all of the normal loss would be allocated to completed production. Alternatively, if losses were detected before the 50% stage, the normal loss would be allocated to completed production and work in progress.

The question is: how should we allocate the normal loss between completed production and work in progress? Several different approaches are advocated, but the most accurate is to apportion the normal loss in the ratio of completed units and incomplete units in progress. In Example 5A.1, 600 units are completed and 300 units are partly complete. It is assumed that the units lost at the inspection were intended to be produced in the same ratio (6/9 to completed production and 3/9 to work in progress). The normal loss is therefore apportioned as follows:

|  | (£) |
|---|---|
| Completed units (600/900 × £712.50) | 475.00 |
| WIP (300/900 × £712.50) | 237.50 |
| | 712.50 |

The cost of completed production and WIP when the loss is detected at the 50% stage is

|  | (£) | (£) |
|---|---|---|
| Completed units (600 × £9.25) | 5550.00 | |
| Share of normal loss | 475.00 | 6025.00 |
| Work in progress: | | |
| Materials (300 × £5) | 1500.00 | |
| Conversion cost (150 × £4.25) | 637.50 | |
| Share of normal loss | £237.50 | 2375.00 |
| | | 8400.00 |

When the lost units have a scrap value, the sales revenue should be deducted from the normal loss, and the net cost should be allocated to units which have passed the inspection point.

## ABNORMAL LOSSES

Where abnormal losses are incurred, the correct procedure is to produce the normal unit cost statement, but with the addition of two separate columns for the units lost; one for normal losses and one for abnormal losses. Consider Example 5A.2.

---

**EXAMPLE 5A.2**

A department with no opening work in progress introduced 1000 units into the process; 600 are completed, 250 are 20% complete, and 150 units are lost consisting of 100 units of normal loss and 50 units of abnormal loss. Losses are detected *upon completion*. Material costs are £8000 (all introduced at the start of the process) and conversion costs are £4000.

---

The unit cost calculations are as follows:

| Element of cost | Total cost (£) | Completed units | Normal loss | Abnormal loss | WIP equiv. units | Total equiv. units | Cost per unit (£) |
|---|---|---|---|---|---|---|---|
| Materials | 8 000 | 600 | 100 | 50 | 250 | 1000 | 8 |
| Conversion cost | 4 000 | 600 | 100 | 50 | 50 | 800 | 5 |
| | 12 000 | | | | | | 13 |

| | (£) | (£) |
|---|---|---|
| Value of work in progress: | | |
| Materials (250 units at £8) | 2000 | |
| Conversion cost (50 units at £5) | 250 | 2 250 |
| Completed units (600 units at £13) | 7800 | |
| Add normal loss (100 units at £13) | 1300 | 9 100 |
| Abnormal loss (50 units at £13) | | 650 |
| | | 12 000 |

You can see that the normal loss has been charged to completed units only. The abnormal loss is charged to a separate account and written off as a period cost to the profit and loss account. The entries in the process account will be as follows:

**Process account**

| | | | |
|---|---|---|---|
| Materials | 8000 | Transfer to next process | 9 100 |
| Conversion cost | 4000 | Abnormal loss written off to | |
| | | profit and loss account | 650 |
| | | Closing work in progress c/fwd | 2 250 |
| | 12 000 | | 12 000 |

Note that there is an argument for allocating the normal loss of £1300 between the completed units and the abnormal loss. If the normal loss is of a significant value then there are strong arguments for doing this, since the normal loss is part of the cost of production. The abnormal loss should therefore be valued at the cost per unit of *normal output*. In the unit cost statement for Example 5A.2 you will see that the completed production is 600 units and the abnormal loss is 50 units. The normal loss of £1300 is therefore apportioned pro rata to completed production and the abnormal loss. The calculations are as follows:

$$\text{completed units } (600/650 \times £1300) = 1200$$
$$\text{abnormal loss} \quad (50/650 \times £1300) = 100$$

The revised value for completed production would then be £10 300 (£9100 + £1200), while for the abnormal loss the value would be £750 (£650 + £100). For most examination questions it is unlikely that you will be expected to allocate the normal loss between completed units and the abnormal loss.

## NORMAL AND ABNORMAL LOSSES WHEN THEY OCCUR PART WAY THROUGH THE PROCESS

This section is more appropriate for an advanced course and may be omitted if you are pursuing an introductory or first level course. In Example 5A.1 we considered a situation where a normal loss was detected at the end of the process. In this section we shall consider a more complex problem when normal and abnormal losses are detected part way through the process. Consider the information presented in Example 5A.3.

The unit cost calculations are as follows:

| (1) Element of cost | (2) Total cost (£) | (3) Completed units | (4) Normal loss | (5) Abnormal loss | (6) WIP equiv. units | (7) Total equiv. units | (8) Cost per unit (£) |
|---|---|---|---|---|---|---|---|
| Previous process cost | 10 000 | 600 | 100 | 50 | 250 | 1000 | 10.000 |
| Materials | 8 000 | 600 | 100 | 50 | 250 | 1000 | 8.000 |
| Conversion cost | 2 900 | 600 | 50 | 25 | 150 | 825 | 3.515 |
| | 20 900 | | | | | | 21.515 |

From this calculation you can see that materials and the previous process cost are 100% complete when the loss is discovered. However, spoilt units will not be processed any further once the loss is detected, and the lost units will be 50% complete in respect of conversion costs. Note that the closing work in progress is 60% complete, and has thus passed the point where the loss is detected. Therefore the normal loss should be allocated between the completed units and work in progress. The cost of the normal loss is

| | (£) |
|---|---|
| Previous process cost (100 units at £10) | 1000 |
| Materials (100 units at £8) | 800 |
| Conversion cost (50 units at £3.515) | 176 |
| | 1976 |

**EXAMPLE 5A.3**

A department with no opening work in progress introduces 1000 units into the process: 600 are completed, 250 are 60% complete and 150 units are lost, consisting of 100 units normal loss and 50 units abnormal loss. Losses are detected *when production is 50% complete*. Material costs are £8000 (all introduced at the start of the process), conversion costs are £2900 and the previous process cost is £10 000.

The normal loss is allocated in the ratio of completed units and units in progress as follows:

|  | (£) |
| --- | --- |
| Completed units  (600/850 × £1976) | 1395 |
| Work in progress (250/850 × £1976) | 581 |
|  | 1976 |

The costs are accounted for as follows:

|  | (£) | (£) |
| --- | --- | --- |
| Value of work in progress: | | |
| Previous process cost (250 units at £10) | 2 500 | |
| Materials (250 units at £8) | 2 000 | |
| Conversion cost (150 units at £3.515) | 527 | |
| Share of normal loss | 581 | 5 608 |
| Completed units: | | |
| 600 units at £21.515 | 12 909 | |
| Share of normal loss | 1 395 | 14 304 |
| Abnormal loss: | | |
| Previous process cost (50 units at £10) | 500 | |
| Materials (50 units at £8) | 400 | |
| Conversion cost (25 units at £3.515) | 88 | 988 |
|  | | 20 900 |

You will remember from our earlier discussion that there is an argument for allocating a share of the normal loss to the abnormal loss. If this approach is adopted, the cost of the normal loss would be apportioned as follows:

| Completed production | 600/900 × normal loss |
| --- | --- |
| WIP | 250/900 × normal loss |
| Abnormal loss | 50/900 × normal loss |

If the short-cut method is applied, the normal loss is automatically allocated between completed units, work in progress and abnormal loss in the ratio of equivalent units (columns 3, 5 and 6 shown in the unit cost calculations) for each element of cost.

## Key Examination Points

Sometimes examination questions do not indicate at what stage in the process the loss occurs. In this situation you are recommended to assume that the loss occurs at the end of the process and allocate the full cost of the normal loss to completed production. Do not forget to state this assumption in your answer. The short-cut method should not be used if the loss occurs at the end of the process, because this method assumes that the loss is to be shared between work in progress and completed units.

If the question indicates the stage when a loss occurs then remember to allocate the loss only to the units which have passed the inspection point.

Where the closing WIP has passed the inspection point, it will be necessary to allocate the normal loss between completed units and the closing WIP.

Process costing questions require many calculations, and there is a possibility that you will make arithmetical errors. Make sure your answer is clearly presented so that the examiner can ascertain whether or not you are using correct methods to calculate the cost per unit. ●●●

## Questions

*Indicates that a suggested solution is to be found in the *Students' Manual*.

### 5.1* Intermediate
AK Chemicals produces high-quality plastic sheeting in a continuous manufacturing operation. All materials are input at the beginning of the process. Conversion costs are incurred evenly throughout the process. A quality control inspection occurs 75% through the manufacturing process, when some units are separated out as inferior quality. The following data are available for December.

| | |
|---|---|
| Materials costs | £90 000 |
| Conversion costs | £70 200 |
| Units started | 40 000 |
| Units completed | 36 000 |

There is no opening or closing work in progress. Past experience indicates that approximately 7.5% of the units started are found to be defective on inspection by quality control.

What is the cost of abnormal loss for December
A £3600
B £4050
C £4680
D £10 800

*ACCA Paper 3*

### 5.2* Intermediate
KL Processing Limited has identified that an abnormal gain of 160 litres occurred in its refining process last week. Normal losses are expected and have a scrap value of £2.00 per litre. All losses are 100% complete as to material cost and 75% complete as to conversion costs.

The company uses the weighted average method of valuation and last week's output was valued using the following costs per equivalent unit:

| | |
|---|---|
| Materials | £9.40 |
| Conversion costs | £11.20 |

The effect on the profit and loss account of last week's abnormal gain is
A Debit £2528
B Debit £2828
C Credit £2528
D Credit £2848
E Credit £3168

*CIMA Stage 2*

### 5.3* Intermediate
The following details relate to the main process of W Limited, a chemical manufacturer:

| | |
|---|---|
| Opening work in progress | 2000 litres, fully complete as to materials and 40% complete as to conversion |
| Material input | 24 000 litres |
| Normal loss is 10% of input | |
| Output to process 2 | 19 500 litres |
| Closing work in progress | 3000 litres, fully complete as to materials and 45% complete as to conversion |

The number of equivalent units to be included in W Limited's calculation of the cost per equivalent unit using a FIFO basis of valuation are:

| | Materials | Conversion |
|---|---|---|
| A | 19 400 | 18 950 |
| B | 20 500 | 20 050 |
| C | 21 600 | 21 150 |
| D | 23 600 | 20 750 |
| E | 23 600 | 21 950 |

*CIMA Stage 2*

## 5.4* Intermediate

Process B had no opening stock. 13 500 units of raw material were transferred in at £4.50 per unit. Additional material at £1.25 per unit was added in process. Labour and overheads were £6.25 per completed unit and £2.50 per unit incomplete.

If 11 750 completed units were transferred out, what was the closing stock in process B?

A   £77 625.00
B   £14 437.50
C   £141 000.00
D   £21 000.00

*CIMA Stage 1*

## 5.5* Intermediate

A chemical process has a normal wastage of 10% of input. In a period, 2500 kgs of material were input and there was an abnormal loss of 75 kgs.

What quantity of good production was achieved?

A   2175 kg
B   2250 kg
C   2325 kg
D   2475 kg

*CIMA Stage 1 Cost Accounting*

## 5.6* Intermediate

KL Processing operates the FIFO method of accounting for opening work in process in its mixing process. The following data relates to April:

| | | |
|---|---|---|
| Opening work in process | 1 000 litres valued at | £1 500 |
| Input | 30 000 litres costing | £15 000 |
| Conversion costs | | £10 000 |
| Output | 24 000 litres | |
| Closing work in process | 3 500 litres | |

Losses in processes are expected to be 10% of period input. They are complete as to input material costs but are discovered after 60% conversion. Losses have a scrap value of £0.20 per litre.

Opening work in process was 100% complete as to input materials, and 70% complete as to conversion. Closing work in process is complete as to input materials and 80% complete as to conversion.

A   The number of material-equivalent units was
   (i)   26 300 litres
   (ii)  26 600 litres
   (iii) 27 000 litres
   (iv)  28 000 litres
   (v)   29 000 litres

B   The number of conversion-equivalent units was
   (i)   26 400 litres
   (ii)  26 600 litres
   (iii) 26 800 litres
   (iv)  27 000 litres
   (v)   27 400 litres

(Total 20 marks)
*CIMA Stage 1 Operational Cost Accounting*

## 5.7 Intermediate

(a)  Describe the distinguishing characteristics of production systems where
   (i)   job costing techniques would be used, and
   (ii)  process costing techniques would be used.                                   (3 marks)
(b)  Job costing produces more accurate product costs than process costing. Critically examine the above statement by contrasting the information requirements, procedures and problems associated with each costing method.

(14 marks)
(Total 17 marks)
*ACCA Level 1 Costing*

## 5.8 Intermediate: Preparation of process accounts with all output fully completed

A product is manufactured by passing through three processes: A, B and C. In process C a by-product is also produced which is then transferred to process D where it is completed. For the first week in October, actual data included:

| | Process A | Process B | Process C | Process D |
|---|---|---|---|---|
| Normal loss of input (%) | 5 | 10 | 5 | 10 |
| Scrap value (£ per unit) | 1.50 | 2.00 | 4.00 | 2.00 |
| Estimated sales value of by-product (£ per unit) | — | — | 8.00 | — |
| Output (units) | 5760 | 5100 | 4370 | — |
| Output of by-product (units) | — | — | 510 | 450 |
| | (£) | (£) | (£) | (£) |
| Direct materials (6000 units) | 12 000 | — | — | — |
| Direct materials added in process | 5 000 | 9000 | 4000 | 220 |
| Direct wages | 4 000 | 6000 | 2000 | 200 |
| Direct expenses | 800 | 1680 | 2260 | 151 |

Budgeted production overhead for the week is £30 500.

Budgeted direct wages for the week are £12 200.

You are required to prepare:

(a) accounts for process A, B, C and D.

(20 marks)

(b) abnormal loss account and abnormal gain account.

(5 marks)

(Total 25 marks)

*CIMA P1 Cost Accounting 2*

## 5.9 Intermediate: Discussion question on methods of apportioning joint costs and the preparation of process accounts with all output fully completed

(a) 'Whilst the ascertainment of product costs could be said to be one of the objectives of cost accounting, where joint products are produced and joint costs incurred, the total cost computed for the product may depend upon the method selected for the apportionment of joint costs, thus making it difficult for management to make decisions about the future of products.'

You are required to discuss the above statement and to state *two* different methods of apportioning joint costs to joint products.

(8 marks)

(b) A company using process costing manufactures a single product which passes through two processes, the output of process 1 becoming the input to process 2. Normal losses and abnormal losses are defective units having a scrap value and cash is received at the end of the period for all such units.

The following information relates to the four-week period of accounting period number 7.

Raw material issued to process 1 was 3000 units at a cost of £5 per unit.

There was no opening or closing work-in-progress but opening and closing stocks of finished goods were £20 000 and £23 000 respectively.

| | Process 1 | Process 2 |
|---|---|---|
| Normal loss as a percentage of input | 10% | 5% |
| Output in units | 2800 | 2600 |
| Scrap value per unit | £2 | £5 |
| Additional components | £1000 | £780 |
| Direct wages incurred | £4000 | £6000 |
| Direct expenses incurred | £10 000 | £14 000 |
| Production overhead as a percentage of direct wages | 75% | 125% |

You are required to present the accounts for
Process 1
Process 2
Finished goods
Normal loss
Abnormal loss
Abnormal gain
Profit and loss (so far as it relates to any of the accounts listed above). (17 marks)

(Total 25 marks)

*CIMA Stage 2 Cost Accounting*

## 5.10* Intermediate: Preparation of process accounts with all output fully completed

A chemical compound is made by raw material being processed through two processes. The output of Process A is passed to Process B where further material is added to the mix. The details of the process costs for the financial period number 10 were as shown below:

**Process A**

| | |
|---|---|
| Direct material | 2000 kilograms at 5 per kg |
| Direct labour | £7200 |
| Process plant time | 140 hours at £60 per hour |

**Process B**

| | |
|---|---|
| Direct material | 1400 kilograms at £12 per kg |
| Direct labour | £4200 |
| Process plant time | 80 hours at £72.50 per hour |

The departmental overhead for Period 10 was £6840 and is absorbed into the costs of each process on direct labour cost.

| | Process A | Process B |
|---|---|---|
| Expected output was | 80% of input | 90% of input |
| Actual output was | 1400 kg | 2620 kg |

Assume no finished stock at the beginning of the period and no work in progress at either the beginning or the end of the period.

Normal loss is contaminated material which is sold as scrap for £0.50 per kg from Process A and £1.825 per kg from Process B, for both of which immediate payment is received.

You are required to prepare the accounts for Period 10, for
(i)   Process A,
(ii)  Process B,
(iii) Normal loss/gain,
(iv)  Abnormal loss/gain,
(v)   Finished goods,
(vi)  Profit and loss (extract).          (15 marks)
*CIMA Stage 2 Cost Accounting*

### 5.11* Intermediate: Equivalent production and no losses

A firm operates a process, the details of which for the period were as follows. There was no opening work-in-progress. During the period 8250 units were received from the previous process at a value of £453 750, labour and overheads were £350 060 and material introduced was £24 750. At the end of the period the closing work-in-progress was 1600 units, which were 100% complete in respect of materials, and 60% complete in respect of labour and overheads. The balance of units were transferred to finished goods.

Requirements:
(a)  Calculate the number of equivalent units produced.          (3 marks)
(b)  Calculate the cost per equivalent unit.          (2 marks)

(c)  Prepare the process account.          (7 marks)
(d)  Distinguish between joint products and by-products, and briefly explain the difference in accounting treatment between them.          (3 marks)
          (Total 15 marks)
*CIMA Stage 1 Cost Accounting and Quantitative Methods*

### 5.12* Intermediate: Equivalent production with no losses

A cleansing agent is manufactured from the input of three ingredients. At 1 December there was no work in progress. During December the ingredients were put into the process in the following quantities:

A    2000 kg at £0.80 per kg
B    3000 kg at £0.50 per kg
C    6000 kg at £0.40 per kg

Additionally, labour working 941 hours and being paid £4 per hour was incurred, and overheads recovered on the basis of 50% of labour cost. There was no loss in the process. Output was 8600 kg.

The remaining items in work in progress were assessed by the company's works manager as follows:

Complete so far as materials were concerned:

One quarter of the items were 60% complete for labour and overheads;

Three-quarters were 25% complete for labour and overheads.

Required:
(a)  A cleansing agent process account, showing clearly the cost of the output and work in progress carried forward.          (16 marks)
(b)  Define the following terms, give examples and explain how they would be accounted for in process costing:
     (i)   By-products          (6 marks)
     (ii)  Abnormal gain          (3 marks)
     (iii) Equivalent units          (3 marks)
          (Total 28 marks)
          *AAT*

### 5.13 Intermediate: Equivalent production and losses in process

Industrial Solvents Limited mixes together three chemicals – A, B and C – in the ratio 3 : 2 : 1 to produce Allklean, a specialised anti-static fluid. The chemicals cost £8, £6 and £3.90 per litre respectively.

In a period, 12 000 litres in total were input to the mixing process. The normal process loss is 5% of input and in the period there was an abnormal loss of 100 litres whilst the completed production was 9500 litres.

There was no opening work-in-progress (WIP) and the closing WIP was 100% complete for materials and 40% complete for labour and overheads. Labour and overheads were £41 280 in total for the period. Materials lost in production are scrapped.

Required:
(a)  Calculate the volume of closing WIP.
    (3 marks)
(b)  Prepare the mixing process account for the period, showing clearly volumes and values.
    (9 marks)
(c)  Briefly explain what changes would be necessary in your account if an abnormal gain were achieved in a period.    (3 marks)
    (Total 15 marks)
    *CIMA Stage 1 Cost Accounting*

### 5.14 Intermediate: Losses in process (weighted average)

(a)  Outline the characteristics of industries in which a process costing system is used and give two examples of such industries.
    (5 marks)
(b)  ATM Chemicals produces product XY by putting it through a single process. You are given the following details for November.

#### Input Costs

| | |
|---|---|
| Materials costs | 25 000 kilos at £2.48 per kilo |
| Labour costs | 8 000 hours at £5.50 per hour |
| Overhead costs | £63 000 |

You are also told the following:
(i)   Normal loss is 4% of input.
(ii)  Scrap value of normal loss is £2.00 per kilo.
(iii) Finished output amounted to 15 000 units.
(iv)  Closing work in progress amounted to 6000 units and was fully complete for material $\frac{2}{3}$ complete for labour and $\frac{1}{2}$ for overheads.
(v)   There was no opening work in progress.
Required:

(i)   Prepare the Process account for the month of November detailing the value of the finished units and the work in progress.    (12 marks)
(ii)  Prepare an Abnormal Loss account.
    (2 marks)
(c)  Distinguish between normal and abnormal losses, their costing treatment and how each loss may be controlled.    (6 marks)
    (Total 25 marks)
    *AAT Cost Accounting and Budgeting*

### 5.15* Intermediate: Losses in process (weighted average)

A company operates expensive process plant to produce a single product from one process. At the beginning of October, 3400 completed units were still in the processing plant, awaiting transfer to finished stock. They were valued as follows:

| | **(£)** |
|---|---|
| Direct material | 25 500 |
| Direct wages | 10 200 |
| Production overhead | 20 400 (200% of direct wages) |

During October, 37 000 further units were put into process and the following costs charged to the process:

| | **(£)** |
|---|---|
| Direct materials | 276 340 |
| Direct wages | 112 000 |
| Production overhead | 224 000 |

36 000 units were transferred to finished stock and 3200 units remained in work-in-progress at the end of October which were complete as to material and half-complete as to labour and production overhead. A loss of 1200 units, being normal, occurred during the process.

The average method of pricing is used.

You are required to
(a)  prepare for the month of October, a statement (or statements) showing
    (i)   production cost per unit in total and by element of cost;
    (ii)  the total cost of production transferred to finished stock;
    (iii) the valuation of closing work-in-progress

in total and by element of cost;

(15 marks)

(b) describe five of the characteristics which distinguish process costing from job costing.

(10 marks)

(Total 25 marks)

*CIMA Stage 2 Cost Accounting*

### 5.16 Intermediate: Losses in process (weighted average)

A company manufactures a product that goes through two processes. You are given the following cost information about the processes for the month of November.

| | Process 1 | Process 2 |
|---|---|---|
| Unit input | 15 000 | — |
| Finished unit input from Process 1 | — | 10 000 |
| Finished unit output to Process 2 | 10 000 | — |
| Finished unit output from Process 2 | — | 9 500 |
| Opening WIP – Units | — | 2 000 |
|     – Value | — | £26 200 |
| Input – Materials | £26 740 | |
|     – Labour | £36 150 | £40 000 |
|     – Overhead | £40 635 | £59 700 |
| Closing WIP – Units | 4 400 | 1 800 |

You are told:

(1) The closing WIP in Process 1 was 80% complete for material, 50% complete for labour and 40% complete for overhead.

(2) The opening WIP in Process 2 was 40% complete for labour and 50% complete for overhead. It had a value of labour £3200, overheads £6000 for work done in Process 2.

(3) The closing WIP in Process 2 was two-thirds complete for labour and 75% complete for overhead.

(4) No further material needed to be added to the units transferred from Process 1.

(5) Normal loss is budgeted at 5% of total input in Process 1 and Process 2. Total input is to be inclusive of any opening WIP.

(6) Normal loss has no scrap value in Process 1 and can be sold for the input value from Process 1, in Process 2.

(7) Abnormal losses have no sales value.

(8) It is company policy to value opening WIP in a process by the weighted average method.

Required:

(a) Prepare accounts for:
  (i) Process 1.
  (ii) Process 2.
  (iii) Normal loss.
  (iv) Any abnormal loss/gain. (19 marks)

(b) Compare and contrast a joint product with a by-product. (6 marks)

(Total 25 marks)

*AAT Cost Accounting and Budgeting*

### 5.17 Intermediate: Losses in process (weighted average)

(a) A company uses a process costing system in which the following terms arise:

conversion costs
work-in-process
equivalent units
normal loss
abnormal loss.

Required:

Provide a definition of each of these terms.

(5 marks)

(b) Explain how you would treat normal and abnormal losses in process costs accounts.

(4 marks)

(c) One of the products manufactured by the company passes through two separate processes. In each process losses, arising from rejected material, occur. In Process 1, normal losses are 20% of input. In Process 2, normal losses are 10% of input. The losses arise at the end of each of the processes. Reject material can be sold. Process 1 reject material can be sold for £1.20 per kilo, and Process 2 reject material for £1.42 per kilo.

Information for a period is as follows:

Process 1:
  Material input 9000 kilos, cost £14 964.
  Direct labour 2450 hours at £3.40 per hour.
  Production overhead £2.60 per direct labour hour.
  Material output 7300 kilos.

Process 2:
  Material input 7300 kilos.
  Direct labour 1000 hours at £3.40 per hour.
  Production overhead £2.90 per direct labour hour.
  Material output 4700 kilos.

At the end of the period 2000 kilos of material were incomplete in Process 2. These were 50% complete as regards direct labour and production overhead.

There was no opening work-in-process in either process, and no closing work-in-process in Process 1.

Required:
Prepare the relevant cost accounts for the period.
(16 marks)

(Total 25 marks)
*ACCA Level 1 Costing*

### 5.18 Intermediate: Losses in process and weighted averages method

ABC plc operates an integrated cost accounting system and has a financial year which ends on 30 September. It operates in a processing industry in which a single product is produced by passing inputs through two sequential processes. A normal loss of 10% of input is expected in each process.

The following account balances have been extracted from its ledger at 31 August:

|  | Debit (£) | Credit (£) |
|---|---|---|
| Process 1 (Materials £4400; Conversion costs £3744) | 8144 | |
| Process 2 (Process 1 £4431; Conversion costs £5250) | 9681 | |
| Abnormal loss | 1400 | |
| Abnormal gain | | 300 |
| Overhead control account | | 250 |
| Sales | | 585 000 |
| Cost of sales | 442 500 | |
| Finished goods stock | 65 000 | |

ABC plc uses the weighted average method of accounting for work in process.

During September the following transactions occurred:

**Process 1**

| materials input | 4000 kg costing £22 000 |
|---|---|
| labour cost | £12 000 |
| transfer to process 2 | 2400 kg |

**Process 2**

| transfer from process 1 | 2400 kg |
|---|---|
| labour cost | £15 000 |
| transfer to finished goods | 2500 kg |

| Overhead costs incurred amounted to | £54 000 |
|---|---|
| Sales to customers were | £52 000 |

Overhead costs are absorbed into process costs on the basis of 150% of labour cost.

The losses which arise in process 1 have no scrap value: those arising in process 2 can be sold for £2 per kg.

Details of opening and closing work in process for the month of September are as follows:

|  | Opening | Closing |
|---|---|---|
| Process 1 | 3000 kg | 3400 kg |
| Process 2 | 2250 kg | 2600 kg |

In both processes closing work in process is fully complete as to material cost and 40% complete as to conversion cost.

Stocks of finished goods at 30 September were valued at cost of £60 000.

Required:
Prepare the ledger accounts for September and the annual profit and loss account of ABC plc. (Commence with the balances given above, balance off and transfer any balances as appropriate.)
(25 marks)
*CIMA Stage 2 Operational Cost Accounting*

### 5.19* Intermediate: Losses in process (weighted average)

Chemical Processors manufacture Wonderchem using two processes, mixing and distillation. The following details relate to the distillation process for a period

No opening work in progress (WIP)

| Input from mixing | 36 000 kg at a cost of | £166 000 |
|---|---|---|
| Labour for period | | £43 800 |
| Overheads for period | | £29 200 |

Closing WIP of 8000 kg, which was 100% complete for materials and 50% complete for labour and overheads.

The normal loss in distillation is 10% of fully complete production. Actual loss in the period was 3600 kg, fully complete, which were scrapped.

Required:
(a) Calculate whether there was a normal or abnormal loss or abnormal gain for the period.
(2 marks)

(b) Prepare the distillation process account for the period, showing clearly weights and values.
(10 marks)
(c) Explain what changes would be required in the accounts if the scrapped production had a resale value, *and* give the accounting entries.
(3 marks)
(Total 15 marks)
*CIMA Stage 1 Cost Accounting*

### 5.20 Intermediate: Process accounts involving an abnormal gain and equivalent production

The following information relates to a manufacturing process for a period:

| | |
|---|---|
| Materials costs | £16 445 |
| Labour and overhead costs | £28 596 |

10 000 units of output were produced by the process in the period, of which 420 failed testing and were scrapped. Scrapped units normally represent 5% of total production output. Testing takes place when production units are 60% complete in terms of labour and overheads. Materials are input at the beginning of the process. All scrapped units were sold in the period for £0.40 per unit.

Required:
Prepare the process accounts for the period, including those for process scrap and abnormal losses/gains.
(12 marks)
*ACCA Foundation Stage Paper 3*

### 5.21* Intermediate: Equivalent production with no losses (FIFO Method)

A company operates a manufacturing process where six people work as a team and are paid a weekly group bonus based upon the actual output of the team compared with output expected.

A basic 37 hour week is worked during which the expected output from the process is 4000 equivalent units of product. Basic pay is £5.00 per hour and the bonus for the group, shared equally, is £0.80 per unit in excess of expected output.

In the week just ended, basic hours were worked on the process. The following additional information is provided for the week:
Opening work in process (1000 units):
Materials £540 (100% complete)
Labour and overheads £355 (50% complete).
During the week:
Materials used £2255
Overheads incurred £1748

Completed production 3800 units
Closing work in process (1300 units)
Materials (100% complete)
Labour and overheads (75% complete).
There are no process losses.
The FIFO method is used to apportion costs.

Required:
(a) Prepare the process account for the week just ended.
(10 marks)
(b) Explain the purpose of the following documents which are used in the control of, and accounting for, the materials used in the process described in part (a)
(i) purchase requisition
(ii) materials (stores) requisition. (4 marks)
(14 marks)
*ACCA Foundation Stage Paper 3*

### 5.22* Intermediate: Preparation of process accounts with output fully completed and a discussion of FIFO and average methods of WIP valuation

(a) Z Ltd manufactures metal cans for use in the food processing industry. The metal is introduced in sheet form at the start of the process. Normal wastage in the form of offcuts is 2% of input. The offcuts can be sold for £0.26 per kilo. Each metal sheet weighs 2 kilos and is expected to yield 80 cans. In addition to wastage through offcuts, 1% of cans manufactured are expected to be rejected. These rejects can also be sold at £0.26 per kilo.

Production, and costs incurred, in the month just completed, were as follows:

| | |
|---|---|
| Production: | 3 100 760 cans |
| Costs incurred: | |
|   Direct materials: | 39 300 metal sheets at £2.50 per sheet |
| Direct labour and overhead: | £33 087 |

There was no opening or closing work in process.

Required:
Prepare the process accounts for the can manufacturing operation for the month just completed.
(15 marks)
(b) Another of the manufacturing operations of Z Ltd involves the continuous processing of raw

materials with the result that, at the end of any period, there are partly completed units of product remaining.

Required:

With reference to the general situation outlined above

(i) explain the concept of equivalent units (3 marks)

(ii) describe, and contrast, the FIFO and average methods of work in process valuation. (7 marks)

(Total 25 marks)

*ACCA Level 1 Costing*

## 5.23* Intermediate: FIFO method and losses in process

The manufacture of one of the products of A Ltd requires three separate processes. In the last of the three processes, costs, production and stock for the month just ended were:

(1) Transfers from Process 2: 180 000 units at a cost of £394 200.

(2) Process 3 costs: materials £110 520, conversion costs £76 506.

(3) Work in process at the beginning of the month: 20 000 units at a cost of £55 160 (based on FIFO pricing method). Units were 70% complete for materials, and 40% complete for conversion costs.

(4) Work in process at the end of the month: 18 000 units which were 90% complete for materials, and 70% complete for conversion costs.

(5) Product is inspected when it is complete. Normally no losses are expected but during the month 60 units were rejected and sold for £1.50 per unit.

Required:

(a) Prepare the Process 3 account for the month just ended. (15 marks)

(b) Explain how, and why, your calculations would be affected if the 60 units lost were treated as normal losses. (5 marks)

(c) Explain how your calculations would be affected by the use of weighted average pricing instead of FIFO. (5 marks)

(Total 25 marks)

*ACCA Cost and Management Accounting 1*

## 5.24 Intermediate: Losses in process (FIFO and weighted average methods)

A company produces a single product from one of its manufacturing processes. The following information of process inputs, outputs and work in process relates to the most recently completed period:

|  | kg |
| --- | --- |
| Opening work in process | 21 700 |
| Materials input | 105 600 |
| Output completed | 92 400 |
| Closing work in process | 28 200 |

The opening and closing work in process are respectively 60% and 50% complete as to conversion costs. Losses occur at the beginning of the process and have a scrap value of £0.45 per kg.

The opening work in process included raw material costs of £56 420 and conversion costs of £30 597. Costs incurred during the period were:

| Materials input | £276 672 |
| Conversion costs | £226 195 |

Required:

(a) Calculate the unit costs of production (£ per kg to four decimal places) using:

(i) the weighted average method of valuation and assuming that all losses are treated as normal;

(ii) the FIFO method of valuation and assuming that normal losses are 5% of materials input. (13 marks)

(b) Prepare the process account for situation (a) (ii) above. (6 marks)

(c) Distinguish between:

(i) joint products, and

(ii) by-products and contrast their treatment in process accounts. (6 marks)

(Total 25 marks)

*ACCA Cost and Management Accounting 1*

## 5.25* Intermediate: FIFO method and losses in process

A company operates several production processes involving the mixing of ingredients to produce bulk animal feedstuffs. One such product is mixed in two separate process operations. The information below is of the costs incurred in, and output from, Process 2 during the period just completed.

**Costs incurred:**

| | £ |
|---|---:|
| Transfers from Process 1 | 187 704 |
| Raw materials costs | 47 972 |
| Conversion costs | 63 176 |
| Opening work in process | 3 009 |

| Production: | Units |
|---|---:|
| Opening work in process | 1 200 |
| (100% complete, apart | |
| from Process 2 | |
| conversion costs which | |
| were 50% complete) | |
| Transfers from Process 1 | 112 000 |
| Completed output | 105 400 |
| Closing work in process | 1 600 |
| (100% complete, apart | |
| from Process 2 | |
| conversion costs which were | |
| 75% complete) | |

Normal wastage of materials (including product transferred from Process 1), which occurs in the early stages of Process 2 (after all materials have been added), is expected to be 5% of input. Process 2 conversion costs are all apportioned to units of good output. Wastage materials have no saleable value.

Required:
(a) Prepare the Process 2 account for the period, using FIFO principles. (15 marks)
(b) Explain how, and why, your calculations would have been different if wastage occurred at the end of the process. (5 marks)
(Total 20 marks)
*ACCA Cost and Management Accounting*

**5.26 Advanced: FIFO method and losses in process**
(a) You are required to explain and discuss the alternative methods of accounting for normal and abnormal spoilage. (8 marks)
(b) Weston Harvey Ltd assembles and finishes trapfoils from bought-in components which are utilized at the beginning of the assembly process. The other assembly costs are incurred evenly throughout that process. When the assembly process is complete, the finishing process is undertaken. Overhead is absorbed into assembly, but not finishing, at the rate of 100% of direct assembly cost.

It is considered normal for some trapfoils to be spoiled during assembly and finishing. Quality control inspection is applied at the conclusion of the finishing process to determine whether units are spoiled.

It is accepted that the spoilage is normal if spoiled units are no more than one-eighteenth of the completed good units produced. Normal spoilage is treated as a product cost, and incorporated into the cost of good production. Any spoilage in excess of this limit is classed as abnormal, and written off as a loss of the period in which it occurs.

Trapfoils are valuable in relation to their weight and size. Despite vigilant security precautions it is common that some units are lost, probably by pilferage. The cost of lost units is written off as a loss of the period in which it occurs. This cost is measured as the cost of the bought-in components plus the assembly process, but no finishing cost is charged.

Weston Harvey uses a FIFO system of costing.

The following data summarize the firm's activities during November:

**Opening work in process:**

| | |
|---|---:|
| Bought-in components | £60 000 |
| Direct assembly cost to 31 October | £25 000 |
| No. of units (on average one-half assembled) | 50 000 |

| Direct costs incurred during November | |
|---|---:|
| Bought-in components received | £120 000 |
| Direct assembly cost | £40 000 |
| Direct finishing cost | £30 000 |

| Production data for November: | Trapfoils |
|---|---:|
| Components received into assembly | 112 000 |
| Good units completed | 90 000 |
| Spoiled units | 10 000 |
| Lost units | 2 000 |

None of the opening work in process had at that stage entered the finishing process. Similarly, nor had any of the closing work in process at the end of the month. The units in the closing work in process were, on average, one-third complete as to assembly; none had entered the finishing process.

You are required:

(i)   to calculate the number of units in the closing work in process;                                    (3 marks)

(ii)  to calculate the number of equivalent units processed in November, distinguishing between bought-in components, assembly and finishing;                                        (6 marks)

(iii) to calculate the number of equivalent units processed in November, subdivided into the amounts for good units produced, spoilage, lost units and closing work in process.

(8 marks)

(Total 25 marks)

*ICAEW Management Accounting*

### 5.27* Advanced: FIFO stock valuation, standard costing and cost-plus pricing

Campex Ltd uses a dyeing and waterproofing process for its fabrics which are later made up into tents and other outdoor pursuit items, or sold to other manufacturers. Each roll of fabric is subject to the same process, with dyeing and waterproofing materials being added at specific times in the process. The direct labour costs are incurred uniformly throughout the process.

Inspection of the fabric for spoilage can take place only at the end of the process when it can be determined whether or not there has been any spoilage. Amounts of up to 10% of good output are acceptable as normal spoilage. Any abnormal spoilage is treated as a period loss. Some spoiled fabric can be reworked and it is saved up until a batch of 500 rolls can be reprocessed.

The reworking costs are charged to process overheads, and any reworked goods will not usually need the full cost of conversion spent on them. The work in progress is valued using the FIFO method.

At the beginning of the month of June the work in progress in the dyeing and waterproofing department was 1000 rolls which were valued at £12 000 direct materials and £4620 direct labour. The work in progress has had all the direct materials added, but was only 60% complete as far as the direct labour was concerned. During the month 5650 rolls were started from new, and 500 rolls were reworked. The rolls being reworked require 60% of direct materials and 50% of direct labour to bring them up to standard. By the end of the month 550 rolls had been found to be spoiled. The work in progress at the end of the month amounted to 800 rolls of which 80% were complete for direct

materials and 40% were complete for direct labour. All other rolls were completed satisfactorily and transferred to stores to await further processing. The costs for June were direct materials £72 085, direct labour £11 718. The departmental overhead recovered was £3.5 for every £1 direct labour, whilst actual overhead expenditure amounted to £34 110 for the month (excluding the reworking costs).

Requirements:

(a)  Prepare a schedule showing the actual equivalent units processed for each cost element in the processing department for the month of June and the costs per roll for the direct material used and the direct labour and applied overheads.                              (7 marks)

(b)  Prepare a schedule showing the allocation of the costs of production to the various cost headings for the month of June, including the value of closing work in progress using the FIFO method.                                (6 marks)

(c)  Discuss the usefulness of converting the system used above to a standard cost based system.                                      (4 marks)

(d)  Comment on the use of the actual costs you have computed above in (a) and (b) for product pricing.                          (4 marks)

(e)  Comment briefly on the implications of using replacement costs in a process costing system including valuation of month end work in progress.                                  (4 marks)

(Total 25 marks)

*ICAEW Paper 2/Management Accounting*

### 5.28 Advanced: Comparison of FIFO and weighted average, stock valuation methods

On 1 October Bland Ltd opened a plant for making verniers. Data for the first two months' operations are shown below:

|  | October (units) | November (units) |
| --- | --- | --- |
| Units started in month | 3900 | 2700 |
| Units completed (all sold) | 2400 | 2400 |
| Closing work in progress | 1500 | 1800 |
|  | (£) | (£) |
| Variable costs: |  |  |
|  Materials | 58 500 | 48 600 |
|  Labour | 36 000 | 21 000 |
| Fixed costs | 63 000 | 63 000 |
| Sales revenue | 112 800 | 120 000 |

At 31 October the units in closing work in progress were 100% complete for materials and 80% complete for labour. At 30 November the units in closing work in progress were 100% complete for materials and 50% complete for labour.

The company's policy for valuation of work in progress is under review. The board of directors decided that two alternative profit and loss statements should be prepared for October and November. One statement would value work in progress on a weighted average cost basis and the other would adopt a first-in, first-out basis. Fixed costs would be absorbed in proportion to actual labour costs in both cases.

For October both bases gave a closing work in progress valuation of £55 500 and a profit of £10 800. When the statements for November were presented to the board the following suggestions were made:

(1) 'We wouldn't have a problem over the valuation basis if we used standard costs.'

(2) 'Standard cost valuation could be misleading for an operation facing volatile costs; all data should be on a current cost basis for management purposes.'

(3) 'It would be simpler and more informative to go to a direct cost valuation basis for management use.'

(4) 'All that management needs is a cash flow report; leave the work in progress valuation to the year-end financial accounts.'

Requirements:

(a) Prepare profit and loss statements for November on the two alternative bases decided by the board of directors, showing workings.
(9 marks)

(b) Explain, with supporting calculations, the differences between the results shown by each statement you have prepared. (6 marks)

(c) Assess the main strengths and weaknesses of each of the suggestions made by the directors,
confining your assessment to matters relating to the effects of work in progress valuation on performance measurement. (10 marks)
(Total 25 marks)
*ICAEW P2 Management Accounting*

## 5.29* Intermediate: Cost control

PC Manufacturing Company operates a process costing system and the following information relates to process A for the month of March:

Opening work in process of 1000 units 40% complete, consisting of £17 400 for direct materials and £10 000 for conversion costs.

Production completed for March was 8200 units with materials added for the month of £162 600 and conversion costs in the month of £173 920.

Closing work in process was 800 units which was 20% complete.

There are no losses in process. All materials are introduced at the start of the process and conversion costs are incurred uniformly throughout the process. Process A is the initial process and the completed production is then transferred to process B.

You are required:

(a) To prepare a schedule of equivalent production and cost per unit and the process account for the month of March.

(b) Assuming that the company operates a standard cost system using the following standards per finished unit:

| | |
|---|---|
| Direct materials | £20 |
| Conversion cost | £23 |

Prepare a performance report for the month of March showing the total variances only for current performance.

# Joint and by-product costing

A distinguishing feature of the production of joint and by-products is that the products are not identifiable as different products until a specific point in the production process is reached. Before this point joint costs are incurred on the production of all products emerging from the joint production process. It is therefore not possible to trace joint costs to individual products.

To meet internal and external profit measurement and inventory valuation requirements, it is necessary to assign all product-related costs (including joint costs) to products so that cost can be allocated to inventories and cost of goods sold. The assignment of joint costs, however, is of little use for decision-making. We shall begin by distinguishing between joint and by-products. This will be followed by an examination of the different methods that can be used to allocate joint costs to products for inventory valuation. We shall then go on to discuss which costs are relevant for decision-making.

## Learning objectives

After studying this chapter, you should be able to:

- distinguish between joint products and by-products;
- explain and identify the split-off point in a joint-cost situation;
- explain the alternative methods of allocating joint costs to products;
- discuss the arguments for and against each of the methods of allocating joint costs to products;
- present relevant financial information for a decision as to whether a product should be sold at a particular stage or further processed;
- describe the accounting treatment of by-products.

# Distinguishing between joint products and by-products

Joint products and by-products arise in situations where the production of one product makes inevitable the production of other products. When a group of individual products is simultaneously produced, and each product has a significant relative sales value, the outputs are usually called **joint products**. Those products that are part of the simultaneous

**FIGURE 6.1** *Production process for joint and by-products.*

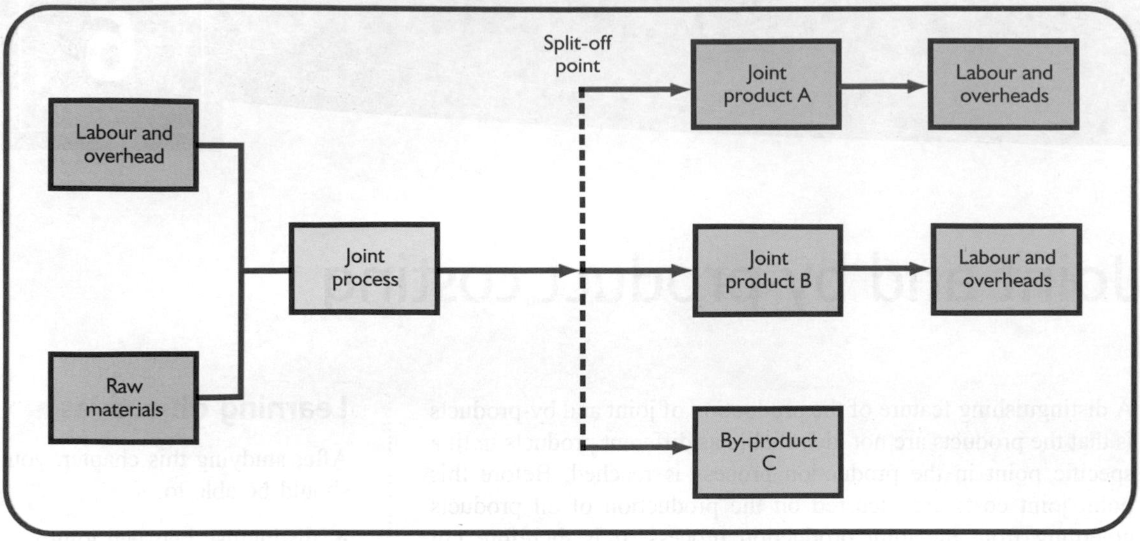

production process and have a minor sales value when compared with the joint products are called **by-products**.

As their name implies, by-products are those products that result incidentally from the main joint products. By-products may have a considerable absolute value, but the crucial classification test is that the sales value is small when compared with the values of the joint products. Joint products are crucial to the commercial viability of an organization, whereas by-products are incidental. In other words, by-products do not usually influence the decision as to whether or not to produce the main product, and they normally have little effect on the prices set for the main (joint) products. Examples of industries that produce both joint and by-products include chemicals, oil refining, mining, flour milling and gas manufacturing.

A distinguishing feature of the production of joint and by-products, is that the products are not identifiable as different individual products until a specific point in the production process is reached, known as the **split-off point**. All products may separate at one time, or different products may emerge at intervals. Before the split-off point, costs cannot be traced to particular products. For example, it is not possible to determine what part of the cost of processing a barrel of crude oil should be allocated to petrol, kerosene or paraffin. After the split-off point, joint products may be sold or subjected to further processing. If the latter is the case, any **further processing costs** can easily be traced to the specific products involved.

Figure 6.1 illustrates a simplified production process for joint and by-products. You will notice from this illustration that, at the split-off point, joint products A and B and by-product C all emerge, and that it is not possible to allocate costs of the joint process directly to the joint products or by-products. After the split-off point, further processing costs are added to the joint products before sale, and these costs can be specifically attributed to the joint products. By-product C in this instance is sold at the split-off point without further processing, although sometimes by-products may be further processed after the split-off point before they are sold on the outside market.

# Methods of allocating joint costs

If all the production for a particular period was sold, the problem of allocating joint costs to products would not exist. Inventory valuations would not be necessary, and the calculation of profit would merely require the deduction of total cost from total sales. However, if inventories are in existence at the end of the period, cost allocation to products are necessary. As any such allocations are bound to be subjective and arbitrary, this area will involve the accountant in making decisions which are among the most difficult to defend. All one can do is to attempt to choose an allocation method that seems to provide a rational and reasonable method of cost distribution. The most frequently used methods that are used to allocate joint costs up to split-off point can be divided into the following two categories:

1. Methods based on physical measures such as weight, volume, etc.
2. Methods assumed to measure the ability to absorb joint costs based on allocating joint costs relative to the market values of the products.

We shall now look at four methods that are used for allocating joint costs using the information given in Example 6.1. In Example 6.1 products X, Y and Z all become finished products at the split-off point. The problem arises as to how much of the £600 000 joint costs should be allocated to each individual product? The £600 000 cannot be specifically identified with any of the individual products, since the products themselves were not separated before the split-off point, but some method must be used to split the £600 000 among the three products so that inventories can be valued and the profit for the period calculated. The first method we shall look at is called the **physical measures method**.

## PHYSICAL MEASURES METHOD

Using this method, the cost allocation is a simple allocation of joint costs in proportion to volume. Each product is assumed to receive similar benefits from the joint cost, and is therefore charged with its proportionate share of the total cost. The cost allocations using this method are as follows:

| Product | Units produced | Proportion to total | Joint costs allocated (£) | Cost per unit (£) |
|---------|----------------|---------------------|----------------------------|-------------------|
| X | 40 000 | $\frac{1}{3}$ | 200 000 | 5 |
| Y | 20 000 | $\frac{1}{6}$ | 100 000 | 5 |
| Z | 60 000 | $\frac{1}{2}$ | 300 000 | 5 |
|   | 120 000 |  | 600 000 |  |

Note that this method assumes that the cost per unit is the same for each of the products. Therefore an alternative method of allocating joint costs is as follows:

$$\text{cost per unit} = £5 \ (£600\,000/120\,000)$$

**EXAMPLE 6.1**

During the month of July the Van Nostrand Company processes a basic raw material through a manufacturing process that yields three products – products X, Y and Z. There were no opening inventories and the products are sold at the split-off point without further processing. We shall initially assume that all of the output is sold during the period. Details of the production process and the sales revenues are given in the following diagram.

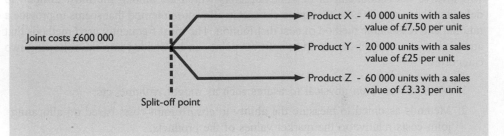

Thus the joint cost allocations are:

$$\text{Product X:} \quad 40\,000 \times £5 = £200\,000$$
$$\text{Product Y:} \quad 20\,000 \times £5 = £100\,000$$
$$\text{Product Z:} \quad 60\,000 \times £5 = £300\,000$$

Where market prices of the joint products differ, the assumptions of identical costs per unit for each joint product will result in some products showing high profits while others may show losses. This can give misleading profit calculations. Let us look at the product profit calculations using the information given in Example 6.1.

| Product | Sales revenue (£) | Total cost (£) | Profit (loss) (£) | Profit/sales (%) |
|---------|-------------------|----------------|-------------------|------------------|
| X | 300 000 | 200 000 | 100 000 | $33\frac{1}{3}$ |
| Y | 500 000 | 100 000 | 400 000 | 80 |
| Z | 200 000 | 300 000 | (100 000) | (50) |
|   | 1 000 000 | 600 000 | 400 000 | 40 |

You will see from these figures that the allocation of the joint costs bears no relationship to the revenue-producing power of the individual products. Product Z is allocated with the largest share of the joint costs but has the lowest total sales revenue; product Y is allocated with the lowest share of the joint costs but has the highest total sales revenue. The physical measures method is not therefore very satisfactory, and its weakness can be further highlighted if we assume that 80% of the production X, Y and Z were sold during the period. The appropriate inventory valuations and corresponding sales value of each product would be as follows:

| Product | Inventory valuations cost[a] (£) | Sales values[a] (£) |
|---|---|---|
| X | 40 000 | 60 000 |
| Y | 20 000 | 100 000 |
| Z | 60 000 | 40 000 |
| | 120 000 | 200 000 |

[a] 20% of total cost and sales revenue.

It appears inappropriate to value the stock of product Z at a price higher than its market value and at a valuation three times higher than that of product Y, when in fact product Y is more valuable in terms of potential sales revenue. A further problem is that the joint products must be measurable by the same unit of measurement. Difficult measurement problems arise in respect of products emerging from the joint process consisting of solids, liquids and gases, and it is necessary to find some common base. For example, in the case of coke, allocations can be made on the basis of theoretical yields extracted from a ton of coke.

The main advantage of using the physical measures method is simplicity, but this is outweighed by its many disadvantages.

## SALES VALUE AT SPLIT-OFF POINT METHOD

When the sales value at split-off point method is used, joint costs are allocated to joint products in proportion to the estimated sales value of production on the assumption that higher selling prices indicate higher costs. To a certain extent, this method could better be described as a means of apportioning profits or losses, according to sales value, rather than a method for allocating costs. Using the information in Example 6.1, the allocations under the sales value method would be as follows:

| Product | Units produced | Sales value (£) | Proportion of sales value to total (%) | Joint costs allocated (£) |
|---|---|---|---|---|
| X | 40 000 | 300 000 | 30 | 180 000 |
| Y | 20 000 | 500 000 | 50 | 300 000 |
| Z | 60 000 | 200 000 | 20 | 120 000 |
| | | 1 000 000 | | 600 000 |

The revised product profit calculations would be as follows:

| Product | Sales revenue (£) | Total cost (£) | Profit (loss) (£) | Profit/sales (%) |
|---|---|---|---|---|
| X | 300 000 | 180 000 | 120 000 | 40 |
| Y | 500 000 | 300 000 | 200 000 | 40 |
| Z | 200 000 | 120 000 | 80 000 | 40 |
| | 1 000 000 | 600 000 | 400 000 | |

If we assume that 80% of the production is sold, the stock valuations would be as follows:

|  | Inventory valuations | |
|---|---|---|
| **Product** | **Cost[a]** | **Sales values[a]** |
| X | 36 000 | 60 000 |
| Y | 60 000 | 100 000 |
| Z | 24 000 | 40 000 |
|  | 120 000 | 200 000 |

[a]20% of total cost and sales revenue.

The sales value method ensures that the inventory valuation does not exceed the net realizable value, but can itself be criticized since it is based on the assumption that sales revenue determines prior costs. For example, an unprofitable product with low sales revenue will be allocated with a small share of joint cost, thus giving the impression that it is generating profits.

In our discussion so far, relating to inventory valuations, we have assumed that inventories represented 20% of total production for each product. Therefore the total inventory valuation was £120 000 for both the physical measures and sales value at split-off methods of allocating joint costs. However, significant differences in the allocation of joint costs to inventories and cost of sales can occur between the two allocation methods. Consider a situation where the proportions of output for each product shown in Example 6.1 is as follows:

|  | Proportion of joint output sold (%) | Proportion of joint output included in the closing inventory (%) |
|---|---|---|
| Product X | 90 | 10 |
| Product Y | 70 | 30 |
| Product Z | 90 | 10 |

Using the joint-cost allocations that we have already computed the allocations to inventories and cost of goods sold are as follows:

|  | **Physical measures method** | | | **Sales value at split-off point method** | | |
|---|---|---|---|---|---|---|
|  | Total joint costs allocated (£) | Allocated to inventories (£) | Allocated to cost of goods sold (£) | Total joint costs allocated (£) | Allocated to inventories (£) | Allocated to cost of goods sold (£) |
| Product X | 200 000 | 20 000 (10%) | 180 000 (90%) | 180 000 | 18 000 (10%) | 162 000 (90%) |
| Product Y | 100 000 | 30 000 (30%) | 70 000 (70%) | 300 000 | 90 000 (30%) | 210 000 (70%) |
| Product Z | 300 000 | 30 000 (10%) | 270 000 (90%) | 120 000 | 12 000 (10%) | 108 000 (90%) |
| Total | 600 000 | 80 000 | 520 000 | 600 000 | 120 000 | 480 000 |

There is a difference of £40 000 between the two methods in the costs allocated to inventories and cost of goods sold. Hence, reported profits will also differ by £40 000. The method chosen to allocate joint costs to products thus has a significant effect both on profit measurement and inventory valuation.

# NET REALIZABLE METHOD

In Example 6.1 we have assumed that all products are sold at the split-off point and that no additional costs are incurred beyond that point. In practice, however, it is likely that joint products will be processed individually beyond the split-off point, and market values may not exist for the products at this stage. To estimate the sales value at the split-off point, it is therefore necessary to use the estimated sales value at the point of sale and work backwards. This method is called the net realizable value method. The net realizable value at split-off point can be estimated by deducting the further processing costs at the point of sale. This approach is illustrated with the data given in Example 6.2 which is the same as Example 6.1 except that further processing costs beyond split-off point are now assumed to exist. You should now refer to Example 6.2.

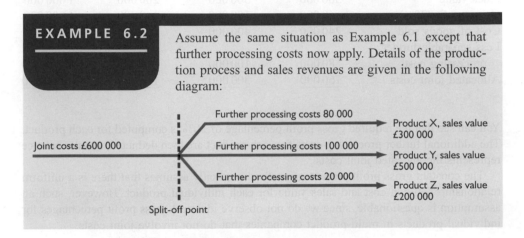

**EXAMPLE 6.2**

Assume the same situation as Example 6.1 except that further processing costs now apply. Details of the production process and sales revenues are given in the following diagram:

Joint costs £600 000

Further processing costs 80 000 → Product X, sales value £300 000

Further processing costs 100 000 → Product Y, sales value £500 000

Further processing costs 20 000 → Product Z, sales value £200 000

Split-off point

The calculation of the net realizable value and the allocation of joint costs using this method is as follows:

| Product | Sales value (£) | Costs beyond split-off point (£) | Estimated net realizable value at split-off point (£) | Proportion to total (%) | Joint costs allocated (£) | Profit (£) | Gross profit (%) |
|---|---|---|---|---|---|---|---|
| X | 300 000 | 80 000 | 220 000 | 27.5 | 165 000 | 55 000 | 18.33 |
| Y | 500 000 | 100 000 | 400 000 | 50.0 | 300 000 | 100 000 | 20.00 |
| Z | 200 000 | 20 000 | 180 000 | 22.5 | 135 000 | 45 000 | 22.50 |
| | 1 000 000 | 200 000 | 800 000 | | 600 000 | 200 000 | 20.00 |

Note that the joint costs are allocated in proportion to each product's net realizable value at split-off point.

# CONSTANT GROSS PROFIT PERCENTAGE METHOD

When the products are subject to further processing after split-off point and the net realizable method is used, the gross profit percentages are different for each product. They are 18.33% for product X, 20% for Y and 22.5% for Z. It could be argued that, since the three products arise from a single productive process, they should earn identical gross profit percentages. The constant gross profit percentage method allocates joint costs so that the overall gross profit percentage is identical for each individual product. From the information contained in Example 6.2 the joint costs would be allocated in such a way that the resulting gross profit percentage for each of the three products is equal to the overall gross profit percentage of 20%. Note that the gross profit percentage is calculated by deducting the *total* costs of the three products (£800 000) from the *total* sales (£1 000 000) and expressing the profit (£200 000) as a percentage of sales. The calculations are as follows:

| | Product X (£) | Product Y (£) | Product Z (£) | Total (£) |
|---|---|---|---|---|
| Sales value | 300 000 | 500 000 | 200 000 | 1 000 000 |
| Gross profit (20%) | 60 000 | 100 000 | 40 000 | 200 000 |
| Cost of goods sold | 240 000 | 400 000 | 160 000 | 800 000 |
| Less separable further processing costs | 80 000 | 100 000 | 20 000 | 200 000 |
| Allocated joint costs | 160 000 | 300 000 | 140 000 | 600 000 |

You can see that the required gross profit percentage of 20% is computed for each product. The additional further processing costs for each product are then deducted, and the balance represents the allocated joint costs.

The constant gross profit percentage method implicitly assumes that there is a uniform relationship between cost and sales value for each individual product. However, such an assumption is questionable, since we do not observe identical gross profit percentages for individual products in multi-product companies that do not involve joint costs.

## COMPARISON OF METHODS

What factors should be considered in selecting the most appropriate method of allocating joint costs? The cause-and-effect criterion, described in Chapter 3, cannot be used because there is no cause-and-effect relationship between the *individual* products and the incurrence of joint costs. Joint costs are caused by *all* products and not by individual products. Where cause-and-effect relationships cannot be established allocations ought to based on the benefits received criterion. If benefits received cannot be measured costs should be allocated based on the principle of equity or fairness. The net realizable method or the sales value at split-off point are the methods that best meet the benefits received criterion. The latter also has the added advantage of simplicity if sales values at the split-off point exists. It is also difficult to estimate the net realizable value in industries where there are numerous subsequent further processing stages and multiple split-off points. Similar measurement problems can also apply with the physical measures methods. In some industries a common denominator for physical measures for each product does not exist. For example, the output of the joint process may consist of a combination of solids, liquids and gases.

The purpose for which joint-cost allocations are used is also important. Besides being required for inventory valuation and profit measurement joint-cost allocations may be used as a mechanism for setting selling prices. For example, some utilities recharge their customers for usage of joint facilities. If market prices do not exist selling prices are likely to be determined by adding a suitable profit margin to the costs allocated to the products. The method used to allocate joint costs will therefore influence product costs, and in turn, the selling price. If external market prices do not exist it is illogical to use sales value methods to allocate joint costs. This would involve what is called circular reasoning because cost allocations determine selling prices, which in turn affect cost allocations, which will also lead to further changes in selling prices and sales revenues. For pricing purposes a physical measures method should be used if external market prices do not exist. What methods do companies actually use? Little empirical evidence exists apart from a UK survey by Slater and Wootton (1984). Their survey findings are presented in Exhibit 6.1. You will see that a physical measures method is most widely used. In practice firms are likely to use a method where the output from the joint

**EXHIBIT 6.1**

*Surveys of company practice*

A survey of UK chemical and oil refining companies by Slater and Wootton (1984) reported the following methods of allocating joint costs:

|  | % |
| --- | --- |
| Physical measures method | 76 |
| Sales value method | 5 |
| Negotiated basis | 19 |
| Other | 14 |

*Note*

The percentages add up to more than 100% because some companies used more than one method.

The analysis by industry indicated that the following methods were used:

| Type of company | Predominant cost allocation method used |
| --- | --- |
| Petrochemicals | Sales value at split-off point or estimated net realizable method |
| Coal processing | Physical measures method |
| Coal chemicals | Physical measures method |
| Oil refining | No allocation of joint costs |

The authors of the survey noted that it was considered by the majority of oil refineries that the complex nature of the process involved, and the vast number of joint product outputs, made it impossible to establish any meaningful cost allocation between products.

process can be measured without too much difficulty. Establishing a common output measure is extremely difficult in some organizations. To overcome this problem they value inventories at their estimated net realizable value minus a normal profit margin.

# Irrelevance of joint cost allocations for decision-making

Our previous discussion has concentrated on the allocation of joint costs for inventory valuation and profit measurement. Joint product costs that have been computed for inventory valuation are entirely inappropriate for decision-making. For decision-making relevant costs should be used – these represent the incremental costs relating to a decision. Therefore costs that will be unaffected by a decision are classed as irrelevant. Joint-cost allocations are thus irrelevant for decision-making. Consider the information presented in Example 6.3.

**EXAMPLE 6.3**

The Adriatic Company incurs joint product costs of £1 000 000 for the production of two joint products, X and Y. Both products can be sold at split-off point. However, if additional costs of £60 000 are incurred on product Y then it can be converted into product Z and sold for £10 per unit. The joint costs and the sales revenue at split-off point are illustrated in the following diagram:

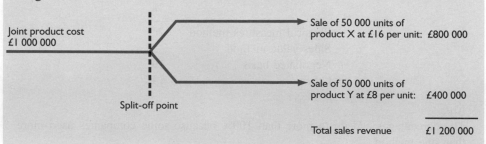

You are requested to advise management whether or not product Y should be converted in product Z.

The joint cost of £1 000 000 will be incurred irrespective of which decision is taken, and is not relevant for this decision. The information which is required for the decision is a comparison of the additional costs with the additional revenues from converting product Y into product Z. The following information should therefore be provided:

| Additional revenue and costs from converting product Y into product Z | (£) |
|---|---:|
| Additional revenues (50 000 × £2) | 100 000 |
| Additional conversion costs | 60 000 |
| Additional profit from conversion | 40 000 |

The proof that profits will increase by £40 000 if conversion takes place is as follows:

| | Convert to product Z (£) | Do not convert (£) |
|---|---:|---:|
| Sales | 1 300 000 | 1 200 000 |
| Total costs | 1 060 000 | 1 000 000 |
| Profits | 240 000 | 200 000 |

The general rule is that it will be profitable to extend the processing of a joint product so long as the additional revenues exceed the additional costs, but note that the variable portion of the joint costs will be relevant for some decisions. For an illustration of a situation where joint variable costs are relevant for decision-making see Example 6.4.

**AR** You can see from this example that the *further* processing variable costs of joint product A and B are £8 and £10 per unit respectively. The fixed portion of the joint costs of £240 000 will remain unchanged even if the customer's order is accepted, and any allocation of these costs should be excluded for decision-making. However, the variable costs of the joint process of £5 per unit will lead to additional costs if the customer's order is accepted, and so should be included in our analysis. Nevertheless, such costs should not be allocated to the products for decision-making. To decide whether or not to accept the offer, we must compare the incremented costs with the incremented revenues.

Unless we are sure that we can sell as much of product A as we produce, we cannot analyse the potential sale of an additional 600 units of product B by comparing the revenue and cost of product B itself. To increase production of product B, we need to incur additional variable costs of £5 per unit of output in the joint production process. As the production of 600 units of product B will lead to an output of 3000 units of product A in the joint process, the variable costs of the joint process will be £18 000 (3600 × £5). The additional costs associated with the production of 600 units of product B will therefore be:

| | |
|---|---:|
| Further processing variable costs of product B | |
| (600 units at £10 per unit) | £6 000 |
| Variable costs of joint process (3600 units at £5 per unit) | £18 000 |
| | £24 000 |

The additional revenue from the sale of 600 units of product B is £15 000 (600 units at £25 per unit). Because of the £18 000 variable cost from the joint process, the additional revenue from the sale of product B cannot cover, by itself, the increase in the total costs of the firm. The company will need to process and sell additional units of product A if the customer's order is to be profitable.

Producing an additional 3000 units of product A will increase the variable costs of product A by £24 000 (3000 units at £8 per unit) after the split-off point. The additional costs arising from acceptance of the customer's order will therefore be

| | |
|---|---:|
| Excess of variable costs over revenues from sale of product B | |
| (£24 000 − £15 000) | £9 000 |
| Variable costs of product A (3000 units at £8) | £24 000 |
| | £33 000 |

To cover these costs, the company must obtain additional sales revenue from product A. If a separate market can be found, the selling price of the 3000 units of product A must be in excess of £11 (£33 000/3000 units) if acceptance of the customer's order is to be profitable. This analysis, of course, assumes that the agreed price will not affect the selling price to existing customers. Alternatively, if the company cannot find a market for the 3000 units of product A at a selling price that is in excess of £11 per unit, it could consider selling the 3000 units at the split-off point rather than after further processing. The company would then have to find a market to cover the £9000 excess of variable costs over revenues from the sale of product B at the split-off point. ●●●

**EXAMPLE 6.4**

The Tivoli Company incurs joint production costs of £300 000 for the production of two joint products, A and B. Both products require further processing before they can be sold. Details of the expected costs and revenues of the joint products are given in the following diagram:

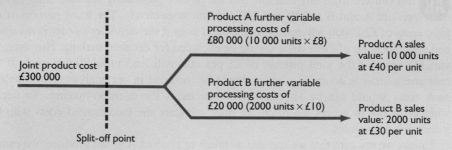

The joint costs of £300 000 consist of £240 000 fixed costs and a variable cost of £5 per unit of output. A new customer has approached the company with an offer to purchase 600 units of product B at a price of £25 per unit. The sale will not affect the market price to the other customers. Should the company accept this offer?

# Accounting for by-products

**By-products** are products that have a minor sales value and that emerge incidentally from the production of the major product. As the major objective of the company is to produce the joint products, it can justifiably be argued that the joint costs should be allocated only to the joint products and that the by-products should not be allocated with any portion of the joint cost that are incurred before the split-off point. Any costs that are incurred in producing by-products after the split-off point can justifiably be charged to the by-product, since such costs are incurred for the benefit of the by-product only.

By-product revenues or by-product net revenues (the sales revenue of the by-product less the additional further processing costs after the split-off point) should be deducted from the cost of the joint products or the main product from which it emerges. Consider Example 6.5

None of the joint costs shown in Example 6.5 is allocated to the by-product but the further processing costs of £5000 (5000 kg × £1) are charged to the by-product. The net revenues from the by-product of £20 000 (sales revenue of £25 000 less further processing costs of £5000) are deducted from the costs of the joint process (£3 020 000). Thus joint costs of £3 000 000 will be allocated to joint products A and B using one of the allocation methods described in this chapter. The accounting entries for the by-product will be as follows:

| | | |
|---|---|---|
| Dr By-product stock (5000 × £4) | 20 000 | |
| Cr Joint process WIP acount | | 20 000 |

**EXAMPLE 6.5**

The Neopolitan Company operates a manufacturing process which produces joint products A and B and by-product C. The joint costs of the manufacturing process are £3 020 000, incurred in the manufacture of:

| | |
|---|---|
| Product A | 30 000 kg |
| Product B | 50 000 kg |
| Product C | 5 000 kg |

By-product C requires further processing at a cost of £1 per kg, after which it can be sold at £5 per kg.

With the net revenue due from the production of the by-product:

| | | |
|---|---|---|
| Dr By-product stock | 5000 | |
| Cr Cash | | 5000 |

With the separable manufacturing costs incurred:

| | | |
|---|---|---|
| Dr Cash | 25 000 | |
| Cr By-product stock | | 25 000 |

With the value of by-products sales for the period.

# By-products, scrap and waste

The terms 'by-products', 'scrap' and 'waste' are used to refer to outputs with little or no value. Because different people use these different terms to refer to the same thing, we shall briefly discuss the distinction between them.

Waste is a term used to describe material that has no value, or even negative value if it has to be disposed of at some cost. Examples include gases, sawdust, smoke and other unsaleable residues from the manufacturing process. Waste presents no accounting problems because it has no sales value, and therefore it is not included in the stock valuation.

By-products, as we have already seen, are those products that have a minor sales value and that emerge incidentally from the production of the major products.

Scrap also emerges as a consequence of the joint production process, but it is distinct from by-products in the sense that it is the leftover part of raw materials, whereas by-products are different from the material that went into the production process. The term 'scrap' is usually limited to material that has some minor sales value. Metal shavings with a minor sales value would normally be classified as scrap. When a product of minor sales value is processed beyond the split-off point, it should be considered as a by-product and not scrap, although the fact that a product will not be processed beyond the split-off point does not necessarily mean that it should be considered as scrap. The major distinguishing feature is that by-products are different from the materials that went into the production process.

The accounting procedures for scrap and by-products are fairly similar, and the accounting treatment which has already been outlined for by-products can also be applied to scrap.

## Self-Assessment Question

You should attempt to answer this question yourself before looking up the suggested answer, which appears on pages 1101–2. If any part of your answer is incorrect, check back carefully to make sure you understand where you went wrong.

(a) Polimur Ltd operates a process that produces three joint products, all in an unrefined condition. The operating results of the process for October 2000 are shown below.
Output from process:

| | |
|---|---|
| Product A | 100 tonnes |
| Product B | 80 tonnes |
| Product C | 80 tonnes |

The month's operating costs were £1 300 000. The closing stocks were 20 tonnes of A, 15 tonnes of B and 5 tonnes of C. The value of the closing stock is calculated by apportioning costs according to weight of output. There were no opening stocks and the balance of the output was sold to a refining company at the following prices:

| | |
|---|---|
| Product A | £5 per kg |
| Product B | £4 per kg |
| Product C | £9 per kg |

Required:

Prepare an operating statement showing the relevant trading results for October 2000.

(6 marks)

(b) The management of Polimur Ltd have been considering a proposal to establish their own refining operations.
The current market prices of the refined products are:

| | |
|---|---|
| Product A | £17 per kg |
| Product B | £14 per kg |
| Product C | £20.50 per kg |

The estimated unit costs of the refining operation are:

| | Product A (£ per kg) | Product B (£ per kg) | Product C (£ per kg) |
|---|---|---|---|
| Direct materials | 0.50 | 0.75 | 2.50 |
| Direct labour | 2.00 | 3.00 | 4.00 |
| Variable overheads | 1.50 | 2.25 | 5.50 |

Prime costs would be variable. Fixed overheads, which would be £700 000 monthly, would be direct to the refining operation. Special equipment is required for refining product B and this would be rented at a cost, not included in the above figures, of £360 000 per month.

187

It may be assumed that there would be no weight loss in the refining process and that the quantity refined each month would be similar to October's output shown in (a) above.

Required:

Prepare a statement that will assist management to evaluate the proposal to commence refining operations. Include any further comments or observations you consider relevant.

(16 marks)

(Total 22 marks)

*ACCA Foundation Costing*

## Summary

The distinguishing feature of joint products and by-products is that they are not separately identifiable as different products before the split-off point. To meet the requirements of financial accounting, it is necessary to trace all product-related costs to products so that costs can be allocated to inventories and to the cost of goods sold. Consequently, joint costs need to be allocated to products. The allocation methods that we have considered are based on physical volume, sales value and gross profit. We have seen that the physical units method can lead to a situation where the recorded joint product cost inventory valuation is in excess of net realizable value, and this method of allocation is not recommended.

We have established that the allocation of joint cost for decision-making is unacceptable. Such decisions should be based on a comparison of the incremental costs with the incremental revenues. This principle was examined in the light of two basic decisions: (1) whether to sell products at the split-off point or to process further; and (2) whether to accept an order below the current selling price.

We have also considered accounting for by-products and noted that by-product net revenues should be deducted from the cost of the joint production process prior to allocating the costs to the individual joint products.

Finally, since the terms 'by-products', 'scrap' and 'waste' are subject to different interpretations, we have considered briefly the distinguishing features of these items.

## Key Terms and Concepts

by-products (p. 174, 184, 185)
constant gross profit percentage method (p. 180)
further processing costs (p. 174)
joint products (p. 173)
net realizable value method (p. 179)

physical measures method (p. 175)
sales value at split-off point method (p. 177)
scrap (p. 185)
split-off point (p. 174)
waste (p. 185)

## Recommended Reading

For a survey of joint-cost allocation methods used by UK chemical and oil refining companies you should read Slater and Wootton (1984). A shorter article (6 pp.) by Cats-Baril *et al.* (1986) describes a system of joint product costing for the production of memory chips of differing quality in the semiconductor industry in the USA. The authors demonstrate how joint-cost allocation is applied, comparing three approaches (one based on market values and two based on physical quantities), and give reasons for supporting the market value approach. For a more detailed discussion of cost allocations in general you should refer to Ahmed and Scapens (1991) or Young (1985).

## Key Examination Points

It is necessary to apportion joint costs to joint products for inventory valuation and profit measurement purposes. Remember that costs calculated for inventory valuation purposes should not be used for decision-making purposes. Examination questions normally require joint product profit calculations and the presentation of information as to whether a product should be sold at the split-off point or further processed. A common mistake with the later requirement is to include joint-cost apportionments. You should compare incremental revenues with incremental costs and indicate that joint costs are not relevant to the decision to sell at the split-off point or process further.

## Questions

*Indicates that a suggested solution is to be found in the *Students' Manual*.

### 6.1* Intermediate

A company operates a process which produces three joint products – K, P and Z. The costs of operating this process during September amounted to £117 000. During the month the output of the three products was:

|   |             |
|---|-------------|
| K | 2000 litres |
| P | 4500 litres |
| Z | 3250 litres |

P is further processed at a cost of £9.00 per litre. The actual loss of the second process was 10% of the input which was normal. Products K and Z are sold without further processing.

The final selling prices of each of the products are:

|   |                  |
|---|------------------|
| K | £20.00 per litre |
| P | £25.00 per litre |
| Z | £18.00 per litre |

Joint costs are attributed to products on the basis of output volume.

The profit attributed to product P was:

A   £6750
B   £12 150
C   £13 500
D   £16 200
E   £18 000

*CIMA Stage 2 Specimen Paper*

### 6.2 Intermediate

(a) Explain briefly the term 'joint products' in the context of process costing.    (2 marks)
(b) Discuss whether, and if so how, joint process costs should be shared amongst joint products. (Assume that no further processing is required after the split-off point.)
    (11 marks)
(c) Explain briefly the concept of 'equivalent units' in process costing.    (4 marks)
    (Total 17 marks)
    *ACCA Level 1 Costing*

### 6.3 Intermediate

(a) Discuss the problems which joint products and by-products pose the management accountant, especially in his attempts to produce useful product profitability reports. Outline the usual accounting treatments of joint and by-products and indicate the extent to which these treatments are effective in overcoming the problems you have discussed. In your answer clearly describe the differences between joint and by-products and provide an example of each.    (14 marks)
(b) A common process produces several joint products. After the common process has been completed each product requires further specific, and directly attributable, expenditure in order to 'finish off' the product and put it in a saleable condition. Specify the conditions under which it is rational to undertake:
    (i)  the common process, and
    (ii) the final 'finishing off' of each of the products which are the output from the common process.
    Illustrate your answer with a single numerical example.    (6 marks)
    (Total 20 marks)
    *ACCA P2 Management Accounting*

## 6.4 Intermediate

Explain how the apportionment of those costs incurred up to the separation point of two or more joint products could give information which is unacceptable for (i) stock valuation and (ii) decision-making. Use figures of your own choice to illustrate your answer. (9 marks)

*ACCA Level 2 Management Accounting*

## 6.5* Intermediate: Preparation of process accounts and apportionment of joint costs

A company manufactures two types of industrial sealant by passing materials through two consecutive processes. The results of operating the two processes during the previous month are shown below:

### Process 1

Costs incurred (£):

| | | |
|---|---|---|
| Materials 7000 kg at £0.50 per kg | 3 500 | |
| Labour and overheads | 4 340 | |

Output (kg):

| | |
|---|---|
| Transferred to Process 2 | 6430 |
| Defective production | 570 |

### Process 2

Cost incurred (£):

| | |
|---|---|
| Labour and overheads | 12 129 |

Output (kg):

| | |
|---|---|
| Type E sealant | 2000 |
| Type F sealant | 4000 |
| By-product | 430 |

It is considered normal for 10% of the total output from process 1 to be defective and all defective output is sold as scrap at £0.40 kg. Losses are not expected in process 2.

There was no work in process at the beginning or end of the month and no opening stocks of sealants.

Sales of the month's output from Process 2 were:

| | |
|---|---|
| Type E sealant | 1100 kg |
| Type F sealant | 3200 kg |
| By-product | 430 kg |

The remainder of the output from Process 2 was in stock at the end of the month.

The selling prices of the products are: Type E sealant £7 per kg and Type F sealant £2.50 per kg. No additional costs are incurred on either of the two main products after the second process. The by-product is sold for £1.80 per kg after being sterilized, at a cost of £0.30 per kg, in a subsequent process. The operating costs of process 2 are reduced by the net income receivable from sales of the by-product.

Required:
(a) Calculate, for the previous month, the cost of the output transferred from process 1 into process 2 and the net cost or saving arising from any abnormal losses or gains in process 1. (6 marks)
(b) Calculate the value of the closing stock of each sealant and the profit earned by each sealant during the previous month using the following methods of apportioning costs to joint products:
    (i) according to weight of output,
    (ii) according to market value of output. (12 marks)
(c) Consider whether apportioning process costs to joint products is useful. Briefly illustrate with examples from your answer to (b) above. (4 marks)
(Total 22 marks)

*ACCA Level 1 Costing*

## 6.6 Intermediate: Accounting for joint and by-products and preparation process accounts

(a) Distinguish between the cost accounting treatment of joint products and of by-products. (3 marks)
(b) A company operates a manufacturing process which produces joint products A and B and by-product C.

Manufacturing costs for a period total £272 926, incurred in the manufacture of:

Product A 16 000 kg (selling price £6.10/kg)
Product B 53 200 kg (selling price £7.50/kg)
Product C 2770 kg (selling price £0.80/kg)

Required:
Calculate the cost per kg (to three decimal places of a pound £) of products A and B in the period, using market values to apportion joint costs. (5 marks)
(c) In another of the company's processes, product X is manufactured using raw materials P and T, which are mixed in the proportions 1 : 2.

Material purchase prices are:

P £5.00 per kg
T £1.60 per kg

Normal weight loss 5% is expected during the process.

In the period just ended 9130 kg of Product X were manufactured from 9660 kg of raw materials. Conversion costs in the period were £23 796. There was no work in progress at the beginning or end of the period.

Required:
Prepare the product X process account for the period. (6 marks)
(Total 14 marks)
*ACCA Foundation Paper 3*

### 6.7* Intermediate: Preparation of joint product account and a decision of further processing

PQR Limited produces two joint products – P and Q – together with a by-product R, from a single main process (process 1). Product P is sold at the point of separation for £5 per kg, whereas product Q is sold for £7 per kg after further processing into product Q2. By-product R is sold without further processing for £1.75 per kg.

Process 1 is closely monitored by a team of chemists, who planned the output per 1000 kg of input materials to be as follows:

Product P   500 kg
Product Q   350 kg
Product R   100 kg
Toxic waste  50 kg

The toxic waste is disposed of at a cost of £1.50 per kg, and arises at the end of processing.

Process 2, which is used for further processing of product Q into product Q2, has the following cost structure:

Fixed costs   £6000 per week
Variable costs  £1.50 per kg processed

The following actual data relate to the first week of accounting period 10:

## Process 1

| | |
|---|---|
| Opening work in process | Nil |
| Materials input | |
| 10 000 kg costing | £15 000 |
| Direct labour | £10 000 |
| Variable overhead | £4000 |
| Fixed overhead | £6000 |

**Outputs:**

| | |
|---|---|
| Product P | 4800 kg |
| Product Q | 3600 kg |
| Product R | 1000 kg |
| Toxic waste | 600 kg |
| Closing work in progress | nil |

## Process 2

| | |
|---|---|
| Opening work in process | nil |
| Input of product Q | 3600 kg |
| Output of product Q2 | 3300 kg |
| Closing work in progress | 300 kg, |
| | 50% converted |

Conversion costs were incurred in accordance with the planned cost structure.

Required:
(a) Prepare the main process account for the first week of period 10 using the final sales value method to attribute pre-separation costs to joint products. (12 marks)
(b) Prepare the toxic waste accounts and process 2 account for the first week of period 10. (9 marks)
(c) Comment on the method used by PQR Limited to attribute pre-separation costs to its joint products. (4 marks)
(d) Advise the management of PQR Limited whether or not, on purely financial grounds, it should continue to process product Q into product Q2:
(i) if product Q could be sold at the point of separation for £4.30 per kg; *and*
(ii) if 60% of the weekly fixed costs of process 2 were avoided by not processing product Q further. (5 marks)
(Total 30 marks)
*CIMA Stage 2 Operational Cost Accounting*

### 6.8* Intermediate: Flow chart and calculation of cost per unit for joint products

A distillation plant, which works continuously, processes 1000 tonnes of raw material each day. The raw material costs £4 per tonne and the plant operating costs per day are £2600. From the input of raw material the following output is produced:

|  | (%) |
| --- | --- |
| Distillate X | 40 |
| Distillate Y | 30 |
| Distillate Z | 20 |
| By-product B | 10 |

From the initial distillation process, Distillate X passes through a heat process which costs £1500 per day and becomes product X which requires blending before sale.

Distillate Y goes through a second distillation process costing £3300 per day and produces 75% of product Y and 25% of product X1.

Distillate Z has a second distillation process costing £2400 per day and produces 60% of product Z and 40% of product X2. The three streams of products X, X1 and X2 are blended, at a cost of £1555 per day to become the saleable final product XXX.

There is no loss of material from any of the processes.

By-product B is sold for £3 per tonne and such proceeds are credited to the process from which the by-product is derived.

Joint costs are apportioned on a physical unit basis.

You are required to:
(a) draw a flow chart, flowing from left to right, to show for one day of production the flow of material and the build up of the operating costs for each product; (18 marks)
(b) present a statement for management showing for *each* of the products XXX, Y and Z, the output for *one* day, the total cost and the unit cost per tonne; (5 marks)
(c) suggest an alternative method for the treatment of the income receivable for by-product B than that followed in this question (figures are not required). (2 marks)
(Total 25 marks)
*CIMA Stage 2 Cost Accounting*

### 6.9 Intermediate: Preparation of joint and by-product process account

XYZ plc, a paint manufacturer, operates a process costing system. The following details related to process 2 for the month of October:

| Opening work in progress | 5000 litres fully complete as to transfers from process 1 and 40% complete as to labour and overhead, valued at £60 000 |
| --- | --- |
| Transfer from process 1 | 65 000 litres valued at cost of £578 500 |
| Direct labour | £101 400 |
| Variable overhead | £80 000 |
| Fixed overhead | £40 000 |
| Normal loss | 5% of volume transferred from process 1, scrap value £2.00 per litre |
| Actual output | 30 000 litres of paint X (a joint product) 25 000 litres of paint Y (a joint product) 7000 litres of by-product Z |
| Closing work in progress | 6000 litres fully complete as to transfers from process 1 and 60% complete as to labour and overhead. |

The final selling price of products X, Y and Z are:

| Paint X | £15.00 per litre |
| --- | --- |
| Paint Y | £18.00 per litre |
| Product Z | £4.00 per litre |

There are no further processing costs associated with either paint X or the by-product, but paint Y requires further processing at a cost of £1.50 per litre.

All three products incur packaging costs of £0.50 per litre before they can be sold.

Required:
(a) Prepare the process 2 account for the month of October, apportioning the common costs between the joint products, based upon their values at the point of separation (20 marks)
(b) Prepare the abnormal loss/gain account, showing clearly the amount to be transferred to the profit and loss account. (4 marks)
(c) Describe one other method of apportioning the common costs between the joint products, *and* explain why it is necessary to make such apportionments, and their usefulness when measuring product profitability.
(6 marks)
(Total 30 marks)
*CIMA Stage 2 Operational Cost Accounting*

## 6.10* Intermediate: Joint cost apportionment and decision on further processing

BK Chemicals produces three joint products in one common process but each product is capable of being further processed separately after the split-off point. The estimated data given below relate to June:

| | Product B | Product K | Product C |
|---|---|---|---|
| Selling price at split-off point (per litre) | £6 | £8 | £9 |
| Selling price after further processing (per litre) | £10 | £20 | £30 |
| Post-separation point costs | £20 000 | £10 000 | £22 500 |
| Output in litres | 3 500 | 2 500 | 2 000 |

Pre-separation point joint costs are estimated to be £40 000 and it is current practice to apportion these to the three products according to litres produced.

You are required:
(i)   to prepare a statement of estimated profit or loss for each product and in total for June if all three products are processed further, and
(ii)  to advise how profits could be maximized if one or more products are sold at the split-off point. Your advice should be supported by a profit statement.                              (11 marks)
*CIMA Stage 2 Cost Accounting*

## 6.11 Intermediate: Joint cost apportionment and a decision on further processing

QR Limited operates a chemical process which produces four different products Q, R, S and T from the input of one raw material plus water. Budget information for the forthcoming financial year is as follows:

| | (£000) |
|---|---|
| Raw materials cost | 268 |
| Initial processing cost | 464 |

| Product | Output in litres | Sales (£1000) | Additional processing cost (£000) |
|---|---|---|---|
| Q | 400 000 | 768 | 160 |
| R | 90 000 | 232 | 128 |
| S | 5 000 | 32 | — |
| T | 9 000 | 240 | 8 |

The company policy is to apportion the costs prior to the split-off point on a method based on net sales value.

Currently, the intention is to sell product S without further processing but to process the other three products after the split-off point. However, it has been proposed that an alternative strategy would be to sell all four products at the split-off point without further processing. If this were done the selling prices obtainable would be as follows:

| | Per litre (£) |
|---|---|
| Q | 1.28 |
| R | 1.60 |
| S | 6.40 |
| T | 20.00 |

You are required:
(a)   to prepare budgeted profit statement showing the profit or loss for each product, and in total, if the current intention is proceeded with;
                                        (10 marks)
(b)   to show the profit or loss by product, and in total, if the alternative strategy were to be adopted;                              (6 marks)
(c)   to recommend what should be done and why, assuming that there is no more profitable alternative use for the plant.
                                         (4 marks)
                                    (Total 20 marks)
*CIMA Stage 2 Cost Accounting*

## 6.12 Intermediate: Joint cost apportionment and decision on further processing

A company manufactures four products from an input of a raw material to process 1. Following this process, product A is processed in process 2, product B in process 3, product C in process 4 and product D in process 5.

The normal loss in process 1 is 10% of input, and there are no expected losses in the other processes. Scrap value in process 1 is £0.50 per litre. The costs incurred in process 1 are apportioned to each product according to the volume of output of each product. Production overhead is absorbed as a percentage of direct wages.

Data in respect of the month of October:

| | Process | | | | | |
| | 1 | 2 | 3 | 4 | 5 | Total |
| --- | --- | --- | --- | --- | --- | --- |
| | (£000) | (£000) | (£000) | (£000) | (£000) | (£000) |
| Direct materials at £1.25 per litre | 100 | | | | | 100 |
| Direct wages | 48 | 12 | 8 | 4 | 16 | 88 |
| Production overhead | | | | | | 66 |

| | Product | | | |
| | A | B | C | D |
| --- | --- | --- | --- | --- |
| Output (litres) | 22 000 | 20 000 | 10 000 | 18 000 |
| Selling price (£) | 4.00 | 3.00 | 2.00 | 5.00 |
| Estimated sales value at end of Process 1 (£) | 2.50 | 2.80 | 1.20 | 3.00 |

You are required to:

(a) calculate the profit or loss for each product for the month, assuming all output is sold at the normal selling price; (4 marks)

(b) suggest and evaluate an alternative production strategy which would optimize profit for the month. It should not be assumed that the output of process 1 can be changed; (12 marks)

(c) suggest to what management should devote its attention, if it is to achieve the potential benefit indicated in (b). (4 marks)
(Total 20 marks)
*CIMA P1 Cost Accounting 2*

**6.13\* Intermediate: Calculation of cost per unit and decision on further processing**
A chemical company carries on production operations in two processes. Materials first pass through process I, where a compound is produced. A loss in weight takes place at the start of processing. The following data, which can be assumed to be representative, relates to the month just ended:

**Quantities (kg):**

| | |
| --- | --- |
| Material input | 200 000 |
| Opening work in process (half processed) | 40 000 |
| Work completed | 160 000 |
| Closing work in process (two-thirds processed) | 30 000 |

**Costs (£):**

| | |
| --- | --- |
| Material input | 75 000 |
| Processing costs | 96 000 |
| Opening work in process: | |
| Materials | 20 000 |
| Processing costs | 12 000 |

Any quantity of the compound can be sold for £1.60 per kg. Alternatively, it can be transferred to process II for further processing and packing to be sold as Starcomp for £2.00 per kg. Further materials are added in process II such that for every kg of compound used, 2 kg of Starcomp result.

Of the 160 000 kg per month of work completed in process I, 40 000 kg are sold as compound and 120 000 kg are passed through process II for sale as Starcomp. Process II has facilities to handle up to 160 000 kg of compound per month if required. The monthly costs incurred in process II (other than the cost of the compound) are:

| | 120 000 kg of compound input | 160 000 kg of compound input |
| --- | --- | --- |
| Materials (£) | 120 000 | 160 000 |
| Processing costs (£) | 120 000 | 140 000 |

Required:

(a) Determine, using the average method, the cost per kg of compound in process I, and the value of both work completed and closing work in process for the month just ended. (11 marks)

(b) Demonstrate that it is worth while further processing 120 000 kg of compound. (5 marks)

(c) Calculate the minimum acceptable selling price per kg, if a potential buyer could be found for the additional output of Starcomp that could be produced with the remaining compound. (6 marks)
(Total 22 marks)
*ACCA Level 1 Costing*

**6.14\* Intermediate: Profitability analysis and a decision on further processing**
C Ltd operates a process which produces three joint products. In the period just ended costs of production totalled £509 640. Output from the process during the period was:

| | |
| --- | --- |
| Product W | 276 000 kilos |
| Product X | 334 000 kilos |
| Product Y | 134 000 kilos |

There were no opening stocks of the three products. Products W and X are sold in this state.

Product Y is subjected to further processing. Sales of Products W and X during the period were:

| | | |
|---|---|---|
| Product W | 255 000 kilos at £0.945 per kilo |
| Product X | 312 000 kilos at £0.890 per kilo |

128 000 kilos of Product Y were further processed during the period. The balance of the period production of the three products W, X and Y remained in stock at the end of the period. The value of closing stock of individual products is calculated by apportioning costs according to weight of output.

The additional costs in the period of further processing Product Y, which is converted into Product Z, were:

| | |
|---|---|
| Direct labour | £10 850 |
| Production overhead | £7 070 |

96 000 kilos of Product Z were produced from the 128 000 kilos of Product Y. A by-product BP is also produced which can be sold for £0.12 per kilo. 8000 kilos of BP were produced and sold in the period.

Sales of Product Z during the period were 94 000 kilos, with a total revenue of £100 110. Opening stock of Product Z was 8000 kilos, valued at £8640. The FIFO method is used for pricing transfers of Product Z to cost of sales.

Selling and administration costs are charged to all main products when sold, at 10% of revenue.

Required:

(a) Prepare a profit and loss account for the period, identifying separately the profitability of each of the three main products.

(14 marks)

(b) C Ltd has now received an offer from another company to purchase the total output of Product Y (i.e. before further processing) for £0.62 per kilo. Calculate the viability of this alternative. (5 marks)

(c) Discuss briefly the methods of, and rationale for, joint cost apportionment. (6 marks)

(Total 25 marks)

*ACCA Level 1 Cost and Management Accounting 1*

**6.15\* Advanced: Calculation of joint product costs and the evaluation of an incremental order**
Rayman Company produces three chemical products, J1X, J2Y and B1Z. Raw materials are processed in a single plant to produce two inter-mediate products, J1 and J2, in fixed proportions. There is no market for these two intermediate products. J1 is processed further through process X to yield the product J1X, product J2 is converted into J2Y by a separate finishing process Y. The Y finishing process produces both J2Y and a waste material, B1, which has no market value. The Rayman Company can convert B1, after additional processing through process Z, into a saleable by-product, B1Z. The company can sell as much B1Z as it can produce at a price of £1.50 per kg.

At normal levels of production and sales, 600 000 kg of the common input material are processed each month. There are 440 000 kg and 110 000 kg respectively, of the intermediate products J1 and J2, produced from this level of input. After the separate finishing processes, fixed proportions of J1X, J2Y and B1Z emerge, as shown below with current market prices (all losses are normal losses):

| Product | Quantity kg | Market Price per kg |
|---|---|---|
| J1X | 400 000 | £2.425 |
| J2Y | 100 000 | £4.50 |
| B1Z | 10 000 | £1.50 |

At these normal volumes, materials and processing costs are as follows:

| | Common Plant Facility | Separate Finishing Processess | | |
|---|---|---|---|---|
| | | X | Y | Z |
| | (£000) | (£000) | (£000) | (£000) |
| Direct materials | 320 | 110 | 15 | 1.0 |
| Direct labour | 150 | 225 | 90 | 5.5 |
| Variable overhead | 30 | 50 | 25 | 0.5 |
| Fixed overhead | 50 | 25 | 5 | 3.0 |
| Total | 550 | 410 | 135 | 10.0 |

Selling and administrative costs are entirely fixed and cannot be traced to any of the three products.

Required:

(a) Draw a diagram which shows the flow of these products, through the processes, label the diagram and show the quantities involved in normal operation. (2 marks)

(b) Calculate the *cost per unit* of the finished products J1X and J2Y and the *total manufacturing profit*, for the month, attributed to each product assuming all joint costs are allocated based on:

   (i)   physical units           (3 marks)

   (ii)  net realizable value     (4 marks)

and comment briefly on the two methods.

                                   (3 marks)

NB All losses are normal losses.

(c)  A new customer has approached Rayman wishing to purchase 10 000 kg of J2Y for £4.00 per kg. This is extra to the present level of business indicated above.

     Advise the management how they may respond to this approach by:

     (i)  Developing a financial evaluation of the offer.                 (4 marks)

     (ii)  Clarifying any assumptions and further questions which may apply.    (4 marks)

                              (Total 20 marks)

*ACCA Paper 8 Managerial Finance*

## 6.16* Advanced: Joint cost apportionment and decision-making

Hawkins Ltd produces two joint products, Boddie and Soull. A further product, Threekeys, is also made as a by-product of one of the processes for making Soull. Each product is sold in bottles of one litre capacity.

It is now January 2001. You are a cost accountant for Hawkins Ltd. You have been instructed to allocate the company's joint costs for 2000 between Boddie and Soull, but *not* to the by-product Threekeys.

During 2000, 2 000 000 litres of a raw material, Necktar, costing £3 000 000, were processed in Department Alpha with no wastage. The processing costs were £1 657 000.

50% of the output of Department Alpha was unfinished Boddie, for which there was no external market. It was transferred to Department Beta, where it was further processed at an additional cost of £8 100 000. Normal wastage by evaporation was 16% of the input of unfinished Boddie. The remaining good output of finished Boddie was sold for £10 per litre in the outside market.

The other 50% of the output from the joint process in Department Alpha was in the form of processed Necktar. It was all transferred to Department Gamma, as there was no outside market for processed Necktar. In Department Gamma it was further processed, with no wastage, at a cost of £30 900 000.

72% of the output of Department Gamma was in the form of unfinished Soull, for which there was no external market. It was transferred to Department Delta, where it was subjected to a finishing process at a further cost of £719 000. Normal spoilage of $16\frac{2}{3}$% of the input to the finishing process was experienced. The spoiled material was disposed of without charge, as effluent. The remaining finished Soull was sold in the outside market for £60 per litre.

The remaining 28% of the output of Department Gamma was in the form of finished Threekeys, the by-product. It was sold in the outside market for £8 per litre, but due to its dangerous nature special delivery costs of £70 000 were incurred in respect of it.

You are required:

(a)  to allocate the appropriate joint costs between Boddie and Soull on the basis of relative sales value, treating the net realizable value of Threekeys as an addition to the sales value of Soull,         (6 marks)

(b)  to prepare a statement showing the profit or loss attributed to each of the three products and the total profit or loss, for 2000, on the basis of the information above and allocating joint costs as in (a) above,     (4 marks)

(c)  to show with reasons whether Hawkins Ltd should continue to produce all three products in 2001, assuming that input/output relationships, prices and sales volumes do not change.

                                 (3 marks)

*ICAEW Management Accounting*

## 6.17 Advanced: Joint cost stock valuation and decision-making

Milo plc has a number of chemical processing plants in the UK. At one of these plants it takes an annual input of 400 000 gallons of raw material A and converts it into two liquid products, B and C.

The standard yield from one gallon of material A is 0.65 gallons of B and 0.3 gallons of C. Product B is processed further, without volume loss, and then sold as product D. Product C has hitherto been sold without further processing. In the year ended 31 July 2000, the cost of material A was £20 per gallon. The selling price of product C was £5 per gallon and transport costs from plant to customer were £74 000.

Negotiations are taking place with Takeup Ltd who would purchase the total production of product C for the years ending 31 July 2001 and 2002 provided it was converted to product E by further processing. It is unlikely that the contract would be renewed after 31 July 2002. New specialized transport costing £120 000 and special vats costing £80 000 will have to be acquired if the contract is to be undertaken. The vats will be installed in part of the existing factory that is presently unused and for which no use has been forecast for the next three years. Both transport and vats will have no residual value at the end of the contract. The company uses straight line depreciation.

Projected data for 2001 and 2002 are as follows:

| | Liquid A | Liquid D | Liquid E |
|---|---|---|---|
| Amount processed (gallons) | 400 000 | | |
| Processing costs (£): | | | |
| Cost of liquid A per gallon | 20 | | |
| Wages to split-off | 400 000 p.a. | | |
| Overheads to split-off | 250 000 p.a. | | |
| Further processing | | | |
| Materials per gallon | | 3.50 | 3.30 |
| Wages per gallon | | 2.50 | 1.70 |
| Overheads | | 52 000 p.a. | 37 000 p.a. |
| Selling costs (£): | | | |
| Total expenses | — | 125 000 p.a. | — |
| Selling price per gallon (£) | | 40.00 | 15.50 |

Total plant administration costs are £95 000 p.a.

You are required to:
(a) Show whether or not Milo plc should accept the contract and produce liquid E in 2001 and 2002. (5 marks)
(b) Prepare a pro forma income statement which can be used to evaluate the performance of the individual products sold, assuming all liquid processed is sold, in the financial year to 31 July 2001,
   (i) assuming liquids D and C are sold,
   (ii) assuming liquids D and E are sold.
   Give reasons for the layout adopted and comment on the apportionment of pre-separation costs. (12 marks)
(c) Calculate, assuming that 10 000 gallons of liquid C remain unsold at 31 July 2000, and using the FIFO basis for inventory valuation, what would be the valuation of:
   (i) the stock of liquid C, and
   (ii) 10 000 gallons of liquid E after conversion from liquid C. (4 marks)

(d) Calculate an inventory valuation at replacement cost of 10 000 gallons of liquid E in stock at 31 July 2001, assuming that the cost of material A is to be increased by 25% from that date; and comment on the advisability of using replacement cost for inventory valuation purposes in the monthly management accounts. (4 marks)
Note: Ignore taxation. (Total 25 marks)
*ICAEW P2 Management Accounting*

## 6.18 Advanced: Cost per unit calculation and decision-making
A chemical company has a contract to supply annually 3600 tonnes of product A at £24 a tonne and 4000 tonnes of product B at £14.50 a tonne. The basic components for these products are obtained from a joint initial distillation process. From this joint distillation a residue is produced which is processed to yield 380 tonnes of by-product Z. By-product Z is sold locally at £5 a tonne and the net income is credited to the joint distillation process.

The budget for the year ending 30 June 2001 includes the following data:

| | | Separable cost | |
|---|---|---|---|
| | Joint Process | Product A | Product B | By-product Z |
| Variable cost per tonne of input (£) | 5 | 11 | 2 | 1 |
| Fixed costs for year (£) | 5000 | 4000 | 8000 | 500 |
| Evaporation loss in process (% of input) | 6 | 10 | 20 | 5 |

Since the budget was compiled it has been decided that an extensive five-week overhaul of the joint distillation plant will be necessary during the year. This will cost an additional £17 000 in repair costs and reduce all production in the year by 10%. Supplies of the products can be imported to meet the contract commitment at a cost of £25 a tonne for A and £15 a tonne for B.

Experiments have also shown that the joint distillation plant operations could be changed during the year such that either:
(i) The output of distillate for product A would increase by 200 tonnes with a corresponding reduction in product B distillate. This change would increase the joint distillation variable costs for the whole of that operation by 2%.
or

(ii) The residue for by-product Z could be mixed with distillate for products A and B proportionate to the present output of these products. By intensifying the subsequent processing for products A and B acceptable quality could be obtained. The intensified operation would increase product A and B separable fixed costs by 5% and increase the evaporation loss for the whole operation to 11% and 21% respectively.

You are required to:
(a) calculate on the basis of the original budget:
  (i) the unit costs of products A and B; and
  (ii) the total profit for the year;
(b) calculate the change in the unit costs of products A and B based on the reduced production;
(c) calculate the profit for the year if the shortfall of production is made up by imported products;
(d) advise management whether either of the alternative distillation operations would improve the profitability calculated under (c) and whether you recommend the use of either.
(30 marks)
*CIMA P3 Management Accounting*

## 6.19* Advanced: Profitability analysis including an apportionment of joint costs and identification of relevant costs/revenues for a price/output decision

A company manufactures two joint products in a single process. One is sold as a garden fertilizer, the other is a synthetic fuel which is sold to external customers but which can also be used to heat greenhouses in which the company grows fruit and vegetables all year round as a subsidiary market venture. Information relating to the previous 12 month period is as follows:
(i) 1 600 000 kilos of garden fertilizer were produced and then sold at £3.00 per kilo. Joint costs are apportioned between the garden fertilizer and the synthetic fuel on a physical units (weight) basis. The fertilizer has a contribution to sales ratio of 40% after such apportionment. There are no direct costs of fertilizer sales or production.
(ii) The synthetic fuel represents 20% of the total weight of output from the manufacturing process. A wholesaler bought 160 000 kilos at £1.40 per kilo under a long-term contract which stipulates that its availability to him will not be reduced below 100 000 kilos per annum. There is no other external market for the fuel. Fixed administrative, selling and

distribution costs incurred specifically as a result of the fuel sales to the wholesaler totalled £40 000. That part of the fuel production which was sold to the wholesaler, incurred additional variable costs for packaging of £1.20 per kilo.
(iii) The remaining synthetic fuel was used to heat the company greenhouses. The greenhouses produced 5 kilos of fruit and vegetables per kilo of fuel. The fruit and vegetables were sold at an average price of £0.50 per kilo. Total direct costs of fruit and vegetable production were £520 000. Direct costs included a fixed labour cost of £100 000 which is avoidable if fruit and vegetable production ceases, the remainder being variable with the quantity produced.

A notional fuel charge of £1.40 per kilo of fuel is made to fruit and vegetable production. This notional charge is in addition to the direct costs detailed above.
(iv) Further company fixed costs were apportioned to the products as follows:

|  | (£) |
| --- | --- |
| Garden fertilizer | 720 000 |
| Synthetic fuel | 18 000 |
| Fruit and vegetables | 90 000 |

The above data were used to produce a profit and loss analysis for the 12 month period for each of three areas of operation viz.
1. Garden fertilizer.
2. Synthetic fuel (including external sales and transfers to the greenhouses at £1.40 per kilo).
3. Fruit and vegetables (incorporating the deduction of any notional charges).

Required:
(a) Prepare a summary statement showing the profit or loss reported in each of the three areas of operation detailed above. (8 marks)
(b) Calculate the percentage reduction in the fixed costs of £40 000 which would have been required before the synthetic fuel sales for the previous 12 month period would have resulted in a net benefit to the company.
(3 marks)
(c) Calculate the net benefit or loss which sales of fruit and vegetables caused the company in the previous 12 month period. (3 marks)
(d) Advise management on the fruit and vegetable price strategy for the coming year if fruit and vegetable production/sales could be expanded according to the following price/demand pattern:

Sales (000 kilos) 1200 1300 1400 1500 1600
Average selling
price/kilo (£)   0.50 0.495 0.485 0.475 0.465

All other costs, prices and quantities will remain unchanged during the coming year. The wholesaler will continue to purchase all available synthetic fuel not used in the greenhouses.

(8 marks)
(Total 22 marks)
*ACCA Level 2 Management Accounting*

## 6.20* Advanced: Calculation of cost per unit, break-even point and recommended selling price

Amongst its products a chemical company markets two concentrated liquid fertilizers – type P for flowers and type Q for vegetables. In 2001 total sales are expected to be restricted by forecast sales of type Q which are limited to 570 000 litres for the year. At this level the plant capacity will be under-utilized by 20%.

The fertilizers are manufactured jointly as follows:

| | |
|---|---|
| Mixing: | Raw materials A and B are mixed together in equal amounts and filtered. After filtering there is a sale-able residue, X, amounting to 5% of the input materials. |
| Distillation: | The mixed materials are heated and there is an evaporation loss of 10%. The remaining liquid distils into one-third each of an extract P, an extract Q and a by-product Y. |
| Blending: | Two parts of raw material C are blended with one part of extract P to form the fertilizer type P. One part of raw material D is blended with one part of extract Q to form the fertilizer type Q. |

Fertilizer type P is filled into 3-litre cans and labelled. Fertilizer type Q is filled into 6-litre preprinted cans. Both are then ready for sale.

The costs involved are as under:

| Raw material | Cost per 100 litres (£) |
|---|---|
| A | 25 |
| B | 12 |
| C | 20 |
| D | 55 |

| Cans | Cost each (£) |
|---|---|
| 3-litre | 0.32 |
| 6-litre | 0.50 |

| Labels | Cost per 1000 (£) |
|---|---|
| For 3-litre cans | 3.33 |

Manufacturing costs:

| | per 100 litres of input processed | | |
|---|---|---|---|
| | Direct wages (£) | Variable overhead (£) | Fixed overhead per year (£) |
| Mixing | 2.75 | 1.00 | 6 000 |
| Distilling | 3.00 | 2.00 | 20 000 |
| Blending | 5.00 | 2.00 | 33 250 |

The residue X and by-product Y are both sold to local companies at £0.03 and £0.04 per litre respectively. Supplies are collected in bulk by the buyers using their own transport. The sales revenue is credited to the process at which the material arises.

Product costs are apportioned entirely to the two main products on the basis of their output from each process.

No inventories of part-finished materials are held at any time.

The fertilizers are sold through agents on the basis of list price less 25%. Of the net selling price, selling and distribution costs amount to $13\frac{1}{3}$% and profit to 20%. Of the selling and distribution costs 70% are variable and the remainder fixed.

You are required to:
(a) calculate separately for the fertilizers type P and type Q for the year 2001:
    (i)   total manufacturing cost,
    (ii)  manufacturing cost per litre,
    (iii) list price per litre,
    (iv)  profit for the year;                     (18 marks)
(b) calculate the break-even price per litre to manufacture and supply an extra 50 000 litres of fertilizer type Q for export and which would incur variable selling and distri-bution costs of £2000;            (8 marks)
(c) state the price you would recommend the

company should quote per litre for this export business, with a brief explanation for your decision. (4 marks)
(Total 30 marks)
*CIMA P3 Management Accounting*

### 6.21 Advanced: Calculation of cost per unit, break-even point and a recommended selling price

A chemical company produces amongst its product range two industrial cleaning fluids, A and B. These products are manufactured jointly. In 2001 total sales are expected to be restricted because home trade outlets for fluid B are limited to 54 000 gallons for the year. At this level plant capacity will be under-utilized by 25%.

From the information given below you are required to:
(a) draw a flow diagram of the operations;
(b) calculate separately for fluids A and B for the year:
    (i) total manufacturing cost;
    (ii) manufacturing cost per gallon;
    (iii) list price per gallon;
    (iv) profit for the year;
(c) calculate the break-even price per gallon to manufacture an extra 3000 gallons of fluid B for export and which would incur selling, distribution and administration costs of £1260;
(d) state the price you would recommend the company should quote per gallon for this export business, with a brief explanation for your decision.

The following data are given:

1. Description of processes

Process 1: Raw materials L and M are mixed together and filtered. There is an evaporation loss of 10%.

Process 2: The mixture from Process 1 is boiled and this reduces the volume by 20%. The remaining liquid distils into 50% extract A, 25% extract B, and 25% by-product C.

Process 3: Two parts of extract A are blended with one part of raw material N, and one part of extract B with one part of raw material N, to form respectively fluids A and B.

Process 4: Fluid A is filled into one-gallon labelled bottles and fluid B into six-

gallon preprinted drums and they are then both ready for sale. One percent wastage in labels occurs in this process.

2. Costs

| | Cost per gallon (£) |
|---|---|
| Raw material L | 0.20 |
| Raw material M | 0.50 |
| Raw material N | 2.00 |

| | Cost (£) |
|---|---|
| Containers: 1-gallon bottles | 0.27 each |
|     6-gallon drums | 5.80 each |
| Bottle labels, per thousand | 2.20 |

| Direct wages: | Per gallon of input processed (£) |
|---|---|
| Process 1 | 0.11 |
| Process 2 | 0.15 |
| Process 3 | 0.20 |
| Process 4 | 0.30 |

Manufacturing overhead:

| Process | Fixed per annum (£) | Variable, per gallon of input processed (£) |
|---|---|---|
| 1 | 6 000 | 0.04 |
| 2 | 20 250 | 0.20 |
| 3 | 19 500 | 0.10 |
| 4 | 14 250 | 0.10 |

By-product C is collected in bulk by a local company which pays £0.50 per gallon for it and the income is credited to process 2.

Process costs are apportioned entirely to the two main products on the basis of their output from each process.

No inventories of part-finished materials are held at any time.

Fluid A is sold through agents on the basis of list price less 20% and fluid B at list price less 33$\frac{1}{3}$%.

Of the net selling price, profit amounts to 8%, selling and distribution costs to 12% and administration costs to 5%.

Taxation should be ignored. (30 marks)
*CIMA P3 Management Accounting*

# Income effects of alternative cost accumulation systems

In the previous chapters we looked at the procedures necessary to ascertain product or job costs for inventory valuation to meet the requirements of external reporting. The approach that we adopted was to allocate all manufacturing cost to products, and to value unsold stocks at their total cost of manufacture. Non-manufacturing costs were not allocated to the products but were charged directly to the profit statement and excluded from the inventory valuation. A costing system based on these principles is known as an absorption or full costing system.

In this chapter we are going to look at an alternative costing system known as variable costing, marginal costing or direct costing. Under this alternative system, only variable manufacturing costs are assigned to products and included in the inventory valuation. Fixed manufacturing costs are not allocated to the product, but are considered as period costs and charged directly to the profit statement. Both absorption costing and variable costing systems are in complete agreement regarding the treatment of non-manufacturing costs as period costs. The disagreement between the proponents of absorption costing and the proponents of variable costing is concerned with whether or not manufacturing fixed overhead should be regarded as a period cost or a product cost. An illustration of the different treatment of fixed manufacturing overhead for both absorption and variable costing systems is shown in Exhibit 7.1.

## Learning objectives

After studying this chapter, you should be able to:

● explain the differences between an absorption costing and a variable costing system;

● prepare profit statements based on a variable costing and absorption costing system;

● explain the difference in profits between variable and absorption costing profit calculations;

● explain the arguments for and against variable and absorption costing;

● distinguish between relevant costing and variable and absorption costing;

● describe the various denominator levels that can be used with an absorption costing system;

● explain how the choice of a denominator level affects reported profits and inventory valuations.

# Problem of terminology

Absorption costing is sometimes referred to as full costing. You can avoid becoming confused by this if you simply remember that absorption costing and full costing are used to refer to a system in which all the fixed manufacturing overheads are allocated to products. The alternative system, which assigns only variable manufacturing costs to products, should correctly be referred to as variable costing, although the terms direct costing and marginal costing are also frequently used. This is unfortunate, since neither direct costs nor marginal costs are quite the same as variable costs. Direct costs are those that can be specifically identified with a product; they include direct labour and materials but in many situations direct labour may not vary in the short term with changes in output. So to use the term 'direct costing' when it specifically includes a non-variable item (that is, direct labour) is not at all appropriate. The term 'marginal costing' is also inappropriate, since economists use this term to describe the cost of producing one additional unit. Applying this definition may lead to fixed costs being included in a situation where the production of an additional unit will result in an increase in fixed costs, for example the appointment of an additional supervisor, or an increase in capacity due to the purchase of an additional machine. Many accountants use the term 'marginal cost' to mean average variable cost. Because marginal cost may be interpreted in different ways by accountants and economists, it is better not to use the term when referring to stock valuation. For all these reasons, we shall be using the term 'variable costing' throughout this book to describe a system of costing where only the variable manufacturing costs are allocated to the product.

# External and internal reporting

Many writers have argued the cases for and against variable costing for inventory valuation for external reporting. One important requirement for external reporting is consistency. It would be unacceptable if companies changed their methods of inventory valuation from year to year. In addition, inter-company comparison would be difficult if some companies valued their stocks on an absorption cost basis while others did so on a variable cost basis. Furthermore, the users of external accounting reports need reassurance that the published financial statements have been prepared in accordance with generally accepted standards of good accounting practice. Therefore there is a strong case for the acceptance of one method of stock valuation for external reporting. In the UK a Statement of Standard Accounting Practice on Stocks and Work in Progress was published by the Accounting Standards Committee (SSAP 9). This states:

> In order to match costs and revenue, cost of stocks and work in progress should comprise that expenditure which has been incurred in the normal course of business in bringing the product or service to its present location and condition. Such costs will include all related production overheads, even though these may accrue on a time basis.

The effect of this statement in SSAP 9 was to require absorption costing for external reporting and for non-manufacturing costs to be treated as period costs. The external financial reporting regulations in most other countries also require that companies adopt absorption costing. One notable exception is Finland where the country's accounting regulations and institutions have not forced companies to adopt absorption costing for external reporting. As a result variable costing is extensively used by Finnish companies (Virtanen *et al.*, 1996). However, it is not widely used in other countries (see Exhibit 7.4).

**EXHIBIT   7.1**

*Absorption
and variable
costing systems
cost*

In spite of the fact that absorption costing is required for
external reporting, the variable costing versus absorption costing debate is still of considerable importance for internal
reporting. Management normally require profit statements at

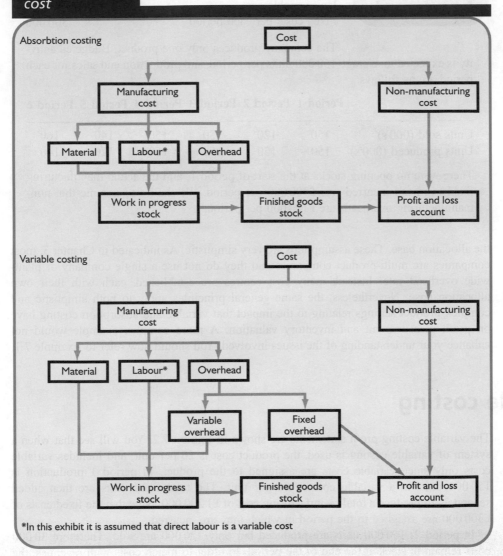

*In this exhibit it is assumed that direct labour is a variable cost

monthly or quarterly intervals, and will no doubt wish to receive separate profit statements
for each major product group or segment of the business. This information is particularly
useful in evaluating the performance of divisional managers. Management must therefore
decide whether absorption costing or variable costing provides the more meaningful
information in assessing the economic and managerial performance of the different
segments of the business.

However, before discussing the arguments for and against absorption and variable
costing, let us look at a simple illustration of both methods using Example 7.1. To keep
things simple we shall assume that the company in this example produces only one product
using a single overhead rate for the company as a whole, with units of output being used as

**EXAMPLE 7.1**

The following information is available for periods 1–6 for the Samuelson Company:

|  | (£) |
|---|---|
| Unit selling price | 10 |
| Unit variable cost | 6 |
| Fixed costs per each period | 300 000 |

The company produces only one product. Budgeted activity is expected to average 150 000 units per period, and production and sales for each period are as follows:

|  | Period 1 | Period 2 | Period 3 | Period 4 | Period 5 | Period 6 |
|---|---|---|---|---|---|---|
| Units sold (000's) | 150 | 120 | 180 | 150 | 140 | 160 |
| Units produced (000's) | 150 | 150 | 150 | 150 | 170 | 140 |

There were no opening stocks at the start of period 1, and the actual manufacturing fixed overhead incurred was £300 000 per period. We shall also assume that non-manufacturing overheads are £100 000 per period.

the allocation base. These assumptions are very simplistic. As indicated in Chapter 3, most companies are multi-product companies and they do not use a single company or plant-wide overhead rate. Instead, many cost centres are established, each with their own allocation base. Nevertheless, the same general principles apply to both simplistic and complex product settings relating to the impact that variable and absorption costing have on profit measurement and inventory valuation. A more complex example would not enhance your understanding of the issues involved. You should now refer to Example 7.1.

# Variable costing

The variable costing profit statements are shown in Exhibit 7.2. You will see that when a system of variable costing is used, the product cost is £6 per unit, and includes variable costs only since variable costs are assigned to the product. In period 1 production is 150 000 units at a variable cost of £6 per unit. The total fixed costs are then added separately to produce a total manufacturing cost of £1 200 000. Note that the fixed costs of £300 000 are assigned to the period in which they are incurred.

In period 2, 150 000 units are produced but only 120 000 are sold. Therefore 30 000 units remain in stock at the end of the period. In order to match costs with revenues, the sales of 120 000 units should be matched with costs for 120 000. As 150 000 units were produced, we need to value the 30 000 units in stock and deduct this sum from the production cost. Using the variable costing system, the 30 000 units in stock are valued at £6 per unit. A closing inventory of £180 000 will then be deducted from the production costs, giving a cost of sales figure of £720 000. Note that the closing inventory valuation does not include any fixed overheads.

The 30 000 units of closing inventory in period 2 becomes the opening inventory for period 3 and therefore an expense for this period. The production cost for the 150 000 units made in period 3 is added to this opening inventory valuation. The overall effect is that costs for 180 000 units are matched against sales for 180 000 units. The profits for periods 4–6 are calculated in the same way.

**EXHIBIT 7.2**

*Variable costing statements*

| | Period 1 (£000's) | Period 2 (£000's) | Period 3 (£000's) | Period 4 (£000's) | Period 5 (£000's) | Period 6 (£000's) |
|---|---|---|---|---|---|---|
| Opening stock | — | — | 180 | — | — | 180 |
| Production cost | 900 | 900 | 900 | 900 | 1020 | 840 |
| Closing stock | — | (180) | — | — | (180) | (60) |
| Cost of sales | 900 | 720 | 1080 | 900 | 840 | 960 |
| Fixed costs | 300 | 300 | 300 | 300 | 300 | 300 |
| Total costs | 1200 | 1020 | 1380 | 1200 | 1140 | 1260 |
| Sales | 1500 | 1200 | 1800 | 1500 | 1400 | 1600 |
| Gross profit | 300 | 180 | 420 | 300 | 260 | 340 |
| Less non-manufacturing costs | 100 | 100 | 100 | 100 | 100 | 100 |
| Net profit | 200 | 80 | 320 | 200 | 160 | 240 |

# Absorption costing

Let us now consider in Exhibit 7.3 the profit calculations when closing stocks are valued on an absorption costing basis. With the absorption costing method, a share of the fixed production overheads are allocated to individual products and are included in the products' production cost. Fixed overheads are assigned to products by establishing overhead absorption rates as described in Chapter 3. To establish the overhead rate we must divide the fixed overheads of £300 000 for the period by an appropriate denominator level. Most companies use an annual budgeted activity measure of the overhead allocation base as the denominator level (we shall discuss the different approaches that can be used for determining denominator levels later in the chapter). Our allocation base in Example 7.1 is units of output and we shall assume that the annual budgeted output is 1 800 000 units giving an average for each monthly period of 150 000 units. Therefore the budgeted fixed overhead rate is £2 per unit (£300 000/150 000 units). The product cost now consists of a variable cost (£6) plus a fixed manufacturing cost (£2), making a total of £8 per unit. Hence, the production cost for period 1 is £1 200 000 (150 000 units at £8).

Now compare the absorption costing statement (Exhibit 7.3) with the variable costing statement (Exhibit 7.2) for period 1. With absorption costing, the fixed cost is included in the production cost figure, whereas with variable costing only the variable cost is included. With variable costing, the fixed cost is allocated separately and is not included in the cost of sales figure. Note also that the closing inventory of 30 000 units for period 2 is valued at £8 per unit in the absorption costing statement, whereas the closing inventory is valued at only £6 in the variable costing statement.

In calculating profits, the matching principle that has been applied in the absorption costing statement is the same way as that described for variable costing. However, complications arise in periods 5 and 6; in period 5, 170 000 units were produced, so the

**EXHIBIT 7.3**

*Absorption costing statements*

production cost of £1 360 000 includes fixed overheads of £340 000 (170 000 units at £2). The total fixed overheads incurred for the period are only £300 000, so £40 000 too much has been allocated. This over recovery of fixed overhead

| | Period 1 (£000's) | Period 2 (£000's) | Period 3 (£000's) | Period 4 (£000's) | Period 5 (£000's) | Period 6 (£000's) |
|---|---|---|---|---|---|---|
| Opening stock | — | — | 240 | — | — | 240 |
| Production cost | 1200 | 1200 | 1200 | 1200 | 1360 | 1120 |
| Closing stock | — | (240) | — | — | (240) | (80) |
| Cost of sales | 1200 | 960 | 1440 | 1200 | 1120 | 1280 |
| Adjustments for under-/(over) recovery of overhead | — | — | — | — | (40) | 20 |
| Total costs | 1200 | 960 | 1440 | 1200 | 1080 | 1300 |
| Sales | 1500 | 1200 | 1800 | 1500 | 1400 | 1600 |
| Gross profit | 300 | 240 | 360 | 300 | 320 | 300 |
| Less non-manufacturing costs | 100 | 100 | 100 | 100 | 100 | 100 |
| Net profit | 200 | 140 | 260 | 200 | 220 | 200 |

is recorded as a period cost adjustment. (A full explanation of under and over recoveries of overheads and the reasons for period cost adjustments was presented in Chapter 3; if you are unsure of this concept, please refer back now to the section headed 'Under and over recovery of overheads'.) Note also that the under or over recovery of fixed overheads is also called volume variance.

In period 6, 140 000 units were produced at a cost of £1 120 000, which included only £280 000 (140 000 units at £2) for fixed overheads. As a result, there is an under recovery of £20 000, which is written off as a period cost. You can see that an under or over recovery of fixed overhead occurs whenever actual production differs from the budged average level of activity of 150 000 units, since the calculation of the fixed overhead rate of £2 per unit was based on the assumption that actual production would be 150 000 units per period. Note that both variable and absorption costing systems do not assign non-manufacturing costs to products for stock valuation.

# Variable costing and absorption costing: a comparison of their impact on profit

A comparison of the variable costing and absorption costing statements produced from the information contained in Example 7.1 reveals the following differences in profit calculations:

(a) The profits calculated under the absorption costing and variable costing systems are identical for periods 1 and 4.

(b) The absorption costing profits are higher than the variable costing profits in periods 2 and 5.

(c) The variable costing profits are higher than the absorption costing profits in periods 3 and 6.

Let us now consider each of these in a little more detail.

## PRODUCTION EQUALS SALES

In periods 1 and 4 the profits are the same for both methods of costing; in both periods production is equal to sales, and inventories will neither increase nor decrease. Therefore if opening inventories exist, the same amount of fixed overhead will be carried forward as an expense to be included in the current period in the opening inventory valuation as will be deducted in the closing inventory valuation from the production cost figure. The overall effect is that, with an absorption costing system, the only fixed overhead that will be included as an expense for the period will be the amount of fixed overhead that is incurred for the period. Thus, whenever sales are equal to production the profits will be the same for both the absorption costing and variable costing systems.

## PRODUCTION EXCEEDS SALES

In periods 2 and 5 the absorption costing system produces higher profits; in both periods production exceeds sales. Profits are higher for absorption costing when production is in excess of sales, because inventories are increasing. The effect of this is that a greater amount of fixed overheads in the closing inventory is being deducted from the expenses of the period than is being brought forward in the opening inventory for the period. For example, in period 2 the opening inventory is zero and no fixed overheads are brought forward from the previous period. However, a closing inventory of 30 000 units means that a £60 000 fixed overhead has to be deducted from the production cost for the period. In other words, only £240 000 is being allocated for fixed overhead with the absorption costing system, whereas the variable costing system allocates the £300 000 fixed overhead incurred for the period. The effect of this is that profits are £60 000 greater with the absorption costing system. As a general rule, if production is in excess of sales, the absorption costing system will show a higher profit than the variable costing system.

## SALES EXCEED PRODUCTION

In periods 3 and 6 the variable costing system produces higher profits; in both periods sales exceed production. When this situation occurs, inventories decline and a greater amount of fixed overheads will need to be brought forward as an expense in the opening inventory than is being deducted in the closing inventory adjustment. For example, with the absorption costing system, in period 6, 30 000 units of opening inventory are brought forward, so that fixed costs of £60 000 are included in the inventory valuation. However, a closing inventory of 10 000 units requires a deduction of £20 000 fixed overheads from the production costs. The overall effect is that an additional £40 000 fixed overheads is included as an expense within the stock movements, and a total of £340 000 fixed overheads is allocated for the period. The variable costing system, on the other hand, would allocate fixed overheads for the period of only £300 000. As a result, profits are £40 000 greater with the variable costing system. As a general rule, if sales are in excess of production, the variable costing system will show a higher profit than the absorption costing system.

## IMPACT OF SALES FLUCTUATIONS

The profit calculations for an absorption costing system can produce some strange results. For example, in period 6 the sales volume has increased but profits have declined, in spite of the fact that both the selling price and the cost structure have remained unchanged. A manager whose performance is being judged in period 6 is likely to have little confidence in an accounting system that shows a decline in profits when sales volume has increased and the cost structure and selling price have not changed. The opposite occurs in period 5. In this period the sales volume declines but profit increases. The situations in periods 5 and 6 arise because the under or over recovery of fixed overhead is treated as a period cost, and such adjustments can at times give a misleading picture of profits.

In contrast, the variable costing profit calculations show that when sales volume increases profit also increases. Alternatively, when sales volume decreases, profit also decreases. These relationships continue as long as the selling price and cost structure remain unchanged. Looking again at the variable costing profit calculations, you will note that profit declines in period 5 when the sales volume declines, and increases in period 6 when the sales volume also increases. The reasons for these changes are that, with a system of variable costing, profit is a function of sales volume only, when the selling price and cost structure remain unchanged. However, with absorption costing, profit is a function of both sales volume and production volume.

# A mathematical model of the profit functions

In Appendix 7.1 the following formula is developed to model the profit function for an absorption costing system when unit costs remain unchanged throughout the period:

$$\text{Absorption costing operating profit} = (usp - uvc - fmohc/ud)us$$
$$+ (fmohc/ud)up - tfc \qquad (7.1)$$

where:

$usp$ = unit selling price
$uvc$ = unit variable cost
$fmohc$ = fixed manufacturing overhead cost for the period
$ud$ = unit denominator level used to calculate the fixed overhead rate
$us$ = units sold
$up$ = units produced
$tfc$ = total fixed costs for the period (i.e. manufacturing + non-manufacturing fixed overheads)

Applying formula 7.1 to the data given in Example 7.1 gives the following profit function:

$$(£10 - £6 - £300\,000/150\,000)us + (£300\,000/150\,000)up - (£400\,000)$$
$$= £2us + £2up - £400\,000$$

Applying the above profit function to periods 4–6 we get:

$$\text{Period } 4 = £2(150\,000) + £2(150\,000) - £400\,000 = £200\,000$$
$$\text{Period } 5 = £2(140\,000) + £2(170\,000) - £400\,000 = £220\,000$$
$$\text{Period } 6 = £2(160\,000) + £2(140\,000) - £400\,000 = £200\,000$$

When production equals sales identical profits with an absorption and variable costing system are reported. Therefore formula 7.1 converts to the following variable costing profit function if we let $us = up$:

$$\text{Variable costing operating profit} = (usp - uvc)us - tfc \qquad (7.2)$$

Using the data given in Example 7.1 the profit function is:

$$£4us - £400\,000$$

Applying the above profit function to periods 4–6 we get:

$$\text{Period } 4 = £4(150\,000) - £400\,000 = £200\,000$$
$$\text{Period } 5 = £4(140\,000) - £400\,000 = £160\,000$$
$$\text{Period } 6 = £4(160\,000) - £400\,000 = £240\,000$$

The difference between the reported operating profits for an absorption costing and a variable costing system can be derived by deducting formulae 7.2 from 7.1 giving:

$$fmohc/ud(up - us) \qquad (7.3)$$

If you look closely at the above term you will see that it represents the inventory change (in units) multiplied by the fixed manufacturing overhead rate. Applying formula 7.3 to period 5 the inventory change $(up - us)$ is 30 000 units (positive) so that absorption costing profits exceed variable costing profits by £60 000 (30 000 units at £2 overhead rate). For an explanation of how formula (7.1) is derived you should refer to Appendix 7.1.

# Some arguments in support of variable costing

## VARIABLE COSTING PROVIDES MORE USEFUL INFORMATION FOR DECISION-MAKING

The separation of fixed and variable costs helps to provide relevant information about costs for making decisions. Relevant costs are required for a variety of short-term decisions, for example whether to make a component internally or to purchase externally, as well as problems relating to product-mix. These decisions will be discussed in Chapter 9. In addition, the estimation of costs for different levels of activities requires that costs be split into their fixed and variable elements. The assumption is that only with a variable costing system will such an analysis of costs be available. It is therefore assumed that projection of future costs and revenues for different activity levels, and the use of relevant cost decision-making techniques, are possible only if a variable costing system is adopted. There is no reason, however, why an absorption costing system cannot be used for profit measurement and inventory valuation and costs can be analysed into their fixed and variable elements for decision-making. The advantage of variable costing is that the analysis of variable and fixed costs is highlighted. (Such an analysis is not a required feature of an absorption costing system.)

# VARIABLE COSTING REMOVES FROM PROFIT THE EFFECT OF INVENTORY CHANGES

We have seen that, with variable costing, profit is a function of sales volume, whereas, with absorption costing, profit is a function of both sales and production. We have also learned, using absorption costing principles, that it is possible for profit to decline when sales volumes increase. Where stock levels are likely to fluctuate significantly, profits may be distorted when they are calculated on an absorption costing basis, since the stock changes will significantly affect the amount of fixed overheads allocated to an accounting period.

Fluctuating stock levels are less likely to occur when one measures profits on an annual basis, but on a monthly or quarterly basis seasonal variations in sales may cause significant fluctuations. As profits are likely to be distorted by an absorption costing system, there are strong arguments for using variable costing methods when profits are measured at frequent intervals. Because frequent profit statements are presented only for management, the argument for variable costing is stronger for management accounting. A survey by Drury *et al.* (1993) relating to 300 UK companies reported that 97% of the companies prepared profit statements at monthly intervals. Financial accounts are presented for public release annually or at half-yearly intervals; because significant changes in stock levels are less likely on an annual basis, the argument for the use of variable costing in financial accounting is not as strong.

A further argument for using variable costing for internal reporting is that the internal profit statements may be used as a basis for measuring managerial performance. Managers may deliberately alter their inventory levels to influence profit when an absorption costing system is used; for example, it is possible for a manager to defer deliberately some of the fixed overhead allocation by unnecessarily increasing stocks over successive periods.

There is a limit, to how long managers can continue to increase stocks, and eventually the situation will arise when it is necessary to reduce them, and the deferred fixed overheads will eventually be allocated to the periods when the inventories are reduced. Nevertheless, there is likely to remain some scope for manipulating profits in the short term. Also senior management can implement control performance measures to guard against such behaviour. For example, the reporting of performance measures that monitor changes in inventory volumes will highlight those situations where managers are manipulating profits by unnecessarily increasing inventory levels.

# VARIABLE COSTING AVOIDS FIXED OVERHEADS BEING CAPITALIZED IN UNSALEABLE STOCKS

In a period when sales demand decreases, a company can end up with surplus stocks on hand. With an absorption costing system, only a portion of the fixed overheads incurred during the period will be allocated as an expense because the remainder of the fixed overhead will be included in the valuation of the surplus stocks. If these surplus stocks cannot be disposed of, the profit calculation for the current period will be misleading, since fixed overheads will have been deferred to later accounting periods. However, there may be some delay before management concludes that the stocks cannot be sold without a very large reduction in the selling price. The stocks will therefore be over-valued, and a stock write-off will be necessary in a later accounting period. The overall effect may be that the current period's profits will be overstated.

# Some arguments in support of absorption costing

## ABSORPTION COSTING DOES NOT UNDERSTATE THE IMPORTANCE OF FIXED COSTS

Some people argue that decisions based on a variable costing system may concentrate only on sales revenues and variable costs and ignore the fact that fixed costs must be met in the long run. For example, if a pricing decision is based on variable costs only, then sales revenue may be insufficient to cover all the costs. It is also argued that the use of an absorption costing system, by allocating fixed costs to a product, ensures that fixed costs will be covered. These arguments are incorrect. Absorption costing will not ensure that fixed costs will be recovered if actual sales volume is less than the estimate used to calculate the fixed overhead rate. For example, consider a situation where fixed costs are £100 000 and an estimated normal activity of 10 000 units is used to calculate the overhead rate. Fixed costs are recovered at £10 per unit. Assume that variable cost is £5 per unit and selling price is set at £20 (total cost plus one-third). If actual sales volume is 5000 units then total sales revenue will be £100 000 and total costs will be £125 000. Total costs therefore exceed total sales revenue. The argument that a variable costing system will cause managers to ignore fixed costs is based on the assumption that such managers are not very bright! A failure to consider fixed costs is due to faulty management and not to a faulty accounting system. Furthermore, using variable costing for inventory valuation and profit measurement still enables full cost information to be extracted for pricing decisions.

## ABSORPTION COSTING AVOIDS FICTITIOUS LOSSES BEING REPORTED

In a business that relies on seasonal sales and in which production is built up outside the sales season to meet demand the full amount of fixed overheads incurred will be charged, in a variable costing system, against sales. However, in those periods where production is being built up for sales in a later season, sales revenue will be low but fixed costs will be recorded as an expense. The result is that losses will be reported during out-of-season periods, and large profits will be reported in the periods when the goods are sold.

By contrast, in an absorption costing system fixed overheads will be deferred and included in the closing inventory valuation, and will be recorded as an expense only in the period in which the goods are sold. Losses are therefore unlikely to be reported in the periods when stocks are being built up. In these circumstances absorption costing appears to provide the more logical profit calculation.

## FIXED OVERHEADS ARE ESSENTIAL FOR PRODUCTION

The proponents of absorption costing argue that the production of goods is not possible if fixed manufacturing costs are not incurred. Consequently, fixed manufacturing overheads should be allocated to units produced and included in the inventory valuation.

## CONSISTENCY WITH EXTERNAL REPORTING

Top management may prefer their internal profit reporting systems to be consistent with the external financial accounting absorption costing systems so that they will be congruent with the measures used by financial markets to appraise overall company performance. In a pilot study of six UK companies Hopper *et al.* (1992) observed that senior managers are primarily interested in financial accounting information because it is perceived as having a major influence on how financial markets evaluate companies and their management. If top management believe that financial accounting information does influence share prices then they are likely to use the same rules and procedures for both internal and external profit measurement and inventory valuation so that managers will focus on the same measures as those used by financial markets. Also the fact that managerial rewards are often linked to external financial measures provides a further motivation to ensure that internal accounting systems do not conflict with external financial accounting reporting requirements.

# The variable costing versus absorption costing debate

**AR** The debate is about whether fixed manufacturing cost are costs of the product made or costs for the period in which they are incurred. The proponents of absorption costing argue that fixed manufacturing costs are a product cost, whereas the proponents of variable costing argue that such costs are a period cost. The period cost argument assumes that fixed manufacturing costs are capacity costs. They are a necessary precondition of production and expire with the passage of time regardless of production activity and they are also incurred for the benefit of operations during a given period of time. This benefit is unchanged by the actual level of operations during the period, and the benefit expires at the end of the period.

The product cost argument is based on the principle that the fixed costs are assigned to the product rather than the period, because it is the product that generates the revenue. The time period is viewed as being purely incidental to the operations of the firm. It is argued that revenue derives from the sale of the product, and therefore all the production costs must be matched with revenue in the period of sale.

## COST OBVIATION CONCEPT

The definition of an asset is critical to the debate. The American Accounting Association defined assets as aggregates of service potentials available for or beneficial to expected operations. One could say that assets have service potentials to the extent that they save costs in the future. This interpretation is called the cost obviation concept, and the proponents of variable costing have used it to argue that variable costing is superior to absorption costing. For example, Wetnight (1958) argued that variable costing meets the future benefit test better than absorption costing in the following way:

> If this test of future benefit is applied to the two methods of costing it can be seen that variable costing most closely meets the requirements. In the first place, there is a future benefit from the incurrence of variable costs. These costs will not need to be incurred in a future period. However, in the case of fixed costs, no

future benefit exists, since these cost will be incurred during the future period, no matter what the level of operations.

Horngren and Sorter (1962), writing on the cost obviation concept, state:

> If the total future cost of an enterprise will be decreased because of the presence of a given cost, the cost is relevant to the future and is an asset; if not, that cost is irrelevant and is expired.

Thus one could argue that the production of goods for stock in one period enables a firm to realize revenue in a future period without re-incurring the variable costs of producing the stock. Alternatively, the availability of stocks in one period does not stop fixed costs being incurred in a future period. Variable costs are therefore relevant to future periods but fixed costs are not. In other words, variable costs are product costs but fixed costs are period costs.

## REVENUE PRODUCTION CONCEPT

Another interpretation of the service potential of an asset is to view an asset in terms of its capacity to contribute to the production of revenue in the future. This is the **revenue production concept**. This interpretation distinguishes between assets and expenses according to whether or not the costs incurred will contribute to the realization of revenue in the future. The revenue production concept assumes that any cost essential in making a product that may reasonably be expected to be sold represents a cost of obtaining sales revenue. Hence these costs should be deferred and included in the inventory valuation so that they may be matched with revenue in the calculation of profit for the period of sale. In other words, the revenue production interpretation of service potential implies adherence to the absorption costing method of valuing inventories.

# Relevant costing

Horngren and Sorter (1962) pursued the cost obviation concept further and presented a theory of inventory valuation based on **relevant costing**. This important contribution moves away from a strict adherence to either variable costing or absorption costing methods for inventory valuation. In some circumstances only variable costs are included in the inventory valuation, while in others both fixed and variable costs are included. The decision on whether fixed manufacturing costs should be included in the inventory valuation is, therefore, not clear-cut, and Horngren and Sorter would argue that it depends on the circumstances.

Horngren and Sorter state that in using relevant costing only one basic assumption is required, and that is that a cost should be carried forward as an asset if and only if it has a favourable economic effect on expected future costs or future revenues. Therefore a cost cannot represent a future benefit if its absence will not influence the obtaining of future revenues or the incurrence of future costs. For example, if an item can be replaced and used in normal operations at zero incremental or opportunity cost, its presence or its physical amount does not represent service potential; in other words, its absence would have no impact on total future costs or revenues. Therefore, if a given cost will not influence either total future revenue or total future costs, it is not an asset.

Sorter and Horngren use an example of a paper manufacturing company with a batch A1 in stock consisting of £40 000 variable costs and £60 000 fixed production overheads. They also assume that if batch A1 was not in hand, a similar batch, A2, could be produced in the next period by utilizing otherwise idle capacity. Therefore no additional fixed costs would have to be incurred, and the total expected incremental costs of batch A2 would be the £40 000 variable production costs. It is also assumed that batches A1 and A2 cannot both be sold. The relevant costing approach would recognize only the £40 000 as representing economic benefit, and the £60 000 fixed cost cannot qualify as an economic good. If batch A1 can be replaced in normal operations at variable cost, its presence or its physical amount represents economic benefit only in the amount of variable costs that will not have to be incurred in the future. In other words, if batch A1 were not on hand, £40 000 would be the only future outlay necessary to restore the enterprise to an equivalent economic position.

Note that the relevant costing approach would support absorption costing if future sales demand exceeded productive capacity (for example, if batch A1 were not in hand, there would be no spare capacity to produce it in the next period), since future sales would be lost for ever because of a shortage of stocks. Production of batch A1 in the current period will therefore change future revenues. Hence the costs of using the capacity (i.e. the fixed costs) have a favourable economic effect on future revenues and should be included in the stock valuation.

Horngren and Sorter provide a further illustration relating to the depreciation of machinery. They argue that if depreciation is most closely related to time expiration (due to obsolescence, technical change, and so on), this depreciation cannot form part of the product cost unless the utilization of a machine in a particular period will make possible future sales that would otherwise be lost for ever. If, on the other hand, depreciation is most closely related to production rather than time, it is properly treated as a product cost because the decision to produce a unit in period 1 rather than in period 2 affects the service potential of the fixed asset. Each decision of this kind affects the asset's useful life, whereas, with time-based depreciation, such a decision has no effect on useful life. ●●●

# Alternative denominator level measures

When absorption costing systems are used estimated fixed overhead rates must be calculated. These rates will be significantly influenced by the choice of the activity level; that is the denominator activity level that is used to calculate the overhead rate. This problem applies only to fixed overheads, and the greater the proportion of fixed overheads in an organization's cost structure the more acute is the problem. Fixed costs arise from situations where resources must be acquired in discrete, not continuous, amounts in such a way that the supply of resources cannot be continuously adjusted to match the usage of resources. For example, a machine might be purchased that provides an annual capacity of 5000 machine hours but changes in sales demand may cause the annual usage to vary from 2500 to 5000 hours. It is not possible to match the supply and usage of the resource and unused capacity will arise in those periods where the resources used are less than the 5000 hours of capacity supplied.

In contrast, variable costs arise in those situations where the supply of resources can be continually adjusted to match the usage of resources. For example, the spending on energy costs associated with running machinery (i.e. the supply and resources) can be immediately reduced by 50% if resources used decline by 50% say, from 5000 hours to 2500 hours. There is no unused capacity in respect of variable costs. Consequently with variable cost the cost per unit of resource used will be constant.

With fixed overheads the cost per unit of resource used will fluctuate with changes in estimates of activity usage because fixed overhead spending remains constant over a wide range of activity. For example, if the estimated annual fixed overheads associated with the machine referred to above are £192 000 and annual activity is estimated to be 5000 hours then the machine hour rate will be £38.40 (£192 000/5000 hours). Alternatively if annual activity is estimated to be 2500 hours then the rate will be £76.80 (£192 000/2500 hours). Therefore the choice of the denominator capacity level can have a profound effect on product cost calculations.

Several choices are available for determining the denominator activity level when calculating overhead rates. Consider the situation described in Example 7.2.

---

**EXAMPLE 7.2**

The Green Company has established a separate cost centre for one of its machines. The annual budgeted fixed overheads assigned to the cost centre are £192 000. Green operates three shifts per day of 8 hours, five days per week for 50 weeks per year (the company closes down for holiday periods for two weeks per year). The maximum machine operating hours are 6000 hours per annum (50 weeks × 24 hrs × 5 days) but because of preventive maintenance the maximum practical operating usage is 5000 hours per annum. It is estimated that normal sales demand over the next three years will result in the machine being required for 4800 hours per annum. However, because of current adverse economic conditions budgeted usage for the coming year is 4000 hours. Assume that actual fixed overheads incurred are identical to the estimated fixed overheads and that there are no opening stocks at the start of the budget period.

---

There are four different denominator activity levels that can be used in Example 7.2. They are:

1. Theoretical maximum capacity of 6000 hours = £32 per hour (£192 000/6000 hours);
2. Practical capacity of 5000 hours = £38.40 per hour (£192 000/5000 hours);
3. Normal average long-run activity of 4800 hours = £40 per hour (£192 000/4800 hours);
4. Budgeted activity of 4000 hours = £48 per hour (£192 000/4000 hours).

Theoretical maximum capacity is a measure of maximum operating capacity based on 100% efficiency with no interruptions for maintenance or other factors. We can reject this measure on the grounds that it represents an activity level that is most unlikely to be achieved. The capacity was acquired with the expectation of supplying a maximum of 5000 hours rather than a theoretical maximum of 6000 hours. This former measure is called practical capacity. Practical capacity represents the maximum capacity that is likely to be supplied by the machine after taking into account unavoidable interruptions arising from machine maintenance and plant holiday closures. In other words, practical capacity is defined as theoretical capacity less activity lost arising from unavoidable interruptions. Normal activity is a measure of capacity required to satisfy average customer demand over a longer term period of, say, approximately three years after taking into account seasonal and cyclical fluctuations. Finally, budgeted activity is the activity level based on the capacity utilization required for the next budget period.

Assuming in Example 7.2 that actual activity and expenditure are identical to budget then, for each of the above denominator activity levels, the annual costs of £192 000 will be allocated as follows:

| | Allocated to products | Volume variance (i.e. cost of unused capacity) | Total |
|---|---|---|---|
| Practical capacity | 4000 hours × £38.40 = £153 600 | 1000 hours × £38.40 = £38 400 | £192 000 |
| Normal activity | 4000 hours × £40 = £160 000 | 800 hours × £40 = £32 000 | £192 000 |
| Budgeted activity | 4000 hours × £48 = £192 000 | Nil | £192 000 |

Note that the overheads allocated to products consist of 4000 hours worked on products during the year multiplied by the appropriate overhead rate. The cost of unused capacity is the under-recovery of overheads arising from actual activity being different from the activity level used to calculate the overhead rate. If practical capacity is used the cost highlights that part of total capacity supplied (5000 hours) that has not been utilized. With normal activity the under-recovery of £32 000 represents the cost of failing to utilize the normal activity of 4800 hours. In Example 7.2 we assumed that actual activity was equivalent to budgeted activity. However, if actual activity is less than budgeted activity then the under-recovery can be interpreted as the cost of failing to achieve budgeted activity.

## IMPACT ON INVENTORY VALUATION OF PROFIT COMPUTATIONS

The choice of an appropriate activity level can have a significant effect on the inventory valuation and profit computation. Assume in Example 7.2 that 90% of the output was sold and the remaining 10% unsold and that there were no inventories at the start of the period. Thus 90% of the overheads allocated to products will be allocated to cost of sales, and 10% will be allocated to inventories. The volume variance arising from the under- or over-recovery of fixed overheads (i.e. the cost of unused capacity) is recorded as a period cost and therefore charged as an expense against the current period. It is not included in the inventory valuation. The computations are as follows:

| | Allocated to cost of sales[a] (£) | Allocated to inventories[b] (£) | Total (£) |
|---|---|---|---|
| Practical capacity | 176 640 | 15 360 | 192 000 |
| Normal activity | 176 000 | 16 000 | 192 000 |
| Budgeted activity | 172 800 | 19 200 | 192 000 |

[a]90% of overhead allocated to products plus cost of unused capacity.
[b]10% of overhead allocated to products.

In the above illustration the choice of the denominator level has not had an important impact on the inventory valuation and the cost of sales (and therefore the profit computation). Nevertheless, the impact can be material when inventories are of significant value. Many service organizations, however, do not hold inventories and just-in-time manufacturing firms aim to maintain minimal inventory levels. In these situations virtually all of the expenses incurred during a period will be recorded as a period expense whatever denominator activity level is selected to calculate the overhead rate. We can therefore conclude that for many organizations the choice of the denominator activity level has little impact on profit measurement and inventory valuation. Therefore the impact of the chosen denominator level depends on the circumstances.

Even where the choice of the denominator level is not of significant importance for profit measurement and inventory valuation it can be of crucial importance for other purposes, such as pricing decisions and managing the cost of unused capacity. Since our objective in this chapter is to focus on the impact of the choice of denominator level on profit measurement and inventory measurement we shall defer a discussion of these other issues until Chapter 10.

Finally, what denominator levels do firms actually use? You will see from Exhibit 7.4 that budgeted activity is the most widely used rate. This preference for budgeted activity probably reflects a preference by firms to allocate fixed manufacturing overheads incurred during a period to products rather than writing off some of the costs as an excess capacity period cost. Also budgeted annual activity is readily available, being determined as part of the annual budgeting process. In contrast, normal activity and practical capacity are not readily available and cannot be precisely determined.

## EXHIBIT 7.4

### Surveys of company practice

Surveys have been undertaken in many countries relating to the use of variable costs and absorption costs. However, these surveys tend to focus on the information that is extracted from the costing system for decision-making rather than the costs that are used for inventory valuation and profit measurement. Many organizations accumulate and use absorption costs for inventory valuation but extract variable costs from the cost system for decision-making. Thus, the use of variable cost for decision-making does not imply that such costs are used for inventory valuation. Surveys that do not clearly indicate the costing method that is used for inventory valuation are therefore not included in the results reported below.

A UK study by Drury *et al.* (1993) indicated the following usage rates for internal profit measurement:

|  | (%) |
| --- | --- |
| Variable costing | 13 |
| Absorption costing | 84 |
| Other | 3 |

A review of surveys of German organizations undertaken by Scherrer (1996) concluded that full costing is the most important system with only 12% of the responding organizations using only a variable costing system.

Similar results were observed in Spain by Saez-Torrecilla *et al.* (1996) who reported a 26% usage rate for variable costing.

In contrast, Virtanen *et al.* (1996) report that variable costing is widely used in Finland mainly because external financial accounting reporting regulations have not forced companies to use absorption costing for external reporting.

Little information is available relating to the denominator activity levels used. A UK study by Drury and Tayles (2000) reported the following usage rates:

|  | (%) |
| --- | --- |
| Budgeted annual activity | 86 |
| Practical capacity | 4 |
| Normal activity | 8 |
| Other | 2 |

## Self-Assessment Question

You should attempt to answer this question yourself before looking up the suggested answer, which appears on pages 1102–5. If any part of your answer is incorrect, check back carefully to make sure you understand where you went wrong.

Bittern Ltd manufactures and sells a single product at a unit selling price of £25. In constant-price-level terms its cost structure is as follows:

Variable costs:
  Production materials    £10 per unit produced
  Distribution            £1 per unit sold
Semi-variable costs:
  Labour                  £5000 per annum, plus £2 per unit produced
Fixed costs:
  Overheads               £5000 per annum

For several years Bittern has operated a system of variable costing for management accounting purposes. It has been decided to review the system and to compare it for management accounting purposes with an absorption costing system.

As part of the review, you have been asked to prepare estimates of Bittern's profits in constant-price-level terms over a three-year period in three different hypothetical situations, and to compare the two types of system generally for management accounting purposes.

(a) In each of the following three sets of hypothetical circumstances, calculate Bittern's profit in each of years $t_1$, $t_2$ and $t_3$, and also in total over the three year period $t_1$ to $t_3$, using first a variable costing system and then a full-cost absorption costing system with fixed cost recovery based on a normal production level of 1000 units per annum:

(i) Stable unit levels of production, sales and inventory

|               | $t_1$ | $t_2$ | $t_3$ |
|---------------|-------|-------|-------|
| Opening stock | 100   | 100   | 100   |
| Production    | 1000  | 1000  | 1000  |
| Sales         | 1000  | 1000  | 1000  |
| Closing stock | 100   | 100   | 100   |

(5 marks)

(ii) Stable unit level of sales, but fluctuating unit levels of production and inventory

|               | $t_1$ | $t_2$ | $t_3$ |
|---------------|-------|-------|-------|
| Opening stock | 100   | 600   | 400   |
| Production    | 1500  | 800   | 700   |
| Sales         | 1000  | 1000  | 1000  |
| Closing stock | 600   | 400   | 100   |

(5 marks)

(iii) Stable unit level of production, but fluctuating unit levels of sales and inventory

|  | $t_1$ | $t_2$ | $t_3$ |
|---|---|---|---|
| Opening stock | 100 | 600 | 400 |
| Production | 1000 | 1000 | 1000 |
| Sales | 500 | 1200 | 1300 |
| Closing stock | 600 | 400 | 100 |

(5 marks)

(Note that all the data in (i)–(iii) are volumes, not values.)

(b) Write a short comparative evaluation of variable and absorption costing systems for management accounting purposes, paying particular attention to profit measurement, and using your answer to (a) to illustrate your arguments if you wish.

(10 marks)

*ICAEW Management Accounting*

## Summary

In this chapter we have examined and compared absorption costing systems and variable costing systems. With an absorption costing system, fixed manufacturing overheads are allocated to the products, and these are included in the inventory valuation. With a variable costing system, only variable manufacturing costs are assigned to the product; fixed manufacturing costs are regarded as period costs and written off to the profit and loss account. Both variable and absorption costing systems treat non-manufacturing overheads as period costs.

Illustrations of the inventory valuations and profit calculations for both systems have been presented, and we noted that when production is equal to sales, both systems yield identical profits. However, when production exceeds sales, absorption costing shows the higher profits. Variable costing yields the higher profits when sales exceed production. Nevertheless, total profits over the life of the business will be the same for both systems. Differences arise merely in the profits attributed to each accounting period.

The proponents of variable costing claim that it provides more useful information for decision-making but it has been argued that similar relevant cost information can easily be provided with an absorption costing system. The major advantage of variable costing is that profit is reflected as a function of sales, whereas in an absorption costing system profit is a function of both sales and production. For example, we have established that, with absorption costing, when all other factors remain unchanged, sales can increase but profit may decline. By contrast, with a variable costing system, when sales increase, profits also increase. A further advantage of variable costing is that fixed overheads are not capitalized in unsaleable stocks.

The arguments that we have considered in support of absorption costing include the following:

1. Absorption costing does not underestimate the importance of fixed costs.

2. Absorption costing avoids fictitious losses being reported.

3. Fixed overheads are essential to production.

4. Internal profit measurement is consistent with external reporting.

Critical to the debate about whether fixed manufacturing costs are product costs or period costs is the definition of an asset. An asset is defined as an aggregate of service potentials, available for, or beneficial to, expected operations. Two interpretations of service potential have been considered: the cost obviation concept and the revenue production concept. The former supports variable costing whereas the latter supports absorption costing.

We have also examined the relevant cost theory of stock valuation. The relevant costing approach emphasizes that the choice of absorption costing or variable costing depends on the particular circumstances, and that one method is not superior for all situations.

We have examined four different levels of measuring activity – that is, theoretical maximum capacity, normal activity, practical capacity and annual budgeted activity. The use of each measure gives us a different overhead rate, which causes product costs, profits and inventory valuations to differ. The under- or over-recovery of overhead also varies, depending on which activity measure is used.

## Key Terms and Concepts

absorption costing (p. 202)
budgeted activity (p. 215)
cost obviation concept (p. 212)
direct costing (p. 202)
full costing (p. 202)
marginal costing (p. 202)
normal activity (p. 215)

period cost adjustment (p. 206)
practical capacity (p. 215)
relevant costing (p. 213)
revenue production concept (p. 213)
theoretical maximum capacity (p. 215)
variable costing (p. 202)
volume variance (p. 206)

# Appendix 7.1: Derivation of the profit function for an absorption costing system

The volume variance (i.e. the under- or over-recovery of fixed manufacturing overhead) is the difference between the unit denominator level ($ud$) used to derive the fixed manufacturing overhead absorption rate and the actual level of production ($up$) multiplied by the fixed manufacturing overhead rate ($fmohc$). Therefore we can express the volume variance (VV) as:

$$VV = (1 - up/ud)fmohc$$

so that:

$$\text{Total cost (TC)} = (uvmc \times us) + (fmohc/ud)us + (uvnmc \times us) + fnmc + (1 - up/ud)fmohc$$
$$TC = (uvc + fmohc/ud)us + fmohc + fnmc - (fmohc/ud)up$$
$$TC = (uvc + fmohc/ud)us - (fmohc/ud)up + tfc$$
$$\text{Operating profit} = (usp - uvc - fmohc/ud)us + (fmohc/ud)up - tfc$$

where:

$uvmc$ = unit variable manufacturing cost
$uvnmc$ = unit variable non-manufacturing cost
$fnmc$ = fixed non-manufacturing cost
$usp$ = unit selling price
$uvc$ = unit variable cost
$fmohc$ = fixed manufacturing overhead cost for the period
$ud$ = unit denominator level used to calculate the fixed overhead rate
$us$ = units sold
$up$ = units produced
$tfc$ = total fixed costs for the period (i.e. manufacturing + non-manufacturing fixed overheads).

## Key Examination Points

A common mistake is for students to calculate *actual* overhead rates when preparing absorption costing profit statements. Normal or budgeted activity should be used to calculate overhead absorption rates, and this rate should be used to calculate the production overhead cost for all periods given in the question. Do not calculate different actual overhead rates for each accounting period.

Remember not to include non-manufacturing overheads in the inventory valuations for both variable and absorption costing. Also note that variable selling overheads will vary with sales and not production. Another common mistake is not to include an adjustment for under/over recovery of fixed overheads when actual production deviates from the normal or budgeted production.

You should note that under/over-recovery of overhead arises only with fixed overheads and when an absorption costing system is used.

## Questions

*Indicates that a suggested solution is to be found in the *Students' Manual*.

### 7.1* Intermediate

Z Limited manufactures a single product, the budgeted selling price and variable cost details of which are as follows:

|  | (£) |
| --- | --- |
| Selling price | 15.00 |
| Variable costs per unit: | |
| Direct materials | 3.50 |
| Direct labour | 4.00 |
| Variable overhead | 2.00 |

Budgeted fixed overhead costs are £60 000 per annum, charged at a constant rate each month. Budgeted production is 30 000 units per annum.

In a month when actual production was 2400 units and exceeded sales by 180 units the profit reported under absorption costing was

A  £6660
B  £7570
C  £7770
D  £8200
E  £8400

*CIMA Stage 2*

### 7.2* Intermediate

A company made 17 500 units at a total cost of £16 each. Three-quarters of the costs were variable and one-quarter fixed. 15 000 units were sold at £25 each. There were no opening stocks.

By how much will the profit calculated using absorption costing principles differ from the profit if marginal costing principles had been used?

A  The absorption costing profit would be £22 500 less.
B  The absorption costing profit would be £10 000 greater.
C  The absorption costing profit would be £135 000 greater.
D  The absorption costing profit would be £10 000 less.

*CIMA Stage 1 Specimen Paper*

### 7.3* Intermediate

A firm had opening stocks and purchases totalling 12 400 kg and closing stocks of 9600 kg. Profits using marginal costing were £76 456 and using absorption costing were £61 056.

What was the fixed overhead absorption rate per kilogram (to the nearest penny)?

A  £1.60
B  £5.50
C  £6.17
D  £6.36

*CIMA Stage 1 Cost Accounting*

### 7.4* Intermediate

Exe Limited makes a single product whose total cost per unit is budgeted to be £45. This includes fixed cost of £8 per unit based on a volume of 10 000 units per period. In a period, sales volume was 9000 units, and production volume was 11 500 units. The actual profit for the same period, calculated using absorption costing, was £42 000.

If the profit statement were prepared using marginal costing, the profit for the period

A  would be £10 000
B  would be £22 000
C  would be £50 000
D  would be £62 000
E  cannot be calculated without more information

*CIMA Stage 1 Operational Cost Accounting*

### 7.5* Intermediate

In a period, opening stocks were 12 600 units and closing stocks 14 100 units. The profit based on marginal costing was £50 400 and profit using absorption costing was £60 150. The fixed overhead absorption rate per unit (to the nearest penny) is

A  £4.00
B  £4.27
C  £4.77
D  £6.50

*CIMA Stage 1 Cost Accounting*

## 7.6 Intermediate

In product costing the costs attributed to each unit of production may be calculated by using either
(i)   absorption costing, or
(ii)  marginal (or direct or variable) costing.
Similarly, in departmental cost or profit reports the fixed costs of overhead or service departments may be allocated to production departments as an integral part of the production departments' costs or else segregated in some form.

Required:
Describe absorption and marginal (or direct or variable) costing and outline the strengths and weaknesses of each method.         (c. 11 marks)
*ACCA P2 Management Accounting*

## 7.7 Intermediate

Discuss the arguments for and against the inclusion of fixed overheads in stock valuation for the purpose of internal profit measurement.

## 7.8 Intermediate: Preparation of variable and absorption costing statements

Solo Limited makes and sells a single product. The following data relate to periods 1 to 4.

|                          | (£)  |
| ------------------------ | ---- |
| Variable cost per unit   | 30   |
| Selling price per unit   | 55   |
| Fixed costs per period   | 6000 |

Normal activity is 500 units and production and sales for the four periods are as follows:

|            | Period 1 units | Period 2 units | Period 3 units | Period 4 units |
| ---------- | -------------- | -------------- | -------------- | -------------- |
| Sales      | 500            | 400            | 550            | 450            |
| Production | 500            | 500            | 450            | 500            |

There were no opening stocks at the start of period 1.

Required:
(a)  Prepare operating statements for EACH of the periods 1 to 4, based on marginal costing principles.                              (4 marks)
(b)  Prepare operating statements for EACH of the periods 1 to 4, based on absorption costing principles.                              (6 marks)
(c)  Comment briefly on the results obtained in each period AND in total by the two systems.
                                              (5 marks)
                                       (Total 15 marks)
*CIMA Stage 1 Cost Accounting*

## 7.9* Intermediate: Preparation of variable costing and absorption costing profit statements and an explanation of the differences in profits

The following data have been extracted from the budgets and standard costs of ABC Limited, a company which manufactures and sells a single product.

|                        | £ per unit |
| ---------------------- | ---------- |
| Selling price          | 45.00      |
| Direct materials cost  | 10.00      |
| Direct wages cost      | 4.00       |
| Variable overhead cost | 2.50       |

Fixed production overhead costs are budgeted at £400 000 per annum. Normal production levels are thought to be 320 000 units per annum.

Budgeted selling and distribution costs are as follows:

| Variable | £1.50 per unit sold |
| -------- | ------------------- |
| Fixed    | £80 000 per annum   |

Budgeted administration costs are £120 000 per annum.

The following pattern of sales and production is expected during the first six months of the year:

|                    | January–March | April–June |
| ------------------ | ------------- | ---------- |
| Sales (units)      | 60 000        | 90 000     |
| Production (units) | 70 000        | 100 000    |

There is to be no stock on 1 January.

You are required
(a)  to prepare profit statements for each of the two quarters, in a columnar format, using
     (i)   marginal costing, and
     (ii)  absorption costing;        (12 marks)
(b)  to reconcile the profits reported for the quarter January–March in your answer to (a) above;
                                              (3 marks)
(c)  to write up the production overhead control account for the quarter to 31 March, using absorption costing principles. Assume that the production overhead costs incurred amounted to £102 400 and the actual production was 74 000 units;                      (3 marks)
(d)  to state and explain briefly the benefits of using marginal costing as the basis of management reporting.        (5 marks)
                                       (Total 23 marks)
*CIMA Stage 1 Accounting*

## 7.10 Intermediate: Preparation of variable and absorption costing systems and CVP analysis

(a) PQ Limited makes and sells a single product, X, and has budgeted the following figures for a one-year period:

Sales, in units              160 000

| | (£) | (£) |
|---|---|---|
| Sales | | 6 400 000 |
| Production costs: | | |
| Variable | 2 560 000 | |
| Fixed | 800 000 | |
| | | |
| Selling, distribution and administration costs: | | |
| Variable | 1 280 000 | |
| Fixed | 1 200 000 | |
| Total costs | | 5 840 000 |
| Net profit | | 560 000 |

Fixed costs are assumed to be incurred evenly throughout the year. At the beginning of the year, there were no stocks of finished goods. In the first quarter of the year, 55 000 units were produced and 40 000 units were sold.

You are required to prepare profit statements for the first quarter, using

(i) marginal costing, and
(ii) absorption costing.    (6 marks)

(b) There is a difference in the profit reported when marginal costing is used compared with when absorption costing is used.

You are required to discuss the above statement and to indicate how each of the following conditions would affect the net profit reported

(i) when sales and production are in balance at standard (or expected) volume,
(ii) when sales exceed production,
(iii) when production exceeds sales.

Use the figures from your answer to (a) above to support your discussion; you should also refer to SSAP 9.    (9 marks)

(c) WF Limited makes and sells a range of plastic garden furniture. These items are sold in sets of one table with four chairs for £80 per set.

The variable costs per set are £20 for manufacturing and £10 for variable selling, distribution and administration.

Direct labour is treated as a fixed cost and the total fixed costs of manufacturing, including depreciation of the plastic-moulding machinery, are £800 000 per annum. Budgeted profit for the forthcoming year is £400 000.

Increased competition has resulted in the management of WF Limited engaging market research consultants. The consultants have recommended three possible strategies, as follows:

| | Reduce selling price per set by % | Expected increase in sales (sets) % |
|---|---|---|
| Strategy 1 | 5 | 10 |
| Strategy 2 | 7.5 | 20 |
| Strategy 3 | 10 | 25 |

You are required to assess the effect on profits of each of the three strategies, and to recommend which strategy, if any, ought to be adopted.    (10 marks)
   (Total 25 marks)
*CIMA Stage 2 Cost Accounting*

## 7.11* Intermediate: Preparation of variable and absorption costing statements as a reconciliation of the profits

The following budgeted profit statement has been prepared using absorption costing principles:

| | January to June | | July to December | |
|---|---|---|---|---|
| | (£000) | (£000) | (£000) | (£000) |
| Sales | | 540 | | 360 |
| Opening stock | 100 | | 160 | |
| Production costs: | | | | |
| Direct materials | 108 | | 36 | |
| Direct labour | 162 | | 54 | |
| Overhead | 90 | | 30 | |
| | 460 | | 280 | |
| Closing stock | 160 | | 80 | |
| | | 300 | | 200 |
| GROSS PROFIT | | 240 | | 160 |
| Production overhead: | | | | |
| (Over)/Under absorption | (12) | | 12 | |
| Selling costs | 50 | | 50 | |
| Distribution costs | 45 | | 40 | |
| Administration costs | 80 | | 80 | |
| | | 163 | | 182 |
| NET PROFIT/(LOSS) | | 77 | | (22) |
| Sales units | | 15 000 | | 10 000 |
| Production units | | 18 000 | | 6000 |

The members of the management team are concerned by the significant change in profitability between the two six-month periods. As management accountant, you have analysed the data upon which the above budget statement has been produced, with the following results:

1. The production overhead cost comprises both a fixed and a variable element, the latter appears to be dependent on the number of units produced. The fixed element of the cost is expected to be incurred at a constant rate throughout the year.
2. The selling costs are fixed.
3. The distribution cost comprises both fixed and variable elements, the latter appears to be dependent on the number of units sold. The fixed element of the cost is expected to be incurred at a constant rate throughout the year.
4. The administration costs are fixed.

Required:

(a) Present the above budgeted profit statement in marginal costing format. (10 marks)
(b) Reconcile EACH of the six-monthly profit/loss values reported respectively under marginal and absorption costing. (4 marks)
(c) Reconcile the six-monthly profit for January to June from the absorption costing statement with the six-monthly loss for July to December from the absorption costing statement. (4 marks)
(d) Calculate the annual number of units required to break even. (3 marks)
(e) Explain briefly the advantages of using marginal costing as the basis of providing managers with information for decision making. (4 marks)

(Total 25 marks)

*CIMA Stage 2 Operational Cost Accounting*

**7.12 Intermediate: Preparation of variable and absorption costing profit statements and comments in support of a variable costing system**

A manufacturer of glass bottles has been affected by competition from plastic bottles and is currently operating at between 65 and 70 per cent of maximum capacity.

The company at present reports profits on an absorption costing basis but with the high fixed costs associated with the glass container industry and a substantial difference between sales volumes and production in some months, the accountant has

been criticized for reporting widely different profits from month to month. To counteract this criticism, he is proposing in future to report profits based on marginal costing and in his proposal to management lists the following reasons for wishing to change:

1. Marginal costing provides for the complete segregation of fixed costs, thus facilitating closer control of production costs.
2. It eliminates the distortion of interim profit statements which occur when there are seasonal fluctuations in sales volume although production is at a fairly constant level.
3. It results in cost information which is more helpful in determining the sales policy necessary to maximise profits.

From the accounting records the following figures were extracted: Standard cost per gross (a gross is 144 bottles and is the cost unit used within the business):

|  | (£) |
| --- | --- |
| Direct materials | 8.00 |
| Direct labour | 7.20 |
| Variable production overhead | 3.36 |
| Total variable production cost | 18.56 |
| Fixed production overhead | 7.52* |
| Total production standard cost | 26.08 |

*The fixed production overhead rate was based on the following computations:

Total annual fixed production overhead was budgeted at £7 584 000 or £632 000 per month.

Production volume was set at 1 008 000 gross bottles or 70 per cent of maximum capacity.

There is a slight difference in budgeted fixed production overhead at different levels of operating:

| Activity level (per cent of maximum capacity) | Amount per month (£000) |
| --- | --- |
| 50–75 | 632 |
| 76–90 | 648 |
| 91–100 | 656 |

You may assume that actual fixed production overhead incurred was as budgeted.

Additional information:

|  | **September** | **October** |
|---|---|---|
| Gross sold | 87 000 | 101 000 |
| Gross produced | 115 000 | 78 000 |
| Sales price, per gross | £32 | £32 |
| Fixed selling costs | £120 000 | £120 000 |
| Fixed administrative costs | £80 000 | £80 000 |

There were no finished goods in stock at 1 September.

You are required

(a) to prepare monthly profit statements for September and October using
    (i) absorption costing; and
    (ii) marginal costing; (16 marks)
(b) to comment briefly on the accountant's three reasons which he listed to support his proposal. (9 marks)
(Total 25 marks)
*CIMA Stage 2 Cost Accounting*

**7.13\* Intermediate: Under/over-recovery of fixed overheads and preparation and reconciliation of absorption and variable costing profit statements**

(a) Discuss the arguments put forward for the use of absorption and marginal costing systems respectively. (8 marks)
(b) The following information is available for a firm producing and selling a single product:

|  | **(£000)** |
|---|---|
| *Budgeted costs* (at normal activity) | |
| Direct materials and labour | 264 |
| Variable production overhead | 48 |
| Fixed production overhead | 144 |
| Variable selling and administration overhead | 24 |
| Fixed selling and administration overhead | 96 |

The overhead absorption rates are based upon normal activity of 240 000 units per period.

During the period just ended 260 000 units of product were produced, and 230 000 units were sold at £3 per unit.

At the beginning of the period 40 000 units were in stock. These were valued at the budgeted costs shown above.

Actual costs incurred were as per budget.

Required:
(i) Calculate the fixed production overhead absorbed during the period, and the extent of any under/over absorption. For both of these calculations you should use absorption costing.
(ii) Calculate profits for the period using absorption costing and marginal costing respectively.
(iii) Reconcile the profit figures which you calculated in (ii) above.
(iv) State the situations in which the profit figures calculated under both absorption costing and marginal costing would be the same.
(17 marks)
(Total 25 marks)
*ACCA Level 1 Costing*

**7.14\* Intermediate: Equivalent production and preparation of variable and absorption costing profit statements**

A new subsidiary of a group of companies was established for the manufacture and sale of Product X. During the first year of operations 90 000 units were sold at £20 per unit. At the end of the year, the closing stocks were 8000 units in finished goods store and 4000 units in work-in-progress which were complete as regards material content but only half complete in respect of labour and overheads. You are to assume that there were no opening stocks. The work-in-progress account had been debited during the year with the following costs:

|  | **(£)** |
|---|---|
| Direct materials | 714 000 |
| Direct labour | 400 000 |
| Variable overhead | 100 000 |
| Fixed overhead | 350 000 |

Selling and administration costs for the year were:

|  | **Variable cost per unit sold (£)** | **Fixed cost (£)** |
|---|---|---|
| Selling | 1.50 | 200 000 |
| Administration | 0.10 | 50 000 |

The accountant of the subsidiary company had prepared a profit statement on the absorption costing principle which showed a profit of £11 000.

The financial controller of the group, however, had prepared a profit statement on a marginal costing basis which showed a loss. Faced with these two profit statements, the director responsible for this particular subsidiary company is confused.

You are required to

(a) prepare a statement showing the equivalent units produced and the production cost of *one* unit of Product X by element of cost and in total; (5 marks)

(b) prepare a profit statement on the absorption costing principle which agrees with the company accountant's statement; (9 marks)

(c) prepare a profit statement on the marginal costing basis; (6 marks)

(d) explain the differences between the two statements given for (b) and (c) above to the director in such a way as to eliminate his confusion and state why both statements may be acceptable. (5 marks)

(Total 25 marks)

*CIMA Stage 2 Cost Accounting*

### 7.15* Intermediate: Preparation of variable and absorption costing profit statements for FIFO and AVECO methods

The following information relates to product J, for quarter 3, which has just ended:

| | Production (units) | Sales (units) | Fixed overheads (£000) | Variable costs (£000) |
|---|---|---|---|---|
| Budget | 40 000 | 38 000 | 300 | 1800 |
| Actual | 46 000 | 42 000 | 318 | 2070 |

The selling price of product J was £72 per unit.

The fixed overheads were absorbed at a predetermined rate per unit.

At the beginning of quarter 3 there was an opening stock of product J of 2000 units, valued at £25 per unit variable costs and £5 per unit fixed overheads.

Required:

(a) (i) Calculate the fixed overhead absorption rate per unit for the last quarter, and present profit statements using FIFO (first in, first out) using:

(ii) absorption costing;

(iii) marginal costing; and

(iv) reconcile and explain the difference between the profits or losses. (12 marks)

(b) Using the same data, present similar statements to those required in part (a). Using the AVECO (average cost) method of valuation, reconcile the profit or loss figures, and comment briefly on the variations between the profits or losses in (a) and (b). (8 marks)

(Total 20 marks)

*ACCA Paper 8 Managerial Finance*

### 7.16 Intermediate: Calculation of overhead absorption rates and an explanation of the differences in profits

A company manufactures a single product with the following variable costs per unit

| | |
|---|---|
| Direct materials | £7.00 |
| Direct labour | £5.50 |
| Manufacturing overhead | £2.00 |

The selling price of the product is £36.00 per unit. Fixed manufacturing costs are expected to be £1 340 000 for a period. Fixed non-manufacturing costs are expected to be £875 000. Fixed manufacturing costs can be analysed as follows:

| Production Department 1 | Production Department 2 | Service Department | General Factory |
|---|---|---|---|
| £380 000 | £465 000 | £265 000 | £230 000 |

'General Factory' costs represent space costs, for example rates, lighting and heating. Space utilization is as follows:

| | |
|---|---|
| Production department 1 | 40% |
| Production department 2 | 50% |
| Service department | 10% |

60% of service department costs are labour related and the remaining 40% machine related.

Normal production department activity is:

| | Direct labour hours | Machine hours | Production units |
|---|---|---|---|
| Department 1 | 80 000 | 2400 | 120 000 |
| Department 2 | 100 000 | 2400 | 120 000 |

Fixed manufacturing overheads are absorbed at a predetermined rate per unit of production for each production department, based upon normal activity.

Required:
(a) Prepare a profit statement for a period using the full absorption costing system described above and showing each element of cost separately. Costs for the period were as per expectation, except for additional expenditure of £20 000 on fixed manufacturing overhead in Production Department 1. Production and sales were 116 000 and 114 000 units respectively for the period. (14 marks)
(b) Prepare a profit statement for the period using marginal costing principles instead. (5 marks)
(c) Contrast the general effect on profit of using absorption and marginal costing systems respectively. (Use the figures calculated in (a) and (b) above to illustrate your answer.) (6 marks)
(Total 25 marks)
*ACCA Cost and Management Accounting 1*

### 7.17* Advanced: Explanation of absorption costing changes in profits and preparation of variable costing profit statements

The Miozip Company operates an absorption costing system which incorporates a factory-wide overhead absorption rate per direct labour hour. For 1999 and 2000 this rate was £2.10 per hour. The fixed factory overhead for 2000 was £600 000 and this would have been fully absorbed if the company had operated at full capacity, which is estimated at 400 000 direct labour hours. Unfortunately, only 200 000 hours were worked in that year so that the overhead was seriously underabsorbed. Fixed factory overheads are expected to be unchanged in 2001 and 2002.

The outcome for 2000 was a loss of £70 000 and the management believed that a major cause of this loss was the low overhead absorption rate which had led the company to quote selling prices which were uneconomic.

For 2001 the overhead absorption rate was increased to £3.60 per direct labour hour and selling prices were raised in line with the established pricing procedures which involve adding a profit mark-up of 50% onto the full factory cost of the company's products. The new selling prices were also charged on the stock of finished goods held at the beginning of 2001.

In December 2001 the company's accountant prepares an estimated Profit and Loss Account for 2001 and a budgeted Profit and Loss Account for 2002. Although sales were considered to be

depressed in 2000, they were even lower in 2001 but, nevertheless, it seems that the company will make a profit for that year. A worrying feature of the estimated accounts is the high level of finished goods stock held and the 2002 budget provides for a reduction in the stock level at 31 December 2002 to the (physical) level existing in January 2000. Budgeted sales for 2002 are set at the 2001 sales level.

The summarised profit statements for the three years to 31 December 2002 are as follows:

**Summarized Profit and Loss Accounts**

| | Actual 2000 (£) | (£) | Estimated 2001 (£) | (£) | Budgeted 2002 (£) | (£) |
|---|---|---|---|---|---|---|
| Sales Revenue | | 1 350 000 | | 1 316 250 | | 1 316 250 |
| Opening Stock of Finished Goods | 100 000 | | 200 000 | | 357 500 | |
| Factory Cost of Production | 1 000 000 | | 975 000 | | 650 000 | |
| | 1 100 000 | | 1 175 000 | | 1 007 500 | |
| *Less*: Closing Stock of Finished Goods | 200 000 | | 357 500 | | 130 000 | |
| Factory Cost of Goods Sold | | 900 000 | | 817 500 | | 877 500 |
| | | 450 000 | | 498 750 | | 438 750 |
| *Less*: Factory Overhead Under-Absorbed | | 300 000 | | 150 000 | | 300 000 |
| | | 150 000 | | 348 750 | | 138 750 |
| Administrative and Financial Costs | | 220 000 | | 220 000 | | 220 000 |
| | Loss | (£70 000) | | £128 750 | Loss | (£81 250) |

(a) You are required to write a short report to the board of Miozip explaining why the budgeted outcome for 2002 is so different from that of 2001 when the sales revenue is the same for both years. (6 marks)
(b) Restate the Profit and Loss Account for 2000, the estimated Profit and Loss Account for 2001 and the Budgeted Profit and Loss Account for 2002 using marginal factory cost for stock valuation purposes. (8 marks)
(c) Comment on the problems which *may* follow from a decision to increase the overhead absorption rate in conditions when cost plus pricing is used and overhead is currently underabsorbed. (3 marks)
(d) Explain why the majority of businesses use full costing systems whilst most management accounting theorists favour marginal costing. (5 marks)

NB Assume in your answers to this question that the value of the £ and the efficiency of the company have been constant over the period under review.

(Total 22 marks)

*ACCA Level 2 Management Accounting*

## 7.18* Advanced: Explanation of absorption costing changes in profits and preparation of variable costing profit statements

Mahler Products has two manufacturing departments each producing a single standardized product. The data for unit cost and selling price of these products are as follows:

| | Department A (£) | Department B (£) |
|---|---|---|
| Direct material cost | 4 | 6 |
| Direct labour cost | 2 | 4 |
| Variable manufacturing overheads | 2 | 4 |
| Fixed manufacturing overheads | 12 | 16 |
| Factory cost | 20 | 30 |
| Profit mark-up | 50% 10 | 25% 7.50 |
| Selling price | 30 | 37.50 |

The factory cost figures are used in the departmental accounts for the valuation of finished goods stock.

The departmental profit and loss accounts have been prepared for the year to 30 June. These are given below separately for the two halves of the year.

Departmental profit and loss accounts – year to 30 June

| | 1 July–31 December Department A (£000) | 1 July–31 December Department B (£000) | 1 January–30 June Department A (£000) | 1 January–30 June Department B (£000) |
|---|---|---|---|---|
| Sales revenue | 300 | 750 | 375 | 675 |
| Manufacturing costs: | | | | |
| Direct material | 52 | 114 | 30 | 132 |
| Direct labour | 26 | 76 | 15 | 88 |
| Variable overheads | 26 | 76 | 15 | 88 |
| Fixed overheads | 132 | 304 | 132 | 304 |
| Factory cost of production | 236 | 570 | 192 | 612 |
| Add Opening stock of finished goods | 60 | 210 | 120 | 180 |
| | 296 | 780 | 312 | 792 |
| Less Closing stock of finished goods | 120 | 180 | 20 | 300 |
| Factory cost of goods sold | 176 | 600 | 292 | 492 |
| Administrative and selling costs | 30 | 100 | 30 | 100 |
| | 206 | 700 | 322 | 592 |
| Net profit | 94 | 50 | 53 | 83 |

The total sales revenue was the same in each six monthly period but in the second half of the year the company increased the sales of department A (which has the higher profit mark-up) and reduced the sales of department B (which has the lower profit mark-up). An increase in company profits for the second six months was anticipated but the profit achieved was £8000 lower for the second half of the year than for the first half. The profit for department A fell by £41 000 while the profit for department B rose by £33 000. There has been no change in prices of inputs or outputs.

You are required:

(a) to explain the situation described in the last paragraph – illustrate your answer with appropriate supporting calculations,     (14 marks)

(b) to redraft the departmental profit and loss accounts using marginal cost to value unsold stock.     (8 marks)

(Total 22 marks)

*ACCA Level 2 Management Accounting*

## 7.19 Advanced: Preparation and comments on variable and absorption costing profit statements

Synchrodot Ltd manufactures two standard products, product 1 selling at £15 and product 2 selling at £18. A standard absorption costing system is in operation and summarised details of the unit cost standards are as follows:

| | Standard Cost Data – Summary Product 1 (£) | Product 2 (£) |
|---|---|---|
| Direct Material Cost | 2 | 3 |
| Direct Labour Cost | 1 | 2 |
| Overhead (Fixed and Variable) | 7 | 9 |
| | £10 | £14 |

The budgeted fixed factory overhead for Synchrodot Ltd is £180 000 (per quarter) for product 1 and £480 000 (per quarter) for product 2. This apportionment to product lines is achieved by using a variety of 'appropriate' bases for individual expense categories, e.g. floor space for rates, number of workstaff for supervisory salaries etc. The fixed overhead is absorbed into production using practical capacity as the basis and any volume variance is written off (or credited) to the

Profit and Loss Account in the quarter in which it occurs. Any planned volume variance in the quarterly budgets is dealt with similarly. The practical capacity per quarter is 30 000 units for product 1 and 60 000 units for product 2.

At the March board meeting the draft budgeted income statement for the April/May/June quarter is presented for consideration. This shows the following:

**Budgeted Income Statement for April May and June**

| | Product 1 | Product 2 |
|---|---|---|
| Budgeted Sales | | |
| Quantity | 30 000 units | 57 000 units |
| Budgeted Production | | |
| Quantity | 24 000 units | 60 000 units |
| Budgeted Sales | | |
| Revenue | £450 000 | £1 026 000 |
| Budgeted Production | | |
| Costs | | |
| Direct Material | £48 000 | £180 000 |
| Direct Labour | 24 000 | 120 000 |
| Factory Overhead | 204 000 | 540 000 |
| | £276 000 | £840 000 |
| *Add*: | | |
| Budgeted opening | | |
| Finished Goods | | |
| Stock at 1 April (8000 units) | 80 000 (3000 units) | 42 000 |
| | £356 000 | £882 000 |
| *Less*: | | |
| Budgeted closing | | |
| finished Goods | | |
| Stock at 30 June (2000 units) | 20 000 (6000 units) | 84 000 |
| Budgeted | | |
| Manufacuring Cost | £336 000 | £798 000 |
| of Budgeted Sales | | |
| Budgeted | | |
| Manufacturing Profit | £114 000 | £228 000 |
| Budgeted | | |
| Administrative and | | |
| Selling Costs (fixed) | 30 000 | 48 000 |
| Budgeted Profit | £84 000 | £180 000 |

The statement causes consternation at the board meeting because it seems to show that product 2 contributes much more profit than product 1 and yet this has not previously been apparent.

The Sales Director is perplexed and he points out that the budgeted sales programme for the forthcoming quarter is identical with that accepted for the current quarter (January/February/March) and yet the budget for the current quarter shows a budgeted profit of £120 000 for each product line and the actual results seem to be in line with the budget.

The Production Director emphasises that identical assumptions, as to unit variable costs, selling prices and manufacturing efficiency, underlie both budgets but there has been a change in the budgeted production pattern. He produces the following table:

| **Budgeted Production** | **Product 1** | **Product 2** |
|---|---|---|
| January/February/ March | 30 000 units | 52 500 units |
| April/May/June | 24 000 units | 60 000 units |

He urges that the company's budgeting procedures be overhauled as he can see no reason why the quarter's profit should be £24 000 up on the previous quarter and why the net profit for product 1 should fall from £4.00 to £2.80 per unit sold, whereas, for product 2 it should rise from £2.11 to £3.16.

You are required:

(a) To reconstruct the company's budget for the January/February/March quarter.   (6 marks)

(b) To restate the budgets (for both quarters) using standard marginal cost as the stock valuation basis.   (8 marks)

(c) To comment on the queries raised by the Sales Director and the Production Director and on the varying profit figures disclosed by the alternative budgets.   (8 marks)

(Total 22 marks)
*ACCA Level 2 Management Accounting*

## 7.20 Advanced: Explanation of difference between absorption and variable costing profit statements

The accountant of Minerva Ltd, a small company manufacturing only one product, wishes to decide how to present the company's monthly management accounts. To date only actual information has been presented on an historic cost basis, with stocks valued at average cost. Standard costs have now been derived for the costs of production. The practical capacity (also known as full capacity) for annual production is 160 000 units, and this has been used as the basis for the allocation of production overheads. Selling and administration fixed overheads have been allocated assuming all 160 000 units are sold. The expected production capacity for 2001 is 140 000 units. It is anticipated now that, for the twelve months to 31 December 2001, production and sales volume will equal 120 000 units, compared to the forecast sales and production volumes of 140 000 units. The standard cost and standard profit per unit based on practical capacity is:

|  | (£ per unit) | (£ per unit) |
|---|---|---|
| Selling price |  | 25.00 |
| Production costs: |  |  |
| Variable | 8.00 |  |
| Fixed | 6.00 |  |
|  | 14.00 |  |
| Variable selling costs | 1.00 | 15.00 |
|  |  | 10.00 |
| Other fixed costs: |  |  |
| Administration | 2.10 |  |
| Selling | 1.20 | 3.30 |
| Standard profit per unit |  | 6.70 |

The accountant has prepared the following three drafts (see below) of Minerva Ltd's profit and loss account for the month of November 2000 using three different accounting methods. The drafts are based on data relating to production, sales and stock for November 2000 which are given below.

### Production and sales quantities November 2000

|  | (units) |
|---|---|
| Opening stock | 20 000 |
| Production | 8 000 |
|  | 28 000 |
| Less Sales | 10 000 |
| Closing stock | 18 000 |

The accountant is trying to choose the best method of presenting the financial information to the directors. The present method is shown under the Actual costs column; the two other methods are based on the standard costs derived above.

The following estimated figures for the month of December 2000 have just come to hand:

Sales 12 000 units at £25

Production 14 000 units

Production costs:
variable £116 000
fixed £90 000

Administration costs £24 500

Selling costs:
variable £12 000
fixed £15 000

**Draft profit and loss accounts for the month ended 30 November 2000**

|  | Actual costs (£000) | (£000) | Absorption cost method (£000) | (£000) | Variable cost method (£000) | (£000) |
|---|---|---|---|---|---|---|
| Sales (10 000 units at £25) | 250 |  | 250 |  | 250 |  |
| Opening stock | 280 |  | 280 |  | 160 |  |
| Production costs: |  |  |  |  |  |  |
| variable | 60 |  | 112ª |  | 64 |  |
| fixed | 66 |  | — |  | — |  |
|  | 406 |  | 392 |  | 224 |  |
| Closing stock | 261 | 145 | 252 | 140 | 144 | 80 |
|  |  | 105 |  | 110 |  | 170 |
| Variable selling costs |  | — |  | — |  | 10 |
| Gross profit/contribution |  | 105 |  | 110 |  | 160 |
| Other expenses: |  |  |  |  |  |  |
| Production – fixed | — |  | — |  | 80 |  |
| Administration – fixed | 23 |  | 21 |  | 28 |  |
| Selling: |  |  |  |  |  |  |
| variable | 11 |  | 10 |  | — |  |
| fixed | 14 | 48 | 12 | 43 | 16 | 124 |
|  |  | 57 |  | 67 |  | 36 |
| Variances |  |  |  |  |  |  |
| Production |  |  |  |  |  |  |
| variable – expenditure |  |  | (4) |  | (4) |  |
| fixed – volume |  |  | 32 |  | — |  |
| – expenditure |  |  | (14) |  | (14) |  |
| Administration – volume |  |  | 7 |  | — |  |
| – expenditure |  |  | (5) |  | (5) |  |
| Selling: |  |  |  |  |  |  |
| variable – expenditure |  |  | 1 |  | 1 |  |
| fixed – volume |  |  | 4 |  | — |  |
| – expenditure |  | — | (2) | 19 | (2) | (24) |
| Net profit |  | 57 |  | 48 |  | 60 |

*Note*
ª Sum of variable and fixed costs.

### Requirements

(a) Prepare a schedule explaining the *main* difference(s) between the net profit figures for November 2000 under the three different allocation methods. (8 marks)

(b) Discuss the relative merits of the two suggested alternative methods as a means of providing useful information to the company's senior management. (8 marks)

(c) Draw up a short report for senior management presenting your recommendations for the choice of method of preparing the monthly accounts, incorporating in your report the profit and loss account for November and the projected profit and loss account for December 2000 as examples of your recommendations. (9 marks)

(Total 25 marks)

*ICAEW P2 Management Accounting*

# PART THREE

# Information for Decision-making

The objective of this Part, which contains seven chapters, is to consider the provision of financial information that will help managers to make better decisions. Chapter 8–12 are concerned mainly with short-term decisions based on the environment of today, and the physical, human and financial resources that are presently available to a firm; these decisions are determined to a considerable extent by the quality of the firm's long-term decisions. An important distinction between the long-term and short-term decisions is that the former cannot easily be reversed whereas the latter can often be changed. The actions that follow short-term decisions are frequently repeated, and it is possible for different actions to be taken in the future. For example, the setting of a particular selling price or product mix can often be changed fairly quickly. With regard to long-term decisions, such as capital investment, which involves, for example, the purchase of new plant and machinery, it is not easy to change a decision in the short term. Resources may only be available for major investments in plant and machinery at lengthy intervals, and it is unlikely that plant replacement decisions will be repeated in the short term.

Chapters 8–12 concentrate mainly on how accounting information can be applied to different forms of short-term decisions. Chapter 8 focuses on what will happen to the financial results if a specific level of activity or volume fluctuates. This information is required for making optimal short-term output decisions. Chapter 9 examines how costs and revenues should be measured for a range of non-routine short-term and long-term decisions. Chapter 10 focuses on an alternative approach for measuring resources consumed by cost objects. This approach is called activity-based costing. Chapter 11 is concerned with profitability analysis and the provision of financial information for pricing decisions. Chapters 8–11 assume a world of certainty, whereas Chapter 12 introduces methods of incorporating uncertainty into the analysis, and the topics covered in Chapters 8–11 are re-examined under conditions of uncertainty.

The final two chapters in this part are concerned with long-term decisions. Chapter 13 looks at the techniques that are used for evaluating capital investment decisions, and introduces the concept of the time value of money. A number of assumptions are made to simplify the discussion, but in Chapter 14 these assumptions are relaxed and we consider how capital investment techniques can be applied to more complex situations.

# Cost–volume–profit analysis

In the previous chapters we have considered how costs should be accumulated for inventory valuation and profit measurement, and we have stressed that costs should be accumulated in a different way for decision-making and cost control. In the next seven chapters we shall look at the presentation of financial information for decision-making. We begin by considering how the management accountant can be of assistance in providing answers to questions about the consequences of following particular courses of action. Such questions might include 'What would be the effect on profits if we reduce our selling price and sell more units?' 'What sales volume is required to meet the additional fixed charges arising from an advertising campaign?' 'Should we pay our sales people on the basis of a salary only, or on the basis of a commission only, or by a combination of the two?' These and other questions can be answered using cost–volume–profit (CVP) analysis.

This is a systematic method of examining the relationship between changes in activity (i.e. output) and changes in total sales revenue, expenses and net profit. As a model of these relationships CVP analysis simplifies the real-world conditions that a firm will face. Like most models, which are abstractions from reality, CVP analysis is subject to a number of underlying assumptions and limitations, which will be discussed later in this chapter; nevertheless, it is a powerful tool for decision-making in certain situations.

This objective of CVP analysis is to establish what will happen to the financial results if a specified level of activity or volume fluctuates. This information is vital to management, since one of the most important variables influencing total sales revenue, total costs and profits is output or volume. For this reason output is given special attention, since knowledge of this relationship will enable management to identify the critical output levels, such as the level at which neither a profit nor a loss will occur (i.e. the break-even point).

CVP analysis is based on the relationship between volume and sales revenue, costs and profit in the short run, the short run normally being a period of one year, or less, in which the output of

## Learning objectives

After studying this chapter, you should be able to:

- describe the differences between the accountant's and the economist's model of cost–volume–profit analysis;

- justify the use of linear cost and revenue functions in the accountant's model;

- apply the mathematical approach to answer questions similar to those listed in Example 8.1;

- construct break-even, contribution and profit–volume graphs;

- identify and explain the assumptions on which cost–volume–profit analysis is based;

- calculate break-even points for multi-product situations.

a firm is restricted to that available from the current operating capacity. In the short run, some inputs can be increased, but others cannot. For example, additional supplies of materials and unskilled labour may be obtained at short notice, but it takes time to expand the capacity of plant and machinery. Thus output is limited in the short run because plant facilities cannot be expanded. It also takes time to reduce capacity, and therefore in the short run a firm must operate on a relatively constant stock of production resources. Furthermore, most of the costs and prices of a firm's products will have already been determined, and the major area of uncertainty will be sales volume. Short-run profitability will therefore be most sensitive to sales volume. CVP analysis thus highlights the effects of changes in sales volume on the level of profits in the short run.

The theoretical relationship between total sales revenue, costs and profits with volume has been developed by economists. We therefore begin this chapter by describing the economist's model of CVP analysis.

# The economist's model

An economist's model of CVP behaviour is presented in Figure 8.1. You will see that the total-revenue line is assumed to be curvilinear, which indicates that the firm is only able to sell increasing quantities of output by reducing the selling price per unit; thus the total revenue line does not increase proportionately with output. To increase the quantity of sales, it is necessary to reduce the unit selling price, which results in the total revenue line rising less steeply, and eventually beginning to decline. This is because the adverse effect of price reductions outweighs the benefits of increased sales volume.

The total cost line AD shows that, between points A and B, total costs rise steeply at first as the firm operates at the lower levels of the volume range. This reflects the difficulties of efficiently operating a plant designed for much larger volume levels. Between points B and C, the total cost line begins to level out and rise less steeply because the firm is now able to operate the plant within the efficient operating range and can take advantage of specialization of labour, and smooth production schedules. In the upper portion of the volume range the total cost line between points C and D rises more and more steeply as the cost per unit increases. This is because the output per direct labour hour declines when the plant is operated beyond the activity level for which it was designed: bottlenecks develop, production schedules become more complex, and plant breakdowns begin to occur. The overall effect is that the cost per unit of output increases and causes the total cost line to rise steeply.

The dashed horizontal line from point A represents the cost of providing the basic operating capacity, and is the economist's interpretation of the total fixed costs of the firm. Note also from Figure 8.1 that the shape of the total revenue line is such that it crosses the total cost line at two points. In other words, there are two output levels at which the total costs are equal to the total revenues; or more simply, there are two break-even points.

It is the shape of the variable cost function in the economist's model that has the most significant influence on the total cost function; this is illustrated in Figure 8.2. The

**FIGURE 8.1** *Economist's cost–volume graph.*

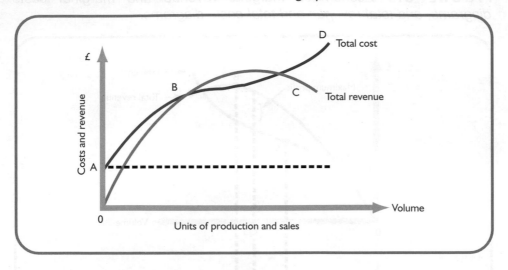

**FIGURE 8.2** *Economist's variable cost function.*

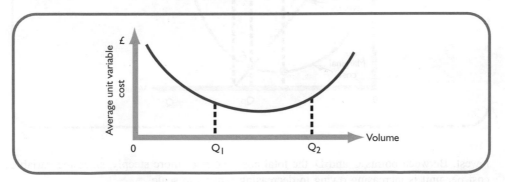

economist assumes that the average *unit* variable cost declines initially, reflecting the fact that, as output expands, a firm is able to obtain bulk discounts on the purchase of raw materials and can benefit from the division of labour; this results in the labour cost per unit being reduced. The economist refers to this situation as **increasing returns to scale**. The fact that *unit* variable cost is higher at lower levels of activity causes the total cost line between points A and B in Figure 8.1 to rise steeply. From Figure 8.2 you can see that the *unit* variable cost levels out between output levels $Q_1$ and $Q_2$ and then gradually begins to rise. This is because the firm is operating at its most efficient output level, and further economies of scale are not possible in the short term. However, beyond output level $Q_2$, the plant is being operated at a higher level than that for which it was intended, and bottlenecks and plant breakdowns occur. The effect of this is that output per direct labour hour declines, and causes the variable cost per unit to increase. The economist describes this situation as **decreasing returns to scale**.

It is the shape of the variable cost function that causes the total cost line to behave in the manner indicated in Figure 8.1. Between points B and C, the total cost line rises less steeply, indicating that the firm is operating in the range where unit variable cost is at its

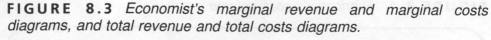

**FIGURE 8.3** *Economist's marginal revenue and marginal costs diagrams, and total revenue and total costs diagrams.*

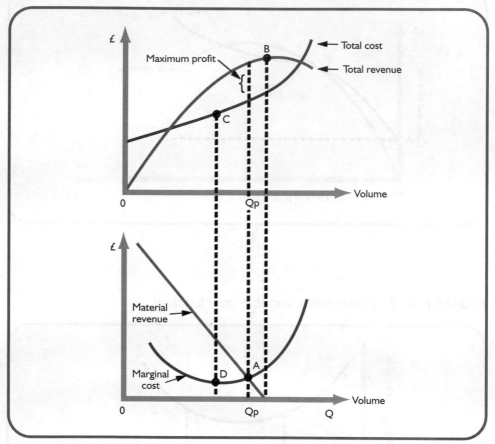

lowest. Between points C and D, the total cost line rises more steeply, since the variable cost per unit is increasing owing to decreasing returns to scale.

## MARGINAL REVENUE AND MARGINAL COST PRESENTATION

The normal presentation of the economist's model is in terms of the marginal revenue and marginal cost curves. Marginal revenue represents the increase in total revenue from the sale of one additional unit. Figure 8.3 is in two parts, with the lower diagram presenting the traditional marginal revenue and marginal cost diagram; the top diagram repeats Figure 8.1. A comparison of the two diagrams in Figure 8.3 enables us to reconcile the traditional marginal revenue and marginal cost diagram with the total cost and total revenue presentation. Economic theory states that the profit maximizing output level is the point at which marginal cost equals marginal revenue. This occurs at Point A on the lower diagram, at output level $Q_p$. Note that in the top diagram this is the point at which the difference between the total revenue and total cost lines is the greatest. The point where total revenue reaches a maximum, point B, is where marginal revenue is equal to zero. Also note that the marginal cost curve reaches a minimum at point D, where the total cost curve (at point C) changes from concave downwards to concave upwards. Let us now compare the accountant's CVP diagram, or break-even model as it is sometimes called, with the economist's model.

# The accountant's cost–volume–profit model

The diagram for the accountant's model is presented in Figure 8.4. Note that the dashed line represents the economist's total cost function, which enables a comparison to be made with the accountant's total cost function. The accountant's diagram assumes a variable cost and a selling price that are constant per unit; this results in a linear relationship (i.e. a straight line) for total revenue and total cost as volume changes. The effect is that there is only one **break-even point** in the diagram, and the profit area widens as volume increases. The most profitable output is therefore at maximum practical capacity. Clearly, the economist's model appears to be more realistic, since it assumes that the total cost curve is non-linear.

## RELEVANT RANGE

The accountants' diagram is not intended to provide an accurate representation of total cost and total revenue throughout all ranges of output. The objective is to represent the behaviour of total cost and revenue over the range of output at which a firm expects to be operating within a short-term planning horizon. This range of output is represented by the output range between points X and Y in Figure 8.4. The term **relevant range** is used to refer to the output range at which the firm expects to be operating within a short-term planning horizon. This relevant range also broadly represents the output levels which the firm has had experience of operating in the past and for which cost information is available.

You can see from Figure 8.4 that, between points X and Y, the shape of the accountant's total cost line is very similar to that of the economist's. This is because the total cost line is only intended to provide a good approximation within the **relevant production range**. Within this range, the accountant assumes that the variable cost per unit is the same throughout the entire range of output, and the total cost line is therefore linear. It would be unwise, however, to make this assumption for production levels outside the relevant range. It would be more appropriate if the accountant's total cost line was presented for the relevant range of output only, and not extended to the vertical axis or to the output levels beyond Y in Figure 8.4.

## FIXED COST FUNCTION

Note also that the accountant's fixed cost function in Figure 8.4 meets the vertical axis at a different point to that at which the economist's total cost line meets the vertical axis. The reason for this can be explained from Figure 8.5. The fixed cost level of 0A may be applicable to, say, activity level $Q_2$ to $Q_3$, but if there were to be a prolonged economic recession then output might fall below $Q_1$, and this could result in redundancies and shutdowns. Therefore fixed costs may be reduced to 0B if there is a prolonged and a significant decline in sales demand. Alternatively, additional fixed costs will be incurred if long-term sales volume is expected to be greater than $Q_3$. Over a longer-term time horizon, the fixed cost line will consist of a series of step functions rather than the horizontal straight line depicted in Figure 8.4. However, since within its short-term planning horizon the firm expects to be operating between output levels $Q_2$ and $Q_3$, it will be committed, in the short term, to fixed costs of 0A; but you should remember that if there was a prolonged economic recession then in the longer term fixed costs may be reduced to 0B.

**FIGURE 8.4** *Accountant's cost–volume–profit diagram.*

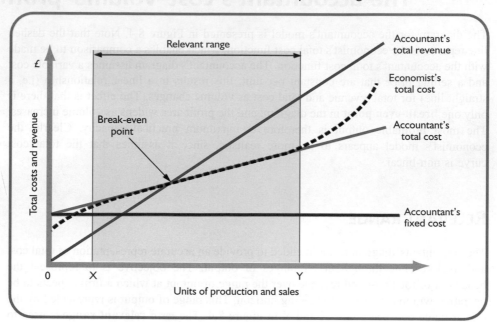

**FIGURE 8.5** *Accountant's fixed costs.*

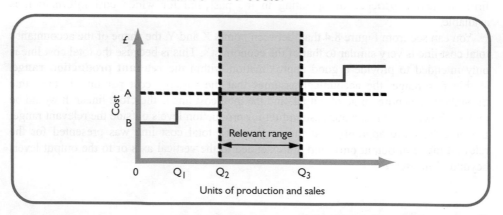

The fixed cost line for output levels below $Q_1$ (i.e. 0B) represents the cost of providing the basic operating capacity, and this line is the equivalent to the point where the economist's total cost line meets the vertical axis in Figure 8.4. Because the accountant assumes that in the short term the firm will operate in the relevant range between $Q_2$ and $Q_3$, the accountant's fixed cost line 0A in Figure 8.5 represents the fixed costs for the relevant output range only, which the firm is committed to in the current period and does not represent the fixed costs that would be incurred at the extreme levels of output beyond the shaded area in Figure 8.5.

## TOTAL REVENUE FUNCTION

Let us now compare the total revenue line for the accountant and the economist. We have seen that the accountant assumes that selling price is constant over the relevant range of output, and therefore the total revenue line is a straight line. The accountant's assumption

**FIGURE 8.6** *Increase in fixed costs.*

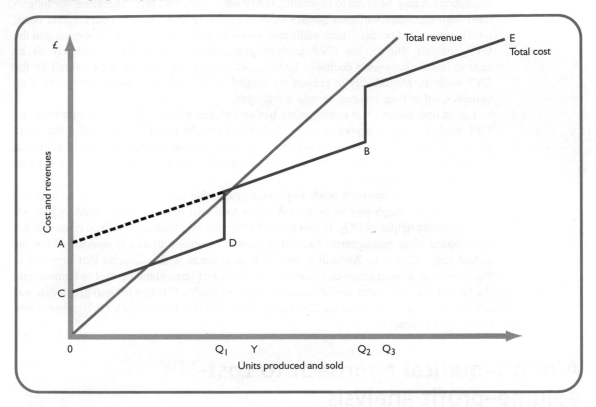

about the revenue line is a realistic one in those firms that operate in industries where selling prices tend to be fixed in the short term. A further factor reinforcing the assumption of a fixed selling price is that competition may take the form of non-price rather than price competition. Moreover, beyond the relevant range, increases in output may only be possible by offering substantial reductions in price. As it is not the intention of firms to operate outside the relevant range, the accountant makes no attempt to produce accurate revenue functions outside this range. It might be more meaningful in Figure 8.4 if the total revenue line was presented for output levels X and Y within the relevant range, instead of being extended to the left and right of these points.

# Application to longer-term time horizons

CVP analysis becomes more complex and questionable if we extend our application to a longer term time horizon. Consider a capacity expansion decision. The expansion of output beyond certain points may require increments of fixed costs such as additional supervision and machinery, the appointment of additional sales persons and the expansion of the firm's distribution facilities. Such increases are incorporated in Figure 8.6. Note from this figure that if the current output level is $OQ_1$ then additional facilities are required, thus increasing fixed costs, if output is to be increased beyond this level. Similarly, additional fixed costs must be incurred to expand output beyond $OQ_2$.

At this point, for a capacity expansion decision, we are moving from beyond the short term to a longer term application of CVP analysis. In the longer term, other factors besides volume are likely to be important. For example, to utilize the additional capacity reductions in selling prices and alternative advertising strategies may be considered. Also consideration may be given to expanding the product range and mix. Therefore, for longer-term decisions other variables besides volume are likely to have an impact on total costs, total revenues and profits. These additional variables cannot be easily incorporated into the CVP analysis. Hence, the CVP analysis presented in Figure 8.6 is unlikely to be appropriate for long-term decisions because other variables, that are not captured by the CVP analysis, are unlikely to remain unchanged. CVP analysis is only appropriate if all variables, other than volume, remain unchanged.

Let us now assume that management has undertaken a detailed analysis, without using CVP analysis, that incorporates all of these other variables and has concluded that extra fixed costs should be incurred to expand output to a maximum level of $OQ_2$ as shown in Figure 8.6. For simplicity we shall also assume that the total cost functions are the same as those described in Figure 8.6.

Once a decision has been made to provide productive capacity equal to a maximum of $OQ_2$, a separate graph may be presented with a total cost function represented by line AB and maximum output of $OQ_2$. In this revised graph the step increases in fixed costs will not be included, since management has already made a decision to aim to operate within the output range $Q_1$ to $Q_2$. Assuming that the total revenue is the same as that depicted in Figure 8.6 the revised graph can now be used as a short-term planning tool to demonstrate the impact that short-term output decisions have on profits. It is this revised graph that was used as a basis for comparing the accountant's and the economist's CVP presentation earlier in this chapter.

# A mathematical approach to cost–volume–profit analysis

Instead of using a diagram to present CVP information, we can use mathematical relationships. The mathematical approach is a quicker and more flexible method of producing the appropriate information than the graphical approach, and is a particularly appropriate form of input to a computer financial model.

When developing a mathematical formula for producing CVP information, you should note that one is assuming that selling price and costs remain constant per unit of output. Such an assumption may be valid for unit selling price and variable cost, but remember that in Chapter 2 we noted that in the short run fixed costs are a constant *total* amount whereas *unit* cost changes with output levels. As a result, profit per *unit* also changes with volume. For example, if fixed costs are £10 000 for a period and output is 10 000 units, the fixed cost will be £1 per unit. Alternatively, if output is 5000 units, the fixed cost will be £2 per unit. Profit per unit will not therefore be constant over varying output levels and it is incorrect to unitize fixed costs for CVP decisions.

We can develop a mathematical formula from the following relationship:

$$\text{net profit} = (\text{units sold} \times \text{unit selling price})$$
$$- [(\text{units sold} \times \text{unit variable cost}) + \text{total fixed costs}]$$

The following symbols can be used to represent the various items in the above equation:

$NP$ = net profit

$x$ = units sold

$P$ = selling price

$b$ = unit variable cost

$a$ = total fixed costs

**EXAMPLE 8.1**

Norvik Enterprises operate in the leisure and entertainment industry and one of its activities is to promote concerts at locations throughout Europe. The company is examining the viability of a concert in Stockholm. Estimated fixed costs are £60 000. These include the fees paid to performers, the hire of the venue and advertising costs. Variable costs consist of the cost of a pre-packed buffet which will be provided by a firm of caterers at a price, which is currently being negotiated, but it is likely to be in the region of £10 per ticket sold. The proposed price for the sale of a ticket is £20. The management of Norvic have requested the following information:

1. The number of tickets that must be sold to break-even (that is, the point at which there is neither a profit or loss).
2. How many tickets must be sold to earn £30 000 profit?
3. What profit would result if 8000 tickets were sold?
4. What selling price would have to be charged to give a profit of £30 000 on sales of 8000 tickets, fixed costs of £60 000 and variable costs of £10 per ticket?
5. How many additional tickets must be sold to cover the extra cost of television advertising of £8000?

The equation can now be expressed in mathematical terms as

$$NP = Px - (a + bx) \tag{8.1}$$

You should now refer to Example 8.1. This example will be used to illustrate the application of the mathematical approach to CVP analysis.

Let us now provide the information requested in Example 8.1.

## 1. BREAK-EVEN POINT IN UNITS (I.E. NUMBER OF TICKETS SOLD)

Since $NP = Px - (a + bx)$, the break-even point is at a level of output $(x)$ where

$$a + bx = Px - NP$$

Substituting the information in Example 8.1, we have

$$60\,000 + 10x = 20x - 0$$
$$60\,000 = 10x$$

and so $x = 6000$ tickets (or £120 000 total sales at £20 per ticket).

An alternative method, called the contribution margin approach, can also be used. Contribution margin is equal to sales minus variable expenses. Because the variable cost per unit and the selling price per unit are assumed to be constant the contribution margin per unit is also assumed to be constant. In Example 8.1 note that each ticket sold generates a contribution of £10, which is available to cover fixed costs and, after they are covered, to contribute to profit. When we have obtained sufficient total contribution to cover fixed costs, the break-even point is achieved, and the alternative formula is

$$\text{break-even point in units} = \frac{\text{fixed costs}}{\text{contribution per unit}}$$

The contribution margin approach can be related to the mathematical formula approach. Consider the penultimate line of the formula approach; it reads

$$£60\,000 = 10x$$

and so

$$x = \frac{£60\,000}{£10}$$

giving the contribution margin formula

$$\frac{\text{fixed costs}}{\text{contribution per unit}}$$

The contribution margin approach is therefore a restatement of the mathematical formula, and either technique can be used; it is a matter of personal preference.

## 2. UNITS TO BE SOLD TO OBTAIN A £30 000 PROFIT

Using the equation $NP = Px - (a + bx)$ and substituting the information in Example 8.1, we have

$$£30\,000 = £20x - (£60\,000 + £10x)$$
$$£90\,000 = £10x$$

and so

$$x = 9000 \text{ tickets}$$

If we apply the contribution margin approach and wish to achieve the desired profit, we must obtain sufficient contribution to cover the fixed costs (i.e. the break-even point) plus a further contribution to cover the desired profit. Hence the equation using the contribution margin approach is

$$\text{units sold for desired profit} = \frac{\text{fixed costs} + \text{desired profit}}{\text{contribution per unit}}$$

This is merely a restatement of the penultimate line of the mathematical formula, which reads

$$£90\,000 = £10\,x$$

and so

$$x = \frac{£90\,000}{£10}$$

## 3. PROFIT FROM THE SALE OF 8000 TICKETS

Substituting in the equation $NP = Px - (a + bx)$, we have

$$NP = £20 \times 8000 - (£60\,000 + £10 \times 8000)$$
$$= £160\,000 - (£60\,000 + £80\,000)$$

and so

$$NP = £20\,000$$

COST–VOLUME–PROFIT ANALYSIS **245**

## 4. SELLING PRICE TO BE CHARGED TO SHOW A PROFIT OF £30000 ON SALES OF 8000 UNITS

Applying the formula for net profit (i.e. Equation 8.1)

$$£30\,000 = 8000P - (£60\,000 + (£10 \times 8000))$$
$$= 8000P - £140\,000$$

giving
$$8000P = £170\,000$$

and
$$P = £21.25 \text{ (i.e. an increase of £1.25 per ticket)}$$

## 5. ADDITIONAL SALES VOLUME TO MEET £8000 ADDITIONAL FIXED ADVERTISING CHARGES

The contribution per unit is £10 and fixed costs will increase by £8000. Therefore an extra 800 tickets must be sold to cover the additional fixed costs of £8000.

## THE PROFIT–VOLUME RATIO

The **profit–volume ratio** is the contribution expressed as a percentage of sales:

$$\text{profit–volume ratio} = \frac{\text{contribution}}{\text{sales revenue}} \times 100$$

In Example 8.1 the contribution is £10 per unit and the selling price is £20 per unit; the profit–volume ratio is 50%. This means that for each £1 sale a contribution of 50p is earned. Because we assume that selling price and contribution per unit are constant, the profit–volume ratio is also assumed to be constant. Given an estimate of total sales revenue, it is possible to use the profit–volume ratio to estimate total contribution. For example, if total sales revenue is estimated to be £200 000, the total contribution will be £100 000 (50% of £200 000). To calculate the profit, we deduct fixed costs of £60 000; thus a profit of £40 000 will be obtained from total sales revenue of £200 000.

## RELEVANT RANGE

It is vital to remember that, as with the mathematical approach, the formulae method can only be used for decisions that result in outcomes within the relevant range. Outside this range the unit selling price and the variable cost are no longer deemed to be constant per unit, and any results obtained from the formulae that fall outside the relevant range will be incorrect. The concept of the relevant range is more appropriate for production settings but it can apply within non-production settings. Returning to Norvic Enterprises in Example 8.1, let us assume that the caterers will increase their charges on a sliding scale up to 4000 tickets sold and further reductions will apply for sales volumes in excess of 12 000 tickets. Thus, the £10 variable cost relates only to a sales volume within a range of 4000–12 000 tickets. Outside this range other costs apply. Also the number of seats made available at the venue is flexible and the hire cost will be reduced for sales of less than 4000 tickets and increased for sales beyond 12 000 tickets. In other words, we will assume that the relevant range is a sales volume of 4000–12 000 tickets and outside this range the results of our CVP analysis do not apply.

# Margin of safety

The margin of safety indicates by how much sales may decrease before a loss occurs. Using Example 8.1, where unit selling price and variable cost were £20 and £10 respectively and fixed costs were £60 000, we noted that the break-even point was 6000 tickets or £120 000 sales value. If sales are expected to be 8000 tickets or £160 000, the margin of safety will be 2000 tickets or £40 000. Alternatively, we can express the margin of safety in a percentage form based on the following ratio:

$$\text{percentage margin of safety} = \frac{\text{expected sales} - \text{break-even sales}}{\text{expected sales}}$$

$$= \frac{£160\,000 - £120\,000}{£160\,000} = 25\%$$

# Constructing the break-even chart

Using the data in Example 8.1, we can construct the break-even chart for Norvik Enterprises (Figure 8.7). In constructing the graph, the fixed costs are plotted as a single horizontal line at the £60 000 level. Variable costs at the rate of £10 per unit of volume are added to the fixed costs to enable the total cost line to be plotted. The total revenue line is plotted at the rate of £20 per unit of volume. The constraints of the relevant range consisting of two vertical lines are then added to the graph: beyond these lines we have little assurance that the CVP relationships are valid.

The point at which the total sales revenue line cuts the total cost line is the point where the concert makes neither a profit nor a loss. This is the break-even point and is 6000 tickets or £120 000 total sales revenue. The distance between the total sales revenue line and the total cost line at a volume below the break-even point represents losses that will occur for various sales levels below 6000 tickets. Similarly, if the company operates at a sales volume above the break-even point, the difference between the total revenue and the total cost lines represents the profit that results from sales levels above 6000 tickets.

# Alternative presentation of cost–volume–profit analysis

## CONTRIBUTION GRAPH

In Figure 8.7 the fixed cost line is drawn parallel to the horizontal axis, and the variable cost is the difference between the total cost line and the fixed cost line. An alternative to Figure 8.7 for the data contained in Example 8.1 is illustrated in Figure 8.8. This alternative presentation is called a contribution graph. In Figure 8.8 the variable cost line is drawn first at £10 per unit of volume. The fixed costs are represented by the difference between the total cost line and the variable cost line. Because fixed costs are assumed to be a constant sum throughout the entire output range, a constant sum of £60 000 for fixed costs is added to the variable cost line, which results in the total cost line being drawn parallel to the variable cost line. The advantage of this form of presentation is that the total contribution is emphasized in the graph, and is represented by the difference between the total sales revenue line and the total variable cost line.

**FIGURE 8.7**  *Break-even chart for Example 8.1.*

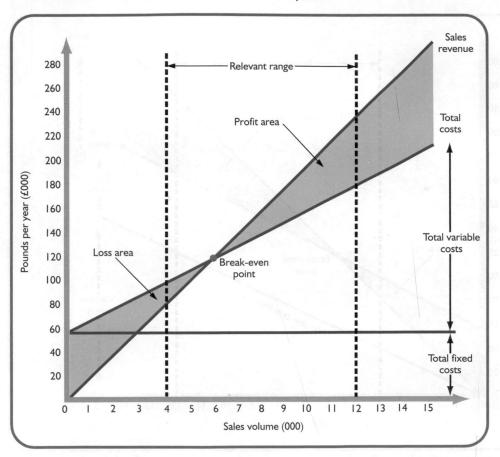

## PROFIT–VOLUME GRAPH

The break-even and contribution charts do not highlight the profit or loss at different volume levels. To ascertain the profit or loss figures from a break-even chart, it is necessary to determine the difference between the total-cost and total-revenue lines. The profit–volume graph is a more convenient method of showing the impact of changes in volume on profit. Such a graph is illustrated in Figure 8.9. The horizontal axis represents the various levels of sales volume, and the profits and losses for the period are recorded on the vertical scale. You will see from Figure 8.9 that profits or losses are plotted for each of the various sales levels, and these points are connected by a profit line. The break-even point occurs at the point where the profit line intersects the horizontal line at a sales volume of 6 000 tickets. If sales are zero, the maximum loss will be the amount of the fixed costs, since a company should not lose more than the amount of the fixed costs that it has incurred. With each unit sold, a contribution of £10 is obtained towards the fixed costs, and the break-even point is at 6000 tickets, when the total contribution exactly equals the total of the fixed costs. With each additional unit sold beyond 6000 tickets, a surplus of £10 per ticket is obtained. If 10 000 tickets are sold, the profit will be £40 000 (4000 tickets at £10 contribution). You can see this relationship between sales and profit at 10 000 tickets from the dotted lines in Figure 8.9.

**FIGURE 8.8** *Contribution chart for Example 8.1.*

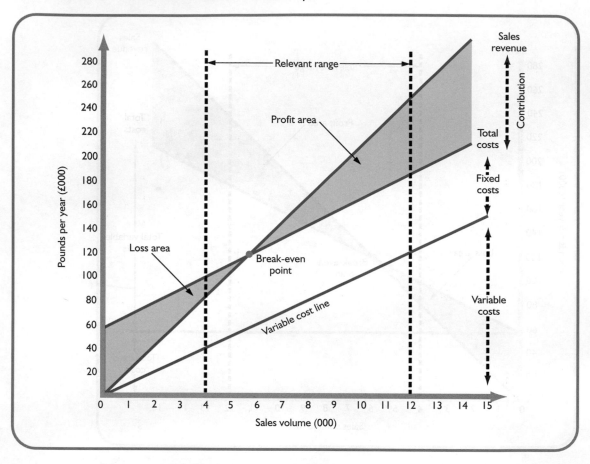

# Cost–volume–profit analysis assumptions

It is essential that anyone preparing or interpreting CVP information is aware of the underlying assumptions on which the information has been prepared. If these assumptions are not recognized, serious errors may result and incorrect conclusions may be drawn from the analysis. We shall now consider these important assumptions. They are as follows:

1. All other variables remain constant.
2. A single product or constant sales mix.
3. Complexity-related fixed costs do not change.
4. Profits are calculated on a variable-costing basis.
5. Total costs and total revenue are linear functions of output.
6. The analysis applies to the relevant range only.
7. Costs can be accurately divided into their fixed and variable elements.
8. The analysis applies only to a short-term time horizon.

**FIGURE 8.9**  *Profit–volume graph for Example 8.1.*

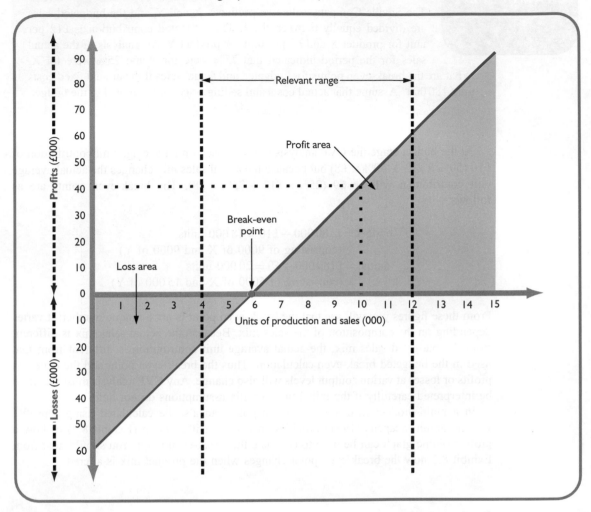

## 1. ALL OTHER VARIABLES REMAIN CONSTANT

It has been assumed that all variables other than the particular one under consideration have remained constant throughout the analysis. In other words, it is assumed that volume is the only factor that will cause costs and revenues to change. However, changes in other variables such as production efficiency, sales mix, price levels and production methods can have an important influence on sales revenue and costs. If significant changes in these other variables occur the CVP analysis presentation will be incorrect.

## 2. SINGLE PRODUCT OR CONSTANT SALES MIX

CVP analysis assumes that either a single product is sold or, if a range of products is sold, that sales will be in accordance with a predetermined sales mix. When a predetermined sales mix is used, it can be depicted in the CVP analysis by assuming average revenues and average variable costs for the given sales mix. Consider the situation described in Example 8.2.

**EXAMPLE 8.2**

The Saville Company sells two products, X and Y, and the budgeted sales are divided equally between them. The estimated contribution is £12 per unit for product X and £8 per unit for product Y. An analysis of the actual sales for the period indicated that 75% were for Y and 25% were for X. What are the break-even points for budgeted and actual sales if the annual fixed costs are £180 000? Assume that actual costs and selling prices are identical to the budget.

At the budget stage the CVP analysis will be based on an average unit contribution of £10 (50% × £12 + 50% × £8) but because the actual sales mix changes the actual average unit contribution will be £9 (25% × £12 + 75% × £8). The break-even points are as follows:

$$\text{budget} = £180\,000 \div £10 = 18\,000 \text{ units}$$
$$\text{(consisting of 9000 of X and 9000 of Y)}$$
$$\text{actual} = £180\,000 \div £9 = 20\,000 \text{ units}$$
$$\text{(consisting of 5000 of X and 15\,000 of Y)}$$

From these figures you will see that the break-even point is not a unique number: it varies depending on the composition of the sales mix. Because the actual sales mix is different from the budgeted sales mix, the actual average unit contribution is different from that used in the budgeted break-even calculation. Thus the break-even point and the expected profits or losses at various output levels will also change. Any CVP analysis must therefore be interpreted carefully if the initial product mix assumptions do not hold.

In a multi-product firm the break-even point can also be calculated using a profit–volume graph. Scapens (1991) provides an excellent illustration (Exhibit 8.1) of how a profit–volume graph can be used to calculate the break-even point. You should note from Exhibit 8.1 how the break-even point changes when the product mix is altered.

## 3. COMPLEXITY-RELATED FIXED COSTS DO NOT CHANGE

CVP analysis assumes that complexity-related costs will remain unchanged. Cooper and Kaplan (1987) illustrate how complexity-related fixed costs can increase as a result of changes in the range of items produced, even though volume remains unchanged. They illustrate the relationship with an example of two identical plants. One plant produces one million units of product A. The second plant produces 100 000 units of A and 900 000 similar units of 199 similar products. The first plant has a simple production environment and requires limited manufacturing support facilities. Set-ups, expediting, inventory movements and schedule activities are minimal. The other plant has a much more complex production management environment. The 200 products must be scheduled through the plant, and this requires frequent set-ups, inventory movements, purchase receipts and inspections. To handle this complexity, the support departments' fixed costs must be larger.

Cooper and Kaplan use the above example to illustrate that many so-called fixed costs vary not with the volume of items manufactured but with range of items produced (i.e. the complexity of the production process). Complexity-related costs do not normally vary significantly in the short term with the volume of production. If a change in volume does not alter the range of products then it is likely that complexity-related fixed costs will not alter, but if volume stays constant and the range of items produced changes then support

**EXHIBIT 8.1**

*Multi-product
CVP analysis
(Scapens, 1991,
pp. 70–71)*

If it is assumed that there are three products, X, Y, and Z, then the CVP chart illustrated in Figure Ex 8.1 could be drawn. This chart was constructed for a total output of V, using an assumed standard product mix for the three products. The total fixed costs of A are not traceable to individual products. At an output of zero the profit earned will amount to −A (i.e. a loss of A), represented by point *k* on the chart. The line *km* represents the profit earned by product X – the slope of the line is determined by the contribution per unit earned on sales of that product. The line *mn* represents the profit earned by product Y, which has a lower contribution per unit than product X. The line *nj* is the profit earned by the least profitable product, i.e. Z. The line joining points *k* and *j* reflects the average profitability of the three products, and each point on that line represents the profit earned for the associated output, assuming that the three products are sold in the standard product mix, i.e. the mix implied in the construction of the chart. Accordingly, the indicated break-even point only applies if the products are sold in that standard product mix. It can be seen clearly from Figure Ex 8.1 that break-even can occur at lower levels of output, provided the proportions of the products are changed. For instance, the point B where the line *kmnj* crosses the horizontal axis indicates a possible break-even point.

The line *kmnj* reflects the amounts of the three products included in a total output of V, using the standard product mix. Break-even at B could be achieved by producing the quantity of product X implied in the total production of V, together with a small amount of product Y. But the necessary combination of X and Y is not a standard product mix. Break-even could also be achieved at point C, provided that only the most profitable product X is produced. Thus, as indicated earlier, if the assumption of a standard product mix is relaxed, there will be no unique break-even point. But, with a standard product mix, a unique break-even point can be determined using CVP analysis, as is illustrated in Figure Ex 8.1.

**FIGURE EX 8.1** *Multi-product CVP chart.*

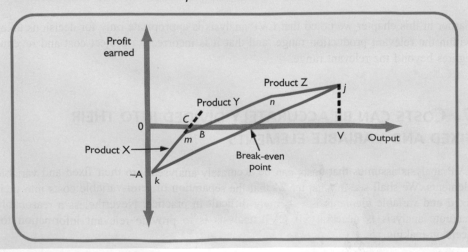

department fixed costs will eventually change because of the increase or decrease in product complexity.

CVP analysis assumptions will be violated if a firm seeks to enhance profitability by product proliferation; that is, by introducing new variants of products based on short-term contribution margins. The CVP analysis will show that profits will increase as sales volume increases and fixed costs remain constant in the short term. The increased product diversity, however, will cause complexity-related fixed costs to increase in future periods, and there is a danger that long-term profits may decline as a result of product proliferation. The CVP analysis incorporates the fixed costs required to handle the diversity and complexity within the current product range, but the costs will remain fixed only if diversity and complexity are not increased further. Thus CVP will not capture the changes in complexity-related costs arising from changes in the range of items produced.

## 4. PROFITS ARE CALCULATED ON A VARIABLE COSTING BASIS

The analysis assumes that the fixed costs incurred during the period are charged as an expense for that period. Therefore variable-costing profit calculations are assumed. If absorption-costing profit calculations are used, it is necessary to assume that production is equal to sales for the analysis to predict absorption costing profits. If this situation does not occur, the inventory levels will change and the fixed overheads allocated for the period will be different from the amount actually incurred during the period. Under absorption costing, only when production equals sales will the amount of fixed overhead incurred be equal to the amount of fixed overhead charged as an expense. For the application of CVP analysis with an absorption costing system you should refer to Appendix 8.1.

## 5. TOTAL COSTS AND TOTAL REVENUE ARE LINEAR FUNCTIONS OF OUTPUT

The analysis assumes that unit variable cost and selling price are constant. This assumption is only likely to be valid within the relevant range of production described on page 239.

## 6. ANALYSIS APPLIES TO RELEVANT RANGE ONLY

Earlier in this chapter we noted that CVP analysis is appropriate only for decisions taken within the relevant production range, and that it is incorrect to project cost and revenue figures beyond the relevant range.

## 7. COSTS CAN BE ACCURATELY DIVIDED INTO THEIR FIXED AND VARIABLE ELEMENTS

CVP analysis assumes that costs can be accurately analysed into their fixed and variable elements. We shall see in Chapter 24 that the separation of semi-variable costs into their fixed and variable elements is extremely difficult in practice. Nevertheless a reasonably accurate analysis is necessary if CVP analysis is to provide relevant information for decision-making.

## 8. THE ANALYSIS APPLIES ONLY TO A SHORT-TERM TIME HORIZON

At the beginning of this chapter we noted that CVP analysis is based on the relationship between volume and sales revenue, costs and profits in the short term, the short term being typically a period of one year. In the short term the costs of providing a firm's operating capacity, such as property taxes and the salaries of senior managers, are likely to be fixed in relation to changes in activity. Decisions on the firm's intended future potential level of operating capacity will determine the amount of capacity costs to be incurred. These decisions will have been made previously as part of the long-term planning process. Once these decisions have been made, they cannot easily be reversed in the short-term. It takes time to significantly expand the capacity of plant and machinery or reduce capacity. Furthermore, plant investment and abandonment decisions should not be based on short-term fluctuations in demand within a particular year. Instead, they should be reviewed periodically as part of the long-term planning process and decisions based on predictions of long-run demand over several years. Thus capacity costs will tend to be fixed in relation to changes of activity within short-term periods such as one year. However, over long-term periods significant changes in volume or product complexity will cause fixed costs to change.

It is therefore assumed that in the short term some costs will be fixed and unaffected by changes in volume whereas other (variable) costs will vary with changes in volume. In the short-run volume is the most important variable influencing total revenue, costs and profit. For this reason volume is given special attention in the form of CVP analysis. You should note, however, that in the long term other variables, besides volume, will cause costs to change. Therefore, the long-term analysis should incorporate other variables, besides volume, and recognize that fixed costs will increase or decrease in steps in response to changes in the explanatory variables.

# Cost–volume–profit analysis and computer applications

The output from a CVP model is only as good as the input. The analysis will include assumptions about sales mix, production efficiency, price levels, total fixed costs, variable costs and selling price per unit. Obviously, our estimates regarding these variables will be subject to varying degrees of uncertainty. In Chapter 12 we shall consider how uncertainty can be incorporated into CVP analysis.

Sensitivity analysis is one approach for coping with changes in the values of the variables. Sensitivity analysis focuses on how a result will be changed if the original estimates or the underlying assumptions change. With regard to CVP analysis, sensitivity analysis answers questions such as the following:

1. What will the profit be if the sales mix changes from that originally predicted?
2. What will the profit be if fixed costs increase by 10% and variable costs decline by 5%?

The widespread use of spreadsheet packages has enabled management accountants to develop CVP computerized models. Managers can now consider alternative plans by keying the information into a computer, which can quickly show changes both graphically and numerically. Thus managers can study various combinations of changes in selling prices, fixed costs, variable costs and product mix, and can react quickly without waiting for formal reports from the management accountant.

## Self-Assessment Questions

You should attempt to answer these questions yourself before looking up the suggested answers, which appear on pages 1105–7. If any part of your answer is incorrect, check back carefully to make sure you understand where you went wrong.

1. Tweed Ltd is a company engaged solely in the manufacture of jumpers, which are bought mainly for sporting activities. Present sales are direct to retailers, but in recent years there has been a steady decline in output because of increased foreign competition. In the last trading year (2001) the accounting report indicated that the company produced the lowest profit for 10 years. The forecast for 2002 indicates that the present deterioration in profits is likely to continue. The company considers that a profit of £80 000 should be achieved to provide an adequate return on capital. The managing director has asked that a review be made of the present pricing and marketing policies. The marketing director has completed this review, and passes the proposals on to you for evaluation and recommendation, together with the profit and loss account for year ending 31 December 2001.

### Tweed Ltd profit and loss account for year ending 31 December 2001

|  | (£) | (£) | (£) |
|---|---:|---:|---:|
| Sales revenue | | | |
| (100 000 jumpers at £10) | | | 1 000 000 |
| Factory cost of goods sold: | | | |
| Direct materials | 100 000 | | |
| Direct labour | 350 000 | | |
| Variable factory overheads | 60 000 | | |
| Fixed factory overheads | 220 000 | 730 000 | |
| Administration overhead | | 140 000 | |
| Selling and distribution overhead | | | |
| Sales commission (2% of sales) | 20 000 | | |
| Delivery costs (variable per unit sold) | 50 000 | | |
| Fixed costs | 40 000 | 110 000 | 980 000 |
| Profit | | | 20 000 |

The information to be submitted to the managing director includes the following three proposals:

(i) To proceed on the basis of analyses of market research studies which indicate that the demand for the jumpers is such that 10% reduction in selling price would increase demand by 40%.

(ii) To proceed with an enquiry that the marketing director has had from a mail order company about the possibility of purchasing 50 000 units annually if the selling price is right. The mail order company would transport the jumpers from Tweed Ltd to its own warehouse, and no sales commission would be paid on these sales by Tweed Ltd. However, if an acceptable price can be negotiated, Tweed Ltd would be expected to contribute £60 000 per annum towards the cost of producing the mail order catalogue. It would also be necessary for Tweed Ltd to provide special additional packaging at a cost of £0.50 per jumper. The marketing director considers that in 2002 the sales from existing business would remain unchanged at 100 000 units, based on a selling price of £10 if the mail order contract is undertaken.

(iii) To proceed on the basis of a view by the marketing director that a 10% price reduction, together with a national advertising campaign costing £30 000 may increase sales to the maximum capacity of 160 000 jumpers.

Required:

(a) The calculation of break-even sales value based on the 2001 accounts.

(b) A financial evaluation of proposal (i) and a calculation of the number of units Tweed Ltd would require to sell at £9 each to earn the target profit of £80 000.

(c) A calculation of the minimum prices that would have to be quoted to the mail order company, first, to ensure that Tweed Ltd would, at least, break even on the mail order contract, secondly, to ensure that the same overall profit is earned as proposal (i) and, thirdly, to ensure that the overall target profit is earned.

(d) A financial evaluation of proposal (iii).

2. (a) A break-even chart is shown below for Windhurst Ltd.

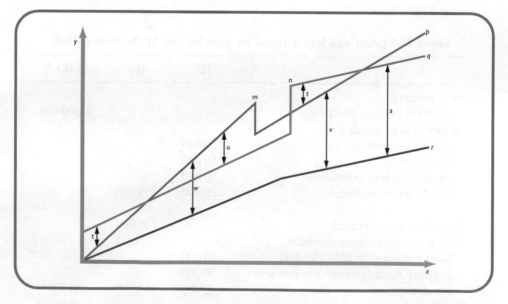

You are required:

(i) to identify the components of the break-even chart labelled *p, q, r, s, t, u, v, w, x* and *y*;
(5 marks)

(ii) to suggest what events are represented at the values of *x* that are labelled *m* and *n* on the chart;
(3 marks)

(iii) to assess the usefulness of break-even analysis to senior management of a small company.
(7 marks)

(b) Hackett Ltd produces gudgeons and bludgeons. The company's budget for 2000 includes the following data:

|  | Gudgeons | Bludgeons |
| --- | --- | --- |
| Unit selling price (£) | 10 | 5 |
| Contribution margin ratio (%) | 40 | 60 |

The budget is designed to show a figure of profit or loss for each product, after apportioning joint fixed costs of £100 000 in proportion to the number of units of each product sold.

For 2000 gudgeons are budgeted to show a profit of £14 000, and bludgeons a loss of £2000. The number of units of each product sold is expected to be equal.

You are required to write a report to the managing director of Hackett Ltd advising him on the basis of the information given whether to implement any of the following three proposals:

(i) to increase the price of bludgeons by 25%, in the expectation that the price elasticity of demand over this range of prices will be unity; (4 marks)

(ii) to make changes to the production process that would reduce the joint fixed costs by 12.5% and increase the variable costs of each product by 10%; (3 marks)

(iii) to introduce both of the above changes. (3 marks)

*ICAEW Management Accounting*

## Summary

CVP analysis has been a core topic in the management accounting education process for over 50 years. It would also appear to be widely used in practice with a recent survey indicating that 86% of Australian firms had adopted the technique (Chenhall and Langfield-Smith, 1998a).

CVP analysis is concerned with examining the relationship between changes in volume and changes in total revenue and costs in the short term. In this chapter we have compared the economist's and accountant's models of CVP behaviour. The major differences are that the total cost and total revenue functions are curvilinear in the economist's model, whereas the accountant's model assumes linear relationships. However, we have noted that the accountant's model was intended to predict CVP behaviour only within the relevant range, where a firm is likely to be operating on constant returns to sale. A comparison of the two models suggested that, within the relevant production range, the total costs and revenue functions are fairly similar.

We have seen that for decision-making a numerical presentation provides more precise information than a graphical one. Given that the cost and revenue functions will already have been determined at the decision-making stage, the major area of uncertainty relates to the actual level of output. The graphical approach provides a useful representation of how costs, revenues and profits will behave for the many possible output levels that may actually materialize.

It is essential when interpreting CVP information that you are aware of the following important assumptions on which the analysis is based:

1. All other variables remain constant.
2. The analysis is based on a single product or constant sales mix.
3. Complexity-related costs do not change.
4. Profits are calculated on a variable-costing basis.
5. Total costs and revenues are a linear function of output.
6. The analysis applies to the relevant range only.
7. Costs can be accurately divided into their fixed and variable elements.
8. The analysis applies only to a short-term time horizon.

In this chapter we have not incorporated uncertainty into the CVP analysis. CVP analysis under conditions of uncertainty will be discussed in the appendix to Chapter 12. You should also note that in Appendix 8.1 CVP analysis is illustrated when profits are measured on an absorption costing basis.

## Key Terms and Concepts

# Appendix 8.1: CVP analysis applied to absorption costing

You will recall from our discussion of CVP analysis assumptions that CVP analysis assumes that profits are measured using a variable costing system, or the special situation where sales volume equals production volume, so that absorption costing profits are equal to variable costing profits. In this appendix we are going to look at how CVP analysis can be adapted to be applied in situations when profits are measured on an absorption costing basis and sales volume does not equal production volume.

Where CVP analysis is used as an input to decision-making the analysis should be based on variable costing principles since inventory movements should not influence the underlying economic reality. However, the outcomes of decisions using CVP analysis are normally not separately reported. Instead, the estimated and actual outcomes arising from the decisions are merged with other activities and incorporated into the monthly budgeting and profit performance reporting system. The monthly profit reporting system in most organizations is based on absorption costing. This can result in situations where the profits reported within the monthly reporting system are different from those predicted by the variable costing CVP analysis. To ascertain how the consequences of decisions will be reported within the monthly reporting system management require CVP analysis based on absorption costing principles.

CVP analysis is more complex with absorption costing because profit is a function of both sales and production whereas with variable costing profit is a function of a single variable (sales volume). To apply CVP analysis to absorption costing the break-even curve will consist of a set of pairs of sales and production and we must assume that one of the variables remains a known, or constant, value.

We shall use the following terms to develop an absorption costing CVP analysis model:

$uvmc$ = unit variable manufacturing cost
$uvnmc$ = unit variable non-manufacturing cost
$fnmc$ = fixed non-manufacturing cost
$usp$ = unit selling price
$uvc$ = unit variable cost
$fmohc$ = fixed manufacturing overhead cost for the period
$ud$ = unit denominator level used to calculate the fixed overhead rate
$us$ = units sold
$up$ = units produced
$tfc$ = total fixed costs for the period (i.e. manufacturing + non-manufacturing fixed overheads)

Our starting point is to develop the profit function for an absorption costing model adopting the same approach as that used in Appendix 7.1. You will recall that the volume variance (i.e. the under- or over-recovery of fixed manufacturing overhead) is the difference between the unit denominator level (*ud*) used to derive the fixed manufacturing overhead absorption rate and the actual level of production (*up*) multiplied by the fixed manufacturing overhead rate. Therefore we can express the volume variance (VV) as:

$$\text{VV} = (1 - up/ud)fmohc$$

so that:

$$\text{Total cost (TC)} = (uvmc \times us) + (fmohc/ud)us + (uvnmc \times us)$$

$$+ fnmc + (1 - up/ud)\,fmohc$$

$$\text{TC} = (uvc + fmohc/ud)us + fmohc + fnmc - (fmohc/ud)up$$

$$\text{TC} = (uvc + fmohc/ud)us - (fmohc/ud)up + tfc$$

$$\therefore \text{Operating profit} = (usp - uvc - fmohc/ud)us + (fmohc/ud)up - tfc$$

Setting profit equal to zero and assuming that production (*up*) is a known, or constant, value the profit function is:

$$0 = (usp - uvc - fmohc/ud)us + (fmohc/ud)up - tfc$$

$$tfc - (fmohc/ud)up = (usp - uvc - fmohc/ud)us$$

therefore the break-even sales volume (*us*) is:

$$\text{BEP}(us) = (tfc - (fmohc/ud)up)/(usp - uvc - fmohc/ud)$$

To illustrate the application of the BEP(*us*) formula we shall use Example 7.1 that we used in the previous chapter. This example is repeated in the form of Example 8A.1. You should now refer to Example 8A.1.

The absorption costing break-even point calculations are as follows:

$$\text{BEP}(us) \text{ Periods } 1\text{–}4 = (£400\,000 - (£300\,000/150\,000)150\,000)/$$
$$(£10 - £6 - £300\,000/150\,000) = 50\,000 \text{ units}$$
$$\text{BEP}(us) \text{ Period } 5 = (£400\,000 - (£300\,000/150\,000)170\,000)/$$
$$(£10 - £6 - £300\,000/150\,000) = 30\,000 \text{ units}$$
$$\text{BEP}(us) \text{ Period } 6 = (£400\,000 - (£300\,000/150\,000)140\,000)/$$
$$(£10 - £6 - £300\,000/150\,000) = 60\,000 \text{ units}$$

Note that the break-even point remains unchanged in periods 1–4 because production is held constant at 150 000 units but changes in periods 5 and 6 because of changes in production. Given that absorption costing profit is a funtion of production volume, besides sales volume, the break-even sales volume changes when production volume changes.

Contrast the variable costing sales volume break-even point with the absorption costing break-even point. The former is 100 000 units (£400 000 fixed costs/£2 unit contribution) for all periods since the same amount of fixed costs are expensed each period whereas with the absorption costing system production volume is significantly in excess of sales volume. Consequently, a large proportion of fixed overheads is deferred to future periods. Hence, the absorption costing break-even point is significantly different from the variable costing break-even point.

The above analysis can be verified by preparing absorption costing profit statements adopting the same approach as that illustrated in Exhibit 7.3 in the previous chapter. If you wish to verify the break-even point calculations, using the break-even sales volumes for each period, do remember to incorporate the opening and closing inventories that will result from the break-even sales volumes.

**EXAMPLE 8A.1**

The following information is available for periods 1–6 for the Samuelson Company:

|  | (£) |
|---|---|
| Unit selling price | 10 |
| Unit variable cost | 6 |
| Fixed costs for each period | 300 000 |

The company produces only one product. Budgeted activity is expected to average 150 000 units per period, and production and sales for each period are as follows:

|  | Period 1 | Period 2 | Period 3 | Period 4 | Period 5 | Period 6 |
|---|---|---|---|---|---|---|
| Units sold (000's) | 150 | 120 | 180 | 150 | 140 | 160 |
| Units produced (000's) | 150 | 150 | 150 | 150 | 170 | 140 |

There were no opening stocks at the start of period 1, and the actual manufacturing fixed overhead incurred was £300 000 per period. We shall also assume that non-manufacturing overheads are £100 000 per period.

The same principles that are used in variable costing CVP analysis to determine the output levels to achieve target profit levels can also be applied here. Adding a target profit to the total fixed costs in the BEP(*us*) formula and assuming that production is held constant at 170 000 units, the sales volume to derive a target profit of £220 000 can be derived. The calculation is:

$$\text{BEP}(us) = (£400\,000 + £220\,000 - (£300\,000/150\,000)170\,000)/$$
$$(£10 - £6 - £300\,000/150\,000) = 140\,000 \text{ units}$$

The above sales volume computation of 140 000 units is based on an assumed production volume of 170 000 units. If you look at the data shown in Example 8A.1 you will see that the production and sales volumes are identical to that of period 5. You should now refer back to Exhibit 7.3 in Chapter 7 and you will be able to verify that a production volume of 170 000 units and a sales volume of 140 000 units does result in a reported profit of £220 000.

The above analysis can also be reversed so that sales volume is a known constant and a break-even production point calculated. Setting operating profit equal to zero and assuming that sales volume (*us*) is known the break-even point production level is:

$$\text{BEP}(up) = (tfc - (usp - uvc - fmohc/un)us)/(fmohc/un)$$

However, since the impact of changes in sales volume is likely to be of greater importance to management we will not illustrate the application of the above BEP(*up*) formula here.

## Key Examination Points

Students experience little difficulty in constructing break-even charts, but many cannot construct profit–volume charts.

Remember that the horizontal axis represents the level of activity while profits/losses are shown on the vertical axis. The maximum loss is at zero activity, and is equal to the fixed costs.

Students also experience difficulty with the following:

1. Coping with multi-product situations.

2. Calculating break-even points when total sales and costs are given but no information is supplied on unit costs.
3. Explaining the assumptions of CVP analysis. For multi-product situations you should base your calculations on the average contribution per unit, using the approach shown in Example 8.2. When unit costs are not given, the break-even point in sales value can be calculated as follows:

$$\text{fixed costs} \times \frac{\text{total estimated sales}}{\text{total estimated contribution}}$$

## Questions

*Indicates that a suggested solution is to be found in the *Students' Manual.*

### 8.1* Intermediate
A company manufactures and sells two products, X and Y. Forecast data for a year are:

|  | Product X | Product Y |
|---|---|---|
| Sales (units) | 80 000 | 20 000 |
| Sales price (per unit) | £12 | £8 |
| Variable cost (per unit) | £8 | £3 |

Annual fixed costs are estimated at £273 000.

What is the break-even point in sales revenue with the current sales mix?
A £570 000
B £606 667
C £679 467
D £728 000
*ACCA Foundation Paper 3 Sample Question*

### 8.2* Intermediate
H Limited manufactures and sells two products, J and K. Annual sales are expected to be in the ratio of J : 1, K : 3. Total annual sales are planned to be £420 000. Product J has a contribution to sales ratio of 40%, whereas that of product K is 50%. Annual fixed costs are estimated to be £120 000.

The budgeted break-even sales value (to the nearest £1000):
A £196 000
B £200 000
C £253 000
D £255 000
E cannot be determined from the above data.
*CIMA Stage 2*

Sometimes a question will give details of costs but not the split into the fixed and variable elements. You can separate the total costs into their fixed and variable elements using the high–low method described in Chapter 24. Alternatively, you can refer to the answer to Question 8.14 and 8.15 in the *Students' Manual* accompanying this book for an illustration of the approach.

### 8.3* Intermediate
The following details relate to product R:

| Level of activity (units) | 1000 (£/unit) | 2000 (£/unit) |
|---|---|---|
| Direct materials | 4.00 | 4.00 |
| Direct labour | 3.00 | 3.00 |
| Production overhead | 3.50 | 2.50 |
| Selling overhead | 1.00 | 0.50 |
|  | 11.50 | 10.00 |

The total fixed cost and variable cost per unit are:

|  | Total fixed cost (£) | Variable cost per unit (£) |
|---|---|---|
| A | 2000 | 1.50 |
| B | 2000 | 7.00 |
| C | 2000 | 8.50 |
| D | 3000 | 7.00 |
| E | 3000 | 8.50 |

*CIMA Stage 2*

### 8.4* Intermediate
Z plc currently sells products Aye, Bee and Cee in equal quantities and at the same selling price per unit. The contribution to sales ratio for product Aye is 40%; for product Bee it is 50% and the total is 48%. If fixed costs are unaffected by mix and are currently 20% of sales, the effect of changing the product mix to:

| Aye | 40% |
| Bee | 25% |
| Cee | 35% |

is that the total contribution/total sales ratio changes to:

A    27.4%
B    45.3%
C    47.4%
D    48.4%
E    68.4%

*CIMA Stage 2*

## 8.5* Intermediate

E plc operates a marginal costing system. For the forthcoming year, variable costs are budgeted to be 60% of sales value and fixed costs are budgeted to be 10% of sales value.

If E plc increases its selling prices by 10%, but if fixed costs, variable costs per unit and sales volume remain unchanged, the effect on E plc's contribution would be:

A    a decrease of 2%;
B    an increase of 5%
C    an increase of 10%
D    an increase of 25%
E    an increase of $66\frac{2}{3}$%.

*CIMA Stage 2*

## 8.6* Intermediate

A Limited has fixed costs of £60 000 per annum. It manufactures a single product which it sells for £20 per unit. Its contribution to sales ratio is 40%.

A Limited's breakeven point in units is:

A    1200
B    1800
C    3000
D    5000
E    7500

*CIMA Stage 2 Specimen Paper*

## 8.7* Intermediate

The following data relate to the overhead expenditure of a contract cleaners at two activity levels:

| Square metres cleaned | 12 750 | 15 100 |
| Overheads | £73 950 | £83 585 |

What is the estimate of the overheads if 16 200 square metres are to be cleaned?

A    £88 095
B    £89 674
C    £93 960
D    £98 095

*CIMA Stage 1*

## 8.8* Intermediate

Z plc makes a single product which it sells for £16 per unit. Fixed costs are £76 800 per month and the product has a contribution to sales ratio of 40%.

In a period when actual sales were £224 000, Z plc's margin of safety, in units, was

A    2000
B    6000
C    8000
D    12 000
E    14 000

*CIMA Stage 2*

## 8.9 Intermediate

Shown below is a typical cost–volume–profit chart:

Required:
(a) Explain to a colleague who is not an accountant the reasons for the change in result on this cost–volume–profit chart from a loss at point (a) to a profit at point (b).         (3 marks)
(b) Identify and critically examine the underlying assumptions of this type of cost–volume–profit analysis and consider whether such analyses are useful to the management of an organization.         (14 marks)
         (Total 17 marks)
*ACCA Level 1 Costing*

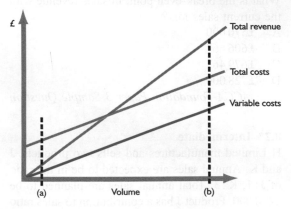

## 8.10 Intermediate

The graphs shown below show cost–volume–profit relationships as they are typically represented in (i) management accounting and (ii) economic theory. In each graph TR = total revenue, TC = total cost, and P = profit. You are required to compare these different representations of cost–volume–profit relationships, identifying, explaining and commenting on points of similarity and also differences. (15 marks)

*ICAEW Management Accounting*

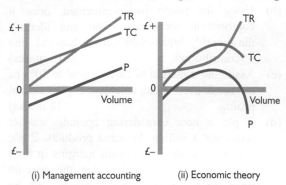

| (i) Management accounting | (ii) Economic theory |

## 8.11 Intermediate

'A break-even chart must be interpreted in the light of the limitations of its underlying assumptions...' (From *Cost Accounting: A Managerial Emphasis*, by C.T. Horngren.)

Required:

(a) Discuss the extent to which the above statement is valid and both describe and briefly appraise the reasons for *five* of the most important underlying assumptions of break-even analysis. (c. 14 marks)

(b) For any *three* of the underlying assumptions provided in answer to (a) above, give an example of circumstances in which that assumption is violated. Indicate the nature of the violation and the extent to which the break-even chart can be adapted to allow for this violation. (c. 6 marks)

(Total 20 marks)

*ACCA P2 Management Accounting*

## 8.12 Advanced

The accountant's approach to cost–volume–profit analysis has been criticized in that, among other matters, it does not deal with the following:

(a) situations where sales volume differs radically from production volume;

(b) situations where the sales revenue and the total cost functions are markedly non-linear;

(c) changes in product mix;

(d) risk and uncertainty.

Explain these objections to the accountant's conventional cost–volume–profit model and suggest how they can be overcome or ameliorated. (17 marks)

*ACCA Level 2 Management Accounting*

## 8.13* Intermediate: Break-even, contribution and profit–volume graph

(a) From the following information you are required to construct:

(i) a break-even chart, showing the break-even point and the margin of safety;

(ii) a chart displaying the contribution level and the profit level;

(iii) a profit–volume chart.

| Sales | 6000 units at |
| | £12 per unit = £72 000 |
| Variable costs | 6000 units at |
| | £7 per unit = £42 000 |
| Fixed costs | = £20 000 |

(9 marks)

(b) State the purposes of each of the three charts in (a) above. (6 marks)

(c) Outline the limitations of break-even analysis. (5 marks)

(d) What are the advantages of graphical presentation of financial data to executives? (2 marks)

(Total 22 marks)

*AAT*

## 8.14* Intermediate: Separation of fixed and variable costs and construction of a break-even graph

A building company constructs a standard unit which sells for £30 000. The company's costs can be readily identifiable between fixed and variable costs.

Budgeted data for the coming six months includes the following:

| | Sales (in units) | Profit £ |
|---|---|---|
| January | 18 | 70 000 |
| February | 20 | 100 000 |
| March | 30 | 250 000 |
| April | 22 | 130 000 |
| May | 24 | 160 000 |
| June | 16 | 40 000 |

You are told that the fixed costs for the six months have been spread evenly over the period under review to arrive at the monthly profit projections.

Required:
(a) Prepare a graph for total sales, costs and output for the six months under review that shows:
   (i) The break-even point in units and revenue.
   (ii) Total fixed costs.
   (iii) The variable cost line.
   (iv) The margin of safety for the total budgeted sales.
                                        (14 marks)
(b) The company is worried about the low level of sales. The sales director says that if the selling price of the unit was reduced by £5000 the company would be able to sell 10% more units. All other costs would remain the same you are told.
   Determine whether the company should reduce the selling price to attract new sales in order to maximize profit. Clearly show any workings.                        (5 marks)
(c) Evaluate whether the assumption that costs are readily identifiable as either fixed or variable throughout a range of production is realistic. Give examples of any alternative classification.                       (6 marks)
                              (Total 25 marks)
              *AAT Cost Accounting and Budgeting*

## 8.15* Intermediate: Separation of fixed and variable costs and construction of a break-even chart

Z plc operates a single retail outlet selling direct to the public. Profit statements for August and September are as follows:

|                          | August | September |
| ------------------------ | ------ | --------- |
| Sales                    | 80 000 | 90 000    |
| Cost of sales            | 50 000 | 55 000    |
| Gross profit             | 30 000 | 35 000    |
| *Less:*                  |        |           |
| Selling and distribution | 8 000  | 9 000     |
| Administration           | 15 000 | 15 000    |
| Net profit               | 7 000  | 11 000    |

Required:
(a) Use the high- and low-points technique to identify the behaviour of:

   (i) cost of sales;
   (ii) selling and distribution costs;
   (iii) administration costs.            (4 marks)
(b) Using the graph paper provided, draw a contribution break-even chart and identify the monthly break-even sales value and area of contribution.                    (10 marks)
(c) Assuming a margin of safety equal to 30% of the break-even value, calculate Z plc's annual profit.                           (2 marks)
(d) Z plc is now considering opening another retail outlet selling the same products. Z plc plans to use the same profit margins in both outlets and has estimated that the specific fixed costs of the second outlet will be £100 000 per annum.
   Z plc also expects that 10% of its annual sales from its existing outlet would transfer to this second outlet if it were to be opened.
   Calculate the annual value of sales required from the new outlet in order to achieve the same annual profit as previously obtained from the single outlet.
                                        (5 marks)
(e) Briefly describe the cost accounting requirements of organizations of this type. (4 marks)
                              (Total 25 marks)
      *Chartered Institute of Management Accountants*
              *Operational Cost Accounting Stage 2*

## 8.16* Intermediate: Profit–volume graph and changes in sales mix

A company produces and sells two products with the following costs:

|                                   | Product X  | Product Y  |
| --------------------------------- | ---------- | ---------- |
| Variable costs<br>(per £ of sales) | £0.45      | £0.6       |
| Fixed costs                       | £1 212 000 | £1 212 000 |
|                                   | per period |            |

Total sales revenue is currently generated by the two products in the following proportions:

|           |     |
| --------- | --- |
| Product X | 70% |
| Product Y | 30% |

Required:
(a) Calculate the break-even sales revenue per period, based on the sales mix assumed above.
                                        (6 marks)

(b) Prepare a profit–volume chart of the above situation for sales revenue up to £4 000 000. Show on the same chart the effect of a change in the sales mix to product X 50%, product Y 50%. Clearly indicate on the chart the break-even point for each situation. (11 marks)

(c) Of the fixed costs £455 000 are attributable to product X. Calculate the sales revenue required on product X in order to recover the attributable fixed costs and provide a net contribution of £700 000 towards general fixed costs and profit. (5 marks)

(Total 22 marks)

*ACCA Level 1 Costing*

## 8.17 Intermediate: Multi-product profit–volume graph

JK Limited has prepared a budget for the next twelve months when it intends to make and sell four products, details of which are shown below:

| Product | Sales in units (thousands) | Selling price per unit (£) | Variable cost per unit (£) |
|---|---|---|---|
| J | 10 | 20 | 14.00 |
| K | 10 | 40 | 8.00 |
| L | 50 | 4 | 4.20 |
| M | 20 | 10 | 7.00 |

Budgeted fixed costs are £240 000 per annum and total assets employed are £570 000.

You are required

(a) to calculate the total contribution earned by each product and their combined total contributions; (2 marks)

(b) to plot the data of your answer to (a) above in the form of a contribution to sales graph (sometimes referred to as a profit–volume graph) *on the graph paper provided*; (6 marks)

(c) to explain your graph to management, to comment on the results shown and to state the break-even point; (4 marks)

(d) to describe briefly three ways in which the overall contribution to sales ratio could be improved. (3 marks)

(Total 15 marks)

*CIMA Stage 2 Cost Accounting*

## 8.18 Intermediate: Break-even chart with increases in fixed costs

(a) Identify and discuss briefly *five* assumptions underlying cost–volume–profit analysis. (10 marks)

(b) A local authority, whose area includes a holiday resort situated on the east coast, operates, for 30 weeks each year, a holiday home which is let to visiting parties of children in care from other authorities. The children are accompanied by their own house mothers who supervise them throughout their holiday. From six to fifteen guests are accepted on terms of £100 per person per week. No differential charges exist for adults and children.

Weekly costs incurred by the host authority are:

| | (£ per guest) |
|---|---|
| Food | 25 |
| Electricity for heating and cooking | 3 |
| Domestic (laundry, cleaning etc.) expenses | 5 |
| Use of minibus | 10 |

Seasonal staff supervise and carry out the necessary duties at the home at a cost of £11 000 for the 30-week period. This provides staffing sufficient for six to ten guests per week but if eleven or more guests are to be accommodated, additional staff at a total cost of £200 per week are engaged for the whole of the 30-week period.

Rent, including rates for the property, is £4000 per annum and the garden of the home is maintained by the council's recreation department which charges a nominal fee of £1000 per annum.

You are required to:

(i) tabulate the appropriate figures in such a way as to show the break-even point(s) and to comment on your figures; (8 marks)

(ii) draw, on the graph paper provided, a chart to illustrate your answer to (b)(i) above. (7 marks)

(Total 25 marks)

*CIMA Cost Accounting Stage 2*

## 8.19* Intermediate: Break-even chart with an increase in fixed costs and incorporating expected values

A manufacturer is considering a new product which could be produced in one of two qualities – Standard or De Luxe. The following estimates have been made:

|  | Standard (£) | De Luxe (£) |
|---|---|---|
| Unit labour cost | 2.00 | 2.50 |
| Unit material cost | 1.50 | 2.00 |
| Unit packaging cost | 1.00 | 2.00 |
| Proposed selling price per unit | 7.00 | 10.00 |
| Budgeted fixed costs per period: |  |  |
| 0–99 999 units | 200 000 | 250 000 |
| 100 000 and above | 350 000 | 400 000 |

At the proposed selling prices, market research indicates the following demand:

**Standard**

| Quantity | Probability |
|---|---|
| 172 000 | 0.1 |
| 160 000 | 0.7 |
| 148 000 | 0.2 |

**De Luxe**

| Quantity | Probability |
|---|---|
| 195 500 | 0.3 |
| 156 500 | 0.5 |
| 109 500 | 0.2 |

You are required

(a) to draw separate break-even charts for *each* quality, showing the break-even points;
(7 marks)

(b) to comment on the position shown by the charts and what guidance they provide for management; (3 marks)

(c) to calculate, for *each* quality, the expected unit sales, expected profits and the margin of safety; (3 marks)

(d) using an appropriate measure of risk, to advise management which quality should be launched. (9 marks)
(Total 22 marks)
*CIMA Stage 3 Management Accounting Techniques*

## 8.20 Intermediate: Analysis of costs into fixed and variable elements and break-even point calculation

(a) 'The analysis of total cost into its behavioural elements is essential for effective cost and management accounting.'

Required
Comment on the statement above, illustrating your answer with examples of cost behaviour patterns.
(5 marks)

(b) The total costs incurred at various output levels, for a process operation in a factory, have been measured as follows:

| Output (units) | Total cost (£) |
|---|---|
| 11 500 | 102 476 |
| 12 000 | 104 730 |
| 12 500 | 106 263 |
| 13 000 | 108 021 |
| 13 500 | 110 727 |
| 14 000 | 113 201 |

Required:
Using the high–low method, analyse the costs of the process operation into fixed and variable components. (4 marks)

(c) Calculate, and comment upon, the break-even output level of the process operation in (b) above, based upon the fixed and variable costs identified and assuming a selling price of £10.60 per unit. (5 marks)
(Total 14 marks)
*ACCA Foundation Paper 3*

## 8.21* Intermediate: Non-graphical CVP analyses

A retailer with a chain of stores is planning product promotions for a future period. The following information relates to a product which is being considered for a four week promotion:

Normal weekly sales (i.e. without promotion), 2400 units at £2.80 per unit.

Normal contribution margin, 45% of normal selling price.

Promotional discount, 20% (i.e. normal selling price reduced by 20% during the promotion).

Expected promotion sales multiplier, 2.5 (i.e.

weekly sales units expected during the promotion is $2.5 \times 2400 = 6000$ units).

Additional fixed costs incurred to run the promotion (i.e. unaffected by the level of promotional sales) are forecast to be £5400. Unit variable costs would be expected to remain at the same level as normal.

Required:
(a) Calculate the expected incremental profit/ (loss) from the promotion.　　(8 marks)
(b) Calculate the sales units multiplier that would be required during the promotion to break even compared with a no-promotion situation.
　　(6 marks)
(c) Describe other factors that should be considered before making a decision regarding the promotion.　　(6 marks)
　　(Total 20 marks)
*ACCA Level 1 – Cost and Management Accounting 1*

## 8.22* Intermediate: Non-graphical CVP analysis and calculation of margin of safety

Z Ltd manufactures and sells three products with the following selling prices and variable costs:

|  | Product A (£/unit) | Product B (£/unit) | Product C (£/unit) |
|---|---|---|---|
| Selling price | 3.00 | 2.45 | 4.00 |
| Variable cost | 1.20 | 1.67 | 2.60 |

The company is considering expenditure on advertising and promotion of Product A. It is hoped that such expenditure, together with a reduction in the selling price of the product, would increase sales. Existing annual sales volume of the three products is:

| Product A |  | 460 000 units |
|---|---|---|
| Product B |  | 1 000 000 units |
| Product C |  | 380 000 units |

If £60 000 per annum was to be invested in advertising and sales promotion, sales of Product A at reduced selling prices would be expected to be:

590 000 units at £2.75 per unit
or 650 000 units at £2.55 per unit

Annual fixed costs are currently £1 710 000 per annum.

Required:
(a) Calculate the current break-even sales revenue of the business.　　(8 marks)
(b) Advise the management of Z Ltd as to whether the expenditure on advertising and promotion, together with selling price reduction, should be introduced on Product A.
　　(6 marks)
(c) Calculate the required unit sales of Product A, at a selling price of £2.75 per unit, in order to justify the expenditure on advertising and promotion.　　(5 marks)
(d) Explain the term 'margin of safety', with particular reference to the circumstances of Z Ltd.　　(6 marks)
　　(Total 25 marks)
*ACCA Level 1 Costing*

## 8.23 Intermediate: Non-graphical CVP analysis and the acceptance of a special order

Video Technology Plc was established in 1987 to assemble video cassette recorders (VCRs). There is now increased competition in its markets and the company expects to find it difficult to make an acceptable profit next year. You have been appointed as an accounting technician at the company, and have been given a copy of the draft budget for the next financial year.

### Draft budget for 12 months to 30 November 2001

|  | (£m) | (£m) |
|---|---|---|
| Sales income |  | 960.0 |
| Cost of sales: |  |  |
| 　Variable assembly materials | 374.4 |  |
| 　Variable labour | 192.0 |  |
| 　Factory overheads – variable | 172.8 |  |
| 　　　　　　　　 – fixed | 43.0 | (782.2) |
|  |  | 177.8 |
| Gross profit |  |  |
| 　Selling overheads – commission | 38.4 |  |
| 　　　　　　　　　 – fixed | 108.0 |  |
| 　Administration overheads – fixed | 20.0 | (166.4) |
| Net profit |  | 11.4 |

The following information is also supplied to you by the company's financial controller, Edward Davies:

1   planned sales for the draft budget in the year to 30 November 2001 are expected to be 25% less than the total of 3.2 million VCR units sold in the year to 30 November 2000;
2   the company operates a Just-In-Time stock control system, which means it holds no stocks of any kind;
3   if more than 3 million VCR units are made and sold, the unit cost of material falls by £4 per unit;
4   sales commission is based on the number of units sold and not on turnover;
5   the draft budget assumes that the factory will only be working at two-thirds of maximum capacity;
6   sales above maximum capacity are not possible.

Edward Davies explains that the Board is not happy with the profit projected in the draft budget, and that the sales director, Anne Williams, has produced three proposals to try and improve matters.

1   Proposal A involves launching an aggressive marketing campaign:
    (i)   this would involve a single additional fixed cost of £14 million for advertising;
    (ii)  there would be a revised commission payment of £18 per unit sold;
    (iii) sales volume would be expected to increase by 10% above the level projected in the draft budget, with no change in the unit selling price.
2   Proposal B involves a 5% reduction in the unit selling price:
    (i)   this is estimated to bring the sales volume back to the level in the year to 30 November 2000.
3   Proposal C involves a 10% reduction in the unit selling price.
    (i)   fixed selling overheads would also be reduced by £45 million;
    (ii)  if proposal C is accepted, the sales director believes sales volume will be 3.8 million units.

Task 1
(a)   For each of the three proposals, calculate the:
      (i)   change in profits compared with the draft budget;
      (ii)  break-even point in units and turnover.
(b)   Recommend which proposal, if any, should be accepted on financial grounds.

(c)   Identify *three* non-financial issues to be considered before a final decision is made.

Edward Davies now tells you that the company is considering a new export order with a proposed selling price of £3 million. He provides you with the following information:
1   The order will require two types of material:
    (i)   material A is in regular use by the company.
          The amount in stock originally cost £0.85 million, but its standard cost is £0.9 million. The amount in stock is sufficient for the order. The current market price of material A to be used in the order is £0.8 million;
    (ii)  material B is no longer used by the company and cannot be used elsewhere if not used on the order.
          The amount in stock originally cost £0.2 million although its current purchase price is £0.3 million. The amount of material B in stock is only half the amount required on the order. If not used on the order, the amount in stock could be sold for £0.1 million;
2   direct labour of £1.0 million will be charged to the order. This includes £0.2 million for idle time, as a result of insufficient orders to keep the workforce fully employed. The company has a policy of no redundancies, and spreads the resulting cost of idle time across all orders;
3   variable factory overheads are expected to be £0.9 million;
4   fixed factory overheads are apportioned against the order at the rate of 50% of variable factory overheads;
5   no sales commission will be paid.

Task 2
Prepare a memo for Edward Davies:
(a)   showing whether or not the order should be accepted at the proposed selling price;
(b)   identifying the technique(s) you have used in reaching this conclusion.

*AAT Technicians Stage*

**8.24\* Intermediate: Changes in sales mix**
XYZ Ltd produces two products and the following budget applies for 2001:

| | Product X (£) | Product Y (£) |
|---|---|---|
| Selling price | 6 | 12 |
| Variable costs | 2 | 4 |
| Contribution margin | 4 | 8 |
| Fixed costs apportioned | £100 000 | £200 000 |
| Units sold | 70 000 | 30 000 |

You are required to calculate the break-even points for each product and the company as a whole and comment on your findings.

## 8.25 Intermediate: Calculation of break-even points based on different product mix assumptions

PE Limited produces and sells two products, P and E. Budgets prepared for the next six months give the following information:

| | Product P per unit £ | Product E per unit £ |
|---|---|---|
| Selling price | 10.00 | 12.00 |
| Variable costs: production and selling | 5.00 | 10.00 |
| Common fixed costs: production and selling for six months | £561 600 | |

(a) You are required, in respect of the forth-coming six months,
   (i) to state what the break-even point in £s will be and the number of each product this figure represents if the two products are sold in the ratio 4P to 3E;   (3 marks)
   (ii) to state the break-even point in £s and the number of products this figure represents if the sales mix changes to 4P to 4E (ignore fractions of products);   (3 marks)
   (iii) to advise the sales manager which product mix should be better, that in (a) (i) above or that in (a) (ii) above, and why;   (2 marks)
   (iv) to advise the sales manager which of the two products should be concentrated on and the reason(s) for your recommendation – assume that whatever can be made can be sold, that both products go through a machining process and that there are only 32 000 machine hours

available, with product P requiring 0.40 hour per unit and product E requiring 0.10 hour per unit.   (2 marks)
(b) You are required to compare and contrast the usefulness of a conventional break-even chart with a contribution break-even chart. Your explanation should include illustrative diagrams drawn within your answer book and not on graph paper.   (5 marks)
   (Total 15 marks)
   *CIMA Stage 2 Cost Accounting*

## 8.26* Intermediate: Calculation of break-even points based on different sales mix assumptions and a product abandonment decision

M Ltd manufactures three products which have the following revenue and costs (£ per unit).

| | Product 1 | 2 | 3 |
|---|---|---|---|
| Selling price | 2.92 | 1.35 | 2.83 |
| Variable costs | 1.61 | 0.72 | 0.96 |
| Fixed costs: | | | |
| Product specific | 0.49 | 0.35 | 0.62 |
| General | 0.46 | 0.46 | 0.46 |

Unit fixed costs are based upon the following annual sales and production volumes (thousand units):

| Product 1 | 2 | 3 |
|---|---|---|
| 98.2 | 42.1 | 111.8 |

Required:
(a) Calculate:
   (i) the break-even point sales (to the nearest £ hundred) of M Ltd based on the current product mix   (9 marks)
   (ii) the number of units of Product 2 (to the nearest hundred) at the break-even point determined in (i) above.   (3 marks)
(b) Comment upon the viability of Product 2.   (8 marks)
   (Total 20 marks)
   *ACCA Cost and Management Accounting 1*

### 8.27* Intermediate: Calculation of sales by individual products to achieve a target contribution

A company manufactures and sells three products which currently have the following annual trading performance:

| (£000) | Product | | |
| --- | --- | --- | --- |
| | A | B | C |
| Sales | 1794 | 3740 | 2950 |
| Production cost of sales | 1242 | 2860 | 1888 |
| Gross profit | 552 | 880 | 1062 |
| Non-production overheads | 460 | 770 | 767 |
| Net profit | 92 | 110 | 295 |
| Sales units (000) | 1150 | 2200 | 2360 |

For each product, units produced and sold were the same in the period.

Fixed production overheads are absorbed at a rate of £0.30 per unit for each product. Non-production overheads include certain costs which vary with activity at a rate of 10% of sales value. The remaining non-production overheads are fixed costs.

Required:
(a) Prepare a statement, in marginal costing format, showing the sales, costs, and profit contribution of each product expressed both in £ per unit (to three decimal places) and also as a % of sales (to one decimal place);

(8 marks)
(b) Calculate, based upon the current mix of sales, the sales required of each product (to the nearest £000) in order to generate a total contribution of £3.75m per annum. (6 marks)
(Total 14 marks)
*ACCA Foundation Stage Paper 3*

### 8.28 Intermediate: Decision-making and non-graphical CVP analysis

York plc was formed three years ago by a group of research scientists to market a new medicine that they had invented. The technology involved in the medicine's manufacture is both complex and expensive. Because of this, the company is faced with a high level of fixed costs.

This is of particular concern to Dr Harper, the company's chief executive. She recently arranged a conference of all management staff to discuss company profitability. Dr Harper showed the managers how average unit cost fell as production volume increased and explained that this was due to the company's heavy fixed cost base. 'It is clear,' she said, 'that as we produce closer to the plant's maximum capacity of 70 000 packs the average cost per pack falls. Producing and selling as close to that limit as possible must be good for company profitability.' The data she used are reproduced below:

| Production volume (packs) | 40 000 | 50 000 | 60 000 | 70 000 |
| --- | --- | --- | --- | --- |
| Average cost per unit[a] | £430 | £388 | £360 | £340 |
| Current sales and production volume: | 65 000 packs | | | |
| Selling price per pack: | £420 | | | |

[a]Defined as the total of fixed and variable costs, divided by the production volume

You are a member of York plc's management accounting team and shortly after the conference you are called to a meeting with Ben Cooper, the company's marketing director. He is interested in knowing how profitability changes with production.

Task 1
Ben Cooper asks you to calculate:
(a) the amount of York plc's fixed costs;
(b) the profit of the company at its current sales volume of 65 000 packs;
(c) the break-even point in units;
(d) the margin of safety expressed as a percentage.

Ben Cooper now tells you of a discussion he has recently had with Dr Harper. Dr Harper had once more emphasized the need to produce as close as possible to the maximum capacity of 70 000 packs. Ben Cooper has the possibility of obtaining an export order for an extra 5000 packs but, because the competition is strong, the selling price would only be £330. Dr Harper has suggested that this order should be rejected as it is below cost and so will reduce company profitability. However, she would be prepared, on this occasion, to sell the packs on a cost basis for £340 each, provided the order was increased to 15 000 packs.

Task 2
Write a memo to Ben Cooper. Your memo should:

(a) calculate the change in profits from accepting the order for 5000 packs at £330;

(b) calculate the change in profits from accepting an order for 15 000 packs at £340;

(c) briefly explain and justify which proposal, if either, should be accepted;

(d) identify *two* non-financial factors which should be taken into account before making a final decision.

*AAT Technicians Stage*

## 8.29* Intermediate: Calculation of break-even points and limiting factor decision-making

You are employed as an accounting technician by Smith, Williams and Jones, a small firm of accountants and registered auditors. One of your clients is Winter plc, a large department store. Judith Howarth, the purchasing director for Winter plc, has gained considerable knowledge about bedding and soft furnishings and is considering acquiring her own business.

She has recently written to you requesting a meeting to discuss the possible purchase of Brita Beds Ltd. Brita Beds has one outlet in Mytown, a small town 100 miles from where Judith works. Enclosed with her letter was Brita Beds' latest profit and loss account. This is reproduced below.

**Brita Beds Ltd**
**Profit and loss account – year to 31 May**

| Sales | (units) | (£) |
|---|---|---|
| Model A | 1620 | 336 960 |
| Model B | 2160 | 758 160 |
| Model C | 1620 | 1 010 880 |
| Turnover | | 2 106 000 |
| Expenses | (£) | |
| Cost of beds | 1 620 000 | |
| Commission | 210 600 | |
| Transport | 216 000 | |
| Rates and insurance | 8 450 | |
| Light heat and power | 10 000 | |
| Assistants' salaries | 40 000 | |
| Manager's salary | 40 000 | 2 145 050 |
| Loss for year | | 39 050 |

Also included in the letter was the following information:

1 Brita Beds sells three types of bed, models A to C inclusive.

2 Selling prices are determined by adding 30%

to the cost of beds.

3 Sales assistants receive a commission of 10% of the selling price for each bed sold.

4 The beds are delivered in consignments of 10 beds at a cost of £400 per delivery. This expense is shown as 'Transport' in the profit and loss account.

5 All other expenses are annual amounts.

6 The mix of models sold is likely to remain constant irrespective of overall sales volume.

Task 1

In preparation for your meeting with Judith Howarth, you are asked to calculate:

(a) the minimum number of beds to be sold if Brita Beds is to avoid making a loss;

(b) the minimum turnover required if Brita Beds it to avoid making a loss.

At the meeting, Judith Howarth provides you with further information:

1 The purchase price of the business is £300 000.

2 Judith has savings of £300 000 currently earning 5% interest per annum, which she can use to aquire Beta Beds.

3 Her current salary is £36 550.

To reduce costs, Judith suggests that she should take over the role of manager as the current one is about to retire. However, she does not want to take a reduction in income. Judith also tells you that she has been carrying out some market research. The results of this are as follows:

1 The number of households in Mytown is currently 44 880

2 Brita Beds Ltd is the only outlet selling beds in Mytown.

3 According to a recent survey, 10% of households change their beds every 9 years, 60% every 10 years and 30% every 11 years.

4 The survey also suggested that there is an average of 2.1 beds per household.

Task 2

Write a letter to Judith Howarth. Your letter should:

(a) identify the profit required to compensate for the loss of salary and interest;

(b) show the number of beds to be sold to achieve that profit;

(c) calculate the likely maximum number of beds that Brita Beds would sell in a year;

(d) use your answers in (a) to (c) to justify

whether or not Judith Howarth should purchase the company and become its manager;

(e) give *two* possible reasons why your estimate of the maximum annual sales volume may prove inaccurate.

On receiving your letter, Judith Howarth decides she would prefer to remain as the purchasing director for Winter plc rather than acquire Brita Beds Ltd. Shortly afterwards, you receive a telephone call from her. Judith explains that Winter plc is redeveloping its premises and that she is concerned about the appropriate sales policy for Winter's bed department while the redevelopment takes place. Although she has a statement of unit profitability, this had been prepared before the start of the redevelopment and had assumed that there would be in excess of 800 square metres of storage space available to the bed department. Storage space is critical as customers demand immediate delivery and are not prepared to wait until the new stock arrives.

The next day, Judith Howarth sends you a letter containing a copy of the original statement of profitability. This is reproduced below:

| Model Monthly demand (beds) | A 35 (£) | B 45 (£) | C 20 (£) |
|---|---|---|---|
| Unit selling price | 240.00 | 448.00 | 672.00 |
| Unit cost per bed | 130.00 | 310.00 | 550.00 |
| Carriage inwards | 20.00 | 20.00 | 20.00 |
| Staff costs | 21.60 | 40.32 | 60.48 |
| Department fixed overheads | 20.00 | 20.00 | 20.00 |
| General fixed overheads | 25.20 | 25.20 | 25.20 |
| Unit profit | 23.20 | 32.48 | (3.68) |
| Storage required per bed (square metres) | 3 | 4 | 5 |

In her letter she asks for your help in preparing a marketing plan which will maximize the profitability of Winter's bed department while the redevelopment takes place. To help you, she has provided you with the following additional information:

1 Currently storage space available totals 300 square metres.
2 Staff costs represent the salaries of the sales staff in the bed department. Their total cost of £3780 per month is apportioned to units on

the basis of planned turnover.
3 Departmental fixed overhead of £2000 per month is directly attributable to the department and is apportioned on the number of beds planned to be sold.
4 General fixed overheads of £2520 are also apportioned on the number of beds planned to be sold. The directors of Winter plc believe this to be a fair apportionment of the store's central fixed overheads.
5 The cost of carriage inwards and the cost of beds vary directly with the number of beds purchased.

Task 3
(a) Prepare a recommended monthly sales schedule in units which will maximize the profitability of Winter plc's bed department.
(b) Calculate the profit that will be reported per month if your recommendation is implemented.

*AAT Technician's Stage*

## 8.30 Intermediate: Marginal costing and absorption costing profit computations and calculation of break-even point for a given sales mix

A company has two products with the following unit costs for a period:

| | Product A (£/unit) | Product B (£/unit) |
|---|---|---|
| Direct materials | 1.20 | 2.03 |
| Direct labour | 1.40 | 1.50 |
| Variable production overheads | 0.70 | 0.80 |
| Fixed production overheads | 1.10 | 1.10 |
| Variable other overheads | 0.15 | 0.20 |
| Fixed other overheads | 0.50 | 0.50 |

Production and sales of the two products for the period were:

| | Product A (000 units) | Product B (000 units) |
|---|---|---|
| Production | 250 | 100 |
| Sales | 225 | 110 |

Production was at normal levels. Unit costs in opening stock were the same as those for the period listed above.

Required:
(a) State whether, and why, absorption or marginal costing would show a higher company profit for the period, and calculate the difference in profit depending upon which method is used. (4 marks)
(b) Calculate the break-even sales revenue for the period (to the nearest £000) based on the above mix of sales. The selling prices of products A and B were £5.70 and £6.90 per unit, respectively. (7 marks)
(Total 11 marks)
*ACCA Foundation Stage Paper 3*

### 8.31* Intermediate: Analysis of change in profit arising from changes in volume and production methods plus sales revenue required to achieve a desired profit

A company has the following summary performance over two accounting periods:

|  | Period 1 (£000) | Period 2 (£000) |
| --- | --- | --- |
| Sales | 902.0 | 1108.1 |
| Variable costs | 360.8 | 398.9 |
| Contribution | 541.2 | 709.2 |
| Fixed costs | 490.5 | 549.0 |
| Net profit | 50.7 | 160.2 |

In period 2 selling prices were 5% higher than in period 1 and cost inflation (affecting both variable and fixed costs) was also 5%.

At the start of period 2 production methods were reorganized. This was the only other factor affecting costs between the two periods (apart from inflation and volume).

Required:
(a) Calculate the percentage increase in sales volume in period 2 compared with period 1. (2 marks)
(b) Calculate the increase in net profit in period 2 compared with period 1, due to:
    (i) volume
    (ii) reorganization of production methods.
    (Calculations should be done at year 1 prices.) (6 marks)
(c) Calculate the sales (to the nearest £000) that

were required in period 2 in order to achieve the same net profit as period 1. (3 marks)
(d) State, and explain, the formula for the calculation of the break-even sales revenue for a period (figures are not required). (3 marks)
(Total 14 marks)
*ACCA Foundation Paper 3*

### 8.32* Intermediate: Decision-making and non-graphical CVP analysis

Fosterjohn Press Ltd is considering launching a new monthly magazine at a selling price of £1 per copy. Sales of the magazine are expected to be 500 000 copies per month, but it is possible that the actual sales could differ quite significantly from this estimate.

Two different methods of producing the magazine are being considered and neither would involve any additional capital expenditure. The estimated production costs for each of the two methods of manufacture, together with the additional marketing and distribution costs of selling the new magazine, are summarized below:

|  | Method A | Method B |
| --- | --- | --- |
| Variable costs | £0.55 per copy | £0.50 per copy |
| Specific fixed costs | £80 000 per month | £120 000 per month |
| Semi-variable costs: | | |

The following estimates have been obtained:

| 350 000 copies | £55 000 per month | £47 500 per month |
| --- | --- | --- |
| 450 000 copies | £65 000 per month | £52 500 per month |
| 650 000 copies | £85 000 per month | £62 500 per month |

It may be assumed that the fixed cost content of the semi-variable costs will remain constant throughout the range of activity shown.

The company currently sells a magazine covering related topics to those that will be included in the new publication and consequently it is anticipated that sales of this existing magazine will be adversely affected. It is estimated that for every ten copies sold of the new publication, sales of the existing magazine will be reduced by one copy.

Sales and cost data of the existing magazine are shown below:

| | |
|---|---|
| Sales | 220 000 copies per month |
| Selling price | £0.85 per copy |
| Variable costs | £0.35 per copy |
| Specific fixed costs | £80 000 per month |

Required:

(a) Calculate, for each production method, the net increase in company profits which will result from the introduction of the new magazine, at each of the following levels of activity:

500 000 copies per month
400 000 copies per month
600 000 copies per month     (12 marks)

(b) Calculate, for each production method, the amount by which sales volume of the new magazine could decline from the anticipated 500 000 copies per month, before the company makes no additional profit from the introduction of the new publication.

(6 marks)

(c) Briefly identify any conclusions which may be drawn from your calculations.     (4 marks)

(Total 22 marks)

*ACCA Foundation Costing*

## 8.33* Intermediate: Decision-making and non-graphical CVP analysis

Mr Belle has recently developed a new improved video cassette and shown below is a summary of a report by a firm of management consultants on the sales potential and production costs of the new cassette.

Sales potential: The sales volume is difficult to predict and will vary with the price, but it is reasonable to assume that at a selling price of £10 per cassette, sales would be between 7500 and 10 000 units per month. Alternatively, if the selling price was reduced to £9 per cassette, sales would be between 12 000 and 18 000 units per month.

Production costs: If production is maintained at or below 10 000 units per month, then variable manufacturing costs would be approximately £8.25 per cassette and fixed costs £12 125 per month. However, if production is planned to exceed 10 000 units per month, then variable costs would be reduced to £7.75 per cassette, but the fixed costs would increase to £16 125 per month.

Mr Belle has been charged £2000 for the report by the management consultants and, in addition, he

has incurred £3000 development costs on the new cassette.

If Mr Belle decides to produce and sell the new cassette it will be necessary for him to use factory premises which he owns, but are leased to a colleague for a rental of £400 per month. Also he will resign from his current post in an electronics firm where he is earning a salary of £1000 per month.

Required:

(a) Identify in the question an example of
    (i)   an opportunity cost,
    (ii)  a sunk cost.     (3 marks)

(b) Making whatever calculations you consider appropriate, analyse the report from the consultants and advise Mr Belle of the potential profitability of the alternatives shown in the report.

Any assumptions considered necessary or matters which may require further investigation or comment should be clearly stated.

(19 marks)
(Total 22 marks)
*ACCA Level 1 Costing*

## 8.34* Advanced: Decision-making and CVP analysis

Bruno Ltd is considering proposals for design changes in one of a range of soft toys. The proposals are as follows:

(a) Eliminate some of the decorative stitching from the toy.

(b) Use plastic eyes instead of glass eyes in the toys (two eyes per toy).

(c) Change the filling material used. It is proposed that scrap fabric left over from the body manufacture be used instead of the synthetic material which is currently used.

The design change proposals have been considered by the management team and the following information has been gathered:

(i)   Plastic eyes will cost £15 per hundred whereas the existing glass eyes cost £20 per hundred. The plastic eyes will be more liable to damage on insertion into the toy. It is estimated that scrap plastic eyes will be 10% of the quantity issued from stores as compared to 5% of issues of glass eyes at present.

(ii)  The synthetic filling material costs £80 per tonne. One tonne of filling is sufficient for 2000 soft toys.

(iii) Scrap fabric to be used as filling material will

need to be cut into smaller pieces before use and this will cost £0.05 per soft toy. There is sufficient scrap fabric for the purpose.

(iv) The elimination of the decorative stitching is expected to reduce the appeal of the product, with an estimated fall in sales by 10% from the current level. It is not felt that the change in eyes or filling material will adversely affect sales volume. The elimination of the stitching will reduce production costs by £0.60 per soft toy.

(v) The current sales level of the soft toy is 300 000 units per annum. Apportioned fixed costs per annum are £450 000. The net profit per soft toy at the current sales level is £3.

Required:

(a) Using the information given in the question, prepare an analysis which shows the estimated effect on annual profit if all three proposals are implemented, and which enables management to check whether each proposal will achieve an annual target profit increase of £25 000. The proposals for plastic eyes and the use of scrap fabric should be evaluated after the stitching elimination proposal has been evaluated.                     (12 marks)

(b) Calculate the percentage reduction in sales due to the stitching elimination at which the implementation of all three design change proposals would result in the same total profit from the toy as that earned before the implementation of the changes in design.
                                                        (8 marks)

(c) Prepare a report which indicates additional information which should be obtained before a final decision is taken with regard to the implementation of the proposals.  (10 marks)
                                                (Total 30 marks)
*ACCA Level 2 Cost and Management*
*Accounting II*

## 8.35 Advanced: CVP analysis based on capacity usage in a leisure centre

A local government authority owns and operates a leisure centre with numerous sporting facilities, residential accommodation, a cafeteria and a sports shop. The summer season lasts for 20 weeks including a peak period of 6 weeks corresponding to the school holidays. The following budgets have been prepared for the next summer season:

*Accommodation*
60 single rooms let on a daily basis.
35 double rooms let on a daily basis at 160% of the single room rate.
Fixed costs £29 900
Variable costs £4 per single room per day and £6.40 per double room per day.

*Sports Centre*
Residential guests each pay £2 per day and casual visitors £3 per day for the use of facilities.
Fixed costs £15 500

*Sports Shop*
Estimated contribution £1 per person per day.
Fixed costs £8250

*Cafeteria*
Estimated contribution £1.50 per person per day.
Fixed costs £12 750

During the summer season the centre is open 7 days a week and the following activity levels are anticipated:
Double rooms fully booked for the whole season.
Single rooms fully booked for the peak period but at only 80% of capacity during the rest of the season.
30 casual visitors per day on average.

You are required to

(a) calculate the charges for single and double rooms assuming that the authority wishes to make a £10 000 profit on accommodation;
                                                        (6 marks)

(b) calculate the anticipated total profit for the leisure centre as a whole for the season;
                                                        (10 marks)

(c) advise the authority whether an offer of £250 000 from a private leisure company to operate the centre for five years is worthwhile, assuming that the authority uses a 10% cost of capital and operations continue as outlined above.                                       (4 marks)
                                                (Total 20 marks)
*CIMA Stage 3 Management Accounting*
*Techniques*

## 8.36* Advanced: CVP analysis and decision-making based on number of holidays to be sold by a hotel

A hotel budget for the forthcoming year shows the following room occupancy:

                                              **Average %**

| January | – March | 45 |
|---------|---------|-----|
| April | – June | 60 |
| July | – September | 90 |
| October | – December | 55 |

Revenue for the year is estimated to be £3 million and arises from three profit centres:

Accommodation* 45%: Restaurant 35%: Bar 20%:
Total 100%

*The accommodation revenue is earned from several different categories of guest, each of which pays a different rate per room.

The three profit centres have the following percentage gross margins:

| | Accommodation (%) | Restaurant (%) | Bar (%) |
|-------------|-----------------|--------------|--------|
| Revenue | 100 | 100 | 100 |
| Wages | 20 | 30 | 15 |
| Cost of sales | – | 40 | 50 |
| Direct costs | 10 | 10 | 5 |
| | 30 | 80 | 70 |
| Gross margin | 70 | 20 | 30 |

Fixed costs for the year are estimated to be £565 000.

Capital employed is £7 million.

As a means of improving the return on capital employed, two suggestions have been made:
(i) to offer special two-night holidays at a reduced price of £25 per night. It is expected that those accepting the offer would spend an amount equal to 40% of the accommodation charge in the restaurant, and 20% in the bar.
(ii) to increase prices. Management is confident that there will be no drop in volume of sales if restaurant prices are increased by 10% and bar prices by 5%. Accommodation prices would also need to be increased.

You are required
(a) to calculate the budgeted return on capital employed before tax; (5 marks)
(b) to calculate
  (i) how many two-night holidays would need to be sold each week in the three off-peak quarters to improve the return on capital employed (ROCE) by a further

4% above the percentage calculated in (a) above; (5 marks)
  (ii) by what percentage the prices of accommodation would need to be increased to achieve the desired increase in ROCE shown in (b) (i) above; (5 marks)
(c) to explain briefly the major problems likely to be encountered with each of the two suggestions and recommend which should be adopted, assuming that they are mutually exclusive. (10 marks)
(Total 25 marks)
*CIMA Stage 4 Management Accounting – Decision Making*

## 8.37* Advanced: CVP analysis and decision-making including a graphical presentation

In the last quarter it is estimated that YNQ will have produced and sold 20 000 units of their main product by the end of the year. At this level of activity it is estimated that the average unit cost will be:

| | (£) |
|-----------------|-----|
| Direct material | 30 |
| Direct labour | 10 |
| Overhead: Fixed | 10 |
| Variable | 10 |
| | 60 |

This is in line with the standards set at the start of the year. The management accountant of YNQ is now preparing the budget for the next year. He has incorporated into his preliminary calculations the following expected cost increases:

| Raw material: | price increase of 20% |
|---------------|----------------------|
| Direct labour: | wage rate increase of 5% |
| Variable overhead: | increase of 5% |
| Fixed overhead: | increase of 25% |

The production manager believes that if a cheaper grade of raw material were to be used, this would enable the direct material cost per unit to be kept to £31.25 for the next year. The cheaper material would, however, lead to a reject rate estimated at 5% of the completed output and it would be necessary to introduce an inspection stage at the end of the manufacturing process to identify the faulty items. The cost of this inspection process would be £40 000 per year (including £10 000 allocation of existing factory overhead).

Established practice has been to reconsider the product's selling price at the time the budget is being prepared. The selling price is normally determined by adding a mark-up of 50% to unit cost. On this basis the product's selling price for last year has been £90 but the sales manager is worried about the implications of continuing the cost-plus 50% rule for next year. He estimates that demand for the product varies with price as follows:

| Price: | £80 | £84 | £88 | £90 | £92 | £96 | £100 |
|---|---|---|---|---|---|---|---|
| Demand (000) | 25 | 23 | 21 | 20 | 19 | 17 | 15 |

(a) You are required to decide whether YNQ should use the regular or the cheaper grade of material and to calculate the best price for the product, the optimal level of production and the profit that this should yield. Comment briefly on the sensitivity of the solution to possible errors in the estimates. (14 marks)

(b) Indicate how one might obtain the answer to part (a) from an appropriately designed cost–volume–profit graph. You should design such a graph as part of your answer but the graph need not be drawn to scale providing that it demonstrates the main features of the approach that you would use. (8 marks)

(Total 22 marks)

*ACCA Level 2 Management Accounting*

## 8.38* Advanced: CVP analysis and changes in product mix

Dingbat Ltd is considering renting additional factory space to make two products, Thingone and Thingtwo. You are the company's management accountant and have prepared the following monthly budget:

| Sales (units) | Thingone 4 000 (£) | Thingtwo 2 000 (£) | Total 6 000 (£) |
|---|---|---|---|
| Sales revenue | 80 000 | 100 000 | 180 000 |
| Variable material and labour costs | (60 000) | (62 000) | (122 000) |
| Fixed production overheads (allocated on direct labour hours) | (9 900) | (18 000) | (27 900) |
| Fixed administration overheads (allocated on sales value) | (1 600) | (2 000) | (3 600) |
| Profit | 8 500 | 18 000 | 26 500 |

The fixed overheads in the budget can only be avoided if neither product is manufactured. Facilities are fully interchangeable between products.

As an alternative to the manual production process assumed in the budget, Dingbat Ltd has the option of adopting a computer-aided process. This process would cut variable costs of production by 15% and increase fixed costs by £12 000 per month.

The management of Dingbat Ltd is confident about the cost forecasts, but there is considerable uncertainty over demand for the new products.

The management believes the company will have to depart from its usual cash sales policy in order to sell Thingtwo. An average of three months credit would be given and bad debts and administration costs would probably amount to 4% of sales revenue for this product.

Both products will be sold at the prices assumed in the budget. Dingbat Ltd has a cost of capital of 2% per month. No stocks will be held.

Requirements:

(a) Calculate the sales revenues at which operations will break-even for each process (manual and computer-aided) and calculate the sales revenues at which Dingbat Ltd will be indifferent between the two processes:

   (i) if Thingone alone is sold; (4 marks)

   (ii) if Thingone and Thingtwo units are sold in the ratio 4:1, with Thingtwo being sold on credit. (6 marks)

(b) Explain the implications of your results with regard to the financial viability of Thingone and Thingtwo. (5 marks)

(c) Discuss the major factors to be considered in the pricing and sales forecasting for new productions. (10 marks)

(Total 25 marks)

*ICAEW P2 Management Accounting*

# Measuring relevant costs and revenues for decision-making

In this chapter we are going to focus on measuring costs and benefits for non-routine decisions. The term 'special studies' is sometimes used to refer to decisions that are not routinely made at frequent intervals. In other words, special studies are undertaken whenever a decision needs to be taken; such as discontinuing a product or a channel of distribution, making a component within the company or buying from an outside supplier, introducing a new product and replacing existing equipment. Special studies require only those costs and revenues that are relevant to the specific alternative courses of action to be reported. The term 'decision-relevant approach' is used to describe the specific costs and benefits that should be reported for special studies. We shall assume that the objective when examining alternative courses of action is to maximize the present value of future net cash inflows. The calculations of present values will be explained in Chapter 13. We also assume for this chapter that future costs and benefits are known with certainty; decision-making under conditions of uncertainty will be considered in Chapter 12. In Chapters 13 and 14 we shall concentrate on the special studies required for capital investment decisions.

It is important that you note at this stage that a decision-relevant approach adopts whichever planning time horizon the decision maker considers appropriate for a given situation. However, it is important not to focus excessively on the short term, since the objective is to maximize long-term net cash inflows. We begin by introducing the concept of relevant cost and applying this principle to special studies relating to the following:

1. special selling price decisions;
2. product-mix decisions when capacity constraints exist;
3. decisions on replacement of equipment;
4. outsourcing (make or buy) decisions;
5. discontinuation decisions.

## Learning objectives

After studying this chapter, you should be able to:

- define relevant and irrelevant costs and revenues;
- explain the importance of qualitative factors;
- distinguish between the relevant and irrelevant costs and revenues for the five decision-making problems described;
- explain why the book value of equipment is irrelevant when making equipment replacement decisions;
- describe the opportunity cost concept;
- understand the misconceptions relating to relevant costs and revenues.

We shall then consider in more detail the specific problems that arise in assessing the relevant costs of materials and labour, and conclude with a comprehensive decision-making problem that consolidates the various aspects of financial information required for decision-making.

The aim of this chapter is to provide you with an understanding of the principles that should be used to identify relevant costs and revenues. It is assumed that relevant costs can be easily measured but, in reality, some indirect relevant costs can be difficult to measure. The measurement of indirect relevant costs for decision-making using activity-based-costing techniques will be examined in the next chapter.

# The meaning of relevance

The **relevant costs** and benefits required for decision-making are only those that will be affected by the decision. Costs and benefits that are independent of a decision are obviously not relevant and need not be considered when making that decision. The relevant financial inputs for decision-making purposes are therefore *future* cash flows, which will differ between the various alternatives being considered. In other words, only **differential** (or **incremental**) **cash flows** should be taken into account, and cash flows that will be the same for all alternatives are irrelevant. Since decision-making is concerned with choosing between future alternative courses of action, and nothing can be done to alter the past, then past costs are not relevant for decision-making. Consider a situation where an individual is uncertain as to whether he or she should purchase a monthly rail ticket to travel to work or use their car. Assuming that the individual will keep the car, whether or not he or she travels to work by train, the cost of the road fund licence and insurance will be irrelevant, since these costs remain the same irrespective of the mode of travel. The cost of petrol will, however, be relevant, since this cost will vary depending on which method of transport is chosen.

# Importance of qualitative factors

In many situations it is difficult to quantify in monetary terms all the important elements of a decision. Those factors that cannot be expressed in monetary terms are classified as **qualitative factors**. A decline in employee morale that results from redundancies arising from a closure decision is an example of a qualitative factor. It is essential that qualitative factors be brought to the attention of management during the decision-making process, since otherwise there may be a danger that a wrong decision will be made. For example, the cost of manufacturing a component internally may be more expensive than purchasing from an outside supplier. However, the decision to purchase from an outside supplier could result in the closing down of the company's facilities for manufacturing the component. The effect of such a decision might lead to redundancies and a decline in employees' morale, which could affect future output. In addition, the company will now be at the mercy of the supplier who might seek to increase prices on subsequent contracts and/or may not always deliver on time. The company may not then be in a position to meet customers' requirements. In turn, this could result in a loss of customer goodwill and a decline in future sales.

It may not be possible to quantify in monetary terms the effect of a decline in employees' morale or loss of customer goodwill, but the accountant in such circumstances should present the relevant quantifiable financial information and draw attention to those qualitative items that may have an impact on future profitability. In circumstances such as those given in the above example management must estimate the likelihood of the supplier failing to meet the company's demand for future supplies and the likely effect on customer goodwill if there is a delay in meeting orders. If the component can be obtained from many suppliers and repeat orders for the company's products are unlikely then the company may give little weighting to these qualitative factors. Alternatively, if the component can be obtained from only one supplier and the company relies heavily on repeat sales to existing customers then the qualitative factors will be of considerable importance. In the latter situation the company may consider that the quantifiable cost savings from purchasing the component from an outside supplier are insufficient to cover the risk of the qualitative factors occurring.

If it is possible qualitative factors should be expressed in quantitative non-financial terms. For example, the increase in percentage of on-time deliveries from a new production process, the reduction in customer waiting time from a decision to invest in additional cash dispensing machines and the reduction in the number of units of defective output delivered to customers arising from an investment in quality inspection are all examples of qualitative factors that can be expressed in non-financial numerical terms.

Let us now move on to apply the relevant cost approach to a variety of decision-making problems. We shall concentrate on measuring the financial outcomes but do remember that qualitative factors should also be taken into account in the decision-making process.

# Special pricing decisions

Special pricing decisions relate to pricing decisions outside the main market. Typically they involve one-time only orders or orders at a price below the prevailing market price. Consider the information presented in Example 9.1.

At first glance it looks as if the order should be rejected since the proposed selling price is less than the total cost of £33. A study of the cost estimates, however, indicates that during the next quarter, the direct labour, manufacturing (i.e. non-variable) fixed overheads and the marketing and distribution costs will remain the same irrespective of whether or not the order is accepted. These costs are therefore irrelevant for this decision. The direct material costs, variable manufacturing overheads and the cost of adding the leisure company's logo will be different if the order is accepted. Hence they are relevant for making the decision. The financial information required for the decision is shown in Exhibit 9.1.

You can see from Exhibit 9.1 that different approaches can be used for presenting relevant cost and revenue information. Cost information can be presented that includes both relevant and irrelevant costs or revenues for all alternatives under consideration. If this approach is adopted the *same* amount for the irrelevant items (i.e. those items that remain unchanged as a result of the decision which are direct labour, manufacturing non-variable overheads and the marketing and distribution costs in our example) are included for all alternatives, thus making them irrelevant to the decision. This information is presented in columns (1) and (2) in Exhibit 9.1. Alternatively, you can present cost information in columns (1) and (2) that excludes the irrelevant costs and revenues because they are identical for both alternatives. A third alternative is to present only the relevant

**EXAMPLE 9.1**

The Caledonian Company is a manufacturer of clothing that sells its output directly to clothing retailers. One of its departments manufactures jumpers. The department has a production capacity of 50 000 jumpers per month. Because of the liquidation of one of its major customers the company has excess capacity. For the next quarter current monthly production and sales volume is expected to be 35 000 jumpers at a selling price of £40 per jumper. Expected costs and revenues for the next month at an activity level of 35 000 jumpers are as follows:

|  | (£) | (£) |
|---|---|---|
| Direct labour | 420 000 | 12 |
| Direct materials | 280 000 | 8 |
| Variable manufacturing overheads | 70 000 | 2 |
| Manufacturing non-variable overheads | 280 000 | 8 |
| Marketing and distribution costs | 105 000 | 3 |
| Total costs | 1 155 000 | 33 |
| Sales | 1 400 000 | 40 |
| Profit | 245 000 | 7 |

Caledonian is expecting an upsurge in demand and considers that the excess capacity is temporary. A company in the leisure industry has offered to buy for its staff 3000 jumpers each month for the next three months at a price of £20 per jumper. The company would collect the jumpers from Caledonian's factory and thus no marketing and distribution costs will be incurred. No subsequent sales to this customer are anticipated. The company would require its company logo inserting on the jumper and Caledonian has predicted that this will cost £1 per jumper. Should Caledonian accept the offer from the company?

(differential) costs. This approach is shown in column (3) of Exhibit 9.1. All of the methods show that the company is better off by £27 000 *per month* if the order is accepted.

Four important factors must be considered before recommending acceptance of the order. Most of these relate to the assumption that there are no long-run implications from accepting the offer at a selling price of £20 per jumper. First, it is assumed that the future selling price will not be affected by selling some of the output at a price below the going market price. If this assumption is incorrect then competitors may engage in similar practices of reducing their selling prices in an attempt to unload spare capacity. This may lead to a fall in the market price, which in turn would lead to a fall in profits from future sales. The loss of future profits may be greater than the short-term gain obtained from accepting special orders at prices below the existing market price. Given that Caledonian has found a customer in a different market from its normal market it is unlikely that the market price would be affected. However, if the customer had been within Caledonian's normal retail market there would be a real danger that the market price would be affected. Secondly, the decision to accept the order prevents the company from accepting other orders that may be obtained during the period at the going price. In other words, it is assumed that no better opportunities will present themselves during the period. Thirdly, it is assumed that the resources have no alternative uses that will yield a contribution to profits in excess of £27 000 *per month*. Finally, it is assumed that the fixed costs are unavoidable for the period under consideration. In other words, we assume that the direct labour force and the fixed overheads cannot be reduced in the short term, or that they are to be retained for an upsurge in demand, which is expected to occur in the longer term.

It is important that great care is taken in presenting financial information for decision-making. For stock valuation the jumpers must be valued at their manufacturing cost of £30.

|  | (1) Do not accept order (£ per month) | (2) Accept order (£ per month) | (3) Difference (relevant costs) (£ per month) |
|---|---|---|---|
| Direct labour | 420 000 | 420 000 |  |
| Direct materials | 280 000 | 304 000 | 24 000 |
| Variable manufacturing overheads | 70 000 | 76 000 | 6 000 |
| Manufacturing non-variable overheads | 280 000 | 280 000 |  |
| Inserting company logo |  | 3 000 | 3 000 |
| Marketing and distribution costs | 105 000 | 105 000 |  |
| Total costs | 1 155 000 | 1 188 000 | 33 000 |
| Sales | 1 400 000 | 1 460 000 | 60 000 |
| Profit per month | 245 000 | 272 000 | 27 000 |

Using this cost would lead to the incorrect decision being taken. For decision-making purposes only future costs that will be relevant to the decision should be included. Costs that have been computed for meeting stock valuation requirements must not therefore be used for decision-making purposes.

When you are trying to establish which costs are relevant to a particular decision you may find that some costs will be relevant in one situation but irrelevant in another. In Example 9.1 we assumed that direct labour was not a relevant cost. The company wishes to retain the direct labour for an expected upsurge in demand and therefore the direct labour cost will be same whether or not the offer is accepted. Alternatively, Caledonian may have had an agreement with its workforce that entitled them to at least three months notice in the event of any redundancies. Therefore, even if Caledonian was not expecting an upsurge in demand direct labour would have been a fixed cost within the three month time horizon. But now let us consider what the relevant cost would be if direct labour consisted of casual labour who are hired on a daily basis. In this situation direct labour will be a relevant cost, since the labour costs will not be incurred if the order is not accepted.

The identification of relevant costs depends on the circumstances. In one situation a cost may be relevant, but in another the same cost may not be relevant. It is not therefore possible to provide a list of costs that would be relevant in particular situations. In each situation you should follow the principle that the relevant costs are future costs that differ among alternatives. The important question to ask when determining the relevant cost is: What difference will it make? The accountant must be aware of all the issues relating to a decision and ascertain full details of the changes that will result, and then proceed to select the relevant financial information to present to management.

## EVALUATION OF A LONGER-TERM ORDER

In Example 9.1 we focused on a short-term time horizon of three months. Capacity cannot easily be altered in the short term and therefore direct labour and fixed costs are likely to be irrelevant costs with respect to short-term decisions. In the longer-term, however, it may be possible to reduce capacity and spending on fixed costs and direct labour. Let us now assume that for Example 9.1 that Caledonian's assumption about an expected upsurge in the market proved to be incorrect and that it estimates that demand in the foreseeable future will remain at 35 000 jumpers *per month*. Given that it has a productive capacity of 50 000 jumpers it has sought to develop a long-term market for the unutilized capacity of 15 000 jumpers. As a result of its experience with the one-time special order with the company in the leisure industry, Caledonian has sought to develop a market with other companies operating in the leisure industry. Assume that this process has resulted in potential customers that are prepared to enter into a contractual agreement for a three year period for a supply of 15 000 jumpers *per month* at an agreed price of £25 per jumper. The cost of inserting the insignia required by each customer would remain unchanged at £1 per jumper. No marketing and distribution costs would be incurred with any of the orders. Caledonian considers that it has investigated all other possibilities to develop a market for the excess capacity. Should it enter into contractual agreements with the suppliers at £25 per jumper?

If Caledonian does not enter into contractual agreement with the suppliers the direct labour required will be made redundant. No redundancy costs will be involved. Further investigations indicate that manufacturing non-variable costs of £70 000 *per month* could be saved if a decision was made to reduce capacity by 15 000 jumpers per month. For example, the rental contracts for some of the machinery will not be renewed. Also some savings will be made in supervisory labour and support costs. Savings in marketing and distribution costs would be £20 000 *per month*. Assume also that if the capacity was reduced factory rearrangements would result in part of the facilities being rented out at £25 000 *per month*.

We are now faced with a longer-term decision where some of the costs that were fixed in the short term can be changed in the longer term. The appropriate financial data for the analysis is shown in Exhibit 9.2. Note that in Exhibit 9.2 the information for an activity of 35 000 jumpers incorporates the changes arising from the capacity reduction whereas the information presented for the same activity level in Exhibit 9.1 is based on the assumption that capacity will be maintained at 50 000 jumpers. Therefore the direct labour cost in Exhibit 9.1 is £420 000 because it represents the labour required to meet demand at full capacity. If capacity is permanently reduced from 50 000 to 35 000 jumpers (i.e. a 30% reduction) it is assumed that direct labour costs will be reduced by 30% from £420 000 to £294 000. This is the amount shown in Exhibit 9.2.

A comparison of the monthly outcomes reported in columns (1) and (2) of Exhibit 9.2 indicates that the company is better off by £31 000 *per month* if it reduces capacity to 35 000 jumpers, assuming that there are no qualitative factors. Instead of presenting the data in columns (1) and (2) you can present only the differential (relevant) costs and revenues shown in column (3). This approach also indicates that the company is better off by £31 000 per month. Note that the entry in column (3) of £25 000 is the lost revenues from the rent of the unutilized capacity if the company accepts the orders. This represents the opportunity cost of accepting the orders. We shall discuss opportunity costs later in the chapter.

In Exhibit 9.2 all of the costs and revenues are relevant to the decision because some of the costs that were fixed in the short term could be changed in the longer term. Therefore whether or not a cost is relevant often depends on the time horizon under consideration.

**EXHIBIT 9.2**

*Evaluation of orders for the unutilized capacity over a three year time horizon*

Thus it is important that the information presented for decision-making relates to the appropriate time horizon. If inappropriate time horizons are selected there is a danger that misleading information will be presented. Remember that our aim should always to maximize *long-term* net cash inflows.

| | (1) Do not accept orders 35 000 (£) | (2) Accept the orders 50 000 (£) | (3) Difference (relevant costs) 15 000 (£) |
|---|---|---|---|
| Monthly sales and production in units | | | |
| Direct labour | 294 000 | 420 000 | 126 000 |
| Direct materials | 280 000 | 400 000 | 120 000 |
| Variable manufacturing overheads | 70 000 | 100 000 | 30 000 |
| Manufacturing non-variable overheads | 210 000 | 280 000 | 70 000 |
| Inserting company logo | | 15 000 | 15 000 |
| Marketing and distribution costs | 85 000 | 105 000 | 20 000 |
| Total costs | 939 000 | 1 320 000 | 381 000 |
| Revenues from rental of facilities | 25 000 | | 25 000 |
| Sales revenues | 1 400 000 | 1 775 000 | (375 000) |
| Profit per month | 486 000 | 455 000 | 31 000 |

# DANGERS OF FOCUSING EXCESSIVELY ON A SHORT-RUN TIME HORIZON

The problems arising from not taking into account the long-term consequences of accepting business that covers short-term incremental costs have been discussed by Kaplan (1990). He illustrates a situation where a company that makes pens has excess capacity, and a salesperson negotiates an order for 20 000 purple pens (a variation to the pens that are currently being made) at a price in excess of the incremental cost. In response to the question 'Should the order be accepted?' Kaplan states:

> take the order. The economics of making the purple pen with the excess capacity are overwhelming. There's no question that if you have excess capacity, the workers are all hired, the technology exists, and you have the product designed, and someone says, let's get an order for 20 000 purple pens, then the relevant consideration is price less the material cost of the purple pens. Don't even worry about the labour cost because you're going to pay them anyway. The second thing we tell them, however, is that they are never to ask us this question again ... Suppose that every month managers see that they have excess capacity to make 20 000 more pens, and salespeople are calling in special orders for turquoise pens, for purple pens with red caps, and other such customised products. Why not accept all these orders based on short-run contribution

margin? The answer is that if they do, then costs that appear fixed in the short-term will start to increase, or expenses currently being incurred will be incapable of being reduced (p. 14).

Kaplan stresses that by utilizing the unused capacity to increase the range of products produced (i.e. different variations of pens in the above example), the production process becomes more complex and consequently the fixed costs of managing the additional complexity will eventually increase. Long-term considerations should therefore always be taken into account when special pricing decisions are being evaluated. In particular, there is a danger that a series of special orders will be evaluated independently as short-term decisions. Consequently, those resources that cannot be adjusted in the short term will be treated as irrelevant for each decision. However, the effect of accepting a series of consecutive special orders over several periods constitutes a long-term decision. If special orders are always evaluated as short-term decisions a situation can arise whereby the decision to reduce capacity is continually deferred. If demand from normal business is considered to be permanently insufficient to utilize existing capacity then a long-term capacity decision is required. This should be based on the long-term approach as illustrated in Exhibit 9.2 and not the short-term approach illustrated in Exhibit 9.1. In other words, this decision should be based on a comparison of the relevant revenues and costs arising from using the excess capacity for special orders with the capacity costs that can be eliminated if the capacity is reduced.

# Product-mix decisions when capacity constraints exist

In the short term sales demand may be in excess of current productivity capacity. For example, output may be restricted by a shortage of skilled labour, materials, equipment or space. When sales demand is in excess of a company's productive capacity, the resources responsible for limiting the output should be identified. These scarce resources are known as limiting factors. Within a short-term time period it is unlikely that production constraints can be removed and additional resources acquired. Where limiting factors apply, profit is maximized when the greatest possible contribution to profit is obtained each time the scarce or limiting factor is used. Consider Example 9.2.

In this situation the company's ability to increase its output and profits/net cash inflows is limited in the short term by the availability of machine capacity. You may think, when first looking at the available information, that the company should give top priority to producing component X, since this yields the highest contribution per unit sold, but this assumption would be incorrect. To produce each unit of component X, 6 scarce machine hours are required, whereas components Y and Z use only 2 hours and 1 hour respectively of scarce machine hours. By concentrating on producing components Y and Z, the company can sell 2000 units of each component and still have some machine capacity left to make component X. If the company concentrates on producing component X it will only be able to meet the maximum sales demand of component X, and will have no machine capacity left to make components Y or Z. The way in which you should determine the optimum production plan is to calculate the contribution per limiting factor for each component and then to rank the components in order of profitability based on this calculation.

**EXAMPLE 9.2**

Rhine Autos is a major European producer of automobiles. A department within one of its divisions supplies component parts to firms operating within the automobile industry. The following information is provided relating to the anticipated demand and the productive capacity for the next quarter in respect of three components that are manufactured within the department:

|  | Component X | Component Y | Component Z |
|---|---|---|---|
| Contribution per unit of output | £12 | £10 | £6 |
| Machine hours required per unit of output | 6 hours | 2 hours | 1 hour |
| Estimated sales demand | 2 000 units | 2000 units | 2000 units |
| Required machine hours for the quarter | 12 000 hours | 4000 hours | 2000 hours |

Because of the breakdown of one of its special purpose machines capacity is limited to 12 000 machine hours for the period, and this is insufficient to meet total sales demand. You have been asked to advise on the mix of products that should be produced during the period.

Using the figures in the present example the result would be as follows:

|  | Component X | Component Y | Component Z |
|---|---|---|---|
| Contribution per unit | £12 | £10 | £6 |
| Machine hours required | 6 hours | 2 hours | 1 hour |
| Contribution per machine hour | £2 | £5 | £6 |
| Ranking | 3 | 2 | 1 |

The company can now allocate the 12 000 scarce machine hours in accordance with the above rankings. The first choice should be to produce as much as possible of component Z. The maximum sales are 2000 units, and production of this quantity will result in the use of 2000 machine hours, thus leaving 10 000 unused hours. The second choice should be to produce as much of component Y as possible. The maximum sales of 2000 units will result in the use of 4000 machine hours. Production of both components Z and Y require 6000 machine hours, leaving a balance of 6000 hours for the production of component X, which will enable 1000 units of component X to be produced.

We can now summarize the allocation of the scarce machine hours:

| Production | Machine hours used | Balance of machine hours available |
|---|---|---|
| 2000 units of Z | 2000 | 10 000 |
| 2000 units of Y | 4000 | 6 000 |
| 1000 units of X | 6000 | — |

This production programme results in the following total contribution:

|  | (£) |
|---|---|
| 2000 units of Z at £6 per unit contribution | 12 000 |
| 2000 units of Y at £10 per unit contribution | 20 000 |
| 1000 units of X at £12 per unit contribution | 12 000 |
| Total contribution | 44 000 |

Always remember that it is necessary to consider other qualitative factors before the production programme is determined. For example, customer goodwill may be lost causing a fall in future sales if the company is unable to supply all three products to, say, 150 of its regular customers. Difficulties may arise in applying this procedure when there is more than one scarce resource. It could not be applied if, for example, labour hours were also scarce and the contribution per labour hour resulted in component Y being ranked first, followed by components X and Z. In this type of situation, where more than one resource is scarce, it is necessary to resort to linear programming methods in order to determine the optimal production programme. The application of linear programming to decision-making when there are several scarce resources will be examined in Chapter 26.

The approach described above can also be applied in non-manufacturing organizations. For example, in a major UK retail store display space is the limiting factor. The store maximizes its short-term profits by allocating shelving space on the basis of contribution per metre of shelving space. For an illustration of a product-mix decision with a capacity constraint within an agricultural setting you should refer to the self-assessment question and answer at the end of this chapter.

The approach outlined in this section applies only to those situations where capacity constraints cannot be removed in the short term. In the longer term additional resources should be acquired if the contribution from the extra capacity exceeds the cost of acquisition. You should note that the principles described in this section have also been applied to a new approach to production management known as the **theory of constraints** and **throughput accounting**. This approach is described in the appendix of this chapter.

# Replacement of equipment – the irrelevance of past costs

Replacement of equipment is a capital investment or long-term decision that requires the use of discounted cash flow procedures. These procedures are discussed in detail in Chapter 13, but one aspect of asset replacement decisions which we will consider at this stage is how to deal with the book value (i.e. the **written-down value**) of old equipment. This is a problem that has been known to cause difficulty, but the correct approach is to apply relevant cost principles (i.e. past or sunk costs are irrelevant for decision-making). We shall now use Example 9.3 to illustrate the irrelevance of the book value of old equipment in a replacement decision. To avoid any possible confusion, it will be assumed here that £1 of cash inflow or outflow in year 1 is equivalent to £1 of cash inflow or outflow in, say, year 3. Such an assumption would in reality be incorrect and you will see why this is so in Chapter 13, but by adopting this assumption at this stage, the replacement problem can be simplified and we can focus our attention on the treatment of the book value of the old equipment in the replacement decision.

You can see from an examination of Example 9.3 that the total costs over a period of three years for each of the alternatives are as follows:

**EXAMPLE 9.3**

A division within Rhine Autos purchased a machine three years ago for £180 000. Depreciation using the straight line basis, assuming a life of six years and with no salvage value, has been recorded each year in the financial accounts. The present written-down value of the equipment is £90 000 and it has a remaining life of three years. Management is considering replacing this machine with a new machine that will reduce the variable operating costs. The new machine will cost £70 000 and will have an expected life of three years with no scrap value. The variable operating costs are £3 per unit of output for the old machine and £2 per unit for the new machine. It is expected that both machines will be operated at a capacity of 20 000 units per annum. The sales revenues from the output of both machines will therefore be identical. The current disposal or sale value of the old machine is £40 000 and it will be zero in three years time.

|  | (1) Retain present machine (£) | (2) Buy replacement machine (£) | (3) Difference (relevant costs/ revenues) (£) |
|---|---|---|---|
| Variable/incremental operating costs: |  |  |  |
| 20 000 units at £3 per unit for 3 years | 180 000 |  |  |
| 20 000 units at £2 per unit for 3 years |  | 120 000 | (60 000) |
| Old machine book value: |  |  |  |
| 3-year annual depreciation charge | 90 000 |  |  |
| Lump sum write-off |  | 90 000 |  |
| Old machine disposal value |  | (40 000) | (40 000) |
| Initial purchase price of new machine |  | 70 000 | 70 000 |
| Total cost | 270 000 | 240 000 | 30 000 |

You can see from the above analysis that the £90 000 book value of the old machine is irrelevant to the decision. Book values are not relevant costs because they are past or sunk costs and are therefore the same for all potential courses of action. If the present machine is retained, three years' depreciation at £30 000 per annum will be written off annually whereas if the new machine is purchased the £90 000 will be written off as a lump sum if it is replaced. Note that depreciation charges for the new machine are not included in the analysis since the cost of purchasing the machine is already included in the analysis. The sum of the annual depreciation charges are equivalent to the purchase cost. Thus, including both items would amount to double counting.

The above analysis shows that the costs of operating the replacement machine are £30 000 less than the costs of operating the existing machine over the three year period. Again there are several different methods of presenting the information. They all show a £30 000 advantage in favour of replacing the machine. You can present the information shown in columns (1) and (2) above, as long as you ensure that the same amount for the irrelevant items is included for all alternatives. Instead, you can present columns (1) and

(2) with the irrelevant item (i.e. the £90 000) omitted or you can present the differential items listed in column (3). However, if you adopt the latter approach you will probably find it more meaningful to restate column (3) as follows:

|  | (£) |
|---|---|
| Savings on variable operating costs (3 years) | 60 000 |
| Sale proceeds of existing machine | 40 000 |
|  | 100 000 |
| Less purchase cost of replacement machine | 70 000 |
| Savings on purchasing replacement machine | 30 000 |

Sometimes managers may make incorrect decisions, and not adopt the relevant cost approach, because of the method that is used to measure managerial performance. This is a major problem area for replacement decisions. For *profit measurement*, rather than the £90 000 book value being written off as a lump sum, it will be offset against the £40 000 sale proceeds of the old machine and written off as a loss on sale of £50 000. Therefore, if the machine is replaced the manager will be faced in the year of replacement with a profit report that includes a loss on sale of £50 000. The manager might be reluctant to take action to publicize such an event, particularly if he, or she, authorized the initial purchase. Furthermore, depreciation for the new machine may also be recorded as an expense in the year of purchase. The overall effect will be that significantly more expenses, and thus lower profits, will be recorded in the year of purchase if the manager makes the correct decision and replaces the machine. The adverse impact on short-term profits of purchasing the new machine will be counter-balanced in later years but if the manager places greater emphasis on short-term results the performance measurement system might motivate him, or her, not to replace the machine.

At this point in time our objective is not to focus on performance measurement. We shall look at how such problems might be overcome when we look at performance measurement in Chapter 20. The important point you should note is that only relevant costs should be incorporated into a financial appraisal. Note that the loss on sale is made up of the lump sum depreciation write-off and the sale proceeds. Only the latter is relevant, and depreciation and any profit or losses on sale of replaced assets, are irrelevant for replacement decisions.

# Outsourcing and make or buy decisions

**Outsourcing** is the process of obtaining goods or services from outside suppliers instead of producing the same goods or providing the same services within the organization. Decisions on whether to produce components or provide services within the organization or to acquire them from outside suppliers are called outsourcing or make or buy decisions. Many organizations outsource some of their activities such as their payroll and purchasing functions or the purchase of speciality components. Increasingly municipal local services such as waste disposal, highways and property maintenance are being outsourced. Consider the information presented in Example 9.4.

At first glance it appears that the component should be outsourced since the purchase price of £30 is less than the current total unit cost of manufacturing. However, the unit costs include some costs that will be unchanged whether or not the components are outsourced. These costs are therefore not relevant to the decision. Assume also that there are no alternative uses of the released capacity if the components are outsourced. The

## EXAMPLE 9.4

## CASE A

One of the divisions within Rhine Autos is currently negotiating with another supplier regarding outsourcing component A that it manufactures. The division currently manufactures 10 000 units per annum of the component. The costs currently assigned to the components are as follows:

| | Total costs of producing 10 000 components (£) | Unit cost (£) |
|---|---|---|
| Direct materials | 120 000 | 12 |
| Direct labour | 100 000 | 10 |
| Variable manufacturing overhead costs (power and utilities) | 10 000 | 1 |
| Fixed manufacturing overhead costs | 80 000 | 8 |
| Share of non-manufacturing overheads | 50 000 | 5 |
| Total costs | 360 000 | 36 |

The above costs are expected to remain unchanged in the foreseeable future if the Rhine Autos division continues to manufacture the components. The supplier has offered to supply 10 000 components per annum at price of £30 per unit guaranteed for a minimum of three years. If Rhine Autos outsources component A the direct labour force currently employed in producing the components will be made redundant. No redundancy costs will be incurred. Direct materials and variable overheads are avoidable if component A is outsourced. Fixed manufacturing overhead costs would be reduced by £10 000 per annum but non-manufacturing costs would remain unchanged. Assume initially that the capacity that is required for component A has no alternative use. Should the Division of Rhine Autos make or buy the component?

## CASE B

Assume now that the extra capacity that will be made available from outsourcing component A can be used to manufacture and sell 10 000 units of part B at a price of £34 per unit. All of the labour force required to manufacture component A would be used to make part B. The variable manufacturing overheads, the fixed manufacturing overheads and non-manufacturing overheads would be the same as the costs incurred for manufacturing component A. The materials required to manufacture component A would not be required but additional materials required for making part B would cost £13 per unit. Should Rhine Autos outsource component A?

appropriate cost information is presented in Exhibit 9.3 (Section A). Alternative approaches to presenting relevant cost and revenue information are presented. In columns (1) and (2) of Exhibit 9.3 cost information is presented that includes both relevant and irrelevant costs for both alternatives under consideration. The same amount for non-manufacturing overheads, which are irrelevant, is included for both alternatives. By including the same amount in both columns the cost is made irrelevant. Alternatively, you can present cost information in columns (1) and (2) that excludes any irrelevant costs and revenues because they are identical for both alternatives. Adopting either approach will result in a difference of £60 000 in favour of making component A.

The third approach is to list only the relevant costs, cost savings and any relevant revenues. This approach is shown in column (3) of Exhibit 9.3. This column represents the differential costs or revenues and it is derived from the differences between columns (1) and (2). In column (3) only the information that is relevant to the decision is presented. You will see that this approach compares the relevant costs of making directly against outsourcing. It indicates that the additional costs of making component A are £240 000 but this enables purchasing costs of £300 000 to be saved. Therefore the company makes a net saving of £60 000 from making the components compared with outsourcing.

**EXHIBIT 9.3**

*Evaluating a make or buy decision*

*Section A – Assuming there is no alternative use of the released capacity*

| | Total cost of continuing to make 10 000 components (1) (£ per annum) | Total cost of buying 10 000 components (2) (£ per annum) | Difference (relevant) (cost) (3) (£ per annum) |
|---|---|---|---|
| Direct materials | 120 000 | | 120 000 |
| Direct labour | 100 000 | | 100 000 |
| Variable manufacturing overhead costs (power and utilities) | 10 000 | | 10 000 |
| Fixed manufacturing overhead costs | 80 000 | 70 000 | 10 000 |
| Non-manufacturing overheads | 50 000 | 50 000 | |
| Outside purchase cost incurred/(saved) | | 300 000 | (300 000) |
| Total costs incurred/(saved) per annum | 360 000 | 420 000 | (60 000) |

Column 3 is easier to interpret if it is restated as two separate alternatives as follows:

| | Relevant cost of making component A (£ per annum) | Relevant cost of outsourcing component A (£ per annum) |
|---|---|---|
| Direct materials | 120 000 | |
| Direct labour | 100 000 | |
| Variable manufacturing overhead costs | 10 000 | |
| Fixed manufacturing overhead costs | 10 000 | |
| Outside purchase cost incurred | | 300 000 |
| | 240 000 | 300 000 |

(Exhibit 9.3 continued)

*Section B – Assuming the released capacity has alternative uses*

| | (1) Make component A and do not make part B (£ per annum) | (2) Buy component A and do not make part B (£ per annum) | (3) Buy component A and make part B (£ per annum) |
|---|---|---|---|
| Direct materials | 120 000 | | 130 000 |
| Direct labour | 100 000 | | 100 000 |
| Variable manufacturing overhead costs | 10 000 | | 10 000 |
| Fixed manufacturing overhead costs | 80 000 | 70 000 | 80 000 |
| Non-manufacturing overheads | 50 000 | 50 000 | 50 000 |
| Outside purchase cost incurred | | 300 000 | 300 000 |
| Revenues from sales of part B | | | (340 000) |
| Total net costs | 360 000 | 420 000 | 330 000 |

*Opportunity cost approach*

| | Relevant cost of making component A (£ per annum) | Relevant cost of outsourcing component A (£ per annum) |
|---|---|---|
| Incremental costs: | | |
| Direct materials | 120 000 | |
| Direct labour | 100 000 | |
| Variable manufacturing overhead costs | 10 000 | |
| Fixed manufacturing overhead costs | 10 000 | |
| | 240 000 | |
| Opportunity cost: profit forgone from allocating capacity to make component A rather than part B | 90 000 | |
| Outside purchase cost incurred | | 300 000 |
| | 330 000 | 300 000 |

However, you will probably find column (3) easier to interpret if it is restated as two separate alternatives as shown in Exhibit 9.3. All of the approaches described in this and the preceding paragraph yield identical results. You can adopt any of them. It is a matter of personal preference.

Let us now re-examine the situation when the extra capacity created from not producing component A has an alternative use. Consider the information presented in Example 9.4 (Case B). The management of Rhine Autos now have three alternatives. They are:

1. Make component A and do not make part B.
2. Outsource component A and do not make part B.
3. Outsource component A and make and sell part B.

It is assumed there is insufficient capacity to make both component A and part B. The appropriate financial information is presented in Exhibit 9.3 (Section B). You will see that, with the exception of non-manufacturing costs, all of the items differ between the alternatives and are therefore relevant to the decision. Again we can omit the non-manufacturing costs from the analysis or include the same amount for all alternatives. Either approach makes them irrelevant. The first two alternatives that do not involve making and selling part B are identical to the alternatives considered in Case A so the information presented in columns (1) and (2) in sections A and B of Exhibit 9.3 are identical. In column 3 of section B the costs incurred in making part B in respect of direct labour, variable and fixed manufacturing overheads and non-manufacturing overheads are identical to the costs incurred in making component A. Therefore the same costs for these items are entered in column 3. However, different materials are required to make part B and the cost of these (10 000 units at £13) are entered in column 3. In addition, the revenues from the sales of part B are entered in column 3. Comparing the three columns in Section B of Exhibit 9.3 indicates that buying component A and using the extra capacity that is created to make part B is the preferred alternative.

The incremental costs of outsourcing are £60 000 more than making component B (see Section A of Exhibit 9.3) but the extra capacity released from outsourcing component A enables Rhine Autos to obtain a profit contribution of £90 000 (£340 000 incremental sales from part B less £250 000 incremental/relevant costs of making part B). The overall outcome is a £30 000 net benefit from outsourcing. Note that the relevant costs of making part B are the same as those of making component A, apart from direct materials, which cost £130 000. In other words, the relevant (incremental) costs of making part B are as follows:

|  | **(£)** |
|---|---|
| Direct materials | 130 000 |
| Direct labour | 100 000 |
| Variable manufacturing overhead costs | 10 000 |
| Fixed manufacturing overhead costs | 10 000 |
|  | 250 000 |

Where the choice of one course of action requires that an alternative course of action is given up the financial benefits that are forgone or sacrificed are known as **opportunity costs**. In other words, opportunity costs represent the lost contribution to profits arising from the best use of the alternative forgone. Opportunity costs only arise when resources are scarce and have alternative uses. In our illustration the capacity allocated to making component A has alternative uses and it is assumed that its best use is to generate a profit contribution of £90 000 in making part B. Thus, manufacturing component A involves an opportunity cost of £90 000 given the circumstances described in Case B in Example 9.4.

Rather than presenting information in the format shown in columns (1) to (3) in Exhibit 9.3 (Section B) you can adopt an opportunity cost approach. This approach is widely adopted in the literature so you ought to be aware of it. The lower part of Exhibit 9.3 (Section B) displays the opportunity cost approach. You will see that only two alternatives are presented – make component A or buy component A. In the alternative for making component A the relevant incremental costs are listed but, given that allocating scarce capacity to making component A means that we have to give up the profit contribution of £90 000 from part B, this opportunity cost is a relevant cost that must be incorporated into the analysis. Therefore the total relevant cost of making component A is the sum of its incremental costs and the opportunity cost, a total of £330 000. This is compared with the outsourcing alternative costs of £300 000. Note that there are no opportunity costs associated with the outsourcing alternative because choosing this alternative does not require the use of a scarce resource or opportunities forgone.

Both the approaches shown in Exhibit 9.3 (Section B) show a £30 000 differential advantage in favour of outsourcing component A and making part B. The first approach explicitly incorporates all three alternatives, whereas the second approach does not explicitly incorporate the second alternative. This alternative is implicitly incorporated within the opportunity cost, being the £90 000 difference between columns (2) and (3). The opportunity cost approach is clearly the more complex approach but you can adopt either approach. Again it is a matter of personal preference.

# Discontinuation decisions

Most organizations periodically analyse profits by one or more cost objects, such as products or services, customers and locations. Periodic profitability analysis provides attention-directing information that highlights those unprofitable activities that require a more detailed appraisal (sometimes referred to as a special study) to ascertain whether or not they should be discontinued. In this section we shall illustrate how the principle of relevant costs can be applied to discontinuation decisions. Consider Example 9.5. You will see that it focuses on a decision whether to discontinue operating a sales territory, but the same principles can also be applied to discontinuing products, services or customers.

In Example 9.5 Euro Company analyses profits by locations. Profits are analysed by regions which are then further analysed by sales territories within each region. It is apparent from Example 9.5 that the Scandinavian region is profitable but the profitability analysis suggests that the Helsinki sales territory is unprofitable. A more detailed study is required to ascertain whether it should be discontinued. Let us assume that this study indicates that:

---

**EXAMPLE 9.5**

The Euro Company is a wholesaler who sells its products to retailers throughout Europe. Euro's headquarters is in Brussels. The company has adopted a regional structure with each region consisting of 3–5 sales territories. Each region has its own regional office and a warehouse which distributes the goods directly to the customers. Each sales territory also has an office where the marketing staff are located. The Scandinavian region consists of three sales territories with offices located in Stockholm, Oslo and Helsinki. The budgeted results for the next quarter are as follows:

| | Stockholm (£000's) | Oslo (£000's) | Helsinki (£000's) | Total (£000's) |
|---|---|---|---|---|
| Cost of goods sold | 800 | 850 | 1000 | 2650 |
| Salespersons salaries | 160 | 200 | 240 | 600 |
| Sales office rent | 60 | 90 | 120 | 270 |
| Depreciation of sales office equipment | 20 | 30 | 40 | 90 |
| Apportionment of warehouse rent | 24 | 24 | 24 | 72 |
| Depreciation of warehouse equipment | 20 | 16 | 22 | 58 |
| Regional and headquarters costs | | | | |
|    Cause-and-effect allocations | 120 | 152 | 186 | 458 |
|    Arbitrary apportionments | 360 | 400 | 340 | 1100 |
| Total costs assigned to each location | 1564 | 1762 | 1972 | 5298 |
| Reported profit | 236 | 238 | (272) | 202 |
| Sales | 1800 | 2000 | 1700 | 5500 |

Assuming that the above results are likely to be typical of future quarterly performance should the Helsinki territory be discontinued?

1. Discontinuing the Helsinki sales territory will eliminate cost of goods sold, salespersons salaries, sales office rent and regional and headquarters expenses arising from cause-and-effect cost allocations.

2. Discontinuing the Helsinki sales territory will have no effect on depreciation of sales office equipment, warehouse rent, depreciation of warehouse equipment and regional and headquarters expenses arising from arbitrary cost allocations.

Note that in the event of discontinuation the sales office will not be required and the rental will be eliminated whereas the warehouse rent relates to the warehouse for the region as a whole and, unless the company moves to a smaller warehouse, the rental will remain unchanged. It is therefore not a relevant cost. Discontinuation will result in the creation of additional space and if the extra space remains unused there are no financial consequences to take into account. However, if the additional space can be sub-let to generate rental income the income would be incorporated as an opportunity cost for the alternative of keeping the Helsinki territory.

Exhibit 9.4. shows the relevant cost computations. Column (1) shows the costs incurred by the company if the sales territory is kept open and column (2) shows the costs that would be incurred if a decision was taken to drop the sales territory. Therefore in column (2) only those costs that would be eliminated are deducted from column (1). You can see that the company will continue to incur some of the costs even if the Helsinki territory is closed and these costs are therefore irrelevant to the decision. Again you can either include, or exclude, the irrelevant costs in columns (1) and (2) as long as you ensure that the same amount of irrelevant costs is included for both alternatives if you adopt the first approach. Both approaches will show that future profits will decline by £154 000 if the Helsinki territory is closed. Alternatively, you can present just

**EXHIBIT 9.4**

*Relevant cost analysis relating to the discontinuation of the Helsinki territory*

| | Total costs and revenues to be assigned | | |
| --- | --- | --- | --- |
| | (1)<br>Keep Helsinki territory open<br>(£000's) | (2)<br>Discontinue Helsinki territory<br>(£000's) | (3)<br>Difference incremental costs and revenues<br>(£000's) |
| Cost of goods sold | 2650 | 1650 | 1000 |
| Salespersons salaries | 600 | 360 | 240 |
| Sales office rent | 270 | 150 | 120 |
| Depreciation of sales office equipment | 90 | 90 | |
| Apportionment of warehouse rent | 72 | 72 | |
| Depreciation of warehouse equipment | 58 | 58 | |
| Regional and headquarters costs | | | |
| Cause-and-effect allocations | 458 | 272 | 186 |
| Arbitrary apportionments | 1100 | 1100 | |
| Total costs to be assigned | 5298 | 3752 | 1546 |
| Reported profit | 202 | 48 | 154 |
| Sales | 5500 | 3800 | 1700 |

the relevant costs and revenues shown in column (3). This approach indicates that keeping the sales territory open results in additional sales revenues of £1 700 000 but additional costs of £1 546 000 are incurred giving a contribution of £154 000 towards fixed costs and profits.

You will have noted that we have assumed that the regional and headquarters costs assigned to the sales territories on the basis of cause-and-effect allocations can be eliminated if the Helsinki territory is discontinued. These are indirect costs that fluctuate in the longer-term according to the demand for them and it is assumed that the selected allocation base, or cost driver, provides a reasonably accurate measure of resources consumed by the sales territories. Cause-and-effect allocation bases assume that if the cause is eliminated or reduced, the effect (i.e. the costs) will be eliminated or reduced. If cost drivers are selected that result in allocations that are inaccurate measures of resources consumed by cost objects (i.e. sales territories) the relevant costs derived from these allocations will be incorrect and incorrect decisions may be made. We shall explore this issue in some detail in the next chapter when we look at activity-based costing.

# Determining the relevant costs of direct materials

So far in this chapter we have assumed, when considering various decisions, that any materials required would not be taken from existing stocks but would be purchased at a later date, and so the estimated purchase price would be the relevant material cost. Where materials are taken from existing stock do remember that the original purchase price represents a past or sunk cost and is therefore irrelevant for decision-making. If the materials are to be replaced then using the materials for a particular activity will necessitate their replacement. Thus, the decision to use the materials on an activity will result in additional acquisition costs compared with the situation if the materials were not used on that particular activity. Therefore the future replacement cost represents the relevant cost of the materials.

Consider now the situation where the materials have no further use apart from being used on a particular activity. If the materials have some realizable value, the use of the materials will result in lost sales revenues, and this lost sales revenue will represent an opportunity cost that must be assigned to the activity. Alternatively, if the materials have no realizable value the relevant cost of the materials will be zero.

# Determining the relevant costs of direct labour

Determining the direct labour costs that are relevant to short-term decisions depends on the circumstances. Where a company has temporary spare capacity and the labour force is to be maintained in the short term, the direct labour cost incurred will remain the same for all alternative decisions. The direct labour cost will therefore be irrelevant for short-term decision-making purposes. Consider now a situation where casual labour is used and where workers can be hired on a daily basis; a company may then adjust the employment of labour to exactly the amount required to meet the production requirements. The labour cost will increase if the company accepts additional work, and will decrease if production is reduced. In this situation the labour cost will be a relevant cost for decision-making purposes.

In a situation where full capacity exists and additional labour supplies are unavailable in the short term, and where no further overtime working is possible, the only way that labour resources could then be obtained for a specific order would be to reduce existing

**EXAMPLE 9.6**

A division of Rhine Autos has received an enquiry from one of its major customers for a special order for a component that will require 1000 skilled labour hours and that will incur other variable costs of £8000. Skilled labour is currently in short supply and if the company accepts the order then it will be necessary to reduce production of component P. Details of the cost per unit and the selling price of component P are as follows:

|  | (£) | (£) |
|---|---|---|
| Selling price |  | 88 |
| Less: Direct labour (4 hours at £10 per hour) | 40 |  |
| Other variable costs | 12 | 52 |
| Contribution to profits |  | 36 |

What is the minimum selling price the company should accept for the special order?

production. This would release labour for the order, but the reduced production would result in a lost contribution, and this lost contribution must be taken into account when ascertaining the relevant cost for the specific order. The relevant labour cost per hour where full capacity exists is therefore the hourly labour rate plus an opportunity cost consisting of the contribution per hour that is lost by accepting the order. Let us consider such a situation in Example 9.6.

In this example the relevant labour cost is £19 per hour, consisting of the hourly wage rate of £10 plus the lost contribution of £9 per hour from component P (the contribution of component P is £36, and requires 4 direct labour hours, resulting in a contribution of £9 per hour). Hence the relevant costs for the special order are as follows:

|  | (£) |
|---|---|
| Variable cost (excluding direct labour) | 8 000 |
| Direct labour (1000 hours at £19 per hour) | 19 000 |
|  | 27 000 |

A selling price of £27 000 takes into account the lost contribution from component P and represents the minimum selling price that the company should accept if it wishes to ensure that future cash flows will remain unchanged. The acceptance of the special order means that production of component P must be reduced by 250 units (1000 hours/4 hours per unit). We can now check that the relevant cost calculation is correct by comparing the contribution from the special order with the contribution that would have been obtained from component P:

|  | Component P (250 units) (£) | Special order (£) |
|---|---|---|
| Sales (250 units at £88 per unit) | 22 000 | 27 000 |
| Less: direct labour (250 units at £40 per unit) | (10 000) | (10 000) |
| variable costs (250 units at £12 per unit) | (3 000) | (8 000) |
| Contribution to profits | 9 000 | 9 000 |

This statement shows that the contribution to profits will be unchanged if the selling price of the special order is equivalent to the relevant cost of the order.

You may have noted that the hourly labour cost will continue whichever alternative is accepted, and you may therefore be concerned that the relevant cost consists of the hourly labour cost plus the lost contribution per hour. The reason for including the hourly labour cost is because a decision to create labour hours by reducing production of other work will result in a loss of sales and incremental/variable costs (excluding labour). That is, there will be a loss of contribution from component P of £76 (£88 selling price less £12 variable costs) before charging the labour costs giving a lost contribution of £19 per labour hour (£76/4 hours) in Example 9.6. This is just another way of saying that the relevant labour cost is the hourly wage rate of £10 plus the lost contribution per hour of £9.

# Misconceptions about relevant costs

Until recently most textbooks have emphasized the contribution approach to decision-making. The term 'contribution' can have different meanings so it is important to precisely define the term. Traditionally contribution has been defined as sales revenues less variable costs. Using this definition the precise term is **variable contribution** which means the contribution that a product (or any other chosen cost object) makes to *all* fixed costs. This was the interpretation given to the term in the previous chapter. Sometimes contribution is defined as sales revenues less variable costs less direct fixed costs. Here the term 'contribution' represents the contribution to *indirect* fixed costs.

The traditional emphasis was on variable contribution for decision-making. This implies that only sales revenues and variable costs are relevant for decision-making and that all fixed costs are irrelevant. This assumption is only correct within a very short-term time horizon. We have seen in the illustrations used in this chapter that those fixed costs that differ among the alternatives are relevant for decision-making. In Example 9.5 the salaries of the salespersons was a relevant cost relating to a decision to discontinue a sales territory. Also variable costs are not always relevant for decision-making. If variable costs are the same for all alternatives they are clearly irrelevant. For example, if two alternative production methods are being considered that require identical direct materials then the direct material cost is irrelevant to both alternatives.

Another misconception is that all direct costs are relevant whereas all indirect costs are irrelevant. If a direct cost is a past/sunk cost it will be irrelevant. In Example 9.5 the depreciation of office equipment was a direct cost to each sales territory but was irrelevant to the discontinuation decision. Some non-variable indirect costs fluctuate according to the demand for them and they may be caused by factors other than volume. For example, a high volume product made in large batches may require less resources from the support activities than a low volume product that is made in small batches. Cost drivers that capture the demand that products place on support activities should be used to allocate indirect costs to products (or other chosen cost objects). If a low or high volume product is discontinued the cost system should accurately measure the reduced resource consumption so that estimates can be made of the costs that can be eliminated. For example, if as a result of a discontinuation decision the demand for the purchase activities is reduced by 10% then we would expect in the longer-term that some of the purchasing costs will be reduced by 10%. Hence, such indirect costs are relevant for decision-making. The measurement of relevant indirect costs for decision-making using activity-based costing systems will be dealt with in the next chapter.

Relevant costs are incremental or differential costs at the company level. You should always focus on the impact decisions will have on the future costs and revenues for the company as a whole and not parts within the company. Consider the arbitrary apportionment of central headquarters costs to the sales territories in Example 9.5. We assumed that the decision to discontinue the Helsinki territory would not affect these central headquarters costs. However, if as a result of the closure assume that the £340 000 costs that were allocated to the Helsinki territory would not be allocated to the Scandinavian region because they are apportioned on the basis of sales revenues. Therefore the costs would be allocated to other regions within the company. Now consider what could happen if the Scandinavian regional manager is responsible for making the decision. He or she might focus only on how the decision affects his or her region rather than the company as a whole. From a regional point of view the £340 000 would be interpreted as an incremental cost whereas from the company point of view it is not an incremental cost. Remember that when determining relevant costs always consider whether the cost is incremental at the company level and not at lower levels within the company.

Finally, always take care when using unit costs. If you turn back to Example 9.1 you will see that the direct labour costs for the period were £420 000 and this was the labour force required for an output level of 50 000 jumpers. However, there was a temporary decline in demand and the labour force was being maintained for the expected resurgence in demand. Current activity was 35 000 jumpers and the current unit labour cost was thus £12 (£420 000/35 000 jumpers). This unit cost only applies at an output level of 35 000 jumpers. At other output levels the unit cost will be different because the labour cost is fixed in the short-term. The example looked at a special one-off order of 3000 jumpers. Given that the labour cost is fixed in the short-term the incremental costs of the order will be zero but there is a real danger that the unit cost of £12 will be mistakenly used giving £36 000 incremental cost (3000 jumpers at a unit cost of £12) for the special one-off order. You can guard against this mistake by only including those future costs that will be incurred for the alternative course of action that is being evaluated.

# A comprehensive example

We shall now conclude this chapter with a comprehensive decision-making problem (Example 9.7) that will enable you to consolidate the various items that have been considered so far. The answer is presented in Exhibit 9.5 adopting an approach that excludes all irrelevant costs and revenues.

---

**EXAMPLE 9.7**

Brown Ltd is a company that has in stock some materials of type XY that cost £75 000 but that are now obsolete and have a scrap value of only £21 000. Other than selling the material for scrap, there are only two alternative uses for them.

*Alternative 1:* Converting the obsolete materials into a specialized product, which would require the following additional work and materials:

| | |
|---|---|
| Material A | 600 units |
| Material B | 1 000 units |
| Direct labour: | |
| 5000 hours unskilled | |
| 5000 hours semi-skilled | |
| 5000 hours highly skilled | 15 000 hours |
| Extra selling and delivery expenses | £27 000 |
| Extra advertising | £18 000 |

The conversion would produce 900 units of saleable product, and these could be sold for £300 per unit.

Material A is already in stock and is widely used within the firm. Although present stocks together with orders already planned will be sufficient to facilitate normal activity, any extra material used by adopting this alternative will necessitate such materials being replaced immediately. Material B is also in stock, but it is unlikely that any additional supplies can be obtained for some considerable time because of an industrial dispute. At the present time material B is normally used in the production of product Z, which sells at £390 per unit and incurs total variable cost (excluding material B) of £210 per unit. Each unit of product Z uses four units of material B.

The details of materials A and B are as follows:

|  | **Material A** (£) | **Material B** (£) |
|---|---|---|
| Acquisition cost at time of purchase | 100 per unit | 10 per unit |
| Net realizable value | 85 per unit | 18 per unit |
| Replacement cost | 90 per unit | — |

*Alternative 2:* Adapting the obsolete materials for use as a substitute for a sub-assembly that is regularly used within the firm. Details of the extra work and materials required are as follows:

| | | |
|---|---|---|
| Material C | | 1000 units |
| Direct labour: | | |
| 4000 hours unskilled | | |
| 1000 hours semi-skilled | | |
| 4000 hours highly skilled | | 9000 hours |

1200 units of the sub-assembly are regularly used per quarter, at a cost of £900 per unit. The adaptation of material XY would reduce the quantity of the sub-assembly purchased from outside the firm to 900 units for the next quarter only. However, since the volume purchased would be reduced, some discount would be lost, and the price of those purchased from outside would increase to £1050 per unit for that quarter.

Material C is not available externally, but is manufactured by Brown Ltd. The 1000 units required would be available from stocks, but would be produced as extra production. The standard cost per unit of material C would be as follows:

|  | (£) |
|---|---|
| Direct labour, 6 hours unskilled labour | 18 |
| Raw materials | 13 |
| Variable overhead, 6 hours at £1 | 6 |
| Fixed overhead, 6 hours at £3 | 18 |
| | 55 |

(Example 9.7 continued)

The wage rates and overhead recovery rates for Brown Ltd are:

| | |
|---|---|
| Variable overhead | £1 per direct labour hour |
| Fixed overhead | £3 per direct labour hour |
| Unskilled labour | £3 per direct labour hour |
| Semi-skilled labour | £4 per direct labour hour |
| Highly skilled labour | £5 per direct labour hour |

The unskilled labour is employed on a casual basis and sufficient labour can be acquired to exactly meet the production requirements. Semi-skilled labour is part of the permanent labour force, but the company has temporary excess supply of this type of labour at the present time. Highly skilled labour is in short supply and cannot be increased significantly in the short term; this labour is presently engaged in meeting the demand for product L, which requires 4 hours of highly skilled labour. The contribution from the sale of one unit of product L is £24.

Given this information, you are required to present cost information advising whether the stocks of material XY should be sold, converted into a specialized product (alternative 1) or adapted for use as a substitute for a sub-assembly (alternative 2).

**EXHIBIT 9.5**

*A comparison of alternatives 1 and 2 with the sale of material XY*

| Alternative 1: Conversion versus immediate sale | (£) | (£) | (£) |
|---|---|---|---|
| 1. Sales revenue (900 units at £300 per unit) | | | 270 000 |
| Less Relevant costs: | | | |
| 2. Material XY opportunity cost | | 21 000 | |
| 3. Material A (600 units at £90) | | 54 000 | |
| 4. Material B (1000 units at £45) | | 45 000 | |
| 5. Direct labour: | | | |
| Unskilled (5000 hrs at £3) | 15 000 | | |
| Semi-skilled | nil | | |
| Highly skilled (5000 hrs at £11) | 55 000 | 70 000 | |
| 6. Variable overheads (15 000 hrs at £1) | | 15 000 | |
| 7. Selling and delivery expenses | | 27 000 | |
| Advertising | | 18 000 | |
| 8. Fixed overheads | | — | 250 000 |
| Excess of relevant revenues | | | 20 000 |

**Alternative 2: Adaptation versus immediate sale**

| | | | |
|---|---|---:|---:|
| 9. Saving on purchase of sub-assembly: | | | |
|    Normal spending (1200 units at £900) | | 1 080 000 | |
|    Revised spending (900 units at £1050) | | 945 000 | 135 000 |
|    Less relevant costs: | | | |
| 2. Material XY opportunity cost | | 21 000 | |
| 10. Material C (1000 units £37) | | 37 000 | |
| 5. Direct labour: | | | |
|    Unskilled (4000 hrs at £3) | 12 000 | | |
|    Semi-skilled | nil | | |
|    Skilled (4000 hrs at £11) | 44 000 | 56 000 | |
| 6. Variable overheads (9000 hrs at £1) | | 9 000 | |
| 8. Fixed overheads | | nil | 123 000 |
|    Net relevant savings | | | 12 000 |

*Notes*

1. There will be additional sales revenue of £270 000 if alternative 1 is chosen.
2. Acceptance of either alternative 1 or 2 will mean a loss of revenue of £21 000 from the sale of the obsolete material XY. This is an opportunity cost, which must be covered whichever alternative is chosen. The original purchase cost of £75 000 for material XY is a sunk cost and is irrelevant.
3. Acceptance of alternative 1 will mean that material A must be replaced at an additional cost of £54 000.
4. Acceptance of alternative 1 will mean that material B will be diverted from the production of product Z. The excess of relevant revenues over relevant cost for product Z is £180 and each unit of product Z uses four units of material. The lost contribution (excluding the cost of material B which is incurred for both alternatives) will therefore be £45 for each unit of material B that is used in converting the raw materials into a specialized product.
5. Unskilled labour can be matched exactly to the company's production requirements. The acceptance of either alternative 1 or 2 will cause the company to incur additional unskilled labour costs of £3 for each hour of unskilled labour that is used. It is assumed that the semi-skilled labour would be retained and that there would be sufficient excess supply for either alternative at no extra cost to the company. In these circumstances semi-skilled labour will not have a relevant cost. Skilled labour is in short supply and can only be obtained by reducing production of product L, resulting in a lost contribution of £24 or £6 per hour of skilled labour. We have already established that the relevant cost for labour that is in short supply is the hourly labour cost plus the lost contribution per hour, so the relevant labour cost here will be £11 per hour. If this point is not clear, refer back now to Example 9.6.
6. It is assumed that for each direct labour hour of input variable overheads will increase by £1. As each alternative uses additional direct labour hours, variable overheads will increase, giving a relevant cost of £1 per direct labour hour.
7. As advertising selling and distribution expenses will be different if alternative 1 is chosen, these costs are clearly relevant to the decision.
8. The company's fixed overheads will remain the same whichever alternative is chosen, and so fixed overheads are not a relevant cost for either alternative.
9. The cost of purchasing the sub-assembly will be reduced by £135 000 if the second alternative is chosen, and so these savings are relevant to the decision.
10. The company will incur additional variable costs of £37 for each unit of material C that is manufactured, so the fixed overheads for material C are not a relevant cost.

When considering a problem such as Example 9.7, there are many different ways in which the information may be presented. The way in which we have dealt with the problem here is to compare each of the two stated alternatives with the other possibility of selling off material XY for its scrap value of £21 000. Exhibit 9.5 sets out the relevant information, and shows that of the three possibilities alternative 1 is to be preferred.

An alternative presentation of this information, which you may prefer, is as follows:

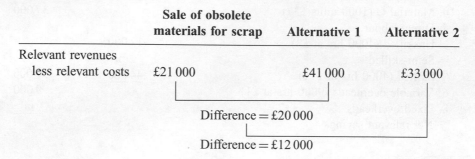

| | Sale of obsolete materials for scrap | Alternative 1 | Alternative 2 |
|---|---|---|---|
| Relevant revenues less relevant costs | £21 000 | £41 000 | £33 000 |

Difference = £20 000

Difference = £12 000

We show here *the sale of the obsolete materials as a separate alternative*, and so the opportunity cost of material XY, amounting to £21 000 (Exhibit 9.5, item 2) is not included in either alternative 1 or 2, since it is brought into the analysis under the heading 'Sale of obsolete materials for scrap' in the above alternative presentation. Consequently, in both alternatives 1 and 2 the relevant revenues less relevant costs figure is increased by £21 000. The differences between alternative 1 and 2 and the sale of the obsolete materials are still, however, £20 000 and £12 000 respectively, which gives an identical result to that obtained in Exhibit 9.5.

## Self-Assessment Questions

You should attempt to answer these questions yourself before looking up the suggested answers, which appear on pages 1108–10. If any part of your answer is incorrect, check back carefully to make sure you understand where you went wrong.

1. A market gardener is planning his production for next season, and he has asked you as a cost accountant, to recommend the optimal mix of vegetable production for the coming year. He has given you the following data relating to the current year.

|  | Potatoes | Turnips | Parsnips | Carrots |
|---|---|---|---|---|
| Area occupied (acres) | 25 | 20 | 30 | 25 |
| Yield per acre (tonnes) | 10 | 8 | 9 | 12 |
| Selling price per tonne (£) | 100 | 125 | 150 | 135 |
| Variable cost per acre (£): |  |  |  |  |
|   Fertilizers | 30 | 25 | 45 | 40 |
|   Seeds | 15 | 20 | 30 | 25 |
|   Pesticides | 25 | 15 | 20 | 25 |
|   Direct wages | 400 | 450 | 500 | 570 |

Fixed overhead per annum £54 000

The land that is being used for the production of carrots and parsnips can be used for either crop, but not for potatoes or turnips. The land being used for potatoes and turnips can be used for either crop, but not for carrots or parsnips. In order to provide an adequate market service, the gardener must produce each year at least 40 tonnes each of potatoes and turnips and 36 tonnes each of parsnips and carrots.

(a) You are required to present a statement to show:
  (i) the profit for the current year;
  (ii) the profit for the production mix that you would recommend.

(b) Assuming that the land could be cultivated in such a way that any of the above crops could be produced and there was no market commitment, you are required to:
  (i) advise the market gardener on which crop he should concentrate his production;
  (ii) calculate the profit if he were to do so;
  (iii) calculate in sterling the break-even point of sales.

(25 marks)
*CIMA Cost Accounting 2*

2. The Aylett Co Ltd has been offered a contract that, if accepted, would significantly increase next year's activity levels. The contract requires the production of 20 000 kg of product X and specifies a contract price of £100 per kg. The resources used in the production of each kg of X include the following:

### Resources per kg of X

| Labour: | |
|---|---|
|   Grade 1 | 2 hours |
|   Grade 2 | 6 hours |
| Materials | |
|   A | 2 units |
|   B | 1 litre |

Grade 1 labour is highly skilled and although it is currently under-utilized in the firm, it is Aylett's policy to continue to pay grade 1 labour in full. Acceptance of the contract would reduce the idle time of grade 1 labour. Idle time payments are treated as non-production overheads.

Grade 2 is unskilled labour with a high turnover, and may be considered a variable cost.

The costs to Aylett of each type of labour are

| | |
|---|---|
| Grade 1 | £4 per hour |
| Grade 2 | £2 per hour |

The materials required to fulfil the contract would be drawn from those materials already in stock. Material A is widely used within the firm, and any usage for this contract will necessitate replacement. Material B was purchased to fulfil an expected order that was not received, if material B is not used for the contract, it will be sold. For accounting purposes FIFO is used. The various values and costs for A and B are

| | A per unit (£) | B per litre (£) |
|---|---|---|
| Book value | 8 | 30 |
| Replacement cost | 10 | 32 |
| Net realizable value | 9 | 25 |

A single recovery rate for fixed factory overheads is used throughout the firm, even though some fixed production overheads could be attributed to single products or departments. The overhead is recovered per productive labour hour, and initial estimates of next year's activity, which excludes the current contract, show fixed production overheads of £600 000 and productive labour hours of 300 000. Acceptance of the contract would increase fixed production overheads by £228 000.

Variable production overheads are accurately estimated at £3 per productive labour hour.

Acceptance of the contract would be expected to encroach on the sales and production of another product, Y, which is also made by Aylett Ltd. It is estimated that sales of Y would then decrease by 5000 units in the next year only. However, this forecast reduction in sales of Y would enable attributable fixed factory overheads of £58 000 to be avoided. Information on Y is as follows:

| | (per unit) |
|---|---|
| Sales price | £70 |
| Labour grade 2 | 4 hours |
| Materials: relevant variable costs | £12 |

All activity undertaken by Aylett is job costed using full, or absorption, costing in order to derive a profit figure for each contract – if the contract for X is accepted, it will be treated as a separate job for routine costing purposes. The decision to accept or reject the contract will be taken in sufficient time to enable its estimated effects to be incorporated in the next year's budgets and also in the calculations carried out to derive the overhead recovery rate to be used in the forthcoming year.

Required:

(a) Advise Aylett on the desirability of the contract. (8 marks)

(b) Show how the contract, if accepted, will be reported on by the routine job costing system used by Aylett. (6 marks)

(c) Briefly explain the reasons for any differences between the figures used in (a) and (b) above. (6 marks)

(Total 20 marks)

*ACCA P2 Management Accounting*

## Summary

In this chapter we have focused on special studies and described the principles involved in determining the relevant cost of alternative courses of action. We have found that a particular cost can be relevant in one situation but irrelevant in another. The important point to note is that relevant costs represent those future costs that will be changed by a particular decision, while irrelevant costs are those that will not be affected by that decision. In the short term total profits will be increased (or total losses decreased) if a course of action is chosen where relevant revenues are in excess of relevant costs. We noted that not all of the important inputs relevant to a decision can always be easily quantified, but that it is essential that any qualitative factors relevant to the decision should

be taken into account in the decision-making process.

We have considered a variety of decision-making problems in the form of Examples 9.1–9.7, the last of which consolidated the various aspects of relevant costs. The important point that you should remember from these examples is that the decision-relevant approach adopts whatever time horizon the decision-maker considers relevant for a given situation. In the short term some costs cannot be avoided, and are therefore irrelevant for decision-making purposes. In the longer term, however, many costs are avoidable, and it is therefore important that decision-makers do not focus excessively on the short term. In the long term revenues must be sufficient to cover all costs.

## Key Terms and Concepts

decision-relevant approach (p. 279)
differential cash flow (p. 280)
incremental cash flow (p. 280)
limiting factor (p. 286)
opportunity cost (p. 294)
optimized prouction technology (p. 308)
outsourcing (p. 290)
qualitative factors (p. 280)

relevant cost (p. 280)
replacement cost (p. 297)
special studies (p. 279)
theory of constraints (pp. 288, 308)
throughput accounting (pp. 288, 310)
written-down value (p. 288).
variable contribution (p. 299)

## Recommended Reading

For a discussion of the arguments for and against using the contribution analysis approach you should refer to the *Journal of Management Accounting Research* (USA) Fall 1990, 1–32, 'Contribution margin analysis: no longer relevant. Strategic cost management: the new paradigm',

which reproduces the contributions from a panel of speakers at the American Accounting Association Annual Meeting: Ferrara (pp. 1–2) Kaplan (pp. 2–15), Shank (pp. 15–21), Horngren (pp. 21–4), Boer (pp. 24–7), together with concluding remarks (pp. 27–32).

# Appendix 9.1: The theory of constraints and throughput accounting

**AR** During the 1980s Goldratt and Cox (1984) advocated a new approach to production management called optimized production technology (OPT). OPT is based on the principle that profits are expanded by increasing the throughput of the plant. The OPT approach determines what prevents throughput being higher by distinguishing between bottleneck and non-bottleneck resources. A bottleneck might be a machine whose capacity limits the throughput of the whole production process. The aim is to identify bottlenecks and remove them or, if this is not possible, ensure that they are fully utilized at all times. Non-bottleneck resources should be scheduled and operated based on constraints within the system, and should not be used to produce more than the bottlenecks can absorb. The OPT philosophy therefore advocates that non-bottleneck resources should not be utilized to 100% of their capacity, since this would merely result in an increase in inventory. Thus idle time in non-bottleneck areas is not considered detrimental to the efficiency of the organization. If it were utilized, it would result in increased inventory without a corresponding increase in throughput for the plant.

With the OPT approach, it is vitally important to schedule all non-bottleneck resources within the manufacturing system based on the constraints of the system (i.e. the bottlenecks). For example, if only 70% of the output of a non-bottleneck resource can be absorbed by the following bottleneck then 30% of the utilization of the non-bottleneck is simply concerned with increasing inventory. It can therefore be argued that by operating at the 70% level, the non-bottleneck resource is achieving 100% efficiency.

Goldratt and Cox (1992) describe the process of maximizing operating profit when faced with bottleneck and non-bottleneck operations as the theory of constraints (TOC). The process involves five steps:

1. identify the system's bottlenecks;
2. decide how to exploit the bottlenecks;
3. subordinate everything else to the decision in step 2;
4. elevate the system's bottlenecks;
5. if, in the previous steps, a bottleneck has been broken go back to step 1.

The first step involves identifying the constraint which restricts output from being expanded. Having identified the bottleneck it becomes the focus of attention since only the bottleneck can restrict or enhance the flow of products. It is therefore essential to ensure that the bottleneck activity is fully utilized. Decisions regarding the optimum mix of products to be produced by the bottleneck activity must be made. Step 3 requires that the optimum production of the bottleneck activity determines the production schedule of the non-bottleneck activities. In other words, the output of the non-bottleneck operations are linked to the needs of the bottleneck activity. There is no point in a non-bottleneck activity supplying more than the bottleneck activity can consume. This would merely result in an increase in WIP inventories and no increase in sales volume. The TOC is a process of continuous improvement to clear the throughput chain of all constraints. Thus, step 4 involves taking action to remove (that is, elevate) the constraint. This might involve replacing a bottleneck machine with a faster one, or increasing the bottleneck efficiency and capacity by providing additional training for a slow worker or changing the design of the product to reduce the processing time required by the activity. When a bottleneck activity has been elevated and replaced by a new bottleneck it is necessary to return to step 1 and repeat the process.

To apply TOC ideas Goldratt and Cox advocate the use of three key measures.

1. *Throughput contribution* which is the rate at which the system generates profit through sales. It is defined as sales less direct materials.
2. *Investments* (inventory) which is the sum of inventories, research and development costs and the costs of equipment and buildings.
3. *Other operational expenses* which include all operating costs (other than direct materials) incurred to earn throughput contribution.

The TOC aims to increase throughput contribution while simultaneously reducing inventory and operational expenses. However, the scope for reducing the latter is limited since they must be maintained at some minimum level for production to take place at all. In other words, operational expenses are assumed to be fixed costs. Goldratt and Cox argue that traditional management accounting is obsessed by the need to reduce operational expenses, which results in a declining spiral of cost-cutting, followed by falling production and a further round of cost-cutting. Instead, they advocate a throughput orientation whereby throughput must be given first priority, inventories second and operational expenses last.

The TOC adopts a short-run time horizon and treats all operating expenses (including direct labour but excluding direct materials) as fixed, thus implying that variable costing should be used for decision-making, profit measurement and inventory valuation. It emphasizes the management of bottleneck activities as the key to improving performance by focusing on the short-run maximization of throughput contribution. Adopting the throughput approach to implement the TOC, however, appears to be merely a restatement of the contribution per limiting factor that was described in this chapter. Consider the situation outlined in Example 9A.1.

You can see from Example 9A.1 that the required machine utilization is as follows:

| Machine | 1 | 112% | $(1800/1600 \times 100)$ |
|---------|---|------|--------------------------|
|         | 2 | 178% | $(2850/1600 \times 100)$ |
|         | 3 | 56%  | $(900/1600 \times 100)$  |

Machine 2 represents the bottleneck activity because it has the highest machine utilization. To ascertain the optimum use of the bottleneck activity we calculate the contribution per hour for machine 2 for each product and rank the products in order of profitability based on this calculation. Using the figures in the present example the result would be as follows:

|                               | Product X | Product Y | Product Z |
|-------------------------------|-----------|-----------|-----------|
| Contribution per unit         | £12       | £10       | £6        |
| Machine 2 hours required      | 9         | 3         | 1.5       |
| Contribution per machine hour | £1.33     | £3.33     | £4        |
| Ranking                       | 3         | 2         | 1         |

The allocation of the 1600 hours for the bottleneck activity is:

|                  | Machine hours used | Balance of hours available |
|------------------|--------------------|----------------------------|
| Production       |                    |                            |
| 200 units of Z   | 300                | 1300                       |
| 200 units of Y   | 600                | 700                        |
| 77 units of X    | 700                | —                          |

**EXAMPLE 9A.1**

A company produces three products using three different machines. The following information is available for a period.

| Product | X | Y | Z | Total |
|---|---|---|---|---|
| Contribution (Sales − direct materials) | £12 | £10 | £6 | |
| Machine hours required per unit: | | | | |
| Machine 1 | 6 | 2 | 1 | |
| Machine 2 | 9 | 3 | 1.5 | |
| Machine 3 | 3 | 1 | 0.5 | |
| Estimated sales demand | 200 | 200 | 200 | |
| Required machine hours | | | | |
| Machine 1 | 1200 | 400 | 200 | 1800 |
| Machine 2 | 1800 | 600 | 450 | 2850 |
| Machine 3 | 600 | 200 | 100 | 900 |

Machine capacity is limited to 1600 hours for each machine.

Following the five step TOC process outlined earlier, action should be taken to remove the constraint. Let us assume that a financial analysis indicates that the purchase of a second 'Type 2' machine is justified. Machine capacity will now be increased by 1600 hours to 3200 hours and Machine 2 will no longer be a constraint. In other words, the bottleneck will have been elevated and Machine 1 will now become the constraint. The above process must now be repeated to determine the optimum output for Machine 1.

Galloway and Waldron (1988) advocate an approach called **throughput accounting** to apply the TOC philosophy. To ascertain the optimum use of the bottleneck activity they rank the products according to a measure they have devised called the throughput accounting (TA) ratio. They define the TA ratio as:

$$\text{TA Ratio} = \frac{\text{Return per factory hour}}{\text{Cost per factory hour}}$$

$$\text{where Return per factory hour} = \frac{\text{Sales price} - \text{Material cost}}{\text{Time on key resource}}$$

$$\text{and Cost per factory hour} = \frac{\text{Total factory cost}}{\text{Total time available on key resource}}$$

Note that sales less direct material cost is equal to throughput contribution, total factory cost is defined in exactly the same way as other operational expenses and return per factory hour is identical to contribution per hour of the bottleneck activity. Let us assume for Example 9A.1 that the total factory cost for the period is £3200. The TA ratios and product rankings for the bottleneck activity (Machine 2), using the data shown in Example 9A.1, are as follows:

|  | Product X | Product Y | Product Z |
|---|---|---|---|
| 1. Return per factory hour | £1.33 | £3.33 | £4 |
| 2. Cost per factory hour (£3200/1600 hours) | £2 | £2 | £2 |
| 3. TA ratio (Row 1/Row 2) | 0.665 | 1.665 | 2 |
| 4. Ranking | 3 | 2 | 1 |

The rankings are identical to the contribution per bottleneck hour calculated earlier. Given that the TA ratio is calculated by dividing the contribution per bottleneck hour (described as return per factory hour) by a constant amount (cost per factory hour) the TA ratio appears merely to represent a restatement of the contribution per limiting factor described in the main body of this chapter.

Goldratt (1993) rejects the use of throughput accounting. He does not advocate any specific accounting practices. Instead, accountants are encouraged to learn TOC ideas and apply them to accounting in ways that suit their own circumstances. However, traditional techniques that have been described in management accounting textbooks for many years, such as linear programming (see Chapter 26) for allocating the optimum use of bottleneck resources and the use of shadow prices for decision-making and variance analysis (see Chapter 19), can be viewed as an attempt to apply TOC ideas. Thus, applying TOC ideas to accounting does not represent a radical innovation in accounting but a move towards the widespread adoption of short-run variable costing techniques. Hence, the same criticisms that have been applied to variable costing can also be made to the application of TOC ideas. That is, all expenses other than direct materials are assumed to be fixed and unavoidable. For a more detailed discussion of the TOC and throughput accounting you should refer to Dugdale and Jones (1998) and Jones and Dugdale (1998). ●●●

## Key Examination Points

A common mistake that students make when presenting information for decision-making is to compare *unit* costs. With this approach, there is a danger that fixed costs will be unitized and treated as variable costs. In most cases you should compare total amounts of costs and revenues rather than unit amounts. Many students do not present the information clearly and concisely. There are many alternative ways of presenting the information, but the simplest approach is to list future costs and revenues for each alternative in a format similar to Exhibit 9.1. You should exclude irrelevant items or ensure that the same amount for irrelevant items is included for each alternative. To determine the amount to be entered for each alternative, you should ask yourself what difference it will make if the alternative is selected.

Never allocate common fixed costs to the alternatives. You should focus on how each alternative will affect future cash flows of the organization. Changes in the apportionment of fixed costs will not alter future cash flows of the company. Remember that if a resource is scarce, your analysis should recommend the alternative that yields the largest contribution per limiting factor.

## Questions

*Indicates that a suggested solution is to be found in the *Students' Manual*.

### 9.1* Intermediate
Z Limited manufactures three products, the selling price and cost details of which are given below:

|  | Product X (£) | Product Y (£) | Product Z (£) |
|---|---|---|---|
| Selling price per unit | 75 | 95 | 95 |

Costs per unit:

| | | | |
|---|---|---|---|
| Direct materials (£5/kg) | 10 | 5 | 15 |
| Direct labour (£4/hour) | 16 | 24 | 20 |
| Variable overhead | 8 | 12 | 10 |
| Fixed overhead | 24 | 36 | 30 |

In a period when direct materials are restricted in supply, the most and the least profitable uses of direct materials are

| | Most profitable | Least profitable |
|---|---|---|
| A | X | Z |
| B | Y | Z |
| C | X | Y |
| D | Z | Y |
| E | Y | X |

*CIMA Stage 2*

### 9.2* Intermediate

Your company regularly uses material X and currently has in stock 600 kg, for which it paid £1500 two weeks ago. At this were to be sold as raw material it could be sold today for £2.00 per kg. You are aware that the material can be bought on the open market for £3.25 per kg, but it must be purchased in quantities of 1000 kg.

You have been asked to determine the relevant cost of 600 kg of material X to be used in a job for a customer. The relevant cost of the 600 kg is:
(a) £1200
(b) £1325
(c) £1825
(d) £1950
(e) £3250

*CIMA Stage 2*

### 9.3* Intermediate

Q plc makes two products – Quone and Qutwo – from the same raw material. The selling price and cost details of these products are as shown below:

| | Quone (£) | Qutwo (£) |
|---|---|---|
| Selling price | 20.00 | 18.00 |
| Direct material (£2.00/kg) | 6.00 | 5.00 |
| Direct labour | 4.00 | 3.00 |
| Variable overhead unit | 2.00 | 1.50 |
| | 12.00 | 9.50 |
| Contribution per unit | 8.00 | 8.50 |

The maximum demand for these products is:

| | |
|---|---|
| Quone | 500 units per week |
| Qutwo | unlimited number of units per week |

If materials were limited to 2000 kg per week, the shadow price (opportunity cost) of these materials would be:
(a) nil;
(b) £2.00 per kg;
(c) £2.66 per kg;
(d) £3.40 per kg;
(e) none of these.

*CIMA Stage 2*

### 9.4* Intermediate

BB Limited makes three components: S, T and U. The following costs have been recorded:

| | Component S Unit cost (£) | Component T Unit cost (£) | Component U Unit cost (£) |
|---|---|---|---|
| Variable cost | 2.50 | 8.00 | 5.00 |
| Fixed cost | 2.00 | 8.30 | 3.75 |
| Total cost | 4.50 | 16.30 | 8.75 |

Another company has offered to supply the components to BB Limited at the following prices:

| | Component S | Component T | Component U |
|---|---|---|---|
| Price each | £4 | £7 | £5.50 |

Which component(s), if any, should BB Limited consider buying in?
(a) Buy in all three components.
(b) Do not buy any.
(c) Buy in S and U.
(d) Buy in T only.

*CIMA Stage 1 Specimen Paper*

### 9.5* Intermediate

M plc makes two products – M1 and M2 – budgeted details of which are as follows:

| | M1 (£) | M2 (£) |
|---|---|---|
| Selling price | 10.00 | 8.00 |
| Costs per unit: | | |
| Direct materials | 2.50 | 3.00 |

| | | |
|---|---|---|
| Direct labour | 1.50 | 1.00 |
| Variable overhead | 0.60 | 0.40 |
| Fixed overhead | 1.20 | 1.00 |
| Profit per unit | 4.20 | 2.60 |

Budgeted production and sales for the year ended 31 December are:

| | |
|---|---|
| Product M1 | 10 000 units |
| Product M2 | 12 500 units |

The fixed overhead shown above comprises both general and specific fixed overhead costs. The general fixed overhead cost has been attributed to units of M1 and M2 on the basis of direct labour cost.

The specific fixed cost totals £2500 per annum and relates to product M2 only.

(a) Both products are available from an external supplier. If M plc could purchase only one of them, the maximum price which should be paid per unit of M1 or M2 instead of internal manufacture would be:

| | **M1** | **M2** |
|---|---|---|
| | **(£)** | **(£)** |
| A | 4.60 | 4.40 |
| B | 4.60 | 4.60 |
| C | 5.80 | 4.40 |
| D | 5.80 | 4.60 |
| E | 5.80 | 5.60 |

(b) If only product M1 were to be made, the number of units to be sold to achieve a profit of £50 000 per annum (to the nearest unit) would be

A  4074;
B  4537;
C  13 333;
D  13 796;
E  none of the above.

*CIMA Stage 2*

### 9.6* Intermediate

A company is considering accepting a one-year contract which will require four skilled employees. The four skilled employees could be recruited on a one-year contract at a cost of £40 000, per employee. The employees would be supervised by an existing manager who earns £60 000 per annum. It is expected that super-vision of the contract would take 10% of the manager's time.

Instead of recruiting new employees, the company could retrain some existing employees who currently earn £30 000 per year. The training would cost £15 000 in total. If these employees were used they would need to be replaced at a total cost of £100 000.

The relevant labour cost of the contract is:

A  £100 000
B  £115 000
C  £135 000
D  £141 000
E  £166 000

*CIMA Stage 2*

### 9.7 Advanced

'I remember being told about the useful decision-making technique of limiting factor analysis (also known as "contribution per unit of the key factor"). If an organisation is prepared to believe that, in the short run, all costs other than direct materials are fixed costs, is this not the same thing that throughput accounting is talking about? Why rename limiting factor analysis as throughput accounting?'

Requirements:

(a) Explain what a limiting (or 'key') factor is and what sort of things can become limiting factors in a business situation. Which of the factors in the scenario could become a limiting factor? (8 marks)

(b) Explain the techniques that have been developed to assist in business decision-making when single or multiple limiting factors are encountered. (7 marks)

(c) Explain the management idea known as throughput accounting. State and justify your opinion on whether or not throughput accounting and limiting factor analysis are the same thing. Briefly comment on whether throughput accounting is likely to be of relevance to SEL. (10 marks)
(Total 25 marks)
*CIMA Stage 3 Management Accounting Applications*

### 9.8* Intermediate: Make or buy decision

The management of Springer plc is considering next year's production and purchase budgets.

One of the components produced by the company, which is incorporated into another product before being sold, has a budgeted manufacturing cost as follows:

|  | (£) |
| --- | --- |
| Direct material | 14 |
| Direct labour | 12 |
| (4 hours at £3 per hour) | |
| Variable overhead | 8 |
| (4 hours at £2 per hour) | |
| Fixed overhead | |
| (4 hours at £5 per hour) | 20 |
| Total cost | 54 per unit |

Trigger plc has offered to supply the above component at a guaranteed price of £50 per unit.

Required:

(a) Considering cost criteria only, advise management whether the above component should be purchased from Trigger plc. Any calculations should be shown and assumptions made, or aspects which may require further investigation should be clearly stated. (6 marks)

(b) Explain how your above advice would be affected by each of the two *separate* situations shown below.

  (i) As a result of recent government legislation if Springer plc continues to manufacture this component the company will incur additional inspection and testing expenses of £56 000 per annum, which are not included in the above budgeted manufacturing costs. (3 marks)

  (ii) Additional labour cannot be recruited and if the above component is not manufactured by Springer plc the direct labour released will be employed in increasing the production of an existing product which is sold for £90 and which has a budgeted manufacturing cost as follows:

|  | (£) |
| --- | --- |
| Direct material | 10 |
| Direct labour | 24 |
| (8 hours at £3 per hour) | |
| Variable overhead | 16 |
| (8 hours at £2 per hour) | |
| Fixed overhead | |
| (8 hours at £5 per hour) | 40 |
|  | 90 per unit |

All calculations should be shown. (4 marks)

(c) The production director of Springer plc recently said:

> 'We must continue to manufacture the component as only one year ago we purchased some special grinding equipment to be used exclusively by this component. The equipment cost £100 000, it cannot be resold or used elsewhere and if we cease production of this component we will have to write off the written down book value which is £80 000.'

Draft a brief reply to the production director commenting on his statement. (4 marks)

(Total 17 marks)

*ACCA Level 1 Costing*

### 9.9 Intermediate: Determining minimum short-term acceptable selling price

Company A expects to have 2000 direct labour hours of manufacturing capacity (in normal time) available over the next two months after completion of current regular orders. It is considering two options in order to utilize the spare capacity. If the available hours are not utilized direct labour costs would not be incurred.

The first option involves the early manufacture of a firm future order which would as a result reduce the currently anticipated need for overtime working in a few months time. The premium for overtime working is 30% of the basic rate of £4.00 per hour, and is charged to production as a direct labour cost. Overheads are charged at £6.00 per direct labour hour. 40% of overhead costs are variable with hours worked.

Alternatively, Company A has just been asked to quote for a one-off job to be completed over the next two months and which would require the following resources:

1. *Raw materials*:

  (i) 960 kg of Material X which has a current weighted average cost in stock of £3.02 per kg and a replacement cost of £3.10 per kg. Material X is used continuously by Company A.

  (ii) 570 kg of Material Y which is in stock at £5.26 per kg. It has a current replacement cost of £5.85 per kg. If used, Material Y would not be replaced. It has no other anticipated use, other than disposal for £2.30 per kg.

  (iii) Other materials costing £3360.

2.  *Direct labour*: 2200 hours.

    Required:
    (a) Establish the minimum quote that could be tendered for the one-off job such that it would increase Company A's profit, compared with the alternative use of spare capacity. (Ignore the interest cost/benefit associated with the different timing of cash flows from the different options.) (12 marks)
    (b) Explain, and provide illustrations of, the following terms:
        (i)   sunk cost, (3 marks)
        (ii)  opportunity cost, (3 marks)
        (iii) incremental cost. (2 marks)
        (Total 20 marks)

*ACCA Level 1 Cost and Management Accounting 1*

### 9.10 Intermediate: Acceptance of a contract

JB Limited is a small specialist manufacturer of electronic components and much of its output is used by the makers of aircraft for both civil and military purposes. One of the few aircraft manufacturers has offered a contract to JB Limited for the supply, over the next twelve months, of 400 identical components.

The data relating to the production of each component is as follows:
(i) Material requirements:

    3 kg material M1 – see note 1 below
    2 kg material P2 – see note 2 below
    1 Part No. 678 – see note 3 below

    *Note 1.* Material M1 is in continuous use by the company. 1000 kg are currently held in stock at a book value of £4.70 per kg but it is known that future purchases will cost £5.50 per kg.

    *Note 2.* 1200 kg of material P2 are held in stock. The original cost of this material was £4.30 per kg but as the material has not been required for the last two years it has been written down to £1.50 per kg scrap value. The only foreseeable alternative use is as a substitute for material P4 (in current use) but this would involve further processing costs of £1.60 per kg. The current cost of material P4 is £3.60 per kg.

    *Note 3.* It is estimated that the Part No. 678 could be bought for £50 each.

(ii) Labour requirements: Each component would require five hours of skilled labour and five hours of semi-skilled. An employee possessing the necessary skills is available and is currently paid £5 per hour. A replacement would, however, have to be obtained at a rate of £4 per hour for the work which would otherwise be done by the skilled employee. The current rate for semi-skilled work is £3 per hour and an additional employee could be appointed for this work.

(iii) Overhead: JB Limited absorbs overhead by a machine hour rate, currently £20 per hour of which £7 is for variable overhead and £13 for fixed overhead. If this contract is undertaken it is estimated that fixed costs will increase for the duration of the contract by £3200. Spare machine capacity is available and each component would require four machine hours.

A price of £145 per component has been suggested by the large company which makes aircraft.

You are required to:
(a) State whether or not the contract should be accepted and support your conclusion with appropriate figures for presentation to management; (16 marks)
(b) comment briefly on *three* factors which management ought to consider and which may influence their decision. (9 marks)
(Total 25 marks)

*CIMA Cost Accounting Stage 2*

### 9.11* Intermediate: Decision on which of two mutually exclusive contracts to accept

A company in the civil engineering industry with headquarters located 22 miles from London undertakes contracts anywhere in the United Kingdom.

The company has had its tender for a job in north-east England accepted at £288 000 and work is due to begin in March. However, the company has also been asked to undertake a contract on the south coast of England. The price offered for this contract is £352 000. Both of the contracts cannot be taken simultaneously because of constraints on staff site management personnel and on plant available. An escape clause enables the company to withdraw from the contract in the north-east, provided notice is given before the end of November and an agreed penalty of £28 000 is paid.

The following estimates have been submitted by the company's quantity surveyor:

## Cost estimates

| | North-east (£) | South coast (£) |
|---|---|---|
| Materials: | | |
| In stock at original cost, Material X | 21 600 | |
| In stock at original cost, Material Y | | 24 800 |
| Firm orders placed at original cost, Material X | 30 400 | |
| Not yet ordered – current cost, Material X | 60 000 | |
| Not yet ordered – current cost, Material Z | | 71 200 |
| Labour – hired locally | 86 000 | 110 000 |
| Site management | 34 000 | 34 000 |
| Staff accommodation and travel for site management | 6 800 | 5 600 |
| Plant on site – depreciation | 9 600 | 12 800 |
| Interest on capital, 8% | 5 120 | 6 400 |
| Total local contract costs | 253 520 | 264 800 |
| Headquarters costs allocated at rate of 5% on total contract costs | 12 676 | 13 240 |
| | 266 196 | 278 040 |
| Contract price | 288 000 | 352 000 |
| Estimated profit | 21 804 | 73 960 |

*Notes:*

1. X, Y and Z are three building materials. Material X is not in common use and would not realize much money if re-sold; however, it could be used on other contracts but only as a substitute for another material currently quoted at 10% less than the original cost of X. The price of Y, a material in common use, has doubled since it was purchased; its net realizable value if re-sold would be its new price less 15% to cover disposal costs. Alternatively it could be kept for use on other contracts in the following financial year.

2. With the construction industry not yet recovered from the recent recession, the company is confident that manual labour, both skilled and unskilled, could be hired locally on a subcontracting basis to meet the needs of each of the contracts.

3. The plant which would be needed for the south coast contract has been owned for some years and £12 800 is the year's depreciation on a straight-line basis. If the north-east contract is undertaken, less plant will be required but the surplus plant will be hired out for the period of the contract at a rental of £6000.

4. It is the company's policy to charge all contracts with notional interest at 8% on estimated working capital involved in contracts. Progress payments would be receivable from the contractee.

5. Salaries and general costs of operating the small headquarters amount to about £108 000 each year. There are usually ten contracts being supervised at the same time.

6. Each of the two contracts is expected to last from March to February which, coincidentally, is the company's financial year.

7. Site management is treated as a fixed cost.

You are required, as the management accountant to the company,

(a) to present comparative statements to show the net benefit to the company of undertaking the more advantageous of the two contracts;

(12 marks)

(b) to explain the reasoning behind the inclusion in (or omission from) your comparative financial statements, of each item given in the cost estimates and the notes relating thereto.

(13 marks)
(Total 25 marks)
*CIMA Stage 2 Cost Accounting*

## 9.12 Intermediate: Preparation of a cost estimate involving the identification of relevant costs

You are the management accountant of a publishing and printing company which has been asked to quote for the production of a programme for the local village fair. The work would be carried out in addition to the normal work of the company. Because of existing commitments, some weekend working would be required to complete the printing of the programme. A trainee accountant has produced the following cost estimate based upon the resources as specified by the production manager:

**(£)**

| | |
|---|---:|
| Direct materials: | |
| paper (book value) | 5 000 |
| inks (purchase price) | 2 400 |
| Direct labour: | |
| skilled 250 hours at £4.00 | 1 000 |
| unskilled 100 hours at £3.50 | 350 |
| Variable overhead | |
| 350 hours at £4.00 | 1 400 |
| Printing press depreciation | |
| 200 hours at £2.50 | 500 |
| Fixed production costs | |
| 350 hours at £6.00 | 2 100 |
| Estimating department costs | 400 |
| | 13 150 |

You are aware that considerable publicity could be obtained for the company if you are able to win this order and the price quoted must be very competitive.

The following are relevant to the cost estimate above:

1. The paper to be used is currently in stock at a value of £5000. It is of an unusual colour which has not been used for some time. The replacement price of the paper is £8000, while the scrap value of that in stock is £2500. The production manager does not foresee any alternative use for the paper if it is not used for the village fair programmes.

2. The inks required are not held in stock. They would have to be purchased in bulk at a cost of £3000. 80% of the ink purchased would be used in printing the programme. No other use is foreseen for the remainder.

3. Skilled direct labour is in short supply, and to accommodate the printing of the programmes, 50% of the time required would be worked at weekends, for which a premium of 25% above the normal hourly rate is paid. The normal hourly rate is £4.00 per hour.

4. Unskilled labour is presently under-utilized, and at present 200 hours per week are recorded as idle time. If the printing work is carried out at a weekend, 25 unskilled hours would have to occur at this time, but the employees concerned would be given two hours' time off (for which they would be paid) in lieu of each hour worked.

5. Variable overhead represents the cost of operating the printing press and binding machines.

6. When not being used by the company, the printing press is hired to outside companies for £6.00 per hour. This earns a contribution of £3.00 per hour. There is unlimited demand for this facility

7. Fixed production costs are those incurred by and absorbed into production, using an hourly rate based on budgeted activity.

8. The cost of the estimating department represents time spent in discussion with the village fair committee concerning the printing of its programme.

Required:
(a) Prepare a revised cost estimate using the opportunity cost approach, showing clearly the minimum price that the company should accept for the order. Give reasons for each resource valuation in your cost estimate.
(16 marks)
(b) Explain why contribution theory is used as a basis for providing information relevant to decision-making. (4 marks)
(c) Explain the relevance of opportunity costs in decision-making. (5 marks)
(Total 25 marks)
*CIMA Stage 2 Operational Costs Accounting*

### 9.13* Intermediate: Calculation of minimum selling price

You have received a request from EXE plc to provide a quotation for the manufacture of a specialized piece of equipment. This would be a one-off order, in excess of normal budgeted production. The following cost estimate has already been prepared:

| | | Note | (£) |
|---|---|:---:|---:|
| Direct materials: | | | |
| Steel | 10 m² at £5.00 per sq. metre | 1 | 50 |
| Brass fittings | | 2 | 20 |
| Direct labour | | | |
| Skilled | 25 hours at £8.00 per hour | 3 | 200 |
| Semi-skilled | 10 hours at £5.00 per hour | 4 | 50 |
| Overhead | 35 hours at £10.00 per hour | 5 | 350 |
| Estimating time | | 6 | 100 |
| | | | 770 |

| Administrative overhead | | |
|---|---|---|
| at 20% of | | |
| production cost | 7 | 154 |
| | | 924 |
| Profit at 25% of | | |
| total cost | 8 | 231 |
| Selling price | | 1155 |

*Notes*:

1. The steel is regularly used, and has a current stock value of £5.00 per sq. metre. There are currently 100 sq. metres in stock. The steel is readily available at a price of £5.50 per sq. metre.
2. The brass fittings would have to be bought specifically for this job: a supplier has quoted the price of £20 for the fittings required.
3. The skilled labour is currently employed by your company and paid at a rate of £8.00 per hour. If this job were undertaken it would be necessary either to work 25 hours overtime which would be paid at time plus one half *or* to reduce production of another product which earns a contribution of £13.00 per hour.
4. The semi-skilled labour currently has sufficient paid idle time to be able to complete this work.
5. The overhead absorption rate includes power costs which are directly related to machine usage. If this job were undertaken, it is estimated that the machine time required would be ten hours. The machines incur power costs of £0.75 per hour. There are no other overhead costs which can be specifically identified with this job.
6. The cost of the estimating time is that attributed to the four hours taken by the engineers to analyse the drawings and determine the cost estimate given above.
7. It is company policy to add 20% on to the production cost as an allowance against administration costs associated with the jobs accepted.
8. This is the standard profit added by your company as part of its pricing policy.

Required:

(a) Prepare, on a relevant cost basis, the lowest cost estimate that could be used as the basis for a quotation. Explain briefly your reasons for using *each* of the values in your estimate.
(12 marks)

(b) There may be a possibility of repeat orders from EXE plc which would occupy part of normal production capacity. What factors need to be considered before quoting for this order?
(7 marks)

(c) When an organisation identifies that it has a single production resource which is in short supply, but is used by more than one product, the optimum production plan is determined by ranking the products according to their contribution per unit of the scarce resource.

Using a numerical example of your own, reconcile this approach with the opportunity cost approach used in (a) above. (6 marks)
(Total 25 marks)
*CIMA Stage Operational Cost Accounting*

**9.14\* Intermediate: Impact of a product abandonment decision and CVP analysis**

(a) Budgeted information for A Ltd for the following period, analysed by product, is shown below:

| | Product I | Product II | Product III |
|---|---|---|---|
| Sales units (000s) | 225 | 376 | 190 |
| Selling price (£ per unit) | 11.00 | 10.50 | 8.00 |
| Variable costs (£ per unit) | 5.80 | 6.00 | 5.20 |
| Attributable fixed costs (£000s) | 275 | 337 | 296 |

General fixed costs, which are apportioned to products as a percentage of sales, are budgeted at £1 668 000.

Required:

(i) Calculate the budgeted profit of A Ltd, and of each of its products. (5 marks)
(ii) Recalculate the budgeted profit of A Ltd on the assumption that Product III is discontinued, with no effect on sales of the other two products. State and justify other assumptions made. (5 marks)
(iii) Additional advertising, to that included in the budget for Product I, is being considered.

Calculate the minimum extra sales units required of Product I to cover additional advertising expenditure of £80 000. Assume that all other existing fixed costs would remain unchanged.
(3 marks)

(iv) Calculate the increase in sales volume of Product II that is necessary in order to compensate for the effect on profit of a 10% reduction in the selling price of the product. State clearly any assumptions made. (5 marks)

(b) Discuss the factors which influence cost behaviour in response to changes in activity. (7 marks)

(Total 25 marks)

*ACCA Cost and Management Accounting 1*

### 9.15* Intermediate: Deleting a segment

A company manufactures and sells a wide range of products. The products are manufactured in various locations and sold in a number of quite separate markets. The company's operations are organised into five divisions which may supply each other as well as selling on the open market.

The following financial information is available concerning the company for the year just ended:

|  | (£000) |
|---|---|
| Sales | 8600 |
| Production cost of sales | 5332 |
| Gross profit | 3268 |
| Other expenses | 2532 |
| Net profit | 736 |

An offer to purchase Division 5, which has been performing poorly, has been received by the company.

The gross profit percentage of sales, earned by Division 5 in the year, was half that earned by the company as a whole. Division 5 sales were 10% of total company sales. Of the production expenses incurred by Division 5, fixed costs were £316 000. Other expenses (i.e. other than production expenses) incurred by the division totalled £156 000, all of which can be regarded as fixed. These include £38 000 apportionment of general company expenses which would not be affected by the decision concerning the possible sale of Division 5.

In the year ahead, if Division 5 is not sold, fixed costs of the division would be expected to increase by 5% and variable costs to remain at the same percentage of sales. Sales would be expected to increase by 10%.

If the division is sold, it is expected that some sales of other divisions would be lost. These would provide a contribution to profits of £20 000 in the year ahead. Also, if the division is sold, the capital sum received could be invested so as to yield a return of £75 000 in the year ahead.

Required:

(a) Calculate whether it would be in the best interests of the company, based upon the expected situation in the year ahead, to sell Division 5. (13 marks)

(b) Discuss other factors that you feel should influence the decision. (7 marks)

(c) Calculate the percentage increase in Division 5 sales required in the year ahead (compared with the current year) for the financial viability of the two alternatives to be the same. (You are to assume that all other factors in the above situation will remain as forecast for the year ahead.) 5 marks)

(Total 25 marks)

*ACCA Level 1 Costing*

### 9.16 Intermediate: Decision on whether to launch a new product

A company is currently manufacturing at only 60% of full practical capacity, in each of its two production departments, due to a reduction in market share. The company is seeking to launch a new product which it is hoped will recover some lost sales.

The estimated direct costs of the new product, Product X, are to be established from the following information:

*Direct materials*:
Every 100 units of the product will require 30 kilos net of Material A. Losses of 10% of materials input are to be expected. Material A costs £5.40 per kilo before discount. A quantity discount of 5% is given on all purchases if the monthly purchase quantity exceeds 25 000 kilos. Other materials are expected to cost £1.34 per unit of Product X.

*Direct labour (per hundred units)*:
Department 1: 40 hours at £4.00 per hour.
Department 2: 15 hours at £4.50 per hour.

Separate overhead absorption rates are established for each production department. Department 1 overheads are absorbed at 130% of direct wages, which is based upon the expected overhead costs and usage of capacity if Product X is launched. The rate in Department 2 is to be established as a rate per direct labour hour also based on expected usage of capacity. The following annual figures for Department 2 are based on full practical capacity:

> Overhead, £5 424 000:
> Direct labour hours, 2 200 000.

Variable overheads in Department 1 are assessed at 40% of direct wages and in Department 2 are £1 980 000 (at full practical capacity).

Non-production overheads are estimated as follows (per unit of Product X):

> Variable, £0.70
> Fixed, £1.95

The selling price for Product X is expected to be £9.95 per unit, with annual sales of 2 400 000 units.

Required:
(a) Determine the estimated cost per unit of Product X. (13 marks)
(b) Comment on the viability of Product X. (7 marks)
(c) Market research indicates that an alternative selling price for Product X could be £9.45 per unit, at which price annual sales would be expected to be 2 900 000 units. Determine, and comment briefly upon, the optimum selling price. (5 marks)
(Total 25 marks)
*ACCA Cost and Management Accounting 1*

### 9.17* Intermediate: Contribution analysis and an outsourcing decision

AZ Transport Group plc comprises three divisions – AZ Buses; AZ Taxis; and Maintenance.

AZ Buses operates a fleet of eight vehicles on four different routes in Ceetown. Each vehicle has a capacity of 30 passengers. There are two vehicles assigned to each route, and each vehicle completes five return journeys per day, for six days each week, for 52 weeks per year.

AZ Buses is considering its plans for year ending 31 December. Data in respect of each route is as follows:

| | Route W | Route X | Route Y | Route Z |
|---|---|---|---|---|
| Return travel distance (km) | 42 | 36 | 44 | 38 |
| Average number of passengers: | | | | |
| Adults | 15 | 10 | 25 | 20 |
| Children | 10 | 8 | 5 | 10 |
| Return journey fares: | | | | |
| Adults | £3.00 | £6.00 | £4.50 | £2.20 |
| Children | £1.50 | £3.00 | £2.25 | £1.10 |

The following cost estimates have been made:

| | |
|---|---|
| Fuel and repairs per kilometre | £0.1875 |
| Drivers' wages per vehicle per work-day | £120 |
| Vehicle fixed cost per annum | £2000 |
| General fixed cost per annum | £300 000 |

Requirements:
(a) Prepare a statement showing the planned contribution of each route and the total contribution and profit of the AZ Buses division for the year ending 31 December. (6 marks)
(b) (i) Calculate the effect on the contribution of route W of increasing the adult fare to £3.75 per return journey if this reduces the number of adult passengers using this route by 20%, and assuming that the ratio of adult to child passengers remains the same. (Assume no change in the child fare.)
(ii) Recommend whether or not AZ Buses should amend the adult fare on route W. (4 marks)
(c) The Maintenance division comprises two fitters who are each paid an annual salary of £15 808, and a transport supervisor who is paid an annual salary of £24 000.

The work of the Maintenance division is to repair and service the buses of the AZ Buses division and the taxis of the AZ Taxis division. In total there are eight buses and six taxis which need to be maintained. Each vehicle requires routine servicing on a regular basis on completion of 4000 kilometres: every two months each vehicle is fully tested for safety. The Maintenance division is also responsible for carrying out any breakdown work, though the amount of regular servicing is only 10% of the Maintenance division's work.

The annual distance travelled by the taxi fleet is 128 000 kilometres.

The projected material costs associated with each service and safety check are £100 and £75 respectively, and the directors of AZ Transport Group plc are concerned over the efficiency and cost of its own Maintenance division. The company invited its local garage to tender for the maintenance contract for its fleet and the quotation received was for £90 000 per annum including parts and labour.

If the maintenance contract is awarded to the local garage then the Maintenance division will be closed down, and the two fitters made redundant with a redundancy payment being made of 6 months' salary to each fitter. The transport supervisor will be retained at the same salary and will be redeployed elsewhere in the Group instead of recruiting a new employee at an annual salary cost of £20 000.

Requirements:
(i) Calculate the cost of the existing maintenance function. (6 marks)
(ii) Advise the directors of AZ Transport Group plc whether to award the maintenance contract to the local garage on financial grounds. (4 marks)
(iii) State clearly the other factors which need to be considered before making such a decision, commenting on any other solutions which you consider may be appropriate. (5 marks)
(Total 25 marks)
*CIMA Stage 2 Operational Cost Accounting*

## 9.18* Intermediate: Limiting factor analysis
Triproduct Limited makes and sells three types of electronic security systems for which the following information is available.
*Standard cost and selling prices per unit*

| Product | Day scan (£) | Night scan (£) | Omni scan (£) |
| --- | --- | --- | --- |
| Materials | 70 | 110 | 155 |
| Manufacturing labour | 40 | 55 | 70 |
| Installation labour | 24 | 32 | 44 |
| Variable overheads | 16 | 20 | 28 |
| Selling price | 250 | 320 | 460 |

Fixed costs for the period are £450 000 and the installation labour, which is highly skilled, is available for 25 000 hours only in a period and is paid £8 per hour.

Both manufacturing and installation labour are variable costs.

The maximum demand for the products is:

| Day scan | Night scan | Omni scan |
| --- | --- | --- |
| 2000 units | 3000 units | 1800 units |

Requirements:
(a) Calculate the shortfall (if any) in hours of installation labour. (2 marks)
(b) Determine the best production plan, assuming that Triproduct Limited wishes to maximise profit. (5 marks)
(c) Calculate the maximum profit that could be achieved from the plan in part (b) above. (3 marks)
(d) Having carried out an investigation of the availability of installation labour, the firm thinks that by offering £12 per hour, additional installation labour would become available and thus overcome the labour shortage.

Requirement:
Based on the results obtained above, advise the firm whether or not to implement this proposal. (5 marks)
(Total 15 marks)
*CIMA Stage 1 Cost Accounting*

## 9.19 Intermediate: Limiting key factors
PDR plc manufactures four products using the same machinery. The following details relate to its products:

| | Product A £ per unit | Product B £ per unit | Product C £ per unit | Product D £ per unit |
| --- | --- | --- | --- | --- |
| Selling price | 28 | 30 | 45 | 42 |
| Direct material | 5 | 6 | 8 | 6 |
| Direct labour | 4 | 4 | 8 | 8 |
| Variable overhead | 3 | 3 | 6 | 6 |
| Fixed overhead* | 8 | 8 | 16 | 16 |
| Profit | 8 | 9 | 7 | 6 |
| Labour hours | 1 | 1 | 2 | 2 |
| Machine hours | 4 | 3 | 4 | 5 |
| | Units | Units | Units | Units |
| Maximum demand per week | 200 | 180 | 250 | 100 |

*Absorbed based on budgeted labour hours of 1000 per week.

There is a maximum of 2000 machine hours available per week.

Requirement:

(a) Determine the production plan which will maximise the weekly profit of PDR plc and prepare a profit statement showing the profit your plan will yield. (10 marks)

(b) The marketing director of PDR plc is concerned at the company's inability to meet the quantity demanded by its customers.

Two alternative strategies are being considered to overcome this:

(i) to increase the number of hours worked using the existing machinery by working overtime. Such overtime would be paid at a premium of 50% above normal labour rates, and variable overhead costs would be expected to increase in proportion to labour costs.

(ii) to buy product B from an overseas supplier at a cost of £19 per unit including carriage. This would need to be re-packaged at a cost of £1 per unit before it could be sold.

Requirement:

Evaluate each of the two alternative strategies and, as management accountant, prepare a report to the marketing director, stating your reasons (quantitative and qualitative) as to which, if either, should be adopted. (15 marks)

(Total 25 marks)

*CIMA Stage 2 Operational Cost Accounting*

## 9.20* Intermediate: Key/limiting factor decision-making

BVX Limited manufactures three garden furniture products – chairs, benches and tables. The budgeted unit cost and resource requirements of each of these items is detailed below:

| | Chair (£) | Bench (£) | Table (£) |
|---|---|---|---|
| Timber cost | 5.00 | 15.00 | 10.00 |
| Direct labour cost | 4.00 | 10.00 | 8.00 |
| Variable overhead cost | 3.00 | 7.50 | 6.00 |
| Fixed overhead cost | 4.50 | 11.25 | 9.00 |
| | 16.50 | 43.75 | 33.00 |
| Budgeted volumes per annum | 4000 | 2000 | 1500 |

These volumes are believed to equal the market demand for these products.

The fixed overhead costs are attributed to the three products on the basis of direct labour hours.

The labour rate is £4.00 per hour.

The cost of the timber is £2.00 per square metre.

The products are made from a specialist timber. A memo from the purchasing manager advises you that because of a problem with the supplier it is to be assumed that this specialist timber is limited in supply to 20 000 square metres per annum.

The sales director has already accepted an order for 500 chairs, 100 benches and 150 tables, which if not supplied would incur a financial penalty of £2000. These quantities are included in the market demand estimates above.

The selling prices of the three products are:

| | |
|---|---|
| Chair | £20.00 |
| Bench | £50.00 |
| Table | £40.00 |

Required:

(a) Determine the optimum production plan *and* state the net profit that this should yield per annum. (10 marks)

(b) Calculate *and* explain the maximum prices which should be paid per sq. metre in order to obtain extra supplies of the timber. (5 marks)

(c) The management team has accused the accountant of using too much jargon.

Prepare a statement which explains the following terms in a way that a multi/disciplinary team of managers would understand. The accountant will use this statement as a briefing paper at the next management meeting. The terms to be explained are:

(i) variable costs;

(ii) relevant costs;

(iii) avoidable costs;

(iv) incremental costs;

(v) opportunity costs. (10 marks)

(Total 25 marks)

*CIMA Operations Cost Accounting Stage 2*

## 9.21* Intermediate: Allocation of scarce capacity

EX Limited is an established supplier of precision parts to a major aircraft manufacturer. It has been offered the choice of making either Part A or Part B for the next period, but not both.

Both parts use the same metal, a titanium alloy, of which 13 000 kilos only are available, at £12.50 per kilo. The parts are made by passing each one through two fully-automatic computer-controlled machine lines – S and T – whose capacities are limited. Target prices have been set and the following data are available for the period:

*Part details*

|  | Part A | Part B |
|---|---|---|
| Maximum call-off (units) | 7000 | 9000 |
| Target price | £145 | £115 |
|  | per unit | per unit |
| Alloy usage | 1.6 kilos | 1.6 kilos |
| Machine times |  |  |
| Line S | 0.6 hours | 0.25 hours |
| Line T | 0.5 hours | 0.55 hours |

*Machine details*

|  | Line S | Line T |
|---|---|---|
| Hours available | 4000 | 4500 |
| Variable overhead | £80 | £100 |
| per machine hour |  |  |

You are required:

(a) to calculate which part should be made during the next period to maximise contribution;

(9 marks)

(b) to calculate the contribution which EX Limited will earn and whether the company will be able to meet the maximum call-off.

(3 marks)

As an alternative to the target prices shown above, the aircraft manufacturer has offered the following alternative arrangement:

Target prices less 10% plus £60 per hour for each unused machine hour.

(c) You are required to decide whether your recommendation in (a) above will be altered and, if so, to calculate the new contribution.

(10 marks)

(Total 22 marks)

*CIMA Stage 3 Management Accounting Techniques*

**9.22 Intermediate: Allocation of scarce capacity and make or buy decision where scarce capacity exists**

PQR Limited is an engineering company engaged in the manufacture of components and finished products.

The company is highly mechanised and each of the components and finished products requires the use of one or more types of machine in its machining department. The following costs and revenues (where appropriate) relate to a single component or unit of the finished product:

|  | Components | | Finished products | |
|---|---|---|---|---|
|  | A | B | C | D |
|  | £ | £ | £ | £ |
| Selling price |  |  | 127 | 161 |
| Direct materials | 8 | 29 | 33 | 38 |
| Direct wages | 10 | 30 | 20 | 25 |
| Variable overhead: |  |  |  |  |
| Drilling | 6 | 3 | 9 | 12 |
| Grinding | 8 | 16 | 4 | 12 |
| Fixed overhead: |  |  |  |  |
| Drilling | 12 | 6 | 18 | 24 |
| Grinding | 10 | 20 | 5 | 15 |
| Total cost | 54 | 104 | 89 | 126 |

*Notes*

1. The labour hour rate is £5 per hour.
2. Overhead absorption rates per machine hour are as follows:

|  | Variable | Fixed |
|---|---|---|
|  | £ | £ |
| Drilling (per hour) | 3 | 6 |
| Grinding (per hour) | 4 | 5 |

3. Components A and B are NOT used in finished products C and D. They are used in the company's other products, none of which use the drilling or grinding machines. The company does not manufacture any other components.

4. The number of machine drilling hours available is limited to 1650 per week. There are 2500 machine grinding hours available per week. These numbers of hours have been used to calculate the absorption rates stated above.

5. The maximum demand in units per week for each of the finished products has been estimated by the marketing director as:

| Product C | 250 units |
|---|---|
| Product D | 500 units |

6. The internal demand for components A and B each week is as follows:

| Component A | 50 units |
|---|---|
| Component B | 100 units |

7. There is no external market for components A and B.

8. PQR Limited has a contract to supply 50 units of each of its finished products to a major customer each week. These quantities are included in the maximum units of demand given in note 5 above.

Requirement:

(a) Calculate the number of units of *each* finished product that PQR Limited should produce in order to maximise its profits, and the profit per week that this should yield. (12 marks)

(b) (i) The production director has now discovered that he can obtain unlimited quantities of components identical to A and B for £50 and £96 per unit respectively.

State whether this information changes the production plan of the company if it wishes to continue to maximise its profits per week. If appropriate, state the revised production plan and the net benefit per week caused by the change to the production plan. (7 marks)

(ii) The solution of problems involving more than one limiting factor requires the use of linear programming.

Explain why this technique must be used in such circumstances, and the steps used to solve such a problem when using the graphical linear programming technique. (6 marks)

(Total 25 marks)

*CIMA Stage 2 Operational Cost Accounting*

## 9.23 Intermediate: Limiting/key factors and a decision whether it is profitable to expand output by overtime

B Ltd manufactures a range of products which are sold to a limited number of wholesale outlets. Four of these products are manufactured in a particular department on common equipment. No other facilities are available for the manufacture of these products.

Owing to greater than expected increases in demand, normal single shift working is rapidly becoming insufficient to meet sales requirements.

Overtime and, in the longer term, expansion of facilities are being considered.

Selling prices and product costs, based on single shift working utilizing practical capacity to the full, are as follows:

|  | Product (£/unit) | | | |
|---|---|---|---|---|
|  | W | X | Y | Z |
| Selling price | 3.650 | 3.900 | 2.250 | 2.950 |
| Product costs: | | | | |
| Direct materials | 0.805 | 0.996 | 0.450 | 0.647 |
| Direct labour | 0.604 | 0.651 | 0.405 | 0.509 |
| Variable manu-facturing o'hd | 0.240 | 0.247 | 0.201 | 0.217 |
| Fixed manufacturing o'hd | 0.855 | 0.950 | 0.475 | 0.760 |
| Variable selling and admin o'hd | 0.216 | 0.216 | 0.216 | 0.216 |
| Fixed selling and admin o'hd | 0.365 | 0.390 | 0.225 | 0.295 |

Fixed manufacturing overheads are absorbed on the basis of machine hours which, at practical capacity, are 2250 per period. Total fixed manufacturing overhead per period is £427 500. Fixed selling and administration overhead, which totals £190 000 per period, is shared amongst products at a rate of 10% of sales.

The sales forecast for the following period (in thousands of units) is:

| Product W | 190 |
|---|---|
| Product X | 125 |
| Product Y | 144 |
| Product Z | 142 |

Overtime could be worked to make up any production shortfall in normal time. Direct labour would be paid at a premium of 50% above basic rate. Other variable costs would be expected to remain unchanged per unit of output. Fixed costs would increase by £24 570 per period.

Required:

(a) If overtime is not worked in the following period, recommend the quantity of each product that should be manufactured in order to maximize profit. (12 marks)

(b) Calculate the expected profit in the following period if overtime is worked as necessary to meet sales requirements. (7 marks)

(c) Consider the factors which should influence the decision whether or not to work overtime in such a situation.                    (6 marks)

(Total 25 marks)

*ACCA Cost and Management Accounting 1*

### 9.24* Intermediate Price/output and key factor decisions

You work as a trainee for a small management consultancy which has been asked to advise a company, Rane Limited, which manufactures and sells a single product. Rane is currently operating at full capacity producing and selling 25 000 units of its product each year. The cost and selling price structure for this level of activity is as follows:

|  | At 25 000 units output | |
|---|---|---|
|  | (£ per unit) | (£ per unit) |
| **Production costs** |  |  |
| Direct material | 14 |  |
| Direct labour | 13 |  |
| Variable production overhead | 4 |  |
| Fixed production overhead | 8 |  |
| Total production cost |  | 39 |
| Selling and distribution overhead: |  |  |
| Sales commission – |  |  |
| 10% of sales value | 6 |  |
| Fixed | 3 |  |
|  |  | 9 |
| Administration overhead: |  |  |
| Fixed |  | 2 |
| Total cost |  | 50 |
| Mark up – 20% |  | 10 |
| Selling price |  | 60 |

A new managing director has recently joined the company and he has engaged your organization to advise on his company's selling price policy. The sales price of £60 has been derived as above from a cost-plus pricing policy. The price was viewed as satisfactory because the resulting demand enabled full capacity operation.

You have been asked to investigate the effect on costs and profit of an increase in the selling price. The marketing department has provided you with the following estimates of sales volumes which could be achieved at the three alternative sales prices under consideration.

| Selling price per unit | £70 | £80 | £90 |
|---|---|---|---|
| Annual sales volume (units) | 20 000 | 16 000 | 11 000 |

You have spent some time estimating the effect that changes in output volume will have on cost behaviour patterns and you have now collected the following information.

Direct material: The loss of bulk discounts means that the direct material cost per unit will increase by 15% for all units produced in the year if activity reduces below 15 000 units per annum.

Direct labour: Savings in bonus payments will reduce labour costs by 10% for all units produced in the year if activity reduces below 20 000 units per annum.

Sales commission: This would continue to be paid at the rate of 10% of sales price.

Fixed production overhead: If annual output volume was below 20 000 units, then a machine rental cost of £10 000 per annum could be saved. This will be the only change in the total expenditure on fixed production overhead.

Fixed selling overhead: A reduction in the part-time sales force would result in a £5000 per annum saving if annual sales volume falls below 24 000 units. This will be the only change in the total expenditure on fixed selling and distribution overhead.

Variable production overhead: There would be no change in the unit cost for variable production overhead.

Administration overhead: The total expenditure on administration overhead would remain unaltered within this range of activity.

Stocks: Rane's product is highly perishable, therefore no stocks are held.

### Task 1

(a) Calculate the annual profit which is earned with the current selling price of £60 per unit.

(b) Prepare a schedule to show the annual profit which would be earned with each of the three alternative selling prices.

### Task 2

Prepare a brief memorandum to your boss, Chris Jones. The memorandum should cover the following points:

(a) Your recommendation as to the selling price which should be charged to maximize Rane limited's annual profits.

(b) *Two* non-financial factors which the management of Rane Limited should consider before planning to operate below full capacity.

Another of your consultancy's clients is a manufacturing company, Shortage Limited, which is experiencing problems in obtaining supplies of a major component. The component is used in all of its four products and there is a labour dispute at the supplier's factory, which is restricting the component's availability.

Supplies will be restricted to 22 400 components for the next period and the company wishes to ensure that the best use is made of the available components. This is the only component used in the four products, and there are no alternatives and no other suppliers.

The components cost £2 each and are used in varying amounts in each of the four products.

Shortage Limited's fixed costs amount to £8000 per period. No stocks are held of finished goods or work in progress.

The following information is available concerning the products.

| Maximum demand per period | Product A 4000 units (£ per unit) | Product B 2500 units (£ per unit) | Product C 3600 units (£ per unit) | Product D 2750 units (£ per unit) |
|---|---|---|---|---|
| Selling price | 14 | 12 | 16 | 17 |
| Component costs | 4 | 2 | 6 | 8 |
| Other variable costs | 7 | 9 | 6 | 4 |

## Task 3

(a) Prepare a recommended production schedule for next period which will maximize Shortage Limited's profit.

(b) Calculate the profit that will be earned in the next period if your recommended production schedule is followed.

*AAT Technicians Stage*

## 9.25* Intermediate: Limiting factor optimum production and the use of simultaneous equations where more than one scarce factor exists

A company manufactures two products (X and Y) in one of its factories. Production capacity is limited to 85 000 machine hours per period. There is no restriction on direct labour hours.

The following information is provided concerning the two products:

| | Product X | Product Y |
|---|---|---|
| Estimated demand (000 units) | 315 | 135 |
| Selling price (per unit) | £11.20 | £15.70 |
| Variable costs (per unit) | £6.30 | £8.70 |
| Fixed costs (per unit) | £4.00 | £7.00 |
| Machine hours (per 000 units) | 160 | 280 |
| Direct labour hours (per 000 units) | 120 | 140 |

Fixed costs are absorbed into unit costs at a rate per machine hour based upon full capacity.

Required:

(a) Calculate the production quantities of Products X and Y which are required per period in order to maximize profit in the situation described above. (5 marks)

(b) Prepare a marginal costing statement in order to establish the total contribution of each product, and the net profit per period, based on selling the quantities calculated in (a) above. (4 marks)

(c) Calculate the production quantities of Products X and Y per period which would fully utilize both machine capacity and direct labour hours, where the available direct labour hours are restricted to 55 000 per period. (The limit of 85 000 machine hours remains.) (5 marks)

(Total 14 marks)

*ACCA Foundation Paper 3*

## 9.26* Advanced: Identification of limiting factors and allocation of scarce capacity where several production constraints exist

Timbcon Ltd has two fully automated machine groups X and Y through which lengths of timber are passed in order to produce decorative lampstand centres. There are production capacity constraints and Timbcon Ltd has decided to produce only one of the two lampstand models, 'Traditional' or 'Modern', in the year to 31 March.

The following forecast information is available for the year to 31 March:

| | 'Traditional' | 'Modern' |
|---|---|---|
| (i) Maximum sales potential (units) | 7400 | 10 000 |
| (ii) Lampstand unit data: | | |
| Selling price | £45 | £40 |

Machine time:

| | group X (hours) | 0.25 | 0.15 |
| | group Y (hours) | 0.20 | 0.225 |

(iii) Machine groups X and Y have maximum operating hours of 1700 and 1920 hours respectively. Lampstand production is the sole use available for production capacity.

(iv) The maximum quantity of timber available is 17 000 metres. Each lampstand requires a two metre length of timber. Timber may be purchased in lengths as required at £2.50 per metre.

(v) Variable machine overhead for machine groups X and Y is estimated at £25 and £30 per machine hour respectively.

(vi) All units are sold in the year in which they are produced.

Required:

(a) Use the above information to determine which of the lampstand centres, 'Traditional' or 'Modern', should be produced and sold in the year to 31 March in order to maximise profit. Your answer should state the number of units to be produced and sold and the resulting contribution. (8 marks)

(b) Timbcon Ltd wish to consider additional sales outlets which would earn contribution at the rate of £20 and £30 per machine hour for machine groups X and Y respectively. Such additional sales outlets would be taken up only to utilise any surplus hours not required for lampstand production.

Prepare figures which show whether 'Traditional' or 'Modern' lampstands should now be produced in order to maximise total contribution in the year to 31 March and state what that contribution would be. (7 marks)

(c) A linear programming model which incorporates the data given in parts (a) and (b) of the question has shown that where Timbcon Ltd is willing to produce and sell both 'Traditional' and 'Modern' lampstands and use any spare capacity for the additional sales outlets detailed in (b) above, the profit maximising mix is the production and sale of 4250 units of each type of lampstand in the year to 31 March.

Prepare a budget analysis showing the total machine hours and timber (metres) required for each lampstand type and in total for the above production/sales mix, the budgeted contribution for each type of lampstand and the total budgeted contribution for Timbcon Ltd in the year to 31 March.
(7 marks)

(d) Suggest ways in which Timbcon Ltd may overcome the capacity constraints which limit the opportunities available to it in the year to 31 March, and indicate the types of costs which may be incurred in overcoming each constraint. (8 marks)
(Total 30 marks)

## 9.27* Advanced: Allocation of scarce resources

A processing company, EF, is extremely busy. It has increased its output and sales from 12 900 kg in quarter 1 to 17 300 kg in quarter 2 but, though demand is still rising, it cannot increase its output more than another 5% from its existing labour force which is now at its maximum.

Data in quarter 2 for its four products were:

| | Product P | Product Q | Product R | Product S |
|---|---|---|---|---|
| Output (kg) | 4560 | 6960 | 3480 | 2300 |
| Selling price (£ per kg) | 16.20 | 11.64 | 9.92 | 13.68 |
| Costs (£ per kg): | | | | |
| Direct labour | 1.96 | 1.30 | 0.99 | 1.70 |
| (at £6 per hour) | | | | |
| Direct materials | 6.52 | 4.90 | 4.10 | 5.42 |
| Direct packaging | 0.84 | 0.74 | 0.56 | 0.70 |
| Fixed overhead | | | | |
| (absorbed on | | | | |
| basis of direct | | | | |
| labour cost) | 3.92 | 2.60 | 1.98 | 3.40 |
| Total | 13.24 | 9.54 | 7.63 | 11.22 |

The XY Company has offered to supply 2000 kg of product Q at a delivered price of 90% of EF's selling price. The company will then be able to produce extra product P in its place up to the plant's total capacity.

You are required to state, with supporting calculations:

(a) whether EF should accept the XY Company's offer; (10 marks)

(b) which would be the most profitable combination of subcontracting 2000 kg of one product at a price of 90% of its selling price and producing extra quantities of another product up to the plant's total capacity. Assume that the market can absorb the extra output and that XY's quality and delivery are acceptable. (15 marks)

*CIMA P3 Management Accounting*

## 9.28 Advanced: Key factor and make or buy decision

A construction company has accepted a contract to lay underground pipework. The contract requires that 2500 m of 10" pipe and 2000 m of 18" pipe be laid each week.

The limiting factor is the availability of specialized equipment. The company owns 15 excavating machines (type A) and 13 lifting and jointing machines (type B). The normal operating time is 40 hours a week but up to 50% overtime is acceptable to the employees.

The time taken to handle each metre of pipe is:

| Size of pipe | Minutes per metre | |
| --- | --- | --- |
| | Machine A | Machine B |
| 10" | 6 | 12 |
| 18" | 18 | 12 |

The costs of operating the machines are:

| | Machine A (£) | Machine B (£) |
| --- | --- | --- |
| Fixed costs, per week, each | 450 | 160 |
| Labour, per crew, per hour: | | |
| up to 40 hours per week | 10 | 12 |
| over 40 hours per week | 15 | 18 |

The costs of materials and supplies per metre are:

| | |
| --- | --- |
| 10" | £10 |
| 18" | £5 |

A subcontractor has offered to lay any quantity of the 10" pipe at £18 per metre and of the 18" pipe at £12 per metre.

You are required to:
(a) calculate the most economical way of undertaking the contract;                    (15 marks)
(b) state the weekly cost involved in your solution to (a) above;                    (5 marks)
(c) comment on the factors that management should consider in reaching a decision whether to adopt the minimum cost solution.
(10 marks)
*CIMA P3 Management Accounting*

## 9.29 Advanced: Allocation of land to four different types of vegetables based on key factor principles

A South American farms 960 hectares of land on which he grows squash, kale, lettuce and beans. Of the total, 680 hectares are suitable for all four vegetables, but the remaining 280 hectares are suitable only for kale and lettuce. Labour for all kinds of farm work is plentiful.

The market requires that all four types of vegetable must be produced with a minimum of 10 000 boxes of any one line. The farmer has decided that the area devoted to any crop should be in terms of complete hectares and not in fractions of a hectare. The only other limitation is that not more than 227 500 boxes of any one crop should be produced.

Data concerning production, market prices and costs are as follows:

| | Squash | Kale | Lettuce | Beans |
| --- | --- | --- | --- | --- |
| *Annual yield* | | | | |
| (boxes per hectare) | 350 | 100 | 70 | 180 |
| | (Pesos) | (Pesos) | (Pesos) | (Pesos) |
| *Costs* | | | | |
| Direct: | | | | |
| Materials per hectare | 476 | 216 | 192 | 312 |
| Labour: | | | | |
| Growing, per hectare | 896 | 608 | 372 | 528 |
| Harvesting and packing, per box | 3.60 | 3.28 | 4.40 | 5.20 |
| Transport, per box | 5.20 | 5.20 | 4.00 | 9.60 |
| *Market price*, per box | 15.38 | 15.87 | 18.38 | 22.27 |

*Fixed overhead* per annum:

| | (Pesos) |
| --- | --- |
| Growing | 122 000 |
| Harvesting | 74 000 |
| Transport | 74 000 |
| General administration | 100 000 |
| Notional rent | 74 000 |

It is possible to make the entire farm viable for all four vegetables if certain drainage work is undertaken. This would involve capital investment and it would have the following effects on direct harvesting costs of some of the vegetables:

| | Capital cost | Change from normal harvesting costs | |
|---|---|---|---|
| | | Squash | Beans |
| | (Pesos) | (Pesos per box) | |
| First lot of 10 hectares | 19 000 total | +1.2 | −1.2 |
| Next lot of 10 hectares | 17 500 total | +1.3 | −1.3 |
| Next lot of 10 hectares | 15 000 total | +1.4 | −1.4 |
| Remaining land (per hectare) | 1 850 | +1.5 | −1.5 |

The farmer is willing to undertake such investment only if he can obtain a return of 15% DCF for a four-year period.

You are required to
(a) advise the farmer, within the given constraints,
  (i) the area to be cultivated with each crop if he is to achieve the largest total profit,
  (13 marks)
  (ii) the amount of this total profit,
  (3 marks)
  (iii) the number of hectares it is worth draining and the use to which they would be put;
  (10 marks)
(b) comment briefly on four of the financial dangers of going ahead with the drainage work.
  (4 marks)

*Notes:* Show all relevant calculations in arriving at your answer. Ignore tax and inflation.

(Total 30 marks)
*CIMA Stage 4 Management Accounting – Decision Making*

## 9.30* Advanced: Optimal production programme, shadow prices and relevant costs for pricing decisions

Rosehip has spare capacity in two of its manufacturing departments – Department 4 and Department 5. A five day week of 40 hours is worked but there is only enough internal work for three days per week so that two days per week (16 hours) could be available in each department. In recent months Rosehip has sold this time to another manufacturer but there is some concern about the profitability of this work.

The accountant has prepared a table giving the hourly operating costs in each department. The summarized figures are as follows:

| | Department 4 (£) | Department 5 (£) |
|---|---|---|
| Power costs | 40 | 60 |
| Labour costs | 40 | 20 |
| Overhead costs | 40 | 40 |
| | 120 | 120 |

The labour force is paid on a time basis and there is no change in the weekly wage bill whether or not the plant is working at full capacity. The overhead figures are taken from the firm's current overhead absorption rates. These rates are designed to absorb all budgeted overhead (fixed and variable) when the departments are operating at 90% of full capacity (assume a 50 week year). The budgeted fixed overhead attributed to Department 4 is £36 000 p.a. and that for Department 5 is £50 400 p.a.

As a short term expedient the company has been selling processing time to another manufacturer who has been paying £70 per hour for time in either department. This customer is very willing to continue this arrangement and to purchase any spare time available but Rosehip is considering the introduction of a new product on a minor scale to absorb the spare capacity.

Each unit of the new product would require 45 minutes in Department 4 and 20 minutes in Department 5. The variable cost of the required input material is £10 per unit. It is considered that:

with a selling price of £100 the demand would be 1500 units p.a.;
with a selling price of £110 the demand would be 1000 units p.a.; and
with a selling price of £120 the demand would be 500 units p.a.

(a) You are required to calculate the best weekly programme for the slack time in the two manufacturing departments, to determine the best price to charge for the new product and to quantify the weekly gain that this programme and this price should yield. (12 marks)
(b) Assume that the new product has been introduced successfully but that the demand for the established main products has now increased so that all available time could now be

absorbed by Rosehip's main-line products. An optimal production plan for the main products has been obtained by linear programming and the optimal LP. tableau shows a shadow price of £76 per hour in Department 4 and of £27 per hour in Department 5. The new product was not considered in this exercise. Discuss the viability of the new product under the new circumstances. (5 marks)

(c) Comment on the relationship between shadow prices and opportunity costs. (5 marks)

(Total 22 marks)

*ACCA Level 2 Management Accounting*

### 9.31* Advanced: Decision relating to the timing of the conversion of a production process

A company extracts exhaust gases from process ovens as part of the manufacturing process. The exhaust gas extraction is implemented by machinery which cost £100 000 when bought five years ago. The machinery is being depreciated at 10% per annum. The extraction of the exhaust gases enhances production output by 10 000 units per annum. This production can be sold at £8 per unit and has variable costs of £3 per unit. The exhaust gas extraction machinery has directly attributable fixed operating costs of £16 000 per annum.

The company is considering the use of the exhaust gases for space heating. The existing space heating is provided by ducted hot air which is heated by equipment with running costs of £10 000 per annum. This equipment could be sold now for £20 000 but would incur dismantling costs of £3000. If retained for one year the equipment could be sold for £18 000 with dismantling costs of £3500.

The conversion to the use of the exhaust gases for space heating would involve the following:

(i) The removal of the existing gas extraction machinery. This could be implemented now at a dismantling cost of £5000 with sale of the machinery for £40 000. Alternatively it could be sold in one year's time for £30 000 with dismantling costs of £5500.

(ii) The leasing of alternative gas extraction equipment at a cost of £4000 per annum with annual fixed running costs of £12 000.

(iii) The conversion would mean the loss of 30% of the production enhancement which the exhaust gas extraction provides for a period of one year only, until the new system is 'run-in'.

(iv) The company has a spare electric motor in store which could be sold to company X for £3500 in one year's time. It could be fitted to the proposed leased gas extraction equipment in order to reduce the impact of the production losses during the running-in period. This course of action would reduce its sales value to company X in one year's time to £2000 and would incur £2500 of fitting and dismantling costs. It would, however, reduce the production enhancement loss from 30% to 10% during the coming year (year 1). This would not be relevant in year 2 because of an anticipated fall in the demand for the product. The electric motor originally cost £5000. If replaced today it would cost £8000. It was purchased for another process which has now been discontinued. It could also be used in a cooling process for one year if modified at a cost of £1000, instead of the company hiring cooling equipment at a cost of £3000 per annum. Because of its modification, the electric motor would have to be disposed of in one year's time at a cost of £250.

Ignore the time value of money.

Required:

(a) Prepare an analysis indicating all the options available for the use of the spare electric motor and the financial implications of each. State which option should be chosen on financial grounds. (8 marks)

(b) Prepare an analysis on an incremental opportunity cost basis in order to decide on financial grounds whether to convert immediately to the use of exhaust gases for space heating or to delay the conversion for one year.

(18 marks)

(Total 26 marks)

*ACCA Paper 9 Information for Control and Decision Making*

### 9.32 Advanced: Relevant costs for a pricing decision

Johnson trades as a chandler at the Savoy Marina. His profit in this business during the year to 30 June was £12 000. Johnson also undertakes occasional contracts to build pleasure cruisers, and is considering the price at which to bid for the contract to build the *Blue Blood* for Mr B.W. Dunn, delivery to be in one year's time. He has no other contract in hand, or under consideration, for at least the next few months.

Johnson expects that if he undertakes the contract he would devote one-quarter of his time to it. To facilitate this he would employ G. Harrison, an unqualified practitioner, to undertake his book-keeping and other paperwork, at a cost of £2000.

He would also have to employ on the contract one supervisor at a cost of £11 000 and two craftsmen at a cost of £8800 each; these costs include Johnson's normal apportionment of the fixed overheads of his business at the rate of 10% of labour cost.

During spells of bad weather one of the craftsmen could be employed for the equivalent of up to three months full-time during the winter in maintenance and painting work in the chandler's business. He would use materials costing £1000. Johnson already has two inclusive quotations from jobbing builders for this maintenance and painting work, one for £2500 and the other for £3500, the work to start immediately.

The equipment which would be used on the *Blue Blood* contract was bought nine years ago for £21 000. Depreciation has been written off on a straight-line basis, assuming a ten-year life and a scrap value of £1000. The current replacement cost of similar new equipment is £60 000, and is expected to be £66 000 in one year's time. Johnson has recently been offered £6000 for the equipment, and considers that in a year's time he would have little difficulty in obtaining £3000 for it. The plant is useful to Johnson only for contract work.

In order to build the *Blue Blood* Johnson will need six types of material, as follows:

| Material code | No. of units In stock | Needed for contract | Price per unit (£) Purchase price of stock items | Current purchase price | Current resale price |
|---|---|---|---|---|---|
| A | 100 | 1000 | 1.10 | 3.00 | 2.00 |
| B | 1 100 | 1000 | 2.00 | 0.90 | 1.00 |
| C | — | 100 | — | 6.00 | — |
| D | 100 | 200 | 4.00 | 3.00 | 2.00 |
| E | 50 000 | 5000 | 0.18 | 0.20 | 0.25 |
| F | 1 000 | 3000 | 0.90 | 2.00 | 1.00 |

Materials B and E are sold regularly in the chandler's business. Material A could be sold to a local sculptor, if not used for the contract. Materials A and E can be used for other purposes, such as property maintenance. Johnson has no other use for materials D and F, the stocks of which are obsolete.

The *Blue Blood* would be built in a yard held on a lease with four years remaining at a fixed annual rental of £5000. It would occupy half of this yard, which is useful to Johnson only for contract work.

Johnson anticipates that the direct expenses of the contract, other than those noted above, would be £6500.

Johnson has recently been offered a one-year appointment at a fee of £15 000 to manage a boat-building firm on the Isle of Wight. If he accepted the offer he would be unable to take on the contract to build *Blue Blood*, or any other contract. He would have to employ a manager to run the chandler's business at an annual cost (including fidelity insurance) of £10 000, and would incur additional personal living costs of £2000.

You are required:

(a) to calculate the price at which Johnson should be willing to take on the contract in order to break even, based exclusively on the information given above; (15 marks)

(b) to set out any further considerations which you think that Johnson should take into account in setting the price at which he would tender for the contract. (10 marks)

Ignore taxation.

*ICAEW Management Accounting*

### 9.33 Advanced: Decision on whether a department should be closed

Shortflower Ltd currently publish, print and distribute a range of catalogues and instruction manuals. The management have now decided to discontinue printing and distribution and concentrate solely on publishing. Longplant Ltd will print and distribute the range of catalogues and instruction manuals on behalf of Shortflower Ltd commencing either at 30 June or 30 November. Longplant Ltd will receive £65 000 per month for a contract which will commence either at 30 June or 30 November.

The results of Shortflower Ltd for a typical month are as follows:

| | Publishing (£000) | Printing (£000) | Distribution (£000) |
|---|---|---|---|
| Salaries and wages | 28 | 18 | 4 |
| Materials and supplies | 5.5 | 31 | 1.1 |
| Occupancy costs | 7 | 8.5 | 1.2 |
| Depreciation | 0.8 | 4.2 | 0.7 |

Other information has been gathered relating to the possible closure proposals:

(i) Two specialist staff from printing will be retained at their present salary of £1500 each per month in order to fulfil a link function with Longplant Ltd. One further staff member will be transferred to publishing to fill a staff vacancy through staff turnover, anticipated in July. This staff member will be paid at his present salary of £1400 per month which is £100 more than that of the staff member who is expected to leave. On closure all other printing and distribution staff will be made redundant and paid an average of two months redundancy pay.

(ii) The printing department has a supply of materials (already paid for) which cost £18 000 and which will be sold to Longplant Ltd for £10 000 if closure takes place on 30 June. Otherwise the material will be used as part of the July printing requirements. The distribution department has a contract to purchase pallets at a cost of £500 per month for July and August. A cancellation clause allows for non-delivery of the pallets for July and August for a one-off payment of £300. Non-delivery for August only will require a payment of £100. If the pallets are taken from the supplier Longplant Ltd has agreed to purchase them at a price of £380 for each month's supply which is available. Pallet costs are included in the distribution material and supplies cost stated for a typical month.

(iii) Company expenditure on apportioned occupancy costs to printing and distribution will be reduced by 15% per month if printing and distribution departments are closed. At present, 30% of printing and 25% of distribution occupancy costs are directly attributable costs which are avoidable on closure, whilst the remainder are apportioned costs.

(iv) Closure of the printing and distribution departments will make it possible to sub-let part of the building for a monthly fee of £2500 when space is available.

(v) Printing plant and machinery has an estimated net book value of £48 000 at 30 June. It is anticipated that it will be sold at a loss of £21 000 on 30 June. If sold on 30 November the prospective buyer will pay £25 000.

(vi) The net book value of distribution vehicles at 30 June is estimated as £80 000. They could be sold to the original supplier at £48 000 on 30 June. The original supplier would purchase the vehicles on 30 November for a price of £44 000.

Required:
Using the above information, prepare a summary to show whether Shortflower Ltd should close the printing and distribution departments on financial grounds on 30 June or on 30 November. Explanatory notes and calculations should be shown. Ignore taxation. (22 marks)

*ACCA Level 2 Cost and Management Accounting II*

**9.34\* Advanced: Decision on whether to subcontract an appliance repair service or do own maintenance**

A company producing and selling a range of consumer durable appliances has its after-sales service work done by local approved sub-contractors.

The company is now considering carrying out all or some of the work itself and it has chosen one area in which to experiment with the new routine.

Some of the appliances are so large and bulky that repair/service work can only be done at the customers' homes. Others are small enough for sub-contractors to take them back to their local repair workshops, repair them, and re-deliver them to the customer. If the company does its own after-sales service, it proposes that customers would bring these smaller items for repair to a local company service centre which would be located and organized to deal with visitors.

There is a *list price to* customers for the labour content of any work done and for materials used. However, the majority of the after-sales service work is done under an annual maintenance contract taken out by customers on purchasing the product; this covers the labour content of any service work to be done, but customers pay for materials used.

Any labour or materials needed in the first six months are provided to the customer free of charge under the company's product guarantee and *subcontractors* are allowed *by the company a fixed sum of 3.5% of the selling price* for each appliance to cover this work. These sums allowed have proved closely in line with the work needed over the past few years. The price structure is:

For materials:

| | |
|---|---|
| Price to sub-contractor: | Company cost plus 10% |
| Price to customer: | Sub-contractor's price plus 25% |

For labour: Price to sub-contractor:

Work done under maintenance contract:

90% of list price

Ad hoc work (i.e. work NOT done under maintenance contract):

85% of list price

Records show that 60% by value of the work has to be carried out at customers' homes, whilst the remainder can be done anywhere appropriate.

The annual income that the company currently receives from sub-contractors for the area in which the experiment is to take place is:

| | | (£) |
|---|---|---|
| Labour | – under maintenance contract | 30 000 |
| | – ad hoc | 12 000 |
| Materials | – under maintenance contract | 18 000 |
| | – ad hoc | 6 000 |
| | | £66 000 |

The company expects the volume of after-sales work to remain the same as last year for the period of the experiment.

The company is considering the following options:

1. Set up a local service centre at which it can service small appliances only.

   Work at customers' houses would continue to be done under sub-contract.

2. Set up a local service centre to act only as a base for its own employees who would only service appliances at customers' homes.

   Servicing of small appliances would continue to be done under sub-contract.

3. Set up a local combined service centre plus base for all work. No work would be sub-contracted.

If the company were to do service work, annual fixed costs are budgeted to be:

| | Option 1 (£000) | Option 2 (£000) | Option 3 (£000) |
|---|---|---|---|
| Establishment costs (rent, rates, light, etc.) | 40 | 15 | 45 |
| Management costs | 20 | 15 | 30 |
| Storage staff costs | 10 | 10 | 15 |
| Transport costs (all vans/cars hired) | 8 | 65 | 70 |
| Repair/service staff | 70 | 180 | 225 |

You are required

(a) to recommend which of the three options the company should adopt from a financial viewpoint; (18 marks)

(b) in relation to the data provided in order to make the recommendation required in (a) above, to comment critically in respect of non-financial features that might favourably or adversely affect the customer. (7 marks)

(Total 25 marks)

*CIMA Stage 4 Management Accounting Decision Making*

# Activity-based costing

The aim of the previous chapter was to provide you with an understanding of the principles that should be used to identify relevant costs and revenues for various types of decisions. It was assumed that relevant costs could easily be measured but, in reality, it was pointed out that indirect relevant costs can be difficult to identify and measure. The measurement of indirect relevant costs for decision-making using activity-based costing (ABC) techniques will be examined in this chapter. The aim of this chapter is to provide you with a conceptual understanding of ABC. Some of the issues explored are complex and therefore much of the content of this chapter is appropriate for a second year management accounting course. If you are pursuing a first year course the content relating to ABC that was presented in Chapter 3 should meet your requirements. In addition, you may wish to read this chapter and omit those sections that are labelled advanced reading.

Our focus will be on an organization's *existing* products or services. There is also a need to manage *future* activities to ensure that only profitable products and services are launched. Here the emphasis is on providing cost information using techniques such as target costing, life cycle costing and value engineering. These issues will be explored in Chapter 22 and the mechanisms for appraising investments in new products, services or locations will be described in Chapters 13 and 14. We shall also defer our discussion of the relevant cost information that is required for pricing decisions until the next chapter.

Unless otherwise stated we shall assume that products are the cost objects but the techniques used, and the principles established, can also be applied to other cost objects such as customers, services and locations. We begin with an examination of the role that a cost accumulation system plays in generating relevant cost information for decision-making.

## Learning objectives

After studying this chapter you should be able to:

- explain the role of a cost accumulation system for generating relevant cost information for decision-making;
- describe the differences between activity-based and traditional costing systems;
- illustrate how traditional costing systems can provide misleading information for decision-making;
- explain each of the four stages involved in designing ABC systems;
- describe the ABC cost hierarchy;
- describe the ABC profitability analysis hierarchy;
- describe the ABC resource consumption model;
- justify the choice of practical capacity as the denominator level for estimating cost driver rates.

# The role of a cost accumulation system in generating relevant cost information for decision-making

There are three main reasons why a cost accumulation system is required to generate relevant cost information for decision-making. They are:

1. many indirect costs are relevant for decision-making;
2. an attention-directing information system is required to identify those potentially unprofitable products that require more detailed special studies;
3. product decisions are not independent.

There is a danger that only those incremental costs that are uniquely attributable to individual products will be classified as relevant for decision-making. Direct costs are transparent and how they will be affected by decisions is clearly observable. In contrast, how indirect costs will be affected by decisions is not clearly observable. There has been a tendency in the past to assume that these costs are fixed and irrelevant for decision-making. In many organizations, however, these are costs that have escalated over the years. The message is clear – they cannot be assumed to be fixed and irrelevant for decision-making.

The costs of many joint resources fluctuate in the long term according to the demand for them. The cost of support functions fall within this category. They include activities such as materials procurement, materials handling, production scheduling, warehousing, expediting and customer order processing. The costs of these activities are either not directly traceable to products, or would involve such detailed tracing, the costs of doing so would far exceed their benefits. Product introduction, discontinuation, redesign and mix decisions determine the demand for support function resources. For example, if a decision results in a 10% reduction in the demand for the resources of a support activity then we would expect, in the long term, for some of the costs of that support activity to decline by 10%. Therefore, to estimate the impact that decisions will have on the support activities (and their future costs) a cost accumulation system is required that assigns indirect costs, using cause-and-effect allocations, to products.

For decision-making it could be argued that relevant costs need only be ascertained when the need arises. For example, why not undertake special studies at periodic intervals to make sure that each product is still profitable? Estimates could be made only when undertaking a special study of those relevant costs that would be avoided if a product was discontinued. This approach is fine for highly simplified situations where an organization only produces a few products and where all relevant costs are uniquely attributable to individual products. However, most organizations produce hundreds of products and the range of potential decisions to explore undertaking special studies is enormous and unmanageable. For example, Kaplan (1990) considers a situation where a company has 100 products and outlines the difficulties of determining which product, or product combinations, should be selected for undertaking special studies. Kaplan states:

> First how do you think about which product you should even think about making a decision on? There are 100 different products to consider. But think about all the combinations of these products: which two products, three products or groupings of 10 or 20 products should be analyzed? It's a simple exercise to calculate that there are $2^{100}$ different combinations of the 100 products ... so there is no way to do an incremental revenue/incremental analysis on all relevant combinations (p. 13).

To cope with the vast number of potential product combinations organizations need attention-directing information to highlight those specific products, or combination of products, that appear to be questionable and which require further detailed special studies to ascertain their viability. Periodic product profitability analysis meets this requirement. A cost accumulation system is therefore required to assign costs to products for periodic profitability analysis.

The third reason for using a cost accumulation system is that many product related decisions are not independent. Consider again those joint resources shared by most products and that fluctuate in the longer term according to the demand for them. If we focus only on individual products and assume that they are independent, decisions will be taken in isolation of decisions made on other products. For joint resources the incremental/avoidable costs relating to a decision to add or drop a single product may be zero. Assuming that 20 products are viewed in this manner then the sum of the incremental costs will be zero. However, if the 20 products are viewed as a whole there may be a significant change in resource usage and incremental costs for those joint resources that fluctuate according to the demand for them.

Cooper (1990b) also argues that decisions should not be viewed independently. He states:

> The decision to drop one product will typically not change 'fixed' overhead spending. In contrast, dropping 50 products might allow considerable changes to be made.
> Stated somewhat tritely, the sum of the parts (the decision to drop individual products) is not equal to the sum of the whole (the realisable savings from having dropped 50 products). To help them make effective decisions, managers require cost systems that provide insights into the whole, not just isolated individual parts (p. 58).

Thus, where product decisions are not independent the multiplication of product costs, that include the cost of joint resources, by the units lost from ceasing production (or additional units from introducing a new product) may provide an approximation of the change in the long term of total company costs arising from the decisions. The rationale for this is that the change in resource consumption will ultimately be followed by a change in the cash flow pattern of the organization because organizations make product introduction or abandonment decisions for many products rather than just a single product. These issues are complex and will be explained in more detail later in the chapter.

# Types of cost systems

Costing systems can vary in terms of which costs are assigned to cost objects and their level of sophistication. Typically cost systems are classified as follows:

1. direct costing systems;
2. traditional absorption costing systems;
3. activity-based costing systems.

Direct costing systems only assign direct costs to cost objects. Hence they report contributions to indirect costs. They are appropriate for decision-making where the cost of those joint resources that fluctuate according to the demand for them are insignificant. Negative or low contribution items should then be highlighted for special studies. An estimate of those indirect costs that are relevant to the decision should be incorporated within the analysis at the special study stage. The disadvantage of direct costing systems is that systems are not in place to measure and assign indirect costs to cost objects. Thus any attempt to incorporate indirect costs into the analysis at the special studies stage must be based on guesswork and arbitrary estimates. Direct costing systems can therefore only be recommended where indirect costs are a low proportion of an organization's total costs.

Both traditional and ABC systems assign indirect costs to cost objects. The major features of these systems were described in Chapter 3 and the assignment of costs to products was illustrated for both systems. In the next section the major features that were described in Chapter 3 are briefly summarized but the assignment of costs to products will not be repeated. If you wish to renew your understanding of the detailed cost assignment process you should refer back to Chapter 3 for an illustration of the application of the two-stage allocation process for both traditional and ABC systems.

# A comparison of traditional and ABC systems

Figure 3.3 was used in Chapter 3 to illustrate the major differences between traditional costing and ABC systems. This diagram is repeated in the form of Figure 10.1 to provide you with an overview of both systems. Both use a two-stage allocation process. In the first stage a traditional system allocates overheads to production and service departments and then reallocates service department costs to the production departments. An ABC system assigns overheads to each major activity (rather than departments). With ABC systems, many activity-based cost centres (alternatively known as cost pools) are established, whereas with traditional systems overheads tend to be pooled by departments, although they are normally described as cost centres.

Activities consist of the aggregation of many different tasks and are described by verbs associated with objects. Typical support activities include: schedule production, set-up machines, move materials, purchase materials, inspect items, process supplier records, expedite and process customer orders. Production process activities include machine products and assemble products. Within the production process, activity cost centres are often identical to the cost centres used by traditional cost systems. Support activities are also sometimes identical to cost centres used by traditional systems, such as when the purchasing department and activity are both treated as cost centres. Overall, however, ABC systems will normally have a greater number of cost centres.

The second stage of the two-stage allocation process allocates costs from cost centres (pools) to products or other chosen cost objects. Traditional costing systems trace overheads to products using a small number of second stage cost drivers, which vary directly with the volume produced. Instead of using the term 'cost driver' the terms 'allocation bases' or 'overhead allocation rates' tend to be used. Direct labour hours and machine hours are the volume bases that are normally used by traditional costing systems. In contrast, ABC systems use many second-stage cost drivers, including non-volume-based drivers, such as the number of production runs for production scheduling and the number of purchase orders for the purchasing activity. A further distinguishing feature is that traditional systems normally allocate service/support costs to production centres. Their costs are merged with the production cost centre costs and thus included within the production centre overhead rates. In contrast, ABC systems tend to establish separate cost driver rates for support centres, and assign the cost of support activities directly to cost objects without any reallocation to production centres.

Therefore the major distinguishing features of ABC systems are that they rely on a greater number of cost centres and second stage drivers. By using a greater number of cost centres and cost drivers that cause activity resource consumption, and assigning activity costs to cost objects on the basis of cost driver usage, ABC systems can more accurately measure the resources consumed by cost objects. Traditional cost systems report less accurate costs because they use cost drivers where no cause-and-effect relationships exist to assign support costs to cost objects.

**FIGURE 10.1** *An illustration of the two-stage allocation process for traditional and activity-based costing systems.*

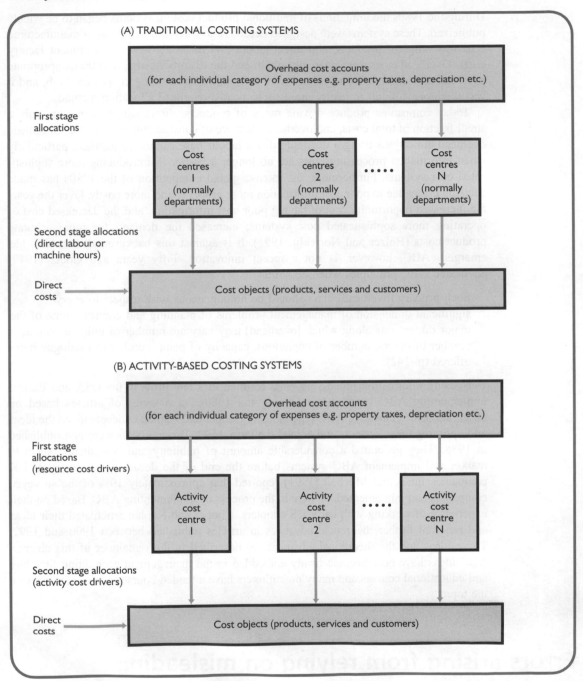

# The emergence of ABC systems

During the 1980s the limitations of traditional product costing systems began to be widely publicized. These systems were designed decades ago when most companies manufactured a narrow range of products, and direct labour and materials were the dominant factory costs. Overhead costs were relatively small, and the distortions arising from inappropriate overhead allocations were not significant. Information processing costs were high, and it was therefore difficult to justify more sophisticated overhead allocation methods.

Today companies produce a wide range of products; direct labour represents only a small fraction of total costs, and overhead costs are of considerable importance. Simplistic overhead allocations using a declining direct labour base cannot be justified, particularly when information processing costs are no longer a barrier to introducing more sophisticated cost systems. Furthermore, the intense global competition of the 1980s has made decision errors due to poor cost information more probable and more costly. Over the years the increased opportunity cost of having poor cost information, and the decreased cost of operating more sophisticated cost systems, increased the demand for more accurate product costs (Holzer and Norreklit, 1991). It is against this background that ABC has emerged. ABC, however, is not a recent innovation. Fifty years ago Goetz (1949) advocated ABC principles when he wrote:

> Each primary [overhead] class should be homogeneous with respect to every significant dimension of management problems of planning and control. Some of the major dimensions along which [overhead] may vary are number of units of output, number of orders, number of operations, capacity of plant, number of catalogue items offered (p. 142).

Decreasing information processing costs resulted in a few firms in the USA and Europe implementing ABC type systems during the 1980s. In a series of articles based on observations of innovative ABC type systems Cooper and Kaplan conceptualized the ideas underpinning these systems and coined the term ABC. These articles were first published in 1988. They generated a considerable amount of publicity and consultants began to market and implement ABC systems before the end of the decade. In a survey of UK companies Innes and Mitchell (1991) reported that approximately 10% of the surveyed companies had implemented, or were in the process of implementing ABC. Based on their experience of working with early US adopters, Cooper and Kaplan articulated their ideas and reported further theoretical advances in articles published between 1990 and 1992. These ideas and the theoretical advances are described in the remainder of this chapter. ABC ideas have now become firmly embedded in the management accounting literature and educational courses and many practitioners have attended courses and conferences on the topic.

# Errors arising from relying on misleading product costs

If a large proportion of an organization's costs are unrelated to volume measures, such as direct labour hours or machine hours, there is a danger that traditional product costing systems will report inaccurate product costs. In particular it is claimed that traditional systems tend to overcost high volume products and undercost low volume products. Consider the information presented in Example 10.1.

**EXAMPLE 10.1**

Assume that the Balearic company has only one overhead cost centre or cost pool. It currently operates a traditional costing system using direct labour hours to allocate overheads to products. The company produces several products, two of which are products HV and LV. Product HV is made in high volumes whereas product LV is made in low volumes. Product HV consumes 30% of the direct labour hours and product LV consumes only 5%. Because of the high volume production product HV can be made in large production batches but the irregular and low level of demand for product LV requires it to be made in small batches. A detailed investigation indicates that the number of batches processed causes the demand for overhead resources. The traditional system is therefore replaced with an ABC system using the number of batches processed as the cost driver. You ascertain that each product accounts for 15% of the batches processed during the period and the overheads assigned to the cost centre that fluctuate in the long term according to the demand for them amount to £1 million. The direct costs and sales revenues assigned to the products are as follows:

|  | Product HV (£) | Product LV (£) |
|---|---|---|
| Direct costs | 310 000 | 40 000 |
| Sales revenues | 600 000 | 150 000 |

Show the product profitability analysis for products HV and LV using the traditional and ABC systems.

The reported product costs and profits for the two products are as follows:

| | Traditional system | | ABC system | |
|---|---|---|---|---|
| | Product HV (£) | Product LV (£) | Product HV (£) | Product LV (£) |
| Direct costs | 310 000 | 40 000 | 310 000 | 40 000 |
| Overheads allocated | 300 000 (30%) | 50 000 (5%) | 150 000 (15%) | 150 000 (15%) |
| Reported profits/(losses) | (10 000) | 60 000 | 140 000 | (40 000) |
| Sales revenues | 600 000 | 150 000 | 600 000 | 150 000 |

Because product HV is a high volume product that consumes 30% of the direct labour hours whereas product LV, the low volume product consumes only 5%, the traditional system that uses direct labour hours as the allocation base allocates six times more overheads to product HV. However, ABC systems recognize that overheads are caused by other factors, besides volume. In our example, all of the overheads are assumed to be volume unrelated. They are caused by the number of batches processed and the ABC system establishes a cause-and-effect allocation relationship by using the number of batches processed as the cost driver. Both products require 15% of the total number of batches so they are allocated with an equal amount of overheads.

With the traditional costing system misleading information is reported. A small loss is reported for product HV and if it were discontinued the costing system mistakenly gives the impression that overheads will decline in the longer term by £300 000. Furthermore, the message from the costing system is to concentrate on the more profitable speciality products like product LV. In reality this strategy would be disastrous because low volume products like product LV are made in small batches and require more people for scheduling production, performing set-ups, inspection of the batches and handling a large number of customer requests for small orders. The long-term effect would be escalating overhead costs.

In contrast, the ABC system allocates overheads on a cause-and-effect basis and more accurately measures the relatively high level of overhead resources consumed by product LV. The message from the profitability analysis is the opposite from the traditional system; that is, product HV is profitable and product LV is unprofitable. If product LV is discontinued, and assuming that the cost driver is the cause of all the overheads then a decision to discontinue product LV should result in the reduction in resource spending on overheads by £150 000.

Example 10.1 is very simplistic. It is assumed that the organization has established only a single cost centre or cost pool, when in reality many will be established with a traditional system, and even more with an ABC system. Furthermore, the data have been deliberately biased to show the superiority of ABC. The aim of the illustration has been to highlight the potential cost of errors that can occur when information extracted from simplistic and inaccurate cost systems is used for decision-making.

# Designing ABC systems

The discussion so far has provided a broad overview of ABC. We shall now examine ABC in more detail by looking at the design of ABC systems. Four steps are involved. They are:

1. identifying the major activities that take place in an organization;
2. assigning costs to cost pools/cost centres for each activity;
3. determining the cost driver for each major activity;
4. assigning the cost of activities to products according to the product's demand for activities.

The first two steps relate to the first stage, and the final two steps to the second stage, of the two-stage allocation process shown in Figure 10.1. Let us now consider each of these stages in more detail.

## STEP 1: IDENTIFYING ACTIVITIES

Activities are composed of the aggregation of units of work or tasks and are described by verbs associated with tasks. For example, purchasing of materials might be identified as a separate activity. This activity consists of the aggregation of many different tasks, such as receiving a purchase request, identifying suppliers, preparing purchase orders, mailing purchase orders and performing follow-ups.

Activities are identified by carrying out an activity analysis. Innes and Mitchell (1995b) suggest that a useful starting point is to examine a physical plan of the workplace (to identify how all work space is being used) and the payroll listings (to ensure all relevant personnel have been taken into account). This examination normally has to be supplemented by a series of interviews with the staff involved, or having staff complete a time sheet for a specific time period explaining how their time is spent. Interviewers will ask managers and employees questions such as what staff work at the location and what tasks are performed by the persons employed at the location.

Many detailed tasks are likely to be identified in the first instance, but after further interviews, the main activities will emerge. The activities chosen should be at a reasonable level of aggregation based on costs versus benefits criteria. For example, rather than classifying purchasing of materials as an activity, each of its constituent tasks could be classified as separate activities. However, this level of decomposition would involve the collection of a vast amount of data and is likely to be too costly for product costing purposes. Alternatively, the purchasing activity might be merged with the materials receiving, storage and issuing activities to form a single materials procurement and handling activity. This is likely to represent too high a level of aggregation because a single cost driver is unlikely to provide a satisfactory determinant of the cost of the activity. For example, selecting the number of purchase orders as a cost driver may provide a good explanation of purchasing costs but may be entirely inappropriate for explaining costs relating to receiving and issuing. Therefore, instead of establishing materials procurement and handling as a single activity it may be preferable to decompose it into three separate activities; namely purchasing, receiving and issuing activities, and establish separate cost drivers for each activity.

In some of the early ABC systems hundreds of separate activity cost centres were established but recent studies suggest that between twenty and thirty activity centres tend to be the norm. The final choice of activities must be a matter of judgement but it is likely to be influenced by factors such as the total cost of the activity centre (it must be of significance to justify separate treatment) and the ability of a single driver to provide a satisfactory determinant of the cost of the activity. Where the latter is not possible further decomposition of the activity will be necessary.

## STEP 2: ASSIGNING COSTS TO ACTIVITY COST CENTRES

After the activities have been identified the cost of resources consumed over a specified period must be assigned to each activity. The aim is to determine how much the organization is spending on each of its activities. Many of the resources will be directly attributable to specific activity centres but others (such as labour and lighting and heating costs) may be indirect and jointly shared by several activities. These costs should be assigned to activities on the basis of cause-and-effect cost drivers, or interviews with staff who can provide reasonable estimates of the resources consumed by different activities. Arbitrary allocations should not be used. The greater the amount of costs traced to activity centres by cost apportionments at this stage the more arbitrary and less reliable will be the product cost information generated by ABC systems. Cause-and-effect cost drivers used at this stage to allocate shared resources to individual activities are called resource cost drivers.

## STEP 3: SELECTING APPROPRIATE COST DRIVERS FOR ASSIGNING THE COST OF ACTIVITIES TO COST OBJECTS

In order to assign the costs attached to each activity cost centre to products a cost driver must be selected for each activity centre. Cost drivers used at this stage are called activity cost drivers. Several factors must be borne in mind when selecting a suitable cost driver. First, it should provide a good explanation of costs in each activity cost pool. Second, a cost driver should be easily measurable, the data should be relatively easy to obtain and be identifiable with products. The costs of measurement should therefore be taken into account.

Activity cost drivers consist of three types.

1. transaction drivers;
2. duration drivers;
3. intensity drivers.

**Transaction drivers**, such as the number of purchase orders processed, number of customer orders processed, number of inspections performed and the number of set-ups undertaken, all count the number of times an activity is performed. Transaction drivers are the least expensive type of cost driver but they are also likely to be the least accurate because they assume that the same quantity of resources is required every time an activity is performed. However, if the variation in the amount of resources required by individual cost objects is not great transaction drivers will provide a reasonably accurate measurement of activity resources consumed. If this condition does not apply then duration cost drivers should be used.

**Duration drivers** represent the amount of time required to perform an activity. Examples of duration drivers include set-up hours and inspection hours. For example, if one product requires a short set-up time and another requires a long time then using set-up hours as the cost driver will more accurately measure activity resource consumption than the transaction driver (number of set-ups) which assumes that an equal amount of activity resources are consumed by both products. Using the number of set-ups will result in the product that requires a long set-up time being undercosted whereas the product that requires a short set-up will be overcosted. This problem can be overcome by using set-up hours as the cost driver, but this will increase the measurement costs.

**Intensity drivers** directly charge for the resources used each time an activity is performed. Whereas duration drivers establish an average hourly rate for performing an activity, intensity drivers involve direct charging based on the actual activity resources committed to a product. For example, if activities require unskilled and skilled personnel a duration driver would establish an average hourly rate to be assigned to products whereas an intensity driver would record the actual or estimated time for each type of personnel and assign the specific resources directly to the products.

Kaplan and Cooper (1998) illustrate how duration and intensity drivers can be simulated by using a weighted index approach. This involves asking individuals to estimate the relative difficulty of performing a task for different types of customers or products. An appropriate numerical scale is used such that standard low complexity products/customers are awarded low scores, medium complexity products/customers are awarded medium scores and highly complex products/customers attract high scores. The aim is to capture the variation in demands for an activity by products or customers without an over-expensive measurement system.

Innes and Mitchell (1995b) provide an illustration of the weighting approach where purchasing is an activity cost centre and the number of purchase orders represent a potential cost driver. Orders are made both domestically and overseas but the overseas orders involve considerably more administrative work. Rather than split the purchasing cost centre into two separate centres (home and overseas purchasing) and have separate cost drivers for each (home purchase orders and overseas purchase orders) the costs of measurement can be reduced by weighting the overseas orders relative to the home orders. For example, after undertaking an assessment of the work required to make the respective orders it might be decided that each overseas order be weighted 1.5 (relative to 1 for a home order) before determining the total weighted volume of the cost driver to be used in calculating the appropriate cost driver rate.

In most situations data will not initially be available relating to the past costs of activities or potential cost driver volumes. To ascertain potential cost drivers interviews will be required with the personnel involved with the specific activities. The interviews will seek to ascertain what causes the particular activity to consume resources and incur costs. The final choice of a cost driver is likely to be based on managerial judgement after taking into account the factors outlined above.

## STEP 4: ASSIGNING THE COST OF THE ACTIVITIES TO PRODUCTS

The final stage involves applying the cost driver rates to products. Therefore the cost driver must be measurable in a way that enables it to be identified with individual products. Thus, if set-up hours are selected as a cost driver, there must be a mechanism for measuring the set-up hours consumed by each product. Alternatively, if the number of set-ups is selected as the cost driver measurements by products are not required since all products that require a set-up are charged with a constant set-up cost. The ease and cost of obtaining data on cost driver consumption by products is therefore a factor that must be considered during the third stage when an appropriate cost driver is being selected.

# Activity hierarchies

Early ABC systems were subject to a number of criticisms, particularly relating to theoretical aspects. As a response to these criticisms a number of theoretical developments emerged during the 1990s.

The first theoretical development was reported by Cooper (1990a) who classified manufacturing activities along a cost hierarchy dimension consisting of:

1. unit-level activities;
2. batch-level activities;
3. product-sustaining activities;
4. facility-sustaining activities.

Unit-level activities are performed each time a unit of the product or service is produced. Expenses in this category include direct labour, direct materials, energy costs and expenses that are consumed in proportion to machine processing time (such as maintenance). Unit-level activities consume resources in proportion to the number of units of production and sales volume. For example, if a firm produces 10% more units it will consume 10% more labour cost, 10 % more machine hours and 10% more energy costs. Typical cost drivers for unit level activities include labour hours, machine hours and the quantity of materials processed. These cost drivers are also used by traditional costing systems. Traditional systems are therefore also appropriate for assigning the costs of unit-level activities to cost objects.

Batch-related activities, such as setting up a machine or processing a purchase order, are performed each time a batch of goods is produced. The cost of batch-related activities varies with the number of batches made, but is common (or fixed) for all units within the batch. For example, set-up resources are consumed when a machine is changed from one product to another. As more batches are produced, more set-up resources are consumed. It costs the same to set-up a machine for 10 or 5000 items. Thus the demands for the set-up resources are independent of the number of units produced after completing the set-up. Similarly, purchasing resources are consumed each time a purchasing order is processed, but the resources consumed are independent of the number of units included in the purchase order. Other examples of batch-related costs include resources devoted to production scheduling, first-item inspection and materials movement. Traditional costing systems treat batch-related expenses as fixed costs. However, the more the batch-related activities are required the more the organization must eventually spend to supply resources to perform these activities. Thus ABC systems provide a mechanism for assigning some of the costs of complexity (such as set-ups, customer ordering and purchasing) to the products or services that cause the activity.

Product-sustaining activities or service-sustaining activities are performed to enable the production and sale of individual products (or services). Examples of product-sustaining activities provided by Kaplan and Cooper (1998) include maintaining and updating product specifications and the technical support provided for individual products and services. Other examples are the resources to prepare and implement engineering change notices (ECNs), to design processes and test routines for individual products, and to perform product enhancements. The costs of product-sustaining activities are incurred irrespective of the number of units of output or the number of batches processed and their expenses will tend to increase as the number of products manufactured is increased. ABC uses product-level bases such as number of active part numbers and number of ECNs to assign these costs to products. Kaplan and Cooper (1998) have extended their ideas to situations where customers are the cost objects with the equivalent term for product-sustaining being customer-sustaining activities. Customer market research and support for an individual customer, or groups of customers if they represent the cost object, are examples of customer-sustaining activities.

The final activity category is facility-sustaining (or business-sustaining) activities. They are performed to support the facility's general manufacturing process and include general administrative staff, plant management and property costs. They are incurred to support the organization as a whole and are common and joint to all products manufactured in the plant. There would have to be a dramatic change in activity, resulting in an expansion or contraction in the size of the plant, for facility-sustaining costs to change. Such events are most unlikely in most organizations. Therefore these costs are not assigned to products since they are unavoidable and irrelevant for most decisions. Instead, they are regarded as common costs to *all* products made in the plant and deducted as a lump sum from the total of the operating margins from *all* products.

# Activity-based costing profitability analysis

**AR** The second theoretical development was first highlighted by Kaplan (1990) and Cooper and Kaplan (1991). They apply the ABC hierarchical activity classification to profitability analysis. In addition, they stress that the reported ABC product costs do not provide information that can be used directly for decision-making. Instead, they report attention-directing information by highlighting those potentially unprofitable products or services that require more detailed special studies. Cooper (1997) has stressed that a major role of ABC is to develop profitability maps (i.e. periodic profitability analysis by cost objects) that are used to focus managerial attention. He argues that because the cost of special studies are high the number performed has to be carefully controlled; hence the need for good attention-directing information. He concludes that the primary value of ABC systems lies in the quality of the profitability analysis generated. Their greater accuracy increases the probability that when the special study is undertaken, its findings will support the message sent by the cost system. In other words, profitable products will be found to be profitable, and unprofitable products will be found to be unprofitable. Traditional cost systems often result in inaccurate profitability analysis resulting in special studies being at odds with the message sent by the cost system. In the extreme the cost system may be ignored.

Kaplan and Cooper (1998) extended cost hierarchies to develop activity-profitability maps by different cost objects. The general principles of activity profitability maps (or profitability analysis) analysed by different cost objects is illustrated in Figure 10.2. This approach categorizes costs according to the causes of their variability at different hierarchical levels. Hierarchies identify the lowest level to which cost can meaningfully be assigned without relying on arbitrary allocations. In Figure 10.2 the lowest hierarchical levels (shown at the top of the diagram) are product, customer and facility contributions and, ignoring the business unit level the highest levels (shown at the bottom of the diagram) are product lines, distribution channels and country profits.

Let us initially focus on products as the cost object. Look at the column for products as the cost object in Figure 10.2. You will see that a unit-level contribution margin is calculated for each *individual* product. This is derived by deducting the cost of unit-level activities from sales revenues. From this unit-level contribution expenses relating to batch-related activities are deducted. Next the cost of product-sustaining activities are deducted. Thus, three different contribution levels are reported at the *individual* product level. Differentiating contributions at these levels provides a better understanding of the implications of product-mix and discontinuation decisions in terms of cost and profit behaviour.

In Figure 10.2 there are two further levels within the product hierarchy. They are the product brand level and the product line level. Some organizations do not market their products by brands and therefore have only one further level within the product hierarchy. A product line consists of a group of similar products. For example, banks have product lines such as savings accounts, lending services, currency services, insurance services and brokering services. Each product line contains individual product variants. The savings product line would include low balance/low interest savings accounts, high balance/high interest accounts, postal savings accounts and other product variants. The lending services product line would include personal loans, house mortgage loans, business loans and other product variants within the product line.

Some organizations market groupings of products within their product lines as separate brands. A typical example of the difference between product brands and product lines is Procter and Gamble who market some of their products within their detergent product line under the Tide label and others without this label.

Where products are marketed by brands, all expenditure relating to a brand, such as management and brand marketing is for the benefit of all products within the brand and not for any specific individual product. Therefore, such brand-sustaining expenses should be attributed to the brand and not to individual products within the brand.

The same reasoning can be applied to the next level in the hierarchy. For example, marketing, research and development and distribution expenses might be incurred for the benefit of the whole product line and not for any specific brands or products within the line. Therefore these product line-sustaining expenses should be attributed to the product line but no attempt should be made to allocate them to individual products or brands. Finally, the profit for the organizational unit as a whole can be determined by deducting facility-sustaining expenses from the sum of the individual product line contributions.

A similar approach to the one described above for products can also be applied to other cost objects. The two final columns shown in Figure 10.2 illustrate how the

**FIGURE 10.2** An illustration of hierarchical profitability analysis.

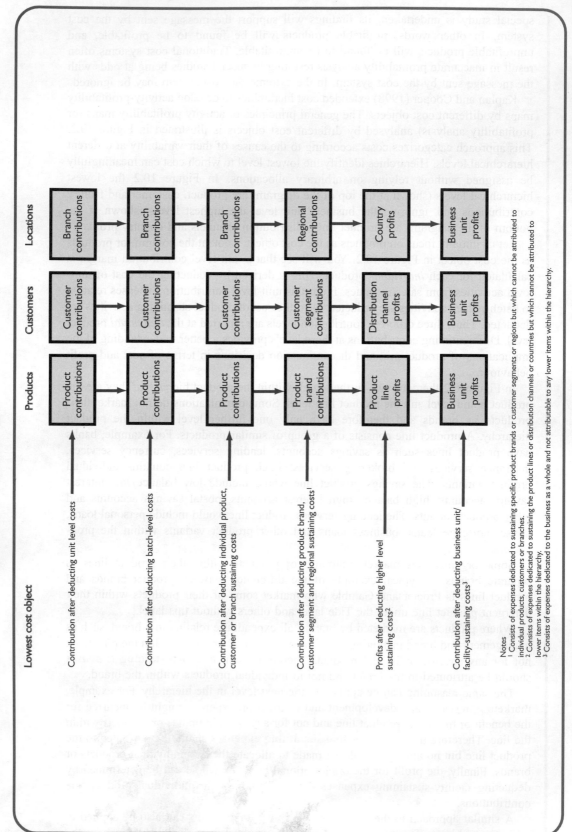

approach can be applied to customers and locations. The aim of ABC hierarchical profitability analysis is to assign all organizational expenses to a particular hierarchical or organizational level where cause-and-effect cost assignments can be established so that arbitrary allocations are non-existent. The hierarchical approach helps to identify the impact on resource consumption by adding or dropping items at each level of the hierarchy. For example, if a brand is dropped activities at the brand level and below (i.e. above the brand profits row in Figure 10.2) which are uniquely associated with the brand will be affected, but higher level activities (i.e. at the product line level) will be unaffected. Similarly, if a product within a particular brand is dropped then all unit, batch and product-sustaining activities uniquely associated with that product will be affected but higher level brand and product-level activities will be unaffected.

# Resource consumption models

The third, and possibly the most important theoretical advance in ABC systems was reported by Cooper and Kaplan (1992) in a paper which emphasized that ABC systems are models of resource consumption. The paper showed how ABC systems measure the cost of using resources and not the cost of supplying resources and highlighted the critical role played by unused capacity. To have a good conceptual grasp of ABC it is essential that you understand the content of this section.

Kaplan (1994) used the following equation to formalize the relationship between activity resources supplied and activity resources used for each activity:

$$\text{Cost of resources supplied} = \text{Cost of resources used} + \text{Cost of unused capacity} \tag{10.1}$$

To illustrate the application of the above formula we shall use Example 10.2. The left-hand side of the above equation indicates that the amount of expenditure on an activity depends on the cost of resources supplied rather than the cost of resources used. Example 10.2 contains data relating to the processing of purchase orders activity in which the equivalent of ten full-time staff are committed to the activity. You will see that the estimated annual cost is £300 000. This represents the cost of resources supplied. This expenditure provides the capacity to process 15 000 purchase orders (i.e. the quantity of resources supplied of the cost driver) per annum. Therefore the estimated cost of processing each purchase order is £20 (£300 000/15 000 orders that can be processed).

Periodic financial accounting profit statements measure the expenses incurred to make resources available (i.e. the cost of resources supplied) whereas ABC systems measure the cost of resources used by individual products, services or customers. During any particular period the number of orders processed will vary. In Example 10.2 it is assumed that the Etna Company expects to process 13 000 purchase orders (i.e. the quantity of resources used). The ABC system will therefore assign £260 000 (13 000 orders at £20 per order) to the parts and materials ordered during the year. This represents the cost of resources used.

The cost of unused capacity represents the difference between the cost of resources supplied and the cost of resources used. Resources have been acquired to enable 15 000 purchase orders to be processed but during the year only 13 000 orders will be processed giving an unused capacity of 2000 purchase orders. Hence the predicted cost of the unused capacity will be £40 000 (2000 orders at £20 per order).

**EXAMPLE 10.2**

The following information relates to the purchasing activity in a division of the Etna Company for the next year:

*(1) Resources supplied*

| | |
|---|---|
| 10 full-time staff at £30 000 per year (including employment costs) | = £300 000 annual activity cost |
| Cost driver | = Number of purchase orders processed |
| Quantity of cost driver supplied per year: (Each member of staff can process 1500 orders per year) | = 15 000 purchase orders |
| Estimated cost driver rate | = £20 per purchase order (£300 000/15 000 orders) |

*(2) Resources used*

| | |
|---|---|
| Estimated number of purchase orders to be processed during the year | = 13 000 |
| Estimated cost of resources used assigned to parts and materials | = £260 000 (13 000 × £20) |

*(3) Cost of unused capacity*

| | |
|---|---|
| Resources supplied (15 000) − Resources used (13 000) at £20 per order | = £40 000 (2000 × £20) |

Unused capacity arises because the supply of some resources has to be acquired in discrete amounts in advance of usage such that the supply cannot be continually adjusted in the short run to match exactly the usage of resources. Typical expenses in this category include the acquisition of equipment or the employment of non-piecework employees. The expenses of supplying these resources are incurred independently of usage in the short run and this independence has led to them being categorized as fixed costs. Kaplan and Cooper (1998) describe such resources as committed resources. In contrast, there are other types of resources whose supply can be continually adjusted to match exactly the usage of resources. For example, materials, casual labour and the supply of energy for running machinery can be continually adjusted to match the exact demand. Thus the cost of supplying these resources will generally equal the cost of resources used and the resources will have no unused capacity. Kaplan and Cooper classify these resources as 'flexible resources' although they have traditionally been categorized as variable costs.

The problem of adjusting the supply of resources to match the usage of resources and eliminating unused capacity therefore applies only to committed resources. Where the cost of supplying resources in the short run is fixed, the quantity used will fluctuate each period based on the activities performed for the output produced. Activity-based systems measure the cost of *using* these resources, even though the cost of supplying them will not vary with short-run usage.

Managers make decisions (for example, changes in output volume and mix, process changes and improvements and changes in product and process design) that result in changes in activity resource usage. Assuming that such decisions result in a decline in the demand for activity resources then the first term on the right-hand side of equation 10.1 will decline (the cost of resources used) but the cost of unused capacity (the second term on the right-hand side of the equation) will increase to offset exactly the lower resource usage cost. To translate the benefits of reduced activity demands into cash flow savings management action is required. They must permanently remove the unused capacity by reducing spending on the supply of the resources. Thus to make a resource variable in the downward direction requires two management decisions – first to reduce the demand for the resource and, second, to lower the spending on the resource.

Demands for activity resources can also increase because of decisions to introduce new products, expand output and create greater product variety. Such decisions can lead to situations where activity resource usage exceeds the supply of resources. In the short term the excess demand might be absorbed by people working longer or faster or delaying production. Eventually, however, additional spending will be required to increase the supply of activity resources. Thus, even if permanent changes in activity resource consumption occur that result in either unused or excess capacity there may be a significant time lag before the supply of activity resources is adjusted to match the revised predicted activity usage. Indeed, there is always a danger that managers may not act to reduce the spending on the supply of resources to match a reduction in demand. They may keep existing resources in place even when there has been a substantial decline in demands for the activities consuming the resources. Consequently, there will be no benefits arising from actions to reduce activity usage. However, if decisions are made based on reported ABC costs it is implicitly assumed that predicted changes in activity resource usage will be translated into equivalent cash flow changes for the resources supplied.

A major feature of ABC systems is therefore that reported product, service or customer costs represent estimates of the cost of resources used. In a period, many decisions are made that affect the usage of resources. It is not feasible to link the required changes in the supply of resources with the change in usage predicted by each *individual* decision. The periodic reporting of both the predicted quantity and the cost of unused capacity for each activity signals the need for management to investigate the potential for reducing the activity resources supplied. In the case of flexible resources cash flow changes will soon follow decisions to reduce activity usage, such as dropping a product, but for committed resources performing one less set-up, ordering one less batch of materials or undertaking one fewer engineering change notice will not result in an automatic reduction in spending. It will create additional capacity and changes in spending on the supply of resources will often be the outcome of the totality of many decisions rather than focusing on a one-off product decision. Such ideas are considered to be of such vital importance by Kaplan and Cooper that they conclude that managing used and unused capacity is the central focus of ABC.

# Selecting the cost driver denominator level

In Example 10.2 there are two potential denominator levels that can be used to establish cost driver rates. They are the capacity supplied (described as **practical capacity**) and the budgeted activity level. If practical capacity is used the cost driver rate will be £20 per purchase order processed (£300 000/15 000 orders) whereas the cost driver rate will be £23.08 (£300 000/13 000 orders) if the budgeted activity level is used as the denominator level.

Support activity costs are caused by the level of capacity that is made available (i.e. the capacity supplied) rather than the budgeted activity level of usage. Therefore the correct denominator activity level to use for calculating activity cost driver rates is practical capacity and not the anticipated activity usage. Furthermore, the use of budgeted activity will mean that the budgeted cost of unused capacity cannot be separately reported. This is the mechanism that is used to translate decisions that result in changes in activity usage into alterations in the supply of resources and thus changes in future spending. Using budgeted activity also means that the cost of unused capacity is also hidden in the cost driver rate and charged to products. Finally, anticipated capacity usage can lead to higher cost driver rates in periods of low sales demand when capacity is being maintained for an expected upsurge in demand. This will result in the cost of unused capacity being assigned to products and the higher cost driver rates will result in an increase in the reported product costs. Hence, there is a danger that bid prices will be increased when demand is depressed and at the time when a firm should be considering lowering prices.

In Example 10.2 practical capacity was measured in human resources which can be acquired and reduced in relatively discrete amounts. Human resources tend to be flexible in the longer term. It is therefore realistic to plan to adjust the practical capacity supplied for an activity to the planned demand for the activity resources. However, physical resources such as machinery and equipment are less flexible because they often can only be acquired in large discrete amounts. It is not possible, even in the longer term, to adjust the supply of capacity resources to exactly match the usage of resources. For example, consider a situation where the maximum demand for a machine might only be 80% of its practical maximum capacity. If the next smaller version of the machine has a capacity of only 60% of the larger machine, the larger machine must be acquired but there will be no expectation of utilizing the practical capacity. In these circumstances Kaplan and Cooper (1998) suggest that if the machine was purchased in the full knowledge that the maximum utilization would be 80% of its potential maximum capacity then the denominator level that should be used for measuring practical capacity is the 80% level. Hence, practical capacity should be defined as 80% of the machine's maximum capacity.

An alternative measure of physical capacity is **normal activity**. We looked at this measure in Chapter 7 when our objective was to focus on the factors which should influence the choice of capacity levels for profit measurement and inventory valuation. Normal activity is defined as the capacity required to satisfy average customer demand over a longer-term period of, say, approximately three years after taking into account seasonal and cyclical fluctuations. In many situations organizations will have invested in physical assets to provide capacity that is required to match long-run demand (i.e. normal activity). In other words, normal activity may be close to the 80% level for the machine quoted in the preceding paragraph. The end result is that a measure of normal capacity may be approximately similar to the measure of practical capacity as defined in the previous paragraph.

The message from the above discussion relating to the choice of denominator levels is that practical capacity ought to be used for measuring human resources. For physical resources it is recommended that the modified measure of practical capacity that has been described, or normal activity, should be used. Budgeted activity is not recommended on the grounds that it is a short-term measure which can lead to fluctuating cost driver rates if budgeted activity varies from period to period. However, a survey by Drury and Tayles (2000) of 186 UK organizations indicated that for both traditional and ABC systems budgeted annual activity was used by 86% of the responding organizations. Only 4% and 8% respectively used practical capacity and normal activity. The preference for budgeted annual activity may reflect the fact that the measure is readily available, being determined as part of the annual budgeting process whereas practical capacity and normal activity are not readily available and cannot be precisely determined. ●●●

# Cost versus benefits considerations

In Chapter 3 it was pointed out that the design of a cost system should be based on cost versus benefit considerations. A sophisticated ABC system will clearly generate the most accurate product costs. However, the cost of implementing and operating an ABC system is significantly more expensive than operating a direct costing or a traditional costing system. In particular, the training and software requirements may prohibit its adoption by small organizations. The partial costs reported by direct costing systems, and the distorted costs reported by traditional systems, may result in significant mistakes in decisions (such as selling unprofitable products or dropping profitable products) arising from the use of this information. If the cost of errors arising from using partial or distorted information generated from using these systems exceeds the additional costs of implementing and operating an ABC system then an ABC system ought to be implemented. In other words ABC must meet the cost/benefit criterion and improvements should be made in the level of sophistication of the costing system up to the point where the marginal cost of improvement equals the marginal benefit from improvement.

The optimal costing system is different for different organizations. A simplistic traditional costing system may report reasonably accurate product costs in organizations that have the following characteristics:

1. low levels of competition;
2. indirect costs that are a low proportion of total costs;
3. a fairly standardized product range all consuming organizational resources in similar proportions.

In contrast, a sophisticated ABC system may be optimal for organizations having following characteristics:

1. intensive competition;
2. indirect costs that are a high proportion of total costs;
3. a diverse range of products, all consuming organizational resources in significantly different proportions.

# Periodic review of an ABC data base

The detailed tracking of costs is unnecessary when ABC information is used for decision-making. A data base should be maintained that is reviewed periodically, say once or twice a year. In addition periodic cost and profitability audits (similar to that illustrated in Figure 10.2) should be undertaken to provide a strategic review of the costs and profitability of a firm's products, customers and sales outlets. The data base and periodic cost and profitability review can be based on either past or future costs. Early adopters, and firms starting off with ABC initially analysed past costs. Besides being historical the disadvantage of this approach is that actual cost driver usage is used as the denominator level to calculate the cost driver rates. Thus cost driver rates and product costs will include the cost of unused capacity. Hence the cost of unused capacity for each activity is not highlighted for management attention. Nevertheless, the information provided for the first time an insight into the resources consumed by products and customers and their profitability based on measuring the resource usage rather than arbitrary allocations.

However, rather than focusing on the past it is preferable to concentrate on the future profitability of products and customers using estimated activity-based costs. It is therefore recommended that an activity-cost data base is maintained at estimated standard costs that are updated on an annual or semi-annual basis.

# ABC in service organizations

Kaplan and Cooper (1998) suggest that service companies are ideal candidates for ABC, even more than manufacturing companies. Their justification for this statement is that most of the costs in service organizations are fixed and indirect. In contrast, manufacturing companies can trace important components (such as direct materials and direct labour) of costs to individual products. Therefore indirect costs are likely to be a much smaller proportion of total costs. Service organizations must also supply most of their resources in advance and fluctuations in the usage of activity resources by individual services and customers does not influence short-term spending to supply the resources. Such costs are treated by traditional costing systems as fixed and irrelevant for most decisions. This resulted in a situation where profitability analysis was not considered helpful for decision-making. Furthermore, until recently many service organizations were either government owned monopolies or operated in a highly regulated, protected and non-competitive environment. These organizations were not subject to any great pressures to improve profitability by identifying and eliminating non-profit making activities. Cost increases could also be absorbed by increasing the prices of services to customers. Little attention was therefore given to developing cost systems that accurately measured the costs and profitability of individual services.

Privatization of government owned monopolies, deregulation, intensive competition and an expanding product range created the need for service organizations to develop management accounting systems that enabled them to understand their cost base and determine the sources of profitability for their products/services, customers and markets. Many service organizations have therefore only recently implemented management accounting systems. They have had the advantage of not having to meet some of the constraints imposed on manufacturing organizations, such as having to meet financial accounting stock valuation requirements or the reluctance to scrap or change existing cost systems that might have become embedded in organizations. Furthermore, service organizations have been implementing new costing systems at the same time as the deficiencies of traditional systems were being widely publicized. Also new insights were beginning to emerge on how cost systems could be viewed as resource consumption models which could be used to make decisions on adjusting the spending on the supply of resources to match resource consumption.

A UK survey by Drury and Tayles (2000) suggests that service organizations are more likely to implement ABC systems. They reported that 51% of the financial and service organizations surveyed, compared with 15% of manufacturing organizations, had implemented ABC. Kaplan and Cooper (1998) illustrate how ABC was applied in The Co-operative Bank, a medium sized UK bank. ABC was used for product and customer profitability analysis. The following are some of the activities and cost drivers that were identified:

| Activity | Cost driver |
| --- | --- |
| Provide ATM services | Number of ATM transactions |
| Clear debit items | Number of debits processed |
| Clear credit items | Number of credits processed |
| Issue chequebooks | Number of chequebooks issued |

Computer processing   Number of computer transactions
Prepare statements of account transactions   Number of statements issued
Administer mortgages   Number of mortgages maintained

Activity costs were allocated to the different savings and loans products based on their demand for the activities using the cost drivers as a measure of resource consumption. Some expenses, such as finance and human resource management, were not assigned to products because they were considered to be for the benefit of the organization as a whole and not attributable to individual products. These business sustaining costs represented approximately 15% of total operating expenses. Profitability analysis was extended to customer segments within product groups. The study revealed that approximately half of the current accounts, particularly those with low balances and high transactions were unprofitable. By identifying the profitable customer segments the marketing function was able to direct its effort to attracting more new customers, and enhancing relationships with those existing customers, whose behaviour would be profitable to the bank.

# ABC cost management applications

Our aim in this chapter has been to look at how ABC can be used to provide information for decision-making by more accurately assigning costs to cost objects, such as products, customers and locations. In addition, ABC can be used for a range of cost management applications. They include cost reduction, activity-based budgeting, performance measurement, benchmarking of activities, process management and business process re-engineering. Figure 10.3 illustrates the product costing and cost management applications of ABC. The vertical box relates to product costing where costs are first assigned to activities and then to cost objects. The horizontal box relates to cost management. Here a process approach is adopted and costs are assigned to activities which then represent the basis for cost management applications. Thus, ABC can be adopted for both product costing and cost management or applied only to product costing or cost management. If ABC is only applied to cost management the second stage of assigning costs from activities to cost objects is omitted.

The decision to implement ABC should not, therefore, be based only on its ability to produce more accurate and relevant decision-making information. Indeed, a survey by Innes and Mitchell (1995a) on ABC applications suggests that the cost management applications tend to outweigh the product costing applications which were central to ABC's initial development. We shall examine ABC applications to cost management in Chapter 22.

# Pitfalls in using ABC information

**AR** Where unit costs are calculated, ABC systems suffer from the same disadvantages as traditional cost systems by suggesting an inappropriate degree of variability. For example, to calculate unit product costs, batch level activity costs are divided by the number of units in the batch and product sustaining costs are divided by the number of products produced. This unitizing approach is an allocation which yields a constant average cost per unit of output which will differ depending on the selected output level. For decision-making there is a danger that what started out as a non-volume-related

**FIGURE 10.3** *Product costing and cost management applications of ABC.*

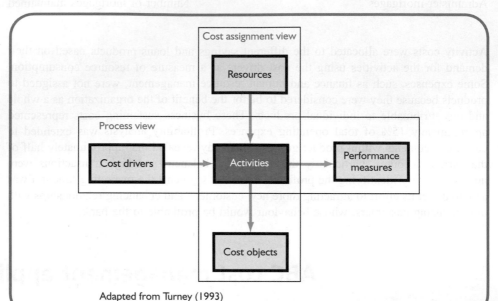

Cost assignment view

Resources

Process view

Cost drivers → Activities → Performance measures

Cost objects

Adapted from Turney (1993)

activity cost will be translated into a cost which varies with production volume. Consider a situation where the cost per set-up is £1000 for a standard batch size of 100 units for a particular part, giving an average set-up cost per part of £10. If a special order requiring the part is received for 50 units then the batch size will differ from the standard batch size and the average cost of the set-up for processing the parts of £10 is not the appropriate cost to use for decision-making. There is a danger that costs of £500 could be assigned to the order. However, if the special order requires one set-up then the activity resources consumed will be £1000 for an additional set-up, and not £500. Care must therefore be taken when using ABC information.

A further problem is that the concept of managing unused capacity is fine for human resources but it does not have the same impact for physical resources, such as the acquisition of plant and equipment. Human resources are more flexible and can be adjusted in small increments. Therefore the supply of resources can more easily be adjusted to the usage of resources. In contrast, physical resources are acquired or removed in lumpy amounts and large increments. If resources are supplied to cover a wide range of activity usage there would have to be a dramatic change in activity for the supply to be changed. Therefore changes in resource usage would tend not to be matched by a change in supply of resources and spending would remain unchanged. Care must therefore be taken to ensure that the cost of human and physical resources are not merged (so that they can be separately reported) when costs are assigned to activity cost centres within the first stage of the two-stage allocation process.

If the changes in physical resource usage arising from potential decisions do not have future cash flow consequences there is unlikely to be a link between resource usage and spending and the future cash flow impact for most decisions will be zero. In other words, the cost of resource usage would be treated as fixed and unavoidable for most decisions which is identical to how these costs would be treated adopting traditional costing systems. Also traditional costing systems accurately trace the cost of unit-level activities to products and facility-sustaining costs cannot accurately be assigned to cost objects by any costing system. Thus, for many organizations the proportion of costs that can be more accurately assigned to cost objects by ABC systems, and that can be expected to have a future cash flow impact, might be quite small. For such organizations this would imply that appropriate cost information extracted from simplistic costing systems may be sufficiently accurate for decision-making purposes. ●●●

**EXHIBIT 10.1**

*Surveys of company practice*

Significant variations in the usage of ABC both within the same country and across different countries have been reported. These differences may arise from the difficulty in precisely defining the difference between traditional costing systems and ABC systems and the specific time period when the surveys were actually undertaken.

Survey evidence suggests that over the last decade there has been an increasing interest in ABC. In the UK, surveys in the early 1990s reported adoption rates around 10% (Innes and Mitchell, 1991; Nicholls, 1992; Drury *et al.*, 1993). Similar adoption rates of 10% were found in Ireland (Clarke, 1992) and 14% in Canada (Armitage and Nicholson, 1993). In the USA Green and Amenkhienan (1992) claimed that 45% of firms used ABC to some extent. More recent surveys suggest higher ABC adoption rates. In the UK reported usage was 20% (Innes and Mitchell, 1995a), 22% (Banerjee and Kane, 1996), 21% (Evans and Ashworth, 1996) and 23% (Drury and Tayles, 2000). In the USA Shim and Stagliano (1997) reported a usage rate of 27%.

Reported usage rates for mainland Europe are 19% in Belgium (Bruggeman *et al.*, 1996) and 6% in Finland in 1992, 11% in 1993 and 24% in 1995 (Virtanen *et al.*, 1996). Low usage rates have been reported in Denmark (Israelsen *et al.*, 1996), Sweden (Ask *et al.*, 1996) and Germany (Scherrer, 1996). Activity-based techniques do not appear to have been adopted in Greece (Ballas and Venieris, 1996), Italy (Barbato *et al.*, 1996) or Spain (Saez-Torrecilla *et al.*, 1996).

Other studies have examined the applications of ABC. Innes and Mitchell (1995) found that cost reduction was the most widely used application. Other widely used applications included product/service pricing, cost modelling and performance measurement/improvement. ABC was used for stock valuation by 29% of ABC adopters thus suggesting that the majority of ABC users have separate systems for stock valuation and management accounting applications.

According to Bjornenak (1997a) there has been little research on who adopts ABC and for what reasons. His survey indicated that 40% of the responding Norwegian companies had adopted ABC as an idea (i.e. they had implemented ABC or planned to do so). Different variables relating to cost structure, competition, existing cost systems, size and product diversity were tested as explanatory factors for the adoption of ABC but only cost structure and size were found to be statistically significant. The UK study by Drury and Tayles indicated that company size and business sector had a significant impact on ABC adoption rates. The adoption rates were 45% for the largest organizations and 51% for financial and service organizations. Although the ABC adopters used significantly more cost pools and cost drivers than the non-adopters most adopters used fewer cost pools and drivers compared with what is recommended in the literature. Approximately, 50% of the ABC adopters used less than 50 cost centres and less than 10 separate types of cost driver rates.

Friedman and Lyne's (1995) case study research of 12 UK companies cited top management support as a significant factor influencing the success or failure of ABC systems. Implementation problems identified by the various studies included the amount of work in setting up the system and data collection, difficulties in identifying activities and selecting cost drivers, lack of resources and inadequate computer software. The benefits reported by the studies included more accurate cost information for product pricing, more accurate profitability analysis, improved cost control and a better understanding of cost causation.

## Self-Assessment Question

You should attempt to answer this question yourself before looking up the suggested answer, which appears on pages 1110-13. If any part of your answer is incorrect, check back carefully to make sure you understand where you went wrong.

The following information provides details of the costs, volume and cost drivers for a particular period in respect of ABC plc, a hypothetical company:

| | Product X | Product Y | Product Z | Total |
|---|---|---|---|---|
| 1. Production and sales (units) | 30 000 | 20 000 | 8000 | |
| 2. Raw material usage (units) | 5 | 5 | 11 | |
| 3. Direct material cost | £25 | £20 | £11 | £1 238 000 |
| 4. Direct labour hours | $1\frac{1}{3}$ | 2 | 1 | 88 000 |
| 5. Machine hours | $1\frac{1}{3}$ | 1 | 2 | 76 000 |
| 6. Direct labour cost | £8 | £12 | £6 | |
| 7. Number of production runs | 3 | 7 | 20 | 30 |
| 8. Number of deliveries | 9 | 3 | 20 | 32 |
| 9. Number of receipts $(2 \times 7)$[a] | 15 | 35 | 220 | 270 |
| 10. Number of production orders | 15 | 10 | 25 | 50 |
| 11. Overhead costs: | | | | |
| Set-up | 30 000 | | | |
| Machines | 760 000 | | | |
| Receiving | 435 000 | | | |
| Packing | 250 000 | | | |
| Engineering | 373 000 | | | |
| | £1 848 000 | | | |

[a]The company operates a just-in-time inventory policy, and receives each component once per production run.

In the past the company has allocated overheads to products on the basis of direct labour hours.

However, the majority of overheads are more closely related to machine hours than direct labour hours.

The company has recently redesigned its cost system by recovering overheads using two volume-related bases: machine hours and a materials handling overhead rate for recovering overheads of the receiving department. Both the current and the previous cost system reported low profit margins for product X, which is the company's highest-selling product. The management accountant has recently attended a conference on activity-based costing, and the overhead costs for the last period have been analysed by the major activities in order to compute activity-based costs.

From the above information you are required to:

(a) Compute the product costs using a traditional volume-related costing system based on the assumptions that:
  (i)   all overheads are recovered on the basis of direct labour hours (i.e. the company's past product costing system);
  (ii)  the overheads of the receiving department are recovered by a materials handling

overhead rate and the remaining overheads are recovered using a machine hour rate (i.e. the company's current costing system).

(b) Compute product costs using an activity-based costing system.

(c) Briefly explain the differences between the product cost computations in (a) and (b).

## Summary

Indirect relevant costs can be difficult to identify and measure. This chapter has shown how ABC systems can identify and measure relevant costs. ABC systems do not report relevant costs for all possible situations but they do provide a superior way of determining relevant costs. The major distinguishing features between ABC and traditional costing systems were compared. ABC systems rely on a greater number of cost centres and second stage cause-and-effect cost drivers. An ABC system involves the following four stages:

1. identify the major activities which take place in an organization;

2. create a cost centre/cost pool for each major activity;

3. determine the cost driver for each major activity;

4. trace the cost of activities to products according to a product's demand (using cost drivers as a measure of demand) for activities.

Early ABC systems were subject to a number of criticisms, particularly relating to theoretical aspects. As a response to these criticisms a number of theoretical developments emerged during the 1990s. The first theoretical development classified manufacturing activities along a cost hierarchy dimension consisting of unit-level, batch-level, product-sustaining and facility-sustaining activities. The second was to apply the cost hierarchy to profitability analysis. The aim is to assign all organizational expenses to a particular hierarchical or organizational level where cause-and-effect cost assignments can be established so that arbitrary allocations are non-existent. It was also emphasized that ABC profitability analysis

provides attention-directing information by high-lighting those potentially unprofitable products or services that require more detailed studies.

The third, and most important, theoretical development, emphasized that ABC systems are models of resource consumption. They measure the cost of *using* resources and not the cost of *supplying* resources. The difference between the cost of resources supplied and the cost of resources used represents the cost of unused capacity. The cost of unused capacity for each activity is the reporting mechanism for identifying the need to adjust the supply of resources to match the usage of resources. However, to translate the benefits of reduced activity demands into cash flow savings management action is required to remove the unused capacity by reducing the spending on the supply of the resources. The ABC resource consumption model requires that practical capacity is used as the denominator level to establish cost driver rates.

ABC must meet the cost/benefit criterion and improvements should be made in the level of sophistication of the costing system up to the point where the marginal cost of improvement equals the marginal benefit from improvement. Sophisticated ABC systems are likely to be optimal in organizations having the following characteristics – intensive competition, a high proportion of indirect costs and a diverse product range.

This chapter has emphasized the conceptual aspects of ABC. For an illustration of the application of ABC and a computation of product costs you should refer to Chapter 3 and the self-assessment question and answer at the end of this chapter. In the next chapter we shall illustrate how ABC information can be used for pricing decisions and customer profitability analysis.

## Key Terms and Concepts

activities (p. 338)
activity cost drivers (p. 343)
batch-related activities (p. 345)

brand-sustaining expenses (p. 347)
business and sustaining activities (p. 346)
committed resources (p. 350)

cost drivers (p. 338)
cost of resources supplied (p. 349)
cost of resources used (p. 349)
cost of unused capacity (p. 349)
customer-sustaining activities (p. 346)
duration drivers (p. 344)
facility-sustaining activities (p. 346)
flexible resources (p. 350)
intensity drivers (p. 344)

models of resource consumption (p. 349)
normal activity (p. 351)
practical capacity (p. 351)
product-line sustaining activities (p. 347)
product-sustaining activities (p. 346)
resource cost drivers (p. 343)
service-sustaining activities (p. 346)
transaction drivers (p. 344)
unit-level activities (p. 345)

## Recommended Reading

Kaplan and Cooper have been the major contributors to the development of activity-based costing. Much of this chapter has therefore drawn off their ideas. For a detailed description of activity-based costing which incorporates all of Kaplan and Cooper's ideas you should consult *Cost and Effect: Using Integrated Systems to Drive Profitability and Performance* (1998). You should refer to the bibliography at the end of this book for the detailed reference.

## Key Examination Points

ABC did not emerge until the late 1980s, and therefore fewer questions have been set on this topic. As a result, only a small number of questions are included in this chapter. It is likely that most questions will require you to compute product costs for a traditional system and an activity-based system and explain the difference between the product costs. It is also likely that examiners will require you to outline the circumstances where ABC systems are likely to prove most beneficial.

## Questions

* Indicates that a suggested solution is to be found in the *Students' Manual*.

### 10.1 Intermediate

The traditional methods of cost allocation, cost apportionment and absorption into products are being challenged by some writers who claim that much information given to management is misleading when these methods of dealing with fixed overheads are used to determine product costs.

You are required to explain what is meant by *cost allocation, cost apportionment* and *absorption* and to describe briefly the alternative approach of *activity-based costing* in order to ascertain total product costs. (15 marks)

*CIMA Stage 2 Cost Accounting*

### 10.2* Intermediate

'It is now fairly widely accepted that conventional cost accounting distorts management's view of business through unrepresentative overhead allocation and inappropriate product costing.

This is because the traditional approach usually absorbs overhead costs across products and orders solely on the basis of the direct labour involved in their manufacture. And as direct labour as a proportion of total manufacturing cost continues to fall, this leads to more and more distortion and misrepresentation of the impact of particular products on total overhead costs.'

(From an article in *The Financial Times*)
You are required to discuss the above and to suggest what approaches are being adopted by management accountants to overcome such criticism. (15 marks)

*CIMA Stage 2 Cost Accounting*

### 10.3 Intermediate

'Attributing direct costs and absorbing overhead costs to the product/service through an activity-based costing approach will result in a better understanding of the true cost of the final output.' (*Source:* a recent CIMA publication on costing in a service environment.)

You are required to explain and comment on the above statement. (15 marks)

*CIMA Stage 2 Cost Accounting*

## 10.4 Advanced

The basic ideas justifying the use of Activity Based Costing (ABC) and Activity Based Budgeting (ABB) are well publicised, and the number of applications has increased. However, there are apparently still significant problems in changing from existing systems.

Requirements:

(a) Explain which characteristics of an organisation, such as its structure, product range, or environment, may make the use of activity based techniques particularly useful. (5 marks)

(b) Explain the problems that may cause an organisation to decide not to use, or to abandon use of, activity based techniques.
(8 marks)

(c) Some categorisations of cost drivers provide hierarchical models:
    (i)   unit-level activities,
    (ii)  batch activities,
    (iii) product sustaining activities,
    (iv)  facility sustaining activities.
    Other analyses focus on 'value adding' and 'non-value adding' activities.

Requirement:

Explain what is meant by 'non-value adding activities', and discuss the usefulness of this form of analysis. (7 marks)
(Total 20 marks)
*CIMA Stage 4 Management Accounting Control Systems*

## 10.5* Advanced

Large service organisations, such as banks and hospitals, used to be noted for their lack of standard costing systems, and their relatively unsophisticated budgeting and control systems compared with large manufacturing organisations. But this is changing and many large service organisations are now revising their use of management accounting techniques.

Requirements:

(a) Explain which features of large-scale service organisations encourage the application of activity-based approaches to the analysis of cost information. (6 marks)

(b) Explain which features of service organisations may create problems for the application of activity-based costing. (4 marks)

(c) Explain the uses for activity-based cost information in service industries. (4 marks)

(d) Many large service organisations were at one time state-owned, but have been privatised. Examples in some countries include electricity supply and telecommunications. They are often regulated. Similar systems of regulation of prices by an independent authority exist in many countries, and are designed to act as a surrogate for market competition in industries where it is difficult to ensure a genuinely competitive market.

Explain which aspects of cost information and systems in service organisations would particularly interest a regulator, and why these features would be of interest. (6 marks)
(Total 20 marks)
*CIMA Stage 4 Management Accounting Control Systems*

## 10.6* Intermediate: Comparison of traditional product costing with ABC

Having attended a CIMA course on activity-based costing (ABC) you decide to experiment by applying the principles of ABC to the four products currently made and sold by your company. Details of the four products and relevant information are given below for one period:

| Product | A | B | C | D |
|---|---|---|---|---|
| Output in units | 120 | 100 | 80 | 120 |
| Costs per unit: | (£) | (£) | (£) | (£) |
| Direct material | 40 | 50 | 30 | 60 |
| Direct labour | 28 | 21 | 14 | 21 |
| Machine hours (per unit) | 4 | 3 | 2 | 3 |

The four products are similar and are usually produced in production runs of 20 units and sold in batches of 10 units.

The production overhead is currently absorbed by using a machine hour rate, and the total of the production overhead for the period has been analysed as follows:

| | (£) |
|---|---|
| Machine department costs (rent, business rates, depreciation and supervision) | 10 430 |
| Set-up costs | 5 250 |
| Stores receiving | 3 600 |
| Inspection/Quality control | 2 100 |
| Materials handling and despatch | 4 620 |

You have ascertained that the 'cost drivers' to be used are as listed below for the overhead costs shown:

| Cost | Cost Driver |
|---|---|
| Set up costs | Number of production runs |
| Stores receiving | Requisitions raised |
| Inspection/Quality control | Number of production runs |
| Materials handling and despatch | Orders executed |

The number of requisitions raised on the stores was 20 for each product and the number of orders executed was 42, each order being for a batch of 10 of a product. You are required

(a) to calculate the total costs for each product if all overhead costs are absorbed on a machine hour basis; (4 marks)

(b) to calculate the total costs for each product, using activity-based costing; (7 marks)

(c) to calculate and list the unit product costs from your figures in (a) and (b) above, to show the differences and to comment briefly on any conclusions which may be drawn which could have pricing and profit implications.

(4 marks)
(Total 15 marks)
*CIMA Stage 2 Cost Accounting*

## 10.7 Intermediate: Calculation of ABC product costs and a discussion of the usefulness of ABC

Trimake Limited makes three main products, using broadly the same production methods and equipment for each. A conventional product costing system is used at present, although an activity-based costing (ABC) system is being considered. Details of the three products for a typical period are:

| | Hours per unit | | Materials per unit | Volumes |
|---|---|---|---|---|
| | Labour hours | Machine hours | £ | Units |
| Product X | $\frac{1}{2}$ | $1\frac{1}{2}$ | 20 | 750 |
| Product Y | $1\frac{1}{2}$ | 1 | 12 | 1250 |
| Product Z | 1 | 3 | 25 | 7000 |

Direct labour costs £6 per hour and production overheads are absorbed on a machine hour basis. The rate for the period is £28 per machine hour.

(a) You are required to calculate the cost per unit for each product using conventional methods.

(4 marks)

Further analysis shows that the total of production overheads can be divided as follows:

| | (%) |
|---|---|
| Costs relating to set-ups | 35 |
| Costs relating to machinery | 20 |
| Costs relating to materials handling | 15 |
| Costs relating to inspection | 30 |
| Total production overhead | 100% |

The following activity volumes are associated with the product line for the period as a whole. Total activities for the period:

| | Number of set-ups | Number of movements of materials | Number of inspections |
|---|---|---|---|
| Product X | 75 | 12 | 150 |
| Product Y | 115 | 21 | 180 |
| Product Z | 480 | 87 | 670 |
| | 670 | 120 | 1000 |

You are required

(b) to calculate the cost per unit for each product using ABC principles; (15 marks)

(c) to comment on the reasons for any differences in the costs in your answers to (a) and (b).

(3 marks)
(Total 22 marks)
*CIMA Stage 3 Management Accounting Techniques*

## 10.8* Intermediate: Preparation of conventional costing and ABC profit statements

The following budgeted information relates to Brunti plc for the forthcoming period:

| | Products | | |
| --- | --- | --- | --- |
| | **XYI** **(000)** | **YZT** **(000)** | **ABW** **(000)** |
| Sales and production (units) | 50 | 40 | 30 |
| | (£) | (£) | (£) |
| Selling price (per unit) | 45 | 95 | 73 |
| Prime cost (per unit) | 32 | 84 | 65 |
| | **Hours** | **Hours** | **Hours** |
| Machine department (machine hours per unit) | 2 | 5 | 4 |
| Assembly department (direct labour hours per unit) | 7 | 3 | 2 |

Overheads allocated and apportioned to production departments (including service cost centre costs) were to be recovered in product costs as follows:

Machine department at
£1.20 per machine hour
Assembly department at
£0.825 per direct labour hour

You ascertain that the above overheads could be re-analysed into 'cost pools' as follows:

| Cost pool | £000 | Cost driver | Quantity for the period |
| --- | --- | --- | --- |
| Machining services | 357 | Machine hours | 420 000 |
| Assembly services | 318 | Direct labour hours | 530 000 |
| Set-up costs | 26 | Set-ups | 520 |
| Order processing | 156 | Customer orders | 32 000 |
| Purchasing | 84 | Suppliers' orders | 11 200 |
| | 941 | | |

You have also been provided with the following estimates for the period:

| | Products | | |
| --- | --- | --- | --- |
| | **XYI** | **YZT** | **ABW** |
| Number of set-ups | 120 | 200 | 200 |
| Customer orders | 8000 | 8000 | 16 000 |
| Suppliers' orders | 3000 | 4000 | 4200 |

Required:
(a) Prepare and present profit statements using:
    (i) conventional absorption costing;
                                            (5 marks)
    (ii) activity-based costing;      (10 marks)
(b) Comment on why activity-based costing is considered to present a fairer valuation of the product cost per unit.      (5 marks)
                                    (Total 20 marks)
        *ACCA Paper 8 Managerial Finance*

### 10.9* Advanced: Computation of ABC and traditional product costs plus a discussion of ABC

Repak Ltd is a warehousing and distribution company which receives products from customers, stores the products and then re-packs them for distribution as required. There are three customers for whom the service is provided – John Ltd, George Ltd and Paul Ltd. The products from all three customers are similar in nature but of varying degrees of fragility. Basic budget information has been gathered for the year to 30 June and is shown in the following table:

| | Products handled (cubic metres) |
| --- | --- |
| John Ltd | 30 000 |
| George Ltd | 45 000 |
| Paul Ltd | 25 000 |
| | Costs (£000) |
| Packaging materials (see note 1) | 1950 |
| Labour – basic | 350 |
| – overtime | 30 |
| Occupancy | 500 |
| Administration and management | 60 |

*Note 1:* Packaging materials are used in re-packing each cubic metre of product for John Ltd, George Ltd and Paul Ltd in the ratio 1 : 2 : 3 respectively. This ratio is linked to the relative fragility of the goods for each customer.

Additional information has been obtained in order to enable unit costs to be prepared for each of the three customers using an activity-based costing approach. The additional information for the year to 30 June has been estimated as follows:
(i) Labour and overhead costs have been identi-

fied as attributable to each of three work centres – receipt and inspection, storage and packing as follows:

### Cost allocation proportions

| | Receipt and inspection % | Storage % | Packing % |
|---|---|---|---|
| Labour – basic | 15 | 10 | 75 |
| – overtime | 50 | 15 | 35 |
| Occupancy | 20 | 60 | 20 |
| Administration and management | 40 | 10 | 50 |

(ii) Studies have revealed that the fragility of different goods affects the receipt and inspection time needed for the products for each customer. Storage required is related to the average size of the basic incoming product units from each customer. The re-packing of goods for distribution is related to the complexity of packaging required by each customer. The relevant requirements per cubic metre of product for each customer have been evaluated as follows:

| | John Ltd | George Ltd | Paul Ltd |
|---|---|---|---|
| Receipt and inspection (minutes) | 5 | 9 | 15 |
| Storage (square metres) | 0·3 | 0·3 | 0·2 |
| Packing (minutes) | 36 | 45 | 60 |

Required:

(a) Calculate the budgeted average cost per cubic metre of packaged products for each customer for each of the following two circumstances:
  (i) where only the basic budget information is to be used, (6 marks)
  (ii) where the additional information enables an activity-based costing approach to be applied. (14 marks)
(b) Comment on the activities and cost drivers which have been identified as relevant for the implementation of activity-based costing by Repak Ltd and discuss ways in which activity-based costing might improve product costing and cost control in Repak Ltd. Make reference to your answer to part (a) of the question, as appropriate.

(10 marks)
(Total 30 marks)
*ACCA Level 2*

### 10.10* Advanced: Comparison of ABC with traditional product costing

(a) In the context of activity-based costing (ABC), it was stated in *Management Accounting – Evolution not Revolution* by Bromwich and Bhimani, that 'Cost drivers attempt to link costs to the scope of output rather than the scale of output thereby generating less arbitrary product costs for decision making.' You are required to explain the terms 'activity-based costing' and 'cost drivers'.

(13 marks)
(b) XYZ plc manufactures four products, namely A, B, C and D, using the same plant and processes. The following information relates to a production period:

| Product | Volume | Material cost per unit | Direct labour per unit | Machine time per unit | Labour cost per unit |
|---|---|---|---|---|---|
| A | 500 | £5 | $\frac{1}{2}$ hour | $\frac{1}{4}$ hour | £3 |
| B | 5000 | £5 | $\frac{1}{2}$ hour | $\frac{1}{4}$ hour | £3 |
| C | 600 | £16 | 2 hours | 1 hour | £12 |
| D | 7000 | £17 | $1\frac{1}{2}$ hours | $1\frac{1}{2}$ hours | £9 |

Total production overhead recorded by the cost accounting system is analysed under the following headings:

Factory overhead applicable to machine-oriented activity is £37 424
  Set-up costs are £4355

The cost of ordering materials is £1920
Handling materials – £7580
Administration for spare parts – £8600.

These overhead costs are absorbed by products on a machine hour rate of £4.80 per hour, giving an overhead cost per product of:

  A = £1.20    B = £1.20    C = £4.80    D = £7.20

However, investigation into the production overhead activities for the period reveals the following totals:

| Product | Number of set-ups | Number of material orders | Number of times material was handled | Number of spare parts |
|---------|-------------------|---------------------------|--------------------------------------|-----------------------|
| A | 1 | 1 | 2 | 2 |
| B | 6 | 4 | 10 | 5 |
| C | 2 | 1 | 3 | 1 |
| D | 8 | 4 | 12 | 4 |

You are required:

(i) to compute an overhead cost per product using activity-based costing, tracing overheads to production units by means of cost drivers. (6 marks)

(ii) to comment briefly on the differences disclosed between overheads traced by the present system and those traced by activity-based costing. (6 marks)

(Total 25 marks)

*CIMA Stage 4 Management Accounting – Control and Audit*

## 10.11 Advanced: Comparison of traditional product costing with ABC

Duo plc produces two products A and B. Each has two components specified as sequentially numbered parts i.e. product A (parts 1 and 2) and product B (parts 3 and 4). Two production departments (machinery and fitting) are supported by five service activities (material procurement, material handling, maintenance, quality control and set up). Product A is a uniform product manufactured each year in 12 monthly high volume production runs. Product B is manufactured in low volume customised batches involving 25 separate production runs each month. Additional information is as follows:

| | Product A | Product B |
|---|---|---|
| Production details: | | |
| Components | Parts 1, 2 | Parts 3, 4 |
| Annual volume produced | 300 000 units | 300 000 units |
| Annual direct labour hours: | | |
| Machinery department | 500 000 DLH | 600 000 DLH |
| Fitting department | 150 000 DLH | 200 000 DLH |

*Overhead Cost Analysis*[a]

| | (£000s) |
|---|---|
| Material handling | 1 500 |
| Material procurement | 2 000 |
| Set-up | 1 500 |
| Maintenance | 2 500 |
| Quality control | 3 000 |
| Machinery (machinery power, depreciation etc.)[b] | 2 500 |
| Fitting (machine, depreciation, power etc.)[b] | 2 000 |
| | 15 000 |

[a] It may be assumed that these represent fairly homogeneous activity-based cost pools.
[b] It is assumed these costs (depreciation, power etc.) are primarily production volume driven and that direct labour hours are an appropriate surrogate measure of this.

*Cost Driver Analysis*

**Annual Cost Driver Volume per Component**

| Cost Driver | Part 1 | Part 2 | Part 3 | Part 4 |
|---|---|---|---|---|
| Material movements | 180 | 160 | 1 000 | 1 200 |
| Number of orders | 200 | 300 | 2 000 | 4 000 |
| Number of set-ups | 12 | 12 | 300 | 300 |
| Maintenance hours | 7 000 | 5 000 | 10 000 | 8 000 |
| Number of inspections | 360 | 360 | 2 400 | 1 000 |
| Direct labour hours | 150 000 | 350 000 | 200 000 | 400 000 |
| Direct labour hours | 50 000 | 100 000 | 60 000 | 140 000 |

You are required to compute the unit costs for products A and B using (i) a traditional volume-based product costing system and (ii) an activity-based costing system.

(Adapted from Innes, J. and Mitchell, F., *Activity Based Costing: A Review with Case Studies, Chartered Institute of Management Accountants*, 1990)

## 10.12 Advanced: Profitability analysis using ABC as traditional cost allocation bases

ABC plc, a group operating retail stores, is compiling its budget statements for the next year. In this exercise revenues and costs at each store A, B and C are predicted. Additionally, all central costs of warehousing and a head office are allocated across the three stores in order to arrive at a total cost and net profit of each store operation.

In earlier years the central costs were allocated in total based on the total sales value of each store. But as a result of dissatisfaction expressed by some store managers alternative methods are to be evaluated.

The predicted results before any re-allocation of central costs are as follows:

|  | A (£000) | B (£000) | C (£000) |
|---|---|---|---|
| Sales | 5000 | 4000 | 3000 |
| Costs of sales | 2800 | 2300 | 1900 |
| Gross margin | 2200 | 1700 | 1100 |
| Local operating expenses | | | |
| Variable | 660 | 730 | 310 |
| Fixed | 700 | 600 | 500 |
| Operating profit | 840 | 370 | 290 |

The central costs which are to be allocated are:

|  | (£000) |
|---|---|
| Warehouse costs: | |
| Depreciation | 100 |
| Storage | 80 |
| Operating and despatch | 120 |
| Delivery | 300 |
| Head office: | |
| Salaries | 200 |
| Advertising | 80 |
| Establishment | 120 |
| Total | 1000 |

The management accountant has carried out discussions with staff at all locations in order to identify more suitable 'cost drivers' of some of the central costs. So far the following has been revealed.

|  | A | B | C |
|---|---|---|---|
| Number of despatches | 550 | 450 | 520 |
| Total delivery distances (thousand miles) | 70 | 50 | 90 |
| Storage space occupied (%) | 40 | 30 | 30 |

1. An analysis of senior management time revealed that 10% of their time was devoted to warehouse issues with the remainder shared equally between the three stores.
2. It was agreed that the only basis on which to allocate the advertising costs was sales revenue.
3. Establishment costs were mainly occupancy costs of senior management.

This analysis has been carried out against a background of developments in the company, for example, automated warehousing and greater integration with suppliers.

Required:
(a) As the management accountant prepare a report for the management of the group which:
   (i) Computes the budgeted net profit of each store based on the *sales value* allocation base originally adopted *and* explains 'cost driver', 'volume' and 'complexity' issues in relation to cost allocation commenting on the possible implications of the dissatisfaction expressed. (6 marks)
   (ii) Computes the budgeted net profit of each store using the additional information provided, discusses the extent to which an improvement has been achieved in the information on the costs and profitability of running the stores and comments on the results. (11 marks)
(b) Explain briefly how regression analysis and coefficient of determination ($r^2$) could be used in confirming the delivery mileage allocation method used in (a) above. (3 marks)
(Total 20 marks)
*ACCA Paper 8 Managerial Finance*

## 10.13 Advanced: Unit cost computation based on traditional and ABC systems

Excel Ltd make and sell two products, VG4U and VG2. Both products are manufactured through two consecutive processes – making and packing. Raw material is input at the commencement of the making process. The following estimated information is available for the period ending 31 March:

(i)

| | Making (£000) | Packing (£000) |
|---|---|---|
| Conversion costs: | | |
| Variable | 350 | 280 |
| Fixed | 210 | 140 |

40% of fixed costs are product specific, the remainder are company fixed costs. Fixed costs will remain unchanged throughout a wide activity range.

(ii) **Product information:**

| | VG4U | VG2 |
|---|---|---|
| Production time per unit: | | |
| Making (minutes) | 5·25 | 5·25 |
| Packing (minutes) | 6 | 4 |
| Production/sales (units) | 5000 | 3000 |
| Selling price per unit (£) | 150 | 180 |
| Direct material cost per unit (£) | 30 | 30 |

(iii) Conversion costs are absorbed by products using estimated time based rates.

Required:
(a) Using the above information,
  (i) calculate unit costs for each product, analysed as relevant. (10 marks)
  (ii) comment on a management suggestion that the production and sale of one of the products should not proceed in the period ending 31 March. (4 marks)
(b) Additional information is gathered for the period ending 31 March as follows:
  (i) The making process consists of two consecutive activities, moulding and trimming. The moulding variable conversion costs are incurred in proportion to the temperature required in the moulds. The variable trimming conversion costs are incurred in proportion to the consistency of the material when it emerges from the moulds. The variable packing process conversion costs are incurred in proportion to the time required for each product. Packing materials (which are part of the variable packing cost) requirement depends on the complexity of packing specified for each product.
  (ii) The proportions of product specific conversion costs (variable and fixed) are analysed as follows:

Making process: moulding (60%); trimming (40%)
Packing process: conversion (70%); packing material (30%)
  (iii) An investigation into the effect of the cost drivers on costs has indicated that the proportions in which the total product specific conversion costs are attributable to VG4U and VG2 are as follows:

| | VG4U | VG2 |
|---|---|---|
| Temperature (moulding) | 2 | 1 |
| Material consistency (trimming) | 2 | 5 |
| Time (packing) | 3 | 2 |
| Packing (complexity) | 1 | 3 |

  (iv) Company fixed costs are apportioned to products at an overall average rate per product unit based on the estimated figures.

Required:
Calculate amended unit costs for each product where activity based costing is used and company fixed costs are apportioned as detailed above.
(12 marks)
(c) Comment on the relevance of the amended unit costs in evaluating the management suggestion that one of the products be discontinued in the period ending 31 March.
(4 marks)
(d) Management wish to achieve an overall net profit margin of 15% on sales in the period ending 31 March in order to meet return on capital targets.

Required:
Explain how target costing may be used in achieving the required return and suggest specific areas of investigation. (5 marks)
(Total 35 marks)
*ACCA Paper 9 Information for Control and Decision Making*

## 10.14* Advanced: ABC product cost computation and discussion relating to ABC, JIT and TQM

During the last 20 years, KL's manufacturing operation has become increasingly automated with computer-controlled robots replacing operatives. KL currently manufactures over 100 products of varying levels of design complexity. A single, plant-wide overhead absorption rate (OAR), based on direct labour hours, is used to absorb overhead costs.

In the quarter ended March, KL's manufacturing overhead costs were:

|  | (£000) |
| --- | --- |
| Equipment operation expenses | 125 |
| Equipment maintenance expenses | 25 |
| Wages paid to technicians | 85 |
| Wages paid to storemen | 35 |
| Wages paid to dispatch staff | 40 |
|  | 310 |

During the quarter, RAPIER Management Consultants were engaged to conduct a review of KL's cost accounting systems. RAPIER's report includes the following statement:

'In KL's circumstances, absorbing overhead costs in individual products on a labour hour absorption basis is meaningless. Overhead costs should be attributed to products using an activity based costing (ABC) system. We have identified the following as being the most significant activities:

(1) receiving component consignments from suppliers
(2) setting up equipment for production runs
(3) quality inspections
(4) dispatching goods orders to customers.

Our research has indicated that, in the short term, KL's overheads are 40% fixed and 60% variable. Approximately half the variable overheads vary in relation to direct labour hours worked and half vary in relation to the number of quality inspections. This model applies only to relatively small changes in the level of output during a period of two years or less.'

Equipment operation and maintenance expenses are apportionable as follows:

- component stores (15%), manufacturing (70%) and goods dispatch (15%).

Technician wages are apportionable as follows:

- equipment maintenance (30%), setting up equipment for production runs (40%) and quality inspections (30%).

During the quarter

- a total of 2000 direct labour hours were worked (paid at £12 per hour),
- 980 component consignments were received from suppliers,
- 1020 production runs were set up,
- 640 quality inspections were carried out, and
- 420 goods orders were dispatched to customers.

*Part One*

KL's production during the quarter included components $r$, $s$ and $t$. The following information is available:

|  | Component r | Component s | Component t |
| --- | --- | --- | --- |
| Direct labour hours worked | 25 | 480 | 50 |
| Direct material costs | £1 200 | £2 900 | £1 800 |
| Component consignments received | 42 | 24 | 28 |
| Production runs | 16 | 18 | 12 |
| Quality inspections | 10 | 8 | 18 |
| Goods orders dispatched | 22 | 85 | 46 |
| Quantity produced | 560 | 12 800 | 2 400 |

In April 2001 a potential customer asked KL to quote for the supply of a new component ($z$) to a given specification. 1000 units of $z$ are to be supplied each quarter for a two-year period. They will be paid for in equal instalments on the last day of each quarter. The job will involve an initial design cost of £40 000 and production will involve 80 direct labour hours, £2000 materials, 20 component consignments, 15 production runs, 30 quality inspections and 4 goods dispatches per quarter.

KL's Sales Director comments:

'Now we have a modern ABC system, we can quote selling prices with confidence. The quarterly charge we quote should be the forecast ABC production cost of the units plus the design cost of the $z$ depreciated on a straight-line basis over the two years of the job – to which we should add a 25% mark-up for profit. We can base our forecast on costs experienced in the quarter ended March.

Requirements:
(a) Calculate the unit cost of components $r$, $s$ and

*t*, using KL's existing cost accounting system (single factory labour hour OAR). (5 marks)

(b) Explain how an ABC system would be developed using the information given. Calculate the unit cost of components *r*, *s* and *t*, using this ABC system. (11 marks)

(c) Calculate the charge per quarter that should be quoted for supply of component *z* in a manner consistent with the Sales Director's comments. Advise KL's management on the merits of this selling price, having regard to factors you consider relevant.

*Note:* KL's cost of capital is 3% per quarter. (9 marks)

*Part Two*

'It is often claimed that ABC provides better information concerning product costs than traditional management accounting techniques. It is also sometimes claimed that ABC provides better information as a guide to decision-making. However, one should treat these claims with caution. ABC may give a different impression of product costs but it is not necessarily a better impression. It may be wiser to try improving the use of traditional techniques before moving to ABC.'

Comment by KL's management accountant on the RAPIER report

Requirements:

(a) Explain the ideas concerning cost behaviour which underpin ABC. Explain why ABC may be better attuned to the modern manufacturing environment than traditional techniques. Explain why KL might or might not obtain a more meaningful impression of product costs through the use of ABC. (10 marks)

(b) Explain how the traditional cost accounting system being used by KL might be improved to provide more meaningful product costs. (6 marks)

(c) Critically appraise the reported claim that ABC gives better information as a guide to decision-making than do traditional product costing techniques. (9 marks)

(Total 25 marks)

*Part Three*

'The *lean enterprise* [characterised by just-in-time (JIT), total quality management (TQM) and supportive supplier relations] is widely considered a better approach to manufacturing. Some have suggested, however, that ABC hinders the spread of the lean enterprise by making apparent the cost of small batch sizes.'

Comment by an academic accountant

Requirements:

(a) Explain the roles that JIT, TQM and supportive supplier relations play in a modern manufacturing management. How might the adoption of such practices improve KL's performance? (10 marks)

(b) Explain what the writer of the above statement means by 'the cost of small batch sizes'. Critically appraise the manner in which this cost is treated by KL's existing (single OAR-based) cost accounting system. Explain the benefits that KL might obtain through a full knowledge and understanding of this cost. (10 marks)

(c) Explain and discuss the extent to which academic research in the area of management accounting is likely to influence the practice of management accounting. (5 marks)

(Total 25 marks)

*CIMA Stage 3 Management Accounting Applications*

# Pricing decisions and profitability analysis

Accounting information is often an important input to pricing decisions. Organizations that sell products or services that are highly customized or differentiated from each other by special features, or who are market leaders, have some discretion in setting selling prices. In these organizations the pricing decision will be influenced by the cost of the product. The cost information that is accumulated and presented is therefore important for pricing decisions. In other organizations prices are set by overall market and supply forces and they have little influence over the selling prices of their products and services. Nevertheless, cost information is still of considerable importance in these organizations for determining the relative profitability of different products and services so that management can determine the target product mix to which its marketing effort should be directed.

In this chapter we shall focus on both of the above situations. We shall consider the role that accounting information plays in determining the selling price by a price setting firm. Where prices are set by the market our emphasis will be on examining the cost information that is required for product-mix decisions. In particular, we shall focus on both product and customer profitability analysis. The content of this chapter is normally applicable only to second year management accounting courses.

The theoretical solution to pricing decisions is derived from economic theory, which explains how the optimal selling price is determined. A knowledge of economic theory provides a suitable framework for considering the cost information that is appropriate for pricing decisions. This chapter therefore begins with a description of economic theory.

## Learning objectives:

After studying this chapter, you should be able to:

- describe how the optimum output and selling price is determined using economic theory;
- calculate the optimum selling price using simple calculus;
- explain the relevant cost information that should be presented in price setting firms for both short-term and long-term decisions;
- describe product and customer profitability analysis and the information that should be included for managing the product and customer mix;
- explain the role that target costing plays in the pricing decision;
- describe the different cost-plus pricing methods for deriving selling prices;
- explain the limitations of cost-plus pricing;
- justify why cost-plus pricing is widely used;
- describe the different pricing policies.

# Economic theory

The central feature of the economic model is the assumption that the firm will attempt to set the selling price at a level where profits are maximized. For **monopolistic/imperfect competition** the model assumes that the lower the price, the larger will be the volume of sales.[1] This relationship is depicted in Figure 11.1, which is known as a demand curve.

Points A and B represent two of many possible price/quantity combinations. You will see that at a price $P_a$, the quantity demanded will be $Q_a$, while at the lower price of $P_b$ the quantity demanded will increase to $Q_b$. The economist describes the sensitivity of demand to changes in price as the **price elasticity of demand**. Demand is elastic when there are substitutes for a product, or when customers do not value the product very highly; the result is that a small increase/decrease in price causes a large decrease/increase in the quantity demanded. Alternatively, demand is inelastic when customers place a high value on the product, or when no close substitutes exist; the result is that a small increase/decrease in price causes only a small decrease/increase in the quantity demanded (see Figure 11.2).

If you compare the two graphs in Figure 11.2, you will see that in (a) an increase in price from $P_A$ to $P_B$ results in only a small reduction in the quantity demanded, whereas in (b) the same increase in price results in a large reduction in the quantity demanded.

## ESTABLISHING THE OPTIMUM SELLING PRICE

The precise quantification of the relationship between the selling price and the quantity demanded is very difficult in practice, but let us assume here that management has produced an estimate of the sales demand at various selling prices, as shown in Exhibit 11.1.

You will note that if the price is reduced from £40 to £38 the total revenue will increase by £18, and that each successive price reduction causes incremental or marginal revenue to increase by successively smaller amounts. This process eventually results in a decline in total revenue when the price per unit is reduced from £30 to £28.

To determine the optimum selling price (i.e. the price at which total profits are maximized), it is also necessary for management to estimate the total costs for each of the sales levels given in Exhibit 11.1; this cost information is set out in Exhibit 11.2.

**EXHIBIT 11.1**

*Estimate of sales demand at different price levels*

| Price (£) | Unit of sales demand | Total revenue (£) | Marginal revenue (£) |
|---|---|---|---|
| 40 | 10 | 400 | |
| 38 | 11 | 418 | 18 |
| 36 | 12 | 432 | 14 |
| 34 | 13 | 442 | 10 |
| 32 | 14 | 448 | 6 |
| 30 | 15 | 450 | 2 |
| 28 | 16 | 448 | − 2 |

**EXHIBIT 11.2**

*Estimate of total costs at different volume levels*

The final stage is to calculate the profit for each sales level and select the most profitable price–volume combination. The profit calculations are obtained by combining the information given in Exhibits 11.1 and 11.2 (see Exhibit 11.3).

You can see from Exhibit 11.3 that profits are maximized at a selling price of £34 when 13 units are sold.

| Price (£) | Demand and output | Total costs (£) | Marginal cost (£) |
|---|---|---|---|
| 40 | 10 | 360 | |
| 38 | 11 | 364 | 4 |
| 36 | 12 | 370 | 6 |
| 34 | 13 | 378 | 8 |
| 32 | 14 | 388 | 10 |
| 30 | 15 | 400 | 12 |
| 28 | 16 | 414 | 14 |

**FIGURE 11.1** *A demand curve.*

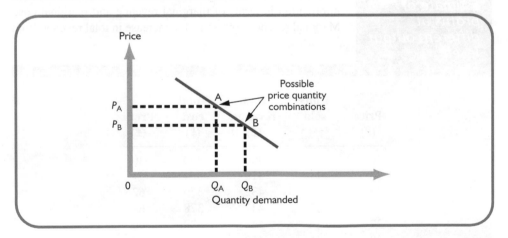

## GRAPHICAL PRESENTATION

Economic theory would normally present the information contained in Exhibits 11.1 to 11.3 in graphical form as shown in Figure 11.3.

The shape of the graphs for the total revenue and the total cost lines is based on the explanations outlined in Chapter 8. If you refer to the top diagram in Figure 11.3, you will see that it indicates that the difference between total revenue and total cost increases as long as total revenue is climbing more rapidly than total cost. When total cost is climbing more rapidly than total revenue (i.e. unit marginal cost exceeds unit marginal revenue), a decision to increase the number of units sold will actually reduce the total profit. The

**FIGURE 11.2** *Price elasticity of demand: (a) inelastic demand; (b) elastic demand.*

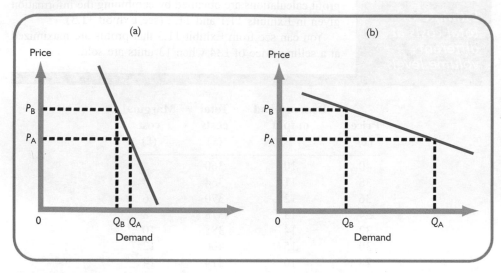

**EXHIBIT 11.3**

*Estimate of profits at different output levels*

difference between total cost and total revenue is the greatest at a volume level of 13 units; the price required to generate this demand is £34 and this is the optimum selling price.

The lower part of Figure 11.3 shows the cost and revenue information in terms of marginal revenue and marginal cost. Marginal revenue represents the increase in total revenue from

| Price (£) | Units sold | Total revenue (£) | Total cost (£) | Profit (£) |
|---|---|---|---|---|
| 40 | 10 | 400 | 360 | 40 |
| 38 | 11 | 418 | 364 | 54 |
| 36 | 12 | 432 | 370 | 62 |
| 34 | 13 | 442 | 378 | 64 |
| 32 | 14 | 448 | 388 | 60 |
| 30 | 15 | 450 | 400 | 50 |
| 28 | 16 | 448 | 414 | 34 |

the sale of one additional unit, and marginal cost represents the increase in total cost when output is increased by one additional unit. Note that the marginal revenue line slopes downwards to the right as demand increases, reflecting the fact that the slope of the total revenue line decreases as demand increases. Similarly, the marginal cost line slopes upwards because of the assumption that total cost increases as output increases.

Exhibit 11.1 and the demand/price curve in the lower part of Figure 11.3 indicates that to increase sales demand from 10 units to 11 units it is necessary to reduce the selling price from £40 to £38. This increases total revenue from £400 to £418, the difference of £18

**FIGURE 11.3** *Economist's model for establishing optimum price. MC, marginal cost; MR, marginal revenue; TC, total cost; TR, total revenue.*

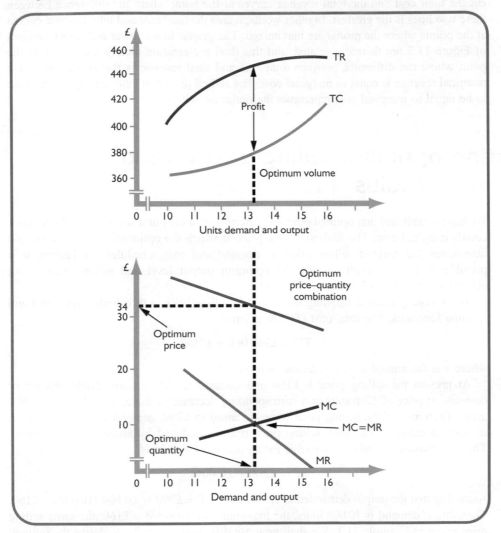

being the marginal revenue of the eleventh unit (shown in the graph as the height of the marginal revenue line at that point). The marginal revenues for the 12th, 13th and 14th units are £14, £10 and £6 respectively. The marginal cost is calculated by assessing the cost of one extra unit (or batch, etc.), and this information is presented in Exhibit 11.2. For example, the marginal cost is £4 for the eleventh unit and £6 for the twelfth unit. The marginal cost is plotted in Figure 11.3, and the optimum price is determined by the intersection of the marginal revenue and marginal cost curves; this is at a price of £34, when sales demand will be 13 units. Note that the intersection of the graphs occurs at a demand just in excess of 13 units. Clearly, we must work in whole units demanded, and therefore the optimal output is 13 units.

The demand curve is also included in the lower part of Figure 11.3, and to obtain the optimum price it is necessary to extend a vertical line upwards from the intersection of the marginal cost and marginal revenue curves. The point where this line cuts the demand curve provides us with the optimum selling price.

Note that if the vertical line at the point of intersection of the marginal cost and marginal revenue curve is extended further upwards into the top part of the graph, it will cut the total cost and the total revenue curves at the point where the difference between these two lines is the greatest. In other words, it cuts the total cost and total revenue curves at the points where the profits are maximized. The graphs in the lower and upper sections of Figure 11.3 are therefore related, and this dual presentation clearly indicates that the point where the difference between total cost and total revenue is the greatest is where marginal revenue is equal to marginal cost. The selling price that causes marginal revenue to be equal to marginal cost represents the optimum selling price.

# Calculating optimum selling prices using differential calculus

We have established that optimal output is determined at the point where marginal revenue equals marginal cost. The highest selling price at which the optimum output can be sold determines the optimal selling price. If demand and cost schedules are known, it is possible to derive simultaneously the optimum output level and selling price using differential calculus. Consider Example 11.1.

The first step when calculating the optimum selling price is to calculate total cost and revenue functions. The total cost (TC) function is

$$TC = £700\,000 + £70x$$

where $x$ is the annual level of demand and output.

At present the selling price is £160 and demand is 10 000 units. Each increase or decrease in price of £2 results in a corresponding decrease or increase in demand of 500 units. Therefore, if the selling price were increased to £200, demand would be zero. To increase demand by one unit, selling price must be reduced by £0.004 (£2/500 units). Thus the maximum selling price (SP) for an output of $x$ units is

$$SP = £200 - £0.004x$$

Assuming that the output demanded is 10 000 units $SP = £200 - £0.004\,(10\,000) = £160$. Therefore if demand is 10 000 units, the maximum selling price is £160, the same selling price given in Example 11.1. We shall now use differential calculus to derive the optimal selling price:

$$TC = £700\,000 + £70x$$

$$SP = £200 - £0.004x$$

Therefore total revenue (TR) for an output of $x$ units $= £200x - £0.004x^2$

$$\text{marginal cost (MC)} = \frac{dTC}{dx} = £70$$

$$\text{marginal revenue (MR)} = \frac{dTR}{dx} = £200 - £0.008x$$

At the optimum output level

$$\frac{dTC}{dx} = \frac{dTR}{dx}$$

**EXAMPLE 11.1**

A division within the Caspian Company sells a single product. Divisional fixed costs are £700 000 per annum and a variable cost of £70 is incurred for each additional unit produced and sold over a very large range of outputs. The current selling price for the product is £160, and at this price 10 000 units are demanded per annum. It is estimated that for each successive increase in price of £2 annual demand will be reduced by 500 units. Alternatively, for each £2 reduction in price demand will increase by 500 units.

Calculate the optimum output and price for the product assuming that if prices are set within each £2 range there will be a proportionate change in demand.

And so

$$£70 = £200 - £0.008x$$

$$x = 162\,500 \text{ units}$$

The highest selling price at which this output can be sold is

$$SP = £200 - £0.004 \, (16\,250)$$

so

$$SP = £135$$

Thus optimum selling price and output are £135 and 162 500 units respectively.

For a more detailed example of setting optimal selling prices using differential calculus you should refer to the self-assesment question and answer at the end of this chapter.

# Difficulties with applying economic theory

Economic theory is extremely difficult to apply in practice. The difficulties can be grouped into three categories. First, economic theory assumes that a firm can estimate a demand curve for its products. Techniques have been developed for estimating demand curves at the industry, or aggregate level for undifferentiated products such as automobiles, coffee and crude oil but consider the difficulties of estimating demand curves below the aggregate level. Most firms have hundreds of different products and varieties, some with complex inter-relationships, and it is therefore an extremely difficult task to estimate demand curves at the individual product level. The problem becomes even more complex when competitive reactions are taken into account since these are likely to impact on the price/demand estimates that have been incorporated in the demand curve.

Secondly, the basic model of economic theory assumes only price influences the quantity demanded. In practice, product quality and packaging, advertising and promotion, the credit terms offered and the after-sales service provided all have an important influence on price. Thus a model that includes only price will fail to capture all of the factors that determine customer demand.

Thirdly, the marginal cost curve for each individual product can only be determined after considerable analysis and the final result may only represent an approximation of the true marginal cost function particularly where significant joint product costs exist. However, whilst an approximation of the cost function may suffice for the application of economic theory the estimation of demand curves for each major product represents the major reason why many firms do not directly apply economic theory in practice.

Nevertheless, economic theory does provide useful insights and stresses the need for managers to think about price/demand relationships, even if the relationships cannot be precisely measured. For example, we shall see that many firms add a profit margin to a product's cost. If managers can identify products or customers where demand is inelastic they can add higher margins to a product's costs. Alternatively, where demand is elastic price changes are likely to be crucial and accurate cost measurement becomes vital. There is a danger where profit margins are reduced to minimal percentage figures that any undercosting of products may result in acceptance of unprofitable business whereas overcosting may result in the loss of profitable business to competitors.

# The role of cost information in pricing decisions

Most organizations need to make decisions about setting or accepting selling prices for their products or services. In some firms prices are set by overall market supply and demand forces and the firm has little or no influence over the selling prices of its products or services. This situation is likely to occur where there are many firms in an industry and there is little to distinguish their products from each other. No one firm can influence prices significantly by its own actions. For example, in commodity markets such as wheat, coffee, rice and sugar prices are set for the market as a whole based on the forces of supply and demand. Also, small firms operating in an industry where prices are set by the dominant market leaders will have little influence over the price of their products or services. Firms that have little or no influence over the prices of their products or services are described as **price takers**.

In contrast firms selling products or services which are highly customized or differentiated from each other by special features, or who are market leaders, have some discretion in setting prices. Here the pricing decision will be influenced by the cost of the product, the actions of competitors and the extent to which customers value the product. We shall describe those firms that have some discretion over setting the selling price of their products or services as **price setters**. In practice, firms may be price setters for some of their products and price takers for others.

Where firms are price setters cost information is often an important input into the pricing decision. Cost information is also of vital importance to price takers in deciding on the output and mix of products and services to which their marketing effort should be directed, given their market prices. For both price takers and price setters the decision time horizon determines the cost information that is relevant for product pricing or output-mix decisions. We shall therefore consider the following four different situations:

1. a price setting firm facing short-run pricing decisions;
2. a price setting firm facing long-run pricing decisions;
3. a price taker firm facing short-run product-mix decisions;
4. a price taker firm facing long-run product-mix decisions.

# A price setting firm facing short-run pricing decisions

Companies can encounter situations where they are faced with the opportunity of bidding for a one-time special order in competition with other suppliers. In this situation only the incremental costs of undertaking the order should be taken into account. It is likely that most of the resources required to fill the order will have already been acquired and the cost of these resources will be incurred whether or not the bid is accepted by the customer. Typically, the incremental costs are likely to consist of:

- extra materials that are required to fulfil the order;
- any extra part-time labour, overtime or other labour costs;
- the extra energy and maintenance costs for the machinery and equipment required to complete the order.

The incremental costs of one-off special orders in service companies are likely to be minimal. For example, the incremental cost of accepting one-off special business for a hotel may consist of only the cost of additional meals, laundering and bathroom facilities. In most cases, incremental costs are likely to be confined to items within unit-level activities. Resources for batch, product and service-sustaining activities are likely to have already been acquired and in most cases no extra costs on the supply of activities are likely to be incurred.

Bids should be made at prices that exceed incremental costs. Any excess of revenues over incremental costs will provide a contribution to committed costs which would not otherwise have been obtained. Given the short-term nature of the decision long-term considerations are likely to be non-existent and, apart from the consideration of bids by competitors, cost data are likely to be the dominant factor in determining the bid price.

Any bid for one-time special orders that is based on covering only short-term incremental costs must meet all of the following conditions:

- Sufficient capacity is available for all resources that are required to fulfil the order. If some resources are fully utilized, opportunity costs (see Chapter 9 for an illustration) of the scarce resources must be covered by the bid price.
- The bid price will not affect the future selling prices and the customer will not expect repeat business to be priced to cover short-term incremental costs.
- The order will utilize unused capacity for only a short period and capacity will be released for use on more profitable opportunities. If more profitable opportunities do not exist and a short-term focus is always adopted to utilize unused capacity then the effect of pricing a series of special orders over several periods to cover incremental costs constitutes a long-term decision. Thus, the situation arises whereby the decision to reduce capacity is continually deferred and short-term incremental costs are used for long-term decisions.

# A price setting firm facing long-run pricing decisions

In the long run firms can adjust the supply of virtually all of their activity resources. Therefore a product or service should be priced to cover all of the resources that are committed to it. If a firm is unable to generate sufficient revenues to cover the long-run costs of all its products, and its business sustaining costs, then it will make losses and will not be able to survive. Setting prices to cover all of the resources that are committed to each individual product (or service) requires a costing system that accurately measures resources consumed by each product. If inaccurate costs are used undercosting or overcosting will occur. In the former situation there is a danger that prices will be set

**EXAMPLE 11.2**

The Kalahari Company has received a request for a price quotation from one of its regular customers for an order of 500 units with the following characteristics:

| | |
|---|---|
| Direct labour per unit produced | 2 hours |
| Direct materials per unit produced | £22 |
| Machine hours per unit produced | 1 hour |
| Number of component and material purchases | 6 |
| Number of production runs for the components prior to assembly | 4 |
| Average set-up time per production run | 3 hours |
| Number of deliveries | 1 |
| Number of customer visits | 2 |
| Engineering design and support | 50 hours |
| Customer support | 50 hours |

Details of the activities required for the order are as follows:

| Activity | Activity cost driver rate |
|---|---|
| Direct labour processing and assembly activities | £10 per labour hour |
| Machine processing | £30 per machine hour |
| Purchasing and receiving materials and components | £100 per purchase order |
| Scheduling production | £250 per production run |
| Setting-up machines | £120 per set-up hour |
| Packaging and delivering orders to customers | £400 per delivery |
| Invoicing and accounts administration | £120 per customer order |
| Marketing and order negotiation | £300 per customer visit |
| Customer support activities including after sales service | £50 per customer service hour |
| Engineering design and support | £80 per engineering hour |

that fail to cover the long-run resources committed to a product. Conversely, with the latter situation profitable business may be lost because overstated product costs have resulted in excessive prices being set that adversely affect sales volumes and revenues. Where firms are price setters there are stronger grounds for justifying the adoption of ABC systems.

The terms **full cost** or **long-run cost** are used to represent the sum of the cost of all those resources that are committed to a product in the long-term. The term is not precisely defined and may include or exclude facility/business sustaining costs. Let us now consider a full cost computation for a product pricing decision using an ABC system. You should now refer to the data presented in Example 11.2.

The estimate of the cost of the resources required to fulfil the order is as follows:

*Unit-level expenses*

| | | |
|---|---|---|
| Direct materials (500 × £22) | 11 000 | |
| Direct labour (500 × 2 hours × £10) | 10 000 | |
| Machining (500 × 1 hour × £30) | 15 000 | 36 000 |

*Batch-level expenses*

| | | |
|---|---|---|
| Purchasing and receiving materials and components (6 × £100) | 600 | |
| Scheduling production (4 production runs × £250) | 1000 | |
| Setting-up machines (4 production runs × 3 hours × £120) | 1440 | |
| Packaging and delivering (1 delivery at £400) | 400 | 3 440 |
| *Product-sustaining expenses* | | |
| Engineering design and support (50 hours × £80) | | 4 000 |
| *Customer-sustaining expenses* | | |
| Marketing and order negotiation (2 visits × £300 per visit) | 600 | |
| Customer support (50 support hours × £50) | 2500 | 3 100 |
| Total cost of resources (excluding facility-sustaining costs) | | 46 540 |

The full cost (excluding facility-sustaining costs) of the order is £46 540. It was pointed out in the previous chapter that facility-sustaining costs are incurred to support the organization as a whole and not for individual products. Therefore they should not be allocated to products for most decisions. Any allocation will be arbitrary. However, such costs must be covered by sales revenues, and for pricing purposes their allocation can be justified as long as they are separately reported.

What allocation base should be used for facility-sustaining costs? The answer is a base that will influence behaviour that the organization wishes to encourage. For example, if the organization has adopted a strategy of standardizing and reducing the number of separate parts maintained it could choose the number of parts as the allocation base. Thus, the facility-sustaining costs allocated to a product would increase with the number of parts used for an order. If a behaviourally desirable allocation base cannot be established then a base should be selected that has a neutral effect and which does not encourage undesirable behaviour. Reporting facility-sustaining costs as a separate category should reduce, or eliminate, the behavioural impact of the chosen allocation base since this provides a clear signal to management that it is an arbitrary allocation, and not a cause-and-effect allocation. We shall look at the behavioural impact of cost drivers in more detail in Chapter 22.

To determine a proposed selling price an appropriate percentage mark-up is added to the estimated cost. In our example facility-sustaining costs have not been allocated to the order. Thus the mark-up that is added should be sufficient to cover a fair share of facility-sustaining costs and provide a profit contribution. Where facility-sustaining costs are allocated a smaller percentage mark-up would be added since the mark-up is required to provide only a profit contribution. Let us assume that the Kalahari Company adds a mark-up of 20%. This would result in a mark-up of £9308 (20% × £46 540) being added to the cost estimate of £46 540, giving a proposed selling price of £55 848. The approach that we have adopted here is called cost-plus pricing. We shall discuss cost-plus pricing and the factors influencing the determination of the profit mark-ups later in the chapter.

Note that the activity-based cost information provides a better understanding of cost behaviour. The batch, product and customer-sustaining costs are unrelated to quantity ordered whereas the unit-level costs are volume related. This provides useful information for salespersons in negotiations with the customer relating to the price and size of the order. Assume that the customer considers purchasing 3000 units, instead of the 500 units originally quoted. If the larger order will enable the company to order 3000 components, instead of 500, and each production run for a component processes 3000 units instead of 500, the batch-level expenses will remain unchanged. Also the cost of the product and customer-sustaining activities will be the same for the larger order but the cost of the unit-level activity resources required will increase by a factor of six because six times the amount of resources will be required for the larger order. Thus the cost of the resources used for an order of 3000 units will be:

|  | (£) |
| --- | --- |
| Unit-level expenses (6 × £36 000[a]) | 216 000 |
| Batch-level expenses | 3 440 |
| Product-sustaining expenses | 4 000 |
| Customer-sustaining expenses | 3 100 |
| Total cost of resources (excluding facility-sustaining costs) | 226 540 |

*Note*
[a]Unit-level expenses for an order of 500 units multiplied by a factor of 6.

The cost per unit for a 500 unit order size is £93.08 (£46 540/500) compared with £75.51 (£226 540/3000) for a 3000 unit order size and the resulting proposed unit selling prices are £111.70 (£93.08 × 120%) and £90.61 (£75.51 × 120%) respectively.

## PRICING NON-CUSTOMIZED PRODUCTS

In Example 11.2 the Kalahari Company was faced with a pricing decision for the sale of a highly customized product to a single customer. The pricing decision would have been based on direct negotiations with the customer for a known quantity. In contrast, a market leader must make a pricing decision, normally for large and unknown volumes, of a single product that is sold to thousands of different customers. To apply cost-plus pricing in this situation an estimate is required of sales volume to determine a unit cost which will determine the cost-plus selling price. This circular process occurs because we are now faced with two unknowns which have a cause-and-effect relationship, namely selling price and sales volume. In this situation it is recommended that cost-plus selling prices are estimated for a range of potential sales volumes. Consider the information presented in Example 11.3 (Case A).

You will see that the Auckland Company has produced estimates of total costs for a range of activity levels. Ideally, the cost estimates should be built up in a manner similar to the activity-based cost estimates that were used by the Kalahari Company in Example 11.2. However, for brevity the cost build-up is not shown. Instead of adding a percentage profit margin the Auckland Company has added a fixed lump sum target profit contribution of £2 million.

The information presented indicates to management the sales volumes, and their accompanying selling prices, that are required to generate the required profit contribution. The unit cost calculation indicates the break-even selling price at each sales volume that is required to cover the cost of the resources committed at that particular volume. Management must assess the likelihood of selling the specified volumes at the designated prices and choose the price which they consider has the highest probability of generating at least the specified sales volume. If none of the sales volumes are likely to be achieved at the designated selling prices management must consider how demand can be stimulated and/or costs reduced to make the product viable. If neither of these, or other strategies, are successful the product should not be launched. The final decision must be based on management judgement and knowledge of the market.

The situation presented in Example 11.3 represents the most extreme example of the lack of market data for making a pricing decision. If we reconsider the pricing decision faced by the company it is likely that similar products are already marketed and information may be available relating to their market shares and sales volumes. Assuming that Auckland's product is differentiated from other similar products a relative comparison should be possible of its strengths and weaknesses and whether customers would be prepared to pay a price in excess of the prices of similar products. It is therefore possible that Auckland may be able to undertake market research to obtain rough approximations of

## EXAMPLE 11.3

*Case A*

The Auckland Company is launching a new product. Sales volume will be dependent on the selling price and customer acceptance but because the product differs substantially from other products within the same product category it has not been possible to obtain any meaningful estimates of price/demand relationships. The best estimate is that demand is likely to range between 100 000 and 200 000 units provided that the selling price is less than £100. Based on this information the company has produced the following cost estimates and selling prices required to generate a target profit contribution of £2 million from the product.

| | | | | | | |
|---|---|---|---|---|---|---|
| Sales volume (000's) | 100 | 120 | 140 | 160 | 180 | 200 |
| Total cost (£000's) | 10 000 | 10 800 | 11 200 | 11 600 | 12 600 | 13 000 |
| Required profit contribution (£000's) | 2 000 | 2 000 | 2 000 | 2 000 | 2 000 | 2 000 |
| Required sales revenues (£000's) | 12 000 | 12 800 | 13 200 | 13 600 | 14 600 | 15 000 |
| Required selling price to achieve target profit contribution (£) | 120.00 | 106.67 | 94.29 | 85.00 | 81.11 | 75.00 |
| Unit cost (£) | 100.00 | 90.00 | 80.00 | 72.50 | 70.00 | 65.00 |

*Case B*

Assume now an alternative scenario for the product in Case A. The same cost schedule applies but the £2 million minimum contribution no longer applies. In addition, Auckland now undertakes market research. Based on this research, and comparisons with similar product types and their current selling prices and sales volumes, estimates of sales demand at different selling prices have been made. These estimates, together with the estimates of total costs obtained in Case A are shown below:

| | | | | | |
|---|---|---|---|---|---|
| Potential selling price | £100 | £90 | £80 | £70 | £60 |
| Estimated sales volume at the potential selling price (000's) | 120 | 140 | 180 | 190 | 200 |
| Estimated total sales revenue (£000's) | 12 000 | 12 600 | 14 400 | 13 300 | 12 000 |
| Estimated total cost (£000's) | 10 800 | 11 200 | 12 600 | 12 800 | 13 000 |
| Estimated profit (loss) contribution (£000s) | 1 200 | 1 400 | 1 800 | 500 | (1 000) |

demand levels at a range of potential selling prices. Let us assume that Auckland adopts this approach, and apart from this, the facts are the same as those given in Example 11.3 (Case A).

Now look at Case B in Example 11.3. The demand estimates are given for a range of selling prices. In addition the projected costs, sales revenues and profit contribution are shown. You can see that profits are maximized at a selling price of £80. The information also shows the effect of pursuing other pricing policies. For example, a lower selling price of £70 might be selected to discourage competition and ensure that a larger share of the market is obtained in the future. Where demand estimates are available ABC cost information should be presented for different potential volume levels and compared with projected sales revenues derived from estimated price/output relationships. Ideally, the cost projections should be based on a life-cycle costing approach to ensure that costs incurred over the whole of a product's life cycle are taken into account in the pricing decision. We shall look at life-cycle costing in Chapter 22.

## TARGET COSTING

Instead of using cost-plus pricing whereby cost is used as the starting point to determine the selling price, target costing is the reverse of this process. With target costing the starting point is the determination of the target selling price. Next a standard or desired profit margin is deducted to get a target cost for the product. The aim is to ensure that the future cost will not be higher than the target cost. The stages involved in target costing can be summarized as follows:

Stage 1: determine the target price which customers will be prepared to pay for the product;

Stage 2: deduct a target profit margin from the target price to determine the target cost;

Stage 3: estimate the actual cost of the product;

Stage 4: if estimated actual cost exceeds the target cost investigate ways of driving down the actual cost to the target cost.

The first stage requires market research to determine the customers' perceived value of the product, its differentiation value relative to competing products and the price of competing products. The target profit margin depends on the planned return on investment for the organization as a whole and profit as a percentage of sales. This is then decomposed into a target profit for each product which is then deducted from the target price to give the target cost. The target cost is compared with the predicted actual cost. If the predicted actual cost is above the target cost intensive efforts are made to close the gap. Product designers focus on modifying the design of the product so that it becomes cheaper to produce. Manufacturing engineers also concentrate on methods of improving production processes and efficiencies.

The aim is to drive the predicted actual cost down to the target cost but if the target cost cannot be achieved at the pre-production stage the product may still be launched if management are confident that the process of continuous improvement and learning curve effects (see Chapter 24) will enable the target cost to be achieved early in the product's life. If this is not possible the product will not be launched.

The major attraction of target costing is that marketing factors and customer research provide the basis for determining selling price whereas cost tends to be the dominant factor with cost-plus pricing. A further attraction is that the approach requires the collaboration of product designers, production engineers, marketing and finance staff whose focus is on managing costs at the product design stage. At this stage costs can be most effectively managed because a decision to committing the firm to incur costs will not have been made.

Target costing is most suited for setting prices for non-customized and high sales volume products. It is also an important mechanism for managing the cost of future products. We shall therefore look at target costing in more detail when we focus on cost management in Chapter 22.

# A price taker firm facing short-run product-mix decisions

Price taking firms may be faced with opportunities of taking on short-term business at a market determined selling price. In this situation the cost information that is required is no different from that of a price setting firm making a short-run pricing decision. In other words, accepting short-term business where the incremental sales revenues exceed incremental short-run costs will provide a contribution towards committed fixed costs which would not otherwise have been obtained. However, such business is acceptable only if the same conditions as those specified for a price setting firm apply. You should remember that these conditions are:

- sufficient capacity is available for all resources that are required from undertaking the business (if some resources are fully utilized, opportunity costs of the scarce resources must be covered by the selling price);
- the company will not commit itself to repeat longer-term business that is priced to cover only short-term incremental costs;
- the order will utilize unused capacity for only a short period and capacity will be released for use on more profitable opportunities.

Besides considering new short-term opportunities organizations may, in certain situations, review their existing product-mix over a short-term time horizon. Consider a situation where a firm has excess capacity which is being retained for an expected upsurge in demand. If committed resources are to be maintained then the product profitability analysis of existing products should be based on a comparison of incremental revenues with short-term incremental costs. The same principle applies as that which applied for accepting new short-term business where spare capacity exists. That is, in the short term products should be retained if their incremental revenues exceed their incremental short-term costs.

Where short-term capacity constraints apply, such that the firm has profitable products whose sales demand exceeds its productive capacity, the product-mix should be based on maximizing contribution per limiting production factor as described in Chapter 9. You may wish to refer back to Example 9.2 for an illustration of this approach. Do note, however, that in the longer-term capacity constraints can be removed.

# A price taker firm facing long-run product-mix decisions

When prices are set by the market a firm has to decide which products to sell given their market prices. In the longer-term a firm can adjust the supply of resources committed to a product. Therefore the sales revenue from a service or product should exceed the cost of all the resources that are committed to it. Hence there is a need to undertake periodic profitability analysis to distinguish between profitable and unprofitable products in order to ensure that only profitable products are sold. Activity-based profitability analysis should be used to evaluate each product's long-run profitability. In the previous chapter Figure 10.2 was used to illustrate ABC hierarchical profitability analysis. This diagram is repeated in the form of Figure 11.4. You will see that where products are the cost object four different hierarchical levels have been identified – the individual products, the product brand groupings, the product line and finally the whole business unit. At the individual product

## FIGURE 11.4

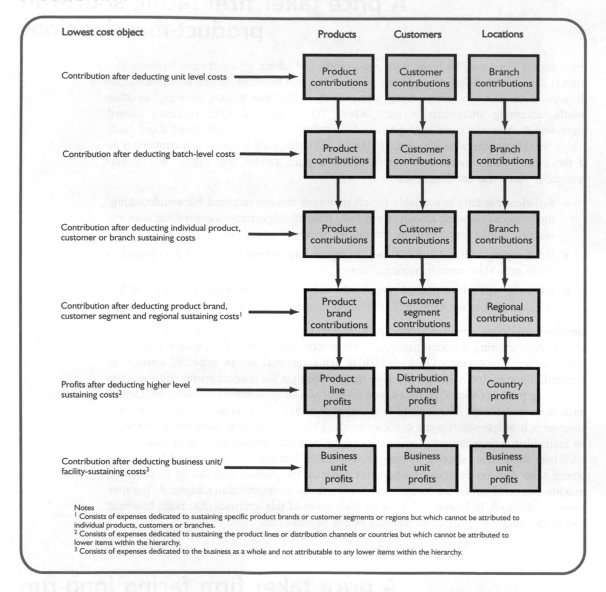

Notes
[1] Consists of expenses dedicated to sustaining specific product brands or customer segments or regions but which cannot be attributed to individual products, customers or branches.
[2] Consists of expenses dedicated to sustaining the product lines or distribution channels or countries but which cannot be attributed to lower items within the hierarchy.
[3] Consists of expenses dedicated to the business as a whole and not attributable to any lower items within the hierarchy.

level all of the resources required for undertaking the unit, batch and product-sustaining activities that are associated with a product would no longer be required if that product were discontinued. Thus, if the product's sales revenues do not exceed the cost of the resources of these activities it should be subject to a special study for a discontinuation decision.

If product groups are marketed as separate brands the next level within the profitability hierarchy is brand profitability. The sum of the individual product profit contributions (that is, sales revenues less the cost of the unit, batch and product-sustaining activities) within a brand must be sufficient to cover those brand-sustaining expenses that can be attributed to the brand but not the individual products within the brand. Thus it is possible for each individual product within the product brand to generate positive contributions but for the brand grouping to be unprofitable because the brand-sustaining expenses exceed the sum of individual product contributions. In these circumstances a special study is required to consider alternative courses of action that can be undertaken to make the brand profitable.

Product line profitability is the next level in the hierarchy in Figure 11.4. The same principle applies. That is, if the product line consists of a number of separate groupings of branded and non-branded products the sum of their contributions (that is, sales revenues less the cost of the unit, batch, product-sustaining and brand-sustaining activities) should exceed those product-line sustaining expenses that are attributable to the product line but not to lower levels within the profit hierarchy. Here a negative profit contribution would signal the need to undertake a major special study to investigate alternative courses of action relating to how the product line can be made profitable. Note that the lower levels within the profit hierarchy are those items below the row entitled 'profits after deducting higher level sustaining costs' shown in Figure 11.4.

The final level in the profitability hierarchy shown in Figure 11.4 relates to the profitability of the business unit as a whole. Here the profit for the business unit can be determined by deducting the facility or business-sustaining expenses that are attributable to the business unit as a whole, but not to lower levels within the hierarchy, from the sum of the product line contributions. Clearly a business must generate profits in the long term if it is to survive.

Most of the decisions are likely to be made at the individual product level. Before discontinuing a product other alternatives or considerations must be taken into account at the special study stage. In some situations it is important to maintain a full product line for marketing reasons. For example, if customers are not offered a full product line to choose from they may migrate to competitors who offer a wider choice. By reporting individual product profitability the cost of maintaining a full product line, being the sum of unprofitable products within the product line, is highlighted. Where maintaining a full product line is not required managers should consider other options before dropping unprofitable products. They should consider re-engineering or redesigning the products to reduce their resource consumption.

If a product cannot be made profitable and it is discontinued do remember our discussion in the previous chapter. That is, dropping products based on ABC information will improve overall profitability only if managers either eliminate the spending on the supply of activity resources that are no longer required to support the discontinued product or redeploy the released resources to produce more of other profitable products. If management does not adopt either of these courses of action the resources will remain in place, the cost of unused capacity will increase and the supply of resources will remain unchanged but sales revenues from the discontinued products will be lost.

The above discussion has concentrated on product profitability analysis. You will see from Figure 11.4 that the same principles can be applied to other cost objects, such as customers or locations. Increasing attention is now being given to customer profitability analysis. Given the importance of this topic we shall consider customer profitability analysis later in the chapter. However, at this stage it is more appropriate to examine cost-plus pricing in more detail.

# Cost-plus pricing

Our earlier discussion relating to short-run and long-run pricing suggested that, where it was virtually impossible to estimate demand, cost-plus pricing should be used. Cost-plus pricing was illustrated using the data presented in Examples 11.2 and 11.3. We shall now look at cost-plus pricing in more detail. Companies use different cost bases and mark-ups to determine their selling prices. Consider the information presented below:

| Cost base | Mark-up percentage | Cost-plus selling price |
|---|---|---|
| | (£) | (£) |
| (1) Direct variable costs | 200 | 250 | 500 |
| (2) Direct non-variable costs | 100 | | |
| (3) Total direct costs | 300 | 70 | 510 |
| (4) Indirect costs | 80 | | |
| (5) Total cost (excluding higher level sustaining costs) | 380 | 40 | 532 |
| (6) Higher level sustaining costs | 60 | | |
| (7) Total cost | 440 | 20 | 528 |

In the above illustration four different cost bases are used. In row (1) only direct variable costs are assigned to products for cost-plus pricing and a high percentage mark-up (250%) is added to cover direct non-variable costs, indirect costs and higher level sustaining costs and also to provide a contribution towards profit. Where products are the cost object higher level sustaining costs would include brand, product line and business-sustaining costs. This approach is best suited to short-term pricing decisions.

The second cost base is row (3). Here a smaller percentage margin (70%) is added to cover indirect costs, the higher level sustaining costs and to provide a contribution to profit. Indirect costs are not therefore assigned to products for cost-plus pricing. This cost base is appropriate if indirect costs are a small percentage of an organization's total costs. The disadvantage of adopting this approach is that the consumption of joint resources by products is not measured. By adding a percentage mark-up to direct costs indirect costs are effectively allocated to products using direct costs as the allocation base. Hence, the approach implicitly uses arbitrary apportionments.

The third cost base adds a lower profit margin (40%) to cover higher level sustaining costs and a profit contribution. This cost base is recommended for long-run pricing and was the approach illustrated in Examples 11.2 and 11.3. Ideally, ABC systems should be used to compute total (full) costs.

The final cost base is row (4) which includes an allocation of all costs but do remember that higher level sustaining costs cannot be allocated to products on a cause-and-effect basis. Some organizations, however, may wish to allocate all costs to products to ensure that all costs are covered in the cost base. The lowest percentage mark-up (20%) is therefore added since the aim is to provide only a profit contribution.

Some manufacturing organizations also use total manufacturing cost as the cost base and add a mark-up to cover non-manufacturing costs and a contribution to profit. The use of this method reflects the fact that many organizations choose to use the same costs as they use for stock valuation for other purposes, including product pricing. Also traditional costing systems are widely used for stock valuation. These systems were not designed to assign non-manufacturing costs to products and organizations. Therefore many organizations do not allocate non-manufacturing costs to products.

## ESTABLISHING TARGET MARK-UP PERCENTAGES

Mark-ups are related to the demand for a product. A firm is able to command a higher mark-up for a product that has a high demand. Mark-ups are also influenced by the elasticity of demand with higher mark-ups being applicable to products which are subject to inelastic demand. Mark-ups are also likely to decrease when competition is intensive. Target mark-up percentages tend to vary from product line to product line to correspond with well-established differences in custom, competitive position and likely demand. For example, luxury goods with a low sales turnover may attract high profit margins whereas non-luxury goods with a high sales turnover may attract low profit margins.

Another approach is to choose a mark-up to earn a **target rate of return on invested capital**. This approach seeks to estimate the amount of investment attributable to a product and then set a price that ensures a satisfactory return on investment for a given volume. For example, assume that cost per unit for a product is £100 and that the annual volume is 10 000 units. If the product requires an investment of £1 million and the target rate of return is 15%, the target mark-up will be

$$\frac{15\% \times £1\,000\,000}{10\,000\,\text{units}} = £15 \text{ per unit}$$

The target price will be £100 plus £15, or £115 per unit. The major problem of applying this approach is that it is difficult to determine the capital invested to support a product. Assets are normally used for many different products and therefore it is necessary to allocate investments in assets to different products. This process is likely to involve arbitrary allocations.

Note that once the target selling price has been calculated, it is rarely adopted without amendment. The price is adjusted upwards or downwards depending on such factors as the future capacity that is available, the extent of competition from other firms, and management's general knowledge of the market. For example, if the price calculation is much lower than that which management considers the customer will be prepared to pay, the price may be increased.

We may ask ourselves the question 'Why should cost-based pricing formulae be used when the final price is likely to be altered by management?' The answer is that cost based pricing formulae provide an initial approximation of the selling price. It is a target price and is important information, although by no means the only information that should be used when the final pricing decision is made. Management should use this information, together with their knowledge of the market and their intended pricing strategies, before the final price is set.

## LIMITATIONS OF COST-PLUS PRICING

The main criticism that has been made against cost-plus pricing is that demand is ignored. The price is set by adding a mark-up to cost, and this may bear no relationship to the price-demand relationship. It is assumed that prices should depend solely on costs. For example, a cost-plus formula may suggest a price of £20 for a product where the demand is 100 000 units, whereas at a price of £25 the demand might be 80 000 units. Assuming that the variable cost for each unit sold is £15, the total contribution will be £500 000 at a selling price of £20, compared with a total contribution of £800 000 at a selling price of £25. Thus cost-plus pricing formulae might lead to incorrect decisions. The following statement made over thirty years ago by Baxter and Oxenfeldt (1961) highlights the major weakness of cost-plus pricing. They state:

> On the other hand, inability to estimate demand accurately scarcely excuses the substitution of cost information for demand information. Crude estimates of demand may serve instead of careful estimates of demand but cost gives remarkably little insight into demand.

It is often claimed that cost-based pricing formulae serve as a pricing 'floor' shielding the seller from a loss. This argument, however, is incorrect since it is quite possible for a firm to lose money even though every product is priced higher than the estimated unit cost. The reason for this is that if sales demand falls below the activity level that was used to calculate the fixed cost per unit, the total sales revenue may be insufficient to cover the total fixed costs. Cost-plus pricing will only ensure that all the costs will be met, and the target profits earned, if the sales volume is equal to, or more than, the activity level that was used to estimate total unit costs.

Consider a hypothetical situation where all of the costs attributable to a product are fixed in the short-term and amount to £1 million. Assume that the cost per unit is £100 derived from an estimated volume of 10 000 units. The selling price is set at £130 using the cost-plus method and a mark-up of 30%. If actual sales volume is 7000 units, sales revenues will be £910 000 compared with total costs of £1 million. Therefore the product will incur a loss of £90 000 even though it is priced above full cost.

## REASONS FOR USING COST-PLUS PRICING

Considering the limitations of cost-plus pricing, why is it that these techniques are frequently used in practice? Baxter and Oxenfeldt (1961) suggest the following reasons:

> They offer a means by which plausible prices can be found with ease and speed, no matter how many products the firm handles. Moreover, its imposing computations look factual and precise, and its prices may well seem more defensible on moral grounds than prices established by other means. Thus a monopolist threatened by a public inquiry might reasonably feel that he is safeguarding his case by cost-plus pricing.

Another major reason for the widespread use of cost-plus pricing methods is that they may help a firm to predict the prices of other firms. For example, if a firm has been operating in an industry where average mark-ups have been 40% in the past, it may be possible to predict that competitors will be adding a 40% mark-up to their costs. Assuming that all the firms in the industry have similar cost structures, it will be possible to predict the price range within which competitors may price their products. If all the firms in an industry price their products in this way, it may encourage price stability.

In response to the main objection that cost-based pricing formulae ignore demand, we have noted that the actual price that is calculated by the formula is rarely adopted without amendments. The price is adjusted upwards or downwards after taking account of the number of sales orders on hand, the extent of competition from other firms, the importance of the customer in terms of future sales, and the policy relating to customer relations. Therefore it is argued that management attempts to adjust the mark-up based on the state of sales demand and other factors which are of vital importance in the pricing decision.

# Pricing policies

Cost information is only one of many variables that must be considered in the pricing decision. The final price that is selected will depend upon the pricing policy of the company. A price-skimming or pricing penetration policy might be selected.

A **price-skimming policy** is an attempt to exploit those sections of the market that are relatively insensitive to price changes. For example, high initial prices may be charged to take advantage of the novelty appeal of a new product when demand is initially inelastic. A skimming pricing policy offers a safeguard against unexpected future increases in costs, or a large fall in demand after the novelty appeal has declined. Once the market becomes saturated, the price can be reduced to attract that part of the market that has not yet been exploited. A skimming pricing policy should not be adopted when a number of close substitutes are already being marketed. Here the demand curve is likely to be elastic, and any price in excess of that being charged for a substitute product by a competitor is likely to lead to a large reduction in sales.

A **penetration pricing policy** is based on the concept of charging low prices initially with the intention of gaining rapid acceptance of the product. Such a policy is appropriate when close substitutes are available or when the market is easy to enter. The low price discourages potential competitors from entering the market and enables a company to establish a large share of the market. This can be achieved more easily when the product is new, than later on when buying habits have become established.

Many products have a **product life cycle** consisting of four stages: introductory, growth, maturity and decline. At the introductory stage the product is launched and there is minimal awareness and acceptance of it. Sales begin to expand rapidly at the growth stage because of introductory promotions and greater customer awareness, but this begins to taper off at the maturity stage as potential new customers are exhausted. At the decline stage sales diminish as the product is gradually replaced with new and better versions.

Sizer (1989) suggests that in the introductory stage it may be appropriate to shade upwards or downwards the price found by normal analysis to create a more favourable demand in future years. For example, he suggests that limited production capacity may rule out low prices. Therefore a higher initial price than that suggested by normal analysis may be set and progressively reduced, if and when (a) price elasticity of demand increases or (b) additional capacity becomes available. Alternatively if there is no production capacity constraint, a lower price than that suggested by normal analysis may be preferred. Such a price may result in a higher sales volume and a slow competitive reaction, which will enable the company to establish a large market share and to earn higher profits in the long term.

At the maturity stage a firm will be less concerned with the future effects of current selling prices and should adopt a selling price that maximizes short-run profits.

# Customer profitability analysis

In the past, management accounting reports have tended to concentrate on analysing profits by products. Increasing attention is now being given to analysing profits by customers using an activity-based costing approach. **Customer profitability analysis** provides important information that can be used to determine which classes of customers should be emphasized or de-emphasized and the price to charge for customer services. Kaplan and Cooper (1998) use Kanthal – a Harvard Business School case study – to illustrate the benefits of customer profitability analysis. Kanthal is a Swedish company that sells electric heating elements. Customer-related selling costs represent 34% of total costs. Until recently, Kanthal allocated these costs on the basis of sales value when special studies of customer profitability analysis were undertaken. An activity-based costing system was introduced that sought to explain the resources consumed by different customers. A detailed study of the resources used to service different types of customers identified two cost drivers:

1. Number of orders placed: each order had a large fixed cost, which did not vary with the quantity of items purchased. Thus a customer who placed 10 orders of 100 items per order generated 10 times more ordering cost than a customer who placed a single order of 1000 units.

2. Non-standard production items: these items were more costly to produce than standard items.

Kanthal estimated the cost per order and the cost of handling standard and non-standard items. A customer profitability analysis was prepared based on the sales for the previous year. This analysis revealed that only 40% of its customers were profitable and a further

**EXAMPLE 11.4**

The Darwin Company has recently adopted customer profitability analysis. It has undertaken a customer profitability review for the past 12 months. Details of the activities and the cost driver rates relating to those expenses that can be attributed to customers are as follows:

| Activity | Cost driver rate |
| --- | --- |
| Sales order processing | £300 per sales order |
| Sales visits | £200 per sales visit |
| Normal delivery costs | £1 per delivery kilometre travelled |
| Special (urgent) deliveries | £500 per special delivery |
| Credit collection costs | 10% per annum on average payment time |

Details relating to four of the firm's customers are as follows:

| Customer | A | B | Y | Z |
| --- | --- | --- | --- | --- |
| Number of sales orders | 200 | 100 | 50 | 30 |
| Number of sales visits | 20 | 10 | 5 | 5 |
| Kilometres per delivery | 300 | 200 | 100 | 50 |
| Number of deliveries | 100 | 50 | 25 | 25 |
| Total delivery kilometres | 30 000 | 10 000 | 2 500 | 1 250 |
| Special (urgent deliveries) | 20 | 5 | 0 | 0 |
| Average collection period (days) | 90 | 30 | 10 | 10 |
| Annual sales | £1 million | £1 million | £0.5 million | £2 million |
| Annual operating profit contribution[a] | £90 000 | £120 000 | £70 000 | £200 000 |

*Note*
[a]Consists of sales revenues less cost of unit-level and batch-related activities

10% lost 120% of the profits. In other words, 10% incurred losses equal to 120% of Kanthal's total profits. Two of the most unprofitable customers turned out to be among the top three in total sales volume. These two companies made many small orders of non-standard items.

Let us now look at an illustration of customer profitability analysis. Consider the information presented in Example 11.4. The profitability analysis in respect of the four customers is as follows:

| | A | B | Y | Z |
| --- | --- | --- | --- | --- |
| Customer attributable costs: | | | | |
| Sales order processing | 60 000 | 30 000 | 15 000 | 9 000 |
| Sales visits | 4 000 | 2 000 | 1 000 | 1 000 |
| Normal deliveries | 30 000 | 10 000 | 2 500 | 1 250 |
| Special (urgent) deliveries | 10 000 | 2 500 | 0 | 0 |
| Credit collection[a] | 24 658 | 8 220 | 1 370 | 5 480 |
| | 128 658 | 52 720 | 19 870 | 16 730 |
| Operating profit contribution | 90 000 | 120 000 | 70 000 | 200 000 |
| Contribution to higher level sustaining expenses | (38 658) | 67 280 | 50 130 | 183 270 |

*Note*
[a](Annual sales revenue × 10%) × (Average collection period/365)

A survey of 187 UK organizations by Drury and Tayles (2000) indicated that 60% used cost-plus pricing. Most of the organizations that used cost-plus pricing indicated that it was applied selectively. It accounted for less than 10% of total sales revenues for 26% of the respondents and more than 50% for 39% of the organizations. Most of the firms (85%) used full cost and the remaining 15% used direct cost as the pricing base. The survey also indicated that 74% analysed profits either by customers or customer categories.

An earlier UK study by Innes and Mitchell (1995a) reported that 50% of the respondents had used customer profitability analysis and a further 12% planned to do so in the future. Of those respondents that ranked customer profitability 60% indicated that the Pareto 80/20 rule broadly applied (that, is 20% of the customers were generating 80% of the profits).

You can see from the above analysis that A and B are high cost to serve whereas Y and Z are low cost to serve customers. Customer A provides a positive operating profit contribution but is unprofitable when customer attributable costs are taken into account. This is because customer A requires more sales orders, sales visits and normal and urgent deliveries than the other customers. In addition, the customer is slow to pay and has higher delivery costs than the other customers. Customer profitability analysis identifies the characteristics of high cost and low cost to serve customers and shows how customer profitability can be increased. The information should be used to persuade high cost to serve customers to modify their buying behaviour away from placing numerous small orders and/or purchasing non-standard items that are costly to make. For example, customer A can be made profitable if action is taken to persuade the customer to place a smaller number of larger quantity orders, avoid special deliveries and reduce the credit period. If unprofitable customers cannot be persuaded to change their buying behaviour selling prices should be increased (or discounts on list prices reduced) to cover the extra resources consumed. Thus ABC is required for customer profitability analysis so that the resources consumed by customers can be accurately measured.

The customer profitability analysis can also be used to rank customers by order of profitability based on **Pareto analysis**. This type of analysis is based on observations by Pareto that a very small proportion of items usually account for the majority of the value. For example, the Darwin Company might find that 20% of the customers account for 80% of the profits. Special attention can then be given to enhancing the relationships with the most profitable customers to ensure that they do not migrate to other competitors. In addition greater emphasis can be given to attracting new customers that have the same attributes as the most profitable customers.

Organizations, such as banks, often with a large customer base in excess of one million customers cannot apply customer profitability analysis at the individual customer level. Instead, they concentrate on customer segment profitability analysis by combining groups of customers into meaningful segments. This enables profitable segments to be highlighted where customer retention is particularly important and provides an input for determining the appropriate marketing strategies for attracting the new customers that have the most profit potential. Segment groupings that are used by banks include income classes, age bands, socio-economic categories and family units.

## Self-Assessment Question

You should attempt to answer this question yourself before looking up the suggested answer, which appears on pages 1113–15. If any part of your answer is incorrect, check back carefully to make sure you understand where you went wrong.

(a) Scott St Cyr wishes to decide whether to lease a new machine to assist in the manufacture of his single product for the coming quarter, and also to decide what price to charge for his product in order to maximize his profit (or minimize his loss).

In the quarter just ended his results were as follows:

|  | (£000) | (£000) |
|---|---|---|
| Sales (200 000 units) |  | 600 |
| Less: Cost of goods sold |  |  |
| Production wages: fixed | 20 |  |
| piecework | 90 |  |
|  | 110 |  |
| Materials | 400 |  |
|  |  | 510 |
| Gross profit |  | 90 |
| Less royalties (£0.50 per unit sold) | 100 |  |
| Less administration (fixed cost) | 30 |  |
|  |  | 130 |
| Loss |  | (40) |

St Cyr expects that, during the coming quarter,

(i) fixed basic wages (£20 000), fixed administration costs (£30 000) and the royalty rate will not change;
(ii) the piecework rate will increase to £0.50 per unit.

Quality control is very difficult and a high proportion of material is spoiled. A new machine has become available that can be delivered immediately. Tests have shown that it will eliminate the quality control problems, resulting in a halving of the usage of materials. It cannot be bought but can be leased for £115 000 per quarter.

The product has a very short shelf life, and is produced only to order. St Cyr estimates that if he were to change the unit selling price, demand for the product would increase by 1000 units per quarter for each one penny (£0.01) decrease in the selling price (so that he would receive orders for 500 000 units if he were to offer them free of charge), and would decrease by 1000 units per quarter for each one penny (£0.01) increase in the unit selling price (so that at a price of £5 his sales would be zero).

You are required to advise Scott St Cyr whether, in the coming quarter, he should lease the new machine and also the price that he should charge for his product, in order to maximize his profit. (15 marks)

(b) Christian Pass Ltd operates in an entirely different industry. However, it also produces to order, and carries no inventory.

Its demand function is estimated to be $P = 100 - 2Q$ (where $P$ is the unit selling price in £ and $Q$ is the quantity demanded in thousands of units).

Its total costs function is estimated to be $C = Q^2 + 10Q + 500$ (where $C$ is the total cost in £000 and $Q$ is as above).

You are required in respect of Christian Pass Ltd to

(i) calculate the output in units that will maximize total profit, and to calculate the corresponding unit selling price, total profit, and total sales revenue. (5 marks)

(ii) calculate the output in units that will maximize total revenues, and to calculate the corresponding unit selling price, total loss, and total sales revenue. (5 marks)

(Total 25 marks)

*ICAEW Management Accounting*

## Summary

Many firms are price takers and do not have to make pricing decisions. Prices are set by overall market supply and demand forces. Here accounting information plays an important role in determining the mix of products to sell, given their market prices. Other firms are price setters. They sell highly customized or differentiated products and have some discretion over setting selling prices. For both price takers and price setters the decision time horizon determines the cost information that is relevant for product pricing or output-mix decisions. The accounting information that is required for the following four situations was therefore described:

1. a price setting firm facing short-run pricing decisions;

2. a price setting firm facing long-run pricing decisions;

3. a price taker firm facing short-run product-mix decisions;

4. a price taker firm facing long-run product-mix decisions.

For long-run pricing decisions cost-plus pricing and target costing were examined and for long-run product- and customer-mix decisions product and customer profitability analysis were described.

The optimal selling price is the price that determines the optimal volume at which total profits are maximized. This is where marginal revenue equals marginal cost. However, optimal selling prices are not easy to determine in practice because of the difficulty in estimating a product demand curve. Consequently many firms use cost-based pricing formulae even though they are subject to a number of limitations. First, demand is ignored and, secondly, the approach requires that some assumption be made about future volume prior to ascertaining the cost and calculating the selling prices. This may lead to an increase in the selling price when demand is declining, and vice versa. Thirdly, there is no guarantee that the total sales revenue will be in excess of total costs, even when each product is priced above 'Cost'.

There are several reasons why cost-based pricing formulae are frequently used in practice. One possible justification is that cost-based pricing methods encourage price stability by enabling firms to predict the prices of their competitors. Also, target mark-ups can be adjusted upwards or downwards according to expected demand, thus ensuring that demand is indirectly taken into account.

## Key Terms and Concepts

cost-plus pricing (p. 381)
customer profitability analysis (p. 391)
full cost (p. 380)
long-run cost (p. 380)
monopolistic/imperfect competition (p. 372)
Pareto analysis (p. 393)
penetration pricing policy (p. 391)

price elasticity of demand (p. 372)
price setters (p. 378)
price-skimming policy (p. 390)
price takers (p. 378)
product life cycle (p. 391)
target costing (p. 384)
target rate of return on invested capital (p. 389)

## Recommended Reading

Sizer (1989) has written extensively on pricing, and you are recommended to read Chapters 11 and 12 of his book. These chapters focus on different pricing policies and the information that management requires to make sound pricing decisions. For a review of the empirical studies on pricing decisions you should read Mills (1988). A more detailed description of target costing can be found in the article by Kato (1993) and the book written by Yoshikawa *et al.* (1993).

## Key Examination Points

Questions in the management accounting examinations requiring the use of differential calculus have been set frequently by ICAEW, occasionally by ACCA and only very rarely by CIMA. You are recommended to attempt Questions 11.18 and 11.19 and check your solutions with the answers in the *Students' Manual* accompanying this book.

Avoid presenting only cost-plus information to recommend a selling price for a product. Wherever possible, incorporate demand estimates and cost estimates in your answer and indicate that the price that maximizes the short-term profits might not maximize long-term profits. You should be prepared to discuss the limitations of cost-plus pricing and indicate why it is widely used in spite of these limitations.

## Questions

*Indicates that a suggested solution is to be found in the *Students' Manual*.

### 11.1* Advanced
Discuss the extent to which cost data is useful in the determination of pricing policy. Explain the advantages and disadvantages of presenting cost data for possible utilization in pricing policy determination using an absorption, rather than a direct, costing basis. (14 marks)

*ACCA P2 Management Accounting*

### 11.2* Advanced
At one of its regular monthly meetings the board of Giant Steps Ltd was discussing its pricing and output policies. Giant Steps Ltd is a multi-product firm, operating in several distinct but related competitive markets. It aims to maximize profits.

You are required to comment critically and concisely on any four of the following six statements which were included in the taped record of the meeting:

(a) Profit is maximized by charging the highest possible price.

(b) The product manager's pricing policy should be to set a price which will maximize demand, by ensuring that contribution per unit is maximized.

(c) Allocation of overheads and joint costs enables management to compare performance between products, projects, or divisions.

(d) Allocation of overheads and joint costs is a way of accountants grabbing power and influence from marketing and production people.

(e) Our management accounts must be consistent with our published external accounts, so we must follow SSAP 9 on overhead allocation.

(f) Expenditure on Research and Development would be a past or sunk cost, and no matter what decision about output or price was eventually made it would have no bearing on the recovery of that expenditure. (12 marks)

*ICAEW Management Accounting*

### 11.3* Advanced
'In providing information to the product manager, the accountant must recognize that decision-making is essentially a process of choosing between competing alternatives, each with its own combination of income and costs; and that the relevant concepts to employ are future incremental costs and revenues and opportunity cost, not full cost which includes past or sunk costs.' (Sizer)

Descriptive studies of pricing decisions taken in practice have, on the other hand, suggested that the inclusion of overhead and joint cost allocations in unit product costs is widespread in connection with the provision of information for this class of decision. Furthermore, these costs are essentially historic costs.

You are required to:

(a) explain the reasoning underlying the above quotation; (10 marks)

(b) suggest reasons why overhead and joint cost allocation is nevertheless widely used in practice in connection with information for pricing decisions; (10 marks)

(c) set out your own views as to the balance of these arguments. (5 marks)

(Total 25 marks)

*ICAEW Management Accounting*

## 11.4 Advanced

A company supplying capital equipment to the engineering industry is part of a large group of diverse companies. It determines its tender prices by adding a standard profit margin as a percentage of its prime cost.

Although it is working at full capacity the group managing director considers the company's annual return on capital employed as inadequate.

You are required, as the group assistant management accountant, to provide him with the following information:

(a) why the return-on-prime-cost (ROPC) approach to tendering would be likely to yield an inadequate return on capital employed; (7 marks)

(b) the steps involved in calculating a return-on capital employed (ROCE) tendering rate for a particular contract; (7 marks)

(c) three problems likely to be encountered in meeting a pre-set profit target on a ROCE basis. (6 marks)

(Total 20 marks)

*CIMA P3 Management Accounting*

## 11.5 Advanced

It has been stated that companies do not have profitable products, only profitable customers. Many companies have placed emphasis on the concept of Customer Account Profitability (CAP) analysis in order to increase their earnings and returns to shareholders. Much of the theory of CAP draws from the view that the main strategic thrust operated by many companies is to encourage the development and sale of new products to existing customers.

Requirements:

(a) Briefly explain the concept of CAP analysis. (5 marks)

(b) Critically appraise the value of CAP analysis as a means of increasing earnings per share and returns to shareholders. (15 marks)

(Total 20 marks)

*CIMA Stage 4 Strategic Management Accounting and Marketing*

## 11.6 Advanced: Discussion of pricing strategies

A producer of high quality executive motor cars has developed a new model which it knows to be very advanced both technically and in style by comparison with the competition in its market segment.

The company's reputation for high quality is well-established and its servicing network in its major markets is excellent. However, its record in timely delivery has not been so good in previous years, though this has been improving considerably.

In the past few years it has introduced annual variations/improvements in its major models. When it launched a major new vehicle some six years ago the recommended retail price was so low in relation to the excellent specification of the car that a tremendous demand built up quickly and a two-year queue for the car developed within six months. Within three months a second-hand model had been sold at an auction for nearly 50% more than the list price and even after a year of production a sizeable premium above list price was being obtained.

The company considers that, in relation to the competition, the proposed new model will be as attractive as was its predecessor six years ago. Control of costs is very good so that accurate cost data for the new model are to hand. For the previous model, the company assessed the long-term targeted annual production level and calculated its prices on that basis. In the first year, production was 30% of that total.

For the present model the company expects that the relationship between first-year production and longer-term annual production will also be about 30%, though the absolute levels in both cases are expected to be higher than previously.

The senior management committee, of which you are a member, has been asked to recommend the pricing approach that the company should adopt for the new model.

You are required

(a) to list the major pricing approaches available in this situation and discuss in some detail the

relative merits and disadvantages to the company of each approach in the context of the new model; (15 marks)
(b) to recommend which approach you would propose, giving your reasons; (5 marks)
(c) to outline briefly in which ways, if any, your answers to (a) and (b) above would differ if, instead of a high quality executive car, you were pricing a new family model of car with some unusual features that the company might introduce. (5 marks)
(Total 25 marks)
*CIMA Stage 4 Management Accounting*
*Decision Making*

## 11.7 Intermediate: Computation of minimum selling price and optimum price from price–demand relationships

In an attempt to win over key customers in the motor industry and to increase its market share, BIL Motor Components plc has decided to charge a price lower than its normal price for component TD463 when selling to the key customers who are being targeted. Details of component TD463's standard costs are as follows:

| | Component TD463 Batch size 200 units | | | |
|---|---|---|---|---|
| | Machine Group 1 (£) | Machine Group 7 (£) | Machine Group 29 (£) | Assembly (£) |
| Materials (per unit) | 26.00 | 17.00 | — | 3.00 |
| Labour (per unit) | 2.00 | 1.60 | 0.75 | 1.20 |
| Variable overheads (per unit) | 0.65 | 0.72 | 0.80 | 0.36 |
| Fixed overheads (per unit) | 3.00 | 2.50 | 1.50 | 0.84 |
| | 31.65 | 21.82 | 3.05 | 5.40 |
| Setting-up costs per batch of 200 units | £10.00 | £6.00 | £4.00 | — |

Required:
(a) Compute the lowest selling price at which one batch of 200 units could be offered, and critically evaluate the adoption of such a pricing policy. (8 marks)
(b) The company is also considering the launch of a new product, component TDX489, and has provided you with the following information:

| | Standard cost per box (£) |
|---|---|
| Variable cost | 6.20 |
| Fixed cost | 1.60 |
| | 7.80 |

Market research forecast of demand:

| Selling price (£) | 13 | 12 | 11 | 10 | 9 |
|---|---|---|---|---|---|
| Demand (boxes) | 5000 | 6000 | 7200 | 11 200 | 13 400 |

The company only has enough production capacity to make 7000 boxes. However, it would be possible to purchase product TDX489 from a subcontractor at £7.75 per box for orders up to 5000 boxes and £7 per box if the orders exceed 5000 boxes.

Required:
Prepare and present a computation which illustrates which price should be selected in order to maximise profits. (8 marks)
(c) Where production capacity is the 'limiting factor', explain briefly the ways in which management can increase it without having to acquire more plant and machinery.
(4 marks)
(Total 20 marks)
*ACCA Paper 8 Managerial Finance*

## 11.8* Intermediate: Calculation of cost-plus selling price and an evaluation of pricing decisions

A firm manufactures two products EXE and WYE in departments dedicated exclusively to them. There are also three service departments, stores, maintenance and administration. No stocks are held as the products deteriorate rapidly.

Direct costs of the products, which are variable in the context of the whole business, are identified to each department. The step-wise apportionment of service department costs to the manufacturing departments is based on estimates of the usage of the service provided. These are expressed as percentages and assumed to be reliable over the current capacity range. The general factory overheads of £3.6m, which are fixed, are apportioned based on floor space occupied. The company establishes product costs based on budgeted volume and marks up these costs by 25% in order to set target selling prices.

Extracts from the budgets for the forthcoming year are provided below:

|  | Annual volume (units) | |
| --- | --- | --- |
|  | EXE | WYE |
| Max capacity | 200 000 | 100 000 |
| Budget | 150 000 | 70 000 |

|  | EXE | WYE | Stores | Mainten- ance | Admin |
| --- | --- | --- | --- | --- | --- |
| *Costs (£m)* |  |  |  |  |  |
| Material | 1.8 | 0.7 | 0.1 | 0.1 |  |
| Other variable | 0.8 | 0.5 | 0.1 | 0.2 | 0.2 |
| *Departmental usage (%)* |  |  |  |  |  |
| Maintenance | 50 | 25 | 25 |  |  |
| Administration | 40 | 30 | 20 | 10 |  |
| Stores | 60 | 40 |  |  |  |
| *Floor space (sq m)* |  |  |  |  |  |
|  | 640 | 480 | 240 | 80 | 160 |

Required:

Workings may be £000 with unit prices to the nearest penny.

(a) Calculate the budgeted selling price of one unit of EXE and WYE based on the usual mark up. (5 marks)

(b) Discuss how the company may respond to each of the following independent events, which represent additional business opportunities.

  (i) an enquiry from an overseas customer for 3000 units only of WYE where a price of £35 per unit is offered

  (ii) an enquiry for 50 000 units of WYE to be supplied in full at regular intervals during the forthcoming year at a price which is equivalent to full cost plus 10%

  In both cases support your discussion with calculations and comment on any assumptions or matters on which you would seek clarification. (11 marks)

(c) Explain the implications of preparing product full costs based on maximum capacity rather than annual budget volume. (4 marks)

(Total 20 marks)

*ACCA Paper 8 Managerial Finance*

**11.9 Advanced: Cost-plus and relevant cost information for pricing decisions**

Josun plc manufactures cereal based foods, including various breakfast cereals under private brand labels. In March the company had been approached by Cohin plc, a large national supermarket chain, to tender for the manufacture and supply of a crunchy style breakfast cereal made from oats, nuts, raisins, etc. The tender required Josun to quote prices for a 1.5 kg packet at three different weekly volumes: 50 000, 60 000 and 70 000. Josun plc had, at present, excess capacity on some of its machines and could make a maximum of 80 000 packets of cereal a week.

Josun's management accountant is asked to prepare a costing for the Cohin tender. The company prepares its tender prices on the basis of full cost plus 15% of cost as a profit margin. The full cost is made up of five elements: raw materials per packet of £0.30p; operating wages £0.12p per packet; manufacturing overheads costed at 200% of operating wages; administration and other corporate overheads at 100% of operating wages; and packaging and transport costing £0.10p per packet. The sales manager has suggested that as an incentive to Cohin, the profit margin be cut on the 60 000 and 70 000 tenders by $\frac{1}{2}$% and 1% to $14\frac{1}{2}$% and 14% respectively. The manufacturing and administration overheads are forecast as fixed at £12 500 per week, unless output drops to 50 000 units or below per week, when a saving of £1000 per week can be made. If no contract is undertaken then all the manufacturing and administration overheads will be saved except for £600 per week. If the tender is accepted the volume produced and sold will be determined by the sales achieved by Cohin.

A week before the Cohin tender is to be presented for negotiation, Josun receives an enquiry from Stamford plc, a rival supermarket chain, to produce, weekly, 60 000 packets of a similar type of breakfast cereal of slightly superior quality at a price of £1.20 per 1.5 kg packet, the quality and mix of the cereal constituents being laid down by Stamford. This product will fill a gap in Stamford's private label range of cereals. The estimated variable costs for this contract would be: raw materials £0.40p per packet, operating labour £0.15p per packet and packaging and transport £0.12p per packet. None of the 80 000 weekly capacity could be used for another product if either of these contracts were taken up.

You are required to:

(a) compute the three selling prices per packet for the Cohin tender using Josun's normal pricing method; (3 marks)

(b) advise Josun, giving your financial reasons, on the relative merits of the two contracts; (6 marks)

(c) discuss the merits of full-cost pricing as a method of arriving at selling prices; (5 marks)

(d) make recommendations to Josun as to the method it might use to derive its selling prices in future; (3 marks)

(e) calculate the expected value of each tender given the following information and recommend which potential customer should receive the greater sales effort. It is estimated that there is a 70% chance of Stamford signing the contract for the weekly production of 60 000 packets, while there is a 20% chance of Cohin not accepting the tender. It is also estimated that the probabilities of Cohin achieving weekly sales volumes of 50 000, 60 000 or 70 000 are 0.3, 0.5 and 0.2 respectively. The two sets of negotiations are completely independent of each other; (4 marks)

(f) provide, with reasons, for each of the two contracts under negotiation, a minimum and a recommended price that Josun could ask for the extra quantity that could be produced under each contract and which would ensure the full utilization of Josun's weekly capacity of 80 000 packets. (4 marks)

(Total 25 marks)

*ICAEW P2 Management Accounting*

**11.10\* Advanced: Limiting factor resource allocation and comparison of marginal revenue to determine optimum output and price**

(a) A manufacturer has three products, A, B, and C. Currently sales, cost and selling price details and processing time requirements are as follows:

| | Product A | Product B | Product C |
|---|---|---|---|
| Annual sales (units) | 6000 | 6000 | 750 |
| Selling price (£) | 20.00 | 31.00 | 39.00 |
| Unit cost (£) | 18.00 | 24.00 | 30.00 |
| Processing time required per unit (hours) | 1 | 1 | 2 |

The firm is working at full capacity (13 500 processing hours per year). Fixed manufactur-

ing overheads are absorbed into unit costs by a charge of 200% of variable cost. This procedure fully absorbs the fixed manufacturing overhead. Assuming that:

(i) processing time can be switched from one product line to another,

(ii) the demand at current selling prices is:

| Product A | Product B | Product C |
|---|---|---|
| 11 000 | 8000 | 2000 |

and

(iii) the selling prices are not to be altered. You are required to calculate the best production programme for the next operating period and to indicate the increase in net profit that this should yield. In addition identify the shadow price of a processing hour. (11 marks)

(b) A review of the selling prices is in progress and it has been estimated that, for each product, an increase in the selling price would result in a fall in demand at the rate of 2000 units for an increase of £1 and similarly, that a decrease of £1 would increase demand by 2000 units. Specifically the following price/demand relationships would apply:

| Product A | | Product B | | Product C | |
|---|---|---|---|---|---|
| Selling price (£) | Estimated demand | Selling price (£) | Estimated demand | Selling price (£) | Estimated demand |
| 24.50 | 2 000 | 34.00 | 2 000 | 39.00 | 2 000 |
| 23.50 | 4 000 | 33.00 | 4 000 | 38.00 | 4 000 |
| 22.50 | 6 000 | 32.00 | 6 000 | 37.00 | 6 000 |
| 21.50 | 8 000 | 31.00 | 8 000 | 36.00 | 8 000 |
| 20.50 | 10 000 | 30.00 | 10 000 | 35.00 | 10 000 |
| 19.50 | 12 000 | 29.00 | 12 000 | 34.00 | 12 000 |
| 18.50 | 14 000 | 28.00 | 14 000 | 33.00 | 14 000 |

From this information you are required to calculate the best selling prices, the revised best production plan *and* the net profit that this plan should produce. (11 marks)

(Total 22 marks)

*ACCA Level 2 Management Accounting*

**11.11 Advanced: Selection of optimal selling price based on demand and cost schedules**

Sniwe plc intend to launch a commemorative product for the 2004 Olympic games onto the

UK market commencing 1 August 2002. The product will have variable costs of £16 per unit.

Production capacity available for the product is sufficient for 2000 units per annum. Sniwe plc has made a policy decision to produce to the maximum available capacity during the year to 31 July 2003.

Demand for the product during the year to 31 July 2003 is expected to be price dependent, as follows:

| Selling price per unit (£) | Annual sales (units) |
|---|---|
| 20 | 2000 |
| 30 | 1600 |
| 40 | 1200 |
| 50 | 1100 |
| 60 | 1000 |
| 70 | 700 |
| 80 | 400 |

It is anticipated that in the year to 31 July 2004 the availability of similar competitor products will lead to a market price of £40 per unit for the product during that year.

During the year to 31 July 2004, Sniwe plc intend to produce only at the activity level required to enable them to satisfy demand, with stocks being run down to zero if possible. This policy is intended as a precaution against a sudden collapse of the market for the product by 31 July 2004.

Required:
(Ignoring tax and the time value of money.)
(a) Determine the launch price at 1 August 2002 which will maximize the net benefit to Sniwe plc during the two year period to 31 July 2004 where the demand potential for the year to 31 July 2004 is estimated as (i) 3600 units and (ii) 1000 units. (12 marks)
(b) Identify which of the launch strategies detailed in (a)(i) and (a)(ii) above will result in unsold stock remaining at 31 July 2004.

Advise management of the minimum price at which such unsold stock should be able to be sold in order to alter the initial launch price strategy which will maximize the net benefit to Sniwe plc over the life of the product. (6 marks)
(c) Comment on any other factors which might influence the initial launch price strategy

where the demand in the year to 31 July 2004 is estimated at 1000 units. (4 marks)
(Total 22 marks)
*ACCA Level 2 Management Accounting*

**11.12\* Advanced: Impact of a change in selling price on profits based on a given elasticity of demand**
You are the management accountant of a medium-sized company. You have been asked to provide budgetary information and advice to the board of directors for a meeting where they will decide the pricing of an important product for the next period.

The following information is available from the records:

| | Previous period (£000) | | Current period (£000) |
|---|---|---|---|
| Sales | | | |
| (100 000 units at £13 each) | 1300 | (106 000 units at £13 each) | 1378.0 |
| Costs | 1000 | | 1077.4 |
| Profit | 300 | | 300.6 |

You find that between the previous and current periods there was 4% general cost inflation and it is forecast that costs will rise a further 6% in the next period. As a matter of policy, the firm did not increase the selling price in the current period although competitors raised their prices by 4% to allow for the increased costs. A survey by economic consultants was commissioned and has found that the demand for the product is elastic with an estimated price elasticity of demand of 1.5. This means that volume would fall by $1\frac{1}{2}$ times the rate of real price increase.

Various options are to be considered by the board and you are required
(a) to show the budgeted position if the firm maintains the £13 selling price for the next period (when it is expected that competitors will increase their prices by 6%); (10 marks)
(b) to show the budgeted position if the firm also raises its price by 6%; (6 marks)
(c) to write a short report to the board, with appropriate figures, recommending whether the firm should maintain the £13 selling price or raise it by 6%; (3 marks)

(d)  to state what assumptions you have used in your answers.    (3 marks)
(Total 22 marks)
*CIMA Stage 3 Management Accounting Techniques*

## 11.13 Advanced: Calculation of elasticity of demand, optimum output and selling price

XYZ is the only manufacturer of a product called the X. The variable cost of producing an X is £1.50 at all levels of output.

During recent months the X has been sold at a unit price of around £6.25. Various small adjustments (up and down) have been made to this price in an attempt to find a profit maximising selling price.

XYZ's Commercial Manager (an economics graduate) has recently commissioned a study by a firm of marketing consultants 'to investigate the demand structure for Xs and in particular to calculate the elasticity of demand for Xs produced by XYZ'. (*Note:* the elasticity of demand for a product is the proportion by which demand changes divided by the proportional price change which causes it.)

The consultants have reported back that at a unit price of £10 there is no demand for Xs but that demand increases by 40 Xs for each 1p (£0.01) that the unit price is reduced below £10. They have also reported that 'when demand is at around half its theoretical maximum the elasticity of demand is approximately 1.'

Upon receiving this report the Commercial Manager makes the following statement:

Recent experiences gained in adjusting the unit selling price of the X suggest that the product has quite an elastic demand structure. Small changes in the unit selling price produce far larger proportionate increases in demand. I find it difficult to accept that the elasticity of demand for the X is 1.

You are required:
(a)  to write a memorandum to the Commercial Manager reconciling the consultants' report with his own observations on the elasticity of demand for the X;    (10 marks)
(b)  to calculate the profit maximising unit selling price for the X (accurate to the nearest penny) and to calculate the elasticity of demand for

the X at that selling price;    (10 marks)
(Total 20 marks)
*CIMA Stage 4 Management Accounting Decision Making*

## 11.14* Advanced: Calculation of cost-plus price and minimum short-run price plus a discussion of cost-plus and relevant cost pricing

Wright is a builder. His business will have spare capacity over the coming six months and he has been investigating two projects.

*Project A*
Wright is tendering for a school extension contract. Normally he prices a contract by adding 100% to direct costs, to cover overheads and profit. He calculates direct costs as the actual cost of materials valued on a first-in-first-out basis, plus the estimated wages of direct labour. But for this contract he has prepared more detailed information.

Four types of material will be needed:

| Material | Quantity (units): Needed for contract | Already in stock | Price per unit: Purchase price of units in stock (£) | Current purchase price (£) | Current resale price (£) |
|---|---|---|---|---|---|
| Z | 1100 | 100 | 7.00 | 10.00 | 8.00 |
| Y | 150 | 200 | 40.00 | 44.00 | 38.00 |
| X | 600 | 300 | 35.00 | 33.00 | 25.00 |
| W | 200 | 400 | 20.00 | 21.00 | 10.00 |

Z and Y are in regular use. Neither X nor W is currently used; X has no foreseeable use in the business, but W could be used on other jobs in place of material currently costing £16 per unit.

The contract will last for six months and requires two craftsmen, whose basic annual wage cost is £16000 each. To complete the contract in time it will also be necessary to pay them a bonus of £700 each. Without the contract they would be retained at their normal pay rates, doing work which will otherwise be done by temporary workers engaged for the contract period at a total cost of £11 800.

Three casual labourers would also be employed specifically for the contract at a cost of £4000 each.

The contract will require two types of equipment: general-purpose equipment already owned by Wright, which will be retained at the end of the contract, and specialized equipment to be purchased second-hand, which will be sold at the end of the contract.

The general-purpose equipment cost £21 000 two years ago and is being depreciated on a straight-line basis over a seven-year life (with assumed zero scrap value). Equivalent new equipment can be purchased currently for £49 000. Second-hand prices for comparable general-purpose equipment, and those for the relevant specialized equipment, are shown below.

| | General-purpose equipment | | Specialized equipment | |
|---|---|---|---|---|
| | Purchase price (£) | Resale price (£) | Purchase price (£) | Resale price (£) |
| Current | 20 000 | 17 200 | 9000 | 7400 |
| After 6 months: | | | | |
| if used for 6 months | 15 000 | 12 600 | 7000 | 5800 |
| if not used | 19 000 | 16 400 | 8000 | 6500 |

The contract will require the use of a yard on which Wright has a four-year lease at a fixed rental of £2000 per year. If Wright does not get the contract the yard will probably remain empty. The contract will also incur administrative expenses estimated at £5000.

*Project B*
If Wright does not get the contract he will buy a building plot for £20 000 and build a house. Building costs will depend on weather conditions:

| Weather condition | A | B | C |
|---|---|---|---|
| Probability | 0.4 | 0.4 | 0.2 |
| Building costs (excluding land) | £60 000 | £80 000 | £95 000 |

Similarly the price obtained for the house will depend on market conditions:

| Market condition | D | E |
|---|---|---|
| Probability | .7 | .3 |
| Sale price (net of selling expenses) | £100 000 | £120 000 |

Wright does not have the resources to undertake both projects.

The costs of his supervision time can be ignored.

Requirements
(a) Ignoring the possibility of undertaking project B, calculate:
   (i) the price at which Wright would tender for the school extension contract if he used his normal pricing method, and
   (ii) the tender price at which you consider Wright would neither gain nor lose by taking the contract.          (10 marks)
(b) Explain, with supporting calculations, how the availability of project B should affect Wright's tender for the school extension contract.          (5 marks)
(c) Discuss the merits and limitations of the pricing methods used above, and identify the circumstances in which they might be appropriate.          (10 marks)
          (Total 25 marks)
          *ICAEW P2 Management Accounting*

**11.15\* Advanced: Recommendation of which market segment to enter and selling price to charge**
AB Ltd is a well-established company producing high quality, technically advanced, electronic equipment.

In an endeavour to diversify, it has identified opportunities in the hi-fi industry. After some preliminary market research it has decided to market a new product that incorporates some of the most advanced techniques available together with a very distinctive design.

AB Ltd's special skill is that it can apply these techniques economically to medium-sized quantities and offer a product of excellent design with an advanced degree of technology.

The new product faces three categories of competition:

| Category | Technology | Design | Quantities sold per annum | Number of models | Retail selling price range (£) |
|---|---|---|---|---|---|
| 1 | Good | Standard | 22 000 | 4 | 600–1050 |
| 2 | Good | Good | 6 000 | 5 | 1450–1900 |
| 3 | Advanced | Good | 750 | 2 | 2500–3000 |

The product will be distributed through a range of specialist retailers who have undertaken not to discount prices. Their commission will be 25% on retail selling price. AB Ltd has also acquired the rights to sell the product under the name of a prestigious hi-fi manufacturer who does not offer this type of product. For this it will pay a royalty of 5% of the retail selling price.

AB Ltd assesses that its direct cost per product will be £670 (excluding the royalty and the retailers' commission) and the annual fixed costs relevant to the project are budgeted at:

|  | (£) |
| --- | --- |
| Production | 250 000 |
| Research and development | 50 000 |
| Marketing | 200 000 |
| Finance and administration | 50 000 |

You are required, from the data provided and making such assumptions as you consider reasonable,

(a) to suggest a range of retail prices (i.e. to the consumer) from which AB Ltd should choose the eventual price for its product. Explain briefly why you have suggested that range of prices; (10 marks)

(b) to select *one* particular price from the range in (a) above that you would recommend AB Ltd to choose. Explain, with any relevant calculations, why you have recommended that price. Mention any assumptions that you have made. (15 marks)

*Note:* The prices suggested should be rounded to the nearest £100.

Ignore VAT (or sales taxes), taxation and inflation.

(Total 25 marks)
*CIMA Stage 4 Management Accounting Decision Making*

## 11.16 Advanced: Calculation of unit costs and optimum selling price

French Ltd is about to commence operations utilizing a simple production process to produce two products X and Y. It is the policy of French to operate the new factory at its maximum output in the first year of operations. Cost and production details estimated for the first year's operations are:

| Product | Production resources per unit Labour hours | Production resources per unit Machine hours | Variable cost per unit Direct labour (£) | Variable cost per unit Direct materials (£) | Fixed production overheads directly attributable to product (£000) | Maximum production (000 units) |
| --- | --- | --- | --- | --- | --- | --- |
| X | 1 | 4 | 5 | 6 | 120 | 40 |
| Y | 8 | 2 | 28 | 16 | 280 | 10 |

There are also general fixed production overheads concerned in the manufacture of both products but which cannot be directly attributed to either. This general fixed production overhead is estimated at £720 000 for the first year of operations. It is thought that the cost structure of the first year will also be operative in the second year.

Both products are new and French is one of the first firms to produce them. Hence in the first year of operations the sales price can be set by French. In the second and subsequent years it is felt that the market for X and Y will have become more settled and French will largely conform to the competitive market prices that will become established. The sales manager has researched the first year's market potential and has estimated sales volumes for various ranges of selling price. The details are:

| Product X Range of per unit sales prices (£)    (£) | Product X Sales volume (000) | Product Y Range of per unit sales prices (£)    (£) | Product Y Sales volume (000) |
| --- | --- | --- | --- |
| Up to 24.00 | 36 | Up to 96.00 | 11 |
| 24.01 to 30.00 | 32 | 96.01 to 108.00 | 10 |
| 30.01 to 36.00 | 18 | 108.01 to 120.00 | 9 |
| 36.01 to 42.00* | 8 | 120.01 to 132.00 | 8 |
|  |  | 132.01 to 144.00 | 7 |
|  |  | 144.01 to 156.00* | 5 |

* Maximum price.

The managing director of French wishes to ascertain the total production cost of X and Y as, he says, 'Until we know the per unit cost of production we cannot properly determine the first year's sales price. Price must always ensure that total cost is covered and there is an element of profit – therefore I feel that the price should be total cost plus 20%. The determination of cost is fairly simple as most costs are clearly attributable to either X or Y. The general factory overhead will probably be allocated to the products in accordance with some measure of usage of factory resources such as labour or machine hours. The choice between labour and machine hours is the only problem in determining the cost of each product – but the problem is minor and so, therefore, is the problem of pricing.'

Required:
(a)  Produce statements showing the effect the cost allocation and pricing methods mentioned by the managing director will have on
  (i)   unit costs,
  (ii)  closing stock values, and
  (iii) disclosed profit for the first year of operation.                            (c. 8 marks)
(b)  Briefly comment on the results in (a) above and advise the managing director on the validity of using the per unit cost figures produced for pricing decisions.   (c. 4 marks)
(c)  Provide appropriate statements to the management of French Ltd which will be of direct relevance in assisting the determination of the optimum prices of X and Y for the first year of operations. The statements should be designed to provide assistance in each of the following, separate, cases:
  (i)   year II demand will be below productive capacity;
  (ii)  year II demand will be substantially in excess of productive capacity.
  In both cases the competitive market sales prices per unit for year II are expected to be
    X – £30 per unit
    Y – £130 per unit
  Clearly specify, and explain, your advice to French for each of the cases described.
  (Ignore taxation and the time value of money.)
                                    (c. 8 marks)
                              (Total 20 marks)
                  *ACCA P2 Management Accounting*

**11.17 Advanced: Calculation of optimal output level adopting a limiting factor approach and the computation of optimum selling prices using differential calculus**
AB p.l.c. makes two products, Alpha and Beta. The company made a £500 000 profit last year and proposes an identical plan for the coming year. The relevant data for last year are summarized in Table 1.

*Table 1: Actuals for last year*

|                                              | Product Alpha | Product Beta |
|----------------------------------------------|--------------:|-------------:|
| Actual production and sales (units)          | 20 000        | 40 000       |
| Total costs per unit                         | £20           | £40          |
| Selling prices per unit (25% on cost)        | £25           | £50          |
| Machining time per unit (hours)              | 2             | 1            |
| Potential demand at above selling prices (units) | 30 000    | 50 000       |

Fixed costs were £480 000 for the year, absorbed on machining hours which were fully utilized for the production achieved.

A new Managing Director has been appointed and he is somewhat sceptical about the plan being proposed. Furthermore, he thinks that additional machining capacity should be installed to remove any production bottlenecks and wonders whether a more flexible pricing policy should be adopted.

Table 2 summarizes the changes in costs involved for the extra capacity and gives price/demand data, supplied by the Marketing Department, applicable to the conditions expected in the next period.

*Table 2: Costs*
Extra machining capacity would increase fixed costs by 10% in total. Variable costs and machining times per unit would remain unchanged.

|                               | Product Alpha | Product Beta |
|-------------------------------|--------------:|-------------:|
| Price/demand data             |               |              |
| Price range (per unit)        | £20–30        | £45–55       |
| Expected demand (000 units)   | 45–15         | 70–30        |

You are required to
(a)  calculate the plan to maximize profits for the coming year based on the data and selling prices in Table 1;                  (7 marks)
(b)  comment on the pricing system for the existing plan used in Table 1;           (3 marks)
(c)  calculate the best selling prices and production plan based on the data in Table 2;
                                          (7 marks)

(d) comment on the methods you have used in part (c) to find the optimum prices and production levels. (3 marks)

Any assumptions made must be clearly stated.

(Total 20 marks)

*CIMA Stage 3 Management Accounting Techniques*

## 11.18* Advanced: Calculation of optimum selling prices using differential calculus

Alvis Taylor has budgeted that output and sales of his single product, flonal, will be 100 000 for the forthcoming year. At this level of activity his unit variable costs are budgeted to be £50 and his unit fixed costs £25. His sales manager estimates that the demand for flonal would increase by 1000 units for every decrease of £1 in unit selling price (and vice-versa), and that at a unit selling price of £200 demand would be nil.

Information about two price increases has just been received from suppliers. One is for materials (which are included in Alvis Taylor's variable costs), and one is for fuel (which is included in his fixed costs). Their effect will be to increase both the variable costs and the fixed costs by 20% in total over the budgeted figures.

Alvis Taylor aims to maximize profits from his business.

You are required, in respect of Alvis Taylor's business:

(a) to calculate, *before the cost inceases*:
  (i) the budgeted contribution and profit at the budgeted level of sales of 100 000 units, and
  (ii) the level of sales at which profits would be maximized, and the amount of those maximum profits, (7 marks)

(b) to show whether and by how much Alvis Taylor should adjust his selling price, in respect of the increases in, respectively:
  (i) fuel costs
  (ii) materials costs, (6 marks)

(c) to show whether and by how much it is worthwhile for Alvis Taylor, following the increases in costs, to spend £1 000 000 on a TV advertising campaign if this were confidently expected to have the effect during the next year (but not beyond then) that demand would still fall by 1000 units for every increase of £1 in unit selling price (and vice-versa), but that it would not fall to nil until the unit selling price was £210, (5 marks)

(d) to comment on the results which you have obtained in (a)–(c) above and on the assumptions underlying them. (7 marks)

(Total 25 marks)

*ICAEW Management Accounting*

## 11.19* Advanced: Calculation of cost-plus selling price and optimum selling price and their impact on profits

Exejet Engineering Ltd manufactures a range of products for the aircraft industry including the Keroklene fuel filter for use in executive jets. A Keroklene fuel filter consists of a pump unit which contains a filter element. The pump unit has a life of five years, after which the entire fuel filter must be scrapped. The fuel filter element must be replaced at the end of each year.

The total market for this type of fuel filter is stable at a level of 2000 units a year, which Exejet shares with several competitors who supply equivalent units. However, customers must purchase replacement filter elements from the supplier of the original equipment as elements are not interchangeable. The supplier who has the largest share of the market has just set its prices for 2002; these include complete fuel filter units at £390 and replacement filter elements at £80 each.

Pump units are manufactured to Exejet's specification by a sub-contractor at a delivered price of £305 each, but the filter elements are made in house. The budgeted cost of manufacturing 1250 filter elements in 2002 has been estimated as follows:

|  | £ |
| --- | --- |
| Direct labour: 1875 hours | 18 750 |
| Materials | 43 750 |
| Variable overhead | 12 500 |
| Fixed overhead | 5 000 |
| Total | 80 000 |

Complete Keroklene fuel filters are sold as a pump unit and a filter element packed together, so no assembly operation is required. Fixed costs associated with the packaging and sale of complete units and replacement elements are budgeted at £7000 for 2002, and are recovered on the basis of the direct labour hours used in the manufacture of filter elements.

Sales of the Keroklene fuel filter in 2001 are expected to be 250 complete units, a figure which has remained stable for several years and which generates a demand for 1000 replacement filter elements each year. Management are confident that the same volume will be maintained in 2002 provided that their traditional pricing policy of full cost plus 5%, rounded up to the nearest pound, is maintained. They also believe that any greater profit margin would render their product uncompetitive in its limited market. However, the new management accountant feels that the 5% margin is too low and not necessarily appropriate for both complete units and replacement elements. He has therefore discussed pricing policy with Exejet's sales manager.

The sales manager's firm opinion is that, given the market leader's prices for 2002, Exejet could capture 40% of the total market for complete units if it priced them at £280, but would lose sales of 5 units for every £1 charged above £280. He also believes that sales for complete fuel filter units would be unaffected by the price charged for replacement filter elements provided this did not exceed the price charged by the market leader by more than 20%. However, if replacement elements were priced at more than 20% above the main competitor's prices then heavy sales losses for complete units would result.

Requirements:
(a) Calculate the selling prices for complete units and replacement elements that would result from the traditional pricing policy. (3 marks)
(b) Assuming that the sales manager's views concerning the effects of price changes are correct, determine the optimum selling prices for both complete units and replacement elements. (7 marks)
(c) Calculate the change in profits that would result from using the new selling prices calculated in (b) above compared with the original prices calculated in (a) above, for each year in the period 2002 to 2004. (5 marks)
(d) Outline any problems you foresee for Exejet in implementing the prices you have calculated in (b) above and suggest how they might be overcome. (5 marks)
(e) Discuss the reasons why many companies appear to determine their selling prices on a 'cost-plus' basis and evaluate the appropriateness of such a practice. (5 marks)
(Total 25 marks)
*ICAEW Management Accounting and Financial Management 2*

## 11.20 Advanced: Calculation of optimum quantity and prices for joint products using differential calculus plus a discussion of joint cost allocations

Nuts plc produces alpha and beta in two stages. The separation process produces crude alpha and beta from a raw material costing £170 per tonne. The cost of the separation process is £100 per tonne of raw material. Each tonne of raw material generates 0.4 tonne of crude alpha and 0.6 tonne of crude beta. Neither product can be sold in its crude state.

The refining process costs £125 per tonne for alpha and £50 per tonne for beta; no weight is lost in refining. The demand functions for refined alpha and refined beta are independent of each other, and the corresponding price equations are:

$$P_A = 1250 - \frac{100 Q_A}{32}$$

$$P_B = 666\tfrac{2}{3} - \frac{100 Q_B}{18}$$

where $P_A$ = price per tonne of refined alpha
$P_B$ = price per tonne of refined beta
$Q_A$ = quantity of refined alpha
$Q_B$ = quantity of refined beta

The company is considering whether any part of the production of crude alpha or crude beta should be treated as a by-product. The by-product would be taken away free of charge by a large-scale pig farming enterprise.

Requirements
(a) If all the output of the separation process is refined and sold:
  (i) calculate the optimal quantity of raw material to be processed and the quantities and prices of the refined products, and
  (ii) determine the 'major' product which is worth refining and the 'minor' product which deserves consideration as a potential by-product, but do not attempt to calculate at this stage how much of the 'minor' product would be refined. (10 marks)
(b) Calculate:
  (i) the optimal quantity of the 'major' product which would be worth producing regardless of the value of the 'minor' product, and
  (ii) the quantity of the resulting 'minor' product that would be worth refining. (6 marks)

(c) Evaluate the principal methods and problems of joint-cost allocation for stock valuation, referring to Nuts plc where appropriate.

(9 marks)

(Total 25 marks)

*ICAEW P2 Management Accounting*

## 11.21 Advanced: Calculation of optimum selling prices using differential calculus

Cassidy Computers plc sells one of its products, a plug-in card for personal computer systems, in both the UK and Ruritania. The relationship between price and demand is different in the two markets, and can be represented as follows:

Home market:  Price (in £) $= 68 - 8Q1$

Export market:  Price (in $) $= 110 - 10Q2$

where $Q1$ is the quantity demanded (in 000) in the home market and $Q2$ is the quantity demanded (in 000) in the export market. The current exchange rate is 2 Ruritanian dollars to the pound.

The variable cost of producing the cards is subject to economies of scale, and can be represented as:

Unit variable cost (in £) $= 19 - Q$ (where $Q = Q1 + Q2$).

Requirements

(a) Calculate the optimum selling price and total contribution made by the product if it can be sold

  (i)  only in the home market

  (ii)  only in the export market

  (iii)  in both markets. (10 marks)

(b) Calculate the optimum selling prices and total contribution made by the product if it can be sold in both markets, but subject to a constraint imposed by the Ruritanian government that the company can sell no more cards in Ruritania than it sells in its home market. How sensitive are the prices to be charged in each market and the total contribution, to changes in the exchange rate over the range $1 = £0.25$ to $1 = £1.00$? (8 marks)

(c) How does the volatility of foreign exchange rates affect the ways in which export sales are priced in practice? (7 marks)

(Total 25 marks)

*ICAEW P2 Management Accounting*

# Decision-making under conditions of risk and uncertainty

In Chapters 8–11 we considered the use of a single representative set of estimates for predicting future costs and revenues when alternative courses of action are followed. For example, in Chapter 11 we used a single representative estimate of demand for each selling price. However, the outcome of a particular decision may be affected by an uncertain environment that cannot be predicted, and a single representative estimate does not therefore convey all the information that might reasonably influence a decision.

Let us now look at a more complicated example; consider a situation where a company has two mutually exclusive potential alternatives, A and B, which each yield receipts of £50 000. The estimated costs of alternative A can be predicted with considerable confidence, and are expected to fall in the range of £40 000–£42 000; £41 000 might be considered a reasonable estimate of cost. The estimate for alternative B is subject to much greater uncertainty, since this alternative requires high-precision work involving operations that are unfamiliar to the company's labour force. The estimated costs are between £35 000 and £45 000, but £40 000 is selected as a representative estimate. If we consider single representative estimates alternative B appears preferable, since the estimated profit is £10 000 compared with an estimated profit of £9000 for alternative A; but a different picture may emerge if we take into account the range of possible outcomes.

Alternative A is expected to yield a profit of between £8000 and £10 000 whereas the range of profits for alternative B is between £5000 and £15 000. Management may consider it preferable to opt for a fairly certain profit of between £8000 and £10 000 for alternative A rather than take the chance of earning a profit of £5000 from alternative B (even though there is the possibility of earning a profit of £15 000 at the other extreme).

This example demonstrates that there is a need to incorporate the uncertainty relating to each alternative into the decision-making process, and in this chapter we shall consider the various

## Learning objectives

After studying this chapter, you should be able to:

- calculate and explain the meaning of expected values;
- explain the role and limitation of standard deviation and coefficient of variation as a measure of risk;
- construct a decision tree when there is a range of alternatives and possible outcomes;
- calculate the value of perfect information;
- apply the maximin, maximax and regret criteria;
- explain the implications of portfolio analysis.

methods of doing this. We shall then look at the application of these methods to pricing decisions and CVP analysis under conditions of uncertainty.

# A decision-making model

It is possible to develop a model of decision-making since all decision problems have some definable structure containing certain basic elements. Figure 12.1 shows the elements of a decision model under conditions of risk and uncertainty.

You can see that a decision model has the following characteristics:

1. An objective or target that a decision-maker is hoping to achieve, for example maximization of profits, or present value of cash flows. The quantification of an objective is often called an **objective function**; it is used to evaluate the alternative courses of action and to provide the basis of choosing the best alternative.

2. The search for alternative courses of action that will enable the objective to be achieved.

3. Because decision problems exist in an uncertain environment, it is necessary to consider those uncontrollable factors that are outside the decision-maker's control and that may occur for each alternative course of action. These uncontrollable factors are called **events** or **states of nature**. For example, in a product launch situation possible states of nature could consist of events such as a similar product being launched by a competitor at a lower price, or no similar product being launched.

4. A set of **outcomes** for the various possible combinations of actions and events. Each outcome is conditionally dependent on a specific course of action and a specific state of nature.

5. A measure of the value or **payoff** of each possible outcome in terms of the decision-maker's objectives. Payoffs are normally expressed in monetary terms such as profits or cash flows, but in some problems we may be interested in other payoffs such as time, market share, and so on.

6. Selection of a course of action.

The essential characteristics of a decision model are illustrated from the information shown in Example 12.1.

The elements of the decision model for Example 12.1 and the hypothetical possible outcomes from each state of nature are illustrated in Figure 12.2. This is known as a **decision tree**. In this diagram we have not measured the value (i.e. the payoff) for each possible course of action, but in the remainder of the chapter we shall look at ways of measuring the payoff where various outcomes are possible. Let us begin by discussing some of the concepts and techniques which are necessary for analysing risk and uncertainty.

# Risk and uncertainty

A distinction is often drawn by decision theorists between risk and uncertainty. **Risk** is applied to a situation where there are several possible outcomes and there is relevant past

**FIGURE 12.1** *A decision-making model under conditions of uncertainty.*

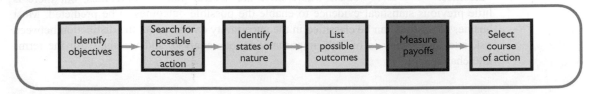

EXAMPLE 12.1

The Pretorian Company is reviewing its marketing policy for the next budget period. It has developed two new products, X and Y, but it only has sufficient resources to launch one of them. The appropriate states of nature relate to the activities of its competitors and are as follows:

1. competitors do nothing;
2. competitors introduce a comparable product;
3. competitors introduce a superior product.

**FIGURE 12.2** *A decision tree.*

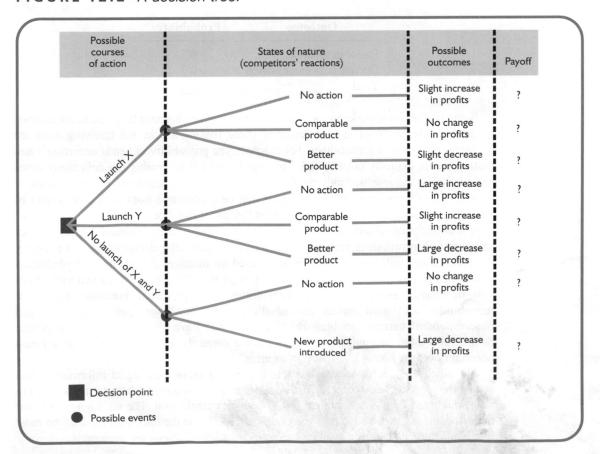

experience to enable statistical evidence to be produced for predicting the possible outcomes. Uncertainty exists where there are several possible outcomes, but there is little previous statistical evidence to enable the possible outcomes to be predicted. Most business decisions can be classified in the uncertainty category, but the distinction between risk and uncertainty is of little importance in our analysis and we shall use the terms interchangeably.

# Probabilities

The likelihood that an event or state of nature will occur is known as its probability, and this is normally expressed in decimal form with a value between 0 and 1. A value of 0 denotes a nil likelihood of occurrence whereas a value of 1 signifies absolute certainty – a definite occurrence. A probability of 0.4 means that the event is expected to occur four times out of ten. The total of the probabilities for events that can possibly occur must sum to 1.0. For example, if a tutor indicates that the probability of a student passing an examination is 0.7 then this means that the student has a 70% chance of passing the examination. Given that the pass/fail alternatives represent an exhaustive listing of all possible outcomes of the event, the probability of not passing the examination is 0.3.

The information can be presented in a probability distribution. A probability distribution is a list of all possible outcomes for an event and the probability that each will occur. The probability distribution for the above illustration is as follows:

| Outcome | Probability |
|---|---|
| Pass examination | 0.7 |
| Do not pass examination | 0.3 |
| Total | 1.0 |

Some probabilities are know as objective probabilities because they can be established mathematically or compiled from historical data. Tossing a coin and throwing a die are examples of objective probabilities. For example, the probability of heads occurring when tossing a coin logically must be 0.5. This can be proved by tossing the coin many times and observing the results. Similarly, the probability of obtaining number 1 when a die is thrown is 0.166 (i.e. one-sixth). This again can be ascertained from logical reasoning or recording the results obtained from repeated throws of the dice.

It is unlikely that objective probabilities can be established for business decisions, since many past observations or repeated experiments for particular decisions are not possible; the probabilities will have to be estimated based on managerial judgement. Probabilities established in this way are known as subjective probabilities because no two individuals will necessarily assign the same probabilities to a particular outcome. Subjective probabilities are based on an individual's expert knowledge, past experience, and observations of current variables which are likely to have an impact on future events. Such probabilities are unlikely to be estimated correctly, but any estimate of a future uncertain event is bound to be subject to error.

The advantage of this approach is that it provides more meaningful information than stating the most likely outcome. Consider, for example, a situation where a tutor is asked to state whether student A and student B will pass an examination. The tutor may reply that both students are expected to pass the examination. This is the tutor's estimate of the most likely outcome. However, the following probability distributions are preferable:

| Outcome | Student A probability | Student B probability |
|---|---|---|
| Pass examination | 0.9 | 0.6 |
| Do not pass examination | 0.1 | 0.4 |
| Total | 1.0 | 1.0 |

Such a probability distribution requires the tutor to specify the degree of confidence in his or her estimate of the likely outcome of a future event. This information is clearly more meaningful than a mere estimate of the most likely outcome that both students are expected to pass the examination, because it indicates that it is most unlikely that A will fail, whereas there is a possibility that B will fail. Let us now apply the principles of probability theory to business decision-making.

# Probability distributions and expected value

The presentation of a probability distribution for each alternative course of action can provide useful additional information to management, since the distribution indicates the degree of uncertainty that exists for each alternative course of action. Probability distributions enable management to consider not only the possible profits (i.e. the payoff) from each alternative course of action but also the amount of uncertainty that applies to each alternative. Let us now consider the situation presented in Example 12.2.

From the probability distributions shown in Example 12.2 you will see that there is a 1 in 10 chance that profits will be £6000 for product A, but there is also a 4 in 10 chance that profits will be £8000. A more useful way of reading the probability distribution is to state that there is a 7 in 10 chance that profits will be £8000 or less. This is obtained by adding together the probabilities for profits of £6000, £7000 and £8000. Similarly, there is a 3 in 10 chance that profits will be £9000 or more.

## EXPECTED VALUES

The **expected value** (sometimes called expected payoff) is calculated by weighting each of the profit levels (i.e. possible outcomes) in Example 12.2 by its associated probability. The sum of these weighted amounts is called the expected value of the probability distribution. In other words, the expected value is the weighted arithmetic mean of the possible outcomes. The expected values of £8000 and £8900 calculated for products A and B take into account a range of possible outcomes rather than using a **single most likely estimate**. For example, the single most likely estimate is the profit level with the highest probability attached to it. For both products A and B in Example 12.2 the single most likely estimate is £8000, which appears to indicate that we may be indifferent as to which product should be made. However the expected value calculation takes into account the possibility that a range of different profits are possible and weights these profits by the probability of their occurrence. The weighted calculation indicates that product B is expected to produce the highest average profits in the future.

The expected value of a decision represents the long-run average outcome that is expected to occur if a particular course of action is undertaken many times. For example, if the decision to make products A and B is repeated on, say, 100 occasions in the future then product A will be expected to give an average profit of £8000 whereas product B would be expected to give an average profit of £8900. The expected values are the averages of the possible outcomes based on management estimates. There is no guarantee that the actual

**EXAMPLE 12.2**

A manager is considering whether to make product A or product B, but only one can be produced. The estimated sales demand for each product is uncertain. A detailed investigation of the possible sales demand for each product gives the following probability distribution of the profits for each product.

**Product A probability distribution**

| (1) Outcome | (2) Estimated probability | (3) Weighted (col. 1 amount × col. 2) (£) |
|---|---|---|
| Profits of £6000 | 0.10 | 600 |
| Profits of £7000 | 0.20 | 1400 |
| Profits of £8000 | 0.40 | 3200 |
| Profits of £9000 | 0.20 | 1800 |
| Profits of £10 000 | 0.10 | 1000 |
| | 1.00 | |
| | Expected value | 8000 |

**Product B probability distribution**

| (1) Outcome | (2) Estimated probability | (3) Weighted (col. 1 amount × col. 2) (£) |
|---|---|---|
| Profits of £4000 | 0.05 | 200 |
| Profits of £6000 | 0.10 | 600 |
| Profits of £8000 | 0.40 | 3200 |
| Profits of £10 000 | 0.25 | 2500 |
| Profits of £12 000 | 0.20 | 2400 |
| | 1.00 | |
| | Expected value | 8900 |

Which product should the company make?

outcome will equal the expected value. Indeed, the expected value for product B does not appear in the probability distribution.

# Measuring the amount of uncertainty

In addition to the expected values of the profits for the various alternatives, management is also interested in the degree of uncertainty of the expected future profits. For example, let us assume that another alternative course of action, say, product C, is added to the alternatives in Example 12.2 and that the probability distribution is as follows:

**Product C probability distribution**

| Outcome | Estimated probability | Weighted amount (£) |
|---|---|---|
| Loss of £4000 | 0.5 | (2 000) |
| Profit of £22 000 | 0.5 | 11 000 |
| | Expected value | 9 000 |

Product C has a higher expected value than either product A or product B, but it is unlikely that management will prefer product C to product B, because of the greater variability of the possible outcomes. In other words, there is a greater degree of uncertainty attached to product C.

The conventional measure of the dispersion of a probability distribution is the **standard deviation**. The standard deviation ($\sigma$) is the square root of the mean of the squared deviations from the expected value and is calculated from the following formula:

$$\sigma = \sqrt{\sum_{x=1}^{n}(A_x - \bar{A})^2 P_x} \qquad (12.1)$$

where $A_x$ are the profit-level observations, $\bar{A}$ is the expected or mean value, $P_x$ is the probability of each outcome, and the summation is over all possible observations, where $n$ is the total number of possibilities.

The square of the standard deviation $\sigma^2$ is known as the statistical variance of the distribution, and should not be confused with the variance from budget or standard cost, which will be discussed in subsequent chapters. The calculations of the standard deviations for products A and B in Example 12.2 are set out in Exhibit 12.1.

If we are comparing the standard deviations of two probability distributions with different expected values, we cannot make a direct comparison. Can you see why this should be so? Consider the following probability distribution for another product, say product D.

**Product D probability distribution**

| Outcome | Estimated probability | Weighted amount (£) |
|---|---|---|
| Profits of £40 000 | 0.05 | 2 000 |
| Profits of £60 000 | 0.10 | 6 000 |
| Profits of £80 000 | 0.40 | 32 000 |
| Profits of £100 000 | 0.25 | 25 000 |
| Profits of £120 000 | 0.20 | 24 000 |
| | Expected value | 89 000 |

The standard deviation for product D is £21 424, but all of the possible outcomes are ten times as large as the corresponding outcomes for product B. The outcomes for product D also have the same pattern of probabilities as product B, and we might conclude that the two projects are equally risky. Nevertheless, the standard deviation for product D is ten times as large as that for product B. This scale effect can be removed be replacing the standard deviation with a relative measure of dispersion. The relative amount of dispersion can be expressed by the **coefficient of variation**, which is simply the standard deviation divided by the expected value. The coefficient of variation for product B is

**EXHIBIT 12.1**

*Calculation of standard deviations*

2142.40/8900 = 0.241 (or 24.1%), and for product D it is also 0.241 (21 424/89 000), thus indicating that the relative amount of dispersion is the same for both products.

### Product A

| (1) Profit (£) | (2) Deviation from expected value, $A_x - \overline{A}$ (£) | (3) Squared deviation $(A_x - \overline{A})^2$ (£) | (4) Probability | (5) Weighted amount (col. 3 × col. 4) (£) |
|---|---|---|---|---|
| 6 000 | −2000 | 4 000 000 | 0.1 | 400 000 |
| 7 000 | −1000 | 1 000 000 | 0.2 | 200 000 |
| 8 000 | 0 | — | 0.4 | — |
| 9 000 | +1000 | 1 000 000 | 0.2 | 200 000 |
| 10 000 | +2000 | 4 000 000 | 0.1 | 400 000 |
| | | Sum of squared deviations | | 1 200 000 |
| | | Standard deviation | | £1095.40 |
| | | Expected value | | £8000 |

### Product B

| (1) Profit (£) | (2) Deviation $A_x - \overline{A}$ (£) | (3) Squared deviation $(A_x - \overline{A})^2$ (£) | (4) Probability | (5) Weighted amount (col. 3 × col. 4) (£) |
|---|---|---|---|---|
| 4 000 | −4900 | 24 010 000 | 0.05 | 1 200 500 |
| 6 000 | −2900 | 8 410 000 | 0.10 | 841 000 |
| 8 000 | −900 | 810 000 | 0.40 | 324 000 |
| 10 000 | 1 100 | 1 210 000 | 0.25 | 302 500 |
| 12 000 | 3100 | 9 610 000 | 0.20 | 1 922 000 |
| | | Sum of squared deviations | | 4 590 000 |
| | | Standard deviation | | £2142.40 |
| | | Expected value | | £8900 |

In our discussion so far we have defined risk in terms of the spread of possible outcomes, so that risk may be large even if all the possible outcomes involve earning high profits. However, the risk attached to possible profits/losses obtained from alternative courses of action is not dispersion *per se* but the possibility of deviations *below* the expected value of the profits. A decision-maker would hardly consider large possible deviations *above* the expected value undesirable. Consider the following probability distributions:

**Product X probability distribution**

| Outcome | Estimated probability | Weighted amount (£) |
|---|---|---|
| Profits of £4000 | 0.1 | 400 |
| Profits of £6000 | 0.3 | 1800 |
| Profits of £8000 | 0.6 | 4800 |
| | Expected value | 7000 |

**Product Y probability distribution**

| Outcome | Estimated probability | Weighted amount (£) |
|---|---|---|
| Profits of £6000 | 0.2 | 1200 |
| Profits of £8000 | 0.5 | 4000 |
| Profits of £12 000 | 0.3 | 3600 |
| | Expected value | 8800 |

The standard deviations are £1342 for X and £2227 for Y, giving coefficients of variations of 0.19 for X and 0.28 for Y. These measures indicate that the estimates of product Y are subject to a greater variability, but product X appears to be the riskier product since the probability of profits being less that £7000 (the expected value of X) is 0.4 for product X but only 0.2 for product Y. Clearly, the standard deviation and coefficient of variation are not perfect measures of risk, but the mathematical complexities of measuring only those deviations below the expected value are formidable for anything beyond the simplest situation. Measures such as expected values, standard deviations or coefficient of variations are used to summarize the characteristics of alternative courses of action, but they are poor substitutes for representing the probability distributions, since they do not provide the decision-maker with all the relevant information. There is an argument for presenting the entire probability distribution directly to the decision-maker. Such an approach is appropriate when management must select one from a small number of alternatives, but in situations where many alternatives need to be considered the examination of many probability distributions is likely to be difficult and time-consuming. In such situations management may have no alternative but to compare the expected values and coefficients of variation.

# Attitudes to risk by individuals

How do we determine whether or not a risky course of action should be undertaken? The answer to this question depends on the decision-maker's attitude to risk. We can identify three possible attitudes: an aversion to risk, a desire for risk and an indifference to risk. Consider two alternatives, A and B, which have the following possible outcomes, depending on the state of the economy (i.e. the state of nature):

**Possible returns**

| State of the economy | A (£) | B (£) |
|---|---|---|
| Recession | 90 | 0 |
| Normal | 100 | 100 |
| Boom | 110 | 200 |

If we assume that the three states of the economy are equally likely then the expected value for each alternative is £100. A **risk-seeker** is one who, given a choice between more or less risky alternatives with identical expected values, prefers the riskier alternative (alternative B). Faced with the same choice, a **risk-averter** would select the less risky alternative (alternative A). The person who is indifferent to risk (**risk neutral**) would be indifferent to both alternatives because they have the same expected values. With regard to investors in general, studies of the securities markets provide convincing evidence that the majority of investors are risk-averse.

Let us now reconsider how useful expected value calculations are for choosing between alternative courses of action. Expected values represent a long-run average solution, but decisions should not be made on the basis of expected values alone, since they do not enable the decision-maker's attitude towards risk to be taken into account. Consider for example, a situation where two individuals play a coin-tossing game, with the loser giving the winner £5000. The expected value to the player who calls heads is as follows:

| Outcome | Cash flow (£) | Probability | Weighted amount (£) |
|---|---|---|---|
| Heads | +5000 | 0.5 | +2500 |
| Tails | −5000 | 0.5 | −2500 |
| | | Expected value | 0 |

The expected value is zero, but this will not be the actual outcome if only one game is played. The expected-value calculation represents the average outcome only if the game is repeated on many occasions. However, because the game is to be played only once, it is unlikely that each player will find the expected value calculation on its own to be a useful calculation for decision-making. In fact, the expected value calculation implies that each player is indifferent to playing the game, but this indifference will only apply if the two players are neutral to risk. However, a risk-averter will find the game most unattractive. As most business managers are unlikely to be neutral towards risk, and business decisions are rarely repeated, it is unwise for decisions to be made solely on the basis of expected values. At the very least, expected values should be supplemented with measures of dispersion and, where possible, decisions should be made after comparing the probability distributions of the various alternative courses of action.

# Decision-tree analysis

In the examples earlier in this chapter we have assumed that profits were uncertain because of the uncertainty of sales demand. In practice, more than one variable may be uncertain (e.g. sales and costs), and also the value of some variables may be dependent on the values of other variables. Many outcomes may therefore be possible, and some outcomes may be

## EXAMPLE 12.3

A company is considering whether to develop and market a new product. Development costs are estimated to be £180 000, and there is a 0.75 probability that the development effort will be successful and a 0.25 probability that the development effort will be unsuccessful. If the development is successful, the product will be marketed, and it is estimated that:

1. if the product is very successful profits will be £540 000;
2. if the product is moderately successful profits will be £100 000;
3. if the product is a failure, there will be a loss of £400 000.

Each of the above profit and loss calculations is after taking into account the development costs of £180 000. The estimated probabilities of each of the above events are as follows:

1. Very successful        0.4
2. Moderately successful  0.3
3. Failure                0.3

dependent on previous outcomes. A useful analytical tool for clarifying the range of alternative courses of action and their possible outcomes is a decision tree.

A decision tree is a diagram showing several possible courses of action and possible events (i.e. states of nature) and the potential outcomes for each course of action. Each alternative course of action or event is represented by a branch, which leads to subsidiary branches for further courses of action or possible events. Decision trees are designed to illustrate the full range of alternatives and events that can occur, under all envisaged conditions. The value of a decision tree is that its logical analysis of a problem enables a complete strategy to be drawn up to cover all eventualities before a firm becomes committed to a scheme. Let us now consider Example 12.3. This will be used to illustrate how decision trees can be applied to decision-making under conditions of uncertainty.

The decision tree for Example 12.3 is set out in Figure 12.3. The boxes indicate the point at which decisions have to be taken, and the branches emanating from it indicate the available alternative courses of action. The circles indicate the points at which there are environmental changes that affect the consequences of prior decisions. The branches from these points indicate the possible types of environment (states of nature) that may occur.

Note that the joint probability of two events occurring together is the probability of one event times the probability of the other event. For example, the probability of the development effort succeeding and the product being very successful consists of the products of the probabilities of these two events, i.e. 0.75 times 0.4, giving a probability of 0.30. Similarly, the probability of the development effort being successful and the product being moderately successful is 0.225 (0.75 × 0.3). The total expected value for the decision to develop the product consists of the sum of all the items in the expected value column on the 'Develop product' branch of the decision tree, i.e. £49 500. If we assume that there are no other alternatives available, other than the decision not to develop, the expected value of £49 500 for developing the product can be compared with the expected value of zero for not developing the product. Decision theory would suggest that the product should be developed because a positive expected value occurs. However, this does not mean that an outcome of £49 500 profit is guaranteed. The expected-value

**FIGURE 12.3** *A simple decision tree.*

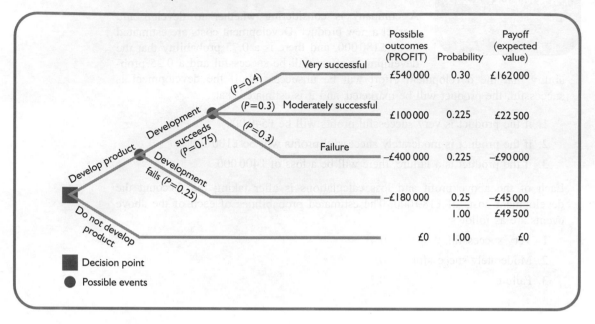

calculation indicates that if the probabilities are correct and this decision was repeated on many occasions an average profit of £49 500 would result.

Unfortunately, the decision will not be repeated on many occasions, and a run of repeated losses could force a company out of business before it has the chance to repeat similar decisions. Management may therefore prefer to examine the following probability distribution for developing the product:

| Outcome | Probability |
|---|---|
| Loss of £400 000 | 0.225 |
| Loss of £180 000 | 0.25 |
| Profit of £100 000 | 0.225 |
| Profit of £540 000 | 0.30 |

Management may decide that the project is too risky, since there is nearly a 0.5 probability of a loss occurring.

The decision tree provides a convenient means of identifying all the possible alternative courses of action and their interdependencies. This approach is particularly useful for assisting in the construction of probability distributions when many combinations of events are possible.

# Cost–volume–profit analysis under conditions of uncertainty

In Chapter 8 our discussion of cost–volume–profit analysis was based on single value estimates. In other words, we assumed that all costs and revenues were known with certainty. Clearly, this assumption is unrealistic, and therefore the traditional CVP model suffers from the limitation of not including any adjustments for risk and uncertainty. You should note, however, that some writers have extended CVP analysis to allow for uncertainty in the parameters of the model. We shall not consider CVP analysis and uncertainty at this stage, since the objective of this chapter is to provide a general explanation of how adjustments for uncertainty can be incorporated into decision models. CVP analysis under conditions of uncertainty is therefore dealt with in the Appendix to this chapter.

# Buying perfect and imperfect information

When a decision-maker is faced with a series of uncertain events that might occur, he or she should consider the possibility of obtaining additional information about which event is likely to occur. This section considers how we can calculate the maximum amount it would be worth paying to acquire additional information from a particular source. The approach we shall take is to compare the expected value of a decision if the information is acquired against the expected value with the absence of the information. The difference represents the maximum amount it is worth paying for the additional information. Consider Example 12.4.

Without the additional information, machine A will be purchased using the expected-value decision rule. If the additional information is obtained then this will give a perfect prediction of the level of demand, and the size of the machine can be matched with the level of demand. Therefore if demand is predicted to be low, machine A will be purchased, whereas if demand is predicted to be high, machine B will be purchased. The revised expected value is

$$(0.5 \times £100\,000) + (0.5 \times £200\,000) = £150\,000$$

You can see that the expected value is calculated by taking the highest profit in the case of low and high demand. When the decision to employ the market consultants is being taken, it is not known which level of demand will be predicted. Therefore the best estimate of the outcome from obtaining the additional information is a 0.5 probability that it will predict a low demand and a 0.5 probability that it will predict a high demand. (These are the probabilities that are currently associated with low and high demand.)

The value of the additional information is ascertained by deducting the expected value without the market survey (£130 000) from the expected value with the survey (£150 000). Thus the additional information increases expected value from £130 000 to £150 000 and the expected value of perfect information is £20 000. As long as the cost of obtaining the information is less than £20 000, the firm of market consultants should be employed.

In the above illustration it was assumed that the additional information would give a 100% accurate prediction of the expected demand. In practice, it is unlikely that *perfect* information is obtainable, but *imperfect* information (for example, predictions of future demand may be only 80% reliable) may still be worth obtaining. However, the value of imperfect information will always be less than the value of perfect information except when both equal zero. This would occur where the additional information would not change the decision. Note that the principles that are applied for calculating the value of imperfect information are the same as those we applied for calculating the value of perfect information, but the calculations are more complex. For an illustration see Scapens (1991).

**EXAMPLE 12.4**

The Boston Company must choose between one of two machines – machine A has low fixed costs and high unit variable costs where-as machine B has high fixed costs and low unit variable costs. Consequently, machine A is most suited to low-level demand whereas machine B is suited to high-level demand. For simplicity assume that there are only two possible demand levels – low and high – and the estimated probability of each of these events is 0.5. The estimated profits for each demand level are as follows:

|           | Low demand (£) | High demand (£) | Expected value (£) |
|-----------|----------------|-----------------|--------------------|
| Machine A | 100 000        | 160 000         | 130 000            |
| Machine B | 10 000         | 200 000         | 105 000            |

There is a possibility of employing a firm of market consultants who would be able to provide a perfect prediction of the actual demand. What is the maximum amount the company should be prepared to pay the consultants for the additional information?

# Maximin, maximax and regret criteria

In some situations it might not be possible to assign meaningful estimates of probabilities to possible outcomes. Where this situation occurs managers might use any of the following criteria to make decisions: maximin, maximax or the criterion of regret.

The assumption underlying the maximin criterion is that the worst possible outcome will always occur and the decision-maker should therefore select the largest payoff under this assumption. Consider the Boston Company in Example 12.4. You can see that the worst outcomes are £100 000 for machine A and £10 000 for machine B. Consequently, machine A should be purchased using the maximin decision rule.

The maximax criterion is the opposite of maximin, and is based on the assumption that the best payoff will occur. Referring again to Example 12.4, the highest payoffs are £160 000 for machine A and £200 000 for machine B. Therefore machine B will be selected under the maximax criterion.

The regret criterion is based on the fact that, having selected an alternative that does not turn out to be the best, the decision-maker will regret not having chosen another alternative when he or she had the opportunity. Thus if in Example 12.4 machine B has been selected on the assumption that the high level of demand would occur, and the high level of demand actually did occur, there would be no regret. However, if machine A has been selected, the company would lose £40 000 (£200 000 – £160 000). This measures the amount of the regret. Similarly, if machine A was selected on the assumption that demand would be low, and the low level of demand actually did occur, there would be no regret; but if machine B was selected, the amount of the regret would be £90 000 (£100 000 – £10 000). This information is summarized in the following regret matrix:

|                   | State of nature      |                       |
|-------------------|----------------------|-----------------------|
|                   | Low demand (£)       | High demand (£)       |
| Choose machine A  | 0                    | 40 000                |
| Choose machine B  | 90 000               | 0                     |

The aim of the regret criterion is to minimize the maximum possible regret. The maximum regret for machine A is £40 000 while that for Machine B is £90 000. Machine A would therefore be selected using the regret criterion.

# Portfolio analysis

It is unwise for a firm to invest all its funds in a single project, since an unfavourable event may occur that will affect this project and have a dramatic effect on the firm's total financial position. A better approach would be for the firm to invest in a number of different projects. If this strategy is followed, an unfavourable event that affects one project may have relatively less effect on the remaining projects and thus have only a small impact on the firm's overall financial position. That is, a firm should not put all of its eggs in one basket, but should try to minimize risk by spreading its investments over a variety of projects.

The collection of investments held by an individual investor or the collection of projects in which a firm invests is known as a portfolio. The objective in selecting a portfolio is to achieve certain desirable characteristics regarding risk and expected return. Let us now consider Example 12.5. From Example 12.5 it can be seen that both the existing activities (umbrella manufacturing) and the proposed new project (ice-cream manufacturing) are risky when considered on their own, but when they are combined, the risk is eliminated because whatever the outcome the cash inflow will be £20 000. Example 12.5 tells us that we should not only consider the risk of individual projects but should also take into account how the risks of potential new projects and existing activities co-vary with each other. Risk is eliminated completely in Example 12.5 because perfect negative correlation (i.e. where the correlation coefficient is $-1$) exists between the cash flows of the proposed project and the cash flows of the existing activities. When the cash flows are perfectly positively correlated (where the correlation is $+1$), risk reduction cannot be achieved when the projects are combined. For all other correlation values risk reduction advantages can be obtained by investing in projects that are not perfectly correlated with existing activites.

## EXAMPLE 12.5

A firm which currently manufactures umbrellas is considering diversifying and investing in the manufacture of ice-cream. The predicted cash flows for the existing activities and the new project are shown below.

| States of nature | Existing activities (Umbrella manufacturing) (£) | Proposed project (Ice-cream manufacturing) (£) | Combination of existing activities and the proposed project (£) |
|---|---|---|---|
| Sunshine | $-40\,000$ | $+60\,000$ | $+20\,000$ |
| Rain | $+60\,000$ | $-40\,000$ | $+20\,000$ |

To simplify the illustration it is assumed that only two states of nature exist (rain or sunshine) and each has a probability of 0.5.

The important point that emerges from the above discussion is that we should not consider the risk of individual projects in isolation but rather the incremental risk that each project will contribute to the overall risk of the firm.

# A more complex illustration

**AR** We shall now use Example 12.6 to illustrate the application of the principles described in this chapter to a more complex situation relating to a pricing decision. To keep things simple Example 12.6 assumes that only three selling prices are being considered and that only sales demand and variable costs are subject to uncertainty. You should now refer to Example 12.6 and then to the decision tree shown in Figure 12.4.

You will see from the decision tree that there are three possible demands and two possible variable costs, giving six possible outcomes for each selling price, and 18 possible outcomes when all three prices are considered. These 18 possible outcomes are included in the decision tree. The expected value for each selling price is calculated by multiplying the contribution to general fixed costs column in Figure 12.4 by the combined probability column for each possible outcome. The probability distribution for each possible selling price has been extracted from the decision tree in Figure 12.4 and is presented in ascending order of contribution in Exhibit 12.2.

---

**EXAMPLE 12.6**

The Sigma Company is introducing a new product. The company has carried out some market research studies and analysed the selling prices of similar types of competitive products that are currently being sold. The information suggests that a selling price of £18, £19 or £20 is appropriate. The company intends to hire machinery to manufacture the product at a cost of £200 000 per annum, but if annual production is in excess of 60 000 units then additional machinery will have to be hired at a cost of £80 000 per annum. The variable cost is expected to be either £5 or £6 per unit produced, depending on the outcome of negotiations with suppliers. The market research department has produced the following estimates of sales demand for each possible selling price. These estimates are based on pessimistic, most likely and optimistic forecasts, and subjective probabilities have been attached to them. The estimates are as follows:

| | £18 | | £19 | | £20 | |
|---|---|---|---|---|---|---|
| | Units sold | Probability | Units sold | Probability | Units sold | Probability |
| Pessimistic | 70 000 | 0.3 | 60 000 | 0.1 | 30 000 | 0.4 |
| Most likely | 80 000 | 0.5 | 70 000 | 0.7 | 60 000 | 0.5 |
| Optimistic | 90 000 | 0.2 | 90 000 | 0.2 | 70 000 | 0.1 |

The probabilities for the unit variable cost are 0.6 for a variable cost of £5 per unit and 0.4 for a variable cost of £6 per unit. The company has also committed itself to an advertising contract of £40 000 per annum.

**FIGURE 12.4**  *Decision tree and probability distributions for various selling prices.*

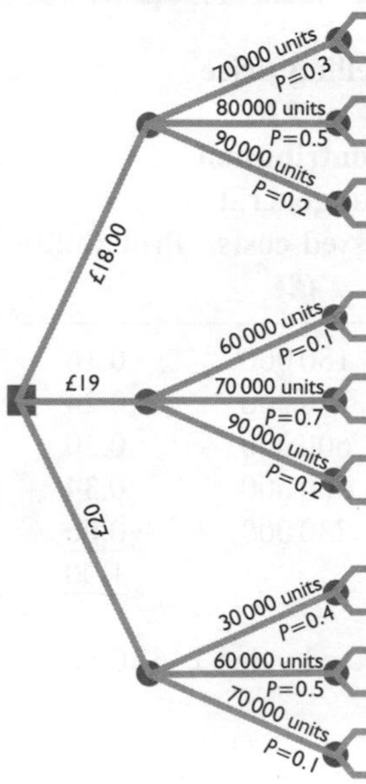

Decision tree branches:

- £18.00 → 70 000 units P=0.3; 80 000 units P=0.5; 90 000 units P=0.2
- £19 → 60 000 units P=0.1; 70 000 units P=0.7; 90 000 units P=0.2
- £20 → 30 000 units P=0.4; 60 000 units P=0.5; 70 000 units P=0.1

| (1) Selling price | (2) Demand | (3) Variable cost | (4) Combined probability (col. 2×col.3) | (5) Total contribution (£) | (6) Hire of machinery (£) | (7) Advertising (£) | (8) Contribution to general fixed costs (col. 5-col.6+7) (£) | (9) Expected value (col. 8×col.4) (£) | Outcome number |
|---|---|---|---|---|---|---|---|---|---|
| | | P=0.6 (£5) | 0.18 | 910000* | 280000 | 40000 | 590000 | 106 200 | 1 |
| | | P=0.4 (£6) | 0.12 | 840000** | 280000 | 40000 | 520000 | 62 400 | 2 |
| | | P=0.6 (£5) | 0.30 | 1040000 | 280000 | 40000 | 720000 | 216000 | 3 |
| | | P=0.4 (£6) | 0.20 | 960000 | 280000 | 40000 | 640000 | 128000 | 4 |
| | | P=0.6 (£5) | 0.12 | 1170000 | 280000 | 40000 | 850000 | 102000 | 5 |
| | | P=0.4 (£6) | 0.08 | 1080000 | 280000 | 40000 | 760000 | 60800 | 6 |
| | | | 1.00 | | | | | 675 400 | |
| | | P=0.6 (£5) | 0.06 | 840000 | 200000 | 40000 | 600000 | 36000 | 7 |
| | | P=0.4 (£6) | 0.04 | 780000 | 200000 | 40000 | 540000 | 21600 | 8 |
| | | P=0.6 (£5) | 0.42 | 980000 | 280000 | 40000 | 660000 | 277200 | 9 |
| | | P=0.4 (£6) | 0.28 | 910000 | 280000 | 40000 | 590000 | 165200 | 10 |
| | | P=0.6 (£5) | 0.12 | 1260000 | 280000 | 40000 | 940000 | 112800 | 11 |
| | | P=0.4 (£6) | 0.08 | 1170000 | 280000 | 40000 | 850000 | 68000 | 12 |
| | | | 1.00 | | | | | 680 800 | |
| | | P=0.6 (£5) | 0.24 | 450000 | 200000 | 40000 | 210000 | 50400 | 13 |
| | | P=0.4 (£6) | 0.16 | 420000 | 200000 | 40000 | 180000 | 28800 | 14 |
| | | P=0.6 (£5) | 0.30 | 900000 | 200000 | 40000 | 660000 | 198000 | 15 |
| | | P=0.4 (£6) | 0.20 | 840000 | 200000 | 40000 | 600000 | 120000 | 16 |
| | | P=0.6 (£5) | 0.06 | 1050000 | 280000 | 40000 | 730000 | 43800 | 17 |
| | | P=0.4 (£6) | 0.04 | 980000 | 280000 | 40000 | 660000 | 26400 | 18 |
| | | | 1.00 | | | | | 467 400 | |

■ Decision point
● Possible events

*70 000 units sales at a unit contribution of £13 (£18 selling price £5 variable cost)
**70 000 units sales at a unit contribution of £12 (£18 selling price less £6 variable cost)

An examination of Exhibit 12.2 indicates that management would be wise not to choose a selling price of £20, since this price gives the lowest expected value. Also, the probability distribution for a selling price of £20 indicates that the probability of a contribution of £210 000 or less is 0.40 compared with zero for a selling price of £18 and £19. However, it may be useful to present salient information from Exhibit 12.2 to management to assist them in deciding whether to choose a selling price of £18 or £19. The following information could be presented:

| | Selling price of £18 | Selling price of £19 |
|---|---|---|
| Probability of a contribution of £590 000 or less | 0.30 | 0.32 |
| Probability of a contribution of £850 000 or more | 0.12 | 0.20 |
| Maximum possible contribution | £850 000 | £940 000 |
| Minimum possible contribution | £520 000 | £540 000 |
| Expected value | £675 400 | £680 000 |

**EXHIBIT 12.2**

*Probability distribution for each possible selling price*

There would be little difference between adopting a selling price of £18 or £19, but a selling price of £19 appears to be slightly more attractive. There are strong arguments for presenting to management all the information contained in Exhibit 12.2 plus the salient information extracted above for selling prices of £18 and £19. This would enable management to choose the selling price with a probability distribution which most closely matches their attitude

| Selling price of £18 | | | Selling price of £19 | | | Selling price of £20 | | |
|---|---|---|---|---|---|---|---|---|
| Out-come | Contribution to general fixed costs (£) | Probability | Out-come | Contribution to general fixed costs (£) | Probability | Out-come | Contribution to general fixed costs (£) | Probability |
| 2 | 520 000 | 0.12 | 8 | 540 000 | 0.04 | 14 | 180 000 | 0.16 |
| 1 | 590 000 | 0.18 | 10 | 590 000 | 0.28 | 13 | 210 000 | 0.24 |
| 4 | 640 000 | 0.20 | 7 | 600 000 | 0.06 | 16 | 600 000 | 0.20 |
| 3 | 720 000 | 0.30 | 9 | 660 000 | 0.42 | 15/18 | 660 000 | 0.34 |
| 6 | 760 000 | 0.08 | 12 | 850 000 | 0.08 | 17 | 730 000 | 0.06 |
| 5 | 850 000 | 0.12 | 11 | 940 000 | 0.12 | | | 1.00 |
| | | 1.00 | | | 1.00 | | | |

Expected value £675 400      Expected value £680 800      Expected value £467 000

towards risk. It is important to note, however, that if a single value estimate approach is adopted that ignores the range of possible outcomes, management will be presented with contribution calculations based on the most likely outcomes, that is, those variables that have the highest probabilities attached to them.

The most likely sales demands and unit variable costs are therefore as follows:

| Selling price (£) | Sales demand (units) | Unit variable cost (£) |
|---|---|---|
| 18 | 80 000 | 5 |
| 19 | 70 000 | 5 |
| 20 | 60 000 | 5 |

The contribution to general fixed costs for the most likely outcomes can be obtained from outcomes 3, 9 and 15 in the decision tree (Figure 12.4), and are as follows:

Selling price of £18      Total contribution of £720 000
Selling price of £19      Total contribution of £660 000
Selling price of £20      Total contribution of £660 000

You will see that a single-value-estimate presentation provides rather misleading information. It appears that a selling price of £20 should be seriously considered and that the highest contribution is obtained from a selling price of £18. The expected value and probability-distribution approach provides a more revealing picture and indicates that management would be unwise to adopt a selling price of £20. Furthermore, a selling price of £19 is shown to be preferable to £18 when all the possible outcomes are considered.

You should also note that Example 12.6 contained only two variables with uncertain values: sales demand and variable cost per unit. In practice, several variables may be uncertain, and this can lead to a decision tree having hundreds of branches, thus causing difficulties in constructing probability distributions on a manual basis. We shall see in Chapter 14 that this problem can be overcome by using a computer and applying simulation techniques. ●●●

## Self-Assessment Question

You should attempt to answer this question yourself before looking up the suggested answer, which appears on pages 1115–17. If any part of your answer is incorrect, check back carefully to make sure you understand where you went wrong.

Central Ltd has developed a new product, and is currently considering the marketing and pricing policy it should employ for this. Specifically, it is considering whether the sales price should be set at £15 per unit or at the higher level of £24 per unit. Sales volumes at these two prices are shown in the following table:

| Sales price £15 per unit | | Sales price £24 per unit | |
|---|---|---|---|
| Forecast sales volume (000) | Probability | Forecast sales volume (000) | Probability |
| 20 | 0.1 | 8 | 0.1 |
| 30 | 0.6 | 16 | 0.3 |
| 40 | 0.3 | 20 | 0.3 |
| | | 24 | 0.3 |

The fixed production costs of the venture will be £38 000.

The level of the advertising and publicity costs will depend on the sales price and the market aimed for. With a sales price of £15 per unit, the advertising and publicity costs will amount to £12 000. With a sales price of £24 per unit, these costs will total £122 000.

Labour and variable overhead costs will amount to £5 per unit produced. Each unit produced requires 2 kg of raw material and the basic cost is expected to be £4 per kg. However, the suppliers of the raw materials are prepared to lower the price in return for a firm agreement to purchase a guaranteed minimum quantity. If Central Ltd contracts to purchase at least 40 000 kg then the price will be reduced to £3.75 per kg for *all* purchases. If Central contracts to purchase a minimum of 60 000 kg then the price will be reduced to £3.50 per kg for all purchases. It is only if Central Ltd guarantees either of the above minimum levels of purchases in advance that the appropriate reduced prices will be operative.

If Central Ltd were to enter into one of the agreements for the supply of raw material and was to find that it did not require to utilize the entire quantity of materials purchased then the excess could be sold. The sales price will depend upon the quantity that is offered for sale. If 16 000 kg or more are sold, the sales price will be £2.90 per kg for all sales. If less than 16 000 kg are offered, the sales price will be only £2.40 per kg.

Irrespective of amount sold, the costs incurred in selling the excess raw materials will be, per kg, as follows:

| | |
|---|---|
| Packaging | £0.30 |
| Delivery | £0.45 |
| Insurance | £0.15 |

Central's management team feels that losses are undesirable, while high expected money values are desirable. Therefore it is considering the utilization of a formula that incorporated both aspects of the outcome to measure the desirability of each strategy. The formula to be used to measure the desirability is:

$$\text{desirability} = L + 3E$$

where $L$ is the lowest outcome of the strategy and $E$ is the expected monetary value of the strategy. The higher this measures, the more desirable the strategy.

The marketing manager seeks the advice of you, the management accountant, to assist in deciding the appropriate strategy. He says 'we need to make two decisions now:

(i) Which price per unit should be charged: £15 or £24?

(ii) Should all purchases of raw materials be at the price of £4 per kg, or should we enter into an agreement for a basic minimum quantity? If we enter into an agreement then what minimum level of purchases should we guarantee?

As you are the management accountant, I expect you to provide me with some useful relevant figures.'

Required:

(a) Provide statements that show the various expected outcomes of each of the choices open to Central Ltd. (10 marks)

(b) Advise on its best choice of strategies if Central Ltd's objective is

    (i)   to maximize the expected monetary value of the outcomes;

    (ii)  to minimize the harm done to the firm if the worst outcome of each choice were to eventuate;

    (iii) to maximize the score on the above mentioned measure of desirability. (6 marks)

(c) Briefly comment on either

    (i)   two other factors that may be relevant in reaching a decision; OR (4 marks)

    (ii)  the decision criteria utilized in (b) above.

(Total 20 marks)

*ACCA P2 Management Accounting*

## Summary

In this chapter we have considered some of the important methods of incorporating risk and uncertainty into the decision-making process. We have established that estimates incorporating a range of possible outcomes with probabilities attached to each outcome are preferable to a single estimate based on the most likely outcome.

The term 'expected value' refers to the weighted average (or mean) outcome of a range of possible values that are assigned to a particular alternative course of action. Because expected values represent a long-run average solution, based on the assumption that decisions are repeated many times, and do not take risk attitudes into account, it has been suggested that decisions should not be taken solely on the basis of expected values.

At the very least expected values should be supplemented by measures of dispersion such as the standard deviation and the coefficient of variation. However, measures of dispersion are imperfect measures of business risk; wherever possible probability distributions for various alternatives should be compared.

Where there are many possible outcomes for various alternatives, and where some outcomes are dependent on previous outcomes, decision trees are a useful tool for analysing each alternative, and we have looked at an illustration of a decision tree for a pricing problem involving two uncertain variables.

Finally, it was pointed out that the degree of uncertainty attached to various alternatives should not be considered in isolation. Instead, how an alternative interacts with existing activities should be considered.

The aim should be to measure the incremented, rather than the total risk, of a project.

## Key Terms and Concepts

coefficient of variation (p. 417)
decision tree (pp. 412, 421)
events (p. 412)
expected value (p. 415)
expected value of perfect information (p. 423)
maximax criterion (p. 424)
maximin criterion (p. 424)
objective function (p. 412)
objective probabilities (p. 414)
outcomes (p. 412)
payoff (p. 412)
portfolio (p. 425)
portfolio analysis (p. 425)

probability (p. 414)
probability distribution (p. 414)
regret criterion (p. 424)
risk (p. 412)
risk-averter (p. 420)
risk neutral (p. 420)
risk-seeker (p. 420)
single most likely estimate (p. 414)
standard deviation (p. 417)
states of nature (p. 412)
subjective probabilities (p. 414)
uncertainty (p. 414)

## Recommended Reading

A more detailed treatment of decision trees can be found in Chapter 4 of Moore and Thomas (1991). For an explanation and illustration of how imperfect information can be valued you should refer to Chapter 7 of Scapens (1991).

# Appendix 12.1 Cost–volume–profit analysis under conditions of uncertainty

**AR** In Chapter 8 we noted that cost–volume–profit analysis suffers from a disadvantage that it does not include adjustments for risk and uncertainty. A possible approach by which uncertainty can be incorporated into the analysis is to apply normal distribution theory. Consider Example 12A.1.

The normal probability distribution for the sales quantity is shown in Figure 12A.1. The probability that actual sales quantity will be greater than 1060 units is shown by the shaded area to the right of 1060 units. Alternatively, the probability that actual sales will be less than 940 units is shown by the shaded area to the left of 940 units. Because the probability distribution for sales quantity is normal, with a mean of 1000 units and a standard deviation of 90 units, and the selling price, the variable costs and the fixed costs are assumed to be certain, the probability distribution for profits will also be normal, with a mean of £4000 and standard deviation of £3600.

The calculations are as follows:[1]

expected profit = expected sales volume (1000 units)

× contribution per unit (£40)

− fixed costs (£36 000)

standard deviation = standard deviation of sales volume (90 units)

× contribution per unit of £40

**EXAMPLE 12A.1**

The selling price of a product for the next accounting period is £100, and the variable cost is estimated to be £60 per unit. The budgeted fixed costs for the period are £36 000. Estimated sales for the period are 1000 units, and it is assumed that the probability distribution for the estimated sales quantity is normal with a standard deviation of 90 units. The selling price, variable cost and total fixed cost are assumed to be certain.

Using normal distribution theory, we can now answer the following questions for Example 12A.1:

1. What is the probability of a loss occurring or of profits being greater than zero?
2. What is the probability of profits being greater than £7600?
3. What is the probability of a loss in excess of £1400?

The questions can be answered by evaluating how many standard deviations each of the possible observations are from the mean:

$$\text{number of standard deviations from the mean} = \frac{X - \text{mean}}{\text{standard deviation}}$$

where $X$ is the outcome in which we are interested. For a profit level of nil the calculation is

$$\text{number of standard deviations from the mean} = \frac{0 - 4000}{3600} = -1.11$$

This calculation indicates that a profit of zero lies $-1.11$ standard deviations from the mean. To determine the probability that profit will be zero or less, we consult the normal probability distribution table in Appendix C at the end of this book. We find from the table that there is a 0.1335 probability that an observation will be less than $-1.11$ standard deviations from the mean of the distribution (Figure 12A.2a). The blue shaded area indicates that 13.35% of the observations will fall to the left of $-1.11$ standard deviations. Therefore the probability of a loss occurring is 13.35% (or 0.1335). The unshaded area indicates that the probability of an observation to the right of $-1.11$ standard deviations from the mean is 86.65% (or 0.8665). Note that the total area under the normal curve is 1.0.

The probability that profits will be in excess of £7600 will result in an observation of one standard deviation from the mean. This is calculated as follows:

$$\frac{7600 - 4000}{3600} = +1.0 \text{ standard deviation}$$

From the normal probability table in Appendix C you will see that the probability of an observation of $+1.0$ standard deviation from the mean is 0.1587, represented by the blue shaded area in Figure 12A.2(b). The probability of profits being greater than £7600 is therefore 15.87%.

Finally, the probability of a loss in excess of £1400 results in an observation of $-1.5$ standard deviations from the mean, calculated as follows:

$$\frac{-1400 - 4000}{3600} = -1.5 \text{ standard deviations}$$

This is represented by the blue shaded area in Figure 14A.2(c). Consequently, the probability of a loss in excess of £1400 is 0.0668.

**FIGURE 12A.1** *Normal distribution for the sales quantity in Example 12A.1.*

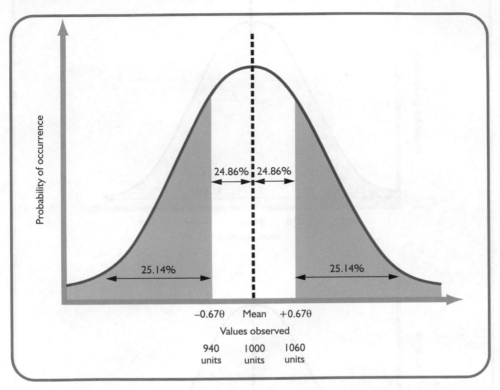

The question now arises as to how this information that we have obtained can be used. The manager knows that the estimated break-even sales are 900 units (£36 000 fixed costs divided by a contribution of £40 per unit) and that the expected sales are 1000 units, giving a profit of £4000. In addition, normal distribution theory enables the following information to be presented:

1. The probability of a loss occurring is 0.1335 and the probability of a profit is 0.8665.
2. The probability of profits being at least £7600 is 0.1587.
3. The probability of a loss in excess of £1400 is 0.0668.

If the manager is comparing this product with other products then this approach will enable him or her to assess the risk involved for each product, as well as to compare the relative break-even points and expected profits. The analysis can be modified to include fixed cost, variable cost and selling price as uncertain variables. The effect of treating these variables as uncertain will lead to an increase in the standard deviation because the variability of the variable cost, fixed cost and selling price will add to the variability of profits. For a description of CVP analysis when more than one variable is uncertain see Jaedicke and Robichek (1964).

## NORMALITY ASSUMPTION

Of vital importance to our discussion so far is the assumption that the distribution of possible outcomes is normal. It is possible to construct an estimate so that it represents a

**FIGURE 12A.2** *Probability distributions for various profit levels.*

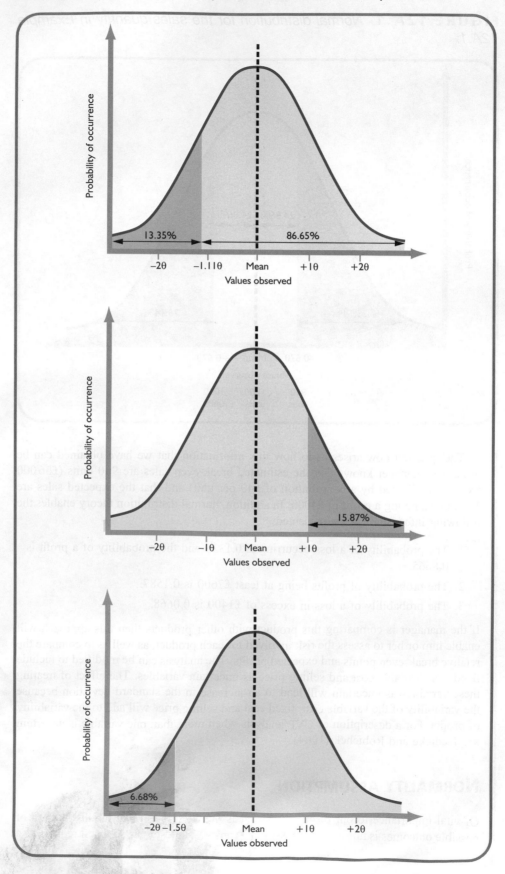

normal distribution. Consider an estimate of future sales quantity for a product. The marketing department are requested to produce an estimate based on the assumption that there is a 50% probability that actual sales will be above or below the estimated sales. Let us assume that this gives an estimated sales volume of 1000 units. Next we ask for an estimate of the quantity on either side of the mean of 1000 that is expected to result in sales quantity falling in this range 50% of the time. Let us assume the estimate is 60 units. In other words, we expect sales to fall within the range of 940 units to 1060 units 50% of the time. From the normal probability tables in Appendix C we know that one-half of the area under the normal curve lies within $\pm 0.67$ standard deviations from the mean (i.e. 1000 units $\pm 60$ units lies within 0.67 standard deviations from the mean). Therefore 0.67 standard deviations represents 60 units. Thus

$$2/3\sigma = 60 \text{ units}$$

$$\sigma = 90 \text{ units}$$

In other words, we have constructed the estimate in such a way that it meets the requirements of a normal distribution. The process can be illustrated by reference to Figure 12A.1.

The normal probability table in Appendix C indicates that the area to the right of $+0.67$ standard deviations from the mean is 25.14%. Similarly, the area to the left of $-0.67$ standard deviations is also 25.14%. The area between the mean and $\pm 0.67$ standard deviations represents the balance and is 49.72% or approximately 50%. In other words, for a normal distribution there is a probability of approximately 0.50 that observations will fall between $\pm 0.67$ standard deviations from the mean.

By ensuring that estimates are established in such a way that they represent a normal distribution, it is possible to estimate probabilities for any possible outcome. However, it is important to note that the resulting probabilities are only as good as the estimates. Like any projection of future outcomes, the projected results are likely to be subject to error. ●●●

## Key Examination Points

When you are faced with problems requiring an evaluation of alternatives with uncertain outcomes, you should calculate expected values and present probability distributions.

Note that expected values on their own are unlikely to be particularly useful and there is a need to supplement this measure with a probability distribution. Avoid calculating standard deviations, since they are rarely required and are a poor substitute for probability distributions.

It is particularly important with this topic that you plan your answer carefully. Once you have started your answer, it is difficult to remedy the situation if you initially adopt the wrong approach. A rough sketch of a decision tree at the start of your answer will force you to analyse the problem and identify all the alternatives and possible outcomes.

Most examination questions on this topic also include a requirement as to whether additional perfect information should be purchased. Do make sure that you understand how to calculate the value of perfect information.

# Questions

*Indicates that a suggested solution is to be found in the *Students' Manual*.

## 12.1 Advanced: Preparation of project statements for different demand levels and calculations of expected profit

Seeprint Limited is negotiating an initial one year contract with an important customer for the supply of a specialized printed colour catalogue at a fixed contract price of £16 per catalogue. Seeprint's normal capacity for producing such catalogues is 50 000 per annum.

Last year Seeprint Limited earned £11 000 profit per month from a number of small accounts requiring specialized colour catalogues. If the contract under negotiation is not undertaken, then a similar profit might be obtained from these customers next year, but, if it is undertaken, there will be no profit from such customers.

The estimated costs of producing colour catalogues of a specialized nature are given below.

The costs below are considered certain with the exception of the direct materials price.

Cost data:

|  | (£) |
| --- | --- |
| Variable costs per catalogue | |
| Direct materials | 4.50 |
| Direct wages | 3.00 |
| Direct expenses | 1.30 |

| Semi-variable costs | Output levels (capacity utilization) | | |
| --- | --- | --- | --- |
|  | 80% | 100% | 120% |
|  | (£) | (£) | (£) |
| Indirect materials | 46 800 | 47 000 | 74 400 |
| Indirect wages | 51 200 | 55 000 | 72 000 |
| Indirect expenses | 6 000 | 8 000 | 9 600 |

Estimated fixed costs per annum:

| | |
| --- | --- |
| Depreciation of specialist equipment | £ 8 000 |
| Supervisory and management salaries | £20 000 |
| Other fixed costs allocated to specialist colour catalogues production | £32 000 |

You are required to:

(a) Tabulate the costs and profits per unit and in total and the annual profits, assuming that the contract orders in the year are: (i) 40 000, (ii) 50 000 and (iii) 60 000 catalogues, at a direct material cost of £4.50 per catalogue. Comment on the tabulation you have prepared.
(10 marks)

(b) Calculate the expected profit for the year if it is assumed that the probability of the total order is:

0.4 for 40 000 catalogues
0.5 for 50 000 catalogues
0.1 for 60 000 catalogues

and that the probability of direct material cost is:

0.5 at £4.50 per catalogue
0.3 at £5.00 per catalogue
0.2 at £5.50 per catalogue.  (6 marks)

(c) Discuss the implications for Seeprint Limited of the acceptance or otherwise of the contract with the important customer.  (6 marks)
(Total 22 marks)
*ACCA Level 2 Management Accounting*

## 12.2* Advanced: Calculation of expected value and the presentation of a probability distribution

The Dunburgh Bus Company operated during the year ended 31 May 2000 with the following results:

(i) Average variable costs were £0·75 per bus mile.
(ii) Total fixed costs were £1 750 000.
(iii) The fare structure per journey was as follows:

| | |
| --- | --- |
| Adults 0 to 3 miles | £0.20 |
| 4 to 5 miles | £0.30 |
| over 5 miles | £0.50 |
| Juveniles (any distance) | £0.15 |
| Senior citizens (any distance) | £0.10 |

(iv) Total passenger journeys paid for were 24 000 000 which represented 60% capacity utilization. The capacity utilized comprised 60% adult, 20% juvenile and 20% senior citizen journeys. The adult journeys were broken down into 0–3 miles: 50%, 4–5 miles: 30%, over 5 miles: 20%.

(v) Twenty routes were operated with four buses per route, each bus covering 150 miles per day for 330 days of the year. The remaining days were taken up with maintenance work on the buses.

(vi) Advertising revenue from displays inside and outside the buses totalled £250 000 for the year. This is a fixed sum from contracts which will apply to each year up to 31 May 2002.

It is anticipated that all costs will increase by 10% due to inflation during the year to 31 May 2001 and that fares will be increased by 5% during the year. Whilst the fare increase of 5% has already been agreed and cannot be altered, it is possible that inflation might differ from the 10% rate anticipated.

Required:

(a) Prepare a statement showing the calculation of the net profit or loss for the year ended 31 May 2000 (5 marks)

(b) Calculate the average percentage capacity utilization at which the company will break even during the forthcoming year to 31 May 2001 if all fares are increased by 5%, cost inflation is 10% as anticipated and the passenger mix and bus operating activity are the same as for the year to 31 May 2000.

(5 marks)

(c) Now assume that management have some doubts about the level of capacity utilization and rate of cost inflation which will apply in the year to 31 May 2001. Other factors are as previously forecast. Revised estimates of the likely levels of capacity utilization and inflation are as follows:

| Capacity utilization | Probability | Inflation | Probability |
|---|---|---|---|
| 70% | 0.1 | 8% | 0.3 |
| 60% | 0.5 | 10% | 0.6 |
| 50% | 0.4 | 12% | 0.1 |

(Capacity utilization rates and inflation rates are independent of each other.)

(i) Calculate the expected value of net profit or loss for the year to 31 May 2001 and show the range of profits or losses which may occur. (9 marks)

(ii) Draw up a table of the possible profits and losses and their probabilities as calculated in (i) for the year ended 31 May 2001 in a way which brings to the attention of management the risks and opportunities which are implied and comment briefly on the figures.

(5 marks)

(d) Comment on factors which have not been incorporated into the model used in (c) above which may affect its usefulness to management in profit forecasting. (6 marks)

(Total 30 marks)

*ACCA Level 2 Cost Accounting II*

### 12.3 Advanced: CVP analysis and uncertainty

(a) The accountant of Laburnum Ltd is preparing documents for a forthcoming meeting of the budget committee. Currently, variable cost is 40% of selling price and total fixed costs are £40 000 per year.

The company uses an historical cost accounting system. There is concern that the level of costs may rise during the ensuing year and the chairman of the budget committee has expressed interest in a probabilistic approach to an investigation of the effect that this will have on historic cost profits. The accountant is attempting to prepare the documents in a way which will be most helpful to the committee members. He has obtained the following estimates from his colleagues:

| | **Average inflation rate over ensuing year** | **Probability** |
|---|---|---|
| Pessimistic | 10% | 0.4 |
| Most likely | 5% | 0.5 |
| Optimistic | 1% | 0.1 |
| | | 1.0 |

| | **Demand at current selling prices** | **Probability** |
|---|---|---|
| Pessimistic | £50 000 | 0.3 |
| Most likely | £75 000 | 0.6 |
| Optimistic | £100 000 | 0.1 |
| | | 1.0 |

The demand figures are given in terms of sales value at the current level of selling prices but it is considered that the company could adjust its selling prices in line with the inflation rate without affecting customer demand in real terms.

Some of the company's fixed costs are contractually fixed and some are apportionments of past costs; of the total fixed costs, an estimated 85% will remain constant irrespective of the inflation rate.

You are required to analyse the foregoing information in a way which you consider will assist management with its budgeting problem. Although you should assume that the directors of Laburnum Ltd are solely interested in the effect of inflation on historic cost profits, you should comment on the validity of the accountant's intended approach. As part of your analysis you are required to calculate:

(i)  the probability of at least breaking even, and

(ii) the probability of achieving a profit of at least £20 000.               (16 marks)

(b)  It can be argued that the use of point estimate probabilities (as above) is too unrealistic because it constrains the demand and cost variables to relatively few values. Briefly describe an alternative simulation approach which might meet this objection.   (6 marks)

                                    (Total 22 marks)
                 *ACCA Level 2 Management Accounting*

## 12.4* Advanced: Pricing decision and the calculation of expected profit and margin of safety

E Ltd manufactures a hedge-trimming device which has been sold at £16 per unit for a number of years. The selling price is to be reviewed and the following information is available on costs and likely demand.

The standard variable cost of manufacture is £10 per unit and an analysis of the cost variances for the past 20 months show the following pattern which the production manager expects to continue in the future.

Adverse variances of +10% of standard variable cost occurred in ten of the months.

Nil variances occurred in six of the months.

Favourable variances of −5% of standard variable cost occurred in four of the months.

*Monthly data*

Fixed costs have been £4 per unit on an average sales level of 20 000 units but these costs are expected to rise in the future and the following estimates have been made for the total fixed cost:

|  | **(£)** |
| --- | --- |
| Optimistic estimate (Probability 0.3) | 82 000 |
| Most likely estimate (Probability 0.5) | 85 000 |
| Pessimistic estimate (Probability 0.2) | 90 000 |

The demand estimates at the two new selling prices being considered are as follows:

| If the selling price/unit is demand would be: | £17 | £18 |
| --- | --- | --- |
| Optimistic estimate (Probability 0.2) | 21 000 units | 19 000 units |
| Most likely estimate (Probability 0.5) | 19 000 units | 17 500 units |
| Pessimistic estimate (Probability 0.3) | 16 500 units | 15 500 units |

It can be assumed that all estimates and probabilities are independent.

You are required to

(a)  advise management, based only on the information given above, whether they should alter the selling price and, if so, the price you would recommend;                        (6 marks)

(b)  calculate the expected profit at the price you recommend and the resulting margin of safety, expressed as a percentage of expected sales;                               (6 marks)

(c)  criticise the method of analysis you have used to deal with the probabilities given in the question;                                   (4 marks)

(d)  describe briefly how computer assistance might improve the analysis.        (4 marks)

                                    (Total 20 marks)
              *CIMA Stage 3 Management Accounting Techniques*

## 12.5* Advanced: Machine hire decision based on uncertain demand and calculation of maximum price to pay for perfect information

Siteraze Ltd is a company which engages in site clearance and site preparation work. Information concerning its operations is as follows:

(i)  It is company policy to hire all plant and machinery required for the implementation of all orders obtained, rather than to purchase its own plant and machinery.

(ii) Siteraze Ltd will enter into an advance hire agreement contract for the coming year at one of three levels – high, medium or low, which correspond to the requirements of a high, medium or low level of orders obtained.

(iii) The level of orders obtained will not be known when the advance hire agreement contract is entered into. A set of probabilities have been estimated by management as to the likelihood of the orders being at a high, medium or low level.

(iv) Where the advance hire agreement entered into is lower than that required for the level of orders actually obtained, a premium rate must be paid to obtain the additional plant and machinery required.

(v) No refund is obtainable where the advance hire agreement for plant and machinery is at a level in excess of that required to satisfy the site clearance and preparation orders actually obtained.

A summary of the information relating to the above points is as follows:

|  |  |  | Plant and machinery hire costs | |
| Level of orders | Turnover (£000) | Probability | Advance hire (£000) | Conversion premium (£000) |
| --- | --- | --- | --- | --- |
| High | 15 000 | 0.25 | 2300 | |
| Medium | 8 500 | 0.45 | 1500 | |
| Low | 4 000 | 0.30 | 1000 | |
| Low to medium | | | | 850 |
| Medium to high | | | | 1300 |
| Low to high | | | | 2150 |

Variable cost (as percentage of turnover) 70%

Required: Using the information given above:

(a) Prepare a summary which shows the forecast net margin earned by Siteraze Ltd for the coming year for each possible outcome.
(6 marks)

(b) On the basis of maximizing expected value, advise Siteraze whether the advance contract for the hire of plant and machinery should be at the low, medium or high level. (5 marks)

(c) Explain how the risk preferences of the management members responsible for the choice of advance plant and machinery hire contract may alter the decision reached in (b) above. (6 marks)

(d) Siteraze Ltd are considering employing a market research consultant who will be able to say with certainty in advance of the placing of the plant and machinery hire contract, which level of site clearance and preparation orders will be obtained. On the basis of expected value, determine the maximum sum which Siteraze Ltd should be willing to pay the consultant for this information.
(5 marks)
(Total 22 marks)
*ACCA Level 2: Cost and Management Accounting 11*

## 12.6 Advanced: Output decision based on expected values

A ticket agent has an arrangement with a concert hall that holds pop concerts on 60 nights a year whereby he receives discounts as follows per concert:

| For purchase of: | He receives a discount of: |
| --- | --- |
| 200 tickets | 20% |
| 300 tickets | 25% |
| 400 tickets | 30% |
| 500 tickets or more | 40% |

Purchases must be in full hundreds. The average price per ticket is £3.

He must decide in advance each year the number of tickets he will purchase. If he has any tickets unsold by the afternoon of the concert he must return them to the box office. If the box office sells any of these he receives 60% of their price.

His sales records over a few years show that for a concert with extremely popular artistes he can be confident of selling 500 tickets, for one with lesser known artistes 350 tickets, and for one with relatively unknown artistes 200 tickets.

His records also show that 10% of tickets he returns are sold by the box office.

His administration costs incurred in selling tickets are the same per concert irrespective of the popularity of the artistes.

There are two possible scenarios in which his sales records can be viewed:

Scenario 1: that, on average, he can expect concerts with lesser known artistes

Scenario 2: that the frequency of concerts will be:

|  | (%) |
|---|---|
| with popular artistes | 45 |
| with lesser known artistes | 30 |
| with unknown artistes | 25 |
|  | 100 |

You are required to calculate:

A. separately for each of Scenarios 1 and 2:
   (a) the expected demand for tickets per concert;
   (b) (i) the level of his purchases of tickets per concert that will give him the largest profit over a long period of time;
       (ii) the profit per concert that this level of purchases of tickets will yield;
B. for Scenario 2 only: the maximum sum per annum that the ticket agent should pay to a pop concert specialist for 100% correct predictions as to the likely success of each concert. (25 marks)

*CIMA P3 Management Accounting*

## 12.7 Advanced: Contracting hotel accommodation based on uncertain demand

Crabbe, the owner of the Ocean Hotel, is concerned about the hotel's finances and has asked your advice. He gives you the following information:

'We have rooms for 80 guests. When the hotel is open, whatever the level of business, we have to meet the following each month:

|  | (£) |
|---|---|
| Staff wages and benefits | 12 500 |
| General overheads (rates, electricity, etc) | 8 000 |
| Depreciation | 2 200 |
| Interest on mortgage and bank loan | 1 800 |
| Repayments on mortgage and bank loan | 2 500 |
| Drawings for my own needs | 1 000 |
|  | 28 000 |

'For our normal business we charge an average of £20 per night for each guest. Each guest-night involves variable costs of £4 for laundry and cleaning. Guests also spend money in the restaurant, which on average brings us another £5 per guest-night after meeting variable costs.

'I need advice on two problems; one concerns the month of September and the other relates to the winter.

(1) 'Normal business in September will depend on weather conditions, and the probabilities of occupancy from normal business are:

| Weather condition | For month of September | | |
|---|---|---|---|
|  | A | B | C |
| Probability | 0.3 | 0.4 | 0.3 |
| Occupancy (total guest-nights) | 1440 | 1680 | 1920 |

'Airtravel Tours has enquired about a block booking at a discount in September. I intend to quote a discount of 40% on our normal guest-night charge. In the restaurant Airtravel's package tourists will only bring us £3 per guest-night after variable costs. Airtravel could take all our capacity, but I have to decide how many guest-nights to offer. The contract will mean that I agree in advance to take the same number of Airtravel tourists every night throughout September. If they won't accept my price, I would be prepared to go as far as a 60% discount.

(2) 'When we come to the winter, trade is usually so bad that we close for three months. We retain only a skeleton staff, costing £1500 per month, and general overheads are reduced from £8000 to £2000. I am trying to find ways of keeping open this winter, but staying open will incur the full monthly outgoings.

'If we remained open for all three months I estimate our basic winter trade at reduced prices, together with income from conferences, would be as follows:

|  | Average number of guests per night | Charge per guest-night (£) | Restaurant revenue per guest-night net of variable costs (£) |
|---|---|---|---|
| Basic winter trade | 12 | 14 | 5 |
| Conferences, etc. | 30 | 13 | 4 |

'Alternatively, I am considering offering a series of language courses. We could not take any other guests, and I estimate the total demand for the three months as follows:

| Market condition | X | Y | Z |
|---|---|---|---|
| Probability | 0.3 | 0.4 | 0.3 |
| Occupancy (total guest-nights) | 2160 | 4320 | 6480 |

'If the courses are offered we shall have to run them for the full three months irrespective of the take-up. The charge per night would be £24, and the revenue from the restaurant net of variable cost would only be £1 per guest-night.

We would have to spend about £5000 per month on tutors, and the courses would also have to be advertised beforehand at a cost of £1500.'

Assume 30-day months throughout.

Requirements:
(a) Calculate the number of guest-nights Crabbe should contract to Airtravel Tours at the quoted 40% discount. (6 marks)
(b) Determine the minimum price per guest-night at which it would be worthwhile for Crabbe to do business with Airtravel, and the maximum number of guest-nights it would be worthwhile to contract at this price. (4 marks)
(c) Assess which of the winter options Crabbe should undertake and state any reservation you may have about your assessment. (9 marks)
(d) Briefly explain the criteria on which you have identified costs to assess Crabbe's business options in requirements (a) to (c). (6 marks)
(Total 25 marks)
*ICAEW P2 Management Accounting*

**12.8\* Advanced: Pricing decisions under conditions of uncertainty**
(a) Allegro Finishes Ltd is about to launch an improved version of its major product – a pocket size chess computer – onto the market. Sales of the original model (at £65 per unit) have been at the rate of 50 000 per annum but it is now planned to withdraw this model and the company is now deciding on its production plans and pricing policy. The standard variable cost of the new model will be £50 which is the same as that of the old, but the company intends to increase the selling price 'to recover the research and

development expenditure that has been incurred'. The research and development costs of the improved model are estimated at £750 000 and the intention is that these should be written off over 3 years. Additionally there are annual fixed overheads of approximately £800 000 allocated to this product line.

The sales director has estimated the maximum annual demand figures that would obtain at three alternative selling prices. These are as follows:

| Selling price (£) | Estimated maximum annual demand (physical units) |
|---|---|
| 70 | 75 000 |
| 80 | 60 000 |
| 90 | 40 000 |

You are required to prepare a cost–volume–profit chart that would assist the management to choose a selling price and the level of output at which to operate. Identify the best price and the best level of output. Outline briefly any reservations that you have with this approach. (5 marks)
(b) With the facts as stated for part (a), now assume the sales director is considering a more sophisticated approach to the problem. He has estimated, for each selling price, an optimistic, a pessimistic and a most likely demand figure and associated probabilities for each of these. For the £90 price the estimates are:

| | Annual demand | Probability of demand |
|---|---|---|
| Pessimistic | 20 000 | 0.2 |
| Most likely | 35 000 | 0.7 |
| Optimistic | 40 000 | 0.1 |
| | | 1.0 |

On the cost side, it is clear that the standard unit variable cost of £50 is an 'ideal' which has rarely been achieved in practice. An analysis of the past 20 months shows that the following pattern of variable cost variances (per unit of output) has arisen: an adverse variance of around £10 arose on occasions,

an adverse variance of around £5 arose on 14 occasions
and a variance of around 0 arose on 2 occasions.

There is no reason to think that the pattern for the improved model will differ significantly from this or that these variances are dependent upon the actual demand level.

From the above, calculate the expected annual profit for a selling price of £90.

(6 marks)

(c) A tabular summary of the result of an analysis of the data for the other two selling prices (£70 and £80) is as follows:

|  | £70 | £80 |
| --- | --- | --- |
| Probability of a loss of £500 000 or more | 0.02 | 0 |
| Probability of a loss of £300 000 or more | 0.07 | 0.05 |
| Probability of a loss of £100 000 or more | 0.61 | 0.08 |
| Probability of break-even or worse | 0.61 | 0.10 |
| Probability of break-even or better | 0.39 | 0.91 |
| Probability of a profit of £100 000 or more | 0.33 | 0.52 |
| Probability of a profit of £300 000 or more | 0.03 | 0.04 |
| Probability of a profit of £500 000 or more | 0 | 0.01 |
| Expected value of profit (loss) | 55 750 | 68 500 |

You are required to compare your calculations in part (b) with the above figures and to write a short memo to the sales director outlining your advice and commenting on the use of subjective discrete probability distributions in problems of this type. (9 marks)

(d) Assume that there is a 10% increase in the fixed overheads allocated to this product line and a decision to write off the research and development costs in one year instead of over 3 years. Indicate the general effect that this would have on your analysis of the problem.

(2 marks)

(Total 22 marks)

*ACCA Level 2 Management Accounting*

## 12.9* Advanced: Expected value comparison of low and high price alternatives

The research and development department of Shale White has produced specifications for two new products for consideration by the company's production director. The director has received detailed costings which can be summarized as follows:

|  | Product newone (£) | Product newtwo (£) |
| --- | --- | --- |
| Direct costs: |  |  |
| Material | 64 | 38 |
| Labour (£3 per hour) | 18 | 6 |
|  | 82 | 44 |
| Factory overheads (£3 per machine hour) | 18 | 6 |
| Total estimated unit cost | 100 | 50 |

The sales department has provided estimates of the probabilities of various levels of demand for two possible selling prices for each product. The details are as follows:

|  | Product newone | Product newtwo |
| --- | --- | --- |
| Low price alternative |  |  |
| Selling price | £120 | £60 |
| Demand estimates: |  |  |
| Pessimistic – probability 0.2 | 1000 | 3000 |
| Most likely – probability 0.5 | 2000 | 4000 |
| Optimistic – probability 0.3 | 3000 | 5000 |
| High price alternative |  |  |
| Selling price | £130 | £70 |
| Demand estimates: |  |  |
| Pessimistic – probability 0.2 | 500 | 1500 |
| Most likely – probability 0.5 | 1000 | 2500 |
| Optimistic – probability 0.3 | 1500 | 3500 |

It would be possible to adopt the low price alternative for product newone together with the high price alternative for newtwo, or the high price alternative for product newone with the low price alternative for newtwo (demand estimates are independent for the two products).

The factory has 60 000 machine hours available during the year. For some years past it has been working at 90% of practical capacity making a standardized product. This product is very profitable and it is only the availability of 6000 hours of spare machine capacity that has made it necessary to search for additional product lines to use the machines fully. The actual level of demand will be known at the time of production.

A statistical study of the behaviour of the factory overhead over the past year has indicated that it can be regarded as a linear function of factory machine time worked. The monthly fixed cost is estimated at £10 000 and the variable cost at £1 per machine hour with a coefficient of correlation of 0.8.

You are required:
(a) to identify the best plan for the utilization of the 6000 machine hours, to comment on the rational selling price alternatives that exist for this plan and to calculate the expected increase in annual profit which would arise for each alternative,                    (17 marks)
(b) to discuss the relevance of regression analysis for problems of this type.                    (5 marks)
                    (Total 22 marks)
*ACCA Level 2 Management Accounting*

## 12.10 Advanced: Pricing and purchase contract decisions based on uncertain demand and calculation of maximum price to pay for perfect information

Z Ltd is considering various product pricing and material purchasing options with regard to a new product it has in development. Estimates of demand and costs are as follows:

| If selling price per unit is | | £15 per unit | £20 per unit |
|---|---|---|---|
| | | Sales volume | Sales volume |
| Forecasts | Probability | (000 units) | (000 units) |
| Optimistic | 0.3 | 36 | 28 |
| Most likely | 0.5 | 28 | 23 |
| Pessimistic | 0.2 | 18 | 13 |
| Variable manufacturing costs (excluding materials) per unit | | £3 | £3 |
| Advertising and selling costs | | £25 000 | £96 000 |
| General fixed costs | | £40 000 | £40 000 |

Each unit requires 3 kg of material and because of storage problems any unused material must be sold at £1 per kg. The sole suppliers of the material offer three purchase options, which must be decided at the outset, as follows:

any quantity at £3 per kg, or

(ii) a price of £2.75 per kg for a minimum quantity of 50 000 kg, or
(iii) a price of £2.50 per kg for a minimum quantity of 70 000 kg.

You are required, assuming that the company is risk neutral, to
(a) prepare calculations to show what pricing and purchasing decisions the company should make, clearly indicating the recommended decisions;                    (15 marks)
(b) calculate the maximum price you would pay for perfect information as to whether the demand would be optimistic or most likely pessimistic.                    (5 marks)
                    (Total 20 marks)
*CIMA Stage 3 Management Accounting Techniques*

## 12.11* Advanced: Pricing decision based on competitor's response

In the market for one of its products, MD and its two major competitors (CN and KL) together account for 95% of total sales.

The quality of MD's products is viewed by customers as being somewhat better than that of its competitors and therefore at similar prices it has an advantage.

During the past year, however, when MD raised its price to £1.2 per litre, competitors kept their prices at £1.0 per litre and MD's sales declined even though the total market grew in volume.

MD is now considering whether to retain or reduce its price for the coming year. Its expectations about its likely volume at various prices charged by itself and its competitors are as follows:

| Prices per litre | | | MD's expected sales |
|---|---|---|---|
| MD (£) | CN (£) | KL (£) | million litres |
| 1.2 | 1.2 | 1.2 | 2.7 |
| 1.2 | 1.2 | 1.1 | 2.3 |
| 1.2 | 1.2 | 1.0 | 2.2 |
| 1.2 | 1.1 | 1.1 | 2.4 |
| 1.2 | 1.1 | 1.0 | 2.2 |
| 1.2 | 1.1 | 1.0 | 2.1 |
| 1.1 | 1.1 | 1.1 | 2.8 |
| 1.1 | 1.0 | 1.0 | 2.4 |
| 1.1 | 1.0 | 1.0 | 2.3 |
| 1.0 | 1.0 | 1.0 | 2.9 |

Experience has shown that CN tends to react to MD's price level and KL tends to react to CN's price level. MD therefore assesses the following probabilities:

| If MD's price per litre is (£) | there is a probability of | that CN's price per litre will be (£) |
|---|---|---|
| 1.2 | 0.2 | 1.2 |
| | 0.4 | 1.1 |
| | 0.4 | 1.0 |
| | 1.0 | |
| 1.1 | 0.3 | 1.1 |
| | 0.7 | 1.0 |
| | 1.0 | |
| 1.0 | 1.0 | 1.0 |

| If CN's price per litre is (£) | there is a probability of | that KL's price per litre will be (£) |
|---|---|---|
| 1.2 | 0.1 | 1.2 |
| | 0.6 | 1.1 |
| | 0.3 | 1.0 |
| | 1.0 | |
| 1.1 | 0.3 | 1.1 |
| | 0.7 | 1.0 |
| | 1.0 | |
| 1.0 | 1.0 | 1.0 |

Costs per litre of the product are as follows:

| | |
|---|---|
| Direct wages | £0.24 |
| Direct materials | £0.12 |
| Departmental expenses: | |
| Indirect wages, maintenance and supplies | $16\frac{2}{3}$% of direct wages |
| Supervision and depreciation | £540 000 per annum |
| General works expenses (allocated) | $16\frac{2}{3}$% of prime cost |
| Selling and administration expenses (allocated) | 50% of manufacturing cost |

You are required to state whether, on the basis of the data given above, it would be most advantageous for MD to fix its price per litre for the coming year at £1.2, £1.1 or £1.0.

Support your answer with relevant calculations.

(20 marks)

*CIMA P3 Management Accounting*

**12.12 Advanced: Selling price decision based on expected values and value of additional information**

Warren Ltd is to produce a new product in a short-term venture which will utilize some obsolete materials and expected spare capacity. The new product will be advertised in quarter I with production and sales taking price in quarter II. No further production or sales are anticipated.

Sales volumes are uncertain but will, to some extent, be a function of sales price. The possible sales volumes and the advertising costs associated with each potential sales price are as follows:

| | Sales price £20 per unit | | Sales price £25 per unit | | Sales price £40 per unit | |
|---|---|---|---|---|---|---|
| | Sales volume units (000) | Probability | Sales volume units (000) | Probability | Sales volume units (000) | Probability |
| | 4 | 0.1 | 2 | 0.1 | 0 | 0.2 |
| | 6 | 0.4 | 5 | 0.2 | 3 | 0.5 |
| | 8 | 0.5 | 6 | 0.2 | 10 | 0.2 |
| | | | 8 | 0.5 | 15 | 0.1 |
| Advertising costs | £20 000 | | £50 000 | | £100 000 | |

The resources used in the production of each unit of the product are:

Production labour:  grade 1  2 hours
grade 2  1 hour

Materials:  X  1 unit
Y  2 units

The normal cost per hour of labour is

grade 1  £2
grade 2  £3

However, before considering the effects of the current venture, there is expected to be 4000 hours of idle time for each grade of labour in quarter II. Idle time is paid at the normal rates.

Material X is in stock at a book value of £8 per unit, but is widely used within the firm and any usage for the purposes of this venture will require replacing. Replacement cost is £9 per unit.

Material Y is obsolete stock. There are 16 000 units in stock at a book value of £3.50 per unit and any stock not used will have to be disposed of at a cost, to Warren, of £2 per unit. Further quantities of Y can be purchased for £4 per unit.

Overhead recovery rates are

| | |
|---|---|
| Variable overhead | £2 per direct labour hour worked |
| Fixed overhead | £3 per direct labour hour worked |

Total fixed overheads will not alter as a result of the current venture.

Feedback from advertising will enable the exact demand to be determined at the end of quarter I and production in quarter II will be set to equal that demand. However, it is necessary to decide now on the sales price in order that it can be incorporated into the advertising campaign.

Required:
(a) Calculate the expected money value of the venture at each sales price and on the basis of this advise Warren of its best course of action.
(12 marks)
(b) Briefly explain why the management of Warren might rationally reject the sales price leading to the highest expected money value and prefer one of the other sales prices.
(4 marks)
(c) It will be possible, for the sales price of £40 per unit only, to ascertain which of the four levels of demand will eventuate. If the indications are that the demand will be low then the advertising campaign can be cancelled at a cost of £10 000 but it would then not be possible to continue the venture at another sales price. This accurate information concerning demand will cost £5000 to obtain.
Indicate whether it is worthwhile obtaining the information and ascertain whether it would alter the advice given in (a) above.
(4 marks)
(Total 20 marks)
*ACCA Level 2 Management Accounting*

## 12.13* Advanced: Expected value, maximin and regret criterion

Stow Health Centre specialises in the provision of sports/exercise and medical/dietary advice to clients. The service is provided on a residential basis and clients stay for whatever number of days suits their needs.

Budgeted estimates for the next year ending 30 June are as follows:

(i) The maximum capacity of the centre is 50 clients per day for 350 days in the year.
(ii) Clients will be invoiced at a fee per day. The budgeted occupancy level will vary with the client fee level per day and is estimated at different percentages of maximum capacity as follows:

| Client fee per day | Occupancy level | Occupancy as percentage of maximum capacity |
|---|---|---|
| £180 | High | 90% |
| £200 | Most likely | 75% |
| £220 | Low | 60% |

(iii) Variable costs are also estimated at one of three levels per client day. The high, most likely and low levels per client day are £95, £85 and £70 respectively.
The range of cost levels reflect only the possible effect of the purchase prices of goods and services.

Required:
(a) Prepare a summary which shows the budgeted contribution earned by Stow Health Centre for the year ended 30 June for each of nine possible outcomes.
(6 marks)
(b) State the client fee strategy for the next year to 30 June which will result from the use of each of the following decision rules: (i) *maximax*; (ii) *maximin*; (iii) *minimax* regret.
Your answer should explain the basis of operation of each rule. Use the information from your answer to (a) as relevant and show any additional working calculations as necessary.
(9 marks)
(c) The probabilities of variable cost levels occurring at the high, most likely and low levels provided in the question are estimated as 0.1, 0.6 and 0.3 respectively.
Using the information available, determine the client fee strategy which will be chosen where maximisation of expected value of contribution is used as the decision basis. (5 marks)
(d) The calculations in (a) to (c) concern contribution levels which may occur given the existing budget.
Stow Health Centre has also budgeted for fixed costs of £1 200 000 for the next year to 30 June.
Discuss ways in which Stow Health Centr

may instigate changes, in ways other than through the client fee rate, which may influence client demand, cost levels and profit.

Your answer should include comment on the existing budget and should incorporate illustrations which relate to each of four additional performance measurement areas appropriate to the changes you discuss. (15 marks)

(Total 35 marks)

*ACCA Paper 9 Information for Control and Decision Making*

### 12.14* Advanced: Expected values, maximin criterion and value of perfect information

Recyc plc is a company which reprocesses factory waste in order to extract good quality aluminium. Information concerning its operations is as follows:

(i) Recyc plc places an advance order each year for chemical X for use in the aluminium extraction process. It will enter into an advance contract for the coming year for chemical X at one of three levels – high, medium or low, which correspond to the requirements of a high, medium or low level of waste available for reprocessing.

(ii) The level of waste available will not be known when the advance order for chemical X is entered into. A set of probabilities have been estimated by management as to the likelihood of the quantity of waste being at a high, medium or low level.

(iii) Where the advance order entered into for chemical X is lower than that required for the level of waste for processing actually received, a discount from the original demand price is allowed by the supplier for the total quantity of chemical X actually required.

(iv) Where the advance order entered into for chemical X is in excess of that required to satisfy the actual level of waste for reprocessing, a penalty payment in excess of the original demand price is payable for the total quantity of chemical X actually required.

A summary of the information relating to the above points is as follows:

| Level of reprocessing | Waste available (000kg) | Probability | Chemical X costs per kg | | |
|---|---|---|---|---|---|
| | | | Advance order (£) | Conversion discount (£) | Conversion premium (£) |
| High | 50 000 | 0.30 | 1.00 | | |
| Medium | 38 000 | 0.50 | 1.20 | | |
| Low | 30 000 | 0.20 | 1.40 | | |

Chemical X: order conversion:

| | |
|---|---|
| Low to medium | 0.10 |
| Medium to high | 0.10 |
| Low to high | 0.15 |
| Medium to low | 0.25 |
| High to medium | 0.25 |
| High to low | 0.60 |

Aluminium is sold at £0.65 per kg. Variable costs (excluding chemical X costs) are 70% of sales revenue.

Aluminium extracted from the waste is 15% of the waste input. Chemical X is added to the reprocessing at the rate of 1 kg per 100 kg of waste.

Required:

(a) Prepare a summary which shows the budgeted contribution earned by Recyc plc for the coming year for each of nine possible outcomes. (14 marks)

(b) On the basis of maximising expected value, advise Recyc plc whether the advance order for chemical X should be at low, medium or high level. (3 marks)

(c) State the contribution for the coming year which corresponds to the use of (i) maximax and (ii) maximin decision criteria, and comment on the risk preference of management which is indicated by each. (6 marks)

(d) Recyc plc are considering employing a consultant who will be able to say with certainty in advance of the placing of the order for chemical X, which level of waste will be available for reprocessing.

On the basis of expected value, determine the maximum sum which Recyc plc should be willing to pay the consultant for this information. (6 marks)

(e) Explain and comment on the steps involved in evaluating the purchase of imperfect information from the consultant in respect of the quantity of waste which will be available for reprocessing. (6 marks)

(Total 35 marks)

*ACCA Paper 9 Information for Control and Decision Making*

### 12.15* Advanced: Decision tree, expected value and maximin criterion

(a) The Alternative Sustenance Company is considering introducing a new franchised product, Wholefood Waffles.

Existing ovens now used for making some of the present 'Half-Baked' range of products could be used instead for baking the Wholefood Waffles. However, new special batch mixing equipment would be needed. This cannot be purchased, but can be hired from the franchiser in three alternative specifications, for batch sizes of 200, 300 and 600 units respectively. The annual cost of hiring the mixing equipment would be £5000, £15 000 and £21 500 respectively.

The 'Half-Baked' product which would be dropped from the range currently earns a contribution of £90 000 per annum, which it is confidently expected could be continued if the product were retained in the range.

The company's marketing manager considers that, at the market price for Wholefood Waffles of £0.40 per unit, it is equally probable that the demand for this product would be 600 000 or 1 000 000 units per annum.

The company's production manager has estimated the variable costs per unit of making Wholefood Waffles and the probabilities of those costs being incurred, as follows:

| Batch size:<br>Cost per<br>unit (pence) | 200 units<br>Probability<br>if annual<br>sales are<br>either<br>600 000<br>or 1 000 000<br>units | 300 units<br>Probability<br>if annual<br>sales are<br>either<br>600 000<br>or 1 000 000<br>units | 600 units<br>Probability<br>if annual<br>sales are<br>600 000<br>units | 600 units<br>Probability<br>if annual<br>sales are<br>1 000 000<br>units |
|---|---|---|---|---|
| £0.20 | 0.1 | 02 | 0.3 | 0.5 |
| £0.25 | 0.1 | 0.5 | 0.1 | 0.2 |
| £0.30 | 0.8 | 0.3 | 0.6 | 0.3 |

You are required:

(i) to draw a decision tree setting out the problem faced by the company,

(12 marks)

(ii) to show in each of the following three independent situations which size of mixing machine, if any, the company should hire:

   (1) to satisfy a 'maximin' (or 'minimax' criterion),

   (2) to maximize the expected value of contribution per annum,

   (3) to minimize the probability of earning an annual contribution of less than £100 000. (7 marks)

(b) You are required to outline briefly the strengths and limitations of the methods of analysis which you have used in part (a) above. (6 marks)

(Total 25 marks)
*ICAEW Management Accounting*

## 12.16 Advanced: Hire of machine based on uncertain demand and value of perfect information

The Ruddle Co. Ltd had planned to install and, with effect from next April, commence operating sophisticated machinery for the production of a new product – product Zed. However, the supplier of the machinery has just announced that delivery of the machinery will be delayed by six months and this will mean that Ruddle will not now be able to undertake production using that machinery until October.

'The first six months of production' stated the commercial manager of Ruddle 'is particularly crucial as we have already contracted to supply several national supermarket groups with whatever quantities of Zed they require during that period at a price of £40 per unit. Their demand is, at this stage, uncertain but would have been well within the capacity of the permanent machinery we were to have installed. The best estimates of the total demand for the first period are thought to be:

| **Estimated demand – first 6 months** | |
|---|---|
| **Quantity<br>(000 units)** | **Probability** |
| 10 | 0.5 |
| 14 | 0.3 |
| 16 | 0.2 |

'Whatever the level of demand, we are going to meet it in full even if it means operating at a loss for the first half year. Therefore I suggest we consider the possibility of hiring equipment on which temporary production can take place.' Details of the only machines which could be hired are:

| | Machine<br>A | Machine<br>B | Machine<br>C |
|---|---|---|---|
| Productive capacity<br>per six month<br>period (units) | 10 000 | 12 000 | 16 000 |
| Variable production<br>cost for each<br>unit produced | £6.5 | £6 | £5 |
| Other 'fixed' costs<br>total for six<br>months | £320 000 | £350 000 | £400 000 |

In addition to the above costs there will be a variable material cost of £5 per unit. For purchases greater than 10 000 units a discount of 20% per unit will be given, but this only applies to the excess over 10 000 units.

Should production capacity be less than demand then Ruddle could subcontract production of up to 6000 units but would be required to supply raw materials. Subcontracting costs are:

up to 4000 units subcontracted – £30 per unit

any excess over 4000 units subcontracted – £35 per unit.

These subcontracting costs relate only to the work carried out by the subcontractor and exclude the costs of raw materials.

The commercial manager makes the following further points, 'Due to the lead time required for setting up production, the choice of which machine to hire must be made before the precise demand is known. However, demand will be known in time for production to be scheduled so that an equal number of units can be produced each month. We will, of course, only produce sufficient to meet demand.'

'We need to decide which machine to hire. However, I wonder whether it would be worthwhile seeking the assistance of a firm of market researchers? Their reputation suggests that they are very accurate and they may be able to inform us whether demand is to be 10, 14 or 16 thousand units.'

Required:
(a) For each of the three machines which could be hired show the possible monetary outcomes and, using expected values, advise Ruddle on its best course of action. (12 marks)
(b) (i) Calculate the maximum amount which it would be worthwhile to pay to the firm of market researchers to ascertain details of demand. (You are required to assume that the market researchers will produce an absolutely accurate forecast and that demand will be exactly equal to one of the three demand figures given.) (4 marks)
(ii) Comment on the view that as perfect information is never obtainable the calculation of the expected value of perfect information is not worthwhile. Briefly explain any uses such a calculation may have. (4 marks)

(Total 20 marks)
Ignore taxation and the time value of money.
*ACCA P2 Management Accounting*

### 12.17 Advanced: Calculation of expected value of perfect and imperfect information

Butterfield Ltd manufactures a single brand of dog-food called 'Lots O' Grissle' (LOG). Sales have stabilized for several years at a level of £20 million per annum at current prices. This level is not expected to change in the foreseeable future (except as indicated below). It is well below the capacity of the plant. The managing director, Mr Rover, is considering how to stimulate growth in the company's turnover and profits. After rejecting all of the alternative possibilities that he can imagine, or that have been suggested to him, he is reviewing a proposal to introduce a new luxury dog-food product. It would be called 'Before Eight Mince' (BEM), and would have a recommended retail price of £0.50 per tin. It would require no new investment, and would incur no additional fixed costs.

Mr Rover has decided that he will undertake this new development only if he can anticipate that it will at least break even in the first year of operation.

(a) Mr Rover estimates that BEM has a 75% chance of gaining acceptance in the marketplace. His best estimate is that if the product gains acceptance it will have sales in the forthcoming year of £3.2 million at retail prices, given a contribution of £1 million after meeting the variable costs of manufacture and distribution. If, on the other hand, the product fails to gain acceptance, sales for the year will, he thinks, be only £800 000 at retail prices, and for various reasons there would be a negative contribution of £400 000 in that year.

You are required to show whether, on the basis of these preliminary estimates, Mr Rover should give the BEM project further consideration. (4 marks)

(b) Mr Rover discusses the new project informally with his sales director, Mr Khoo Chee Khoo, who suggests that some of the sales achieved for the new product would cause lost sales of LOG. In terms of retail values he estimates the likelihood of this as follows:

There is a 50% chance that sales of LOG will fall by half of the sales of BEM.

There is a 25% chance that sales of LOG will fall by one-quarter of the sales of BEM.

There is a 25% chance that sales of LOG will fall by three-quarters of the sales of BEM.

The contribution margin ratio of LOG is 25% at all relevant levels of sales and output. You are required to show whether, after accepting these further estimates, Mr Rover should give the BEM project further consideration.                                   (5 marks)

(c) Mr Rover wonders also whether, before attempting to proceed any further, he should have some market research undertaken. He approaches Delphi Associates, a firm of market research consultants for whom he has a high regard. On previous occasions he has found them to be always right in their forecasts, and he considers that their advice will give him as near perfect information as it is possible to get. He decides to ask Delphi to advise him only on whether or not BEM will gain acceptance in the marketplace in the sense in which he has defined it; he will back Mr Khoo Chee Khoo's judgement about the effects of the introduction of BEM on the sales of LOG. If Delphi advise him that the product will not be accepted he will not proceed further. Delphi have told him that their fee for this work would be £100 000.

You are required to show whether Mr Rover should instruct Delphi Associates to carry out the market research proposals.
                                   (5 marks)

(d) Preliminary discussions with Delphi suggest that Delphi's forecast will not be entirely reliable. They believe that, if they indicate that BEM will gain acceptance, there is only a 90% chance that they will be right; and, if they indicate failure to gain acceptance, there is only a 70% chance that they will be right. This implies a 75% chance overall that Delphi will indicate acceptance, in line with Mr Rover's estimate.

You are required to show the maximum amount that Mr Rover should be prepared to pay Delphi to undertake the market research, given the new estimates of the reliability of their advice.                        (5 marks)

(e) You are required to outline briefly the strengths and limitations of your methods of analysis in (a)–(d) above.      (6 marks)
*ICAEW Management Accounting*

## 12.18* Advanced: Expected net present value and decision whether to abandon a project after one year

A company is considering a project involving the outlay of £300 000 which it estimates will generate cash flows over its 2-year life at the probabilities shown in the following table:

### Cash flows for project Year 1

| Cash flow (£) | Probability |
| --- | --- |
| 100 000 | 0.25 |
| 200 000 | 0.50 |
| 300 000 | 0.25 |
| | 1.00 |

### Year 2

| If cash flow in Year 1 is: (£) | there is a probability of: | that cash flow in Year 2 will be: (£) |
| --- | --- | --- |
| 100 000 | 0.25 | Nil |
| | 0.50 | 100 000 |
| | 0.25 | 200 000 |
| | 1.00 | |
| 200 000 | 0.25 | 100 000 |
| | 0.50 | 200 000 |
| | 0.25 | 300 000 |
| | 1.00 | |
| 300 000 | 0.25 | 200 000 |
| | 0.50 | 300 000 |
| | 0.25 | 350 000 |
| | 1.00 | |

*Note*: All cash flows should be treated as being received at the end of the year.

It has a choice of undertaking this project at either of two sites (A or B) whose costs are identical and are included in the above outlay. In terms of the technology of the project itself, the location will have no effect on the outcome.

If the company chooses site B it has the facility to abandon the project at the end of the first year and to sell the site to an interested purchaser for £150 000. This facility is not available at site A.

The company's investment criterion for this type of project is 10% DCF. Its policy would be to abandon the project on site B and to sell the site at the end of year 1 if its expected future cash flows for year 2 were less than the disposal value.

You are required to:

(a) calculate the NPV of the project on site A; (7 marks)

(b) (i) explain, based on the data given, the specific circumstances in which the company would abandon the project on site B;

(ii) calculate the NPV of the project on site B taking account of the abandonment facility; (14 marks)

(c) calculate the financial effect of the facility for abandoning the project on site B, stating whether it is positive or negative. (4 marks)

Ignore tax and inflation.

*CIMA P3 Management Accounting*

# 13

# Capital investment decisions: 1

Capital investment decisions are those decisions that involve current outlays in return for a stream of benefits in future years. It is true to say that all of the firm's expenditures are made in expectation of realizing future benefits. The distinguishing feature between short-term decisions and capital investment (long-term) decisions is time. Generally, we can classify short-term decisions as those that involve a relatively short time horizon, say one year, from the commitment of funds to the receipt of the benefits. On the other hand, capital investment decisions are those decisions where a significant period of time elapses between the outlay and the recoupment of the investment. We shall see that this commitment of funds for a significant period of time involves an interest cost, which must be brought into the analysis. With short-term decisions, funds are committed only for short periods of time, and the interest cost is normally so small that it can be ignored.

Capital investment decisions normally represent the most important decisions that an organization makes, since they commit a substantial proportion of a firm's resources to actions that are likely to be irreversible. Such decisions are applicable to all sectors of society. Business firms' investment decisions include investments in plant and machinery, research and development, advertising and warehouse facilities. Investment decisions in the public sector include new roads, schools and airports. Individuals' investment decisions include house-buying and the purchase of consumer durables. In this and the following chapter we shall examine the economic evaluation of the desirability of investment proposals. We shall concentrate on the investment decisions of business firms, but the same principles, with modifications, apply to individuals, and the public sector.

To simplify the introduction to capital investment decision, we shall assume initially that all cash inflows and outflows are known with certainty, and that sufficient funds are available to undertake all profitable investments. We will also assume a world where there are no taxes and where there is an absence of inflation. These factors will be brought into the analysis in the next chapter.

## Learning objectives

After studying this chapter, you should be able to:

- explain the opportunity cost of an investment;
- distinguish between compounding and discounting;
- explain the concept of net present value (NPV) and internal rate of return (IRR);
- calculate NPV, IRR, payback period and accounting rate of return;
- justify the superiority of NPV over the IRR;
- explain the limitations of payback and the accounting rate of return methods;
- describe the effect of performance measurement on capital investment decisions.

# Objectives of capital budgeting

Capital investment decisions are part of the capital budgeting process, which is concerned with decision-making in the following areas:

1. determining which specific investment projects the firm should accept;
2. determining the total amount of capital expenditure which the firm should undertake;
3. determining how this portfolio of projects should be financed.

Each of the above decisions should be evaluated on the basis of their estimated contribution towards the achievement of the goals of the organization. Organizations may pursue a variety of goals, for example maximization of profits, maximization of sales, survival of the firm, achieving a satisfactory level of profits and obtaining the largest possible share of the market. The two most important goals appear to be profitability and survival of the firm. A firm that invests in risky projects takes a chance that these projects may be unsuccessful. The acceptance of risky projects thus lowers the probability that a firm will be able to survive in the future.

The theory of capital budgeting reconciles the goals of survival and profitability by assuming that management takes as its goal the maximization of the market value of the shareholders' wealth via the maximization of the market value of ordinary shares. We shall see that this is equivalent to the maximization of the present value of future net cash inflows.

If the maximization of shareholders' funds is the firm's objective, the important goals of profitability and survival can be combined into a single measure. Let us assume that a firm is considering investing in a new product, which may increase the return on investment, but is also risky and may be unsuccessful, and may lead to a lower return on investment or even bankruptcy. If the stock market believes that the probability of the increased return outweighs the increase in risk, it is likely that the share price will rise if the investment is undertaken. Alternatively, if the stock market considers that the riskiness outweighs the increase in expected returns, one would expect the share price to fall. Therefore, defining the objectives of the firm in terms of the market value of the ordinary shares incorporates the efforts by management to seek an optimum balance between risk and profitability.

# A decision-making model for capital investment decisions

To give a better understanding of capital investment decisions, we shall now consider how they fit into the overall framework for decision-making. In Figure 13.1 the decision-making model presented in Chapter 12 has been adapted to incorporate capital investment decisions.

Let us now examine each of these stages more closely. Stage 1 indicates that the objectives or goals of the organization must be determined, and the targets which the company wishes to achieve must be established. The quantification of the objective is known as the objective function. We have noted already in this chapter that the objective function of capital budgeting is to maximize shareholders' wealth via the maximization of the market value of ordinary shares.

The second stage involves a search for investment opportunities. Potential investment projects are not just born – someone has to suggest them. Without a creative search for

**FIGURE 13.1**  *A decision-making model for capital investment decisions.*

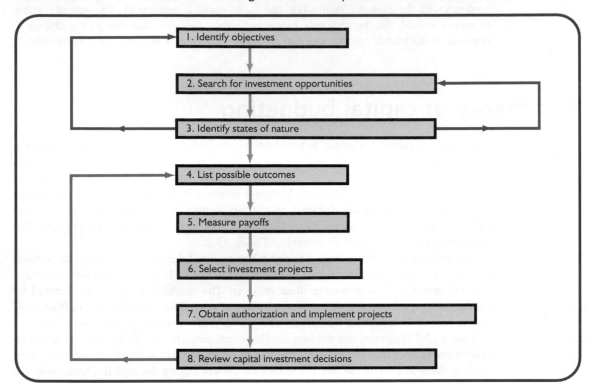

new investment opportunities, even the most sophisticated evaluation techniques are worthless. A firm's prosperity depends far more on its ability to create investments rather than on its ability to appraise them. Thus it is important that a firm scans the environment for potential opportunities or takes action to protect itself against potential threats. This process is closely linked to the strategies of an organization. We shall look at this process in more detail in Chapter 15

The third stage in the decision process is to gather data about the possible future environments (states of nature) that may affect the outcomes of the projects. Examples of possible states of nature include economic boom, high inflation, recession and so on. In this chapter we shall assume that certainty prevails, so that the outcome of a project is known. Only one state of nature is therefore possible. In the next chapter we shall consider capital investment decisions under conditions of uncertainty.

After the states of nature have been identified, the fourth and fifth stages are to list the possible outcomes for each state of nature, and measure the payoff of each possible outcome in terms of the objective of maximizing shareholders' funds. These stages are examined in detail in this and the following chapter.

Stage 6 in the process is to select the investment projects that will give the maximum payoff and to include them in the firm's long-term plan. The formulation of the long-term plan is discussed in Chapter 15. When a project is included in a firm's long-term plan, it does not necessarily mean that authorization has been given to implement the project. The authorization process and the procedure for reviewing capital investment decisions (stages 7 and 8) will be discussed further in the next chapter.

The arrowed lines in Figure 13.1 linking the various stages in the process represent 'feedback loops'. They signify that the process is continuous and dynamic. In other words, capital investment decisions should be continually reviewed to see if the actual results conform with the expected results (i.e. the list of possible outcomes). The potential states of nature should also be regularly monitored, since this may indicate that a change is required in the search process and that the target objective function should be revised.

# The theory of capital budgeting

The theory of capital budgeting is based on the economic theory of the firm by applying the principle that the firm should operate at the point where marginal cost is equal to marginal revenue. When this rule is applied to capital budgeting decisions, the value of shareholders' wealth is maximized. Marginal revenue is represented by the percentage return on investment, while marginal cost is represented by the marginal cost of capital (MCC). By cost of capital we mean the cost of the funds to finance the projects. The application of this theory is illustrated in Figure 13.2.

The horizontal axis measures the total funds invested during a year, while the vertical axis shows both the percentage rate of return on the available projects and the percentage cost of capital used in financing these projects. The available projects are denoted by bands. For example, project A requires an outlay of £5 million and provides a 20% rate of return, project B requires a £2 million outlay and yields a return of 16% and so on.

Figure 13.2 illustrates that the firm should accept projects A to D because the return on investment is in excess of the cost of capital, and that projects E and F should be rejected because the return on investment is less than the cost of raising the capital. Throughout this chapter, we are assuming that the cost of capital is constant (i.e. the MCC curve is constant) and that the acceptance of any project does not alter the risk of the firm as perceived by the suppliers of capital. These assumptions enable the firm's financing decision to be held constant so that we can concentrate on the investment decision. Note that the cost of capital is consistent at 12%.

**FIGURE 13.2** *Determining the total amounts of capital expenditure that a firm should undertake.*

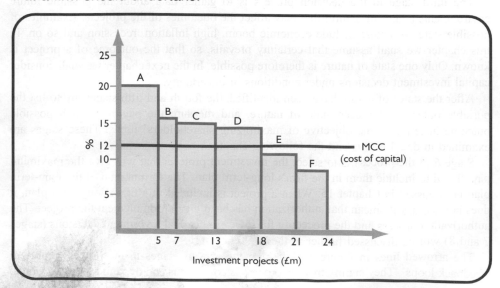

# The opportunity cost of an investment

You will recall that in Chapter 1 we adopted the view that, broadly, firms seek to maximize the present value of future net cash inflows. It is therefore important that you acquire an intuitive understanding of the term 'present value'.

Any individual can invest in securities traded in financial markets. If you prefer to avoid risk, you can invest in government securities, which will yield a *fixed* return. On the other hand, you may prefer to invest in *risky* securities such as the ordinary shares of companies quoted on the stock exchange. If you invest in the ordinary shares of a company, you will find that the return will vary from year to year, depending on the performance of the company and its future expectations. Investors normally prefer to avoid risk if possible, and will generally invest in risky securities only if they believe that they will obtain a greater return for the increased risk. Suppose that risk-free gilt-edged securities issued by the government yield a return of 10%. You will therefore be prepared to invest in ordinary shares only if you expect the return to be greater than 10%; let us assume that you require an *expected* return of 15% to induce you to invest in ordinary shares in preference to a risk-free security. Note that expected return means the average return. You would expect to earn, on average, 15%, but in some years you might earn more and in others considerably less.

Suppose you invest in company X ordinary shares. Would you want company X to invest your money in a capital project that gives less than 15%? Surely not, assuming the project has the same risk as the alternative investments in shares of other companies that are yielding a return of 15%. You would prefer company X to invest in other companies' ordinary shares at 15% or, alternatively, to repay your investment so that you could invest yourself at 15%.

The rates of return that are available from investments in securities in financial markets such as ordinary shares and government gilt-edged securities represent the opportunity cost of an investment in capital projects; that is, if cash is invested in the capital project, it cannot be invested elsewhere to earn a return. A firm should therefore invest in capital projects only if they yield a return in excess of the opportunity cost of the investment. The opportunity cost of the investment is also known as the minimum required rate of return, cost of capital, discount rate or interest rate.

The return on securities traded in financial markets provides us with the opportunity costs, that is the required rates of return available on securities. The expected returns that investors require from the ordinary shares of different companies vary because some companies' shares are more risky than others. The greater the risk, the greater the expected returns. Consider Figure 13.3. You can see that as the risk of a security increases the return that investors require to compensate for the extra risk increases. Consequently, investors will expect to receive a return in excess of 15% if they invest in securities that have a higher risk than company X ordinary shares. If this return was not forthcoming, investors would not purchase high-risk securities. It is therefore important that companies investing in high-risk capital projects earn higher returns to compensate investors for this risk. You can also see that a risk-free security such as a gilt-edged government security yields the lowest return, i.e. 10%. Consequently, if a firm invests in a project with zero risk, it should earn a return in excess of 10%. If the project does not yield this return and no other projects are available then the funds earmarked for the project should be repaid to the shareholders as dividends. The shareholders could then invest the funds themselves at 10%.

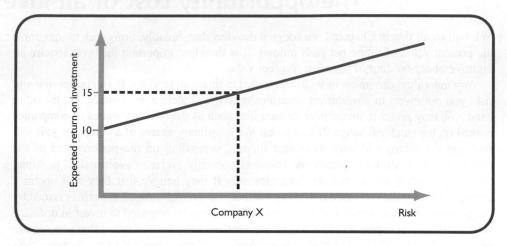

**FIGURE 13.3** *Risk–return trade-off.*

# Compounding and discounting

Our objective is to calculate and compare returns on an investment in a capital project with an alternative equal risk investment in securities traded in the financial markets. This comparison is made using a technique called discounted cash flow (DCF) analysis. Because a DCF analysis is the opposite of the concept of compounding interest, we shall initially focus on compound interest calculations.

Suppose you are investing £100 000 in a risk-free security yielding a return of 10% payable at the end of each year. Exhibit 13.1 shows that if the interest is reinvested, your investment will accumulate to £146 410 by the end of year 4. Period 0 in the first column of Exhibit 13.1 means that no time has elapsed or the time is *now*, period 1 means one year later, and so on. The values in Exhibit 13.1 can also be obtained by using the formula:

$$FV_n = V_0 (1 + K)^n \qquad (13.1)$$

**EXHIBIT 13.1**

*The value of £100 000 invested at 10%, compounded annually, for four years*

| End of year | Interest earned (£) | Total investment (£) |
|---|---|---|
| 0 | | 100 000 |
| | 0.10 × 100 000 | 10 000 |
| 1 | | 110 000 |
| | 0.10 × 110 000 | 11 000 |
| 2 | | 121 000 |
| | 0.10 × 121 000 | 12 100 |
| 3 | | 133 100 |
| | 0.10 × 133 100 | 13 310 |
| 4 | | 146 410 |

where $FV_n$ denotes the future value of an investment in $n$ years, $V_0$ denotes the amount invested at the beginning of the period (year 0), $K$ denotes the rate of return on the investment and $n$ denotes the number of years for which the money is invested. The calculation for £100 000 invested at 10% for two years is

$$FV_2 = £100\,000\,(1 + 0.10)^2 = £121\,000$$

In Exhibit 13.1 all of the year-end values are equal as far as the time value of money is concerned. For example, £121 000 received at the end of year 2 is equivalent to £100 000 received today and invested at 10%. Similarly, £133 100 received at the end of year 3 is equivalent to £121 000 received at the end of year 2, since £121 000 can be invested at the end of year 2 to accumulate to £133 100. Unfortunately, none of the amounts are directly comparable at any single moment in time, because each amount is expressed at a different point in time.

When making capital investment decisions, we must convert cash inflows and outflows for different years into a common value. This is achieved by converting the cash flows into their respective values at the same point in time. Mathematically, any point in time can be chosen, since all four figures in Exhibit 13.1 are equal to £100 000 at year 0, £110 000 at year 1, £121 000 at year 2, and so on. However, it is preferable to choose the point in time at which the decision is taken, and this is the present time or year 0. All of the values in Exhibit 13.1 can therefore be expressed in values at the present time (i.e. 'present value') of £100 000.

The process of converting cash to be received in the future into a value at the present time by the use of an interest rate is termed discounting and the resulting present value is the discounted present value. Compounding is the opposite of discounting, since it is the future value of present value cash flows. Equation (13.1) for calculating future values can be rearranged to produce the present value formula:

$$V_0 \text{ (present value)} = \frac{FV_n}{(1 + K)^n} \tag{13.2}$$

By applying this equation, the calculation for £121 000 received at the end of year 2 can be expressed as

$$\text{present value} = \frac{£121\,000}{(1 + 0.10)^2} = £100\,000$$

You should now be aware that £1 received today is not equal to £1 received one year from today. No rational person will be equally satisfied with receiving £1 a year from now as opposed to receiving it today, because money received today can be used to earn interest over the ensuing year. Thus one year from now an investor can have the original £1 plus one year's interest on it. For example, if the interest rate is 10% each £1 invested now will yield £1.10 one year from now. That is, £1 received today is equal to £1.10 one year from today at 10% interest. Alternatively, £1 one year from today is equal to £0.9091 today, its present value because £0.9091, plus 10% interest for one year amounts to £1. The concept that £1 received in the future is not equal to £1 received today is known as the time value of money.

We shall now consider five different methods of appraising capital investments: the net present value, internal rate of return, profitability index, accounting rate of return and payback methods. We shall see that the first three methods take into account the time value of money whereas the accounting rate of return and payback methods ignore this factor.

# The concept of net present value

By using discounted cash flow techniques and calculating present values, we can compare the return on an investment in capital projects with an alternative equal risk investment in securities traded in the financial market. Suppose a firm is considering four projects (all of which are risk-free) shown in Exhibit 13.2. You can see that each of the projects is identical with the investment in the risk-free security shown in Exhibit 13.1 because you can cash in this investment for £110 000 in year 1, £121 000 in year 2, £133 100 in year 3 and £146 410 in year 4. In other words your potential cash receipts from the risk-free security are identical to the net cash flows for projects A, B, C and D shown in Exhibit 13.2. Consequently, the firm should be indifferent as to whether it uses the funds to invest in the projects or invests the funds in securities of identical risk traded in the financial markets.

The most straightforward way of determining whether a project yields a return in excess of the alternative equal risk investment in traded securities is to calculate the net present value (NPV). This is the present value of the net cash inflows less the project's initial investment outlay. If the rate of return from the project is greater than the return from an equivalent risk investment in securities traded in the financial market, the NPV will be positive. Alternatively, if the rate of return is lower, the NPV will be negative. A positive NPV therefore indicates that an investment should be accepted, while a negative value indicates that it should be rejected. A zero NPV calculation indicates that the firm should be indifferent to whether the project is accepted or rejected.

You can see that the present value of each of the projects shown in Exhibit 13.2 is £100 000. You should now deduct the investment cost of £100 000 to calculate the project's NPV. The NPV for each project is zero. The firm should therefore be indifferent to whether it accepts any of the projects or invests the funds in an equivalent risk-free security. This was our conclusion when we compared the cash flows of the projects with the investments in a risk-free security shown in Exhibit 13.1.

You can see that it is better for the firm to invest in any of the projects shown in Exhibit 13.2 if their initial investment outlays are less than £100 000. This is because we have to pay £100 000 to obtain an equivalent stream of cash flows from a security traded in the financial markets. Conversely, we should reject the investment in the projects if their initial investment outlays are greater than £100 000. You should now see that the NPV rule leads to a direct comparison of a project with an equivalent risk security traded in the financial market.

**EXHIBIT 13.2**

*Evaluation of four risk-free projects*

| | A (£) | B (£) | C (£) | D (£) |
|---|---|---|---|---|
| Project investment outlay | 100 000 | 100 000 | 100 000 | 100 000 |
| End of year cash flows: | | | | |
| Year 1 | 110 000 | 0 | 0 | 0 |
| 2 | 0 | 121 000 | 0 | 0 |
| 3 | 0 | 0 | 133 100 | 0 |
| 4 | 0 | 0 | 0 | 146 410 |
| present value = | $\dfrac{110\,000}{1.10}$ | $\dfrac{121\,000}{(1.10)^2}$ | $\dfrac{133\,000}{(1.10)^3}$ | $\dfrac{146\,410}{(1.10)^4}$ |
| | = 100 000 | = 100 000 | = 100 000 | = 100 000 |

Given that the present value of the net cash inflows for each project is £100 000, their NPVs will be positive (thus signifying acceptance) if the initial investment outlay is less than £100 000 and negative (thus signifying rejection) if the initial outlay is greater than £100 000.

# Calculating net present values

You should now have an intuitive understanding of the NPV rule. We shall now learn how to calculate NPVs. The NPV can be expressed as:

$$NPV = \frac{FV_1}{1+K} + \frac{FV_2}{(1+K)^2} + \frac{FV_3}{(1+K)^3} + \cdots + \frac{FV_n}{(1+K)^n} - I_0 \qquad (13.3)$$

where $I_0$ represents the investment outlay and $FV$ represents the future values received in years 1 to $n$. The rate of return $K$ used is the return available on an equivalent risk security in the financial market. Consider the situation in Example 13.1.

---

**EXAMPLE 13.1**

The Bothnia Company is evaluating two projects with an expected life of three years and an investment outlay of £1 million. The estimated net cash inflows for each project are as follows:

|  | Project A (£) | Project B (£) |
|---|---|---|
| Year 1 | 300 000 | 600 000 |
| Year 2 | 1 000 000 | 600 000 |
| Year 3 | 400 000 | 600 000 |

The opportunity cost of capital for both projects is 10%. You are required to calculate the net present value for each project.

---

The net present value calculation for Project A is:

$$NPV = \frac{£300\,000}{(1.10)} + \frac{£1\,000\,000}{(1.10)^2} + \frac{£400\,000}{(1.10)^3} - £1\,000\,000 = +£399\,700$$

Alternatively, the net present value can be calculated by referring to a published table of present values. You will find examples of such a table if you refer to Appendix A (see pages 1080–3). To use the table, simply find the discount factors by referring to each year of the cash flows and the appropriate interest rate.

For example, if you refer to year 1 in Appendix A, and the 10% column, this will show a discount factor of 0.9091. For years 2 and 3 the discount factors are 0.8264 and 0.7513. You then multiply the cash flows by the discount factors to find the present value of the cash flows. The calculation is as follows:

| Year | Amount (£) | Discount factor | Present value (£) |
|------|-----------|-----------------|-------------------|
| 1 | 300 | 0.9091 | 272 730 |
| 2 | 1000 | 0.8264 | 826 400 |
| 3 | 400 | 0.7513 | 300 520 |
| | | | 1 399 650 |
| | | Less initial outlay | 1 000 000 |
| | | Net present value | 399 650 |

The difference between the two calculations is due to rounding differences.

Note that the discount factors in the present value table are based on £1 received in *n* years time calculated according to the present value formula (equation 13.2). For example, £1 received in years 1, 2 and 3 when the interest rate is 10% is calculated as follows:

$$\text{Year } 1 = £1/1.10 = 0.9091$$
$$\text{Year } 2 = £1(1.10)^2 = 0.8264$$
$$\text{Year } 3 = £1(1.10)^3 = 0.7513$$

The positive net present value from the investment indicates the increase in the market value of the shareholders' funds which should occur once the stock market becomes aware of the acceptance of the project. The net present value also represents the potential increase in present consumption that the project makes available to the ordinary shareholders, after any funds used have been repaid with interest. For example, assume that the firm finances the investment of £1 million in Example13.1 by borrowing £1 399 700 at 10% and repays the loan and interest out of the project's proceeds as they occur. You can see from the repayment schedule in Exhibit 13.3 that £399 700 received from the loan is available for current consumption, and the remaining £1 000 000 can be invested in the project. The cash flows from the project are just sufficient to repay the loan. Therefore acceptance of the project enables the ordinary shareholders' present consumption to be increased by the net present value of £399 700. Hence the acceptance of all available projects with a positive net present value should lead to the maximization of shareholders' wealth.

Let us now calculate the net present value for Project B. When the annual cash flows are constant, the calculation of the net present value is simplified. The discount factors when the cash flows are the same each year (that is, an annuity) are set out in Appendix B (see pages 1084–7). We need to find the discount factor for 10% for three years. If you refer to Appendix B, you will see that it is 2.487. The NPV is calculated as follows:

| Annual cash inflow | Discount factor | Present value (£) |
|--------------------|-----------------|-------------------|
| £600 000 | 2.487 | 1 492 200 |
| | Less investment cost | 1 000 000 |
| | Net present value | 492 200 |

You will see that the total present value for the period is calculated by multiplying the cash inflow by the discount factor. It is important to note that the annuity tables shown in Appendix B can only be applied when the annual cash flows are the same each year.

# The internal rate of return

The **internal rate of return (IRR)** is an alternative technique for use in making capital investment decisions that also takes into account the time value of money. The internal rate of return represents the true interest rate earned on an investment over the course of its economic life. This measure is sometimes referred to as the discounted rate of return.

**EXHIBIT 13.3**

*The pattern of cash flows assuming that the loan is repaid out of the proceeds of the project*

The internal rate of return is the interest rate $K$ that when used to discount all cash flows resulting from an investment, will equate the present value of the cash receipts to the present value of the cash outlays. In other words, it is the discount rate that will cause the net present value of an investment to be zero. Alternatively, the internal rate of return can be described as the maximum cost of capital that can be applied to finance a project without causing harm to the shareholders. The internal

| Year | Loan outstanding at start of year (1) (£) | Interest at 10% (2) (£) | Total amount owed before repayment (3) = (1)+(2) (£) | Proceeds from project (4) (£) | Loan outstanding at year end (5) = (3)−(4) (£) |
|---|---|---|---|---|---|
| 1 | 1 399 700 | 139 970 | 1 539 670 | 300 000 | 1 239 670 |
| 2 | 1 239 670 | 123 967 | 1 363 637 | 1 000 000 | 363 637 |
| 3 | 363 637 | 36 363 | 400 000 | 400 000 | 0 |

rate of return is found by solving for the value of $K$ from the following formula:

$$I_0 = \frac{FV_1}{1+K} + \frac{FV_2}{(1+K)^2} + \frac{FV_3}{(1+K)^3} + \cdots + \frac{FV_n}{(1+K)^n} \qquad (13.4)$$

It is easier, however, to use the discount tables. Let us now calculate the internal rate of return for Project A in Example 13.1.

The IRR can be found by trial and error by using a number of discount factors until the NPV equals zero. For example, if we use a 25% discount factor, we get a positive NPV of £84 800. We must therefore try a higher figure. Applying 35% gives a negative NPV of £66 530. We know then that the NPV will be zero somewhere between 25% and 35%. In fact, the IRR is approximately 30%, as indicated in the following calculation:

| Year | Net cash flow (£) | Discount factor (30%) | Present value of cash flow (£) |
|---|---|---|---|
| 1 | 300 000 | 0.7692 | 230 760 |
| 2 | 1 000 000 | 0.5917 | 591 700 |
| 3 | 400 000 | 0.4552 | 182 080 |
| | | Net present value | 1 004 540 |
| | | Less initial outlay | 1 000 000 |
| | | Net present value | 4 540 |

It is claimed that the calculation of the IRR does not require the prior specification of the cost of capital. The decision rule is that if the IRR is greater than the opportunity cost of capital, the investment is profitable and will yield a positive NPV. Alternatively, if the IRR is less than the cost of capital, the investment is unprofitable and will result in a negative

NPV. Therefore any interpretation of the significance of the IRR will still require that we estimate the cost of capital. The calculation of the IRR is illustrated in Figure 13.4.

The dots in the graph represent the NPV at different discount rates. The point where the line joining the dots cuts the horizontal axis indicates the IRR (the point at which the NPV is zero). Figure 13.4 indicates that the IRR is 30%, and you can see from this diagram that the interpolation method can be used to calculate the IRR without carrying out trial and error calculations. When we use interpolation, we infer the missing term (in this case the discount rate at which NPV is zero) from a known series of numbers. For example, at a discount rate of 25% the NPV is +£84 800 and for a discount rate of 35% the NPV is −£66 530. The total distance between these points is £151 330 (+£84 800 and −£66 530). The calculation for the approximate IRR is therefore

$$25\% + \frac{84\,800}{151\,330} \times (35\% - 25\%) = 30.60\%$$

In other words, if you move down line A in Figure 13.4 from a discount rate of 25% by £84 800, you will reach the point at which NPV is zero. The distance between the two points on line A is £151 330, and we are given the discount rates of 25% and 35% for these points. Therefore 84 800/151 330 represents the distance that we must move between these two points for the NPV to be zero. This distance in terms of the discount rate is 5.60% (84 800/151 330), which, when added to the starting point of 25%, produces an IRR of 30.60%. The formula using the interpolation method is as follows:

$$A + \frac{C}{C - D}(B - A) \tag{13.5}$$

where $A$ is the discount rate of the low trial, $B$ is the discount rate of the high trial, $C$ is the NPV of cash inflow of the low trial and $D$ is the NPV of cash inflow of the high trial. Thus

$$25\% + \left[ \frac{84\,800}{84\,800 - (-66\,530)} \times 10\% \right]$$

$$= 25\% + \left[ \frac{84\,800}{151\,330} \times 10\% \right]$$

$$= 30.60\%$$

Note that the interpolation method only gives an approximation of the IRR. The greater the distance between any two points that have a positive and a negative NPV, the less accurate is the IRR calculation. Consider line B in Figure 13.4. The point where it cuts the horizontal axis is approximately 33%, whereas the actual IRR is 30.60%.

The calculation of the IRR is easier when the cash flows are of a constant amount each year. Let us now calculate the internal rate of return for project B in Example 13.1. Because the cash flows are equal each year, we can use the annuity table in Appendix B. When the cash flows are discounted at the IRR, the NPV will be zero. The IRR will therefore be at the point where

$$[\text{annual cash flow}] \times \left[ \begin{matrix} \text{discount factor for number of years} \\ \text{for which cash flow is received} \end{matrix} \right] - \left[ \begin{matrix} \text{investment} \\ \text{cost} \end{matrix} \right] = 0$$

Rearranging this formula, the internal rate of return will be at the point where

$$\text{discount factor} = \frac{\text{investment cost}}{\text{annual cash flow}}$$

Substituting the figures for project B in Example 13.1,

$$\text{discount factor} = \frac{£1\,000\,000}{£600\,000} = 1.666$$

**FIGURE 13.4**  *Interpretation of the internal rate of return.*

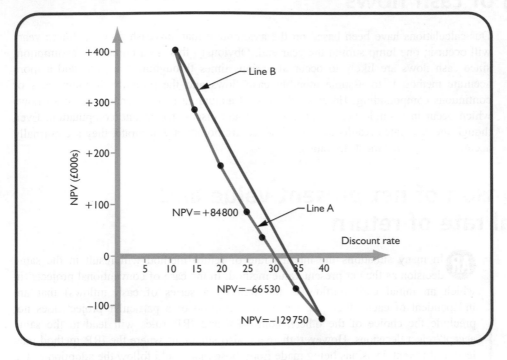

We now examine the entries for year 3 in Appendix B to find the figures closest to 1.666. They are 1.673 (entered in the 36% column) and 1.652 (entered in the 37% column). We can therefore conclude that the IRR is between 36% and 37%. However, because the cost of capital is 10%, an accurate calculation is unnecessary; the IRR is far in excess of the cost of capital.

The calculation of the IRR can be rather tedious (as the cited examples show), but the trial-and-error approach can be programmed for fast and accurate solution by a computer. The calculation problems are no longer a justification for preferring the NPV method of investment appraisal. Nevertheless, there are theoretical justifications, which we shall discuss later in this chapter, that support the NPV method.

# Relevant cash flows

Investment decisions, like all other decisions, should be analysed in terms of the cash flows that can be directly attributable to them. These cash flows should include the incremental cash flows that will occur in the future following acceptance of the investment. The cash flows will include cash inflows and outflows, or the inflows may be represented by savings in cash outflows. For example, a decision to purchase new machinery may generate cash savings in the form of reduced out-of-pocket operating costs. For all practical purposes such cost savings are equivalent to cash receipts.

It is important to note that depreciation is not included in the cash flow estimates for capital investment decisions, since it is a non-cash expense. This is because the capital investment cost of the asset to be depreciated is included as a cash outflow at the start of the project, and depreciation is merely an accounting method for apportioning the capital costs to the relevant accounting periods. Any inclusion of depreciation will lead to double counting.

# Timing of cash flows

Our calculations have been based on the assumption that any cash flows in future years will occur in one lump sum at the year end. Obviously, this is an unrealistic assumption, since cash flows are likely to occur at various times throughout the year, and a more accurate method is to assume monthly cash flows and the monthly discount rates or continuous compounding. However, the use of annual cash flows enables all cash flows which occur in a single year to be combined and discounted in one computation. Even though the calculated results that are obtained are not strictly accurate, they are normally accurate enough for most decisions.

# Comparison of net present value and internal rate of return

**AR** In many situations the internal rate of return method will result in the same decision as the net present value method. In the case of conventional projects (in which an initial cash outflow is followed by a series of cash inflows) that are independent of each other (i.e. where the selection of a particular project does not preclude the choice of the other), both NPV and IRR rules will lead to the same accept/reject decisions. However, there are also situations where the IRR method may lead to different decisions being made from those that would follow the adoption of the NPV procedure.

## MUTUALLY EXCLUSIVE PROJECTS

Where projects are mutually exclusive, it is possible for the NPV and the IRR methods to suggest different rankings as to which project should be given priority. Mutually exclusive projects exist where the acceptance of one project excludes the acceptance of another project, for example the choice of one of several possible factory locations, or the choice of one of many different possible machines. Example 13.2 illustrates how the

---

**EXAMPLE 13.2**

The Bothnia Company is also evaluating two alternative mutually exclusive methods of improving the marketing of its products which it has described as project X and project Y. The estimated incremental cash flows from each alternative are as follows:

| | Initial Investment outlay (£) | Net inflow at the end of years 1–3 (£) | | |
| --- | --- | --- | --- | --- |
| | | 1 | 2 | 3 |
| Project X | 700 000 | 343 000 | 343 000 | 343 000 |
| Project Y | 1 200 000 | 552 000 | 552 000 | 552 000 |

The company's estimated cost of capital is 10%. Which project should the company accept?

**FIGURE 13.5** *Net present values at different discount rates for projects X and Y (Example 13.2).*

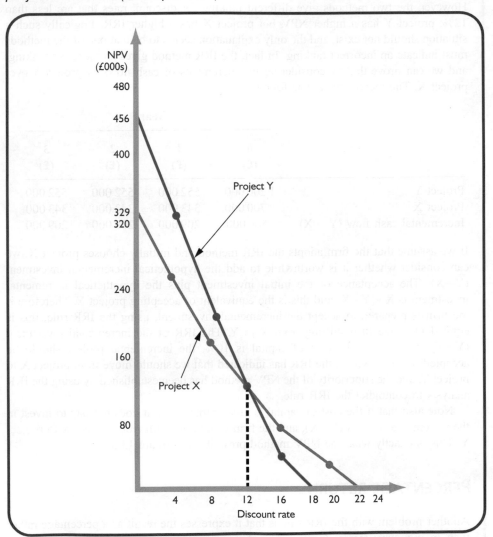

application of the IRR and the NPV rules can lead to different decisions.

The NPV and IRR calculations are as follows:

|            | IRR<br>(%) | NPV<br>(£) |
|------------|:----:|:-------:|
| Project X  | 22   | 153 041 |
| Project Y  | 18   | 172 824 |

You can see that the IRR ranks X first, but the NPV rate ranks Y first. If the projects were independent, this would be irrelevant, since both would be accepted and the firm would be indifferent as to the order in which they were accepted. However, in the case of mutually exclusive projects the ranking is crucial, since only one project can be accepted and we cannot be indifferent to the outcome of applying the NPV and the IRR rules. The reasons for the different rankings are shown in Figure 13.5.

The NPV ranking depends on the discount rate used. For a discount rate greater than 12% no contradictions arise, since both the NPV and the IRR rules rank X first. However, the two methods give different ranking for discount rates that are less than 12%: project Y has a higher NPV, but project X has a higher IRR. Logically such a situation should not exist, and the only explanation seems to be that one of the methods must indicate an incorrect ranking. In fact, the IRR method gives an incorrect ranking, and we can prove this by considering the increments of cash flows of project Y over project X. The increments are as follows:

| | Years | | | |
| --- | --- | --- | --- | --- |
| | 0 (£) | 1 (£) | 2 (£) | 3 (£) |
| Project Y | 1 200 000 | 552 000 | 552 000 | 552 000 |
| Project X | 700 000 | 343 000 | 343 000 | 343 000 |
| Incremental cash flow (Y – X) | 500 000 | 209 000 | 209 000 | 209 000 |

If we assume that the firm adopts the IRR method and initially chooses project X, we can consider whether it is worthwhile to add the hypothetical incremental investment (Y−X). The acceptance of the initial investment plus the hypothetical incremental investment is X+(Y−X) and this is the equivalent of accepting project Y. Therefore if the firm is prepared to accept the incremental investment, using the IRR rule, this is equivalent to the firm shifting from X to Y. The IRR of the incremental investment (Y−X) is 12%. As the cost of capital is 10%, the incremental project should be accepted. In other words, the IRR has indicated that we should move from project X to project Y, and the superiority of the NPV method has been established by using the IRR analysis to contradict the IRR rule.

Note also that if the cost of capital is greater than 12%, it does not pay to invest in the incremental project (Y−X), and the firm should not shift from project X to project Y. This is exactly what the NPV method prescribes in Figure 13.5.

## PERCENTAGE RETURNS

Another problem with the IRR rule is that it expresses the result as a percentage rather than in monetary terms. Comparison of percentage returns can be misleading; for example, compare an investment of £10 000 that yields a return of 50% with an investment of £100 000 that yields a return of 25%. If only one of the investments can be undertaken, the first investment will yield £5000 but the second will yield £25 000. If we assume that the cost of capital is 10%, and that no other suitable investments are available, any surplus funds will be invested at the cost of capital. Choosing the first investment will leave a further £90 000 to be invested, but this can only be invested at 10%, yielding a return of £9000. Adding this to the return of £5000 from the £10 000 investment gives a total return of £14 000. Clearly, the second investment, which yields a return of £25 000, is preferable. Thus, if the objective is to maximize the firm's wealth then NPV provides the correct measure.

## REINVESTMENT ASSUMPTIONS

The assumption concerning the reinvestment of interim cash flows from the acceptance of projects provides another reason for supporting the superiority of the NPV method.

The implicit assumption if the NPV method is adopted is that the cash flows generated from an investment will be reinvested at the cost of capital (i.e. the discount rate). However, the IRR method makes a different implicit assumption about the reinvestment of the cash flows. It assumes that all the proceeds from a project can be reinvested to earn a return equal to the IRR of the original project. In Example 13.2 the NPV method assumes that the annual cash inflows of £343 000 for project X will be reinvested at a cost of capital of 10%, whereas the IRR method assumes that they will be reinvested at 22%. In theory, a firm will have accepted all projects which offer a return in excess of the cost of capital, and any other funds that become available can only be reinvested at the cost of capital. This is the assumption that is implicit in the NPV rule.

## UNCONVENTIONAL CASH FLOWS

Where a project has unconventional cash flows, the IRR has a technical shortcoming. Most projects have conventional cash flows that consist of an initial negative cash flow followed by positive cash inflows in later years. In this situation the algebraic sign changes, being negative at the start and positive in all future periods. If the sign of the net cash flows changes in successive periods, it is possible for the calculations to produce as many internal rates of return as there are sign changes. While multiple rates of return are mathematically possible, only one rate of return is economically significant in determining whether or not the investment is profitable.

Fortunately, the majority of investment decisions consist of conventional cash flows that produce a single IRR calculation. However, the problem cannot be ignored, since unconventional cash flows are possible and, if the decision-maker is unaware of the situation, serious errors may occur at the decision-making stage. Example 13.3 illustrates a situation where two internal rates of return occur.

---

**EXAMPLE 13.3**

The Bothnia Company has the following series of cash flows for a specific project:

Year 0      − £400 000 (Investment outlay)
Year 1      + £1 020 000 (Net cash inflows)
Year 2      − £630 000 (Environmental and disposal costs)

You are required to calculate the internal rate of return.

---

You will find that the cash flows in Example 13.3 give internal rates of return of 5% and 50%. The effect of multiple rates of return on the NPV calculations is illustrated in Figure 13.6.

When the cost of capital is between 5% and 50%, the NPV is positive and, following the NPV rule, the project should be accepted. However, if the IRR calculation of 5% is used, the project may be incorrectly rejected if the cost of capital is in excess of 5%. You can see that the graph of the NPV in Figure 13.6 indicates that this is an incorrect decision when the cost of capital is between 5% and 50%. Alternatively, if the IRR of 50% is used, this will lead to the same decision being made as if the NPV rule were

**FIGURE 13.6** *Net present values for unconventional cash flows.*

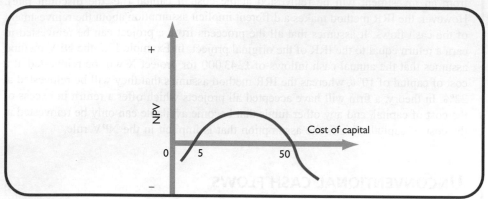

adopted, provided that the cost of capital is greater than 5%. Note that the NPV is negative if the cost of capital is less than 5%. ●●●

# Profitability index

The **profitability index** is the third method of evaluating capital investment proposals that takes into account the time value of money. The method is simply a variation of the NPV method, and it is computed by dividing the present value of the cash proceeds by the initial cost of the investment. If the profitability index is less than 1, the investment should be rejected. Conversely, if it is greater than 1, the investment should be accepted. This method is consistent with the NPV method, since the index can only be less than 1 when the NPV is negative. Similarly, an index greater than 1 only arises when the NPV is positive.

In the case of independent projects and where the company is not restricted from accepting profitable projects because of the shortage of funds the profitability index will yield the same acceptance–rejection decision as the NPV method. For mutually exclusive investments the profitability index will not always result in the same rankings as the NPV method. Consider the following situation, where projects C and D are mutually exclusive:

|  | PV of cash flow (£) | Initial investment outlay (£) | Profitability index |
|---|---|---|---|
| Project C | 100 000 | 50 000 | 2.0 |
| Project D | 180 000 | 100 000 | 1.8 |

According to the profitability index, project C is to be preferred, but, given that only one of these two projects can be chosen, project D should be the one. This is because D gives the largest absolute NPV. Therefore the profitability index is a weak measure for selecting between mutually exclusive investment projects in a situation when a company can accept all investments that yield a positive NPV. However, we shall see in the next chapter that when a firm cannot accept all of those projects with positive NPVs because of the unavailability of funds, the profitability index can be a useful method for determining how the scarce funds can best be allocated.

# Techniques that ignore the time value of money

In addition to those methods that take into account the time value of money two other methods that ignore this factor are frequently used in practice. These are the payback method and the accounting rate of return method. Methods that ignore the time value of money are theoretically weak, and they will not necessarily lead to the maximization of the market value of ordinary shares. Nevertheless, the fact that they are frequently used in practice means that we should be aware of their limitations.

# Payback method

The payback method is one of the simplest and most frequently used methods of capital investment appraisal. It is defined as the length of time that is required for a stream of cash proceeds from an investment to recover the original cash outlay required by the investment. If the stream of cash flows from the investment is constant each year, the payback period can be calculated by dividing the total initial cash outlay by the amount of the expected annual cash proceeds. Therefore if an investment requires an initial outlay of £60 000 and is expected to produce annual cash inflows of £20 000 per year for five years, the payback period will be £60 000 divided by £20 000, or three years. If the stream of expected proceeds is not constant from year to year, the payback period is determined by adding up the cash inflows expected in successive years until the total is equal to the original outlay. Example 13.4 illustrates two projects, A and B, that require the same initial outlay of £50 000 but that display different time profiles of benefits.

In Example 13.4 project A pays back its initial investment cost in three years, whereas project B pays back its initial cost in four years. However, project B has a higher NPV, and the payback method incorrectly ranks project A in preference to project B. Two obvious deficiencies are apparent from these calculations. First, the payback method does not take into account cash flows that are earned after the payback date and, secondly, it fails to take into account the differences in the timing of the proceeds which are earned before the payback date. Payback computations ignore the important fact that future cash receipts cannot be validly compared with an initial outlay until they are discounted to their present values.

## EXAMPLE 13.4

The cash flows and NPV calculations for two projects are as follows:

|  | Project A | | Project B | |
| --- | --- | --- | --- | --- |
|  | (£) | (£) | (£) | (£) |
| Initial cost |  | 50 000 |  | 50 000 |
| Cash inflows |  |  |  |  |
| Year 1 | 10 000 |  | 10 000 |  |
| Year 2 | 20 000 |  | 10 000 |  |
| Year 3 | 20 000 |  | 10 000 |  |
| Year 4 | 20 000 |  | 20 000 |  |
| Year 5 | 10 000 |  | 30 000 |  |
| Year 6 | — |  | 30 000 |  |
| Year 7 | — | 80 000 | 30 000 | 140 000 |
| NRV at a 10% cost capital |  | 10 500 |  | 39 460 |

**EXAMPLE 13.5**

The cash flows and NPV calculation for project C are as follows:

|  | (£) | (£) |
|---|---|---|
| Initial cost | | 50 000 |
| Cash outflows | | |
| Year 1 | 10 000 | |
| Year 2 | 20 000 | |
| Year 3 | 20 000 | |
| Year 4 | 3 500 | |
| Year 5 | 3 500 | |
| Year 6 | 3 500 | |
| Year 7 | 3 500 | 64 000 |
| NPV (at 10% cost of capital) | | (−1036) |

Not only does the payback period incorrectly rank project A in preference to project B, but the method can also result in the acceptance of projects that have a negative NPV. Consider the cash flows for project C in Example 13.5.

The payback period for project C is three years, and if this was within the time limit set by management, the project would be accepted in spite of its negative NPV. Note also that the payback method would rank project C in preference to project B in Example 13.4, despite the fact that B would yield a positive NPV.

The payback period can only be a valid indicator of the time that an investment requires to pay for itself, if all cash flows are first discounted to their present values and the discounted values are then used to calculate the payback period. This adjustment gives rise to what is known as the adjusted or discounted payback method. Even when such an adjustment is made, the adjusted payback method cannot be a complete measure of an investment's profitability. It can estimate whether an investment is likely to be profitable, but it cannot estimate how profitable the investment will be.

Despite the theoretical limitations of the payback method it is the method most widely used in practice (see Exhibit 13.4). Why, then, is payback the most widely applied formal investment appraisal technique? It is a particularly useful approach for ranking projects where a firm faces liquidity constraints and requires a fast repayment of investments. The payback method may also be appropriate in situations where risky investments are made in uncertain markets that are subject to fast design and product changes or where future cash flows are extremely difficult to predict. The payback method assumes that risk is time-related: the longer the period, the greater the chance of failure. By concentrating on the early cash flows, payback uses data in which managers have greater confidence. The justification for this is that cash flows tend to be correlated over time. Thus if cash flows are below the expected level in the early years, this pattern will often continue. The payback method is also frequently used in conjunction with the NPV or IRR methods. It serves as a simple first-level screening device that identifies those projects that should be subject to more rigorous investigation. A further attraction of payback is that it is easily understood by all levels of management and provides an important summary measure: how quickly will the project recover its initial outlay? Ideally, the payback method should be used in conjunction with the NPV method, and the cash flows discounted before the payback period is calculated.

## EXHIBIT 13.4

### Surveys of practice

Surveys conducted by Pike relating to the investment appraisal techniques by 100 large UK companies between 1975 and 1992 provide an indication of the changing trends in practice in large UK companies. Pike's findings relating to the percentage of firms using different appraisal methods are as follows:

|  | 1975 % | 1981 % | 1986 % | 1992 % |
|---|---|---|---|---|
| Payback | 73 | 81 | 92 | 94 |
| Accounting rate of return | 51 | 49 | 56 | 50 |
| DCF methods (IRR or NPV) | 58 | 68 | 84 | 88 |
| Internal rate of return (IRR) | 44 | 57 | 75 | 81 |
| Net present value (NPV) | 32 | 39 | 68 | 74 |

*Source*: Pike (1996)

A study of 300 UK manufacturing organizations by Drury *et al.* (1993) sought to ascertain the extent to which particular techniques were used. The figures below indicate the percentage of firms that often or always used a particular technique:

|  | All organizations % | Smallest organizations % | Largest organizations % |
|---|---|---|---|
| Payback (unadjusted) | 63 | 56 | 55 |
| Discounted payback | 42 | 30 | 48 |
| Accounting rate of return | 41 | 35 | 53 |
| Internal rate of return | 57 | 30 | 85 |
| Net present value | 43 | 23 | 80 |

Few studies have been undertaken in mainland Europe. The following usage rates relate to surveys undertaken in the USA and Belgium. For comparative purposes Pike's UK study is also listed :

|  | UK[a] % | USA[b] % | Belgium[c] % |
|---|---|---|---|
| Payback | 94 | 72 | 50 |
| Accounting rate of return | 50 | 65 | 65 |
| Internal rate of return | 81 | 91 | 77 |
| Net present value | 74 | 88 | 60 |
| Discounted payback |  | 65 | 68 |

[a] Pike (1996)
[b] Trahan and Gitman (1995)
[c] Dardenne (1998)

It is apparent from the above surveys that firms use a combination of appraisal methods. The studies by Pike indicate a trend in the increasing usage of discount rates. The Drury *et al.* study suggests that larger organizations use net present value and internal rate of return to a greater extent than the smaller organizations. The Drury *et al.* study also asked the respondents to rank the appraisal methods in order of importance for evaluating major projects. The larger organizations ranked internal rate of return first, followed by payback and net present value whereas the smaller organizations ranked payback first, internal rate of return second and intuitive management judgement third.

The use of the accounting rate of return probably reflects the fact that it is a widely used external financial accounting measure by financial markets and managers therefore wish to assess what impact a project will have on the external reporting of this measure. Also it is a widely used measure for evaluating managerial performance.

# Accounting rate of return

The **accounting rate of return** (also known as the **return on investment** and **return on capital employed**) is calculated by dividing the average annual profits from a project into the average investment cost. It differs from other methods in that profits rather than cash flows are used. The use of this method results from the wide use of the return on investment measure in financial statement analysis.

When the average annual net profits are calculated, only additional revenues and costs that follow from the investment are included in the calculation. The average annual net profit is therefore calculated by dividing the difference between incremental revenues and costs by the estimated life of the investment. The incremental costs include either the *net* investment cost or the total depreciation charges, these figures being identical. The average investment figure that is used in the calculation depends on the method employed to calculate depreciation. If straight-line depreciation is used, it is presumed that investment will decline in a linear fashion as the asset ages. The average investment under this assumption is one-half of the amount of the initial investment plus one-half of the scrap value at the end of the project's life[1].

For example, the three projects described in Examples 13.4 and 13.5 for which the payback period was computed required an initial outlay of £50 000. If we assume that the projects have no scrap values and that straight-line depreciation is used, the average investment for each project will be £25 000. The calculation of the accounting rate of return for each of these projects is as follows:

$$\text{accounting rate of return} = \frac{\text{average annual profits}}{\text{average investment}}$$

$$\text{project A} = \frac{6\,000}{25\,000} = 24\%$$

$$\text{project B} = \frac{12\,857}{25\,000} = 51\%$$

$$\text{project C} = \frac{2\,000}{25\,000} = 8\%$$

For project A the total profit over its five-year life is £30 000, giving an average annual profit of £6000. The average annual profits for projects B and C are calculated in a similar manner.

It follows that the accounting rate of return is superior to the payback method in one respect; that is, it allows for differences in the useful lives of the assets being compared. For example, the calculations set out above reflect the high earnings of project B over the whole life of the project, and consequently it is ranked in preference to project A. Also, projects A and C have the same payback periods, but the accounting rate of return correctly indicates that project A is preferable to project C.

However, the accounting rate of return suffers from the serious defect that it ignores the time value of money. When the method is used in relation to a project where the cash inflows do not occur until near the end of its life, it will show the same accounting rate of return as it would for a project where the cash inflows occur early in its life, providing that the average cash inflows are the same. For this reason the accounting rate of return cannot be recommended.

# The effect of performance measurement on capital investment decisions

The way that the performance of a manager is measured is likely to have a profound effect on the decisions he or she will make. There is a danger that, because of the way performance is measured, a manager may be motivated to take the wrong decision and not follow the NPV rule. Consider the information presented in Exhibit 13.5 in respect of the net cash inflows and the annual reported profits or losses for projects J and K. The figures without the parentheses refer to the cash inflows whereas the figures within the parentheses refer to annual reported profit. You will see that the total cash inflows over the five year lives for projects J and K are £11 million and £5 million respectively. Both projects require an initial outlay of £5 million. Assuming a cost of capital of 10% project J will have a positive NPV and project K will have a negative NPV.

If the straight line method of depreciation is used the annual depreciation for both projects will be £1 million (£5 million investment cost/5 years). Therefore the reported profits are derived from deducting the annual depreciation charge from the annual net cash inflows. For decision-making the focus is on the entire life of the projects. Our objective is to ascertain whether the present value of the cash inflows exceeds the present value of the cash outflows over the entire life of a project, and not allocate the NPV to different accounting periods as indicated by the dashed vertical lines in Figure 13.5. In other words we require an answer to the question will the project add value?

In contrast, a company is required to report on its performance externally at annual intervals and managerial performance is also often evaluated on an annual or more frequent basis. Evaluating managerial performance at the end of the five year project lives is clearly too long a time scale since managers are unlikely to remain in the same job for such lengthy periods. Therefore, for performance evaluation we must measure a project's outcomes at periodic intervals throughout its life. You will see that this process results in losses being reported for Project J in its early years, even though it has a positive NPV. There is a danger that a manager who is anxious to improve his or her short-term performance might reject project J even though it has a positive impact on the performance measure in the long-term.

The reverse may happen with project K. This has a favourable impact on the short-term profit performance measure in years one and two but a negative impact in the longer-term so the manager might accept the project to improve his or her short-term performance measure.

It is thus important to avoid an excessive focus on short-term profitability measures since this can have a negative impact on long-term profitability. Emphasis should also be given to measuring a manager's contribution to an organization's long-term objectives. These issues are discussed in

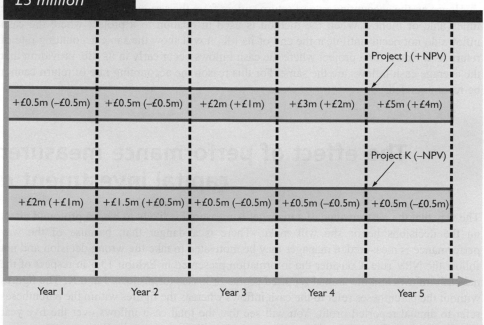

**EXHIBIT 13.5**

*Annual net cash inflows (profits/losses) for two projects each with an initial outlay of £5 million*

| Project J (+NPV) | | | | |
|---|---|---|---|---|
| +£0.5m (−£0.5m) | +£0.5m (−£0.5m) | +£2m (+£1m) | +£3m (+£2m) | +£5m (+£4m) |

| Project K (−NPV) | | | | |
|---|---|---|---|---|
| +£2m (+£1m) | +£1.5m (+£0.5m) | +£0.5m (−£0.5m) | +£0.5m (−£0.5m) | +£0.5m (−£0.5m) |

| Year 1 | Year 2 | Year 3 | Year 4 | Year 5 |

Chapter 20 when we shall look at performance measurement in more detail. However, at this point you should note that the way in which managerial performance is measured will influence their decisions and may motivate them to work in their own best interests, even when this is not in the best interest of the organization.

# Qualitative factors

Not all investment projects can be described completely in terms of monetary costs and benefits (e.g. a new cafeteria for the employees or the installation of safety equipment). Nevertheless, the procedures described in this chapter may be useful by making the value placed by management on quantitative factors explicit. For example, if the present value of the cash outlays for a project is £100 000 and the benefits from the project are difficult to quantify, management must make a value judgement as to whether or not the benefits are in excess of £100 000. In the case of capital expenditure on facilities for employees, or expenditure to avoid unpleasant environmental effects from the company's manufacturing process, one can take the view that the present value of the cash outlays represents the cost to shareholders of the pursuit of goals other than the maximization of shareholders' funds. In other words, ordinary shareholders, as a group in the bargaining coalition, should know how much the pursuit of other goals is costing them.

Capital investment decisions are particularly difficult in non-profit organizations such as national and local government organizations, since it is not always possible to quantify the costs and benefits of a project. Cost–benefit analysis (CBA), which is an investment appraisal technique for analysing and measuring the costs and benefits to the community of capital projects, has been developed to resolve this problem, and it seeks to determine the incidence of costs and benefits between different sectors of the community. CBA attempts to take into account all the costs and benefits that accrue from a project by defining the costs and benefits in much wider terms than those that would be included in traditional accounting measures. A wider range of factors is therefore included in the analysis than those that would be incorporated in the traditional accounting investment appraisal. For example, when CBA was applied to the appraisal of a new metro service in London attempts were made to set a monetary value on the travelling time saved by users.

There is also a danger that those aspects of a new investment that are difficult to quantify may be omitted from the financial appraisal. This applies particularly to investments in advanced manufacturing technologies that yield benefits such as improved quality and delivery times and a greater flexibility that provides the potential for low cost production of high-variety, low-volume goods. Various commentators have criticized financial appraisal techniques because they fail to take such qualitative aspects into account. They claim that an over-emphasis on the quantitative aspects has inhibited investment in advanced manufacturing technologies.

The difficulty in quantifying the cash flows is no excuse for omitting them from the analysis. A bad estimate is better than no estimate at all. One approach that has been suggested for overcoming these difficulties is not to attempt to place a value on those benefits that are difficult to quantify. Instead, the process can be reversed by estimating how large these benefits must be in order to justify the proposed investment. Assume that a project with an estimated life of 10 years and a cost of capital of 20% has a negative NPV of £1 million. To achieve a positive NPV, or in other words to obtain the required rate of return of 20%, additional cash flows would need to be achieved that when discounted at 20%, would amount to at least £1 million. The project lasts for 10 years, and the discount factor for an annuity over 10 years at 20% is 4.192. Therefore the additional cash flows from the benefits that have not been quantified must be greater than £238 550 per annum (note that £1 million divided by an annuity factor (Appendix B) for ten years at 20% (4.192) equals £238 550) in order to justify the proposed investment. Discussions should then take place to consider whether benefits that have not been quantified, such as improved flexibility, rapid customer service and market adaptability, are worth more than £238 550 per year.

## Self-Assessment Question

You should attempt to answer this question yourself before looking up the suggested answer, which appears on pages 1117–19. If any part of your answer is incorrect, check back carefully to make sure you understand where you went wrong.

Stadler is an ambitious young executive who has recently been appointed to the position of financial director of Paradis plc, a small listed company. Stadler regards this appointment as a temporary one, enabling him to gain experience before moving to a larger organization. His intention is to leave Paradis plc in three years time, with its share price standing high. As a consequence, he is particularly concerned that the reported profits of Paradis plc should be as high as possible in his third and final year with the company.

Paradis plc has recently raised £350 000 from a rights issue, and the directors are considering three ways of using these funds. Three projects (A, B and C) are being considered, each involving the immediate purchase of equipment costing £350 000. One project only can be undertaken, and the equipment for each project will have a useful life equal to that of the project, with no scrap value. Stadler favours project C because it is expected to show the highest accounting profit in the third year. However, he does not wish to reveal his real reasons for favouring project C, and so, in his report to the chairman, he recommends project C because it shows the highest internal rate of return. The following summary is taken from his report:

| Project | Net cash flows (£000) Years | | | | | | | | | Internal rate of return (%) |
|---|---|---|---|---|---|---|---|---|---|---|
| | 0 | 1 | 2 | 3 | 4 | 5 | 6 | 7 | 8 | |
| A | −350 | 100 | 110 | 104 | 112 | 138 | 160 | 180 | — | 27.5 |
| B | −350 | 40 | 100 | 210 | 260 | 160 | — | — | — | 26.4 |
| C | −350 | 200 | 150 | 240 | 40 | — | — | — | — | 33.0 |

The chairman of the company is accustomed to projects being appraised in terms of payback and accounting rate of return, and he is consequently suspicious of the use of internal rate of return as a method of project selection. Accordingly, the chairman has asked for an independent report on the choice of project. The company's cost of capital is 20% and a policy of straight-line depreciation is used to write off the cost of equipment in the financial statements.

Requirements:

(a) Calculate the payback period for each project. (3 marks)

(b) Calculate the accounting rate of return for each project. (5 marks)

(c) Prepare a report for the chairman with supporting calculations indicating which project should be preferred by the ordinary shareholders of Paradis plc.

(12 marks)

(d) Discuss the assumptions about the reactions of the stock market that are implicit in Stadler's choice of project C. (5 marks)

*Note*: ignore taxation. (Total 25 marks)

*ICAEW P2 Financial Management*

## Summary

In this chapter we have noted that capital investment decisions are of vital importance, since they involve the commitment of large sums of money and they affect the whole conduct of the business for many future years. The commitment of funds for long periods of time entails a large interest cost, which must be incorporated into the analysis. We have seen that the rate of return that is required by investors can be incorporated by converting future cash flows to their present values. For business firms the rate of return includes a risk-free interest rate plus a risk premium to compensate for uncertainty. For certain cash flows, which we have assumed in this chapter, the required rate of return is the risk-free rate.

The objective of capital budgeting is to maximize shareholders' wealth, and this is achieved by the acceptance of all projects that yield positive net present values. Three alternative methods of evaluating capital investment decisions that take into account the time value of money have been examined: the net present value, the internal rate of return and the profitability index methods. We have seen that neither the internal rate of return nor the profitability index can guarantee that the correct decision will be made when there is a choice between several mutually exclusive projects. In addition, the internal rate of return is theoretically unsound regarding the reinvestment assumptions of the interim cash flows. A further point is that more than one internal rate of return is possible in situations where mid-project negative unconventional cash flows occur. The net present value method is therefore recommended where a firm can obtain sufficient funds to accept all the projects with positive net present values.

Finally, we have considered the payback and accounting rate of return methods for evaluating capital investment decisions, since these are frequently used in practice, but because neither incorporates the time value of money, we must conclude that they are theoretically unsound.

## Key Terms and Concepts

accounting rate of return (p. 474)
capital budgeting (p. 454)
compounding interest (p. 458)
cost–benefit analysis (p. 477)
cost of capital (pp. 456,457)
discounted cash flow (p. 458)
discounted payback method (p. 472)
discounted present value (p. 459)
discounting (p. 459)
discount rate (p. 457)
discount rate of return (p. 462)
interest rate (p. 457)

internal rate of return (p. 462)
minimum required rate of return (p. 457)
mutually exclusive projects (p. 466)
net present value (p. 460)
opportunity cost of an investment (p. 457)
payback method (p. 471)
present value (p. 459)
profitability index (p. 470)
return on capital employed (p. 474)
return on investment (p. 474)
risk-free gilt-edged securities (p. 457)
time value of money (p. 459)

## Recommended Reading

The financing of capital projects is normally part of a corporate finance course. If you wish to undertake further reading relating to the financing of capital investments you should refer to Pike and Neale (1999) or Brealey and Myers (1999). For a discussion of the issues relating to appraising investments in advanced manufacturing technologies you should read the publications by Currie (1990, 1991a,b) and Sizer and Motteram, Chapter 15 (1996).

## Key Examination Points

A common mistake is a failure to distinguish between relevant and irrelevant cash flows. Remember to include only incremental cash flows in a DCF analysis. Depreciation and reapportionments of overheads should not be included.

Another common error is to use the wrong present-value table. With unequal annual cash flows, use Appendix A (the discount factors will be less that 1), and if the cash flows are the same each year, use Appendix B (the discount factors will be greater than 1 from year 2 onwards). If you are required to evaluate mutually exclusive projects, use NPV, since IRR can give incorrect rankings. Where IRR calculations are required, check that the cash flows are conventional. For unconventional cash flows it is necessary to calculate more than one IRR. Normally, very accurate calculations of the IRR will not be required, and an approximate answer using the interpolation method should be appropriate.

## Questions

* Indicates that a suggested solution is to be found in the *Students' Manual*.

### 13.1  Advanced
The evidence of many recent studies suggests that there are major differences between current theories of investment appraisal and the methods which firms actually use in evaluating long-term investments.

You are required to:

(a) present theoretical arguments for the choice of net present value as the best method of investment appraisal;

(b) explain why in practice other methods of evaluating investment projects have proved to be more popular with decision-makers than the net present value method.

### 13.2*  Intermediate: IRR calculation
A machine with a purchase price of £14 000 is estimated to eliminate manual operations costing £4000 per year. The machine will last five years and have no residual value at the end of its life.

You are required to calculate:

(a) the discounted cash flow (DCF) rate of return;

(b) the level of annual saving necessary to achieve a 12% DCF return;

(c) the net present value if the cost of capital is 10%.

### 13.3  Intermediate: Payback, accounting rate of return and NPV calculations plus a discussion of qualitative factors
The following information relates to three possible capital expenditure projects. Because of capital rationing only one project can be accepted.

|  | Project | | |
|  | A | B | C |
| --- | --- | --- | --- |
| Initial Cost | £200 000 | £230 000 | £180 000 |
| Expected Life | 5 years | 5 years | 4 years |
| Scrap value expected | £10 000 | £15 000 | £8 000 |
| Expected Cash Inflows | (£) | (£) | (£) |
| End Year 1 | 80 000 | 100 000 | 55 000 |
| 2 | 70 000 | 70 000 | 65 000 |
| 3 | 65 000 | 50 000 | 95 000 |
| 4 | 60 000 | 50 000 | 100 000 |
| 5 | 55 000 | 50 000 | |

The company estimates its cost of capital is 18%. Calculate

(a) The pay back period for each project.
(4 marks)

(b) The Accounting Rate of Return for each project.
(4 marks)

(c) The Net present value of each project.
(8 marks)

(d) Which project should be accepted – give reasons.
(5 marks)

(e) Explain the factors management would need to consider: in addition to the financial factors before making a final decision on a project.

(4 marks)

(Total 25 marks)

*AAT Stage 3 Cost Accounting and Budgeting*

**13.4\* Discussion of alternative investment appraisal techniques and the calculation of payback and NPV for two mutually exclusive projects**

(a) Explain why Net Present Value is considered technically superior to Payback and Accounting Rate of Return as an investment appraisal technique even though the latter are said to be easier to understand by management. Highlight the strengths of the Net Present Value method and the weaknesses of the other two methods.

(8 marks)

(b) Your company has the option to invest in projects T and R but finance is only available to invest in one of them.

You are given the following projected data:

| Project | T £ | R £ |
|---|---|---|
| Initial Cost | 70 000 | 60 000 |
| Profits: Year 1 | 15 000 | 20 000 |
| Year 2 | 18 000 | 25 000 |
| Year 3 | 20 000 | (50 000) |
| Year 4 | 32 000 | 10 000 |
| Year 5 | 18 000 | 3 000 |
| Year 6 | | 2 000 |

You are told:

(1) All cash flows take place at the end of the year apart from the original investment in the project which takes place at the beginning of the project.

(2) Project T machinery is to be disposed of at the end of year 5 with a scrap value of £10 000.

(3) Project R machinery is to be disposed of at the end of year 3 with a nil scrap value and replaced with new project machinery that will cost £75 000.

(4) The cost of this additional machinery has been deducted in arriving at the profit projections for R for year 3. It is projected that it will last for three years and have a nil scrap value.

(5) The company's policy is to depreciate its assets on a straight line basis.

(6) The discount rate to be used by the company is 14%.

Required:

(i) If investment was to be made in project R determine whether the machinery should be replaced at the end of year 3.

(4 marks)

(ii) Calculate for projects T and R, taking into consideration your decision in (i) above:

(a) Payback period

(b) Net present value and advise which project should be invested in, stating your reasons. (10 marks)

(c) Explain what the discount rate of 14% represents and state two ways how it might have been arrived at. (3 marks)

(Total 25 marks)

*AAT Cost Accounting and Budgeting*

**13.5\* Intermediate**

An investment project has the following expected cash flows over its economic life of three years:

| | (£) |
|---|---|
| Year 0 | (142 700) |
| 1 | 51 000 |
| 2 | 62 000 |
| 3 | 73 000 |

Required:

(i) Calculate the net present value (NPV) of the project at discount rates of 0%, 10% and 20% respectively.

(ii) Draw a graph of the project NPVs calculated in (i) and use the graph to estimate, and clearly indicate, the project internal rate of return (IRR) to the nearest integer percentage.

(8 marks)

*ACCA Foundation Stage Paper 3*

**13.6 Intermediate: Calculation of payback, NPV and ARR for mutually exclusive projects**

Your company is considering investing in its own transport fleet. The present position is that carriage is contracted to an outside organization. The life of the transport fleet would be five years, after which time the vehicles would have to be disposed of.

The cost to your company of using the outside organization for its carriage needs is £250 000 for this year. This cost, it is projected, will rise 10% per annum over the life of the project. The initial cost of the transport fleet would be £750 000 and it is estimated that the following costs would be incurred over the next five years:

| | Drivers' Costs (£) | Repairs & Maintenance (£) | Other Costs (£) |
|---|---|---|---|
| Year 1 | 33 000 | 8 000 | 130 000 |
| Year 2 | 35 000 | 13 000 | 135 000 |
| Year 3 | 36 000 | 15 000 | 140 000 |
| Year 4 | 38 000 | 16 000 | 136 000 |
| Year 5 | 40 000 | 18 000 | 142 000 |

Other costs include depreciation. It is projected that the fleet would be sold for £150 000 at the end of year 5. It has been agreed to depreciate the fleet on a straight line basis.

To raise funds for the project your company is proposing to raise a long-term loan at 12% interest rate per annum.

You are told that there is an alternative project that could be invested in using the funds raised, which has the following projected results:

> Payback = 3 years
> Accounting rate of return = 30%
> Net present value = £140 000.

As funds are limited, investment can only be made in one project.

*Note:* The transport fleet would be purchased at the beginning of the project and all other expenditure would be incurred at the end of each relevant year.

Required:
(a) Prepare a table showing the net cash savings to be made by the firm over the life of the transport fleet project. (5 marks)
(b) Calculate the following for the transport fleet project:
  (i) Payback period
  (ii) Accounting rate of return
  (iii) Net present value (13 marks)
(c) Write a short report to the Investment Manager in your company outlining whether investment should be committed to the transport fleet or the alternative project outlined. Clearly state the reasons for your decision.

(7 marks)
(Total 25 marks)
*AAT Cost Accounting and Budgeting*

### 13.7 Intermediate: NPV and payback calculations

You are employed as the assistant accountant in your company and you are currently working on an appraisal of a project to purchase a new machine. The machine will cost £55 000 and will have a useful life of three years. You have already estimated the cash flows from the project and their taxation effect, and the results of your estimates can be summarized as follows:

| | Year 1 | Year 2 | Year 3 |
|---|---|---|---|
| Post-tax cash inflow | £18 000 | £29 000 | £31 000 |

Your company uses a post-tax cost of capital of 8% to appraise all projects of this type.

Task 1
(a) Calculate the net present value of the proposal to purchase the machine. Ignore the effects of inflation and assume that all cash flows occur at the end of the year.
(b) Calculate the payback period for the investment in the machine.

Task 2
The marketing director has asked you to let her know as soon as you have completed your appraisal of the project. She has asked you to provide her with some explanation of your calculations and of how taxation affects the proposal.

Prepare a memorandum to the marketing director which answers her queries. Your memorandum should contain the following:

(a) your recommendation concerning the proposal;
(b) an explanation of the meaning of the net present value and the payback period;
(c) an explanation of the effects of taxation on the cash flows arising from capital expenditure.
*AAT Technicians Stage*

### 13.8 Intermediate: Present value of purchasing or renting machinery

The Portsmere Hospital operates its own laundry. Last year the laundry processed 120 000 kilograms of washing and this year the total is forecast to grow to 132 000 kilograms. This growth in laundry processed is forecast to continue at the same percentage rate for the next seven years. Because of this, the hospital must immediately replace its existing laundry equipment. Currently, it is considering two options, the purchase of machine A or the rental of machine B. Information on both options is given below:

### Machine A – purchase

| | |
|---|---|
| Annual capacity (kilograms) | £180 000 |
| Material cost per kilogram | £2.00 |
| Labour cost per kilogram | £3.00 |
| Fixed costs per annum | £20 000 |
| Life of machine | 3 years |
| Capital cost | £60 000 |
| Depreciation per annum | £20 000 |

### Machine B – rent

| | |
|---|---|
| Annual capacity (kilograms) | £170 000 |
| Material cost per kilogram | £1.80 |
| Labour cost per kilogram | £3.40 |
| Fixed costs per annum | £18 000 |
| Rental per annum | £20 000 |
| Rental agreement | 3 years |
| Depreciation per annum | nil |

Other information:

1. The hospital is able to call on an outside laundry if there is either a breakdown or any other reason why the washing cannot be undertaken in-house. The charge would be £10 per kilogram of washing.
2. Machine A, if purchased, would have to be paid for immediately. All other cash flows can be assumed to occur at the end of the year.
3. Machine A will have no residual value at any time.
4. The existing laundry equipment could be sold for £10 000 cash.
5. The fixed costs are a direct cost of operating the laundry.
6. The hospital's discount rate for projects of this nature is 15%.

Task 1
You are an accounting technician employed by the Portsmere Hospital and you are asked to write a brief report to its chief executive. Your report should:

(a) evaluate the two options for operating the laundry, using discounted cash flow techniques;
(b) recommend the preferred option and identify *one* possible non-financial benefit;
(c) justify your treatment of the £10 000 cash value of the existing equipment;
(d) explain what is meant by discounted cashflow.

*Note*:
Inflation can be ignored.

*AAT Technicians Stage*

### 13.9* Intermediate: Calculation of break-even point involving PV calculations

CD is an aviation company engaged in providing transport services to tour operators and industrial customers. CD's cost of money is 10%.

CD is considering the acquisition of three new aircraft which have a cost price of £2 000 000 each. Each aircraft has a useful life of five years, requires an overhaul (costing £600 000) at the end of the third year of its life, incurs fixed operating costs of £100 000 per year and has nil residual value at the end of its useful life.

If an aircraft is purchased and fully utilised then it flies for 2400 hours per year and generates an expected contribution of £1 600 000 per year.

As an alternative to buying an aircraft, it is possible to rent it via a broker. The terms of the rental are a fixed fee of £250 000 per year (payable annually in advance) and a variable charge of £361 per flying hour (calculated and paid annually in arrears). If an aircraft is rented, then CD will avoid fixed operating and overhaul costs. However, CD will incur the same variable operating costs regardless of whether the aircraft is purchased or rented.

Requirements:
(a) Advise CD on the minimum average flying hours per year required in order to
   - make renting an aircraft a viable proposition,
   - make buying an aircraft a viable proposition,
   and advise CD on the average flying hours per year required in order to make buying and renting an aircraft equally viable propositions.
   (15 marks)
(b) Advise CD as to how many aircraft it should acquire, and how it should acquire them (purchase or rent) on the basis of a flying

hour requirement forecast of 5750 hours per year for five years.

Support your advice with a full financial analysis.

*Note:* You may ignore tax and inflation.

(10 marks)

(Total 25 marks)

*CIMA Stage 3 Management Accounting Applications*

### 13.10* Intermediate: Calculation of NPVs of two projects

In the manufacture of a company's range of products, the processes give rise to two main types of waste material.

Type A is the outcome of the company's original processes. This waste is sold at £2 per tonne, but this amount is treated as sundry income and no allowance for this is made in calculating product costs.

Type B is the outcome of newer processes in the company's manufacturing activity. It is classified as hazardous, has needed one employee costing £9000 per year specially employed to organise its handling in the factory, and has required special containers whose current resale value is assessed at £18 000. At present the company pays a contractor £14 per tonne for its collection and disposal.

Company management has been concerned with both types of waste and after much research has developed the following proposals.

*Type A waste*

This could be further processed by installing plant and equipment costing £20 000 and incurring extra direct costs of £2.50 per tonne and extra fixed costs of £10 000 per annum.

Extra space would be needed, but this could be obtained by taking up some of the space currently used as a free car park for employees. The apportioned rental cost of that land is £2500 per annum and a 'compensation' payment totalling £500 per annum would need to be paid to those employees who would lose their car-parking facilities.

The selling price of the processed waste would be £12.50 per tonne and the quantity available would be 2000 tonnes per annum.

*Type B waste*

Using brand-new technology, this could be further processed into a non-hazardous product by installing a plant costing £120 000 on existing factory space whose apportioned rental cost is £12 500 per annum.

This plant cost includes a pipeline that would eliminate any special handling of the hazardous waste. Extra direct costs would be £13.50 per tonne and extra fixed costs of £20 000 per annum would be incurred.

The new product would be saleable to a limited number of customers only, but the company has been able to get the option of a contract for two years' sales renewable for a further two years. This would be at a price of £11 per tonne and the output over the next few years is expected to be 4000 tonnes per year.

For Type A waste project, the board wants to achieve an 8% DCF return over four years. For Type B waste project, it wants a 15% DCF return over six years.

You are required

(a) to recommend whether the company should invest in either or both of the two projects.
  Give supporting figures and comments.
  Assume that no capital rationing exists.

(20 marks)

(b) to explain briefly in respect of Type B waste project what major reservations (apart from the cost and investment figures) you might have about the project, irrespective of whether you recommend it in (a) above.    (5 marks)
  Ignore inflation and taxation.

(Total 25 marks)

*CIMA Stage 4 Management Accounting Decision Making*

### 13.11 Advanced: Comparison of NPV and IRR

Using the discounted cash flow yield (internal rate of return) for evaluating investment opportunities has the basic weakness that it does not give attention to the amount of the capital investment, in that a return of 20% on an investment of £1000 may be given a higher ranking than a return of 15% on an investment of £10 000.

Comment in general on the above statement and refer in particular to the problem of giving priorities to (ranking) investment proposals.

Your answers should make use of the following information.

| | Project A cash flow (£) | Project B cash flow (£) |
|---|---|---|
| Year 0 (Capital investments) | 1000 | 10 000 |
| 1 Cash flows | 240 | 2 300 |
| 2 Cash flows | 288 | 2 640 |
| 3 Cash flows | 346 | 3 040 |
| 4 Cash flows | 414 | 3 500 |
| 5 Cash flows | 498 | 4 020 |
| Cost of capital | 10% | 10% |

Taxation can be ignored.

(20 marks)
*ACCA P3 Financial Management*

### 13.12*Advanced: Accounting Rate of Return

Armcliff Ltd is a division of Shevin plc which requires each of its divisions to achieve a rate of return on capital employed of at least 10% p.a. For this purpose, capital employed is defined as fixed capital and investment in stocks. This rate or return is also applied as a hurdle rate for new investment projects. Divisions have limited borrowing powers and all capital projects are centrally funded.

The following is an extract from Armcliff's divisional accounts:

**Profit and loss account for the year ended 31 December**

| | (£m) |
|---|---|
| Turnover | 120 |
| Cost of sales | (100) |
| Operating profit | 20 |

**Assets employed as at 31 December 1994**

| | (£m) | (£m) |
|---|---|---|
| Fixed (net): | | 75 |
| Current assets (inc. stocks £25m) | 45 | |
| Current liabilities: | (32) | 13 |
| Net capital employed | | 88 |

Armcliff's production engineers wish to invest in a new computer-controlled press. The equipment cost is £14m. The residual value is expected to be £2m after four years operation, when the equipment will be shipped to a customer in South America.

The new machine is capable of improving the quality of the existing product and also of produ-

cing a higher volume. The firm's marketing team is confident of selling the increased volume by extending the credit period. The expected additional sales are:

| | |
|---|---|
| Year 1 | 2 000 000 units |
| Year 2 | 1 800 000 units |
| Year 3 | 1 600 000 units |
| Year 4 | 1 600 000 units |

Sales volume is expected to fall over time due to emerging competitive pressures. Competition will also necessitate a reduction in price by £0.5 each year from the £5 per unit proposed in the first year. Operating costs are expected to be steady at £1 per unit, and allocation of overheads (none of which are affected by the new project) by the central finance department is set at £0.75 per unit.

Higher production levels will require additional investment in stocks of £0.5m, which would be held at this level until the final stages of operation of the project. Customers at present settle accounts after 90 days on average.

Required:
(a) Determine whether the proposed capital investment is attractive to Armcliff, using the average rate of return on capital method, as defined as average profit-to-average capital employed, ignoring debtors and creditors.
[Note: Ignore taxes] (7 marks)
(b) (i) Suggest *three* problems which arise with the use of the average return method for appraising new investment. (3 marks)
    (ii) In view of the problems associated with the ARR method, why do companies continue to use it in project appraisal? (3 marks)

(Total 13 marks)
*ACCA Paper 8 Managerial Finance*

### 13.13* Advanced: NPV calculation and identification of incremental cash flows

LKL plc is a manufacturer of sports equipment and is proposing to start project VZ, a new product line. This project would be for the four years from the start of year 20X1 to the end of 20X4. There would be no production of the new product after 20X4.

You have recently joined the company's accounting and finance team and have been provided with the following information relating to the project:

*Capital expenditure*

A feasibility study costing £45 000 was completed and paid for last year. This study recommended that the company buy new plant and machinery costing £1 640 000 to be paid for at the start of the project. The machinery and plant would be depreciated at 20% of cost per annum and sold during year 20X5 for £242 000 receivable at the end of 20X5.

As a result of the proposed project it was also recommended that an old machine be sold for cash at the start of the project for its book value of £16 000. This machine had been scheduled to be sold for cash at the end of 20X2 for its book value of £12 000.

*Other data relating to the new product line*:

| | 20X1 (£000) | 20X2 (£000) | 20X3 (£000) | 20X4 (£000) |
|---|---|---|---|---|
| Sales | 1000 | 1300 | 1500 | 1800 |
| Debtors (at the year end) | 84 | 115 | 140 | 160 |
| Lost contribution on existing products | 30 | 40 | 40 | 36 |
| Purchases | 400 | 500 | 580 | 620 |
| Creditors (at the year end) | 80 | 100 | 110 | 120 |
| Payments to sub-contractors, including prepayments of | 60 5 | 90 10 | 80 8 | 80 8 |
| Net tax payable associated with this project | 96 | 142 | 174 | 275 |

*Fixed overheads and advertising:*

| | | | | |
|---|---|---|---|---|
| With new line | 1330 | 1100 | 990 | 900 |
| Without new line | 1200 | 1000 | 900 | 800 |

*Notes*

● The year-end debtors and creditors are received and paid in the following year.

● The next tax payable has taken into account the effect of any capital allowances. There is a one year time-lag in the payment of tax.

● The company's cost of capital is a constant 10% per annum.

● It can be assumed that operating cash flows occur at the year end.

● Apart from the data and information supplied there are no other financial implications after 20X4.

*Labour costs*

From the start of the project, three employees currently working in another department and earning £12 000 each would be transferred to work on the new product line, and an employee currently earning £20 000 would be promoted to work on the new line at a salary of £30 000 per annum. The effect on the transfer of employees from the other department to the project is included in the lost contribution figures given above.

As a direct result of introducing the new product line, four employees in another department currently earning £10 000 each would have to be made redundant at the end of 20X1 and paid redundancy pay of £15 500 each at the end of 20X2.

Agreement had been reached with the trade unions for wages and salaries to be increased by 5% each year from the start of 20X2.

*Material costs*

Material XNT which is already in stock, and for which the company has no other use, cost the company £6400 last year, and can be used in the manufacture of the new product. If it is not used the company would have to dispose of it at a cost to the company of £2000 in 20X1.

Material XPZ is also in stock and will be used on the new line. It cost the company £11 500 some years ago. The company has no other use for it, but could sell it on the open market for £3000 in 20X1.

Required

(a) Prepare and present a cash flow budget for project VZ, for the period 20X1 and 20X5 and calculate the net present value of the project.                                      (14 marks)

(b) Write a short report for the board of directors which:

(i) explains why certain figures which were provided in (a) were excluded from your cash flow budget, and

(ii) advises them on whether or not the project should be undertaken, and lists other factors which would also need to be considered.          (7 marks)

*ACCA Paper 8 Managerial Finance*

**13.14\* Advanced: Comparison of NPV and IRR and relationship between profits and NPV**
Khan Ltd is an importer of novelty products. The directors are considering whether to introduce a new product, expected to have a very short

economic life. Two alternative methods of promoting the new product are available, details of which are as follows:

Alternative 1 would involve heavy initial advertising and the employment of a large number of agents. The directors expect that an immediate cash outflow of £100 000 would be required (the cost of advertising) which would produce a net cash inflow after one year of £255 000. Agents' commission, amounting to £157 500, would have to be paid at the end of two years.

Alternative 2 would involve a lower outlay on advertising (£50 000, payable immediately), and no use of agents. It would produce net cash inflows of zero after one year and £42 000 at the end of each of the subsequent two years.

Mr Court, a director of Khan Ltd, comments, 'I generally favour the payback method for choosing between investment alternatives such as these. However, I am worried that the advertising expenditure under the second alternative will reduce our reported profit next year by an amount not compensated by any net revenues from sale of the product in that year. For that reason I do not think we should even consider the second alternative.'

The cost of capital of Khan Ltd is 20% per annum. The directors do not expect capital or any other resource to be in short supply during the next three years.

You are required to:
(a) calculate the net present values and estimate the internal rates of return of the two methods of promoting the new product; (10 marks)
(b) advise the directors of Khan Ltd which, if either, method of promotion they should adopt, explaining the reasons for your advice and noting any additional information you think would be helpful in making the decision; (8 marks)
(c) comment on the views expressed by Mr Court. (7 marks)
Ignore taxation.

*ICAEW Financial Management*

**13.15\* Advanced: Calculation of NPV and IRR, a discussion of the inconsistency in ranking and a calculation of the cost of capital at which the ranking changes**

A company is considering which of two mutually exclusive projects it should undertake. The finance director thinks that the project with the higher NPV should be chosen whereas the managing director thinks that the one with the higher IRR should be undertaken especially as both projects have the same initial outlay and length of life. The company anticipates a cost of capital of 10% and the net after tax cash flows of the projects are as follows:

|  | Project X (£000) | Project Y (£000) |
| --- | --- | --- |
| Year 0 | −200 | −200 |
| 1 | 35 | 218 |
| 2 | 80 | 10 |
| 3 | 90 | 10 |
| 4 | 75 | 4 |
| 5 | 20 | 3 |

You are required to:
(a) calculate the NPV and IRR of each project; (6 marks)
(b) recommend, with reasons, which project you would undertake (if either); (4 marks)
(c) explain the inconsistency in ranking of the two projects in view of the remarks of the directors; (4 marks)
(d) identify the cost of capital at which your recommendation in (b) would be reversed. (6 marks)
(Total 20 marks)

*CIMA Stage 3 Management Accounting Techniques*

**13.16 Advanced: Calculation of NPV and additional cash flows which will result in a zero NPV**

Losrock Housing Association is considering the implementation of a refurbishment programme on one of its housing estates which would reduce maintenance and heating costs and enable a rent increase to be made.

Relevant data are as follows:
(i) Number of houses: 300.
(ii) Annual maintenance cost per house: £300. This will be reduced by 25% on completion of the refurbishment of each house.
(iii) Annual heating cost per house: £500. This will be reduced by 30% on completion of the refurbishment of each house.
(iv) Annual rental income per house: £2100. This will be increased by 15% on completion of the refurbishment of each house.

(v) Two contractors A and B have each quoted a price of £2000 per house to implement the refurbishment work.

(vi) The quoted completion profiles for each contractor are as follows:

| | Number of houses refurbished | | |
| | Year 1 | Year 2 | Year 3 |
|---|---|---|---|
| Contractor A | 90 | 90 | 120 |
| Contractor B | 150 | 90 | 60 |

(vii) Contractor A requires £100 000 at the commencement of the work and the balance of the contract price in proportion to the number of houses completed in each of years 1 to 3. Contractor B requires £300 000 at the commencement of the work and the balance of the contract price in proportion to the number of houses completed in each of years 1 to 3.

(viii) An eight year period from the commencement of the work should be used as the time horizon for the evaluation of the viability of the refurbishment programme.

Assume that all events and cash flows arise at year end points. Savings and rent increases will commence in the year following refurbishment. Ignore taxation.

Required:

(a) Prepare financial summaries and hence advise management whether to accept the quote from contractor A or contractor B in each of the following situations:
   (i) ignoring the discounting of cash flows; and
   (ii) where the cost of capital is determined as 14% and the discount factors given in appendix 1 are available. (14 marks)

(b) For contractor A only, calculate the maximum refurbishment price per house at which the work would be acceptable to Losrock Housing Association on financial grounds using discounted cash flows as the decision base, where the initial payment remains at £100 000 and the balance is paid in proportion to the houses completed in each of years 1 to 3. (5 marks)

(c) Suggest additional information relating to maintenance and heating costs which might affect the acceptability of the existing quotes per house where discounted cash flows are used as the decision base. (3 marks)
(Total 22 marks)
*ACCA Level 2 Management Accounting*

### 13.17* Advanced: Evaluation of a proposed investment of computer integrated manufacturing equipment and a discussion of NPV and ARR

Abert, the production manager of Blom plc, a manufacturer of precision tools, has recently attended a major international exhibition on Computer Integrated Manufacturing (CIM). He has read of the improvements in product quality and profitability achieved by companies which have switched to this new technology. In particular, his Japanese competitors are believed to use CIM equipment extensively. Abert is sufficiently concerned about his company's future to commission a report from Saint-Foix Ltd, a vendor of CIM equipment, as to the appropriateness of utilising CIM for all his manufacturing operations.

The report, which has recently been prepared, suggests that the following costs and benefits will accrue to Blom plc as a result of investing in an appropriate CIM system:

(1) *Costs of implementing CIM*
   (i) Capital equipment costs will be £40m. The equipment will have an estimated life of 10 years, after which time its disposal value will be £10m.
   (ii) Proper use of the equipment will require the substantial re-training of current employees. As a result of the necessary changes in the production process, and the time spent on retraining, Blom plc will lose production (and sales) in its first two years of implementation. The lost production (and sales) will cost the company £10m per annum.
   (iii) The annual costs of writing software and maintaining the computer equipment will be £4m.

(2) *Benefits of implementing CIM*
   (i) The use of CIM will enhance the quality of Blom plc's products. This will lead to less reworking of products, and a consequent reduction in warranty costs. The annual cost savings are expected to be £12m per annum.

(ii) The CIM equipment will use less floor space than the existing machinery. As a result one existing factory will no longer be needed. It is estimated that the factory can be let at an annual rental of £2m.

(iii) Better planning and flow of work will result in an immediate reduction in the existing levels of working capital from £13m to £8m.

The directors of Blom plc currently require all investments to generate a positive net present value at a cost of capital of 15% *and* to show an accounting rate of return in the first year of at least 15%. You may assume that all cash flows arise at the end of the year, except for those relating to the equipment and re-training costs, and the reduction in working capital. It is Blom plc's intention to capitalise re-training costs for management accounting purposes. Requirements:

(a) Determine whether Blom plc should invest in the CIM technology on the basis of its existing investment criteria. (10 marks)

(b) Discuss possible reasons as to why Blom plc currently requires its long-term investments to meet both the net present value *and* the accounting rate of return criteria. (8 marks)

(c) Discuss the additional factors Blom plc should consider when deciding whether to switch to CIM technology. (7 marks)

(Total 25 marks)

*ICAEW P2 Financial Management*

### 13.18* Advanced: Calculation of minimum selling price of a machine based on PV of future cash flows

FG Ltd has two machines used on a contract for a large customer, LC Ltd. Each machine can produce the same product and has a capacity of 40 000 units per year, but each has different characteristics resulting in the following total annual costs at different production levels which must be in lots of 10 000 units:

| Annual production level (units) | Annual total costs Machine X (£000) | Machine Y (£000) |
|---|---|---|
| Nil | 52* | 65* |
| 10 000 | 105 | 108 |
| 20 000 | 132 | 122 |
| 30 000 | 148 | 131 |
| 40 000 | 174 | 204 |

*This figure includes:

Direct materials

Direct labour ⎫ usable in other sections of the
Direct expenses ⎬ company if the machine were
⎭ disposed of

Depreciation £8000 p.a.

Apportioned production overhead £12 000 p.a.

The contract price to LC Ltd is £6.00 per unit. The company's cost of capital is 13%.

FG Ltd expects that sales will end in five years' time and that the quantities required by LC Ltd will average 75% of its present total capacity.

FG Ltd has received an invitation to sell either of the machines to an overseas organization and must decide whether it should do so and, if so, at what price. If it retains either or both machines, each is expected to have a scrap value of £20 000 in five years' time. If one of the machines is sold to the overseas organization, FG Ltd will not have to pay any penalty to LC Ltd on account of any shortfall in delivery.

You are required

(a) to set out a table from 10 000 to 80 000 units to show which machine or combination of machines should be used at each level to yield minimum costs to FG Ltd; (7 marks)

(b) to recommend to FG Ltd

(i) which level of total unit sales will yield the largest profit, (3 marks)

(ii) which machine it should offer to the overseas company and the minimum price at which it should offer that machine (to the nearest £1000 upwards); (9 marks)

Show your supporting calculations.

(c) assuming that the price at (b) (ii) above is acceptable, to explain briefly *three* major factors that FG Ltd should consider when making its eventual decision. (6 marks)

Ignore taxation.

(Total 25 marks)

*CIMA Stage 4 Management Accounting – Decision Making*

### 13.19 Advanced: Replacement decision and the conflict between decision-making and performance evaluation models

Paragon Products plc has a factory which manufactures a wide range of plastic household utensils. One of these is a plastic brush which is made from a special raw material used only for this purpose.

The brush is moulded on a purpose-built machine which was installed in January 1997 at a cost of £210 000 with an expected useful life of 7 years. This machine was assumed to have zero scrap value at the end of its life and was depreciated on the same straight line basis that the company used for all equipment.

Recently an improved machine has become available, at a price of £130 000, which requires two men to operate it rather than the five men required by the existing machine. It also uses a coarser grade of raw material costing £70 per tonne (1000 kg), compared with £75 per tonne for the present material. Further, it would use only 60% of the power consumed by the existing machine. However, it has an expected life of only three years and an expected scrap value of £10 000.

The factory manager is considering replacing the existing machine immediately with the new one as the suppliers have offered him £40 000 for the existing machine, which is substantially more than could be obtained on the second hand market, provided the new machine is installed by 1 January 2001. Unfortunately this would leave stocks of the old raw material sufficient to make 40 000 brushes which could not be used and which would fetch only £25 per tonne on resale.

The brush department is treated as a profit centre. Current production amounts to 200 000 brushes a year which are sold at a wholesale price of £1 each. The production of each brush uses 2 kg of the raw material, consumes 1 kW hour of electricity costing £0.05, and incurs direct labour costs amounting to £0.25 per brush. Overhead costs amount to £60 000 per annum and include £10 000 relating to supervision costs which vary according to the number of employees. The men no longer required to operate the new machine could be found employment elsewhere in the factory and would be paid their current wage although they would be performing less skilled work normally paid at 80% of their current rate.

Requirements:
(a) Evaluate the proposal to replace the existing machine with the new model, ignoring the time value of money in your analysis.
(10 marks)
(b) Construct brush department profit and loss accounts for each alternative for 2001, 2002 and 2003. Indicate how the factory manager's

decision might be influenced by these figures.
(8 marks)
(c) Explain how your analysis would be affected if the new machine had a longer expected life and the time value of money was to be taken into account. (7 marks)
(Total 25 marks)
Note: Ignore taxation.
*ICAEW P2 Management Accounting*

**13.20\* Advanced: Calculation of target sales required to meet the objectives specified by the Management Board of a theatre**
A theatre with some surplus accommodation proposes to extend its catering facilities to provide light meals to its patrons.

The Management Board is prepared to make initial funds available to cover capital costs. It requires that these be repaid over a period of five years at a rate of interest of 14%.

The capital costs are estimated at £60 000 for equipment that will have a life of five years and no residual value. Running costs of staff, etc. will be £20 000 in the first year, increasing by £2000 in each subsequent year. The Board proposes to charge £5000 per annum for lighting, heating and other property expenses, and wants a nominal £2500 per annum to cover any unforeseen contingencies. Apart from this, the Board is not looking for any profit, as such, from the extension of these facilities, because it believes that this will enable more theatre seats to be sold. It is proposed that costs should be recovered by setting prices for the food at double the direct costs.

It is not expected that the full sales level will be reached until Year 3. The proportions of that level estimated to be reached in Years 1 and 2 are 35% and 65% respectively.

You are required to
(a) calculate the sales that need to be achieved in *each* of the *five* years to meet the Board's targets; (13 marks)
(b) comment briefly on *five* aspects of the proposals that you consider merit further investigation. (7 marks)
Ignore taxation and inflation.
(Total 20 marks)
*CIMA Stage 4 Management Accounting – Decision Making*

### 13.21 Advanced: Calculation of a contract price involving monthly discounting and compounding

Franzl is a contract engineer working for a division of a large construction company. He is responsible for the negotiation of contract prices and the subsequent collection of instalment monies from customers. It is company policy to achieve a mark-up of at least 10% on the direct production costs of a contract, but there is no company policy on the speed of customer payment. Franzl usually attempts to persuade customers to pay in six-monthly instalments in arrears.

Franzl is presently engaged in deciding upon the minimum acceptable price for contract K491, which will last for 24 months. He has estimated that the following direct production costs will be incurred:

| | (£) |
|---|---|
| Raw material | 168 000 |
| Labour | 120 000 |
| Plant depreciation | 18 400 |
| Equipment rental | 30 000 |
| | 336 400 |

On the basis of these costs Franzl estimates that the minimum contract price should be £370 000. The raw material and labour costs are expected to arise evenly over the period of the contract and to be paid monthly in arrears. Plant depreciation has been calculated as the difference between the cost of the new plant (£32 400) which will be purchased for the contract and its realizable value (£14 000) at the end of contract. Special equipment will be rented for the first year of the contract, the rent being paid in two six-monthly instalments in advance. The contract will be financed from head office funds, on which interest of 1% per month is charged or credited according to whether the construction division is a net borrower or net lender.

Requirements:
(a) Calculate the net present value of contract K491 assuming that Franzl's minimum price and normal payment terms are accepted.

(5 marks)

(b) Assuming that the customer agrees to pay the instalments in advance rather than arrears, calculate the new contract price and mark-up that Franzl could accept so as to leave the net present value of the contract unchanged.

(5 marks)

(c) Prepare two statements to show that the eventual cash surpluses generated in (a) and (b) are identical. The statements need show *only* the total cash received and paid for each category of revenue and expense. (6 marks)

(d) Discuss the factors that should influence the tender price for a long-term contract.

(9 marks)
(Total 25 marks)

Note: Ignore taxation.

*ICAEW Financial Management*

# Capital investment decisions: 2

In the previous chapter the major techniques that can be used for evaluating capital investment decisions were introduced and their relative merits were assessed. To simplify the discussion, we made a number of assumptions: first, that cash inflows and outflows were known with certainty; secondly that sufficient funds were available to enable acceptance of all those projects with positive net present values; thirdly, that firms operated in an environment where there was no taxation and no inflation; and finally, that the cost of capital was the risk-free rate.

In this chapter we shall relax these assumptions and discuss how capital investment techniques can be applied to more complicated situations. Therefore, this chapter is more applicable to a second-year management accounting course. In addition, we shall consider the various methods of administering and controlling capital expenditures.

## Learning objectives

After studying this chapter, you should be able to:

- evaluate mutually exclusive projects with unequal lives;

- explain capital rationing and select the optimum combination of investments when capital is rationed for a single period;

- calculate the incremental taxation payments arising from a proposed investment;

- describe the two approaches for adjusting for inflation when appraising capital projects;

- explain how risk-adjusted discount rates are calculated;

- explain the uses and limitations of traditional risk measures;

- describe the procedures for reviewing and controlling capital investments.

# The evaluation of mutually exclusive investments with unequal lives

The application of the net present value method is complicated when a choice must be made between two or more projects, where the projects have unequal lives. A perfect comparison requires knowledge about future alternatives that will be available for the period of the difference in the lives of the projects that are being considered. Let us look at the situation in Example 14.1.

In Example 14.1 it is assumed that both machines produce exactly the same output. Therefore only cash outflows will be considered, because revenue cash inflows are assumed to be the same whichever alternative is selected. Consequently our objective is to choose the alternative with the lower present value of cash outflows. Revenue cash inflows should only be included in the analysis if they differ for each alternative. Suppose we compute the present value (PV) of the cash outflows for each alternative.

**End of year cash flows (£000)**

| Machine | Year 0 | Year 1 | Year 2 | Year 3 | PV at 10% |
|---------|--------|--------|--------|--------|-----------|
| X | 1200 | 240 | 240 | 240 | 1796.832 |
| Y | 600 | 360 | 360 | | 1224.78 |

Machine Y appears to be the more acceptable alternative, but the analysis is incomplete because we must consider what will happen at the end of year 2 if machine Y is chosen. For example, if the life of the task to be performed by the machines is in excess of three years, it will be necessary to replace machine Y at the end of year 2; whereas if machine X is chosen, replacement will be deferred until the end of year 3. We shall consider the following methods of evaluating projects with unequal lives:

1. Evaluate the alternatives over an interval equal to the lowest common multiple of the lives of the alternatives under consideration.

2. Equivalent annual cost method by which the cash flows are converted into an equivalent annual annuity.

3. Estimate a terminal value for one of the alternatives.

## 1. LOWEST COMMON MULTIPLE METHOD

Assume that the life of the task to be performed by the machines is a considerable period of time, say in excess of six years. Consequently, both machines will be replaced at the end of their useful lives. If machine X is replaced by an identical machine then it will be replaced every three years, whereas machine Y will be replaced every two years. A correct analysis therefore requires that a sequence of decisions be evaluated over a common time horizon so that the analysis of each alternative will be comparable. The common time horizon can be determined by setting the time horizon equal to the lowest common multiple of the lives of the alternatives under consideration. In Example 14.1, where the lives of the alternatives are two and three years, the lowest common multiple is six years. The analysis for the sequence of replacements over a six-year period is as follows:

**EXAMPLE 14.1**

The Bothnia Company is choosing between two machines, X and Y. They are designed differently but have identical capacity and do exactly the same job. Machine X costs £1 200 000 and will last three years, costing £240 000 per year to run. Machine Y is a cheaper model costing £600 000 but will last only two years and costs £360 000 per year to run. The cost of capital is 10%. Which machine should the firm purchase?

|  | End-of-year cash flows (£000) | | | | | | |
|---|---|---|---|---|---|---|---|
|  | **0** | **1** | **2** | **3** | **4** | **5** | **6** |
| Sequence of type X machines | | | | | | | |
| Capital investment | 1200 | | | 1200 | | | |
| Operating costs | | 240 | 240 | 240 | 240 | 240 | 240 |
| PV at 10% | −3146.76 | | | | | | |
| Sequence of type Y machines | | | | | | | |
| Capital investment | 600 | | 600 | | 600 | | |
| Operating costs | | 360 | 360 | 360 | 360 | 360 | 360 |
| PV at 10% | −3073.44 | | | | | | |

By year 6 machine X is replaced twice and machine Y three times. At this point the alternatives are comparable, and a replacement must be made in year 6 regardless of the initial choice of X or Y. We can therefore compare the present value of the cost of these two sequences of machines. Thus it is better to invest in a sequence of type Y machines, since this alternative has the lowest present value of cash outflows. Note that another decision must be made in year 6. This will depend on the sequence of machines that is then available and how much longer is the life of the task that is to be performed by the machines.

## 2. EQUIVALENT ANNUAL COST METHOD

Comparing projects over a span of time equal to the lowest common multiple of their individual life spans is often tedious. Instead, we can use the second method – the equivalent annual cost method. The costs for the different lives of machines X and Y are made comparable if they are converted into an equivalent annuity. The present value of the costs of machine X is £1 796 832 for a three-year time horizon and £3 146 760 for a six-year time horizon. The equivalent annual costs for the machine can be solved from the following formula:

$$\text{present value of costs} = \text{equivalent annual cost} \times \text{annuity factor for } N \text{ years of } R\%$$

(14.1)

Solving for the equivalent annual cost, we have

$$\text{equivalent annual cost} = \frac{\text{present value of costs}}{\text{annuity factor for } N \text{ years at } R\%}$$

(14.2)

Using the data for machine X, the equivalent annual cost is

$$\frac{£1\,796\,832}{2.4869} = £722\,519 \text{ (using a 3-year time horizon)}$$

or

$$\frac{£3\,146\,760}{4.3553} = £722\,519 \text{ (using a 6-year time horizon)}$$

The present values in the above calculations are obtained from our earlier calculations for three- and six-year time horizons. The annuity factors are obtained from annuity (i.e. cumulative discount) tables shown in Appendix B for three and six years and a 10% discount rate. We get the same equivalent annual costs for both time horizons. To simplify calculations, we can always use the first purchase in the sequence to calculate the equivalent annual cost.

What does the equivalent annual cost represent? Merely that the sequence of machine X cash flows is exactly like a sequence of cash flows of £722 519 a year. Calculating the equivalent annual cost for machine Y, you will find that it is £705 678 a year. A stream of machine X cash flows is the costlier; therefore we should select machine Y. Using this method, our decision rule is to choose the machine with the lower annual equivalent cost.

Note that when we used the common time horizon method the present value of a sequence of machine Xs was £3 146 760 compared with £3 073 440 for a sequence of machine Ys; a present value cost saving of £73 320 in favour of machine Y. The equivalent annual cost saving for machine Y was £16 841 (£722 519 − £705 678). If we discount this saving for a time horizon of six years, the present value is £73 320, the same as the saving we calculated using the lowest common multiple method.

The equivalent annual cost method simplifies handling different multiples of lives. For example, if two alternative machines have lives of three and eight years respectively, the least common time horizon method requires combined calculations over 24 years. In contrast, the equivalent annual cost method only requires calculations for the initial life of each machine. You should note, however, that the equivalent annual cost method should only be used when there is a sequence of identical replacements for each alternative and this process continues until a common time horizon is reached.

## 3. ESTIMATE TERMINAL VALUES

Consider a situation where machines A and B have lives of six and eight years respectively. Assume that the life of the task to be performed by the machines is ten years. Because the task life is shorter than the lowest common multiple (24 years), we cannot use either of the first two methods. An alternative approach is to assume that each machine will be replaced once (machine X at the end of year 6 and machine Y at the end of year 8) and incorporate estimates of the disposal values into the analysis for both machines at the end of the 10 year task life.

# Capital rationing

In our previous discussions it has been suggested that all investments with positive net present values should be undertaken. For mutually exclusive projects the project with the highest net present value should be chosen. However, situations may occur where there are insufficient funds available to enable a firm to undertake all those projects that yield a positive net present value. The situation is described as **capital rationing**.

Capital rationing occurs whenever there is a budget ceiling, or a market constraint on the amount of funds that can be invested during a specific period of time. For various reasons top management may pursue a policy of limiting the amount of funds available for investment in any one period. Such policies may apply to firms that finance all their capital investment with internal funds. Alternatively, in a large decentralized organization top management may limit the funds available to the divisional managers for investment. Such restrictions on available funds may be for various reasons. For example, top management may be reluctant to issue additional share capital because they may be concerned that this will lead to outsiders gaining control of the business, or because a share issue may lead to a dilution of earnings per share. Alternatively, they may be reluctant to raise additional debt capital beyond a certain point because they do not wish to be committed to large fixed interest payments. Note that whenever a firm adopts a policy that restricts funds available for investment, such a policy may be less than optimal, as the firm may reject projects with a positive net present value and forgo opportunities that would have enhanced the market value of the firm.

The term '**soft capital rationing**' is often used to refer to situations where, for various reasons the firm *internally* imposes a budget ceiling on the amount of capital expenditure. On the other hand, where the amount of capital investment is restricted because of *external* constraints such as the inability to obtain funds from the financial markets, the term '**hard capital rationing**' is used.

Whenever capital rationing exists, management should allocate the limited available capital in a way that maximizes the NPVs of the firm. Thus it is necessary to rank all investment opportunities so that the NPV can be maximized from the use of the available funds. The analytical techniques used must therefore be capable of ranking the various alternatives or of determining the optimal combination of investments that meet the constraint of limited capital. Ranking in terms of absolute NPVs will normally give incorrect results, since this method leads to the selection of large projects, each of which has a high individual NPV but that have in total a lower NPV than a large number of smaller projects with lower individual NPVs. For example, the ranking of projects by NPV will favour a project that yields an NPV of £1000, for an investment of £10 000, over two projects of £5000 that each yield an individual NPV of £800. Clearly, if funds are restricted to £10 000, it is better to accept the two smaller projects, which will yield a total NPV of £1600. Consider the situation presented in Example 14.2.

Our aim is to select the projects in descending order of profitability until the investment funds of £20 million have been exhausted. If we use the net present value method of ranking, the following projects will be selected:

| Projects selected in order of ranking | Investment cost (£m) | New present value (£m) |
|---|---|---|
| C | 5 | 2.575 |
| D | 10 | 2.350 |
| G | 5 | 0.900 |
| | Total net present value | 5.825 |

If, on the other hand, we adopt the profitability index method of ranking, the selected projects will be as follows:

**EXAMPLE 14.2**

A division of the Bothnia Company that operates under the constraint of capital rationing has identified seven independent investments from which to choose. The company has £20 million available for capital investment during the current period. Which projects should the company choose? The net present values and profitability index ratios for each of the projects are as follows:

| Projects | Investment required (£m) | Present value, PV (£m) | Net present value (£m) | Profitability index, PV/ investment cost | Ranking as per NPVs | Ranking as per profitability index |
|---|---|---|---|---|---|---|
| A | 2.5 | 3.25 | 0.75 | 1.30 | 6 | 2 |
| B | 10.0 | 10.825 | 0.825 | 1.08 | 5 | 6 |
| C | 5.0 | 7.575 | 2.575 | 1.51 | 1 | 1 |
| D | 10.0 | 12.35 | 2.35 | 1.23 | 2 | 3 |
| E | 12.5 | 13.35 | 0.85 | 1.07 | 4 | 7 |
| F | 2.5 | 3.0 | 0.5 | 1.20 | 7 | 4 |
| G | 5.0 | 5.9 | 0.9 | 1.18 | 3 | 5 |

| Projects selected in order of ranking | Investment cost (£m) | Net present value (£) |
|---|---|---|
| C | 5.0 | 2.575 |
| A | 2.5 | 0.750 |
| D | 10.0 | 2.350 |
| F | 2.5 | 0.500 |
| | Total net present value | 6.175 |

You can see that the ranking of projects by the profitability index gives the highest NPV.

Our discussion so far has assumed that investment funds are restricted for one period only. This is most unlikely. Also, the cost of certain investment projects may be spread over several periods. In addition, a one-period analysis does not take into account the intermediate cash flows generated by a project. Some projects may provide relatively high cash flows in the early years, and these can then be used to increase the availability of funds for investment in further projects in those early years. We should therefore consider more than just a one-period constraint in the allocation of limited capital to investment projects. To cope with such problems, it is necessary to use mathematical techniques, but we shall defer our discussion of the application of such techniques until Chapter 26.

# Taxation and investment decisions

In our discussions so far we have ignored the impact of taxation. Taxation rules differ between countries but in most countries similar principles tend to apply relating to the taxation allowances available on capital investment expenditure. Companies rarely pay taxes on the profits that are disclosed in their annual published accounts, since certain expenses that are deducted in the published accounts are not allowable deductions for taxation purposes. For example, depreciation is not an allowable deduction; instead, taxation legislation enables capital allowances (also known as writing-down allowances or depreciation tax shields) to be claimed on capital expenditure that is incurred on plant and machinery and other fixed assets. Capital allowances represent standardized depreciation allowances granted by the tax authorities. These allowances vary from country to country but their common aim is to enable the *net* cost of assets to be deducted as an allowable expense, either throughout their economic life or on an accelerated basis which is shorter than an asset's economic life.

Taxation laws in different countries typically specify the amount of capital expenditure that is allowable (sometimes this exceeds the cost of the asset where a government wishes to stimulate investment), the time period over which the capital allowances can be claimed and the depreciation method to be employed. Currently in the UK, companies can claim annual capital allowances of 25% on the written-down value of plant and equipment based on the reducing balance method of depreciation. Different percentage capital allowances are also available on other assets such as industrial buildings where an allowance of 4% per annum based on straight line depreciation can be claimed.[1]

Let us now consider how taxation affects the NPV calculations. You will see that the calculation must include the incremental tax cash flows arising from the investment. Consider the information presented in Example 14.3.

The first stage is to calculate the annual writing down allowances (i.e. the capital allowances). The calculations are as follows:

| End of year | Annual writing-down allowance (£) | Written-down value (£) |
|---|---|---|
| 0 | 0 | 1 000 000 |
| 1 | 250 000 (25% × £1 000 000) | 750 000 |
| 2 | 187 500 (25% × £750 000) | 562 500 |
| 3 | 140 630 (25% × £562 500) | 421 870 |
| 4 | 105 470 (25% × £421 870) | 316 400 |
|   | 683 600 | |

Next we calculate the additional taxable profits arising from the project. The calculations are as follows:

|  | Year 1 (£) | Year 2 (£) | Year 3 (£) | Year 4 (£) |
|---|---|---|---|---|
| Incremental annual profits | 500 000 | 500 000 | 500 000 | 500 000 |
| Less annual writing-down allowance | 250 000 | 187 500 | 140 630 | 105 470 |
| Incremental taxable profits | 250 000 | 312 500 | 359 370 | 394 530 |
| Incremental tax at 35% | 87 500 | 109 370 | 125 780 | 138 090 |

You can see that for each year the incremental tax payment is calculated as follows:

corporate tax rate × (incremental cash flows − capital allowance)

Note that depreciation charges should not be included in the calculation of incremental cash flows. We must now consider the timing of the taxation payments. In the UK taxation

**EXAMPLE 14.3**

The Sentosa Company operates in Ruratania where investments in plant and machinery are eligible for 25% annual writing-down allowances on the written-down value using the reducing balance method of depreciation. The corporate tax rate is 35%. The company is considering whether to purchase some machinery which will cost £1 million and which is expected to result in additional net cash inflows of £500 000 per annum for four years. It is anticipated that the machinery will be sold at the end of year 4 for its written-down value for taxation purposes. Assume a one year lag in the payment of taxes. Calculate the net present value.

payments vary depending on the end of the accounting year, but they are generally paid approximately one year after the end of the company's accounting year. We shall apply this rule to our example. This means that the tax payment of £87 500 for year 1 will be paid at the end of year 2, £109 370 tax will be paid at the end of year 3 and so on.

The incremental tax payments are now included in the NPV calculation:

| Year | Cash flow (£) | Taxation | Net cash flow (£) | Discount factor | Present value (£) |
|---|---|---|---|---|---|
| 0 | −1 000 000 | 0 | −1 000 000 | 1.0000 | −1 000 000 |
| 1 | +500 000 | 0 | +500 000 | 0.9091 | +454 550 |
| 2 | +500 000 | −87 500 | +412 500 | 0.8264 | +348 090 |
| 3 | +500 000 | −109 370 | +390 630 | 0.7513 | +293 480 |
| 4 | +500 000⎫ +316,400[a]⎭ | −125 780 | +690 620 | 0.6830 | +471 690 |
| 5 | 0 | −138 090 | −138 090 | 0.6209 | −85 740 |
| | | | | Net present value | +482 070 |

[a]Sale of machinery for written down value of £316 400.

The taxation rules in most countries allow capital allowances to be claimed on the *net* cost of the asset. In our example the machine will be purchased for £1 million and the estimated realizable value at the end of its life is its written-down value of £316 400. Therefore the estimated net cost of the machine is £683 600. You will see from the above calculations that the total of the writing-down allowances amount to the net cost. How would the analysis change if the estimated realizable value for the machine was different from its written-down value, say £450 000? The company will have claimed allowances of £683 600 but the estimated net cost of the machine is £550 000 (£1 million − £450 000 estimated net realizable value). Therefore excess allowances of £133 600 (£683 600− £550 000) will have been claimed and an adjustment must be made at the end of year 4 so that the tax authorities can claim back the excess allowance. This adjustment is called a balancing charge.

Note that the above calculation of taxable profits for year 4 will now be as follows:
Incremental annual profits

500 000

Less annual writing-down allowance(105 470)
Add balancing charge

133 600

Incremental taxable profits

528 130

Incremental taxation at 35%

184 845

An alternative calculation is to assume that a writing-down allowance will not be claimed in year 4. The balancing charge is now calculated by deducting the written-down value at the end of year 3 of £421 870 from the *actual* sales value at the time of sale (i.e. £450 000 sale proceeds). The balancing charge is now £28 130. This is the same as the net charge incorporated in the above calculation (£133 600 − £105 470 = £28 130). You can adopt either method. It is a matter of personal preference.

Let us now assume that the estimated disposal value is less than the written-down value for tax purposes, say £250 000. The net investment cost is £750 000 (£1 000 000 − £250 000), but you will see that our calculations at the start of this section indicate that estimated taxation capital allowances of £683 600 will have been claimed by the end of year 4. Therefore an adjustment of £66 400 (£750 000 − £683 600) must be made at the end of year 4 to reflect the fact that insufficient capital allowances have been claimed. This adjustment is called a balancing allowance.

Thus in year 4 the total capital allowance will consist of an annual writing-down allowance of £105 470 plus a balancing allowance of £66 400, giving a total of £171 870. Taxable profits for year 4 are now £328 130 (500 000 − £171 870), and tax at the rate of 35% on these profits will be paid at the end of year 5.

Do note that in the UK, and some other countries, it is possible to combine similar types of assets into asset pools and purchases and sales of assets are added to the pool so that balancing allowances and charges on individual assets do not arise. However, similar outcomes are likely to occur. Accordingly, it is essential when appraising investment proposals to be fully aware of the specific taxation legislation that applies so that you can precisely determine the taxation impact. In most cases taxation is likely to have an important effect on the NPV calculation.

# The effect of inflation on capital investment appraisal

**AR** In the 1970s the annual rate of inflation in many European countries exceeded 10%. What impact does inflation have on capital investment decisions? We shall see that inflation affects future cash flows and the return that shareholders require on the investment (i.e. the discount rate). The discount rate consists of the required rate of return on a riskless investment plus a risk premium that is related to a project's risk. Inflation affects both the risk-free interest rate and the risk premium. How does inflation affect the risk-free interest rate? According to Fisher (1930), interest rates quoted on risk-free investments such as treasury bills fully reflect anticipated inflation. Note that interest rates quoted on securities are known as nominal or money rates of interest, whereas the real rate of interest represents the rate of interest that would be required in the absence of inflation. Fisher proposed the following equation relating to the nominal rate of interest to the real rate of interest and the rate of inflation:

$$\left(1 + \frac{\text{nominal rate}}{\text{of interest}}\right) = \left(1 + \frac{\text{real rate}}{\text{of interest}}\right) \times \left(1 + \frac{\text{expected rate}}{\text{of inflation}}\right) \qquad (14.3)$$

Suppose that the real rate of interest is expected to be 2% and the anticipated rate of inflation 8%. Applying Fisher's equation, the nominal or money rate of interest would be

$$(1 + 0.02)(1 + 0.08) = 1.1016$$

The nominal rate of interest would therefore be 10.16%. In the absence of inflation, an individual who invests £100 in a risk-free security will require a 2% return of £102 to compensate for the time value of money. Assuming that the expected rate of inflation is 8%, then to maintain the return of £102 in real terms this return will have to grow by 8% to £110.16 (i.e. £102 + 8%). Therefore a real rate of interest of 2% requires a nominal rate of interest of 10.16% when the expected rate of inflation is 8%.

Inflation also affects future cash flows. For example, assume that you expect a cash flow of £100 in one year's time when there is no inflation. Now assume that that the predicted annual inflation rate is 10%. Your expected cash flow at the end of the year will now be £110, instead of £100. However, you will be no better off as a result of the 10% increase in cash flows. Assume that you can buy physical goods, say widgets, at £1 each when there is no inflation so that at the end of the year you can buy 100 widgets. With an annual inflation rate of 10% the cost of a widget will increase to £1.10 and your cash flow will be £110, but your purchasing power will remain unchanged because you will still only be able to buy 100 widgets.

The increase in cash flows from £100 to £110 is an illusion because it is offset by a decline in the purchasing power of the monetary unit. Rather than expressing cash flows in year one monetary units it is more meaningful to express the cash flows in today's purchasing power or monetary unit (that is, in real cash flows). Thus, £110 receivable at the end of year one is equivalent to £100 in today's purchasing power. When cash flows are expressed in monetary units at the time when they are received they are described as nominal cash flows whereas cash flows expressed in today's (that is, time zero) purchasing power are known as real cash flows. Therefore the £110 cash flow is a nominal cash flow but if it is expressed in today's purchasing power it will be equivalent to a real cash flow of £100.

Real cash flows can be converted to nominal cash flows using the following formula:

Nominal cash flow = Real cash flow $(1 +$ the anticipated rate of inflation$)^n$    (14.4)

where $n =$ the number of periods that the cash flows are subject to inflation.

Alternatively, we can rearrange formula (14.4) to restate it in terms of real cash flows:

Real cash flow = Nominal cash flow $(1 +$ the anticipated rate of inflation$)^n$    (14.5)

Therefore if a real cash flow expressed in today's purchasing power is £100 and the anticipated annual rate of inflation is 10% then the nominal value at the end of year 2 will be:

$$£100(1 + 0.10)^2 = £121$$

or a nominal cash flow of £121 receivable at the end of year 2 will be equivalent to a real cash flow of:

$$£121/(1 + 0.10)^2 = £100$$

The average rate of inflation for all goods and services traded in an economy is known as the general rate of inflation. Assume that your cash flow of £100 has increased at exactly the same rate as the general rate of inflation (in other words, the general rate of inflation is 10%). Therefore your purchasing power has remained unchanged and you will be no better or worse off if all your cash flows increase at the general rate of inflation. Indeed, we would expect the same result to apply when we calculate NPVs. If project cash flows increase at exactly the same rate as the general rate of inflation we would expect NPV to be identical to what the NPV would be if there was no inflation. Consider Example 14.4.

**EXAMPLE 14.4**

A division within the Bothnia Company is considering whether to undertake a project that will cost £1 million and will have the following cash inflows:

| | |
|---|---|
| Year 1 | £600 000 |
| Year 2 | £400 000 |
| Year 3 | £1 000 000 |

The cost of capital is 10% and the expected rate of inflation is zero. Ignore taxation. Calculate the net present value.

You should recall from Chapter 13 that the NPV can be expressed in formula terms as:

$$\frac{FV_1}{1+K} + \frac{FV_2}{(1+K)^2} + \frac{FV_3}{(1+K)^3} + \cdots + \frac{FV_n}{(1+K)^n} - I_0$$

where $FV_n$ are future values, $K$ is the cost of capital and $I_0$ is the initial investment cost. The NPV calculation is

$$\frac{£600\,000}{1.10} + \frac{£400\,000}{(1.10)^2} + \frac{£1\,000\,000}{(1.10)^3} - £1\,000\,000 = £627\,347$$

Let us now adjust Example 14.4 and incorporate the effects of inflation. Suppose that an annual inflation rate of 8% is expected during the three years of the project. In this situation the stock market data that are used to calculate the rate of return required by investors will include a premium for anticipated inflation. Hence this premium will be incorporated in the required rate of return on the project (i.e. the applicable cost of capital for the project). The revised required rate of return (RRR) is calculated using Fisher's formula:

$$1 + \text{nominal RRR} = [1 + \text{real RRR} (0.10)] \times [1 + \text{rate of inflation}(0.08)]$$
$$= (1 + 0.10)(1 + 0.08)$$
$$= 1.188$$

Therefore the RRR is now 18.8%. It is also necessary to adjust the cash flows for inflation. The revised NPV calculation is

$$\frac{£600\,000(1.08)}{(1.10)(1.08)} + \frac{£400\,000(1.08)^2}{(1.10)^2(1.08)^2} + \frac{£1\,000\,000(1.08)^3}{(1.10)^3(1.08)^3} - £1\,000\,000 = £627\,347$$

You can see in the numerator of the NPV calculation that the real cash flows are adjusted at the compound rate of inflation of 8%. In the denominators of the calculation Fisher's equation is shown to calculate the discount rate assuming an expected inflation rate of 8%. Consequently, the inflation factors of 1.08 cancel out. Therefore if the cash flows and the required rate of return are subject to the same rate of inflation then the project's NPV will be unaffected by expected changes in the level of inflation. For example, if inflation is now expected to be 5% instead of 8% then the inflation factor of 1.08 in the numerator and denominator of the NPV calculation would be replaced by 1.05. However, the revised inflation factors would still cancel out, and NPV would remain unchanged.

Looking at the NPV calculation, you should see that there are two correct approaches for adjusting for inflation which will lead to the same answer. They are:

Method 1: Predict *nominal cash flows* (i.e. adjust the cash flows for inflation) and use a *nominal discount rate*.

Method 2: Predict *real cash flows* at today's prices and use a *real discount rate*.

You will have noted that the approach outlined above used Method 1. Can you see that if we use Method 2 the inflation factors of 1.08 will be omitted from the above NPV calculation but the NPV will remain unchanged? The NPV calculation will thus be identical to the calculation shown earlier, which assumed zero inflation.

The correct treatment of inflation therefore requires that the assumptions about inflation that enter the cash flow forecasts are consistent with those that enter into the discount rate calculation. You must avoid the mistakes that are commonly made of discounting real cash flows at nominal discount rates or the discounting of nominal cash flows at real discount rates.

If *all* cash flows increase at the same rate as the general level of inflation, we could estimate cash flows in todays (*current*) prices, since such estimates would represent real cash flows. In other words, cash flows would be estimated without considering inflation. Applying the real discount rate would result in the correct treatment of inflation. However, the taxation rules in many countries can result in taxation cash flows not increasing at the general rate of inflation. This is because capital allowances remain constant, and thus taxation cash flows will not change in line with inflation. When cash flows do not increase at the general rate of inflation, we cannot use current price estimates to represent real cash flows. Real cash flows can then only be estimated by first expressing them in nominal terms and deflating them by the general rate of inflation. Because of these difficulties, you are recommended to use Method 1 if all of the cash flows do not increase at the same rate as the general level of inflation.

# Calculating risk-adjusted discount rates

In Chapter 13 we noted that a company should only invest in new projects if the returns are greater than those that the shareholders could obtain from investing in securities of the same risk traded in the financial markets. If we can measure the returns that investors require for different levels of risk, we can use these rates of return as the discount rates for calculating net present values.

Exhibit 14.1 shows the *average* returns from investing in government long-term gilt-edged securities and ordinary shares. Investing in government gilt-edged securities is virtually risk-free, but investing in ordinary shares is risky.[2] There is a possibility that you could earn very low or very high returns. You can see from Exhibit 14.1 that the safest investment gives the lowest average rate of return.

The average return on ordinary shares represents the average return that you would have obtained if you invested in all the companies listed on the UK stock exchange. This investment is described as investing in the **market portfolio**. It is unlikely that any investor could invest in the market portfolio, but it is possible to invest in a portfolio of shares (or a unit trust) that in terms of risk and return is virtually identical with the market portfolio.

From Exhibit 14.1 you can see that in the past investors who invested in the market portfolio obtained on average a return of 8.1% (13% − 4.9%) in excess of the risk-free investment. This extra return is called the **risk premium**. Suppose a firm has a project that in terms of risk is identical with the market portfolio. What is the *current* required

**EXHIBIT 14.1**

*Returns of risk
of different
types of security*

|  | Annual average return (%) |
|---|---|
| UK 1923–80 | |
|     Long-term gilts | 4.9 |
|     Ordinary shares | 13.0 |

*Source*: London Business School, Risk Measurement
Service, July–September 1981.

rate of return on this project? We calculate this by taking the current interest rate on gilt-edged securities (called the risk-free rate) and adding the average past risk premium of 8.1%. Assume that the current interest rate is 9%. The required rate of return (RRR) is calculated as follows:

$$\begin{array}{l} \text{RRR on an equivalent} \\ \text{investment to the market portfolio} \end{array} = \begin{array}{l} \text{risk-free} \\ \text{rate (9\%)} \end{array} + \begin{array}{l} \text{average past risk} \\ \text{premium (8.1\%)} \end{array} \qquad (14.6)$$

Therefore the project's cash flows should be discounted at 17.1% and a project that is risk free should be discounted at the same rate as that available from investing in government securities (i.e. 9%).

We have now established two benchmarks: the discount rate for risk-free projects and the discount rate for investments that have a risk equivalent to the market portfolio. However, we have not established how discount rates can be estimated for projects that do not fall into these categories. To do this, we must consider the relationship between risk and return.

Let us consider the risk and return from holding the market portfolio. Assume that the expected return from holding the market portfolio is 17% and the risk-free rate of interest is 9%. Therefore the risk premium required for holding the market portfolio is 8%. We shall also assume that the standard deviation from investing in the market portfolio is 16% and that from investing in the risk-free security is zero. These risk–return relationships are plotted in Figure 14.1. Note that the return on the market portfolio is represented by $R_m$ and the return on the risk-free security as $R_f$.

You can see that an investor can invest in any portfolio that falls on the line between points $R_f$ and $R_m$. For example, if you invest in portfolio X consisting of £500 in the market portfolio and £500 in the risk-free investment, your *expected* return will be 13% (£500 at 9% plus £500 at 17%). Note that the standard deviation from investing in portfolio X is

$$\left( \begin{array}{l} 1/2 \times \text{standard deviation of} \\ \text{risk-free security (0)} \end{array} \right) + \left( \begin{array}{l} 1/2 \times \text{standard deviation of} \\ \text{market portfolio (16\%)} \end{array} \right) = 8\% \qquad (14.7)$$

In other words, investing in portfolio X is half as risky as investing in the market portfolio. We can now establish a formula for calculating the *expected* return on

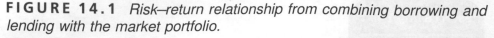

**FIGURE 14.1** *Risk–return relationship from combining borrowing and lending with the market portfolio.*

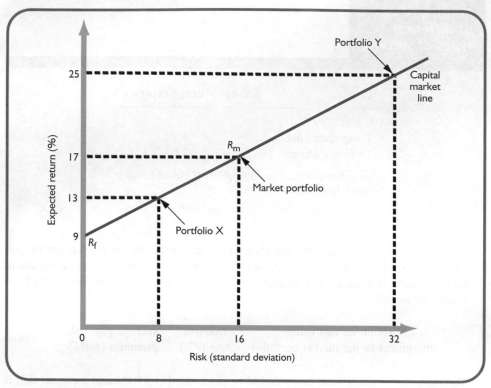

portfolios of different levels of risk:

$$\text{expected return} = \frac{\text{risk-free}}{\text{return}} + \left(\text{risk premium} \times \frac{\text{risk of selected portfolio}}{\text{risk of market portfolio}}\right) \quad (14.8)$$

$$= 9 + (8\% \times 8/16) = 13$$

Using this formula, we can calculate the expected return for any point along the line $R_f$ to $R_m$ in Figure 14.1. How can you invest in a portfolio that falls on the line above $R_m$? Such a position is achieved by borrowing and investing your funds in the market portfolio. Suppose you invest £1000 of your own funds and borrow £1000 at the risk-free rate of 9% and invest the combined funds of £2000 in the market portfolio. We shall call this portfolio Y. Your *expected* annual return will be £340 from investing in the market portfolio (£2000 × 17%) less £90 interest on the £1000 loan. Therefore your return will be £250 from investing £1000 of your own funds, i.e. 25%. However, this is the *expected* return, and there is a possibility that the return on the market portfolio could be zero, but you would have to repay the borrowed funds. In other words, by borrowing you increase the variability of your potential returns and therefore the standard deviation. The calculation of the standard deviation for portfolio Y is

$$\frac{(\pounds2000 \times 16\%) - (\pounds1000 \times 0\%)}{\pounds1000} = 32\%$$

We can also use equation (14.8) to calculate the expected return on portfolio Y. It is

$$9\% + (8\% \times 32/16) = 25\%$$

We have now established that an investor can achieve any point along the sloping line in Figure 14.1 by combining lending (i.e. investing in the risk-free security) and

**FIGURE 14.2**  *Risk–return relationship expressed in terms of beta.*

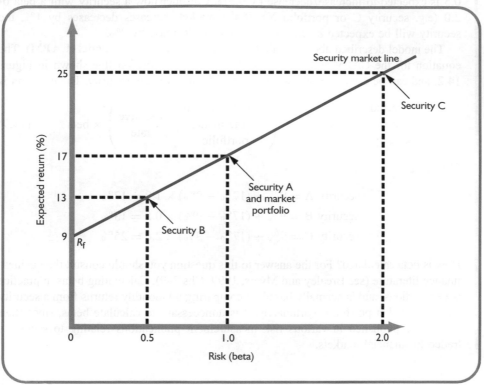

investing in the market portfolio or borrowing and investing in the market portfolio. The sloping line shown in Figure 14.1 that indicates the risk return relationship from combining lending or borrowing with the market portfolio is called the capital market line.

The market portfolio can now be used as a benchmark for determining the expected return on *individual* securities, rather than portfolios of securities. Consider three securities – the ordinary shares of companies A, B and C. Let us assume that, relative to the variability of the market portfolio, the risk of security A is identical, B is half as risky and C is twice as risky. In other words, in terms of risk, security A is identical with the market portfolio, B is equivalent to portfolio X and C is equivalent to portfolio Y. Consequently the required rates of return are 17% for A, 13% for B and 25% for C.

The returns available from combining investing in the market portfolio with borrowing and lending represent the most efficient investment portfolios, and determines the risk/return relationships for all securities traded in the market. The relationship between the risk of a security and the risk of the market portfolio is called beta. The beta of the market portfolio is 1.0, and the beta of a security that is half as risky as the market is 0.5 whereas the beta of a security that is twice as risky as the market portfolio is 2.0. The relationship between risk (measured in terms of beta) and expected return is shown by the sloping line in Figure 14.2 This sloping line is called the security market line.

Beta measures the sensitivity of the return on a security with market movements. For example, if the return on the market portfolio increased by 10%, the *expected* return on portfolio X and security B will be expected to increase by 5%. Similarly, if the return on the market portfolio decreased by 10%, the *expected* return on portfolio X and security B will be expected to decline by 5%. Both portfolio X and security B have a beta of 0.5, and this indicates that for a market increase/decrease of 1% any security with a beta of 0.5 is expected to increase/decrease by 0.5%. Consider now a security with a beta of 2.0 (e.g. security C or portfolio Y). If the market increases/decreases by 1%, the security will be expected *on average* to increase/decrease by 2%.

The model described above is called the **capital asset pricing model (CAPM)**. The equation for the CAPM is the equation for the security market line shown in Figure 14.2, and can be used to establish the expected return on any security. The equation is

$$\begin{array}{c}\text{expected}\\\text{return on a}\\\text{security}\end{array} = \begin{array}{c}\text{risk-free}\\\text{rate}\end{array} + \left( \begin{array}{c}\text{expected return}\\\text{on the market}\\\text{portfolio}\end{array} - \begin{array}{c}\text{risk-free}\\\text{rate}\end{array} \right) \times \text{beta} \qquad (14.9)$$

Therefore

$$\text{security A} = 9\% + (17\% - 9\%) \times 1.0 = 17\%$$
$$\text{security B} = 9\% + (17\% - 9\%) \times 0.5 = 13\%$$
$$\text{security C} = 9\% + (17\% - 9\%) \times 2.0 = 25\%$$

How is beta calculated? For the answer to this question you should consult the business finance literature (see Brealey and Myers, 1999, Chs 7–9). Calculating betas in practice is very tedious, and is normally based on comparing 60 monthly returns from a security with the market portfolio. Fortunately, it is unnecessary to calculate betas, since their values are published in various risk measurement publications relating to securities traded in financial markets.

# Calculating the required rates of returns on a firm's securities

You should now know how to calculate the required rates of returns for securities: simply multiply the average risk premium from investing in the market portfolio (8% shown in Exhibit 14.1) by the beta for the security, and add this to the current interest rate on gilt-edged securities. The required rate of return is the cost of capital or discount rate, which should be used to calculate the NPVs of projects that are just as risky as the firm's existing business.[3] For projects that are more or less risky than a firm's existing business it will be necessary to use the beta of companies that specialise in the projects being evaluated. For a detailed explanation of this approach you should refer to Brealey and Myers (1999, Ch. 9) or Pike and Neale (1999, Ch. 12).

# Weighted average cost of capital

So far we have considered how to calculate the required rate of return on ordinary shares (i.e. equity capital). However, most companies are likely to be financed by a combination of debt and equity capital. These companies aim to maintain target proportions of debt and equity.

The cost of *new* debt capital is simply the after tax interest cost of raising new debt. Assume that the after tax cost of new debt capital is 10% and the required rate of return on equity capital is 18% and that the company intends to maintain a capital structure of 50% debt and 50% equity. The overall cost of capital for the company is calculated as follows:

$$= \left( \begin{array}{c} \text{proportion of debt capital} \\ \times \text{ cost of debt capital} \\ (0.5 \times 10\%) \end{array} \right) + \left( \begin{array}{c} \text{proportion of equity capital} \\ \times \text{ cost of equity capital} \\ (0.5 \times 18\%) \end{array} \right) = 14\%$$

(14.10)

The overall cost of capital is also called the weighted average cost of capital. Can we use the weighted average cost of capital as the discount rate to calculate a project's NPV? The answer is yes, provided that the project is of equivalent risk to the firm's existing assets and the firm intends to maintain its target capital structure of 50% debt and 50% equity.

In practice, a firm will not finance every single project with 50% debt and 50% equity. For example, project X costing £5 million might be all equity financed. The firm should maintain its target capital structure by issuing debt to finance future projects of £5 million. In this way the firm maintains its target capital structure. Therefore the weighted average cost of capital that should be used for evaluating investment proposals should be an incremental cost based on the firm's target capital structure. Do not use the specific cost of the funds that have been used to finance the project.

We have now established how to calculate the discount rate for projects that are of similar risk to the firm's existing assets and to incorporate the financing aspects. You should estimate the required rate of return on a firm's shares using the capital asset pricing model and use this return as an input to estimate the weighted average cost of capital.

# Traditional methods of measuring risk

In this section we shall consider some of the traditional methods used by companies to measure the risk of a project. These measures were developed before we knew how to introduce risk into the calculation of NPV using the capital asset pricing model. Because these methods continue to be used, it is important that you understand their limitations. We shall consider the following methods of quantifying risk:

1. standard deviations and probability distributions;
2. simulation;
3. sensitivity analysis.

## 1. STANDARD DEVIATION AND PROBABILITY DISTRIBUTIONS

In Chapter 12 we discussed standard deviations, the coefficient of variation and probability distributions as methods of comparing the risk characteristics of various alternative courses of action. We shall now consider how these methods can be used to assess the risk of various capital projects. Consider the situation presented in Example 14.5.

The expected values of the cash flows can be used to calculate the project's expected net present value by adding together the discounted net present values of the expected values for each year. That is,

$$\text{Expected NPV} = \frac{£20\,000}{1.10} + \frac{£5000}{(1.10)^2} + \frac{£0}{(1.10)^3} - £20\,000 = £2314$$

**EXAMPLE 14.5**

A firm is considering a capital investment proposal that requires an immediate cash outlay of £20 000. The project has an estimated life of three years and the forecast cash flows and their estimated probabilities are as follows:

| | Year 1 | | Year 2 | | Year 3 |
|---|---|---|---|---|---|
| Probability | Net Cash flow (£) | Probability | Net Cash flow (£) | Probability | Net Cash flow (£) |
| 0.10 | 10 000 | 0.10 | (−5 000) | 0.10 | (−10 000) |
| 0.25 | 15 000 | 0.25 | 0 | 0.25 | (−5 000) |
| 0.30 | 20 000 | 0.30 | 5 000 | 0.30 | 0 |
| 0.25 | 25 000 | 0.25 | 10 000 | 0.25 | 5 000 |
| 0.10 | 30 000 | 0.10 | 15 000 | 0.10 | 10 000 |
| Expected value | 20 000 | Expected value | 5 000 | Expected value | 0 |

The operating cash flows in any one year do not depend on the operating cash flows of previous years. The risk-free cost of capital is 10%.

One method of describing the uncertainty associated with this project is to construct the entire probability distribution for the project's NPV. Unfortunately, the calculations are rather tedious, since there are 125 possibilities (i.e. $5^3$) in Example 14.5. We could summarize the 125 possibilities in a probability distribution of several possible outcomes, but the 125 NPVs must still initially be calculated. To avoid all these calculations, an indication of the risk may be obtained by calculating the standard deviation of the NPV. The formula for the calculation of the variance of the NPV is given below. The standard deviation is the square root of the variance.

$$V_P = \sum_{t=0}^{n} \frac{V_t}{(1+r)^{2t}} \qquad (14.11)$$

where $V_p$ is the variance of the project's NPV and $V_t$ is the variance of the project's cash flow in year $t$. The discount factor is squared so that it is in the same terms as the variance of the cash flows. The cash flow variances for each of the three years are £32 500 000[4]. The variances are identical because the probability distributions have the same dispersion about their expected values. Let us now apply equation (14.9) to calculate the variance of the project's NPV:

$$V_P = \frac{£32\,500\,000}{(1.10)^2} + \frac{£32\,500\,000}{(1.10)^4} + \frac{£32\,500\,000}{(1.10)^6} = £67\,402\,844$$

The standard deviation is the square root of the variance (i.e. £8210), so the expected value of the NPV of the project is £2314 and the standard deviation about the expected NPV is £8210. Note that the risk-free rate has been used in the above calculations. Our objective is to measure the risk of investment proposals, but if we use a discount rate which embodies a premium for risk then this would result in an adjustment for risk within the discounting process and would lead to double counting and the prejudging of risk.

It is difficult to interpret expected NPVs and the standard deviations. The expected NPV and standard deviation for the project in Example 14.5 are £2314 and £8210 respectively. However, we have no means of ascertaining whether an NPV of £2314 is sufficient to compensate for the risk involved (i.e. a standard deviation of £8210). Consider also a situation where the firm has a second, alternative project that has an expected NPV of £5000 with a standard deviation of £10 000. Assume that the two projects are mutually exclusive. It is unclear from the analysis whether the increase in the expected NPV of £2686 is sufficient to justify the increase in risk (i.e. an increase in standard deviation of £1790). In contrast, the capital asset pricing model incorporates risk in the discounting process and clearly indicates whether a project's return is in excess of the risk adjusted return required by shareholders.

## 2. SIMULATION

To produce a probability distribution for the possible NPVs in Example 14.5, it is necessary to construct a decision tree with 125 different outcomes, even though the example was based on some very simple assumptions. In practice, it may be necessary to produce separate probabilities for alternative sales revenue outcomes, different items of costs, and different possible life spans. Consequently, a decision tree will consist of thousands of different branches. In addition, the cash flows may be correlated over the years; for example, if a new product is successful in the early years then it is also likely to be successful in later years. When the cash flows are correlated over time, the standard deviation calculation in equation (14.9) will not give a correct calculation of the variation of the project's NVP.

A way in which these problems can be overcome is to use Monte Carlo simulation analysis. We can use Example 14.5 to illustrate the simulation process. The first step is to construct a probability distribution for each factor that influences the capital investment decision, for example market share, selling price, operating costs and the useful life of the facilities. For Example 14.5 we shall only use probability distributions for the cash flows in each year of the project's life. The next step is to assign numbers (from 1 to 100) to the cash flows in the probability distributions to exactly match their respective probabilities. This is achieved by working upwards cumulatively from the lowest to the highest cash flow values and assigning numbers that will correspond to probability groupings. The numbers for the cash flows in Example 14.5 for each year are as follows:

| Year 1 | | Year 2 | | Year 3 | |
|---|---|---|---|---|---|
| Assigned numbers | Cash flow (£) | Assigned numbers | Cash flow (£) | Assigned numbers | Cash flow (£) |
| 1–10 | 10 000 | 1–10 | (−5 000) | 1–10 | (−10 000) |
| 11–35 | 15 000 | 11–35 | 0 | 11–35 | (−5 000) |
| 36–65 | 20 000 | 36–65 | 5 000 | 36–65 | 0 |
| 66–90 | 25 000 | 66–90 | 10 000 | 66–90 | 5 000 |
| 91–100 | 30 000 | 91–100 | 15 000 | 91–100 | 10 000 |

For year 1 the selection of a number at random between 1 and 10 obtained from between 1 and 100 has a probability of 0.1. In the above schedule this represents a cash flow of £10 000. Similarly, the selection of a number at random between 11 and 35 has a probability of 0.25, and this represents a cash flow of £15 000. Numbers have been assigned to cash flows so that when numbers are selected at random the cash flows have exactly the same probability of being selected as is indicated in their respective probability distribution in Example 14.5.

Simulation trials are now carried out by computer. The computer selects one number at random for each of the relevant distributions (i.e. each probability distribution for years 1–3 in our example) and produces an estimated NPV. For example, if random numbers of 26, 8 and 85 respectively are selected for each of the three distributions for each year, this will indicate cash flows of +£15 000 in year 1, −£5000 in year 2 and +£5000 in year 3 and the resulting NPV will be calculated. This particular NPV is only one of a particular combination of values from a computer run. The computer will select many other sets of random numbers, convert them into cash flows and compute other NPVs repeatedly, for perhaps several thousand trials. A count is kept of the number of times each NPV is computed; and when the computer run has been completed, it can be programmed to produce an expected value, probability distribution and standard deviation. A graph of the probability distribution can also be plotted.

Note that the cash flows for each computer run are discounted at the risk-free rate for the reasons described earlier (namely to avoid double counting and prejudging risk). It is therefore very difficult to interpret the probability distribution of NPVs discounted at the risk-free rate. We still lack a clear-cut answer to the basic question: should the project be accepted or rejected?

The advantage of simulation analysis is that it compels decision-makers to look carefully at the relationships between the factors affecting the cash flows. Brealey and Myers (1999) conclude:

> By considering a detailed Monte Carlo simulation model, you will get a better understanding of how a project works and what could go wrong with it. You will have confirmed, or improved, your forecasts of future cash flows, and your calculations of project NPV will be more confident... Don't use simulation just to generate a distribution of NPVs. Use it to understand the project, forecast its expected cash flows, and assess its risk. Then calculate the NPV the old fashioned way, by discounting expected cash flows at a discount rate appropriate for the project's risk.

Computer simulation is not always feasible for risk analysis. The technique requires that probability distributions be established for a number of variables such as sales volume, selling prices, various input prices and asset lives. Therefore full-scale simulation may only be appropriate for the most important projects that involve large sums of money.

# 3. SENSITIVITY ANALYSIS

Sensitivity analysis enables managers to assess how responsive the NPV is to changes in the variables which are used to calculate it. Figure 14.3 illustrates that the NPV calculation is dependent on several independent variables, all of which are uncertain. The approach requires that the NPVs are calculated under alternative assumptions to determine how sensitive they are to changing conditions.

The application of sensitivity analysis can indicate those variables to which the NPV is most sensitive, and the extent to which these variables may change before the investment results in a negative NPV. In other words, sensitivity analysis indicates why a project might fail. Management should review any critical variables to assess whether or not there is a strong possibility of events occurring which will lead to a negative NPV. Management should also pay particular attention to controlling those variables to which NPV is particularly sensitive, once the decision has been taken to accept the investment. Sensitivity analysis is illustrated with Example 14.6.

**FIGURE 14.3** *Sensitivity of NPV to changes in independent variables.*

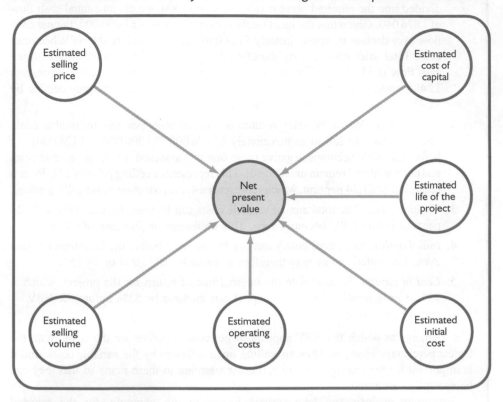

One of the divisions of the Bothnia Company is considering the purchase of a new machine, and estimates of the most likely cash flows are as follows:

|  | Year 0 (£) | Year 1 (£) | Year 2 (£) | Year 3 (£) |
|---|---|---|---|---|
| Initial outlay | −2 000 000 |  |  |  |
| Cash inflows |  |  |  |  |
| (100 000 units at £30 per unit) |  | 3 000 000 | 3 000 000 | 3 000 000 |
| Variable costs |  | 2 000 000 | 2 000 000 | 2 000 000 |
| Net cash flows | −2 000 000 | +1 000 000 | +1 000 000 | +1 000 000 |

The cost of capital is 15% and the net present value is £2 830 000.

Some of the variables referred to in Example 14.6 to which sensitivity analysis can be applied are as follows.

1. *Sales volume*: The net cash flows will have to fall to £876 040 (£2 000 000/2.283 discount factor) for the NPV to be zero, because it will be zero when the present value of the future cash flows is equal to the investment cost of £2 000 000. As the cash flows are equal each year, the cumulative discount tables in Appendix B can

be used. The discount factor for 15% and year 3 is 2.283. If the discount factor is divided into the required present value of £2 000 000, we get an annual cash flow of £876 040. Given that the most likely *net* cash flow is +£1 000 000, the *net* cash flow may decline by approximately £124 000 each year before the NPV becomes zero. Total sales revenue may therefore decline by £372 000 (assuming that net cash flow is 33.1/3% of sales). At a selling price of £30 per unit, this represents 12 400 units, or alternatively we may state that the sales volume may decline by 12.4% before the NPV becomes negative.

2. *Selling price:* When the sales volume is 100 000 units per annum, total annual sales revenue can fall to approximately £2 876 000 (£3 000 000 − £124 000) before the NPV becomes negative (note that it is assumed that total variable costs and units sold will remain unchanged). This represents a selling price of £28.76, or a reduction of £1.24 per unit, which represents a 4.1% reduction in the selling price.

3. *Variable costs:* The total annual variable costs can increase by £124 000 or £1.24 per unit before NPV becomes zero. This represents an increase of 6.2%.

4. *Initial outlay*: The initial outlay can rise by the NPV before the investment breaks even. The initial outlay may therefore increase by £283 000 or 14.15%.

5. *Cost of capital*: We calculate the internal rate of return for the project, which is 23%. Consequently, the cost of capital can increase by 53% before the NPV becomes negative.

The elements to which the NPV appears to be most sensitive are the items with the lowest percentage changes. They are selling price followed by the variable costs, and it is important for the manager to pay particular attention to these items so that they can be carefully monitored.

Sensitivity analysis can take various forms. In our example, for the selected variables, we focused on the extent to which each could change for NPV to become zero. Another form of sensitivity analysis is to examine the impact on NPV of a specified percentage change in a selected variable. For example, what is the impact on NPV if sales volume falls by 10%? A third approach is to examine the impact on NPV of pessimistic, most likely and optimistic estimates for each selected variable.

Sensitivity analysis has a number of serious limitations. In particular, the method requires that changes in each key variable be isolated, but management is more interested in the combination of the effect of changes in two or more key variables. In addition, the method gives no indication of the probability of key variables or a combination of these variables occurring. For example, the sensitivity analysis may indicate that one key variable may change by 25% and another may change by 10%. This suggests that we should concentrate on the latter, but if the former has a probability of occurring of 0.5 and the latter has a probability of 0.01 then clearly the key variable change of 25% is more important. You will see from Exhibit 14.2 (Surveys of company practice) that sensitivity analysis is the most frequently used formal risk measurement technique.

# A summary of risk measurement techniques

There are three different approaches that can be adopted to measure the risk of a project. Project risk can be measured by viewing the investment:

1. As part of a well-diversified investment portfolio held by shareholders (i.e. a *capital asset pricing model approach*).

2. On its own and ignoring its relationship with either the shareholders' or the firm's other investments (i.e. a *stand-alone risk measure*).

3. As part of the firm's total investment in assets (i.e. *corporate portfolio risk measure*).

We adopted the capital asset pricing model (CAPM) approach when we described the method of computing risk-adjusted discount rates. With this approach, risk is measured by comparing the risk of a project relative to the market portfolio. Investors are assumed to hold an efficiently diversified portfolio (this can normally be achieved by investing in about 15 securities) that approximates the market portfolio. The CAPM approach assumes that the *overall* risk incurred by shareholders falls into two categories:

1. Specific (diversifiable) risk, which is specific to an *individual* company such as the impact on cash flows arising from a new competitor entering the market or when a technological change makes one of the firm's major products obsolete.

2. Market (non-diversifiable) risk, which is due to macroeconomic factors that affect the returns of *all* companies, such as changes in interest or corporate tax rates or changes in overall consumer demand.

The *CAPM approach* assumes that specific risk is irrelevant in determining the returns required by shareholders because they can diversify it away (and thus avoid it) by investing in a well-diversified portfolio of securities. Consider a situation where you invest in a company whose main activity is ice-cream manufacturing. You will be exposed to specific company risk, since a rainy summer will adversely affect the company's profitability and share price. You can eliminate much of this specific risk by also investing in a company that manufactures rainwear, assuming that a rainy summer will have a favourable impact on company profitability and share price. By investing in a well-diversified portfolio of securities, an unfavourable event affecting the value of any one company in the portfolio will have a small impact on the value of the entire portfolio because much of the investment will be unaffected by the occurrence of the event.

If investors do hold well-diversified portfolios (and the major investors such as the financial institutions certainly do) then the market will only reward investors for bearing risk that cannot be avoided (i.e. market risk). The CAPM approach measures the *market* risk of a project relative to the market portfolio. This is expressed in the form of the beta measure, which can then be used to derive the *expected* returns for different levels of market risk (Figure 14.2). The CAPM approach implies that investors are saying: 'These are the *expected* returns that can be obtained from securities traded in financial markets for different levels of *market* risk. If you (the firm) can invest in projects that earn returns in excess of returns available from securities with the same level of market risk then invest the funds on my behalf.'

The *stand-alone risk measurement approach* measures the *total* risk of a project in isolation from either the shareholders' or the firm's other investments. The standard deviation, probability distributions and simulation methods described earlier are stand-alone measures of risk. They measure the dispersion of the outcomes for a specific project, but do not distinguish between specific and market risk. If only market risk is rewarded by the stock market then stand-alone risk measures will be inappropriate, since they include specific firm risk that is not rewarded by the stock market. A further problem is that stand-alone risk measures merely measure risk. They do not provide a basis for determining the rates of return required for different levels of risk.

The *corporate portfolio risk measurement approach* measures the incremental risk arising from the acceptance of a project. The incremental risk may not be the same as

**EXAMPLE 14.7**

Assume that a firm operates in an environment in which there are only two potential states of nature. There is an equal probability that each state of nature will occur. The estimated cash flow from the existing projects and a proposed investment project are as follows:

| | Existing projects (£) | Proposed project (£) | Existing projects combined with proposed project (£) |
|---|---|---|---|
| State of nature 1 | −40 000 | +20 000 | −20 000 |
| State of nature 2 | +60 000 | −10 000 | +50 000 |
| Expected value | +10 000 | +5000 | +15 000 |
| Standard deviation | 50 000 | 15 000 | 35 000 |

the individual risk of a project measured on a stand-alone approach. For example, the standard deviation of the cash flows from the firm's existing assets might be £100 000 and the standard deviation of the cash flows of a proposed project £60 000 on a stand-alone basis. If the proposed project is not highly correlated with the firm's existing projects, it is possible that the total standard deviation of the cash flows from the firm's assets might increase to, say, £120 000. Thus the incremental standard deviation arising from the acceptance of the project is only £20 000 whereas the stand-alone measure is £60 000.

You can see why stand-alone risk can differ from incremental risk by considering Example 14.7.

The stand-alone standard deviation of the cash flows from the proposed project is +£15 000 but the incremental standard deviation of the cash flow is −£15 000 (£35 000 − £50 000). Thus acceptance of the project *reduces* the dispersion of the total cash flows of the firm, and therefore has risk reduction properties. However, when viewed on a stand-alone basis the proposed project appears to involve a high level of risk. The analysis suggests that we should not focus on the risk of individual projects in isolation, but we should consider the impact of a project on the total risk of the firm.

The corporate portfolio risk approach can merely measure incremental risk. As with stand-alone measures, there is no mechanism for determining the required rate of return for different levels of risk. It is also extremely difficult to compute the standard deviation from the firm's existing assets and thus measure incremental risk. In Example 14.7 we illustrated how diversification by the firm can reduce risk. However, shareholders can do this themselves by investing in well-diversified portfolios. The firm has reduced specific (diversifiable) risk, but if investors can do this themselves then risk reduction by the firm will be of no value. The corporate portfolio approach therefore fails to distinguish between specific and market risk.

Finally, you should note that, unlike the other methods described in this chapter, sensitivity analysis does not measure risk. It shows the impact on NPV from making alternative assumptions in the variables that were used to calculate it, and can also be used to indicate the extent to which each variable can change before the investment results in a negative NPV. Sensitivity analysis should be used to complement the CAPM risk-adjusted discount approach. Its real value is that it helps managers to delve into the cash flow estimates and understand what could go wrong and what opportunities are available to modify the project. ●●●

# Authorization of capital investment proposals

It is essential to implement a sound system for approving capital investment proposals. Capital investment decisions frequently require the commitment of a large amount of funds for many years, and, once approval has been obtained and initial outlays have been incurred, there is normally no turning back on the decision. A detailed scrutiny of capital investment proposals by top management is therefore essential. A procedure should be implemented that encourages managers to submit investment proposals, since only by managers constantly reviewing future opportunities and threats can a company prosper in the long term. However, approval should not be merely a rubber-stamping of the managers' proposals, since there is a danger that a manager's favourite proposals will be implemented when they do not provide a sound financial return. It is important that top management should establish a capital investment approval procedure that both encourages managers to submit capital investment proposals and ensures that such proposals meet the long-term objectives of the company. An example of a capital investment approval procedure is illustrated in Figure 14.4, although in practice such a procedure is likely to exist only in large firms.

## INITIATION OF PROPOSALS

The originator of a proposal should make a request for a capital appropriation for those projects that seem to have merit. The request should include a description of the proposal, the reasons for making it, and an estimate of the costs, benefits and economic life. The originator should obtain the assistance of the accounting department, which should provide a financial evaluation of the proposal. If the proposal does not meet the financial criteria then it will probably proceed no further, but not all desirable proposals lend themselves to financial evaluation because of the difficulty in quantifying the benefits (consider, for example, expenditure on social facilities for the employees, or pollution control devices). With these kinds of projects, management will have to make a value judgement as to whether the benefits exceed the present value of the outlays.

## INITIAL APPROVAL OF THE PROPOSAL

When the financial evaluation has been completed, the proposal, together with its financial evaluation, should be submitted to a top management committee consisting of the heads of various functions such as production, marketing, finance, research and development, and so on. At this stage there will be much discussion and additional information such as sensitivity analysis or other information about the risk of the project may be requested. The committee will then either approve or reject the proposal. Minor proposals, which require only a small initial cash outlay, may not require the approval of the top management committee. The managers themselves or their superiors may be able to approve such projects. However, approval will normally be subject to the proposals meeting the company's normal profitability standards. Such projects should also be subject to **post-completion audits** (i.e. a comparison of budgeted and actual cash flows). Approval by the top management team of a request indicates only that the proposal fits into the company's programme; it does not carry with it authorization to proceed immediately with the proposal.

**FIGURE 14.4** *Authorization of capital investment procedure.*

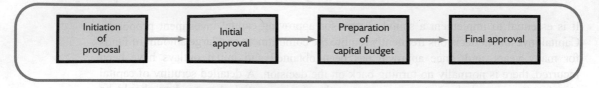

## PREPARATION OF THE ANNUAL CAPITAL BUDGET

The accountant will normally prepare this budget, but will have to work closely with the top management capital expenditure approval committee. In the capital budget projects are often classified under the following headings:

(a) cost reduction and replacement;

(b) expansion of existing product lines;

(c) new product lines;

(d) health and safety;

(e) other.

Within these classifications, individual projects may be listed in what is believed to be their order of merit, and estimated cash inflows and outflows should be analysed by years, or quarters, so that their impact on the funds of each time period can be shown. A blanket amount is normally included for the total of smaller projects which are not listed individually. The capital budget should be reviewed by a top management review committee, and it will ultimately be approved, perhaps after some revision and resubmissions. When approving the capital budget, an overall view should be taken; for example, the committee should consider whether the overall mix of proposed projects fits in with the required financial return and risk profile of the company.

## FINAL APPROVAL

Approval of the capital budget will normally mean that a project is approved in principle; but, before a project can be undertaken, it is necessary to submit a final authorization request that spells out the proposal in more detail and includes an agreed price quotation. Final approval may be obtained from the top management approval committee or lower levels of management, depending on the cost and the importance of the project.

# Review of capital investment decisions

When the capital investment decision has been made, it is important to implement a sound system for reviewing and controlling the capital expenditure. The review should consist in the following:

1. control over the amount of the expenditure before the project is operational;

2. a post-completion audit of the operating cash inflows and outflows.

# CONTROLLING CAPITAL EXPENDITURE

Capital expenditure is difficult to control because each investment is usually unique, and therefore no predetermined standards or past experience will be available for establishing what the cash outflows should be. When the actual capital expenditure costs are different from the amount originally estimated, the difference may be due to an incorrect original estimate and/or inefficiency in controlling the actual costs. Unfortunately, it is very difficult, and sometimes impossible, to isolate a variance (i.e. the difference between the actual and the estimated expenditure) into a forecasting element and an efficiency element. However, the originator of a project will have prepared an estimate and defended it at the approval stage. This estimate forms a major component in determining whether or not the project should be approved, and there are sound reasons for comparing this estimate with the actual expenditures and requiring the individual responsible to explain any variances. This comparison may also indicate inefficiencies that will enable action to be taken to avoid overspending on the uncompleted part of the project. In addition, a comparison of actual costs with estimated costs will provide an incentive for the proposers of future projects to make careful estimates, and will also provide an incentive to control the costs and the date of completion.

Comparisons should take place at periodic intervals during the installation and construction stage of the project. Reports should be prepared giving details of the percentage completion, over- or under-spending relative to the stage of completion, the estimated costs to complete compared with the original estimate, the time taken compared with the estimate for the current stage of completion, and also the estimated completion date compared with the original estimate. This information will enable management to take corrective cost-saving action such as changing the construction schedule.

# POST-COMPLETION AUDIT OF CASH FLOWS

When the investment is in operation, the actual results should be compared with the estimated results that were included in the investment proposal. The comparison should be based on the same method of evaluation as was used in making the investment decision. Whenever possible, actual cash flows plus estimated cash flows for the remainder of the project's life should be compared with the cash flows that were included in the original estimate. However, the feasibility of making such a comparison will depend on the ease and cost of estimating future cash flows.

The problem is that normally no pre-set standards or past information will be available as to what the cash inflows and outflows should be, and a comparison of actual and estimated cash flows will be difficult to evaluate. Furthermore, except for the very large projects, the portion of cash flows that stem from a specific capital investment is very difficult to isolate. All one can do in such situations is to scrutinize carefully the investment at the approval stage and incorporate the estimated results into departmental operating budgets. Although the results of individual projects cannot be isolated, their combined effect can be examined as part of the conventional periodic performance review.

A post-audit of capital investment decisions is a very difficult task, and any past investment decisions that have proved to be wrong should not be interpreted in isolation. It is important to remind oneself that capital investment decisions are made under uncertainty. For example, a good decision may turn out to be unsuccessful yet may still have been the correct decision in the light of the information and alternatives available at the time. We would agree that a manager should undertake a project that costs £100 000 and has a 0.9 probability of a positive NPV of £20 000 and a 0.1 probability of a negative NPV of £5000. However, if the event with a 0.1 prob-ability occurred, a post-completion audit would suggest that the investment has been undesirable.

Lister (1983) suggests that 'post-mortems' may be viewed with disfavour in industry on the grounds that they discourage initiative and produce a policy of over-caution. There is a danger that managers will submit only safe investment proposals. The problem is likely to be reduced if managers know their selections will be fairly judged.

In spite of all the problems a post-audit comparison should be undertaken. A record of past performance and mistakes is one way of improving future performance and ensuring that fewer mistakes are made. In addition, the fact that the proposers of capital investment projects are aware that their estimates will be compared with actual results encourages them to exercise restraint and submit more thorough and realistic appraisals of future investment projects. You will see from the survey evidence relating to large UK companies (see Exhibit 14.2) that the majority of companies conducted some form of ex-post monitoring of their capital investment decisions.

## EXHIBIT 14.2

*Surveys of company practice*

Surveys conducted by Pike (1996) on the use of risk analysis techniques by 100 large UK companies between 1975 and 1992 provide an indication of the changing trends in practice in large UK companies. Pike's findings are as follows:

|  | 1975 % | 1980 % | 1986 % | 1992 % |
|---|---|---|---|---|
| Sensitivity analysis | 28 | 42 | 71 | 86 |
| Best/worse case analysis | N/A | N/A | 93 | 85 |
| Reduced payback period | 25 | 30 | 51 | 69 |
| Risk adjusted discount rate | 37 | 41 | 61 | 64 |
| Probability analysis | 9 | 10 | 40 | 47 |
| Beta analysis (based on the CAPM) | — | — | 16 | 20 |

*Source*: Pike (1996)

A USA study by Trahan and Gitman (1995) reported that 52% adjusted the discount rate and 72% used sensitivity analysis.

The UK study of 300 UK manufacturing organizations by Drury *et al.* (1993) sought to ascertain the extent to which particular risk adjustment techniques were used. The figures below indicate the percentage of firms that often or always used a particular technique:

| | |
|---|---|
| Require a shorter payback period | 37 |
| Increase/decrease discount rate | 18 |
| Probability analysis | 14 |
| Monte Carlo simulation | 1 |
| Sensitivity analysis | 51 |
| Conservative cash flow forecasts | 32 |
| Beta analysis (based on the CAPM) | 1 |

Dardenne (1998) reported that 42% of Belgian companies regularly used sensitivity analysis, 16% regularly used the simulation approach and 35% raised the discount rate.

The Drury *et al.* (1993) study also examined the methods that firms used to incorporate inflation into the investment appraisal. They reported that 44% of the responding firms incorrectly discounted real cash flows at a nominal discount rate and a further 11% incorrectly discounted nominal cash flows at a real discount rate.

In terms of post audits a UK survey by Neale and Holmes (1988) indicated that 48% of large quoted UK companies adopted post-audits and a later study by Neale and Holmes (1991) reported that this rate had increased to 77%, with about half the firms having adopted post-audits between 1986 and 1990.

The conclusions that emerge from the above studies is that there has been a dramatic increase over the years in the usage of formal risk analysis techniques and that the CAPM approach is not widely used in practice.

## Self-Assessment Questions

You should attempt to answer these questions yourself before looking up the suggested answers, which appear on pages 1119–22. If any part of your answer is incorrect, check back carefully to make sure you understand where you went wrong.

1. Assume that you have been appointed finance director of Breckall plc. The company is considering investing in the production of an electronic security device, with an expected market life of five years.

   The previous finance director has undertaken an analysis of the proposed project; the main features of his analysis are shown below. He has recommended that the project should not be undertaken because the estimated annual accounting rate of return is only 12.3%.

### Proposed electronic security device project

|  | Year 0 (£000) | Year 1 (£000) | Year 2 (£000) | Year 3 (£000) | Year 4 (£000) | Year 5 (£000) |
|---|---|---|---|---|---|---|
| Investment in depreciable fixed assets | 4500 | | | | | |
| Cumulative investment in working capital | 300 | 400 | 500 | 600 | 700 | 700 |
| Sales | | 3500 | 4900 | 5320 | 5740 | 5320 |
| Materials | | 535 | 750 | 900 | 1050 | 900 |
| Labour | | 1070 | 1500 | 1800 | 2100 | 1800 |
| Overhead | | 50 | 100 | 100 | 100 | 100 |
| Interest | | 576 | 576 | 576 | 576 | 576 |
| Depreciation | | 900 | 900 | 900 | 900 | 900 |
|  | | 3131 | 3826 | 4276 | 4726 | 4276 |
| Taxable profit | | 369 | 1074 | 1044 | 1014 | 1044 |
| Taxation | | 129 | 376 | 365 | 355 | 365 |
| Profit after tax | | 240 | 698 | 679 | 659 | 679 |

Total initial investment is £4 800 000
Average annual after tax profit is £591 000

All the above cash flow and profit estimates have been prepared in terms of present day costs and prices, since the previous finance director assumed that the sales price could be increased to compensate for any increase in costs.

   You have available the following additional information:

(a) Selling prices, working capital requirements and overhead expenses are expected to increase by 5% per year.

(b) Material costs and labour costs are expected to increase by 10% per year.

(c) Capital allowances (tax depreciation) are allowable for taxation purposes against profits at 25% per year on a reducing balance basis.

(d) Taxation on profits is at a rate of 35%, payable one year in arrears.

(e) The fixed assets have no expected salvage value at the end of five years.

(f) The company's real after-tax weighted average cost of capital is estimated to be 8% per year, and nominal after-tax weighted average cost of capital 15% per year.

Assume that all receipts and payments arise at the end of the year to which they relate, except those in year 0, which occur immediately.

Required:

(a) Estimate the net present value of the proposed project. State clearly any assumptions that you make. (13 marks)

(b) Calculate by how much the discount rate would have to change to result in a net present value of approximately zero. (4 marks)

(c) Describe how sensitivity analysis might be used to assist in assessing this project. What are the weaknesses of sensitivity analysis in capital investment appraisal? Briefly outline alternative techniques of incorporating risk into capital investment appraisal. (8 marks)

(Total 25 marks)

*ACCA Level 3 Financial Management*

2. Ceder Ltd has details of two machines that could fulfil the company's future production plans. Only one of these will be purchased.

The 'standard' model costs £50 000, and the 'de luxe' £88 000, payable immediately. Both machines would require the input of £10 000 working capital throughout their working lives, and both have no expected scrap value at the end of their expected working lives of 4 years for the standard machine and 6 years for the de luxe machine.

The forecast pre-tax operating net cash flows (£) associated with the two machines are

| | **Years hence** | | | | | |
|---|---|---|---|---|---|---|
| | 1 | 2 | 3 | 4 | 5 | 6 |
| Standard | 20 500 | 22 860 | 24 210 | 23 410 | | |
| De luxe | 32 030 | 26 110 | 25 380 | 25 940 | 38 560 | 35 100 |

The de luxe machine has only recently been introduced to the market, and has not been fully tested in operating conditions. Because of the higher risk involved, the appropriate discount rate for the de luxe machine is believed to be 14% per year, 2% higher than the discount rate for the standard machine.

The company is proposing to finance the purchase of either machine with a term loan at a fixed interest rate of 11% per year.

Taxation at 35% is payable on operating cash flows one year in arrears, and capital allowances are available at 25% per year on a reducing balance basis.

Required:

(a) For both the standard and the de luxe machines calculate:
  (i) payback period;
  (ii) net present value.
  Recommend, with reasons, which of the two machines Ceder Ltd should purchase. (Relevant calculations must be shown.) (13 marks)

(b) Surveys have shown that the accounting rate of return and payback period are widely used by companies in the capital investment decision process. Suggest reasons for the widespread use of these investment appraisal techniques. (6 marks)

(Total 25 marks)

*ACCA Level 3 Financial Management*

## Summary

In this chapter we have discussed how capital investment techniques can be applied to more complicated situations. We have seen that when a choice must be made between mutually exclusive investments with unequal lives, it is necessary to compare the projects over equal time periods. One method is to convert the time periods into a common time horizon and assume the replacement of identical assets.

Capital rationing applies to a situation where there is a constraint on the amount of funds that can be invested during a specific period of time. In this situation the net present value is maximized by adopting the profitability index method of ranking and selecting projects up to the amount of the investment funds available.

When taxation is included in the capital investment evaluation, the cash flows from a project must be reduced by the amount of taxation paid on these cash flows. In addition, the investment cost must be reduced by the taxation saving arising from the capital allowance. Because taxation payments do not occur at the same times as the associated cash inflows or outflows, the precise timing of the taxation payment must be identified.

The net present value calculations can be adjusted in two basic ways to take inflation into account. First, a discount rate can be used, based on the market-determined required rate of return, which includes an allowance for inflation. Remember that cash flows must also be adjusted for inflation. Secondly, the anticipated rate of inflation can be excluded from the discount rate, and the cash flows can be expressed in real terms. When cash flows are subject to uncertainly, they should be discounted at a risk-adjusted discount rate using the capital asset pricing model. Several traditional methods exist for quantifying risk: standard deviations of NPV, simulation and sensitivity analysis. However, traditional risk measures involve discounting the cash flows at the risk-free rate. Therefore they fail to deal with the risk/return trade-off and do not provide a clear cut answer to the basic question: Should the project be accepted or rejected?

In the final section we have considered alternative methods, of authorizing and reviewing capital investment decisions. In spite of the difficulties involved in carrying out a post-audit review of capital investment decisions, such a review is necessary so that lessons can be learned from past mistakes and to discourage the proposers of capital investment projects from submitting over-optimistic estimates.

## Key Terms and Concepts

balancing allowance (p. 501)
balancing charge (p. 500)
beta (p. 507)
capital allowances (p. 499)
capital asset pricing model (pp. 508, 515)
capital market line (p. 507)
capital rationing (p. 497)
depreciation tax shields (p. 499)
equivalent annual cost method (p. 495)
expected net present value (p. 509)
general rate of inflation (p. 502)
hard capital rationing (p. 497)
lowest common multiple method (p. 494)
market (non-diversifiable) risk (p. 515)

market portfolio (p. 504)
Monte Carlo simulation analysis (p. 511)
nominal and money interest rates (p. 501)
nominal cash flows (p. 502)
post-completion audit (p. 517)
real cash flows (p. 502)
real rate of interest (p. 501)
risk premium (p. 504)
security market line (p. 507)
sensitivity analysis (p. 512)
soft capital rationing (p. 497)
specific (diversifiable) risk (p. 515)
weighted average cost of capital (p. 509)
writing-down allowances (p. 499)

## Recommended Reading

This chapter has provided an outline of the capital asset pricing model and the calculation of risk-adjusted discount rate. These topics are dealt with in more depth in the business finance literature. You should refer to Brealey and Myers (1999, Chs 7–10) for a description of the capital asset pricing model and risk-adjusted discount rates. For a discussion of the differences between company, divisional and project cost of capital and an explanation of how project discount rates can be calculated when project risk is different from average

overall firm risk see Pike and Neale (1999, Ch. 12) You should refer to Neale and Holmes (1991) for a more detailed explanation of post-completion audits.

## Key Examination Points

A common error is for students to include depreciation and apportioned overheads in the DCF analysis. Remember that only incremental cash flows should be included in the analysis. Where a question includes taxation, you should separately calculate the incremental taxable profits and then work out the tax payment. You should then include the tax payment in the DCF analysis. Incremental taxable profits are normally incremental cash flows less capital allowances on the project. To simplify the calculations, questions sometimes indicate that capital allowances should be calculated on a straight-line depreciation method.

Do not use accounting profits instead of taxable

profits to work out the tax payment. Taxable profits are calculated by adding back depreciation to accounting profits and then deducting capital allowances. Make sure that you include any balancing allowance or charge and disposal value in the DCF analysis if the asset is sold.

With inflation, you should discount nominal cash flows at the nominal discount rate. Most questions give the nominal discount rate (also called the money discount rate). You should then adjust the cash flows for inflation. If you are required to choose between alternative projects, check that they have equal lives. If not, use one of the methods described in this chapter.

## Questions

*Indicates that a suggested solution is to be found in the *Students' Manual*.

### 14.1 Advanced

You have been appointed as chief management accountant of a well-established company with a brief to improve the quality of information supplied for management decision-making. As a first task you have decided to examine the system used for providing information for capital investment decisions. You find that discounted cash flow techniques are used but in a mechanical fashion with no apparent understanding of the figures produced. The most recent example of an investment appraisal produced by the accounting department showed a positive net present value of £35 000 for a five-year life project when discounted at 14% which you are informed 'was the rate charged on the bank loan raised to finance the investment'. You note that the appraisal did not include any consideration of the effects of inflation nor was there any form of risk analysis.

You are required to:

(a) explain the meaning of a positive net present value of £35 000; (4 marks)

(b) comment on the appropriateness or otherwise of the discounting rate used; (4 marks)

(c) state whether you agree with the treatment of inflation and, if not, explain how you would deal with inflation in investment appraisals; (6 marks)

(d) explain what is meant by 'risk analysis' and describe ways this could be carried out in investment appraisals and what benefits (if any) this would bring. (6 marks)

(Total 20 marks)

*CIMA Stage 3 Management Accounting Techniques Pilot Paper*

### 14.2 Advanced

In the context of capital budgeting, you are required to explain:

(a) the meaning of 'beta'; (4 marks)

(b) the function of 'beta' in the capital asset pricing model; (4 marks)

(c) what one might do to overcome the difficulty that 'beta' for a proposed capital expenditure project is not necessarily the same as that for the company as a whole; (8 marks)

(d) the major limitations to the use of the capital asset pricing model for the purposes of (c) above. (4 marks)

(Total 20 marks)

*CIMA Stage 4 Management Accounting – Decision-Making Pilot Paper*

### 14.3 Advanced

Describe and discuss the important stages that should be followed when a company wishes to develop and implement a new programme of capital investment.

Do *not* confine your discussion to the nature and use of evaluation techniques in the appraisal of capital investments. (25 marks)

*ACCA Level 3 Financial Management*

### 14.4* Intermediate: Computation of NPV and tax payable

Sound Equipment Ltd was formed five years ago to manufacture parts for hi-fi equipment. Most of its customers were individuals wanting to assemble their own systems. Recently, however, the company has embarked on a policy of expansion and has been approached by JBZ plc, a multinational manufacturer of consumer electronics. JBZ has offered Sound Equipment Ltd a contract to build an amplifier for its latest consumer product. If accepted, the contract will increase Sound Equipment's turnover by 20%.

JBZ's offer is a fixed price contract over three years, although it is possible for Sound Equipment to apply for subsequent contracts. The contract will involve Sound Equipment purchasing a specialist machine for £150 000. Although the machine has a 10-year life, it would be written off over the three years of the initial contract as it can only be used in the manufacture of the amplifier for JBZ.

The production director of Sound Equipment has already prepared a financial appraisal of the proposal. This is reproduced below. With a capital cost of £150 000 and total profits of £60 300, the production director has calculated the return on capital employed as 40.2%. As this is greater than Sound Equipment's cost of capital of 18%, the production director is recommending that the board accepts the contract.

| | Year 1 (£) | Year 2 (£) | Year 3 (£) | Total (£) |
|---|---|---|---|---|
| Turnover | 180 000 | 180 000 | 180 000 | 540 000 |
| Materials | 60 000 | 60 000 | 60 000 | 180 000 |
| Labour | 40 000 | 40 000 | 40 000 | 120 000 |
| Depreciation | 50 000 | 50 000 | 50 000 | 150 000 |
| Pre-tax profit | 30 000 | 30 000 | 30 000 | 90 000 |
| Corporation tax at 33% | 9 900 | 9 900 | 9 900 | 29 700 |
| After-tax profit | 20 100 | 20 100 | 20 100 | 60 300 |

You are employed as the assistant accountant to Sound Equipment Ltd and report to John Green, the financial director, who asks you to carry out a full financial appraisal of the proposed contract. He feels that the production director's presentation is inappropriate. He provides you with the following additional information:

- Sound Equipment pays corporation tax at the rate of 33%;
- the machine will qualify for a 25% writing-down allowance on the reducing balance;
- the machine will have no further use other than in manufacturing the amplifier for JBZ;
- on ending the contract with JBZ, any outstanding capital allowances can be claimed as a balancing allowance;
- the company's cost of capital is 18%;
- the cost of materials and labour is forecast to increase by 5% per annum for years 2 and 3.

John Green reminds you that Sound Equipment operates a just-in-time stock policy and that production will be delivered immediately to JBZ, who will, under the terms of the contract, immediately pay for the deliveries. He also reminds you that suppliers are paid immediately on receipt of goods and that employees are also paid immediately.

Write a report to the financial director. Your report should:

(a) use the net present value technique to identify whether or not the initial three-year contract is worthwhile;

(b) explain your approach to taxation in your appraisal;

(c) identify *one* other factor to be considered before making a final decision.

*Notes*:
For the purpose of this task, you may assume the following:

- the machine would be purchased at the beginning of the accounting year;
- there is a one-year delay in paying corporation tax;
- all cashflows other than the purchase of the machine occur at the end of each year;
- Sound Equipment has no other assets on which to claim capital allowances.

*AAT Technicians Stage*

## 14.5 Intermediate: NPV calculation and taxation

*Data*

Tilsley Ltd manufactures motor vehicle components. It is considering introducing a new product. Helen Foster, the production director, has already prepared the following projections for this proposal:

| | **Year** | | | |
| | **1** | **2** | **3** | **4** |
| | **(£000)** | **(£000)** | **(£000)** | **(£000)** |
| Sales | 8 750 | 12 250 | 13 300 | 14 350 |
| Direct materials | 1 340 | 1 875 | 2 250 | 2 625 |
| Direct labour | 2 675 | 3 750 | 4 500 | 5 250 |
| Direct overheads | 185 | 250 | 250 | 250 |
| Depreciation | 2 500 | 2 500 | 2 500 | 2 500 |
| Interest | 1 012 | 1 012 | 1 012 | 1 012 |
| Profit before tax | 1 038 | 2 863 | 2 788 | 2 713 |
| Corporation tax @ 30% | 311 | 859 | 836 | 814 |
| Profit after tax | 727 | 2 004 | 1952 | 1 899 |

Helen Foster has recommended to the board that the project is not worthwhile because the cumulative after tax profit over the four years is less than the capital cost of the project.

As an assistant accountant at the company you have been asked by Philip Knowles, the chief accountant, to carry out a full financial appraisal of the proposal. He does not agree with Helen Foster's analysis, and provides you with the following information:

- the initial capital investment and working capital will be incurred at the beginning of the

first year. All other receipts and payments will occur at the end of each year.

- the equipment will cost £10 million;
- additional working capital of £1 million;
- this additional working capital will be recovered in full as cash at the end of the four-year period;
- the equipment will qualify for a 25% per annum reducing balance writing down allowance;
- any outstanding capital allowances at the end of the project can be claimed as a balancing allowance;
- at the end of the four-year period the equipment will be scrapped, with no expected residual value;
- the additional working capital required does not qualify for capital allowances, nor is it an allowable expense in calculating taxable profit;
- Tilsley Ltd pays corporation tax at 30% of chargeable profits;
- there is a one-year delay in paying tax;
- the company's cost of capital is 17%.

*Task*

Write a report to Philip Knowles. Your report should:

(a) evaluate the project using net present value techniques;

(b) recommend whether the project is worthwhile;

(c) explain how you have treated taxation in your appraisal;

(d) give *three* reasons why your analysis is different from that produced by Helen Foster, the production director.

*Notes*:
Risk and inflation can be ignored.

*AAT Technicians Stage*

## 14.6* Advanced: Relevant cash flows and taxation plus a calculation of the weighted average cost of capital

Ceely plc is evaluating a high risk project in a new industry. The company is temporarily short of accountants, and has asked an unqualified trainee to produce a draft financial evaluation of the project. This draft is shown below:

|  | (£000) | | | | | | |
|---|---|---|---|---|---|---|---|
| Year[1] | 0 | 1 | 2 | 3 | 4 | 5 | 6 |
| *Cash outflows* | | | | | | | |
| Long term capital: | | | | | | | |
|   Land and buildings | 500 | 600 | | | | | |
|   Plant and machinery | 700 | 1700 | | | | | |
| Working capital | | | | | | | |
|   (cumulative | | | | | | | |
|   requirement) | 230 | 570 | 680 | 700 | 720 | 740 | 740 |
| Sales | | 2950 | 3820 | 5200 | 5400 | 5600 | 5800 |
| Direct costs: | | | | | | | |
|   Materials | | 487 | 630 | 858 | 891 | 924 | 957 |
|   Labour | | 805 | 1043 | 1420 | 1474 | 1529 | 1583 |
|   Selling and | | 207 | 267 | 364 | 378 | 392 | 406 |
|   distribution | | | | | | | |
| | | 1499 | 1940 | 2642 | 2743 | 2845 | 2946 |
| Overheads | | 370 | 480 | 630 | 642 | 655 | 660 |
| Interest | | 214 | 610 | 610 | 610 | 610 | 610 |
| Depreciation | | 240 | 700 | 700 | 700 | 700 | 460 |
| Total cost | | 2323 | 3730 | 4582 | 4695 | 4810 | 4676 |
| Net profit before tax | | 627 | 90 | 618 | 705 | 790 | 1124 |
| Taxation at 40% | | 251 | 36 | 247 | 282 | 316 | 450 |
| Net profit after | | 376 | 54 | 371 | 423 | 474 | 674 |
|   taxation | | | | | | | |
| Net cash flows | (1200) | (1924) | 54 | 371 | 423 | 474 | 674 |
| Cash flows | | | | | | | |
|   discounted | | | | | | | |
|   at 30% per year | (1200) | (1480) | 32 | 169 | 148 | 124 | 140 |

The net present value is – £2 067 000

Conclusion: The project is not financially viable and should not be undertaken.

*Notes*:

[1] Year 0 is the present time, year 1 one year in the future etc.

Cash flows have been discounted at a high rate because of the high risk of the project.

Assume that you have been engaged as a financial consultant to Ceely plc. The following additional information is made available to you.

(i)    The company has a six year planning horizon for capital investments. The value of the investment at the end of six years is estimated to be five times the after tax operating cash flows of the sixth year.

(ii)   The project would be financed by two 15% debentures, one issued almost immediately and one in a year's time. The debentures would both have a maturity of 10 years.

(iii)  50% of the overheads would be incurred as a direct result of undertaking this project.

(iv)  Corporate taxation is at the rate of 40% payable one year in arrears.

(v)   Tax allowable depreciation is on a straight-line basis at a rate of 20% per year on the full historic cost of depreciable fixed assets. Land and buildings are not depreciable fixed assets and their total value is expected to be £1.1 million at the end of year six.

(vi)  The company is listed on the USM. Its current share price is £2.73, and its equity beta coefficient value is 1.1.

(vii)  The yield on Treasury Bills is 12% per year, and the average total yield from companies forming the Financial Times Actuaries All Share Index is 20% per year.

(viii) Interest rates are not expected to change significantly.

(ix)  The equity beta value of a company whose major activity is the manufacture of a similar product to that proposed in Ceely's new project is 1.5. Both companies have gearing levels of 60% equity and 40% debt (by market values). Ceely's gearing includes the new debenture issues.

Required:

(a)  Modify the draft financial evaluation of the project, where appropriate, to produce a revised estimate of the net present value of the project. Recommend whether the project should be accepted, and briefly discuss any reservations you have about the accuracy of your revised appraisal. State clearly any assumptions that you make.    (20 marks)

(b)  You are later told that the draft cash flow estimates did not include the effects of changing prices. Discuss whether, on the basis of this new information, any further amendments to your analysis might be necessary.   (5 marks)

(Total 25 marks)

*ACCA Level 3 Financial Management*

## 14.7 Advanced: Calculation of IRR and incremental yield involving identification of relevant cash flows

LF Ltd wishes to manufacture a new product. The company is evaluating two mutually exclusive machines, the Reclo and the Bunger. Each machine is expected to have a working life of four years, and is capable of a maximum annual output of 150 000 units.

Cost estimates associated with the two machines include:

| | Reclo £000 | Bunger £000 |
|---|---|---|
| Purchase price | 175 | 90 |
| Scrap value | 10 | 9 |
| Incremental working capital | 40 | 40 |
| Maintenance (per year) | 40 (20 in year 1) | |
| Supervisor | 20 | |
| Allocated central overhead | 35 | |
| Labour costs (per unit) | £1.30 | |
| Material costs (per unit) | £0.80 | |

The Reclo requires 120 square metres of operating space. LF Ltd currently pays £35 per square metre to rent a factory which has adequate spare space for the new product. There is no alternative use for this spare space. £5000 has been spent on a feasibility survey of the Reclo.

The marketing department will charge a fee of £75 000 per year for promoting the product, which will be incorporated into existing plans for catalogues and advertising. Two new salesmen will be employed by the marketing department solely for the new product, at a cost of £22 500 per year each. There are no other incremental marketing costs.

The selling price in year one is expected to be £3.50 per unit, with annual production and sales estimated at 130 000 units throughout the four year period. Prices and costs after the first year are expected to rise by 5% per year. Working capital will be increased by this amount from year one onwards.

Taxation is payable at 25% per year one year in arrears and a writing-down allowance of 25% per year is available on a reducing balance basis.

The company's accountant has already estimated the taxable operating cash flows (sales less relevant labour costs, materials costs etc., but before taking into account any writing-down allowances) of the second machine, the Bunger. These are:

| | **Bunger – £000** | | | |
|---|---|---|---|---|
| **Year** | **1** | **2** | **3** | **4** |
| Taxable operating cash flows | 50 | 53 | 55 | 59 |

Required:
(a) Calculate the expected internal rate of return (IRR) of each of the machines.
State clearly any assumptions that you make. (14 marks)
(b) Evaluate, using the incremental yield method, which, if either, of the two machines should be selected. (6 marks)
(c) Explain briefly why the internal rate of return is regarded as a relatively poor method of investment appraisal. (5 marks)
(Total 25 marks)
*ACCA Level 3 Financial Management*

**14.8\* Advanced: Single period capital rationing**
Banden Ltd is a highly geared company that wishes to expand its operations. Six possible capital investments have been identified, but the company only has access to a total of £620 000. The projects

are not divisible and may not be postponed until a future period. After the projects end it is unlikely that similar investment opportunities will occur.

**Expected net cash inflows (including salvage value)**

| Project | Year 1 (£) | 2 (£) | 3 (£) | 4 (£) | 5 (£) | Initial Outlay (£) |
|---|---|---|---|---|---|---|
| A | 70 000 | 70 000 | 70 000 | 70 000 | 70 000 | 246 000 |
| B | 75 000 | 87 000 | 64 000 | | | 180 000 |
| C | 48 000 | 48 000 | 63 000 | 73 000 | | 175 000 |
| D | 62 000 | 62 000 | 62 000 | 62 000 | | 180 000 |
| E | 40 000 | 50 000 | 60 000 | 70 000 | 40 000 | 180 000 |
| F | 35 000 | 82 000 | 82 000 | | | 150 000 |

Projects A and E are mutually exclusive. All projects are believed to be of similar risk to the company's existing capital investments.

Any surplus funds may be invested in the money market to earn a return of 9% per year. The money market may be assumed to be an efficient market.

Banden's cost of capital is 12% per year.

Required:
(a) Calculate:
  (i) The expected net present value;
  (ii) The expected profitability index associated with each of the six projects, and rank the projects according to both of these investment appraisal methods.
  Explain briefly why these rankings differ. (8 marks)
(b) Give reasoned advice to Banden Ltd recommending which projects should be selected. (6 marks)
(c) A director of the company has suggested that using the company's normal cost of capital might not be appropriate in a capital rationing situation. Explain whether you agree with the director. (4 marks)
(d) The director has also suggested the use of linear or integer programming to assist with the selection of projects. Discuss the advantages and disadvantages of these mathematical programming methods to Banden Ltd. (7 marks)
(Total 25 marks)
*ACCA Level 3 Financial Management*

**14.9 Advanced: Net present value calculation for the replacement of a machine and a discussion of the conflict between ROI and NPV**
Eckard plc is a large, all-equity financed, divisionalized textile company whose shares are listed on

the London Stock Exchange. It has a current cost of capital of 15%. The annual performance of its four divisions is assessed by their return on investment (ROI), i.e. net profit after tax divided by the closing level of capital employed. It is expected that the overall ROI for the company for the year ending 31 December 2000 will be 18%, with the towelling division having the highest ROI of 25%. The towelling division has a young, ambitious managing director who is anxious to maintain its ROI for the next two years, by which time he expects to be able to obtain a more prestigious job either within Eckard plc or elsewhere. He has recently turned down a proposal by his division's finance director to replace an old machine with a more modern one, on the grounds that the old one has an estimated useful life of four years and should be kept for that period. The finance director has appealed to the main board of directors of Eckard plc to reverse her managing director's decision.

The following estimates have been prepared by the finance director for the new machine:

*Investment cost*: £256 000, payable on 2 January 2001.

*Expected life*: four years to 31 December 2004.

*Disposal value*: equal to its tax written down value on 1 January 2004 and receivable on 31 December 2004.

*Expected cash flow savings*: £60 000 in 2001, rising by 10% in each of the next three years. These cash flows can be assumed to occur at the end of the year in which they arise.

*Tax position*: the company is expected to pay 35% corporation tax over the next four years. The machine is eligible for a 25% per annum writing down allowance. Corporation tax can be assumed to be paid 12 months after the accounting year-end on 31 December. No provision for deferred tax is considered to be necessary.

*Old machine to be replaced*: this would be sold on 2 January 2001 with an accounting net book value of £50 000 and a tax written down value of nil. Sale proceeds would be £40 000, which would give rise to a balancing charge. If retained for a further four years, the disposal value would be zero.

*Relevant accounting policies*: the company uses the straight-line depreciation method with a full year's depreciation being charged in both the year of acquisition and the year of disposal. The capital employed figure for the division comprises all assets excluding cash.

Requirements

(a) Calculate the net present value to Eckard plc of the proposed replacement of the old machine by the new one. (8 marks)

(b) Calculate, for the years 2001 and 2002 only, the effect of the decision to replace the old machine on the ROI of the towelling division. (7 marks)

(c) Prepare a report for the main board of directors recommending whether the new machine should be purchased. Your report should include a discussion of the effects that performance measurement systems can have on capital investment decisions. (10 marks)

(Total 25 marks)

*ICAEW P2 Financial Management*

### 14.10* Advanced: Timing of replacement decision

XYZ plc uses 10 very old injection moulding machines, which are of a type which are no longer obtainable. It is proposed that they be replaced by 4 'new model' machines with the same total capacity.

The old machines have a further life of 3 years and will have no salvage value at that time – the present salvage value averages £5000 per machine. Annual operating costs are £10 000 per machine.

Each new machine, which has a life of 7 years, costs £52 000 and is expected to have an end of life scrap value of £4000. Total annual operating costs are £15 000 per machine.

The 6 operators who would be released following replacement of the old machines would be redeployed within the firm thereby saving some additional external recruitment.

There is the possibility that the installation of the new machines would entail modifications, costing £60 000, to the factory building.

An appropriate discount rate suitable for the appraisal of all cash flows relevant to this decision is 12%.

Required:

Ignoring the possibility of modifications to the factory building determine whether the old machines should be replaced now or operated for a further 3 years.

Indicate how the costs of modifying the factory building should be included in the analysis.

Specify any assumptions and outline the

deficiencies inherent in your analysis. Taxation may be ignored. (12 marks)

*ACCA Level 3 Financial Management*

### 14.11 Advanced: Determining the optimum replacement period for a fleet of taxis

Eltern plc is an unlisted company with a turnover of £6 million which runs a small fleet of taxis as part of its business. The managers of the company wish to estimate how regularly to replace the taxis. The fleet costs a total of £55 000 and the company has just purchased a new fleet. Operating costs and maintenance costs increase as the taxis get older. Estimates of these costs and the likely resale value of the fleet at the end of various years are presented below.

| Year | 1 (£) | 2 (£) | 3 (£) | 4 (£) | 5 (£) |
|---|---|---|---|---|---|
| Operating costs | 23 000 | 24 500 | 26 000 | 28 000 | 44 000 |
| Maintenance costs | 6 800 | 9 200 | 13 000 | 17 000 | 28 000 |
| Resale value | 35 000 | 24 000 | 12 000 | 2 000 | 200 |

The company's cost of capital is 13% per year.

Required:

(a) Evaluate how regularly the company should replace its fleet of taxis. Assume all cash flows occur at the year end and are after taxation (where relevant). Inflation may be ignored. (10 marks)

(b) Briefly discuss the main problems of this type of evaluation. (4 marks)

*ACCA Level 3 Financial Management*

### 14.12* Advanced: Evaluation of projects with unequal lives

A2Z p.l.c. supports the concept of terotechnology or life cycle costing for new investment decisions covering its engineering activities. The financial side of this philosophy is now well established and its principles extended to all other areas of decision making.

The company is to replace a number of its machines and the Production Manager is torn between the Exe machine, a more expensive machine with a life of 12 years, and the Wye machine with an estimated life of 6 years. If the Wye machine is chosen it is likely that it would be replaced at the end of 6 years by another Wye machine. The pattern of maintenance and running costs differs between the two types of machine and relevant data are shown below.

| | Exe (£) | Wye (£) |
|---|---|---|
| Purchase price | 19 000 | 13 000 |
| Trade-in value | 3 000 | 3 000 |
| Annual repair costs | 2 000 | 2 600 |
| Overhaul costs | 4 000 (at year 8) | 2 000 (at year 4) |
| Estimated financing costs averaged over machine life | 10% p.a. | 10% p.a. |

You are required to

(a) recommend, with supporting figures, which machine to purchase, stating any assumptions made; (10 marks)

(b) describe an appropriate method of comparing replacement proposals with unequal lives; (4 marks)

(c) describe life cycle costing and give the benefits that are likely to accrue from its use. Support your answer with examples of changes in practice that could occur from adopting this philosophy. (6 marks)

(Total 20 marks)

*CIMA Stage 3 Management Accounting Techniques*

### 14.13 Advanced: Relevant cash flows and taxation plus unequal lives

Pavgrange plc is considering expanding its operations. The company accountant has produced *pro forma* profit and loss accounts for the next three years assuming that:

(a) The company undertakes no new investment.

(b) The company invests in Project 1.

(c) The company invests in Project 2.

Both projects have expected lives of three years, and the projects are mutually exclusive.

The *pro forma* accounts are shown below:

(a) *No new investment*

| Years | 1 (£000) | 2 (£000) | 3 (£000) |
|---|---|---|---|
| Sales | 6500 | 6950 | 7460 |
| Operating costs | 4300 | 4650 | 5070 |
| Depreciation | 960 | 720 | 540 |
| Interest | 780 | 800 | 800 |
| Profit before tax | 460 | 780 | 1050 |
| Taxation | 161 | 273 | 367 |
| Profit after tax | 299 | 507 | 683 |
| Dividends | 200 | 200 | 230 |
| Retained earnings | 99 | 307 | 453 |

(b) *Investment in Project 1*

| Years | 1 (£000) | 2 (£000) | 3 (£000) |
|---|---|---|---|
| Sales | 7340 | 8790 | 9636 |
| Operating costs | 4869 | 5620 | 6385 |
| Depreciation | 1460 | 1095 | 821 |
| Interest | 1000 | 1030 | 1030 |
| Profit before tax | 11 | 1045 | 1400 |
| Taxation | 4 | 366 | 490 |
| Profit after tax | 7 | 679 | 910 |
| Dividends | 200 | 200 | 230 |
| Retained earnings | (193) | 479 | 680 |

(c) *Investment in Project 2*

| Years | 1 (£000) | 2 (£000) | 3 (£000) |
|---|---|---|---|
| Sales | 8430 | 9826 | 11 314 |
| Operating costs | 5680 | 6470 | 7230 |
| Depreciation | 1835 | 1376 | 1032 |
| Interest | 1165 | 1205 | 1205 |
| Profit before tax | (250) | 775 | 1847 |
| Taxation | 0 | 184 | 646 |
| Profit after tax | (250) | 591 | 1201 |
| Dividends | 200 | 200 | 230 |
| Retained earnings | (450) | 391 | 971 |

The initial outlay for Project 1 is £2 million and for Project 2 £3½ million.

Tax allowable depreciation is at the rate of 25% on a reducing balance basis. The company does not expect to acquire or dispose of any fixed assets during the next three years other than in connection with Projects 1 or 2. Any investment in Project 1 or 2 would commence at the start of the company's next financial year.

The expected salvage value associated with the investments at the end of three years is £750 000 for Project 1, and £1 500 000 for Project 2.

Corporate taxes are levied at the rate of 35% and are payable one year in arrears.

Pavgrange would finance either investment with a three year term loan at a gross interest payment of 11% per year. The company's weighted average cost of capital is estimated to be 8% per annum.

Required:

(a) Advise the company which project (if either) it should undertake. Give the reasons for your choice and support it with calculations.
(12 marks)

(b) What further information might be helpful to the company accountant in the evaluation of these investments? (3 marks)

(c) If Project 1 had been for four years duration rather than three years, and the new net cash flows of the project (after tax and allowing for the scrap value) for years four and five were £77 000 and (£188 000) respectively, evaluate whether your advice to Pavgrange would change. (5 marks)

(d) Explain why the payback period and the internal rate of return might not lead to the correct decision when appraising mutually exclusive capital investments. (5 marks)

(Total 25 marks)

*ACCA Level 3 Financial Management*

**14.14\* Advanced: Inflation adjustments and sensitivity analysis**

(a) Burley plc, a manufacturer of building products, mainly supplies the wholesale trade. It has recently suffered falling demand due to economic recession, and thus has spare capacity. It now perceives an opportunity to produce designer ceramic tiles for the home improvement market. It has already paid £0.5m for development expenditure, market research and a feasibility study.

The initial analysis reveals scope for selling 150 000 boxes per annum over a five-year period at a price of £20 per box. Estimated operating costs, largely based on experience, are as follows:

Cost per box of tiles (£) (at today's prices):

| | |
|---|---|
| Material cost | 8.00 |
| Direct labour | 2.00 |
| Variable overhead | 1.50 |
| Fixed overhead (allocated) | 1.50 |
| Distribution, etc. | 2.00 |

Production can take place in existing facilities although initial re-design and set-up costs would be £2m after allowing for all relevant tax reliefs. Returns from the project would be taxed at 33%.

Burley's shareholders require a nominal return of 14% per annum after tax, which includes allowance for generally-expected inflation of 5.5% per annum. It can be assumed that all operating cash flows occur at year ends.

Required:
Assess the financial desirability of this venture in *real* terms, finding both the Net Present Value and the Internal Rate of Return to the nearest 1%) offered by the project.
*Note*: Assume no tax delay. (7 marks)

(b) Briefly explain the purpose of sensitivity analysis in relation to project appraisal, indicating the drawbacks with this procedure.
(6 marks)

(c) Determine the values of
  (i) price
  (ii) volume
at which the project's NPV becomes zero. Discuss your results, suggesting appropriate management action. (7 marks)
(Total 20 marks)
*ACCA Paper 8 Managerial Finance*

**14.15\* Advanced: Adjusting cash flows for inflation and identification of relevant cash flows**
Ramelton plc is a large entirely equity financed engineering company, whose financial year ends on 31 December.

The company's objective is to maximise shareholder's wealth, and it generates sufficient taxable profits to relieve all capital allowances at the earliest opportunity.

Currently one of the company's divisional managers has to fulfil a particular contract, and he can do this in one of two ways.

Under the first (Proposal 1), he can purchase plant and machinery; while under the second (Proposal 2), he can use a machine already owned by the company.

The end-year operating net cash inflows in nominal (i.e. money) terms and before corporation tax are as follows:

| | 2001 £ | 2002 £ | 2003 £ |
|---|---|---|---|
| Proposal 1 | 40 000 | 55 000 | 70 000 |
| Proposal 2 | 70 000 | 70 000 | — |

*Proposal 1*
Under the first proposal the company will incur an outlay of £62 500 on 31 December 2000 for the purchase of plant and machinery.

The labour force required under this proposal will have to be recruited locally, and budgeted wages have been taken into account in preparing the estimates of future nominal net cash inflows given above.

The plant and machinery is expected to be scrapped on 31 December 2003, the nominal cash proceeds at that date being projected as £5000.

*Proposal 2*
The second proposal covers a two year period from 31 December 2000. It will require the company to use a machine which was purchased for £150 000 a number of years ago when 100% first year capital allowances were available and which is therefore fully written down for tax purposes. The company has no current use for the machine, and its net realisable value at 31 December 2000 is £50 000.

However, if retained unused there would be no incremental costs of keeping it, and it would be sold on 1 January 2002 for an estimated £60 000 in nominal money terms. If used under the second proposal, the expected residual value of the machine would be zero at the end of the two year period.

The labour force required under the second proposal would be recruited from elsewhere within the company, and in end-year nominal cash flow terms would be paid £20 000 and £21 600 respectively for 2001 and 2002. However, the staff that would have to be taken on in other divisions to replace those switched over to the new project would in corresponding end-year nominal cash flow terms cost £22 000 for 2001 and £23 760 for 2002.

The end-year nominal net cash inflows of £70 000 for both 2001 and 2002 which are associated with the second proposal are after deducting the remuneration of the work force actually employed on the scheme.

*Working capital requirements*
Working capital requirements in nominal money terms at the beginning of each year are estimated at 10% of the end-year operating net cash inflows referred to in the table above.

The working capital funds will be released when a proposal is completed.

There are no tax effects associated with changes in working capital.

*Other information*
Expected annual inflation rates over the next four calendar years are:

| 2001 | 2002 | 2003 | 2004 |
|------|------|------|------|
| 10%  | 8%   | 6%   | 5%   |

The company's real cost of capital is estimated at 10% per annum and is expected to remain at that rate for the foreseeable future.

The corporation is expected to be 50% over the planning period, tax being payable twelve months after the accounting year end to which it relates.

The annual writing down allowance for plant and machinery is 20% reducing balance. A full writing down allowance is given in the year of acquisition, but none in the year of disposal. Any balancing charges or allowances are calculated for individual assets (i.e. they are not part of the general pool for tax purposes).

Requirements:
(a) Calculate the net present value at 31 December 2000 of each of the two mutually exclusive projects; and                                    (15 marks)
(b) indicate briefly any reservations you might have in basing an investment decision on these figures.
                                                              (3 marks)

*Note*: Calculate to the nearest £.
Show all calculations clearly.
Repetition of a project is not possible.
                                              (Total 18 marks)
*ICAEW Management Accounting and Financial Management 1*

### 14.16 Advanced: Adjusting cash flows for inflation and the calculation of NPV and ROI
The general manager of the nationalized postal service of a small country, Zedland, wishes to introduce a new service. This service would offer same-day delivery of letters and parcels posted before 10 am within a distance of 150 kilometres. The service would require 100 new vans costing $8000 each and 20 trucks costing $18 000 each. 180 new workers would be employed at an average annual wage of $13 000 and five managers at average annual salaries of $20 000 would be moved from their existing duties, where they would not be replaced.

Two postal rates are proposed. In the first year of operation letters will cost $0.525 and parcels $5.25. Market research undertaken at a cost of $50 000 forecasts that demand will average 15 000 letters per working day and 500 parcels per working day during the first year, and 20 000 letters per day and 750 parcels per day thereafter. There is a five day working week. Annual running and maintenance costs on similar new vans and trucks are currently estimated in the first year of operation to be $2000 per van and $4000 per truck respectively. These costs will increase by 20% per year (excluding the effects of inflation). Vehicles are depreciated over a five year period on a straight-line basis. Depreciation is tax allowable and the vehicles will have negligible scrap value at the end of five years. Advertising in year one will cost $500 000 and in year two $250 000. There will be no advertising after year two. Existing premises will be used for the new service but additional costs of $150 000 per year will be incurred.

All the above cost data are current estimates and exclude any inflation effects. Wage and salary costs and all other costs are expected to rise because of inflation by approximately 5% per year during the five year planning horizon of the postal service. The government of Zedland will not permit annual price increases within nationalized industries to exceed the level of inflation.

Nationalized industries are normally required by the government to earn at least an annual after tax return of 5% on average investment and to achieve, on average, at least zero net present value on their investments.

The new service would be financed half with internally generated funds and half by borrowing on the capital market at an interest rate of 12% per year. The opportunity cost of capital for the postal service is estimated to be 14% per year. Corporate taxes in Zedland, to which the postal service is subject, are at the rate of 30% for annual profits of up to $500 000 and 40% for the balance in excess of $500 000. Tax is payable one year in arrears. All transactions may be assumed to be on a cash basis and to occur at the end of the year with the exception of the initial investment which would be required almost immediately.

Required:

(a) Acting as an independent consultant prepare a report advising whether the new postal service should be introduced. Include in your report a discussion of other factors that might need to be taken into account before a final decision was made with respect to the introduction of the new postal service.

State clearly any assumptions that you make. (18 marks)

(b) Monte Carlo simulation has been suggested as a possible method of estimating the net present value of a project. Briefly assess the advantages and disadvantages of using this technique in investment appraisal. (7 marks)

(Total 25 marks)

*ACCA Level 3 Financial Management*

## 14.17 Advanced: Calculation of discounted payback and NPV incorporating inflation, tax and financing costs

The board of directors of Portand Ltd are considering two *mutually exclusive* investments each of which is expected to have a life of five years. The company does not have the physical capacity to undertake both investments. The first investment is relatively capital intensive whilst the second is relatively labour intensive.

Forecast profits of the two investments are:

*Investment 1 (requires four new workers)*

**(£000)**

| Year | 0 | 1 | 2 | 3 | 4 | 5 |
|---|---|---|---|---|---|---|
| Initial cost | (500) | | | | | |
| Projected sales | | 400 | 450 | 500 | 550 | 600 |
| Production costs | | 260 | 300 | 350 | 450 | 500 |
| Finance charges | | 21 | 21 | 21 | 21 | 21 |
| Depreciation[1] | | 125 | 94 | 70 | 53 | 40 |
| Profit before tax | | (6) | 35 | 59 | 26 | 39 |
| Average profit before tax £30 600. | | | | | | |

*Investment 2 (requires nine new workers)*

**(£000)**

| Year | 0 | 1 | 2 | 3 | 4 | 5 |
|---|---|---|---|---|---|---|
| Initial cost | (175) | | | | | |
| Projected sales | | 500 | 600 | 640 | 640 | 700 |
| Production costs | | 460 | 520 | 550 | 590 | 630 |
| Depreciation[1] | | 44 | 33 | 25 | 18 | 14 |
| Profit before tax | | (4) | 47 | 65 | 32 | 56 |
| Average profit before tax £39 200. | | | | | | |

[1]Depreciation is a tax allowable expense and is at 25% per year on a reducing balance basis. Both investments are of similar risk to the company's existing operations.

*Additional information*

(i) Tax and depreciation allowances are payable/receivable one year in arrears. Tax is at 25% per year.

(ii) Investment 2 would be financed from internal funds, which the managing director states have no cost to the company. Investment 1 would be financed by internal funds plus a £150 000 14% fixed rate term loan.

(iii) The data contains no adjustments for price changes. These have been ignored by the board of directors as both sales and production costs are expected to increase by 9% per year, after year one.

(iv) The company's real overall cost of capital is 7% per year and the inflation rate is expected to be 8% per year for the foreseeable future.

(v) All cash flows may be assumed to occur at the end of the year unless otherwise stated.

(vi) The company currently receives interest of 10% per year on short-term money market deposits of £350 000.

(vii) Both investments are expected to have negligible scrap value at the end of five years.

Director A favours Investment 2 as it has a larger average profit.

Director B favours Investment 1 which she believes has a quicker discounted payback period, based upon cash flows.

Director C argues that the company can make £35 000 per year on its money market investments and that, when risk is taken into account, there is little point in investing in either project.

Required:

(a) Discuss the validity of the arguments of each of Directors A, B and C with respect to the decision to select Investment 1, Investment 2 or neither. (7 marks)

(b) Verify whether or not Director B is correct in stating that Investment 1 has the quicker discounted payback period.

Evaluate which investment, if any, should be selected. All calculations must be shown. Marks will not be deducted for sensible rounding. State clearly any assumptions that you make. (14 marks)

(c) Discuss briefly what non-financial factors might influence the choice of investment. (4 marks)

(Total 25 marks)

*ACCA Level 3 Financial Management*

### 14.18* Advanced: Calculation of the internal rate of return using the interpolation method and a discussion of asset betas

Amble plc is evaluating the manufacture of a new consumer product. The product can be introduced quickly, and has an expected life of four years before it is replaced by a more efficient model. Costs associated with the product are expected to be:

*Direct costs* (per unit)

Labour:

3.5 skilled labour hours at £5 per hour
4 unskilled labour hours at £3 per hour

Materials:

6 kilos of material Z at £1.46 per kilo
Three units of component P at £4.80 per unit
One unit of component Q at £6.40
Other variable costs: £2.10 per unit

*Indirect costs*

Apportionment of management salaries £105 000 per year

Tax allowable depreciation of machinery £213 000 per year

Selling expenses (not including any salaries) £166 000 per year

Apportionment of head office costs £50 000 per year

Rental of buildings £100 000 per year

Interest charges £104 000 per year

Other overheads £70 000 per year (including apportionment of building rates £20 000. NB rates are a local tax on property).

If the new product is introduced it will be manufactured in an existing factory, and will have no effect on rates payable. The factory could be rented for £120 000 per year (not including rates), to another company if the product is not introduced.

New machinery costing £864 000 will be required. The machinery is to be depreciated on a straight-line basis over four years, and has an expected salvage value of £12 000 after four years. The machinery will be financed by a four year fixed rate bank loan at an interest rate of 12% per year. Additional working capital requirements may be ignored.

The product will require two additional managers to be recruited at an annual gross cost of £25 000 each, and one manager currently costing £20 000 will be moved from another factory where he will be replaced by a deputy manager at a cost of £17 000 per year. 70 000 kilos of material Z are already in stock and are not required for other production. The realisable value of the material is £99 000.

The price per unit of the product in the first year will be £110, and demand is projected at 12 000, 17 500, 18 000 and 18 500 units in years 1 to 4 respectively.

The inflation rate is expected to be approximately 5% per year, and prices will be increased in line with inflation. Wage and salary costs are expected to increase by 7% per year, and all other costs (including rent) by 5% per year. No price or cost increases are expected in the first year of production.

Corporate tax is at the rate of 35% payable in the year the profit occurs. Assume that all sales and costs are on a cash basis and occur at the end of the year, except for the initial purchase of machinery which would take place immediately. No stocks will be held at the end of any year.

Required:

(a) Calculate the expected internal rate of return (IRR) associated with the manufacture of the new product. (15 marks)

(b) What is meant by an asset beta?

If you were told that the company's asset beta is 1.2, the market return is 15% and the risk free rate is 8% discuss whether you would recommend introducing the new product. (5 marks)

(c) Amble is worried that the government might increase corporate tax rates.

Show by how much the tax rate would have to change before the project is not financially viable. A discount rate of 17% per year may be assumed for part (c).          (5 marks)
(Total 25 marks)
*ACCA Level 3 Financial Management*

**14.19\* Advanced: NPV calculation, choice of discount rate and sensitivity analysis**
The managing director of Tigwood Ltd believes that a market exists for 'microbooks'. He has proposed that the company should market 100 best-selling books on microfiche which can be read using a special microfiche reader that is connected to a television screen. A microfiche containing an entire book can be purchased from a photographic company at 40% of the average production cost of best-selling paperback books.

It is estimated that the average cost of producing paperback books is £1.50, and the average selling price of paperbacks is £3.95 each. Copyright fees of 20% of the average selling price of the paperback books would be payable to the publishers of the paperbacks plus an initial lump sum which is still being negotiated, but is expected to be £1.5 million. No tax allowances are available on this lump sum payment. An agreement with the publishers would be signed for a period of six years. Additional variable costs of staffing, handling and marketing are 20 pence per microfiche, and fixed costs are negligible.

Tigwood Ltd has spent £100 000 on market research, and expects sales to be 1 500 000 units per year at an initial unit price of £2.

The microfiche reader would be produced and marketed by another company.

Tigwood would finance the venture with a bank loan at an interest rate of 16% per year. The company's money (nominal) cost of equity and real cost of equity are estimated to be 23% per year and 12.6% per year respectively. Tigwood's money weighted average cost of capital and real weighted average cost of capital are 18% per year and 8% per year respectively. The risk free rate of interest is 11% per year and the market return is 17% per year.

Corporate tax is at the rate of 35%, payable in the year the profit occurs. All cash flows may be assumed to be at the year end, unless otherwise stated.

Required
(a) Calculate the expected net present value of the microbooks project.          (5 marks)
(b) Explain the reasons for your choice of discount rate in your answer to part (a). Discuss whether this rate is likely to be the most appropriate rate to use in the analysis of the proposed project.          (5 marks)
(c) (i) Using sensitivity analysis, estimate by what percentage each of the following would have to change before the project was no longer expected to be viable:
– initial outlay
– annual contribution
– the life of the agreement
– the discount rate.
(ii) What are the limitations of this sensitivity analysis?          (10 marks)
(d) What further information would be useful to help the company decide whether to undertake the microbook project?          (5 marks)
(Total 25 marks)
*ACCA Level 3 Financial Management*

**14.20 Advanced: Sensitivity analysis and alternative methods of adjusting for risk**
Parsifal Ltd is a private company whose ordinary shares are all held by its directors. The chairman has recently been impressed by the arguments advanced by a computer salesman, who has told him that Parsifal will be able to install a fully operational computer system for £161 500. This new system will provide all the data currently being prepared by a local data-processing service. This local service has a current annual cost of £46 000. According to the salesman, annual maintenance costs will be only £2000 and if properly maintained the equipment can be expected to last 'indefinitely'.

The chairman has asked the company accountant to evaluate whether purchase of the computer system is worthwhile. The accountant has spoken to a friend who works for a firm of management consultants. She has told him that Parsifal would probably have to employ two additional members of staff at a total cost of about £15 000 per annum and that there would be increased stationery and other related costs of approximately £4000 per annum if Parsifal purchased the computer system. She also estimates that the useful life of the system would be between 6 and 10 years, depending upon the rate of technological change and changes in the pattern of the business of Parsifal. The system would have no scrap or resale value at the end of its useful life.

The company accountant has prepared a net present value calculation by assuming that all the annual costs and savings were expressed in real terms and that the company had a real cost of capital of 5% per annum. He chose this course of action because he did not know either the expected rate of inflation of the cash flows or the cost of capital of Parsifal Ltd. All cash flows, except the initial cost of the system, will arise at the end of the year to which they relate.

You are required to:
(a) estimate, using the company accountant's assumptions, the life of the system which produces a zero net present value, (3 marks)
(b) estimate the internal real rate of return arising from purchase of the computer system, assuming that the system will last:
  (i)  for 6 years, and
  (ii) indefinitely, (5 marks)
(c) estimate the value of the annual running costs (maintenance, extra staff, stationery and other related costs) that will produce a net present value of zero, assuming that the system will last for 10 years, (3 marks)
(d) discuss how the company accountant should incorporate the information from parts (a), (b) and (c) above in his recommendation to the directors of Parsifal Ltd as to whether the proposed computer system should be purchased, (7 marks)
(e) discuss how the company accountant could improve the quality of his advice. (7 marks)
(Total 25 marks)

Ignore taxation

*ICAEW P2 Financial Management*

### 14.21* Advanced: Expected NPV calculation and taxes on cashflows

Blackwater plc, a manufacturer of speciality chemicals, has been reported to the anti-pollution authorities on several occasions in recent years, and fined substantial amounts for making excessive toxic discharges into local rivers. Both the environmental lobby and Blackwaters shareholders demand that it clean up its operations.

It is estimated that the total fines it may incur over the next four years can be summarised by the following probability distribution (all figures are expressed in present values):

| Level of fine | Probability |
| --- | --- |
| £0.5m | 0.3 |
| £1.4m | 0.5 |
| £2.0m | 0.2 |

Filta & Strayne Ltd (FSL), a firm of environmental consultants, has advised that new equipment costing £1m can be installed to virtually eliminate illegal discharges. Unlike fines, expenditure on pollution control equipment is tax-allowable via a 25% writing-down allowance (reducing balance). The rate of corporate tax is 33%, paid with a one-year delay. The equipment will have no resale value after its expected four-year working life, but can be in full working order immediately prior to Blackwater's next financial year.

A European Union Common Pollution Policy grant of 25% of gross expenditure is available, but with payment delayed by a year. Immediately on receipt of the grant from the EU, Blackwater will pay 20% of the grant to FSL as commission. These transactions have no tax implications for Blackwater.

A disadvantage of the new equipment is that it will raise production costs by £30 per tonne over its operating life. Current production is 10 000 tonnes per annum, but is expected to grow by 5% per annum compound. It can be assumed that other production costs and product price are constant over the next four years. No change in working capital is envisaged.

Blackwater applies a discount rate of 12% after all taxes to investment projects of this nature. All cash inflows and outflows occur at year ends.

Required:
(a) Calculate the expected net present value of the investment assuming a four-year operating period.
  Briefly comment on your results. (12 marks)
(b) Write a memorandum to Blackwater's management as to the desirability of the project, taking into account both financial and non-financial criteria. (8 marks)
(Total 20 marks)

*ACCA Paper 8 Managerial Finance*

## 14.22 Advanced: Calculation of expected net present value plus a discussion of whether expected values is an appropriate way of evaluating risk

Galuppi plc is considering whether to scrap some highly specialized old plant or to refurbish it for the production of drive mechanisms, sales of which will last for only three years. Scrapping the plant will yield £25 000 immediately, whereas refurbishment will require an immediate outlay of £375 000.

Each drive mechanism will sell for £50 and, if manufactured entirely by Galuppi plc, give a contribution at current prices of £10. All internal company costs and selling prices are predicted to increase from the start of each year by 5%. Refurbishment of the plant will also entail fixed costs of £10 000, £12 500 and £15 000 for the first, second and third years respectively.

Estimates of product demand depend on different economic conditions. Three have been identified as follows:

| Economic condition | Probability of occurrence | Demand in the first year (units) |
|---|---|---|
| A | 0.25 | 10 000 |
| B | 0.45 | 15 000 |
| C | 0.3 | 20 000 |

Demand in subsequent years is expected to increase at 20% per annum, regardless of the initial level demanded.

The plant can produce up to 20 000 drive mechanisms per year, but Galuppi plc can supply more by contracting to buy partially completed mechanisms from an overseas supplier at a fixed price of £20 per unit. To convert a partially completed mechanism into the finished product requires additional work amounting, at current prices, to £25 per unit. For a variety of reasons the supplier is only willing to negotiate contracts in batches of 2000 units.

All contracts to purchase the partially completed units must be signed one year in advance, and payment made by Galuppi plc at the start of the year in which they are to be used.

Galuppi plc has a cost of capital of 15% per annum, and you may assume that all cash flows arise at the end of the year, unless you are told otherwise.

Requirements:
(a) Determine whether refurbishment of the plant is worthwhile. (17 marks)

(b) Discuss whether the expected value method is an appropriate way of evaluating the different risks inherent in the refurbishment decision of Galuppi plc. (8 marks)
(Total 25 marks)
*ICAEW P2 Financial Management*

## 14.23* Advanced: Expected net present value and value of additional information

The directors of Astros plc are considering the purchase and exploitation of a disused tin mine which is being offered for sale for £50 000. A review of the mine's history shows that the total amount of pure tin that can be extracted depends upon the type of rock formations in the area and that only the following three possibilities exist:

| Rock type | Total tin output | Probability |
|---|---|---|
| A | 240 tonnes | 0.4 |
| B | 120 tonnes | 0.4 |
| C | 72 tonnes | 0.2 |

If Astros purchases the mine, the first year of ownership will be spent in making the mine and associated smelting plants operational, at a cost of £95 000 payable at the end of the year. Production will start at the beginning of the second year of ownership, when the output of pure tin will be 2 tonnes per month, whatever the type of rock formations. This production rate will remain unchanged until the mine is exhausted. During the first year of production, the directors expect that the resale value of the tin will be £9900 per tonne and that labour and other production costs will be £187 000. These revenues and costs are expected to rise by 10% per annum in subsequent years. These cash flows can be assumed to occur at the end of the year in which they arise.

Special mining equipment will also be purchased at the beginning of the first year of production at a cost of £48 000. This equipment will be sold immediately on the cessation of production, at an amount expected to equal its purchase price, less £200 for every tonne of tin produced during its life. Other revenues from the sale of the mine at the end of production are expected to equal the closure costs exactly.

Astros plc has received permission from the present owners of the mine to carry out a geological survey of the area. The survey would cost £10 000 and would reveal for certain the type of rock formations in the area and hence how much tin could be produced from the mine.

Astros plc has a money cost of capital of 21% per annum for this type of project.

You are required to:

(a) calculate the expected net present value of purchasing the mine, assuming that the geological survey is *not* undertaken, (15 marks)

(b) advise the directors of Astros plc whether or not they should commission the geological survey. (10 marks)

Ignore taxation.

(Total 25 marks)
*ICAEW P2 Financial Management*

## 14.24 Advanced: Calculation of NPV from incomplete data involving taxation, financing costs and identification of relevant cash flows and cost of capital

An unqualified colleague has recently been moved to another office whilst part way through a job. His working notes on a capital investment project have been given to you.

**AXT project (working draft)**
**(£000)**

| | Year 0 | 1 | 2 | 3 | 4 |
|---|---|---|---|---|---|
| Sales | | | 4500 | 5300 | 6000 |
| *Outflows* | | | | | |
| Materials | | 200 | 850 | 1200 | 1320 |
| Wages | | 180 | 960 | 1200 | 1360 |
| Salaries | | | 50 | 110 | 130 | 150 |
| Head office overhead | | 85 | 90 | 95 | 100 |
| Other fixed costs | | 20 | 400 | 420 | 440 |
| Market research | 110 | | | | |
| Warehouse rent | | 40 | 40 | 40 | 40 |
| Opportunity costs: | | | | | |
|   Labour | | 80 | 80 | | |
|   Warehouse space | | 60 | 60 | 60 | 60 |
|   Exports | | 110 | 110 | 110 | 110 |
| Interest | | 70 | 286 | 286 | 286 |
| Tax allowable depreciation | | 135 | 391 | 293 | 220 |
| Profit before tax | (110) | (1030) | 1123 | 1466 | 1914 |
| Tax | (36) | (340) | 371 | 484 | 632 |
| Other outflows | | | | | |
|   Land | 300 | | | | |
|   Building | 240 | 510 | | | |
|   Machinery | | 650 | | | (80) |
| Total working capital | | 400 | 440 | 460 | 480 |
| Net flows | (614) | (2250) | 312 | 522 | 882 |

*Working notes*:

(i) The investment will be financed by a 12% fixed rate term loan, £540 000 to be drawn

down immediately, £1 560 000 to be drawn down at the end of year one.

(ii) Working capital of £480 000 is expected to be returned in full in year five.

(iii) Highly skilled labour would need to be taken from other jobs losing £80 000 per year post-tax contributions for two years. These workers could not be replaced in the other jobs.

(iv) The warehouse space could be rented to another company for £60 000 per year if not used for this investment.

(v) The project will result in a reduction in existing exports of another product, causing pre-tax contributions to fall by £110 000 per year.

(vi) One manager, at an initial year one salary of £25 000 per year (increasing by 5% per year) will be transferred from another division. If he had not been transferred he would have been made redundant at an immediate after tax cost to the company of £40 000. This manager is additional to the salaries shown in the working draft.

(vii) Data includes the estimated effects of inflation on costs and prices wherever relevant.

(viii) Head office cash flows for overhead will increase by £40 000 as a result of the project in year one, rising by £5000 per year after year one.

(ix) Tax is at a rate of 33% per year payable one year in arrears. The company has other profitable projects.

(x) Tax allowable depreciation is 2.5% per year straight line on buildings and 25% per year reducing balance on machinery.

(xi) Land and buildings are expected to increase in value by 5% per year.

(xii) The company's cost of capital is 16%.

(xiii) Company equity beta is 1.3
Company asset beta is 1.1
Average equity beta of companies in the same industry as the new AXT project is 1.5
Average asset beta of companies in the same industry as the new AXT project is 1.2
The market return is 15% per year and the risk free rate 6% per year.

(xiv) Company gearing:
Book value 60% equity, 40% debt
Market value 76% equity, 24% debt.

(xv) The market research survey was undertaken last month.

(xvi) The company has a time horizon of three years of sales for evaluating this investment.

Required:
(a) Using the working draft and any other relevant information, complete the appraisal of the AXT project.

There are no arithmetic errors in the working draft, but there might be errors of principle that result in incorrect data.

State clearly any assumptions that you make. (20 marks)

(b) Discuss possible limitations of net present value as the decision criterion for a capital investment. (5 marks)

(Total 25 marks)

*ACCA Level 3 Financial Management*

# Information for Planning, Control and Performance Measurement

The objective in this section is to consider the implementation of decisions through the planning and control process. Planning involves systematically looking at the future, so that decisions can be made today which will bring the company its desired results. Control can be defined as the process of measuring and correcting actual performance to ensure that plans for implementing the chosen course of action are carried out.

Part Four contains seven chapters. Chapter 15 considers the role of budgeting within the planning process and the relationship between the long-range plan and the budgeting process. The budgeting process in profit-oriented organizations is compared with that in non-profit organizations.

Chapters 16–19 are concerned with the control process. To fully understand the role that management accounting control systems play in the control process, it is necessary to be aware of how they relate to the entire array of control mechanisms used by organizations. Chapter 16 describes the different types of controls that are used by companies. The elements of management accounting control systems are described within the context of the overall control process. To design effective management accounting control systems it is necessary to consider the circumstances in which they will be used. There is no universally best management accounting control system which can be applied to all organizations. The applicability of a management accounting control system is contingent on the circumstances faced by organizations. Chapter 17 describes the contingency theory of management accounting. In addition, the role of management accounting is examined within a social, organizational and political context. Chapters 18 and 19 focus on the technical aspects of accounting control systems. They describe the major features of a standard costing system: a system that enables the differences between the planned and actual outcomes to be analysed in detail. Chapter 18 describes the operation of a standard costing system and explains the procedure for calculating the variances. Chapter 19 examines the difficulties that arise from using standard costing in today's environment, and looks at some suggestions for overcoming them.

Chapters 20 and 21 examine the special problems of control and measuring performance of divisions and other decentralized units within an organization. Chapter 20 considers how divisional financial performance measures might be devised which will motivate managers to pursue overall organizational goals. Chapter 21 focuses on the transfer pricing problem and examines how transfer prices can be established that will motivate managers to make optimal decisions and also ensure that the performance measures derived from using the transfer prices represent a fair reflection of managerial performance.

# 15

# The budgeting process

In the previous seven chapters we have considered how management accounting can assist managers in making decisions. The actions that follow managerial decisions normally involve several aspects of the business, such as the marketing, production, purchasing and finance functions, and it is important that management should coordinate these various interrelated aspects of decision-making. If they fail to do this, there is a danger that managers may each make decisions that they believe are in the best interests of the organization when, in fact, taken together they are not; for example, the marketing department may introduce a promotional campaign that is designed to increase sales demand to a level beyond that which the production department can handle. The various activities within a company should be coordinated by the preparation of plans of actions for future periods. These detailed plans are usually referred to as budgets.

Our objective in this chapter is to focus on the planning process within a business organization and to consider the role of budgeting within this process. What do we mean by planning? Planning is the design of a desired future and of effective ways of bringing it about (Ackoff, 1981). A distinction is normally made between short-term planning (budgeting) and long-range planning, alternatively known as strategic or corporate planning. How is long-range planning distinguished from other forms of planning? Sizer (1989) defines long-range planning as a systematic and formalized process for purposely directing and controlling future operations towards desired objectives for periods extending beyond one year. Short-term planning or budgeting, on the other hand, must accept the environment of today, and the physical, human and financial resources at present available to the firm. These are to a considerable extent determined by the quality of the firm's long-range planning efforts.

## Learning objectives

After studying this chapter, you should be able to:

- explain how budgeting fits into the overall framework of decision-making, planning and control;
- describe the six different purposes of budgets;
- describe the various stages in the budget process;
- prepare functional and master budgets;
- describe the limitations of incremental budgeting;
- describe activity-based budgeting;
- explain the role of budgeting and planning, programming budgeting systems in non-profit organizations;
- describe zero-base budgeting.

# Stages in the planning process

To help you understand the budgetary process we shall begin by looking at how it fits into an overall framework of planning, decision-making and control. A model of this process is presented in Figure 15.1. The framework outlined in this model will be used to illustrate the role of long-term and short-term planning within the overall planning and control process. The first stage involves establishing the objectives of the organization.

## STAGE 1: ESTABLISHING OBJECTIVES

Establishing objectives is an essential pre-requisite of the planning process. In all organizations employees must have a good understanding of what the organization is trying to achieve. Strategic or long-range planning therefore begins with the specification of the objectives towards which future operations should be directed. The attainment of objectives should be measurable in some way and ideally people should be motivated by them. Johnson and Scholes (1999) distinguish between three different objectives, which form a hierarchy: the 'mission' of an organization, corporate objectives and unit objectives.

The mission of an organization describes in very general terms the broad purpose and reason for an organization's existence, the nature of the business(es) it is in and the customers it seeks to serve and satisfy. It is a visionary projection of the central and overriding concepts on which the organization is based. Objectives tend to be more specific, and represent desired states or results to be achieved.

Corporate objectives relate to the organization as a whole. They are normally measurable and are expressed in financial terms such as desired profits or sales levels, return on capital employed, rates of growth or market share. Corporate objectives are normally formulated by members of the board of directors and handed down to senior managers. It is important that senior managers in an organization understand clearly where their company is going and why and how their own role contributes to the attainment of corporate objectives. Once the overall objectives of the organization have been established they must be broken down into subsidiary objectives relating to areas such as product range, market segmentation, customer service and so on. Objectives must also be developed for the different parts of an organization. Unit objectives relate to the specific objectives of individual units within the organization, such as a division or one company within a holding company. Corporate objectives are normally set for the organization as a whole and are then translated into unit objectives, which become the targets for the individual units. You should note that the expression aims is sometimes used as an alternative to mission and the term goals is synonymous with objectives.

## STAGE 2: IDENTIFY POTENTIAL STRATEGIES

The next stage shown in Figure 15.1 is to identify a range of possible courses of action (or strategies) that might enable the company's objectives to be achieved. The corporate strategy literature advocates that, prior to developing strategies, it is necessary to undertake a strategic analysis to become better informed about the organization's present strategic situation. This involves understanding the company's present position, its strengths and weaknesses and its opportunities and risks.

Having undertaken a strategic analysis, the next stage is to identify alternative strategies. The identification of strategies should take into account the following:

**FIGURE 15.1** *The role of long- and short-term planning within the planning, decision-making and control process.*

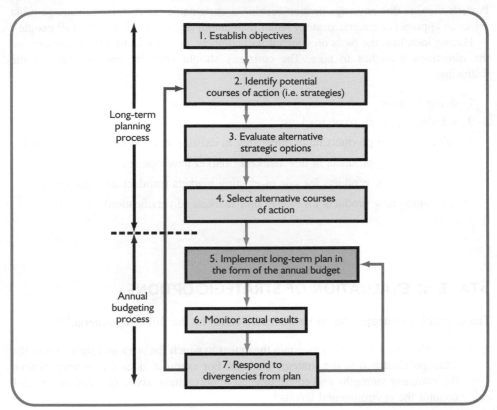

1. the generic strategy to be pursued (i.e. the basis on which the organization will compete or sustain excellence).
2. the alternative directions in which the organization may wish to develop.

An organization should determine the basis on which it will compete and/or sustain a superior level of performance (i.e. the generic strategy that it will follow). The purpose is to ensure that deliberate choices are made regarding the type of competitive advantage it wishes to attain. Porter (1985) has identified three **generic strategies** that an organization can follow:

1. *cost leadership*, whereby the organization aims to be the lowest cost producer within the industry;
2. *differentiation*, through which the organization seeks some unique dimension in its product/service that is valued by consumers, and which can command a premium price;
3. *focus*, whereby the organization determines the way in which the strategy is focused at particular parts of the market. For example, a product or service may be aimed at a particular buyer group, segment of the product line or smaller geographical area. An organization that adopts a focused strategy aimed at narrow segments of the market to the exclusion of others also needs to determine whether within the segment it will compete through cost leadership or differentiation. Small companies often follow very focused or *niche* strategies by becoming so specialized in meeting the needs of

a very small part of the market that they are secure against competition from large organizations.

Porter's view is that any organization seeking a sustainable competitive advantage must select an appropriate generic strategy rather than attempting to be 'all things to all people'.

Having identified the basis on which it will compete, an organization should determine the directions it wishes to take. The company should consider one or more of the following:

1. doing nothing;
2. withdrawing from some markets;
3. selling existing products more effectively in existing markets (market penetration);
4. selling existing products in new markets (market development);
5. developing new products for sale in existing markets (product development);
6. developing new products for sale in new markets (diversification).

## STAGE 3: EVALUATION OF STRATEGIC OPTIONS

The alternative strategies should be examined based on the following criteria:[1]

1. *suitability*, which seeks to ascertain the extent to which the proposed strategies fit the situation identified in the strategic analysis. For example, does the strategy exploit the company strengths and environmental opportunities, avoid the weaknesses and counter the environmental threats?
2. *feasibility*, which focuses on whether the strategy can be implemented in resource terms. For example, can the strategy be funded? Can the necessary market position be achieved? Can the company cope with the competitive reactions?
3. *acceptability*, which is concerned with whether a particular strategy is acceptable. For example, will it be sufficiently profitable? Is the level of risk acceptable?

The above criteria represent a broad framework of general criteria against which strategic options can be judged. The criteria narrow down the options to be considered for a detailed evaluation. The evaluation of the options should be based on the approaches described in Chapters 13 and 14 and will not be repeated here. Management should select those strategic options that have the greatest potential for achieving the company's objectives. There could be just one strategy chosen or several.

## STAGE 4: SELECT COURSE OF ACTION

When management has selected those strategic options that have the greatest potential for achieving the company's objectives, long-term plans should be created to implement the strategies. A **long-term plan** is a statement of the preliminary targets and activities required by an organization to achieve its strategic plans together with a broad estimate for each year of the resources required.

Because long-term planning involves 'looking into the future' for several years ahead the plans tend to be uncertain, general in nature, imprecise and subject to change.

## STAGE 5: IMPLEMENTATION OF THE LONG-TERM PLANS

Budgeting is concerned with the implementation of the long-term plan for the year ahead. Because of the shorter planning horizon budgets are more precise and detailed. Budgets are a clear indication of what is expected to be achieved during the budget period whereas long-term plans represent the broad directions that top management intend to follow.

The budget is not something that originates 'from nothing' each year – it is developed within the context of ongoing business and is ruled by previous decisions that have been taken within the long-term planning process. When the activities are initially approved for inclusion in the long-term plan, they are based on uncertain estimates that are projected for several years. These proposals must be reviewed and revised in the light of more recent information. This review and revision process frequently takes place as part of the annual budgeting process, and it may result in important decisions being taken on possible activity adjustments within the current budget period. The budgeting process cannot therefore be viewed as being purely concerned with the current year – it must be considered as an integrated part of the long-term planning process.

## STAGES 6 AND 7: MONITOR ACTUAL OUTCOMES RESPOND TO DIVERGENCIES FROM PLANNED OUTCOMES

The final stages in the decision-making, planning and control process outlined in Figure 15.1 are to compare the actual and the planned outcomes, and to respond to any divergencies from the plan. These stages represent the control process of budgeting, but a detailed discussion of this process will be deferred until Chapter 16. Let us now consider the short-term budgeting process in more detail.

# The multiple functions of budgets

Budgets serve a number of useful purposes. They include:

1. *planning* annual operations;
2. *coordinating* the activities of the various parts of the organization and ensuring that the parts are in harmony with each other;
3. *communicating* plans to the various responsibility centre managers;
4. *motivating* managers to strive to achieve the organizational goals;
5. *controlling* activities;
6. *evaluating* the performance of managers.

Let us now examine each of these six factors.

## PLANNING

The major planning decisions will already have been made as part of the long-term planning process. However, the annual budgeting process leads to the refinement of those plans, since managers must produce detailed plans for the implementation of the long-range plan. Without the annual budgeting process, the pressures of day-to-day operating problems may tempt managers not to plan for future operations. The budgeting process ensures that managers do plan for future operations, and that they consider how conditions in the next year might change and what steps they should take now to respond to these changed conditions. This process encourages managers to anticipate problems before they arise, and hasty decisions that are made on the spur of the moment, based on expediency rather than reasoned judgement, will be minimized.

## COORDINATION

The budget serves as a vehicle through which the actions of the different parts of an organization can be brought together and reconciled into a common plan. Without any guidance, managers may each make their own decisions, believing that they are working in the best interests of the organization. For example, the purchasing manager may prefer to place large orders so as to obtain large discounts; the production manager will be concerned with avoiding high stock levels; and the accountant will be concerned with the impact of the decision on the cash resources of the business. It is the aim of budgeting to reconcile these differences for the good of the organization as a whole, rather than for the benefit of any individual area. Budgeting therefore compels managers to examine the relationship between their own operations and those of other departments, and, in the process, to identify and resolve conflicts.

## COMMUNICATION

If an organization is to function effectively, there must be definite lines of communication so that all the parts will be kept fully informed of the plans and the policies, and constraints, to which the organization is expected to conform. Everyone in the organization should have a clear understanding of the part they are expected to play in achieving the annual budget. This process will ensure that the appropriate individuals are made accountable for implementing the budget. Through the budget, top management communicates its expectations to lower level management, so that all members of the organization may understand these expectations and can coordinate their activities to attain them. It is not just the budget itself that facilitates communication – much vital information is communicated in the actual act of preparing it.

## MOTIVATION

The budget can be a useful device for influencing managerial behaviour and motivating managers to perform in line with the organizational objectives. A budget provides a standard that under certain circumstances, a manager may be motivated to strive to achieve. However, budgets can also encourage inefficiency and conflict between managers. If individuals have actively participated in preparing the budget, and it is used as a tool to assist managers in managing their departments, it can act as a strong motivational device by providing a challenge. Alternatively, if the budget is dictated from above, and imposes a threat rather than a challenge, it may be resisted and do more harm than good. We shall discuss the dysfunctional motivational consequence of budgets in Chapter 16.

## CONTROL

A budget assists managers in managing and controlling the activities for which they are responsible. By comparing the actual results with the budgeted amounts for different categories of expenses, managers can ascertain which costs do not conform to the original plan and thus require their attention. This process enables management to operate a system of **management by exception** which means that a manager's attention and effort can be concentrated on significant deviations from the expected results. By investigating the reasons for the deviations, managers may be able to identify inefficiencies such as the purchase of inferior quality materials. When the reasons for the inefficiencies have been found, appropriate control action should be taken to remedy the situation.

## PERFORMANCE EVALUATION

A manager's performance is often evaluated by measuring his or her success in meeting the budgets. In some companies bonuses are awarded on the basis of an employee's ability to achieve the targets specified in the periodic budgets, or promotion may be partly dependent upon a manager's budget record. In addition, the manager may wish to evaluate his or her own performance. The budget thus provides a useful means of informing managers of how well they are performing in meeting targets that they have previously helped to set. The use of budgets as a method of performance evaluation also influences human behaviour, and for this reason we shall consider the behavioural aspects of performance evaluation in Chapter 16.

# Conflicting roles of budgets

Because a single budget system is normally used to serve several purposes there is a danger that they may conflict with each other. For instance the planning and motivation roles may be in conflict with each other. Demanding budgets that may not be achieved may be appropriate to motivate maximum performance, but they are unsuitable for planning purposes. For these a budget should be set based on easier targets that are expected to be met.

There is also a conflict between the planning and performance evaluation roles. For planning purposes budgets are set in advance of the budget period based on an anticipated set of circumstances or environment. Performance evaluation should be based on a comparison of actual performance with an adjusted budget to reflect the circumstances under which managers actually operated. In practice, many firms compare actual performance with the original budget (adjusted to the actual level of activity, i.e. a flexible budget), but if the circumstances envisaged when the original budget was set have changed then there will be a planning and evaluation conflict.

# The budget period

The conventional approach is that once per year the manager of each budget centre prepares a detailed budget for one year. The budget is divided into either twelve monthly or thirteen four-weekly periods for control purposes.

An alternative approach is for the annual budget to be broken down by months for the first three months, and by quarters for the remaining nine months. The quarterly budgets are then developed on a monthly basis as the year proceeds. For example, during the first quarter, the monthly budgets for the second quarter will be prepared; and during the second quarter, the monthly budgets for the third quarter will be prepared. The quarterly budgets may also be reviewed as the year unfolds. For example, during the first quarter, the budget for the next three quarters may be changed as new information becomes available. A new budget for a fifth quarter will also be prepared. This process is known as continuous or rolling budgeting, and ensures that a twelve month budget is always available by adding a quarter in the future as the quarter just ended is dropped. Contrast this with a budget prepared once per year. As the year goes by, the period for which a budget is available will shorten until the budget for next year is prepared. Rolling budgets also ensure that planning is not something that takes place once a year when the budget is being formulated. Instead, budgeting is a continuous process, and managers are encouraged to constantly look ahead and review future plans. Furthermore, it is likely that actual performance will be compared with a more realistic target, because budgets are being constantly reviewed and updated.

Irrespective of whether the budget is prepared on an annual or a continuous basis, it is important that monthly or four-weekly budgets be used for *control* purposes.

# Administration of the budgeting process

It is important that suitable administration procedures be introduced to ensure that the budget process works effectively. In practice, the procedures should be tailor-made to the requirements of the organization, but as a general rule a firm should ensure that procedures are established for approving the budgets and that the appropriate staff support is available for assisting managers in preparing their budgets.

## THE BUDGET COMMITTEE

The budget committee should consist of high-level executives who represent the major segments of the business. Its major task is to ensure that budgets are realistically established and that they are coordinated satisfactorily. The normal procedure is for the functional heads to present their budget to the committee for approval. If the budget does not reflect a reasonable level of performance, it will not be approved and the functional head will be required to adjust the budget and re-submit it for approval. It is important that the person whose performance is being measured should agree that the revised budget can be achieved; otherwise, if it is considered to be impossible to achieve, it will not act as a motivational device. If budget revisions are made, the budgetees should at least feel that they were given a fair hearing by the committee. We shall discuss budget negotiation in more detail later in this chapter.

The budget committee should appoint a budget officer, who will normally be the accountant. The role of the budget officer is to coordinate the individual budgets into a budget for the whole organization, so that the budget committee and the budgetee can see the impact of an individual budget on the organization as a whole.

## ACCOUNTING STAFF

The accounting staff will normally assist managers in the preparation of their budgets; they will, for example, circulate and advise on the instructions about budget preparation, provide past information that may be useful for preparing the present budget, and ensure that managers submit their budgets on time. The accounting staff do not determine the content of the various budgets, but they do provide a valuable advisory and clerical service for the line managers.

## BUDGET MANUAL

A budget manual should be prepared by the accountant. It will describe the objectives and procedures involved in the budgeting process and will provide a useful reference source for managers responsible for budget preparation. In addition, the manual may include a timetable specifying the order in which the budgets should be prepared and the dates when they should be presented to the budget committee. The manual should be circulated to all individuals who are responsible for preparing budgets.

# Stages in the budgeting process

The important stages are as follows:

1. communicating details of budget policy and guidelines to those people responsible for the preparation of budgets;
2. determining the factor that restricts output;
3. preparation of the sales budget;
4. initial preparation of various budgets;
5. negotiation of budgets with superiors;
6. coordination and review of budgets;
7. final acceptance of budgets;
8. ongoing review of budgets.

Let us now consider each of these stages in more detail.

## COMMUNICATING DETAILS OF THE BUDGET POLICY

Many decisions affecting the budget year will have been taken previously as part of the long-term planning process. The long-range plan is therefore the starting point for the preparation of the annual budget. Thus top management must communicate the policy effects of the long-term plan to those responsible for preparing the current year's budgets. Policy effects might include planned changes in sales mix, or the expansion or contraction of certain activities. In addition, other important guidelines that are to govern the preparation of the budget should be specified – for example the allowances that are to be made for price and wage increases, and the expected changes in productivity. Also, any expected changes in industry demand and output should be communicated by top management to the managers responsible for budget preparation. It is essential that all managers be made aware of the policy of top management for implementing the long-term plan in the current year's budget so that common guidelines can be established. The process also indicates to the managers responsible for preparing the budgets how they should respond to any expected environmental changes.

## DETERMINING THE FACTOR THAT RESTRICTS PERFORMANCE

In every organization there is some factor that restricts performance for a given period. In the majority of organizations this factor is sales demand. However, it is possible for production capacity to restrict performance when sales demand is in excess of available capacity. Prior to the preparation of the budgets, it is necessary for top management to determine the factor that restricts performance, since this factor determines the point at which the annual budgeting process should begin.

## PREPARATION OF THE SALES BUDGET

The volume of sales and the sales mix determine the level of a company's operations, when sales demand is the factor that restricts output. For this reason, the sales budget is the most important plan in the annual budgeting process. This budget is also the most difficult plan to produce, because total sales revenue depends on the actions of customers. In addition, sales demand may be influenced by the state of the economy or the actions of competitors.

## INITIAL PREPARATION OF BUDGETS

The managers who are responsible for meeting the budgeted performance should prepare the budget for those areas for which they are responsible. The preparation of the budget should be a 'bottom-up' process. This means that the budget should originate at the lowest levels of management and be refined and coordinated at higher levels. The justification for this approach is that it enables managers to participate in the preparation of their budgets and increases the probability that they will accept the budget and strive to achieve the budget targets.

There is no single way in which the appropriate quantity for a particular budget item is determined. Past data may be used as the starting point for producing the budgets, but this does not mean that budgeting is based on the assumption that what has happened in the past will occur in the future. Changes in future conditions must be taken into account, but past information may provide useful guidance for the future. In addition, managers may look to the guidelines provided by top management for determining the content of their budgets. For example, the guidelines may provide specific instructions as to the content of their budgets and the permitted changes that can be made in the prices of purchases of materials and services. For production activities standard costs may be used as the basis for costing activity volumes which are planned in the budget.

## NEGOTIATION OF BUDGETS

To implement a participative approach to budgeting, the budget should be originated at the lowest level of management. The managers at this level should submit their budget to their superiors for approval. The superior should then incorporate this budget with other budgets for which he or she is responsible and then submit this budget for approval to his or her superior. The manager who is the superior then becomes the budgetee at the next higher

**FIGURE 15.2** *An illustration of budgets moving up the organization hierarchy.*

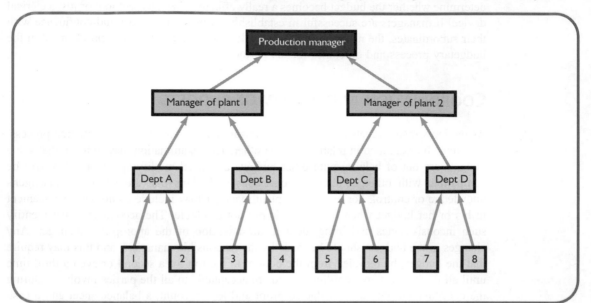

level. The process is illustrated in Figure 15.2. Sizer (1989) describes this approach as a two-way process of a top-down statement of objectives and strategies, bottom-up budget preparation and top-down approval by senior management.

The lower-level managers are represented by boxes 1–8. Managers 1 and 2 will prepare their budgets in accordance with the budget policy and the guidelines laid down by top management. The managers will submit their budget to their supervisor, who is in charge of the whole department (department A). Once these budgets have been agreed by the manager of department A, they will be combined by the departmental manager, who will then present this budget to his or her superior (manager of plant 1) for approval. The manager of plant 1 is also responsible for department B, and will combine the agreed budgets for departments A and B before presenting the combined budget to his or her supervisor (the production manager). The production manager will merge the budget for plants 1 and 2, and this final budget will represent the production budget that will be presented to the budget committee for approval.

At each of these stages the budgets will be negotiated between the budgetees and their superiors, and eventually they will be agreed by both parties. Hence the figures that are included in the budget are the result of a bargaining process between a manager and his or her superior. It is important that the budgetees should participate in arriving at the final budget and that the superior does not revise the budget without giving full consideration to the subordinates' arguments for including any of the budgeted items. Otherwise, real participation will not be taking place, and it is unlikely that the subordinate will be motivated to achieve a budget that he or she did not accept.

It is also necessary to be watchful that budgetees do not deliberately attempt to obtain approval for easily attainable budgets, or attempt to deliberately understate budgets in the hope that the budget that is finally agreed will represent an easily attainable target. It is equally unsatisfactory for a superior to impose difficult targets in the hope that an authoritarian approach will produce the desired results. The desired results may be achieved in the short term, but only at the cost of a loss of morale and increased labour turnover in the future.

The negotiation process is of vital importance in the budgeting process, and can determine whether the budget becomes a really effective management tool or just a clerical device. If managers are successful in establishing a position of trust and confidence with their subordinates, the negotiation process will produce a meaningful improvement in the budgetary process and outcomes for the period.

## COORDINATION AND REVIEW OF BUDGETS

As the individual budgets move up the organizational hierarchy in the negotiation process, they must be examined in relation to each other. This examination may indicate that some budgets are out of balance with other budgets and need modifying so that they will be compatible with other conditions, constraints and plans that are beyond a manager's knowledge or control. For example, a plant manager may include equipment replacement in his or her budget when funds are simply not available. The accountant must identify such inconsistencies and bring them to the attention of the appropriate manager. Any changes in the budgets should be made by the responsible managers, and this may require that the budgets be recycled from the bottom to the top for a second or even a third time until all the budgets are coordinated and are acceptable to all the parties involved. During the coordination process, a budgeted profit and loss account, a balance sheet and a cash flow statement should be prepared to ensure that all the parts combine to produce an acceptable whole. Otherwise, further adjustments and budget recycling will be necessary until the budgeted profit and loss account, the balance sheet and the cash flow statement prove to be acceptable.

## FINAL ACCEPTANCE OF THE BUDGETS

When all the budgets are in harmony with each other, they are summarized into a **master budget** consisting of a budgeted profit and loss account, a balance sheet and a cash flow statement. After the master budget has been approved, the budgets are then passed down through the organization to the appropriate responsibility centres. The approval of the master budget is the authority for the manager of each responsibility centre to carry out the plans contained in each budget.

## BUDGET REVIEW

The budget process should not stop when the budgets have been agreed. Periodically, the actual results should be compared with the budgeted results. These comparisons should be made on a monthly basis and a report sent to the appropriate budgetees in the first week of the following month, so that it has the maximum motivational impact. This will enable management to identify the items that are not proceeding according to plan and to investigate the reasons for the differences. If these differences are within the control of management, corrective action can be taken to avoid similar inefficiencies occurring again in the future. However, the differences may be due to the fact that the budget was unrealistic to begin with, or that the actual conditions during the budget year were different from those anticipated; the budget for the remainder of the year would than be invalid.

During the budget year, the budget committee should periodically evaluate the actual performance and reappraise the company's future plans. If there are any changes in the actual conditions from those originally expected, this will normally mean that the budget plans should be adjusted. This revised budget then represents a revised statement of formal operating plans for the remaining portion of the budget period. The important point to note is that the budgetary process does not end for the current year once the budget has begun; budgeting should be seen as a continuous and dynamic process.

# A detailed illustration

Let us now look at an illustration of the procedure for constructing budgets in a manufacturing company, using the information contained in Example 15.1. Note that the level of detail included here is much less than that which would be presented in practice. A truly realistic illustration would fill many pages, with detailed budgets being analysed in various ways. We shall consider an annual budget, whereas a realistic illustration would analyse the annual budget into twelve monthly periods. Monthly analysis would considerably increase the size of the illustration, but would not give any further insight into the basic concepts or procedures. In addition, we shall assume in this example that the budgets are prepared for only two responsibility centres (namely departments 1 and 2). In practice, many responsibility centres are likely to exist.

# Sales budget

The sales budget shows the quantities of each product that the company plans to sell and the intended selling price. It provides the predictions of total revenue from which cash receipts from customers will be estimated, and it also supplies the basic data for constructing budgets for production costs, and for selling, distribution and administrative expenses. The sales budget is therefore the foundation of all other budgets, since all expenditure is ultimately dependent on the volume of sales. If the sales budget is not accurate, the other budget estimates will be unreliable. We will assume that the Enterprise Company has completed a marketing analysis and that the following annual sales budget is based on the result:

### Schedule 1 – Sales budget for year ending 200X

| Product | Units sold | Selling price (£) | Total revenue (£) |
|---|---|---|---|
| Alpha | 8500 | 100 | 850 000 |
| Sigma | 1600 | 140 | 224 000 |
| | | | 1074 000 |

Schedule 1 represents the *total* sales budget for the year. In practice, the *total* sales budget will be supported by detailed *subsidiary* sales budgets where sales are analysed by areas of responsibility, such as sales territories, and into monthly periods analysed by products. The detailed *subsidiary* sales budget could be set out as shown on page 560.

**EXAMPLE 15.1**

The Enterprise Company manufactures two products, known as alpha and sigma. Alpha is produced in department 1 and sigma in department 2. The following information is available for 200X.

Standard material and labour costs:

|  | (£) |
| --- | --- |
| Material X | 1.80 per unit |
| Material Y | 4.00 per unit |
| Direct labour | 3.00 per hour |

Overhead is recovered on a direct labour hour basis.

The standard material and labour usage for each product is as follows:

|  | Model alpha | Model sigma |
| --- | --- | --- |
| Material X | 10 units | 8 units |
| Material Y | 5 units | 9 units |
| Direct labour | 10 hours | 15 hours |

The balance sheet for the previous year end 200X was as follows:

|  | (£) | (£) | (£) |
| --- | --- | --- | --- |
| Fixed assets: | | | |
| Land | | 42 500 | |
| Buildings and equipment | 323 000 | | |
| Less depreciation | 63 750 | 259 250 | 301 750 |
| Current assets: | | | |
| Stocks, finished goods | 24 769 | | |
| raw materials | 47 300 | | |
| Debtors | 72 250 | | |
| Cash | 8 500 | | |
|  | 152 819 | | |
| Less current liabilities | | | |
| Creditors | 62 200 | | 90 619 |
| Net assets | | | 392 369 |
| Represented by shareholder's interest: | | | |
| 300 000 ordinary shares of £1 each | | 300 000 | |
| Reserves | | 92 369 | |
|  | | | 392 369 |

Other relevant data is as follows for the year 200X:

|  | Finished product | |
| --- | --- | --- |
|  | Model alpha | Model sigma |
| Forecast sales (units) | 8500 | 1600 |
| Selling price per unit | £100 | £140 |
| Ending inventory required (units) | 1870 | 90 |
| Beginning inventory (units) | 170 | 85 |

| | Direct material | |
|---|---|---|
| | **Material X** | **Material Y** |
| Beginning inventory (units) | 8500 | 8000 |
| Ending inventory required (units) | 10 200 | 1700 |

| | **Department 1** **(£)** | **Department 2** **(£)** |
|---|---|---|
| Budgeted variable overhead rates | | |
| (per direct labour hour): | | |
| Indirect materials | 0.30 | 0.20 |
| Indirect labour | 0.30 | 0.30 |
| Power (variable portion) | 0.15 | 0.10 |
| Maintenance (variable portion) | 0.05 | 0.10 |
| | | |
| Budgeted fixed overheads | | |
| Depreciation | 25 000 | 20 000 |
| Supervision | 25 000 | 10 000 |
| Power (fixed portion) | 10 000 | 500 |
| Maintenance (fixed portion) | 11 400 | 799 |
| | | **(£)** |

| | |
|---|---|
| Estimated non-manufacturing overheads: | |
| Stationery etc. (Administration) | 1000 |
| Salaries | |
| Sales | 18 500 |
| Office | 7000 |
| Commissions | 15 000 |
| Car expenses (Sales) | 5500 |
| Advertising | 20 000 |
| Miscellaneous (Office) | 2000 |
| | 69 000 |

Budgeted cash flows are as follows:

| | **Quarter 1** **(£)** | **Quarter 2** **(£)** | **Quarter 3** **(£)** | **Quarter 4** **(£)** |
|---|---|---|---|---|
| Receipts from customers | 250 000 | 300 000 | 280 000 | 246 250 |
| Payments: | | | | |
| Materials | 100 000 | 120 000 | 110 000 | 136 996 |
| Payments for wages | 100 000 | 110 000 | 120 000 | 161 547 |
| Other costs and expenses | 30 000 | 25 000 | 18 004 | 3 409 |

You are required to prepare a master budget for the year 200X and the following budgets:

1. sales budget
2. production budget
3. direct materials usage budget

4.  direct materials purchase budget
5.  direct labour budget
6.  factory overhead budget
7.  selling and administration budget
8.  cash budget

Note that with the detailed subsidiary monthly budgets the total budgeted sales of £1 074 000 is analysed by each sales territory for each month of the budget period. The detailed analysis assumes that sales are divided among the four sales territories as follows:

|  | **Alpha** | **Sigma** |
|---|---|---|
| North | 3000 units | 500 units |
| South | 2500 units | 600 units |
| East | 1000 units | 200 units |
| West | 2000 units | 300 units |
|  | 8500 units | 1600 units |

**Detailed monthly budgets for North, South, East and West sales territories**

|  |  | **North** | | **South** | | **East** | | **West** | | **Total** | |
|---|---|---|---|---|---|---|---|---|---|---|---|
|  |  | **Units** | **Value (£)** | **Units** | **Value (£)** | **Units** | **Value (£)** | **Units** | **Value (£)** | **Units** | **Value (£)** |
| Month 1 | Alpha |  |  |  |  |  |  |  |  |  |  |
|  | Sigma |  | ——— |  | ——— |  | ——— |  | ——— |  | ——— |
|  | Total |  | ——— |  | ——— |  | ——— |  | ——— |  | ——— |
| Month 2 |  |  |  |  |  |  |  |  |  |  |  |
| Month 3 |  |  |  |  |  |  |  |  |  |  |  |
| Month 4 |  |  |  |  |  |  |  |  |  |  |  |
| Month 5 |  |  |  |  |  |  |  |  |  |  |  |
| Month 6 |  |  |  |  |  |  |  |  |  |  |  |
| Month 7 |  |  |  |  |  |  |  |  |  |  |  |
| Month 8 |  |  |  |  |  |  |  |  |  |  |  |
| Month 9 |  |  |  |  |  |  |  |  |  |  |  |
| Month 10 |  |  |  |  |  |  |  |  |  |  |  |
| Month 11 |  |  |  |  |  |  |  |  |  |  |  |
| Month 12 |  |  |  |  |  |  |  |  |  |  |  |
| Total months 1–12 | Alpha | 3000 | 300 000 | 2500 | 250 000 | 1000 | 100 000 | 2000 | 200 000 | 8500 | 850 000 |
|  | Sigma | 500 | 70 000 | 600 | 84 000 | 200 | 28 000 | 300 | 42 000 | 1600 | 224 000 |
|  |  |  | 370 000 |  | 334 000 |  | 128 000 |  | 242 000 |  | 1074 000 |

# Production budget and budgeted stock levels

When the sales budget has been completed, the next stage is to prepare the production budget. This budget is expressed in *quantities only* and is the responsibility of the production manager. The objective is to ensure that production is sufficient to meet sales demand and that economic stock levels are maintained. The production budget (schedule 2) for the year will be as follows:

**Schedule 2 – Annual production budget**

|  | Department 1 (alpha) | Department 2 (sigma) |
|---|---|---|
| Units to be sold | 8 500 | 1600 |
| Planned closing stock | 1 870 | 90 |
| Total units required for sales and stocks | 10 370 | 1690 |
| Less planned opening stocks | 170 | 85 |
| Units to be produced | 10 200 | 1605 |

The total production for each department should also be analysed on a monthly basis.

# Direct materials usage budget

The supervisors of departments 1 and 2 will prepare estimates of the materials which are required to meet the production budget. The materials usage budget for the year will be as follows:

**Schedule 3 – Annual direct material usage budget**

|  | Department 1 | | | Department 2 | | | Total units | Total unit price (£) | Total (£) |
|---|---|---|---|---|---|---|---|---|---|
|  | Units | Unit price (£) | Total (£) | Units | Unit price (£) | Total (£) |  |  |  |
| Material X | 102 000[a] | 1.80 | 183 600 | 12 840[c] | 1.80 | 23 112 | 114 840 | 1.80 | 206 712 |
| Material Y | 51 000[b] | 4.00 | 204 000 | 14 445[d] | 4.00 | 57 780 | 65 445 | 4.00 | 261 780 |
|  |  |  | 387 600 |  |  | 80 892 |  |  | 468 492 |

[a] 10 200 units production at 10 units per unit of production.
[b] 10 200 units production at 5 units per unit of production.
[c] 1605 units production at 8 units per unit of production.
[d] 1605 units production at 9 units per unit of production.

# Direct materials purchase budget

The direct materials purchase budget is the responsibility of the purchasing manager, since it will be he or she who is responsible for obtaining the planned quantities of raw materials to meet the production requirements. The objective is to purchase these materials at the right time at the planned purchase price. In addition, it is necessary to take into account the planned raw material stock levels. The annual materials purchase budget for the year will be as follows:

### Schedule 4 – Direct materials purchase budget

|  | Material X (units) | Material Y (units) |
|---|---|---|
| Quantity necessary to meet production requirements as per material usage budget | 114 840 | 65 445 |
| Planned closing stock | 10 200 | 1 700 |
|  | 125 040 | 67 145 |
| Less planned opening stock | 8 500 | 8 000 |
| Total units to be purchased | 116 540 | 59 145 |
| Planned unit purchase price | £1.80 | £4 |
| Total purchases | £209 772 | £236 580 |

Note that this budget is a summary budget for the year, but for detailed planning and control it will be necessary to analyse the annual budget on a monthly basis.

# Direct labour budget

The direct labour budget is the responsibility of the respective managers of departments 1 and 2. They will prepare estimates of the departments' labour hours required to meet the planned production. Where different grades of labour exist, these should be specified separately in the budget. The budget rate per hour should be determined by the industrial relations department. The direct labour budget will be as follows:

### Schedule 5 – Annual direct labour budget

|  | Department 1 | Department 2 | Total |
|---|---|---|---|
| Budgeted production (units) | 10 200 | 1 605 |  |
| Hours per unit | 10 | 15 |  |
| Total budgeted hours | 102 000 | 24 075 | 126 075 |
| Budgeted wage rate per hour | £3 | £3 |  |
| Total wages | £306 000 | £72 225 | £378 225 |

# Factory overhead budget

The factory overhead budget is also the responsibility of the respective production department managers. The total of the overhead budget will depend on the behaviour of the costs of the individual overhead items in relation to the anticipated level of production. The overheads must also be analysed according to whether they are controllable or non-controllable for the purpose of cost control. The factory overhead budget will be as follows:

**Schedule 6 – Annual factory overhead budget**
**Anticipated activity – 102 000 direct labour hours (department 1)**
**24 075 direct labour hours (department 2)**

| | Variable overhead rate per direct labour hour | | Overheads | | Total |
|---|---|---|---|---|---|
| | Department 1 (£) | Department 2 (£) | Department 1 (£) | Department 2 (£) | (£) |
| Controllable overheads: | | | | | |
| Indirect material | 0.30 | 0.20 | 30 600 | 4 815 | |
| Indirect labour | 0.30 | 0.30 | 30 600 | 7 222 | |
| Power (variable portion) | 0.15 | 0.10 | 15 300 | 2 407 | |
| Maintenance (variable portion) | 0.05 | 0.10 | 5 100 | 2 407 | |
| | | | 81 600 | 16 851 | 98 451 |
| Non-controllable overheads: | | | | | |
| Depreciation | | | 25 000 | 20 000 | |
| Supervision | | | 25 000 | 10 000 | |
| Power (fixed portion) | | | 10 000 | 500 | |
| Maintenance (fixed portion) | | | 11 400 | 799 | |
| | | | 71 400 | 31 299 | 102 699 |
| Total overhead | | | 153 000 | 48 150 | 201 150 |
| Budgeted departmental overhead rate | | | £1.50[a] | 2.00[b] | |

[a] £153 000 total overheads divided by 102 000 direct labour hours.
[b] £48 150 total overheads divided by 24 075 direct labour hours.

The budgeted expenditure for the variable overhead items is determined by multiplying the budgeted direct labour hours for each department by the budgeted variable overhead rate per hour. It is assumed that all variable overheads vary in relation to direct labour hours.

# Selling and administration budget

The selling and administration budgets have been combined here to simplify the presentation. In practice, separate budgets should be prepared: the sales manager will be responsible for the selling budget, the distribution manager will be responsible for the distribution expenses and the chief administrative officer will be responsible for the administration budget.

**Schedule 7 – Annual selling and administration budget**

| | (£) | (£) |
|---|---|---|
| Selling: | | |
| Salaries | 18 500 | |
| Commission | 15 000 | |
| Car expenses | 5 500 | |

|  |  |  |
|---|---:|---:|
| Advertising | 20 000 | 59 000 |
| Administration: | | |
| Stationery | 1 000 | |
| Salaries | 7 000 | |
| Miscellaneous | 2 000 | 10 000 |
| | | 69 000 |

# Departmental budgets

For cost control the direct labour budget, materials usage budget and factory overhead budget are combined into separate departmental budgets. These budgets are normally broken down into twelve separate monthly budgets, and the actual monthly expenditure is compared with the budgeted amounts for each of the items concerned. This comparison is used for judging how effective managers are in controlling the expenditure for which they are responsible. The departmental budget for department 1 will be as follows:

**Department 1 – Annual departmental operating budget**

|  | (£) | Budget (£) | Actual (£) |
|---|---:|---:|---:|
| Direct labour (from schedule 5): | | | |
| 102 000 hours at £3 | | 306 000 | |
| Direct materials (from schedule 3): | | | |
| 102 000 units of material X at £1.80 per unit | 183 600 | | |
| 51 000 units of material Y at £4 per unit | 204 000 | 387 600 | |
| Controllable overheads (from schedule 6): | | | |
| Indirect materials | 30 600 | | |
| Indirect labour | 30 600 | | |
| Power (variable portion) | 15 300 | | |
| Maintenance (variable portion) | 5 100 | 81 600 | |
| Uncontrollable overheads (from schedule 6): | | | |
| Depreciation | 25 000 | | |
| Supervision | 25 000 | | |
| Power (fixed portion) | 10 000 | | |
| Maintenance (fixed portion) | 11 400 | 71 400 | |
| | | 846 600 | |

# Master budget

When all the budgets have been prepared, the budgeted profit and loss account and balance sheet provide the overall picture of the planned performance for the budget period.

**Budgeted profit and loss account for the year ending 200X**

|  | (£) | (£) |
|---|---:|---:|
| Sales (schedule 1) | | 1 074 000 |
| Opening stock of raw materials (from opening balance sheet) | 47 300 | |
| Purchases (schedule 4) | 446 352[a] | |
| | 493 652 | |

| | | |
|---|---:|---:|
| Less closing stock of raw materials (schedule 4) | | 25 160[b] |
| Cost of raw materials consumed | | 468 492 |
| Direct labour (schedule 5) | | 378 225 |
| Factory overheads (schedule 6) | | 201 150 |
| Total manufacturing cost | | 1 047 867 |
| Add opening stock of finished goods (from opening balance sheet) | 24 769 | |
| Less closing stock of finished goods | 166 496[c] | |
| | | (141 727) |
| Cost of sales | | 906 140 |
| Gross profit | | 167 860 |
| Selling and administration expenses (schedule 7) | | 69 000 |
| Budgeted operating profit for the year | | 98 860 |

[a]£209 772 (X) + £236 580 (Y) from schedule 4.
[b]10 200 units at £1.80 plus 1700 units at £4 from schedule 4.
[c]1870 units of alpha valued at £83 per unit, 90 units of sigma valued at £125.40 per unit. The product unit costs are calculated as follows:

| | Alpha | | Sigma | |
|---|---:|---:|---:|---:|
| | Units | (£) | Units | (£) |
| Direct materials | | | | |
| X | 10 | 18.00 | 8 | 14.40 |
| Y | 5 | 20.00 | 9 | 36.00 |
| Direct labour | 10 | 30.00 | 15 | 45.00 |
| Factory overheads: | | | | |
| Department 1 | 10 | 15.00 | — | — |
| Department 2 | — | — | 15 | 30.00 |
| | | 83.00 | | 125.40 |

### Budgeted balance sheet as at 31 December

| | (£) | (£) |
|---|---:|---:|
| Fixed assets: | | |
| Land | | 42 500 |
| Building and equipment | 323 000 | |
| Less depreciation[a] | 108 750 | 214 250 |
| | | 256 750 |
| Current assets: | | |
| Raw material stock | 25 160 | |
| Finished good stock | 166 496 | |
| Debtors[b] | 70 000 | |
| Cash[c] | 49 794 | |
| | 311 450 | |
| Current liabilities: | | |
| Creditors[d] | 76 971 | 234 479 |
| | | 491 229 |

Represented by shareholders' interest:

| | | |
|---|---:|---:|
| 300 000 ordinary shares of £1 each | 300 000 | |
| Reserves | 92 369 | |
| Profit and loss account | 98 860 | 491 229 |

[a]£63 750 + £45 000 (schedule 6) = £108 750.
[b]£72 250 opening balance + £1 074 000 sales − £1 076 250 cash.
[c]Closing balance as per cash budget.
[d]£62 200 opening balance + £446 352 purchases + £35 415 indirect materials − £466 996 cash.

# Cash budgets

The objective of the **cash budget** is to ensure that sufficient cash is available at all times to meet the level of operations that are outlined in the various budgets. The cash budget for Example 15.1 is presented below and is analysed by quarters, but in practice monthly or weekly budgets will be necessary. Because cash budgeting is subject to uncertainty, it is necessary to provide for more than the minimum amount required, to allow for some margin of error in planning. Cash budgets can help a firm to avoid cash balances that are surplus to its requirements by enabling management to take steps in advance to invest the surplus cash in short-term investments. Alternatively, cash deficiencies can be identified in advance, and steps can be taken to ensure that bank loans will be available to meet any temporary cash deficiencies. For example, by looking at the cash budget for the Enterprise Company, management may consider that the cash balances are higher than necessary in the second and third quarters of the year, and they may invest part of the cash balance in short-term investments.

The overall aim should be to manage the cash of the firm to attain maximum cash availability and maximum interest income on any idle funds.

### Cash budget for year ending 200X

| | Quarter 1 (£) | Quarter 2 (£) | Quarter 3 (£) | Quarter 4 (£) | Total (£) |
|---|---:|---:|---:|---:|---:|
| Opening balance | 8 500 | 28 500 | 73 500 | 105 496 | 8 500 |
| Receipts from debtors | 250 000 | 300 000 | 280 000 | 246 250 | 1 076 250 |
| | 258 500 | 328 500 | 353 500 | 351 746 | 1 084 750 |
| Payments: | | | | | |
| Purchase of materials | 100 000 | 120 000 | 110 000 | 136 996 | 466 996 |
| Payment of wages | 100 000 | 110 000 | 120 000 | 161 547 | 491 547 |
| Other costs and expenses | 30 000 | 25 000 | 18 004 | 3 409 | 76 413 |
| | 230 000 | 255 000 | 248 004 | 301 952 | 1 034 956 |
| Closing balance | 28 500 | 73 500 | 105 496 | 49 794 | 49 794 |

# Final review

The budgeted profit and loss account, the balance sheet and the cash budget will be submitted by the accountant to the budget committee, together with a number of budgeted financial ratios such as the return on capital employed, working capital, liquidity and gearing ratios. If these ratios prove to be acceptable, the budgets will be approved. In Example 15.1 the return on capital employed is approximately 20%, but the working capital ratio is over 4:1, so management should consider alternative ways of reducing investment in working capital before finally approving the budgets.

# Computerized budgeting

In the past, budgeting was a task dreaded by many management accountants. You will have noted from Example 15.1 that many numerical manipulations are necessary to prepare the budget. In the real world the process is far more complex, and, as the budget is being formulated, it is altered many times since some budgets are found to be out of balance with each other or the master budget proves to be unacceptable.

In today's world, the budgeting process is computerized instead of being primarily concerned with numerical manipulations, the accounting staff can now become more involved in the real planning process. Computer-based financial models normally consist of mathematical statements of inputs and outputs. By simply altering the mathematical statements budgets can be quickly revised with little effort. However, the major advantage of computerized budgeting is that management can evaluate many different options before the budget is finally agreed. Establishing a model enables 'What-if?' analysis to be employed. For example, answers to the following questions can be displayed in the form of a master budget: What if sales increase or decrease by 10%? What if unit costs increase or decrease by 5%? What if the credit terms for sales were reduced from 30 to 20 days?

In addition, computerized models can incorporate actual results, period by period, and carry out the necessary calculations to produce budgetary *control* reports. It is also possible to adjust the budgets for the remainder of the year when it is clear that the circumstances on which the budget was originally set have changed.

# Activity-based budgeting

**AR** The conventional approach to budgeting works fine for unit level activity costs where the consumption of resources varies proportionately with the volume of the final output of products or services. However, for those indirect costs and support activities where there are no clearly defined input–output relationships, and the consumption of resources does not vary with the final output of products or services, conventional budgets merely serve as authorization levels for certain levels of spending for each budgeted item of expense. Budgets that are not based on well-understood relationships between activities and costs are poor indicators of performance and performance reporting normally implies little more than checking whether the budget has been exceeded. Conventional budgets therefore provide little relevant information for managing the costs of support activities.

With conventional budgeting indirect costs and support activities are prepared on an incremental basis. This means that existing operations and the current budgeted allowance for existing activities are taken as the starting point for preparing the next annual budget. The base is then adjusted for changes (such as changes in product mix, volumes and prices) which are expected to occur during the new budget period. This approach is called **incremental budgeting**, since the budget process is concerned mainly with the increment in operations or expenditure that will occur during the forthcoming budget period. For example, the allowance for budgeted expenses may be based on the previous budgeted allowance plus an increase to cover higher prices caused by inflation. The major disadvantage of the incremental approach is that the majority of expenditure, which is associated with the 'base level' of activity, remains unchanged. Thus, the cost of non-unit level activities become fixed and past inefficiencies and waste inherent in the current way of doing things is perpetuated.

To manage costs more effectively organizations that have implemented activity-based costing (ABC) have also adopted **activity-based budgeting (ABB)**. The aim of ABB is to authorize the supply of only those resources that are needed to perform activities required to meet the budgeted production and sales volume. Whereas ABC assigns resource expenses to activities and then uses activity cost drivers to assign activity costs to cost objects (such as products, services or customers), ABB is the reverse of this process. Cost objects are the starting point. Their budgeted output determines the necessary activities which are then used to estimate the resources that are required for the budget period. ABB involves the following stages:

1. estimate the production and sales volume by individual products and customers;
2. estimate the demand for organizational activities;
3. determine the resources that are required to perform organizational activities;
4. estimate for each resource the quantity that must be supplied to meet the demand;
5. take action to adjust the capacity of resources to match the projected supply.

The first stage is identical to conventional budgeting. Details of budgeted production and sales volumes for individual products and customer types will be contained in the sales and production budgets. Next, ABC extends conventional budgeting to support activities such as ordering, receiving, scheduling production and processing customers' orders. To implement ABB a knowledge of the activities that are necessary to produce and sell the products and services and service customers is essential. Estimates of the quantity of activity cost drivers must be derived for each activity. For example, the number of purchase orders, the number of receipts, the number of set-ups and the number of customer orders processed are estimated using the same approach as that used by conventional budgeting to determine the quantity of direct labour and materials that are incorporated into the direct labour and materials purchase budgets. Standard cost data incorporating a bill of activities is maintained for each product indicating the different activities, and the quantity of activity drivers that are required, to produce a specified number of products. Such documentation provides the basic information for building up the activity-based budgets.

The third stage is to estimate the resources that are required for performing the quantity of activity drivers demanded. In particular, estimates are required of each type of resource, and their quantities required, to meet the demanded quantity of activities. For example, if the number of customer orders to be processed is estimated to be 5000 and each order takes 30 minutes processing time then 2500 labour hours of the customer processing activity must be supplied.

Next, the resources demanded (derived from the third stage) are converted into an estimate of the total resources that must be supplied for each type of resource used by an activity. The quantity of resources supplied depends on the cost behaviour of the resource. For flexible resources where the supply can be matched exactly to meet demand, such as direct materials and energy costs, the quantity of resources supplied will be identical to the quantity demanded. For example, if customer processing were a flexible resource exactly 2500 hours would be purchased. However, a more likely assumption is that customer processing labour will be a step cost function in relation to the volume of the activity (see Chapter 2 for a description of step cost functions). Assuming that each person employed is contracted to work 1500 hours per year then 1.67 persons (2500/1500) represents the quantity of resources required, but because resources must be acquired in uneven amounts, two persons must be employed. For other resources, such as equipment, resources will tend to be fixed and committed over a very wide range of volume for the activity. As long as demand is less than the capacity supplied by the committed resource no additional spending will be required.

The final stage is to compare the estimates of the quantity of resources to be supplied for each resource with the quantity of resources that are currently committed. If the estimated supply of a resource exceeds the current capacity additional spending must be authorized within the budgeting process to acquire additional resources. Alternatively, if the demand for resources is less than the projected supply, the budgeting process should result in management taking action to either redeploy or reduce those resources that are no longer required.

Exhibit 15.1 illustrates an activity-based budget for an order receiving process or department. You will see that the budget is presented in a matrix format with the major activities being shown for each of the columns and the resource inputs are listed by rows. The cost driver activity levels are also highlighted. A major feature of ABB is the enhanced visibility arising from showing the outcomes, in terms of cost drivers, from the budgeted expenditure. This information is particularly useful for planning and estimating future expenditure.

Let us now look at how ABB can be applied using the information presented in Exhibit 15.1. Assume that ABB stages one and two as outlined above result in an estimated annual demand of 2800 orders for the processing of the receipt of the standard customers' order activity. For the staff salaries (that is, the processing of customers' orders labour resource) assume that each member of staff can process on average 50 orders per month, or 600 per year. Therefore 4.67 (2800 orders/600 orders) persons are required for the supply of this resource (that is, stage three as outlined above). The fourth stage converts the 4.67 staff resources into the amount that must be supplied, that is 5 members of staff. Let us assume that the current capacity or supply of resources committed to the activity is 6 members of staff at £25 000 per annum, giving a total annual cost of £150 000. Management is therefore made aware that staff resources can be reduced by £25 000 per annum by transferring one member of staff to other activities where staff resources need to be expanded or, more drastically, making them redundant.

Some of the other resource expenses (such as office supplies and telephone expenses) listed in Exhibit 15.1 for the processing of customers' order activity represent flexible resources which are likely to vary in the short-term with the number of orders processed. Assuming that the budget for the forthcoming period represents 80% of the number of orders processed during the previous budget period then the budget for those resource expenses that vary in the short-term with the number of orders processed should be reduced by 20%.

With conventional budgeting the budgeted expenses for the forthcoming budget for support activities are normally based on the previous year's budget plus an adjustment for inflation. Support costs are therefore considered to be fixed in relation to activity volume. In contrast, ABB provides a framework for understanding the amount of resources that are required to achieve the budgeted level of activity. By comparing the amount of resources that are required with the amount of resources that are in place, upwards or downwards adjustments can be made during the budget setting phase.

Periodically actual results should be compared with a budget adjusted (flexed) to the actual output for the activities (in terms of cost drivers) to highlight both in financial and non-financial terms those activities with major discrepancies from budget. Assume that practical capacity for salaries for the processing of customers' standard orders activity was set at 3000 orders (5 staff at 600 orders per member of staff), even though budgeted activity was only 2800 orders, and the actual number of orders processed

**EXHIBIT 15.1**

*Activity-based budget for an order receiving process*

during the period was 2500 orders. Also assume that the actual resources committed to the activity in respect of salaries was £125 000 (all fixed in the short term). The following information should be presented in the performance report:

| Activities → | Handle import goods | Execute express orders | Special Deliveries | Distribution administration | Order receiving (standard products) | Order receiving (non-standard products) | Execute rush orders | Total cost |
|---|---|---|---|---|---|---|---|---|
| *Resource expense accounts:* | | | | | | | | |
| Office supplies | | | | | | | | |
| Telephone expenses | | | | | | | | |
| Salaries | | | | | | | | |
| Travel | | | | | | | | |
| Training | | | | | | | | |
| | | | | | | | | |
| Total cost | | | | | | | | |
| | | | | | | | | |
| Activity cost driver → measures | Number of customs documents | Number of customer bills | Number of letters of credit | Number of consignment notes | Number of standard orders | Number of non-standard orders | Number of rush orders | |

Flexed budget based on the number of orders processed
(2500 orders at £41.67)                                                    104 175
Budgeted unused capacity (3000 − 2800) × £41.67                      8 334
Actual unplanned unused capacity (2800 − 2500) × £41.67        12 491
                                                                                    125 000

The cost driver rate of £41.67 per order processed is calculated by dividing the £125 000 budgeted cost of supplying the resources by the capacity supplied (3000 orders). The above activity performance information highlights for management attention the potential reduction in the supply of resources of £20 825 (£8334 expected and £12 491 unexpected) or, alternatively, the additional business that can be accommodated with the existing supply of resources.

A survey of UK organizations by Innes and Mitchell (1995a) found that 20% of the respondents used the activity-based approach for budgeting and 76% of these users rated the ability to set more realistic budgets as the most important benefit from ABB. Other benefits identified by the survey respondents included the better identification of resource needs and the identification of budget slack. In a later survey of organizations in the financial services sector Innes and Mitchell (1997) found that these organizations also derived similar benefits from ABB. ●●●

# The budgeting process in non-profit-making organizations

The budgeting process in a non-profit-making organization normally begins with the managers of the various activities calculating the expected costs of maintaining current ongoing activities and then adding to those costs any further developments of the services that are considered desirable. For example, the education, health, housing and social services departments of a municipal authority will propose specific activities and related costs for the coming year. These budgets are coordinated by the accounting department into an overall budget proposal.

The available resources for financing the proposed level of public services should be sufficient to cover the total costs of such services. In the case of a municipal authority the resources will be raised by local taxes and government grants. Similar procedures are followed by churches, hospitals, charities and other non-profit-making organizations, in that they produce estimates for undertaking their activities and then find the means to finance them, or reduce the activities to realistic levels so that they can be financed from available financial resources.

One difficulty encountered in non-profit-making organizations is that precise objectives are difficult to define in a quantifiable way, and the actual accomplishments are even more difficult to measure. In most situations outputs cannot be measured in monetary terms. By 'outputs' we mean the quality and amount of the services rendered. In profit-oriented organizations output can be measured in terms of sales revenues. The effect of this is that budgets in non-profit organizations, tend to be mainly concerned with the input of resources (i.e. expenditure), whereas budgets in profit organizations focus on the relationships between inputs (expenditure) and outputs (sales revenue). In non-profit organizations there is not the same emphasis on what was intended to be achieved for a given input of resources. The budgeting process tends to compare what is happening in cash input terms with the estimated cash inputs. In other words, there is little emphasis on measures of managerial performance in terms of the results achieved. The reason for this is that there is no clear relationship between resource inputs and the benefits flowing from the use of these resources. However, we shall see that increasing efforts have been made in recent years to overcome these deficiencies by developing measures of output that can be used to compare budgeted and actual accomplishments.

## LINE ITEM BUDGETS

The traditional format for budgets in non-profit organizations is referred to as **line item budgets**. A line item budget is one in which the expenditures are expressed in considerable detail, but the activities being undertaken are given little attention. In other words, line item budgeting shows the nature of the spending but not the purpose. A typical line item budget is illustrated in Exhibit 15.2.

The amounts in this type of budget are frequently established on the basis of historical costs that have been adjusted for anticipated changes in costs and activity levels. When they are compared with the actual expenditures, line item budgets provide a basis for comparing whether or not the authorized budgeted expenditure has been exceeded or whether underspending has occurred. Note that data for the current year and for the previous year are included to indicate how the proposed budget differs from current spending patterns. However, such line item budgets fail to identify the costs of *activities* and the *programmes* to be implemented. In addition, compliance with line item budgets

**EXHIBIT 15.2**

*Typical line item budget*

provides no assurance that resources are used wisely, effectively or efficiently in financing the various activities in a non-profit organization.

| | Actual 20X2 (£) | Original budget 20X3 (£) | Revised budget 20X3 (£) | Proposed budget 20X4 (£) |
|---|---|---|---|---|
| Employees | 1 292 000 | 1 400 000 | 1 441 000 | 1 830 000 |
| Premises | 3 239 | 12 000 | 10 800 | 14 200 |
| Supplies and services | 34 735 | 43 200 | 44 900 | 147 700 |
| Transport | 25 778 | 28 500 | 28 700 | 30 700 |
| Establishment expenses | 123 691 | 120 000 | 116 000 | 158 600 |
| Agency charges | 10 120 | 10 000 | 9 800 | 13 300 |
| Financing charges | 2 357 | 2 700 | 2 800 | 114 800 |
| Other expenses | 1 260 | 1 350 | 1 400 | 1 600 |
| | 1 493 180 | 1 617 750 | 1 655 400 | 2 310 900 |

## PLANNING, PROGRAMMING BUDGETING SYSTEMS

Non-profit organizations have found line item budgets to be unsatisfactory mainly because they fail to provide information on planned and actual accomplishments. In addition, such budgets do not provide information on the efficiency with which the organization's activities have been performed, or its effectiveness in achieving its objectives. A further deficiency with line item budgets is that they fail to provide a sound basis for deciding how the available resources should be allocated. Planning, programming budgeting systems (PPBS) are intended to overcome these deficiencies.

The aim of PPBS is to enable the management of a non-profit organization to make more informed decisions about the allocation of resources to meet the overall objectives of the organization. First, overall objectives are established. Secondly, the programmes that might achieve these objectives are identified. Finally the costs and benefits of each programme are determined so that budget allocations can be made on the basis of the cost–benefits of the different programmes. PPBS is the counterpart of the long-term planning process operated in profit-oriented organizations. We can relate PPBS to the long-term planning process outlined in Figure 15.1 for profit-oriented companies. The first stage in the process of PPBS is to review the organizational objectives for the activities which it performs (i.e. stage 1 in Figure 15.1). Stage 2 involves identifying programmes that can be undertaken to achieve the organization's objectives, for instance, extending childcare facilities, improvement of health care for senior citizens and the extension of nursery facilities (see Exhibit 15.3 for an illustration of a childcare programme). The third stage involves identifying and evaluating alternative methods of achieving the objectives for each specific programme. Such a comparison and evaluation will show the costs of each alternative course of action and the benefits which result. The final stage (stage 4) is to select the appropriate programmes on the basis of cost–benefit principles. At this stage it would be useful if the programmes could be ranked, but this is extremely difficult. It is

| EXHIBIT 15.3 | therefore necessary for a subjective judgement to be made by the top management of the organization on the amount of resources to be allocated to the various programmes. |
|---|---|
| *Illustration of a childcare programme* | PPBS involves the preparation of a *long-term* corporate plan that clearly establishes the objectives that the organiza- |

- The construction of three new kindergartens.
- The repair and extension of five existing kindergartens.
- The employment of ten new nursery school teachers.
- The establishment of a child-minding scheme that is based in the homes of mothers with young children of their own.
- The setting up of an occasional childcare centre.
- The introduction of an hourly baby-sitting service.

*Source:* Wilson and Chua (1993).

tion aims to achieve. These objectives do not necessarily follow the existing organizational structure. For example, one objective of a local authority may be the care of the elderly. The following services may contribute to this objective:

1. provision of sheltered accommodation;
2. erection of aged-persons dwellings;
3. provision of domestic health services;
4. provision of home nursing services;
5. provision of social and recreational facilities.

The provision of these activities may be undertaken by separate departments, such as housing, health and social services. However, PPBS relates the estimates of total costs to the care of the elderly programme, rather than relating costs to the various departments. A programme budget cuts across departmental barriers by providing estimates of the programme for the provision of the elderly rather than these estimates being included within the three budgets for each of the housing, health and social welfare departments.

PPBS forces management to identify the activities, functions or programmes to be provided, thereby establishing a basis for evaluating their worthiness. In addition, PPBS provides information that will enable management to assess the effectiveness of its plans; for example, is the provision of the services for the elderly as well developed as it should be for an expenditure of X thousand pounds? The programme structure should correspond to the principal objectives of the organization and enable management to focus on the organization's outputs (the objectives to be achieved) rather than just the inputs (the resources available to be used). Hence a more effective allocation of scarce resources can be achieved. Within the overall programme budget, apart from the main objectives of the programme, there will be a series of sub-objectives reaching down to the lower levels of management.

Because the programme structure is unlikely to match the organization's structure, a particular individual must be made responsible for controlling and supervising the programme. Anthony and Young (1988) suggest that one possibility is to adopt a matrix type of organizational structure, with a matrix consisting of programme managers in one dimension and functionally organized responsibility centres in the other. This process is illustrated in Figure 15.3. The programmes are represented by horizontal bars and the

**FIGURE 15.3** *A matrix organizational structure.*

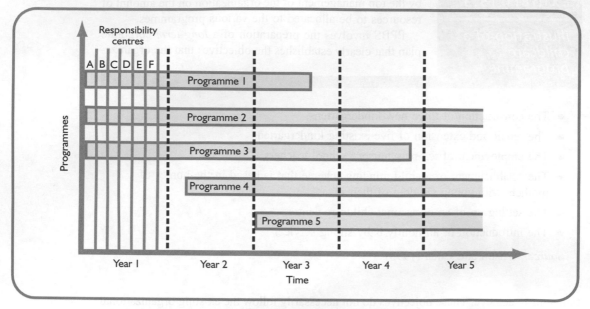

budgets by vertical dashed lines. The budget for year 1 has been analysed by six responsibility centres (A to F). Such an organizational structure requires that the budgeted and the actual accomplishments be compared by *programmes*. In addition information must be accumulated by department or responsibility centre (i.e. responsibility centres A to F in Figure 15.3) and line item budgets must be used for controlling expenditure. Note that the budgeting process in this illustration focuses on a single year, whereas PPBS focuses on activities extending over a period of several years. A budget is, in effect, one slice of the organization's programmes where costs are related to departments or responsibility centres, rather than programmes.

In the 1960s and early 1970s efforts were made to implement PPBS into US government budgeting, but by the mid 1970s the attempt had been abandoned. Pendlebury (1996) concludes that efforts to implement PPBS failed because much of the data that were required on outputs were unobtainable. He states:

> Although the philosophy behind PPBS was good, practical difficulties and organizational realities led to its demise. One influence that it did have, however, and that still remains, is to have reinforced the advantages of a programme structure. In other words even though programme impacts might not be measurable and the establishment of cost/benefit relationships not possible, the budget might at least show the proposed spending on different activities or programmes (page 287).

# Zero-based budgeting

Zero-based budgeting (also known as priority-based budgeting) emerged in the late 1960s as an attempt to overcome the limitations of incremental budgets. This approach requires that all activities are justified and prioritized before decisions are taken relating to the amount of resources allocated to each activity. Besides adopting a 'zero-based' approach zero-base budgeting (ZBB) also focuses on programmes or activities instead of functional departments based on line-items which is a feature of traditional budgeting.

ZBB works from the premise that projected expenditure for existing programmes should start from base zero, with each year's budgets being compiled as if the programmes were being launched for the first time. The budgetees should present their requirements for appropriations in such a fashion that all funds can be allocated on the basis of cost–benefit or some similar kind of evaluative analysis. The cost–benefit approach is an attempt to ensure 'value for money'; it questions long-standing assumptions and serves as a tool for systematically examining and perhaps abandoning any unproductive projects.

ZBB is best suited to discretionary costs and support activities. With **discretionary costs** management has some discretion as to the amount it will budget for the particular activity in question. Examples of discretionary costs include advertising, research and development and training costs. There is no optimum relationship between inputs (as measured by the costs) and outputs (measured by revenues or some other objective function) for these costs. Furthermore, they are not predetermined by some previous commitment. In effect, management can determine what quantity of service it wishes to purchase and there is no established method for determining the appropriate amount to be spent in particular periods. ZBB has mostly been applied in local and government organizations where the predominant costs are of a discretionary nature. In contrast, direct production and service costs, where input–output relationships exist, are more suited to traditional budgeting using standard costs.

ZBB involves the following three stages:

- a description of each organizational activity in a decision package;
- the evaluation and ranking of decision packages in order of priority;
- allocation of resources based on order of priority up to the spending cut-off level.

**Decision packages** are identified for each decision unit. Decision units represent separate programmes or groups of activities that an organization undertakes. A decision package represents the operation of a particular programme with incremental packages reflecting different levels of effort that may be expended on a specific function. One package is usually prepared at the 'base' level for each programme. This package represents the minimum level of service or support consistent with the organization's objectives. Service or support higher than the base level is described in one or more incremental packages. For example, managers might be asked to specify the base package in terms of level of service that can be provided at 70% of the current cost level and incremental packages identify higher activity or cost levels.

Once the decision packages have been completed, management is ready to start to review the process. To determine how much to spend and where to spend it, management will rank all packages in order of decreasing benefits to the organization. Theoretically, once management has set the budgeted level of spending, the packages should be accepted down to the spending level based on cost–benefit principles.

The benefits of ZBB over traditional methods of budgeting are claimed to be as follows:

1. Traditional budgeting tends to extrapolate the past by adding a percentage increase to the current year. ZBB avoids the deficiencies of incremental budgeting and represents a move towards the allocation of resources by need or benefit. Thus, unlike traditional budgeting the level of funding is not taken for granted.

2. ZBB creates a questioning attitude rather than one that assumes that current practice represents value for money.

3. ZBB focuses attention on outputs in relation to value for money.

ZBB was first applied in Texas Instruments in 1969. It quickly became one of the fashionable management tools of the 1970s and, according to Phyrr (1976), there were 100 the USA in the early 1970s, including the State of Georgia whose governor was ex-president Jimmy Carter. When he became the US President, he directed that all federal agencies adopt ZBB.

During the 1970s many articles on ZBB were published but they declined rapidly towards the end of the decade, and by the 1980s they had become a rarity. ZBB has never achieved the widespread adoption that its proponents envisaged. The major reason for its lack of success would appear to be that it is too costly and time-consuming. The process of identifying decision packages and determining their purpose, cost and benefits is extremely time-consuming. Furthermore, there are often too many decision packages to evaluate and there is frequently insufficient information to enable them to be ranked.

Research suggests that many organizations tend to approximate the principles of ZBB rather than applying the full-scale approach outlined in the literature. For example, it does not have to be applied throughout the organization. It can be applied selectively to those areas about which management is most concerned and used as a one-off cost reduction programme. Some of the benefits of ZBB can be captured by using priority-based incremental budgets. Priority incremental budgets require managers to specify what incremental activities or changes would occur if their budgets were increased or decreased by a specified percentage (say 10%). Budget allocations are made by comparing the change in costs with the change in benefits. Priority incremental budgets thus represent an economical compromise between ZBB and incremental budgeting.

# Self-Assessment Question

You should attempt to answer this question yourself before looking up the suggested answer, which appears on pages 1123–4. If any part of your answer is incorrect, check back carefully to make sure you understand where you went wrong.

R Limited manufactures three products A, B and C.

You are required:

(a) Using the information given below, to prepare budgets for the month of January for
   (i) sales in quantity and value, including total value;
   (ii) production quantities;
   (iii) material usage in quantities;
   (iv) material purchases in quantity and value, including total value;
   (Note that particular attention should be paid to your layout of the budgets.)

(b) To explain the term 'principal budget factor' and state what it was assumed to be in (a).

| Product | Quantity (units) | Price each (£) |
|---|---|---|
| Sales: | | |
| A | 1000 | 100 |
| B | 2000 | 120 |
| C | 1500 | 140 |

Materials used in the company's products:

| Material | M1 | M2 | M3 |
|---|---|---|---|
| Unit cost | £4 | £6 | £9 |

| Quantities used in: | M1 (units) | M2 (units) | M3 (units) |
|---|---|---|---|
| Product A | 4 | 2 | – |
| Product B | 3 | 3 | 2 |
| Product C | 2 | 1 | 1 |

| Finished stocks: | Product A (units) | Product B (units) | Product C (units) |
|---|---|---|---|
| Quantities | | | |
| 1st January | 1000 | 1500 | 500 |
| 31st January | 1100 | 1650 | 550 |

| Material stocks: | M1 (units) | M2 (units) | M3 (units) |
|---|---|---|---|
| 1st January | 26 000 | 20 000 | 12 000 |
| 31st January | 31 200 | 24 000 | 14 400 |

(20 marks)

*CIMA Cost Accounting 1*

## Summary

Every organization needs to plan and consider how to confront future potential risks and opportunities. In most organizations this process is formalized by preparing annual budgets and monitoring performance against the budgets. Budgets are merely a collection of plans and forecasts. They reflect the financial implications of business plans, identifying the amount, quantity and timing of resources needed.

The annual budget should be set within the context of longer-term plans, which are likely to exist even if they have not been made explicit. Long-term planning involves strategic planning over several years and the identification of the basic strategy of the firm (i.e. the future direction the organization will take) and the gaps which exist between the future needs and present capabilities. A long-term plan is a statement of the preliminary targets and activities required by an organization to achieve its strategic plans together with a broad estimate for each year of the resources required. Because long-term planning involves 'looking into the future' for several years ahead, the plans tend to be uncertain, general in nature, imprecise and subject to change.

Annual budgeting is concerned with the implementation of the long-term plan for the year ahead. Before the annual budgeting process is begun, top management must communicate the policy effects of the long-term plan to those responsible for preparing the current year's budgets. Normally, the sales budget is the first to be prepared, and this supplies the basic data for producing the remaining budgets. The managers responsible for meeting budgeted performance should prepare the budgets for those areas for which they are responsible and submit them to their superiors for approval. As the budgets move up the organizational hierarchy, they must be examined in relation to each other to ensure that all the parts combine to produce an acceptable whole. When all the budgets are in mutual harmony, they will be summarized into a master budget consisting of a budgeted profit and loss account, a balance sheet and a cash flow statement. The approval of the master budget will constitute authority for the managers of each responsibility centre to carry out the plans contained in each budget. The process should not stop when all the budgets have been agreed; periodically, the actual results should be compared with the budget and remedial action taken to ensure that the results conform to plan. Budgeting is a continuous and dynamic process, and should not end once the annual budget has been prepared.

With conventional budgeting the budgeted expenses for the forthcoming budget for support activities are normally based on the previous year's budget plus an adjustment for inflation. Support costs are therefore considered to be fixed in relation to activity volume. In contrast, activity-based budgeting provides a framework for understanding the amount of resources that are required to achieve the budgeted level of activity. By comparing the amount of resources that are required with the amount of resources that are in place, upwards or downwards adjustments can be made during the budget setting phase.

In non-profit organizations the annual budgeting process compares budgeted and actual inputs, but does not provide information on the efficiency with which activities have been performed, or the effectiveness in achieving objectives. PPBS attempts to overcome these deficiencies. It is a long-term planning process and is the counterpart of the long-term planning process in profit-oriented companies. Incremental budgeting is a system of preparing annual budgets that takes the current level of operating activity as the starting point for preparing the next annual budget. This base is then adjusted for the changes expected to occur during the new budget period. An alternative approach is that of zero-base budgeting where the projected expenditure for preparing the next annual budget for existing programmes starts from base zero.

## Key Terms and Concepts

activity-based budgeting (p. 568)
aims (p. 546)
budgeting (p. 549)
budgets (p. 545)
cash budgets (p. 566)

continuous budgeting (p. 552)
corporate objectives (p. 546)
corporate planning (p. 545)
decision package (p. 575)
discretionary costs (p. 575)

## Recommended Reading

In this chapter we have provided a very brief summary of the process for selecting alternative strategies. A detailed explanation of strategy formulation can be found in the corporate strategy literature. Predominant texts on this area include Johnson and Scholes (1999) and Thompson (1997). For a more detailed discussion of budgeting in the public sector see Pendlebury (1996).

## Key Examination Points

Examination questions on budgeting frequently require the preparation of functional or cash budgets. A common mistake is to incorrectly deduct closing stocks and add opening stocks when preparing production and material purchase budgets. Examination questions are also set frequently on zero-base budgeting (ZBB). Do make sure that you can describe and discuss the advantages and disadvantages of ZBB.

## Questions

*Indicates that a suggested solution is to be found in the *Students' Manual*.

### 15.1 Intermediate
Outline:
(a) the objectives of budgetary planning and control systems; (7 marks)
(b) the organization required for the preparation of a master budget. (10 marks)

(Total 17 marks)
*ACCA Level 1 Costing*

### 15.2 Intermediate
The preparation of budgets is a lengthy process which requires great care if the ultimate master budget is to be useful for the purposes of management control within an organization.
You are required:
(a) to identify and to explain briefly the stages involved in the preparation of budgets identifying separately the roles of managers and the budget committee; (8 marks)
(b) to explain how the use of spreadsheets may improve the efficiency of the budget preparation process. (7 marks)

(Total 15 marks)
*CIMA Stage 1 Accounting*

### 15.3 Advanced
What is zero-base budgeting and how does it differ from other more traditional forms of budgeting? Discuss the applicability of zero-base budgeting to profit-orientated organizations.
*ACCA Level 2 Management Accounting*

### 15.4* Advanced
You are the management accountant of a group of companies and your managing director has asked you to explore the possibilities of introducing a zero-base budgeting system experimentally in one of the operating companies in place of its existing orthodox system. You are required to prepare notes for a paper for submission to the board that sets out:
(a) how zero-base budgeting would work within the company chosen; (6 marks)

(b) what advantages it might offer over the existing system; (5 marks)

(c) what problems might be faced in introducing a zero-base budgeting scheme; (5 marks)

(d) the features you would look for in selecting the operating company for the introduction in order to obtain the most beneficial results from the experiment. (4 marks)

(Total 20 marks)

*CIMA P3 Management Accounting*

### 15.5 Advanced

The chief executive of your organization has recently seen a reference to zero-base budgeting. He has asked for more details of the technique.

You are required to prepare a report for him explaining:

(a) what zero-base budgeting is and to which areas it can best be applied;

(b) what advantages the technique has over traditional type budgeting systems; and

(c) how the organization might introduce such a technique. (20 marks)

*CIMA P3 Management Accounting*

### 15.6 Advanced

Prepare brief notes about zero-base budgeting covering the following topics:

(a) what zero-base budgeting means;

(b) how zero-base budgeting would operate;

(c) what problems might be met in introducing zero-base budgeting;

(d) what special advantages could be expected from zero-base budgeting, as compared with more traditional budgeting methods, for an organization operating in an economic recession. (20 marks)

*CIMA P3 Management Accounting*

### 15.7* Advanced

(a) '... corporate planning and budgeting are complementary, rather than the former superseding the latter.'

Compare the aims and main features of 'corporate planning' and 'budgeting' systems. (12 marks)

(b) The aims of zero-base budgeting have been described recently in the following terms: 'Zero-base budgeting is a general management tool that can provide a systematic way to evaluate all operations and programmes; a means of establishing a working structure to recognise priorities and performance measures for current and future plans; in essence, a methodology for the continual redirection of resources into the highest priority programmes, and to explicitly identify tradeoffs among long-term growth, current operations, and profit needs.'

Explain how a system of zero-base budgeting works, and to assess its likely success in attaining the aims set out above. (13 marks)

*ICAEW Management Accounting*

### 15.8 Advanced

A budgetary planning and control system may include many individual budgets which are integrated into a 'master budget'.

You are required to outline and briefly explain with reasons the steps which should normally be taken in the preparation of master budgets in a manufacturing company, indicating the main budgets which you think should normally be prepared. (12 marks)

*ICAEW Management Accounting*

### 15.9 Advanced

The managing director of your company believes that the existing annual budget system is costly to operate and produces unsatisfactory results due to: long preparation period;

business decisions being made throughout the year;

unpredictable changes in the rate of general inflation;

sudden changes in the availability and price of raw materials.

He has read about rolling budgets and wonders whether these might be more useful for his decision-making.

You are required, as the management accountant, to prepare a paper for him covering the following areas.

(a) a brief explanation of rolling budgets;
(4 marks)

(b) how a rolling budget system would operate;
(4 marks)

(c) *three* significant advantages of a rolling budget system; (6 marks)

(d) *three* problems likely to be encountered in using a rolling budget system (6 marks)

*CIMA P3 Management Accounting*

### 15.10* Advanced

A company that has hitherto prepared its operating budgets on a single target level of performance is considering changing to one of the following:

(i) a three-level budget;

(ii) a decision tree analysis leading to a calculation of joint probabilities of budget levels;

(iii) a simulation of probabilities of budget levels (probably computer-based).

You are required to:

(a) explain briefly the method of constructing budgets for (i), (ii) and (iii) above;

(b) comment briefly on the advantages that would result from choosing:

method (i) over the existing method;

method (ii) over method (i);

method (iii) over method (ii). (20 marks)

*CIMA P3 Management Accounting*

## 15.11* Advanced

Various attempts have been made in the public sector to achieve a more stable, long-term planning base in contrast to the traditional short-term annual budgeting approach, with its emphasis on 'flexibility'.

You are required to:

(a) explain the deficiencies of the traditional approach to planning which led to the attempts to introduce PPBS (programme budgeting); (6 marks)

(b) give an illustration of how a PPBS plan could be drawn up in respect of one sector of public authority activity; (8 marks)

(c) discuss the problems which have made it difficult in practice to introduce PPBS.

(6 marks)

(Total 20 marks)

*CIMA Stage 4: Management Accounting –*
*Control and Audit*
*Pilot Paper*

## 15.12 Advanced

Explain the specific roles of planning, motivation and evaluation in a system of budgetary control.

(7 marks)

*ACCA Level 2 Management Accounting*

## 15.13* Advanced

Traditional budgeting systems are incremental in nature and tend to focus on cost centres. Activity based budgeting links strategic planning to overall performance measurement aiming at continuous improvement.

(a) Explain the weaknesses of an incremental budgeting system. (5 marks)

(b) Describe the main features of an activity based budgeting system and comment on the advantages claimed for its use. (10 marks)

(Total 15 marks)

*ACCA Paper 9 Information for Control*
*and Decision Making*

## 15.14*Advanced

Budgeting has been criticised as

● a cumbersome process which occupies considerable management time;

● concentrating unduly on short-term financial control;

● having undesirable effects on the motivation of managers;

● emphasising formal organisation structure.

Requirements:

(a) Explain these criticisms. (8 marks)

(b) Explain what changes can be made in response to these criticisms to improve the budgeting process. (12 marks)

(Total 20 marks)

*CIMA Stage 4 Management Accounting*
*Control Systems*

## 15.15 Intermediate: Preparation of functional budgets

X plc manufactures Product X using three different raw materials. The product details are as follows:

### Selling price per unit £250

| | | |
|---|---|---|
| Material A | 3 kgs | material price £3.50 per kg |
| Material B | 2 kgs | material price £5.00 per kg |
| Material C | 4 kgs | material price £4.50 per kg |
| Direct labour | 8 hours | labour rate £8.00 per hour |

The company is considering its budgets for next year and has made the following estimates of sales demand for Product X for July to October:

| July | August | September | October |
|---|---|---|---|
| 400 units | 300 units | 600 units | 450 units |

It is company policy to hold stocks of finished goods at the end of each month equal to 50% of the following month's sales demand, and it is expected that the stock at the start of the budget period will meet this policy.

At the end of the production process the products are tested: it is usual for 10% of those tested to be faulty. It is not possible to rectify these faulty units.

Raw material stocks are expected to be as follows on 1 July:

| | |
|---|---|
| Material A | 1000 kgs |
| Material B | 400 kgs |
| Material C | 600 kgs |

Stocks are to be increased by 20% in July, and then remain at their new level for the foreseeable future.

Labour is paid on an hourly rate based on attendance. In addition to the unit direct labour hours shown above, 20% of *attendance time* is spent on tasks which support production activity.

Requirements:
(a) Prepare the following budgets for the quarter from July to September inclusive:
  (i)   sales budget in quantity and value;
  (ii)  production budget in units;
  (iii) raw material usage budget in kgs;
  (iv)  raw material purchases budget in kgs and value;
  (v)   labour requirements budget in hours and value.                        (16 marks)
(b) Explain the term '*principal budget factor*' and why its identification is an important part of the budget preparation process.    (3 marks)
(c) Explain clearly, using data from part (a) above, how you would construct a spreadsheet to produce the labour requirements budget for August. Include a specimen cell layout diagram containing formulae which would illustrate the basis for the spreadsheet.
                                            (6 marks)
                                     (Total 25 marks)
      *CIMA Stage 2 Operational cost accounting*

## 15.16 Intermediate: Preparation of functional budgets

D Limited is preparing its annual budgets for the year to 31 December 2001. It manufactures and sells one product, which has a selling price of £150. The marketing director believes that the price can be increased to £160 with effect from 1 July 2001 and that at this price the sales volume for each quarter of 2001 will be as follows:

**Sales volume**

| | |
|---|---|
| Quarter 1 | 40 000 |
| Quarter 2 | 50 000 |
| Quarter 3 | 30 000 |
| Quarter 4 | 45 000 |

Sales for each quarter of 2002 are expected to be 40 000 units.

Each unit of the finished product which is manufactured requires four units of component R and three units of component T, together with a body shell S. These items are purchased from an outside supplier. Currently prices are:

| | |
|---|---|
| Component R | £8.00 each |
| Component T | £5.00 each |
| Shell S | £30.00 each |

The components are expected to increase in price by 10% with effect from 1 April 2001; no change is expected in the price of the shell.

Assembly of the shell and components into the finished product requires 6 labour hours: labour is currently paid £5.00 per hour. A 4% increase in wage costs is anticipated to take effect from 1 October 2001.

Variable overhead costs are expected to be £10 per unit for the whole of 2001; fixed production overhead costs are expected to be £240 000 for the year, and are absorbed on a per unit basis. Stocks on 31 December 2000 are expected to be as follows:

| | |
|---|---|
| Finished units | 9000 units |
| Component R | 3000 units |
| Component T | 5500 units |
| Shell S | 500 units |

Closing stocks at the end of each quarter are to be as follows:

| | |
|---|---|
| Finished units | 10% of next quarter's sales |
| Component R | 20% of next quarter's production requirements |
| Component T | 15% of next quarter's production requirements |
| Shell S | 10% of next quarter's production requirements |

Requirement:
(a) Prepare the following budgets of D Limited for the year ending 31 December 2001, showing values for each quarter and the year in total:
  (i)   sales budget (in £s and units)
  (ii)  production budget (in units)
  (iii) material usage budget (in units)
  (iv)  production cost budget (in £s).
                                            (15 marks)

(b) Sales are often considered to be the principal budget factor of an organisation.

Requirement:
Explain the meaning of the 'principal budget factor' and, assuming that it is sales, explain how sales may be forecast making appropriate reference to the use of statistical techniques and the use of microcomputers. (10 marks)
(Total 25 marks)
*CIMA Stage 2 Operational Cost Accounting*

### 15.17* Intermediate: Calculation of sales to achieve target profit and preparation of functional budgets

There is a continuing demand for three sub-assemblies – A, B, and C – made and sold by MW Limited. Sales are in the ratios of A 1, B 2, C 4 and selling prices are A £215, B £250, C £300.

Each sub-assembly consists of a copper frame onto which are fixed the same components but in differing quantities as follows:

| Sub-assembly | Frame | Component D | Component E | Component F |
|---|---|---|---|---|
| A | 1 | 5 | 1 | 4 |
| B | 1 | 1 | 7 | 5 |
| C | 1 | 3 | 5 | 1 |
| Buying in costs, per unit | £20 | £8 | £5 | £3 |

Operation times by labour for each sub-assembly are:

| Sub-assembly | Skilled hours | Unskilled hours |
|---|---|---|
| A | 2 | 2 |
| B | $1\frac{1}{2}$ | 2 |
| C | $1\frac{1}{2}$ | 3 |

The skilled labour is paid £6 per hour and unskilled £4.50 per hour. The skilled labour is located in a machining department and the unskilled labour in an assembly department. A five-day week of $37\frac{1}{2}$ hours is worked and each accounting period is for four weeks.

Variable overhead per sub-assembly is A £5, B £4 and C £3.50. At the end of the current year, stocks are expected to be as shown below but because interest rates have increased and the company utilises a bank overdraft for working capital purposes, it is planned to effect a 10% reduction in all finished sub-assemblies and

bought-in stocks during Period 1 of the forthcoming year.

Forecast stocks at current year end:

| Sub-assembly | | Copper frames | 1 000 |
|---|---|---|---|
| A | 300 | Component D | 4 000 |
| B | 700 | Component E | 10 000 |
| C | 1 600 | Component F | 4 000 |

Work-in-progress stocks are to be ignored.

Overhead for the forthcoming year is budgeted to be Production £728 000, Selling and Distribution £364 000 and Administration £338 000. These costs, all fixed, are expected to be incurred evenly throughout the year and are treated as period costs.

Within Period 1 it is planned to sell one thirteenth of the annual requirements which are to be the sales necessary to achieve the company profit target of £6.5 million before tax.

You are required:
(a) to prepare budgets in respect of Period 1 of the forthcoming year for
  (i) sales, in quantities and value;
  (ii) production, in quantities only;
  (iii) materials usage, in quantities;
  (iv) materials purchases, in quantities and value;
  (v) manpower budget, i.e. numbers of people needed in each of the machining department and the assembly department; (20 marks)
(b) to discuss the factors to be considered if the bought-in stocks were to be reduced to one week's requirements – this has been proposed by the purchasing officer but resisted by the production director. (5 marks)
(Total 25 marks)
*CIMA Stage 2 Cost Accounting*

### 15.18* Intermediate: Preparation of functional budgets

*Data*
Wilmslow Ltd makes two products, the Alpha and the Beta. Both products use the same material and labour but in different amounts. The company divides its year into four quarters, each of twelve weeks. Each week consists of five days and each day comprises 7 hours.

You are employed as the management accountant to Wilmslow Ltd and you originally prepared a budget for quarter 3, the twelve weeks to 17 September. The basic data for that budget is reproduced below.

**Original budgetary data: quarter 3
12 weeks to 17 September**

| Product | Alpha | Beta |
|---|---|---|
| Estimated demand | 1800 units | 2100 units |
| Material per unit | 8 kilograms | 12 kilograms |
| Labour per unit | 3 hours | 6 hours |

Since the budget was prepared, three developments have taken place.

1. The company has begun to use linear regression and seasonal variations to forecast sales demand. Because of this, the estimated demand for quarter 3 has been revised to 2000 Alphas and 2400 Betas.
2. As a result of the revised sales forecasting, you have developed more precise estimates of sales and closing stock levels.
   - The sales volume of both the Alpha and Beta in quarter 4 (th twelve weeks ending 10 December) will be 20% more than in the revised budget for quarter 3 as a result of seasonal variations.
   - The closing stock of finished Alphas at the end of quarter 3 should represent 5 days sales for quarter 4.
   - The closing stock of finished Betas at the end of quarter 3 should represent 10 days sales for quarter 4.
   - Production in quarter 4 of both Alpha and Beta is planned to be 20% more than in the revised budget for quarter 3. The closing stock of materials at the end of quarter 3 should be sufficient for 20 days production in quarter 4.
3. New equipment has been installed. The workforce is not familiar with the equipment. Because of this, for quarter 3, they will only be working at 80% of the efficiency assumed in the original budgetary data.

   Other data from your original budget which has not changed is reproduced below:

   - 50 production employees work a 35 hour week and are each paid £210 per week;
   - overtime is paid for at £9 per hour;
   - the cost of material is £10 per kilogram;

- opening stocks at the beginning of quarter 3 are as follows:
- finished Alphas          500 units
- finished Betas          600 units
- material          12 000 kilograms
- there will not be any work in progress at any time.

*Task 1*

The production director of Wilmslow Ltd wants to schedule production for quarter 3 (the twelve weeks ending 17 September) and asks you to use the revised information to prepare the following:
(a) the revised production budget for Alphas and Betas;
(b) the material purchases budget in kilograms;
(c) a statement showing the cost of the material purchases;
(d) the labour budget in hours;
(e) a statement showing the cost of labour.

*Data*

Margaret Brown is the financial director of Wilmslow Ltd. She is not convinced that the use of linear regression, even when adjusted for seasonal variations, is the best way of forecasting sales volumes for Wilmslow Ltd.

The quality of sales forecasting is an agenda item for the next meeting of the Board of Directors and she asks for your advice.

*Task 2*

Write a *brief* memo to Margaret Brown. Your memo should:
(a) identify *two* limitations of the use of linear regression as a forecasting technique;
(b) suggest *two* other ways of sales forecasting.
*AAT Contribution to the planning and allocation of resources*

**15.19 Intermediate: Preparation of functions budgets, cash budget and master budget**
The budgeted balance sheet data of Kwan Tong Umbago Ltd is as follows:

**1 March**

| | Cost (£) | Depreciation to date (£) | Net (£) |
|---|---|---|---|
| Fixed assets | | | |
| Land and buildings | 500 000 | — | 500 000 |
| Machinery and equipment | 124 000 | 84 500 | 39 500 |

| Motor vehicles | 42 000 | 16 400 | 25 600 |
|---|---|---|---|
| | 666 000 | 100 900 | 565 100 |

*Working capital:*
*Current assets*

| | | |
|---|---|---|
| Stock of raw materials (100 units) | 4320 | |
| Stock of finished goods (110 units)ª | 10 450 | |
| Debtors (January £7680 February £10 400) | 18 080 | |
| Cash and bank | 6 790 | |
| | 39 640 | |

*Less current liabilities*

| | | |
|---|---|---|
| Creditors (raw materials) | 3 900 | 35 740 |
| | | 600 840 |

*Represented by*:

| | | |
|---|---|---|
| Ordinary share capital (fully paid) £1 shares | 500 000 | |
| Share premium | 60 000 | |
| Profit and loss account | 40 840 | |
| | | 600 840 |

ªThe stock of finished goods was valued at marginal cost

The estimates for the next four-month period are as follows:

| | March | April | May | June |
|---|---|---|---|---|
| Sales (units) | 80 | 84 | 96 | 94 |
| Production (units) | 70 | 75 | 90 | 90 |
| Purchases of raw materials (units) | 80 | 80 | 85 | 85 |
| Wages and variable overheads at £65 per unit | £4550 | £4875 | £5850 | £5850 |
| Fixed overheads | £1200 | £1200 | £1200 | £1200 |

The company intends to sell each unit for £219 and has estimated that it will have to pay £45 per unit for raw materials. One unit of raw material is needed for each unit of finished product.

All sales and purchases of raw materials are on credit. Debtors are allowed two months' credit and suppliers of raw materials are paid after one month's credit. The wages, variable overheads and fixed overheads are paid in the month in which they are incurred.

Cash from a loan secured on the land and buildings of £120 000 at an interest rate of 7.5% is due to be received on 1 May. Machinery costing £112 000 will be received in May and paid for in June.

The loan interest is payable half yearly from September onwards. An interim dividend to 31 March of £12 500 will be paid in June.

Depreciation for the four months, including that on the new machinery is:

| | |
|---|---|
| Machinery and equipment | £15 733 |
| Motor vehicles | £3 500 |

The company uses the FIFO method of stock valuation. Ignore taxation.

Required:

(a) Calculate and present the raw materials budget and finished goods budget in terms of units, for each month from March to June inclusive.                (5 marks)

(b) Calculate the corresponding sales budgets, the production cost budgets and the budgeted closing debtors, creditors and stocks in terms of value.                (5 marks)

(c) Prepare and present a cash budget for each of the four months.                (6 marks)

(d) Prepare a master budget, i.e. a budgeted trading and profit and loss account, for the four months to 30 June, and budgeted balance sheet as at 30 June.                (10 marks)

(e) Advise the company about possible ways in which it can improve its cash management.
(9 marks)
(Total 35 marks)
*ACCA Paper 8 Managerial Finance*

**15.20\* Intermediate: Budget preparation and comments on sales forecasting methods**

You have recently been appointed as the management accountant to Alderley Ltd, a small company manufacturing two products, the Elgar and the Holst. Both products use the same type of material and labour but in different proportions. In the past, the company has had poor control over its working capital. To remedy this, you have recommended to the directors that a budgetary control system be introduced. This proposal has, now, been agreed.

Because Alderley Ltd's production and sales are spread evenly over the year, it was agreed that the annual budget should be broken down into four periods, each of 13 weeks, and commencing with the 13 weeks ending 4 April. To help you in this task, the sales and production directors have provided you with the following information:

1. Marketing and production data

|  | Elgar | Holst |
| --- | --- | --- |
| Budgeted sales for 13 weeks (units) | 845 | 1235 |
| Material content per unit (kilograms) | 7 | 8 |
| Labour per unit (standard hours) | 8 | 5 |

2. Production labour

The 24 production employees work a 37-hour, five-day week and are paid £8 per hour. Any hours in excess of this involve Alderley in paying an overtime premium of 25%. Because of technical problems, which will continue over the next 13 weeks, employees are only able to work at 95% efficiency compared to standard.

3. Purchasing and opening stocks

The production director believes that raw material will cost £12 per kilogram over the budget period. He also plans to revise the amount of stock being kept. He estimates that the stock levels at the commencement of the budget period will be as follows:

| Raw materials | Elgar | Holst |
| --- | --- | --- |
| 2328 kilograms | 163 units | 361 units |

4. Closing stocks

At the end of the 13-week period closing stocks are planned to change. On the assumption that production and sales volumes for the second budget period will be similar to those in the first period:

- raw material stocks should be sufficient for 13 days' production;
- finished stocks of the Elgar should be equivalent to 6 days' sales volume;
- finished stocks of the Holst should be equivalent to 14 days sales volume.

*Task 1*

Prepare in the form of a statement the following information for the 13-week period to 4 April:

(a) the production budget in units for the Elgar and Holst;
(b) the purchasing budget for Alderley Ltd in units;
(c) the cost of purchases for the period;
(d) the production labour budget for Alderley Ltd in hours;

(e) the cost of production labour for the period.

*Note*: Assume a five-day week for both sales and production.

The managing director of Alderley Ltd, Alan Dunn, has also only recently been appointed. He is keen to develop the company and has already agreed to two new products being developed. These will be launched in eighteen months' time. While talking to you about the budget, he mentions that the quality of sales forecasting will need to improve if the company is to grow rapidly. Currently, the budgeted sales figure is found by initially adding 5% to the previous year's sales volume and then revising the figure following discussions with the marketing director. He believes this approach is increasingly inadequate and now requires a more systematic approach.

A few days later, Alan Dunn sends you a memo. In that memo, he identifies three possible strategies for increasing sales volume. They are:

- more sales to existing customers;
- the development of new markets;
- the development of new products.

He asks for your help in forecasting likely sales volumes from these sources.

*Task 2*

Write a brief memo to Alan Dunn. Your memo should:

(a) identify *four* ways of forecasting future sales volume;
(b) show how each of your four ways of forecasting can be applied to *one* of the sales strategies identified by Alan Dunn and justify your choice;
(c) give *two* reasons why forecasting methods might not prove to be accurate.

*AAT Technicians Stage*

**15.21 Intermediate: Preparation of cash budgets**
The following data and estimates are available for ABC Limited for June, July and August.

|  | June (£) | July (£) | August (£) |
| --- | --- | --- | --- |
| Sales | 45 000 | 50 000 | 60 000 |
| Wages | 12 000 | 13 000 | 14 500 |
| Overheads | 8 500 | 9 500 | 9 000 |

The following information is available regarding direct materials:

| | June (£) | July (£) | August (£) | September (£) |
|---|---|---|---|---|
| Opening stock | 5000 | 3500 | 6000 | 4000 |
| Material usage | 8000 | 9000 | 10000 | |

*Notes*:
1. 10% of sales are for cash, the balance is received the following month. The amount received in June for May's sales is £29 500.
2. Wages are paid in the month they are incurred.
3. Overheads include £1500 per month for depreciation. Overheads are settled the month following. £6500 is to be paid in June for May's overheads.
4. Purchases of direct materials are paid for in the month purchased.
5. The opening cash balance in June is £11 750.
6. A tax bill of £25 000 is to be paid in July.

Required:
(a) Calculate the amount of direct material purchases in *each* of the months of June, July and August. (3 marks)
(b) Prepare cash budgets for June, July and August. (9 marks)
(c) Describe briefly the advantages of preparing cash budgets. (3 marks)
(Total marks 15)
*CIMA Stage 1 Cost Accounting*

## 15.22* Intermediate: Preparation of cash budgets and calculation of stock, debtor and creditor balances

In the near future a company will purchase a manufacturing business for £315 000, this price to include goodwill (£150 000), equipment and fittings (£120 000), and stock of raw materials and finished goods (£45 000). A delivery van will be purchased for £15 000 as soon as the business purchase is completed. The delivery van will be paid for in the second month of operations.

The following forecasts have been made for the business following purchase:
(i) Sales (before discounts) of the business's single product, at a mark-up of 60% on production cost, will be:

| Month | 1 | 2 | 3 | 4 | 5 | 6 |
|---|---|---|---|---|---|---|
| (£000) | 96 | 96 | 92 | 96 | 100 | 104 |

25% of sales will be for cash; the remainder will be on credit, for settlement in the month following that of sale. A discount of 10% will be given to selected credit customers, who represent 25% of gross sales.
(ii) Production cost will be £5.00 per unit. The production cost will be made up of:

| | |
|---|---|
| raw materials | £2.50 |
| direct labour | £1.50 |
| fixed overhead | £1.00 |

(iii) Production will be arranged so that closing stock at the end of any month is sufficient to meet sales requirements in the following month. A value of £30 000 is placed on the stock of finished goods which was acquired on purchase of the business. This valuation is based on the forecast of production cost per unit given in (ii) above.
(iv) The single raw material will be purchased so that stock at the end of a month is sufficient to meet half of the following month's production requirements. Raw material stock acquired on purchase of the business (£15 000) is valued at the cost per unit which is forecast as given in (ii) above. Raw materials will be purchased on one month's credit.
(v) Costs of direct labour will be met as they are incurred in production.
(vi) The fixed production overhead rate of £1.00 per unit is based upon a forecast of the first year's production of 150 000 units. This rate includes depreciation of equipment and fittings on a straight-line basis over the next five years.
(vii) Selling and administration overheads are all fixed, and will be £208 000 in the first year. These overheads include depreciation of the delivery van at 30% per annum on a reducing balance basis. All fixed overheads will be incurred on a regular basis, with the exception of rent and rates. £25 000 is payable for the year ahead in month one for rent and rates.

Required:
(a) Prepare a monthly cash budget. You should include the business purchase and the first four months of operations following purchase. (17 marks)
(b) Calculate the stock, debtor, and creditor balances at the end of the four month

period. Comment briefly upon the liquidity situation. (8 marks)
(Total 25 marks)
*ACCA Level 1 Costing*

### 15.23* Intermediate: Preparation of cash budgets

A redundant manager who received compensation of £80 000 decides to commence business on 4 January, manufacturing a product for which he knows there is a ready market. He intends to employ some of his former workers who were also made redundant but they will not all commence on 4 January. Suitable premises have been found to rent and second-hand machinery costing £60 000 has been bought out of the £80 000. This machinery has an estimated life of five years from January and no residual value.

*Other data*
1. Production will begin on 4 January and 25% of the following month's sales will be manufactured in January. Each month thereafter the production will consist of 75% of the current month's sales and 25% of the following month's sales.
2. Estimated sales are

| | (units) | (£) |
|---|---|---|
| January | Nil | Nil |
| February | 3200 | 80 000 |
| March | 3600 | 90 000 |
| April | 4000 | 100 000 |
| May | 4000 | 100 000 |

3. Variable production cost per unit

| | (£) |
|---|---|
| Direct materials | 7 |
| Direct wages | 6 |
| Variable overhead | 2 |
| | 15 |

4. Raw material stocks costing £10 000 have been purchased (out of the manager's £80 000) to enable production to commence and it is intended to buy, each month, 50% of the materials required for the following month's production requirements. The other 50% will be purchased in the month of production. Payment will be made 30 days after purchase.

5. Direct workers have agreed to have their wages paid into bank accounts on the seventh working day of each month in respect of the previous month's earnings.
6. Variable production overhead: 60% is to be paid in the month following the month it was incurred and 40% is to be paid one month later.
7. Fixed overheads are £4000 per month. One quarter of this is paid in the month incurred, one half in the following month, and the remainder represents depreciation on the second-hand machinery.
8. Amounts receivable: a 5% cash discount is allowed for payment in the current month and 20% of each month's sales qualify for this discount. 50% of each month's sales are received in the following month, 20% in the third month and 8% in the fourth month. The balance of 2% represents anticipated bad debts.

You are required to:
(a) (i) prepare a cash budget for each of the first four months, assuming that overdraft facilities will be available, (17 marks)
(ii) state the amount receivable from customers in May; (4 marks)
(b) describe briefly the benefits to cash budgeting from the use of a particular type of software package. (4 marks)
(Total 25 marks)
*CIMA Stage 2 Cost Accounting 2*

### 15.24 Intermediate: Preparation of cash budgets

A company is to carry out a major modernization of its factory commencing in two weeks time. During the modernization, which is expected to take four weeks to complete, no production of the company's single product will be possible.

The following additional information is available:
(i) *Sales/Debtors*: Demand for the product at £100 per unit is expected to continue at 800 units per week, the level of sales achieved for the last four weeks, for one further week. It is then expected to reduce to 700 units per week for three weeks, before rising to a level of 900 units per week where it is expected to remain for several weeks.

All sales are on credit, 50% being received in cash in the week following the week of sale and 50% in the week after that.

(ii) *Production/Finished goods stock*: Production will be at a level of 1200 units per week for the next two weeks. Finished goods stock is 2800 units at the beginning of week 1.

(iii) *Raw material stock*: Raw material stock is £36 000 at the beginning of week 1. This will be increased by the end of week 1 to £40 000 and reduced to £10 000 by the end of week 2.

(iv) *Costs*

|  | (£ per unit) |
| --- | --- |
| Variable: | |
| Raw material | 35 |
| Direct labour | 20 |
| Overhead | 10 |
| Fixed: | |
| Overhead | 25 |

Fixed overheads have been apportioned to units on the basis of the normal output level of 800 units per week and include depreciation of £4000 per week.

In addition to the above unit costs, overtime premiums of £5000 per week will be incurred in weeks 1 and 2. During the modernization variable costs will be avoided, apart from direct labour which will be incurred at the level equivalent to 800 units production per week. Outlays on fixed overheads will be reduced by £4000 per week.

(v) *Payments:* Creditors for raw materials, which stand at £27 000 at the beginning of week 1, are paid in the week following purchase. All other payments are made in the week in which the liability is incurred.

(vi) *Liquidity:* The company has a bank overdraft balance of £39 000 at the beginning of week 1 and an overdraft limit of £50 000.

The company is anxious to establish the liquidity situation over the modernization period, excluding the requirements for finance for the modernization itself.

Required:

(a) Prepare a weekly cash budget covering the six-week period up to the planned completion of the modernization. (15 marks)

(b) Comment briefly upon any matters concerning the liquidity situation which you feel should be drawn to the attention of management. (7 marks)

(Total 22 marks)

*ACCA Level 1 Costing*

### 15.25* Intermediate: Preparation of cash budgets

The management of Beck plc have been informed that the union representing the direct production workers at one of their factories, where a standard product is produced, intends to call a strike. The accountant has been asked to advise the management of the effect the strike will have on cash flow.

The following data has been made available:

|  | Week 1 | Week 2 | Week 3 |
| --- | --- | --- | --- |
| Budgeted sales | 400 units | 500 units | 400 units |
| Budgeted production | 600 units | 400 units | Nil |

The strike will commence at the beginning of week 3 and it should be assumed that it will continue for at least four weeks. Sales at 400 units per week will continue to be made during the period of the strike until stocks of finished goods are exhausted. Production will stop at the end of week 2. The current stock level of finished goods is 600 units. Stocks of work in progress are not carried.

The selling price of the product is £60 and the budgeted manufacturing cost is made up as follows:

|  | (£) |
| --- | --- |
| Direct materials | 15 |
| Direct wages | 7 |
| Variable overheads | 8 |
| Fixed overheads | 18 |
| Total | £48 |

Direct wages are regarded as a variable cost. The company operates a full absorption costing system and the fixed overhead absorption rate is based upon a budgeted fixed overhead of £9000 per week. Included in the total fixed overheads is £700 per week for depreciation of equipment. During the period of the strike direct wages and variable overheads would not be incurred and the cash expended on fixed overheads would be reduced by £1500 per week.

The current stock of raw materials are worth £7500; it is intended that these stocks should increase to £11 000 by the end of week 1 and then remain at this level during the period of the strike. *All direct materials are paid for one week after they have been received. Direct wages are paid one week in arrears. It should be assumed that all relevant overheads are paid for immediately the expense is incurred.* All sales are on credit, 70% of the sales value is received in cash from the debtors at the end of the first week after the sales have been made and the balance at the end of the second week.

The current amount outstanding to material suppliers is £8000 and direct wage accruals amount to £3200. Both of these will be paid in week 1. The current balance owing from debtors is £31 200, of which £24 000 will be received during week 1 and the remainder during week 2. The current balance of cash at bank and in hand is £1000.

Required:

(a) (i) Prepare a cash budget for weeks 1 to 6 showing the balance of cash at the end of each week together with a suitable analysis of the receipts and payments during each week. (13 marks)

(ii) Comment upon any matters arising from the cash budget which you consider should be brought to management's attention. (4 marks)

(b) Explain why the reported profit figure for a period does not normally represent the amount of cash generated in that period.

(5 marks)
(Total 22 marks)
*ACCA Level 1 Costing*

**15.26 Advanced: Preparation of a cash budget and a decision whether to close a department and sub contract**

The Rosrock Housing Association has two types of housing estate in the Rosburgh area (A and B).

The following information is available:

(i) The association has its own squad of painters who carry out painting and decorating work on the housing estates. The estimated cost for each house in which the work will be done in 2001 is as follows: Painting

|  | (£) |
| --- | --- |
| (a) Direct material cost | 75 |
| (b) Direct labour cost | 270 |

(c) In 2001 overhead cost is absorbed at 20% on direct material cost plus 100%

on direct labour cost. Only 30% of material related overhead and 33$\frac{1}{3}$% of labour related overhead is variable, the remainder is fixed overhead and the absorption rate is arrived at using the budgeted number of houses which require painting and decorating each year.

(d) Fixed overhead may be analysed into:
1. Items avoidable on cessation of the service 30%
2. Depreciation of equipment and premises 20%
3. Apportionment of head office costs 50%

(e) Direct material and direct labour cost are wholly variable.

(ii) The total number of houses of each type and the percentage requiring painting and decorating each year is as follows:

|  | Estate Type A | Estate Type B |
| --- | --- | --- |
| Total number of houses | 500 | 600 |
| Percentage of houses requiring maintenance each year: | 30% | 20% |

(iii) Where relevant, all future costs are expected to increase each year by a fixed percentage of the previous year's level due to changes in prices and wage rates as follows:

| Direct material cost | 5% |
| --- | --- |
| Direct labour cost | 7% |
| Overhead cost | 6% |

(iv) Forecast balances at 31 December 2000 and other cash flow timing information is as follows:

(a) Creditors for materials: £2100. Credit purchases are 90% of purchases, the remainder being cash purchases. The credit purchases outstanding at a year end are estimated at 10% of the annual materials purchased on credit. There are no materials on hand on 31 December 2000.

(b) Labour costs accrued: £2800. Labour costs outstanding at a year end are estimated at 4% of the annual total earnings for the year.

(c) Creditors for variable overheads: £600. Variable overheads are paid 60% in the month of incidence and 40% in the month following. Variable overheads are deemed to accrue evenly each month throughout the year.

(d) Fixed overheads are paid in twelve equal amounts with no accruals or prepayments.

Required:

(a) Prepare a cash budget for the existing painting and decorating function for the period 1 January 2001 to 31 December 2003 which shows the cash flows for each of the years 2001, 2002 and 2003. (Calculations should be rounded to the nearest whole £.)  (14 marks)

(b) An outside company has offered to undertake all painting and decorating work for a three year period 2001 to 2003 for a fixed fee of £135 000 per annum.

  (i) Calculate whether the offer should be accepted on financial grounds using the information available in the question.

    (2 marks)

  (ii) List and comment upon other factors which should be taken into account by Rosrock Housing Association management when considering this offer.

    (6 marks)

    (Total 22 marks)

*ACCA Level 2 Cost and Management Accounting*

### 15.27 Intermediate: Direct labour budget and labour cost accounting

A company, which manufactures a range of consumer products, is preparing the direct labour budget for one of its factories. Three products are manufactured in the factory. Each product passes through two stages: filling and packing.

Direct labour efficiency standards are set for each stage. The standards are based upon the number of units expected to be manufactured per hour of direct labour. Current standards are:

| | Product 1 (units/hour) | Product 2 (units/hour) | Product 3 (units/hour) |
|---|---|---|---|
| Filling | 125 | 300 | 250 |
| Packing | 95 | 100 | 95 |

Budgeted sales of the three products are:

| | |
|---|---|
| Product 1 | 850 000 units |
| Product 2 | 1 500 000 units |
| Product 3 | 510 000 units |

Production will be at the same level each month, and will be sufficient to enable finished goods stocks at the end of the budget year to be:

| | |
|---|---|
| Product 1 | 200 000 units |
| Product 2 | 255 000 units |
| Product 3 | 70 000 units |

Stocks at the beginning of the budget year are expected to be:

| | |
|---|---|
| Product 1 | 100 000 units |
| Product 2 | 210 000 units |
| Product 3 | 105 000 units |

After completion of the filling stage, 5% of the output of Products 1 and 3 is expected to be rejected and destroyed. The cost of such rejects is treated as a normal loss.

A single direct labour hour rate is established for the factory as a whole. The total payroll cost of direct labour personnel is included in the direct labour rate. Hours of direct labour personnel are budgeted to be split as follows:

| | % of Total time |
|---|---|
| Direct work | 80 |
| Holidays (other, than public holidays) | 7 |
| Sickness | 3 |
| Idle time | 4 |
| Cleaning | 3 |
| Training | 3 |
| | 100% |

All direct labour personnel are employed on a full-time basis to work a basic 35 hour, 5 day, week. Overtime is to be budgeted at an average of 3 hours per employee, per week. Overtime is paid at a premium of 25% over the basic hourly rate of £4 per hour. There will be 250 possible working days during the year. You are to assume that employees are paid for exactly 52 weeks in the year.

Required:

Calculate:

(a) The number of full-time direct employees required during the budget year.  (14 marks)

(b) The direct labour rate (£ per hour, to 2 decimal places).  (5 marks)

(c) The direct labour cost for each product (pence per unit to 2 decimal places).  (6 marks)

    (Total 25 marks)

*ACCA Level 1 Costing*

# Management control systems

Control is the process of ensuring that a firm's activities conform to its plan and that its objectives are achieved. There can be no control without objectives and plans, since these predetermine and specify the desirable behaviour and set out the procedures that should be followed by members of the organization to ensure that a firm is operated in a desired manner.

Drucker (1964) distinguishes between 'controls' and 'control'. Controls are measurement and information, whereas control means direction. In other words, 'controls' are purely a means to an end; the end is control. 'Control' is the function that makes sure that actual work is done to fulfil the original intention, and 'controls' are used to provide information to assist in determining the control action to be taken. For example, material costs may be greater than budget. 'Controls' will indicate that costs exceed budget and that this may be because the purchase of inferior quality materials causes excessive wastage. 'Control' is the action that is taken to purchase the correct quality materials in the future to reduce excessive wastage.

'Controls' encompasses all the methods and procedures that direct employees towards achieving the organization objectives. Many different control mechanisms are used in organizations and the management accounting control system represents only one aspect of the various control mechanisms that companies use to control their managers and employees. To fully understand the role that management accounting control systems play in the control process, it is necessary to be aware of how they relate to the entire array of control mechanisms used by organizations.

This chapter begins by describing the different types of controls that are used by companies. The elements of management accounting control systems will then be described within the context of the overall control process.

## Learning objectives:

After studying this chapter you should be able to:

- describe the three different types of controls used in organizations;
- describe a cybernetic control system;
- distinguish between feedback and feed-forward controls;
- explain the potential harmful side-effects of the different types of controls;
- define the four different types of responsibility centres;
- explain the different elements of management accounting control systems;
- describe the controllability principle and the methods of implementing it;
- describe the different types of financial performance targets and the effects of their level of difficulty on motivation and performance;
- describe the influence of participation in the budgeting process;
- distinguish between the three different styles of evaluating performance and identify the circumstances when a particular style is most appropriate.

# Control at different organizational levels

Control is applied at different levels within an organization. Merchant (1998) distinguishes between strategic control and management control. Strategic control has an external focus. The emphasis is on how a firm, given its strengths and weaknesses and limitations can compete with other firms in the same industry. We shall explore some of these issues in Chapter 23 within the context of strategic management accounting. In this, and the next four chapters, our emphasis will be on management control systems which consist of a collection of control mechanisms that primarily have an internal focus. The aim of management control systems is to influence employee behaviours in desirable ways in order to increase the probability that an organization's objectives will be achieved.

# Different types of controls

Companies use many different control mechanisms to cope with the problem of organizational control. To make sense of the vast number of controls that are used we shall classify them into three categories using approaches that have been adopted by Ouchi (1979) and Merchant (1998). They are:

1. action (or behavioural) controls;
2. personnel and cultural (or clan and social) controls;
3. results (or output) controls.

The terms in parentheses refer to the classification used by Ouchi whereas the other terms refer to the categories specified by Merchant. Because the classifications used by both authors are compatible we shall use the terms interchangeably.

## ACTION OR BEHAVIOURAL CONTROLS

Behavioural controls involve observing the actions of individuals as they go about their work. They are appropriate where cause and effect relationships are well understood, so that if the correct means are followed, the desired outcomes will occur. Under these circumstances effective control can be achieved by having superiors watch and guide the actions of subordinates. For example, if the foreman watches the workers on the assembly line and ensures that the work is done exactly as prescribed then the expected quality and quantity of work should ensue.

Instead of using the term behavioural controls Merchant uses the term action controls. He defines action controls as applying to those situations where the actions themselves are the focus of controls. They are usable and effective only when managers know what actions are desirable (or undesirable) and have the ability to make sure that the desirable actions occur (or that the undesirable actions do not occur). Forms of action controls described by Merchant include behavioural constraints, preaction reviews and action accountability.

The aim of *behavioural constraints* is to prevent people from doing things that should not be done. They include physical constraints, such as computer passwords that restrict accessing or updating information sources to authorized personnel, and administrative constraints. Imposing ceilings on the amount of capital expenditure that managers may authorize is an example of an administrative constraint. For example, managers at lower levels may be able to authorize capital expenditure below £10 000 within a total annual budget of, say, £100 000. The aim is to ensure that only those personnel with the necessary expertise and authority can authorize major expenditure and that such expenditure remains under their control.

*Preaction reviews* involve the scrutiny and approval of action plans of the individuals being controlled before they can undertake a course of action. Examples include the approval by municipal authorities of plans for the construction of properties prior to building commencing or the approval by a tutor of a dissertation plan prior to the student being authorized to embark on the dissertation.

*Action accountability* involves defining actions that are acceptable or unacceptable, observing the actions and rewarding acceptable or punishing unacceptable actions. Examples of action accountability include establishing work rules and procedures and company codes of conduct that employees must follow. Line item budgets that were described in the previous chapter are another form of action accountability whereby an upper limit on an expense category is given for the budget period. If managers exceed these limits they are held accountable and are required to justify their actions. The purpose of action accountability is to set limits on employee behaviour. Direct observation of employees' actions by superiors to ensure that they are following prescribed rules represents the main form of ensuring action accountability. Other forms include internal audits which involve checks on transaction records and compliance with pre-set action standards.

Action/behavioural controls can only be used effectively when managers know what actions are desirable (or undesirable). In other words, they are appropriate only when cause-and-effect work relationships are well understood such as when a supervisor can observe the actions of workers on a production line to ensure that work is done exactly as prescribed. In contrast, the application of action controls is limited where the work of employees is complex and uncertain and cause-and-effect relationships cannot be precisely described. For action controls to be effective a second requirement must also be met. Managers must also be able to ensure that desired actions are taken. There must be some means of action tracking so that managers can distinguish between good and bad actions. If both of the above conditions do not apply then action controls are inappropriate.

Action controls that focus on *preventing* undesirable behaviour are the ideal form of control because their aim is to prevent the behaviour from occurring. They are preferable to *detection* controls that are applied after the occurrence of the actions because they avoid the costs of undesirable behaviour. Nevertheless, detection controls can still be useful if they are applied in a timely manner so that they can lead to the early cessation of undesirable actions. Their existence also discourages individuals from engaging in such actions.

## PERSONNEL, CULTURAL AND SOCIAL CONTROLS

Clan and social controls are the second types of controls described by Ouchi. **Clan controls** are based on the belief that by fostering a strong sense of solidarity and commitment towards organizational goals people can become immersed in the interests of the organization. Macintosh (1985) illustrates an extreme example of clan controls by describing the exploits of the Japanese *kamikaze* pilots during World War II. He describes how each pilot fervently believed his individual interests were served best by complete personal immersion in the needs of Japan and the Emperor. It was understood that each pilot would sacrifice himself and his plane by crashing into an enemy warship. National ruin without resistance represented public disgrace. These beliefs were shared by each pilot.

The main feature of clan controls is the high degree of employee discipline attained through the dedication of each individual to the interests of the whole. At a less extreme level clan controls can be viewed as corporate cultures or a special form of social control such as the selection of people who have already been socialized into adopting particular norms and patterns of behaviour to perform particular tasks. For example, if the only staff promoted to managerial level are those who display a high commitment to the firm's objectives then the need for other forms of controls can be reduced, provided that the managers are committed to achieving the 'right' objectives.

Merchant adopts a similar approach to Ouchi and classifies personnel and cultural controls as a second form of control. He defines personnel controls as helping employees do a good job by building on employees' natural tendencies to control themselves. In particular, they ensure that the employees have the capabilities (in terms of intelligence, qualifications and experience) and the resources needed to do a good job. Merchant identifies three major methods of implementing personnel controls. They are selection and placement, training and job design and the provision of the necessary resources. Selection and placement involves finding the right people to do a specified job. Training can be used to ensure that employees know how to perform the assigned tasks and to make them fully aware of the results and actions that is expected from them. Job design entails designing jobs in such a way that enable employees to undertake their tasks with a high degree of success. This requires that jobs are not made too complex, onerous or badly defined so that employees do not know what is expected of them.

Cultural controls represent a set of values, social norms and beliefs that are shared by members of the organization and that influence their actions. Cultural controls are exercised by individuals over one another – for example, procedures used by groups within an organization to regulate performance of their own members and to bring them into line when they deviate from group norms. It is apparent from the above description that cultural controls are virtually the same as social controls.

Merchant suggest that a number of methods can be employed to shape culture and thus effect cultural controls. They include codes of conduct, group based rewards, and interorganizational transfers. Codes of conduct are formal written documents that incorporate general statements of corporate values and commitments to stakeholders and ways in which top management would like the organization to function. They are designed to indicate to employees what behaviours are expected in the absence of clearly defined rules or controls. Group based rewards consist of rewards based on collective achievements such as group bonuses and profit sharing schemes. They encourage mutual-monitoring by members of the group and reduce measurement costs because individual performance does not have to be measured. Interorganizational transfers involve moving managers between different functions and divisions in order to give them a better understanding of the organization as a whole. This practice is frequently used by Japanese firms to improve their sense of belonging to an organization rather than to the sub-units and also to ensure that managers are aware of the problems experienced by different parts of the organization.

In recent years working practices have begun to change and managers are now relying on people closest to the operating processes and customers to take actions without authorization from superiors. This approach is known as employee empowerment and places greater emphasis on shared organizational values for ensuring that everyone is acting in the organization's best interests. A strong internal firm culture can decrease the need for other control mechanisms since employee beliefs and norms are more likely to coincide with firm goals. They can also be used to some extent in many different organizational settings and are less costly to operate than other types of controls. They also tend to have less harmful side-effects than other control mechanisms.

# RESULTS OR OUTPUT CONTROLS

Output or results controls involve collecting and reporting information about the outcomes of work effort. The major advantage of results controls is that senior managers do not have to be knowledgeable about the means required to achieve the desired results or be involved in directly observing the actions of subordinates. They merely rely on output reports to ascertain whether or not the desired outcomes have been achieved. Accounting control systems can be described as a form of output controls. They are mostly defined in monetary terms such as revenues, costs, profits and ratios such as return on investment. Results measures also include non-accounting measures such as the number of units of defective production, the number of loan applications processed or ratio measures such as the number of customer deliveries on time as a percentage of total deliveries.

Results controls involve the following stages:

1. establishing results (i.e. performance) measures that minimize undesirable behaviour;
2. establishing performance targets;
3. measuring performance;
4. providing rewards or punishment.

Ideally *desirable behaviour should improve the performance measure and undesirable behaviour should have a detrimental effect* on the measure. A performance measure that is not a good indicator of what is desirable to achieve the organization's objectives might actually encourage employees to take actions that are detrimental to the organization. The term 'What you measure is what you get' can apply whereby employees concentrate on improving the performance measures even when they are aware that their actions are not in the firm's best interests. For example, a divisional manager whose current return on investment (ROI) is 30% might reject a project which yields an ROI of 25% because it will lower the division's average ROI, even though the project has a positive NPV, and acceptance is in the best interests of the organization.

Without a *pre-set performance target* individuals do not know what to aim for. Various research studies suggest that the existence of a clearly defined quantitative target is likely to motivate higher performance than vague statements such as 'do your best'. It is also difficult for employees or their superiors to interpret performance unless actual performance can be compared against predetermined standards.

Ability to measure some outputs effectively constrains the use of results measures. In the previous chapter you will remember that it was pointed out that the outputs in non-profit organizations are extremely difficult to measure and inhibit the use of results controls. Another example relates to *measuring the performance* of support departments. Consider a personnel department. The accomplishments of the department can be difficult to measure and other forms of control might be preferable. Merchant suggests that to evoke the right behaviours results measures should be precise, objective, timely and understandable.

Whilst 100% accuracy is not essential, measurements should be sufficiently accurate for the purpose required. If measures are not sufficiently precise they will have little information value and may lead to managers misevaluating performance. Measures should also be objective and free from bias. Where performance is self-measured and reported there is a danger that measures will be biased. Objectivity can be increased by performance being measured by people who are independent of the process being measured. Timeliness relates to the time lag between actual performance and the reporting of the results. Significant delays in reporting will result in the measures losing most of their motivational impact and a lengthy delay in taking remedial action when outcomes deviate from target. Finally, measures should be understandable by the individuals whose behaviours are being controlled. If measures are not understandable it is unlikely that managers will know how their actions will effect the measure and there is a danger that the measures will lose their motivational impact.

For results measures to work effectively the individuals whose behaviours are being controlled must be able to control and influence the results. Where factors outside the control of the individuals affect the results measures it is difficult to determine whether the results are the outcome of actions taken or from the impact of uncontrollable factors. If uncontrollable factors cannot be separated from controllable factors results controls measures are unlikely to provide useful information for evaluating the actions taken. Note also that if the outcomes of desirable behaviours are offset by the impact of uncontrollable factors results measures will lose their motivational impact and create the impression that the results measures are unjust. The term **controllability principle** is used to refer to the extent that individuals whose behaviours are being controlled can influence the results controls measures. We shall examine the controllability principle in more detail later in this chapter.

Employees are encouraged to achieve organizational goals by having *rewards (or punishments)* linked to their success (or failure) in achieving the results measures. Oganizational rewards include salary increases, bonuses, promotions and recognition. Employees can also derive intrinsic rewards through a sense of accomplishment and achievement. Punishments include demotions, failure to obtain the rewards and possibly the loss of one's job.

# Cybernetic control systems

The traditional approach in the management control literature has been to view results controls as a simple cybernetic system. In describing this process authors often use a mechanical model such as a thermostat that controls a central heating system as a resemblance. This process is illustrated in Figure 16.1. You will see that the control system consists of the following elements:

1. The process (the room's temperature) is continually monitored by an automatic regulator (the thermostat).
2. Deviations from a predetermined level (the desired temperature) are identified by the automatic regulator.
3. Corrective actions are started if the output is not equal to the predetermined level. The automatic regulator causes the input to be adjusted by turning the heater on if the temperature falls below a predetermined level. The heater is turned off when the output (temperature) corresponds with the predetermined level.

The output of the process is monitored, and whenever it varies from the predetermined level, the input is automatically adjusted. Emmanuel *et al.* (1990) state that four conditions must be satisfied before any process can be said to be controlled. First, objectives for the process being controlled must exist. Without an aim or purpose control has no meaning. Secondly, the output of the process must be measurable in terms of the dimensions defined by the objectives. In other words, there must be some mechanism for ascertaining whether the process is attaining its objectives. Thirdly, a predictive model of the process being controlled is required so that causes for the non-attainment can be identified and proposed

**FIGURE 16.1** *A cybernetic control system.*

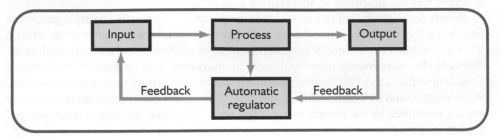

corrective actions evaluated. Finally, there must be a capability for taking action so that deviations from objectives can be reduced. Emmanuel *et al*. stress that if any of these conditions are not met the process cannot be considered to be 'in control'.

Result controls resemble the thermostat control model. Standards of performance are determined, measurement systems monitor performance, comparisons are made between the standard and actual performance and feedback provides information on the variances. Note that the term variance is used to describe the difference the standard and actual performance of the actions that are being measured.

# Feedback and feed-forward controls

The cybernetic system of control described in Figure 16.1 is that of feedback control. Feedback control involves monitoring outputs achieved against desired outputs and taking whatever corrective action is necessary if a deviation exists. In feed-forward control instead of actual outputs being compared against desired outputs, predictions are made of what outputs are expected to be at some future time. If these expectations differ from what is desired, control actions are taken that will minimize these differences. The objective is for control to be achieved before any deviations from desired outputs actually occur. In other words, with feed-forward controls likely errors can be anticipated and steps taken to avoid them, whereas with feedback controls actual errors are identified after the event and corrective action is taken to implement future actions to achieve the desired outputs.

Feed-forward control requires the use of a predictive model that is sufficiently accurate to ensure that control action will improve the situation and not cause it to deteriorate further. A major limitation of feedback control is that errors are allowed to occur. This is not a significant problem when there is a short time lag between the occurrence of an error and the identification and implementation of corrective action. Feed-forward control is therefore preferable when a significant time lag occurs. The budgeting process is a feed-forward control system. To the extent that outcomes fall short of what is desired, alternatives are considered until a budget is produced that is expected to achieve what is desired. The comparison of actual results with budget, in identifying variances and taking remedial action to ensure that future outcomes will conform with budgeted outcomes is an illustration of a feedback control system. Thus accounting control systems consist of both feedback and feed-forward controls.

# Harmful side-effects of controls

Harmful side-effects occur when the controls motivate employees to engage in behaviour that is not organizationally desirable. In this situation the control system leads to a lack of goal congruence. Alternatively, when controls motivate behaviour that is organizationally desirable they are described as encouraging goal congruence.

*Results controls* can lead to a lack of goal congruence if the results that are required can only be partially specified. Here there is a danger that employees will concentrate only on what is monitored by the control system, regardless of whether or not it is organizationally desirable. In other words, they will seek to maximize their individual performance according to the rules of the control system irrespective of whether their actions contribute to the organization's objectives. In addition, they may ignore other important areas, if they are not monitored by the control system. The term 'What you measure is what you get' applies in these circumstances.

Figure 16.2, derived from Otley (1987) illustrates the problems that can arise when the required results can only be partially specified. You will see that those aspects of behaviour on which subordinates are likely to concentrate to achieve their personal goals (circle B) do not necessarily correspond with those necessary for achieving the wider organizational goals (circle A). In an ideal system the measured behaviour (represented by circle C) should completely cover the area of desired behaviour (represented by circle A). Therefore if a manager maximizes the performance measure, he or she will also maximize his or her contribution to the goals of the organization. In other words, the performance measures encourage goal congruence. In practice, it is unlikely that perfect performance measures can be constructed that measure all desirable organizational behaviour, and so it is unlikely that all of circle C will cover circle A. Assuming that managers desire the rewards offered by circle C, their actual behaviour (represented by circle B) will be altered to include more of circle C and, to the extent that C coincides with A, more of circle A.

However, organizational performance will be improved only to the extent that the performance measure is a good indicator of what is desirable to achieve the firm's goals. Unfortunately, performance measures are not perfect and, as an ideal measure of overall performance, is unlikely to exist. Some measures may encourage goal congruence or organizationally desirable behaviour (the part of circle C that coincides with A), but other measures will not encourage goal congruence (the part of circle C that does not coincide with A). Consequently, there is a danger that subordinates will concentrate only on what is measured, regardless of whether or not it is organizationally desirable. Furthermore, actual behaviour may be modified so that desired results appear to be obtained, although they may have been achieved in an undesirable manner which is detrimental to the firm.

There is also a tendency for results controls to focus mainly on controlling behaviours that are quantifiable and easily measurable and ignore those behaviours that are less quantifiable. For example, less attention may be given to employee morale and welfare, personnel development or public responsibility because actions relating to these areas are difficult to quantify. A possible solution is to develop appropriate surrogate measures such as conducting attitude surveys to measure employee welfare. However, care must be taken not to overuse results measures in circumstances where the results that are required cannot be specified in quantitative terms. Instead, other types of controls should be used.

The evidence suggests that data manipulation is common with results controls (Merchant, 1990). Data manipulation occurs where individuals try and distort the data in order to improve the performance measure. For example, where individuals have some influence in the setting of performance targets there is a danger that they will seek to obtain easier targets by deliberately underperforming so that their targets will not be increased in the forthcoming period. Merchant (1990) also reported the widespread use of shifting funds between different budget items in order to avoid adverse budget variances.

Another harmful side effect of controls is that they can cause negative attitudes towards the control system. If controls are applied too rigorously they can result in job-related tensions, conflict and a deterioration in relationships with managers. To a certain extent people do not like being subject to controls so that negative attitudes may be unavoidable.

**FIGURE 16.2** *The measurement reward process with imperfect measures.*

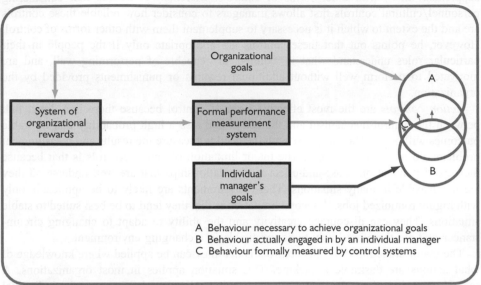

A  Behaviour necessary to achieve organizational goals
B  Behaviour actually engaged in by an individual manager
C  Behaviour formally measured by control systems

Nevertheless, they can be minimized if care is taken in designing control systems. Results controls can cause negative attitudes when targets are set which are considered to be too difficult and unachievable. Negative attitudes can also be exacerbated by a failure to apply the controllability principle. Performance evaluations are likely to be considered unfair where managers are held accountable for outcomes over which they have little control. Another potential cause of negative attitudes is the way in which results controls are applied. If they are applied in an insensitive and rigid manner and used mainly as punitive devices they are likely to provoke negative reactions. The way that a control system is applied can be just as important as the design issues in determining the success of a control system. Negative attitudes are likely to be the cause of many of the harmful side-effects that have been described above. Thus, if the negative attitudes can be minimized the harmful side-effects are likely to be minimized.

A lack of goal congruence can also occur with other types of controls. For example, *action controls* in the form of standard operating procedures and the imposition of work rules encourage employees to routinize their jobs rather than being creative and responding to changing circumstances. In a stable environment where there is complete knowledge relating to what actions are required action controls can be used to establish required working practices without causing incongruent behaviour. There is, however, a danger that action controls may cause a lack of goal congruence if they are used in a changing environment. Cultural controls can also lead to a lack of goal congruence where the behavioural norms shared by the group members, or group-based rewards, do not coincide with firm goals.

# Advantages and disadvantages of different types of controls

Merchant (1998) suggests that when deciding on the control alternatives managers should start by considering whether *personnel* or *cultural controls* will be sufficient. He suggests that they are worthy of first consideration because they have relatively few harmful side-effects. Also in small organizations they may be completely effective without the need to supplement them with other forms of controls. Merchant concludes that considering personnel/cultural controls first allows managers to consider how reliable these controls are and the extent to which it is necessary to supplement them with other forms of control. However, he points out that these controls are appropriate only if the people in their particular roles understand what is required, are capable of performing well, and are motivated to perform well without additional rewards or punishments provided by the organization.

*Action controls* are the most effective form of control because there is a direct link between the control mechanism and the action and also a high probability that desirable outcomes will occur. They dispense with the need to measure the results and measurement problems do not therefore apply. The major limitation of action controls is that because they are dependent on cause-and-effect work relationships that are well understood they are not feasible in many situations. These requirements are likely to be applicable only with highly routinized jobs. A second limitation is that they tend to be best suited to stable situations. They can discourage creativity and the ability to adapt to changing circumstances and are therefore likely to be unsuitable in a changing environment.

The major attraction of *results controls* is that they can be applied where knowledge of what actions are desirable is lacking. This situation applies in most organizations. A second attraction of results controls is that their application does not restrict individual autonomy. The focus is on the outcomes thus giving individuals the freedom to determine how they can best achieve the outcomes. Individuals are not burdened with having to follow prescribed rules and procedures.

The major disadvantages of results controls have already been discussed. In many cases the results required can only be partially specified, there can be difficulties in separating controllable and uncontrollable factors and measurement problems in the form of precision, objectivity, timeliness and understandability may inhibit their ability to satisfactorily measure performance.

# Management accounting control systems

To enable you to understand the role that management accounting control systems play within the overall control process this chapter has initially adopted a broad approach to describing management control systems. We shall now concentrate on management accounting control systems which represent the predominant controls in most organizations.

Why are accounting controls the predominant controls? There are several reasons. First, all organizations need to express and aggregate the results of a wide range of dissimilar activities using a common measure. The monetary measure meets this requirement. Second, profitability and liquidity are essential to the success of all organizations and financial measures relating to these and other areas are closely monitored by stakeholders. It is therefore natural that managers will wish to monitor performance in monetary terms. Third, financial measures also enable a common decision rule to be applied by all managers when considering alternative courses of action. That is, a course of action will normally benefit a firm only if it results in an improvement in its financial performance. Fourth, measuring results in financial terms enables managers to be given more autonomy. Focusing on the outcomes of managerial actions, summarized in financial terms, gives managers the freedom to take whatever actions they consider to be appropriate to achieve the desired results. Finally, outputs expressed in financial terms continue to be effective in uncertain environments even when it is unclear what course of action should be taken. Financial results provide a mechanism to indicate whether the actions benefited the organization.

# Responsibility centres

The complex environment in which most businesses operate today makes it virtually impossible for most firms to be controlled centrally. This is because it is not possible for central management to have all the relevant information and time to determine the detailed plans for all the organization. Some degree of decentralization is essential for all but the smallest firms. Organizations decentralize by creating responsibility centres. A responsibility centre may be defined as a unit of a firm where an individual manager is held responsible for the unit's performance. There are four types of responsibility centres. They are:

1. cost or expense centres;
2. revenue centres;
3. profit centres;
4. investment centres.

The creation of responsibility centres is a fundamental part of management accounting control systems. It is therefore important that you can distinguish between the various forms of responsibility centres.

## COST OR EXPENSE CENTRES

**Cost** or **expense centres** are responsibility centres whose managers are normally accountable for only those costs that are under their control. We can distinguish between two types of cost centres – standard cost centres and discretionary cost centres. The main features of **standard cost centres** are that output can be measured and the input required to produce each unit of output can be specified. Control is exercised by comparing the standard cost (that is, the cost of the inputs that *should* have been consumed in producing the output) with the cost that was *actually* incurred. The difference between the actual cost and the standard cost is described as the **variance**. Standard cost centres and variance analysis will be discussed extensively in Chapters 18 and 19.

Standard cost centres are best suited to units within manufacturing firms but they can also be established in service industries such as units within banks, where output can be measured in terms of the number of cheques or the number of loan applications processed, and there are also well defined input–output relationships. Although cost centre managers are not accountable for sales revenues they can affect the amount of sales revenue generated if quality standards are not met and outputs are not produced according to schedule. Therefore quality and timeliness performance measures are also required besides financial measures.

**Discretionary expense centres** are those responsibility cost centres where output cannot be measured in financial terms and there are no clearly observable relationships between inputs (the resources consumed) and the outputs (the results achieved). Control normally takes the form of ensuring that actual expenditure adheres to budgeted expenditure for each expense category and also ensuring that the tasks assigned to each centre have been successfully accomplished. Examples of discretionary centres include advertising and publicity and research and development departments. You should note that in discretionary centres underspending against budget may not necessarily be a good thing since this may result in a lower level of service than that originally planned by management. For example, underspending on research and development may indicate that the amount to be spent on research and development has not been followed. One of the major problems arising in discretionary expense centres is measuring the effectiveness of expenditures. For example, the marketing support department may not have exceeded an advertising budget but this does not mean that the advertising expenditure has been effective. The advertising may have been incorrectly timed, it may have been directed to the wrong audience, or it may have contained the wrong message. Determining the effectiveness and efficiency of discretionary expense centres is one of the most difficult areas of management control.

## REVENUE CENTRES

Revenue centres are responsibility centres where managers are accountable only for financial outputs in the form of generating sales revenues. Typical examples of revenue centres are where regional sales managers are accountable for sales within their regions. In some organizations revenue centres acquire finished goods from a manufacturing division and are responsible for selling and distributing these goods. Where managers are evaluated solely on the basis of sales revenues there is a danger that they may concentrate on maximizing sales revenues at the expense of profitability. This can occur when all sales are not equally profitable and managers can achieve higher sales revenues by promoting low-profit products.

Revenue centre managers may also be held accountable for selling expenses, such as salesperson salaries, commissions and order-getting costs. They are not, however, made accountable for the cost of the goods and services that they sell. Revenue centres can be distinguished from profit centres by the fact that revenue centres are accountable for only a small proportion of the total costs of manufacturing and selling products and services, namely selling costs, whereas profit centre managers are responsible for the majority of the costs including both manufacturing and selling costs.

## PROFIT CENTRES

Both cost and revenue centre managers have limited decision-making authority. Cost centre managers are accountable only for managing inputs of their centres and decisions relating to outputs are made by other units within the firm. Revenue centres are accountable for selling the products or services but they have no control over their manufacture. A significant increase in managerial autonomy occurs when unit managers are given responsibility for both production and sales. In this situation managers are normally free to set selling prices, choose which markets to sell in, make product-mix and output decisions and select suppliers. Units within an organization whose managers are accountable for both revenues and costs are called profit centres.

In practice many firms create profit centres that do not conform to the above requirements. They are more limited in scope and can be described as pseudo-profit centres. For example, selling units might be made profit centres by charging the units with the standard cost of the products or services sold, thus making the unit manager accountable for gross margin. Making selling units pseudo-profit centres overcomes a major limitation of revenue centres whereby managers can be motivated to maximize sales revenues rather than profits.

Sometimes manufacturing and administrative units that supply products or services to other units are allocated sales revenues derived from internal transfer prices that are established for the goods or services. If established external market prices can be used as a benchmark for setting the transfer prices and the buying units can outsource their purchases, rather than buying internally, then the selling units are likely to have some influence over the revenues generated and thus resemble true profit centres. If these conditions do not apply and inter-unit trading is not subject to external competitive forces the responsibility centres will be merely pseudo-profit centres. You should note, however, that many profit centres do in fact derive most, or sometimes all, of their revenues by selling their products or services to other units within the same firm.

## INVESTMENT CENTRES

Investment centres are responsibility centres whose managers are responsible for both sales revenues and costs and, in addition, have responsibility and authority to make working capital and capital investment decisions. Typical investment centre performance measures include return on investment and economic value added. These measures are influenced by revenues, costs and assets employed and thus reflect the responsibility that managers have for both generating profits and managing the investment base.

Investment centres represent the highest level of managerial autonomy. They include the company as a whole, operating subsidiaries, operating groups and divisions. You will find that many firms are not precise in their terminology and call their investment centres profit centres. Profit and investment centres will be discussed extensively in Chapter 20.

# The nature of management accounting control systems

Management accounting control systems have two core elements. The first is the formal planning processes such as budgeting and long-term planning that were described in the previous chapter. These processes are used for establishing performance expectations for evaluating performance. The second is responsibility accounting which involves the creation of responsibility centres. Responsibility centres enable accountability for financial results and outcomes to be allocated to individuals throughout the organization. The objective of responsibility accounting is to accumulate costs and revenues for each individual responsibility centre so that the deviations from a performance target (typically the budget) can be attributed to the individual who is accountable for the responsibility centre. For each responsibility centre the process involves setting a performance target, measuring performance, comparing performance against the target, analysing the variances and taking action where significant variances exist between actual and target performance. Financial performance targets for profit or investment centres are typically in terms of profits, return on investment or economic value added whereas performance targets for cost centres are defined in terms of costs.

Responsibility accounting is implemented by issuing performance reports at frequent intervals (normally monthly) that inform responsibility centre managers of the deviations from budgets for which they are accountable and are required to take action. An example of a performance report issued to a cost centre manager is presented in the lower section of Exhibit 16.1. You should note that at successively higher levels of management less detailed information is reported. You can see from the upper sections of Exhibit 16.1 that

**EXHIBIT 16.1**

*Responsibility accounting monthly performance reports*

the information is condensed and summarized as the results relating to the responsibility centre are reported at higher levels. Exhibit 16.1 only includes financial information. In addition non-financial measures such as those relating to quality and timeliness may be reported. We shall look at non-financial measures in more detail in Chapter 23.

### Performance report to managing director

| | | Budget | | Variance[a] F (A) | |
| | | Current month (£) | Year to date (£) | This month (£) | Year to date (£) |
|---|---|---|---|---|---|
| Managing director | Factory A | 453 900 | 6 386 640 | 80 000(A) | 98 000(A) |
| | Factory B | X | X | X | X |
| | Factory C | X | X | X | X |
| | Administration costs | X | X | X | X |
| | Selling costs | X | X | X | X |
| | Distribution costs | X | X | X | X |
| | | 2 500 000 | 30 000 000 | 400 000(A) | 600 000(A) |

### Performance report to production manager of factory A

| | | Budget | | Variance F (A) | |
| | | Current month | Year to date | This month | Year to date |
|---|---|---|---|---|---|
| Production manager | Works manager's office | X | X | X | X |
| | Machining department 1 | 165 600 | 717 600 | 32 760(A) | 89 180(A) |
| | Machining department 2 | X | X | X | X |
| | Assembly department | X | X | X | X |
| | Finishing department | X | X | X | X |
| | | 453 900 | 6 386 640 | 80 000(A) | 98 000(A) |

### Performance report to head of responsibility centre

| | | Budget | | Variance F (A) | |
| | | Current month | Year to date | This month | Year to date |
|---|---|---|---|---|---|
| Head of responsibility centre | Direct materials | X | X | X | X |
| | Direct labour | X | X | X | X |
| | Indirect labour | X | X | X | X |
| | Indirect materials | X | X | X | X |
| | Power | X | X | X | X |
| | Maintenance | X | X | X | X |
| | Idle time | X | X | X | X |
| | Other | X | X | X | X |
| | | 165 600 | 717 600 | 32 760(A) | 89 180(A) |

[a]F indicates a favourable variance (actual cost less than budgeted cost) and (A) indicates an adverse budget (actual cost greater than budget cost). Note that, at the lowest level of reporting, the responsibility centre head's performance report contains detailed information on operating costs. At successively higher levels of management less detail is reported. For example, the managing director's information on the control of activities consists of examining those variances that represent significant departures from the budget for each factory and functional area of the business and requesting explanations from the appropriate managers.

Responsibility accounting involves:

- distinguishing between those items which managers can control and for which they should be held accountable and those items over which they have no control and for which they are not held accountable;
- determining how challenging the financial targets should be;
- determining how much influence managers should have in the setting of financial targets.

We shall now examine each of these items in detail.

# The controllability principle

Responsibility accounting is based on the application of the controllability principle which means that it is appropriate to charge to an area of responsibility only those costs that are significantly influenced by the manager of that responsibility centre. The controllability principle can be implemented by either eliminating the uncontrollable items from the areas for which managers are held accountable or calculating their effects so that the reports distinguish between controllable and uncontrollable items.

Applying the controllability principle is difficult in practice because many areas do not fit neatly into either controllable and uncontrollable categories. Instead, they are partially controllable. For example, even when outcomes may be affected by occurrences outside a manager's control; such as competitors' actions, price changes and supply shortages, managers can take action to reduce their adverse effects. They can substitute alternative materials where the prices of raw materials change or they can monitor and respond to competitors' actions. If these factors are categorized as uncontrollables managers will be motivated not to try and influence them. A further problem is that even when a factor is clearly uncontrollable, it is difficult to measure in order to highlight its impact on the reported outcomes.

Merchant (1989) identifies two possible errors when dealing with the effects of uncontrollable factors. First, managers may not be protected from the effects of uncontrollables when they should be and second they may be protected when they should not be protected. If incorrect judgements are made about the treatment of uncontrollables the benefits derived from the responsibility accounting system will be substantially reduced because of the motivational, evaluation and morale problems that can result.

Three arguments are suggested by Merchant for not making employees accountable for the effects of factors they cannot completely control. First, most employees are risk averse and prefer their performance-dependent rewards to result directly from their efforts and not to be influenced by factors they cannot completely control. To compensate them for the risks firms have to provide employees with higher expected rewards. If they fail to do so they will bear other costs such as an inability to employ talented employees and low employee motivation.

Second, firms will bear the costs of some employee behaviours arising from their actions to reduce their exposure to uncontrollable factors which may be at the expense of corporate profitability. For example, they may avoid risky projects where the expected value of the benefits exceed the expected costs or protect themselves against the effects of uncontrollable factors by creating budgetary slack. Budgetary slack relates to the process by which managers seek to obtain budget targets that can be easily achieved by understating revenues and/or overstating costs. Studies by Schiff and Lewin (1970) and Osni

(1973) suggest that many managers seek to obtain slack within the budget negotiation process.

Third, firms will bear the costs of lost time, as employees whose performances are evaluated by measures that are influenced by uncontrollable factors tend to feel that their evaluations are unjust and spend their time disputing the results, at the expense of doing their jobs. In addition, negative attitudes towards the management accounting control system are likely to be exacerbated.

## TYPES OF UNCONTROLLABLE FACTORS

Merchant (1998) identifies three types of uncontrollable factors. They are:

1. economic and competitive factors;
2. acts of nature;
3. interdependencies.

Both revenues and costs are affected by *economic and competitive factors*. Changes in customers' tastes, competitors' actions, business cycles and changing government regulations and foreign exchange rates affect sales revenues. Costs are affected by items such as changes in input prices, interest and foreign exchange rates, government regulations and taxes. Although these items appear to be uncontrollable managers can respond to these changes to relieve their negative impacts. For example, they can respond to changes in customers' tastes by developing new products or redesigning existing products. They can respond to changes in exchange rates by changing their sources of supply and selling in different countries. Responding to such changes is an important part of a manager's job. Therefore most management accounting control systems do not shield managers completely from economic and competitive factors although they may not be required to bear all of the risk.

*Acts of nature* are usually large, one-time events with effects on performance that are beyond the ability of managers to anticipate. Examples are disasters such as fires, floods, riots, tornadoes, accidents and machine breakdowns. Most organizations protect managers from the adverse consequences of acts of nature by not making them accountable for them provided that the events are considered to be clearly uncontrollable. However, controllability can be an issue where accidents or machine breakdowns are avoidable. Also the extent of uncontrollability becomes questionable where managers have failed in their responsibility to reduce the adverse consequences of such events by not purchasing insurance protection.

The third type of uncontrollable relates to *interdependence* whereby a responsibility centre is not completely self-contained so that the outcomes are affected by other units within the organization. Merchant classifies interdependencies by three types; pooled, sequential and reciprocal.

*Pooled interdependencies* apply when responsibility centres use common firm resources such as shared administrative activities. Pooled interdependence is low when responsibility centres are relatively self-contained so that use of pooled resources has little impact on a unit's performance. The users of pooled resources should not have to bear any higher costs arising from the bad performance of the shared resource pools. Managers can be protected from inefficiencies of the shared resource pools to a certain extent by negotiations during the annual budgeting process whereby the quantities and amounts of services are agreed. Responsibility centre managers are charged with their usage of pooled resources at the budgeted rate and do not bear the cost of any inefficiencies incurred by the pooled resource centres during the current budget period. If the pooled resource centre cannot deliver the specified quantity or quality of service the responsibility centre users should have the freedom to find alternative sources of supply. If this is not possible they should not be held accountable for any extra costs incurred or loss of revenues.

*Sequential interdependencies* exist when the outputs of one unit are the inputs of another unit whereas *reciprocal interdependencies* exist in diversified organizations when a responsibility centre produces outputs that are used by other units and the responsibility centre also uses inputs from these units. Firms deal with both types of interdependencies by establishing a transfer pricing system that aims to approximate the conditions found in external competitive markets so that they resemble the economic and competitive variables described at the beginning of this section. Therefore they should be subject to the same treatment described for these variables. We shall examine the transfer pricing issues in Chapter 21.

Merchant identifies one other type of interdependency. This is where the results are affected by the intervention of higher-level managers. This can occur when decisions are imposed on a manager or where a proposed course of action that requires higher level approval is not ratified such as a change in working practices or initiating training courses. If such actions have been imposed on a manager the impact on the outcomes should ideally be adjusted for and treated as an uncontrollable event.

## DEALING WITH THE DISTORTING EFFECTS OF UNCONTROLLABLE FACTORS BEFORE THE MEASUREMENT PERIOD

Management can attempt to deal with the distorting effects of uncontrollables by making adjustments either before or after the measurement period. Uncontrollable and controllable factors can be determined prior to the measurement period by specifying which budget line items are to be regarded as controllable and uncontrollable. Uncontrollable items can either be excluded from performance reports or shown in a separate section within the performance report so that they are clearly distinguishable from controllable items. The latter approach has the advantage of drawing managerial attention to those costs that a company incurs to support their activities. Managers may be able to indirectly influence these costs if they are made aware of the sums involved.

How do we distinguish between controllable and uncontrollable items? Merchant suggests that the following general rule should be applied to all employees – 'Hold employees accountable for the performance areas you want them to pay attention to.' Applying this rule explains why some organizations assign the costs of shared resource pools, such as administrative costs relating to personnel and data processing departments, to responsibility centres. Assigning these costs authorizes managers of the user responsibility centres to question the amount of the costs and the quantity and quality of services supplied. In addition, responsibility centres are discouraged from making unnecessary requests for the use of these services when they are aware that increases in costs will be assigned to the users of the services.

Care must be taken, however, in making responsibility heads accountable for many areas for which they do not have a significant influence. The additional costs arising from the harmful side-effects described earlier will be incurred and these must be offset against the benefits discussed above.

The second method that managers use for dealing with uncontrollable factors prior to the measurement period is by insuring against uncontrollable events. Typical insurable events include product and employee liability insurance and insurance against theft, damages, accidents, fire and floods.

# DEALING WITH THE DISTORTING EFFECTS OF UNCONTROLLABLE FACTORS AFTER THE MEASUREMENT PERIOD

Merchant identifies four methods of removing the effects of uncontrollable factors from the results measures after the measurement period and before the rewards are assigned. They are:

1. variance analysis;
2. flexible performance standards;
3. relative performance evaluations;
4. subjective performance evaluations.

Variance analysis seeks to analyse the factors that cause the actual results to differ from pre-determined budgeted targets. In particular, variance analysis helps to distinguish between controllable and uncontrollable items and identify those individuals who are accountable for the variances. For example, variances analysed by each type of cost, and by their price and quantity effects, enables variances to be traced to accountable individuals and also to isolate those variances that are due to uncontrollable factors. Variance analysis will be discussed extensively in Chapters 18 and 19.

Flexible performance standards apply when targets are adjusted to reflect variations in uncontrollable factors arising from the circumstances not envisaged when the targets were set. The most widely used flexible performance standard is to use flexible budgets whereby the uncontrollable volume effects on cost behaviour are removed from the manager's performance reports. Because some costs vary with changes in the level of activity, it is essential when applying the controllability principle to take into account the variability of costs. For example, if the actual level of activity is greater than the budgeted level of activity then those costs that vary with activity will be greater than the budgeted costs purely because of changes in activity. Let us consider the simplified situation presented in Example 16.1.

---

**EXAMPLE 16.1**

An item of expense that is included in the budget for a responsibility centre varies directly in relation to activity at an estimated cost of £5 per unit of output. The budgeted monthly level of activity was 20 000 units and the actual level of activity was 24 000 units at a cost of £105 000.

---

Assuming that the increase in activity was due to an increase in sales volume greater than that anticipated when the budget was set then the increases in costs arising from the volume change are beyond the control of the responsibility centre manager. It is clearly inappropriate to compare actual *variable* costs of £105 000 from an activity level of 24 000 units with budgeted *variable* costs of £100 000 from an activity level of 20 000 units. This would incorrectly suggest an overspending of £5000. If managers are to be made responsible for their costs, it is essential that they are responsible for performance under the conditions in which they worked, and not for a performance based on conditions when the budget was drawn up. In other words, it is misleading to compare actual costs at one level of activity with budgeted costs at another level of activity. At the end of the period the original budget must be adjusted to the actual level of activity to take into account the impact of the uncontrollable volume change on costs. This procedure is called flexible budgeting. In Example 16.1 the performance report should be as follows:

| Budgeted expenditure | Actual expenditure |
|---|---|
| (flexed to 24 000 units) | (24 000 units) |
| £120 000 | £105 000 |

The budget is adjusted to reflect what the costs should have been for an actual activity of 24 000 units. This indicates that the manager has incurred £15 000 less expenditure than would have been expected for the actual level of activity, and a favourable variance of £15 000 should be recorded on the performance report, not an adverse variance of £5000, which would have been recorded if the original budget had not been adjusted.

In Example 16.1 it was assumed that there was only one variable item of expense, but in practice the budget will include many different expenses including fixed, semi-variable and variable expenses. You should note that fixed expenses do not vary in the short-term with activity and therefore the budget should remain unchanged for these expenses. The budget should be flexed only for variable and semi-variable expenses.

Budgets may also be adjusted to reflect other uncontrollable factors besides volume changes. Budgets are normally set based on the environment that is anticipated during the budget setting process. If the budget targets are then used throughout the duration of the annual budget period for performance evaluation the managers will be held accountable for uncontrollable factors arising from forecasting errors. To remove the managerial exposure to uncontrollable risks arising from forecasting errors *ex post* budget adjustments can be made whereby the budget is adjusted to the environmental and economic conditions that the manager's actually faced during the period. An alternative view is that a manager's job is to respond to such uncertainties and that the uncontrollable effects should not be removed from the performance evaluation. This view has greater merit where managers have participated in the forecasting process. A further problem is that it is time-consuming and costly to isolate the effects of unforeseen events. The uncontrollable factors arising from forecasting errors can be substantially reduced by using the system of continuous or rolling budgets that was described in the previous chapter.

Relative performance evaluation relates to the situations where the performance of a responsibility centre is evaluated relative to the performance of similar centres within the same company or to similar units outside the organization. To be effective responsibility centres must perform similar tasks and face similar environmental and business conditions with the units that they are being benchmarked against. Such relative comparisons with units facing similar environmental conditions neutralizes the uncontrollable factors because they are in effect held constant when making the relative comparisons. The major difficulty relating to relative performance evaluations is finding benchmark units that face similar conditions and uncertainties.

Instead of making the formal and quantitative adjustments that are a feature of the methods that have been described so far subjective judgements are made in the evaluation process based on the knowledge of the outcome measures and the circumstances faced by the responsibility centre heads. The major advantage of subjective evaluations is that they can alleviate some of the defects of the measures used by accounting control systems. The disadvantages of subjective evaluations are that they are not objective, they tend not to provide the person being evaluated with a clear indication of how performance has been evaluated, they can create conflict with superiors resulting in a loss of morale and a decline in motivation and they are expensive in terms of management time.

The major problem arising from all of the methods described above is that managers may not have a clear idea of exactly what they are aiming for. Hence, the benefits of having pre-determined standards will be removed.

## GUIDELINES FOR APPLYING THE CONTROLLABILITY PRINCIPLE

Dealing with uncontrollables represents one of the most difficult areas for the design and operation of management accounting control systems. The following guidelines published by the Report of the Committee of Cost Concepts and Standards in the United States in 1956 still continues to provide useful guidance:

1. If a manager *can control the quantity and price paid* for a service then the manager is responsible for all the expenditure incurred for the service.

2. If the manager *can control the quantity of the service but not the price paid* for the service then only that amount of difference between actual and budgeted expenditure that is due to usage should be identified with the manager.

3. If the manager *cannot control either the quantity or the price paid* for the service then the expenditure is uncontrollable and should not be identified with the manager.

An example of the latter situation is when the costs of an industrial relations department are apportioned to a department on some arbitrary basis; such arbitrary apportionments are likely to result in an allocation of expenses that the managers of responsibility centres may not be able to influence. In addition to the above guidelines Merchants's general rule should also be used as a guide – 'Hold employees accountable for the performance areas you want them to pay attention to.'

# Setting financial performance targets

There is substantial evidence from a large number of studies that the existence of a defined, quantitative goal or target is likely to motivate higher levels of performance than when no such target is stated. People perform better when they have a clearly defined goal to aim for and are aware of the standards that will be used to interpret their performance. There are three approaches that can be used to set financial targets. They are targets derived from engineering studies of input–output relationships, targets derived from historical data and targets derived from negotiations between superiors and subordinates.

**Engineered targets** can be used when there are clearly defined and stable input–output relationships such that the inputs required can be estimated directly from product specifications. For example, in a fast-food restaurant for a given output of hamburgers it is possible to estimate the inputs required because there is a physical relationship between the ingredients such as meats, buns, condiments and packaging and the number of hamburgers made. Input–output relationships can also be established for labour by closely observing the processes to determine the quantity of labour that will be required for a given output.

Where clearly defined input–output relationships do not exist other approaches must be used to set financial targets. One approach is to use **historical targets** derived directly from the results of previous periods. Previous results plus an increase for expected price changes may form the basis for setting the targets or an improvement factor may be incorporated into the estimate, such as previous period costs less a reduction of 10%. The disadvantage of using historical targets is that they may include past inefficiencies or may encourage employees to underperform if the outcome of efficient performance in a previous period is used as a basis for setting a more demanding target in the next period.

**Negotiated targets** are set based on negotiations between superiors and subordinates. The major advantage of negotiated targets is that they address the information asymmetry gap that can exist between superior and subordinate. This gap arises because subordinates have more information than their superiors on the relationships between outputs and inputs and the constraints that exist at the operating level, whereas superiors have a broader view of the organization as a whole and the resource constraints that apply. Negotiated targets enable the information asymmetry gap to be reduced so that the targets set incorporate the constraints applying at both the operational level and the firm as a whole. You should refer back to the previous chapter for a more detailed discussion of the negotiation process.

Targets vary in their level of difficulty and the chosen level has a significant effect on motivation and performance. Targets are considered to be moderately difficult or (highly achievable) when they are set at the average level of performance for a given task. According to Merchant (1990) most companies set their annual profit budgets targets at levels that are highly achievable. Their budgets are set to be challenging but achievable 80–90 per cent of the time by an effective management team working at a consistently high level of effort. Targets set at levels above average are labelled as difficult, tight or high, and those set below average are classed as easy, loose or low (Chow, 1983).

The research evidence suggests that setting specific difficult budget targets leads to higher task performance than setting specific moderate or easy targets (Stedry and Kay, 1966; Hofstede, 1968; Chow, 1983). However, Hirst (1987) has advocated that the benefits arising from setting specific difficult budget goals are dependent on the level of task uncertainty. He suggests that where task uncertainty is low, setting specific difficult budget goals will promote performance, and the subsequent use of difficult budget goals to evaluate performance will minimize the incidence of dysfunctional behaviour, such as falsifying accounting information. In contrast, where task uncertainty is high, the beneficial effects arising from setting specific difficult goals are less likely to occur, and subsequent use of these difficult goals will promote dysfunctional behaviour.

Merchant (1998) also suggests that the level of budget difficulty should be related to task uncertainty. He suggests that difficult targets may be implemented when engineered targets are set because the link between effort and results is direct. There is also a high probability that a performance problem exists when the inputs consumed exceed the engineered target. He also suggests that difficult targets can be used when historical targets are set if the processes being controlled are stable over time. Difficult targets are, however, inappropriate when important assumptions about the future must be made to set the targets or if negotiation is used.

## THE EFFECT OF THE LEVEL OF BUDGET DIFFICULTY ON MOTIVATION AND PERFORMANCE

The fact that a financial target represents a specific quantitative goal gives it a strong motivational potential, but the targets set must be accepted if managers are to be motivated to achieve higher levels of performance. Unfortunately, it is not possible to specify exactly the optimal degree of difficulty for financial targets, since task uncertainty and cultural, organizational and personality factors all affect an individual manager's reaction to a financial target.

Figure 16.3 derived from Otley (1987) shows the theoretical relationship between budget difficulty, aspiration levels and performance. Note that the **aspiration level** relates to the personal goal of the budgetee (that is, the person who is responsible for the budget). In other words, it is the level of performance that they hope to attain. You will see from Figure 16.3 that as the level of budget difficulty is increased both the budgetees' aspiration level and performance increases. However, there becomes a point where the budget is perceived as impossible to achieve and the aspiration level and performance decline dramatically. It can be seen from Figure 16.3 that the budget level that motivates the best

**FIGURE 16.3** *The effect of budget difficulty on performance. Source: Otley (1987).*

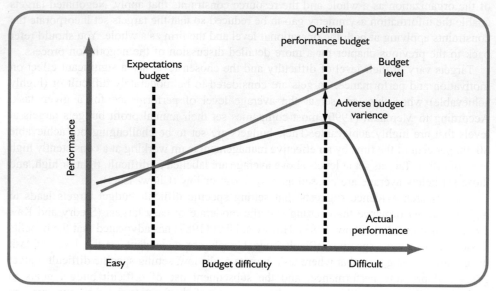

**FIGURE 16.4** *The effect of budget levels on aspiration.*

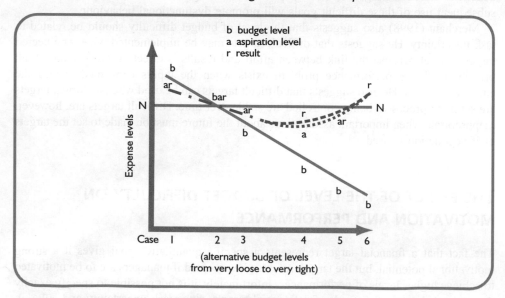

level of performance may not be achievable. In contrast, the budget that is expected to be achieved (that is, the expectations budget in Figure 16.3) motivates a lower level of performance.

Hofstede (1968) adopted a similar approach to illustrate a hypothesized relationship between the level of difficulty of an expense budget, the aspiration level and performance. His work is still relevant today. Hofstede uses the diagram reproduced in Figure 16.4 to illustrate an expense budget, where the level of expense is shown on the vertical axis and the degree of tightness of the budget is shown on the horizontal axis, going from very loose on the left to very tight on the right. The budget, aspiration levels and actual results are denoted by the letters b, a and r. In the absence of a budget the expense level is assumed to be N, and the diagram shows what will happen if we consider various alternative budget levels from very loose (case 1) to very tight (case 6). In case 1 the budget is too loose (i.e. above level N). The budgetee will not find the budget very challenging, and will set a higher aspiration level (lower than the budgeted cost) but still above N. The result r will be equal to the aspiration level.

In case 2 the budget is equal to N, and the aspiration level and the result coincide with the budget; the budget will not influence performance. In case 3, the budget is below N, and the budgetee responds by altering his aspiration level to below N but not to the budgeted level of expenditure. Because the aspiration level is not too difficult, the actual result will be equal to the aspiration level. In case 4 the budget is tighter still, and this results in an improvement in the aspiration level. However, since the budget and aspiration level are so tight, there is a strong possibility that the actual result will not be as good as the aspiration level. Therefore r is shown to be above a, but the highest level of performance will be achieved at this point. In case 5 the budget is very tight. The budgetee sees this is almost impossible, and sets an aspiration level that is easier than case 4. In this situation the actual result will be equal to the aspiration level. In case 6 the budget is so tight that the budgetee will regard it as impossible. He or she will stop trying, and will not attempt to set an aspiration level. The effect of this approach is that the actual result will be worse than that which would have been achieved had no budget been set.

A close examination of Figure 16.4 indicates that budgets do not always lead to improved performance. In cases 1 and 6 the budgets do more harm than good, and improvements occur only in cases 3 and 4. The problem is further complicated by the fact that failure to achieve the budget is likely to lead to a lowering of aspiration levels. Therefore in case 4, where the actual result is worse than the aspiration level, the budgetee might respond by setting a less ambitious aspiration level next time. The effect may be that case 4 will shift to case 5.

Hofstede's conclusions concerning budget difficulties were as follows:

1. Budgets have no motivational effect unless they are accepted by the managers involved as their own personal targets.

2. Up to the point where the budget target is no longer accepted, the more demanding the budget target the better the results achieved.

3. Demanding budgets are also seen as more relevant than less difficult targets, but negative attitudes result if they are seen as too difficult.

4. Acceptance of budgets is facilitated when good upward communication exists. The use of departmental meetings was found helpful in encouraging managers to accept budget targets.

5. Managers' reactions to budget targets were affected both by their own personality (some managers intensely disliked budgets that they thought they would not achieve) and by more general cultural and organizational norms.

An interesting implication of the hypothesized relationships is that the budget level that motivates the best performance is unlikely to be achieved much of the time (case 4 in Figure 16.4 or the optimal performance budget in Figure 16.3). However, a budget that is usually achieved will motivate a lower level of performance (cases 1 and 2 in Figure 16.4 or the expectations budget in Figure 16.3). Therefore if budgets are to be set at a level that will motivate individuals to achieve maximum performance, adverse budget variances are to be expected. In such a situation it is essential that adverse budget variances are not used by management as a punitive device, since this is likely to encourage budgetees to attempt to obtain looser budgets by either underperforming or deliberately negotiating easily attainable budgets. This may lead to fewer adverse variances, but also to poorer overall performance.

To motivate the best level of actual performance, demanding budgets should be set and small adverse variances should be regarded as a healthy sign and not as something to be avoided. If budgets are always achieved with no adverse variances, this indicates that the standards are too loose to motivate the best possible results.

## ARGUMENTS IN FAVOUR OF SETTING HIGHLY ACHIEVABLE BUDGETS

It appears from our previous discussion that tight budgets should be established to motivate maximum performance, although this may mean that the budget has a high probability of not being achieved. Otley (1987) suggests that the optimum point may be at the point where individuals perceive there is significantly less than a 50 % chance of target achievement. However, budgets are not used purely as a motivational device to maximize performance. They are also used for planning purposes and it is most unlikely that tight budgets will be suitable for planning purposes. Why? Tight budgets that have a high probability of not being achieved are most unsuitable for cash budgeting and for harmonizing the company plans in the form of a master budget. Because of this conflict, it has been suggested that separate budgets should be used for planning and for motivation purposes. The counter argument to this is that budgetees may react unfavourably to a situation where they believe that one budget is used to evaluate their performance and a second looser budget is used by top management.

Most companies use the same budgets for planning and motivational purposes (Umapathy, 1987). If only one set of budgets is used it is most unlikely that one set can, at the same time, perfectly meet both the planning and the motivational requirements. A compromise is required whereby the targets that can be used for planning purposes are not so easy that they have no motivational impact. Merchant (1990) suggests that highly achievable budgets that are achievable 80–90 per cent of the time require managers to be working consistently at a high level of effort to meet this requirement.

Highly achievable budgets also have a number of other advantages. The theoretical models such as those illustrated in Figures 16.3 and 16.4 ignore the psychological impact of failure. For example, Merchant (1998) points out that when managers fail to achieve their budget targets they live with that failure for an entire year and that this can result in a prolonged period of discouragement and depression that can be quite costly to the organization. In contrast, highly achievable budgets provide managers with a sense of achievement and self-esteem which can be beneficial to the organization in terms of increased levels of commitment and aspirations. Highly achievable budgets also shield managers from unexpected adverse circumstances which were not anticipated when the budget was set. Hence, they are less likely to look for excuses for failure to achieve the budget. Instead, they promote an increase in commitment to achieving the budgets.

Rewards such as bonuses, promotions and job security are normally linked to budget achievement so that the costs of failing to meet budget targets can be high. The greater the probability of the failure to meet budget targets the greater is the probability that managers will be motivated to distort their performance by engaging in behaviour that will result in the harmful side-effects described earlier in this chapter. You should be able to recall that they include manipulation of data, negative attitudes and deliberately underperforming so that targets will not be increased in the forthcoming periods. Adopting targets that are highly achievable alleviates these harmful side-effects.

The disadvantage of adopting highly achievable budget targets is that aspiration levels and performance may not be maximized. To encourage managers to maximize perform-ance when highly achievable standards are adopted, rewards can be given for achieving the budget, and additional rewards can also be given relating to the extent to which they exceed the budget. Managers therefore have incentives not to merely achieve the budget but to exceed it.

# Participation in the budgeting and target setting process

**Participation** relates to the extent that subordinates or budgetees are able to influence the figures that are incorporated in their budgets or targets. Participation is sometimes referred to as **bottom-up budget setting** whereas a non-participatory approach whereby subordinates have little influence on the target setting process is sometimes called **top-down budget setting**.

Allowing individuals to participate in the setting of performance targets has several advantages. First, individuals are more likely to accept the targets and be committed to achieving them if they have been involved in the target setting process. Second, participation can reduce the information asymmetry gap that applies when standards are imposed from above. Earlier in this chapter it was pointed out that subordinates have more information than their superiors on the relationships between outputs and inputs and the constraints that exist at the operating level whereas the superiors have a broader view of the organization as a whole and the resource constraints that apply. This information sharing process enables more effective targets to be set that attempt to deal with both operational and organizational constraints. Finally, imposed standards can encourage negative attitudes and result in demotivation and alienation. This in turn can lead to a rejection of the targets and poor performance. Hofstede (1968) presents the diagram shown in Figure 16.5 to illustrate the relationship between participation in standard setting and performance. The diagram indicates that participation is seen as affecting performance in three ways. First, allowing a manager to participate in budget setting improves his or her attitude towards the budget system and this should reduce some of the dysfunctional behavioural consequences. Secondly, a manager who has had an influence on setting a standard is likely to see the standard as more relevant than one that has been imposed upon him or her. This should increase the likelihood of the budget being accepted by the subordinate, and therefore becomes a target. Thirdly, performance is also affected by the potential for improved communication and control that stems from the use of participative methods. This should also lead to better and more relevant standards. Note that both relevance and attitude affect motivation, and this in turn should lead to improved performance.

## FACTORS INFLUENCING THE EFFECTIVENESS OF PARTICIPATION

Participation has been advocated by many writers as a means of making tasks more challenging and giving individuals a greater sense of responsibility. For many years participation in decision-making was thought to be a panacea for effective organizational effort but this school of thought was later challenged. The debate has never been resolved. The believers have never been able to demonstrate that participation really does have a positive effect on productivity and the sceptics have never been able to prove the opposite (Macintosh, 1985). The empirical studies have presented conflicting evidence on the usefulness of participation in the management process. For every study indicating that participation leads to better attitudes and improved performance, an alternative frequently exists suggesting the opposite.

**FIGURE 16.5** *Hofstede's model of the relationship between participation in standard setting and performance.*

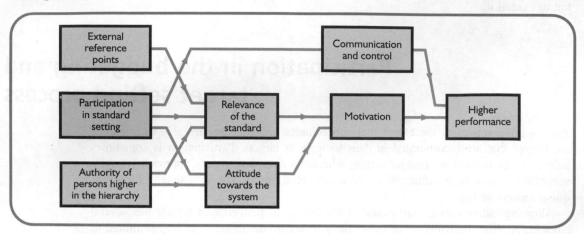

A number of studies investigating the role of participation within the budgeting context have been undertaken. In a study of foremen of a large industrial company, Milani (1975) showed that participation was positively associated with attitudes towards both job and company, and Collins (1978) found a similar association with attitude towards the budgetary system. Kenis (1979), in a survey study of department managers and supervisors, found participation positively and significantly associated with performance. However, Milani (1975) found only a weak positive association between participation and performance.

Because of the conflicting findings relating to the effectiveness of participation research has tended to concentrate on studying how various factors influence the effectiveness of participation. In a classic study Vroom (1960) demonstrated that personality variables can have an important influence on the effectiveness of participation. He identified authoritarianism as an important factor conditioning the relationship between participation and performance. Vroom found that highly authoritarian people with a low need for independence were unaffected by participative approaches, and that high participation was effective only for individuals who were low on the authoritarianism measure.

Hopwood (1978) suggests that greater satisfaction might therefore be obtained when both superior and subordinate expectations are identical with authoritarian supervisors in charge of subordinates with authoritarian expectations, and more participative supervisors in charge of subordinates who are more appreciative of participative approaches. Hopwood also identifies the importance of the work situation in determining the appropriateness of participation. He states:

> In highly programmed, environmentally and technologically constrained areas, where speed and detailed control are essential for efficiency, participative approaches may have much less to offer from the point of view of the more economic aspects of organizational effectiveness... In contrast, in areas where flexibility, innovation and the capacity to deal with unanticipated problems are important, participation in decision-making may offer a more immediate and more narrowly economic payoff than more authoritarian styles.

Brownell (1981) examined the role of the personality variable, locus of control (i.e. the degree to which individuals feel they have control over their own destiny), and its effect on the participation–performance relationship. Budgetary participation was found to have a positive effect on those individuals who felt they had a large degree of control over their destiny, but a negative effect on those who felt that their destinies were controlled by luck, chance or fate. Brownell suggests that when an organization has discretion over the level of budgetary participation afforded to its members, role descriptions should be modified (specifically in regard to participation) to suit the individual characteristics of the role occupants. For example, participation appears to have a positive motivational effect only upon those managers who are confident in their ability to cope with the many factors influencing job performance. Conversely, managers who lack confidence are likely to find that participation only serves to increase their feelings of stress and tension due to uncertainty.

Licata *et al.* (1986) examined the relationship between superior and subordinates. The results of their experiment supported the hypothesis that superiors who felt they had a large degree of control over their destiny were willing to allow greater participation than superiors who felt their destinies were controlled by luck, chance or fate.

Mia (1989) examined how job difficulty interacts with participation to influence managerial performance. Performance was found to be high when the amount of participation was proportionate to the level of job difficulty. In contrast, performance was found to be low when the amount of participation was disproportionate to the level of job difficulty. Thus a congruence (good fit) between the level of participation and job difficulty appeared to be a pre-condition for effective participation (in terms of performance). Mia's findings suggest that participation in budgeting as a tool for improving performance should be used selectively. In cases where perceived job difficulty is high, encouraging managers to participate in budgeting is likely to improve their performance. On the other hand, in cases where perceived job difficulty is low, encouraging managers to participate in budgeting is unlikely to improve their performance. Mia concludes that in such cases prescribed rules, programmes, policies and standards may be more effective in the pursuit of improved performance.

The evidence from the various studies suggests that participative styles of management will not necessarily be more effective than other styles, and that participative methods should be used with care. It is therefore necessary to identify those situations where there is evidence that participative methods are effective, rather than to introduce universal application into organizations. Participation must be used selectively; but if it is used in the right circumstances, it has an enormous potential for encouraging the commitment to organizational goals, improving attitudes towards the budgeting system, and increasing subsequent performance. Note, however, at this stage that there are some limitations on the positive effects of participation in standard setting and circumstances where top-down budget setting is preferable. They are:

1. Performance is measured by precisely the same standard that the budgetee has been involved in setting. This gives the budgetee the opportunity to negotiate lower targets that increase the probability of target achievement and the accompanying rewards. Therefore an improvement in performance – in terms of comparison with the budget – may result merely from a lowering of the standard. Ideally external reference points should be available, since this can provide an indication as to whether the participation process leads to low performance because of loose standards.

2. Personality traits of the participants may limit the benefits of participation. For example, the evidence appears to indicate that authoritarians and persons of weak independence needs may well perform better on standards set by a higher authority.

3. Participation by itself is not adequate in ensuring commitment to standards. The

manager must also believe that he or she can significantly influence the results and be given the necessary feedback about them.

4. A top-down approach to budget setting is likely to be preferable where a process is highly programmable, and there are clear and stable input–output relationships, so that engineered studies can be used to set the targets. Here there is no need to negotiate targets using a bottom-up process.

5. Where a company has a large number of homogeneous units (such as many similar retailing outlets) operating in a stable environment, relative comparisons of the units can be made for performance evaluation. In these circumstances it is inappropriate for each unit to be involved in setting the targets. It is preferable for a top-down approach to be adopted so that a uniform policy can be established for setting the targets.

# Side-effects arising from using accounting information for performance evaluation

Earlier in this chapter we discussed some of the harmful side-effects that can arise from the use of results controls. Some of these effects can be due to the ways in which the output measures are used. A number of studies have been undertaken that examine the side-effects arising from the ways that accounting information is used in performance evaluation.

Hofstede (1968) found that stress on the actual results in performance evaluation led to more extensive use of budgetary information, and this made the budget more relevant. However, this stress was also associated with a feeling that the performance appraisal was unjust; to overcome this problem, the correct balance must be established when the budget performance is evaluated. Too much stress on the results leads to a feeling of injustice, but too little stress leads to a budget being of little relevance and a poor motivation device. Hofstede suggests that a balance maybe obtained by good upwards communication from one's subordinates, and by using the budget in a supportive and flexible manner; this will allow the subordinates adequate scope for creativity.

A more detailed study on how budgets are used in performance evaluation was undertaken by Hopwood (1976), based on observations in a manufacturing division of a large US company. Three distinct styles of using budget and actual cost information in performance evaluation were observed and were described as follows:

1. **Budget-constrained style:** Despite the many problems in using accounting data as comprehensive measures of managerial performance, the evaluation is based primarily upon the cost centre head's ability continually to meet the budget on a short-term basis. This criterion of performance is stressed at the expense of other valued and important criteria, and a cost centre head will tend to receive an unfavourable evaluation if his or her actual costs exceed the budgeted costs, regardless of other considerations. Budget data are therefore used in a rigid manner in performance evaluation.

2. **Profit-conscious style:** The performance of the cost centre head is evaluated on the basis of his or her ability to increase the general effectiveness of his or her unit's operations in relation to the long-term goals of the organization. One important aspect of this at the cost centre level is the head's concern with the minimization of long-run costs. The accounting data must be used with some care and in a rather

flexible manner, with the emphasis for performance evaluation in contributing to long-term profitability.

3. **Non-accounting style**: Accounting data plays a relatively unimportant part in the supervisor's evaluation of the cost centre head's performance.

Emmanuel *et al.* (1990) state that

> The three styles of evaluation are distinguished by the way in which extrinsic rewards are associated with budget achievement. In the rigid (budget constrained) style there is a clear-cut relationship; not achieving budget targets results in punishment, whereas achievement results in rewards. In the flexible (profit conscious) style, the relationship depends on other factors; given good reasons for over-spending, non-attainment of the budget can still result in rewards, whereas the attainment of the budget in undesirable ways may result in punishment. In the non-accounting style, the budget is relatively unimportant because rewards and punishment are not directly associated with its attainment. (Page 179.)

Hopwood observed that, while the accounting data clearly indicated whether a person had been successful in meeting the budget, the data did not necessarily indicate whether a manager was behaving so as to minimize long-term costs. To assess this ability, the data has to be used with discretion, and where necessary supplemented with information from other sources. Hopwood identified such an approach as consistent with a profit-conscious style, which emphasizes the wider use of accounting information rather than just a rigid analysis of the reported variances.

The evidence from Hopwood's study indicated that both the budget-constrained and the profit-conscious styles of evaluation led to a higher degree of involvement with costs than the non-accounting style. Only the profit-conscious style, however, succeeded in attaining this involvement without incurring either emotional costs for the managers in charge of the cost centres or defensive behaviour that was undesirable from the company's point of view.

The budget-constrained style gave rise to a belief that the evaluation was unjust, and caused widespread worry and tension on the job. Hopwood provides evidence of manipulation and undesirable decision behaviour as methods of relieving tension when a budget-constrained style of evaluation is used. In addition, the manager's relationships with the budget-constrained supervisors were allowed to deteriorate, and the rigid emphasis on the short-term budget results also highlighted the interdependent nature of their tasks, so that the immediate instrumental concerns permeated the pattern of social relationships among colleagues. For example, managers went out to improve their own reports, regardless of the detrimental effects on the organization, and then tried to pass on the responsibility by blaming their colleagues. In contrast, Hopwood found that the profit-conscious style avoided these problems, while at the same time it ensured that there was an active involvement with the financial aspects of the operations. A summary of the effect of the three styles of evaluation is given in Exhibit 16.2.

Hopwood's study was based on cost centres having a high degree of interdependence. Rigid measures of performance become less appropriate as the degree of interdependence increases, and therefore the managers used the accounting information in a more flexible manner to ensure that the information remained effective. Otley (1978) replicated Hopwood's study in a British firm that consisted of profit centres with a high degree of independence and where accounting information represented a more adequate basis of performance evaluation. He found no significant differences in the levels of job tension and performance reported by managers evaluated on styles initially used by Hopwood. Three explanations were offered for the differences in results. First, Otley's managers were said to operate more independently of other units within the same organization than Hopwood's managers. Second, Otley's managers were profit centre managers whereas

Hopwood's were cost centre managers. Finally, Hopwood's managers operated in a less predictable environment than Otley's.

Otley suggested a style-context framework to reconcile the differences in results between his study and that of Hopwood. The style dimension consisted of a high and low emphasis on budget data in performance evaluation. The context dimension consisted of managerial interdependency[1] (high and low) and task uncertainty[2] (also high and low). Otley's framework suggested that when managers face high levels of interdependency or uncertainty, they may perceive themselves as having less than full control over performance outcomes. Using budget data in a rigid manner in such situations may be dysfunctional for performance, since a rigid use of budget data assumes that most of the factors that have an effect on task outcomes are within the control of the managers being evaluated (Ansari, 1979). On the other hand, Imoisili (1989) suggests that a rigid use of budget data may be more acceptable to managers if they perceive they are able to exercise control over their performance outcomes. This would be the case with tasks characterized by low uncertainty or interdependency. In other words, it is not budget style *per se* that may lead to higher stress or lower performance. Rather, it is the mismatch of budget style and task contexts that may enhance stress or reduce managerial performance (Imoisili, 1989).

Hirst (1981) has also argued that medium to high reliance on accounting performance measures will minimize dysfunctional behaviour in situations of low task uncertainty, whereas only a medium to low reliance is appropriate in conditions of high uncertainty. Govindarajan (1984) also suggests that managers are likely to be evaluated in a more subjective manner if their unit faces a high degree of uncertainty.

**EXHIBIT 16.2**

*Hopwood's findings on the effect of different styles of evaluating budget performance*

|  | Style of evaluation | | |
| --- | --- | --- | --- |
|  | Budget-constrained | Profit-conscious | Non-accounting |
| Involvement with costs | High | High | Low |
| Job-related tension | High | Medium | Medium |
| Manipulation of accounting information | Extensive | Little | Little |
| Relations with superior | Poor | Good | Good |
| Relations with colleagues | Poor | Good | Good |

## Self-Assessment Questions

You should attempt to answer these questions yourself before looking up the suggested answers, which appear on pages 1124–5. If any part of your answer is incorrect, check back carefully to make sure you understand where you went wrong.

1. The Victoria Hospital is located in a holiday resort that attracts visitors to such an extent that the population of the area is trebled for the summer months of June, July and August. From past experience, this influx of visitors doubles the activity of the hospital during these months. The annual budget for the hospital's laundry department is broken down into four quarters, namely April–June, July–September, October–December and January–March, by dividing the annual budgeted figures by four. The budgeting work has been done for the current year by the secretary of the hospital using the previous year's figures and adding 16%. It is realized by the Hospital Authority that management information for control purposes needs to be improved, and you have been recruited to help to introduce a system of responsibility accounting.

You are required, from the information given, to:

(a) comment on the way in which the quarterly budgets have been prepared and to suggest improvements that could be introduced when preparing the budgets for 2001/2002;

(b) state what information you would like to flow from the actual against budget comparison (note that calculated figures are *not* required);

(c) state the amendments that would be needed to the current practice of budgeting and reporting to enable the report shown below to be used as a measure of the efficiency of the laundry manager.

### Victoria Hospital – Laundry department
### Report for quarter ended 30 September 2000

|  | Budget | Actual |
|---|---|---|
| Patients days | 9 000 | 12 000 |
| Weight processed (kgs) | 180 000 | 240 000 |
|  | (£) | (£) |
| Costs: |  |  |
| Wages | 8 800 | 12 320 |
| Overtime premium | 1 400 | 2 100 |
| Detergents and other supplies | 1800 | 2 700 |
| Water, water softening and heating | 2 000 | 2 500 |
| Maintenance | 1 000 | 1 500 |
| Depreciation of plant | 2 000 | 2 000 |
| Manager's salary | 1 250 | 1 500 |
| Overhead, apportioned: |  |  |
| for occupancy | 4 000 | 4 250 |
| for administration | 5 000 | 5 750 |

(15 marks)

*CIMA Cost Accounting 1*

2. A manufacturing company has the following budgeted costs for one month which are based on a normal capacity level of 40 000 hours.

A departmental overhead absorption rate of £4.40 per hour has been calculated, as follows:

| | Fixed (£000) | Variable per hour (£) |
|---|---|---|
| Overhead: | | |
| Management and supervision | 30 | — |
| Shift premium | — | 0.10 |
| National Insurance and pension costs | 6 | 0.22 |
| Inspection | 20 | 0.25 |
| Consumable supplies | 6 | 0.18 |
| Power for machinery | — | 0.20 |
| Lighting and heating | 4 | — |
| Rates | 9 | — |
| Repairs and maintenance | 8 | 0.15 |
| Materials handling | 10 | 0.30 |
| Depreciation of machinery | 15 | — |
| Production administration | 12 | — |
| | 120 | |
| Overhead rate per hour: Variable | | 1.40 |
| Fixed | | 3.00 |
| Total | | £4.40 |

During the month of April, the company actually worked 36 000 hours producing 36 000 standard hours of production and incurred the following overhead costs:

| | (£000) |
|---|---|
| Management and supervision | 30.0 |
| Shift premium | 4.0 |
| National Insurance and pension costs | 15.0 |
| Inspection | 28.0 |
| Consumable supplies | 12.7 |
| Power for machinery | 7.8 |
| Lighting and heating | 4.2 |
| Rates | 9.0 |
| Repairs and maintenance | 15.1 |
| Materials handling | 21.4 |
| Depreciation of machinery | 15.0 |
| Production administration | 11.5 |
| Idle time | 1.6 |
| | 175.3 |

You are required to:

(a) prepare a statement showing for April the flexible budget for the month, the actual costs and the variance for each overhead item;

(b) comment on each variance of £1000 or more by suggesting possible reasons for the variances reported;

(c) state, for control purposes, with reasons to support your conclusions:
    (i) whether (b) above is adequate; and
    (ii) whether the statement prepared in respect of the request in (a) above could be improved, and if so, how.

*CIMA Stage 2 Cost Accounting*
*Pilot Paper*

## Summary

The aim of management control systems is to influence employee behaviours in desirable ways in order to increase the probability that an organization's objectives will be achieved. Companies use many different control mechanisms to cope with the problem of organizational control. To fully understand the role that management accounting control systems play in the control process, it is necessary to be aware of how they relate to the entire array of control mechanisms used by firms.

We therefore initially examined the different types of controls that are used by firms. Three different categories were identified – action/behavioural controls, personnel and cultural controls and results/output controls. With action controls the actions themselves are the focus of controls. They are usable and effective only when managers know what actions are desirable (or undesirable) and have the ability to make sure that the desirable actions occur (or that the undesirable actions do not occur). Personnel controls help employees do a good job by building on employees' natural tendencies to control themselves. They include selection and placement, training and job design. Cultural controls represent a set of values, social norms and beliefs that are shared by members of the organization and that influence their actions. Output or results controls involve collecting and reporting information about the outcomes of work effort. They involve the following stages – establishing results and performance targets, measuring performance and providing rewards or punishments based on an employee's ability to achieve the performance target.

Results controls can promote a number of harmful side effects. They can lead to a lack of goal congruence when employees seek to achieve the performance targets in a way that is not organizationally desirable. They can also lead to data manipulation and negative attitudes which can result in a decline in morale and a lack of motivation.

The creation of responsibility centres is a fundamental part of management accounting control systems. Four different types of responsibility centres were described. They were cost (or expense) centres, revenue centres, profit centres and investment centres. Management accounting control systems have two core elements. The first, is the formal planning processes such as budgeting and long-term planning. These processes are used for establishing performance expectations for evaluating performance. The second is responsibility accounting which involves the creation of responsibility centres. Responsibility centres enable accountability for financial results/outcomes to be allocated to individuals throughout the firm. The objective of responsibility accounting is to accumulate costs and revenues for each individual responsibility centre so that the deviations from a performance target can be attributed to the individual who is accountable. For each responsibility centre the process involves setting a performance target, measuring performance, comparing performance against the target, analysing the variances and taking action where significant variances exist between actual and target performance.

Responsibility accounting involves:

1. distinguishing between those items which managers can control and for which they should be held accountable and those items over which they have no control and for which they are not held accountable;
2. determining how challenging the financial targets should be;
3. determining how much influence managers should have in the setting of financial targets.

The controllability principle states that it is appropriate to charge to an area of responsibility only those costs that are significantly influenced by the manager of that responsibility centre. Different types of uncontrollables were explained and methods of dealing with them, either before or after the measurement period, were described. The general rule that should be applied is to hold employees accountable for the performance area you want them to pay attention to.

Different types of financial performance targets have been described and the impact of their level of difficulty on motivation and performance examined. Highly achievable targets were recommended because they could be used for planning purposes and they also had a motivational impact.

Participation or bottom-up budget setting was compared with top-down budget setting. The bene-fits arising from participation in the budget process were outlined and the empirical studies summarized. It was concluded that participation must be used selectively; but if it is used in the right circumstances, it has an enormous potential for encouraging commitment to organizational goals, improving attitudes towards the budgeting system, and increasing subsequent performance.

Finally, we examined the side-effects arising from the ways that accounting information is used in performance evaluation. Three different styles of performance evaluation were described (a budget-constrained, profit conscious and non-accounting style) and the circumstances where a specific style was recommended were identified.

## Key Terms and Concepts

action controls (p. 594)
aspiration level (p. 613)
behavioural controls (p. 594)
bottom-up budget setting (p. 617)
budgetary slack (p. 607)
budget-constrained style (p. 620)
clan controls (p. 595)
control (p. 593)
controllability principle (pp. 598, 607)
controls (p. 593)
cost centres (p. 603)
cultural controls (p. 596)
cybernetic system (p. 598)
discretionary expense centres (p. 603)
engineered targets (p. 612)
expense centres (p. 603)
*ex post* budget adjustments (p. 611)
feedback control (p. 599)
feed-forward control (p. 599)
flexible budgets (p. 610)
goal congruence (p. 600)

historical targets (p. 612)
investment centres (p. 605)
management control systems (p. 594)
negotiated targets (p. 612)
non-accounting style (p. 621)
output controls (p. 597)
participation (p. 617)
personnel controls (p. 596)
profit centres (p. 604)
profit-conscious style (p. 620)
relative performance evaluation (p. 611)
responsibility accounting (p. 605)
results controls (p. 597)
revenue centres (p. 604)
social control (p. 596)
standard cost centres (p. 603)
strategic control (p. 594)
subjective judgements (p. 611)
top-down budget setting (p. 617)
variance (pp. 599, 603)
variance analysis (p. 610)

## Recommended Reading

For a detailed study of the controllability principle you should refer to Merchant (1989). There are a number of important textbooks that specialize in management control. If you wish to study manage-ment control in more depth you are recommended to read Merchant (1998). For a discussion of performance measurement in the service industries you should refer to Fitzgerald and Moon (1996).

## Key Examination Points

A common error is to compare actual performance against an unflexed budget. Remember to flex the budget on output and not input. Questions relating to this chapter tend to ask you to present a performance report. It is important that you distin-guish between controllable and non-controllable expenses and stress the need to incorporate non-financial measures.

# Questions

*Indicates that a suggested solution is to be found in the *Students' Manual*.

### 16.1* Intermediate

(a) Identify and explain the essential elements of an effective cost control system. (13 marks)

(b) Outline possible problems which may be encountered as a result of the introduction of a system of cost control into an organization. (4 marks)

(Total 17 marks)

### 16.2 Intermediate

You have applied for the position of assistant accountant in a company manufacturing a range of products with a sales turnover of £12 million per annum and employing approximately 300 employees. As part of the selection process you are asked to spend half an hour preparing a report, to be addressed to the managing director, on the topic of 'cost control'.

You are required to write the report which should deal with what is meant by 'cost control', its purpose and the techniques which you believe would be useful within this particular company.

(20 marks)

*CIMA Foundation Cost Accounting 1*

### 16.3 Intermediate

Outline the main features of a responsibility accounting system. (6 marks)

*ACCA Level 2 Management Accounting*

### 16.4 Intermediate

Explain the meaning of each of the undernoted terms, comment on their likely impact on cash budgeting and profit planning and suggest ways in which any adverse effects of each may be reduced.

(a) Budgetary slack. (7 marks)

(b) Incremental budgets. (7 marks)

(c) Fixed budgets. (6 marks)

(Total 20 marks)

*ACCA Level 2 Cost and Management Accounting II*

### 16.5 Advanced

(a) Discuss the use of the following as aids to *each* of planning and control:

(i) rolling budgets

(ii) flexible budgets

(iii) planning and operational variances.

(9 marks)

(b) Discuss the extent to which the incidence of budgetary slack is likely to be affected by the use of each of the techniques listed in (a).

(6 marks)

(Total 15 marks)

*ACCA Paper 9 Information for Control and Decision Making*

### 16.6 Advanced

In the context of budgetary control, certain costs are not amenable to the use of flexible budgets. These include some costs which are often called 'discretionary' (or 'programmed').

You are required to explain:

(a) the nature of discretionary (or programmed) costs and give *two* examples;

(b) how the treatment of these costs differs from that of other types of cost in the process of preparing and using budgets for control purposes. (20 marks)

*CIMA P3 Management Accounting*

### 16.7* Advanced

A local government authority is organized so that some operating departments (e.g. building, transport, printing, catering) supply services to several functional departments (e.g. education, recreational facilities, road works, fire service). At present the total cost of each service department is allocated on a simple proportional basis to user departments.

As an aid to cost control the authority has decided to charge the user departments for these services on the basis of cost or market price whichever is the lower.

You are required to:

(a) indicate the benefits likely to arise from this decision;

(b) outline the problems you expect may be encountered in putting the decision into practice;

(c) state how these problems might be overcome. (20 marks)

*CIMA P3 Management Accounting*

### 16.8* Advanced

A major feature of the world economy is the high proportion of employment in service industries, and the development of large service organisations such as banks, insurance companies, and hotel groups.

You are required to explain:

(a) how and why control of a large service organisation differs from that of a large manufacturing organisation; (8 marks)

(b) the problems of tracing costs to products in service industries and the uses of the cost information that can be obtained; (6 marks)

(c) how the control of quality in service industries differs from that in manufacturing industry, and suggest three appropriate measures for quality in a large-scale competitive service organisation. Indicate briefly how the measurements would be made. *(Possible examples of such industries include banks, insurance companies and large professional firms, but an organisation in another industry may be selected: the choice should be indicated.)* (6 marks)
(Total 20 marks)
*CIMA Stage 4 Management Accounting – Control and Audit*

**16.9\* Advanced**
One of the major practical difficulties of applying a financial reporting and control system based on flexible budgeting to a service or overhead department is in identifying and measuring an appropriate unit of activity with which to 'flex' the budget.

Required:

(a) Describe and comment on the desirable attributes of such a measure in the context of a valid application of flexible budgeting to a service centre or to a cost centre where standard costing is not applicable.
(c. 8 marks)

(b) Explain the difficulties in obtaining such a measure. (c. 6 marks)

(c) List three suitable measures of activity, indicating the circumstances in which each would be suitable and the circumstances in which each of them would be misleading or unsuitable. (c. 6 marks)
(Total 20 marks)
*ACCA P2 Management Accounting*

**16.10\* Advanced**
(a) Budgetary controls have been likened to a system of thermostatic control.
  (i) In what respects is the analogy inappropriate? (10 marks)

  (ii) What are the matters raised in (a) (i) above that need to be considered when setting a structure for an effective budgetary control system? (8 marks)

(b) Describe the pre-conditions which should exist if budget variance analysis is to be of value to an organization. (7 marks)
(Total 25 marks)
*CIMA Stage 4 – Control and Audit*

**16.11\* Advanced**
One common approach to organisational control theory is to look at the model of a cybernetic system. This is often illustrated by a diagram of a thermostat mechanism.

You are required:

(a) to explain the limitations of the simple feedback control this model illustrates, as an explanation of the working of organisational control systems;
*Note:* A diagram is *not* required. (7 marks)

(b) to explain
  (i) the required conditions (pre-requisites) for the existence of control in an organisation, which are often derived from this approach to control theory; (5 marks)

  (ii) the difficulties of applying control in a not-for-profit organisation (NPO). (8 marks)
(Total 20 marks)
*CIMA Stage 4 Management Accounting – Control and Audit May 1994*

**16.12 Advanced**
'Textbooks on accounting often describe management information and financial control systems as if they work in exactly the same way as machine control systems. Many accountants appear to assume that they do work in this way. The problem is that business operations do not function like machines. Unless a financial control system is very well designed and managed, then it can easily distort the functioning of a business operation.'
*One comment on the design and use of financial control systems*

Requirements
Having regard to this comment,
(a) • explain the concepts of management information system design, and the role that

such systems play in the financial control of business operations;

- explain the role that performance evaluation plays in a management information system;
- compare and contrast output controls and input controls in the context of a management information system; (11 marks)

(b) explain

- the manner in which management information systems can distort the functioning of the business operations they are meant to serve;
- the action that might be taken by the chartered management accountant in order to avoid such distortion; (9 marks)

(c) explain how the use of PCs, spreadsheets and databases contributes to the cost-effectiveness of management information systems.

(5 marks)
(Total 25 marks)
*CIMA Stage 3 Management Accounting Applications*

### 16.13 Advanced

(a) In the context of budgeting, provide definitions for *four* of the following terms:
aspiration level;
budgetary slack;
feedback;
zero-base budgeting;
responsibility accounting. (8 marks)

(b) Discuss the motivational implications of the level of efficiency assumed in establishing a budget. (9 marks)

(Total 17 marks)
*ACCA Level 2 Management Accounting*

### 16.14 Advanced

In the context of budgeting, describe the meaning of and write notes on *four* of the following terms:
Feedback control;
Feedforward control;
Budgetary slack;
Aspiration level;
Control limits;
Noise. (17 marks)
*ACCA Level 2 Management Accounting*

### 16.15* Advanced

You are required, within the context of budgetary control, to:

(a) explain the specific roles of planning, motivation and evaluation; (7 marks)

(b) describe how these roles may conflict with each other; (7 marks)

(c) give *three* examples of ways by which the management accountant may resolve the conflict described in (b). (6 marks)
*CIMA P3 Management Accounting*

### 16.16* Advanced

(a) Explain the ways in which the attitudes and behaviour of managers in a company are liable to pose more threat to the success of its budgetary control system than are minor technical inadequacies that may be in the system. (15 marks)

(b) Explain briefly what the management accountant can do to minimise the disruptive effects of such attitudes and behaviour. (5 marks)
*CIMA P3 Management Accounting*

### 16.17* Advanced

What are the behavioural aspects which should be borne in mind by those who are designing and operating standard costing and budgetary control systems? (20 marks)
*CIMA Cost Accounting 2*

### 16.18* Advanced

One purpose of management accounting is to influence managers' behaviour so that their resulting actions will yield a maximum benefit to the employing organization. In the context of this objective, you are required to discuss:

(a) how budgets can cause behavioural conflict;

(b) how this behavioural conflict may be overcome;

(c) the importance of the feedback of information; and

(d) the purpose of goal congruence. (20 marks)
*CIMA P3 Management Accounting*

### 16.19* Advanced

In his study of 'The Impact of Budgets on People', published in 1952, C. Argyris reported *inter alia* the following comment by a financial controller on the practice of participation in the setting of budgets in his company:

'We bring in the supervisors of budget areas, we tell them that we want their frank opinion, but most of them just sit there and nod their heads. We know they're not coming out with exactly how they feel. I guess budgets scare them.'

You are required to suggest reasons why managers may be reluctant to participate fully in setting budgets, and to suggest also unwanted side effects which may arise from the imposition of budgets by senior management. (13 marks)
*ICAEW Management Accounting*

### 16.20* Advanced

Several assumptions are commonly made by accountants when preparing or interpreting budgetary information.

You are required to explain why each of the following five assumptions might be made by accountants when designing a system of budgeting, and to set out in each case also any arguments which, in your view, raise legitimate doubts about their validity:

(a) budgeted performance should be reasonably attainable but not too loose, (5 marks)
(b) participation by managers in the budget-setting process leads to better performance, (5 marks)
(c) management by exception is the most effective system of routine reporting, (5 marks)
(d) a manager's budget reports should exclude all matters which are not completely under his control, (5 marks)
(e) budget statements should include only matters which can be easily and accurately measured in monetary terms. (5 marks)
(Total 25 marks)
*ICAEW Management Accounting*

### 16.21* Advanced

The level of efficiency assumed in the setting of standards has important motivational implications – Discuss. (8 marks)
*ACCA Level 2 Management Accounting*

### 16.22* Advanced

In discussing the standard setting process for use within budgetary control and/or standard costing systems, the following has been written: 'The level of standards appears to play a role in achievement motivation . . .'

Required:
(a) Briefly distinguish between the motivational and managerial reporting objectives of both budgetary control and standard costing. Describe the extent to which these two objectives place conflicting demands on the stan-

dard of performance utilized in such systems. (6 marks)
(b) Describe three levels of efficiency which may be incorporated in the standards used in budgetary control and/or standard costing systems. Outline the main advantages and disadvantages of each of the three levels described. (6 marks)
(c) Discuss the advantages and disadvantages of involving employees in the standard setting process. (8 marks)
(Total 20 marks)
*ACCA P2 Management Accounting*

### 16.23* Advanced

You are required to:
(i) discuss the factors that are likely to cause managers to submit budget estimates of sales and costs that do not represent their best estimates or expectations of what will actually occur, (8 marks)
(ii) suggest, as a budget accountant, what procedures you would advise in order to minimize the likelihood of such biased estimates arising. (4 marks)
*ICAEW Management Accounting*

### 16.24 Advanced

'Budgeting is too often looked upon from a purely mechanistic viewpoint. The human factors in budgeting are more important than the accounting techniques. The success of a budgetary system depends upon its acceptance by the company members who are affected by the budgets.'

Discuss the validity of the above statement from the viewpoint of both the planning and the control aspects of budgeting. In the course of your discussion present at least one practical illustration to support your conclusions. (20 marks)
*ACCA P2 Management Accounting*

### 16.25 Advanced

'The major reason for introducing budgetary control and standard costing systems is to influence human behaviour and to motivate the managers to achieve the goals of the organization. However, the accounting literature provides many illustrations of accounting control systems that fail to give sufficient attention to influencing human behaviour towards the achievement of organization goals.'

You are required:

(a) To identify and discuss four situations where accounting control systems might not motivate desirable behaviour.

(b) To briefly discuss the improvements you would suggest in order to ensure that some of the dysfunctional behavioural consequences of accounting control systems are avoided.

### 16.26 Advanced

'The final impact which any accounting system has on managerial and employee behaviour is dependent not only upon its design and technical characteristics but also in the precise manner in which the resulting information is used...' (A. Hopwood, *Accounting and Human Behaviour*).

Discuss this statement in relation to budgeting and standard costing.

### 16.27 Advanced

'Motivation is the over-riding consideration that should influence management in formulating and using performance measures, and in designing management control systems.'

Discuss this statement in relation to the design and implementation of budgetary control systems.

### 16.28 Advanced

(a) Discuss the behavioural arguments for and against involving those members of management who are responsible for the implementation of the budget in the annual budget setting process. (10 marks)

(b) Explain how the methods by which annual budgets are formulated might help to overcome behavioural factors likely to limit the efficiency and effectiveness of the budget. (7 marks)
(Total 17 marks)

### 16.29* Advanced

The typical budgetary control system in practice does not encourage *goal congruence*, contains *budgetary slack*, ignores the *aspiration levels* of participants and attempts to control operations by *feedback*, when *feedforward* is likely to be more effective; in summary the typical budgetary control system is likely to have dysfunctional effects.

You are required to

(a) explain briefly *each* of the *six* terms in italics; (6 marks)

(b) describe how the major dysfunctional effects of budgeting could be avoided. (11 marks)
(Total 17 marks)
*CIMA Stage 3 Management Accounting Techniques*

### 16.30 Advanced

(a) An extensive literature on the behavioural aspects of budgeting discusses the propensity of managers to create budgetary slack.

You are required to explain three ways in which managers may attempt to create budgetary slack, and how senior managers can identify these attempts to distort the budgetary system. (6 marks)

(b) Managerial behaviour can be quite different from that discussed in (a).

You are required to explain circumstances in which managers may be motivated to set themselves very high, possibly unachievable budgets. (6 marks)

(c) Sections (a) and (b) above are examples of differing managerial behaviour in disparate situations. There are theories which attempt to explain the consequences for the design of management accounting systems of disparate situations, one of which is contingency theory.

You are required to explain

- the contingency theory of management accounting
- the effects of environmental uncertainty on the choice of managerial control systems and on information systems for managerial control. (13 marks)
(Total 25 marks)
*CIMA Stage 4 Management Accounting – Control and Audit*

### 16.31 Advanced

An article in *Management Accounting* concluded that there will always be some budgetary padding in any organisation.

Requirements:

(a) As Management Accountant, write a report to your Finance Director, explaining what steps can be taken by you, and by senior management when approving budgets, to minimise budgetary slack. (8 marks)

(b) The Finance Director, having read the report referred to in part (a), discussed the problem with the Managing Director and suggested that appropriate action be taken to reduce budgetary slack.

The Managing Director expressed doubts, stating that in his opinion removing all budget padding could cause considerable problems.

Requirement:
Explain the arguments that can be advanced for accepting some budgetary slack, and the advantages of this to the manager being appraised and to the organisation. Discuss whether the budget review and approval process should permit managers to build in some budgetary slack.

(12 marks)

(Total 20 marks)

*CIMA Stage 4 Management Accounting Control Systems*

### 16.32 Intermediate: Flexible budgets and the motivational role of budgets

Club Atlantic is an all-weather holiday complex providing holidays throughout the year. The fee charged to guests is fully inclusive of accommodation and all meals. However, because the holiday industry is so competitive, Club Atlantic is only able to generate profits by maintaining strict financial control of all activities.

The club's restaurant is one area where there is a constant need to monitor costs. Susan Green is the manager of the restaurant. At the beginning of each year she is given an annual budget which is then broken down into months. Each month she receives a statement monitoring actual costs against the annual budget and highlighting any variances. The statement for the month ended 31 October is reproduced below along with a list of assumptions:

#### Club Atlantic Restaurant Performance Statement
#### Month to 31 October

| | Actual | Budget | Variance (over)/ under |
|---|---|---|---|
| Number of guest days | 11 160 | 9 600 | (1560) |
| | (£) | (£) | (£) |
| Food | 20 500 | 20 160 | (340) |
| Cleaning materials | 2 232 | 1 920 | (312) |
| Heat, light and power | 2 050 | 2 400 | 350 |
| Catering wages | 8 400 | 7 200 | (1200) |
| Rent rates, insurance and depreciation | 1 860 | 1 800 | (60) |
| | 35 042 | 33 480 | (1562) |

Assumptions:

(a) The budget has been calculated on the basis of a 30-day calendar month with the cost of rents, insurance and depreciation being an apportionment of the fixed annual charge.

(b) The budgeted catering wages assume that:
   (i) there is one member of the catering staff for every forty guests staying at the complex;
   (ii) the daily cost of a member of the catering staff is £30.

(c) All other budgeted costs are variable costs based on the number of guest days.

*Task 1*

Using the data above, prepare a revised performance statement using flexible budgeting. Your statement should show both the revised budget and the revised variances. Club Atlantic uses the existing budgets and performance statements to motivate its managers as well as for financial control. If manages keep expenses below budget they receive a bonus in addition to their salaries. A colleague of Susan is Brian Hilton. Brian is in charge of the swimming pool and golf course, both of which have high levels of fixed costs. Each month he manages to keep expenses below budget and in return enjoys regular bonuses. Under the current reporting system, Susan Green only rarely receives a bonus.

At a recent meeting with Club Atlantic's directors Susan Green expressed concern that the performance statement was not a valid reflection of her management of the restaurant. You are currently employed by Hall and Co., the club's auditors, and the directors of Club Atlantic have asked you to advice them whether there is any justification for Susan Green's concern.

At the meeting with the Club's directors, you were asked the following questions:

(a) Do budgets motivate managers to achieve objectives?

(b) Does motivating managers lead to improved performance?

(c) Does the current method of reporting performance motivate Susan Green and Brian Hilton to be more efficient?

*Task 2*

Write a *brief* letter to the directors of Club Atlantic addressing their question and justifying your answers.

*Note:* You should make use of the data given in this task plus your findings in Task 1.

*AAT Technicians Stage*

## 16.33 Intermediate: Criticism and redrafting of a performance report

(a) The following report has been prepared, relating to one product for March. This has been sent to the appropriate product manager as part of PDC Limited's monitoring procedures.

### Monthly variance report – March 1

| | Actual | Budget | Variance | % |
|---|---|---|---|---|
| Production volume (units) | 9 905 | 10 000 | 95 A | 0.95 A |
| Sales volume (units) | 9 500 | 10 000 | 500 A | 5.00 A |
| Sales revenue (£) | 27 700 | 30 000 | 2300 A | 7.67 A |
| Direct material (kg) | 9 800 | 10 000 | 200 F | 2.00 F |
| Direct material (£) | 9 600 | 10 000 | 400 F | 4.00 F |
| Direct labour (hours) | 2 500 | 2 400 | 100 A | 4.17 A |
| Direct labour (£) | 8 500 | 8 400 | 100 A | 1.19 A |
| Contribution (£) | 9 600 | 11 600 | 2000 A | 17.24 A |

The product manager has complained that the report ignores the principle of flexible budgeting and is unfair.

Required:

Prepare a report addressed to the management team which comments critically on the monthly variance report. Include as an appendix to your report the layout of a revised monthly variance report which will be more useful to the product manager. Include row and column headings, but do *not* calculate the contents of the report. (15 marks)

(b) Explain the differences between budgetary control and standard costing/variance analysis. In what circumstances would an organization find it beneficial to operate both of these cost control systems? (5 marks)

(Total 20 marks)

*CIMA Operational Cost Accounting Stage 2*

## 16.34* Intermediate: Preparation of flexible budgets based on an analysis of past cost behaviour and an adjustment for inflation

TJ Limited is in an industry sector which is recovering from the recent recession. The directors of the company hope next year to be operating at 85% of capacity, although currently the company is operating at only 65% of capacity. 65% of capacity represents output of 10 000 units of the single product which is produced and sold. One hundred direct workers are employed on production for 200 000 hours in the current year.

The flexed budgets for the current year are:

| Capacity level | 55% (£) | 65% (£) | 75% (£) |
|---|---|---|---|
| Direct materials | 846 200 | 1 000 000 | 1 153 800 |
| Direct wages | 1 480 850 | 1 750 000 | 2 019 150 |
| Production overhead | 596 170 | 650 000 | 703 830 |
| Selling and distribution overhead | 192 310 | 200 000 | 207 690 |
| Administration overhead | 120 000 | 120 000 | 120 000 |
| Total costs | 3 235 530 | 3 720 000 | 4 204 470 |

Profit in any year is budgeted to be $16\frac{2}{3}\%$ of sales.

The following percentage increases in costs are expected for next year

| | Increase % |
|---|---|
| Direct materials | 6 |
| Direct wages | 3 |
| Variable production overhead | 7 |
| Variable selling and distribution overhead | 7 |
| Fixed production overhead | 10 |
| Fixed selling and distribution overhead | 7.5 |
| Administration overhead | 10 |

You are required:

(a) to prepare for next year a flexible budget statement on the assumption that the company operates at 85% of capacity; your statement should show both contribution and profit; (14 marks)

(b) to discuss briefly three problems which may arise from the change in capacity level; (6 marks)

(c) to state who is likely to serve on a budget committee operated by TJ Limited and explain the purpose of such a committee. (5 marks)

(Total 25 marks)

*CIMA Stage 2 Cost Accounting*

## 16.35 Intermediate: Preparation of flexible budgets and an explanation of variances

You have been provided with the following operating statement, which represents an attempt to compare the actual performance for the quarter which has just ended with the budget:

| | Budget | Actual | Variance |
|---|---|---|---|
| Number of units sold (000s) | 640 | 720 | 80 |
| | £000 | £000 | £000 |
| Sales | 1024 | 1071 | 47 |
| Cost of sales (all variable) | | | |
| Materials | 168 | 144 | |
| Labour | 240 | 288 | |
| Overheads | 32 | 36 | |
| | 440 | 468 | (28) |
| Fixed labour cost | 100 | 94 | 6 |
| Selling and distribution costs: | | | |
| Fixed | 72 | 83 | (11) |
| Variable | 144 | 153 | (9) |
| Administration costs: | | | |
| Fixed | 184 | 176 | 8 |
| Variable | 48 | 54 | (6) |
| | 548 | 560 | (12) |
| Net profit | 36 | 43 | 7 |

Required:

(a) Using a flexible budgeting approach, re-draft the operating statement so as to provide a more realistic indication of the variances and comment briefly on the possible reasons (other than inflation) why they have occurred. (12 marks)

(b) Explain why the original operating statement was of little use to management. (2 marks)

(c) Discuss the problems associated with the forecasting of figures which are to be used in flexible budgeting. (6 marks)

(Total 20 marks)

*ACCA Paper 8 Managerial Finance*

## 16.36* Intermediate: Preparation of a flexible budget performance report

The Viking Smelting Company established a division, called the reclamation division, two years ago, to extract silver from jewellers' waste materials. The waste materials are processed in a furnace, enabling silver to be recovered. The silver is then further processed into finished products by three other divisions within the company.

A performance report is prepared each month for the reclamation division which is then discussed by the management team. Sharon Houghton, the newly appointed financial controller of the reclamation division, has recently prepared her first report for the four weeks to 31 May. This is shown below:

**Performance Report Reclamation Division**
**4 weeks to 31 May**

| | Actual | Budget | Variance | Comments |
|---|---|---|---|---|
| Production (tonnes) | 200 | 250 | 50 (F)[a] | |
| | (£) | (£) | (£) | |
| Wages and social security costs | 46 133 | 45 586 | 547 (A) | Overspend |
| Fuel | 15 500 | 18 750 | 3250 (F) | |
| Consumables | 2 100 | 2 500 | 400 (F) | |
| Power | 1 590 | 1 750 | 160 (F) | |
| Divisional overheads | 21 000 | 20 000 | 1 000 (A) | Overspend |
| Plant maintenance | 6 900 | 5 950 | 950 (A) | Overspend |
| Central services | 7 300 | 6 850 | 450 (A) | Overspend |
| Total | 100 523 | 101 386 | 863 (F) | |

[a] (A) = adverse, (F) = favourable

In preparing the budgeted figures, the following assumptions were made for May:

- the reclamation division was to employ four teams of six production employees;
- each employee was to work a basic 42-hour week and be paid £7.50 per hour for the four weeks of May;
- social security and other employment costs were estimated at 40% of basic wages;
- a bonus, shared amongst the production employees, was payable if production exceeded 150 tonnes. This varied depending on the output achieved;

1. if output was between 150 and 199 tonnes, the bonus was £3 per tonne produced;
2. if output was between 200 and 249 tonnes, the bonus was £8 per tonne produced;
3. if output exceeded 249 tonnes the bonus was £13 per tonne produced;

- the cost of fuel was £75 per tonne;
- consumables were £10 per tonne;
- power comprised a fixed charge of £500 per four weeks plus £5 per tonne for every tonne produced;
- overheads directly attributable to the division were £20 000;

- plant maintenance was to be apportioned to divisions on the basis of the capital values of each division;
- the cost of Viking's central services was to be shared equally by all four divisions.

You are the deputy financial controller of the reclamation division. After attending her first monthly meeting with the board of the reclamation division, Sharon Houghton arranges a meeting with you. She is concerned about a number of issues, one of them being that the current report does not clearly identify those expenses and variances which are the direct responsibility of the reclamation division.

*Task 1*

Sharon Houghton asks you to prepare a flexible budget report for the reclamation division for May in a form consistent with responsibility accounting.

On receiving your revised report. Sharon tells you about the other questions raised at the management meeting when the original report was presented. These are summarized below:

(i) Why are the budget figures based on 2-year-old data taken from the proposal recommending the establishment of the reclamation division?

(ii) Should the budget data be based on what we were proposing to do or what we actually did do?

(iii) is it true that the less we produce the more favourable our variances will be?

(iv) Why is there so much maintenance in a new division with modern equipment and why should we be charged with the actual costs of the maintenance department even when they overspend?

(v) Could the comments, explaining the variances, be improved?

(vi) Should all the variances be investigated?

(vii) Does showing the cost of central services on the divisional performance report help control these costs and motivate the divisional managers?

*Task 2*

Prepare a memo for the management of the reclamation division. Your memo should:

(a) answer their queries and justify your comments;

(b) highlight the main objective of your revised performance report developed in Task 1 and

give two advantages of it over the original report

*AAT Technicians Stage*

## 16.37* Intermediate: Sales forecasting removing seasonal variations, flexible budgets and budget preparation

You work as the assistant to the management accountant for Henry Limited, a medium-sized manufacturing company. One of its products, product P, has been very successful in recent years, showing a steadily increasing trend in sales volumes. Sales volumes for the four quarters of last year were as follows:

|  | Quarter 1 | Quarter 2 | Quarter 3 | Quarter 4 |
|---|---|---|---|---|
| Actual sales volume (units) | 420 000 | 450 000 | 475 000 | 475 000 |

A new assistant has recently joined the marketing department and she has asked you for help in understanding the terminology which is used in preparing sales forecasts and analysing sales trends. She has said: 'My main problem is that I do not see why my boss is so enthusiastic about the growth in product P's sales volume. It looks to me as though the rate of growth is really slowing down and has actually stopped in quarter 4. I am told that I should be looking at the deseasonalized or seasonally adjusted sales data but I do not understand what is meant by this.'

You have found that product P's sales are subject to the following seasonal variations:

|  | Quarter 1 | Quarter 2 | Quarter 3 | Quarter 4 |
|---|---|---|---|---|
| Seasonal variation (units) | +25 000 | +15 000 | 0 | −40 000 |

*Task 1*

(a) Adjust for the seasonal variations to calculate deseasonalized or seasonally adjusted sales volume (i.e. the trend figures) for each quarter of last year.

(b) Assuming that the trend and seasonal variations will continue, forecast the sales volumes for each of the four quarters of next year.

## Task 2

Prepare a memorandum to the marketing assistant which explains:

(a) what is meant by seasonal variations and deseaonalized or seasonally adjusted data;

(b) how they can be useful in analysing a time series and preparing forecasts.

Use the figures for product P's sales to illustrate your explanations.

## Task 3

Using the additional data below, prepare a further memorandum to the marketing assistant which explains the following:

(a) why fixed budgets are useful for planning but flexible budgets may be more useful to enable management to exercise reflective control over distribution costs,

(b) *two* possible activity indicators which could be used as a basis for flexing the budget for distribution costs,

(c) how a flexible budget cost allowance is calculated and used for control purposes. Use your own examples and figures where appropriate to illustrate your explanations.

Additional data:

The marketing assistant has now approached you for more help in understanding the company's planning and control systems. She has been talking with the distribution manager, who has tried to explain how flexible budgets are used to control distribution costs within Henry Limited. She makes the following comment. 'I thought that budgets were supposed to provide a target to plan our activities and against which to monitor our costs. How can we possibly plan and control our costs if we simply change the budgets when activity levels alter?'

Product Q is another product which is manufactured and sold by Henry Limited. In the process of preparing budgetary plans for next year the following information has been made available to you.

1. Forecast sales units of product Q for the year = 18 135 units.

2. Closing stocks of finished units of product Q at the end of next year will be increased by 15% from their opening level of 1200 units.

3. All units are subject to quality control check. The budget plans are to allow for 1% of all units checked to be rejected and scrapped at the end of the process. All closing stocks will have passed this quality control check.

4. Five direct labour hours are to be worked for each unit of product Q processed, including those which are scrapped after the quality control check. Of the total hours to be paid for, 7.5% are budgeted to be idle time.

5. The standard hourly rate of pay for direct employees is £6 per hour.

6. Material M is used in the manufacture of product Q. One finished unit of producing Q contains 9 kg of M but there is a wastage of 10% of input of material M due to evaporation and spillage during the process.

7. By the end of next year stocks of material M are to be increased by 12% from their opening level of 8000 kg. During the year a loss of 1000 kg is expected due to deterioration of the material in store.

## Task 4

Prepare the following budgets for the forthcoming year:

(a) production budget for product Q, in units;

(b) direct labour budget for product Q, in hours and in £;

(c) material usage budget for material M, in kg;

(d) material purchases budget for material M, in kg.

## Task 5

The supplier of material M was warned that available supplies will be below the amount indicated in your budget for Task 4 part (d) above. Explain the implications of this shortage and suggest *four* possible actions which could be taken to overcome the problem. For each suggestion, identify any problems which may arise.

*AAT Technicians Stage*

## 16.38* Intermediate: Preparation of flexible budgets

*Data*

Rivermede Ltd makes a single product called the Fasta. Last year, Steven Jones, the managing director of Rivermede Ltd, attended a course on budgetary control. As a result, he agreed to revise the way budgets were prepared in the company. Rather than imposing targets for managers, he encouraged participation by senior managers in the preparation of budgets.

An initial budget was prepared but Mike Fisher, the sales director, felt that the budgeted sales volume was set too high. He explained that setting too high a budgeted sales volume would mean his sales staff would be de-motivated because they would not be able to achieve that sales volume. Steven Jones agreed to use the revised sales volume suggested by Mike Fisher.

Both the initial and revised budgets are reproduced below complete with the actual results for the year ended 31 May.

**Rivermede Ltd – budgeted and actual costs for the year ended 31 May**

| Fast production and sales (units) | Original budget 24 000 (£) | Revised budget 20 000 (£) | Actual results 22 000 (£) | Variances from revised budget 2000 (£) | (F) |
|---|---|---|---|---|---|
| Variable costs | | | | | |
| Material | 216 000 | 180 000 | 206 800 | 26 800 | (A) |
| Labour | 288 000 | 240 000 | 255 200 | 15 200 | (A) |
| Semi-variable costs | | | | | |
| Heat, light and power | 31 000 | 27 000 | 33 400 | 6400 | (A) |
| Fixed costs | | | | | |
| Rent, rates and depreciation | 40 000 | 40 000 | 38 000 | 2 000 | (F) |
| | 575 000 | 487 000 | 533 400 | 46 400 | (A) |

Assumptions in the two budgets
1. No change in input prices
2. No change in the quantity of variable inputs per Fasta

As the management accountant at Rivermede Ltd, one of your tasks is to check that invoices have been properly coded. On checking the actual invoices for heat, light and power for the year to 31 May, you find that one invoice for £7520 had been incorrectly coded. The invoice should have been coded to materials.

*Task 1*
(a) Using the information in the original and revised budgets, identify:
   ● the variable cost of material and labour per Fasta;
   ● the fixed and unit variable cost within heat, light and power.
(b) Prepare a flexible budget, including variances, for Rivermede Ltd after correcting for the miscoding of the invoice.

*Data*
On receiving your flexible budget statement, Steven Jones states that the total adverse variance

is much less than the £46 400 shown in the original statement. He also draws your attention to the actual sales volume being greater than in the revised budget. He believes these results show that a participative approach to budgeting is better for the company and wants to discuss this belief at the next board meeting. Before doing so, Steven Jones asked for your comments.

*Task 2*
Write a memo to Steven Jones. Your memo should:
(a) *briefly* explain why the flexible budgeting variances differ from those in the original statement given in the data to task 1;
(b) give *two* reasons why a favourable cost variance may have arisen other than through the introduction of participative budgeting;
(c) give *two* reasons why the actual sales volume compared with the revised budget's sales volume may not be a measure of improved motivation following the introduction of participative budgeting.

*AAT Technicians Stage*

### 16.39* Intermediate: Demand forecasts and preparation of flexible budgets
*Data*
Happy Holidays Ltd sells holidays to Xanadu through newspaper advertisements. Tourist are flown each week of the holiday season to Xanadu, where they take a 10 day touring holiday. In 2000, Happy Holidays began to use the least-squares regression formula to help forecast the demand for its holidays.

You are employed by Happy Holidays as an accounting technician in the financial controller's department. A colleague of yours has recently used the least-squares regression formula on a spreadsheet to estimate the demand for holidays per year. The resulting formula was:

$$y = 640 + 40x$$

where $y$ is the annual demand and $x$ is the year. The data started with the number of holidays sold in 1993 and was identified in the formula as year 1. In each subsequent year the value of $x$ increases by 1 so, for example, 1998 was year 6. To obtain the *weekly* demand the result is divided by 25, the number of weeks Happy Holidays operates in Xanadu.

*Task 1*
(a) Use the least-squares regression formula developed by your colleague to estimate the

weekly demand for holidays in Xanadu for 2001.

(b) In preparation for a budget meeting with the financial controller, draft a *brief* note. Your note should identify *three* weaknesses of the least-squares regression formula in forecasting the weekly demand for holidays in Xanadu.

### Data

The budget and actual costs for holidays to Xanadu for the 10 days ended 27 November 2000 is reproduced below.

**Happy Holidays Ltd Cost Statement**
**10 days ended 27 November 2000**

|  | Fixed Budget (£) | Actual (£) | Variances (£) |
|---|---|---|---|
| Aircraft seats | 18 000 | 18 600 | 600 A |
| Coach hire | 5 000 | 4 700 | 300 F |
| Hotel rooms | 14 000 | 14 200 | 200 A |
| Meals | 4 800 | 4 600 | 200 F |
| Tour guide | 1 800 | 1 700 | 100 F |
| Advertising | 2 000 | 1 800 | 200 F |
| Total costs | 45 600 | 45 600 | 0 |

Key: A = adverse, F = favourable

The financial controller gives you the following additional information:

Cost and volume information
- each holiday lasts 10 days;
- meals and hotel rooms are provided for each of the 10 days;
- the airline charges £450 per return flight per passenger for each holiday but the airline will only sell seats at this reduced price if Happy Holidays purchases seta in blocks of 20;
- the costs of coach hire, the tour guide and advertising are fixed costs;
- the cost of meals was budgeted at £12 per tourist per day;
- the cost of a single room was budgeted at £60 per day;
- the cost of a double room was budgeted at £70 per day;
- 38 tourists travelled on the holiday requiring 17 double rooms and 4 single rooms;

Sales information
- the price of a holiday is £250 more if using a single room.

### Task 2

Write a memo to the financial controller. Your memo should:

(a) take account of the cost and volume information to prepare a revised cost statement using flexible budgeting and identifying any variances;

(b) state and justify which of the two cost statements is more useful for management control of costs;

(c) identify *three* factors to be taken into account in deciding whether or not to investigate individual variances.

*AAT Technicians Stage*

### 16.40 Intermediate: Responsibility centre performance reports

#### Data

Jim Smith has recently been appointed as the Head Teacher of Mayfield School in Midshire. The age of the pupils ranges from 11 years to 18 years. For many years, Midshire County Council was responsible for preparing and reporting on the school budget. From June, however, these responsibilities passed to the Head Teacher of Mayfield School.

You have recently accepted a part-time appointment as the accountant to Mayfield School, although your previous accounting experience has been gained in commercial organisations. Jim Smith is hoping that you will be able to apply that experience to improving the financial reporting procedures at Mayfield School.

The last budget statement prepared by Midshire County Council is reproduced below. It covers the ten months to the end of May and all figures refer to cash *payments* made.

**Midshire County Council Mayfield School**
**Statement of school expenditure against budget: 10 months ending May**

|  | Expenditure to date | Budget to date | Under/over spend | Total budget for year |
|---|---|---|---|---|
| Teachers – full-time | 1 680 250 | 1 682 500 | 2250 Cr | 2 019 000 |
| Teachers – part-time | 35 238 | 34 600 | 638 | 41 520 |
| Other employee expenses | 5 792 | 15 000 | 9 208 Cr | 18 000 |
| Administrative staff | 69 137 | 68 450 | 687 | 82 140 |
| Caretaker and cleaning | 49 267 | 57 205 | 7 938 Cr | 68 646 |
| Resources (books, etc.) | 120 673 | 100 000 | 20 673 | 120 000 |
| Repairs and maintenance | 458 | 0 | 458 | 0 |
| Lighting and heating | 59 720 | 66 720 | 7 000 Cr | 80 064 |
| Rates | 23 826 | 19 855 | 3 971 | 23 826 |
| Fixed assets: furniture and equipment | 84 721 | 100 000 | 15 279 Cr | 120 000 |
| Stationery, postage and phone | 1 945 | 0 | 1 945 | 0 |
| Miscellaneous expenses | 9 450 | 6 750 | 2 700 | 8 100 |
| Total | 2 140 477 | 2 151 080 | 10 603 Cr | 2 581 296 |

*Task 1*

Write a memo to Jim Smith. Your memo should:

(a) identify *four* weaknesses of the existing statement as a management report;

(b) include an improved *outline* statement format showing revised column headings and a more meaningful classification of costs which will help Jim Smith to manage his school effectively (figures are not required);

(c) give *two* advantages of your proposed format over the existing format.

*Data*

The income of Mayfield School is based on the number of pupils at the school. Jim Smith provides you with the following breakdown of student numbers.

**Mayfield School:**
**Student numbers as at 31 May**

| School year | Age range | Current number of pupils |
|---|---|---|
| 1 | 11–12 | 300 |
| 2 | 12–13 | 350 |
| 3 | 13–14 | 325 |
| 4 | 14–15 | 360 |
| 5 | 15–16 | 380 |
| 6 | 16–17 | 240 |
| 7 | 17–18 | 220 |
| Total number of students | | 2175 |

Jim also provides you with the following information relating to existing pupils:

- pupils move up one school-year at the end of July;
- for those pupils entering year 6, there is an option to leave the school. As a result only 80% of the current school-year 5 pupils go on to enter school-year 6;
- of those currently in school-year 6 only 95% continue into school-year 7;
- pupils currently in school-year 7 leave to go on to higher education or employment;
- the annual income per pupil is £1200 in years 1 to 5 and £1500 in years 6 to 7.

The new year 1 pupils come from the final year at four junior schools. Not all pupils, however, elect to go to Mayfield School. Jim has investigated this matter and derived accurate estimates of the proportion of final year pupils at each of the four junior schools who go on to attend Mayfield School.

The number of pupils in the final year at each of the four junior schools is given below along with Jim's estimate of the proportion likely to choose Mayfield School.

| Junior School | Number in final year at 31 May | Proportion choosing Mayfield School |
|---|---|---|
| Ranmoor | 60 | 0.9 |
| Hallamshire | 120 | 0.8 |
| Broomhill | 140 | 0.9 |
| Endcliffe | 80 | 0.5 |

*Task 2*

(a) Forecast the number of pupils and the income of Mayfield School for the next year from August to July

(b) Assuming expenditure next year is 5% more than the current annual budgeted expenditure, calculate the budgeted surplus or deficit of Mayfield School for next year.

*AAT Technicians Stage*

### 16.41 Advanced: Design of a management control system

Maxcafe Ltd sold its own brand of coffee throughout the UK. Sales policies, purchasing and the direction of the company was handled from head office in London. The company operated three roasting plants in Glasgow, Hull and Bristol. Each plant had profit and loss responsibility and the plant manager was paid a bonus on the basis of a percentage on gross margin. Monthly operating statements were prepared for each plant by head office and the following statement is a monthly report for the Glasgow plant:

**Operating statement**
**Glasgow plant**
**April**

| | (£) |
|---|---|
| Net sales | 1 489 240 |
| Less: Cost of sales | |
| Special coffee | 747 320 |
| – at contract cost | |
| Roasting and grinding: | |
| Labour | 76 440 |
| Fuel | 49 560 |
| Manufacturing expenses | 67 240 |
| | 193 240 |

Packaging:

| | | |
|---|---:|---:|
| Container | 169 240 | |
| Packing carton | 18 280 | |
| Labour | 24 520 | |
| Manufacturing expenses | 50 880 | 262 920 |
| Total manufacturing cost | | 1 203 480 |
| Gross margin on sales | | 285 760 |

Each month the plant manager was given a production schedule for the current month and a tentative schedule for the next month. Credit collection and payment was done by Head Office. The procurement of special coffee for roasting operations was also handled by the purchasing department at Head Office. The objective of the purchasing department was to ensure that any one of forty grades of special coffee was available for the roasting plants.

Based on estimated sales budgets, purchase commitments were made that would provide for delivery in 3 to 15 months from the date that contracts for purchases were made. While it was possible to purchase from local brokers for immediate delivery, such purchases were more costly than purchases made for delivery in the country of origin and hence these 'spot' purchases were kept to a minimum. A most important factor was the market 'know-how' of the purchasing department, who must judge whether the market trend was up or down and make commitments accordingly.

The result was that the purchasing department was buying a range of coffees for advance delivery at special dates. At the time of actual delivery, the sales of the company's coffee might not be going as anticipated when the purchase commitment was made. The difference between actual deliveries and current requirements was handled through either 'spot' sales of surplus special grades or 'spot' purchases when actual sales demand of the completed coffee brands was greater than the estimated sales.

In accounting for coffee purchases a separate record was maintained for each purchase contract. This record was charged with coffee purchased and import and transport expenses, with the result that a net cost per bag was developed for each purchase. The established policy was to treat each contract on an individual basis. When special coffee was delivered to a plant, a charge was made for the cost represented by the contracts which covered that particular delivery of coffee, with no element of profit or loss. When special coffee was sold to outsiders, the sales were likewise costed on a specific contract basis with a resulting profit or loss on these transactions.

For the past several years there has been some dissatisfaction on the part of plant managers with the method of computing gross margins subject to bonuses. This had finally led to a request from the managing director to the accountant to study the whole method of reporting on results of *plant operations* and the *purchasing operation*.

Required:
(a) An explanation to the managing director indicating any weaknesses of the current control system, and
(b) an explanation of what changes you consider should be made in the present reporting and control system.

## 16.42* Advanced: Recommendations for improvements to a performance report and a review of the management control system

Your firm has been consulted by the managing director of Inzone plc, which owns a chain of retail stores. Each store has departments selling furniture, tableware and kitchenware. Departmental managers are responsible to a store manager, who is in turn responsible to head office (HO).

All goods for sale are ordered centrally and stores sell at prices fixed by HO. Store managers (aided by departmental managers) order stocks from HO and stores are charged interest based on month-end stock levels. HO appoints all permanent staff and sets all pay levels. Store managers can engage or dismiss temporary workers, and are responsible for store running expenses.

The introduction to Inzone plc's management accounting manual states:

'Budgeting starts three months before the budget year, with product sales projections which are developed by HO buyers in consultation with each store's departmental managers. Expense budgets, adjusted for expected inflation, are then prepared by HO for each store. Inzone plc's accounting year is divided into 13 four-weekly control periods, and the budgeted sales and expenses are assigned to periods with due regard to seasonal factors. The budgets are completed one month before the year begins on 1st January.

'All HO expenses are recharged to stores in order to give the clearest indication of the "bottom line" profit of each store. These HO costs are mainly buying expenses, which are recharged to stores according to their square footage.

'Store reports comparing actual results with budgets are on the desks of HO and store management one week after the end of each control period. Significant variations in performance are then investigated, and appropriate action taken.'

Ms Lewis is manager of an Inzone plc store. She is eligible for a bonus equal to 5% of the amount by which her store's 'bottom-line' profit exceeds the year's budget. However, Ms Lewis sees no chance of a bonus this year, because major roadworks near the store are disrupting trade. Her store report for the four weeks ending 21 June is as follows:

| | Actual (£) | Budget (£) |
|---|---|---|
| Sales | 98 850 | 110 000 |
| Costs: | | |
| Cost of goods (including stock losses) | 63 100 | 70 200 |
| Wages and salaries | 5 300 | 5 500 |
| Rent | 11 000 | 11 000 |
| Depreciation of store fittings | 500 | 500 |
| Distribution costs | 4 220 | 4 500 |
| Other store running expenses | 1 970 | 2 000 |
| Interest charge on stocks | 3 410 | 3 500 |
| Store's share of HO costs | 2 050 | 2 000 |
| Store profit | 7 300 | 10 800 |
| | 98 850 | 110 000 |
| Stocks held at end of period | 341 000 | 350 000 |
| Store fittings at written down value | 58 000 | 58 000 |

Requirements:

(a) Make recommendations for the improvement of Inzone plc's store report, briefly justifying each recommendation. (11 marks)

(b) Prepare a report for the managing director of Inzone plc reviewing the company's responsibility delegation, identifying the major strengths and weaknesses of Inzone plc's management control system, and recommend-

ing any changes you consider appropriate.
(14 marks)
(Total 25 marks)
*ICAEW P2 Management Accounting*

### 16.43 Advanced: Comments on an existing performance measurement and bonus system and recommendations for improvement

1. You are the group management accountant of a large divisionalised group.

There has been extensive board discussion of the existing system of rewarding Divisional General Managers with substantial bonuses based on the comparison of the divisional profit with budget.

The scheme is simple: the divisional profit (PBIT) is compared with the budget for the year. If budget is not achieved no bonus is paid. If budget is achieved a bonus of 20% of salary is earned. If twice budgeted profit is achieved, a bonus of 100% of salary is paid, which is the upper limit of the bonus scheme. Intermediate achievements are calculated pro rata.

The Finance Director has been asked to prepare a number of reports on the issues involved, and has asked you to prepare some of these.

He has decided to use the results for Division X as an example on which the various discussions could be based. A schedule of summary available data is given below.

**Division X**
**Summary of management accounting data**

| | Strategic plan 2001 Prepared Aug 2000 | Budget 2001 Prepared Oct 2000 | Latest estimate 2001 Prepared April 2001 |
|---|---|---|---|
| Sales of units by Division X | 35 000 | 36 000 | 35 800 |
| Sales | 28 000 | 28 800 | 28 100 |
| Marginal costs | 14 350 | 15 300 | 14 900 |
| Fixed factory cost | 6 500 | 6 800 | 7 200 |
| Product development | 2 000 | 2 000 | 1 400 |
| Marketing | 3 500 | 3 200 | 2 600 |
| PBIT | 1 650 | 1 500 | 2 000 |

Division X manufactures and sells branded consumer durables in competitive markets. High expenditure is required on product development and advertising, as the maintenance of market share depends on a flow of well-promoted new models.

Reliable statistics on market size are available annually. Based on the market size for 2000, where stronger than anticipated growth had occurred, a revised market estimate of 165 000 units for 2001 is agreed by group and divisional staff in May 2001. This is a significant increase on the estimate of 150 000 units made in May 2000 and used since.

The Divisional General Manager has commented that action now, almost half way through the year, is unlikely to produce significant results during this year. However, had he known last year, at the time of producing the budget, that the market was growing faster, he could have taken the necessary action to maintain the strategic plan market share. The actions would have been

- cutting prices by £10 per unit below the price at present charged and used in the latest estimate for 2001,
- increasing marketing expenditure by £300 000 compared with the strategic plan.

The Group Managing Director, commenting on the same data, said that the Divisional General Manager could have maintained both strategic plan market share and selling prices by an alternative approach.

The approach, he thought, should have been

- maintaining expenditure on product development and marketing at 20% of sales over the years,
- spending his time controlling production costs instead of worrying about annual bonuses.

You are required:
(a) to analyse and comment on the results of Division X, making appropriate comparisons with Budget, with Plan and with new available data. Present the results in such a form that the Board can easily understand the problems involved; (17 marks)
(b) to comment on the advantages and problems of the existing bonus system for the Divisional General Manager and the way in which the present bonus scheme may motivate the Divisional General Manager; (8 marks)

(c) to make specific proposals, showing calculations if appropriate, for an alternative bonus scheme, reflecting your analysis in (a).
(8 marks)

A non-executive director has commented that he can understand the case for linking executive directors' rewards to group results. He is not convinced that this should be extended to divisional managers, and certainly not to senior managers below this level in divisions and head office.

(d) Explain and discuss the case for extending bonus schemes widely throughout the organisation. (7 marks)
(Total 40 marks)
*CIMA Stage 4 Management Accounting – Control and Audit*

### 16.44 Advanced: Budget use and performance reporting

A new private hospital of 100 beds was opened to receive patients on 2 January though many senior staff members including the supervisor of the laundry department had been *in situ* for some time previously. The first three months were expected to be a settling-in period; the hospital facilities being used to full capacity only in the second and subsequent quarters.

In May the supervisor of the laundry department received her first quarterly performance report from the hospital administrator, together with an explanatory memorandum. Copies of both documents are set out below.

The supervisor had never seen the original budget, nor had she been informed that there would be a quarterly performance report. She knew she was responsible for her department and had made every endeavour to run it as efficiently as possible. It had been made clear to her that there would be a slow build up in the number of patients accepted by the hospital and so she would need only 3 members of staff, but she had had to take on a fourth during the quarter due to the extra work. This extra hiring had been anticipated for May, not late February.

Rockingham Private Patients Hospital Ltd
MEMORANDUM                              30 April
To: All Department Heads/Supervisors
From: Hospital Administrator

Attached is the Quarterly Performance Report for your department. The hospital has adopted a responsibility accounting system so you will be receiving one of these reports quarterly. Responsibility accounting means that you are accountable for ensuring that the expenses of running your department are kept in line with the budget. Each report compares the actual expenses of running your department for the quarter with our budget for the same period. The difference between the actual and forecast will be highlighted so that you can identify the important variations from budget and take corrective action to get back on budget. Any variation in excess of 5% from budget should be investigated and an explanatory memo sent to me giving reasons for the variations and the proposed corrective actions.

**Performance report – laundry department**
**3 Months to 31 March**

| | Actual | Budget | Variation (Over)/ Under | % Variation |
|---|---|---|---|---|
| Patient days | 8 000 | 6 500 | (1 500) | (23) |
| Weight of laundry processed (kg) | 101 170 | 81 250 | (19 920) | (24.5) |
| | (£) | (£) | (£) | |
| Department expenses | | | | |
| Wages | 4 125 | 3 450 | (675) | (19.5) |
| Supervisor salary | 1 490 | 1 495 | 5 | — |
| Washing materials | 920 | 770 | (150) | (19.5) |
| Heating and power | 560 | 510 | (50) | (10) |
| Equipment depreciation | 250 | 250 | — | – |
| Allocated administration costs | 2 460 | 2 000 | (460) | (23) |
| Equipment maintenance | 10 | 45 | 35 | 78 |
| | 9 815 | 8 520 | (1 295) | (15) |

Comment: We need to have a discussion about the overexpenditure of the department.

You are required to:
(a) discuss in detail the various possible effects on the behaviour of the laundry supervisor of the way that her budget was prepared and the form and content of the performance report, having in mind the published research findings in this area, (15 marks)
(b) re-draft, giving explanations, the performance report and supporting memorandum in a way which, in your opinion, would make them

more effective management tools. (10 marks)
(Total 25 marks)
*ICAEW P2 Management Accounting*

## 16.45* Advanced: Impact of aggregating budget estimates and budget bias

Devonshire Dairies plc sells a range of dairy products on a national basis through a direct sales force organized into four geographical regions. In December the sales director had received sales budgets for the next year from his four regional managers, and was concerned that they appeared to represent very different standards of attainment. He also thought it unlikely that the national budget (i.e. the sum of the four regional budgets) could be achieved, and so had made his own estimates of the sales revenue he expected each division to obtain, as shown below:

| Region | Sales revenue budgets submitted (£m) | Sales director's own estimates (£m) |
|---|---|---|
| Northern | 5.7 | 5.0 |
| Southern | 10.9 | 10.0 |
| Eastern | 7.9 | 8.0 |
| Western | 7.5 | 7.0 |
| Total | 32.0 | 30.0 |

The sales director recognized that his estimates were subject to some uncertainty due to random events, and believed this could be adequately modelled by assuming that they represented the means of normal distributions having a standard deviation of £1 million for each region and that actual sales in each region were statistically independent of each other. However, he was reluctant to amend the budgets submitted to him as he could see the motivational advantages in letting each regional sales manager aim for a target which he had set for himself, and to which he was committed.

Requirements
(a) Calculate the probability of each sales region achieving at least the budget submitted by its regional manager, on the assumption that the sales director's model is correct. Also calculate the probability that the total of the budget submissions will be at least achieved, and comment on your results. (10 marks)

(b) Discuss the reasons why managers may submit budgets that differ from their superiors' estimates of outcomes. What action would you recommend the sales director to take in this case? (8 marks)

(c) The company is considering implementing a system of performance-related pay whereby managers who achieve their annual sales budgets are rewarded by the payment of an annual bonus equivalent to one month's salary. Discuss the impact such a system could have on the operation of the budgeting system, and suggest ways in which the proposed bonus system could be amended to minimize any adverse effects. (7 marks)

(Total 25 marks)

*ICAEW P2 Management Accounting*

## 16.46 Advanced: Aspiration levels

Individual performance measurement is likely to be related to the aspiration level of the individual and the timing and level of the target set.

Discuss the above statement in the context of each of Tables 1 and 2. The tables provide illustrations expressed in terms of output, of the results of two separate studies linking targets, aspiration levels and achievement. (15 marks)

Table 1

| | | Actual achievement (units) | | |
|---|---|---|---|---|
| Target | Target Units | Aspiration level set by individual before knowing target | Aspiration level set by individual after knowing target | Average |
| Implicit | not quoted | 53 | 57 | 55 |
| Explicit: low | 35 | 45 | 44 | 44.5 |
| Explicit medium | 50 | 54 | 54 | 54 |
| Explicit: high | 70 | 40 | 60 | 50 |

Table 2

| Target (units) | Aspiration level of individual (where target is known) (units) | Actual achieved (units) |
|---|---|---|
| 70 | 80 | 80 |
| 90 | 90 | 90 |
| 110 | 100 | 100 |

| 130 | 120 | 112 |
| 150 | 110 | 90 |
| 180 | nil | 80 |

*ACCA Paper 9 Information for Control and Decision Making*

## 16.47 Advanced: Advantages and disadvantages of participation and comments on a new performance measurement and evaluation system

Incorporated Finance plc is a finance company having one hundred branch offices in major towns and cities throughout the UK. These offer a variety of hire purchase and loan facilities to personal customers both directly and through schemes operated on behalf of major retailers. The main function of the branches is to sell loans and to ensure that repayments are collected; the head office is responsible for raising the capital required, which it provides to branches at a current rate of interest.

Each year branch managers are invited to provide estimates of the following items for the forthcoming year, as the start of the budgetary process:

Value of new loans (by category e.g. direct, retail, motor)

Margin percentage (i.e. loan rate of interest less cost of capital provided by head office)

Gross margin (i.e. value of new loans × margin percentage)

Branch operating expenses

Net margin (i.e. gross margin less operating expenses)

The main branch expenses relate to the cost of sales and administrative staff, and to the cost of renting and maintaining branch premises, but also include the cost of bad debts on outstanding loans.

These estimates are then passed to headquarters by area and regional managers and are used, together with other information such as that relating to general economic conditions, to set an overall company budget. This is then broken down by headquarters into regional figures; regional managers then set the area budgets and area managers finally set branch budgets. However, a common complaint of branch managers is that the budgets they are set often bear little resemblance to the estimates they originally submitted.

Budget targets are set for the five items specified above, with managers receiving a bonus based on the average percentage achievement of all five targets, weighted equally.

Requirements

(a)  Discuss the advantages and disadvantages of allowing managers to participate in budget-setting, and suggest how Incorporated Finance plc should operate its budgetary system.

(15 marks)

(b)  The managing director is considering changing the performance evaluation and bonus scheme so that branch managers are set only a net margin target. Prepare a report for him outlining the advantages and disadvantages of making such a change.          (10 marks)

(Total 25 marks)

*ICAEW P2 Management Accounting*

# Contingency theory and organizational and social aspects of management accounting

In the previous chapter the major features of management accounting control systems were described. To design effective management accounting control systems it is necessary to consider the circumstances in which they will be used. It should be apparent from the discussion in the previous chapter that there is no universally best management accounting control system which can be applied to all organizations. The applicability of a management accounting control system is contingent on the circumstances faced by organizations. This approach is known as the **contingency theory** approach to management accounting. A widely used contingency theory definition is that provided by Otley (1980). He states:

> The contingency approach to management accounting is based on the premise that there is no universally appropriate accounting system applicable to all organisations in all circumstances. Rather a contingency theory attempts to identify specific aspects of an accounting system that are associated with certain defined circumstances and to demonstrate an appropriate matching. (Page 413.)

This chapter, all of which you should regard as advanced reading, will examine the contingency theory approach. In addition, the different roles that management accounting information plays in organizations will also be considered. In particular, the wider social and political roles of management accounting are discussed. We begin with a discussion of contingency theory.

## Learning objectives

After reading this chapter, you should be able to:

- describe the contingency theory of management accounting;

- provide illustrations of the relationship between the five broad contingent factors described in Exhibit 17.1 and features of the management accounting system;

- explain the circumstances when behavioural, output and clan controls should be used;

- describe the three different types of assessment and scorekeeping (efficiency, effectiveness and social tests) and explain the circumstances where each of them should be used;

- distinguish between programmed and non-programmed decisions;

- describe the ideal and actual uses of accounting information for decision-making in relation to a combination of uncertainty of objectives and uncertainty of cause-and-effect relationships;

● explain the different 'roles' or 'purposes' for which management accounting information is used within organizations.

# Contingent factors

**AR** The contingency theory approach advocates that there is no one 'best' design for a management accounting information system, but that 'it all depends' upon the situational factors. The situational factors represent the contingent factors or the contingent variables. Because each organization is unique the potential range of situations or contingent factors is enormous and it is impossible to study each one separately. To overcome this problem contingency factors are classified into categories which appear to make sense in terms of explaining differences in management accounting information systems.

Exhibit 17.1 lists the major contingent factors, divided into five broad categories, that have been examined in the literature. The list of factors is not exhaustive and there is a vast amount of literature relating to the impact of each of these factors on management accounting information systems. A discussion of each factor is not possible within a general purpose management accounting textbook. How some of the factors listed in Exhibit 17.1 affect management accounting control systems have been briefly discussed in the previous chapter. This chapter will attempt to provide a broad overview of the contingency theory studies and examine in more detail some of the studies that are of particular relevance to the content of this book.

The contingency theory literature has two strands – empirical and theoretical. The empirical literature has sought to investigate the relationship between some hypothesized contingent factors and the existence of certain features of the management accounting system. Difficult measurement problems apply and it has therefore been difficult to establish definitive findings. In addition to the empirically based literature there has also been a theoretical strand that has speculated on the nature of a contingency theory of management accounting information systems.

Another important feature of the literature is that it focuses on either management accounting information systems, management control systems in general or management accounting control systems. Although this chapter is primarily concerned with management accounting control systems it will also look at some of the contingency studies relating to management accounting information systems that incorporate aspects of accounting information for both decision-making and control. Where this applies the term management accounting information system will be used. Some of the studies relate to management control systems in general but, given that the management accounting control system is a major component of this system, these studies are also relevant to the study of management accounting.

**EXHIBIT
17.1**

*Contingent
factors
grouped by
major
categories*

*1. The external environment*
Uncertain and certain
Static and dynamic
Simple and complex
Turbulent and calm

*2. Competitive strategy and strategic mission*
Low cost and differentiation
Defender and prospector
Product life cycle (build, hold, harvest and divest)

*3. Technology*
Small batch, large batch, process production, mass production
Interdependence (pooled, sequential, reciprocal)

*4. Business unit, firm and industry variables*
Firm size
Firm diversification (single product, related diversified and unrelated
    diversified)
Organizational structure
Industry variables

*5. Knowledge and observability factors*
Knowledge of the transformation process
Outcome (output) observability
Behaviour (effort) observability

*(Adapted from Fisher, 1995)*

## THE EXTERNAL ENVIRONMENT

The first broad category listed in Exhibit 17.1 consists of variables relating to the
external environment. Most of the variables within this category are concerned with the
level of uncertainty. Khandwalla (1972) examined the effect that the type of *competition*
faced by a firm has on its use of management controls and concluded that competition,
in particular product competition, was an important factor influencing the usage of
sophisticated formal controls.

An empirical study of eight firms in the USA by Govindarajan (1984) supported the
hypothesis that superiors in business units which face higher *environmental uncertainty*
use a more subjective performance appraisal approach whereas superiors of business

units that face lower environmental uncertainty use a more formula-based performance evaluation approach. A formula-based approach was defined as an evaluation based solely on meeting various levels of financial performance.

The rationale for the hypothesis is that performance evaluation presupposes targets, and for targets to remain valid standards for subsequent performance appraisal, one must be able to predict the conditions that will exist during the coming year. It is possible to predict these conditions more accurately under stable environmental conditions than under dynamic and changing conditions. Thus, the greater the environmental uncertainty, the more difficult it is to prepare satisfactory targets which could then become the basis for performance evaluation. In addition, although managers have control over their actions they do not have control over the states of nature which combine with their actions to result in outcomes. In a situation with high environmental uncertainty, financial data alone will not, therefore, adequately reflect managerial performance whereas such data would be adequate for a situation with low environmental uncertainty.

Govindarajan related his findings to those of Hopwood (1976) and Otley (1978) described in the final section of the previous chapter. He suggests that Otley studied units which might have operated in relatively stable environmental conditions whereas Hopwood examined units which might have operated in relatively uncertain environmental conditions. Govindarajan concludes that, in the light of his findings, it is not surprising that Hopwood found dysfunctional effects for the budget constrained style of performance evaluation whereas Otley did not. In other words, a budget constrained style was synonymous with a formula-based, rigid evaluation style and this style was inappropriate in units facing an uncertain environment. Therefore there was a mismatch and this caused the dysfunctional side-effects.

Chenhall and Morris (1985) and Gul and Chia (1994) provide evidence to suggest that the greater the *perceived environmental uncertainty* the greater the need for more sophisticated management accounting information that has a broad scope. Broad scope was defined as information that was external, non-financial and future oriented whereas narrow scope relates to internal, financial and historical information. The results from the study by Gul and Chia suggest that decentralization, and the availability of broad scope management accounting information, was associated with higher managerial performance under conditions of perceived environmental uncertainty.

## COMPETITIVE STRATEGY AND STRATEGIC MISSION

Competitive strategy describes how a business chooses to compete in its industry and tries to achieve a competitive advantage relative to its competitors. Strategic mission can be defined across a continuum from the early to the late stages of a product's life cycle from build, hold, harvest and divest.

The research relating to corporate strategy has focused mainly on classifications proposed by Porter (1985) and Miles and Snow (1978). Most of the contingency theory research that has addressed Porter's strategy variables has examined the control differences between business units pursuing *low-cost* and *differentiation strategies*. A low cost strategy involves offering relatively standardized, undifferentiated products with an attempt to obtain high volume and routinized tasks to exploit economies of scale. A differentiation strategy involves the creation of something that is perceived by customers as being unique and valuable.

Miles and Snow distinguish between *defenders* and *prospectors*. Defenders operate in relatively stable areas, have limited product lines and employ a mass production routine technology. They compete through making operations efficient through cost, quality and service leadership, and engage in little product or market research. Prospectors compete through new product innovations and market development and are constantly looking for new market opportunities. Hence, they face a more uncertain task environment.

Merchant (1998) concludes that business units following a low-cost strategy, or those defending existing businesses, should control their lower level employees' behaviours through standardized operating procedures designed to maximize efficiency. For motivating managers their results measures should emphasize cost reductions and budget achievement. Alternatively, business units competing on the basis of differentiation and those prospecting for new markets, should have a more participative decision-making environment and should reward employees and managers based on any of a number of non-financial indicators, such as product innovation, market development, customer service and growth, as well as secondarily financial measures such as budget achievement. Simons (1987) found that business units that follow a defender strategy tend to place a greater emphasis on the use of financial measures (e.g. short-term budget targets) for compensating financial managers. Ittner *et al.* (1997) also found that the use of non-financial measures for determining executives' bonuses increases with the extent to which firms follow an innovation-oriented prospector strategy.

A study by Chenhall and Langfield-Smith (1998b) relating to a survey 78 Australian companies hypothesized that higher performing firms that place a strong emphasis on product differentiation strategies will gain high benefits from the following management techniques and management accounting practices:

- quality systems;
- integrating systems;
- team-based structures;
- human resource management policies;
- balanced performance measures;
- benchmarking;
- strategic planning techniques.

To implement product differentiation strategies successfully, companies may employ manufacturing techniques which enhance their ability to persuade their customers that their products are of high quality. Therefore quality systems, such as statistical process control (see Chapter 22) may be used to provide a way to detect and correct process variations that may influence product quality.

The effective implementation of customer focused strategies may require employees at the operational level to adopt a strong customer orientation. Employees are more likely to develop a customer focus if a high degree of empowerment is encouraged. Two broad approaches are identified as being conducive to employee empowerment. First, team-based structures may be introduced to encourage employees to take ownership of customer-focused initiatives. Second, a range of human resource management policies may be introduced to establish a work environment that encourages employees to share the organization's customer-focused orientation. These include encouraging a participative culture, and providing focused training. In other words, effective implementation of customer strategies suggests that the personnel and cultural controls that were described in the previous chapter should be emphasized.

Balanced performance measurement systems provide a balanced focus on various aspects of differentiation strategies by linking measures of customer satisfaction (such as timely and reliable delivery) with other measures of key production strategies (such as cycle time and throughput rates) and also emphasizing financial outcomes. This balanced performance measurement approach is known as the balanced scorecard and represents an attempt to develop a broader and integrated set of financial and non-financial performance measures that provide a comprehensive view of the performance of the business. The balanced scorecard will be dealt with extensively in Chapter 23. Overall the results provided support for the proposed associations, described above.

Chenhall and Langfield-Smith also hypothesized that higher performing firms that place a strong emphasis on low price strategies will gain high benefits from the following management techniques and management accounting practices:

- improving existing practices;
- manufacturing innovations;
- traditional accounting techniques;
- activity-based techniques.

To achieve cost efficiencies companies may focus on improving existing processes. This may involve reorganizing existing processes in order to improve efficiency and reduce waste. In addition, companies may reduce costs by outsourcing when external firms can supply at a lower cost. The type of formal performance measures appropriate for firms emphasizing low price strategies will focus mainly on controlling costs. Traditional management accounting techniques, such as budget performance measures and variance analysis, may be particularly suitable for these companies. Activity-based techniques are considered to be appropriate for companies pursuing a low cost strategy because they are a powerful mechanism for helping managers understand how their firms' activities affect costs. They also provide useful information for reducing costs by redesigning business processes. The results also provided support for the associations specified above relating to the second hypothesis.

In terms of the product life cycle Govindarajan and Gupta (1985) found that business units following a build strategy rely more on non-financial measures of performance (such as new product development, market share, research and development and personnel development) for determining managers' bonuses.

# FIRM TECHNOLOGY AND INTERDEPENDENCE

Firm technology and interdependence includes Woodward's (1965) classification of technology into *small batch*, *large batch*, *process production* and *mass production categories*. The nature of the production process determines the type of costing system with process costing being used in process production and mass production technologies and job costing being used in batch production technologies.

In the previous chapter *pooled*, *sequential* and *reciprocal interdependencies* were described. Pooled interdependencies apply when responsibility centres use common resources, such as shared administrative units. Pooled interdependence is low when responsibility centres are relatively self-contained so that use of pooled resources has little impact on a unit's performance. Therefore unsophisticated methods can be used for assigning the costs of pooled resources to the user responsibility centres. However, where pooled interdependence is high management accounting control systems must address the issue of how to protect managers from being assigned the costs of the inefficiencies incurred by the shared resource pools. You should refer back to the previous chapter (page 612) for a discussion of the methods that can be adopted. Sequential interdependencies exist when the outputs of one unit are the inputs of another unit whereas reciprocal interdependencies exist in diversified organizations when a responsibility centre produces outputs that are used by other units and the responsibility centre also uses inputs from these units. Both types of interdependencies create the need to establish a transfer pricing system that aims to approximate the conditions found in external competitive markets.

# FIRM SIZE, INDUSTRY TYPE, FIRM DIVERSIFICATION AND FIRM STRUCTURE

Studies indicate a positive relationship between *company size* and management accounting system sophistication. In particular, studies of ABC adoption rates have shown that adoption is much higher in larger organizations (Innes and Mitchell, 1995a; Bjornenak, 1997a). A possible reason for this is that larger organizations have relatively greater access to resources to experiment with the introduction of more sophisticated systems. Several surveys have also indicated that an important factor limiting the implementation of more sophisticated management accounting systems is the prohibitive cost (Innes and Mitchell, 1995a; Shields, 1995). As larger organizations have more resources to develop innovative systems it is also more likely that they will be able to implement more sophisticated costing systems.

Control systems have been shown to differ by *industry type*. For example, controls differ in the manufacturing sector that have a large number of standard cost centres that rely extensively on detailed variance analysis. In contrast, costs in non-manufacturing industries tend to be mostly of a discretionary nature. You will remember from the previous chapter that different approaches were required for cost control in discretionary cost centres.

According to Chandler (1962) a diversification strategy can either be related or unrelated to a firm's existing products. With a *related diversification strategy* firms do not veer far from their core business activity. They diversify in order to obtain the benefits of economies of scope arising from relationships among the divisions. Firms pursuing an *unrelated diversification strategy* do not restrict their activities to their core business. A firm should adopt a management control system that is consistent with its diversification strategy. Because of the high interdependence among sub-units that exists when a firm pursues a related diversification strategy Merchant (1998) suggests that they should take advantage of this interdependence by using several features. First, they should rely on elaborate planning and budgeting systems requiring large amounts of interpersonal communication in order to encourage their managers to keep their interrelated activities coordinated so that they can find and exploit synergy. Second, they should also encourage coordination by using performance-dependent incentive compensation systems that base rewards to some extent on group performance. Third, they should devote considerable resources to solving transfer pricing problems so that they do not inhibit coordination. We shall focus on transfer pricing in Chapter 21.

The top-level corporate management of an organization with unrelated businesses are unable to remain informed about all of the activities of their diverse business units. Decentralization of decision-making to lower levels in the organization and a heavy reliance on financial controls are common responses to the information asymmetry. In particular, unrelated diversification leads to the creation of profit and investment centre responsibility structures and a greater reliance on the financial results controls, such as return on investment and economic value added, rather than other types of controls. Because corporate management do not have a detailed knowledge of the activities of the business units they are likely to judge their performance objectively and not rely on subjective evaluations. Lower-level managers will tend to be under considerable pressure to achieve financial performance although they will have a relatively high level of autonomy in terms of how they might achieve the financial targets.

There is evidence to suggest that the *structure of an organization* affects the manner in which budgetary information is best used. Hopwood's (1976) study, discussed in the previous chapter, indicated that a rigid budget constrained style of evaluation was associated with high degrees of job-related tension and dysfunctional behaviour (such as the manipulation of accounting data) whereas the more flexible profit-conscious style had no such associations. Adopting a universal approach suggests that a flexible profit conscious style is likely to lead to more effective organizational performance. A subsequent study by Otley (1978) yielded contradictory results and suggested that a rigid style was more likely to lead to a better performance than the more flexible style.

A comparison of the two findings indicates an important situational difference which suggests a contingent explanation. Hopwood's study was based on responsibility cost centres that were highly interdependent whereas Otley's study involved profit centres which were independent of each other. The contingency theory explanation is that an appropriate style of budget use depends upon the degree of interdependence that exists between responsibility centres. Because budgetary measures of performance are less appropriate as the degree of interdependence increases, managers tend to use the budgetary information in a more flexible manner. In contrast, in highly independent units where managers perceive themselves as having more control over their performance outcomes a rigid budget constrained style of evaluation is more appropriate.

## KNOWLEDGE AND OBSERVABLILITY FACTORS

The final category in Exhibit 17.1 consists of knowledge and observablility factors. Four areas that fall within this category will be examined in detail since they are of particular relevance to the content of this book. The first relates to the type controls that are appropriate in relation to the knowledge of the transformation process and the ability to measure output. The second examines the appropriate type of performance assessment and scorekeeping in relation to the extent to which task cause-and-effect relationships are well understood and the uncertainty concerning an organization's goals. Programmability of decisions, that is the extent to which a decision is sufficiently well understood for reliable predictions of the decision outcomes to be made, is the third area. Here we shall look how programmability influences the type of controls that should be used. The final area examines the relationship between accounting information and uncertainty about objectives and the uncertainty about cause-and-effect relationships.

# Types of controls in relation to the transformation process and output measurement

Ouchi (1979) considered the circumstances when behavioural, output and social controls should be employed. These controls were described in the previous chapter. You should be able to recall that behavioural controls involve observing the actions of individuals, output controls involve collecting and reporting information about the outcome of the work effort and social controls are concerned with the selection of

**FIGURE 17.1**  *Uncertainty situations and control measurements.*

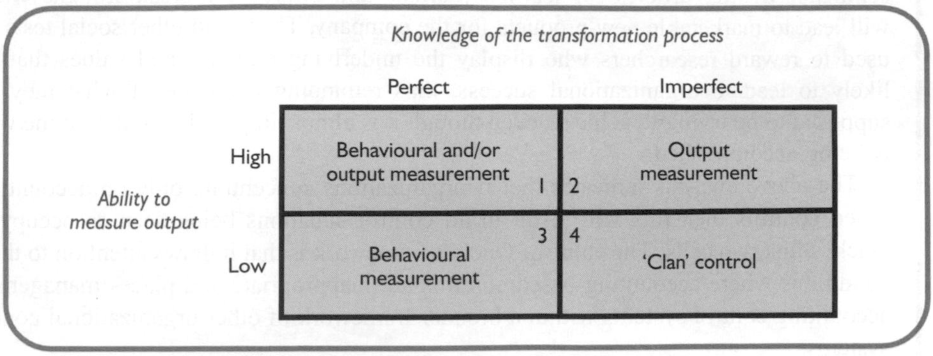

people who have already been socialized into adopting particular norms and patterns of behaviour to perform particular tasks. Ouchi identified two basic conditions. First, the ability to measure outputs and second, knowledge of the transformation process. He combined these elements to derive a matrix containing four control situations. This matrix is reproduced in Figure 17.1.

The first cell shown in Figure 17.1 describes a situation where knowledge of the transformation process is perfect (i.e. task knowledge is high) and output measures are available. In this situation it is possible to measure both output and behaviour and so both behavioural and output controls are appropriate. An illustration of the conditions outlined in the first cell is in a production department where the process can be controlled by the foreman monitoring the actions of each of the employees. Alternatively, if it is possible to measure the output of each employee, control can be exercised by relying on information derived from reports relating to production qualities, spoilage and the efficiency of each worker.

In cell 2 the ability to measure output is high but knowledge of the transformation process is imperfect. Therefore observing behaviour is not beneficial and output control mechanisms are most appropriate. A good example of this type of situation is that described by Macintosh (1985). He illustrates a situation where a financial services company is selling life assurance. We do not know the 'correct' way of selling life assurance and it is not possible to create a set of rules which, if followed, would ensure success. However, the results of sales efforts, measured in terms of life assurance cover and premiums, can easily be measured. In this situation output controls should be used.

In cell 3 where the ability to measure output is low but knowledge of the transformation process is perfect, emphasis should shift from output to behavioural controls. Ouchi relates this situation to a tin can plant where it is impossible to measure the output of any individual working on the assembly line. Therefore output controls cannot be used. The technology, however, is well understood and supervisors can monitor both the actions of each employee and the workings of the machines to see if they accord with the proper action. If they do, they know without relying on output measures that the right quantity and quality of tin cans are coming off the assembly line. Behavioural controls are therefore appropriate in this situation.

Finally, in cell 4 the ability to measure output is low and knowledge of the transformation process is imperfect. Under these conditions neither behavioural nor output controls are appropriate and Ouchi advocates the use of clan controls or corporate cultures as the most appropriate mode. He illustrates the use of clan controls in a multi-billion dollar corporation that runs a research laboratory. The controls focused on the recruitment of only a few selected individuals, each of whom had been through a schooling and professionalization process which has taught them to internalize the desired values. This process includes encouraging attendance at seminars, writing articles for learned journals and awards for breakthroughs which will lead to marketable new products for the company. These and other social tests are used to reward researchers who display the underlying attitudes and values that are likely to lead to organizational success, thus reminding everyone of what they are supposed to be trying to achieve, even though it is almost impossible to determine what is being accomplished.

The above analysis indicates that if organizations concentrate only on accounting-based controls then this will result in all control situations being seen as occupying Ouchi's first two cells. The value of Ouchi's framework is that it draws attention to those conditions where accounting-based controls are inappropriate and places management accounting control systems within a broader framework of other organizational control systems.

# Scorekeeping and uncertainty

In the previous section we looked at a framework used by Ouchi that identified the different circumstances where different types of controls should be used. Adopting a similar approach Macintosh (1985) uses a framework developed by Thompson (1967) that deals with the appropriate type of assessment and scorekeeping for different types of uncertainty.

The framework, reproduced in Figure 17.2, concentrates on the interaction of two antecedent conditions: task instrumentality and beliefs about the clarity of the organization's ends (goals), mission and purpose. **Task instrumentality** refers to the available means for task accomplishment. It is a continuum; at one end (represented by cells 1 and 3 in Figure 17.2) the ways of doing the work are well understood so that actions produce highly predictable results. An example falling within this category is an engineering factory where the correct sequencing of operations is well understood, the precise machine tolerances can be specified and the optimum inputs of labour and materials can be specified with a high degree of certainty.

At the other end of the continuum (cells 2 and 4) the optimum ways of doing the work are not known and the effect of actions cannot be predicted with any degree of certainty. For example, the sales revenues generated by a marketing department cannot be directly related to specific courses of action. The effect of pricing decisions, choice of distribution channels or methods of advertising cannot be traced directly to specific sales transactions. The actions of competitors and changes in the external economic environment also have a significant but indeterminate influence over the outcome.

The second area of uncertainty relates to beliefs about the organization's ends, mission and purpose. This is also a continuum. At one end (cells 1 and 2) goals are objectively determined and there are clear-cut preferences over other possible goals. For example, profit is preferable to market share, health is preferred to illness and wealth to poverty. The direction for improvement is also obvious moving from market share to profit and from poverty to wealth. When there is general agreement on one clear-cut end, goals can be viewed as being unambiguous.

At the other end of the continuum (cells 3 and 4) goals are ambiguous and involve a choice between two or more dimensions. Using Macintosh's illustration it is not merely a matter of health over illness, but rather a choice of health or wealth. Furthermore, there can also be shades of health and shades of wealth involved in the choice. In these circumstances there is no general agreement about which end(s) are preferred and goals are therefore ambiguous.

**FIGURE 17.2** *Assessment situations and appropriate tests.*

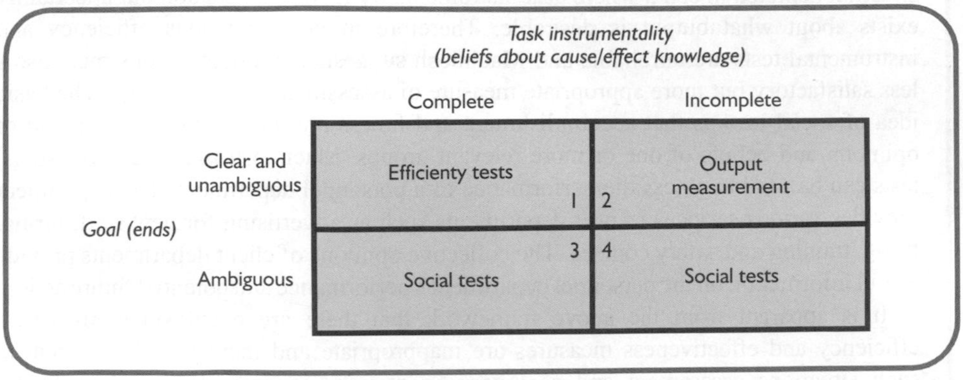

|  | | Task instrumentality (beliefs about cause/effect knowledge) | |
| --- | --- | --- | --- |
|  | | Complete | Incomplete |
| Goal (ends) | Clear and unambiguous | Efficienty tests    1 | 2    Output measurement |
|  | Ambiguous | 3    Social tests | 4    Social tests |

Macintosh combined the two continuums and used their extreme values to derive the four assessment situations depicted in Figure 17.2. In cell 1 where task instrumentality is well understood and goals are clear and unambiguous the optimum economic relationship between inputs and outputs can be derived. In such circumstances scorekeeping and assessment can rely on **efficiency tests**. Efficiency is concerned with achieving a given result with a minimum use of resources or, alternatively, achieving the maximum amount of output from a given level of input resources. Thus, efficiency measures imply that we have a means of determining the minimum resources necessary to produce a given effect or the maximum output that should be derived from a given level of resources. Efficiency measures, such as standard costing efficiency variances (discussed in the next chapter), are widely used accounting performance measures. However, the accuracy and usefulness of such measures is dependent on tasks being well understood and goals being clear and unambiguous.

In cell 2 uncertainty exists in relation to cause and effect knowledge such that the relationship of inputs and outputs cannot be ascertained with any degree of certainty. It is therefore not possible to determine whether the desired result has been achieved efficiently. However, goals are clear and unambiguous so we can ascertain whether the actions achieved the desired state. In these circumstances the scorekeeping question should concentrate on **effectiveness tests**.

With measures of effectiveness the focus is on whether or not the action resulted in the desired goal. Thus, effectiveness is concerned with the attainment of objectives; an action being effective if it achieves what it was intended to achieve. Efficiency is often confused with effectiveness. An action may be effective, but inefficient in that the result could have been achieved with fewer resources. Conversely, actions can be efficient but not effective. For example, output may be produced efficiently at minimum cost but this is ineffective if demand is depressed so that the output must be sold below cost.

Macintosh describes those tests that are intended to ascertain whether actions achieve the desired goals as **instrumental tests**. He illustrates how such tests are widely used in the public sector with scorekeeping being based on simple bottom-line assessments such as the ability to achieve the desired outputs for levels of employment, inflation and interest rates. Most large industrial organizations divide themselves into separate self-contained segments or divisions and use instrumental tests to measure the effectiveness of each division. Performance is deemed satisfactory if predetermined target profits are met. However, it is impossible to establish the level of optimum profits, or determine the extent to which profits may have been influenced by external factors, such as general changes in the economy.

In cells 3 and 4 goals are ambiguous. Efficiency measures can be computed for the situation depicted in cell 3 where task instrumentality is well understood but uncertainty exists about what output is desirable. Therefore in both situations efficiency and instrumental tests are unreliable and Macintosh suggests that organizations must use a less satisfactory but more appropriate measure of assessment: the social test. The basic idea of social tests is that accomplishment and fitness are judged by the collection of opinions and beliefs of one or more relevant groups. Macintosh illustrates how social tests can be used to assess the performance of a personnel department. The department provides various services to user departments such as advertising for new staff, hiring, firing, training and safety courses. The collective opinions of client departments provide useful information on the personnel department's performance and potential future action.

It is apparent from the above framework that there are many situations where efficiency and effectiveness measures are inappropriate and there is a danger that in such situations assessment and scorekeeping may be ignored. If the management accounting function is to continue to represent the dominant scorekeeping function in an organization it is important that it expands scorekeeping beyond measures of efficiency and effectiveness and gathers, stores and reports information on opinions and beliefs of relevant social groups within the organization.

# Programmed and non-programmed decisions

Emmanuel *et al.* (1990) distinguish between programmed and non-programmed decisions. They define a programmed decision as one where the decision situation is sufficiently well understood for a reliable prediction of the decision outcome to be made. Programmed decisions are equivalent to the situations outlined in cell 1 of Figures 17.1 and 17.2 where knowledge of the transformation process is high and task instrumentality is well understood so that the optimum relationship between inputs and outputs can be derived. Because input–output relationships are well understood detailed line item budgets specifying an appropriate level of spending for each item of expenditure can be prepared. Variance analysis can be used as a tool to control spending of each item of expenditure. Behavioural controls and output controls in the form of efficiency tests can also be applied to programmed situations.

A non-programmed decision is defined by Emmanuel *et al.* as one that has to rely on the judgement of managers because there is no formal mechanism for predicting likely outcomes. In non-programmed decisions, the causal relationships are less well understood so that it is possible only to instruct a manager as to what he or she is expected to achieve. Managers can be held responsible for results; but how they are to be attained must be left to their discretion. Thus non-programmed decisions are equivalent to situations where knowledge of the transformation process and task cause-and-effect relationships are incomplete (that is, cells 2 and 4 in Figures 17.1 and 17.2). Where the ability to measure output is high and goals are clear and unambiguous then output controls should be used and scorekeeping measures should consist of instrumental tests.

# Acounting information, decision-making and uncertainty

Earl and Hopwood (1981) and Burchell *et al.* (1980) examined the relationship between accounting information and decision-making. They use a framework developed from

**FIGURE 17.3** *Uncertainty decision-making and ideal information systems.*

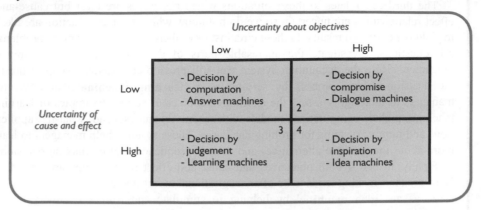

earlier work by Thompson and Tuden (1959) that characterized various states of uncertainty and, as a consequence, a range of possible approaches to decision-making. The framework, reproduced in Figure 17.3, distinguishes between uncertainty over the objectives (or disagreement which has the same effects at the organizational level) for organizational action and uncertainty over the patterns of cause and effect relations that determine the consequences of action. Earl and Hopwood contrast the potentially useful roles that accounting systems should play (that is, their ideal uses) with their actual uses.

## IDEAL USES

By referring to cell 1 in Figure 17.3 you will see that objectives are clear and undisputed and the consequences of action (i.e. the cause-and-effect relationship) are presumed to be known. In such circumstances it is possible to compute whether the consequences of action being considered will not satisfy objectives. Tasks can be programmed and algorithms, formulae and predetermined rules can be derived and decisions can be made by computation. Here accounting information systems can serve as 'answer machines' to provide solutions to problems. Examples of accounting systems fulfilling this role include standard costing systems, discounted cash flow, linear programming and economic order inventory models. For these situations the accounting information system provides information that enables a clear and optimal decision to be made.

In cell 2 objectives are uncertain but cause-and-effect relationships are assumed to be known. Uncertainty over objectives may arise because they are simply unstated or, in a rapidly changing environment, there may be disagreement and conflict over which objectives should take precedence. Where objectives are uncertain Thompson and Tuden suggest that decision-making is a political rather than a computational process with a range of interests being articulated and the outcome being determined by bargaining and compromise.

In these circumstances decision-making should be orientated towards opening up and maintaining channels of communication. Accounting information systems can facilitate this process by helping managers to develop and argue different points of view which are conflicting, but consistent with the underlying facts (Boland, 1979). Here the accounting system should serve as a 'dialogue machine' designed to encourage exploration and debate, rather than providing answers.

The third cell relates to those situations where objectives are clear but cause-and-effect relationships are uncertain so we do not know which courses of action are likely to yield the optimum results. In these circumstances there is a need to explore problems, ask questions, investigate the analysable parts of decisions and finally resort to judgement. Here the accounting system can still provide considerable support during the decision-making process by serving as a 'learning machine' that helps the managers to thoroughly assess the alternative courses of action. Examples of learning machines include computerized models with sensitivity analysis and 'what-if?' applications and inquiry systems for probing databases. These systems help managers to learn more about the possible alternatives and their consequences before making decisions.

Finally, in cell 4 both objectives and cause-and-effect relationships are uncertain. Here decision-making tends to be of an inspirational nature and accounting systems can serve as an 'idea machine' by helping to stimulate and trigger creativity during brainstorming sessions where any idea is given serious consideration. It has been suggested that in changing environmental conditions semi-confusing accounting systems can be designed deliberately to shake organizations out of rigid behaviour patterns (Hedberg and Jonsson, 1978).

## ACTUAL USES

The above analysis suggests that decision-making requirements and the role of information systems should vary with the nature of the underlying uncertainty. However, in practice accounting information systems do not always follow the ideal uses depicted in Figure 17.3. There are no problems in cell 1 where objectives are certain and cause-and-effect relationships are well understood. Here decisions are programmable and the accounting information system can be used to generate answers.

In cell 2 where uncertainty over objectives applies but cause-and-effect relationships are well understood we find that 'ammunition machines' are used instead of dialogue and compromise. In these situations political processes are important and accounting information is often used as ammunition through which interested parties seek to promote their own vested interests. Traditional management accounting systems are often used as ammunition machines. Reports containing only financial information are used to reduce multiple objectives to a single goal when, in reality organizational needs also include marketing, engineering and human relations aspects (Macintosh, 1994). By focusing on only one objective, information systems can be exploited to further the political ambitions of particular vested interest groups (Dirsmith and Jablonsky, 1979).

Macintosh illustrates how different parties can use the same information by quoting an example from politics where various parties try and influence the law-making in legislative assemblies. Using the same data base, one party develops an information system which supports a reduction in government meddling in the economy, while another using the very same data base, develops information which indicates the need for an increase in government planning. Ammunition machines are dangerous because they override the need for constructive dialogue and compromise.

In cell 3 learning machines are required but answer machines are often used instead. This situation can arise when accounting information is presented in such a way that it ignores or masks uncertainty when cause-and-effect relationships are uncertain. For example there is a danger that techniques, such as probability and risk analysis models which have been designed to incorporate uncertainty into the analysis, may produce answers that inadvertently create an aura of relative certainty. If these techniques are used purely as answer machines there is a possibility that opportunities to stimulate learning and exploit uncertainty will be lost (Macintosh, 1994).

Finally, in cell 4 where both objectives and cause-and-effect relationships are uncertain we often find that instead of using accounting information systems as idea machines they are used as 'rationalization machines' that seek to justify and legitimize actions that have already been decided upon. For example, Bower (1970) has suggested that capital budgeting procedures are often used to justify decisions that have already been made, rather than as an aid to decision-making. Rationalization machines sometimes can have legitimate uses such as when it is appropriate to justify to others that decisions are being taken rationally. Accounting systems, however, should not be used to discourage creativity or always encourage the maintenance of the status quo.

The message from the analysis above is that the role of accounting information systems should be dependent on the type of uncertainty involved for the particular decision. An over-emphasis on formal systems and technical problems is inconsistent with the realities of organizational information flows. Unless accounting information system managers abandon their traditional narrow and technical perspective they will continue to be isolated from substantive organizational processes (Macintosh, 1985).

# Purposes of management accounting

You should be aware from reading the previous section that management accounting information can be used for several different purposes. Drawing off earlier work by Earl and Hopwood (1981), Burchell *et al.* (1980) and Chua (1988), Kelly and Pratt (1992) review the different 'roles' or 'purposes' of management accounting. They include:

1.  a rational/instrumental purpose;
2.  a symbolic purpose;
3.  a political/bargaining purpose;
4.  a legitimate/retrospective rationalizing purpose;
5.  a repressive/dominating/ideological purpose.

## A RATIONAL/INSTRUMENTAL PURPOSE

The conventional wisdom of management accounting, as portrayed in most management accounting textbooks, is derived from neo-classical economic theory. It is assumed that decision-making involves the formulation of goals (usually based on profit maximization), the identification of alternative courses of action, the evaluation of alternatives and a rational choice based on clearly defined criteria. The role of management accounting is to aid rational economic decision-making. The writings of Burchell *et al.* (1980) and Earl and Hopwood (1981), described in the previous section, suggest that when task instrumentality is well understood and objectives are clear, rational decision-making models can provide an accurate description of actual practice. In many situations, however, the assumption of rational economic decision-making does not reflect actual real world behaviour. For example, Cooper (1980) states:

Within a business context, it is perhaps unsurprising that the techniques that have been developed from neo-classical marginal theory are rarely implemented. Many managers recognise the simplistic and partial nature of the models and therefore have little confidence in the level of their prescriptions.

As long ago as 1959, Simon drew attention to the many problems inherent in attempting to explain the organizational decision-making process purely in economic terms. He concluded that the normative microeconomist does not need a theory of human behaviour: he wants to know how people *ought* to behave, not how they *do* behave. Simon also attacked one of the most fundamental assumptions of neo-classical economics; that is that people are rational economic decision-makers. He argues that business people are content to find a plan that provides satisfactory profits rather than to maximize profits. Because the business environment is too complex to understand in its entirety and people can deal with only a limited amount of information at any one time (Simon uses the term 'bounded rationality' to describe these constraints) they tend to search for solutions only until the first acceptable solution is found rather than continuing to search until the *best* solution is found.

It is also argued that the problem of resolving conflict between multiple goals is simplified by pursuing one goal at a time. At any one time, a particular goal is seen as being of prime importance, and action is taken to try and attain it. As time progresses other goals that have been neglected become of prime importance and attention is devoted to them in turn. This sequential attention to goals is a means of avoiding computing trade-offs between mutually exclusive goals and such behaviour has been described by Lindblom (1959) as 'muddling through'. Rather than the rational decision-making model this type of behaviour may be a more accurate description of actual behaviour in many organizations.

Other influential work based on bounded rationality is that of Cohen, March and Olsen (1972) who developed a garbage can model of decision-making in organizations that do not have clearly defined goals. They suggest that decisions are made in terms of the relatively random interaction of problems, solutions, participants and choice opportunities. A choice opportunity is modelled as a garbage can into which various problems and solutions are dumped by organizational participants.

Organizational life is seen as a continuous stream of problems that interact with an independent stream of possible solutions in an almost random manner. A given solution is chosen because it happens to be available and perceived at the time at which the problem emerges. This can result in solutions looking for problems as well as the more normal view of problems seeking solutions. Participants come and go and only chance attaches them to any particular decision opportunity. Choices are made only when problems, solutions and participants combine in such a way to make action possible.

In reviewing the garbage can model Ezzamel and Hart (1987) point out that in some cases goals may be pre-existent, well-ordered and antecedent to action. In these cases the emphasis is on interpreting actions and relating them to goals. In many cases, however, goals may be fluid, vague and ill-defined and discovered or reformulated as a consequence of action. The link between goals and actions will be ambiguous or even non-existent in these circumstances. In such cases emphasis is likely to shift from a preoccupation with ensuring that actions are consistent with goals to a concern with the processes through which actions are taken and possibly legitimized.

The conclusion that emerges from the literature is that where objectives can be clearly specified and input–output relationships are well understood, rational decision-making may represent a reasonable approximation to real world behaviour. In many situations, however, rationality is imperfect and actual behaviour is inconsistent with that assumed by neo-classical economic theory. To obtain a more complete understanding of management accounting there is a need to expand our knowledge, beyond adopting a universal theory that assumes rational decision-making, to approaches that incorporate what actually happens in practice. In the remaining part of this chapter we shall consider alternative roles that management accounting play in organizations.

## A SYMBOLIC PURPOSE

Organizations and managers gather and process far more information than they can possibly use for decision-making (Feldman and March, 1981). Furthermore, much of the information they collect is totally unconnected with decisions. The observations by Feldman and March that organizations overinvest in the amount of information they gather and process is in marked contrast to conventional wisdom which suggests that managers will collect and process information only if its marginal cost is less than its incremental value.

Why do managers collect more information than they need for decision-making? The answer is that information represents a means of signalling to others inside and outside the organization that decisions are being taken rationally and that managers in the organization are accountable. It is a representation to others of one's competence and is a symbol for all to see that one believes in intelligent choice. Accounting systems may be adopted ceremonially in order to convince the environment of the legitimacy and rationality of organizational activities.

Organizations without formal accounting systems are vulnerable to claims that they are negligent (Cooper *et al.*, 1981). Thus managers can find value in accounting information systems for symbolic purposes even when the information has little or no relation to decision-making. In its most extreme form it is more important to be perceived as being rational rather than actually being rational (Kelly and Pratt, 1992).

There is a mythical belief in Western society that more information leads to better decisions. Therefore the more information that a manager processes, the more impressive he or she is likely to be to others. Thus managers can establish their legitimacy, enhance their reputation and inspire confidence in others by displaying their command and use of the accounting information system. Therefore management accounting information can have a value to managers far beyond its worth as a basis for action (Macintosh, 1994).

Mackintosh also draws attention to the fact that managers use management accounting information for defensive purposes. There is a widespread practice within many organizations of criticizing decisions after the event. Because decisions are made under uncertainty a good decision may turn out to be unsuccessful yet it may still have been the correct one in the light of the information and alternatives available at the time. Furthermore, managers may be criticized on the grounds that they should have collected more information prior to making the decision. To protect themselves against such criticisms, and to defend their actions, managers protect their interests by collecting all the information available before making a decision.

## A POLITICAL/BARGAINING PURPOSE

Various writers have drawn attention to the fact that accounting information is widely used to achieve political power or a bargaining advantage. You will have already noted earlier in this chapter that when objectives are uncertain accounting information is often used as an ammunition machine through which interested parties seek to promote their own vested interests. Burchell *et al.* (1980) state:

> Rather than creating a basis for dialogue and interchange where objectives are uncertain or in dispute, accounting systems are often used to articulate and promote particular interest positions and values ... Organizations are arenas in which people and groups participate with a diversity of interests with political processes being endemic features of organizational life ... The design of information and processing systems are also implicated in the management of these political processes... The powerful are helped to observe the less powerful but not vice versa ... Moreover by influencing the accepted language of negotiation and debate, accounting systems can help to shape what is regarded as problematic, what can be deemed a credible solution and, perhaps most important of all, the criteria which are used for selection. For rather than being solely orientated towards the provision of information for decision-making, accounting systems can influence the criteria by which other information is sifted, marshalled and evaluated. (Page 17.)

Cooper *et al.* (1981) also draw attention to the role of accounting systems as reflections of power and tools of internal disputes. Pfeffer and Salancik (1974) observed that university budget allocations can be understood in terms of the relative power of departments, such power deriving from research reputations and ability to generate external funds. Wildavsky (1974) cites numerous examples of the political aspects of budgeting at the government level, many of which have ready parallels with both public and business organizations. For example, he cites situations where successful arguments for funding are based on ignorance of sunk costs, and where combining budget estimates enables 'pet projects' to be slipped through the review process. Macintosh (1994) also concludes that management accounting and control systems are vitally involved in relations of domination and power. He states that

> command over them is a key allocation resource used by upper-level executives to hold dominion over the organization's physical and technical assets. The master budget, for example, contains the detailed and all-encompassing blueprint for resource allocation for the entire organization and is a powerful lever in terms of ability to make a difference, to get things done and to dominate the organization. (Page 175.)

The various studies that have examined the use of accounting information to achieve political power or a bargaining position have concluded that accounting systems are a significant component of the power system in the organization. In addition, these studies have also contributed to a wider understanding of how accounting operates in an organizational context and the ways in which accounting can be used by interested parties to reinterpret and modify existing perceptions of reality.

# A LEGITIMATING/RETROSPECTIVE RATIONALIZING PURPOSE

This role relates to the use of accounting information to justify and legitimize actions that have already been decided upon. This role was briefly discussed when we considered how accounting information can be used as a 'rationalization machine'.

Weick (1969) maintains that the sequence whereby actions precede goals may well be a more accurate portrayal of organizational functioning than the more traditional goal–action paradigm. If goals are discovered through action and we make sense of actions retrospectively the notion of a budget as a quantified statement about future actions, as reflected by the conventional wisdom of management accounting, simply does not hold (Cooper *et al.*, 1981). Rather as part of the rationalization process of retrospective goal discovery, it appears that by performing the budget process an organization may be discovering its goals instead of achieving them because the exercise often involves looking backwards prior to extrapolation into the future. The budget process may be interpreted as a means of justifying past actions and making them appear sensible.

Attention has already been drawn to the observation by Bower (1970) that a major use of capital budgeting procedures is to justify decisions already made, rather than simply providing information prior to taking a particular decision. Similarly, Dirsmith and Jablonsky (1979) and Covaleski and Dirsmith (1980) suggest from their studies of budgetary systems in the governmental and health sectors, that systems such as planned programmed budgeting and management by objectives and budgets are used in large part to provide an appearance of rationality and a legitimation of activities. Earl and Hopwood (1981) and Burchell *et al.* (1980) also cite numerous instances in which managers utilize accounting data as *ex post* justification rather than as informational input. Cooper *et al.* (1981) state:

> Accounting systems which record and report the results of activities provide an authoritative means of explaining the past and thereby providing a guide to the future. Such observations have led to the suggestion that sophisticated accounting systems may, rather than aiding efficiency itself, instead provide a dramatisation of efficiency, maintaining a rational facade and thus providing a respectable identity for an organization. In general the processes associated with accounting in organizations may be interpreted as a way of facilitating what has happened in the past and attaching meaning to previous actions. Future actions may then be justified by the same explanations which have helped to make sense of previous action. The rituals of accounting may provide the legitimation for continuing current organizational activities. (Page 181.)

In summary, Cooper *et al.* provide an insight into how accounting information can act as signals and symbols which can be used to endow past actions and decisions with legitimacy. In particular, they demonstrate that in organizations characterized by ambiguous goals and uncertain technologies (they refer to this situation as an organized anarchy) accounting systems represent an *ex post* rationalization of actions, rather than an *ex ante* statement of organization goals. In addition, they also highlight the role that accounting systems, and in particular budgets, play in providing a rationalization of behaviour rather than a decisional input.

# A REPRESSIVE/DOMINATING/IDEOLOGICAL PURPOSE

This role is based on the labour process perspective of management control which views management accounting systems as playing a crucial role in preserving capitalist and class-based systems of domination. The labour process perspective sees management accounting as contributing to the institutional subordination of labour through a language that serves to legitimate sectional interests and which like other forms of management control has been fashioned largely to meet the perceived interests of capital (Hopper *et al.*, 1987). Puxty (1993) describes how management accounting and control systems developed during early capitalism to secure control over recalcitrant labour developed into sophisticated control mechanisms designed to ensure the institutionalized subordination of labour to the needs of capital.

The labour process scholars depict management accounting, supported with management science techniques, as a way for owners to deprive workers of the technical and financial knowledge of the production process, treat them as commodities and pressure them for even more productivity. Owners also use accounting systems as a way to legitimate grabbing the lion's share of any surplus value accruing to the enterprise (Mackintosh, 1994). Reviewing the literature relating to the repressive/dominating role of accounting Kelly and Pratt (1992) conclude that the labour process perspective views the managers of capital as being assessed, not in terms of how well they serve the labour entrusted to them, but how well they protect the interests of the absentee owners of the capital. In order to serve this end it is necessary for managers to initiate a surveillance system to monitor the performance of de-skilled labour.

The distinctly Marxist perspective adopted by labour process scholars arises from their concern with the role that accounting plays in the processes of social reproduction characteristics of advanced capitalism. In the hands of its more committed advocates the labour process perspective is an unashamedly partial perspective on work and organizations. It sets out from the premise that in a capitalist society work and employment, the organization and industrial relations are all shaped and structured to serve the interests of the capitalist class. The study of these aspects of social order is intended to demonstrate the substance of the founding assumption of this perspective (Roslender, 1992).

## Summary

The contingency theory approach to management accounting advocates that there is no universally best management accounting control system which can be applied to all organizations, but that 'it all depends' upon the situational factors. The situational factors represent the contingent factors or the contingent variables. Because each organization is unique the potential range of situations, or contingent factors, is enormous and it is impossible to study each one separately. To overcome this problem contingency factors are classified by categories which appear to make sense in terms of describing differences in management accounting systems. The contingency factors were divided into five broad categories. They were:

1. the external environment;

2. the competitive strategy and strategic mission;

3. firm technology and interdependence;

4. business unit, firm and industry variables;

5. knowledge and observability factors.

Within each category several contingent variables were identified and a brief summary was provided that explained their impact on the management control system.

In addition, contingency frameworks developed by Ouchi (1979), Macintosh (1985) and Burchell et al. (1980) were described. Ouchi developed a framework that identified the circumstances when a particular type of control ought to be employed. This framework is dependent on two basic conditions: first, the ability to measure outputs and, second, knowledge of the transformation process. The framework combines these two elements in a matrix that contains four control situations. Where knowledge of the transformation process is near perfect behavioural controls can be used. Alternatively, output controls are most appropriate if knowledge of the transformation process is imperfect but the ability to measure output is high. Where there is low ability to measure outputs coupled with imperfect knowledge of the transformation process, neither behaviour nor output controls are appropriate. Here clan controls are the most appropriate mode.

Macintosh (1985) presented a framework, similar to that used by Ouchi, that focuses on the appropriate type of assessment for different types of uncertainty. The framework is based on the interaction of two basic conditions: task instrumentality (the extent to which the ways of doing work are well understood) and beliefs about the clarity of organization goals. Where goals are clear and unambiguous and task instrumentality is well understood, so that the optimum economic relationship between inputs and outputs can be derived, scorekeeping and assessment can rely on efficiency tests. Alternatively, where task instrumentality is not well understood but goals are clear and unambiguous we can ascertain whether the actions achieved the desired result. In these circumstances the scorekeeping question should focus on measures of effectiveness. Where goals are ambiguous both efficiency and effectiveness measures are unreliable and Macintosh advocates the use of a less satisfactory but more appropriate measure of assessment, the social test. With social tests the performance of a department is based on the collective opinions and beliefs of one or more user groups.

Burchell et al. use a framework that distinguishes between uncertainty over the objectives for organizational action and uncertainty over the patterns of cause-and-effect relations that determine the consequences of action. When objectives are clear and the patterns of cause-and-effect relationships are known, tasks can be programmed and decisions can be made by computation. Here accounting systems can serve as 'answer machines' to provide solutions to problems. The second situation relates to where objectives are uncertain but cause-and-effect relations are still known. Accounting systems should serve as a 'dialogue machine' by providing information that helps managers to develop and argue different points of view. However, in these circumstances accounting information is often used as an 'ammunition machine' whereby interested parties seek to promote their own vested interests.

The third situation applies to where objectives are clear but cause-and-effect relations are uncertain. Here there is a need to explore problems and use accounting systems as learning machines by providing information that helps managers to assess thoroughly the alternative courses of action. Examples include sensitivity analysis and inquiry systems for probing data bases. In practice, however, accounting information is often used as an answer machine instead of a learning machine. For example, accounting information is often presented in such a way that it ignores or masks uncertainty.

The final situation relates to where both objectives and cause-and-effect relationships are uncertain. In these circumstances decision-making tends to be of an inspirational nature and accounting systems can serve as an 'idea machine' by helping to stimulate and trigger creativity. Instead, we often find that accounting information systems are used as 'rationalization machines' that seek to justify and legitimize actions that have already been decided upon.

In the final part of the chapter the different 'roles' or 'purposes' of management accounting were examined. Five different purposes were discussed:

1. a rational/instrumental purpose;
2. a symbolic purpose;
3. a political/bargaining purpose;
4. a legitimate/retrospective rationalizing purpose;
5. a repressive/dominating/ideological purpose.

The conventional wisdom of management accounting is derived from neo-classical economic theory. It is assumed that the role of management accounting is to aid rational economic decision-making. In many situations, however, rationality is imperfect and actual behaviour is inconsistent with that assumed by neo-classical theory. Accounting systems may also be adopted ceremonially in order to convince the environment of the legitimacy and rationality of organizational activities. Thus managers can find value in accounting information systems for symbolic purposes even when the information has little or no relation to decision-making. Accounting information is also used for political purposes. Interested parties use the information to promote their own vested interests to achieve political power or a bargaining position. The legitimizing/rationalizing purpose of accounting relates to the use of accounting information to justify and legitimize actions that have already been decided upon rather than as a decisional input. In other words, accounting systems can represent an *ex post* rationalization of actions, rather than an *ex ante* statement of organizational goals. The repressive/dominating/ideological purpose is based on the labour process perspective which views management accounting as contributing to the institutional subordination of labour through a language that serves to legitimize sectional interests and that has been fashioned largely to meet the perceived interests of capital.

The conventional wisdom of management accounting, grounded in neo-classical economic theory does not, by itself, provide an adequate explanation of management accounting practice because it ignores the socio-political forces that have influenced accounting practices. Alternative approaches to understanding management accounting practice in its political and organizational contexts have been presented. There now exists a multiplicity of 'ways of seeing' management accounting that provide different insights and add richness to the literature. Any attempt to privilege one approach over another is problematical, and can be grounded only in value judgements (Kelly and Pratt, 1992). ●●●

## Key Terms and Concepts

ammunition machine (p. 660)
answer machine (p. 659)
behavioural controls (p. 654)
bounded rationality (p. 662)
clan controls (p. 655)
contingency theory (p. 647)
dialogue machine (p. 660)

effectiveness tests (p. 657)
efficiency tests (p. 657)
garbage-can model of decision-making (p. 662)
idea machine (p. 660)
instrumental tests (p. 657)
learning machine (p. 660)
non-programmed decision (p. 658)

output controls (p. 654)
programmed decision (p. 658)
rationalization machine (p. 661)

social control (p. 654)
social test (p. 658)
task instrumentality (p. 656)

## Recommended Reading

There are several textbooks that focus mainly on the organizational and social aspects of management accounting. You are recommended to read either Emmanuel *et al.* (1990), Macintosh (1985), Macintosh (1994), Ezzamel and Hart (1987) or Roslender (1992). For a more in-depth understanding of some of the issues discussed in this chapter you should refer to the articles by Burchell *et al.* (1980), Cooper *et al.* (1981) and Kelly and Pratt (1992).

## Key Examination Points

Most professional examining bodies rarely examine the content of this chapter. However, the content is likely to be examined in those courses that focus on management accounting within a wider social and organizational context. Examination questions are likely to consist of essays and be somewhat ill-defined. There will be no ideal answer. You should concentrate on reading widely and relating the literature to the question that is asked.

## Questions

### 17.1 Advanced

(a) Contingency theory has frequently been used to explain variations in the functioning of organizations. It has been criticised on a number of grounds, including whether sufficient attention has been given to people and culture.

Requirement:
Explain and discuss from a management control perspective, the criticism that contingency theory pays insufficient attention to the people in organizations and to organizational culture. (10 marks)

(b) Some organizations have long-standing practices of promoting from existing staff, as a consequence of which they rarely recruit outsiders to any senior position. Staff turnover is very low. Other organizations have frequent management and structural changes, and often recruit senior managers from outside the organization.

Requirement:
Explain the differences in control systems and approaches to management control that could be expected with these alternative practices.

*CIMA Stage 4*
*Management Accounting Control Systems*

### 17.2 Advanced

Conventional approaches to the study of the organizational process emphasize economic reality, order and planned action as the basis of manager-ial decision-making. Outline the major limitations inherent in such a viewpoint, highlighted by research studies, and discuss the implications of your analysis for the management accountant.

### 17.3 Advanced

It has been argued that the further introduction of technical management accounting controls in the public sector and not-for-profit sector are doomed to failure. Evaluate possible grounds of such an argument.

### 17.4 Advanced

Describe the contingency theory of management accounting and discuss the relationship between various contingent factors and features of the management accounting system.

### 17.5 Advanced

Describe the different types of controls that can be used in organizations and discuss the factors that influence the choice of specific types of controls.

### 17.6 Advanced

Discuss the different 'roles' or 'purposes' for which management accounting information is used within organizations.

### 17.7 Advanced

Management accounting information is rarely used in the ways that are depicted in textbooks. Discuss.

### 17.8 Advanced

There is no universally best management accounting control system which can be applied to all organizations. Discuss.

# Standard costing and variance analysis 1

In the previous two chapters the major features of management accounting control systems have been examined. Chapter 16 concentrated on the different types of controls used by companies so that the elements of management accounting control systems could be described within the context of the overall control process. Because there is no universally best management accounting control system that can be applied to all organizations Chapter 17 considered the relationship between contingent, or situational factors, and certain features of management accounting control systems. Both chapters adopted a broad approach to control and the detailed procedures of financial controls were not examined. In this, and the next two chapters we shall focus on the detailed financial controls that are used by organizations.

In this chapter we shall consider a financial control system that enables the deviations from budget to be analysed in detail, thus enabling costs to be controlled more effectively. This system of control is called standard costing. In particular, we shall examine how a standard costing system operates and how the variances are calculated. In the next chapter we shall consider some of the criticisms made against standard costing variance analysis, and look at various ways of overcoming the problems that arise. Standard costing systems are applied in standard cost centres which were described in Chapter 16. You will recall that the main features of standard cost centres are that output can be measured and the input required to produce each unit of output can be specified. In addition, the sales variances that are described in this chapter can also be applied in revenue centres. In Chapter 20 we shall look at financial controls that are appropriate for measuring profit and investment centre performance.

Standard costs are predetermined costs; they are target costs that should be incurred under efficient operating conditions. They are not the same as budgeted costs. A budget relates to an entire activity or operation; a standard presents the same information on a per unit basis. A standard therefore provides cost expectations per unit of activity and a budget provides the cost expectation for the total activity. If the budget output for a product is for 10 000 units and the standard cost is £3 per unit, budgeted cost will be

## Learning objectives

After studying this chapter, you should be able to:

- explain how standard costs are set;
- explain the meaning of standard hours produced;
- define basic, ideal and currently attainable standards;
- explain how a standard costing system operates;
- calculate labour, material, overhead and sales margin variances and reconcile actual profit with budgeted profit;
- identify the causes of labour, material, overhead and sales margin variances;
- construct a departmental performance report;
- distinguish between standard variable costing and standard absorption costing.

£30 000. We shall see that establishing standard costs for each unit produced enables a detailed analysis to be made of the difference between the budgeted cost and the actual cost so that costs can be controlled more effectively.

In the first part of the chapter (pages 672–94) we shall concentrate on those variances that are likely to be useful for cost control purposes. The final part describes those variances that are required for financial accounting purposes but that are not particularly useful for cost control. If your course does not relate to the disposition of variances for financial accounting purposes, you can omit pages 694–700.

# Operation of a standard costing system

Standard costing is most suited to an organization whose activities consist of a series of *common* or *repetitive* operations and the input required to produce each unit of output can be specified. It is therefore relevant in manufacturing companies, since the processes involved are often of a repetitive nature. Standard costing procedures can also be applied in service industries such as units within banks, where output can be measured in terms of the number of cheques or the number of loan applications processed, and there are also well-defined input–output relationships. Standard costing cannot, however, be applied to activities of a non-repetitive nature, since there is no basis for observing repetitive operations and consequently standards cannot be set.

A standard costing system can be applied to organizations that produce many different products, as long as production consists of a series of common operations. For example, if the output from a factory is the result of five common operations, it is possible to produce many different product variations from these operations. It is therefore possible that a large product range may result from a small number of common operations. Thus standard costs should be developed for repetitive operations and product standard costs are derived simply by combining the standard costs from the operations which are necessary to make the product. This process is illustrated in Exhibit 18.1.

It is assumed that the standard costs are £20, £30, £40 and £50 for each of the operations 1 to 4. The standard cost for *product* 100 is therefore £110, which consists of £20 for operation 1, plus £40 and £50 for operations 3 and 4. The standard costs for each of the other products are calculated in a similar manner. In addition, the total standard cost for the total output of each operation for the period has been calculated. For example, six items of operation number 1 have been completed, giving a total standard cost of £120 for this operation (six items at £20 each). Three items of operation 2 have been completed, giving a total standard cost of £90, and so on.

## VARIANCES ALLOCATED TO RESPONSIBILITY CENTRES

You can see from Exhibit 18.1 that different responsibility centres are responsible for each operation. Consequently, there is no point in comparing the actual cost of *product* 100 with the standard cost of £110 for the purposes of control, since responsibility centres A, C and D are responsible for the variance. None of the responsibility centres is solely answerable for the variance. Cost control requires that responsibility centres be identified with the

EXHIBIT 18.1

*Standard costs analysed by operations and products*

standard cost for the output achieved. Therefore if the actual costs for responsibility centre A are compared with the standard cost of £120 for the production of the six items, the manager of this responsibility centre will be answerable for the full amount of the variance. Only by comparing total

| Responsibility centre | Operation no. and standard cost | | Products | | | | | | | Total standard cost (£) | Actual cost |
|---|---|---|---|---|---|---|---|---|---|---|---|
| | No. | (£) | 100 | 101 | 102 | 103 | 104 | 105 | 106 | | |
| A | 1 | 20 | ✓ | ✓ | | ✓ | ✓ | ✓ | ✓ | 120 | |
| B | 2 | 30 | | ✓ | | ✓ | ✓ | ✓ | | 90 | |
| C | 3 | 40 | ✓ | | ✓ | | ✓ | | | 120 | |
| D | 4 | 50 | ✓ | ✓ | ✓ | | | | ✓ | 200 | |
| Standard product cost | | | £110 | £100 | £90 | £50 | £60 | £50 | £70 | 530 | |

actual costs with total standard costs *for each operation or responsibility centre* for a period can control be effectively achieved. A comparison of standard *product* costs with actual costs that involves several different responsibility centres is clearly inappropriate.

Figure 18.1 provides an overview of the operation of a standard costing system. You will see that the standard costs for the actual output for a particular period are traced to the managers of responsibility centres who are responsible for the various operations. The actual costs for the same period are also charged to the responsibility centres. Standard and actual costs are compared and the variance is reported. For example, if the actual cost for the output of the six items produced in responsibility centre A during the period is £220 and the standard cost is £120 (Exhibit 18.1), a variance of £100 will be reported.

## DETAILED ANALYSIS OF VARIANCES

You can see from Figure 18.1 that the operation of a standard costing system also enables a detailed analysis of the variances to be reported. For example, variances for each responsibility centre can be identified by each element of cost and analysed according to the price and quantity content. The accountant assists managers by pinpointing where the variances have arisen and the responsibility managers can undertake to carry out the appropriate investigations to identify the reasons for the variance. For example, the accountant might identify the reason for a direct materials variance as being excessive usage of a certain material in a particular process, but the responsibility centre manager must investigate this process and identify the reasons for the excessive usage. Such an investigation should result in appropriate remedial action being taken or, if it is found that the variance is due to a permanent change in the standard, the standard should be changed.

**FIGURE 18.1** *An overview of a standard costing sytem.*

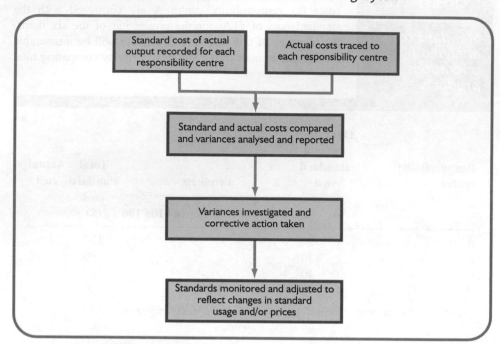

## ACTUAL PRODUCT COSTS NOT REQUIRED

It is questionable whether the allocation of actual costs to products serves any useful purpose. Because standard costs represent *future* target costs, they are preferable to actual *past* costs for decision-making. Also, the external financial accounting regulations in most countries specify that if standard product costs provide a reasonable approximation of actual product costs, they are acceptable for inventory valuation calculations for external reporting.

There are therefore strong arguments for not producing actual product costs when a standard costing system exists, since this will lead to large clerical savings. However, it must be stressed that actual costs must be accumulated periodically for each operation or responsibility centre, so that comparisons can be made with standard costs. Nevertheless, there will be considerably fewer responsibility centres than products, and the accumulation of actual costs is therefore much less time consuming.

## COMPARISONS AFTER THE EVENT

It may be argued that there is little point in comparing actual performance with standard performance, because such comparisons can only be made after the event. Nevertheless, if people know in advance that their performance is going to be judged, they are likely to act differently from the way they would have done if they were aware that their performance was not going to be measured. Furthermore, even though it is not possible for a manager to change his or her performance after the event, an analysis of how well a person has performed in the past may indicate – both to the person concerned and his or her superior – ways of obtaining better performance in the future.

# Establishing cost standards

Control over costs is best effected through action at the point where the costs are incurred. Hence the standards should be set for the quantities of material, labour and services to be consumed in performing an *operation*, rather than the complete *product* cost standards. Variances from these standards should be reported to show causes and responsibilities for deviations from standard. Product cost standards are derived by listing and adding the standard costs of operations required to produce a particular product. For example, if you refer to Exhibit 18.1 you will see that the standard cost of product 100 is £110 and is derived from the sum of the standard costs of operations 1, 3 and 4.

There are two approaches that can be used to set standard costs. First, past historical records can be used to estimate labour and material usage. Secondly, standards can be set based on **engineering studies**. With engineering studies a detailed study of each operation is undertaken based on careful specifications of materials, labour and equipment and on controlled observations of operations. If historical records are used to set standards, there is a danger that the latter will include past inefficiencies. With this approach, standards are set based on average past performance for the same or similar operations. Known excess usage of labour or materials should be eliminated or the standards may be tightened by an arbitrary percentage reduction in the quantity of resources required. The disadvantage of this method is that, unlike the engineering method, it does not focus attention on finding the best combination of resources, production methods and product quality. Nevertheless, standards derived from average historical usage do appear to be widely used in practice. (See Exhibit 18.3.)

Let us now consider how standards are established using the engineering studies approach.

## DIRECT MATERIAL STANDARDS

These are based on product specifications derived from an intensive study of the input quantity necessary for each operation. This study should establish the most suitable materials for each product, based on product design and quality policy, and also the optimal quantity that should be used after taking into account any wastage or loss that is considered inevitable in the production process. Material quantity standards are usually recorded on a **bill of materials**. This describes and states the required quantity of materials for each operation to complete the product. A separate bill of materials is maintained for each product. The standard material product cost is then found by multiplying the standard quantities by the appropriate standard prices.

The standard prices are obtained from the purchasing department. The standard material prices are based on the assumption that the purchasing department has carried out a suitable search of alternative suppliers and has selected suppliers who can provide the required quantity of sound quality materials at the most competitive price. Normally, price standards take into account the advantages to be obtained by determining the most economical order quantity and quantity discounts, best method of delivery and the most favourable credit terms. However, consideration should also be given to vendor reliability with respect to material quality and meeting scheduled delivery dates. Standard prices then provide a suitable base against which actual prices paid for materials can be evaluated.

## DIRECT LABOUR STANDARDS

To set labour standards, activities should be analysed by the different operations. Each operation is studied and an allowed time computed, usually after carrying out a time and motion study. The normal procedure for such a study is to analyse each operation to eliminate any unnecessary elements and to determine the most efficient production method. The most efficient methods of production, equipment and operating conditions are then standardized. This is followed by time measurements that are made to determine the number of standard hours required by an average worker to complete the job. Unavoidable delays such as machine breakdowns and routine maintenance are included in the standard time. Wage rate standards are normally either a matter of company policy or the result of negotiations between management and unions. The agreed wage rates are applied to the standard time allowed to determine the standard labour cost for each operation.

## OVERHEAD STANDARDS

The procedure for establishing standard manufacturing overhead rates for a standard costing system is the same as that which is used for establishing predetermined overhead rates as described in Chapter 3. Separate rates for fixed and variable overheads are essential for planning and control. Normally the standard overhead rate will be based on a rate per direct labour hour or machine hour of input.

Fixed overheads are largely independent of changes in activity, and remain constant over wide ranges of activity in the short term. It is therefore inappropriate for short-term cost control purposes to unitize fixed overheads to derive a fixed overhead rate per unit of activity. However, in order to meet the external financial reporting stock valuation requirements, fixed manufacturing overheads must be traced to products. It is therefore necessary to unitize fixed overheads for stock valuation purposes.

The main difference with the treatment of overheads under a standard costing system as opposed to a non-standard costing system is that the product overhead cost is based on the hourly overhead rates multiplied by the *standard hours* (that is, hours which should have been used) rather than the *actual hours* used.

At this stage it is that it is appropriate if we summarize the approach that should be used to establish cost standards. Control over costs is best effected through action at the point where they are incurred. Hence standards should be set for labour, materials and variable overheads consumed in performing an *operation*. For stock valuation purposes it is necessary to establish *product cost* standards. Standard manufacturing product costs consist of the total of the standard costs of operations required to produce the product plus the product's standard fixed overhead cost. A standard cost card should be maintained for each product and operation. A typical product standard cost card is illustrated in Exhibit 18.2. In most organizations standard cost cards are now stored on a computer. Standards should be continuously reviewed, and, where significant changes in production methods or input prices occur, they should be changed in order to ensure that standards reflect current targets. We shall discuss how the learning curve can be applied in standard setting in Chapter 24.

## STANDARD HOURS PRODUCED

It is not possible to measure *output* in terms of units produced for a department making several different products or operations. For example, if a department produces 100 units of product X, 200 units of product Y and 300 units of product Z, it is not possible to add the production of these items together, since they are not homogeneous. This problem can be overcome by ascertaining the amount of time, working under efficient conditions, it should take to make each product. This time calculation is called **standard hours**

**EXHIBIT 18.2**

*An illustration of a standard cost card*

produced. In other words, standard hours are an *output* measure that can act as a common denominator for adding together the production of unlike items.

Let us assume that the following standard times are established for the production of one unit of each product:

---

Date standard set ........................                     Product: Sigma

*Direct materials*

| Operation no. | Item code | Quantity (kg) | Standard price (£) | Department A | B | C | D | Totals (£) |
|---|---|---|---|---|---|---|---|---|
| 1 | 5.001 | 5 | 3 | £15 | | | | |
| 2 | 7.003 | 4 | 4 | | £16 | | | |
| | | | | | | | | 31 |

*Direct labour*

| Operation no. | Standard hours | Standard rate (£) | | | | |
|---|---|---|---|---|---|---|
| 1 | 7 | 9 | £63 | | | |
| 2 | 8 | 9 | | £72 | | |
| | | | | | | 135 |

*Factory overhead*

| Department | Standard hours | Standard rate (£) | | | |
|---|---|---|---|---|---|
| B | 7 | 3 | £21 | | |
| C | 8 | 4 | | £32 | |
| | | | | | 53 |
| Total manufacturing cost per unit (£) | | | | | 219 |

---

| Product X | 5 standard hours |
|---|---|
| Product Y | 2 standard hours |
| Product Z | 3 standard hours |

This means that it should take 5 hours to produce one unit of product X under efficient production conditions. Similar comments apply to products Y and Z. The production for the department will be calculated in standard hours as follows:

| Product | Standard time per unit produced (hours) | Actual output (units) | Standard hours produced |
|---|---|---|---|
| X | 5 | 100 | 500 |
| Y | 2 | 200 | 400 |
| Z | 3 | 300 | 900 |
| | | | 1800 |

Remember that standard hours produced is an output measure, and flexible budget allowances should be based on this. In the illustration we should expect the *output* of 1800 standard hours to take 1800 direct labour hours of *input* if the department works at the prescribed level of efficiency. The department will be inefficient if 1800 standard hours of output are produced using, say, 2000 direct labour hours of input. The flexible budget allowance should therefore be based on 1800 standard hours produced to ensure that no extra allowance is given for the 200 excess hours of input. Otherwise, a manager will obtain a higher budget allowance through being inefficient.

# Types of cost standards

The determination of standard costs raises the problem of how demanding the standards should be. Should they represent ideal or faultless performance or should they represent easily attainable performance? Standards are normally classified into three broad categories:

1. basic cost standards;
2. ideal standards;
3. currently attainable standards.

## BASIC COST STANDARDS

Basic cost standards represent constant standards that are left unchanged over long periods. The main advantage of basic standards is that a base is provided for a comparison with actual costs through a period of years with the same standard, and efficiency trends can be established over time. When changes occur in methods of production, price levels or other relevant factors, basic standards are not very useful, since they do not represent *current* target costs. For this reason basic cost standards are seldom used.

## IDEAL STANDARDS

Ideal standards represent perfect performance. Ideal standard costs are the minimum costs that are possible under the most efficient operating conditions. Ideal standards are unlikely to be used in practice because they may have an adverse impact on employee motivation. Such standards constitute goals to be aimed for rather than performance that can currently be achieved.

## CURRENTLY ATTAINABLE STANDARD COSTS

These standards represent those costs that should be incurred under efficient operating conditions. They are standards that are difficult, but not impossible, to achieve. Attainable standards are easier to achieve than ideal standards because allowances are made for normal spoilage, machine breakdowns and lost time. The fact that these standards represent a target that can be achieved under efficient conditions, but which is also viewed as being neither too easy to achieve nor impossible to achieve, provides the best norm to which actual costs should be compared. Attainable standards can vary in terms of the level of difficulty. For example, if tight attainable standards are set over a given time period, there might only be a 70% probability that the standard will be attained. On the other hand, looser attainable standards might be set with a probability of 90% attainment. Attainable standards are equivalent to highly achievable standards described in Chapter 16.

Attainable standards that are likely to be achieved are preferable for planning and budgeting. It is preferable to prepare the master budget and cash budget using these standards. Clearly, it is inappropriate to use standards that may not be achieved for planning purposes. Hence attainable standards that are likely to be achieved lead to economies, since they can be used for both *planning* and *control*. However, easily attainable standards are unlikely to provide a challenging target that will motivate higher levels of efficiency.

For an indication of the types of cost standards that companies actually use you should refer to Exhibit 18.3.

## PURPOSES OF STANDARD COSTING

Standard costing systems are widely used because they provide cost information for many different purposes such as the following.

- Providing a prediction of future costs that can be used for *decision-making purposes*. Standard costs can be derived from either traditional or activity-based costing systems. Because standard costs represent *future* target costs based on the elimination of avoidable inefficiencies they are preferable to estimates based on adjusted past costs which may incorporate inefficiencies. For example, in markets where competitive prices do not exist products may be priced on a bid basis. In these situations standard costs provide more appropriate information because efficient competitors will seek to eliminate avoidable costs. It is therefore unwise to assume that inefficiencies are recoverable within the bid price.

- Providing a *challenging target* which individuals are motivated to achieve. For example research evidence suggests that the existence of a defined quantitative goal or target is likely to motivate higher levels of performance than would be achieved if no such target was set.

- Assisting in *setting budgets* and evaluating managerial performance. Standard costs are particularly valuable for budgeting because a reliable and convenient source of data is provided for converting budgeted production into physical and monetary resource requirements. Budgetary preparation time is considerably reduced if standard costs are available because the standard costs of operations and products can be readily built up into total costs of any budgeted volume and product mix.

- Acting as a *control device* by highlighting those activities which do not conform to plan and thus alerting managers to those situations that may be 'out of control' and in need of corrective action. With a standard costing system variances are analysed in great detail such as by element of cost, price and quantity. Useful feedback is therefore provided in pinpointing the areas where variances have arisen.

- Simplifying the task of tracing costs to products for *profit measurement and inventory valuation* purposes. Besides preparing annual financial accounting profit statements most organizations also prepare monthly internal profit statements. If actual costs are used a considerable amount of time is required in tracking costs so that monthly costs can be allocated between cost of sales and inventories. A data processing system is required which can track monthly costs in a resource efficient manner. Standard costing systems meet this requirement You will see from Figure 18.2 that product costs are maintained at standard cost. Inventories and cost of goods sold are recorded at standard cost and a conversion to actual cost is made by writing off all variances arising during the period as a period cost. Note that the variances from standard cost are extracted by comparing actual with standard costs at the responsibility centre level, and not at the product level, so that actual costs are not assigned to individual products.

**EXHIBIT 18.3**

*Surveys of company practice*

Since its introduction in the early 1900s standard costing has flourished and is now one of the most widely used management accounting techniques. Three independently conducted surveys of USA practice indicate highly consistent figures in terms of adopting standard costing systems. Cress and Pettijohn (1985) and Schwarzbach (1985) report an 85% adoption rate, while Cornick *et al.* (1988), found that 86% of the surveyed firms used a standard costing system. A Japanese survey by Scarborough *et al.* (1991) reported a 65% adoption rate. Surveys of UK companies by Drury *et al.* (1993) and New Zealand companies by Guilding *et al.* (1998) report adoption rates of 76% and 73% respectively.

In relation to the methods to set labour and material standards Drury *et al.* reported the following usage rates:

| | Extent of use (%) | | | | |
| --- | --- | --- | --- | --- | --- |
| | **Never** | **Rarely** | **Sometimes** | **Often** | **Always** |
| Standards based on design/ engineering studies | 18 | 11 | 19 | 31 | 21 |
| Observations based on trial runs | 18 | 16 | 36 | 25 | 5 |
| Work study techniques | 21 | 18 | 19 | 21 | 21 |
| Average of historic usage | 22 | 11 | 23 | 35 | 9 |

In the USA Lauderman and Schaeberle (1983) reported that 43% of the respondents used average historic usage, 67% used engineering studies, 11% used trial runs under controlled conditions and 15% used other methods. The results add up to more than 100% because some companies used more than one method.

Drury *et al.* also reported that the following types of standards were employed:

| | |
| --- | --- |
| Maximum efficiency standards | 5% |
| Achievable but difficult to attain standards | 44% |
| Average past performance standards | 46% |
| Other | 5% |

# Variance analysis

It is possible to compute variances simply by committing to memory a series of variance formulae. If you adopt this approach, however, it will not help you to understand what a

**EXAMPLE
18.1**

Alpha manufacturing company produces a single product, which is known as sigma. The product requires a single operation, and the standard cost for this operation is presented in the following standard cost card:

| *Standard cost card for product sigma* | (£) |
|---|---|
| Direct materials: | |
| 2 kg of A at £10 per kg | 20.00 |
| 1 kg of B at £15 per kg | 15.00 |
| Direct labour (3 hours at £9 per hour) | 27.00 |
| Variable overhead (3 hours at £2 per direct labour hour) | 6.00 |
| Total standard variable cost | 68.00 |
| Standard contribution margin | 20.00 |
| Standard selling price | 88.00 |

Alpha Ltd plan to produce 10 000 units of sigma in the month of April, and the budgeted costs based on the information contained in the standard cost card are as follows:

*Budget based on the above standard costs and an output of 10 000 units*

| | (£) | (£) | (£) |
|---|---|---|---|
| Sales (10 000 units of sigma at £88 per unit) | | | 880 000 |
| Direct materials: | | | |
| A: 20 000 kg at £10 per kg | 200 000 | | |
| B: 10 000 kg at £15 per kg | 150 000 | 350 000 | |
| Direct labour (30 000 hours at £9 per hour) | | 270 000 | |
| Variable overheads (30 000 hours at £2 per direct labour hour) | | 60 000 | 680 000 |
| Budgeted contribution | | | 200 000 |
| Fixed overheads | | | 120 000 |
| Budgeted profit | | | 80 000 |

Annual budgeted fixed overheads are £1 440 000 and are assumed to be incurred evenly throughout the year. The company uses a variable costing system for internal profit measurement purposes.

The actual results for April are:

| | (£) | (£) |
|---|---|---|
| Sales (9000 units at £90) | | 810 000 |
| Direct materials: | | |
| A: 19 000 kg at £11 per kg | 209 000 | |
| B: 10 100 kg at £14 per kg | 141 400 | |
| Direct labour (28 500 hours at £9.60 per hour) | 273 600 | |
| Variable overheads | 52 000 | 676 000 |
| Contribution | | 134 000 |
| Fixed overheads | | 116 000 |
| Profit | | 18 000 |

Manufacturing overheads are charged to production on the basis of direct labour hours. Actual production and sales for the period were 9000 units.

**FIGURE 18.2** *Standard costs for inventory valuation and profit measurement.*

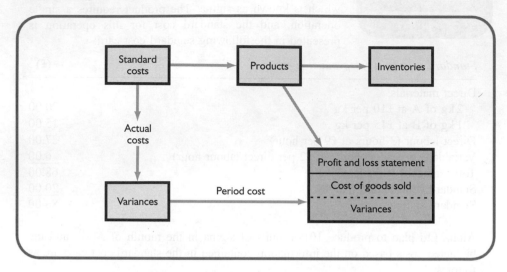

variance is intended to depict and what the relevant variables represent. In our discussion of each variance we shall therefore concentrate on the fundamental meaning of the variance, so that you can logically deduce the variance formulae as we go along.

All of the variances presented in this chapter are illustrated from the information contained in Example 18.1 on page 681. Note that the level of detail presented is highly simplified. A truly realistic situation would involve many products, operations and responsibility centres but would not give any further insights into the basic concepts or procedures.

Figure 18.3 shows the breakdown of the profit variance (the difference between budgeted and actual profit) into the component cost and revenue variances that can be calculated for a standard variable costing system. We shall now calculate the variances set out in Figure 18.3 using the data presented in Example 18.1.

# Material variances

The costs of the materials which are used in a manufactured product are determined by two basic factors: the price paid for the materials, and the quantity of materials used in production. This gives rise to the possibility that the actual cost will differ from the standard cost because the *actual quantity* of materials used will be different from the *standard quantity* and/or that the *actual price* paid will be different from the *standard price*. We can therefore calculate a material usage and a material price variance.

# Material price variances

The starting point for calculating this variance is simply to compare the standard price per unit of materials with the actual price per unit. In Example 18.1 the standard price for material A was £10 per kg, but the actual price paid was £11 per kg. The price variance is £1 per kg. This is of little consequence if the excess purchase price has been paid only for a small number of units or purchases. But the consequences are important if the excess

**FIGURE 18.3** *Variance analysis for a variable costing system.*

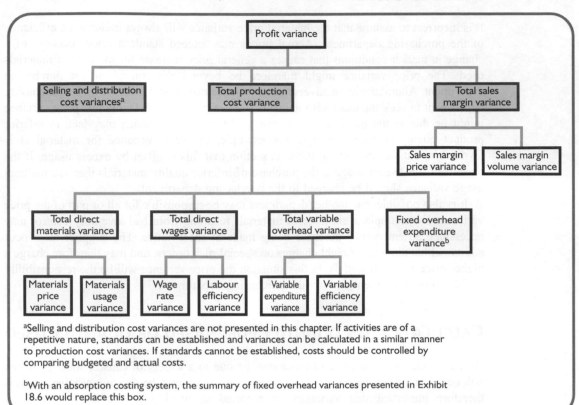

ªSelling and distribution cost variances are not presented in this chapter. If activities are of a repetitive nature, standards can be established and variances can be calculated in a similar manner to production cost variances. If standards cannot be established, costs should be controlled by comparing budgeted and actual costs.

ᵇWith an absorption costing system, the summary of fixed overhead variances presented in Exhibit 18.6 would replace this box.

purchase price has been paid for a large number of units, since the effect of the variance will be greater.

The difference between the standard material price and the actual price per unit should therefore be multiplied by the quantity of materials purchased. For material A the price variance is £1 per unit; but since 19 000 kg were purchased, the excess price was paid out 19 000 times. Hence the total material price variance is £19 000 adverse. The formula for the material price variance now follows logically:

the **material price variance** is equal to the difference between the standard price (SP) and the actual price (AP) per unit of materials multiplied by the quantity of materials purchased (QP):

$$(SP - AP) \times QP$$

For material B the standard price is £15, compared with an actual price of £14 giving a £1 saving per kg. As 10 100 kg were purchased, the total price variance will be £10 100 (10 100 kg at £1). The variance for material B is favourable and that for material A is adverse. The normal procedure is to present the amount of the variances followed by symbols A or F to indicate either adverse or favourable variances.

## POSSIBLE CAUSES

It is incorrect to assume that the material price variance will always indicate the efficiency of the purchasing department. Actual prices may exceed standard prices because of a change in market conditions that causes a general price increase for the type of materials used. The price variance might therefore be beyond the control of the purchasing department. Alternatively, an adverse price variance may reflect a failure by the purchasing department to seek the most advantageous sources of supply. A favourable price variance might be due to the purchase of inferior quality materials, which may lead to inferior product quality or more wastage. For example, the price variance for material B is favourable, but we shall see in the next section that this is offset by excess usage. If the reason for this excess usage is the purchase of inferior quality materials then the material usage variance should be charged to the purchasing department.

It is also possible that another department may be responsible for all or part of the price variance. For example, a shortage of materials resulting from bad inventory control may necessitate an emergency purchase being made at short notice. The supplier may incur additional handling and freight charges on special rush orders, and may therefore charge a higher price for the materials. In this situation the price variance will be the responsibility of the stores department and not the purchasing department.

## CALCULATION ON QUANTITY PURCHASED OR QUANTITY USED

We have noted that the price variance may be due to a variety of causes, some of which will be beyond a company's control, but others of which may be due to inefficiencies. It is therefore important that variances be reported as quickly as possible so that any inefficiencies can be identified and remedial action taken. A problem occurs, however, with material purchases in that the time of purchase and the time of usage may not be the same: materials may be purchased in one period and used in a subsequent period. For example, if 10 000 units of a material are purchased in period 1 at a price of £1 per unit over standard and 2000 units are used in each of periods 1 to 5, the following alternatives are available for calculating the price variance:

1. The full amount of the price variance of £10 000 is reported in *period 1* with quantity being defined as the *quantity purchased*.
2. The price variance is calculated with quantity being defined as the *quantity used*. The unit price variance of £1 is multiplied by the quantity used (i.e. 2000 units), which means that a price variance of £2000 will be reported for each of *periods 1 to 5*.

Method 1 is recommended, because the price variance can be reported in the period in which it is incurred, and reporting of the total variance is not delayed until months later when the materials are used. For the sake of simplicity we shall assume in Example 18.1 that the actual purchases are identical with the actual usage.

# Material usage variance

The starting point for calculating this variance is simply to compare the standard quantity that should have been used with the actual quantity which has been used. In Example 18.1 the standard usage for the production of one unit of sigma is 2 kg for material A. As 9000 units of sigma are produced, 18 000 kg of material A should have been used; however, 19 000 kg are actually used, which means there has been an excess usage of 1000 kg.

The importance of this excess usage depends on the price of the materials. For example, if the price is £0.01 per kg then an excess usage of 1000 kg will not be very significant, but if the price is £10 per unit then an excess usage of 1000 kg will be very significant. It follows that to assess the importance of the excess usage, the variance should be expressed in monetary terms.

## CALCULATION BASED ON STANDARD PRICE OR ACTUAL PRICE

Should the standard material price per kg or the actual material price per kg be used to calculate the variance? The answer is the standard price. If the *actual* material price is used, the usage variance will be affected by the efficiency of the purchasing department, since any excess purchase price will be assigned to the excess usage. It is therefore necessary to remove the price effects from the usage variance calculation, and this is achieved by valuing the variance at the standard price. Hence the 1000 kg excess usage of material A is multiplied by the standard price of £10 per unit, which gives an adverse usage variance of £10 000. The formula for the variance is

the **material usage variance** is equal to the difference between the standard quantity (SQ) required for actual production and the actual quantity (AQ) used multiplied by the standard material price (SP):

$$(SQ - AQ) \times SP$$

For material B the standard quantity is 9000 kg, but 10 100 kg have been used. The excess usage of 1100 kg is multiplied by the standard price of £15 per kg, which gives an adverse variance of £16 500. Note that the principles of flexible budgeting also apply here, with *standard quantity being based on actual production and not budgeted production*. This ensures that a manager is evaluated under the conditions in which he or she actually worked and not those envisaged at the time the budget was prepared.

## POSSIBLE CAUSES

The material usage variance is normally controllable by the manager of the appropriate production responsibility centre. Common causes of material usage variances include the careless handling of materials by production personnel, the purchase of inferior quality materials, pilferage, changes in quality control requirements, or changes in methods of production. Separate material usage variances should be calculated for each type of material used and allocated to each responsibility centre.

# Joint price usage variance

**AR** Note that the analysis of the material variance into the price and usage elements is not theoretically correct, since there may be a joint mutual price/quantity effect. The following information is extracted from Example 18.1 for material A:

1. 18 000 kg of material A are required, at a standard price of £10 per kg.

2. 19 000 kg are used, at a price of £11 per kg.

The purchasing officer might readily accept responsibility for the price variance of £1 per kg for 18 000 kg, but may claim that the extra 1000 kg at £1 is more the responsibility of the production foreman. It may be argued that if the foreman had produced in accordance with the standard then the extra 1000 kg would not have been needed.

The foreman, on the other hand, will accept responsibility for the 1000 kg excess usage at a standard price of £10, but will argue that he should not be held accountable for the additional purchase price of £1 per unit.

One possible way of dealing with this would be to report the joint price/quantity variance of £1000 (1000 kg at £1) separately and not charge it to either manager. In other words, the original price variance of £19 000 would be analysed as follows:

|  | (£) |
|---|---|
| 1. Pure price variance (18 000 kg at £1 per kg) | 18 000A |
| 2. Joint price/quantity variance (1 000 kg at £1 per kg) | 1 000A |
|  | 19 000A |

The importance of this refinement depends on the significance of the joint variance and the purpose for which price variances are used. For example, if the purchasing officer is paid a bonus depending upon the value of the variance then conflict may arise where the purchasing officer's bonus is reduced because of the impact of an adverse joint price/quantity variance.

Most textbooks recommend that the material price variance be calculated by multiplying the difference between the standard and actual prices by the actual quantity, rather than the standard quantity. Adopting this approach results in the joint price/quantity variance being assigned to the materials price variance. This approach can be justified on the ground that the purchasing manager ought to be responsible for the efficient purchase of all material requirements, irrespective of whether or not the materials are used efficiently by the production departments. ●●●

# Total material variance

From Figure 18.3 you will see that this variance is the total variance before it is analysed into the price and usage elements. The formula for the variance is

the **total material variance** is the difference between the standard material cost (SC) for the actual production and the actual cost (AC):

$$SC - AC$$

For material A the standard material cost is £20 per unit, giving a total standard material cost of £180 000. The actual cost is £209 000, and therefore the variance is £29 000 adverse. The price variance of £19 000 plus the usage variance of £10 000 agrees with the total material variance. Similarly, the total material variance for material B is £6400, consisting of a favourable price variance of £10 100 and an adverse usage variance of £16 500.

Note that if the price variance is calculated on the actual quantity *purchased* instead of the actual quantity *used*, the price variance plus the usage variance will agree with the total variance only when the quantity purchased is equal to the quantity which is used in the particular accounting period. Reconciling the price and usage variance with the total variance is merely a reconciliation exercise, and you should not be concerned if reconciliation of the sub-variances with the total variance is not possible.

# Labour variances

The cost of labour is determined by the price paid for labour and the quantity of labour used. Thus a price and quantity variance will also arise for labour. Unlike materials, labour cannot be stored, because the purchase and usage of labour normally takes place at the same time. Hence the actual quantity of hours *purchased* will be equal to the actual quantity of hours *used* for each period. For this reason the price variance plus the quantity variance should agree with the total labour variance.

# Wage rate variance

This variance is calculated by comparing the standard price per hour with the actual price paid per hour. In Example 18.1 the standard wage rate per hour is £9 and the actual wage rate is £9.60 per hour, giving a wage rate variance of £0.60 per hour. To determine the importance of the variance, it is necessary to ascertain how many times the excess payment of £0.60 per hour is paid. As 28 500 labour hours are used, we multiply 28 500 hours by £0.60. This gives an adverse wage rate variance of £17 100. The formula for the wage rate variance is

the **wage rate variance** is equal to the difference between the standard wage rate per hour (SR) and the actual wage rate (AR) multiplied by the actual number of hours worked (AH):

$$(SR - AR) \times AH$$

Note the similarity between this variance and the material price variance. Both variances multiply the difference between the standard price and the actual price paid for a unit of a resource by the actual quantity of resources used.

## POSSIBLE CAUSES

The wage rate variance may be due to a negotiated increase in wage rates not yet having been reflected in the standard wage rate. In a situation such as this the variance cannot be regarded as controllable. Labour rate variances may also occur because a standard is used that represents a single average rate for a given operation performed by workers who are paid at several different rates. In this situation part of all of the variance may be due to the assignment of skilled labour to work that is normally performed by unskilled labour. The variance may then be regarded as the responsibility of the foreman, because he should have matched the appropriate grade of labour to the task at hand. However, the wage rate variance is probably the one that is least subject to control by management. In most cases the variance is due to wage rate standards not being kept in line with changes in actual wage rates, and for this reason it is not normally controllable by departmental managers.

# Labour efficiency variance

The labour efficiency variance represents the quantity variance for direct labour. The quantity of labour that should be used for the actual output is expressed in terms of *standard hours produced*. In Example 18.1 the standard time for the production of one unit of sigma is 3 hours. Thus a production level of 9000 units results in an output of 27 000 standard hours. In other words, working at the prescribed level of efficiency, it should take 27 000 hours to produce 9000 units. However, 28 500 direct labour hours are actually required to produce this output, which means that 1500 excess direct labour hours are used. We multiply the excess direct labour hours by the *standard* wage rate to calculate the variance. This gives an adverse variance of £13 500. The formula for calculating the labour efficiency variance is

the labour efficiency variance is equal to the difference between the standard labour hours for actual production (SH) and the actual labour hours worked (AH) during the period multiplied by the standard wage rate per hour (SR):

$$(SH - AH) \times SR$$

This variance is similar to the material usage variance. Both variances multiply the difference between the standard quantity and actual quantity of resources consumed by the standard price.

## POSSIBLE CAUSES

The labour efficiency variance is normally controllable by the manager of the appropriate production responsibility centre and may be due to a variety of reasons. For example, the use of inferior quality materials, different grades of labour, failure to maintain machinery in proper condition, the introduction of new equipment or tools and changes in the production processes will all affect the efficiency of labour. An efficiency variance may not always be controllable by the production foreman; it may be due, for example, to poor production scheduling by the planning department, or to a change in quality control standards.

# Total labour variance

From Figure 18.3 you will see that this variance represents the total variance before analysis into the price and quantity elements. The formula for the variance is

the total labour variance is the difference between the standard labour cost (SC) for the actual production and the actual labour cost (AC):

$$SC - AC$$

In Example 18.1 the actual production was 9000 units, and, with a standard labour cost of £27 per unit, the standard cost is £243 000. The actual cost is £273 600, which gives an adverse variance of £30 600. This consists of a wage rate variance of £17 100 and a labour efficiency variance of £13 500.

# Variable overhead variances

A total variable overhead variance is calculated in the same way as the total direct labour and material variances. In Example 18.1 the output is 9000 units and the standard variable overhead cost is £6 *per unit* produced. The standard cost of production for variable overheads is thus £54 000. The actual variable overheads incurred are £52 000, giving a favourable variance of £2000. The formula for the variance is

the total variable overhead variance is the difference between the standard variable overheads charged to production (SC) and the actual variable overheads incurred (AC):

$$SC - AC$$

Where variable overheads vary with direct labour or machine hours of *input* the total variable overhead variance will be due to one or both of the following:

1. A *price* variance arising from actual expenditure being different from budgeted expenditure.
2. A *quantity* variance arising from actual direct labour or machine hours of input being different from the hours of input, which *should* have been used.

These reasons give rise to the two sub-variances, which are shown in Figure 18.3: the variable overhead expenditure variance and the variable overhead efficiency variance.

# Variable overhead expenditure variance

To compare the actual overhead expenditure with the budgeted expenditure, it is necessary to flex the budget. Because it is assumed in Example 18.1 that variable overheads will vary with direct labour hours of *input* the budget is flexed on this basis. Actual variable overhead expenditure is £52 000, resulting from 28 500 direct labour hours of input. For this level of activity variable overheads of £57 000, which consist of 28 500 input hours at £2 per hour, should have been spent. Spending was £5000 less than it should have been, and the result is a favourable variance.

If we compare the budgeted and the actual overhead costs for 28 500 direct labour hours of input, we shall ensure that any efficiency content is removed from the variance. This means that any difference must be due to actual variable overhead spending being different from the budgeted variable overhead spending. The formula for the variance is

the variable overhead expenditure variance is equal to the difference between the budgeted flexed variable overheads (BFVO) for the actual direct labour hours of input and the actual variable overhead costs incurred (AVO):

$$BFVO - AVO$$

## POSSIBLE CAUSES

The variable overhead expenditure variance on its own is not very informative. Any meaningful analysis of this variance requires a comparison of the actual expenditure for each individual item of variable overhead expenditure against the budget. If you refer to the performance report presented in Exhibit 18.8 on page 701, you can see how the £5000 variable overhead expenditure variance can be analysed by individual items of expenditure.

# Variable overhead efficiency variance

The variable overhead efficiency variance arises because 28 500 direct labour hours of input were required to produce 9000 units. Working at the prescribed level of efficiency, it should take 27 000 hours to produce 9000 units of output. Therefore an extra 1500 direct labour hours of input were required. Because variable overheads are assumed to vary with direct labour hours of input, an additional £3000 (1500 hours at £2) variable overheads will be incurred. The formula for the variance is

the **variable overhead efficiency variance** is the difference between the standard hours of output (SH) and the actual hours of input (AH) for the period multiplied by the standard variable overhead rate (SR):

$$(SH - AH) \times SR$$

You should note that if it is assumed that variable overheads vary with direct labour hours of input, this variance is identical to the labour efficiency variance. Consequently, the reasons for the variance are the same as those described previously for the labour efficiency variance. If you refer again to Figure 18.3, you will see that the variable overhead expenditure variance (£5000 favourable) plus the variable efficiency variance (£3000 adverse) add up to the total variable overhead variance of £2000 favourable.

# Similarities between materials, labour and overhead variances

So far, we have calculated price and quantity variances for direct material, direct labour and variable overheads. You will have noted the similarities between the computations of the three quantity and price variances. For example, we calculated the quantity variances (i.e. material usage, labour efficiency and variable overhead efficiency variances) by multiplying the difference between the standard quantity (SQ) of resources consumed for the actual production and the actual quantity (AQ) of resources consumed by the standard price (SP) per unit of the resource. The quantity variances can be formulated as

$$(SQ - AQ) \times SP$$

The price variances (i.e. material price, wage rate and variable overhead expenditure variances) were calculated by multiplying the difference between the standard price (SP) and the actual price (AP) per unit of a resource by the actual quantity (AQ) of resources acquired/used. The price variances can be formulated as

$$(SP - AP) \times AQ$$

This can be re-expressed as

$$(AQ \times SP) - (AQ \times AP)$$

Note that the first term in this formula (with AQ representing actual hours) is equivalent to the budgeted flexed variable overheads that we used to calculate the variable overhead expenditure variance. The last term represents the actual cost of the resources consumed.

We can therefore calculate all the price and quantity variances illustrated so far in this chapter by applying the formulae outlined above.

# Fixed overhead expenditure or spending variance

With a variable costing system, fixed manufacturing overheads are not unitized and allocated to products. Instead, the total fixed overheads for the period are charged as an expense to the period in which they are incurred. Fixed overheads are assumed to remain unchanged in response to changes in the level of activity, but they may change in response to other factors. For example, price increases may cause expenditure on fixed overheads to increase. The fixed overhead expenditure variance therefore explains the difference between budgeted fixed overheads and the actual fixed overheads incurred. The formula for the variance is the **fixed overhead expenditure variance** is the difference between the budgeted fixed overheads (BFO) and the actual fixed overhead (AFO) spending:

$$BFO - AFO$$

In Example 18.1 budgeted fixed overhead expenditure is £120 000 and actual fixed overhead spending £116 000. Therefore the fixed overhead expenditure variance is £4000. Whenever the actual fixed overheads are less than the budgeted fixed overheads, the variance will be favourable. The total of the fixed overhead expenditure variance on its own is not particularly informative. Any meaningful analysis of this variance requires a comparison of the actual expenditure for each individual item of fixed overhead expenditure against the budget. The difference may be due to a variety of causes, such as changes in salaries paid to supervisors, or the appointment of additional supervisors. Only by comparing individual items of expenditure and ascertaining the reasons for the variances, can one determine whether the variance is controllable or uncontrollable. Generally, this variance is likely to be uncontrollable in the short term.

# Sales variances

Sales variances can be used to analyse the performance of the sales function or revenue centres on broadly similar terms to those for manufacturing costs. The most significant feature of sales variance calculations is that they are calculated in terms of profit or contribution margins rather than sales values. Consider Example 18.2.

You will see that when the variances are calculated on the basis of sales *value*, it is necessary to compare the budgeted sales *value* of £110 000 with the actual sales of £120 000. This gives a favourable variance of £10 000. This calculation, however, ignores the impact of the sales effort on profit. The budgeted profit contribution is £40 000, which consists of 10 000 units at £4 per unit, but the actual impact of the sales effort in terms of profit margins indicates a profit contribution of £36 000, which consists of 12 000 units at £3 per unit, indicating an adverse variance of £4000. If we examine Example 18.2, we can see that the selling prices have been reduced, and that this has led not only to an increase in the total sales revenue but also to a reduction in total profits. The objective of the selling function is to influence favourably total profits. Thus a more meaningful performance measure will be obtained by comparing the results of the sales function in terms of profit or contribution margins rather than sales revenues.

**EXAMPLE 18.2**

The budgeted sales for a company are 10 000 units at £11 per unit. The standard cost per unit is £7. Actual sales are 12 000 units at £10 per unit and the actual cost per unit is £7.

Note that with a standard absorption costing system, *profit* margins are used (selling price less total unit manufacturing cost), whereas with a standard variable costing system, *contribution* margins (selling price less unit manufacturing variable cost) are used to calculate the variances.

Let us now calculate the sales variances for a standard variable costing system from the information contained in Example 18.1.

# Total sales margin variance

Where a variable costing approach is adopted, the total sales *margin* variance seeks to identify the influence of the sales function on the difference between budget and actual profit contribution. In Example 18.1 the budgeted profit contribution is £200 000, which consists of budgeted sales of 10 000 units at a contribution of £20 per unit. This is compared with the contribution from the actual sales volume of 9000 units. Because the sales function is responsible for the sales volume and the unit selling price, but not the unit manufacturing costs, the standard cost of sales and not the actual cost of sales is deducted from the actual sales revenue. The calculation of *actual* contribution for ascertaining the total sales margin variance will therefore be as follows:

|  | **(£)** |
|---|---|
| Actual sales revenue (9000 units at £90) | 810 000 |
| *Standard* variable cost of sales for actual sales volume (9000 units at £68) | 612 000 |
| Actual profit contribution margin | 198 000 |

To calculate the total sales margin variance, we compare the budgeted contribution of £200 000 with the actual contribution of £198 000. This gives an adverse variance of £2000 because the actual contribution is less that the budgeted profit contribution.

The formula for calculating the variance is as follows:

the **total sales margin variance** is the difference between the actual contribution (AC) and the budgeted contribution (BC) (both based on standard unit costs):

$$AC - BC$$

Using the standard cost to calculate both the budgeted and the actual contribution ensures that the production variances do not distort the calculation of the sales variances. The effect of using standard costs throughout the contribution margin calculations means that the sales variances arise because of changes in those variables controlled by the sales function (i.e. selling prices and sales quantity). Consequently, Figure 18.3 indicates that it is possible to analyse the total sales margin variance into two sub-variances – a sales margin price variance and a sales margin volume variance.

# Sales margin price variance

In Example 18.1 the actual selling price is £90 but the budgeted selling price is £88. With a standard unit variable cost of £68, the change in selling price has led to an increase in the contribution margin from £20 per unit to £22 per unit. Because the actual sales volume is 9000 units, the increase in the selling price means that an increased contribution margin is obtained 9000 times, giving a favourable sales margin price variance of £18000. The formula for calculating the variance is

the **sales margin price variance** is the difference between the actual contribution margin (AM) and the standard margin (SM) (both based on standard unit costs) multiplied by the actual sales volume (AV):

$$(AM - SM) \times AV$$

# Sales margin volume variance

To ascertain the effect of changes in the sales volume on the difference between the budgeted and the actual contribution, we must compare the budgeted sales volume with the actual sales volume. The budgeted sales are 10000 units but the actual sales are 9000 units, and to enable us to determine the impact of this reduction in sales volume on profit, we must multiply the 1000 units by the standard contribution margin of £20. This gives an adverse variance of £20000.

The use of the standard margin (standard selling price less standard cost) ensures that the standard selling price is used in the calculation, and the volume variance will not be affected by any *changes* in the actual selling prices. The formula for calculating the variance is

the **sales margin volume variance** is the difference between the actual sales volume (AV) and the budgeted volume (BV) multiplied by the standard contribution margin (SM):

$$(AV - BV) \times SM$$

# Difficulties in interpreting sales margin variances

The favourable sales margin price variance of £18000 plus the adverse volume variance of £20000 add up to the total adverse sales margin variance of £2000. It may be argued that it is not very meaningful to analyse the total sales margin variance into price and volume components, since changes in selling prices are likely to affect sales volume. Consequently, a favourable price variance will tend to be associated with an adverse volume variance, and vice versa. It may be unrealistic to sell more than the budgeted volume when selling prices have increased.

A further problem with sales variances is that the variances may arise from external factors and may not be controllable by management. For example, changes in selling prices may be the result of a response to changes in selling prices of competitors. Alternatively, a reduction in both selling prices and sales volume may be the result of an economic recession that was not foreseen when the budget was prepared. Manufacturing variances are not influenced as much by external factors, and for this reason management are likely to focus most of their attention on the control of the manufacturing variances. Nevertheless, sales margin variances provide useful information that enables the budgeted profit to be reconciled with the actual profit. However, for control and performance appraisal it is preferable to compare actual market share with target market share for each product. In addition, the trend in market shares should be monitored and selling prices should be compared with competitors' prices.

# Reconciling budgeted profit and actual profit

Top management will be interested in the reason for the actual profit being different from the budgeted profit. By adding the favourable production and sales variances to the budgeted profit and deducting the adverse variances, the reconciliation of budgeted and actual profit shown in Exhibit 18.4 can be presented in respect of Example 18.1.

Example 18.1 assumes that Alpha Ltd produces a single product consisting of a single operation and that the activities are performed by one responsibility centre. In practice, most companies make many products, which require operations to be carried out in different responsibility centres. A reconciliation statement such as that presented in Exhibit 18.4 will therefore normally represent a summary of the variances for many responsibility centres. The reconciliation statement thus represents a broad picture to top management that explains the major reasons for any difference between the budgeted and actual profits.

# Standard absorption costing

The external financial accounting regulations in most countries require that companies should value inventories at full absorption manufacturing cost. The effect of this is that fixed overheads should be allocated to products and included in the closing inventory valuations. With the variable costing system, fixed overheads are not allocated to products. Instead, the total fixed costs are charged as an expense to the period in which they are incurred. (For a discussion of the differences between variable and absorption costing systems you should refer back to Chapter 7.) With an absorption costing system, an additional fixed overhead variance is calculated. This variance is called a **volume variance**. In addition, the sales margin variances must be expressed in unit *profit* margins instead of *contribution* margins. These variances are not particularly useful for control purposes. If your course does not relate to the disposition of variances to meet financial accounting requirements, you can omit pages 694–700.

With a standard absorption costing system, predetermined fixed overhead rates are established by dividing annual budgeted fixed overheads by the budgeted annual level of activity. We shall assume that in respect of Example 18.1, budgeted annual fixed overheads are £1 440 000 (£120 000 per month) and budgeted annual activity is 120 000 units (10 000 units per month). The fixed overhead rate per *unit* of output is calculated as follows:

$$\frac{\text{budgeted fixed overheads (£1 440 000)}}{\text{budgeted activity (120 000 units)}} = £12 \text{ per unit of sigma produced}$$

We have noted earlier in this chapter that in most situations more than one product will be produced. Where different products are produced, units of output should be converted to standard hours. In Example 18.1 the output of one unit of sigma requires 3 direct labour hours. Therefore, the budgeted output in standard hours is 360 000 hours (120 000 × 3 hours). The fixed overhead rate per standard hour of output is

$$\frac{\text{budgeted fixed overheads } (£1\,440\,000\,)}{\text{budgeted standard hours } (360\,000\,)} = £4 \text{ per standard hour}$$

By multiplying the number of hours required to produce one unit of Sigma by £4 per hour, we also get a fixed overhead allocation of £12 for one unit of Sigma (3 hours × £4). For the remainder of this chapter output will be measured in terms of standard hours produced.

We shall assume that production is expected to occur evenly throughout the year. Monthly budgeted production *output* is therefore 10 000 units, or 30 000 standard direct labour hours. At the planning stage an input of 30 000 direct

**EXHIBIT 18.4**

*Reconciliation of budgeted and actual profits for a standard variable costing system*

| | (£) | (£) | (£) |
|---|---|---|---|
| Budgeted net profit | | | 80 000 |
| Sales variances: | | | |
|    Sales margin price | 18 000F | | |
|    Sales margin volume | 20 000A | 2 000A | |
| Direct cost variances: | | | |
|    Material: Price | 8 900A | | |
|            Usage | 26 500A | 35 400A | |
|    Labour:  Rate | 17 100A | | |
|            Efficiency | 13 500A | 30 600A | |
| Manufacturing overhead variances: | | | |
|    Fixed overhead expenditure | 4 000F | | |
|    Variable overhead expenditure | 5 000F | | |
|    Variable overhead efficiency | 3 000A | 6 000F | 62 000A |
| Actual profit | | | 18 000 |

labour hours (10 000 × 3 hours) will also be planned as the company will budget at the level of efficiency specified in the calculation of the product standard cost. Thus the budgeted hours of input and the budgeted hours of output (i.e. the standard hours produced) will be the same at the planning stage. In contrast, the *actual* hours of input may differ from the *actual* standard hours of output. In Example 18.1 the actual direct labour hours of input are 28 500, and 27 000 standard hours were actually produced.

With an absorption costing system, fixed overheads of £108 000 (27 000 standard hours of output at a standard rate of £4 per hour) will have been charged to products for the month of April. Actual fixed overhead expenditure was £116 000. Therefore, £8000 has not been allocated to products. In other words, there has been an under-recovery of fixed overheads. Where the fixed overheads allocated to products exceeds the overhead incurred, there will be an over-recovery of fixed overheads. The under- or over-recovery of fixed overheads represents the total fixed overhead variance for the period. The total fixed overhead variance is calculated using a formula similar to those for the total direct labour and total direct materials variances:

the total fixed overhead variance is the difference between the standard fixed overhead charged to production (SC) and the actual fixed overhead incurred (AC):

$$SC(£108\,000) - AC(£116\,000) = £8000A$$

Note that the standard cost for the actual production can be calculated by measuring production in standard hours of output (27 000 hours × £4 per hour) or units of output (9000 units × £12 per unit).

The under- or over-recovery of fixed overheads (i.e. the fixed overhead variance) arises because the fixed overhead rate is calculated by dividing *budgeted* fixed overheads by *budgeted* output. If actual output or fixed overhead expenditure differs from budget, an under- or over-recovery of fixed overheads will arise. In other words, the under- or over-recovery may be due to the following:

1. A fixed overhead expenditure variance of £4000 arising from actual *expenditure* (£116 000) being different from budgeted *expenditure* (£120 000).
2. A fixed overhead volume variance arising from actual *production* differing from budgeted production.

The fixed overhead expenditure variance also occurs with a variable costing system. The favourable variance of £4000 was explained earlier in this chapter. The volume variance arises only when inventories are valued on an absorption costing basis.

# Volume variance

This variance seeks to identify the portion of the total fixed overhead variance that is due to actual production being different from budgeted production. In Example 18.1 the standard fixed overhead rate of £4 per hour is calculated on the basis of a normal activity of 30 000 standard hours per month. Only when actual standard hours produced are 30 000 will the budgeted monthly fixed overheads of £120 000 be exactly recovered. Actual output, however, is only 27 000 standard hours. The fact that the actual production is 3000 standard hours less than the budgeted output hours will lead to a failure to recover £12 000 fixed overhead (3000 hours at £4 fixed overhead rate per hour). The formula for the variance is

the volume variance is the difference between actual production (AP) and budgeted production (BP) for a period multiplied by the standard fixed overhead rate (SR):

$$(AP - BP) \times SR$$

The volume variance reflects the fact that fixed overheads do not fluctuate in relation to output in the short term. Whenever actual production is less than budgeted production, the fixed overhead charged to production will be less than the budgeted cost, and the volume variance will be adverse. Conversely, if the actual production is greater than the budgeted production, the volume variance will be favourable.

## SUNK COST

Information indicating that actual production is 3000 standard hours less than budgeted production is useful to management, but to attach a fixed overhead rate to this figure is of little value for control because fixed costs represent sunk costs. The volume variance of

£12 000 does not reflect the cost of the facilities that remain idle, since the fixed overhead cost will not change if production declines – at least in the short term. A cost of lost output only occurs if a firm has demand for the lost output. In this situation it is more meaningful to measure the cost of the lost output in terms of the lost contribution from a failure to produce the budgeted output. We shall consider this approach in the next chapter.

## POSSIBLE CAUSES

Changes in production volume from the amount budgeted may be caused by shifts in demand for products, labour disputes, material shortages, poor production scheduling, machine breakdowns, labour efficiency and poor production quality. Some of these factors may be controllable by production or sales management, while others may not.

When the adverse volume variance of £12 000 is netted with the favourable expenditure variance of £4000, the result is equal to the total fixed overhead adverse variance of £8000. It is also possible to analyse the volume variance into two further sub-variances – the volume efficiency variance and the capacity variance.

# Volume efficiency variance

**AR** If we wish to identify the reasons for the volume variance, we may ask why the actual production was different from the budgeted production. One possible reason may be that the labour force worked at a different level of efficiency from that anticipated in the budget.

The actual number of direct labour hours of input was 28 500. Hence one would have expected 28 500 hours of output (i.e. standard hours produced) from this input, but only 27 000 standard hours were actually produced. Thus one reason for the failure to meet the budgeted output was that output in standard hours was 1500 hours less than it should have been. If the labour force had worked at the prescribed level of efficiency, an additional 1500 standard hours would have been produced, and this would have led to a total of £6000 (£1500 hours at £4 per standard hour) fixed overheads being absorbed. The inefficiency of labour is therefore one of the reasons why the actual production was less than the budgeted production, and this gives an adverse variance of £6000. The formula for the variance is

the **volume efficiency variance** is the difference between the standard hours of output (SH) and the actual hours of input (AH) for the period multiplied by the standard fixed overhead rate (SR):

$$(SH - AH) \times SR$$

You may have noted that the physical content of this variance is a measure of labour efficiency and is identical with the labour efficiency variance. Consequently, the reasons for this variance will be identical with those previously described for the labour efficiency variance. Note also that since this variance is a sub-variance of the volume variance, the same comments apply as to the usefulness of attaching a value for fixed overheads, because fixed overheads represent sunk costs. Total fixed overhead will not change because of the efficiency of labour. Again it would be better to measure this variance in terms of the lost contribution arising from lost sales.

# Volume capacity variance

This variance indicates the second reason why the actual production might be different from the budgeted production. The budget is based on the assumption that the direct labour hours of input will be 30 000 hours, but the actual hours of input are 28 500 hours. The difference of 1500 hours reflects the fact that the company has failed to utilize the planned capacity. If we assume that the 1500 hours would have been worked at the prescribed level of efficiency, an additional 1500 standard hours could have been produced and an additional £6000 fixed overhead could have been absorbed. Hence the capacity variance is £6000 adverse.

Whereas the volume efficiency variance indicated a failure to utilize capacity *efficiently*, the volume capacity variance indicates a failure to utilize capacity *at all*. The formula is

the **volume capacity variance** is the difference between the actual hours of input (AH) and the budgeted hours of input (BH) for the period multiplied by the standard fixed overhead rate (SR):

$$(AH - BH) \times SR$$

A failure to achieve the budgeted capacity may be for a variety of reasons. Machine breakdowns, material shortages, poor production scheduling, labour disputes and a reduction in sales demand are all possible causes of an adverse volume capacity variance. Again it is better to express this variance in terms of lost contribution from lost sales caused by a failure to utilize the capacity. It is not very meaningful to attach fixed costs to the variance, since the total fixed costs will not be affected by a failure to utilize capacity.

# Summary of fixed overhead variances

The volume efficiency variance is £6000 adverse, and the volume capacity variance is also £6000 adverse. When these two variances are added together, they agree with the fixed overhead volume variance of £12 000. Exhibit 18.5 summarizes how the volume variance is analysed according to capacity and efficiency.

The actual *output* was 3000 hours less than the budget, giving an adverse volume variance. The capacity variance indicates that one reason for failing to meet the budgeted output was that 1500 hours of *capacity* were not utilized. In addition, those 28 500 hours that were utilized only led to 27 000 hours of output. An inefficient use of 1500 hours capacity therefore provides a second explanation as to why the budgeted output was not achieved. A fixed overhead rate of £4 per hour is applied to the physical quantity of the variances, so that fixed overhead variances may be presented in monetary terms. Exhibit 18.6 summarizes the variances we have calculated in this section.

In Example 18.1 we have assumed that fixed overheads are allocated to products on a direct labour hour basis. In automated production departments fixed overheads ought to be allocated on the basis of machine hours. Where machine hours are used as an allocation base, output should be measured in standard machine hours and the fixed overhead variances calculated by replacing direct labour hours with machine hours.

We have noted that, with an absorption costing system, fixed overheads are allocated to products, and this process creates a fixed overhead volume variance. The volume

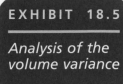

## EXHIBIT 18.5

*Analysis of the volume variance*

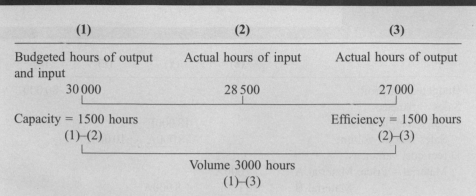

|  | (1) | (2) | (3) |
| --- | --- | --- | --- |
|  | Budgeted hours of output and input | Actual hours of input | Actual hours of output |
|  | 30 000 | 28 500 | 27 000 |

Capacity = 1500 hours
(1)–(2)

Efficiency = 1500 hours
(2)–(3)

Volume 3000 hours
(1)–(3)

## EXHIBIT 18.6

*Diagram of fixed overhead variances*

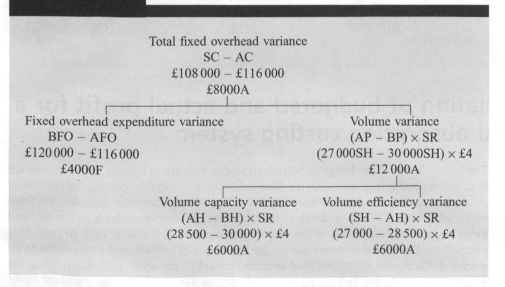

Total fixed overhead variance
SC − AC
£108 000 − £116 000
£8000A

Fixed overhead expenditure variance
BFO − AFO
£120 000 − £116 000
£4000F

Volume variance
(AP − BP) × SR
(27 000SH − 30 000SH) × £4
£12 000A

Volume capacity variance
(AH − BH) × SR
(28 500 − 30 000) × £4
£6000A

Volume efficiency variance
(SH − AH) × SR
(27 000 − 28 500) × £4
£6000A

variance is not particularly useful for cost control purposes, but we shall see in Chapter 19 that the variance is required to meet the profit measurement requirements of financial accounting. Traditionally, the volume variance is analysed further to ascertain the two sub-variances – the volume efficiency and capacity variance – but it is questionable whether these variances provide any meaningful information for control purposes.

Where inventories are valued on a variable costing system, fixed overheads are not allocated to products, and therefore a volume variance will not occur. However, a fixed overhead expenditure variance will arise with both variable and absorption costing systems. ●●●

**EXHIBIT 18.7**

*Reconciliation of budgeted*

| | (£) | (£) | (£) | (£) |
|---|---|---|---|---|
| Budgeted net profit | | | | 80 000 |
| Sales variances: | | | | |
| Sales margin price | | 18 000F | | |
| Sales margin volume | | 8 000A | 10 000F | |
| Direct cost variances: | | | | |
| Material – Price: Material A | 19 000A | | | |
| Material B | 10 100F | 8 900A | | |
| – Usage: Material A | 10 000A | | | |
| Material B | 16 500A | 26 500A | 35 400A | |
| Labour – Rate | | 17 100A | | |
| Efficiency | | 13 500A | 30 600A | |
| Manufacturing overhead variances: | | | | |
| Fixed – Expenditure | 4 000F | | | |
| Volume | 12 000A | 8 000A | | |
| Variable – Expenditure | 5 000F | | | |
| Efficiency | 3 000A | 2 000F | 6 000A | 62 000A |
| Actual profit | | | | 18 000 |

# Reconciliation of budgeted and actual profit for a standard absorption costing system

The reconciliation of the budgeted and actual profits is shown in Exhibit 18.7. You will see that the reconciliation statement is identical with the variable costing reconciliation statement, apart from the fact that the absorption costing statement includes the fixed overhead volume variance and values the sales margin volume variance at the standard profit margin per unit instead of the contribution per unit. If you refer back to page 681, you will see that the contribution margin for Sigma is £20 per unit sold whereas the profit margin per unit after deducting fixed overhead cost (£12 per unit) is £8. Multiplying the difference in budgeted and actual sales volumes of 1000 units by the standard profit margin gives a sales volume margin variance of £8000. Note that the sales margin price variance is identical for both systems.

# Performance reports

The managers of responsibility centres will require a more detailed analysis of the variances to enable them to exercise control, and detailed performance reports should be prepared at monthly or weekly intervals to bring to their attention any significant

**EXHIBIT 18.8**

*A typical departmental performance report*

## DEPARTMENTAL PERFORMANCE REPORT

| | | |
|---|---|---|
| Department............................. | Actual production | 27 000 standard hours |
| Period............. April 20XX ......... | Actual working hours | 28 500 hours |
| | Budgeted hours | 30 000 hours |

Control ratios: Efficiency 94.7%    Capacity 95%    Volume 90%

### DIRECT MATERIALS

| Type | Standard quantity | Actual quantity | Difference | Standard price | Usage variance | Reason |
|---|---|---|---|---|---|---|
| A | 18 000 kg | 19 000 | 1000 | £10.00 | £10 000A | |
| B | 9 000 kg | 10 100 | 1100 | £15.00 | £16 500A | |

### DIRECT LABOUR

| Grade | Standard hours | Actual hours | Difference | Standard cost | Actual cost | Total variance | Analysis Efficiency | Rate | Reason |
|---|---|---|---|---|---|---|---|---|---|
| | 27 000 | 28 500 | 1500 | £243 000 | £273 600 | £30 600 | £13 500A | £17 100A | |

### OVERHEADS

| | Allowed cost | Actual cost | Expenditure variance | Reason | | Variable overhead efficiency variance (hours) | (£) |
|---|---|---|---|---|---|---|---|
| Controllable costs (variable): | | | | | | | |
| Indirect labour | | | | | Difference | | |
| Power | | | | | between | 1500 | 3000A |
| Maintenance | | | | | standard | | |
| Indirect materials | | | | | hours and | | |
| | | | | | actual | | |
| | | | | | hours at £2 | | |
| | | | | | per hour | | |
| Total | £57 000 | £52 000 | £5000F | | | 1500 | 3000A |
| Uncontrollable costs (fixed): | | | | | | | |
| Lighting and heating | | | | | | | |
| Depreciation | | | | | | | |
| Supervision | | | | | | | |
| | £120 000 | 116 000 | 4000F | | | | |

| SUMMARY | Variances (£) | | Variances as a % of a standard cost | |
|---|---|---|---|---|
| | This month (£) | Cumulative (£) | This month (%) | Cumulative (%) |
| Direct materials usage | 26 500A | | | |
| Direct labour: | | | | |
| Efficiency | 13 500A | | | |
| Wage rate | 17 100A | | | |
| Controllable overheads: | | | | |
| Expenditure | 5 000F | | | |
| Variable overhead | 3 000A | | | |
| Total | 55 100A | | | |

Comments:

variances. A typical performance report based on the information contained in Example 18.1 is presented in Exhibit 18.8. A departmental performance report should include only those items that the responsibility manager can control or influence. The material price and wage rate variances and the monetary amount of the volume variance are *not* presented, since these are not considered to be within the control of the manager of the responsibility centre. However, the volume variance and the two sub-variances (capacity and efficiency) are restated in non-monetary terms in Exhibit 18.8. You can see that these variances have been replaced by the following three control ratios:

$$\text{production volume ratio} = \frac{\text{standard hours of actual output (27 000)}}{\text{budgeted hours of output (30 000)}} \times 100$$

$$= 90\%$$

$$\text{production efficiency ratio} = \frac{\text{standard hours of actual output (27 000)}}{\text{actual hours worked (28 500)}} \times 100$$

$$= 94.7\%$$

$$\text{capacity usage ratio} = \frac{\text{actual hours worked (28 500)}}{\text{budgeted hours of input (30 000)}} \times 100$$

$$= 95\%$$

You can interpret these ratios in the same way as was described for the equivalent monetary variances. The ratios merely represent the replacement of an *absolute* monetary measure with a *relative* performance measure.

A comparison of current variances with those of previous periods and/or with those of the year to date is presented in the summary of the performance report. This information is often useful in establishing a framework within which current variances can be evaluated.

In addition to weekly or monthly performance reports, the manager of a responsibility centre should receive daily reports on those variances that are controllable on a daily basis. This normally applies to material usage and labour efficiency. For these variances the weekly or monthly performance reports will provide a summary of the information that has previously been reported on a daily basis.

In addition to weekly or monthly performance reports, the manager of a responsibility centre should receive daily reports on those variances that are controllable on a daily basis. This normally applies to material usage and labour efficiency. For these variances the weekly or monthly performance reports will provide a summary of the information that has previously been reported on a daily basis.

## Self-Assessment Questions

You should attempt to answer these questions yourself before looking up the suggested answers, which appear on pages 1126–7. If any part of your answer is incorrect, check back carefully to make sure you understand where you went wrong.

1. BS Limited manufactures one standard product and operates a system of variance accounting using a fixed budget. As assistant management accountant, you are responsible for preparing the monthly operating statements. Data from the budget, the standard product cost and actual data for the month ended 31 October are given below.

   Using the data given, you are required to prepare the operating statement for the month ended 31 October to show the budgeted profit; the variances for direct materials, direct wages, overhead and sales, each analysed into causes; and actual profit.

   Budgeted and standard cost data:

   Budgeted sales and production for the month: 10 000 units
      Standard cost for each unit of product:
      Direct material:     X:     10 kg at £1 per kg
                     Y:     5 kg at £5 pe  kg
      Direct wages:           5 hours at £3 per hour
      Fixed production overhead is absorbed at 200% of direct wages
      Budgeted sales price has been calculated to give a profit of 20% of sales price

   Actual data for month ended 31 October:

   Production: 9500 units sold at a price of 10% higher than that budgeted
   Direct materials consumed:
      X:     96 000 kg at £1.20 per kg
      Y:     48 000 kg at £4.70 per kg
   Direct wages incurred 46 000 hours at £3.20 per hour
   Fixed production overhead incurred £290 000

   (30 marks)
   *CIMA Cost Accounting 2*

2. The following data relate to actual output, costs and variances for the four-weekly accounting period number 4 of a company that makes only one product. Opening and closing work in progress figures were the same.

| | **(£000)** |
| --- | --- |
| Actual production of product XY | 18 000 units |
| Actual costs incurred: | |
|   Direct materials purchased and used (150 000 kg) | 210 |
|   Direct wages for 32 000 hours | 136 |
|   Variable production overhead | 38 |

|  | **(£000)** |
|---|---|
| Variances: | |
| Direct materials price | 15 F |
| Direct materials usage | 9 A |
| Direct labour rate | 8 A |
| Direct labour efficiency | 16 F |
| Variable production overhead expenditure | 6 A |
| Variable production overhead efficiency | 4 F |

Variable production overhead varies with labour hours worked.
A standard marginal costing system is operated.

You are required to:

(a) present a standard product cost sheet for one unit of product XY,    (16 marks)
(b) describe briefly *three* types of standard that can be used for a standard costing system, stating which is usually preferred in practice and why.    (9 marks)
(Total 25 marks)
*CIMA Cost Accounting Stage 2*

## Summary

In this chapter we have explained the variance computations for a standard variable and a standard absorption costing system. With a standard variable costing system, fixed overheads are not allocated to products. Sales margin variances are therefore reported in terms of contribution margins and a single fixed overhead variance, that is, the fixed overhead expenditure variance is reported. With a standard absorption costing system, fixed overheads are allocated to products, and this process leads to the creation of a fixed overhead volume variance and the reporting of sales margin variances measured in terms of profit margins. The fixed overhead volume variance is not particularly helpful for cost control purposes, but this variance is required for financial accounting purposes.

To enable you to review your understanding of variance calculations, the formulae for the variances that we have considered in this chapter are summarized below. In each case the formula is arranged so that a positive variance is favourable and a negative variance unfavourable. The following variances are reported for both variable and absorption standard costing systems.

*Materials and labour*

1. Material price variance = (standard price per unit of material – actual price) × quantity of materials purchased

2. Material usage variance = (standard quantity of materials for actual production – actual quantity used) × standard price per unit

3. Total materials cost variance = (actual production × standard material cost per unit of production) – actual materials cost

4. Wage rate variance = (standard wage rate per hour – actual wage rate) × actual labour hours worked

5. Labour efficiency = (standard quantity of variance labour hours for actual production – actual labour hours) × standard wage rate

6. Total labour cost = (actual production × variance standard labour cost per unit of production) – actual labour cost

*Fixed production overhead*

7. Fixed overhead = budgeted fixed expenditure overheads – actual fixed overheads

*Variable production overhead*

8. Variable overhead = (budgeted variable expenditure overheads for actual variance input volume – actual variable overhead cost)

9. Variable overhead = (standard quantity of efficiency input hours for actual variance production – actual input hours) × variable overhead rate

10. Total variable = (actual production × overhead variance standard variable overhead rate per unit) – actual variable overhead cost

*Sales margins*

11. Sales margin = (actual unit price variance contribution margin* – standard unit contribution margin) × actual sales volume

(*Contribution margins are used with a variable standard costing system whereas profit margins are used with an absorption costing system. With both systems, actual margins are calculated by deducting *standard* costs from actual selling price.)

12. Sales margin = (actual sales volume – volume variance budgeted sales volume) × standard contribution margin

13. Total sales margin = total actual variance contribution – total budgeted contribution

*With a standard absorption costing system the following additional variances can be reported:*

14. Fixed overhead = (actual production – volume variance budgeted production) × standard fixed overhead rate

15. Volume efficiency = (standard quantity of variance input hours for actual production – actual input hours) × standard fixed overhead rate

16. Volume capacity = (actual hours of input variance – budgeted hours of input) × standard fixed overhead rate

17. Total fixed = (actual production × overhead variance standard fixed overhead rate per unit) – actual fixed overhead cost

## Key Terms and Concepts

## Key Examination Points

A common error that students make is to calculate variances based on the original fixed budget. Remember to flex the budget. Therefore the starting point when answering a standard costing question should be to calculate actual production. If more than one product is produced, output should be expressed in standard hours. If standard overhead rates are not given, you can calculate the rates by dividing budgeted fixed and variable overheads by the budgeted output. Remember that output can be measured by units produced or standard hours produced. Make sure you are consistent and use overhead rates per standard hours if production is measured in standard hours, or overhead rates per

unit produced if output is measured in terms of units produced. You should always express output in standard hours if the question requires the calculation of overhead efficiency variances.

Frequently questions are set that give you the variances but require calculations of actual costs and inputs (see Questions 18.26–18.30). Students who calculate variances simply by committing to memory a series of variance formulae experience difficulties in answering these questions. Make sure you understand how the variances are calculated, and check with the *Students' Manual* your answers to Questions 18.26, 18.28 and 18.30.

## Questions

*Indicates that a suggested solution is to be found in the *Students' Manual*.

### 18.1* Intermediate

During a period, 17 500 labour hours were worked at a standard cost of £6.50 per hour. The labour efficiency variance was £7800 favourable.

How many standard hours were produced?

|   |        |
|---|--------|
| A | 1 200  |
| B | 16 300 |
| C | 17 500 |
| D | 18 700 |

### 18.2* Intermediate

T plc uses a standard costing system, which is material stock account being maintained at standard costs. The following details have been extracted from the standard cost card in respect of direct materials:

8 kg at £0.80/kg = £6.40 per unit
Budgeted production in April was 850 units.

The following details relate to actual materials purchased and issued to production during April, when actual production was 870 units:

| Materials purchased | 8200 kg costing £6888 |
|---|---|
| Materials issued to production | 7150 kg |

Which of the following correctly states the material price and usage variance to be reported?

|   | Price | Usage |
|---|-------|-------|
| A | £286 (A) | £152 (A) |
| B | £286 (A) | £280 (A) |
| C | £286 (A) | £294 (A) |
| D | £328 (A) | £152 (A) |
| E | £328 (A) | £280 (A) |

*CIMA Stage 2*

## 18.3* Intermediate

PQ Limited operates a standard costing system for its only product. The standard cost card is as follows:

| | |
|---|---|
| Direct material (4 kg at £2/kg) | £8.00 |
| Direct labour (4 hours at £4/hour) | £16.00 |
| Variable overhead (4 hours at £3/hour) | £12.00 |
| Fixed overhead (4 hours at £5/hour) | £20.00 |

Fixed overheads are absorbed on the basis of labour hours. Fixed overhead costs are budgeted at £12 000 per annum, arising at a constant rate during the year.

Activity in period 3 is budgeted to be 10% of total activity for the year. Actual production during period 3 was 500 units, with actual fixed overhead costs incurred being £9800 and actual hours worked being 1970.

The fixed overhead expenditure variance for period 3 was:

| | |
|---|---|
| A | £2200 (F) |
| B | £200 (F) |
| C | £50 (F) |
| D | £200 (A) |
| E | £2200 (A) |

*CIMA Stage 2*

## 18.4* Intermediate

QR Limited uses a standard absorption costing system. The following details have been extracted from its budget for April:

| | |
|---|---|
| Fixed production overhead cost | £48 000 |
| Production (units) | 4 800 |

In April the fixed production overhead cost was under-absorbed by £8000 and the fixed production overhead expenditure variance was £2000 adverse.

The actual number of units produced was:

| | |
|---|---|
| A | 3800 |
| B | 4000 |
| C | 4200 |
| D | 5400 |
| E | 5800 |

*CIMA Stage 2*

## 18.5* Intermediate

F Limited has the following budget and actual data:

| | |
|---|---|
| Budget fixed overhead cost | £100 000 |
| Budget production (units) | 20 000 |
| Actual fixed overhead cost | £110 000 |
| Actual production (units) | 19 500 |

The fixed overhead volume variance:

| | |
|---|---|
| A | is £500 adverse; |
| B | is £2500 adverse; |
| C | is £10 000 adverse; |
| D | is £17 500 adverse; |
| E | cannot be calculated from the data given. |

*CIMA Stage 2 Specimen Paper*

## 18.6* Intermediate

J Limited operates a standard cost accounting system. The following information has been extracted from its standard cost card and budgets:

| | |
|---|---|
| Budgeted sales volume | 5000 units |
| Budgeted selling price | £10.00 per unit |
| Standard variable cost | £5.60 per unit |
| Standard total cost | £7.50 per unit |

If it used a standard marginal cost accounting system and its actual sales were 4500 units at a selling price of £12.00, its sales volume variance would be:

| | |
|---|---|
| A | £1250 adverse |
| B | £2200 adverse |
| C | £2250 adverse |
| D | £3200 adverse |
| E | £5000 adverse |

*CIMA Stage 2 Specimen Paper*

## 18.7* Intermediate

In a period, 11 280 kg of material were used at a total standard cost of £46 248. The material usage variance was £492 adverse.

What was the standard allowed weight of material for the period?

| | |
|---|---|
| A | 11 520 kg |
| B | 11 280 kg |
| C | 11 394 kg |
| D | 11 160 kg |

*CIMA Stage 1 Specimen Paper*

## 18.8* Intermediate

S plc has the following fixed overhead cost data for October:

| | |
|---|---|
| Budgeted cost | £100 000 |
| Actual cost | £101 400 |
| Budget output | 10 000 standard hours |
| Actual output | 9 000 standard hours |
| Actual efficiency | 96% |

The values of over-absorption/under-absorption caused by volume and expenditure effects are:

| | Volume | Expenditure |
|---|---|---|
| A | £7 650 under | £1 400 under |
| B | £7 650 under | £7 650 under |
| C | £10 000 under | £1 400 under |
| D | £10 000 under | £7 650 under |
| E | £10 000 under | £11 400 under |

*CIMA Stage 2*

## 18.9* Intermediate

The following information relates to R plc for October:

Bought 7800 kg of material R at a total cost of £16 380
Stocks of material R increased by 440 kg
Stocks of material R are valued using standard purchase price
Material price variance was £1170 adverse

The standard price per kg for material R is:

| | |
|---|---|
| A | £1.95 |
| B | £2.10 |
| C | £2.23 |
| D | £2.25 |
| E | £2.38 |

*CIMA Stage 2*

## 18.10* Intermediate

P Limited has the following data relating to its budgeted sales for October:

| | |
|---|---|
| Budgeted sales | £100 000 |
| Budgeted selling price per unit | £8.00 |
| Budgeted contribution per unit | £4.00 |
| Budgeted profit per unit | £2.50 |

During October actual sales were 11 000 units for a sales revenue of £99 000.

P Limited uses an absorption costing system.
The sales variances reported for October were:

| | Price | Volume |
|---|---|---|
| A | £11 000 F | £3 750 A |
| B | £11 000 F | £6 000 A |
| C | £11 000 A | £6 000 A |
| D | £12 500 F | £12 000 A |
| E | £12 500 A | £12 000 A |

*CIMA Stage 2*

## 18.11* Intermediate

The following details have been extracted from a standard cost card of X plc:

| | Product X |
|---|---|
| Direct labour: | 4 hours at £5.40 per hour |

During October the budgeted production was 5000 units of product X and the actual production was 4650 units of product X. Actual hours worked were 19 100 and the actual direct labour cost amounted to £98 350.

The labour variances reported were:

| | Rate | Efficiency |
|---|---|---|
| A | £9650 F | £4860 F |
| B | £9650 F | £2700 A |
| C | £4790 F | £2575 A |
| D | £4790 F | £4860 F |
| E | £4790 F | £2700 A |

*CIMA Stage 2*

## 18.12* Intermediate

In a period, 5792 units were made with a standard labour allowance of 6.5 hours per unit at £5 per hour. Actual wages were £6 per hour and there was an adverse efficiency variance of £36 000.

How many labour hours were actually worked?

| | |
|---|---|
| A | 30 448 |
| B | 31 648 |
| C | 43 648 |
| D | 44 848 |

*CIMA Stage 1*

## 18.13 Intermediate: Flexible budgets and computation of labour and material variances

(a) JB plc operates a standard marginal cost accounting system. Information relating to product J, which is made in one of the company departments, is given below:

| Product J | Standard marginal product cost Unit (£) |
|---|---|
| Direct material | |
| 6 kilograms at £4 per kg | 24 |
| Direct labour | |
| 1 hour at £7 per hour | 7 |
| Variable production overhead[a] | 3 |
| | 34 |

[a]Variable production overhead varies with units produced

Budgeted fixed production overhead, per month: £100 000.

Budgeted production for product J: 20 000 units per month.

Actual production and costs for *month 6* were as follows:

| Units of J produced | 18 500 |
|---|---|
| | (£) |
| Direct materials purchased and used: 113 500 kg | 442 650 |
| Direct labour: 17 800 hours | 129 940 |
| Variable production overhead incurred | 58 800 |
| Fixed production overhead incurred | 104 000 |
| | 735 390 |

You are required to:

(i) prepare a columnar statement showing, by element of cost, the:
   (i) original budget;
   (ii) flexed budget;
   (iii) actual;
   (iv) total variances; (9 marks)

(ii) subdivide the variances for direct material and direct labour shown in your answer to (a) (i)–(iv) above to be more informative for managerial purposes. (4 marks)

(b) Explain the meaning and use of a 'rolling forecast'. (2 marks)

(Total 15 marks)
*CIMA State 2 Cost Accounting*

## 18.14* Intermediate: Computation of labour and material variances for a hotel

You work as the assistant to the management accountant for a major hotel chain, Stately Hotels plc. The new manager of one of the largest hotels in the chain, the Regent Hotel, is experimenting with the use of standard costing to plan and control the costs of preparing and cleaning the hotel bedrooms.

Two of the costs involved in this activity are cleaning labour and the supply of presentation soap packs.

*Cleaning labour:*
Part-time staff are employed to clean and prepare the bedrooms for customers. The employees are paid for the number of hours that they work, which fluctuates on a daily basis depending on how many rooms need to be prepared each day.

The employees are paid a standard hourly rate for weekday work and a higher hourly rate at the weekend. The standard cost control system is based on an average of these two rates, at £3.60 per hour.

The standard time allowed for cleaning and preparing a bedroom is fifteen minutes.

*Presentation soap packs:*
A presentation soap pack is left in each room every night. The packs contain soap, bubble bath, shower gel, hand lotion etc. Most customers use the packs or take them home with them, but many do not. The standard usage of packs used for planning and control purposes is one pack per room night.

The packs are purchased from a number of different suppliers and the standard price is £1.20 per pack. Stocks of packs are valued in the accounts at standard price.

*Actual results for May:*
During May 8400 rooms were cleaned and prepared. The following data were recorded for cleaning labour and soap packs.

Cleaning labour paid for:
| Weekday labour | 1850 hours at £3 per hour |
|---|---|
| Weekend labour | 700 hours at £4.50 per hour |
| | 2550 |

Presentation soap packs purchased and used:

> 6530 packs at £1.20 each
> 920 packs at £1.30 each
> 1130 packs at £1.40 each
> 8580

*Task*

(a) Using the data above, calculate the following cost variances for May:
  (i) soap pack price;
  (ii) soap pack usage;
  (iii) cleaning labour rate;
  (iv) cleaning labour utilization or efficiency.
(b) Suggest one possible cause for each of the variances which you have calculated, and outline any management action which may be necessary.

*AAT Technicians Stage*

### 18.15* Intermediate: Computation of labour and material variances and reconciliation statements

Malton Ltd operates a standard marginal costing system. As the recently appointed management accountant to Malton's Eastern division, you have responsibility for the preparation of that division's monthly cost reports. The standard cost report uses variances to reconcile the actual marginal cost of production to its standard cost.

The Eastern division is managed by Richard Hill. The division only makes one product, the Beta. Budgeted Beta production for May was 8000 units, although actual production was 9500 units.

In order to prepare the standard cost report for May, you have asked a member of your staff to obtain standard and actual cost details for the month of May. This information is reproduced below:

| | Unit standard cost | | | Actual details for May | | |
|---|---|---|---|---|---|---|
| | Quantity | Unit price | Cost per Beta (£) | | Quantity | Total cost (£) |
| Material | 8 litres | £20 | 160 | Material | 78 000 litres | 1 599 000 |
| Labour | 4 hours | £6 | 24 | Labour | 39 000 hours | 249 600 |
| | | | 184 | | | 1 848 600 |

*Task 1*

(a) Calculate the following:
  (i) the material price variance;
  (ii) the material usage variance;
  (iii) the labour rate variance;

  (iv) the labour efficiency variance (sometimes called the utilization variance);
(b) Prepare a standard costing statement reconciling the actual marginal cost of production with the standard marginal cost of production.

After Richard Hill has received your standard costing statement, you visit him to discuss the variances and their implications. Richard, however, raises a number of queries with you. He makes the following points:

- An index measuring material prices stood at 247.2 for May but at 240.0 when the standard for the material price was set.
- The Eastern division is budgeted to run at its normal capacity of 8000 units of production per month, but during May it had to manufacture an additional 1500 Betas to meet a special order agreed at short notice by Melton's sales director.
- Because of the short notice, the normal supplier of the raw material was unable to meet the extra demand and so additional materials had to be acquired from another supplier at a price per litre of £22.
- This extra material was not up to the normal specification, resulting in 20% of the special purchase being scrapped *prior* to being issued to production.
- The work force could only produce the special order on time by working overtime on the 1500 Betas at a 50% premium.

*Task 2*

(a) Calculate the amounts within the material price variance, the material usage variance and the labour rate variance which arise from producing the special order.
(b) (i) Estimate the revised standard price for materials based on the change in the material price index.
  (ii) For the 8000 units of normal production, use your answer in (b) (i) to estimate how much of the price variance calculated in Task 1 is caused by the general change in prices.
(c) Using your answers to parts (a) and (b) of this task, prepare a revised standard costing statement. The revised statement should subdivide the variances prepared in Task 1 into those elements controllable by Richard Hill and those elements caused by factors outside his divisional control.

(d) Write a *brief* note to Richard Hill justifying your treatment of the elements you believe are outside his control and suggesting what action should be taken by the company.

*AAT Technicians Stage*

## 18.16* Intermediate: Reconciliation of actual and budgeted profit (including overhead variances)

A local restaurant has been examining the profitability of its set menu. At the beginning of the year the selling price was based on the following predicted costs:

|  |  | (£) |
|---|---|---|
| Starter | Soup of the day | |
|  | 100 grams of mushrooms @ £3.00 per kg | 0.30 |
|  | Cream and other ingredients | 0.20 |
| Main course | Roast beef | |
|  | Beef 0.10 kgs @ £15.00 per kg | 1.50 |
|  | Potatoes 0.2 kgs @ £0.25 per kg | 0.05 |
|  | Vegetables 0.3 kgs @ £0.90 per kg | 0.27 |
|  | Other ingredients and accompaniments | 0.23 |
| Dessert | Fresh tropical fruit salad | |
|  | Fresh fruit 0.15 kgs @ £3.00 per kg | 0.45 |

The selling price was set at £7.50, which produced an overall gross profit of 60%.

During October the number of set menus sold was 860 instead of the 750 budgeted: this increase was achieved by reducing the selling price to £7.00. During the same period an analysis of the direct costs incurred showed:

|  | (£) |
|---|---|
| 90 kgs of mushrooms | 300 |
| Cream and other ingredients | 160 |
| 70 kgs of beef | 1148 |
| 180 kgs of potatoes | 40 |
| 270 kgs of vegetables | 250 |
| Other ingredients and accompaniments | 200 |
| 140 kgs of fresh fruit | 450 |

There was no stock of ingredients at the beginning or end of the month.

Requirements:
(a) Calculate the budgeted profit for the month of October. (2 marks)
(b) Calculate the actual profit for the month of October. (3 marks)
(c) Prepare a statement which reconciles your answers to (a) and (b) above, showing the variances in as much detail as possible. (14 marks)
(d) Prepare a report, addressed to the restaurant manager, which identifies the two most significant variances, and comments on their possible causes. (6 marks)

(Total 25 marks)

*CIMA State 2 Operational Cost Accounting*

## 18.17 Intermediate: Reconciliation of standard and actual cost for a variable costing system

*Data*

You are employed as the assistant management accountant in the group accountant's office of Hampstead plc. Hampstead recently acquired Finchley Ltd, a small company making a specialist product called the Alpha. Standard marginal costing is used by all the companies within the group and, from 1 August, Finchley Ltd will also be required to use standard marginal costing in its management reports. Part of your job is to manage the implementation of standard marginal costing at Finchley Ltd.

John Wade, the managing director of Finchley, is not clear how the change will help him as a manager. He has always found Finchley's existing absorption costing system sufficient. By way of example, he shows you a summary of its management accounts for the three months to 31 May. These are reproduced below.

**Statement of budgeted and actual cost of Alpha Production – 3 months ended 31 May**

| Alpha production (units) | Actual 10 000 | | Budget 12 000 | | Variance |
|---|---|---|---|---|---|
|  | Inputs | (£) | Inputs | (£) | (£) |
| Materials | 32 000 metres | 377 600 | 36 000 metres | 432 000 | 54 400 |
| Labour | 70 000 hours | 422 800 | 72 000 hours | 450 000 | 27 200 |
| Fixed overhead absorbed | | 330 000 | | 396 000 | 66 000 |
| Fixed overhead unabsorbed | | 75 000 | | 0 | (75 000) |
| | | 1 205 400 | | 1 278 000 | 72 600 |

John Wade is not convinced that standard marginal costing will help him to manage Finchley. 'My current system tells me all I need to know,' he said. 'As you can see, we are £72 600 below budget which is really excellent given that we lost production as a result of a serious machine breakdown.'

To help John Wade understand the benefits of standard marginal costing, you agree to prepare a statement for the three months ended 31 May reconciling the standard cost of production to the actual cost of production.

### Task 1

(a) Use the budget data to determine:
   (i) the standard marginal cost per Alpha; and
   (ii) the standard cost of actual Alpha production for the three months to 31 May.
(b) Calculate the following variances:
   (i) material price variance;
   (ii) material usage variance;
   (iii) labour rate variance;
   (iv) labour efficiency variance;
   (v) fixed overhead expenditure variance.
(c) Write a *short* memo to John Wade. Your memo should:
   (i) include a statement reconciling the actual cost of production to the standard cost of production;
   (ii) give *two* reasons why your variances might differ from those in his original management accounting statement despite using the same basic data;
   (iii) *briefly* discuss *one* further reason why your reconciliation statement provides improved management information.

### Data

On receiving your memo, John Wade informs you that:
- the machine breakdown resulted in the workforce having to be paid for 12 000 hours even though no production took place;
- an index of material prices stood at 466.70 when the budget was prepared but at 420.03 when the material was purchased.

### Task 2

Using this new information, prepare a revised statement reconciling the standard cost of production to the actual cost of production. Your statement should subdivide:

- both the labour variances into those parts arising from the machine breakdown and

those parts arising from normal production; and
- the material price variance into that part due to the change in the index and that part arising for other reasons.

### Data

Barnet Ltd is another small company owned by Hampstead plc. Barnet operates a job costing system making a specialist, expensive piece of hospital equipment.

### Existing system

Currently, employees are assigned to individual jobs and materials are requisitioned from stores as needed. The standard and actual costs of labour and material are recorded for each job. These job costs are totalled to produce the marginal cost of production. Fixed production costs – including the cost of storekeeping and inspection of deliveries and finished equipment – are then added to determine the standard and actual cost of production. Any costs of remedial work are included in the materials and labour for each job.

### Proposed system

Carol Johnson, the chief executive of Barnet, has recently been to a seminar on modern manufacturing techniques. As a result, she is considering introducing Just-in-Time stock deliveries and Total Quality Management. Barnet would offer suppliers a long-term contract at a fixed price but suppliers would have to guarantee the quality of their materials.

In addition, she proposes that the workforce is organised as a single team with flexible work practices. This would mean employees helping each other as necessary, with no employee being allocated a particular job. If a job was delayed, the workforce would work overtime without payment in order for the job to be completed on time. In exchange, employees would be guaranteed a fixed weekly wage and time off when production was slack to make up for any overtime incurred.

### Cost of quality

Carol has asked to meet you to discuss the implications of her proposals on the existing accounting system. She is particularly concerned to monitor the *cost of quality*. This is defined as the total of all costs incurred in preventing defects plus those costs involved in remedying defects once they have occurred. It is a single figure measuring all the explicit costs of quality – that is, those costs collected within the accounting system.

*Task 3*

In preparation for the meeting, produce *brief* notes. Your notes should:

(a) identify *four* general headings (or classifications) which make up the *cost of quality*;

(b) give *one* example of a type of cost likely to be found within each category;

(c) assuming Carol Johnson's proposals are accepted, state, with reasons, whether or not:
   (i) a standard marginal costing system would still be of help to the managers;
   (ii) it would still be meaningful to collect costs by each individual job;

(d) identify *one* cost saving in Carol Johnson's proposals which would not be recorded in the existing costing system.

*AAT Technicians Stage*

### 18.18* Intermediate: Variance analysis and reconciliation of budgeted and actual profit

The Perseus Co. Ltd, a medium-sized company, produces a single produce in its one overseas factory. For control purposes, a standard costing system was recently introduced and is now in operation.

The standards set for the month of May were as follows:

| | |
|---|---|
| Production and sales | 16 000 units |
| Selling price (per unit) | £140 |
| Materials | |
| Material 007 | 6 kilos per unit at £12.25 per kilo |
| Material XL90 | 3 kilos per unit at £3.20 per kilo |
| Labour | 4.5 hours per unit at £8.40 per hour |

Overheads (all fixed) at £86 400 per month are not absorbed into the product costs.

The actual data for the month of May, are as follows:

Produced 15 400 units, which were sold at £138.25 each.

Materials

Used 98 560 kilos of material 007 at a total cost of £1 256 640

Used 42 350 kilos of material XL90 at a total cost of £132 979

Labour

Paid an actual rate of £8.65 per hour to the labour force. The total amount paid out amounted to £612 766

Overheads (all fixed) £96 840

Required:

(a) Prepare a standard costing profit statement, and a profit statement based on actual figures for the month of May. (6 marks)

(b) Prepare a statement of the variances which reconcile the actual with the standard profit or loss figure. (9 marks)

(c) Explain briefly the possible reasons for inter-relationships between material variances and labour variances. (5 marks)

(Total 20 marks)

*ACCA Paper 8 Management Finance*

### 18.19 Intermediate: Calculation of labour, material and overhead variances and reconciliation of budgeted and actual profit

You are the management accountant of T plc. The following computer printout shows details relating to April:

| | Actual | Budget |
|---|---|---|
| Sales volume | 4900 units | 5000 units |
| Selling price per unit | £11.00 | £10.00 |
| Production volume | 5400 units | 5000 units |
| Direct materials | | |
| kgs | 10 600 | 10 000 |
| price per kg | £0.60 | £0.50 |
| Direct labour | | |
| hours per unit | 0.55 | 0.50 |
| rate per hour | £3.80 | £4.00 |
| Fixed overhead: | | |
| Production | £10 300 | £10 000 |
| Administration | £3 100 | £3 000 |

T plc uses a standard absorption costing system.

There was no opening or closing work-in-progress.

Requirements:

(a) Prepare a statement which reconciles the budgeted profit with the actual profit for April, showing individual variances in as much detail as the above data permit
(20 marks)

(b) Explain briefly the possible causes of
   (i) the material usage variance;
   (ii) the labour rate variance; and

(iii) the sales volume profit variance.

(6 marks)

(c) Explain the meaning and relevance of inter-dependence of variances when reporting to managers. (4 marks)

(Total 30 marks)

*CIMA Stage 2 Operational Cost Accounting*

### 18.20 Intermediate: Computation of fixed overhead variances

A manufacturing company has provided you with the following data, which relate to component RYX for the period which has just ended:

| | Budget | Actual |
|---|---|---|
| Number of labour hours | 8 400 | 7 980 |
| Production units | 1 200 | 1 100 |
| Overhead cost (all fixed) | £22 260 | £25 536 |

Overheads are absorbed at a rate per standard labour hour.

Required:

(a) (i) Calculate the fixed production overhead cost variance and the following subsidiary variances:

   expenditure
   efficiency
   capacity

(ii) Provide a summary statement of these four variances. (7 marks)

(b) Briefly discuss the possible reasons why adverse fixed production overhead expenditure, efficiency and capacity variances occur. (10 marks)

(c) Briefly discuss two examples of interrelationships between the fixed production overhead efficiency variances and the material and labour variances. (3 marks)

(Total 20 marks)

*ACCA Paper 8 Managerial Finance*

### 18.21 Intermediate: Labour and overhead variances and export wage rate analysis

*Data*

The Eastern Division of Countryside Communications plc assembles a single product, the Beta. The Eastern Division has a fixed price contract with the supplier of the materials used in the Beta. The contract also specifies that the materials should be free of any faults. Because of these clauses in the contract, the Eastern Division has no material variances when reporting any differences between standard and actual production.

You have recently accepted the position of assistant management accountant in the Eastern Division. One of your tasks is to report variances in production costs on a four-weekly basis. Fixed overheads are absorbed on the basis of standard labour hours. A colleague provides you with the following data:

**Standard costs and budgeted production – four weeks ended 27 November**

| | Quantity | Unit price | Standard cost per Beta |
|---|---|---|---|
| Material | 30 metres | £12.00 | £360.00 |
| Labour | 10 hours | £5.25 | £52.50 |
| Fixed overhead | 10 hours | £15.75 | £157.50 |
| Standard cost per Beta | | | £570.00 |
| Budgeted production | 1200 Betas | £570.00 | £684 000 |

**Actual production – four weeks ended 27 November**

| | Quantity | Total cost |
|---|---|---|
| Actual cost of material | 31 200 metres | £374 400 |
| Actual cost of labour | 11 440 hours | £59 488 |
| Actual fixed cost overheads | | £207 000 |
| Actual cost of actual production | | £640 888 |
| Actual production | 1040 Betas | |

*Task 1*

(a) Calculate the following variances:

   (i) the labour rate variance;
   (ii) the labour efficiency variance (sometimes called the utilisation variance);
   (iii) the fixed overhead expenditure variance (sometimes known as the price variance);
   (iv) the fixed overhead volume variance;
   (v) the fixed overhead capacity variance;
   (vi) the fixed overhead efficiency variance (sometimes known as the usage variance).

(b) Prepare a statement reconciling the standard cost of actual production with the actual cost of actual production.

*Data*

When the Eastern Division's budget for the four weeks ended 27 November was originally prepared, a national index of labour rates stood at 102.00. In preparing the budget, Eastern Division had allowed for a 5% increase in labour rates. For the actual four weeks ended 27 November, the index stood at 104.04.

Because of this, Ann Green, Eastern Division's production director, is having difficulty understanding the meaning of the labour rate variance calculated in task 1.

*Task 2*

Write a memo to Ann Green. Your memo should:
(a) identify the original labour rate before allowing for the 5% increase;
(b) calculate the revised standard hourly rate using the index of 104.04;
(c) subdivide the labour rate variance calculated in task 1(a) into that part due to the change in the index and that part arising for other reasons;
(d) *briefly* interpret the possible meaning of these two subdivisions of the labour rate variance;
(e) give *two* reasons why the index of labour rates might not be valid in explaining part of the labour rate variance;
(f) *briefly* explain the meaning of the following variances calculated in task 1 and for *each* variance suggest *one* reason why it may have occurred;
  (i) the fixed overhead expenditure (or price) variance;
  (ii) the fixed overhead capacity variance;
  (iii) the fixed overhead efficiency (or usage) variance.

*AAT Technicians Stage*

## 18.22 Intermediate: Discussion and calculation of overhead variances

(a) Explain fully how the variances between actual and standard production overhead costs may be analysed, where overhead absorption is based upon separate direct labour hour rates for variable and fixed overheads. (12 marks)
(b) Calculate fixed production overhead variances in as much detail as possible, in the following situation:

| | Budget | Actual |
|---|---|---|
| Fixed overhead (£) | 246 000 | 259 000 |
| Direct labour (hours) | 123 000 | 141 000 |
| Output (units) | 615 000 | (see below) |

The company operates a process costing system. At the beginning of the period 42 000 half completed units were in stock. During the period 680 000 units were completed and 50 000 half completed units remained in stock at the end of the period.

(13 marks)
(Total 25 marks)
*ACCA Level 1 Costing*

## 18.23* Intermediate: Calculation of labour, material and overhead variances

The summary production budget of a factory with a single product for a four week period is as follows:

| | |
|---|---|
| Production quantity | 240 000 units |
| Production costs: | |
| Material: | 336 000 kg at £4.10 per kg |
| Direct labour: | 216 000 hours at £4.50 per hour |
| Variable overheads: | £475 200 |
| Fixed overheads: | £1 521 600 |

Variable overheads are absorbed at a predetermined direct labour hour rate. Fixed overheads are absorbed at a predetermined rate per unit of output.

During the four week period the actual production was 220 000 units which incurred the following costs:

Material: 313 060 kg costing £1 245 980
Direct labour: 194 920 hours costing £886 886
Variable overheads: £433 700
Fixed overheads: £1 501 240

Required:
(a) Calculate the cost variances for the period.
(12 marks)
(b) Give reasons in each case why the direct labour efficiency, variable overhead efficiency and fixed overhead volume variances may have arisen. (8 marks)
(Total 20 marks)
*ACCA Level 1*
*Cost and Management Accounting 1*

## 18.24* Intermediate: Computation of variable overhead variances

The following details have been extracted from the standard cost card for product X:

|  | (£/unit) |
| --- | --- |
| Variable overhead | |
| 4 machine hours at £8.00/hour | 32.00 |
| 2 labour hours at £4.00/hour | 8.00 |
| Fixed overhead | 20.00 |

During October 5450 units of the product were made compared to a budgeted production target of 5500 units. The actual overhead costs incurred were:

| | |
| --- | --- |
| Machine-related variable overhead | £176 000 |
| Labour-related variable overhead | £42 000 |
| Fixed overhead | £109 000 |

The actual number of machine hours was 22 000 and the actual number of labour hours was 10 800.

Required:
(a) Calculate the overhead cost variances in as much detail as possible from the data provided. (12 marks)
(b) Explain the meaning of, and give possible causes for, the variable overhead variances which you have calculated. (8 marks)
(c) Explain the benefits of using multiple activity bases for variable overhead absorption.
(5 marks)
(Total 25 marks)
*CIMA Stage 2 Operational Cost Accounting*

## 18.25* Intermediate: Variance analysis and reconciliation of standard with actual cost

SK Limited makes and sells a single product 'Jay' for which the standard cost is as follows:

| | | £ per unit |
| --- | --- | --- |
| Direct materials | 4 kilograms at £12.00 per kg | 48.00 |
| Direct labour | 5 hours at £7.00 per hour | 35.00 |
| Variable production overhead | 5 hours at £2.00 per hour | 10.00 |
| Fixed production overhead | 5 hours at £10.00 per hour | 50.00 |
| | | 143.00 |

The variable production overhead is deemed to vary with the hours worked.

Overhead is absorbed into production on the basis of standard hours of production and the normal volume of production for the period just ended was 20 000 units (100 000 standard hours of production).

For the period under consideration, the actual results were:

| Production of 'Jay' | 18 000 units (£) |
| --- | --- |
| Direct material used – 76 000 kgs at a cost of | 836 000 |
| Direct labour cost incurred – for 84 000 hours worked | 604 800 |
| Variable production overhead incurred | 172 000 |
| Fixed production overhead incurred | 1 030 000 |

You are required
(a) to calculate and show, by element of cost, the standard cost for the output for the period;
(2 marks)
(b) to calculate and list the relevant variances in a way which reconciles the standard cost with the actual cost (*Note*: Fixed production overhead sub-variances of capacity and volume efficiency (productivity) are *not* required).
(9 marks)
(c) to comment briefly on the usefulness to management of statements such as that given in your answer to (b) above. (4 marks)
(Total 15 marks)
*CIMA Stage 2 Cost Accounting*

## 18.26* Intermediate: Material price and usage variances and calculation of material price and usage working backwards from variances

AB Ltd manufactures a range of products. One of the products, Product M, requires the use of materials X and Y. Standard material costs for the manufacture of an item of product M in period 1 included:

Material X: 9 kilos at 1.20 per kilo

Total purchases of material X in period 1, for use in all products, were 142 000 kilos, costing £171 820. 16 270 kilos were used in the period in the manufacture of 1790 units of product M.

In period 2 the standard price of material X was increased by 6%, whilst the standard usage of the material in product M was left unchanged. 147 400 kilos of material X were purchased in period 2 at a favourable price variance of £1031.80. A favourable usage variance of 0.5% of standard occurred on material X in the manufacture of product M in the period.

Required:
(a)  Calculate:
   (i)   the total price variance on purchases of material X in period 1;        (2 marks)
   (ii)  the material X usage variance arising from the manufacture of product M in period 1;        (3 marks)
   (iii) the actual cost inflation of material X from period 1 to period 2 (calculate as a percentage increase to one decimal place);        (5 marks)
   (iv)  the percentage change in actual usage of material X per unit of product M from period 1 to period 2 (calculate to one decimal place).        (5 marks)
(b)  Describe, and contrast, the different types of standards that may be set for raw material usage and labour efficiency.
                                    (10 marks)
                              (Total 25 marks)
   *ACCA Cost and Management Accounting 1*

### 18.27 Intermediate: Calculation of actual input data working back from variances

The following profit reconciliation statement has been prepared by the management accountant of ABC Limited for March:

|  | | (£) |
|---|---|---|
| Budgeted profit | | 30 000 |
| Sales volume profit variance | | 5 250A |
| Selling price variance | | 6 375F |
| | | 31 125 |

| Cost variances: | A | F |
|---|---|---|
| | (£) | (£) |
| Material: | | |
| price | 1 985 | |
| usage | | 400 |
| Labour: | | |
| rate | | 9 800 |
| efficiency | 4 000 | |

| Variable overhead: | | |
|---|---|---|
| expenditure | | 1 000 |
| efficiency | 1 500 | |
| Fixed overhead: | | |
| expenditure | | 500 |
| volume | 24 500 | |
| | 31 985 | 11 700 |

|  |  |
|---|---|
| | 20 285A |
| Actual profit | 10 840 |

The standard cost card for the company's only product is as follows:

|  |  | (£) |
|---|---|---|
| Materials | 5 litres at £0.20 | 1.00 |
| Labour | 4 hours at £4.00 | 16.00 |
| Variable overhead | 4 hours at £1.50 | 6.00 |
| Fixed overhead | 4 hours at £3.50 | 14.00 |
| | | 37.00 |
| Standard profit | | 3.00 |
| Standard selling price | | 40.00 |

The following information is also available:
1.  There was no change in the level of finished goods stock during the month.
2.  Budgeted production and sales volumes for March were equal.
3.  Stocks of materials, which are valued at standard price, decreased by 800 litres during the month.
4.  The actual labour rate was £0.28 lower than the standard hourly rate.

Required:
(a)  Calculate the following:
   (i)   the actual production/sales volume;
                                    (4 marks)
   (ii)  the actual number of hours worked;
                                    (4 marks)
   (iii) the actual quantity of materials purchased;        (4 marks)
   (iv)  the actual variable overhead cost incurred;        (2 marks)
   (v)   the actual fixed overhead cost incurred.
                                    (2 marks)
(b)  ABC Limited uses a standard costing system whereas other organizations use a system of budgetary control. Explain the reasons why a system of budgetary control is often preferred to the use of standard costing in non-manufacturing environments.        (9 marks)
                              (Total 25 marks)

*CIMA Stage 2 Operational Cost Accounting*

## 18.28* Intermediate: Calculation of actual quantities working backwards from variances

The following profit reconciliation statement summarizes the performance of one of SEW's products for March.

|  | (£) |
|---|---|
| Budgeted profit | 4250 |
| Sales volume variance | 850A |
| Standard profit on actual sales | 3400 |
| Selling price variance | 4000A |
|  | (600) |

| Cost variances: | Adverse | Favourable |
|---|---|---|
|  | (£) | (£) |
| Direct material price |  | 1000 |
| Direct material usage | 150 |  |
| Direct labour rate | 200 |  |
| Direct labour efficiency | 150 |  |
| Variable overhead expenditure | 600 |  |
| Variable overhead efficiency | 75 |  |
| Fixed overhead efficiency | 2500 |  |
| Fixed overhead volume |  | 150 |
| Actual profit | 1175 | 3650 | 2475F |
|  |  |  | 1875 |

The budget for the same period contained the following data:

| Sales volume | 1500 units |
|---|---|
| Sales revenue | £20 000 |
| Production volume | 1500 units |
| Direct materials purchased | 750 kg |
| Direct materials used | 750 kg |
| Direct material cost | £4 500 |
| Direct labour hours | 1125 |
| Direct labour cost | £4 500 |
| Variable overhead cost | £2 250 |
| Fixed overhead cost | £4 500 |

Additional information:
- Stocks of raw materials and finished goods are valued at standard cost.
- During the month the actual number of units produced was 1550.

- The actual sales revenue was £12 000.
- The direct materials purchased were 1000 kg.

Required:
(a) Calculate
   (i)   the actual sales volume;
   (ii)  the actual quantity of materials used;
   (iii) the actual direct material cost;
   (iv)  the actual direct labour hours;
   (v)   the actual direct labour cost;
   (vi)  the actual variable overhead cost;
   (vii) the actual fixed overhead cost.
                                    (19 marks)
(b) Explain the possible causes of the direct materials usage variance, direct labour rate variance and sales volume variance.
                                    (6 marks)
                              (Total 25 marks)
*CIMA Operational Cost Accounting Stage 2*

## 18.29 Intermediate: Calculation of inputs working backwards from variances

The following data have been collected for the month of April by a company which operates a standard absorption costing system:

| Actual production of product EM | 600 units |
|---|---|
| Actual costs incurred: | (£) |
| Direct material E   660 metres | 6 270 |
| Direct material M  200 metres | 650 |
| Direct wages      3200 hours | 23 200 |
| Variable production overhead (which varied with hours worked) | 6 720 |
| Fixed production overhead | 27 000 |
| Variances | (£) |
| Direct material price: |  |
| Material E | 330 F |
| Material M | 50 A |
| Direct material usage: |  |
| Material E | 600 A |
| Material M | nil |
| Direct labour rate | 800 A |
| Direct labour efficiency | 1400 A |
| Variable production overhead: |  |
| expenditure | 320 A |
| efficiency | 400 A |
| Fixed production overhead: |  |
| expenditure | 500 F |
| volume | 2500 F |

Opening and closing work in progress figures were identical, so can be ignored.

You are required to:

(a) prepare for the month of April a statement of total standard costs for product EM; (3 marks)

(b) prepare a standard product cost sheet for one unit of product EM; (7 marks)

(c) calculate the number of units of product EM which were budgeted for April; (2 marks)

(d) state how the material and labour cost standards for product EM would originally have been determined. (3 marks)

(Total 15 marks)

*CIMA Stage 2 Cost Accounting*

## 18.30* Intermediate: Calculation of labour variances and actual material inputs working backwards from variances

A company manufactures two components in one of its factories. Material A is one of several materials used in the manufacture of both components.

The standard direct labour hours per unit of production and budgeted production quantities for a 13 week period were:

| | Standard direct labour hours | Budgeted production quantities |
|---|---|---|
| Component X | 0.40 hours | 36 000 units |
| Component Y | 0.56 hours | 22 000 units |

The standard wage rate for all direct workers was £5.00 per hour. Throughout the 13-week period 53 direct workers were employed, working a standard 40-hour week.

The following actual information for the 13-week period is available:

Production:
Component X, 35 000 units
Component Y, 25 000 units
Direct wages paid, £138 500
Material A purchases, 47 000 kilos costing £85 110
Material A price variance, £430 F
Material A usage (component X), 33 426 kilos
Material A usage variance (component X), £320.32 A

Required:

(a) Calculate the direct labour variances for the period; (5 marks)

(b) Calculate the standard purchase price for material A for the period and the standard usage of material A per unit of production of component X. (8 marks)

(c) Describe the steps, and information, required to establish the material purchase quantity budget for material A for a period. (7 marks)

(Total 20 marks)

*ACCA Cost and Management Accounting 1*

## 18.31* Intermediate: Comparison of absorption and marginal costing variances

You have been provided with the following data for S plc for September:

| Accounting method: Variances: | Absorption (£) | Marginal (£) |
|---|---|---|
| Selling price | 1900 (A) | 1900 (A) |
| Sales volume | 4500 (A) | 7500 (A) |
| Fixed overhead expenditure | 2500 (F) | 2500 (F) |
| Fixed overhead volume | 1800 (A) | n/a |

During September production and sales volumes were as follows:

| | Sales | Production |
|---|---|---|
| Budget | 10 000 | 10 000 |
| Actual | 9 500 | 9 700 |

Required:

(a) Calculate:
(i) the standard contribution per unit;
(ii) the standard profit per unit;
(iii) the actual fixed overhead cost total. (9 marks)

(b) Using the information presented above, explain why different variances are calculated depending upon the choice of marginal or absorption costing. (8 marks)

(c) Explain the meaning of the fixed overhead volume variance and its usefulness to management. (5 marks)

(d) Fixed overhead absorption rates are often calculated using a single measure of activity. It is suggested that fixed overhead costs should be attributed to cost units using multiple measures of activity (activity-based costing).

Explain 'activity-based costing' and how it may provide useful information to managers.

(Your answer should refer to both the setting of cost driver rates and subsequent overhead cost control.) (8 marks)

(Total 30 marks)

*CIMA Operational Cost Accounting Stage 2*

### 18.32* Intermediate: Calculation of production ratios

NAB Limited has produced the following figures relating to production for the week ended 21 May:

| | Production (in units) | |
| | Budgeted | Actual |
| --- | --- | --- |
| Product A | 400 | 400 |
| Product B | 400 | 300 |
| Product C | 100 | 140 |

Standard production times were:

| | Standard hours per unit |
| --- | --- |
| Product A | 5.0 |
| Product B | 2.5 |
| Product C | 1.0 |

During the week 2800 hours were worked on production.

You are required:

(a) (i) to calculate the production volume ratio and the efficiency ratio for the week ended 21 May; (4 marks)

(ii) to explain the significance of the two ratios you have calculated and to state which variances may be related to each of the ratios; (5 marks)

(b) to explain the three measures of capacity referred to in the following statement:

During the recent recession, increased attention was paid to 'practical capacity' and 'budgeted capacity' because few manufacturing companies could anticipate working again at 'full capacity'.

(6 marks)

(Total 15 marks)

*CIMA Stage 2 Cost Accounting*

### 18.33* Advanced: Preparation of an operating control statement and the calculation of labour, material and overhead variances

The following statement has been produced for presentation to the general manager of Department X.

**Month ended 31 October**

| | Original budget (£) | Actual result (£) | Variance (£) |
| --- | --- | --- | --- |
| Sales | 600 000 | 550 000 | (50 000) |
| Direct materials | 150 000 | 130 000 | 20 000 |
| Direct labour | 200 000 | 189 000 | 11 000 |
| Production overhead: | | | |
| Variable with direct labour | 50 000 | 46 000 | 4 000 |
| Fixed | 25 000 | 29 000 | (4 000) |
| Variable selling overhead | 75 000 | 72 000 | 3 000 |
| Fixed selling overhead | 50 000 | 46 000 | 4 000 |
| Total costs | 550 000 | 512 000 | 38 000 |
| Profit | 50 000 | 38 000 | (12 000) |
| Direct labour hours | 50 000 | 47 500 | |
| Sales and production units | 5 000 | 4 500 | |

*Note*: There are no opening and closing stocks.

The general manager says that this type of statement does not provide much relevant information for him. He also thought that the profit for the month would be well up to budget and was surprised to see a large adverse profit variance.

You are required to

(a) re-draft the above statement in a form which would be more relevant for the general manager; (6 marks)

(b) calculate all sales, material, labour and overhead variances and reconcile to the statement produced in (a); (9 marks)

(c) produce a short report explaining the principles upon which your re-drafted statement is based and what information it provides.

(7 marks)

(Total 22 marks)

*CIMA Stage 3 Management Accounting Techniques*

### 18.34 Advanced: Preparation of an operating control statement and the computation of labour, material and overhead variances

(a) A factory is planning to produce and sell 8000 units of product P during the next 4-week operating period.

Its standard product unit and total costs are as follows:

| | Costs per unit (£) | Total costs (£) |
|---|---|---|
| Direct material | | |
| 1.111 units at £5.40/unit | 6.00 | 48 000 |
| Direct labour | | |
| 0.6 hours at £5.00/hour | 3.00 | 24 000 |
| Variable overhead | | |
| 0.6 hours at £0.50/hour | 0.30 | 2 400 |
| Fixed overhead | 5.95 | 47 600 |

The product sells for £16.50/unit.

The following details relate to the actual results for the 4-week period:

| | |
|---|---|
| Actual orders received for the 4-week period: | 8200 units |
| Actual sales: | 7500 units |
| Actual production: | 7500 units |
| Units of direct material purchased and issued into production: | 7750 units |
| Direct material price per unit: | £5.60 |
| Direct labour hours: | 4700 |
| Direct labour rate (per hour): | £5.25 |

Total overhead expenditure amounted to £49 000 of which variable overhead was £2150.

You are required to

(i) produce an Operating Control Statement which analyses the budget: actual comparisons for the four-week period;
(7 marks)

(ii) arrange the results you have produced in a way which will improve management's understanding and interpretation of their meaning, explaining the basis of the presentation you have adopted.
(8 marks)

(b) Some consider that the key to fair assessment of management performance is provided by the concept of controllability, i.e. measurements should be based on factors over which management has control. However, identifying controllability may raise complex issues.

You are required to discuss the management accounting problems which arise in attributing performance to managers in a manner which recognizes controllability.
(10 marks)
(Total 25 marks)
*CIMA Stage 4 Management Accounting – Control and Audit*

### 18.35 Advanced: Variance calculations and reconciliation of budgeted and actual profit

Bamfram plc is a well established manufacturer of a specialized product, a Wallop, which has the following specifications for production:

| Components | Standard quantity | Standard price (£) |
|---|---|---|
| WALS | 15 | 60 |
| LOPS | 8 | 75 |

The standard direct labour hours to produce a Wallop at the standard wage rate of £10.50 per hour has been established at 60 hours per Wallop.

The annual fixed overhead budget is divided into calendar months with equal production per month. The budgeted annual fixed overheads are £504 000 for the budgeted output of 2400 Wallops per annum.

Mr Jones, a marketing person, is now the managing director of Bamfram plc and must report to the board of directors later this day and he seeks your advice in respect of the following operating information for the month of May:

| | (£) | (£) |
|---|---|---|
| Sales | | 504 000 |
| Cost of sales: | | |
| Direct materials | 281 520 | |
| Direct labour | 112 320 | |
| | 393 840 | |
| Fixed production overheads | 42 600 | |
| | | 436 440 |
| Gross profit | | 67 560 |
| Administration expenses | | 11 150 |
| Selling and distribution expenses | | 17 290 |
| Net profit | | 39 120 |

The sales manager informs Mr Jones that despite adverse trading conditions his sales staff have been able to sell 180 Wallops at the expected standard selling price.

The production manager along with the purchasing department manager are also pleased that prices for components have been stable for the whole of the current year and they are able to provide the following information:

Stocks for May are as follows:

|  | 1 May | 31 May |
| --- | --- | --- |
| Component WALS | 600 | 750 |
| Component LOPS | 920 | 450 |

The actual number of direct labour hours worked in May was 11 700, considerably less than the production manager had budgeted. Further, the purchasing manager advised that WALS had cost £171 000 at a price of £57 per unit in the month of May and 1000 LOPS had been acquired for £81 000.

Mr Jones, eager to please the board of directors, requests you, as the newly appointed management accountant, to prepare appropriate statements to highlight the following information which is to be presented to the board:

(a) The standard product cost of a Wallop.

(3 marks)

(b) (i) The direct material variances for both price and usage for each component used in the month of May assuming that prices were stable throughout the relevant period.

(ii) The direct labour efficiency and wage rate variances for the month of May.

(iii) The fixed production overhead expenditure and volume variances.

*Note*: You may assume that during the month of May there is no change in the level of finished goods stocks.

(10 marks)

(c) A detailed reconciliation statement of the standard gross profit with the actual gross profit for the month of May. (4 marks)

(d) Draft a brief report for Mr Jones that he could present to the board of directors on the usefulness, or otherwise, of the statement you have prepared in your answer to (c) above.

(5 marks)

(Total 22 marks)

*ACCA Level 2 Management Accounting*

## 18.36* Advanced: Reconciliation of budgeted and actual profits

The Britten Co. Ltd manufactures a variety of products of basically similar composition. Production is carried out by subjecting the various raw materials to a number of standardized operations, each major series of operations being carried out in a different department. All products are subjected to the same initial processing which is carried out in departments A, B and C; the order and extent of further processing then depending upon the type of end product to be produced.

It has been decided that a standard costing system could be usefully employed within Britten and a pilot scheme is to be operated for six months based initially only on department B, the second department in the initial common series of operations. If the pilot scheme produces useful results then a management accountant will be employed and the system would be incorporated as appropriate throughout the whole firm.

The standard cost per unit of output of department B is:

|  | (£) | (£) |
| --- | --- | --- |
| Direct labour (14 hours at £2 per hour) |  | 28 |
| Direct materials: |  |  |
| (i) output of department A (3 kg at £9 per kg) | 27 |  |
| (ii) acquired by and directly input to department B material X (4 kg at £5 per kg) | 20 | 47 |
| Variable overhead (at £1 per direct labour hour worked) |  | 14 |
| Fixed production overheads: |  |  |
| (i) directly incurred by department B (note 1) manufacturing overhead (per unit) | 3 |  |
| (ii) allocated to department B general factory overhead (per unit) | 8 | 11 |
| Standard cost per unit |  | £100 |

In the first month of operation of the pilot study (month 7 of the financial year), department B had no work in progress at the beginning and the end of the month. The actual costs allocated to department B in the first month of operation were:

|  | (£) | (£) |

| Direct labour (6500 hours) | | 14 000 |
| --- | --- | --- |
| Direct materials: | | |
| (i) output of department A (1400 kg) (note 2) | 21 000 | |
| (ii) material X (1900 kg) | 11 500 | 32 500 |
| Variable overhead | | 8 000 |
| Fixed overhead: | | |
| (i) directly incurred manufacturing overhead | 1 600 | |
| (ii) allocated to department B (note 3) | 2 900 | 4 500 |
| | | £59 000 |

*Note 1* Based on normal monthly production of 400 units.
*Note 2* Actual cost of output of department A.
*Note 3* Based on the actual expenditure on joint manufacturing overheads and allocated to departments in accordance with labour hours worked.

The production manager feels that the actual costs of £59 000 for production of 500 units indicates considerable inefficiency on the part of department B. He says, 'I was right to request that the pilot standard costing system be carried out in department B as I have suspected that they are inefficient and careless – this overspending of £9000 proves I am right.'

Required:
(a) Prepare a brief statement which clearly indicates the reasons for the performance of department B and the extent to which that performance is attributable to department B. The statement should utilize variance analysis to the extent it is applicable and relevant.
(14 marks)
(b) Comment on the way the pilot standard costing system is currently being operated and suggest how its operation might be improved during the study period. (6 marks)
(Total 20 marks)
*ACCA P2 Management Accounting*

**18.37 Advanced: Computation of variances and the reconciliation of budgeted and actual profits for a taxi firm**
Tardy Taxis operates a fleet of taxis in a provincial town. In planning its operations for November it estimated that it would carry fare-paying passengers for 40 000 miles at an average price of £1 per mile. However, past experience suggested that the total miles run would amount to 250% of the fare-

paid miles. At the beginning of November it employed ten drivers and decided that this number would be adequate for the month ahead.
The following cost estimates were available:

| | |
| --- | --- |
| Employment costs of a driver | £1000 per month |
| Fuel costs | £0.08 per mile run |
| Variable overhead costs | £0.05 per mile run |
| Fixed overhead costs | £9000 per month |

In November revenue of £36 100 was generated by carrying passengers for 38 000 miles. The total actual mileage was 105 000 miles. Other costs amounted to:

| | |
| --- | --- |
| Employment costs of drivers | £9600 |
| Fuel costs | £8820 |
| Variable overhead costs | £5040 |
| Fixed overhead costs | £9300 |

The saving in the cost of drivers was due to one driver leaving during the month; she was not replaced until early December.

Requirements:
(a) Prepare a budgeted and actual profit and loss account for November, indicating the total profit variance. (6 marks)
(b) Using a flexible budget approach, construct a set of detailed variances to explain the total profit variance as effectively as possible. Present your analysis in a report to the owner of Tardy Taxis including suggested reasons for the variances. (14 marks)
(c) Outline any further variances you think would improve your explanation, indicating the additional information you would require to produce these. (5 marks)
(Total 25 marks)
*ICAEW P2 Management Accounting*

**18.38\* Advanced: Comparison of variable and absorption standard costing**
Chimera Ltd makes chimes, one of a variety of products. These products pass through several production processes.
The first process is moulding and the standard costs for moulding chimes are as follows:

**Standard costs
per unit**

| | (£) |
|---|---|
| Direct material X  7 kg at £7.00 per kg | 49.00 |
| Direct labour      5 hours at £5 per hour | 25.00 |
| Overhead (fixed    5 hours at £6.60 | 33.00 |
| and variable)           per hour | 107.00 |

The overhead allocation rate is based on direct labour hours and comprises an allowance for both fixed and variable overhead costs. With the aid of regression analysis the fixed element of overhead costs has been estimated at £9000 per week, and the variable element of overhead costs has been estimated at £0.60 per direct labour hour. The accounting records do not separate actual overhead costs between their fixed and variable elements.

The moulding department occupies its own premises, and all of the department's overhead costs can be regarded as being the responsibility of the departmental manager.

In week 27 the department moulded 294 chimes, and actual costs incurred were:

| | |
|---|---|
| Direct material X (2030 kg used) | £14 125 |
| Direct labour (1520 hours worked) | £7 854 |
| Overhead expenditure | £10 200 |

The 1520 hours worked by direct labour included 40 hours overtime, which is paid at 50% above normal pay rates.

Requirements:
(a) Prepare a report for the moulding department manager on the results of the moulding department for week 27, presenting information in a way which you consider to be most useful. (9 marks)
(b) Discuss the treatment of overheads adopted in your report and describe an alternative treatment, contrasting its use with the method adopted in your report. (6 marks)
(c) Describe the approaches used for determining standards for direct costs and assess their main strengths and weaknesses. (10 marks)
(Total 25 marks)
*ICAEW P2 Management Accounting*

**18.39 Advanced: Calculation of sales variances on an absorption and variable costing basis and reconciliation of actual with budgeted margin**
Claylock Ltd make and sell a single product. The company operates a standard cost system and the following information is available for period 5:

(i) Standard product cost per unit:

| | (£) |
|---|---|
| Direct material 8 kilos at £5.40 per kilo | 43.20 |
| Direct labour 2.5 hours at £4.50 per hour | 11.25 |
| Fixed production overhead | 17.00 |

(ii) The standard selling price per unit is £90.

(iii) Direct labour hours worked total 12 000 hours. Labour productivity in comparison to standard was 90%.

(iv) 42 000 kilos of direct material were purchased at £5.60 per kilo. Issues from stores to production totalled 36 000 kilos during the period.

(v) Stocks of finished goods rose from nil to 300 units during the period. It was budgeted that all units produced would be sold during the period.

(vi) Stocks of raw materials and finished goods are valued at standard cost.

(vii) Summary operating statement for period 5:

| | | (£) |
|---|---|---|
| Budgeted sales revenue | | 450 000 |
| Sales volume variance | | 88 200 (A) |
| Standard sales revenue | | 361 800 |
| *Less*: Standard cost of sales | | 287 229 |
| Standard production margin | | 74 571 |

| | (F) | (A) | | |
|---|---|---|---|---|
| Variance analysis: | (£) | (£) | | |
| Sales price | 30 150 | | | |
| Direct material cost | | 16 176 | | |
| Fixed overhead volume | | 11 560 | | |
| Fixed overhead expenditure | 1 500 | | | |
| | 31 650 | 27 736 | 3 914 (F) | |
| Actual production margin | | | 78 485 | |

*Note*: (F) = favourable (A) = adverse.

Required:
(a) Determine the values of the sales volume variance when it is expressed alternatively in terms of: standard revenue; standard production margin; and standard contribution. Discuss which valuation, when combined with the sales price variance, provides a measure of whether the sales variance have resulted in a net cash benefit to the company. (9 marks)

(b) Analyse the direct material cost variance into relevant sub-variances and comment on the method by which material usage is valued by Claylock Ltd. (7 marks)

(c) Analyse the fixed overhead volume variance into two sub-variances and comment on the relevance of each sub-variance as perceived by adherents of absorption costing.

(7 marks)

(d) Prepare an operating statement for period 5 which amends the statement given in the question into standard marginal cost format. Explain the reason for any difference in the actual production margin from that reported under the present system. Comment also on any changes in the variances reported in the amended statement.

(7 marks)
(Total 30 marks)
*ACCA Level 2 Cost and Management Accounting II*

# Standard costing and variance analysis 2: further aspects

In the previous chapter we examined the principles of standard costing variance analysis. We are now going to consider how the material usage and the sales margin volume variance can be further analysed, and look at the accounting entries that are necessary to record the variances. We shall then turn our attention to considering more meaningful approaches to variance analysis and identify the factors that should be taken into account in deciding whether or not it is worthwile investigating variances. Finally, we shall consider the future role of standard costing and examine the implications of ABC for traditional flexible budgeting and variance analysis.

With the exception of the accounting entries for a standard costing system all of the topics covered in this chapter are more appropriate to a second-year management accounting course. It is recommended that you read the relevant topics appropriate to your course of study rather than reading the chapter from start to finish. However, the sections relating to the future role of standard costing and the implications of ABC for traditional variance analysis should be regarded as essential reading for all second-year management accounting students.

## Learning objectives

After studying this chapter, you should be able to:

● calculate material mix and yield and sales mix and quantity variances;

● explain the criticisms of sales margin variances;

● prepare a set of accounts for a standard costing system;

● calculate planning and operating variances;

● explain the need for an *ex post* variance analysis and an opportunity cost approach for analysing variances;

● explain the methods that can be used to determine whether or not a variance should be investigated;

● comment on the future role of standard costing;

● explain the implications of ABC for traditional variance analysis.

## Direct materials mix and yield variances

**AR** In many industries, particularly of the process type, it is possible to vary the mix of input materials and affect the yield. Where it is possible to combine two or more raw materials, input standards should be established to indicate the target mix of materials required to produce a unit, or a specified number of units, of output. Laboratory and engineering studies are necessary in order to determine the standard mix. The costs of the different material mixes are estimated, and a standard mix is determined based on the mix of materials that minimizes the cost per unit of output but still meets the quality requirements. Trade-offs may occur. For example, cost increases arising from using better quality materials may be offset by a higher yield, or vice versa.

By deviating from the standard mix of input materials, operating managers can affect the yield and cost per unit of output. Such deviations can occur as a result of a conscious response to changes in material prices, or alternatively may arise from inefficiencies and a failure to adhere to the standard mix. By computing mix and yield variances, we can provide an indication of the cost of deviating from the standard mix.

## MIX VARIANCE

The material mix variance arises when the mix of materials used differs from the predetermined mix included in the calculation of the standard cost of an operation. If the mixture is varied so that a larger than standard proportion of more expensive materials is used, there will be an unfavourable variance. When a larger proportion of cheaper materials is included in the mixture, there will be a favourable variance. Consider Example 19.1.

The total input for the period is 100 000 litres, and, using the standard mix, an input of 50 000 litres of X (5/10 × 100 000), 30 000 litres of Y (3/10 × 100 000) and 20 000 litres of Z (2/10 × 100 000) should have been used. However, 53 000 litres of X, 28 000 litres of Y and 19 000 litres of Z were used. Therefore 3000 additional litres of X at a standard price of £7 per litre were substituted for 2000 litres of Y (at a standard price of £5 per litre) and 1000 litres of Z (at a standard price of £2 per litre). An adverse material mix variance of £9000 will therefore be reported. The formula for the material mix variance is as follows:

(actual quantity in standard mix proportions − actual quantity used) × standard price

If we apply this formula, the calculation is as follows:

*Actual usage in standard proportions:*

|  |  | (£) |
| --- | --- | --- |
| X = 50 000 litres (5/10 × 100 000) at | £7 | 350 000 |
| Y = 30 000 litres (3/10 × 100 000) at | £5 | 150 000 |
| Z = 20 000 litres (2/10 × 100 000) at | £2 | 40 000 |
|  |  | 540 000 |

*Actual usage in actual proportions:*

|  | (£) |
| --- | --- |
| X = 53 000 litres at £7 | 371 000 |
| Y = 28 000 litres at £5 | 140 000 |
| Z = 19 000 litres at £2 | 38 000 |
|  | 549 000 |
| mix variance = | £9 000 A |

**EXAMPLE   19.1**

The Milano company has established the following standard mix for producing 9 litres of product A:

|  | (£) |
| --- | --- |
| 5 litres of material X at £7 per litre | 35 |
| 3 litres of material Y at £5 per litre | 15 |
| 2 litres of material Z at £2 per litre | 4 |
|  | £54 |

A standard loss of 10% of input is expected to occur. Actual input was

|  | (£) |
| --- | --- |
| 53 000 litres of material X at £7 per litre | 371 000 |
| 28 000 litres of material Y at £5.30 per litre | 148 400 |
| 19 000 litres of material Z at £2.20 per litre | 41 800 |
| 100 000 | £561 200 |

Actual output for the period was 92 700 litres of product A.

Note that standard prices are used to calculate the mix variance to ensure that the price effects are removed from the calculation. An adverse mix variance will result from substituting more expensive higher quality materials for cheaper materials. Substituting more expensive materials may result in a boost in output and a favourable yield variance. On the other hand, a favourable mix variance will result from substituting cheaper materials for more expensive materials – but this may not always be in a company's best interests, since the quality of the product may suffer or output might be reduced. Generally, the use of a less expensive mix of inputs will mean the production of fewer units of output than standard. This may be because of excessive evaporation of the input units, an increase in rejects due to imperfections in the lower quality inputs, or other similar factors. To analyse the effect of changes in the quantity of outputs from a given mix of inputs, a yield variance can be calculated. It is important that the standard mix be continuously reviewed and adjusted where necessary, since price changes may lead to a revised standard mix.

## DIRECT MATERIALS YIELD VARIANCE

The **materials yield variance** arises because there is a difference between the standard output for a given level of inputs and the actual output attained. In Example 19.1 an input of 100 000 litres should have given an output of 90 000 litres of product A. (Every 10 litres of input should produce 9 litres of output.) In fact, 92 700 litres were produced, which means that the output was 2700 litres greater than standard. This output is valued at the average standard cost per unit of *output*, which is calculated as follows.

Each 10 litres of *input* is expected to yield 9 litres of *output*.
The standard cost for this output is £54.
Therefore the standard cost for one litre of *output* = £54 × 1/9 = £6.

The yield variance will be £6 × 2700 = £16 200F. The formula is as follows:

(actual yield − standard yield from actual input of material)

× standard cost per unit of output

= (92 700 litres − 90 000 litres) × £6 = £16 200F

An adverse yield variance may arise from a failure to follow standard procedures. For example, in the steel industry a yield variance may indicate that the practice that was followed for pouring molten metal may have been different from that which was determined as being the most efficient when the standard yield was calculated. Alternatively, the use of inferior quality materials may result in an adverse yield variance.

The material mix variance in Example 19.1 is £9000 adverse, while the material yield variance is £16 200 favourable. There was a trade-off in the material mix, which boosted the yield. This trade-off may have arisen because the prices of materials Y and Z have increased whereas the actual price paid for material X is identical with the standard price. The manager of the production process may have responded to the different relative prices by substituting material X (the most expensive material) for materials Y and Z. This substitution process has resulted in an adverse mix variance and a favourable yield variance. Note, however, that actual material cost per unit of output is £6.05 (£561 200/92 700 litres) whereas the standard cost per unit is £6 (£54/9 litres). You will find that this difference has been partly caused by an adverse material price variance of £12 200.

At this stage you should be aware that materials price, mix and yield variances are inter-related and that individual variances should not be interpreted in isolation. Inter-dependencies should be recognized. You should also note that changes in relative input prices of materials will affect the optimal standard mix and yield of materials. Where significant changes in input prices occur, the actual mix and yield should be compared with a revised *ex post* standard mix and yield. We shall discuss the *ex post* approach later in this chapter.

## MATERIAL USAGE VARIANCE

The material usage variance consists of the mix variance and the yield variance. The material usage variance is therefore a favourable variance of £7200, consisting of an adverse mix variance of £9000 and a favourable yield variance of £16 200. To calculate the material usage variance, we compare the standard quantity of materials for the actual production with the actual quantity of materials used and multiply by the standard material prices in the normal way. The calculations are as follows:

*Standard quality for actual production at standard prices:*

Actual production of 92 700 litres requires an input of 103 000 litres (92 700 × 10/9), consisting of

| | (£) |
|---|---|
| 51 500 litres of X (103 000 × 5/10) at £7 per litre | = 360 500 |
| 30 900 litres of Y (103 000 × 3/10) at £5 per litre | = 154 500 |
| 20 600 litres of Z (103 000 × 2/10) at £2 per litre | = 41 200 |
| | 556 200 (i) |

*Actual quantity at standard prices:*

|  | (£) |
|---|---|
| 53 000 litres at X at £7 per litre | = 371 000 |
| 28 000 litres of Y at £5 per litre | = 140 000 |
| 19 000 litres of Z at £2 per litre | = 38 000 |
|  | 549 000 (ii) |
| Material usage variance (i) – (ii) | = £7 200 F |

Note that the standard quantity for actual production at standard prices can also be calculated by multiplying the actual output by the standard cost per unit of output (92 700 × £6 = £556 200).

## SUMMARY OF MATERIAL VARIANCES

The total material variance and the price variances are calculated using the approaches described in the previous chapter. The calculations are as follows:

Total material variance:

| Standard cost for actual production (92 700 × £6) | = £556 200 |
|---|---|
| – Actual cost | (£561 200) |
|  | = £5 000 A |

Material price variances, (standard price – actual price) × actual quantity:

| Material X = (£7 – £7) × 53 000 | = 0 |
|---|---|
| Material Y = (£5 – £5.30) × 28 000 | = £8 400 A |
| Material Z = (£2 – £2.20) × 19 000 | = £3 800 A |
|  | £12 200 A |

We have already noted that these variances may be inter-related. The manager of the production process may have responded to the price increases by varying the mix of inputs, which in turn may affect the yield of the process. The decomposition of the total material variance into price, mix and yield components highlights different aspects of the production process and provides additional insights to help managers to attain the optimum combination of materials input.

You should note that mix and yield variances are appropriate only to those production processes where managers have the discretion to vary the mix of materials and deviate from engineered input–output relationships. Where managers control each input on an individual basis and have no discretion regarding the substitution of materials, it is inappropriate to calculate mix and yield variances. For example, there is often a predetermined mix of components needed for the assembly of washing machines, television sets and vacuum cleaners. In these production processes deviations from standard usage are related to efficiency of material usage rather than to changes in the physical mix of material inputs.

The same approach as that used to determine material mix and yield variances can also be applied to direct labour where it is possible to combine two or more grades of labour to perform specific operations. Given that the variance calculations for labour mix and yield variances are identical with the procedures described in this section, the computations will not be illustrated.

**EXAMPLE 19.2**

The budgeted sales for the Milano company for a period were

|  | Units | Unit contribution margin (£) | Total contribution (£) |
|---|---|---|---|
| Product X | 8 000 (40%) | 20 | 160 000 |
| Y | 7 000 (35%) | 12 | 84 000 |
| Z | 5 000 (25%) | 9 | 45 000 |
|  | 20 000 |  | 289 000 |

and the actual sales were

|  | Units (£) | Unit contribution margin (£) | Total contribution |
|---|---|---|---|
| Product X | 6 000 | 20 | 120 000 |
| Y | 7 000 | 12 | 84 000 |
| Z | 9 000 | 9 | 81 000 |
|  | 22 000 |  | 285 000 |

You are required to calculate the sales margin variances.

# Sales mix and sales quantity variances

Where a company sells several different products that have different profit margins, the sales volume margin variance can be divided into a sales quantity (sometimes called a sales yield variance) and sales mix variance. This division is commonly advocated in textbooks. The quantity variance measures the effect of changes in physical volume on total profits, and the mix variance measures the impact arising from the actual sales mix being different from the budgeted sales mix. The variances can be measured either in terms of contribution margins or profit margins. However, contribution margins are recommended because changes in sales volume affect profits by the contribution per unit sold and not the profit per unit sold. Let us now calculate the sales margin mix and quantity variances. Consider Example 19.2.

The total sales margin variance is £4000 adverse, and is calculated by comparing the difference between the budgeted total contribution and the actual contribution. Contribution margins for the three products were exactly as budgeted. The total sales margin for the period therefore consists of a zero sales margin price variance and an adverse sales margin volume variance of £4000. Even through more units were sold than anticipated (22 000 rather than the budgeted 20 000), and budgeted and actual contribution margins were the same, the sales volume variance is £4000 adverse. The reasons for this arises from having sold fewer units of product X, the high margin product, and more units of product Z, which has the lowest margin.

We can explain how the sales volume margin variance was affected by the change in sales mix by calculating the sales margin mix variance. The formula for calculating this variance is

> (actual sales quantity − actual sales quantity in budgeted proportions)
>     × standard margin

If we apply this formula, we will obtain the following calculations:

|  | Actual sales quantity | Actual sales in budgeted proportions | Difference | Standard margin (£) | Sales margin mix variance (£) |
|---|---|---|---|---|---|
| Product X | 6 000 (27%) | 8 800 (40%) = | − 2800 | 20 | 56 000A |
| Y | 7 000 (32%) | 7 700 (35%) = | − 700 | 12 | 8 400A |
| Z | 9 000 (41%) | 5 500 (25%) = | + 3500 | 9 | 31 500 F |
|  | 22 000 | 22 000 |  |  | 32 900A |

To compute the sales quantity component of the sales volume variance, we compare the budgeted and actual sales volumes (holding the product mix constant). The formula for calculating the sales quantity variance is

> (actual sales quantity in budgeted proportion − budgeted sales quantity)
>     × standard margin

Applying this formula gives the following calculations:

|  | Actual sales in budgeted proportions | Budgeted sales quantity | Difference | Standard margin (£) | Sales margin quantity variance (£) |
|---|---|---|---|---|---|
| Product X | 8 800 | 8 000 | + 800 | 20 | 16 000F |
| Y | 7 700 | 7 000 | + 700 | 12 | 8 400F |
| Z | 5 500 | 5 000 | + 500 | 9 | 4 500F |
|  | 22 000 | 20 000 |  |  | 28 900F |

The sales quantity variance is sometimes further divided into a market size and a market share variance. A summary of the sales margin variances is presented in Figure 19.1. Before considering the market size and market share variances, we shall discuss the sales variances we have calculated so far in respect of Example 19.2.

By separating the sales volume variance into quantity and mix variances, we can explain how the sales volume variance is affected by a shift in the total physical volume of sales and a shift in the relative mix of products. The sales volume quantity variance indicates that if the original planned sales mix of 40% of X, 35% of Y and 25% of Z had been maintained then, for the actual sales volume of 22 000 units, profits would have increased by £28 900. In other words, the sales volume variance would have been £28 900 favourable instead of £4000 adverse. However, because the actual sales mix was not in accordance with the budgeted sales mix, an adverse mix variance of £32 900 occurred. The adverse sales mix variance has arisen because of an increase in the percentage of units sold of product Z, which has the lowest contribution margin, and a decrease in the percentage sold of units of product X, which has the highest contribution margin. An adverse mix variance will occur whenever there is an increase in the percentage sold of units with below average contribution margins or a decrease in

**FIGURE 19.1** *Summary of sales variances.*

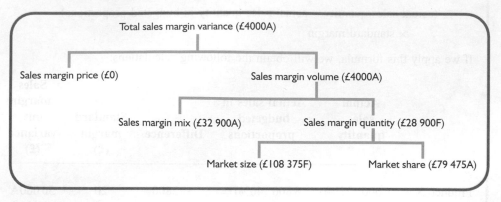

the percentage sold of units with above average contribution margins. The division of the sales volume variance into quantity and mix components demonstrates that increasing or maximizing sales volume may not be as desirable as promoting the sales of the most desirable mix of products.

## MARKET SIZE AND SHARE VARIANCES

Where published industry sales statistics are readily available, it is possible to divide the sales quantity variance into a component due to changes in market size and a component due to changes in market share. Suppose that the budgeted industry sales volume for the illustrative company in Example 19.2 was 200 000 units and a market share of 10% was predicted. Assume also that the actual industry sales volume was 275 000 units and the company obtained a market share of 8 per cent (8% × 275 000 = 22 000 units). The formulae and calculations of the **market size** and **market share variances** are as follows:

$$\begin{array}{l} \text{market size} \\ \text{variance} \end{array} = \begin{bmatrix} \text{budgeted} \\ \text{market} \\ \text{share} \\ \text{percentage} \end{bmatrix} \times \begin{bmatrix} \text{actual} & \text{budgeted} \\ \text{industry} & \text{industry} \\ \text{sales} & - & \text{sales} \\ \text{volume} & \text{volume} \\ \text{in units} & \text{in units} \end{bmatrix} \times \begin{bmatrix} \text{budgeted} \\ \text{average} \\ \text{contribution} \\ \text{margin} \\ \text{per unit} \end{bmatrix}$$

$$= 10\% \times (275\,000 - 200\,000) \times £14.45*$$
$$= £108\,375F$$

(*budgeted company total contribution (£289 000)/budgeted sales volume in units (20000))

$$\begin{array}{l} \text{market share} \\ \text{variance} \end{array} = \begin{bmatrix} \text{actual} & \text{budgeted} \\ \text{market} & \text{market} \\ \text{share} & - & \text{share} \\ \text{percentage} & \text{percentage} \end{bmatrix} \times \begin{bmatrix} \text{actual} & \text{budgeted} \\ \text{industry} & \text{average} \\ \text{sales} & \times & \text{contribution} \\ \text{volume} & \text{margin} \\ \text{in units} & \text{per unit} \end{bmatrix}$$

$$= (8\% - 10\%) \times 275\,000 \times £14.45$$
$$= £79\,475A$$

The market size variance indicates that an additional contribution of £108 375 was expected, given that the market expanded from 200 000 to 275 000 units. However, the company did not attain the predicted market share of 10%. Instead, a market share of only 8% was attained, and the 2% decline in market share resulted in a failure to obtain a contribution of £79 475. Hence the sum of the market size variance (£108 375F) and the market share variance (£79 475A) equals the sales margin quantity variance of £28 900.

Using the budgeted average contribution per unit in the formulae for the market size and share variances implies that we are assuming that budgeted and actual industry sales mix is the same as company's sales mix of 40% of X, 35% of Y and 25% of Z. Market size and share variances provide more meaningful information where the market size for each individual product can be ascertained.

## CRITICISMS OF SALES MARGIN VARIANCES

Sales margin price and volume variances and the decomposition of the volume variance into mix and yield variances are commonly advocated in textbooks. However, some writers (e.g. Manes, 1983) question the usefulness of sales variance analysis on the grounds that in an imperfectly competitive market structure, prices and quantities are interrelated. Given price elasticity, the logical consequence of lower/higher sales prices is higher/lower volume. Thus the relevant variances and analysis based on these variances are also interrelated. Consequently, it is argued that sales margin variance analysis does not generate any meaningful results.

Several writers have also argued that it is inappropriate to separate the sales volume variance into mix and quantity variances. Bastable and Bao (1988) illustrate two different approaches advocated in the literature to calculate mix and yield variances. The first approach calculates weights in terms of physical quantities whereas the second uses sales dollars. Bastable and Bao show that the two approaches generate divergent results in many situations. Because of this deficiency they argue that decomposing the sales volume variance into mix and quantity variances is misleading and has the potential for more harm than good.

Gibson (1990) advocates that mix and quantity variances provide useful information only where there is an identifiable relationship between the products sold and these relationships are incorporated into the planning process. Where relationships between products are not expected, the budgeted contribution for a period is derived from *separate* estimates of physical volumes and prices of each product. The mix that emerges from the combination of the separate estimates for each product does not constitute a planned mix. Gibson therefore argues that providing management with mix and quantity variances, where there is no identified relationship between the sales volume of individual products, is misleading because it incorrectly implies that a possible cause of the sales volume variance is a change in mix. The only possible 'causes' that require investigation are simply deviations from planned volumes for the individual products. Gibson (1990) provides the following examples of situations where identifiable relationships exist:

the sale, by the firm of a number of similar products (differentiated by single characteristics such as size) where sales of individual products are *expected* to vary proportionally with total sales; the sale of complementary products (where increased sales of one product are *expected* to result in increased sales in another); the sale of product substitutes (where increased sales of one product are expected to result in decreased sales of another); and the sale of heterogeneous products, the

> quantities of which are limited by factors of production (for example, where the sale of products with lower contribution margins per limiting resource factor is made only if products with higher contribution margins cannot be sold). (Page 38.)

Gibson identifies two possible situations where a planned relationship between the sales of products could be incorporated into the planning model. The first relates to where the total sales of individual products are expected to occur in a constant mix, such as different sizes of a particular product. In this situation management would be interested in how the volume variance has been affected by deviations from the planned mix. The second relates to situations where sales of products in a group are expected to vary in proportion to sales of a 'critical' product, such as where other products are complementary to, or substitutes for, the 'critical' product. ●●●

# Recording standard costs in the accounts

Standard costs can be used for planning, control, motivation and decision-making purposes without being entered into the books. However, the incorporation of standard costs into the cost accounting system greatly simplifies the task of tracing costs for inventory valuation and saves a considerable amount of data processing time. For example, if raw material stocks are valued at standard cost, the stock records may be maintained in terms of physical quantities only. The value of raw materials stock may be obtained simply by multiplying the physical quantity of raw materials in stock by the standard cost per unit. This avoids the need to record stocks on a first-in, first-out or average cost basis. The financial accounting regulations in most countries specify that inventory valuations based on standard costs may be included in externally published financial statements, provided the standard costs used are current and attainable. Most companies that have established standard costs therefore incorporate them into their cost accounting recording system.

Variations exist in the data accumulation methods adopted for recording standard costs, but these variations are merely procedural and the actual inventory valuations and profit calculations will be the same whichever method is adopted. In this chapter we shall illustrate a standard absorption costing system that values all inventories at standard cost, and all entries that are recorded in the inventory accounts will therefore be at *standard prices*. Any differences between standard costs and actual costs are debited or credited to variance accounts. Adverse variances will appear as debit balances, since they are additional costs in excess of standard. Conversely, favourable variances will appear as credit balances. Only production variances are recorded, and sales variances are not entered in the accounts.

Let us now consider the cost accounting records, for Example 18.1, which was presented in the previous chapter. We shall assume that the company operates an integrated cost accounting system. The variances recorded in the accounts will be those we calculated in Chapter 18, and we need not therefore explain them again here – but if you cannot remember the variance calculations, turn back now to Chapter 18 to refresh your memory. To keep things simple and to avoid confusion, we shall now repeat Example 18.1 and the reconciliation of actual and budgeted profits for this example (which was Exhibit 18.7 in the previous chapter).

Let us now consider the accounting entries for Example 18.1. The appropriate ledger entries are presented in Exhibit 19.1. Each ledger entry and journal entry has been labelled with numbers from 1 to 13 to try to give you a clear understanding of each accounting entry.

## EXAMPLE 18.1

*[From Chapter 18]*

Alpha manufacturing company produces a single product, which is known as sigma. The product requires a single operation, and the standard cost for this operation is presented in the following standard cost card:

| Standard cost card for product sigma | (£) |
| --- | --- |
| Direct materials: | |
| 2 kg of A at £10 per kg | 20.00 |
| 1 kg of B at £15 per kg | 15.00 |
| Direct labour (3 hours at £9 per hour) | 27.00 |
| Variable overhead (3 hours at £2 per direct labour hour) | 6.00 |
| Total standard variable cost | 68.00 |
| Standard contribution margin | 20.00 |
| Standard selling price | 88.00 |

Alpha Ltd plan to produce 10 000 units of sigma in the month of April, and the budgeted costs based on the information contained in the standard cost card are as follows:

*Budget based on the above standard costs and an output of 10 000 units*

| | (£) | (£) | (£) |
| --- | --- | --- | --- |
| Sales (10 000 units of sigma at £88 per unit) | | | 880 000 |
| Direct materials: | | | |
| A: 20 000 kg at £10 per kg | 200 000 | | |
| B: 10 000 kg at £15 per kg | 150 000 | 350 000 | |
| Direct labour (30 000 hours | | | |
| at £9 per hour) | | 270 000 | |
| Variable overheads (30 000 hours | | | |
| at £2 per direct labour hour) | | 60 000 | 680 000 |
| Budgeted contribution | | | 200 000 |
| Fixed overheads | | | 120 000 |
| Budgeted profit | | | 80 000 |

Annual budgeted fixed overheads are £1 440 000 and are assumed to be incurred evenly throughout the year. The company uses a variable costing system for internal profit measurement purposes.

The actual results for April are:

| | (£) | (£) |
| --- | --- | --- |
| Sales (9000 units at £90) | | 810 000 |
| Direct materials: | | |
| A: 19 000 kg at £11 per kg | 209 000 | |
| B: 10 100 kg at £14 per kg | 141 400 | |
| Direct labour (28 500 hours at £9.60 per hour) | 273 600 | |
| Variable overheads | 52 000 | 676 000 |
| Contribution | | 134 000 |
| Fixed overheads | | 116 000 |
| Profit | | 18 000 |

Manufacturing overheads are charged to production on the basis of direct labour hours. Actual production and sales for the period were 9000 units.

**EXHIBIT 18.7**

*(from Chapter 18)*

*Reconciliation of budgeted and actual profits for April*

## PURCHASE OF MATERIALS

19 000 kg of raw material A at £11 per kg and 10 100 kg of raw material B at £14 per kg were purchased. This gives a total purchase cost of £209 000 for A and £141 400 for B. The standard prices were £10 per kg for A and £5

| | (£) | (£) | (£) | (£) |
|---|---|---|---|---|
| Budgeted net profit | | | | 80 000 |
| Sales variances: | | | | |
| Sales margin price | | 18 000 F | | |
| Sales margin volume | | 8 000 A | 10 000 F | |
| Direct cost variances | | | | |
| Material – Price: Material A | 19 000 A | | | |
| Material B | 10 100 F | 8900 A | | |
| Usage: Material A | 10 000 A | | | |
| Material B | 16 500 A | 26 500 A | 35 400 A | |
| Labour – Rate | | 17 100 A | | |
| Efficiency | | 13 500 A | 30 600 A | |
| Manufacturing overhead variances | | | | |
| Fixed – Expenditure | 4000 F | | | |
| Volume | 12 000 A | 8 000 A | | |
| Variable – Expenditure | 5000 F | | | |
| Efficiency | 3000 A | 2 000 F | 6 000 A | 62 000 A |
| Actual profit | | | | 18 000 |

per kg for B. The accounting entries for material A are

| | | |
|---|---|---|
| 1. Dr Stores ledger control account (AQ × SP) | 190 000 | |
| 1. Dr Material price variance account | 19 000 | |
| 1. Cr Creditors control account (AQ × AP) | | 209 000 |

You will see that the stores ledger control account is debited with the standard price (SP) for the actual quantity purchased (AQ), and the actual price (AP) to be paid is credited to the creditors control account. The difference is the material price variance. The accounting entries for material B are

| | | |
|---|---|---|
| 2. Dr Stores ledger control account (AQ × SP) | 151 500 | |
| 2. Cr Material price variance account | | 10 100 |
| 2. Cr Creditors (AQ × AP) | | 141 400 |

## USAGE OF MATERIALS

19 000 kg of A and 10 100 kg of B were actually issued, and the standard usage (SQ) was 18 000 and 9000 kg at standard prices of £10 and £15. The accounting entries for material A are

| | | |
|---|---|---|
| 3. Dr Work in progress (SQ × SP) | 180 000 | |
| 3. Dr Material usage variance | 10 000 | |
| 3. Cr Stores ledger control account (AQ × SP) | | 190 000 |

Work in progress is debited with the standard quantity of materials at the standard price and the stores ledger account is credited with the actual quantity issued at the standard price. The difference is the material usage variance. The accounting entries for material B are

| | | |
|---|---|---|
| 4. Dr Work in progress (SQ × SP) | 135 000 | |
| 4. Dr Material usage variance | 16 500 | |
| 4. Cr Stores ledger control account (AQ × SP) | | 151 500 |

## DIRECT WAGES

The actual hours worked were 28 500 hours for the month. The standard hours produced were 27 000. The actual wage rate paid was £9.60 per hour, compared with a standard rate of £9 per hour. The actual wages cost is recorded in the same way in a standard costing system as an actual costing system. The accounting entry for the actual wages paid is

| | | |
|---|---|---|
| 5. Dr Wages control account | 273 600 | |
| 5. Cr Wages accrued account | | 273 600 |

The wages control account is then cleared as follows:

| | | |
|---|---|---|
| 6. Dr Work in progress (SQ × SP) | 243 000 | 243 000 |
| 6. Cr Wages control account | 17 100 | |
| 6. Dr Wage rate variance | 13 500 | |
| 6. Dr Labour efficiency variance | | 30 600 |
| 6. Cr Wages control account | | |

and the work in progress account is debited with the
The wages control account ... s produced times the standard wage rate). The wage rate
standard cost (i.e. difference accounts are debited, since they are both adverse variances
and labour efcount) between the actual wages cost (recorded as a debit in the
and account). and the standard wages cost (recorded as a credit in the wa...

## MANUFACTURING OVERHEAD COSTS INCURRED overheads and

verhead incurred
The actual manufacturing overhead incurred is £52 000 .n an actual costing
£116 000 for fixed overheads. The accounting entri...
are recorded in the same way in a standard cos...
system. That is,

|  | | |
|---|---|---|
| 7. Dr Factory variable overhead control account | 52 000 | |
| 7. Dr Factory fixed overhead control account | 116 000 | |
| 7. Cr Expense creditors | | 168 000 |

## ABSORPTION OF MANUFACTURING OVERHEADS AND RECORDING THE VARIANCES

Work in progress is debited with the standard manufacturing overhead cost for the output produced. The standard overhead rates were £4 per standard hour for fixed overhead and £2 per standard hour for variable overheads. The actual output was 27 000 standard hours. The standard fixed overhead cost is therefore £108 000 (27 000 standard hours at £4 per hour) and the variable overhead cost is £54 000. The accounting entries for fixed overheads are

|  | | |
|---|---|---|
| 8. Dr Work in progress (SQ × SP) | 108 000 | |
| 8. Dr Volume variance | 12 000 | |
| 8. Cr Factory fixed overhead control account | | 120 000 |
| 8. Dr Factory fixed overhead control account | 4 000 | |
| 8. Cr Fixed overhead expenditure variance | | 4 000 |

You will see that the debit of £108 000 to the work in progress account and the corresponding credit to the factory fixed overhead control account represents the standard fixed overhead cost of production. The difference between the debit entry of £116 000 in the factory fixed overhead control account in Exhibit 19.1 for the *actual* fixed overheads incurred, and the credit entry of £108 000 for the *standard* fixed overhead cost of production is the total fixed overhead variance, which consists of an adverse volume variance of £12 000 and a favourable expenditure variance of £4000. This is recorded as a debit to the volume variance account and a credit to the expenditure variance account. The accounting entries for variable overheads are

|  | | |
|---|---|---|
| 9. Dr Work in progress account (SQ × SP) | 54 000 | |
| 9. Dr Variable overhead efficiency variance | 3 000 | |
| 9. Cr Factory variable overhead control account | | 57 000 |
| 9. Dr Factory variable overhead control account | 5 000 | |
| 9. Cr Variable overhead expenditure variance account | | 5 000 |

The same principles apply with variable overheads and the corresponding credit to the factory variable overhead control account of £54 000 is the standard variable overhead cost of production. The debit to work in progress account of £52 000 in the factory variable overhead account in Exhibit between the debit entry overheads incurred and the credit entry of £54 000 for the *standard* actual variable of production is the total variable overhead variance, which consists overhead cost efficiency variance of £3000 and a favourable expenditure variance of £5overhead cost adverse

## CON...N OF PRODUCTION

In Exhibit N is £720 000. cost of production amount recorded on the debit side of the work in progress account opening or closing stocks, this represents the total standard which consists of 9000 units at £80 per unit. When the

**EXHIBIT 19.1**

*Accounting entries for a standard costing system*

### Stores ledger control account

| | | | |
|---|---:|---|---:|
| 1. Creditors (material A) | 190 000 | 3. Work in progress (material A) | 180 000 |
| 2. Creditors (material B) | 151 500 | | |
| | | 3. Material usage variance (material A) | 10 000 |
| | | 4. Work in progress (material B) | 135 000 |
| | | 4. Material usage variance (material B) | 16 500 |
| | 341 500 | | 341 500 |

### Creditors control account

| | | | |
|---|---:|---|---:|
| 2. Material price variance (material B) | 10 100 | 1. Stores ledger control (material A) | 190 000 |
| | | 1. Material price variance (material A) | 19 000 |
| | | 2. Stores ledger control (material B) | 151 500 |

### Variance accounts

| | | | |
|---|---:|---|---:|
| 1. Creditors (material A) | 19 000 | 2. Creditors (material price B) | 10 100 |
| 3. Stores ledger control (material A usage) | 10 000 | 8. Fixed factory overhead (expenditure) | 4 000 |
| 4. Stores ledger control (material B usage) | 16 500 | 9. Variable factory overhead (expenditure) | 5 000 |
| 6. Wages control (wage rate) | 17 100 | | 19 100 |
| 6. Wages control (lab. effic'y) | 13 500 | 13. Costing P + L a/c (balance) | 72 000 |
| 8. Fixed factory overhead (volume) | 12 000 | | |
| 9. Variable factory overhead (effic'y) | 3 000 | | |
| | 91 100 | | 91 100 |

### Work in progress control account

| | | | |
|---|---:|---|---:|
| 3. Stores ledger (material A) | 180 000 | 10. Finished goods stock account | 720 000 |
| 4. Stores ledger (material B) | 135 000 | | |
| 6. Wages control | 243 000 | | |
| 8. Fixed factory overhead | 108 000 | | |
| 9. Variable factory overhead | 54 000 | | |
| | 720 000 | | 720 000 |

### Wages control account

| | | | | |
|---|---|---|---|---|
| 5. Wages accrued account | 273 600 | 6. WIP | | 243 000 |
| | | 6. Wage rate variance | | 17 100 |
| | | 6. Labour efficiency variance | | 13 500 |
| | 273 600 | | | 273 600 |

### Fixed factory overhead control account

| | | | |
|---|---|---|---|
| 7. Expense creditors | 116 000 | 8. WIP | 108 000 |
| 8. Expenditure variance | 4 000 | 8. Volume variance | 12 000 |
| | 120 000 | | 120 000 |

### Variable factory overhead control account

| | | | |
|---|---|---|---|
| 7. Expense creditors | 52 000 | 9. WIP | 54 000 |
| 9. Expenditure | 5 000 | 9. Efficiency variance | 3 000 |
| | 57 000 | | 57 000 |

### Finished goods stock control account

| | | | |
|---|---|---|---|
| 10. WIP | 720 000 | 12. Cost of sales | 720 000 |

### Cost of sales account

| | | | |
|---|---|---|---|
| 12. Finish goods stock | 720 000 | 13. Costing P + L a/c | 720 000 |

### Costing P + L Account

| | | | |
|---|---|---|---|
| 12. Cost of sales at standard cost | 720 000 | 11. Sales | 810 000 |
| 13. Variance account (net variances) | 72 000 | | |
| Profit for period | 18 000 | | |
| | 810 000 | | 810 000 |

completed production is transferred from work in progress to finished goods stock, the accounting entries will be as follows:

| | | |
|---|---|---|
| 10. Dr Finished stock account | 720 000 | |
| 10. Cr Work in progress account | | 720 000 |

Because there are no opening or closing stocks, both the work in progress account and the stores ledger account will show a nil balance.

## SALES

Sales variances are not recorded in the accounts, so actual sales of £810 000 for 9000 units will be recorded as

| | | |
|---|---|---|
| 11. Dr Debtors | 810 000 | |
| 11. Cr Sales | | 810 000 |

As all the production for the period has been sold, there will be no closing stock of finished goods, and the standard cost of production for the 9000 units will be transferred from the finished goods account to the cost of sales account:

|  |  |  |  |
|---|---|---|---|
| 12. Dr Cost of sales account | | 288 000 | |
| 12. Cr Finished goods account | | | 288 000 |

Finally, the cost of sales account and the variance accounts will be closed by a transfer to the costing profit and loss account (the item labelled 13 in Exhibit 19.1). The balance of the costing profit and loss account will be the *actual* profit for the period.

## CALCULATION OF PROFIT

To calculate the profit, we must add the adverse variances and deduct the favourable variances from the standard cost of sales, which is obtained from the cost of sales account. This calculation gives the actual cost of sales for the period, which is then deducted from the actual sales to produce the actual profit for the period. The calculations are as follows:

|  | (£) | (£) | (£) |
|---|---|---|---|
| Sales | | | 810 000 |
| Less standard cost of sales | | 720 000 | |
| Plus adverse variances: | | | |
| Material A price variance | 19 000 | | |
| Material usage variance | 26 500 | | |
| Wage rate variance | 17 100 | | |
| Labour efficiency variance | 13 500 | | |
| Volume variance | 12 000 | | |
| Variable overhead efficiency variance | 3 000 | 91 100 | |
| | | 811 100 | |
| Less favourable variances: | | | |
| Material B price variance | 10 100 | | |
| Fixed overhead expenditure variance | 4 000 | | |
| Variable overhead expenditure variance | 5 000 | 19 100 | |
| Actual cost of sales | | | 792 000 |
| Actual profit | | | 18 000 |

# Accounting disposition of variances

At the end of an accounting period a decision must be made as to how the variances that have arisen during the period should be treated in the accounts. Variance may be disposed of in either of the following ways:

1. Adopt the approach illustrated in Exhibit 19.1 and charge the variances as expenses to the period in which they arise. With this approach, inventories are valued at standard cost.

2. Allocate the variances between inventories and cost of goods sold.

If standards are current and attainable then charging the total amount of the variances for the period to the profit and loss account is recommended, since the variances are likely to represent efficiencies or inefficiencies. This approach is justified on the grounds that the cost of inefficient operations is not recoverable in the selling price, and should not therefore be deferred and included in the inventory valuation, but should be charged to the period in which the inefficiency occurred.

Where standards are not current, the second method can be used and variances allocated between inventories and cost of goods sold. The effect is to include with the cost of inventories the portion of the variance that is applicable to the stocks in inventory, and thereby to arrive at the approximate actual cost of these stocks. In practice, a company may treat different types of variances in different ways. Some may be written off in their entirety against the current period, while others may be divided between inventories and cost of goods sold. For example, price variances are frequently not controllable by a firm because they can arise following changes in the external market prices. It can therefore be argued that those price variances that are unavoidable should be allocated between inventories and cost of goods sold.

To illustrate the method of allocating variances between inventories and cost of goods sold, consider a situation where the percentages of cost elements in the inventories and cost of goods sold are as follows:

|  | Materials (%) | Labour (%) | Factory overhead (%) |
|---|---|---|---|
| Raw material stocks | 20 | — | — |
| Work in progress | 10 | 15 | 20 |
| Finished goods stocks | 15 | 25 | 30 |
| Cost of goods sold | 55 | 60 | 50 |
|  | 100 | 100 | 100 |

Assume that the following variances for a particular period are to be allocated between inventories and cost of goods sold:

|  | (£) |
|---|---|
| Material price | 30 000 |
| Wage rate | 20 000 |
| Overhead expenditure | 10 000 |

The variances would be allocated as follows:

|  | Material price (£) | Wage rate (£) | Overhead expenditure (£) | Total (£) |
|---|---|---|---|---|
| Raw material stocks | 6 000 | — | — | 6 000 |
| Work in progress | 3 000 | 3 000 | 2 000 | 8 000 |
| Finished goods stocks | 4 500 | 5 000 | 3 000 | 12 500 |
| Cost of goods sold | 16 500 | 12 000 | 5 000 | 33 500 |
|  | 30 000 | 20 000 | 10 000 | 60 000 |

At the end of the period the above figures are allocated to the cost of sales and inventory control accounts, but the subsidiary inventory accounts and records are not adjusted. At the beginning of the next period the inventory allocations are reversed (by crediting the inventory accounts and debiting the variance accounts) in order to return beginning inventories to standard costs. At the end of that period the amounts reversed plus new variances are allocated in the same manner as before, based on the standard cost of ending inventory and cost of goods sold balances. For a further illustration relating to the accounting disposition of variances you should refer to the answer to 19.19 in the *Students' Manual* accompanying this book.

# *Ex post* variance analysis

**AR** Standard costing variance analysis has some recognized disadvantages. Most of the problems centre around the comparison of actual performance with the standard. If the standard is weak then the comparison is also likely to be weak. Standards or plans are normally based on the environment that is anticipated when the targets are set. However, Demski (1977) has argued that if the environment is different from that anticipated, actual performance should be compared with a standard which reflects these changed conditions (i.e. an *ex post* **variance analysis approach**). Clearly, to measure managerial performance, we should compare like with like and compare actual results with adjusted standards based on the conditions that managers actually operated during the period. Let us now apply this principle to a selection of cost variances. For a more detailed discussion of the items covered in the foregoing section you should refer to the answers to Questions 19.25 and 19.26 in the *Students' Manual* accompanying this book.

Consider Example 19.3.

The conventional material price variance is £1800 adverse (10 000 units at £0.18). However, this variance consists of an adverse planning variance of £2000 that is due to incorrect estimates of the target buying price and a favourable purchasing efficiency (operational) variance of £200. The planning variance is calculated as follows:

> **purchasing planning variance**
> = (original target price − general market price at the time of purchase)
>   × quantity purchased
> = (£5 − £5.20) × 10 000
> = £2000 A

This planning variance is not controllable, but it does provide useful feedback information to management on how successful they are in forecasting material prices, thus helping managers to improve their future estimates of material prices.

The efficiency of the purchasing department is assessed by a purchasing efficiency variance. This variance measures the purchasing department's efficiency for the conditions that actually prevailed and is calculated as follows:

> **purchasing efficiency variance**
> = (general market price − actual price paid) × quantity purchased
> = (£5.20 − £5.18) × 10 000
> = £200F

---

**EXAMPLE 19.3**

The standard cost per unit of raw material was estimated to be £5 per unit. The general market price at the time of purchase was £5.20 per unit and the actual price paid was £5.18 per unit. 10 000 units of the raw materials were purchased during the period.

Hence the conventional price variance of £1800 adverse can be divided into an *uncontrollable* adverse material planning variance of £2000 and a *controllable* favourable purchasing efficiency variance of £200. This analysis give a clearer indication of the efficiency of the purchasing function, and avoids including an adverse uncontrollable planning variance in performance reports. If an adverse price variance of £1800 is reported, this is likely to lead to dysfunctional motivation effects if the purchasing department have performed the purchasing function efficiently.

In practice, standard prices are often set on an annual basis, with the target representing the average for the year. Price changes will occur throughout the year, and it is unlikely that the actual prices paid for the materials will be equal to the average for the year as a whole even if actual prices are equal to the prices used to set the average standard price. Consequently, with rising prices actual prices will be less than the average earlier in the year (showing favourable variances) and above average standard later in the year (showing adverse variances).

This problem can be overcome by calculating separate purchasing planning and efficiency variances.

## MATERIAL USAGE VARIANCE

Part of the material usage variance may also be due to uncontrollable environmental changes. For example, materials may be in short supply and it may be necessary to purchase inferior substitute materials. The material usage variance should therefore be based on a comparison of actual usage with an adjusted standard that takes account of the change in environmental conditions. The difference between the original standard and the adjusted standard represents an uncontrollable planning variance. Example 19.4 illustrates the analysis of the material usage variance.

The conventional analysis would report an adverse material usage variance of £200 (200 kg at £1), but this is misleading if all or part of this variance is due to uncontrollable environmental changes. When the standard is adjusted to take into account the changed conditions, the standard quantity is 6 kg per unit, which gives a *revised* standard of 1500 kg for an output of 250 units. The difference between this revised standard and the original standard quantity of 1250 kg (250 units at 5 kg per unit) represents the **uncontrollable planning variance** due to environmental changes. The uncontrollable planning variance is therefore £250 adverse, and is calculated as follows:

$$\text{(original standard quantity} - \text{revised standard quantity)} \times \text{standard price}$$
$$= (1250 - 1500) \times £1$$

---

**EXAMPLE 19.4**

The standard quantity of materials per unit of production for a product is 5 kg. Actual production for the period was 250 units and actual material usage was 1450 kg. The standard cost per kg of materials was £1. Because of a shortage of skilled labour, it has been necessary to use unskilled labour and it is estimated that this will increase the material usage by 20%.

The revised **controllable usage variance** is the difference between the standard quantity of 1500 kg, based on the revised standard usage, and the actual usage of 1450 kg. Hence the controllable usage variance will be £50 favourable.

The conventional material usage variance of £200 adverse has been divided into an uncontrollable adverse planning variance of £250 and a revised controllable usage variance of £50 favourable. This approach produces variance calculations that provide a truer representation of a manager's performance and avoids any uncontrollable elements being included in the material usage variance.

## LABOUR VARIANCES

The criticisms we have identified for the material variances are also applicable to the labour variances. For example, the labour efficiency and wage rate variances should be adjusted to reflect changes in the environmental conditions that prevailed during the period. A situation where this might occur is when unskilled labour is substituted for skilled labour because of conditions in the labour market. It is necessary in these circumstances to adjust the standard and separate the labour efficiency and wage rate variances into the following components:

- an uncontrollable planning variance due to environmental changes;
- a controllable efficiency and wage rate variance.

The variance should be calculated in a similar manner to that described for material variances.

## SALES VARIANCES

The conventional sales volume variance reports the difference between actual and budgeted sales priced at the budgeted contribution per unit. This variance merely indicates whether sales volume is greater or less than expected. It does not indicate how well sales management has performed. In order to appraise the performance of sales management, actual sales volume should be compared with an *ex post* estimate that reflects the market conditions prevailing during the period.

Consider a situation where the budgeted sales are 100 000 units at a standard contribution of £100 per unit. Assume that actual sales are 110 000 units and that actual selling price is identical with the budgeted selling price. The conventional approach would report a favourable sales volume variance of £1m (10 000 units at £100 contribution per unit). However, the market size was greater than expected and, if the company had attained its target market share for the period, sales volume should have been 120 000 units. In other words, the *ex post* standard sales volume is 120 000 units. Actual sales volume is 10 000 units less than would have been expected after the circumstances prevailing during the period are taken into account. The *ex post* variance approach would therefore report an adverse sales volume appraisal variance of £1m (10 000 units × £100). Conversely, if the total market demand had fallen because of reasons outside the control of sales management, actual sales volume would be assessed against a more realistic lower standard.

The difference between the original budgeted sales volume of 100 000 units and the *ex post* budgeted sales volume of 120 000 units, priced at the budgeted contribution, represents the planning variance. A planning variance of £2m (20 000 units at a contribution of £100 per unit) would therefore be reported. The sum of the planning variance (2m favourable) and the *ex post* sales volume variance (£1m adverse) equals the conventional sales volume variance.

The *ex post* approach provides an opportunity cost view of the performance of sales management by reporting a forgone contribution of £1m. The conventional approach reports a favourable performance, whereas the *ex post* approach reports that sales management has under-performed by indicating the cost to the company of neglected opportunities. The conventional variance is irrelevant, since it merely indicates whether or not sales management has beaten an obsolete target.

In our illustration we have assumed that actual selling price was equal to the budgeted selling price. A zero sales price variance would therefore be reported, and the sales volume variance would be equal to the *total* sales margin variance. It is questionable whether separating the total sales margin variance into a volume and a price variance provides any meaningful extra information. We noted earlier in this chapter that selling prices and sales volumes are inter-related and that the logical consequence of lower/higher selling price is higher/lower sales volume. It is therefore recommended that only the total sales margin variance be reported. The variance should be separated into planning and appraisal elements using the following formulae:

Total sales margin variance (planing element):
  *ex post* budgeted sales volume × (*ex post* selling price − standard cost)
    − original budgeted sales volume × (budgeted selling price − standard cost)

Total sales margin variance (appraisal element):
  actual sales volume × (actual selling price − standard cost)
    − *ex post* budgeted sales volume × (*ex post* selling price − standard cost)

The *ex post* budgeted sales volume for a particular product can be determined by estimating the total market sales volume for the period and then multiplying this estimate by the target percentage market share. Where industry statistics are published, this calculation should be based on actual total industry sales volume.

Where a company markets several different product lines, separate variances should be calculated for each. Mix variances should only be reported where there are identifiable relationships between the volumes of each product sold and these relationships are incorporated into the budgeting process.

# Variance analysis and the opportunity cost of scarce resources

We shall now consider situations where production resources are scarce. Thus any failure to use the scarce resources efficiently results in forgone profits that should be included in the appropriate variance analysis calculations. To keep things simple at this stage, we shall assume that only one production resource is scarce, the *ex post* standard is identical with the original standard and actual and budgeted input prices are identical. An overview of the analysis is given in Figure 19.2.

Figure 19.2 illustrates a situation where a company uses a single resource that is restricted to 4000 units. Each unit of output consumes 4 units of input of the resource. Therefore budgeted output is limited to 1000 units (i.e. OB in the figure). The budgeted cost per unit of output is £4 (4 units of input at £1 per unit), and the budgeted and actual selling price is £10 per unit of output. Budgeted total contribution for the period is

**FIGURE 19.2** *Variance analysis and the opportunity cost of scarce resources.*

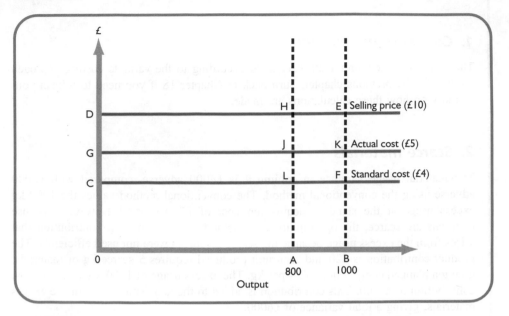

therefore £6000 (1000 units at £6), and is indicated by the area CDEF in the diagram. Assume that the actual consumption of the scarce resource is 5 units, instead of 4. Hence the actual cost per unit of output is £5 and is represented by the horizontal line GK. Maximum output will therefore be 800 units (4000/5 units), represented by OA in the diagram, and the actual profit will be £4000 (800 units at an actual contribution of £5 per unit), indicated by the area GDHJ. The difference between the budgeted and actual profit is £2000 (represented by the area HEFL, plus the area CGJL).

Conventional variance analysis would report an adverse *usage* cost variance of £800 (800 units × £1), equivalent to the area CGJL, and an adverse sales volume variance of £1200 (200 units at a contribution of £6 per unit), represented by the area HEFL. However, the failure to achieve the budgeted optimum output is due to the inefficient usage of the scarce resource. The forgone contribution should be charged to the manager responsible for controlling the usage of the scarce resource – not the sales manager – because the failure to achieve the budgeted sales is due to a failure to use the scarce resource efficiently. As a general rule, where resources are scarce, the usage variance (800 units) should be priced at the acquisition cost (£1 per unit) plus the budgeted contribution per unit of the scarce resource (£6 per unit of output/4 units of input). The conventional approach prices variances for scarce resources at their acquisition cost.

The above analysis is based on the assumption that any lost sales are lost for ever. However, if the lost sales volume can be made up in later periods, the real opportunity cost arising from a failure to use scarce resources efficiently would consist of the lost interest arising from the delay in receiving the net cash inflows, and not the foregone contribution.

In order to provide a clearer understanding of the computation of variances when resources are scarce, we shall compute the variances for the situation outlined in Example 19.5. An analysis of the variances and a reconciliation of the budgeted and actual profits is presented in Exhibit 19.2. Note that Example 19.5 has been designed so that all the price variances are zero. This will enable us to concentrate on the quantity variances. Let us now consider each of the columns in Exhibit 19.2.

## 1. Conventional method

The variances in column 1 are calculated according to the variable costing approach outlined in the previous chapter. Turn back to Chapter 18 if you need to refresh your memory on how these calculations are made.

## 2. Scarce materials

The material usage variance in column 2 is £6000 adverse, compared with £2000 adverse using the conventional method. The conventional method values the 1000 kg excess usage at the standard acquisition cost of £2 per unit.[1] However, because materials are scarce, the opportunity cost method includes the lost contribution that arises from the excess usage because the scarce resources were not used efficiently. The product contribution is £20 and each unit produced requires 5 scarce kg of materials, giving a planned contribution of £4 per kg. The excess usage of 1000 kg leads to a lost contribution of £4000. This contribution is added to the acquisition cost for the excess materials, giving a total variance of £6000.

Because labour hours are not scarce, the labour variances are identical with those from the conventional method. The computation of the sales margin volume variance, however, is different from the conventional method because the failure to achieve budgeted sales is due to a failure to use the scarce materials efficiently. Hence the cost should be charged to the responsible production manager and not the sales manager.

## 3. Scarce labour

Because it is assumed that materials are no longer scarce, the materials usage variance in column 3 is identical with the conventional method calculation in column 1. Since labour hours are scarce, the acquisition cost will not reflect the true economic cost for the labour efficiency variance. The conventional approach values the 800 excess hours at the standard acquisition cost of £9 per hour, but the opportunity cost method in column 3 adds the lost contribution from the excess usage of 800 scarce labour hours.[2] The product contribution is £20 and each unit produced required 4 scarce labour hours, so each labour hour is planned to yield a £5 contribution. Thus the 800 excess labour hours lead to a £4000 lost contribution. This lost contribution of £4000 is added to the acquisition cost for the excess labour hours, giving a variance of £11 200.

## 4. No scarce inputs

Where there are no scarce production inputs, the failure to achieve the budgeted sales volume is the responsibility of the sales manager. The lost sales volume of 200 units results in a lost contribution of £20 per unit, giving an adverse sales volume variance of £4000. In this situation there is no lost contribution arising from the inefficient use of resources, which are not scarce. Cost variances should therefore be priced at their standard acquisition cost. We can conclude that where production inputs are not scarce, and the *ex post* standards are identical with the original standards, variances should be reported adopting the conventional approach illustrated in column 1.

**EXAMPLE 19.5**

XYZ Ltd manufacture a single product, the standards of which are as follows:

|  | (£) | (£) |
|---|---|---|
| Standard per unit |  |  |
| Standard selling price |  | 72 |
| Less standard cost |  |  |
| Material (5 kg at £2 per kg) | 10 |  |
| Labour (4 hours at £9 per hour) | 36 |  |
| Variable overheads (4 hours at £1.50 per hour)[a] | 6 | 52 |
| Standard contribution |  | 20 |

[a]Variable overheads are assumed to vary with direct labour hours

The following information relates to the previous month's activities.

|  | Budget | Actual |
|---|---|---|
| Production and sales | 2000 units | 1800 units |
| Direct materials | 10 000 kg at £2 per kg | 10 000 kg at £2 per kg |
| Direct labour | 8000 hours at £9 per hour | 8000 hours at £9 per hour |
| Variable overheads | £12 000 | £12 000 |
| Fixed overheads | £12 000 | £12 000 |
| Profit | £28 000 | £13 600 |

The actual selling price was identical with the budgeted selling price and there were no opening or closing stocks during the period.

You are required to calculate the variances and reconcile the budgeted and actual profit for each of the following methods:

1. The traditional (or conventional) method.
2. The relevant cost method assuming *materials* are the limiting factor and materials are restricted to 10 000 kg for the period.
3. The relevant cost method assuming *labour hours* are the limiting factor and labour hours are restricted to 8000 hours for the period.
4. The relevant cost method assuming there are no scarce inputs.

## CONCLUSION

There are strong arguments for valuing variances at their opportunity cost. This approach requires that scarce resources be identified in advance of production, but this is not easy to do in practice. In addition, the approach must rely on linear programming techniques when more than one scarce resource exists. (Multiple resource constraints are discussed in Chapter 26.) The important points that you should note from this discussion are, first, that if quantity variances are valued at the acquisition cost of resources, this may not be a true reflection of the correct economic cost. Secondly, standard costing variance analysis must not be viewed as a mechanical procedure, but rather as an intelligent approach to charging the controllable economic cost of the difference between actual and target performance to responsible individuals.

**EXHIBIT 19.2**

*Variance analysis using a conventional and opportunity cost approach*

| | (1) Conventional method (£) | (2) Scarce materials (£) | (3) Scarce labour hours (£) |
|---|---|---|---|
| Budgeted profit | 28 000 | 28 000 | 28 000 |
| Direct material usage variance | 2 000A | 6 000A | 2 000A |
| Labour efficiency variance | 7 200A | 7 200A | 11 200A |
| Variable overhead efficiency | 1 200A | 1 200A | 1 200A |
| Sales margin volume | 4 000A | Nil | Nil |
| Actual profit | 13 600 | 13 600 | 13 600 |

# The investigation of variances

In Chapter 18 we noted that a standard costing system consists of the following:

1. setting standards for each operation;
2. comparing actual with standard performance;
3. analysing and reporting variances arising from the difference between actual and standard performance;
4. investigating significant variances and taking appropriate corrective action.

In the final stage of this process management must decide which variances should be investigated. They could adopt a policy of investigating every reported variance. Such a policy would, however, be very expensive and time-consuming, and would lead to investigating some variances that would not result in improvements in operations even if the cause of the variance was determined. If, on the other hand, management do not investigate reported variances, the control function would be ignored. The optimal policy lies somewhere between these two extremes. In other words, the objective is to investigate only those variances that yield benefits in excess of the cost of investigation.

We shall now consider some of the cost variance investigation models developed in the accounting literature. These models can be classified into the following categories.

1. *Simple rule of thumb models* based on arbitrary criteria such as investigating if the absolute size of a variance is greater than a certain amount or if the ratio of the variance to the total standard cost exceeds some predetermined percentage.
2. *Statistical models* that compute the probability that a given variance comes from an in-control distribution but that does not take into account the costs and benefits of investigation.

3. *Statistical decision models* that take into account the cost and benefits of investigation.

To help you to understand the variance investigation models, we shall start by considering the reasons why actual performance might differ from standard performance.

# Types of variances

There are several reasons why actual performance might differ from standard performance. A variance may arise simply as a result of an error in measuring the actual outcome. A second cause relates to standards becoming out of date because of changes in production conditions. Thirdly, variances can result from efficient or inefficient operations. Finally, variances can be due to random or chance fluctuations for which no cause can be found.

## MEASUREMENT ERRORS

The recorded amounts for actual costs or actual usage may differ from the actual amounts. For example, labour hours for a particular operation may be incorrectly added up or indirect labour costs might be incorrectly classified as a direct labour cost. Unless an investigation leads to an improvement in the accuracy of the recording system, it is unlikely that any benefits will be obtained where the cause is found to be due to measurement errors.

## OUT-OF-DATE STANDARDS

Where frequent changes in prices of inputs occur, there is a danger that standard prices may be out of date. Consequently any investigation of price variances will indicate a general change in market prices rather than any efficiencies or inefficiencies in acquiring the resources. Standards can also become out of date where operations are subject to frequent technological changes or fail to take into account learning-curve effects. Investigation of variances falling into this category will provide feedback on the inaccuracy of the standards and highlight the need to update the standard. Where standards are revised, it may be necessary to alter some of the firm's output or input decisions. Ideally, standards ought to be frequently reviewed and, where appropriate, updated in order to minimize variances being reported that are due to standards being out of date.

## OUT-OF-CONTROL OPERATIONS

Variances may result from inefficient operations due to a failure to follow prescribed procedures, faulty machinery or human errors. Investigation of variances in this category should pinpoint the cause of the inefficiency and lead to corrective action to eliminate the inefficiency being repeated.

## RANDOM OR UNCONTROLLABLE FACTORS

These occur when a particular process is performed by the same worker under the same conditions, yet performance varies. When no known cause is present to account for this variability, it is said to be due to **random or uncontrollable factors**. A standard is determined from a series of observations of a particular operation. It is most unlikely that repeated observations of this operation will yield the same result, even if the operation consists of the same worker repeating the same task under identical conditions. The correct approach is to choose a representative reading from these observations to determine a standard. Frequently, the representative reading that is chosen is the average or some other measure of central tendency. The important point to note is that one summary reading has been chosen to represent the standard when in reality a range of outcomes is possible when the process is *under control*. Any observation that differs from the chosen standard when the process is under control can be described as a random uncontrollable variation around the standard.

Any investigation of variances due to random uncontrollable factors will involve a cost, and will not yield any benefits because no assignable cause for the variance is present. Furthermore, those variances arising from **assignable causes** (such as inaccurate data, out of date standards or out-of-control operations) do not necessarily warrant investigation. For example, such variances may only be worthy of investigation if the benefits expected from the investigation exceed the costs of searching for and correcting the sources of the variance.

Variances may therefore be due to the following causes:

1. random uncontrollable factors when the operation is under control;
2. assignable causes, but with the costs of investigation exceeding the benefits;
3. assignable causes, but with the benefits from investigation exceeding the cost of investigation.

A perfect cost investigation model would investigate only those variances falling in the third category.

# Simple rule of thumb cost investigation models

In many companies managers use simple models based on arbitrary criteria such as investigating if the absolute size of a variance is greater than a certain amount or if the variance exceeds the standard cost by some predetermined percentage (say 10%). For example, if the standard usage for a particular component was 10 kilos and the actual output for a period was 1000 components then the variance would not be investigated if actual usage was between 9000 and 11 000 kilos.

The advantages of using simple arbitrary rules are their simplicity and ease of implementation. There are, however, several disadvantages. Simple rule of thumb models do not adequately take into account the statistical significance of the reported variances or consider the costs and benefits of an investigation. For example, investigating all variances that exceed the standard cost by a fixed percentage can lead to investigating many variances of small amounts.

Some of these difficulties can be overcome by applying different percentages or amounts for different expense items as the basis for the investigation decision. For example, smaller percentages might be used as a signal to investigate key expense items, and a higher percentage applied to less important items of expense. Nevertheless, such approaches still do not adequately take into account the statistical significance of the reported variances, or balance the cost and benefits of investigation. Instead, they rely on managerial judgement and intuition in selecting the 'cut-off' values.

# Statistical models not incorporating costs and benefits of investigation

A number of cost variance investigation models have been proposed in the accounting literature that determine the statistical probability that a variance comes from an in-control distribution. An investigation is undertaken when the probability that an observation comes from an in-control distribution falls below some arbitrarily determined probability level. The statistical models that we shall consider assume that two mutually exclusive states are possible. One state assumes that the system is 'in control' and a variance is simply due to random fluctuations around the expected outcome. The second possible state is that the system is in some way 'out of control' and corrective action can be taken to remedy the situation. We shall also assume that the 'in-control' state can be expressed in the form of a known probability distribution such as a normal one.

## DETERMINING PROBABILITIES

Consider a situation where the standard material usage for a particular operation has been derived from the average (i.e. the expected value) of a series of past observations made under 'close' supervision to ensure they reflected operations under normal efficiency. The average usage is 10 kg per unit of output. We shall assume that the actual observations were normally distributed with a standard deviation of 1 kg. Suppose that the actual material usage for a period was 12 000 kg and that output was 1000 units. Thus average usage was 12 kg per unit of output. We can ascertain the probability of observing an average usage of 12 kg or more when the process is under control by applying normal distribution theory. An observation of an average usage of 12 kg per unit of output is 2 standard deviations from the expected value, where, for a normal distribution,

$$Z = \frac{\text{actual usage (12 kg)} - \text{expected usage (10 kg)}}{\text{standard deviation (1 kg)}} = 2.0$$

A table of areas under the normal distribution (see Appendix C shown on page 1088) indicates that there is a probability of 0.02275 that an observation from that distribution will occur at least 2 standard deviations above the mean. This is illustrated in Figure 19.3. The shaded area indicates that 2.275% of the area under the curve falls to the right of 2 standard deviations from the mean. Thus the probability of actual material usage per unit of output being 12 kg or more when the operation is under control is 2.275%. It is very unlikely that the observation comes from a distribution with a mean of 10 kg and a standard deviation of 1 kg. In other words, it is likely that this observation comes from another distribution and that the material usage for the period is out of control.

Where the standard is derived from a small number of observations, we only have an estimate of the standard deviation, rather than the true standard deviation, and the deviation from the mean follows a *t*-distribution rather than a normal distribution. The *t*-distribution has more dispersion than the normal distribution so as to allow for the

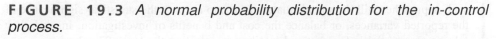

**FIGURE 19.3** *A normal probability distribution for the in-control process.*

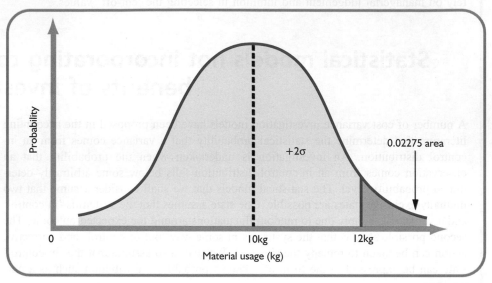

additional uncertainty that exists where an estimate is used instead of the true standard deviation. However, as the number of observations increases, to about 30, the values of a *t*-distribution shown on a *t*-table approach the values on a table for a normal distribution. Assume that the mean and the standard deviation were derived from 10 observations when the process was under control. The probability that a random variable having a *t*-distribution with 9 degrees of freedom ($n - 1$) will exceed 2 standard deviations from the mean is still small, equal to approximately 0.025 (or 1 chance in 40).[3] Therefore it is still likely that the observation comes from another distribution, and thus the material usage for the period is out of control.

## STATISTICAL CONTROL CHARTS

Variances can be monitored by recording the number of standard deviations each observation is from the mean of the in-control distribution (10 kg in our illustration) on a statistical control chart. **Statistical quality control charts** are widely used as a quality control technique to test whether a batch of produced items is within pre-set tolerance limits. Usually samples from a particular production process are taken at hourly or daily intervals. The mean, and sometimes the range, of the sampled items are calculated and plotted on a quality control chart (Figure 19.4). A control chart is a graph of a series of past observations (which can be a single observation, a mean or a range of samples) in which each observation is plotted relative to pre-set points on the expected distribution. Only observations beyond specified pre-set control limits are regarded as worthy of investigation.

The control limits are set based on a series of past observations of a process when it is under control, and thus working efficiently. It is assumed that the past observations can be represented by a normal distribution.

The past observations are used to estimate the population mean and the population standard deviation $\sigma$. Assuming that the distribution of possible outcomes is normal, then, when the process is under control, we should expect

**FIGURE 19.4**  *Statistical quality control charts.*

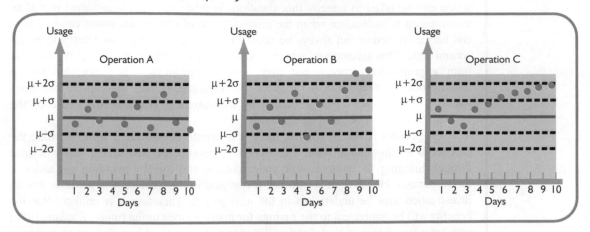

68.27% of the observations to fall within the range $+1\sigma$ from the mean;
95.45% of the observations to fall within the range $+2\sigma$ from the mean;
99.8% of the observations to fall within the range $+3\sigma$ from the mean.

Control limits are now set. For example, if control limits are set based on two standard deviations from the mean then this would indicate 4.55% (100% – 95.45%) of future observations would result from pure chance when the process is under control. Therefore there is a high probability that an observation outside the 2 control limits is out of control.

Figure 19.4 shows three control charts, with the outer horizontal lines representing a possible control limit of $2\sigma$, so that all observations outside this range are investigated. You will see that for operation A the process is deemed to be in control because all observations fall within the control limits. For operation B the last two observations suggest that the operation is out of control. Therefore both observations should be investigated. With operation C the observations would not prompt an investigation because all the observations are within the control limits. However, the last six observations show a steadily increasing usage in excess of the mean, and the process may be out of control. Statistical procedures (called casum procedures) that consider the trend in recent usage as well as daily usage can also be used.

Statistical quality control is used mainly for product or quality control purposes, but within a standard costing context, statistical control charts can be used to monitor accounting variances. For example, labour usage and material usage could be plotted on a control chart on a hourly or daily basis for each operation. This process would consist of sampling the output from an operation and plotting on the chart the mean usage of resources per unit for the sample output.

# Decision models with costs and benefits of investigation

Statistical decision models have been extended to incorporate the costs and benefits of investigation. A simple decision theory single-period model for the investigation of variances was advocated by Bierman *et al.* (1977). The model assumes that two mutually exclusive states are possible. One state assumes that the system is in control and a variance is simply due to a random fluctuation around the expected outcome. The second possible state is that the system is in some way out of control and corrective action can be taken to remedy this situation. In other words, it is assumed that if an investigation is undertaken when the process is out of control, the cause can be found and corrective action can always be taken to ensure that the process returns to its in-control state. This assumption is more appropriate for controlling the quality of output from a production process, but may not be appropriate when extended to the investigation of standard cost variances. For example, it does not capture situations where the investigation was signalled by measurement errors or the cause of the variance was due to out of date standards.

If the process is out of control, there is a benefit $B$ associated with returning the process to its 'in-control' state. This benefit represents the cost saving that will arise through bringing the system back under control and thereby avoiding variances in future periods. However, if we do not investigate in this period, it is possible that an investigation may be undertaken in the next period. Therefore it is unlikely that the benefits will be equivalent to the savings for many periods in the future. Kaplan (1982) concludes that $B$ should be defined as the expected one-period benefit from operating in control rather than out of control, recognizing that this will underestimate the actual benefits.

A cost of $C$ will be incurred when an investigation is undertaken. This cost includes the manager's time spent on investigation, the cost of interrupting the production process, and the cost of correcting the process. We shall assume that the costs to correct of an investigation that discovers that the process is 'out of control' are identical with the costs associated with finding that the process is 'in control'. However, the model can be easily modified to incorporate the incremental correction costs if the process is found to be out of control.

To illustrate a one-period model let us assume that the incremental cost of investigating the material usage variance in our earlier illustration (see page 757) is £100. Assume also that the estimated benefit $B$ from investigating a variance and taking corrective action is £400. We can therefore develop a simple decision rule: investigate if the expected benefit is greater than the expected cost. Denoting by $P$ the probability that the process is *out* of control, the expected benefit can be expressed as

$$\text{expected benefit} = PB + (1 - P)B$$
$$= PB + (1 - P)0$$
$$= PB$$

The probability that the system is *in* control is $1 - P$, and the benefit arising from investigating an 'in-control' situation is zero. Therefore $PB$ represents the expected benefit of investigating a variance. Assuming that the cost of investigation $C$ is known with certainty, the decision rule is to investigate if

$$PB > C, \text{ or } P > C/B$$

In our example we should investigate if

$$P > 100/400 = 0.25$$

The model requires an estimate of $P$, the probability that the process is out of control. Bierman *et al.* (1977) have suggested that the probabilities could be determined by computing the probability that a particular observation, such as a variance, comes from an 'in-control' distribution. They also assume that the 'in-control' state can be expressed in the form of a known probability distribution such as a normal distribution. Consider our earlier example shown on page 757, where the expected usage based on actual observation when the process in control was 10 kg per unit of output with a standard deviation of 1 kg. We noted that the recorded actual average usage of 12 kg for a particular period exceeded the mean of the distribution by 2 standard deviations. We referred to a normal probability table to ascertain that the probability of an observation of 12 kg (or larger) was 0.02275 (2.275%).[4] The probability of the process being out of control is 1 minus the probability of being in control.[5]

Thus $P = 1 - 0.02275 = 0.97725$. Recall that we ascertained that the variance should be investigated if the probability that the process is out of control is in excess of 0.25. The process should therefore be investigated. Instead of using the cost–benefit ratio $C/B$, we can ascertain whether

$$PB > C:$$
$$PB = 0.97725 \times £400 = £391$$
$$C = £100$$

Therefore the *expected value* of the benefits from investigation, $PB$, exceeds the cost of the investigation, $C$, and the variance should be investigated.

A major problem with decision theory models concerns the difficulty in determining the cost of investigation $C$ and the benefits arising from the investigation $B$. Note that $B$ is defined as the present value of the costs that will be incurred if an investigation is not made now. In situations where the inefficiency will be repeated there will be many opportunities in the future to correct the process, and the discounted future costs, assuming no future investigation, will be an overestimate of $B$. We have noted that Kaplan (1982) concludes that $B$ should be defined as the expected one-period benefit from operating in control rather than out of control, but recognizing that this will be an underestimate of the actual benefits. It is also assumed that when an out-of-control situation is discovered, action can be taken so that the process will be in-control. In many situations the variance may have been caused by a permanent change in the process, such as a change in the production process or in raw material availability. In such instances the investigation will not exceed the expected benefit, since future operations will remain at the current cost level. The cost–benefit variance investigation model does not take such factors into account. Some benefits will be derived, however, since standards can be altered to reflect the permanent changes in the production process. This should lead to improvements in planning and control in future periods.

Problems also arise with determining the cost of investigating variances. The cost of an investigation will vary, depending upon the cause of the variance. Some assignable causes will be detected before others, depending upon the ordering of the stages in the investigation procedure. If the variance is not due to an assignable cause, the cost of investigation will be higher because the investigation must eliminate all other causes before it can be established that the variance is not due to an assignable cause. Also, *additional* costs of carrying out the investigation may not be incurred, since they may be carried out by existing staff at no extra cost to the organization. However, some opportunity cost is likely to be involved because of alternative work forgone while the investigation is being undertaken.

# Quantity variances

Finally, it is important to note that the application of statistical techniques that incorporate random variations is only applicable to quantity variances – that is, labour efficiency and material usage variances. There is a fundamental difference between these variances and price variances. Efficiency cannot be predetermined in the

**EXHIBIT 19.3**

*Survey of company practice*

A USA survey by Lauderman and Schaeberle (1983) and two UK surveys (Puxty and Lyall, 1990; Drury *et al.*, 1993) indicate that the statistical models outlined in this chapter are rarely used and also that some firms use more than one method to determine when variances should be investigated.

| | Lauderman and Schaeberle (1983) (%) | Puxty and Lyall (1990) (%) |
|---|---|---|
| Decision based on managerial judgement | 72 | 81 |
| Variances investigated beyond a certain monetary amount | 54 | 36 |
| Variances investigated beyond a certain percentage | 43 | 26 |
| Investigation based on statistical decision rules | 4 | — |
| Variances investigated in all cases | — | 9 |
| (— no details reported) | | |

| *Drury* et al. *(1993) survey* | Extent to which method used | | | | |
| | Never (%) | Rarely (%) | Sometimes (%) | Often (%) | Always (%) |
|---|---|---|---|---|---|
| Decision based on managerial judgement | 8 | 5 | 12 | 53 | 22 |
| Investigation where a variance exceeds a specific amount | 12 | 17 | 31 | 34 | 6 |
| Investigation where a variance exceeds a given percentage of standard | 15 | 18 | 31 | 29 | 7 |
| Statistical basis using control charts or other statistical models | 60 | 25 | 12 | 2 | 1 |

same way as material prices and wage rates: first, because of the random variations inherent in the human element; and, secondly, because the resulting non-uniformity is more pronounced. One does not expect actual results to be equal to standard where the human element is involved, since some variances may be expected to occur even when no assignable cause is present. For this reason, statistical techniques should be applied only to quantity variances. For an indication of the extent to which statistical models are used in practice you should refer to Exhibit 19.3.

# Criticisms of standard costing

Standard costing systems were developed to meet the needs of a business environment drastically different from that which exists today. The usefulness of standard costing variance analysis in a modern business environment has been questioned and several writers have predicted its demise because of the following:

● the changing cost structure;
● inconsistency with modern management approaches;
● over-emphasizes the importance of direct labour;
● delay in feedback reporting.

## IMPACT OF THE CHANGING COST STRUCTURE

It is claimed that overhead costs have become the dominant factory costs, direct labour costs have diminished in importance and that most of a firm's costs have become fixed in the short-term. Given that standard costing is a mechanism that is most suited to the control of direct and variable costs, but not fixed or indirect costs, its usefulness has been questioned. However, recent surveys in many different countries have reported remarkably similar results in terms of cost structures. They all report that direct costs and overheads averaged approximately 75% and 25% respectively of total manufacturing costs with average direct labour costs varying from 10–15% of total manufacturing cost.

Clearly the claim by some commentators that overheads are the dominant factory costs is not supported by the survey evidence. Direct materials are the dominant costs in most manufacturing organizations and account for, on average, approximately 60% of total manufacturing costs. Direct labour costs are now of much less importance and tend to be fixed in the short-term. Direct materials and variable overheads (e.g. energy costs for running the machines) are now the only short-term variable costs. Thus, standard costing variance analysis for control purposes would appear to be only appropriate for direct materials and variable overheads, the latter being a small proportion of total manufacturing costs. However, the reporting of direct labour variances at periodic intervals is probably justified since efficiencies/inefficiencies in resource consumption are highlighted and provide useful feedback information for re-deploying labour or ensuring that in the longer-term changes in resource consumption are translated into changes in spending on the supply of direct labour resources.

## INCONSISTENCY WITH MODERN MANAGEMENT APPROACHES

In recent years many organizations have adopted new management approaches that focus on minimizing inventories, zero defective production, delivery of high quality products and services and a process of continuous improvement. Critics claim that variance analysis does not support today's management philosophy. For example, if purchase price variances are used to evaluate the performance of the purchasing function, it is likely that purchasing management will be motivated to focus entirely on obtaining the materials at the lowest possible prices even if this results in:

● the use of many suppliers (all of them selected on the basis of price);
● larger quantity purchases, thus resulting in larger inventories;

- delivery of lower quality goods;
- indifference to attaining on-time delivery.

Today, companies wish to focus on performance measures which emphasize all the factors important to the purchasing function, such as quality and reliability of suppliers, and not just price. Nevertheless, material price variances still have an important role to play.

It is also claimed that using the volume variance to measure unutilized capacity motivates managers to expand output and thus increase inventories. This is inconsistent with a philosophy of minimizing inventories. Favourable volume variances are reported whenever actual production exceeds budgeted production and therefore profit centre managers can manipulate monthly profits by expanding output and increasing profits. Attention has already been drawn to the fact that volume variances are inappropriate for short-term cost control and performance measurement purposes. If volume variances are being used for these purposes then the problem arises because of the faulty application, rather than the inadequacies, of standard costing.

Volume variances are required to meet financial accounting requirements. Even if standard costing is abandoned the under- or over-recovery of overheads is necessary to meet conventional absorption costing profit measurement requirements. It is therefore inappropriate to single out standard costing variance analysis as being responsible for the excess production. The solution is to replace absorption costing with a standard variable costing system for monthly internal reporting.

To compete successfully in today's global competitive environment organizations are adopting a philosophy of continuous improvement, an ongoing process that involves a continuous search to reduce costs, eliminate inefficiencies and improve the quality and performance of activities that increase customer satisfaction. It is claimed that when standards are set, a climate is created whereby the standards represent targets to be achieved and maintained, rather than a philosophy of continuous improvement. Standard costing can be made more consistent with a continuous improvement philosophy if variances are used to monitor the trend in performance and giving more emphasis to the rate of change in performance. In addition, standards should also be regularly reviewed and tightened as improvements occur.

## OVER-EMPHASIS ON DIRECT LABOUR

Some writers have criticized variance analysis on the grounds that it encourages too much attention to be focused on direct labour when direct labour has diminished in importance and is only a small proportion of total factory costs. Surveys, however, indicate that direct labour is the most widely used overhead allocation base. To reduce their allocated costs managers are motivated to reduce direct labour hours since this is the basis on which the overheads are allocated to cost centres. This process overstates the importance of direct labour and directs attention away from controlling escalating overhead costs. This overemphasis on direct labour arises, not from any inadequacies of standard costing, but from the faulty application of standard costing by focusing excessively on volume variances for short-term cost control and performance evaluation. Attention has already been drawn to the fact that volume variances should be used for meeting financial accounting requirements and not for cost control.

## DELAYED FEEDBACK REPORTING

A further criticism of variance reporting is that performance reports often arrive too late to be of value in controlling production operations. Performance reports are normally prepared weekly or monthly but such a lengthy time lag is not helpful for the daily control of operations. For operational control purposes labour and material quantity variances should be reported in physical terms in 'real time'. For example, most companies now use 'on line' computers to collect information at the point of manufacture so that variances can be reported and fed into the system instantaneously. Summary variance reports can still be prepared at appropriate periodic intervals if management wish to monitor deviations from standard and examine the trend in reported variances.

# The future role of standard costing

Critics of standard costing question the relevance of traditional variance analysis for cost control and performance appraisal in today's manufacturing and competitive environment. Nevertheless, standard costing systems continue to be widely used. This is because standard costing systems provide cost information for many other purposes besides cost control and performance evaluation. Standard costs and variance analysis would still be required for other purposes; particularly inventory valuation, profit measurement and decision-making even if they were abandoned for cost control and performance evaluation. For example, the detailed tracking of costs is unnecessary for decision-making purposes. Product costs for decision-making should be extracted from a data base of standard costs reviewed periodically (say once or twice a year). A periodic cost audit should be undertaken to provide a strategic review of the standard costs and profitability of a firm's products. The review provides attention-directing information for signalling the need for more detailed studies to make cost reduction, discontinuation, redesign or outsourcing decisions. Standard costs thus provide the basis for such decisions and can be derived from a database of either traditional or activity-based systems.

Many organizations have adapted their variance reporting system to report on those variables that are particularly important to them. These variables are company specific and cannot be found in textbooks. For example, some organizations that pursue a zero production defects policy have sought to measure the cost of quality by reporting quality variances. They define the quality variance as the standard cost of the output that does not meet specification. In traditional variance analysis this variance is buried in the efficiency variances of the various inputs. To illustrate the computation of the variances we shall simplify it by ignoring direct labour and overhead variances and concentrate on direct materials and assume that the standard usage for the production of a product is 5 kg and the standard price is £10 per kg. Actual usage for an output of 5000 units (of which 400 were defective) was 24 800 kg. Traditional variance would report an adverse usage variance of £18 000, being the difference between the standard quantity of 23 000 kg for the good output of 4600 units and the actual usage of 24 800 kg priced at £10 per kg. The variance analysis is modified to report an adverse quality variance of £20 000 (400 defective units × 5 kgs × £10) and a favourable usage variance of £2000 reflecting the fact that only 24 800 kg were used to produce 5000 units with a standard usage of 25 000 kg. The fact that 400 units were defective is reflected in the quality variance.

In recent years there has been a shift from using variances generated from a standard costing system as the foundation for short-term cost control and performance measurement to treating them as one among a broader set of measures. Greater emphasis is now being placed on the frequent reporting of non-financial measures that provide feedback on the key variables required to compete successfully in today's competitive environment. These non-financial measures focus on such factors as quality, reliability, flexibility, after-sales service, customer satisfaction and delivery performance. Recognition is also being given to the fact that periodic short-term reporting may be inappropriate for controlling those costs that are fixed in the short-run but variable in the longer-term. Attention has already been drawn to the fact that variance reporting for long-term variable costs should be at less frequent intervals. However, standard costing on its own is insufficient for controlling these costs. Special cost reduction exercises (i.e. *kaizen* costing) for existing products, target costing for future products and activity-based cost management are now being increasingly used to manage future costs. In particular, an awareness that a significant proportion of a product's costs are determined by decisions made early in a product's life cycle has resulted in greater attention being given to feed-forward controls and managing the costs at the design stage rather than after production has commenced. The management of long-run variable costs using the above techniques will be examined in Chapter 22.

Most of the criticisms that have been levelled at standard costing relate to cost control and performance measurement. It remains to be seen whether standard costing will decline in importance as a cost control and a performance evaluation mechanism. The survey evidence, however, suggests that practitioners do consider that it is an important mechanism for controlling costs. A UK survey by Drury *et al.* (1993) reported that 76% of the responding organizations operated a standard costing system. When asked how important standard costing was for cost control and performance evaluation, 72% of the respondents whose organizations operated a standard costing system stated that it was 'above average' or of 'vital importance'.

## THE ROLE OF STANDARD COSTING WHEN ABC HAS BEEN IMPLEMENTED

For those organizations that have implemented activity-based systems standard costing still has an important role to play in controlling the costs of unit-level activities. Unit-level activities can be defined as those activities that are performed each time a unit of product or service is produced. These activities consume resources in proportion to the number of units produced. For example, if a firm produces 10% more units, it will consume 10% more labour cost, 10% more materials, 10% more machine hours and 10% more energy costs. Expenses in this category include direct labour, direct materials, energy costs and expenses that are consumed in proportion to machine processing times (such as machine maintenance). Therefore traditional variance analysis can be applied for direct labour, direct materials and those variable overheads that vary with output, machine hours and direct labour hours.

Variance analysis is most suited to controlling the costs of unit-level activities but it can also provide meaningful information for managing those overhead costs that are fixed in the short-term but variable in the longer-term if traditional volume-based cost drivers are replaced with activity-based cost drivers that better reflect the causes of resource consumption. Variance analysis, however, cannot be used to manage all overhead costs. It is inappropriate for the control of facility-sustaining (infrastructure) costs because the costs of these resources do not fluctuate in the longer-term according to the demand for them.

Mak and Roush (1994) and Kaplan (1994b) have considered how variance analysis can be applied to incorporate activity costs and cost drivers for those overheads that are fixed in the short-term but variable in the long-term. The data presented in Example 19.6 illustrates their ideas relating to ABC overhead variance analysis for a set-up activity. You will see from this example that budgeted fixed costs of £80 000 provide a practical capacity to perform 2000 set-ups during the period. Assuming that the number of set-ups has been identified as the appropriate cost driver a cost of £40 per set-up (£80 000/2000) will be charged to products. For a discussion of the reasons for basing the cost driver rate on practical capacity, rather than budgeted usage, refer back to Chapter 10 (pages 351–352). Since budgeted capacity usage is 1600 set-ups not all of the capacity provided (2000 set-ups) will be used, and a budgeted cost of unused capacity of £16 000 (400 × £40), will be highlighted during the budget process. The actual number of set-ups performed was 1500 compared with a budget of 1600 and an unexpected capacity utilization variance of £4000 (100 × £40) will be reported at the end of the period. The traditional spending (expenditure) variance is £10 000, being the difference between budgeted and actual fixed costs incurred. We can now reconcile the fixed set-up expenses charged to products with the actual expenses incurred that are recorded in the financial accounts:

|  | £ |
|---|---|
| Set-up expenses charged to products (1500 × £40) | 60 000 |
| Budgeted unused capacity variance (400 × £40) | 16 000A |
| Capacity utilization variance (100 × £40) | 4 000A |
| Expenditure variance | 10 000F |
| Total actual expenses | 70 000 |

The above capacity variances highlight resources or using the surplus resources to ...ed) and thus signals the opportunity for attention the £20 000 unused such as reducing.

generate additional... it is assumed that the variable set-up costs, such as the cost of In Ex... in the set-up activity, varies with the number of set-ups. The variable cost ...rate of £25 per set-up has been calculated by dividing the budgeted variable cost of £40 000 by the budgeted number of set-ups of 1600. Note that the budgeted variable cost per set-up will be £25 for all activity levels. Thus the estimated set-up costs at the practical capacity of 2000 set-ups would be £50 000 (2500 × £25) but the cost per set-up would remain at £25. To calculate the set-up variable cost variance we must flex the budget. The actual number of set-ups performed were 1500 and the flexible budget allowance is £37 500 (1500 × £25). Actual expenditure is £39 000 and therefore an adverse variable cost variance of £1500 will be reported. The reconciliation between the variable set-up expenses charged to products and the actual expenses incurred is as follows:

|  |  |
|---|---|
| Variable set-up expenses charged to products (1500 × £25) | 37 500 |
| Variable overhead variance | 1 500A |
| Total actual expenses | 39 000 |

**EXAMPLE 19.6**

Assume the following information for the set-up activity for a period:

**Budget**

Activity level: 1600 set-ups
Practical capacity supplied: 2000 set-ups
Total fixed costs: £80 000
Total variable costs: £40 000
Cost driver rates (variables): £25 per set-up
(fixed): £40 per set-up

**Actual**

Total fixed costs:    £70 000
Total variable costs: £39 000

Number of set-ups 1500

In Example 19.6 we assumed that the number of set-ups was the cost driver. If set-ups take varying amounts of time they will not represent an homogeneous measure of output and thus may not provide a satisfactory measure of the cost of activity. To overcome this problem it may be preferable to use the number of set-up hours as the cost driver. Let us now assume in Example 19.6 that the cost driver is set-up hours and that the quantity of set-up hours is the same throughout as the number of set-ups. Therefore the variance analysis based on set-up hours will be identical to the variances that were computed when the number of set-ups was the cost driver.

Where cost drivers that capture the duration of the activity are used Mak and Roush (1994) advocate the reporting of separate efficiency variances for each activity. Assume in Example 19.6 that the standard activity level for the actual number of set-ups performed during the period was 1500 hours but the actual number of set-up hours required was 1660. The standard activity level represents the number of set-up hours that should have been required for the actual number of set-ups. The difference between the standard and actual set-up hours thus arises because of efficiencies/inefficiencies in performing the activity. The actual number of set-up hours then involves an extra 160 set-up hours (1660 − 1500). Assuming that variable costs vary with the number of set-up hours then involves costs vary with the £4000 (160 hours × £25). In addition, a favourable resulted in variance of £2500 will be reported. This figure is derived in a manner the traditional analysis by deducting the actual variable overhead expenditure of the from the flexible budget based on actual set-up hours (1660 × £25 = £41 500). Note that the sum of the efficiency variance (£4000A) and the expenditure variance (£2500F) is the same as the variable overhead variance of £1500 reported when the number of set-ups were used as the cost driver.

It is also possible to compute a capacity utilization and efficiency variance for fixed overheads. The efficiency variance is calculated by multiplying the 160 excess set-up hours by the fixed cost driver rate. Therefore an adverse efficiency variance of £6400 (160 × £40) and a favourable capacity utilization variance of £2400 (60 × £40) will be reported. The capacity utilization variance reflects the fact that the actual set-up capacity utilized was 60 hours in excess of the budget (assumed to be 1600 hours) but this was offset by the inefficiency in performing the activity which resulted in 160 hours in excess of requirements being utilized. The sum of the efficiency variance (£6400A) and the revised capacity utilization variance (£2400F) is identical to the capacity utilization variance reported when the number of set-ups was used as the cost driver.

The capacity utilization and efficiency variances relating to activity fixed costs are not particularly useful for short-term cost management. Mak and Roush conclude that they are more useful in a multi-period context whereby recurring adverse capacity variances (unused capacity) indicate the potential cost savings which can result from eliminating excess capacity. ●●●

## Self-Assessment Question

You should attempt to answer this question yourself before looking up the suggested answer, which appears on pages 1128–30. If any part of your answer is incorrect, check back carefully to make sure you understand where you went wrong.

Bronte Ltd manufactures a single product, a laminated kitchen unit with a standard cost of £80 made up as follows:

|  | (£) |
| --- | --- |
| Direct materials (15 sq. metres at £3 per sq. metre) | 45 |
| Direct labour (5 hours at £4 per hour) | 20 |
| Variable overheads (5 hours at £2 per hour) | 10 |
| Fixed overheads (5 hours at £1 per hour) | 5 |
|  | 80 |

The standard selling price of the kitchen unit is £100. The monthly budget projects production and sales of 1000 units. Actual figures for the month of April are as follows:

Sales 1200 units at £102
Production 1400 units
Direct materials 22 000 sq. metres at £4 per sq. metre
Direct wages 6800 hours at £5
Variable overheads £11 000
Fixed overheads £6000

You are required to prepare:

(a) a trading account reconciling actual and budgeted profit and showing all the appropriate variances; (13 marks)

(b) ledger accounts in respect of the above transactions.

*ICAEW Accounting Techniques**

(*The original examination question did not include part (b).)

## Summary

In some production processes it is possible to vary the mix of materials used to make the final product. We have seen in this chapter that any deviations from the standard mix will lead to a mix variance. A favourable mix variance will result when cheaper materials are substituted for more expensive ones. This may not always be in the company's best interest, since product quality may suffer or output may be reduced, leading to an adverse yield variance. The yield variance arises because there is a difference between the standard output for a given level of input and the actual output attained.

Part of the sales margin volume variance may be accounted for because the actual sales mix differs from the budgeted sales mix. This element can be isolated by calculating a sales margin mix variance.

One of the criticisms of standard costing is that standards are normally based on the environment that was anticipated when the targets were set. To overcome this problem, whenever the actual environment is different from the anticipated environment, performance should be compared with a standard that reflects the changed conditions. One possible solution is to analyse the variance so that a planning or forecasting variance is extracted. This variance provides management with useful feed-back information on how successful they are in predicting target costs. The price or usage variance should then be calculated based on a revised target for the conditions under which the managers operated during a period.

Another criticism of standard costing is that the variances are calculated using standard acquisition costs, and in some cases acquisition costs do not represent the economic cost for the excess usage of resources. In such situations it is preferable to value the quantity variances incorporating the opportunity cost of scarce resources.

The decision to investigate a variance should depend on whether the expected benefits are likely to exceed the costs of carrying out the investigation. Variances may be due to the following causes:

1. Random uncontrollable variances when the operation is under control.

2. Assignable causes but the costs of investigation exceed the benefits.

3. Assignable causes but the benefits from investigation exceed the costs of investigation.

We should aim to investigate only those variances that fall into the final category.

Finally, the future role of standard costing was examined. It was pointed out that standard costing can be used either with traditional or ABC systems and computations of overhead variances using activity-based cost drivers were illustrated.

## Key Terms and Concepts

assignable causes (p. 756)
controllable usage variance (p. 749)
*ex post* variance analysis (p. 747)
market share variance (p. 736)
market size variance (p. 736)
material mix variance (p. 730)
materials yield variance (p. 731)
purchasing efficiency variance (p. 747)
purchasing planning variance (p. 747)

random uncontrollable factors (p. 756)
sales margin mix variance (p. 734)
sales margin price variance (p. 734)
sales margin volume variance (p. 734)
sales quantity variance (p. 735)
statistical quality control charts (p. 758)
total sales margin variance (p. 734)
uncontrollable planning variance (p. 748)

## Recommended Reading

For a review of the research literature relating to variance investigation models you should refer to Scapens (1991, ch. 6) and Sen (1998). For further reading on ABC variance analysis see Kaplan (1994a) and Mak and Roush (1994, 1996). The future role of standard costing is addressed in the article by Cheatham and Cheatham (1996).

## Key Examination Points

Questions on accounting entries for a standard costing system, variance investigation models and calculating planning and operating variance are frequently included in advanced management accounting examinations. Make sure you under-stand these topics and attempt the questions for the chapter that relate to these topics. You should compare your answers with the answers in the *Students' Manual*.

# Questions

*Indicates that a suggested solution is to be found in the *Students' Manual*.

## 19.1* Advanced

(a) In high technology small batch manufacture, accountants sometimes take the view that standard costing cannot be applied. The move into high technology is generally accompanied by a shift away from labour-dominated to capital-intensive processes.

   You are required to appraise the application of standard costing in the circumstance described above. (12 marks)

(b) In order to secure and direct employee motivation towards the achievement of a firm's goals, it may be considered that budget centres should be created at the lowest defined management level.

   You are required to discuss the advantages and disadvantages of creating budget centres at such a level. (12 marks)
(Total 24 marks)
*CIMA Stage 4 Management Accounting – Control and Audit*

## 19.2 Advanced

Variance analysis involves the separation of individual cost variances into component parts. The benefit that may be derived from variance analysis depends on the interpretation and investigation of the component variances. A company has recently been carrying out a study on its use of variance analysis.

Requirement:

Explain, with the aid of simple numeric examples, for each of the following variance analysis exercises,
- their logic, purpose and limitation; and
- how the management accountant should go about investigating the component variances disclosed.

(a) The separation of the fixed overhead volume variance into capacity utilisation and efficiency components. (9 marks)
(b) The separation of the materials usage variance into materials mixture and materials yield components. (8 marks)
(c) The separation of the labour rate variance into planning and operational components. (8 marks)
(Total 25 marks)

*CIMA Stage 3 Management Accounting Applications*

## 19.3* Advanced

In recent years, writers have argued that standard costing and variance analysis should not be used for cost control and performance evaluation purposes in today's manufacturing world. Its use, they argue, is likely to induce behaviour which is inconsistent with the strategic manufacturing objectives that companies need to achieve in order to survive in today's intensely competitive international economic environment.

Requirements:

(a) Explain the arguments referred to in the above paragraph concerning the relevance of standard costing and variance analysis. (10 marks)
(b) Explain the arguments in favour of the relevance of standard costing and variance analysis in the modern manufacturing environment. (8 marks)
(c) Suggest methods that might be used by management accountants to control costs and evaluate efficiency as alternatives or complements to standard costing and variance analysis. (7 marks)
(Total 25 marks)
*CIMA Stage 3 Management Accounting Applications*

## 19.4 Advanced

In the new industrial environment, the usefulness of standard costing is being challenged, and new approaches sought.

   One approach, pioneered by the Japanese, is to replace standard costs by target costs.

You are required

(a) to describe the problems associated with standard costing in the new industrial environment; (6 marks)
(b) to explain what target costs are, and how they are developed and used; (6 marks)
(c) to contrast standard and target costs. (5 marks)
(Total 17 marks)
*CIMA Management Accounting Techniques*

## 19.5* Advanced

(a) The investigation of a variance is a fundamental element in the effective exercise of control through budgetary control and standard costing systems. The systems for identifying the variances may be well defined and detailed yet the procedures adopted to determine whether to pursue the investigation of variances may well not be formalized.

Critically examine this situation, discussing possible effective approaches to the investigation of variances. (15 marks)

(b) Explain the major motivational factors which influence managers in their actions to eliminate variances from budget. (10 marks)

(Total 25 marks)

*CIMA Stage 4 Management Accounting Control and Audit*

### 19.6 Advanced

Variance investigation decisions are normally explained in textbooks by simple models, which assume the availability of a significant amount of information.

An example of this approach is:

The managers estimate the probability of any variance being due to a controllable, and therefore correctable, cause at 25%. They estimate the cost of investigating a variance at £1400, and the cost of correcting the cause of a correctable variance at £400. The investigation process is regarded as 100%, reliable in that a correctable cause of the variance will be found if it exists.

Managers estimate the loss due to not investigating, and hence not discovering, a correctable cause of the variance, averages 75% of the size of the variance. For example, the loss from the failure to discover a correctable £4000 variance would be £3000.

Requirement:
(a) Calculate the minimum size of variance that would justify investigation. (8 marks)
In addition to the approach described above, alternative approaches exist to decide whether to investigate variances by using criteria related to the absolute size of the variance, and criteria based on the percentage from standard.

Requirement:
(b) (i) Explain why these approaches are taken rather than the approach described in (a) above.

(ii) Comment on the appropriateness of the alternative approaches described above.

(12 marks)

(Total 20 marks)

*CIMA Stage 4 Management Accounting Control Systems*

### 19.7 Advanced

(a) Specify and explain the factors to be considered in determining whether to investigate a variance which has been routinely reported as part of a standard costing system. (12 marks)

(b) Describe how accumulated production variances should be treated at the end of an accounting period. (8 marks)

(Total 20 marks)

*ACCA P2 Management Accounting*

### 19.8* Advanced

(a) Outline the factors a management accountant should consider when deciding whether or not to investigate variances revealed in standard costing and budgetary control systems.

(b) Indicate briefly what action the management accountant can take to improve the chances of achieving positive results from investigating variances. (20 marks)

*CIMA P3 Management Accounting*

### 19.9* Advanced

Explain:

(a) the problems concerning control of operations that a manufacturing company can be expected to experience in using a standard costing system during periods of rapid inflation;

(b) three methods by which the company could try to overcome the problems to which you have referred in your answer to (a) above, indicating the shortcomings of each method.

(20 marks)

*CIMA P3 Management Accounting*

### 19.10* Intermediate: Accounting entries for a standard costing system

A company uses Material Z in several of its manufacturing processes. On 1 November, 9000 kilos of the material were in stock. These materials cost £9630 when purchased. Receipts and issues of Material Z during November were:

*Receipts*

4 November, 10 000 kilos costing £10 530

23 November, 8000 kilos costing £8480

*Issues*

2 November, 2000 kilos to Process 1

7 November, 4500 kilos to Process 2

20 November, 4000 kilos to Process 1

27 November, 6000 kilos to Process 3

The company operates a standard costing system. The standard cost of Material Z during November was £1.04 per kilo.

Process 1 is exclusively concerned with the production of Product X. Production information for November is as follows:

Opening work-in-process, 6000 units
– complete as to materials; 50% complete for direct labour and overheads.

Completed units, 9970.

Closing work-in-process, 8000 units
– complete as to materials; 75% complete for direct labour and overheads.

The standard cost per unit of Product X comprises the following:

Material Z, 0.5 kilos at £1.04 per kilo

Direct labour, 0.1 hours at £4.80 per hour

Overhead, absorbed on direct labour hours at £5.00 per hour.

Costs (other than Material Z) incurred in Process 1 during November were:

Direct labour, 1340 hours at £4.80 per hour

Overheads, £6680.

Required:

(a) Prepare the stock account and material price variance account for Material Z for the month of November on the assumption that:

(i) The material price variance is identified on purchase of material.

(ii) The material price variance is identified at the time of issue of material to production (assume that the weighted average pricing method is used).

(9 marks)

(b) State which of the above two methods, (a) (i) or (a) (ii), you would prefer. State briefly the reasons for your preference. (4 marks)

(c) Prepare the account for Process 1 for the month of November. (Assume that Material Z is charged to the process at standard price.)

(12 marks)

(Total 25 marks)

*ACCA Level 1 Costing*

## 19.11* Intermediate: Calculation of labour, material and overhead variances plus appropriate accounting entries

JC Limited produces and sells one product only, Product J, the standard cost for which is as follows for one unit.

|  | (£) |
|---|---|
| Direct material X – 10 kilograms at £20 | 200 |
| Direct material Y – 5 litres at £6 | 30 |
| Direct wages – 5 hours at £6 | 30 |
| Fixed production overhead | 50 |
| Total standard cost | 310 |
| Standard gross profit | 90 |
| Standard selling price | 400 |

The fixed production overhead is based on an expected annual output of 10 800 units produced at an even flow throughout the year; assume each calendar month is equal. Fixed production overhead is absorbed on direct labour hours.

During April, the first month of the financial year, the following were the actual results for an actual production of 800 units.

|  |  | (£) |
|---|---|---|
| Sales on credit: | | 320 000 |
| 800 units at £400 | | |
| Direct materials: | | |
| X 7800 kilogrammes | 159 900 | |
| Y 4300 litres | 23 650 | |
| Direct wages: 4200 hours | 24 150 | |
| Fixed production overhead | 47 000 | |
| | | 254 700 |
| Gross profit | | 65 300 |

The material price variance is extracted at the time of receipt and the raw materials stores control is maintained at standard prices. The purchases, bought on credit, during the month of April were:

X 9000 kilograms at £20.50 per kg from K Limited

Y 5000 litres at £5.50 per litre from C p.l.c.

Assume no opening stocks.

Wages owing for March brought forward were £6000.

Wages paid during April (net) £20 150.

Deductions from wages owing to the Inland Revenue for PAYE and NI were £5000 and the wages accrued for April were £5000.

The fixed production overhead of £47 000 was made up of expense creditors of £33 000, none of which was paid in April, and depreciation of £14 000.

The company operates an integrated accounting system.

You are required to
(a) (i) calculate price and usage variances for each material,
   (ii) calculate labour rate and efficiency variances,
   (iii) calculate fixed production overhead expenditure, efficiency and volume variances; (9 marks)
(b) show all the accounting entries in T accounts for the month of April – the work-in-progress account should be maintained at standard cost and each balance on the separate variance accounts is to be transferred to a Profit and Loss Account which you are also required to show; (18 marks)
(c) explain the reason for the difference between the actual gross profit given in the question and the profit shown in your profit and loss account. (3 marks)
(Total 30 marks)
*CIMA Stage 2 Cost Accounting*

### 19.12 Intermediate: Calculation of variances and accounting entries for an interlocking standard costing system

B Ltd manufactures a single product in one of its factories. Information relating to the month just ended is as follows:
(i) Standard cost per hundred units:

|  | (£) |
| --- | --- |
| Raw materials: 15 kilos at £7 per kilo | 105 |
| Direct labour: 10 hours at £6 per hour | 60 |
| Variable production overhead: | |
| 10 hours at £5 per hour | 50 |
|  | 215 |

(ii) 226 000 units of the product were completed and transferred to finished goods stock.
(iii) 34 900 kilos of raw material were purchased in the month at a cost of £245 900.
(iv) Direct wages were £138 545 representing 22 900 hours' work.
(v) Variable production overheads of £113 800 were incurred.

(vi) Fixed production overheads of £196 800 were incurred.
(vii) Stocks at the beginning and end of the month were:

|  | Opening Stock | Closing Stock |
| --- | --- | --- |
| Raw materials | 16 200 kilos | 16 800 kilos |
| Work in progress | — | 4000 units, (complete as to raw materials but only 50% complete as to direct labour and overhead) |
| Finished goods | 278 000 units | 286 000 units |

Raw materials, work in progress, and finished goods stocks are maintained at standard cost. You should assume that no stock discrepancies or losses occurred during the month just ended.

Required:
(a) Prepare the cost ledger accounts relating to the above information in B Ltd's interlocking accounting system. Marginal costing principles are employed in the cost ledger. (17 marks)
(b) Explain and contrast the different types of standards that may be set as a benchmark for performance measurement. (8 marks)
(Total 25 marks)
*ACCA Cost and Management Accounting 1*

### 19.13 Intermediate: Accounting entries for a standard costing system

Fischer Ltd manufactures a range of chess sets, and operates a standard costing system. Information relating to the 'Spassky' design for the month of March is as follows:
(1) Standard costs per 100 sets

|  | (£) |
| --- | --- |
| Raw materials: | |
| Plaster of Paris, 20 kg at £8 per kg | 160 |
| Paint, 1/2 litre at £30 per litre | 15 |
| Direct wages, $2\frac{1}{2}$ hours at £10 per hour | 25 |
| Fixed production overheads, | |
| 400% of direct wages | 100 |
|  | 300 |

(2) Standard selling price per set  £3.80

(3) Raw materials, work in progress and finished goods stock records are maintained at standard cost.

(4) Stock levels at the beginning and end of March were as follows:

|  | 1 March | 31 March |
|---|---|---|
| Plaster of Paris | 2800 kg | 2780 kg |
| Paint | 140 litres | 170 litres |
| Finished sets | 900 sets | 1100 sets |

There was no work in progress at either date.

(5) Budgeted production and sales during the month were 30 000 sets. Actual sales, all made at standard selling price, and actual production were 28 400 and 28 600 sets respectively.

(6) Raw materials purchased during the month were 5400 kg of plaster of Paris at a cost of £43 200 and 173 litres of paint at a cost of £5800.

(7) Direct wages were 730 hours at an average rate of £11 per hour.

(8) Fixed production overheads amounted to £34 120.

Requirement:

Prepare for the month of March:

(a) the cost ledger accounts for raw materials, work in progress and finished goods;

(10 marks)

(b) (i) budget trading statement,
(ii) standard cost trading statement,
(iii) financial trading statement, and
(iv) a reconciliation between these statements identifying all relevant variances.

(14 marks)

(Total 24 marks)

*ICAEW Accounting Techniques*

### 19.14 Intermediate: Accounting entries for a standard process costing system

A firm produces a plastic feedstock using a process form of manufacture. The firm operates in an industry where the market price fluctuates and the firm adjusts output levels, period by period, in an attempt to maximise profit which is its objective. Standard costing is used in the factory and the following information is available.

Process 2 receives input from process 1 and, after processing, transfers the output to finished goods. For a given period, the opening work-in-process for process 2 was 600 barrels which had the following values:

|  | Value (£) | Percentage complete |
|---|---|---|
| Input material (from process 1) | 3 000 | 100 |
| Process 2 material introduced | 6 000 | 50 |
| Process 2 labour | 1 800 | 30 |
| Process 2 overhead | 2 700 | 30 |
|  | £13 500 | |

During the period, 3700 barrels were received from process 1 and at the end of the period, the closing work-in-progress was at the following stages of completion:

|  | Percentage completion |
|---|---|
| Input material | 100 |
| Process 2 material introduced | 50 |
| Process 2 labour | 40 |
| Process 2 overhead | 40 |

The following standard variable costs have been established for process 2:

|  | Standard variable cost per barrel (£) |
|---|---|
| Input material (standard cost process 1) | 5 |
| Process 2 material | 20 |
| Labour | 10 |
| Overhead | 15 |
|  | £50 |

During the period, actual costs for process 2 were

|  | (£) |
|---|---|
| Material | 79 500 |
| Labour | 39 150 |
| Overhead | 60 200 |
|  | £178 850 |

In addition you are advised that the following theoretical functions have been derived:

Total cost $(£) = 100\,000 + 20Q + 0.005Q^2$
Price per barrel $(£) = 76 - 0.002Q$

where $Q$ represents the number of barrels.

You are required to
(a) determine the theoretical production level which will maximize profit; (6 marks)
(b) prepare the process 2 account assuming that the calculated production level is achieved; (7 marks)
(c) prepare the accounts for process 2 material, labour and overhead showing clearly the variance in each account.

(7 marks)
(Total 20 marks)
*CIMA Stage 3 Management Accounting Techniques*

### 19.15* Advanced: Material mix and yield variances

Acca-chem Co plc manufacture a single product, product W, and have provided you with the following information which relates to the period which has just ended:

**Standard cost per batch of product W**

| Materials: | Kilos | Price per kilo (£) | Total (£) |
|---|---|---|---|
| F | 15 | 4 | 60 |
| G | 12 | 3 | 36 |
| H | 8 | 6 | 48 |
| | 35 | | 144 |
| *Less*: Standard loss | 3 | | |
| Standard yield | 32 | | |

| Labour: | Hours | Rate per hour (£) | |
|---|---|---|---|
| Department P | 4 | 10 | 40 |
| Department Q | 2 | 6 | 12 |
| | | | 196 |

Budgeted sales for the period are 4096 kilos at £16 per kilo. There were no budgeted opening or closing stocks of product W.

The actual materials and labour used for 120 batches were:

| Materials: | Kilos | Price per kilo (£) | Total (£) |
|---|---|---|---|
| F | 1680 | 4.25 | 7 140 |
| G | 1650 | 2.80 | 4 620 |
| H | 870 | 6.40 | 5 568 |
| | 4200 | | 17 328 |
| *Less*: Actual loss | 552 | | |
| Actual yield | 3648 | | |

| Labour: | Hours | Rate per hour (£) | |
|---|---|---|---|
| Department P | 600 | 10.60 | 6 360 |
| Department Q | 270 | 5.60 | 1 512 |
| | | | 25 200 |

All of the production of W was sold during the period for £16.75 per kilo.

Required:
(a) Calculate the following material variances:
   − price
   − usage
   − mix
   − yield. (5 marks)
(b) Prepare an analysis of the material mix and price variances for each of the materials used. (3 marks)
(c) Calculate the following labour variances:
   − cost
   − efficiency
   − rate
   for each of the production departments. (4 marks)
(d) Calculate the sales variances. (3 marks)
(e) Comment on your findings to help explain what has happened to the yield variance. (5 marks)
(Total 20 marks)
*ACCA Paper 8 Managerial Finance*

### 19.16* Advanced: Labour mix and yield variances

A large manufacturing company with a diverse range of products is developing the use of standard costing throughout its divisions. A full standard costing system has already been implemented in Division A, including the use of mix and yield material variances, and attention has now turned to Division B where the main problem concerns labour.

Division B makes highly complex work stations which incorporate material handling, automatic controls and robotics. Manufacture is a team effort and the team specified for work station No. 26 comprises:

2 supervisors paid £8 per hour
10 fitters paid £6 per hour
6 electricians paid £6 per hour
2 electronics engineers paid £7 per hour
4 labourers paid £4 per hour

Output is measured in standard hours and 90 standard hours are expected for every 100 clock hours. During a period the following data were recorded:

| | Actual hours | Actual pay (£) |
|---|---|---|
| Supervisors | 170 | 1 394 |
| Fitters | 820 | 4 920 |
| Electricians | 420 | 2 562 |
| Electronics engineers | 230 | 1 725 |
| Labourers | 280 | 1 120 |
| Total | 1920 | £11 721 |

1650 standard hours were produced.

The factory director of Division B is anxious to gain the maximum information possible from the standard costing system. He sees no reason why the normal labour efficiency variance could not be divided into sub-variances in order to show separately the effects of non-standard team composition and team productivity in a similar fashion to the material usage variance which can be sub-divided into mix and yield variances.

You are required
(a) to calculate the labour rate variance;
(3 marks)
(b) to calculate
  (i) the team composition variance,
  (ii) the team productivity variance and
  (iii) labour efficiency variance; (11 marks)
(c) to comment on the meaning of the variances calculated in (b) and their weaknesses.
(6 marks)
(Total 20 marks)
*CIMA Stage 3 Management Accounting Techniques*

## 19.17 Advanced: Mix variances and reconciliation as actual and budgeted profit

A company operates a number of hairdressing establishments which are managed on a franchise arrangement. The franchisor offers support using a PC package which deals with profit budgeting and control information.

Budget extracts of one franchisee for November are shown below analysed by male and female clients. For the purposes of budget projections average revenue rates are used. At the month end these are compared with the average monthly rates actually achieved using variance analysis. Sales price, sales quantity, sales mix and cost variances are routinely produced in order to compare the budget and actual results.

Staff working in this business are paid on a commission basis in order to act as an incentive to attract and retain clients. The labour rate variance is based on the commission payments, any basic pay is part of the monthly fixed cost.

*Budget*

| | Male | Female |
|---|---|---|
| Clients | 4000 | 1000 |
| | (£) | (£) |
| Average revenue (per client) | 7.5 | 18.0 |
| Average commission (per client) | 3.0 | 10.0 |
| Total monthly fixed cost | £20 000 | |

*Actual results*

| | Male | Female |
|---|---|---|
| Clients | 2000 | 2000 |
| | (£) | (£) |
| Average revenue (per client) | 8.0 | 20.0 |
| Average commission (per client) | 3.5 | 11.0 |
| Total monthly fixed cost | £24 000 | |

Required:
(a) Reconcile the budgeted and actual profit for November by calculating appropriate price, quantity, mix and cost variances, presenting the information in good form. You should adopt a contribution style, with mix variances based on units (i.e. clients). (10 marks)
(b) Write a short memorandum to the manager of the business commenting on the result in (a) above. (4 marks)
(c) Comment on the limitations associated with generating sales variances as in (a) above.
(6 marks)
(Total 20 marks)
*ACCA Paper 8 Managerial Finance*

**19.18\* Advanced: Mix variances and reconciliation of actual and budgeted profit**

The budgeted income statement for one of the products of Derwen plc for the month of May was as follows:

**Budgeted income statement – May**

| | (£) | (£) | (£) |
|---|---|---|---|
| Sales revenue: | | | |
| 10 000 units at £5 | | | 50 000 |
| Production costs: | | | |
| Budgeted production | | | |
| 10 000 units | | | |
| Direct materials: | | | |
| Material | | | |
| A (5000 kg at £0.30) | 1 500 | | |
| B (5000 kg at £0.70) | 3 500 | | |
| | | 5 000 | |
| Direct labour: | | | |
| Skilled | 13 500 | | |
| (4500 hours at £3.00) | | | |
| Semi-skilled | 6 500 | | |
| (2600 hours at £2.50) | | | |
| | | 20 000 | |
| Overhead cost: | | | |
| Fixed | 10 000 | | |
| Variable | 5 000 | | |
| (10 000 units at £0.50) | | | |
| | | 40 000 | |
| Add Opening stock | | | |
| (1000 units at £4) | | 4 000 | |
| | | 44 000 | |
| Deduct Closing stock | | 4 000 | |
| (1000 units at £4) | | | |
| Cost of goods sold | | | 40 000 |
| Budgeted profit | | | 10 000 |

During May production and sales were both above budget and the following income statement was prepared:

**Income statement – May**

| | | (£) |
|---|---|---|
| Sales revenue: | | |
| 7000 units at £5 | | 35 000 |
| 4000 units at £4.75 | | 19 000 |
| | | 54 000 |
| Production costs: | | |
| Actual production | | |
| 12 000 units | | |

Direct materials:

| Material | | |
|---|---|---|
| A (8000 kg at £0.20) | 1 600 | |
| B (5000 kg at £0.80) | 4 000 | |
| | | 5 600 |

Direct labour:

| | | |
|---|---|---|
| Skilled | 17 700 | |
| (6000 hours at £2.95) | | |
| Semi-skilled | 8 190 | |
| (3150 hours at £2.60) | | |
| | | 25 890 |

Overhead cost:

| | | |
|---|---|---|
| Fixed | 9 010 | |
| Variable | 7 500 | |
| (12 000 units at £0.625) | | |
| | | 48 000 |
| Add Opening stock | | 4 000 |
| (1000 units at £4) | | |
| | | 52 000 |
| Deduct Closing stock | | 8 000 |
| (2000 units at £4) | | |
| Cost of goods sold | | 44 000 |
| 'Actual' profit | | 10 000 |

In the above statement stock is valued at the standard cost of £4 per unit.

There is general satisfaction because the budgeted profit level has been achieved but you have been asked to prepare a standard costing statement analysing the differences between the budget and the actual performance. In your analysis, include calculations of the sales volume and sales price variances and the following cost variances: direct material price, mix, yield and usage variances; direct labour rate, mix, productivity and efficiency variances: and overhead spending and volume variances. (17 marks)

Provide a commentary on the variances and give your views on their usefulness. (5 marks)

(Total 22 marks)

*ACCA Level 2 Management Accounting*

**19.19\* Advanced: Accounting disposition of variances**

(a) Mingus Ltd produces granoids. It revises its cost standards annually in September for the year commencing 1 December.

At a normal annual volume of output of 40 000 granoids its standard costs, including overheads, for the year to 30 November 2001 were:

| Cost | Standard | Per unit (£) | Total (£000) |
|---|---|---|---|
| Direct materials | 5 kg at £10 per kg | 50 | 2000 |
| Direct labour | 2 hrs at £5 per hr | 10 | 400 |
| Variable overheads | £1 per kg of direct material | 5 | 200 |
| Fixed overheads | £5 per hr of direct labour | 10 | 400 |
| | | 75 | 3000 |

The actual expenditure incurred in that year to produce an actual output of 50 000 granoids was:

| Cost | Total expenditure (£000) | Further details |
|---|---|---|
| Direct materials | 2880 | 320 000 kg at £9 per kg |
| Direct labour | 540 | 90 000 hr at £6 per hr |
| Variable overheads | 280 | |
| Fixed overheads | 380 | |
| | 4080 | |

Due to an industrial dispute in 2000 there was no stockholding of materials, work in progress, or completed granoids at 1 December 2000. At 30 November 2001 there was an inventory of 10 000 completed granoids, but no work in progress, and no raw materials inventory.

You are required to calculate in each case the balance which would remain in the finished goods inventory account if each of the following six costing systems were used:
(i) actual absorption costing,
(ii) standard absorption costing with variances written off,
(iii) standard absorption costing with variances pro-rated between cost of sales and inventory,
(iv) actual direct costing,
(v) standard direct costing with variances written off,
(vi) standard direct costing with variances pro-rated between cost of sales and inventory. (10 marks)
(b) You are required to comment briefly in general terms on the main effects of applying to inventory valuation the various costing systems set out above, referring to your calculations in part (a) if you wish. (5 marks)
(c) Overhead cost absorption may be used in connection with various other matters. You are required to discuss the use of overhead cost absorption procedures for either
(i) pricing, or
(ii) control of costs. (10 marks)
(Total 25 marks)
*ICAEW Management Accounting*

**19.20\* Advanced: Sales mix and quantity variances and planning and operating variances**
Milbao plc make and sell three types of electronic game for which the following budget/standard information and actual information is available for a four-week period:

| Model | Budget sales (units) | Standard unit data | | Actual sales (units) |
|---|---|---|---|---|
| | | Selling price (£) | Variable cost (£) | |
| Superb | 30 000 | 100 | 40 | 36 000 |
| Excellent | 50 000 | 80 | 25 | 42 000 |
| Good | 20 000 | 70 | 22 | 18 000 |

Budgeted fixed costs are £2 500 000 for the four-week period. Budgeted fixed costs should be changed to product units at an overall budgeted average cost unit where it is relevant to do so.

Required:
(a) Calculate the sales volume variance for each model and in total for the four-week period where (i) turnover (ii) contribution and (iii) net profit is used as the variance valuation base. (9 marks)
(b) Discuss the relative merits of each of the valuation bases of the sales volume variance calculated in (a) above. (6 marks)
(c) Calculate the *total* sales quantity and sales mix variances for Milbao plc for the four-week period, using contribution as the valuation base. (Individual model variances are not required.) (4 marks)
(d) Comment on why the individual model variances for sales mix and sales quantity may provide misleading information to management. (No calculations are required.) (4 marks)

(e) The following additional information is available for the four-week period:

1. The actual selling price and variable costs of Milbao plc are 10% and 5% lower respectively, than the original budget/standard.

2. General market prices have fallen by 6% from the original standard. Short-term strategy by Milbao plc accounts for the residual fall in selling price.

3. 3% of the variable cost reduction from the original budget/standard is due to an over-estimation of a wage award, the remainder (i.e. 2%) is due to short-term operational improvements.

(i) Prepare a summary for a four-week period for model 'Superb' *only*, which reconciles original budget contribution with actual contribution where planning and operational variances are taken into consideration. (8 marks)

(ii) Comment on the usefulness to management of planning and operational variance analysis in feedback and feed-forward control. (4 marks)
(Total 35 marks)
*ACCA Paper 9 Information for Control and Decision Making*

## 19.21* Advanced: Planning and operating variances plus mix and yield variances

County Preserves produce jams, marmalade and preserves. All products are produced in a similar fashion; the fruits are low temperature cooked in a vacuum process and then blended with glucose syrup with added citric acid and pectin to help setting.

Margins are tight and the firm operates a system of standard costing for each batch of jam.

The standard cost data for a batch of raspberry jam are:

| | |
|---|---|
| Fruit extract | 400 kg at £0.16 per kg |
| Glucose syrup | 700 kg at £0.10 per kg |
| Pectin | 99 kg at £0.332 per kg |
| Citric acid | 1 kg at £2.00 per kg |
| Labour | 18 hrs at £3.25 per hour |

Standard processing loss 3%.

The summer proved disastrous for the raspberry crop with a late frost and cool, cloudy conditions at the ripening period, resulting in a low national yield. As a consequence, normal prices in the trade were £0.19 per kg for fruit extract although good buying could achieve some savings. The impact of exchange rates on imports of sugar has caused the price of syrup to increase by 20%.

The actual results for the batch were:

| | |
|---|---|
| Fruit extract | 428 kg at £0.18 per kg |
| Glucose syrup | 742 kg at £0.12 per kg |
| Pectin | 125 kg at £0.328 per kg |
| Citric acid | 1 kg at £0.95 per kg |
| Labour | 20 hrs at £3.00 per hour |

Actual output was 1164 kg of raspberry jam.

You are required to

(a) calculate the ingredients planning variances that are deemed uncontrollable; (4 marks)

(b) calculate the ingredients operating variances that are deemed controllable; (4 marks)

(c) comment on the advantages and disadvantages of variance analysis using planning and operating variances; (4 marks)

(d) calculate the mixture and yield variances; (5 marks)

(e) calculate the total variance for the batch. (3 marks)
(Total 20 marks)
*CIMA Stage 3 Management Accounting Techniques*

## 19.22 Advanced: Detailed variance analysis (including revision variances) plus an explanation of the meaning of operating statement variances

Tungach Ltd make and sell a single product. Demand for the product exceeds the expected production capacity of Tungach Ltd. The holding of stocks of the finished product is avoided if possible because the physical nature of the product is such that it deteriorates quickly and stocks may become unsaleable.

A standard marginal cost system is in operation. Feedback reporting takes planning and operational variances into consideration.

The management accountant has produced the following operating statement for period 9:

**Tungach Ltd**
**Operating Statement – Period 9**

| | (£) | (£) |
|---|---|---|
| Original budgeted contribution | | 36 000 |
| Revision variances: | | |
| Material usage | 9 600(A) | |
| Material price | 3 600(F) | |
| Wage rate | 1 600(F) | 4 400(A) |
| Revised budgeted contribution | | 31 600 |
| Sales volume variance: | | |
| Causal factor | | |
| Extra capacity | 4 740    (F) | |
| Productivity drop | 987.5  (A) | |
| Idle time | 592.5  (A) | |
| Stock increase | 2 370    (A) | 790(F) |
| Revised standard contribution for sales achieved | | 32 390 |
| Other variances: | | |
| Material usage | 900(F) | |
| Material price | 3 120(A) | |
| Labour efficiency | 1 075(A) | |
| Labour idle time | 645(A) | |
| Wage rate | 2 760(A) | |
| | | 6 700(A) |
| Actual contribution | | 25 690 |

(F) = favourable    (A) = adverse

Other data are available as follows:
(i)   The original standard contribution per product unit as determined at period 1 was:

| | (£) | (£) |
|---|---|---|
| Selling price | | 30 |
| Less: Direct material 1.5 kilos at £8 | 12 | |
| Direct labour 2 hours at £4.50 | 9 | 21 |
| Contribution | | 9 |

(ii)  A permanent change in the product specification was implemented from period 7 onwards. It was estimated that this change would require 20% additional material per product unit. The current efficient price of the material has settled at £7.50 per kilo.
(iii) Actual direct material used during period 9 was 7800 kilos at £7.90 per kilo. Any residual variances are due to operational problems.
(iv) The original standard wage rate overestimated

the degree of trade union pressure during negotiations and was £0.20 higher than the rate subsequently agreed. Tungach Ltd made a short-term operational decision to pay the workforce at £4.60 per hour during periods 7 to 9 in an attempt to minimise the drop in efficiency likely because of the product specification change. Management succeeded in extending the production capacity during period 9 and the total labour hours paid for were 9200 hours. These included 150 hours of idle time.
(v)  Budgeted production and sales quantity
(period 9)                                            4000 units
Actual sales quantity (period 9)    4100 units
Actual production quantity
(period 9)                                            4400 units
(vi) Stocks of finished goods are valued at the current efficient standard cost.

Required:
(a)  Prepare detailed figures showing how the material and labour variances in the operating statement have been calculated.    (8 marks)
(b)  Prepare detailed figures showing how the sales volume variance has been calculated for each causal factor shown in the operating statement.    (6 marks)
(c)  Prepare a report to the management of Tungach Ltd explaining the meaning and relevance of the figures given in the operating statement for period 9. The report should contain specific comments for any two of the sales volume variance causal factors and any two of the 'other variances'. The comments should suggest possible reasons for each variance, the management member likely to be answerable for each variance and possible corrective action.    (8 marks)
(Total 22 marks)
*ACCA Level 2 Management Accounting*

**19.23 Advanced: Reconciliation of budgeted and actual profit including operating and planning variances plus an interpretation of the reconciliation statement**
Casement Ltd makes windows with two types of frame: plastic and mahogany. Products using the two types of materials are made in separate premises under the supervision of separate production managers.

Data for the three months ended 30 November are shown below.

| Sales units | Plastic | | Mahogany | | Totals | |
|---|---|---|---|---|---|---|
| | Budget | Actual | Budget | Actual | Budget | Actual |
| | 3000 | 2500 | 1000 | 1250 | 4000 | 3750 |
| | (£000) | (£000) | (£000) | (£000) | (£000) | (£000) |
| Sales revenue | 660 | 520 | 340 | 460 | 1000 | 980 |
| Materials | (147) | (120) | (131) | (160) | (278) | (280) |
| Labour | (108) | (105) | (84) | (85) | (192) | (190) |
| Fixed production overheads | (162) | (166) | (79) | (83) | (241) | (249) |
| Sales commissions | (33) | (26) | (17) | (23) | (50) | (49) |
| Other selling and administration costs | | | | | (128) | (133) |
| Net profit | | | | | 111 | 79 |

Casement Ltd sells to a wide variety of users, so that window sizes and shapes vary widely; consequently a square metre of window is adopted as the standard unit for pricing and costing.

Sales budgets were based on the expectation that the company's share of the regional market in windows would be 12%. The Window Federation's quarterly report reveals that sales in the regional market totalled 25 000 units in the three months ended 30 November. The managing director of Casement Ltd is concerned that the company's sales and profit are below budget; she wants a full analysis of sales variances as well as an analysis of the cost variances which can be obtained from the data.

Labour costs comprise the wages of shop-floor employees who receive a fixed wage for a 40-hour week; no overtime is worked. Production managers receive a fixed monthly salary which is included in production overheads, plus an annual personal performance bonus (excluded from the above data) which is decided by the board of directors at the end of each year. Sales representatives are paid a monthly retainer plus commission of 5% on all sales.

The management of Casement Ltd is keen to improve performance and is reviewing the company's reward structure. One possibility which is under consideration is that the company should adopt a profit-related pay scheme. The scheme would replace all the existing arrangements and would give every employee a basic remuneration equal to 90% of his or her earnings last year. In addition every employee would receive a share in the company's profit; on the basis of the past year's trading this payment would amount to about 17% of basic remuneration for each employee.

Requirements

(a) Prepare a variance report for the managing director on the results for the quarter ended 30 November, providing market share and market volume (or size) variances, sales mix variance and basic cost variances, from the available information. (10 marks)

(b) Interpret your results in part (a) for the benefit of the managing director. (7 marks)

(c) Examine the issues (excluding taxation) which should be considered by the management of Casement Ltd in relation to the company's reward structure, with particular reference to the proposal to move to a profit-related pay scheme. (8 marks)

(Total 25 marks)

*ICAEW P2 Management Accounting*

## 19.24 Advanced: Labour planning and operating variances

A standard costing and budgetary control system which provides management with a range of planning and operational variances for each four week accounting period should facilitate improved feedback control information which may then be used for improved feedforward control.

(a) Explain the meaning of the terms planning and operational variances, feedback control and feedforward control. (6 marks)

(b) Explain and illustrate with reference to direct labour cost variances, ways in which a planning and operational variance analysis could provide management with

   (i) additional feedback control information and

   (ii) additional feedforward control information. (14 marks)

Use the following direct labour cost information for any illustrative content of your answer.

Original standard per product unit: 0.4 hours

Original wage rate per hour: £4

Budget output per month: 1000 units

Actual results for January:

Output: 1000 units; direct labour hours incurred: 420 hours at £4.50 per hour.

At the end of January it has been established that the original standard time allowance per unit was understated by 10%. In addition, the completion of negotiations with the trade union has resulted in a wage rate of £4.25 being agreed from 1 January.

(20 marks)

*ACCA Level 2 Cost Accounting II*

## 19.25* Advanced: Planning and operating variances

A year ago Kenp Ltd entered the market for the manufacture and sale of a revolutionary insulating material. The budgeted production and sales volumes were 1000 units. The originally estimated sales price and standard costs for this new product were:

|  | (£) | (£) |
|---|---|---|
| Standard sales price (per unit) | | 100 |
| Standard costs (per unit) | | |
| Raw materials (Aye 10 kg at £5) | 50 | |
| Labour (6 hours at £4) | 24 | 74 |
| Standard contribution (per unit) | | £26 |

Actual results were:

| | First year's results | |
|---|---|---|
| | (£000) | (£000) |
| Sales (1000 units) | | 158 |
| Production costs (1000 units) | | |
| Raw materials (Aye 10 800 kg) | 97.2 | |
| Labour (5800 hours) | 34.8 | 132 |
| Actual contribution | | £26 |

'Throughout the year we attempted to operate as efficiently as possible, given the prevailing conditions' stated the managing director. 'Although in total the performance agreed with budget, in every detailed respect, expect volume, there were large differences. These were due, mainly, to the tremendous success of the new insulating material which created increased demand both for the product itself and all the manufacturing resources used in its production. This then resulted in price rises all round.'

'Sales were made at what was felt to be the highest feasible price but, it was later discovered, our competitors sold for £165 per unit and we could have equalled this price. Labour costs rose dramatically with increased demand for the specialist skills required to produce the product and the general market rate was £6.25 per hour – although Kenp always paid below the general market rate whenever possible.'

'Raw material Aye was chosen as it appeared cheaper than the alternative material Bee which could have been used. The costs which were expected at the time the budget was prepared were (per kg): Aye, £5 and Bee, £6. However, the market prices relating to efficient purchases of the materials during the year were:

Aye £8.50 per kg, and
Bee £7.00 per kg.

Therefore it would have been more appropriate to use Bee, but as production plans were based on Aye it was Aye that was used.'

'It is not proposed to request a variance analysis for the first year's results as most of the deviations from budget were caused by the new product's great success and this could not have been fully anticipated and planned for. In any event the final contribution was equal to that originally budgeted so operations must have been fully efficient.'

Required:

(a) Compute the traditional variances for the first year's operations. (5 marks)

(b) Prepare an analysis of variances for the first year's operations which will be useful in the circumstances of Kenp Ltd. The analysis should indicate the extent to which the variances were due to operational efficiency or planning causes. (10 marks)

(c) Using, for illustration, a comparison of the raw material variances computed in (a) and (b) above, briefly outline two major advantages and two major disadvantages of the approach applied in part (b) over the traditional approach. (5 marks)

(Total 20 marks)

*ACCA P2 Management Accounting*

## 19.26* Advanced: Planning and operating variances

POV Ltd uses a standard costing system to control and report upon the production of its single product.

An abstract from the original standard cost card of the product is as follows:

| | (£) | (£) |
|---|---|---|
| Selling price per unit | | 200 |
| *less:* 4 kgs materials @ £20 per kg | 80 | |
| 6 hours labour @ £7 per hour | 42 | 122 |
| Contribution per unit | | 78 |

For Period 3, 2500 units were budgeted to be produced and sold but the actual production and sales were 2850 units.

The following information was also available:

(i) At the commencement of Period 3 the normal material became unobtainable and it was necessary to use an alternative. Unfortunately, 0.5 kg per unit extra was required and it was thought that the material would be more difficult to work with. The price of the alternative was expected to be £16.50 per kg. In the event, actual usage was 12 450 kgs at £18 per kg.

(ii) Weather conditions unexpectedly improved for the period with the result that a £0.50 per hour bad weather bonus, which had been allowed for in the original standard, did not have to be paid. Because of the difficulties expected with the alternative material, management agreed to pay the workers £8 per hour for Period 3 only. During the period 18 800 hours were paid for.

After using conventional variances for some time, POV Ltd is contemplating extending its system to include planning and operational variances.

You are required:

(a) to prepare a statement reconciling budgeted contribution for the period with actual contribution, using conventional material and labour variances; (4 marks)

(b) to prepare a similar reconciliation statement using planning and operational variances; (14 marks)

(c) to explain the meaning of the variances shown in statement (b). (4 marks)

(Total 22 marks)

*CIMA Stage 3 Management Accounting Techniques*

### 19.27 Advanced: Relevant cost approach to variance analysis

Blue Ltd manufactures a single product, the standards of which are as follows:

|  | (£) | (£) |
|---|---|---|
| Standards per unit: |  |  |
| Standard selling price |  | 268 |
| Less Standard cost: |  |  |
| Materials (16 units at £4) | 64 |  |
| Labour (4 hours at £3) | 12 |  |
| *Overheads (4 hours at £24) | 96 | 172 |
| Standard profit |  | 96 |

*Total overhead costs are allocated on the basis of budgeted direct labour hours. The following information relates to last month's activities:

|  | Budgeted | Actual |
|---|---|---|
| Production and sales | 600 units | 500 units |
| Direct labour | 2400 hours at £3 | 2300 hours at £3 |
| Fixed overheads | £19 200 | £20 000 |
| Variable | £38 400 | £40 400 |
| Materials | 9600 units at £4 per unit | 9600 units at £4 per unit |

The actual selling price was identical to the budgeted selling price and there was no opening or closing stocks during the period.

(a) You are required to calculate the variances and reconcile the budgeted and actual profit for each of the following methods:

(i) The traditional method.

(ii) The opportunity cost method assuming *materials* are the limiting factor and materials are restricted to 9600 units for the period.

(iii) The opportunity cost method assuming *labour hours* are the limiting factor and labour hours are restricted to 2400 hours for the period.

(iv) The opportunity cost method assuming there are *no scarce inputs*.

(b) Briefly explain and comment on any differences between your answers to (a) (i) to (a) (iv) above.

### 19.28* Advanced: Variable costing reconciliation of budgeted and actual contribution and a discussion of the role of standard costing in a modern manufacturing environment

XYZ Ltd makes a single product and uses standard marginal costing. The standard cost data for the product are:

| Standard cost data per unit | (£) |
|---|---|
| Selling price | 175 |
| Direct materials (8 kgs at £2) | 16 |
| Direct labour (4 hours at £5) | 20 |
| Variable overhead (4 hours @ £15) | 60 |
| = Marginal cost | 96 |

The average production volume per period is 500 units but during Period 6 only 450 units were made and sold. At the end of the period the following variance statement was prepared.

| Results for period 6 | | | | |
|---|---|---|---|---|
| | Budget (500 units) (£) | | Actual (450 units) (£) | Variances (£) |
| Sales | 87 500 | | 83 250 | 4 250 Adv |
| *Less:* Marginal cost | | | | |
| Direct materials | 8 000 | (3690 kgs used) | 7 650 | 350 Fav |
| Direct labour | 10 000 | (1840 hours worked) | 8 100 | 1 900 Fav |
| Variable overheads | 30 000 | | 28 350 | 1 650 Fav |
| = Marginal cost | 48 000 | | 44 100 | |
| Contribution | 39 500 | | 39 150 | 350 Adv |
| *Less:* Fixed costs | 25 000 | | 24 650 | 350 Fav |
| = Profit | 14 500 | | 14 500 | — |

After studying the above report, the General Manager expressed surprise that all the cost variances were favourable as he understood that there had been some production problems. Furthermore, the Sales Manager had told him that he had been able to make some excellent sales during the period which seemed at odds with the statement.

You are required:

(a) to reconcile budgeted contribution to actual contribution, adjust for fixed cost, and disclose the actual profit;    (14 marks)

(b) to explain briefly why your revised presentation differs from the original statement.    (3 marks)

(c) The General Manager mentions that he has seen an article stating that standard costing is becoming less useful in modern factories. He is puzzled by this and wonders whether the company should stop using the technique.

You are required to prepare a reply to the General Manager explaining what the article refers to, and giving your opinion whether standard costing should continue to be used within the company.    (5 marks)

(Total 22 marks)

*CIMA Stage 3 Management Accounting Techniques*

**19.29\* Advanced: Traditional and activity-based variance analysis**

Frolin Chemicals Ltd produces FDN. The standard ingredients of 1 kg of FDN are:

| | |
|---|---|
| 0.65 kg of ingredient F | @ £4.00 per kg |
| 0.30 kg of ingredient D | @ £6.00 per kg |
| 0.20 kg of ingredient N | @ £2.50 per kg |
| 1.15 kg | |

Production of 4000 kg of FDN was budgeted for April. The production of FDN is entirely automated and production costs attributed to FDN production comprise only direct materials and overheads. The FDN production operation works on a JIT basis and no ingredient or FDN inventories are held.

Overheads were budgeted for April for the FDN production operation as follows:

| Activity | | Total amount |
|---|---|---|
| Receipt of deliveries from suppliers | (standard delivery quantity is 460 kg) | £4 000 |
| Despatch of goods to customers | (standard despatch quantity is 100 kg) | £8 000 |
| | | £12 000 |

In April, 4200 kg of FDN were produced and cost details were as follows:

● *Materials used*:

2840 kg of F, 1210 kg of D and 860 kg of N total cost    £20 380

● *Actual overhead costs*:

12 supplier deliveries (cost £4800) were made, and 38 customer despatches (cost £7800) were processed.

Frolin Chemicals Ltd's budget committee met recently to discuss the preparation of the financial control report for April, and the following discussion occurred:

*Chief Accountant*: 'The overheads do not vary directly with output and are therefore by definition "fixed". They should be analysed and reported accordingly.'

*Management Accountant*: 'The overheads do not vary with output, but they are certainly not fixed. They should be analysed and reported on an activity basis.'

Requirements:

Having regard to this discussion,

(a) prepare a variance analysis for FDN production costs in April: separate the material cost variance into price, mixture and yield components; separate the overhead cost variance into expenditure, capacity and efficiency components using consumption of ingredient F as the overhead absorption base;(11 marks)

(b) prepare a variance analysis for FDN production overhead costs in April on an activity basis;    (9 marks)

(c) explain how, in the design of an activity-based costing system, you would identify and select the most appropriate activities and cost drivers. (5 marks)

(Total 25 marks)

*CIMA Stage 3 Management Accounting Applications*

## 19.30 Advanced: Performance reports for sales and product managers

Zits Ltd makes two models for rotary lawn mowers, the Quicut and the Powacut. The company has a sales director and reporting to her, two product managers, each responsible for the profitability of one of the two models. The company's financial year ended on 31 March. The budgeted and actual results for the two models for the year ended on 31 March are given below:

| | Quicut | | Powacut | | Total | |
|---|---|---|---|---|---|---|
| | Budget | Actual | Budget | Actual | Budget | Actual |
| Sales volume (000 units) | 240 | 280 | 120 | 110 | 360 | 390 |
| | (£000) | (£000) | (£000) | (£000) | (£000) | (£000) |
| Sales revenue | 28 800 | 32 200 | 24 000 | 24 200 | 52 800 | 56 400 |
| Costs: | | | | | | |
| Variable | 9 600 | 11 480 | 7 200 | 6 820 | 16 800 | 18 300 |
| Traceable fixed manufacturing | 8 200 | 7 600 | 6 800 | 6 800 | 15 000 | 14 400 |
| Period costs: | | | | | | |
| Manufacturing | | | | | 5 700 | 6 000 |
| Administration and selling | | | | | 4 300 | 4 500 |
| | | | | | 41 800 | 43 200 |
| Net Profit before Tax | | | | | £11 000 | £13 200 |

The accountant had drawn up a series of flexed budgets at the beginning of the year should the actual volume differ from budget. The variable costs were unchanged, but the budgeted fixed costs, assuming a constant sales mix, for the different output ranges were as given below:

| Output range (000 units) | 300–360 (£000) | 361–420 (£000) |
|---|---|---|
| Traceable fixed manufacturing costs | 15 000 | 16 000 |
| Period cost – manufacturing | 5 700 | 6 000 |
| – administration and selling | 4 300 | 4 500 |
| | £25 000 | £26 500 |

The sales director has just received information from the trade association that industry rotary lawn mower sales for the twelve months ended on 31 March were 1.3 million units as against a forecast of 1.0 million.

Requirements:

(a) Prepare a schedule of variances which will be helpful to the sales director, and a schedule of more detailed variances which will be appropriate to the two product managers who are treated as profit centres. (16 marks)

(b) Discuss the results scheduled in (a) above identifying which of the variances are planning and which are operating variances. (9 marks)

(Total 25 marks)

*ICAEW Management Accounting*

## 19.31 Advanced: Investigation of variances

(a) Describe and comment briefly on the basis and limitations of the control chart approach to variance investigation decisions. (6 marks)

(b) The following analysis is available for the month of April for Department A:

| | (£) |
|---|---|
| Standard direct material | 72 000 |
| Material usage variance | 4 500 unfavourable |
| Material mix variance | 2 500 unfavourable |

The following estimates have also been made for Department A:

| | (£) |
|---|---|
| Estimated cost of investigating the total material variance | 1 000 |
| Estimated cost of correcting the total variance if investigated and found to be out of control | 2 000 |
| Estimated cost of permitting out-of-control material variances to continue | 10 000 |

Maximum Probability of a given total variance:

| Probability | 0.99 | 0.98 | 0.96 | 0.93 | 0.89 | 0.85 | 0.8 | 0.75 |
|---|---|---|---|---|---|---|---|---|
| Total Variance £000 | 1 | 2 | 3 | 4 | 5 | 6 | 7 | 8 |

You are required to determine, using a payoff table, whether the variance should be investigated. (6 marks)

(c)  You are uncertain of the estimated probability in (b). Calculate the probability estimate at which you would be indifferent between investigating and not investigating the variance.

(6 marks)

(d)  Discuss the use of mathematical models for the variance investigation decision. (7 marks)

(Total 25 marks)

*CIMA Stage 4 Management Accounting –*
*Control and Audit*

**19.32\*  Advanced: Investigation of variances**

(a)  The Secure Locke Company operates a system of standard costing, which it uses amongst other things as the basis for calculating certain management bonuses.

In September the Company's production of 100 000 keys was in accordance with budget. The standard quantity of material used in each key is one unit; the standard price is £0.05 per unit. In September 105 000 units of material were used, at an actual purchase price of £45 per thousand units (which was also the replacement cost).

The materials buyer is given a bonus of 10% of any favourable materials price variance. The production manager is given a bonus of 10% of any favourable materials quantity variance.

You are required:

(i)  to calculate the materials cost variances for September;  (4 marks)

(ii)  to record all relevant bookkeeping entries in journal form;  (2 marks)

(iii)  to evaluate the bonus system from the view-points of the buyer, the production manager, and the company.  (6 marks)

(b)  In October there was an adverse materials quantity variance of £500. A decision has to be made as to whether to investigate the key-making process to determine whether it is out of control.

On the basis of past experience the cost of an investigation is estimated at £50. The cost of correcting the process if it is found to be out of control is estimated at £100. The probability that the process is out of control is estimated at .50.

You are required:

(i)  to calculate the minimum present value of the expected savings that would have to be made in future months in order to justify making an investigation;

(6 marks)

(ii)  to suggest why the monthly cost savings arising from a systematic investigation are unlikely to be as great as the adverse materials variance of £500 which was experienced in the month of October;

(3 marks)

(iii)  to calculate, if the expected present value of cost savings were *first* £600 and *second* £250, the respective levels of probability that the process was out of control, at which the management would be indifferent about whether to conduct an investigation.  (4 marks)

*ICAEW Management Accounting*

**19.33\*  Advanced: Investigation of variances**

From past experience a company operating a standard cost system has accumulated the following information in relation to variances in its monthly management accounts:

Percentage of total number of variances

(1)  Its variances fall into two categories:

| Category 1: those which are not worth investigating | 64 |
| Category 2: those which are worth investigating | 36 |
| | 100 |

(2)  Of Category 2, corrective action has eliminated 70% of the variances, but the remainder have continued.

(3)  The cost of investigation averages £350 and that of correcting variances averages £550.

(4)  The average size of any variance not corrected is £525 per month and the company's policy is to assess the present value of such costs at 2% per month for a period of five months.

You are required to:

(a)  prepare *two* decision trees, to represent the position if an investigation is:

(i)  carried out;

(ii)  not carried out;  (12 marks)

(b)  recommend, with supporting calculations, whether or not the company should follow a policy of investigating variances as a matter of routine;  (3 marks)

(c) explain briefly *two* types of circumstance that would give rise to variances in Category 1 and *two* to those in Category 2; (6 marks)

(d) mention any *one* variation in the information used that you feel would be beneficial to the company if you wished to improve the quality of the decision-making rule recommended in (b) above. Explain briefly why you have suggested it.

(4 marks)

*CIMA P3 Management Accounting*

# Divisional financial performance measures

Large companies produce and sell a wide variety of products throughout the world. Because of the complexity of their operations, it is difficult for top management to directly control operations. It may therefore be appropriate to divide a company into separate self-contained segments or divisions and to allow divisional managers to operate with a great deal of independence. A divisional manager has responsibility for both the production and marketing activities of the division. The danger in creating autonomous divisions is that divisional managers might not pursue goals that are in the best interests of the company as a whole. The objective of this chapter is to consider financial performance measures that will motivate managers to pursue those goals that will best benefit the company as a whole. In other words, the objective is to develop performance measures that will achieve goal congruence.

In this chapter we shall focus on financial measures of divisional performance. However, financial measures cannot adequately measure all those factors that are critical to the success of a division. Emphasis should also be given to reporting key non-financial measures relating to such areas as competitiveness, product leadership, quality, delivery performance, innovation and flexibility to respond to changes in demand. In particular, performance measures should be developed that support the objectives and competitive strategies of the organization. Divisional financial performance measures should therefore be seen as one of a range of measures that should be used to measure and control divisional performance.

## Learning objectives

After studying this chapter, you should be able to:

- distinguish between functional and divisionalized organizational structures;
- explain the factors that should be considered in designing financial performance measures for evaluating divisional managers;
- explain why it is preferable to distinguish between managerial and economic performance;
- explain the meaning of return on investment, residual income and economic value added;
- compute economic value added;
- illustrate how performance measures may conflict with the net present value decision model;
- justify the use of a risk-adjusted discount rate for determining the divisional cost of capital;
- explain why it is important to include additional non-financial measures when evaluating divisional performance.

# Functional and divisionalized organizational structures

A **functional organizational structure** is one in which all activities of a similar type within a company are placed under the control of the appropriate departmental head. A simplified organization chart for a functional organizational structure is illustrated in Figure 20.1(a). It is assumed that the company illustrated consists of five separate departments – production, marketing, financial administration, purchasing and research and development. In a typical functional organization none of the managers of the five departments is responsible for more than a part of the process of acquiring the raw materials, converting them into finished products, selling to customers, and administering the financial aspects of this process. For example, the production department is responsible for the manufacture of all products at a minimum cost, and of satisfactory quality, and to meet the delivery dates requested by the marketing department. The marketing department is responsible for the total sales revenue and any costs associated with selling and distributing the products, but not for the total profit. The purchasing department is responsible for purchasing supplies at a minimum cost and of satisfactory quality so that the production requirements can be met.

You will see from Figure 20.1 that the marketing function is a revenue centre and the remaining departments are cost centres. Revenues and costs (including the cost of investments) are combined together only at the chief executive, or corporate level, which is classified as an investment centre.

Let us now consider Figure 20.1(b), which shows a **divisionalized organizational structure**, which is split up into divisions in accordance with the products which are made. You will see from the diagram that each divisional manager is responsible for all of the operations relating to his or her particular product. To reflect this greater autonomy each division is either an investment centre or a profit centre. To simplify the presentation it is assumed that all of the divisions in Figure 20.1(a) are investment centres (we shall discuss the factors influencing the choice of investment or profit centres later in the chapter). Note that within each division there are multiple cost and revenue centres and also that a functional structure is applied within each division. Figure 20.1(b) shows a simplified illustration of a divisionalized organizational structure. In practice, however, only part of a company may be divisionalized. For example, activities such as research and development, industrial relations, and general administration may be structured centrally on a functional basis with a responsibility for providing services to all of the divisions.

The distinguishing feature between the functional structure (Figure 20.1a) and the divisionalized structure (Figure 20.1b) is that in the functional structure only the organization as a whole is an investment centre and below this level a functional structure applies throughout. In contrast, in a divisionalized structure the organization is divided into separate investment or profit centres and a functional structure applies below this level.

Generally, a divisionalized organizational structure will lead to a decentralization of the decision-making process. For example, divisional managers will normally be free to set selling prices, choose which market to sell in, make product mix and output decisions, and select suppliers (this may include buying from other divisions within the company or from other companies). In a functional organizational structure pricing, product mix and output decisions will be made by central management. Consequently, the functional managers in a centralized organization will have far less independence than divisional managers. One way to express the difference between the two organizational structures is to say that the divisional managers have profit responsibility. They are responsible for generating revenues, controlling costs and earning a satisfactory return on the capital invested in

**FIGURE 20.1** *A functional and divisionalized organizational structure.*

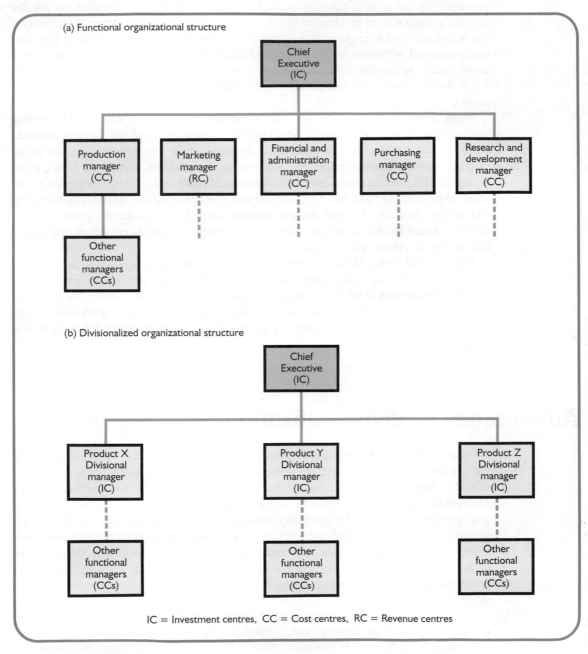

(a) Functional organizational structure

Chief Executive (IC)

Production manager (CC)

Marketing manager (RC)

Financial and administration manager (CC)

Purchasing manager (CC)

Research and development manager (CC)

Other functional managers (CCs)

(b) Divisionalized organizational structure

Chief Executive (IC)

Product X Divisional manager (IC)

Product Y Divisional manager (IC)

Product Z Divisional manager (IC)

Other functional managers (CCs)

Other functional managers (CCs)

Other functional managers (CCs)

IC = Investment centres, CC = Cost centres, RC = Revenue centres

their operations. The managers of the functional organizational structure do not have profit responsibility. For example, in Figure 20.1(a) the production manager has no control over sources of supply, selling prices, or product mix and output decisions.

# Profit centres and investment centres

The creation of separate divisions may lead to the delegation of different degrees of authority; for example, in some organizations a divisional manager may, in addition to having authority to make decisions on sources of supply and choice of markets, also have responsibility for making capital investment decisions. Where this situation occurs, the division is known as an **investment centre**. Alternatively, where a manager cannot control the investment and is responsible only for the profits obtained from operating the fixed assets assigned to him or her by corporate headquarters, the segment is referred to as a **profit centre**. In contrast, the term **cost centre** is used to describe a responsibility centre in a functional organizational structure where a manager is responsible for costs but not profits.

Many firms attempt to simulate a divisionalized profit centre structure by creating separate manufacturing and marketing divisions in which the supplying division produces a product and transfers it to the marketing division, which then sells the product in the external market. Transfer prices are assigned to the products transferred between the divisions. This practice creates pseudo-divisionalized profit centres. Separate profits can be reported for each division, but the divisional managers have limited authority for sourcing and pricing decisions. To meet the true requirements of a divisionalized profit centre, a division should be able to sell the majority of its output to outside customers and should also be free to choose the sources of supply.

Ezzamel and Hilton (1980) investigated the degree of autonomy allowed to divisional managers in 129 large UK companies. They found that divisional managers enjoyed substantial discretion in taking operating decisions relating to output, selling prices, setting credit terms, advertising and purchasing policies. However, close supervision by top management in choosing capital projects and specifying capital expenditures in the annual budget was observed.

# Advantages of divisionalization

Divisionalization can improve the decision-making process both from the point of view of the quality of the decision and the speed of the decision. The quality of the decisions should be improved because decisions can be made by the person who is familiar with the situation and who should therefore be able to make more informed judgements than central management who cannot be intimately acquainted with all the activities of the various segments of the business. Speedier decisions should also occur because information does not have to pass along the chain of command to and from top management. Decisions can be made on the spot by those who are familiar with the product lines and production processes and who can react to changes in local conditions in a speedy and efficient manner.

In addition, delegation of responsibility to divisional managers provides them with greater freedom, thus making their activities more challenging and providing the opportunity to achieve self-fulfilment. This process should mean that motivation and efficiency will be increased not just at the divisional manager level but throughout the whole division. A study by Dittman and Ferris (1978) of the attitudes of managers in companies in the USA found that those managers in charge of profit centres had greater job satisfaction than the managers of cost centres. They conclude that wherever possible, system designers ought to try to construct profit centres for organizational units.

Another important reason for adopting a divisionalized structure is that the distribution of decision-making responsibility to divisions frees top management from detailed involvement in day-to-day operations, and enables them to devote more effort to strategic planning. It is also claimed that divisions can provide an excellent training ground for future members of top management by enabling trainee managers to acquire the basic managerial skills and experience in an environment that is less complex than managing the company as a whole.

# Disadvantages of divisionalization

If a company is divisionalized, there is a danger that divisions may compete with each other excessively and that divisional managers may be encouraged to take action which will increase their own profits at the expense of the profits of other divisions. This may adversely affect co-operation between the divisions and lead to a lack of harmony in achieving the overall organizational goals of the company. This in turn may lead to a reduction in total company profits.

It is also claimed that the costs of activities that are common to all divisions may be greater for a divisionalized structure than for a centralized structure. For example, a large central accounting department in a centralized organizational structure may be less costly to operate than separate accounting departments for each division within a divisionalized structure. If top management are contemplating a divisionalized structure, it is important that they assess whether the additional benefits will exceed the additional costs.

A further argument against divisionalization is that top management loses some control by delegating decision-making to divisional managers. It is argued that a series of control reports is not as effective as detailed knowledge of a company's activities. However, with a good system of performance evaluation together with appropriate control information, top management should be able to effectively control operations.

# Pre-requisites for successful divisionalization

A divisionalized structure is most suited to companies engaged in several dissimilar activities. The reason is that it is difficult for top management to be intimately acquainted with all the diverse activities of the various segments of the business. On the other hand, when the major activities of a company are closely related, these activities should be carefully coordinated, and this coordination is more easily achieved in a centralized organizational structure. The results from a number of surveys suggest that divisionalization is more common in companies having diversified activities than when single or related activities are undertaken (Ezzamel and Hilton, 1980).

For successful divisionalization it is important that the activities of a division be as independent as possible of other activities. However, Solomons (1965) argues that even though substantial independence of divisions from each other is a necessary condition for divisionalization, if carried to the limit it would destroy the very idea that such divisions are an integral part of any single business. Divisions should be more than investments – they should contribute not only to the success of the company but to the success of each other.

According to Solomons, a further condition for the success of divisionalization is that the relations between divisions should be regulated so that no one division, by seeking its own profit, can reduce that of the company as a whole. He states that this is not the same as seeking profit at the expense of other divisions, but the amount that a division adds to its own profit must exceed the loss that it inflicts on another division. Unfortunately, conflicts between divisions do arise, and one of the important tasks of the accountant is to design an accounting control system that will discourage a division from improving its own profit at the expense of the company as a whole.

# Distinguishing between the managerial and economic performance of the division

Before discussing the factors to be considered in determining how divisional profitability should be measured, we must decide whether the primary purpose is to measure the performance of the division or that of the divisional manager. The messages transmitted from these two measures may be quite different. For example, a manager may be assigned to an ailing division to improve performance, and might succeed in substantially improving the performance of the division. However, the division might still be unprofitable because of industry factors, such as overcapacity and a declining market. The future of the division might be uncertain, but the divisional manager may well be promoted as a result of the outstanding managerial performance. Conversely, a division might report significant profits but, because of management deficiencies, the performance may be unsatisfactory when the favourable economic environment is taken into account.

If the purpose is to evaluate the divisional manager then only those items directly controllable by the manager should be included in the profitability measure. Thus all allocations of indirect costs, such as central service and central administration costs, which are not controllable by divisional managers, ought not to be included in the profitability measure. Such costs can only be controlled where they are incurred; which means that they can be controlled only by central service managers and central management.

Corporate headquarters, however, will also be interested in evaluating a division's economic performance for decision-making purposes, such as expansion, contraction and divestment decisions. In this situation a measure that includes only those amounts directly controllable by the divisional manager would overstate the economic performance of the division. This overstatement occurs because, if the divisions were independent companies, they would have to incur the costs of those services provided by head office. Therefore, to measure the economic performance of the division many items that the divisional manager cannot influence, such as interest expenses, taxes and the allocation of central administrative staff expenses, should be included in the profitability measure.

# Alternative divisional profit measures

There are strong arguments for computing two measures of divisional profitability – one to evaluate managerial performance and the other to evaluate the economic performance of the division. In this chapter we shall focus on both these measures. The most common measures of divisional profitability are return on investment (that is, profit as a percentage of the investment in a division) residual income and economic value added. The reported divisional profit is a component of each of these measures. At this stage we shall restrict our attention purely to problems that are encountered with divisional profit measurement before turning our attention to the above three common measures of divisional profitability.

Exhibit 20.1 presents a divisional profit statement. You can see that there are four different profit measures that we can use to measure divisional performance. We shall focus initially on measuring *managerial* performance. The **variable short-run contribution margin** is inappropriate for performance evaluation, because it does not include fixed costs that are controllable by the divisional manager. For example, a manager may not be motivated to control non-variable labour costs or equipment rentals, since they fall below the variable short-run contribution line and are not included in the performance measure.

EXHIBIT 20.1

*Alternative divisional profit measures*

The **controllable contribution** is computed by deducting from total divisional revenues all those costs that are controllable by the division manager. This measure therefore includes controllable fixed costs such as non-variable

| | |
|---|---|
| Sales to outside customers | xxx |
| Transfers to other divisions | xxx |
| Total sales revenue | xxx |
| Less variable costs | xxx |
| 1. *Variable short-run contribution margin* | xxx |
| Less controllable fixed costs | xxx |
| 2. *Controllable contribution* | xxx |
| Less non-controllable avoidable costs | xxx |
| 3. *Divisional contribution* | xxx |
| Less allocated corporate expenses | xxx |
| 4. *Divisional net profit before taxes* | xxx |

labour, equipment rental and the cost of utilities. These costs are fixed in the short term, but in the longer term the divisional manager has the option of reducing them by altering the scale of operations or reducing the complexity and diversity of product lines and distribution channels. Where a division is a profit centre, depreciation is not a controllable cost, since the manager does not have authority to make capital investment decisions. Depreciation, however, should be deemed to be a controllable expense for an investment centre in respect of those assets that are controllable by the divisional manager.

Controllable contribution is the most appropriate measure of a divisional manager's performance, since it measures the ability of managers to use the resources under their control effectively. It should not be interpreted in isolation if it is used directly to evaluate the performance of a divisional manager. Instead, the controllable contribution reported by a division should be evaluated relative to a budgeted performance, so that market conditions can be taken into account.

In practice, it is extremely difficult to distinguish between controllable and non-controllable costs. However, three situations can be identified that will assist us in overcoming this problem. Where a division is completely free to shop around for a service and there is no rule requiring the division to obtain the service from within the company, the expense is clearly controllable. Alternatively, a division may not be free to choose an outside source of supply for the service in question, but it may be able to decide how much of this service is utilized. In this latter situation the quantity is controllable by the division but the price is not. An appropriate solution here is for the division to be charged with the actual quantity at the standard or budgeted cost for the service that has been obtained. Thus any difference between the budget and actual performance would relate solely to excess usage by the division recorded at the standard price. Finally, the division may not be free to decide on either the quantity of the service it utilizes or the price it will be charged. Industrial relations costs may fall into this category. Here the divisions have no choice but to accept an apportioned cost for the benefits they have received (such apportionments may be made for external reporting purposes). In situations like this, the costs charged to the division for the service can only be regarded as a non-controllable item of divisional overhead. Another general rule that can be applied for distinguishing between controllable and non-controllable costs is to follow the guideline suggested by Merchant (1998) – that is, hold managers accountable for those costs that you want them to pay attention to.

Controllable contribution provides an incomplete measure of the *economic* performance of a division, since it does not include those costs that are attributable to the division but which are not controllable by the divisional manager. For example, depreciation of divisional assets, and head office finance and legal staff who are assigned to providing services for specific divisions, would fall into this category. These expenses would be avoidable if a decision were taken to close the division. Those non-controllable expenses that are attributable to a division, and which would be avoidable if the division was closed, are deducted from controllable contribution to derive the **divisional contribution**. This is clearly a useful figure for evaluating the *economic* contribution of the division, since it represents the contribution that a division is making to corporate profits and overheads. It should not be used, however, to evaluate managerial performance, since it includes costs that are not controllable by divisional managers.

Many companies allocate all corporate general and administrative expenses to divisions to derive a **divisional net profit before taxes**. From a theoretical point of view, it is difficult to justify such allocations since they tend to be arbitrary and do not have any connection with the manner in which divisional activities influence the level of these corporate expenses. Divisional contribution would therefore seem to be the most appropriate measure of divisions' *economic* performance, since it is not distorted by arbitrary allocations. We have noted, however, that corporate headquarters may wish to compare a division's economic performance with that of comparable firms operating in the same industry. The divisional contribution would overstate the performance of the division, because if the division were independent, it would have to incur the costs of those services performed by head office. The apportioned head office costs are an approximation of the costs that the division would have to incur if it traded as a separate company. Consequently, companies may prefer to use divisional net profit when comparing the performance of a division with similar companies.

For the reasons mentioned above, divisional net profit is not a satisfactory measure for evaluating *managerial* performance. Despite the many theoretical arguments against divisional net profit, the empirical evidence indicates that this measure is used widely to evaluate both divisional *economic* and *managerial* performance (Reece and Cool, 1978; Fremgen and Liao, 1981; Ramadan, 1989; Skinner, 1990; Drury *et al.*, 1993). In the Fremgen and Liao survey respondents were asked why they allocated indirect costs. The most important managerial performance evaluation reason was to 'remind profit centre managers that indirect costs exist and that profit centre earnings must be adequate to cover a share of these costs'. The counter-argument to this is that if central management wishes to inform managers that divisions must be profitable enough to cover not only their own operations but corporate expenses as well, it is preferable to set a high budgeted controllable contribution target that takes account of these factors. Divisional managers can then concentrate on increasing controllable contribution by focusing on those costs and revenues that are under their control and not be concerned with costs that they cannot control.

A further reason for cost allocations cited in the surveys by Fremgen and Liao and Skinner was that by allocating central overhead costs to divisions, divisional managers are made aware of these costs, so they will exert pressure on central management to minimize the costs of central staff departments. There is also some evidence to suggest that companies hold managers accountable for divisional net profit because this is equivalent to the measure that financial markets focus on to evaluate the performance of the company as a whole (Joseph *et al.*, 1996). Top management therefore require their divisional managers to concentrate on the same measures as those used by financial markets.

# Return on investment

Instead of focusing purely on the absolute size of a division's profits, most organizations focus on the return on investment (ROI) of a division. ROI expresses divisional profit as a percentage of the assets employed in the division. Assets employed can be defined as total divisional assets, assets controllable by the divisional manager or net assets. We shall consider the alternative measures of assets employed later in the chapter.

ROI is the most widely used financial measure of divisional performance. Why? Consider a situation where division A earns a profit of £1 million and division B a profit of £2 million. Can we conclude that Division B is more profitable than Division A? The answer is no, since we should consider whether the divisions are returning a sufficiently high return on the capital invested in the division. Assume that £4 million capital is invested in division A and £20 million in division B. Division A's ROI is 25% (£1m/£4m) whereas the return for division B is 10% (£2m/£20m). Capital invested has alternative uses, and corporate management will wish to ascertain whether the returns being earned on the capital invested in a particular division exceeds the division's opportunity cost of capital (i.e. the returns available from the alternative use of the capital). If, in the above illustration, the return available on similar investments to that in division B is 15% then the economic viability of division B is questionable if profitability cannot be improved. In contrast, the ROI measure suggests that division A is very profitable.

ROI provides a useful overall approximation on the success of a firm's past investment policy by providing a summary measure of the *ex post* return on capital invested. Kaplan and Atkinson (1998) also draw attention to the fact that, without some form of measurement of the *ex post* returns on capital, there is little incentive for accurate estimates of future cash flows during the capital budgeting process. Measuring returns on invested capital also focuses managers' attention on the impact of levels of working capital (particularly stocks and debtors) on the ROI.

Another feature of the ROI is that it can be used as a common denominator for comparing the returns of dissimilar businesses, such as other divisions within the group or outside competitors. ROI has been widely used for many years in all types of organizations so that most managers understand what the measure reflects and consider it to be of considerable importance.

Despite the widespread use of ROI, a number of problems exist when this measure is used to evaluate the performance of divisional managers. For example, it is possible that divisional ROI can be increased by actions that will make the company as a whole worse off, and conversely, actions that decrease the divisional ROI may make the company as a whole better off. In other words, evaluating divisional managers on the basis of ROI may not encourage goal congruence. Consider the following example:

|                                | Division X   | Division Y     |
| ------------------------------ | ------------ | -------------- |
| Investment project available   | £10 million  | £10 million    |
| Controllable contribution      | £2 million   | £1.3 million   |
| Return on the proposed project | 20%          | 13%            |
| ROI of divisions at present    | 25%          | 9%             |

It is assumed that neither project will result in any changes in non-controllable costs and that the overall cost of capital for the company is 15%. The manager of division X would be reluctant to invest the additional £10 million because the return on the proposed project is 20%, and this would reduce the existing overall ROI of 25%. On the other hand, the manager of division Y would wish to invest the £10 million because the return on the proposed project of 13% is in excess of the present return of 9%, and it would increase the division's overall ROI. Consequently, the managers of both divisions would make decisions that would not be in the best interests of the company. The company should accept only those projects where the return is in excess of the cost of capital of 15%, but the manager of division X would reject a potential return of 20% and the manager of division Y would accept a potential return of 13%. ROI can therefore lead to a lack of goal congruence.

Managers can also be motivated to make incorrect asset disposal decisions. Consider the situation where the manager of division X has an asset that generates a return of 19% and the manager of division Y has an asset that yields a return of 12%. The manager of division X can increase ROI by disposing of the asset, whereas the ROI of division Y will decline if the asset is sold. Asset disposals are appropriate where assets earn a return less than the cost of capital. Hence the asset in division X should be kept and division Y's asset sold (assuming that the assets can be sold for their book values). Both managers can therefore increase their ROI by making decisions that are not in the best interest of the company.

# Residual income

To overcome some of the dysfunctional consequences of ROI, the residual income approach can be used. For the purpose of evaluating the performance of *divisional managers*, residual income is defined as controllable contribution less a cost of capital charge on the investment controllable by the divisional manager. For evaluating the *economic performance* of the division residual income can be defined as divisional contribution (see Exhibit 20.1) less a cost of capital charge on the total investment in assets employed by the division. If residual income is used to measure the managerial performance of investment centres, there is a greater probability that managers will be encouraged, when acting in their own best interests, also to act in the best interests of the company. Returning to our previous illustration in respect of the investment decision for divisions X and Y, the residual income calculations are as follows:

|  | Division X (£) | Division Y (£) |
|---|---|---|
| Proposed investment | 10 million | 10 million |
| Controllable contribution | 2 million | 1.3 million |
| Cost of capital charge (15% of the investment cost) | 1.5 million | 1.5 million |
| Residual income | 0.5 million | − 0.2 million |

This calculation indicates that the residual income of division X will increase and that of division Y will decrease if both managers accept the project. Therefore the manager of division X would invest, whereas the manager of division Y would not. These actions are in the best interests of the company as a whole.

Residual income would also encourage both managers to make the correct asset disposal decisions. Consider again the asset disposal example in the previous section. The manager of division X would avoid a cost of capital charge of 15% on the asset by disposing of it, but this would also result in a loss of the return of 19%. In contrast, the manager of division Y would also avoid a cost of capital charge of 15% on the asset, but would lose a return of 12%. Therefore the residual income measure would lead to the manager of division Y disposing of the asset and the manager of division X retaining the asset.

A further reason cited in favour of residual income over the ROI measure is that residual income is more flexible, because different cost of capital percentage rates can be applied to investments that have different levels of risk. Not only will the cost of capital of divisions that have different levels of risk differ – so may the risk and cost of capital of assets within the same division. The residual income measure enables different risk-adjusted capital costs to be incorporated in the calculation, whereas the ROI cannot incorporate these differences.

Residual income suffers from the disadvantages of being an absolute measure, which means that it is difficult to compare the performance of a division with that of other divisions or companies of a different size. For example, a large division is more likely to earn a larger residual income than a small division. To overcome this deficiency, targeted or budgeted levels of residual income should be set for each division that are consistent with asset size and the market conditions of the divisions.

In the case of profit centres, where divisional managers are not authorized to make capital investment decisions and where they cannot influence the investment in working capital, ROI is a satisfactory performance measure, because if the return on investment is maximized on a fixed quantity of capital, the absolute return itself will also be maximized. However, in the case of investment centres, or profit centres where managers can significantly influence the investment in working capital, ROI appears to be an unsatisfactory method of measuring managerial performance, and in these circumstances the residual income is preferable.

Surveys of methods used by companies to evaluate the performance of divisional managers indicate a strong preference for ROI over residual income. For example, the UK survey by Drury *et al.* (1993) reported that the following measures were used:

|  | (%) |
| --- | --- |
| A target ROI set by the group | 55 |
| Residual income | 20 |
| A target profit *before* charging interest on investment | 61 |
| A target cash flow figure | 43 |

Why is ROI preferred to residual income? Skinner (1990) found evidence to suggest that firms prefer to use ROI because, being a ratio, it can be used for inter-division and inter-firm comparisons. ROI for a division can be compared with the return from other divisions within the group or with whole companies outside the group, whereas absolute monetary measures such as residual income are not appropriate in making such comparisons. A second possible reason for the preference for ROI is that 'outsiders' tend to use ROI as a measure of a company's overall performance. Corporate managers therefore want their divisional managers to focus on ROI so that their performance measure is congruent with outsiders' measure of the company's overall economic performance. A further reason, suggested by Kaplan and Atkinson (1998), is that managers find percentage measures of profitability such as ROI more convenient, since they enable a division's profitability to be compared with other financial measures (such as inflation rates, interest rates, and the ROI rates of other divisions and comparable companies outside the group).

# Economic value added (EVA$^{(TM)}$)

During the 1990s residual income has been refined and renamed as economic value added (EVA$^{(TM)}$) by the Stern Stewart consulting organization and they have registered EVA$^{(TM)}$ as their trademark. An article in an issue of *Fortune* magazine (1993) described the apparent success that many companies had derived from using EVA$^{(TM)}$ to motivate and evaluate corporate and divisional managers. *The Economist* (1997) reported that more than 300 firms world-wide had adopted EVA$^{(TM)}$ including Coca-Cola, AT&T, ICL, Boots and the Burton Group.

The EVA$^{(TM)}$ concept extends the traditional residual income measure by incorporating adjustments to the divisional financial performance measure for distortions introduced by generally accepted accounting principles (GAAP). EVA$^{(TM)}$ can be defined as:

$$EVA^{(TM)} = \text{Conventional divisional profit} \pm \text{accounting adjustments} - \text{cost of capital charge on divisional assets}$$

Our earlier discussion relating to which of the conventional alternative divisional profit measures listed in Exhibit 20.1 should be used also applies here. There are strong theoretical arguments for using controllable contribution as the divisional profit measure for *managerial* performance and divisional contribution for measuring *economic* performance. Many companies, however, use divisional net profit (after allocated costs) to evaluate both divisional managerial and economic performance.

Adjustments are made to the chosen conventional divisional profit measure in order to replace historic accounting data with a measure of economic profit and asset values. Stern Stewart have stated that they have developed approximately 160 accounting adjustments that may need to be made to convert the conventional accounting profit into a sound measure of EVA$^{(TM)}$ but they have indicated that most organizations will only need to use about 10 of the adjustments. These adjustments result in the capitalization of many discretionary expenditures, such as research and development, marketing and advertising, by spreading these costs over the periods in which the benefits are received. Therefore adopting EVA$^{(TM)}$ should reduce some of the harmful side-effects arising from using financial measures that were discussed in Chapter 16. This is because managers will not bear the full costs of the discretionary expenditures in the period in which they are incurred if the expenses are capitalized. Also because it is a restatement of the residual income measure, compared with ROI, EVA$^{(TM)}$ is more likely to encourage goal congruence in terms of asset acquisition and disposal decisions. Managers are also made aware that capital has a cost and they are thus encouraged to dispose of underutilized assets that do not generate sufficient income to cover their cost of capital.

Stern Stewart developed EVA$^{(TM)}$ with the aim of producing an overall financial measure that encourages senior managers to concentrate on the delivery of shareholder value. They consider that the aim of managers of companies, whose shares are traded in the stock market, should be to maximize shareholder value. It is therefore important that the key financial measure that is used to measure divisional or company performance should be congruent with shareholder value. Stern Stewart claim that, compared with other financial measures, EVA$^{(TM)}$ is more likely to meet this requirement and also to reduce dysfunctional behaviour.

There are a number of issues that apply to ROI, residual income or its replacement (EVA$^{(TM)}$). They concern determining which assets should be included in a division's asset base, and the adjustments that should be made to financial accounting practices to derive managerial information that is closer to economic reality.

# Determining which assets should be included in the investment base

We must determine which assets to include in a division's asset base to compute both ROI and EVA$^{(TM)}$. (Note that for the remainder of the chapter we shall use the term EVA$^{(TM)}$ to incorporate residual income.) If the purpose is to evaluate the performance of the divisional manager then only those assets that can be directly traced to the division and that are controllable by the divisional manager should be included in the asset base. Assets managed by central headquarters should not be included. For example, if debtors and cash are administered centrally, they should not be included as part of the asset base. On the other hand, if a divisional manager can influence these amounts, they should be included in the investment base. If they were not included, divisional managers could improve their profits by granting over-generous credit terms to customers; they would obtain the rewards of the additional sales without being charged with any cost for the additional capital that would be tied up in debtors.

Any liabilities that are within the control of the division should be deducted from the asset base. For example, a division may finance its investment in stocks by the use of trade creditors; this liability for creditors should therefore be deducted. The term controllable investment is used to refer to the net asset base that is controllable by divisional managers. Our overall aim in analysing controllable and non-controllable investment is to produce performance measures that will encourage a manager to behave in the best interests of the organization and also to provide a good approximation of managerial performance. It is therefore appropriate to include in the investment base only those assets that a manager can influence, and any arbitrary apportionments should be excluded.

If the purpose is to evaluate the economic performance of the division, the profitability of the division will be overstated if controllable investment is used. This is because a division could not operate without the benefit of corporate assets such as buildings, cash and debtors managed at the corporate level. These assets would be included in the investment base if the divisions were separate independent companies. Therefore many divisionalized companies allocate corporate assets to divisions when comparing divisional profitability with comparable firms in the same industry.

# The impact of inflation

Both ROI and EVA$^{(TM)}$ are likely to be distorted if there is no attempt to adjust for inflation. This is because cash costs and revenues are measured in current prices, whereas fixed assets and depreciation charges are measured in historical prices of the year in which the assets were acquired. Depreciation and fixed assets should be adjusted by a price index to reflect inflationary price movements. If these adjustments are not made then both depreciation and fixed assets will be understated. Therefore divisional profits will be overstated and the divisional investment will be understated. The combination of overstated profits and understated investment causes ROI and EVA$^{(TM)}$ to be overstated. The increased ROI and EVA$^{(TM)}$ result from a failure to adjust for inflationary price changes, and do not represent an increase in economic wealth. A discussion of the alternative accounting approaches for incorporating inflationary price changes is outside the scope of this book. Readers interested in this topic should refer to financial accounting textbooks such as Lee (1996).

# The impact of depreciation

It is common to find fixed assets valued at either their original cost or their written down value for the purpose of calculating return on investment and EVA$^{(TM)}$, but both of these valuation methods are weak. Consider, for example, an investment in an asset of £1 million with a life of five years with annual cash flows of £350 000 and a cost of capital of 10%.

This investment has a positive NPV of £326 850, and should be accepted. You can see from Exhibit 20.2 that the annual profit is £150 000 when straight line depreciation is used. If the asset is *valued at original cost*, there will be a return of 15% per annum for five years. This will understate the true return, because the economic valuation is unlikely to remain at £1 million each year for five years and then immediately fall to zero. If ROI is based on the *written-down value*, you can see from Exhibit 20.2 that the investment base will decline each year – and, with constant profits, the effect will be to show a steady increase in return on investment. This steady increase in return on investment will suggest an improvement in managerial performance when the economic facts indicate that performance has remained unchanged over the five-year period.

Similar inconsistencies will also occur if the EVA$^{(TM)}$ method is used. If the asset is valued at the original cost, EVA$^{(TM)}$ of £50 000 will be reported each year (£150 000 profit – (10% cost of capital × 1 million)). On the other hand, if the cost of capital charge is based on the written-down value of the asset, the investment base will decline each year, and EVA$^{(TM)}$ will increase.

Exhibit 20.2 serves to illustrate that if asset written-down values are used to determine the division's investment base, managers can improve their ROI or EVA$^{(TM)}$ by postponing new investments and operating with older assets with low written-down values. In contrast, divisional managers who invest in new equipment will have a lower ROI or EVA$^{(TM)}$. This situation arises because financial accounting depreciation methods (including the reducing balance method) produce lower profitability measures in the earlier years of an asset's life.

To overcome this problem, it has been suggested that ROI or EVA$^{(TM)}$ calculations should be based on the original cost (i.e. gross book value) of the assets. When assets are measured at gross book value, managers will have an incentive to replace existing assets with new assets. This is because the increase in the investment base is only the difference between the original cost of the old asset and the purchase cost of the new asset. This difference is likely to be significantly less than the incremental cash flow (purchase cost less sale proceeds of the old asset) of the new asset. Managers may therefore be motivated to replace old assets with new ones that have a negative NPV.

To overcome the problems created by using financial accounting depreciation methods, alternative depreciation models have been recommended. These methods are discussed in the Appendix to this chapter. The theoretically correct solution to the problem is to value assets at their economic cost (i.e. the present value of future net cash inflows) but this presents serious practical difficulties. An appropriate solution to the practical problems is to value assets at their replacement cost (see Lee, 1996 for a discussion of this topic). Although this method is conceptually distinct from the present value method of valuation, it may provide answers which are reasonable approximations of what would be obtained using a present value approach. In addition, replacement cost is conceptually superior to the historical cost method of asset valuation. It follows that the depreciation charge on controllable investment based on replacement cost is preferable to a charge based on historical cost. The ROI and EVA$^{(TM)}$ would then be calculated on controllable investment valued at replacement cost.

# The effect of performance measurement on capital investment decisions

**AR** Capital investment decisions are the most important decisions that a divisional manager will have to make. We noted in Chapter 13 that these decisions should be taken on the basis of the net present value (NPV) decision rule. The way in which the

**EXHIBIT 20.2**

*Profitability measures using straight-line depreciation*

performance of the divisional manager is measured, however, is likely to have a profound effect on the decisions that he or she will make. There is a danger that, because of the way in which divisional performance is measured, the manager may be motivated to take the wrong decision and not follow the NPV rule. We noted

|  | 1 (£) | 2 (£) | 3 (£) | 4 (£) | 5 (£) |
|---|---|---|---|---|---|
| Net cash flow | 350 000 | 350 000 | 350 000 | 350 000 | 350 000 |
| Depreciation | 200 000 | 200 000 | 200 000 | 200 000 | 200 000 |
| Profit | 150 000 | 150 000 | 150 000 | 150 000 | 150 000 |
| Cost of capital (10% of WDV) | 100 000 | 80 000 | 60 000 | 40 000 | 20 000 |
| EVA$^{((TM))}$ | 50 000 | 70 000 | 90 000 | 110 000 | 130 000 |
| Opening WDV of the asset | 1 000 000 | 800 000 | 600 000 | 400 000 | 200 000 |
| ROI | 15% | 18.75% | 25% | 37.5% | 75% |

in an earlier example (page 800) that the residual income (or EVA$^{(TM)}$) method of evaluation appeared to encourage a divisional manager to make capital investment decisions that are consistent with the NPV rule, but there is no guarantee that this or any other financial measure will in fact motivate the manager to act
in this way. Consider the information presented in Exhibit 20.3, which relates to three mutually exclusive projects: X, Y and Z.

Applying the NPV rule, the manager should choose project X in preference to project Z, and should reject project Y.

## PROFITS AND RETURN ON INVESTMENT

Divisional managers are likely to estimate the outcomes from alternative investments and choose the investment that maximizes their performance measure. Exhibit 20.4 shows the estimated profits and ROI's for projects X, Y and Z. The calculations in Exhibit 20.4 are based on the net cash flows for each year presented in Exhibit 20.3, less straight-line depreciation of £287 000 per year. The ROI is calculated on the *opening* written-down value at the start of the year. From the calculation in Exhibit 20.4 you will see that a manager who is anxious to improve his or her *short-term* performance will choose project Y if he or she is evaluated on total profits or return on investment, since project Y earns the largest profits and ROI in year 1; but project Y has a negative net present value, and should be rejected. Alternatively, a manager who assesses the impact of the project on his or her performance measure *over the three years* will choose project Z, because this yields the highest total profits and average ROI.

## ECONOMIC VALUE ADDED (EVA$^{(TM)}$ )

Let us now consider whether the EVA$^{(TM)}$ calculations are consistent with the NPV calculations. Exhibit 20.5 presents the estimated EVA$^{(TM)}$ calculations for project X.

The total present value of EVA$^{(TM)}$ for project X is £77 000 and this is identical with the NPV of project X which was calculated in Exhibit 20.3. EVA$^{(TM)}$ is therefore the long-term counterpart of the discounted NPV. Thus, given that maximizing NPV is equivalent to maximizing shareholder value, then maximizing the present value of EVA$^{(TM)}$ is also equivalent to maximizing shareholder value and Stern Stewart's claim that EVA$^{(TM)}$ is congruent

|  | X (£000s) | Y (£000s) | Z (£000s) |
|---|---|---|---|
| Machine cost initial outlay (time zero) | 861 | 861 | 861 |
| Estimated net cash flow (year 1) | 250 | 390 | 50 |
| Estimated net cash flow (year 2) | 370 | 250 | 50 |
| Estimated net cash flow (year 3) | 540 | 330 | 1100 |
| Estimated net present value at 10% cost of capital[a] | 77 | (52) | 52 |
| Ranking on the basis of NPV | 1 | 3 | 2 |

*Note*
[a] The net present value calculations are to the nearest £000.

with shareholder value would appear to be justified. Consequently, if divisional managers are evaluated on the basis of the long-run present value of EVA$^{(TM)}$, their capital investment decisions should be consistent with the decisions that would be taken using the NPV rule.

However, there is no guarantee that the short-run EVA$^{(TM)}$ measure will be consistent with the longer-run measure if conventional depreciation methods are used. To ensure consistency with the long-run measure and NPV an adjustment must be made within the EVA$^{(TM)}$ accountancy adjustments so that depreciation is based on economic values and not historic book values. For

| Profits | X (£000s) | Y (£000s) | Z (£000s) |
|---|---|---|---|
| Year 1 | (37) | 103 | (237) |
| Year 2 | 83 | (37) | (237) |
| Year 3 | 253 | 43 | 813 |
| Total profits | 299 | 109 | 339 |

| ROI | X (%) | Y (%) | Z (%) |
|---|---|---|---|
| Year 1 | (4.3) | 11.9 | (27.5) |
| Year 2 | 14.5 | (6.4) | (41.3) |
| Year 3 | 88.1 | 15.0 | 283.2 |
| Average | 32.8 | 6.8 | 71.5 |

**EXHIBIT 20.5**

*Estimated EVA$^{(TM)}$ calculations for project X$^a$*

| | Year 1 (£000s) | Year 2 (£000s) | Year 3 (£000s) | Total (£000s) |
|---|---|---|---|---|
| Profit before interest | (37) | 83 | 253 | |
| 10% interest on opening written-down value | 86 | 57 | 29 | |
| EVA$^{(TM)}$ | (123) | 26 | 224 | |
| PV of EVA$^{(TM)}$ | (112) | 21 | 168 | 77 |

*Note*
$^a$ All calculations are to the nearest £000

example, if conventional depreciation is used the EVA$^{(TM)}$ for year 1 for each of the projects will be as follows:

| | (£000s) |
|---|---|
| Project X | (−123) |
| Project Y | 17 |
| Project Z | (−323) |

The *short-term* measure of EVA$^{(TM)}$ may lead to acceptance of project Y. In addition, a manager concerned about a possible deterioration in his or her expected EVA$^{(TM)}$ may reject project X even when he or she is aware that acceptance will mean an increase in long-term EVA$^{(TM)}$.

Let us now repeat the facts that we have established in our discussion so far. Decisions taken on the basis of a project's impact on divisional profit and return on investment are not consistent with the NPV rule. If managerial performance is evaluated on this basis of either of these two measures, there is a danger that managers will make decisions that will improve their own performance measure, even if such decisions are not in the best interests of the organization. The present value of EVA$^{(TM)}$ is the long-run counterpart of the discounted NPV, but the short-run measure may not signal the same decision as the long-run measure. Hence there is a need to establish a short-term measure of EVA$^{(TM)}$ that signals the same decision as the long-run measure. If this can be achieved and managers are evaluated on this basis, decisions based on improving their own short-term performance will be consistent with decisions taken using the NPV rule. In the Appendix to this chapter alternative depreciation models are explained that ensure that the short-term EVA$^{(TM)}$ measure does not conflict with the long-term measure and that are therefore consistent with the NPV rule. These models are not widely used in practice. The theoretical conclusion reached in the Appendix is that a comparison of budgeted and actual cash flows is the most appropriate method of measuring divisional performance, but, for various reasons, managers may prefer to use accounting methods based on the accruals concept. Where accruals based accounting is employed, the EVA$^{(TM)}$ approach should be used to measure managerial performance.[2]

# Determining the divisional cost of capital charge

To calculate NPV and EVA$^{(TM)}$, we must ascertain the cost of capital for each division. The use of a single corporate cost of capital that is applied to all divisions within the group appears to be widespread in computing EVA$^{(TM)}$. The survey by Drury *et al.* (1993) reported that 74% of the firms used the same cost of capital for all divisions within the group. The use of a uniform cost of capital is probably due to the fact that divisional managers consider this to be a fairer method of comparing their results with other divisions. In addition, it is claimed that the use of uniform rates avoids friction and has a more favourable impact on the morale of managers.

It appears, however, that the use of a uniform cost of capital may lead to incorrect decisions. The theory of business finance supports the use of a different cost of capital being used for different divisions. The various divisions of a company can be viewed as a collection of different investments whose income streams result from different risks. In Chapter 14 we established that the cost of capital is a function of risk, and, since various divisions face different risks, a different cost of capital should be used for each division, based on the relative investment risk of each division.

Figure 20.2 shows how the use of a uniform company cost of capital for appraising capital investments can lead to incorrect decisions. The horizontal line AC represents the overall cost of capital of the company and the sloping line BD represents the risk-adjusted cost of capital. If the overall cost of capital is used as a discount rate then only those projects that yield an internal rate of return in excess of AC (which is equivalent to having a positive NPV at this cost of capital) will be accepted. You can see that low-risk projects that yield an internal rate of return in excess of the risk-adjusted discount rate (i.e. those that fall in area X) will be *incorrectly* rejected. Projects falling in this area will have a negative NPV when discounted at the company's overall cost of capital (AC) but a positive NPV when discounted at the risk adjusted cost of capital. Furthermore if an overall cost of capital is used, there is a danger that high-risk projects that yield a lower return than the risk-adjusted discount rate (i.e. projects that fall in area Y) will be incorrectly accepted.

To establish the cost of capital to be used for each division, quoted companies should be identified that are engaged solely in the same line of business as the division. The cost of capital of the identified companies can then be used as an approximation of the division's cost of capital. A full discussion of the appropriate cost of capital that should be used is beyond the scope of this book, but for a detailed discussion of this topic you should refer to Pike and Neale (1999, ch. 12). The important point to note when measuring managerial performance is that we have attempted to establish a measure that is consistent with the NPV rule. If the chosen measure requires that a manager be charged with the cost of capital on the division investment (i.e. EVA$^{(TM)}$), the cost of capital which is used in this calculation should be the same rate as that used for capital investment decisions. Only by using the same cost of capital can the success of a manager's past investment decisions be truly established. ●●●

# Addressing the dysfunctional consequences of short-term financial performance measures

The primary objective of profit-making organizations is to maximize shareholder value. Therefore performance measures should be based on the value created by each division.

**FIGURE 20.2** *Risk-adjusted discount rates.*

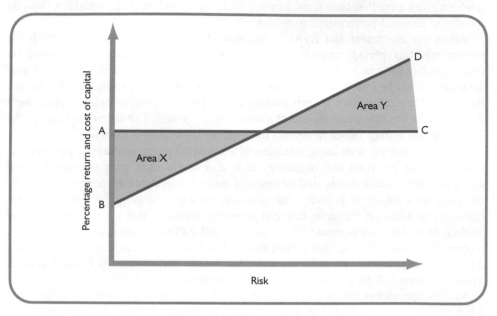

Unfortunately, direct measures of value creation are not possible because the shares for only the business as a whole are traded on the stockmarket. It is not possible to derive stock market values at the segmental or business unit level of an organization. Instead, most firms use accounting profit or ROI measures as a surrogate for changes in market values. Also, even if market measures could be derived, they may not be ideal performance measures because they are affected by many factors that managers cannot control (such as changes in investor expectations, interest rate changes and rumours). In contrast, accounting performance measures are not affected to the same extent by some of the uncontrollable factors that cause the volatile changes in share values.

Unfortunately, using accounting measures such as ROI or EVA$^{(TM)}$ as performance measures can encourage managers to become short-term oriented. For example, it has been shown that in the short term managers can improve both of these measures, by rejecting profitable long-term investments. By not making the investments, they can reduce expenses in the current period and not suffer the lost revenues until future periods. Managers can also boost their performance measure in a particular period by destroying customer and employee goodwill. For example, they can force employees to work excessive overtime towards the end of a measurement period so that goods can be delivered and their sales revenues and profits reported for the period. If the products are of lower quality, customer satisfaction (and future sales) may diminish. In addition, the effects of increased work pressure may result in staff absenteeism, demotivation and increased labour turnover. These harmful effects are unlikely to have much impact on the financial performance measure in the short term and will only become apparent in future periods. You will also remember from Chapter 7 that where profits are measured on an absorption costing basis it is possible to defer expenses to future reporting periods, and increase profits, by deliberately increasing inventories.

Consider also the situation where two divisional managers using exactly the same amount of investment produce exactly the same EVA$^{(TM)}$ or ROI. Does this mean that their performances are the same? The answer is no. Even though their performance measures would be identical this does not mean their performances are the same. One manager may have built up customer goodwill by offering excellent customer service, and also have paid great attention to training, education, research and development, etc., while another may not have given these items any consideration. Differences such as these would not show up initially in financial performance measures.

Return on investment and EVA$^{(TM)}$ are short-run concepts that deal only with the current reporting period, whereas managerial performance measures should focus on future results that can be expected because of present actions. Ideally, divisional performance should be evaluated on the basis of economic income by estimating future cash flows and discounting them to their present value. This calculation could be made for a division at the beginning and the end of a measurement period. The difference between the beginning and ending values represents the estimate of economic income.

The main problem with using estimates of economic income to evaluate performance is that it lacks precision and objectivity It is also inconsistent with external financial accounting information that is used by financial markets to evaluate the performance of the company as a whole. It is likely that corporate managers may prefer their divisional managers to focus on the same financial reporting measures that are used by financial markets to evaluate the company as a whole. A final difficulty with measuring economic income is that the individual that is most knowledgeable and in the best position to provide the cash flow estimates is usually the individual whose performance is being evaluated. Thus, managers will be tempted to bias their estimates.

Various approaches can be used to overcome the short-term orientation that can arise when accounting profit-related measures are used to evaluate divisional performance. One possibility is to improve the accounting measures. EVA$^{(TM)}$ represents such an approach. If you refer back to the formula for calculating EVA$^{(TM)}$ you will see that it is computed by making accounting adjustments to the conventional divisional profit calculation. These adjustments, such as capitalizing research and development and advertising expenditure, represent an attempt to approximate economic income. Incorporating a cost of capital charge is also a further attempt to approximate economic income. However, it should be noted that conventional accounting profits are the starting point for calculating EVA$^{(TM)}$ and these are based on historic costs, and not future cash flows, so that EVA$^{(TM)}$ can only provide a rough approximation of economic income.

Another alternative for reducing the short-term orientation, and increasing congruence of accounting measures with economic income is to lengthen the measurement period. The longer the measurement period, the more congruent accounting measures of performance are with economic income. For example, profits over a three-year measurement period are a better indicator of economic income than profits over a six-monthly period. The disadvantage of lengthening the measurement period is that rewards are tied to the performance evaluation, and if they are provided a long time after actions are taken, there is a danger that they will lose much of their motivational effects.

Probably the most widely used approach to mitigate against the dysfunctional consequnces that can arise from relying excessively on financial measures is to supplement them with non-financial measures that measure those factors that are critical to the long-term success and profits of the organization. These measures focus on areas such as competitiveness, product leadership, productivity, quality, delivery performance, innovation and flexibility in responding to changes in demand. If managers focus excessively on the short-term, the benefits from improved short-term financial performance may be counter-balanced by a deterioration in the non-financial measures. Such non-financial measures should provide a broad indication of the contribution of a divisional manager's current actions to the long-term success of the organization.

The incorporation of non-financial measures creates the need to link financial and non-financial measures of performance. In particular, there is a need for a balanced set of measures that provide both short-term performance pressure and also leading indicators of future financial performance from current actions. The balanced scorecard emerged in the

1990s to meet these requirements. The balanced scorecard will be covered extensively in Chapter 23 but at this stage you should note that the financial performance evaluation measures discussed in this chapter ought to be seen as one of the elements within the balanced scorecard. Divisional performance evaluation should be based on a combination of financial and non-financial measures using the balanced scorecard approach.

## Self-Assessment Question

You should attempt to answer this question yourself before looking up the suggested answer, which appears on pages 1130–1. If any part of your answer is incorrect, check back carefully to make sure you understand where you went wrong.

Theta Ltd compares the performance of its subsidiaries by return on capital employed (ROCE), using the following formula.

> Profit:             Depreciation is calculated on a straight-line basis.
> Losses on sale of assets are charged against profit in the year of the sale.
>
> Capital employed: Net current assets – at the average value throughout the year.
> Fixed assets – at original cost less accumulated depreciation as at the end of the year.

Theta Ltd, whose cost of capital is 14% per annum, is considering acquiring Alpha Ltd, whose performance has been calculated on a similar basis to that shown above except that fixed assets are valued at original cost.

During the past year, apart from normal trading, Alpha Ltd was involved in the following separate transactions:

(a) It bought equipment on 1 November 2000 (the start of its financial year) at a cost of £120 000. Resulting savings were £35 000 for the year; these are expected to continue at that level throughout the six-year expected life of the asset, after which it will have no scrap value.

(b) On 1 November 2000 it sold a piece of equipment that had cost £200 000 when bought exactly three years earlier. The expected life was four years, with no scrap value. This equipment has been making a contribution to profit of £30 000 per annum before depreciation, and realized £20 000 on sale.

(c) It negotiated a bank overdraft of £20 000 for the year to take advantage of quick payment discounts offered by creditors; this reduced costs by £4000 per annum.

(d) To improve liquidity, it reduced stocks by an average of £25 000 throughout the year. This resulted in reduced sales with a reduction of £6000 per annum contribution.

The financial position of Alpha Ltd for the year from 1 November 1999 to 31 October 2000 *excluding the outcomes of transactions (a)–(d)* above, was as follows:

|  | (£000) |
|---|---|
| Profit for the year | 225 |
| Fixed assets: | |
| Original cost | 1000 |
| Accumulated depreciation | 475 |
| Net current assets (average for the year) | 250 |

You are required to:

(a) Calculate the ROCE of Alpha Ltd using its present basis of calculation:
   (i) if none of the transactions (A)–(D) had taken place;
   (ii) if transaction (A) had taken place by not (B), (C) or (D);

(iii) if transaction (B) had taken place but not (A), (C), or (D);
(iv) if transaction (C) had taken place but not (A), (B) or (D);
(v) if transaction (D) had taken place but not (A), (B) or (C).

(b) Calculate the ROCE as in (a) (i)–(v) above using Theta Ltd's basis of calculation.

(c) Explain briefly whether there would have been any lack of goal congruence between Theta Ltd and the management of Alpha Ltd (assuming that Alpha Ltd has been acquired by Theta Ltd on 1 November 1999 and that Theta Ltd's basis of calculation was used) in respect of

(i) transaction (A);
(ii) transaction (B).

Taxation is to be ignored.

(25 marks)
*CIMA P3 Management Accounting*

## Summary

The major organizational device for maximizing decentralization is the creation of divisions. These may consist of investment centres or profit centres. In an investment centre a divisional manager can significantly influence the size of the investment, whereas in a profit centre managers are only responsible for obtaining profits from the assets that are assigned to them. The major challenge to the accountant is to design performance measures that create a situation where managers acting in their own best interests also act in the best interests of the company as a whole.

The most common methods of measuring divisional performance are absolute profits, profit expressed as a percentage of investment (ROI) and residual income. During the 1990s residual income was replaced by the economic value added (EVA$^{(TM)}$) measure. EVA$^{(TM)}$ extends the traditional residual income measure by incorporating adjustments to the conventional divisional profit measure for distortions introduced by generally accepted accounting principles.

ROI suffers from the disadvantage that the managers of those divisions with an existing ROI in excess of the cost of capital may incorrectly reject projects with positive NPVs. Similarly, managers with an existing ROI that is lower than the cost of capital may accept projects with returns that are less than the cost of capital. ROI is therefore an unsatisfactory method of measuring managerial performance in investment centres or those profit centres where a manager can significantly influence the amount invested in working capital.

In the long-run, the EVA$^{(TM)}$ method leads to a calculation that is consistent with the net present value rule, but if conventional accounting methods of depreciation are used, the short-term EVA$^{(TM)}$ calculation may not motivate a decision that is consistent to the NPV rule. This problem can be resolved (see the Appendix to this chapter) by using the annuity method of depreciation if the project's annual cash flows are constant. When the annual cash flows fluctuate, this method does not ensure that the short-term measure is consistent with the NPV rule. This problem can be overcome (see the Appendix) by making depreciation a balancing figure, but such an approach is unlikely to be acceptable. One possible solution is to compare the budgeted and actual cash flows, which is equivalent to comparing budgeted and actual EVAs$^{(TM)}$.

The choice is between using accounting methods that will lead to decisions that maximize NPV more often than other methods, or comparing budgeted and actual cash flows. If the former approach is chosen, it appears that EVA$^{(TM)}$ is the most appropriate financial measure, and performance should be evaluated based on a comparison of budgeted and actual EVA$^{(TM)}$.

The dysfunctional effects of focusing on short-term performance will be minimized if financial measures of performance are supplemented with non-financial performance measures that provide a broad indication of the contribution of a divisional manager's current actions to the long-term success of the organization. The balanced scorecard emerged in the 1990s to provide a balanced set of financial and non-financial measures in order to obtain a comprehensive view of a business. The financial performance evaluation measures discussed in this chapter ought to be seen as one of the elements within the balanced scorecard. Divi-sional performance evaluation should therefore be based on a combination of financial and non-financial measures using the balanced scorecard approach.

## Key Terms and Concepts

annuity method of depreciation (p. 817)
balanced scorecard (p. 810)
controllable contribution (p. 797)
controllable investment (p. 803)
cost centre (p. 794)
divisional contribution (p. 798)
divisional net profit before taxes (p. 798)
divisionalized organizational structure (p. 792)
economic value added (EVA$^{TM}$) (p. 801)

functional organizational structure (p. 792)
investment centre (p. 794)
profit centre (p. 794)
residual income (p. 800)
return on investment (ROI) (p. 799)
risk-adjusted cost of capital (p. 808)
single corporate cost of capital (p. 808)
variable short-run contribution margin (p. 796)

## Recommended Reading

You should refer to Egginton (1995) for a review of the methods that seek to ensure that periodic residual income (EVA$^{TM}$ ) measures are consistent with the NPV rule. For further reading on economic value added you should refer to Stewart (1991, 1994 and 1995) and the articles in *Fortune* (The Real Key to Creating Wealth – 20 September 1993) and *The Economist* (Valuing companies: A star to sail by? – 2 August 1997, pp. 61–3).

# Appendix 20.1: Reconciling short- and long-term residual income EVA$^{(TM)}$ measures

**AR** In this Appendix alternative depreciation models are examined that seek to ensure that the short-term residual income measure does not conflict with the long-term measure.

## VALUING ASSETS AT NPV OF FUTURE CASH FLOWS

It is not easy to design a short-term measure of performance that does not conflict with decisions based on the NPV rule. One approach is to value the assets at the present value of the future cash flows. This is illustrated in Exhibit 20A.1 in respect of the information presented in Exhibit 20.3 in the main body of this chapter for project X.

You will see that the asset is valued at £938 000 at the start, and because it is purchased for £861 000, an immediate profit of £77 000 is recognized. This is identical with the NPV calculated in Exhibit 20.3. EVA$^{(TM)}$ of zero will then be recorded for the next three years. This approach recognizes that the firm will be better off at the time of the acquisition by £77 000. However, because of the difficulty of valuing an asset at the present value of future cash flows, and writing the asset up in value above cost at the start, it is unlikely that this approach will be acceptable to accountants and managers.

**EXHIBIT 20A.1**

*Effect of valuing assets at NPV of future cash flows (000s)[a]*

| | (£000s) |
|---|---|
| Value of asset at start (£) $(250 \times 0.909) + (370 \times 0.826) + (540 \times 0.751) = 938$ | |
| Value at end of year 1 (£) $(370 \times 0.909) + (540 \times 0.826)$ $= 782$ | |
| Value at end of year 2 (£) $(540 \times 0.909)$ $= 491$ | |
| Value at end of year 3 (£) $= \text{nil}$ | |

| | Year 1 (£000) | Year 2 (£000) | Year 3 (£000) |
|---|---|---|---|
| Cash inflow | 250 | 370 | 540 |
| Depreciation | 156[a] | 291 | 491 |
| Profit before interest | 94 | 79 | 49 |
| Interest (at 10%) | 94[c] | 79 | 49 |
| EVA(TM) | — | — | — |

[a]All calculations are to the nearest (£000s)
[b]Value at start (£938) less value at end of year 1 (£782)
[c]Calculated on opening written-down value (10% of £938)

**EXAMPLE 20A.1**

A division has the opportunity to acquire a new machine for £100 000. The machine is expected to produce cash savings of £29 000 every year for five years. The cost of capital is 10%.

The net present value for the new machine is £9939 and is calculated as follows:

| | (£) |
|---|---|
| Investment cost | 100 000 |
| Present value of cash savings | |
| $(29\,000 \times 3.791)$ | 109 939 |
| Net present value | 9 939 |

The EVA(TM) for year 1 using the straight-line method of depreciation is:

| | (£) | (£) |
|---|---|---|
| Annual cash inflow | | 29 000 |
| Less Depreciation | 20 000 | |
| Interest on capital (10% of £100 000) | 10 000 | 30 000 |
| EVA(TM) | | (1 000) |

**EXHIBIT 20A.2**

*Capital repayment schedule*

| Year | Annual repayment (1) (£) | 10% interest on capital outstanding (2) (£) | Capital repayment (3) = (1) − (2) (£) | Capital outstanding (4) = (4) − (3) (£) |
|------|------|------|------|------|
| 0 | | | | 100 000 |
| 1 | 26 380 | 10 000 | 16 380 | 83 620 |
| 2 | 26 380 | 8 362 | 18 018 | 65 602 |
| 3 | 26 380 | 6 560 | 19 820 | 45 782 |
| 4 | 26 380 | 4 578 | 21 802 | 23 980 |
| 5 | 26 380 | 2 398 | 23 982 | (2) |

## ANNUITY DEPRECIATION

When the cash inflows are constant and the annuity method of depreciation is used, the short-term EVA$^{(TM)}$ will also be constant. In addition, the total present value of the EVA$^{(TM)}$ will be equal to the NPV calculation. In other words, decisions taken on the basis of the short-term measure will be consistent with decisions taken on the basis of the long-term measure or the NPV rule. Let us illustrate the procedure using the annuity method of depreciation. Consider Example 20.A1.

There is a danger that this project will be rejected on the basis of the first year's EVA$^{(TM)}$ calculation if the straight-line method of depreciation is used.

If we use the annuity method of depreciation, the annual depreciation will be equivalent to the capital element of an annuity required to redeem £100 000 borrowed at 10% over five years.

If you refer to Appendix D (see page 1089), you will see that the capital recovery factor for five years at 10% is 0.2638 for £1; look at the entry in the five-year row and the 10% column. A repayment of £26 380 per annum is therefore required to repay £100 000 borrowed for five years. The repayment schedule is set out in Exhibit 20A.2.

The £100 000 will be repaid with interest, and the capital repayment column represents the annual depreciation charge. The EVA$^{(TM)}$ calculation using this depreciation charge is shown in Exhibit 20A.3.

The annual cash inflow is constant, and the EVA$^{(TM)}$ is also constant at £2620 per annum for five years. The present value of £2620, which is received annually for five years, is equal to the net present value calculation of £9939. The short-term measure should therefore lead to decisions being made that are consistent with decisions that would be taken on the basis of NPV calculations, when the cash inflows are constant and the annuity method of depreciation is used. A manager will undertake the machinery purchase, even if he or she places great emphasis on the impact of the purchase on the first year's performance. The manager may, however, reject the purchase if straight-line depreciation is used because a negative figure for EVA$^{(TM)}$ is reported.

**EXHIBIT 20A.3**

*EVA(TM) calculation*

| Year | Opening written down value (1) (£) | Cash inflow (2) (£) | Depreciation (3) (£) | Interest on capital (10%) (4) (£) | EVA(TM) (2) − [(3) + (4)] (5) (£) |
|---|---|---|---|---|---|
| 1 | 100 000 | 29 000 | 16 380 | 10 000 | 2620 |
| 2 | 83 620 | 29 000 | 18 018 | 8 362 | 2620 |
| 3 | 65 602 | 29 000 | 19 820 | 6 560 | 2620 |
| 4 | 45 782 | 29 000 | 21 802 | 4 578 | 2620 |
| 5 | 23 980 | 29 000 | 23 982 | 2 398 | 2620 |

**EXAMPLE 20A.2**

A division has the opportunity to acquire a new machine for £100 000. The machine has expected cash savings of £145 000 over five years. The timing of the expected cash savings is as follows:

| | (£) |
|---|---|
| Year 1 | 20 000 |
| Year 2 | 25 000 |
| Year 3 | 50 000 |
| Year 4 | 40 000 |
| Year 5 | 10 000 |

The cost of capital is 10% and the NPV is £9938.

**EXHIBIT 20A.4**

*EVA(TM) with unequal cash flows*

| Year | Opening written-down value (£) | Cash inflow (£) | Depreciation (£) | Interest on capital (£) | EVA(TM) (£) |
|---|---|---|---|---|---|
| 1 | 100 000 | 20 000 | 16 380 | 10 000 | (6 380) |
| 2 | 83 620 | 25 000 | 18 018 | 8 362 | (1 380) |
| 3 | 65 602 | 50 000 | 19 820 | 6 560 | 23 620 |
| 4 | 45 782 | 40 000 | 21 802 | 4 578 | 13 620 |
| 5 | 23 980 | 10 000 | 23 982 | 2 398 | (16 380) |

## EXHIBIT 20A.5

*Depreciation based on interest deducted from cash flows*

| Year | Cash inflow (1) (£) | Capital outstanding (written-down value) (2) (£) | Interest (10%) (3) (£) | Depreciation (4) = (1) − (3) (£) | EVA$^{(TM)}$ (5) = (1) − [(3) + (4)] (£) |
|------|------|------|------|------|------|
| 0 | | 100 000 | | | |
| 1 | 20 000 | 90 000 | 10 000 | 10 000 | 0 |
| 2 | 25 000 | 74 000 | 9 000 | 16 000 | 0 |
| 3 | 50 000 | 31 400 | 7 400 | 42 600 | 0 |
| 4 | 40 000 | 0 | 3 140 | 31 400 | 5 460 |
| 5 | 10 000 | 0 | 0 | 0 | 10 000 |

## UNEVEN CASH FLOWS

Unfortunately, the annuity method of depreciation only produces a short-term measure that will lead to decisions consistent with the NPV rule when the net cash inflows are equal each year. Example 20.A1 has been amended so that the total net cash inflows of £145 000 fluctuate between years. All other items remain unchanged. The revised problem is presented in Example 20A.2.

The EVA$^{(TM)}$ for this example, using the annuity method of depreciation that was calculated in Exhibit 20A.2, is presented in Exhibit 20A.4.

The present value of the EVA$^{(TM)}$ in Exhibit 20A.4 is £9938, which is identical with the NPV calculation. There is, however, a danger that the manager may reject the investment because of the negative EVA$^{(TM)}$ calculations in years 1 and 2. This means that *the short-term EVA$^{(TM)}$ measure may be in conflict with the NPV rule when the annuity method of depreciation is used and unequal cash flows occur.*

Tomkins (1975) shows that it is possible to construct a depreciation schedule that avoids negative or EVA$^{(TM)}$ calculations and that will motivate managers to accept projects yielding positive NPVs. He suggests that, instead of using the annuity method of depreciation, a depreciation figure should be calculated by deducting the interest on the written-down value of the asset from the expected cash inflows for the year, instead of deducting it from the annuity required to redeem the loan. This procedure is illustrated in Exhibit 20A.5.

You will see that the interest is calculated on the opening written-down value. For example, the £9000 interest charge for year 2 is based on 10% of the opening written-down value for year 2 of £90 000. (This is represented by the written-down value at the end of year 1.) Depreciation is then calculated by deducting interest from the cash inflow. In year 4 the depreciation charge is limited to the written-down value of £31 400. The effect of the depreciation charge being based on a deduction of interest from the cash flow means that EVA$^{(TM)}$ is zero each year until the asset is completely written off. Any cash inflows received after this point will result in a positive EVA$^{(TM)}$ calculation.

The present value of the EVA$^{(TM)}$ in years 4 and 5 is £9931, compared with the capital investment net present value calculation of £9938.

If a divisional manager is evaluated with EVA$^{(TM)}$ calculated in the manner illustrated in Exhibit 20A.5, he or she will recognize that in the short term EVA$^{(TM)}$ will remain unchanged, and that by years 4 and 5 the benefits will be reflected in the performance measure. The manager will be motivated to accept the project. It remains doubtful, though, whether widespread adoption of this method can be achieved, since the depreciation is merely a balancing figure that does not conform to any of the usual notions of depreciation. The calculations also indicate that the EVA$^{(TM)}$ does not become positive until the initial investment cost topped up with interest cost has been recovered. Tomkins suggests that a better description of the concept would be capital surplus rather than residual income.

## COMPARISON OF ACTUAL WITH BUDGET

When considering performance evaluation, the *actual* EVA$^{(TM)}$ must be compared with a *predetermined* standard such as budgeted EVA$^{(TM)}$. If we use the procedure suggested in Exhibit 20A.5, however, we shall obtain a zero EVA$^{(TM)}$ calculation in the early years of a project's life for both the actual and budgeted results. Consequently, there are no benefits to be derived from making such a comparison between budgeted and actual EVA$^{(TM)}$. Tomkins suggests that the relevant yardstick of performance in this situation is a comparison between the budgeted capital outstanding at the end of the year and the actual capital outstanding. Any difference, though, between budgeted and actual capital outstanding can only result from actual cash flows being different from budgeted cash flows, since both interest and depreciation charges will be dependent on actual cash flows.[3] Tomkins therefore concludes that calculating residual income (and therefore EVA$^{(TM)}$) and comparing budgeted and actual capital outstanding is only an elaborate way of achieving what can be attained far more simply merely by comparing actual cash flows with those budgeted in the capital investment proposals.

It appears that the choice is between using an accounting method based on the accruals concept, which will lead to the correct decision more often than other methods, or comparing budgeted and actual cash flows. If the former method is preferred, EVA$^{(TM)}$ is the most appropriate method of measuring the performance of divisional managers. ●●●

## Key Examination Points

Most examination questions include a comparison of residual income (RI) (or EVA$^{(TM)}$) and return on investment (ROI). Make sure you can calculate these measures and discuss the merits and deficiencies of RI and ROI. You should emphasize that when evaluating short-term divisional performance, it is virtually impossible to capture in one financial measure all the variables required to measure the performance of a divisional manager. It is also necessary to include in the performance reports other non-financial performance measures.

Typical examination questions require you to consider whether a manager will undertake various transactions when he or she is evaluated on RI/EVA$^{(TM)}$ or ROI. A typical requirement is to compare the change in RI or ROI when the assets are valued at original cost or written-down value. Note that neither method of valuation is satisfactory (you should therefore pay particular attention to the section on 'The Impact of Depreciation' (see pages 803–4)). For each transaction you should state which course of action is in the best interests of the company as a whole. You should then state which course of action is likely to maximize a manager's performance rating. Goal congruence will only exist when actions that are in the best interests of the company also lead to an improvement in the performance measures used to evaluate the divisional managers.

## Questions

*Indicates that a suggested solution is to be found in the *Students' Manual*.

### 20.1* Advanced

(a) 'Because of the possibility of goal incongruence, an optimal plan can only be achieved if divisional budgets are constructed by a central planning department, but this means that divisional independence is a pseudo-independence.'

Discuss the problems of establishing divisional budgets in the light of this quotation.

(9 marks)

(b) 'Head Office' will require a division to submit regular reports of its performance.

Describe, discuss and compare three measures of divisional operating performance that might feature in such reports. (8 marks)

*ACCA Level 2 Management Accounting*

### 20.2 Advanced

A large organisation, with a well-developed cost centre system, is considering the introduction of profit centres and/or investment centres throughout the organisation, where appropriate. As management accountant, you will be providing technical advice and assistance for the proposed scheme.

You are required:

(a) to describe the main characteristics and objectives of profit centres and investment centres;

(4 marks)

(b) to explain what conditions are necessary for the successful introduction of such centres;

(5 marks)

(c) to describe the main behavioural and control consequences which may arise if such centres are introduced; (4 marks)

(d) to compare two performance appraisal measures that might be used if investment centres are introduced. (4 marks)

*CIMA Stage 3 Management Accounting Techniques*

### 20.3 Advanced

From an accounting perspective an organizational unit of an accounting entity may be a cost centre or a profit centre or an investment centre. Explain

Economic value added is a recent development and is likely to feature more prominently (instead of residual income) in future examinations.

these categories, describe the strengths and weaknesses of each and conditions in which each would be most appropriate if the aim is to develop efficient planning and control procedures.

(7 marks)

*ACCA Level 2 Management Accounting*

### 20.4* Advanced

A long-established, highly centralized company has grown to the extent that its chief executive, despite having a good supporting team, is finding difficulty in keeping up with the many decisions of importance in the company.

Consideration is therefore being given to reorganizing the company into profit centres. These would be product divisions, headed by a divisional managing director, who would be responsible for all the division's activities relating to its products.

You are required to explain, in outline:

(a) the types of decision areas that should be transferred to the new divisional managing directors if such a reorganization is to achieve its objectives;

(b) the types of decision areas that might reasonably be retained at company head office;

(c) the management accounting problems that might be expected to arise in introducing effective profit centre control. (20 marks)

*CIMA P3 Management Accounting*

### 20.5 Advanced

Divisionalization is a common form of organizational arrangement but there is some diversity of opinion as to the best measure of divisional performance.

Discuss this topic and describe and compare the main performance measures that have been suggested. (17 marks)

*ACCA Level 2 Management Accounting*

### 20.6 Advanced

Critically discuss the methods of evaluating the performance of managers of divisionalized companies. What factors should be considered in designing control systems for evaluating divisional profit performances?

## 20.7 Advanced

'In the control of divisional operations within a large company, conflicts often arise between the aims of the organization as a whole and the aspirations of the individual divisions.'

What forms may these conflicts take, and how would you expect the finance function to assist in the resolution of such conflicts?

## 20.8* Advanced

A recently formed group of companies is proposing to use a single return on capital employed (ROCE) rate as an index of the performance of its operating companies which differ considerably from one another in size and type of activities.

It is, however, particularly concerned that the evaluations it makes from the use of this rate should be valid in terms of measurement of performance.

You are required to:

(a) mention *four* considerations in calculating the ROCE rate to which the group will need to attend, to ensure that its intentions are achieved; for each consideration give an example of the type of problem that can arise; (8 marks)

(b) mention *three* types of circumstance in which a single ROCE rate might not be an adequate measure of performance and, for each, explain what should be done to supplement the interpretation of the results of the single ROCE rate. (12 marks)

*CIMA P3 Management Accounting*

## 20.9* Advanced

Residual Income and Return on Investment are commonly used measures of performance. However, they are frequently criticised for placing too great an emphasis on the achievement of short-term results, possibly damaging longer-term performance.

You are required to discuss

(a) the issues involved in the long-term:short-term conflict referred to in the above statement; (11 marks)

(b) suggestions which have been made to reconcile this difference. (11 marks)

(Total 22 marks)

*CIMA Stage 4 Management Accounting –
Control and Audit*

## 20.10* Advanced

(a) Explain the meaning of each of the under-noted measures which may be used for divisional performance measurement and investment decision-making. Discuss the advantages and problems associated with the use of each.

(i) Return on capital employed.

(ii) Residual income.

(iii) Discounted future earnings. (9 marks)

(b) Comment on the reasons why the measures listed in (a) above may give conflicting investment decision responses when applied to the same set of data. Use the following figures to illustrate the conflicting responses which may arise:

Additional investment of £60 000 for a 6 year life with nil residual value.

Average net profit per year: £9000 (after depreciation).

Cost of capital: 14%.

Existing capital employed: £300 000 with ROCE of 20%. (8 marks)

(Solutions should ignore taxation implications.)

(Total 17 marks)

*ACCA Level 2 Management Accounting*

## 20.11 Advanced

Divisionalised structures are normal in large firms, and occur even when centralised structures would be feasible.

Requirements:

(a) Explain and discuss the arguments for divisionalised structures in large firms. (6 marks)

(b) Explain the costs and potential inefficiencies of a divisionalised structure. (6 marks)

(c) Explain how adoption of a divisionalised structure changes the role of top management and their control of subordinates. (8 marks)

(Total 20 marks)

*CIMA Stage 4 Management
Accounting Control Systems*

## 20.12 Advanced: Accounting, motivational and ethical issues arising from divisional actions

Within a large group, divisional managers are paid a bonus which can represent a large proportion of their annual earnings. The bonus is paid when the budgeted divisional profit for the financial year is achieved or exceeded.

Meetings of divisional boards are held monthly and attended by the senior management of the division, and senior members of group management.

With the aid of the financial year approaching, there had been discussion in all divisional board meetings of forecast profit for the year, and whether budgeted profit would be achieved. In three board meetings, for divisions which were having difficulty in achieving budgeted profits, the following divisional actions had been discussed. In each case, the amounts involved would have been material in determining whether the division would achieve its budget:

- Division A had severely cut spending on training, and postponed routine re-painting of premises.

- Division B had re-negotiated a contract for consultancy services. It was in the process of installing Total Quality Management (TQM) systems, and had originally agreed to pay progress payments to the consultants, and had budgeted to make these payments. It had re-negotiated that the consultancy would invoice the division with the total cost only when the work was completed in the next financial year.

- Division C had persuaded some major customers to take early delivery, in the current financial year, of products originally ordered for delivery early in the next financial year. This would ensure virtually nil stock at year end.

Requirement:
Discuss the financial accounting, budgeting, ethical and motivational issues which arise from these divisional actions.

Comment on whether any group management action is necessary.                (20 marks)
*CIMA Stage 4 Management Accounting Control Systems*

### 20.13 Advanced: Establishing a system of divisional performance measurement in a hospital

(a) Briefly explain how the measurement of divisional performance differs when assessing the achievement of strategic targets as distinct from operational targets.        (5 marks)

(b) J is a hospital which supplies a wide range of healthcare services. The government has created a competitive internal market for healthcare by separating the function of service delivery from purchasing. The government provides funds for local health organisations to identify healthcare needs and to purchase services from different organisations which actually supply the service. The service suppliers are mainly hospitals.

J is service supplier and has established contracts with some purchasing organisations. The healthcare purchasing organisations are free to contract with any supplier for the provision of their healthcare requirements.

Previously, J was organised and controlled on the basis of functional responsibility. This meant that each specialist patient function, such as medical, nursing and pharmacy services, was led by a manager who held operational and financial responsibility for its activities throughout the hospital. J now operates a system of control based on devolved financial accountability. Divisions comprising different functions have been established and are responsible for particular categories of patient care such as general medical or general surgical services. Each division is managed by a senior medical officer.

J's Board recognises that it exists in a competitive environment. It believes there is a need to introduce a system of divisional appraisal. This measures performance against strategic as well as operational targets, using both financial and non-financial criteria. The Board is concerned to develop a system which improves the motivation of divisional managers. This will encourage them to accept responsibility for achieving strategic as well as operational organisational targets. In particular, the Board wishes to encourage more contractual work to supply services to healthcare purchasing organisations from both within and outside its local geographical area. It is a clear aim of the Board that a cultural change in the management of the organisation will result from the implementation of such a system.

Requirement:
Discuss the issues which the Board of J should take into consideration in establishing a system of performance measurement for divisional managers in order to ensure the attainment of its strategic targets.                (15 marks)
(Total 20 marks)
*CIMA Stage 4 Strategic Management Accounting and Marketing*

### 20.14* Advanced: Impact of various transactions on ROCE and a discussion whether ROCE leads to goal congruence

G Limited, one of the subsidiaries of GAP Group p.l.c., produces the following condensed data in respect of its budgeted performance for the year to 31 December:

|  | (£000) |
|---|---|
| Profit | 330 |
| Fixed assets: | |
| Original cost | 1500 |
| Accumulated depreciation | 720 |
| (as at 31 December) | |
| Net current assets (average for the year) | 375 |

In addition, it is considering carrying out the following separate non-routine transactions:

A.  It would offer its customers cash discounts that would cost £8000 per annum.

   This would reduce the level of its debtors by an average of £30 000 over the year. This sum would be used to increase the dividend to GAP Group p.l.c. payable at the end of the year.

B.  It would increase its average stocks by £40 000 throughout the year and reduce by that amount the dividend payable to GAP Group p.l.c. at the end of the year.

   This is expected to yield an increased contribution of £15 000 per annum resulting from larger sales.

C.  At the start of the year it would sell for £35 000 a fixed asset that originally cost £300 000 and which has been depreciated by 4/5ths of its expected life.

   If not sold, this asset would be expected to earn a profit contribution of £45 000 during the year.

D.  At the start of the year it would buy for £180 000 plant that would achieve reductions of £52 500 per annum in revenue costs. This plant would have a life of five years, after which it would have no resale value.

The chief accountant of GAP Group p.l.c. has the task of recommending to the Group management committee whether the non-routine transactions should go ahead. The Group's investment criterion is to earn 15% DCF and where no time period is specified, four years is the period assumed.

In measuring the comparative performance of its subsidiaries, GAP Group p.l.c. uses return on capital employed (ROCE) calculated on the following basis:

Profit: Depreciation of fixed assets is calculated on a straight-line basis. Profit or loss on sale of assets is respectively added to or deducted from operating profits in the year of sale.

Capital employed:

Fixed assets: Valued at original cost less accumulated depreciation as at the end of the year.

Net current assets: At the average value for the year.

You are required

(a)  as managing director of G Ltd, to recommend whether *each* of the *four* non-routine transactions (A to D) should independently go ahead;
   (8 marks)

(b)  as chief accountant of GAP Group p.l.c.,

   (i)  to state whether you expect there to be goal congruence between G Limited and GAP Group p.l.c. in respect of *each* of the *four* non-routine transactions considered separately;   (8 marks)

   (ii)  to state whether you would support a proposal to substitute a Group ROCE investment criterion in place of the existing DCF investment criterion.
   (4 marks)

*Note*: You should give supporting calculations and/or explanations in each part of your answer. Ignore taxation.

(Total 20 marks)
*CIMA Stage 4 Management Accounting – Decision Making*

### 20.15 Advanced: Impact of various transactions on divisional performance measures

XYZ plc operates a divisional organisation structure. The performance of each division is assessed on the basis of the Return on Capital Employed (ROCE) that it generates.

For this purpose the ROCE of a division is calculated by dividing its 'trading profit' for the year by the 'book value of net assets' that it is using at the end of the year. Trading profit is the profit earned excluding extraordinary items. Book value of net assets excludes any cash, bank account balance or overdraft because XYZ plc uses a common bank account (under the control of its head office) for all divisions.

At the start of every year each division is given a target ROCE. If the target is achieved or exceeded then the divisional executives are given a large salary bonus at the end of the year.

In 2000, XYZ plc's division A was given a target ROCE of 15%. On 15 December 2000 A's divisional manager receives a forecast that trading profit for 2000 would be £120 000 and net assets employed at the end of 2000 would be £820 000. This would give an ROCE of 14.6% which is slightly below A's target.

The divisional manager immediately circulates a memorandum to his fellow executives inviting proposals to deal with the problem. By the end of the day he has received the following proposals from those executives (all of whom will lose their salary bonus if the ROCE target is not achieved):

(i) *from the Works Manager:* that £100 000 should be invested in new equipment resulting in cost savings of £18 000 per year over the next fifteen years;

(ii) *from the Chief Accountant:* that payment of a £42 000 trade debt owed to a supplier due on 16 December 2000 be deferred until 1 January 2001. This would result in a £1000 default penalty becoming immediately due;

(iii) *from the Sales Manager:* that £1500 additional production expenses be incurred and paid in order to bring completion of an order forward to 29 December 2000 from its previous scheduled date of 3 January 2001. This would allow the customer to be invoiced in December, thereby boosting 2000 profits by £6000, but would not accelerate customer payment due on 1 February 2001;

(iv) *from the Head of Internal Audit:* that a regional plant producing a particular product be closed allowing immediate sale for £120 000 of premises having a book value of £90 000. This would result in £50 000 immediate redundancy payments and a reduction in profit of £12 600 per year over the next fifteen years;

(a) You are required to assess *each* of the above *four* proposals having regard to
– their effect on divisional performance in 2000 and 2001 as measured by XYZ plc's

existing criteria;
– their intrinsic commercial merits;
– any ethical matters that you consider relevant.
You should ignore taxation and inflation.

(20 marks)

(b) You are required to discuss what action XYZ plc's Finance Director should take when the situation at division A and the above four proposals are brought to his attention.

(5 marks)

(Total 25 marks)

*CIMA Stage 4 Management Accounting – Decision Making*

## 20.16 Advanced: Calculation of NPV and ROI and a discussion as to whether goal congruence exists plus a further discussion relating to resolving the conflict between decision-making and performance evaluation models

J plc's business is organized into divisions. For operating purposes, each division is regarded as an investment centre, with divisional managers enjoying substantial autonomy in their selection of investment projects. Divisional managers are rewarded via a remuneration package which is linked to a Return on Investment (ROI) performance measure. The ROI calculation is based on the net book value of assets at the beginning of the year. Although there is a high degree of autonomy in investment selection, approval to go ahead has to be obtained from group management at the head office in order to release the finance.

Division X is currently investigating three independent investment proposals. If they appear acceptable, it wishes to assign each a priority in the event that funds may not be available to cover all three. Group finance staff assess the cost of capital to the company at 15%.

The details of the three proposals are:

| | Project A (£000) | Project B (£000) | Project C (£000) |
|---|---|---|---|
| Initial cash outlay on fixed assets | 60 | 60 | 60 |
| Net cash inflow in year 1 | 21 | 25 | 10 |
| Net cash inflow in year 2 | 21 | 20 | 20 |
| Net cash inflow in year 3 | 21 | 20 | 30 |
| Net cash inflow in year 4 | 21 | 15 | 40 |

Ignore tax and residual values.

Depreciation is straight-line over asset life, which is four years in each case.

You are required
(a) to give an appraisal of the *three* investment proposals from a divisional and from a company point of view; (13 marks)
(b) to explain any divergence between these two points of view and to demonstrate techniques by which the views of both the division and the company can be brought into line.
(12 marks)
(Total 25 marks)
*CIMA Stage 4 Management Accounting – Control and Audit*

## 20.17 Advanced: Merits and problems associated with three proposed divisional performance measures

Sliced Bread plc is a divisionalized company. Among its divisions are Grain and Bakery. Grain's operations include granaries, milling and dealings in the grain markets; Bakery operates a number of bakeries.

The following data relate to the year ended 30 November:

| | Grain (£000) | Bakery (£000) |
|---|---|---|
| Sales | 44 000 | 25 900 |
| Gain on sale of plant | — | 900 |
| | 44 000 | 26 800 |
| Direct labour | 8 700 | 7 950 |
| Direct materials | 25 600 | 10 200 |
| Depreciation | 700 | 1 100 |
| Divisional overheads | 5 300 | 4 550 |
| Head office costs (allocated) | 440 | 268 |
| | 40 740 | 24 068 |

| | Grain (£000) | Bakery (£000) |
|---|---|---|
| Fixed assets (at cost less accumulated depreciation) | 7000 | 9000 |
| Stocks | 6350 | 1800 |
| Trade debtors | 4000 | 2100 |
| Cash at bank | 1500 | — |
| Bank overdraft | — | 750 |
| Trade creditors | 3000 | 2150 |

Divisional managements (DMs) are given authority to spend up to £20 000 on capital items as long as total spending remains within an amount provided for small projects in the annual budget. Larger projects, as well as sales of assets with book values in excess of £20 000, must be submitted to central management (CM). All day-to-day operations are delegated to DMs, whose performance is monitored with the aid of budgets and reports.

The basis for appraising DM performance is currently under review. At present divisions are treated as investment centres for DM performance appraisal, but there is disagreement as to whether return on capital employed or residual income is the better measure. An alternative suggestion has been made that DM performance should be appraised on the basis of controllable profit; this measure would exclude depreciation and gains or losses on sale of assets, treating investment in fixed assets as a CM responsibility.

The cost of capital of Sliced Bread plc is 15% per annum.

Requirements
(a) Calculate for both divisions the three measures (return on capital employed, residual income and controllable profit) which are being considered by Sliced Bread plc, and state any assumptions or reservations about the data you have used in your calculations.
(5 marks)
(b) Examine the merits and problems of Sliced Bread plc's three contemplated approaches to DM performance appraisal, and briefly suggest how CM could determine the required level of performance in each case.
(15 marks)
(c) Discuss briefly whether further measures are needed for the effective appraisal of DM performance.
(5 marks)
(Total 25 marks)

## 20.18* Advanced: Conflict between NPV and performance measurement

Linamix is the chemicals division of a large industrial corporation. George Elton, the divisional general manager, is about to purchase new plant in order to manufacture a new product. He can buy either the Aromatic or the Zoman plant, each of which have the same capacity and expected four year life, but which differ in their capital costs and expected net cash flows, as shown below:

|  | Aromatic | Zoman |
| --- | --- | --- |
| Initial capital investment | £6 400 000 | £5 200 000 |
| Net cash flows (before tax) | | |
| 2001 | £2 400 000 | £2 600 000 |
| 2002 | £2 400 000 | £2 200 000 |
| 2003 | £2 400 000 | £1 500 000 |
| 2004 | £2 400 000 | £1 000 000 |
| Net present value (@ 16% p.a.) | £ 315 634 | £ 189 615 |

In the above calculations it has been assumed that the plant will be installed and paid for by the end of December 2000, and that the net cash flows accrue at the end of each calendar year. Neither plant is expected to have a residual value after decommissioning costs.

Like all other divisional managers in the corporation, Elton is expected to generate a before tax return on his divisional investment in excess of 16% p.a., which he is currently just managing to achieve. Anything less than a 16% return would make him ineligible for a performance bonus and may reduce his pension when he retires in early 2003. In calculating divisional returns, divisional assets are valued at net book values at the beginning of the year. Depreciation is charged on a straight line basis.

Requirements:

(a) Explain, with appropriate calculations, why neither return on investment nor residual income would motivate Elton to invest in the process showing the higher net present value. To what extent can the use of alternative accounting techniques assist in reconciling the conflict between using accounting-based performance measures and discounted cash flow investment appraisal techniques?

(12 marks)

(b) Managers tend to use post-tax cash flows to evaluate investment opportunities, but to evaluate divisional and managerial performance on the basis of pre-tax profits. Explain why this is so and discuss the potential problems that can arise, including suggestions as to how such problems can be overcome. (8 marks)

(c) Discuss what steps can be taken to avoid dysfunctional behaviour which is motivated by accounting-based performance targets.

(5 marks)

(Total 25 marks)

*ICAEW Management Accounting and Financial Management 2*

**20.19 Advanced: Discussion of residual income and ROI and the problems with using these measures to evaluate a speculative new division operating in a high technology industry**

Indico Ltd is a well established company which has operated in a sound but static market for many years where it has been the dominant supplier. Over the past three years it has diversified into three new product areas which are unrelated to each other and to the original business.

Indico Ltd has organised the operation of its four activities on a divisional basis with four divisional general managers having overall responsibility for all aspects of running each business except for finance. All finance is provided centrally with routine accounting and cash management, including invoicing, debt collection and bill payments, being handled by the Head Office. Head Office operating costs were £1 million in 2000. The total capital employed at mid-2000 amounted to £50 million, of which £20 million was debt capital financed at an average annual interest rate of 10%. Head Office assets comprise 50% fixed assets and 50% working capital. To date, the company has financed its expansion without raising additional equity capital, but it may soon require to do so if further expansion is undertaken. It has estimated that the cost of new equity capital would be 20% per annum. No new investment was undertaken in 2000 pending a review of the performance of each division.

The results for the divisions for the year to 31 December 2000 are as follows:

| | Division | | | |
| --- | --- | --- | --- | --- |
| | A (£m) | B (£m) | C (£m) | D (£m) |
| Sales | 110.0 | 31.0 | 18.0 | 13.0 |
| Trading profit | 2.0 | 1.1 | 1.2 | 0.5 |
| Exchange gain (1) | 2.0 | — | — | — |
| Profit after currency movement | 4.0 | 1.1 | 1.2 | 0.5 |
| Exceptional charge (2) | — | — | (1.8) | — |
| Profit/(loss) after exceptional charges | 4.0 | 1.1 | (0.6) | 0.5 |
| Group interest charge (3) | (1.1) | (0.3) | (0.2) | (0.1) |
| Net divisional profit/(loss) | 2.9 | 0.8 | (0.8) | 0.4 |

| | | | | |
|---|---|---|---|---|
| Depreciation charged above | 3.0 | 1.0 | 2.0 | 0.4 |
| Net assets (at year end) | 23.5 | 9.5 | 4.0 | 1.8 |

(1) The exchange gain represents the difference between the original sterling value of an overseas contract and the eventual receipts in sterling.

(2) The exceptional charge relates to the closure of a factory in January 2000.

(3) Group interest is purely a notional charge from Head Office based on a percentage of sales.

Requirements

(a) Calculate the return on investment and residual income for each division, ignoring the Head Office costs and stating any assumptions you consider appropriate. Explain how this information is useful in evaluating divisional performance, and outline the main standards of comparison you would use. (13 marks)

(b) Explain how you would deal with the Head Office costs in measuring divisional performance within Indico Ltd. (4 marks)

(c) Discuss the problems arising from using return on investment and residual income to evaluate a speculative new division operating in a high technology industry. State how you could improve these measures to enable better divisional comparisons to be made. (8 marks)
(Total 25 marks)
*ICAEW P2 Management Accounting*

## 20.20* Advanced: Appropriate performance measures for different goals

The executive directors and the seven divisional managers of Kant Ltd spent a long weekend at a country house debating the company's goals. They concluded that Kant had multiple goals, and that the performance of senior managers should be assessed in terms of all of them.

The goals identified were:

(i) to generate a reasonable financial return for shareholders;

(ii) to maintain a high market share;

(iii) to increase productivity annually;

(iv) to offer an up-to-date product range of high quality and proven reliability;

(v) to be known as responsible employers;

(vi) to acknowledge social responsibilities;

(vii) to grow and survive autonomously.

The finance director was asked to prepare a follow-up paper, setting-out some of the implications of these ideas. He has asked you, as his personal assistant, to prepare comments on certain issues for his consideration.

You are required to set out briefly, with reasons:

(a) suitable measures of performance for each of the stated goals for which you consider this to be possible. (18 marks)

(b) an outline of your view as to whether any of the stated goals can be considered to be sufficiently general to incorporate all of the others. (7 marks)
(Total 25 marks)
*ICAEW Management Accounting*

## 20.21 Advanced: Performance reporting and a discussion of key measurement issues for a divisionalized company

A recently incorporated power company, set up after the privatisation of the electricity and coal industries, owns the following assets:

An electricity generating station, capable of being fuelled either by coal or by oil.

Three coal mines, located some ten to twenty miles from the generating station, connected to a coal preparation plant.

A coal preparation plant, which takes the coal from the three mines and cleans it into a form suitable for use in the generating plant. As a by-product, a quantity of high quality coal is produced which can be sold on the industrial market. The plant has a rail link to the generating station.

The electricity generated is distributed via power lines owned by a separate company, which has an obligation to provide the distribution service on pre-set terms. The market for electricity is highly competitive with demand varying both by the time of day (in the short-term) and by season of the year (in the medium-term).

The power company is in the process of developing a management accounting system which will be used to provide information to assist in setting electricity tariffs for customers and to hold managers within the company accountable for their performance. Initially there are five main operating units, with a manager responsible for each, namely the generating station, the three coal mines and the coal preparation plant.

Requirements

(a) Outline, using pro-forma (i.e. without figures) reports where necessary, the accounting statements you would recommend as a basis for the evaluation of the performance of each of the unit managers.                    (10 marks)

(b) Discuss the key measurement issues that need to be resolved in designing such a responsibility accounting system.                    (8 marks)

(c) Explain how the information required for tariff-setting purposes might differ from that used for performance evaluation.    (7 marks)

(Total 25 marks)

*ICAEW P2 Management Accounting*

## 20.22 Advanced: Discussion relating to historical and current cost asset valuations for performance evaluation

A group of companies has hitherto used historical costing in the performance evaluation of its investment centres.

Whilst a few of those investment centres (class A) have replaced their fixed assets fairly regularly, the majority (class B) have, amongst their fixed assets, plant and equipment bought at a fairly even rate over the past 25 years. During that time their manufacturing technologies have changed very little, but these technologies are expected to change much more rapidly in the near future.

The group now wishes to evaluate its investment centres on a current cost basis.

You are required to prepare notes for a paper for the executive management committee to show

(a) the impact for performance evaluation of the difference between class A and class B investment centres that are likely to result from the change to a current cost basis in respect of
   (i)  their depreciation charges,    (7 marks)
   (ii) their relative standing as measured by their return on capital employed;

   (7 marks)

(b) what steps would be needed to revalue the plant and equipment.    (6 marks)

(Total 20 marks)

*CIMA Stage 4 Management Accounting –*
*Decision making*

## 20.23 Advanced: Calculations of residual income using straight line and annuity depreciation

(a) Meldo Division is part of a vertically integrated group where all divisions sell externally and transfer goods to other divisions within the group. Meldo Division management performance is measured using controllable profit before tax as the performance measurement criterion.

   (i)  Show the cost and revenue elements which should be included in the calculation of controllable divisional profit before tax.                    (3 marks)

   (ii) Discuss ways in which the degree of autonomy allowed to Meldo Division may affect the absolute value of controllable profit reported.    (9 marks)

(b) Kitbul Division management performance is measured using controllable residual income as the performance criterion.

   Explain why the management of Kitbul Division may make a different decision about an additional investment opportunity where residual income is measured using:
   (i)  straight-line depreciation or
   (ii) annuity depreciation based on the cost of capital rate of the division.

   Use the following investment information to illustrate your answer:

   Investment of £900 000 with a three year life and nil residual value.

   Net cash inflow each year of £380 000.

   Cost of capital is 10%. Imputed interest is calculated on the written-down value of the investment at the start of each year.

   Present value of an annuity of £1 for three years at 10% interest is £2.487.    (8 marks)

(Total 20 marks)

*ACCA Level 2 Cost Accounting II*

## 20.24* Advanced: Calculation and comparison of ROI and residual income using straight line and annuity methods of depreciation

The CP division of R p.l.c. had budgeted a net profit before tax of £3 million per annum over the period of the foreseeable future, based on a net capital employed of £10 million.

Plant replacement anticipated over this period is expected to be approximately equal to the annual depreciation each year. These figures compare well with the organization's required rate of return of 20% before tax.

CP's management is currently considering a substantial expansion of its manufacturing capacity to cope with the forecast demands of a new customer. The customer is prepared to offer a five-year contract providing CP with annual sales of £2 million.

In order to meet this contract, a total additional capital outlay of £2 million is envisaged, being £1.5 million of new fixed assets plus £0.5 million working capital. A five-year plant life is expected.

Operating costs on the contract are estimated to be £1.35 million per annum, excluding depreciation.

This is considered to be a low-risk venture as the contract would be firm for five years and the manufacturing processes are well understood within CP.

You are required

(a) to calculate the impact of accepting the contract on the CP divisional Return on Capital Employed (ROCE) and Residual Income (RI), indicating whether it would be attractive to CP's management; (8 marks)

(b) to repeat (a) using annuity depreciation for the newly acquired plant; (7 marks)

(c) to explain the basis of the calculations in the statements you have produced and discuss the suitability of each method in directing divisional management toward the achievement of corporate goals. (10 marks)

(Total 25 marks)

*CIMA Stage 4 – Control and Audit*

### 20.25* Advanced: Calculation and comparison of ROI and RI using straight line and annuity depreciation

Alpha division of a retailing group has five years remaining on a lease for premises in which it sells self-assembly furniture. Management are considering the investment of £600 000 on immediate improvements to the interior of the premises in order to stimulate sales by creating a more effective selling environment.

The following information is available:

(i) The expected increased sales revenue following the improvements is £500 000 per annum. The average contribution: sales ratio is expected to be 40%.

(ii) The cost of capital is 16% and the division has a target return on capital employed of 20%,

using the net book value of the investment at the beginning of the year in its calculation.

(iii) At the end of the five year period the premises improvements will have a nil residual value.

Required:

(a) Prepare *two* summary statements for the proposal for years 1 to 5, showing residual income and return on capital employed for each year. Statement 1 should incorporate straight-line depreciation. Statement 2 should incorporate annuity depreciation at 16%. (12 marks)

(b) Management staff turnover at Alpha division is high. The division's investment decisions and management performance measurement are currently based on the figures for the first year of a proposal.

(i) Comment on the use of the figures from statements 1 and 2 in (a) above as decision-making and management performance measures.

(ii) Calculate the net present value (NPV) of the premises improvement proposal and comment on its compatibility with residual income as a decision-making measure for the proposal's acceptance or rejection. (8 marks)

(c) An alternative forecast of the increase in sales revenue per annum from the premises improvement proposal is as follows:

| Year: | 1 | 2 | 3 | 4 | 5 |
|---|---|---|---|---|---|
| Increased sales revenue (£000) | 700 | 500 | 500 | 300 | 200 |

All other factors remain as stated in the question.

(i) Calculate year 1 values for residual income and return on capital employed where (1) straight-line depreciation and (2) annuity depreciation at 16% are used in the calculations.

(ii) Calculate the net present value of the proposal.

(iii) Comment on management's evaluation of the amended proposal in comparison with the original proposal using the range of measures calculated in (a), (b) and (c). (10 marks)

(Total 30 marks)

*ACCA Level 2 Cost and Management Accounting II*

**20.26 Advanced: Divisional performance measurement using different methods of asset valuation plus non-financial measures**

(a) When a previously centralized organization decides to decentralize a major part of its planning and control functions to a series of independent divisional operating units, the nature of and flow of accounting and other information will require redefinition.

You are required to

(i) identify the main problems faced at the level of both central and divisional management in carrying out their planning and control functions which arise from the changes in the flow of information resulting from decentralization;
(5 marks)

(ii) explain the purposes which performance measures serve in the context of the problems identified in (i). (5 marks)

(b) The new managing director of the ABC Hotels group intends to conduct a survey of financial performance in each region of the country in which the group operates. Initially, a pilot study is to be carried out in the Midshires region.

He discovers that the available accounting information is based on historical cost, with management performance in each hotel measured as a return on investment (ROI). However, the practice has been that the group finance director requires requests for additional investment funds to be evaluated using the discounted cash flow (DCF) criterion.

The managing director has asked you, as the group's financial advisor, to see whether the existing information provides an adequate basis for the evaluation of the group's investments and its divisional performance. As part of the investigation, you have produced the following information, using the company's existing accounting information and your own estimates, relating to the year ended June 2000:

**Midshire region**

|  | Hotel X | Hotel Y | Hotel Z |
|---|---|---|---|
| Value of investment: | (£m) | (£m) | (£m) |
| Historical cost | 2.0 | 2.3 | 3.5 |
| Current cost | 4.5 | 3.5 | 4.6 |
| Disposal value | 7.2 | 3.8 | 4.5 |
| Operating income | 0.8 | 0.4 | 0.5 |
| Year in which hotel opened | 1987 | 1995 | 1997 |

The 'investment' includes land, buildings and the hotel fixtures and fittings.

The historical cost valuation is net of accumulated depreciation.

The current cost valuation is the current cost of replacing the buildings and facilities to their present standard at current prices. It includes an indexation of the cost of land for the general increase in prices.

You are also informed that the group recently asked hotel managers to put forward proposals to improve and modernise their facilities.

A minimum 12% DCF rate of return was to be used to evaluate each proposal, a rate which the company's brokers affirm would be seen as a satisfactory return.

Details of the proposals from the Midshire region hotels were:

|  | Hotel X (£000) | Hotel Y (£000) | Hotel Z (£000) |
|---|---|---|---|
| Investment cost | 500 | 730 | 800 |
| Annual cash operating income | 67 | 90 | 155 |

You are required to advise on:

(i) the current and prospective future financial position of the Midshire region hotels; (10 marks)

(ii) additional information which may be used to supplement the general rate of return measures in the evaluation of the hotels' managements. (5 marks)
(Total 25 marks)
*CIMA Stage 4 Management Accounting – Control and Audit*

**20.27\* Advanced: Economic valued added approach to divisional performance measurement**
The most recent published results for V plc are shown below:

|  | **Published (£m)** |
|---|---|
| Profit before tax for year ending 31 December | 13.6 |

*Summary consolidated balance sheet at 31 December*

| | |
|---|---|
| Fixed assets | 35.9 |
| Current assets | 137.2 |
| *Less*: Current liabilities | (95.7) |
| Net current assets | 41.5 |
| Total assets *less* current liabilities | 77.4 |
| Borrowings | (15.0) |
| Deferred tax provisions | (7.6) |
| Net assets | 54.8 |
| Capital and reserves | 54.8 |

An analyst working for a stockbroker has taken these published results, made the adjustments shown below, and has reported his conclusion that 'the management of V plc is destroying value'.

*Analyst's adjustments to profit before tax:*

| | **(£m)** |
|---|---|
| Profit before tax | 13.6 |
| *Adjustments* | |
| *Add*: Interest paid (net) | 1.6 |
| R&D (Research and Development) | 2.1 |
| Advertising | 2.3 |
| Amortisation of goodwill | 1.3 |
| *Less*: Taxation paid | (4.8) |
| Adjusted profit | 16.1 |

*Analyst's adjustments to summary consolidated balance sheet at 31 December*

| | **(£m)** | |
|---|---|---|
| Capital and reserves | 54.8 | |
| *Adjustments* | | |
| *Add*: Borrowings | 15.0 | |
| Deferred tax provisions | 7.6 | |
| R&D | 17.4 | Last 7 years' expenditure |
| Advertising | 10.5 | Last 5 years' expenditure |
| Goodwill | 40.7 | Written off against reserves on acquisitions in previous years |

| | |
|---|---|
| Adjusted capital employed | 146.0 |
| Required return | 17.5  12% cost of capital |
| Adjusted profit | 16.1 |
| Value destroyed | 1.4 |

The Chairman of V plc has obtained a copy of the analyst's report.

Requirement:
(a) Explain, as management accountant of V plc, in a report to your Chairman, the principles of the approach taken by the analyst. Comment on the treatment of the specific adjustments to R&D, Advertising, Interest and Borrowings and Goodwill. (12 marks)
(b) Having read your report, the Chairman wishes to know which division or divisions are 'destroying value', when the current internal statements show satisfactory returns on investment (ROIs). The following summary statement is available:

**Divisional performance, year ending 31 December**

| | Division A (Retail) (£m) | Division B (Manufacturing) (£m) | Division C (Services) (£m) | Head office (£m) | Total (£m) |
|---|---|---|---|---|---|
| Turnover | 81.7 | 63.2 | 231.8 | — | 376.7 |
| Profit before interest and tax | 5.7 | 5.6 | 5.8 | (1.9) | 15.2 |
| Total assets *less* current liabilities | 27.1 | 23.9 | 23.2 | 3.2 | 77.4 |
| ROI | 21.0% | 23.4% | 25.0% | | |

Some of the adjustments made by the analyst can be related to specific divisions:
- Advertising relates entirely to Division A (Retail)
- R&D relates entirely to Division B (Manufacturing)
- Goodwill write-offs relate to
  Division B (Manufacturing) £10.3m
  Division C (Services) £30.4m
- The deferred tax relates to
  Division B (Manufacturing) £1.4m
  Division C (Services) £6.2m
- Borrowings and interest, per divisional accounts, are:

| | Division A (Retail) (£m) | Division B (Mfg) (£m) | Division C (Services) (£m) | Head office (£m) | Total (£m) |
|---|---|---|---|---|---|
| Borrowings | — | 6.6 | 6.9 | 1.5 | 15.0 |
| Interest paid/(received) | (0.4) | 0.7 | 0.9 | 0.4 | 1.6 |

Requirement:

Explain, with appropriate comment, in a report to the Chairman, where 'value is being destroyed'. Your report should include

- a statement of divisional performance,
- an explanation of any adjustments you make,
- a statement and explanation of the assumptions made, and
- comment on the limitations of the answers reached.                                        (20 marks)

(c) The use of ROI has often been criticised as emphasising short-term profit, but many companies continue to use the measure. Explain the role of ROI in managing business performance, and how the potential problems of short-termism may be overcome.

(8 marks)

(Total 40 marks)

*CIMA State 4 Management Accounting Control Systems*

## 20.28 Advanced: Impact of transactions on divisional performance measures and various issues relating to divisional performance measurement

*Scenario*

Frantisek Precision Engineering plc (FPE) is an engineering company which makes tools and equipment for a wide range of applications. FPE has twelve operating divisions, each of which is responsible for a particular product group. In the past, divisional performance has been assessed on the basis of Residual Income (RI). RI is calculated by making a finance charge (at bank base rate + 2%) on net assets (excluding cash) as at the end of the year to each division.

Rapier Management Consultants have recently been engaged to review the management accounting systems of FPE. In regard to the performance evaluation system, Rapier have reported as follows:

RI is a very partial and imperfect performance indicator. What you need is a more comprehensive system which reflects the mission, strategy and technology of each individual division. Further, executives should each be paid a performance bonus linked to an indicator which relates to their own personal effectiveness.

FPE's Directors provisionally accepted the Rapier recommendation and have carried out a pilot scheme in the diving equipment (DE) division. DE division manufactures assorted equipment

used by sport and industrial divers. Safety is a critical factor in this sector. Customers will not readily accept new products, design features and technologies, and therefore many remain unexploited.

At the start of 2000, Rapier designed a performance evaluation system for DE division as follows:

| Factor | Calculated |
| --- | --- |
| Return on Capital Employed (ROCE) | Operating profit for the year divided by book value of net assets (excluding cash) at the end of the year. |
| Cash conversion period (CCP) | Number of days' debtors plus days' stock minus days' creditors outstanding at the end of the year. |
| Strategy | Number of new products and major design features (innovations) successfully brought to market. |

Under the terms of DE's new performance evaluation system, the bases of bonuses for individual divisional managers are:

| | |
| --- | --- |
| ROCE over 10% | Chief Executive, Production Manager, Sales Manager |
| CCP less than 40 days | Accountant, Office Manager |
| More than 4 innovations | Chief Executive, Design Manager |

DE division's accounting office currently consists of four employees. The division does not have its own bank account. All main accounting systems are operated by FPE's Head Office. DE's accounting staff draw information from the main accounting system in order to prepare weekly budgetary control reports which are submitted to Head Office. The reports prompt regular visits by Head Office accountants to investigate reported cost variances.

*Part One*

In November 2000, DE's Accountant predicts that DE's results for 2000 will be as follows:

| | 2000 | | End 2000 |
| --- | --- | --- | --- |
| Sales | £6 900 000 | Stock | £530 000 |
| Purchases | £2 920 000 | Debtors | £1 035 000 |
| Operating profit | £450 000 | Creditors | £320 000 |
| Number of innovations | 4 | Net assets | £4 800 000 |

The Accountant further forecasts that in the absence of some change in policy or new investment, the corresponding figures for 2001 and end-2001 will be similar to those shown above for 2000. Upon receiving this forecast, DE division's Chief Executive convenes a meeting of his managers to discuss strategy for the rest of 2000 and for 2001. Several proposals are made, including:

*From the Office Manager:*

I propose that we immediately dispose of £160 000 of stock at cost and defer a creditor payment of £180 000 due 16 December 2000 until 2 January 2001. The first measure will reduce profit by £16 500 a year from 2001 onwards. The second measure will incur an immediate £2000 penalty.

*From the Production Manager:*

I recommend we invest £400 000 in new equipment, either immediately or in early 2001. This will increase operation profit by £25 000 per year for eight years and the equipment will have a residual value of £40 000 at the end of its life.

*From the Design Manager:*

I propose we introduce a new electronic digital depth gauge to the market. This will involve an initial investment of £100 000 in new equipment, either immediately or in early 2001, which will have a life of at least ten years. Sales will have to be on 6 months' 'buy or return' credit in order to overcome market resistance. I forecast that the new depth gauge will generate £20 000 extra operating profit per year with purchases, sales, stock and creditors all increasing in proportion.

Requirements:
(a)  Explain the impact of each proposal on the reported performance of DE division in 2000 and 2001, having regard to the new performance evaluation criteria stated in the Scenario.
  State whether or not each proposal is likely to be acceptable to members of DE management.
(15 marks)
(b)  State your views (supported by financial evaluation) on the inherent merits of each proposal, having regard to factors you consider relevant.
(10 marks)

*Note*: Where relevant, you may assume that depreciation is on a straight-line basis and DCF evaluation is carried out using an 8% discount rate and 10-year time horizon.

*Part Two*

A great deal of management accounting practice (including divisional performance evaluation) can be carried out with varying degrees of sophistication. Many new techniques have been developed in recent years. The degree of sophistication adopted in any case is partly influenced by the imagination and knowledge of the management accountant, and partly by the availability of management information technology.

Requirements:
(a)  In the light of this quotation, state your views on the advantages and disadvantages to FPE of using a firm of consultants to advise on the design of management accounting systems.
  Explain your opinion on the merits of the statement quoted above.
(10 marks)
(b)  Explain the main purpose of divisional organisation and the main features of the management accounting systems that are used to support it.
(5 marks)
(c)  Explain the changes that might be required in the management accounting operation of DE division if that division became an independent business.
(10 marks)

*Part Three*

There is nothing inherently wrong with the factors used in DE's new performance evaluation system. The problem is what those factors are used for – in particular, their use as a basis for management remuneration. For one thing, almost any factor is highly vulnerable to manipulation: for another thing, they can seriously distort business decision making.

Requirements:
Having regard to this statement,
(a)  explain the strengths and weaknesses of RI and ROCE as divisional business performance indicators as far as FPE is concerned;
(5 marks)
(b)  comment critically on the statement made by Rapier (quoted in the Scenario). In particular,

explain the problems connected with linking management pay to performance, and the measures that management accountants might take to deal with these problems;

(7 marks)

(c) explain what JIT philosophy is, in the light of a proposal to adopt just-in-time (JIT) practices in the DE division. Write a report for FPE management on whether or not DE division's Production Manager should be paid a bonus linked to CCP instead of one linked to ROCE (see Scenario), in the light of the proposal to adopt JIT practices in the DE division.

(13 marks)

*CIMA State 3 Management Accounting*
*Applications*

# Transfer pricing in divisionalized companies

In the previous chapter alternative financial measures for evaluating divisional performance were examined. However, all of the financial measure outcomes will be significantly affected when divisions transfer goods and services to each other. The established transfer price is a cost to the receiving division and revenue to the supplying division, which means that whatever transfer price is set, will affect the profitability of each division. In addition, this transfer price will also significantly influence each division's input and output decisions, and thus total company profits.

In this chapter we shall examine the various approaches that can be adopted to arrive at transfer prices between divisions. Although our focus will be on transfer pricing between divisions (i.e. profit or investment centres) transfer pricing can also apply between cost centres (typically support/service centres) or from cost centres to profit/investment centres. The same basic principles apply as those that apply between divisions, the only difference being that there is no need for a profit element to be included in the transfer price to reimburse the supplying cost centre. A more rigorous economic analysis of the transfer pricing problem is provided in the Appendix at the end of this chapter.

## Learning objectives:

After studying this chapter, you should be able to:

- describe the different purposes of a transfer pricing system;
- describe the five different transfer pricing methods;
- explain why the correct transfer price is the external market price when there is a perfectly competitive market for the intermediate product;
- explain why cost-plus transfer prices will not result in the optimum output being achieved;
- explain the two methods of transfer pricing that have been advocated to resolve the conflicts between decision-making, performance evaluation and autonomy objectives;
- explain the domestic transfer pricing recommendations;
- describe the additional factors that must be considered when setting transfer prices for multinational transactions;
- calculate optimum output and transfer prices when there is an imperfect market or no market for the intermediate product.

# Purposes of transfer pricing

A transfer pricing system is required to meet the following purposes:
1. To provide information that motivates divisional managers to make good economic decisions. This will happen when actions that divisional managers take to improve the reported profit of their divisions also improves the profit of the company as a whole.
2. To provide information that is useful for evaluating the managerial and economic performance of the divisions.
3. To intentionally move profits between divisions or locations.
4. To ensure that divisional autonomy is not undermined.

## PROVIDING INFORMATION FOR MAKING GOOD ECONOMIC DECISIONS

Goods transferred from the supplying division to the receiving division are known as **intermediate products**. The products sold by a receiving division to the outside world are known as **final products**. The objective of the receiving division is to subject the intermediate product to further processing before it is sold as a final product in the outside market. The transfer price of the intermediate product represents a cost to the receiving division and a revenue to the supplying division. Therefore transfer prices are used to determine how much of the intermediate product will be produced by the supplying division and how much will be acquired by the receiving division. In a centralized company the decision as to whether an intermediate product should be sold or processed further is determined by comparing the incremental cost of, and the revenues from, further processing. In a divisionalized organization structure, however, the manager of the receiving division will treat the price at which the intermediate product is transferred as an incremental cost, and this may lead to incorrect decisions being made.

For example, let us assume that the incremental cost of the intermediate product is £100, and the additional further processing costs of the receiving division are £60. The incremental cost of producing the final product will therefore be £160. Let us also assume that the supplying division has a temporary excess capacity which is being maintained in order to meet an expected resurgence in demand and that the market price of the final product is £200. To simplify the illustration, we assume there is no market for the intermediate product. The correct short-term decision would be to convert the intermediate product into the final product. In a centralized company this decision would be taken, but in a divisionalized organization structure where the transfer price for the intermediate product is £150 based on full cost plus a profit margin, the incremental cost of the receiving division will be £210 (£150 + £60). The divisional manager would therefore incorrectly decide not to purchase the intermediate product for further processing. This problem can be overcome if the transfer price is set at the incremental cost of the supplying division, which in this example is £100.

## EVALUATING MANAGERIAL PERFORMANCE

When goods are transferred from one division to another, the revenue of the supplying division becomes a cost of the receiving division. Consequently, the prices at which goods are transferred can influence each division's reported profits, and there is a danger that an unsound transfer price will result in a misleading performance measure that may cause divisional managers to believe that the transfer price is affecting their performance rather unfairly. This may lead to disagreement and negative motivational consequences.

## CONFLICT OF OBJECTIVES

Unfortunately, no single transfer price is likely to perfectly serve all of the four specified purposes. They often conflict and managers are forced to make trade-offs. In particular, the decision-making and the performance evaluation purposes may conflict with each other. For example, in some situations the transfer price that motivates the short-run optimal economic decision is marginal cost. If the supplier has excess capacity, this cost will probably equal variable cost. The supplying division will fail to cover any of its fixed costs when transfers are made at variable cost, and will therefore report a loss. Furthermore, if a transfer price equal to variable cost (£100 in the above example) is imposed on the manager of the supplying division, the concept of divisional autonomy and decentralization is undermined. On the other hand, a transfer price that may be satisfactory for evaluating divisional performance (£150 in the above example) may lead divisions to make suboptimal decisions when viewed from the overall company perspective.

# Alternative transfer pricing methods

There are five primary types of transfer prices that companies can use to transfer goods and services.

1.  **Market-based transfer prices:** These are usually based on the listed price of an identical or similar products or services, the actual price the supplying division sells the intermediate product to external customers (possibly less a discount that reflects the lower selling costs for inter-group transfers), or the price a competitor is offering.
2.  **Marginal cost transfer prices:** Most accountants assume that marginal cost can be approximated by short-run variable cost which is interpreted as direct costs plus variable indirect costs.
3.  **Full cost transfer prices:** The terms full cost or long-run cost are used to represent the sum of the cost of all of those resources that are committed to a product or service in the long-term. Some firms add an arbitrary mark-up to variable costs in order to cover fixed costs and thus approximate full costs. Such an approach is likely to result in an inaccurate estimate of full cost.
4.  **Cost-plus a mark-up transfer prices:** With cost-based transfer prices the supplying divisions do not make any profits on the products or services transferred. Therefore they are not suitable for performance measurement. To overcome this problem a mark-up is added to enable the supplying divisions to earn a profit on inter-divisional transfers.
5.  **Negotiated transfer prices:** In some cases transfer prices are negotiated between the managers of the supplying and receiving divisions. Information about the market prices and marginal or full costs often provide an input into these negotiations, although there is no requirement that they must do so.

Exhibit 21.1 shows the results of surveys of the primary transfer pricing methods used in various countries. This exhibit shows that in the USA transfer prices are used by the vast majority of the firms surveyed. It is apparent from all of the surveys that a small minority (less than 10%) transfer at marginal or variable cost. A significant proportion of firms use each of the other methods with the largest proportions transferring goods or services at

**EXHIBIT 21.1**

*Surveys of company practice*

The studies listed below relate to surveys of transfer pricing practices in various countries. It is apparent from these surveys that variable/marginal costs are not widely used, whereas full cost or full cost plus a mark-up are used extensively. Market price methods are also widely used.

*Australian and Canadian Surveys*

| | Australia Joye and Blayney (1991) | Canada Tang (1992) |
|---|---|---|
| Market price-based | 13% | 34% |
| Cost-based: | | |
|     Variable Costs | | 6 |
|     Full costs | | 37 |
|     Other | | 3 |
| Total | 65 | 46 |
| Negotiated | 11 | 18 |
| Other | 11 | 2 |
| | 100 | 100 |

The Canadian survey asked the respondents to name the dominant objective of the transfer pricing system. Approximately 50% stated that it was performance evaluation and one third stated that it was for profit maximization of the consolidated firm.

*UK Survey (Drury et al., 1993)*

| | Extent of use | | |
|---|---|---|---|
| | Never/rarely | Sometimes | Often/always |
| Unit variable cost | 94% | 4% | 2% |
| Unit full cost | 66 | 13 | 21 |
| Unit variable cost-plus mark-up | 83 | 6 | 11 |
| Unit full cost-plus mark-up | 55 | 18 | 27 |
| Marginal/incremental cost | 93 | 6 | 1 |
| Market price/adjusted market price | 53 | 14 | 33 |
| Negotiated | 41 | 29 | 30 |
| Lump sum payment plus cost per unit transferred | 95 | 4 | 1 |

*USA Survey (Borkowski, 1990)*

| | | |
|---|---|---|
| **Number of Companies Participating** | **215** | |
| **Percentage Using Transfer Prices** | **89.6%** | |

Percentage using transfers on following bases
Market price

| | | |
|---|---|---|
| Full market price | 20.2 | |
| Adjusted market price | <u>12.5</u> | 32.7 |
| Negotiated | | |
| To external price | 13.6 | |
| To manufacturing costs | 3.0 | |
| With no restrictions | <u>6.0</u> | 22.6 |
| Full cost | | |
| Standard | 14.3 | |
| Actual | 7.1 | |
| Plus profit based on cost | 14.9 | |
| Plus fixed profit | 2.4 | |
| Other | <u>2.4</u> | 41.1 |
| Variable cost | | |
| Standard | 2.4 | |
| Actual | 0.6 | |
| Plus contribution based on cost | 0.6 | |
| Plus fixed contribution | 0.0 | |
| Plus opportunity cost | <u>0.0</u> | 3.6 |
| Marginal (incremental) cost | 0.0 | |
| Mathematical/programming models | 0.0 | |
| Dual pricing | <u>0.0</u> | |
| Total | | <u>100.00</u> |

market prices or either full cost or full cost plus a mark-up. The following sections describe in detail each of the transfer pricing methods and the circumstances when they are appropriate.

# Market-based transfer prices

In most circumstances, where a perfectly competitive market for an intermediate product exists it is optimal for both decision-making and performance evaluation purposes to set transfer prices at competitive market prices. A perfectly competitive market exists where the product is homogeneous and no individual buyer or seller can affect the market prices.

When transfers are recorded at market prices divisional performance is more likely to represent the real economic contribution of the division to total company profits. If the supplying division did not exist, the intermediate product would have to be purchased on the outside market at the current market price. Alternatively, if the receiving division did not exist, the intermediate product would have to be sold on the outside market at the current market price. Divisional profits are therefore likely to be similar to the profits that would be calculated if the divisions were separate organizations. Consequently, divisional profitability can be compared directly with the profitability of similar companies operating in the same type of business.

In a perfectly competitive market the supplying division should supply as much as the receiving division requires at the current market price, so long as the incremental cost is lower than the market price. If this supply is insufficient to meet the receiving division's demand, it must obtain additional supplies by purchasing from an outside supplier at the current market price. Alternatively, if the supplying division produces more of the intermediate product than the receiving division requires, the excess can be sold to the outside market at the current market price.

Where the selling costs for internal transfers of the intermediate product are identical with those that arise from sales in the outside market, it will not matter whether the supplying division's output is sold internally or externally. To illustrate this we shall consider two alternatives. First, assume initially that the output of the supplying division is sold *externally* and that the receiving division purchases its requirements *externally*. Now consider a second situation where the output of the intermediate product is transferred *internally* at the market price and is not sold on the outside market. You should now refer to Exhibit 21.2. The aim of this diagram is to show that divisional and total profits are not affected, whichever of these two alternatives is chosen.

Exhibit 21.2 illustrates a situation where the receiving division sells 1000 units of the final product in the external market. The incremental costs for the production of 1000 units of the intermediate product are £5000, with a market price for the output of £8000. The incremental costs of the receiving division for the additional processing of the 1000 units of the intermediate product are £4000. This output can be sold for £18 000. You will see that it does not matter whether the intermediate product is transferred internally or sold externally – profits of each division and total company profits remain unchanged.

This of course assumes that the supplying division can sell all its output either internally or externally at the going market price. If this were not the case then it would be necessary to instruct the receiving division to purchase from the supplying division the quantity that it is prepared to supply at the market price. This is because the receiving division is indifferent to whether it purchases the intermediate product from the supplying division or from the external market.

If the supplying division cannot make a profit in the long run at the current outside market price then the company will be better off not to produce the product internally but to obtain its supply from the external market. Similarly, if the receiving division cannot make a long-run profit when transfers are made at the current market price, it should cease processing this product, and the supplying division should be allowed to sell all its output to the external market. Where there is a competitive market for the intermediate product, the market price can be used to allow the decisions of the supplying and receiving division to be made independently of each other.

## THE EFFECT OF SELLING EXPENSES

In practice, it is likely that total company profits will be different when the intermediate product is acquired internally or externally. The supplying division will incur selling expenses when selling the intermediate product on the external market, but such expenses will not be incurred on inter-divisional transfers. If the transfer price is set at the current market price, the receiving division will be indifferent to whether the intermediate product is obtained internally or externally. However, if the receiving division purchases the intermediate product externally, the company will be worse off to the extent of the selling expenses incurred by the supplying division in disposing of its output on the external market. In practice, many companies modify the market price rule for pricing inter-divisional transfers and deduct a margin to take account of the savings in selling and collection expenses.

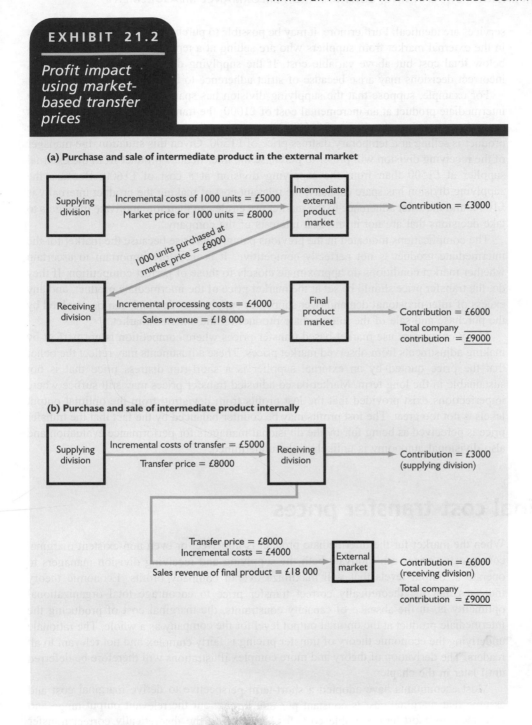

**EXHIBIT 21.2**

*Profit impact using market-based transfer prices*

**(a) Purchase and sale of intermediate product in the external market**

Supplying division →
Incremental costs of 1000 units = £5000
Market price for 1000 units = £8000
→ Intermediate external product market → Contribution = £3000

1000 units purchased at market price = £8000

Receiving division →
Incremental processing costs = £4000
Sales revenue = £18 000
→ Final product market → Contribution = £6000

Total company contribution = £9000

**(b) Purchase and sale of intermediate product internally**

Supplying division →
Incremental costs of transfer = £5000
Transfer price = £8000
→ Receiving division → Contribution = £3000 (supplying division)

Transfer price = £8000
Incremental costs = £4000
Sales revenue of final product = £18 000
→ External market → Contribution = £6000 (receiving division)

Total company contribution = £9000

# OTHER MARKET IMPERFECTIONS

One of the major problems with using market prices is that the market is unlikely to be perfectly competitive. In addition, the transferred product may have special characteristics that differentiate it from other varieties of the same product. The market price for the intermediate product is appropriate only when quality, delivery, discounts and back-up services are identical. Furthermore, it may be possible to purchase the intermediate product in the external market from suppliers who are selling at a temporary distress price that is below total cost but above variable cost. If the supplying division has excess capacity, incorrect decisions may arise because of strict adherence to the market price rule.

For example, suppose that the supplying division has spare capacity and produces an intermediate product at an incremental cost of £1000; the transfer price for this product is set at the external market price of £1600. Now suppose that a supplier of the intermediate product is selling at a temporary distress price of £1500. Given this situation, the manager of the receiving division will prefer to purchase the intermediate product from the external supplier at £1500 than from the supplying division at a cost of £1600. Because the supplying division has spare capacity, the relevant cost of making the product internally is £1000, and the strict adherence to the market price rule can therefore motivate managers to take decisions that are not in the best interests of the company.

The complications indicated in the previous paragraphs arise because the market for the intermediate product is not perfectly competitive. It is therefore important to ascertain whether market conditions do approximate closely to those of perfect competition. If they do, the transfer price should be set at the market price of the intermediate product, and any excess of inter-divisional demand over supply, or supply over demand, can be resolved by the purchase and sale of the intermediate product on the external market.

Many companies use market-based transfer prices where competition is not perfect by making adjustments from observed market prices. These adjustments may reflect the belief that the price quoted by an external supplier is a short-run distress price that is not sustainable in the long term. Market-based adjusted transfer prices may still suffice where imperfections exist provided that the lost profits from deviating from the optimal output levels is not too great. The lost profits may be counter-balanced by the fact that the transfer price is perceived as being fair by the divisional managers for performance evaluation and also divisional autonomy is unlikely to be undermined.

# Marginal cost transfer prices

When the market for the intermediate product is imperfect or even non-existent marginal cost transfer prices can motivate both the supplying and receiving division managers to operate at output levels that will maximize overall company profits. Economic theory indicates that the theoretically correct transfer price to encourage total organizational optimality is, in the absence of capacity constraints, the marginal cost of producing the intermediate product at the optimal output level for the company as a whole. The rationale underlying the economic theory of transfer pricing is fairly complex and not relevant to all readers. The derivation of theory and more complex illustrations will therefore be deferred until later in the chapter.

Most accountants have adopted a short-term perspective to derive marginal cost and assume that marginal cost is constant per unit throughout the relevant output range and equivalent to short-term variable cost. In this situation the theoretically correct transfer price can be interpreted as being equivalent to the variable cost of the supplying division of providing an intermediate product or service. However, using short-term variable cost is only optimal when a short-term perspective is adopted.

Figure 21.1 illustrates how setting transfer prices at marginal cost will provide information that will motivate the divisional managers to operate at output levels that will maximize overall company profits. This diagram assumes that marginal cost is equal to variable cost and constant throughout the entire production range. It therefore relates to a short-term time horizon. To keep things simple we shall assume that there is no market

**FIGURE 21.1** *A comparison of marginal cost and full cost or cost-plus transfer pricing.*

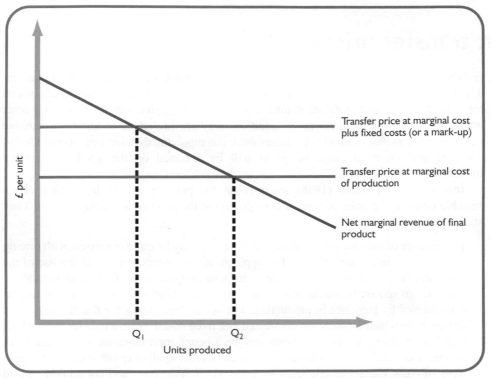

for the intermediate product. Note also that the net marginal revenue curve of the final product declines to reflect the fact that to sell more the price must be lowered. The term **net marginal revenue** refers to the marginal revenue of the final product less the marginal conversion costs (excluding the transfer price) incurred by the receiving division. The supplying division will purchase the intermediate product up to the point where net marginal revenue equals its marginal costs, as reflected by the transfer price. It will therefore be the optimal output from the overall company perspective ($Q_2$) only if the transfer price is set at the marginal cost of the intermediate product or service. If a higher price is set (as indicated by the green line) to cover full cost, or a mark-up is added to marginal cost, then the supplying division will restrict output to the sub-optimal level $Q_1$.

It is apparent from the surveys of company practice shown in Exhibit 21.1 that less than 10% of the companies transfer goods and services at marginal cost. The major reason for its low use is that when marginal cost is interpreted as being equivalent to variable cost it does not support the profit or investment responsibility structure because it provides poor information for evaluating the performance of either the supplying or receiving divisions. The supplying division will record losses on the capacity allocated to inter-divisional transfers because it bears the full cost of production but only receives revenues that cover variable cost. Conversely the profit of the receiving division will be overstated because it will not bear any of the fixed capacity costs of the supplying division.

A further problem is that marginal costs may not be constant over the entire range of output because step increases in fixed costs can occur. Measuring marginal cost is also difficult in practice beyond a short-term period. The low usage of marginal cost transfer prices suggests that managers reject the short-term interpretation of approximating marginal costs with variable costs. Instead, they view product-related decisions as long-range decisions that must reflect long-run pricing considerations and therefore the appropriate marginal cost to use is long-run marginal cost. We shall examine how long-run marginal cost can be derived later in the chapter.

# Full cost transfer prices

Exhibit 21.1 shows that full costs or full cost plus a mark-up are widely used in practice. Their attraction is that, as indicated above, managers view product-related decisions as long-run decisions and therefore require a measure of long-run marginal cost. Full costs attempt to meet this requirement. In addition, they are preferable to short-run variable costs for performance evaluation purposes since the supplying division can recover the full costs of production, although no profit will be obtained on the goods or services transferred.

Tomkins and McAulay (1996) suggest that the practice of transfer pricing above variable cost may be quite consistent with pricing at the economist's marginal cost. They state:

> The practice of transfer pricing above variable cost may be quite consistent with pricing at the economist's marginal cost. The apparent inconsistency may lie in the use of the accountant's variable cost as a surrogate for true marginal cost. To take an obvious example, an economist would argue that marginal cost includes extra wear and tear on plant caused by increases in production. The accountant allows for this through depreciation which is nearly always treated as a fixed cost. Hence, a transfer price which includes an absorption of fixed costs may be a better approximation of true marginal cost than is variable cost. The same argument can be applied to other costs. If some types of costs, e.g. set-up costs, are included within fixed costs and not properly traced to their causal transaction, variable costs in the accounts are being understated if that transaction in turn is a function of output levels, albeit not in the usual proportionate relationship. Hence, the full allocated cost approach may be a better approximation to true marginal cost. Of course, it would be better to establish more accurately what the nature of all the cost functions are and relate them to their specific transactions and thence to changes in output levels. This is the argument behind activity-based costing. This form of argument leads Kaplan and Atkinson (1989) to suggest that activity-based costing may provide the unifying concept that would enable a practical full cost system to conform with economic theory. (Page 355.)

The major problem with full cost transfer prices is that they are derived from traditional costing systems which, as was pointed out in Chapter 10, can provide poor estimates of long-run marginal costs. Ideally, full cost transfer prices should be derived from an activity-based costing system. We shall consider how long-run marginal costs can be derived using activity-based costs later in the chapter. In addition, a further problem with full cost transfer prices is that they do not provide an incentive for the supplying division to transfer goods and services internally because they do not include a profit margin. If internal transfers are a significant part of the supplying division's business, they will understate the division's profits.

# Cost-plus a mark-up transfer prices

Cost-plus a mark-up transfer prices represent an attempt to meet the performance evaluation purpose of transfer pricing by enabling the supplying divisions to obtain a profit on the goods and services transferred. Where full cost is used as the cost base the mark-up is intended to provide a profit margin for the supplying division. Sometimes variable costs are used as the cost base and the mark-up is intended to cover both fixed costs and a profit contribution. Where such an approach is adopted the estimate of full cost will be even more inaccurate than traditional costing systems.

Because they include a margin in excess of either short-run or long-run variable cost, transfer prices based on cost-plus a mark-up will cause inter-divisional transfers to be less than the optimal level for the company as a whole. You will see why if you refer back to Figure 21.1. The green horizontal line in this diagram represents the transfer price and at this price the receiving division manager will restrict output to $OQ_1$ compared to the optimal output level of $OQ_2$.

A further problem arises if we extend our analysis beyond two divisions to several divisions. If the first division in the process transfers goods to the second division at cost plus 20%, and the goods received from the second division are further processed and transferred at cost plus 20% to a third division, and so on, then the percentage margin becomes enormous by the time a mark-up is added by the final division in the process. Similar situations will also arise where the cost of shared resources, such as central administrative costs, are assigned to divisions and their costs are incorporated into the products or services that are transferred between several divisions such that the output cost of one division becomes the input costs of other divisions.

# Negotiated transfer prices

The difficulties encountered in establishing a sound system of transfer pricing have led to suggestions that negotiated transfer prices should be used. Negotiated transfer prices are most appropriate in situations where some market imperfections exist for the intermediate product, particularly when there are different selling costs for internal and external sales, or where there exist several different market prices. When there are such imperfections in the market, the respective divisional managers must have the freedom to buy and sell outside the company to enable them to engage in a bargaining process. It is claimed that if this is the case then the friction and bad feeling that may arise from a centrally controlled market transfer price will be eliminated without incurring a mis-allocation of resources.

There are strong arguments for believing that in certain situations, if divisions are allowed to bargain freely with each other, they will usually make decisions that will maximize total company profits – this is of course assuming that managers are competent and know how to use the accounting information. For negotiation to work effectively it is important that managers have equal bargaining power. If the receiving division has many sourcing possibilities for the intermediate product or service, but the supplying division has limited outlets, the bargaining power of the managers will be unequal. Unequal bargaining power can also occur if the transfers are a relatively small proportion of the business for one of the divisions and a relatively large proportion of the business of the other. The manager of the division where transfers are a small proportion of business has considerably more bargaining power because he, or she, will not suffer serious consequences if agreement is not reached on the proposed inter-divisional transfers.

The behavioural literature also supports the use of negotiated transfer prices. Watson and Baumler (1975) advocate that negotiated transfer prices can help to resolve conflicts between organizational sub-units. They argue that mathematically elegant solutions to the transfer pricing problem may be less than ideal in behavioural terms because decentralization is sacrificed to optimize a numerical solution. Lawrence and Lorsch's (1986) research evidence indicated that successful firms facing uncertain environments were able effectively to resolve inter-departmental conflict, and the most important means of resolving this conflict was by confrontation (i.e. negotiation). Watson and Baumler therefore argue that if the appropriate conflict resolution process is negotiation, the transfer price should be the one arrived at in this way. In particular, they argue that if the requisite degree of decentralization is achievable and there is a problem in obtaining adequate integration between the divisions then one integrative tool that is available is a system of negotiated transfer prices.

The situation may arise where divisional managers cannot agree on a mutually satisfactory transfer price, or where one division refuses to deal with another division. Central headquarters may then have to resolve the dispute, but the difficulty here is that the managers involved can no longer be said to have complete responsibility for the activities of their divisions. This not only raises immediate behavioural problems with respect to morale and motivation, but it also means that, when divisional performance is evaluated, the managers will be held responsible for the results of decisions that they did not make. The overall effect is a breakdown in decentralized profit responsibility and a move towards centralized decision-making. Nevertheless, the support and involvement of top management must be available to mediate the occasional unresolvable dispute or to intervene when it sees that the bargaining process is leading to suboptimal decisions.

It is important to note that negotiated transfer prices are inappropriate where there is a perfect market for the intermediate product, since in a perfect market situation transfer prices can be based on the competitive market price without the need for the managers to engage in a negotiating process. At the other extreme, where there is no market for the intermediate product, it is most unlikely that managers can engage in meaningful negotiation. Negotiated transfer prices are therefore best suited to situations where there is an imperfect external market for the intermediate product or service. Negotiated transfer prices do, however, suffer from the following limitations:

- because the agreed transfer price can depend on the negotiating skills and bargaining power of the managers involved, the final outcome may not be close to being optimal;

- they can lead to conflict between divisions and the resolution of such conflicts may require top management to mediate;

- measurement of divisional profitability can be dependent on the negotiating skills of managers, who may have unequal bargaining power;

- they are time-consuming for the managers involved, particularly where a large number of transactions are involved.

Even if negotiated prices do not result in an optimum output level, the motivational advantages of giving managers full independence over their input and output decisions may lead to increased profits that outweigh the loss of profits from negotiated non-optimal transfer prices.

# An illustration of transfer pricing

The data used in Example 21.1 will now be used to illustrate the impact that transfer prices can have on divisional profitability and decision-making. You should now refer to Example 21.1.

At *the full cost plus a mark-up transfer price* of £35 the profit computations for each division will be as follows:

*Oslo Division (Supplying division)*

| Output level (units) | Transfer price revenues | Variable costs | Fixed costs | Total profit/(loss) |
|---|---|---|---|---|
| 1000 | 35 000 | 11 000 | 60 000 | (36 000) |
| 2000 | 70 000 | 22 000 | 60 000 | (12 000) |
| 3000 | 105 000 | 33 000 | 60 000 | 12 000 |
| 4000 | 140 000 | 44 000 | 60 000 | 36 000 |
| 5000 | 175 000 | 55 000 | 60 000 | 60 000 |
| 6000 | 210 000 | 66 000 | 60 000 | 84 000 |

*Bergen Division (Receiving division)*

| Output level (units) | Total revenues | Variable costs | Total cost of transfers | Fixed costs | Total profit/(loss) |
|---|---|---|---|---|---|
| 1000 | 100 000 | 7 000 | 35 000 | 90 000 | (32 000) |
| 2000 | 180 000 | 14 000 | 70 000 | 90 000 | 6 000 |
| 3000 | 240 000 | 21 000 | 105 000 | 90 000 | 24 000 |
| 4000 | 280 000 | 28 000 | 140 000 | 90 000 | 22 000 |
| 5000 | 300 000 | 35 000 | 175 000 | 90 000 | 0 |
| 6000 | 300 000 | 42 000 | 210 000 | 90 000 | (42 000) |

**EXAMPLE 21.1**

The Oslo division and the Bergen division are divisions within the Baltic Group. One of the products manufactured by the Oslo division is an intermediate product for which there is no external market. This intermediate product is transferred to the Bergen division where it is converted into a final product for sale on the external market. One unit of the intermediate product is used in the production of the final product. The expected units of the final product which the Bergen division estimates it can sell at various selling prices are as follows:

| Net selling price (£) | Quantity sold Units |
|---|---|
| 100 | 1000 |
| 90 | 2000 |
| 80 | 3000 |
| 70 | 4000 |
| 60 | 5000 |
| 50 | 6000 |

The costs of each division are as follows:

| (£) | Oslo (£) | Bergen (£) |
|---|---|---|
| Variable cost per unit | 11 | 7 |
| Fixed costs attributable to the products | 60 000 | 90 000 |

The transfer price of the intermediate product has been set at £35 based on a full cost plus a mark-up.

The supplying division maximizes profits at an output level of 6000 units whereas the receiving division maximizes profits at an output level of 3000 units. The receiving division will therefore purchase 3000 units from the supplying division. This is because the Bergen division will compare its net marginal revenue with the transfer price and expand output as long as the net marginal revenue of the additional output exceeds the transfer price. Remember that net marginal revenue was defined as the marginal revenue from the sale of the final product less the marginal conversion costs (excluding the transfer price). The calculations are as follows:

| Units | Net marginal revenue(£) |
|---|---|
| 1000 | 93 000 (100 000 − 7000) |
| 2000 | 73 000 (80 000 − 7000) |
| 3000 | 53 000 (60 000 − 7000) |
| 4000 | 33 000 (40 000 − 7000) |
| 5000 | 13 000 (20 000 − 7000) |
| 6000 | −7 000 (0 − 7 000) |

Faced with a transfer price of £35 000 per 1000 units the Bergen division will not expand output beyond 3000 units because the transfer price paid for each batch exceeds the net marginal revenue.

Let us now look at the profit at the different output levels for the company as a whole. Note that these calculations do not incorporate the transfer price since it represents inter-company trading with the revenue from the supplying division cancelling out the cost incurred by the receiving division.

*Whole company profit computations*

| Output level (units) | Total revenues | Company variable costs | Company fixed costs | Company profit/(loss) |
|---|---|---|---|---|
| 1000 | 100 000 | 18 000 | 150 000 | (68 000) |
| 2000 | 180 000 | 36 000 | 150 000 | (6 000) |
| 3000 | 240 000 | 54 000 | 150 000 | 36 000 |
| 4000 | 280 000 | 72 000 | 150 000 | 58 000 |
| 5000 | 300 000 | 90 000 | 150 000 | 60 000 |
| 6000 | 300 000 | 108 000 | 150 000 | 42 000 |

The profit maximizing output for the company as a whole is 5000 units. Therefore the current transfer pricing system does not motivate the divisional managers to operate at the optimum output level for the company as a whole.

To induce overall company optimality the *transfer price must be set at the marginal cost of the supplying division*, which over the time horizon and output levels under consideration, is the unit variable cost of £11 per unit. Therefore the transfer price for each batch of 1000 units would be £11 000. The receiving division will expand output as long as net marginal revenue exceeds the transfer price. Now look at the net marginal revenue that we calculated for the receiving division. You will see that the net marginal revenue from expanding output from 4000 to 5000 units is £13 000 and the transfer price that the receiving division must pay to acquire this batch of 1000 units is £11 000. Therefore expanding the output will increase the profits of the supplying division. Will the manager of the receiving division be motivated to expand output from 5000 to 6000 units? The answer is no because the net marginal revenue (−£7000) is less than the transfer price of purchasing the 1000 units.

Setting the transfer price at the unit marginal (variable) cost of the supplying division will motivate the divisional managers to operate at the optimum output level for the company as a whole provided that the supplying division manager is instructed to meet the demand of the receiving division at this transfer price. Although the variable cost transfer price encourages overall company optimality it is a poor measure of divisional performance. The supplying division manager will be credited with transfer price revenues of £11 000 per 1000 units. If you look back at the profit computations for the Oslo division you will see that the transfer price revenues will be identical to the variable cost column and therefore a loss equal to the fixed costs of £60 000 will be reported for all output levels. In the short-term the fixed costs are unavoidable and therefore the divisional manager is no worse off since these fixed costs will be still incurred but in the longer-term some, or all of them, may be avoidable and the manager would not wish to produce the intermediate product. The performance measure will overstate the performance of the receiving division because all of the contribution (sales less variable costs) from the sale of the final product will be credited to the manager of the receiving division.

Let us now consider a *full cost transfer price without the mark-up*. We need to estimate unit fixed costs at the planning stage for making decisions relating to output levels. You will also recall from Chapter 3 that it was pointed out that pre-determined fixed overhead rates should be established. Let us assume that the 5000 units optimal output level for the company as a whole is used to determine the fixed overhead rate per unit. Therefore the fixed cost per unit for the intermediate product will be £12 per unit (£60 000 fixed costs/5 000 units) giving a full cost of £23 (£11 variable cost plus £12 fixed cost). If the transfer price is set at £23 per unit (i.e. £23 000 per 1000 batch) the receiving division manager will expand output as long as net marginal revenues exceeds the transfer price. If you refer to the net marginal revenue schedule you will see that the receiving division manager will choose to purchase 4000 units. The manager will choose not to expand output to the 5000 units optimal level for the company as a whole because the transfer cost of £23 000 exceeds the net marginal revenue of £13 000. Also at the selected output level of 4000 units the total transfer price revenues of the receiving division will be £92 000 (4000 units at £23) but you will see from the profit calculations for the Oslo division that the total costs are £104 000 (£44 000 + £60 000). Therefore the supplying division will report a loss because all of its fixed costs have not been recovered. Hence the transfer price is suitable for neither performance evaluation nor ensuring that optimal output decisions are made.

Would the managers be able to *negotiate a transfer price* that meets the decision-making and performance evaluation requirements? If the manager of the supplying division cannot avoid the fixed costs in the short-run he or she will have no bargaining power because there is no external market for the intermediate product and would accept any price as long as it is not below variable cost. Meaningful negotiation is not possible. If the fixed costs are avoidable the manager has some negotiating power since he or she can avoid £90 000 by not producing the intermediate product. The manager will try and negotiate a selling price in excess of full cost. If an output level of 5000 units is used to calculate the full cost the unit cost from our earlier calculations was £23 and the manager will try and negotiate a price in excess of £23. If you examine the net marginal revenue of the receiving division you will see that the manager of the receiving division will not expand output to 5000 units if the transfer price is set above £23 per unit. As indicated earlier negotiation is only likely to work when there is an external market for the intermediate market.

We can conclude from this illustration that to ensure overall company optimality the transfer price must be set at the marginal cost of the supplying division. Our analysis has focused on the short term, a period during which we have considered that fixed costs are irrelevant and unavoidable. In the longer term fixed costs are relevant and avoidable and thus represent a marginal cost that should be considered for decision-making. Thus for long-term decisions marginal cost should incorporate avoidable fixed costs but we have noted in earlier chapters that they should not be unitized since this is misleading because it gives the impression that they are variable with output. To incorporate avoidable fixed costs within long-run marginal cost they should be added as a lump-sum to short-run marginal (variable) costs. This is a feature of one of the proposals that we shall look at in the next section.

# Proposals for resolving transfer pricing conflicts

Our discussion so far has indicated that in the absence of a perfect market for the intermediate product none of the transfer pricing methods can perfectly meet both the decision-making and performance evaluation requirements and also not undermine divisional autonomy. It has been suggested that if the external market for the intermediate product does not approximate closely those of perfect competition, then if long-run marginal cost can be accurately estimated, transfers at marginal cost should motivate decisions that are optimal from the overall company's perspective. However, transfers at marginal cost are unsuitable for performance evaluation since they do not provide an incentive for the supplying division to transfer goods and services internally. This is because they do not contain a profit margin for the supplying division. Central head-quarters intervention may be necessary to instruct the supplying division to meet the receiving division's demand at the marginal cost of the transfers. Thus, divisional autonomy will be undermined. Transferring at cost-plus a mark-up creates the opposite conflict. Here the transfer price meets the performance evaluation requirement but will not induce managers to make optimal decisions.

To resolve the above conflicts the following transfer pricing methods have been suggested:

1. adopt a dual-rate transfer pricing system;
2. transfer at a marginal cost plus a fixed lump-sum fee.

## DUAL-RATE TRANSFER PRICING SYSTEM

**Dual-rate transfer pricing** uses two separate transfer prices to price each inter-divisional transaction. For example, the supplying division may receive the full cost plus a mark-up on each transaction and the receiving division may be charged at the marginal cost of the transfers. The former transfer price is intended to approximate the market price of the goods or services transferred. Exhibit 21.3, which relates to inter-divisional trading between two divisions in respect of 100 000 units on an intermediate product, is used to illustrate the application of a dual-rate transfer pricing system. You will see that if the transfer price is set at the supplying division's marginal cost of £10 per unit for the intermediate product, the supplying division will be credited with a zero contribution from the transfers, and all of the total contribution of £1 million from inter-divisional trading will be assigned to the receiving division.

Dual-rate transfer pricing can be implemented by setting the transfer price to be charged to the receiving division at the marginal cost of the supplying division (£10 per unit). To keep things simple here, the transfer price that the supplying division receives is set at marginal cost plus 50%, giving a price of £15. It is assumed that the mark-up added will be sufficient to cover the supplying division's fixed costs and also provide a profit contribution. Therefore the receiving division manager will use the marginal cost of the supplying division which should ensure that decisions are made that are optimal from the company's perspective. The transfer price should also meet the performance evaluation requirements of the supplying division since each unit transferred generates a profit. Thus the supplying division manager is motivated to transfer the intermediate product internally. The reported outcomes for each division using the above dual-rate transfer prices, and the information shown in Exhibit 21.3 would be as follows:

| Supplying division | (£) | Receiving division | (£) |
|---|---|---|---|
| Transfers to the supplying division at £15 (100 000 units at £10 plus 50%) | 1 500 000 | Sales of the final product at £50 (100 000 units) | 5 000 000 |
| Less: marginal processing costs | 1 000 000 | Less marginal costs: | |
| | | Supplying division transfers (100 000 units at £10) | (1 000 000) |
| | | Conversion costs (100 000 units at £30) | (3 000 000) |
| Profit contribution | 500 000 | Profit contribution | 1 000 000 |

Note that the contribution for the company as a whole is less than the sum of the divisional profits by £500 000, but this can be resolved by a simple accounting adjustment.

Dual-rate transfer prices are not widely used in practice for several reasons. First, the use of different transfer prices causes confusion, particularly when the transfers spread beyond two divisions. Secondly, they are considered to be artificial. Thirdly, they reduce divisional incentives to compete effectively. For example, the supplying division can easily generate internal sales to the receiving divisions when they are charged at marginal cost. This protects them from competition and gives them little incentive to improve their productivity. Finally, top-level managers do not like to double count internal profits because this can result in misleading information and create a false impression of divisional profits. Furthermore, the inter-divisional profits can be considerably in excess of total company profits where a sequence of transfers involves several divisions. At the extreme all of the divisions may report profits when the company as a whole is losing money.

**EXHIBIT 21.3**

*Projected financial statement from inter-group trading*

| | (£) | (£) |
|---|---|---|
| Sale of final product: 100 000 units at £50 | | 5 000 000 |
| Marginal costs: | | |
| Supplying division processing costs (100 000 units at £10) | 1 000 000 | |
| Receiving division conversion costs (100 000 units at £30) | 3 000 000 | 4 000 000 |
| Total contribution from inter-divisional trading | | 1 000 000 |

## MARGINAL COSTS PLUS A FIXED LUMP-SUM FEE

A solution that has been proposed where the market for the intermediate product is imperfect or non-existent, and where the supplying division has no capacity constraints, is to price all transfers at the short-run marginal cost and for the supplying division to also charge the receiving division a fixed fee for the privilege of obtaining these transfers at short-run marginal cost. This approach is sometimes described as a **two-part transfer pricing system**. With this system, the receiving division acquires additional units of the intermediate product at the marginal cost of production. Therefore when it equates its marginal costs with its marginal revenues to determine the optimum profit-maximizing output level, it will use the appropriate marginal costs of the supplying division. The supplying division can recover its fixed costs and earn a profit on the inter-divisional transfers through the fixed fee charged each period. The fixed fee is intended to compensate the supplying division for tying up some of its fixed capacity for providing products or services that are transferred internally. The fixed fee should cover a share of fixed costs of the supplying division and also provide a return on capital. For example, it can be based on the receiving division's budgeted use of the average capacity of the supplying division. Therefore if a particular receiving division plans to use 25% of a supplying division's average capacity, the division would be charged 25% of the fixed costs plus a further charge to reflect the required return on capital. The fixed fee plus the short-run marginal cost represents an estimate of long-run marginal cost.

The advantage of this approach is that transfers will be made at the marginal cost of the supplying division, and both divisions should also be able to report profits from inter-divisional trading. Furthermore, the receiving divisions are made aware, and charged for the full cost of obtaining intermediate products from other divisions, through the two components of the two-part transfer pricing system. It also stimulates planning, communication and coordination amongst the divisions because the supplying and receiving divisions must agree on the capacity requirements in order to determine the bases for the fixed fee.

If you refer back to Example 21.1 you will see that this proposal would result in a transfer price at the short-run marginal (variable) cost of £11 per unit for the intermediate product plus a fixed fee lump-sum payment of £60 000 to cover the fixed costs of the capacity allocated to producing the intermediate product. In addition, a fixed sum to reflect the required return on the capital employed would be added to the £60 000. Adopting this approach the receiving division will use the short-run variable cost to equate with its net marginal revenue and choose to purchase the optimal output level for the company as a whole (5000 units). For longer-term decisions the receiving division will made aware that the revenues must be sufficient to cover the full cost of producing the intermediate product (£11 unit variable cost plus £60 000 fixed costs plus the opportunity cost of capital). When the lump-sum fixed fee is added to the short-run transfer price you will see that the supplying division will report a profit at all output levels.

**AR** Kaplan and Cooper (1998) advocate this approach using an activity-based costing (ABC) system to calculate long-run marginal cost. The short-run element of the marginal cost consists of the cost of the supplying division's unit-level and batch-level activities assigned to the intermediate product or service. You should be able to recall from Chapter 10 that unit-level activities consume resources in proportion to the number of units of production and sales volume and typically include direct labour and material costs. Batch-level activities, such as setting-up a machine or processing a purchase order, are performed each time a batch of goods is produced. Therefore the costs of batch-related activities vary with the number of batches made. They are treated as fixed costs by traditional costing systems.

The fixed fee is added to approximate long-run marginal cost. It consists of an annual fee derived from the product-related and facility-sustaining costs. Remember from Chapter 10 that product-sustaining costs are performed to enable the production and sale of individual products (or services) and include the technical support provided for individual products or services. Facility-sustaining costs are the costs incurred to support a facility's manufacturing process and include general administrative, plant management and property costs. The fixed fee should be based on the user's planned use of the supplying division's products and facilities. For example, if a receiving division plans to use 20% of the average capacity of the supplying division and 30% of the output of a particular product then the fixed fee would be 20% of the facility-sustaining costs plus 30% of the product's sustaining costs.

The prepaid capacity would be reserved for the user paying for that capacity. Kaplan and Atkinson (1998) suggest that the approach has two desirable economic traits. First, in the short-run, transfers will take place at short-run marginal costs (which consist of unit and batch-related costs) as specified by economic theory. Second, managers will be more honest in negotiations at the capacity acquisition stage. If they overstate their estimated requirements in order to ensure adequate capacity for their own use, they will pay a higher fixed fee. Alternatively, if they understate their estimated requirements, to reduce their fixed fee, they may not have sufficient capacity for their needs as the capacity may have been reserved for others who have expressed a willingness to pay for the capacity. When capacity expectations are not realized there is a danger that capacity allocations based on expectations may no longer be assigned to their most profitable current uses. This problem can be overcome by allowing divisions to subcontract with each other so that divisions facing better opportunities can rent the excess capacity from other divisions that they have previously reserved. ●●●

# Domestic transfer pricing recommendations

This chapter has described the various approaches that can be adopted to arrive at transfer prices for transactions between different units within an organization and the circumstances where they are appropriate. The following is a summary of the recommendations that can be derived from our discussion of the different transfer pricing methods:

1. Where a competitive market exists for the intermediate product, the market price (less any adjustments to reflect additional selling and distribution and collection expenses to outside customers) should be used as the transfer price. To ensure overall company optimality it will also be necessary, where the supplying division has excess capacity, to instruct the receiving division to purchase from the supplying division the quantity that it is prepared to supply at the market price.

2. Where no external market exists for the intermediate product, transfers should be made at the long-run marginal cost of producing a product or delivering a service. The long-run marginal cost should consist of two elements – a short-run marginal cost per unit of the product or service transferred and a fixed lump-sum fee based on the receiving division's budgeted use of the average capacity of the supplying division. Ideally, the short-run marginal cost should consist of the unit and batch level activities derived from an ABC system. If a traditional costing system is used unit variable cost (including the cost of direct labour) should be used as an approximation of short-run marginal cost. The lump-sum fixed fee, assuming an ABC system, should consist of an annual fee based on the planned usage of the supplying division's products and facility-sustaining resources. If a traditional costing system is used the fixed fee should cover a share of the supplying division's fixed costs. The fixed fee should include an opportunity cost of capital in terms of a required return on the capital employed. The short-run marginal cost per unit plus the lump-sum fixed fee ensures that the receiving division incorporates the full costs

of the supplying division's resources required to produce the intermediate product and also motivates the supplying divisions because they are reimbursed for the capacity utilized.

3. Where an imperfect market for the intermediate product or service exists and a small number of products, or transactions, are involved, a negotiated transfer pricing system is likely to be the most suitable method. Here some form of external benchmark price is likely to be available to enable a meaningful bargaining process to take place between the supplying and receiving divisional managers.

4. Where cost-based transfer prices are used standard costs, and not actual costs, per unit of output should be used. If actual costs are used the supplying divisions will be able to pass on the cost of any inefficiencies to the receiving divisions. Using standard costs ensures that the cost of inefficiencies are allocated to the supplying divisions.

# International transfer pricing

So far we have concentrated on domestic transfer pricing. International transfer pricing is concerned with the prices that an organization uses to transfer products between divisions in different countries. The rise of multinational organizations introduces additional issues that must be considered when setting transfer prices.

When the supplying and the receiving divisions are located in different countries with different taxation rates, and the taxation rates in one country are much lower than those in the other, it would be in the company's interest if most of the profits were allocated to the division operating in the low taxation country. For example, consider an organization that manufactures products in Country A, which has a marginal tax rate of 25% and sells those products to country B, which has a marginal tax rate of 40%. It is in the company's best interests to locate most of its profits in country A, where the tax rate is lowest. Therefore it will wish to use the highest possible transfer price so that the receiving division operating in a country B will have higher costs and report lower profits whereas the supplying division operating in country A will be credited with higher revenues and thus report the higher profits. In many multinational organizations, the taxation issues outweigh other transfer pricing issues and the dominant consideration in the setting of transfer prices is the minimization of global taxes.

Taxation authorities in each country are aware that companies can use the transfer pricing system to manipulate the taxable profits that are declared in different countries and investigate the transfer pricing mechanisms of companies to ensure that they are not using the transfer pricing system to avoid paying local taxes. For example, in the UK the Income and Corporate Taxes Act 1988, Section 770 and the Finance Act 1998 (Chapter 36 – Schedules 16 and 17) deal with international transfer pricing issues. In an attempt to provide a world-wide consensus on the pricing of international intra-firm transactions the Organization for Economic Co-operation and Development issued a guideline statement in 1995 (OECD, Paris, 1995). This document is important because the taxation authorities in most countries have used it as the basis for regulating transfer pricing behaviour of international intra-firm transactions. The OECD guidelines are based on the arms length price principle which relates to the price that would have resulted if the prices actually used had been between two unrelated parties. The arms length principle can be implemented using one of the following methods:

1. the comparable uncontrolled price method (which uses externally verified prices of similar transactions involving unrelated prices);

2. the resale price method (which deducts a percentage from the selling price from the final product to allow for profit);

3. the cost-plus method.

The OECD guidelines state that, whenever possible the comparable uncontrolled price method should be used and if there is no market price preference should be given to cost-plus. Where the cost-plus method is used considerable variations in costing practices exist that provide some flexibility for a company to engage in opportunistic behaviour to reduce their taxation burden when determining the cost-plus transfer price.

It would appear that multinational companies should use two transfer pricing systems – one for internal purposes based on our discussion in the earlier part of this chapter and another for taxation purposes. However, evidence of two transfer pricing systems is likely to attract the attention of the taxation authorities. It is easier for companies to claim that they are not manipulating profits to evade taxes if they use the same transfer pricing method for taxation and internal purposes. For this reason, and the greater simplicity, multinational companies tend to use the same transfer pricing method for both domestic and international transfers.

Transfer pricing can also have an impact on import duties and dividend repatriations. Import duties can be minimized by transferring products at low prices to a division located in a country with high import duties. Some countries also restrict the repatriation of income and dividends. By increasing the transfer prices of goods transferred into divisions operating with these restrictions, it is possible to increase the funds repatriated without appearing to violate dividend restrictions.

# Economic theory of transfer pricing

Throughout this chapter it has been pointed out that economic theory indicates that the theoretically correct transfer price to encourage total organizational optimality is, in the absence of capacity constraints, the marginal cost of producing the intermediate product at the optimal output level for the company as a whole. No attempt has been made to explain or illustrate the theory because the explanation is fairly complex and a knowledge of the theory is not essential for you to understand the transfer pricing mechanisms described in this chapter. Indeed, it is unlikely to form part of the curriculum for many readers. However, for those readers pursuing advanced courses for the examinations of the professional accountancy bodies an understanding of economic theory is essential. Questions relating to an understanding of theory are frequently included in the examinations of the professional accountancy bodies (see for example Questions 21.17–21.22 at the end of the chapter). If you are not pursing the examinations of the professional accountancy bodies, and your curriculum does not require a detailed understanding of economic theory, you may wish to omit this section.

## SETTING TRANSFER PRICES WHEN THERE IS NO MARKET FOR THE INTERMEDIATE PRODUCT

To simplify the presentation we shall initially assume there is no market for the intermediate product. In this situation a responsibility centre may still be classified as a profit or investment centre if it has other activities which involve external sales, and is not dependent on sales revenues only from internal transfers.

Besides applying to situations where there is no market for the intermediate product, the theoretically correct transfer price (that is, the marginal cost of producing the intermediate product for the optimal output for the company as a whole) also applies to situations where there is an imperfect market for the intermediate product.

Assuming that there is no market for the intermediate product the optimal output for the company as a whole is the level at which:

$$\left(\begin{array}{c}\text{marginal cost of}\\\text{supplying division}\end{array}\right) + \left(\begin{array}{c}\text{marginal cost of}\\\text{receiving division}\end{array}\right) = \left(\begin{array}{c}\text{marginal revenue}\\\text{of receiving division}\end{array}\right) \quad (21.1)$$

This equation can be re-written as

$$\left(\begin{array}{c}\text{marginal cost of}\\\text{supplying division}\end{array}\right) = \left(\begin{array}{c}\text{marginal revenue of}\\\text{receiving division}\end{array}\right) - \left(\begin{array}{c}\text{marginal cost of}\\\text{receiving division}\end{array}\right) \quad (21.2)$$

The right hand side of equation (27.2) is known as **net marginal revenue**. This is defined as the marginal revenue derived by the receiving division from the sale of an additional unit less the marginal cost of converting the intermediate product into the final product; so the net marginal revenue therefore excludes the transfer price. The optimum output level can therefore be re-expressed as the output level where

$$\begin{array}{c}\text{marginal cost of}\\\text{the supplying division}\end{array} = \begin{array}{c}\text{net marginal revenue of}\\\text{the receiving division}\end{array}$$

This transfer pricing rule is illustrated in Exhibit 21.4.[1] To simplify the analysis, we shall assume that output can be produced and sold only in 1000-unit batches. You can see that the optimal output level where marginal cost equals net marginal revenue is 7000 units. At this output level profits for the company as a whole are maximized (see column 7). The theoretically correct transfer price for batches of 1000 units is the marginal cost of the supplying division at this output level (i.e. £4000). The receiving division will compare this transfer price with its net marginal revenue (column 6 in Exhibit 21.4) for each output level, and will be motivated to expand output up to the level where the transfer price equals its net marginal revenue (i.e. 7000 units). The transfer price of £4000 will also induce the supplying division to produce 7000 units. At an output level below 7000 units the supplying division will be motivated to expand output, because the transfer price received from the receiving division will be in excess of its marginal cost. However, the supplying division will not be motivated to produce beyond 7000 units, since the marginal cost will be in excess of the transfer price.

The profits for each division at the various output levels based on a transfer price of £4000 per batch of 1000 units are presented in Exhibit 21.5. You can see that at the optimal transfer price both divisions will arrive at the correct optimal solution. In other words, they will be motivated to operate at output levels that will maximize overall company profits. Note that overall company profits and divisional profits are maximized at an output level of 6000 or 7000 units. This is because marginal cost equals net marginal revenue when output is expanded from 6000 to 7000 units. Overall company profits therefore remain unchanged. A graphic illustration of a situation where no market exists for the intermediate product is presented in the Appendix to this chapter.

Earlier in this chapter it was pointed out that most accountants assume that marginal cost is constant per unit of output within the relevant output range. In other words, for *short-term* output decisions marginal cost is usually interpreted as being equivalent to variable cost per unit of output.

*Assume that in Exhibit 21.4 marginal cost is equivalent to variable cost and is £6000 per batch of 1000 units.* In other words, the marginal cost (column 3 in Exhibit 21.4) would be £6000 for all output levels, and the total cost column would increase in increments of £6000. The optimum output level will be at 5000 units, the level at which

**EXHIBIT 21.4**

*Optimum transfer price for an imperfect final market and no market for the intermediate product*

marginal cost equals net marginal revenue. Where marginal cost is constant, the marginal cost of producing the intermediate product at the optimum output level will be equivalent to variable cost. Therefore, in the absence of capacity constraints, the theoretically correct transfer price will be equivalent to variable cost per unit of output assuming that marginal cost is constant throughout the entire output range. Applying this rule to Exhibit 21.4, the correct transfer price is £6000 per batch.

| | Suppling division | | | | Receiving division | | |
|---|---|---|---|---|---|---|---|
| (1) | (2) | (3) | (4) | (5) | (6) | (7) |
| | | | | | Net | Overall |
| Units produced | Total cost (£) | Marginal cost (£) | Units produced | Total net revenue (£)[a] | marginal revenue (£) | company profit (loss): (5)–(2) (£) |
| 1 000 | 4 000 | 4 000 | 1 000 | 10 000 | 10 000 | 6 000 |
| 2 000 | 7 000 | 3 000 | 2 000 | 19 000 | 9 000 | 12 000 |
| 3 000 | 10 000 | 3 000 | 3 000 | 27 000 | 8 000 | 17 000 |
| 4 000 | 11 000 | 1 000 | 4 000 | 34 000 | 7 000 | 23 000 |
| 5 000 | 13 000 | 2 000 | 5 000 | 40 000 | 6 000 | 27 000 |
| 6 000 | 15 000 | 2 000 | 6 000 | 45 000 | 5 000 | 30 000 |
| 7 000 | 19 000 | 4 000 | 7 000 | 49 000 | 4 000 | 30 000 |
| 8 000 | 24 000 | 5 000 | 8 000 | 52 000 | 3 000 | 28 000 |
| 9 000 | 31 000 | 7 000 | 9 000 | 54 000 | 2 000 | 23 000 |
| 10 000 | 39 000 | 8 000 | 10 000 | 55 000 | 1 000 | 16 000 |
| 11 000 | 48 000 | 9 000 | 11 000 | 55 000 | 0 | 7 000 |
| 12 000 | 58 000 | 10 000 | 12 000 | 54 000 | –1 000 | (4 000) |

[a]Net revenue is defined as total revenue from the sale of the final product less the conversion costs incurred. It does not include the transfer price.

At a transfer price of £6000 per batch the manager of the receiving division will expand output until the transfer price is equal to its net marginal revenue. Hence the receiving division will be motivated to produce 5000 units, which is the optimal output level of the company as a whole. However, the supplying division will be indifferent to the amount it supplies to the receiving division if transfers are priced at a variable cost of £6000 per batch, because it will earn a zero contribution on each batch transferred. On the other hand, all of the total company contribution of £10 000 (£40 000 net revenue less £30 000 total cost of the supplying division) arising from inter-divisional trading will be allocated to the receiving division.

This example illustrates the conflicts between the role of a transfer price in motivating optimal decisions and its role in evaluating divisional performance. Where marginal cost is equal to variable costs, the theoretically correct transfer price that motivates optimizing behaviour results in the supplying division earning zero contribution and failing to recover any of its fixed costs on the inter-divisional transfers. Note, however, that where marginal cost is not constant the supplying division will report profits arising from inter-dimensional trading (see Exhibit 21.5).

**EXHIBIT 21.5**

*Reported profits at a transfer price of £4000 per batch*

| | Supplying division | | | | Receiving division | | |
|---|---|---|---|---|---|---|---|
| Units produced | Total cost (£) | Transfer price received (£) | Profit (loss) (£) | Total net revenue (£) | Transfer price paid (£) | Profit (loss) (£) | Total company profit (loss) (£) |
| 1 000 | 4 000 | 4 000 | 0 | 10 000 | 4 000 | 6 000 | 6 000 |
| 2 000 | 7 000 | 8 000 | 1 000 | 19 000 | 8 000 | 11 000 | 12 000 |
| 3 000 | 10 000 | 12 000 | 2 000 | 27 000 | 12 000 | 15 000 | 17 000 |
| 4 000 | 11 000 | 16 000 | 5 000 | 34 000 | 16 000 | 18 000 | 23 000 |
| 5 000 | 13 000 | 20 000 | 7 000 | 40 000 | 20 000 | 20 000 | 27 000 |
| 6 000 | 15 000 | 24 000 | 9 000 | 45 000 | 24 000 | 21 000 | 30 000 |
| 7 000 | 19 000 | 28 000 | 9 000 | 49 000 | 28 000 | 21 000 | 30 000 |
| 8 000 | 24 000 | 32 000 | 8 000 | 52 000 | 32 000 | 20 000 | 28 000 |
| 9 000 | 31 000 | 36 000 | 5 000 | 54 000 | 36 000 | 18 000 | 23 000 |
| 10 000 | 39 000 | 40 000 | 1 000 | 55 000 | 40 000 | 15 000 | 16 000 |
| 11 000 | 48 000 | 44 000 | (4 000) | 55 000 | 44 000 | 11 000 | 7 000 |
| 12 000 | 58 000 | 48 000 | (10 000) | 54 000 | 48 000 | 6 000 | (4 000) |

## IMPERFECT MARKET FOR THE INTERMEDIATE PRODUCT

Where there is an imperfect market for the intermediate product, we can apply the same approach that we used to derive transfer prices when there was no market for the intermediate product. The theoretically correct transfer price, in the absence of capacity constraints, is therefore the marginal cost of producing the intermediate product at the optimal output level for the company as a whole. Consider Exhibit 21.6.

Column 4 shows the marginal revenue that can be obtained from selling the intermediate product in the external market, and column 6 shows the net marginal revenue from converting the intermediate product into a final product and selling in the external final product market.

To determine the optimal output level, we must allocate the output of the intermediate product between sales in the intermediate product market and the final product market. The sale of the first unit in the intermediate external market gives a marginal revenue (MR) of £40 compared with a net marginal revenue (NMR) of £35 if the first unit is transferred to the receiving division and sold as a final product. Consequently, the first unit of output of the supplying division should be sold in the intermediate external market. The second unit of output should also be sold in the intermediate market because the MR of £37 is in excess of the NMR of £35 if the unit is sold as a final product. The third unit of output of the intermediate product should be sold in the final product market, since the NMR of £35 is in excess of the MR of £34 that can be obtained from selling in the intermediate market. The fourth unit of output

**EXHIBIT 21.6**

*Optimum transfer price for an imperfect intermediate market*

yields a MR of £34 if sold in the intermediate market, compared with £33.50 if sold in the final product market. Therefore the fourth unit should be allocated to the intermediate market. The remaining output of the supplying division should be allocated in a similar manner.

| | Supplying division | | | Receiving division | |
|---|---|---|---|---|---|
| (1) | (2) | (3) | (4) | (5) | (6) |
| Units produced | Total cost (£) | Marginal cost (£) | Marginal revenue (£) | Units produced | Net marginal revenue (£) |
| 1 | 19 | 19 | 40 (1) | 1 | 35.00 (3) |
| 2 | 37 | 18 | 37 (2) | 2 | 33.50 (5) |
| 3 | 54 | 17 | 34 (4) | 3 | 32.00 (6) |
| 4 | 69 | 15 | 31 (7) | 4 | 30.50 (8) |
| 5 | 83 | 14 | 28 (10) | 5 | 29.00 (9) |
| 6 | 98 | 15 | 25 (13) | 6 | 27.50 (11) |
| 7 | 114 | 16 | 22 | 7 | 26.00 (12) |
| 8 | 132 | 18 | 19 | 8 | 24.50 |
| 9 | 152 | 20 | 16 | 9 | 23.00 |
| 10 | 175 | 23 | 13 | 10 | 21.50 |
| 11 | 202 | 27 | 10 | 11 | 20.00 |
| 12 | 234 | 32 | 7 | 12 | 18.50 |
| 13 | 271 | 37 | 4 | 13 | 17.00 |

The numbers in parentheses in columns 4 and 6 of Exhibit 21.6 refer to the ranking of the 13 units of output of the supplying division on the basis of MR from the sale of the intermediate product and NMR from the sale of the final product. The allocation of the output of the supplying division based on these rankings is shown in column 3 of Exhibit 21.7.

We can now determine the optimal output for the company as a whole by comparing the marginal cost of the supplying division (column 2 of Exhibit 21.7) with the MR/NMR derived from either selling the intermediate product or converting it into a final product for sale (column 4 of Exhibit 21.7). By comparing these two columns, you will see that the optimal output is 11 units. The twelfth unit should not be produced, because the marginal cost of the supplying division is in excess of the MR/NMR that can be obtained from its most profitable use.

The theoretically correct transfer price is the marginal cost of the supplying division at the optimal output level (i.e. £27). To be more precise, the optimal output level is just in excess of 11 units, and the marginal cost will be between £27 and £27.50 at the optimal output level. In other words, if we were to graph the data in Exhibit 21.7, the marginal cost and MR/NMR schedules would intersect at a point above £27 and below £27.50. Therefore the transfer price should be set at any point between £27.01 and £27.49.

If you refer to column 4 of Exhibit 21.6, you will see that if the transfer price is set between £27.01 and £27.49 then the manager of the supplying division will choose to sell the first 5 units of the intermediate product on the external market (this is because marginal revenue is in excess of the transfer price) and transfer the remaining output to

**EXHIBIT 21.7**

*Allocation of output of supplying division between intermediate and external market*

the receiving division (this is because the transfer price is in excess of marginal revenue). You will also see that the manager of the supplying division will select an output level of 11 units based on the principle that he or she will not manufacture any units when the marginal cost is in excess of the transfer price.

If the transfer price is set between £27.01 and £27.49, the manager of the receiving division will choose to sell 6 units (see column 6 of Exhibit

| (1)<br>Output<br>(units) | (2)<br>Marginal cost<br>of supplying<br>division<br>(£) | (3)<br>Allocation per<br>ranking in<br>Exhibit 21.6 | (4)<br>Marginal revenue/<br>net marginal<br>revenue<br>(£) |
|---|---|---|---|
| 1 | 19 | Intermediate market | 40.00 |
| 2 | 18 | Intermediate market | 37.00 |
| 3 | 17 | Final market | 35.00 |
| 4 | 15 | Intermediate market | 34.00 |
| 5 | 14 | Final market | 33.50 |
| 6 | 15 | Final market | 32.00 |
| 7 | 16 | Intermediate market | 31.00 |
| 8 | 18 | Final market | 30.50 |
| 9 | 20 | Final market | 29.00 |
| 10 | 23 | Intermediate market | 28.00 |
| 11 | 27 | Final market | 27.50 |
| 12 | 32 | No allocation | 26.00 |

21.6) because NMR is in excess of the transfer price. A transfer price set within this range will therefore induce the supplying division to produce 11 units, sell 5 units to the external market and transfer 6 units to the receiving division; the receiving division will also wish to purchase 6 units from the supplying division. This is identical with the optimal output schedule for the company as a whole shown in Exhibit 21.7.

What would be the correct transfer price if the marginal cost per unit of the intermediate product was constant throughout the entire output range (i.e. marginal cost equals variable cost)? The answer is that applying the marginal cost rule will result in the transfer price being set at the variable cost per unit of the supplying division. You can see that if the variable/marginal cost of the supplying division was £29 throughout the entire output schedule in Exhibits 21.6 and 21.7 then applying the above procedure would result in the transfer price being set at £29.

A graphical illustration of how the optimal transfer price is derived when there is an imperfect market for the intermediate product is presented in Figure 21A.4 in the Appendix to this chapter.

## CAPACITY CONSTRAINTS

When there is a capacity constraint, a transfer price based on the marginal cost rule will not ensure that the optimum output levels are achieved. For example, let us assume that in Exhibits 21.6 and 21.7 the capacity of the supplying division is restricted to 6 units.

You will see from the ranking (see columns 4 and 6 of Exhibit 21.6) that the scarce capacity of 6 units should be allocated so that 3 units are transferred to the receiving division and 3 units are sold on the intermediate external market. However, column 4 of Exhibit 21.6 indicates that at a transfer price between £27.01 and £27.49 the supplying division will maximize its own profits by selling 5 units of the intermediate product in the external market and transferring 1 unit to the receiving division. Alternatively, by referring to column 6, you will see that the receiving division will maximize its own profits by taking the entire output of 6 units from the supplying division and selling them as final products.[2] This situation will also apply if the transfer price is set at the marginal cost of the supplying division at the capacity level of 6 units.

Both divisions pursuing their own best interests in isolation will not therefore arrive at the optimal company solution – that is, the sale of 3 units of the intermediate product and 3 units of the final product. A conflict occurs because what is in the best interests of a specific division is not in the best interests of the company as a whole. One way of ensuring that the optimal solution is achieved is for central headquarters to obtain information from the supplying and the receiving divisions and to work out the optimal production programme for each division. However, such an approach strikes at the very heart of the transfer price problem, because the optimal production programme has been achieved by an infringement of divisional autonomy. ●●●

## Summary

Let us now summarize our findings where there is an imperfect market for the intermediate product. Where the supplying division has no capacity constraints, the theoretically correct transfer price is the marginal cost of producing the intermediate product at the optimal output level for the company as a whole. Where unit marginal cost is constant (and thus equals variable cost) and fixed costs remain unchanged, this rule will give a transfer price equal to the variable cost per unit of the supplying division. However, when capacity constraints apply and the profit maximizing output cannot be achieved, transfer prices based on marginal cost will not ensure that optimal output is achieved, and in this situation it may be necessary for staff at the central headquarters to establish the optimum production programme for each division based on the output derived from a linear programming model. The application of linear programming to management accounting is presented in Chapter 26.

## Self-Assessment Question

You should attempt to answer this question yourself before looking up the suggested answer, which appears on pages 1131–3. If any part of your answer is incorrect, check back carefully to make sure you understand where you went wrong.

Enormous Engineering (EE) plc is a large multidivisional engineering company having interests in a wide variety of product markets. The Industrial Products Division (IPD) sells component parts to consumer appliance manufacturers, both inside and outside the company. One such part, a motor unit, it sells solely to external customers, but buys the motor itself internally from the Electric Motor Division. The Electric Motor Division (EMD) makes the motor to IPD specifications and it does not expect to be able to sell it to any other customers.

In preparing the 2001 budgets IPD estimated the number of motor units it expects to be able to sell at various prices as follows:

| Price (ex works) (£) | Quantity sold (units) |
|---|---|
| 50 | 1000 |
| 40 | 2000 |
| 35 | 3000 |
| 30 | 4000 |
| 25 | 6000 |
| 20 | 8000 |

It then sought a quotation from EMD, who offered to supply the motors at £16 each based on the following estimate:

| | (£) |
|---|---|
| Materials and bought-in parts | 2 |
| Direct labour costs | 4 |
| Factory overhead (150% of direct labour costs) | 6 |
| Total factory cost | 12 |
| Profit margin (33$\frac{1}{3}$% on factory cost) | 4 |
| Quoted price | £16 |

Factory overhead costs are fixed. All other costs are variable.

Although it considered the price quoted to be on the high side, IPD nevertheless believed that it could still sell the completed unit at a profit because it incurred costs of only £4 (material £1 and direct labour £3) on each unit made. It therefore placed an order for the coming year.

On reviewing the budget for 2001 the finance director of EE noted that the projected sales of the motor unit were considerably less than those for the previous year, which was disappointing as both divisions concerned were working well below their capacities. On making enquiries he was told by IPD that the price reduction required to sell more units would reduce rather than increase profit and that the main problem was the high price

865

charged by EMD. EMD stated that they required the high price in order to meet their target profit margin for the year, and that any reduction would erode their pricing policy.
You are required to:

(a) develop tabulations for each division, and for the company as a whole, that indicate the anticipated effect of IPD selling the motor unit at each of the prices listed,

(10 marks)

(b) (i) show the selling price which IPD should select in order to maximize its own divisional profit on the motor unit, (2 marks)

(ii) show the selling price which would be in the best interest of EE as a whole, (2 marks)

(iii) explain why this latter price is not selected by IPD, (1 mark)

(c) state:

(i) what changes you would advise making to the transfer pricing system so that it will motivate divisional managers to make better decisions in future, (5 marks)

(ii) what transfer price will ensure overall optimality in this situation. (5 marks)

(Total 25 marks)
*ICAEW Management Accounting*

## Summary

A transfer pricing system is required for meeting the following purposes:

1. to provide information that motivates divisional managers to make good economic decisions.

2. to provide information that is useful for evaluating performance of the managerial and economic performance of the divisions;

3. to intentionally move profits between divisions or locations;

4. to ensure that divisional autonomy is not undermined.

It is unlikely that a single transfer price can be established that perfectly serves all four purposes. The following five primary transfer pricing methods were described:

1. market-based transfer prices;

2. marginal cost transfer prices;

3. full cost transfer prices;

4. cost-plus a mark-up transfer prices;

5. negotiated transfer prices.

In most circumstances, where there is a perfectly competitive market for an intermediate product it is optimal for both decision-making and performance evaluation purposes to set transfer prices at the competitive market prices. If there is no external market for the intermediate product or the market is imperfect, marginal cost transfer prices will motivate both supplying and receiving divisions to operate at output levels that will maximize overall company profits. However, marginal cost transfer prices are unsatisfactory for performance evaluation because the supplying division will record losses equal to the fixed costs allocated to the intermediate product and the profits of the receiving division will be overstated. Full cost and cost-plus a mark-up transfer prices do not motivate managers to choose the optimal output levels.

To overcome the decision-making and performance evaluation conflicts that occur with the cost-based transfer pricing methods two proposals were examined – a dual-rate transfer pricing system and a two-part transfer pricing system involving a marginal cost plus a lump-sum fee. The latter method was recommended where there is no market for the intermediate product.

Attention was drawn to the fact that where divisions operate in different countries taxation implications can be a dominant influence. The aim is to set transfer prices at levels which will ensure that most of the profits are allocated to divisions operating in low taxation countries. However, taxation authorities in each country are aware that companies can use the transfer pricing system to manipulate the taxable profits that are declared in different countries and investigate the transfer pricing mechanisms of companies to ensure that they are not using the transfer pricing system to avoid paying local taxes.

Finally, the economic theory of transfer pricing was described. A more rigorous economic analysis of transfer pricing is illustrated graphically in the Appendix to this chapter.

## Key Terms and Concepts

dual-rate transfer pricing (p. 852)
cost-plus a mark-up transfer prices (p. 839)
final products (p. 838)
full cost transfer prices (p. 839)
intermediate products (p. 838)
marginal cost transfer prices (p. 839)

market-based transfer prices (p. 839)
negotiated transfer prices (p. 839)
net marginal revenue (pp. 845, 858)
perfectly competitive market (p. 841)
two-part transfer pricing system (p. 854)

## Recommended Reading

It is possible to develop transfer pricing models that are more elaborate than those introduced in this chapter. For a review of these models you should refer to Tomkins (1973). Adelberg (1986) and Charles (1985) develop some of the points considered in this chapter. Adelberg (1986) focuses on how a dual transfer pricing system can promote goal congruence, motivation and a sound performance evaluation. Charles (1985a, b) provides further illustrations of how optimal transfer prices are set. In addition to adopting an approach similar to the method explained in this chapter, he also shows how optimal transfer prices can be set using differential calculus. Both articles are less than four pages, and you should find them useful for revision. For a discussion of multinational transfer pricing see Chapters 4 and 5 of Emmanuel and Mehafdi (1994). Finally, you should refer to Emmanuel and Mehafdi (1994) if you wish to consult a book that focuses entirely on transfer pricing.

# Appendix 21.1: Economic analysis of transfer pricing

**AR** It is difficult to discuss the economic analysis of transfer pricing in purely verbal terms without some loss of rigour. To overcome this difficulty, a number of theoretical transfer pricing models applicable to different situations are presented in diagrammatic form in this Appendix.[3] These are based upon principles first suggested by Hirshleifer (1956) and Gould (1964). For simplicity, we shall assume that the company consists of only two divisions: a supplying division and a receiving division. The theoretically correct transfer price that will induce divisions to arrive at the optimum output for the company as a whole, when operating in their own best interests, is presented in the foregoing analysis.

## PERFECT EXTERNAL MARKET FOR THE INTERMEDIATE PRODUCT

In our previous discussion in the main body of the chapter we established that where a perfect market for an intermediate product exists, the correct transfer price is the intermediate external market price. This situation is presented in Figure 21A.1.

**FIGURE 21A.1** *Perfect external market for the intermediate product.*

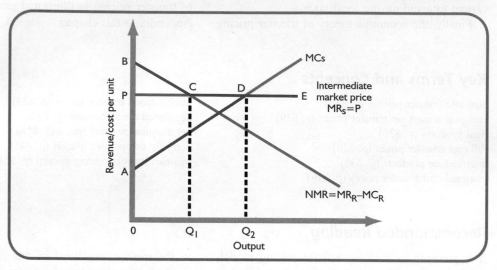

The external market price for the intermediate product is OP, and, because the external market for the intermediate product is assumed to be perfect, the marginal revenue for the intermediate product ($MR_S$) is constant and is represented by the horizontal line PE. The NMR line refers to the net marginal revenue of the receiving division, and consists of the marginal revenue of the receiving division ($MR_R$) less the marginal conversion cost ($MC_R$) but excludes the transfer price paid to the supplying division.

The transfer price will be set equal to the market price of the intermediate product on the external perfect market at OP. At this transfer price the receiving division will require quantity $OQ_1$ (this is where NMR is equal to the transfer price) and will be indifferent as to whether it obtains this supply from the supplying division or the external market. The supplying division will also be indifferent as to whether it sells this quantity to the receiving division or the external market. However, the supplying division will wish to sell a total quantity of $OQ_2$, and will sell an additional quantity $Q_1Q_2$ externally if it supplies $OQ_1$ internally. (Total quantity $OQ_2$ is where the marginal cost of the supplying division ($MC_S$) is equal to its marginal revenue ($MR_S$).) Note that the NMR schedule for the company as a whole is BCDE, and the most profitable output is where it intersects the company's marginal cost schedule ADE at point D. This requires an output of $OQ_2$, which is identical with the amount produced by the supplying division.

A transfer price of OP, which is equal to the market price of the intermediate product, will mean that the divisions will achieve the total company's optimal output, and it will also allow them to deal with each other as they please.

## A PERFECT MARKET FOR THE INTERMEDIATE PRODUCT AND THE PRESENT OF SELLING COSTS

Gould (1964) considers the situation where a company incurs transportation and selling costs such that there might be a difference between the net price received for the sale of the intermediate product externally and the price at which the product is

**FIGURE 21A.2** *Perfect external market for the intermediate product.*

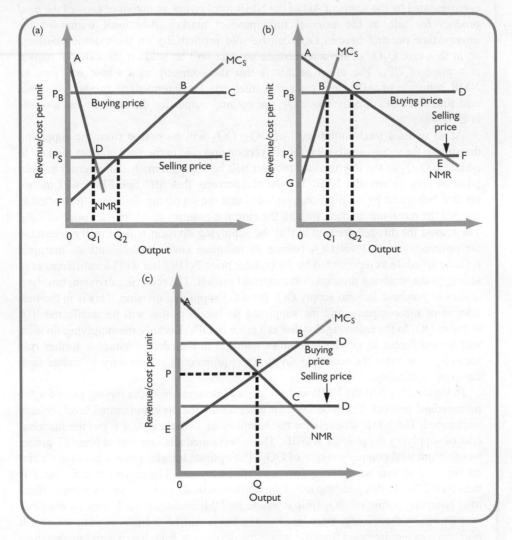

purchased on the external market. Also, if the intermediate product is transferred internally, some selling costs might be avoided. Under these circumstances an optimal production policy may not be achieved if the divisions are allowed to ignore each other's request for the transfer of intermediate products.

Figure 21A.2 contains information identical with that presented in Figure 21A.1, with the exception that the market price line is replaced by two lines – a buying price and a selling price. Figure 21A.2(a) represents the situation where the NMR and $MC_S$ lines intersect below the net selling price for the intermediate product. You will see that it is cheaper for the company to manufacture the intermediate product internally so long as the marginal cost of the supplying division ($MC_S$) is below the buying price of the intermediate product on the external market. Beyond B it is cheaper to purchase the intermediate product on the external market. The company as a whole therefore faces a marginal cost schedule equal to FBC.

So long as the company can obtain a larger marginal revenue by converting the intermediate product into the final product, it should do so. This situation applies so long as the NMR line lies above the net selling price for the intermediate product. This is represented by the segment AD of the NMR line, giving an output of $OQ_1$ of the *final* product for sale in the external final product market. Additional output of the intermediate product beyond $OQ_1$ can be sold profitability on the external markets; so in this case $Q_1Q_2$ of the intermediate product will be sold on the external market at a price of $OP_s$. The effect of this is that the company as a whole will face an NMR schedule of ADE, and since this intersects the intermediate product marginal cost function FBC directly above $Q_2$, the optimal output for the company as a whole is $OQ_2$.

At an optimal total output level of $OQ_2$, $OQ_1$ will be passed from the supplying division to the receiving division for conversion and sale in the final product market. In addition, $Q_1Q_2$ of the intermediate product will be sold externally. An internal transfer price of $OP_S$ (where the NMR line ADE intersects that MC line FBC) will induce optimal behaviour by the divisions, provided that the supplying division is instructed to provide the receiving division with all the output it requires at the transfer price of $OP_S$. The reason for this requirement is that the supplying division will correctly determine the optimum output level $OQ_2$ (where its marginal cost schedule cuts its marginal revenue schedule as represented by the transfer price $P_SDE$), but will be indifferent as to selling to the receiving division or the external market. The receiving division, however, wishes to purchase its total supply $OQ_1$ from the supplying division. This is in the best interest of the company, and the supplying division's profits will be unaffected if it supplies $OQ_1$ to the receiving division at a price of $OP_S$. Because the supplying division will be indifferent as to who it supplies with the intermediate product, a further rule requiring it to meet the receiving division's requirements is necessary to ensure total company optimality.

In Figure 21A.2(b) the NMR and $MC_S$ lines intersect above the buying price for the intermediate product. The procedure for determining the optimum output level remains unchanged. The NMR schedule for the company as a whole is ACEF and the marginal cost of supplying the product is GBD. These two schedules intersect at point C, giving an optimum total company output of $OQ_2$. The optimal transfer price is given at a point on the vertical axis where these two schedules intersect. The correct transfer price is therefore $OP_B$. At this price the receiving division will also wish to produce the optimal total company output of $OQ_2$ (this is where its NMR schedule ACE cuts its marginal cost shown by the transfer price line $P_BCD$), but it will be indifferent as to whether it purchases its requirements from the supplying division or from the external market. The supplying division will want to produce $OQ_1$ to sell to the receiving division at the transfer price $OP_B$, and this will be in the best interest of the company, since the marginal cost of production is lower than the external purchase price. Because the receiving division is indifferent as to whether it purchases the intermediate product from the supplying division or from the external market, the receiving division must be instructed to purchase from the supplying division the quantity that it is prepared to supply at the transfer price $OP_B$. This will be quantity $OQ_1$, and the receiving division will then obtain its additional supplies (i.e. $Q_1Q_2$) on the external market.

In Figure 21A.2(c) the NMR and $MC_S$ lines intersect between the buying and selling price for the intermediate product. Here the NMR and the marginal cost of supplying intersect at point F, giving an optimal output for the total company of OQ. The transfer price is determined at the point on the vertical axis where these two points intersect. The correct transfer price is therefore OP. At this price there is no need for additional instructions to be given to the supplying or the receiving division about dealing with each other, since each division will prefer to deal internally, and no sales or purchases will be made in the external intermediate product market.

**FIGURE 21A.3** *No external market for the intermediate product.*

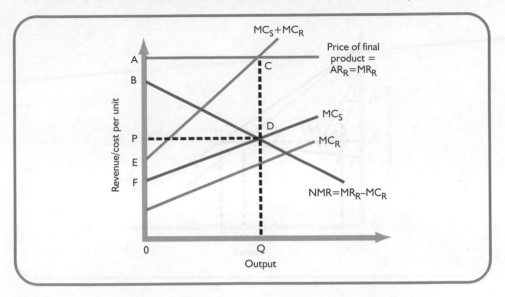

## NO EXTERNAL MARKET FOR THE INTERMEDIATE PRODUCT AND A PERFECT MARKET FOR THE FINAL PRODUCT

This situation is illustrated in Figure 21A.3. The marginal costs of the supplying and receiving divisions are represented by $MC_S$ and $MC_R$. The marginal cost schedule for the company as a whole is represented by $MC_S + MC_R$. The marginal revenue function for the final product is also shown, and is presented by $MR_R$. As it is assumed that the market for the final product is perfect, the marginal revenue line is horizontal and equal to the average revenue. The net marginal revenue for the receiving division is represented by NMR, and is ascertained by deducting the marginal cost of the receiving division (excluding the cost of purchasing from the supplying division) from the marginal revenue of the receiving division.

The optimum output level for the company as a whole is where the marginal revenue for the company, shown by the horizontal $MR_R$ line, intersects the marginal cost line for the whole company, represented by $MC_S + MC_R$. This indicates an optimum output of OQ, and the maximum profit that results is the area ACE. The transfer price at which the supplying division wishes to sell OQ to the receiving division and also the price at which the receiving division wishes to purchase this amount is determined at the point on the vertical axis where the $MC_S$ and the NMR lines intersect. The correct transfer price is therefore OP (i.e. the marginal cost of the supplying division at the optimum output level). The supplying division will view the horizontal transfer price line PD as its marginal revenue schedule, and will wish to produce OQ for transfer to the receiving division. The receiving division will want to purchase for conversion to the final product the quantity of output at which the transfer price will be equal to its net marginal revenue. This is also quantity OQ. So both divisions will want quantity OQ to be transferred between them, and the sum of their respective profits will be equal to the total company's maximum profit. The supplying division's profit is represented by the area FDP and the receiving division's profit by the area BDP, which together equal BDF; the area BDF is equal to the area ACE that represents total company profits.

**FIGURE 21A.4** *Imperfect market for the intermediate product.*

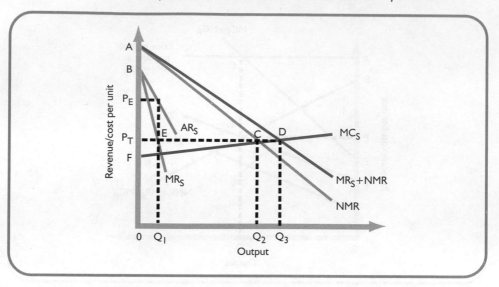

## IMPERFECT MARKET FOR THE INTERMEDIATE PRODUCT

In an imperfect market the quantity of the intermediate product that is sold externally will influence the market price, and the marginal revenue for the sale of the intermediate product ($MR_S$) will decline as output increases (Figure 21A.4). The marginal cost and marginal revenue schedules for the company as a whole are represented by the $MC_S$ and $MR_S + NMR$ schedules. The latter represents the marginal revenue of the supplying division plus the net marginal revenue of the receiving division. The optimum output for the company as a whole will therefore occur where the $MC_S$ and $MR_S + NMR$ schedules intersect; that is, at level $OQ_3$.

The optimal transfer price that induces the supplying and receiving divisions to operate in this output level is shown by the point on the vertical axis where the $MC_S$ and the $MR_S + NMR$ schedules intersect. The correct transfer price is therefore $OP_T$ (i.e. the MC of the supplying division at the optimum output level). At this price the receiving division will view the horizontal line $P_TD$ as its marginal cost of supply and require output $OQ_2$ from the supplying division. At this point its NMR schedule intersects the horizontal line $P_TD$. The supplying division will face a marginal revenue schedule equal to BED (it will prefer to sell at a transfer price $P_T$ beyond point E, since this is in excess of the marginal revenue line below E). This means that the supplying division will prefer to sell $OQ_1$ of the intermediate product on the external market at a price $OP_E$ (the selling price at which its marginal revenue line is equal to or above E). In addition, the supplying division will wish to supply $Q_1Q_3$ at the transfer price $OP_T$ to the receiving division. This will give a total output by the supplying division of $OQ_3$ (i.e. the optimal output for the company as a whole), being the quantity of output at which its marginal cost $MC_S$ is equal to its marginal revenue BED. This is consistent with the receiving division's demand for $OQ_2$, because $OQ_1$ is equal to $Q_2Q_3$. Therefore, $OQ_2$ equals $Q_1Q_3$. ●●●

## Key Examination Points

When discussing a transfer pricing system, you should indicate that the proposed system should motivate managers to make correct decisions, provide a reasonable measure of performance and ensure that divisional autonomy is not undermined. It is not possible for a single transfer price to meet all three of these requirements. Most examination questions require you to recommend an optimal transfer price. It is particularly important that you understand how optimal transfer prices should be set when there is an imperfect market or no market for the intermediate product.

## Questions

*Indicates that a suggested solution is to be found in the *Students' Manual.*

### 21.1* Advanced
The production director of a company is concerned with the problem of measuring the efficiency of process managers. In the production department there are six processes and all products processed pass through a combination of these processes. One specific area of investigation is the measurement of output values which involves the use of transfer prices.

You have been asked by the production director to tabulate the advantages and disadvantages of using each of the following systems of transfer pricing as related to process costing:
(a)  absorption cost;
(b)  marginal cost;
(c)  cost plus profit;
(d)  standard cost.                        (20 marks)
*CIMA P1 Cost Accounting 2*

### 21.2* Advanced
It has been argued that full cost is an inappropriate basis for setting transfer prices. Outline the objections which can be levied at this basis.   (9 marks)
*ACCA Level 2 Management Accounting*

### 21.3 Advanced
(a)  Outline and discuss the main objectives of a transfer pricing system.          (5 marks)
(b)  Consider the advantages and disadvantages of
     (i)   market price-based transfer prices; and
     (ii)  cost-based transfer prices.
     Outline the main variants that exist under each heading.                         (9 marks)
(c)  Discuss the relevance of linear programming to the setting of transfer prices.   (3 marks)
                                  (Total 17 marks)
*ACCA Level 2 Management Accounting*

### 21.4* Advanced
(a)  Transfers between processes in a manufacturing company can be made at (i) cost or (ii) sales value at the point of transfer.
     Discuss how each of the above methods might be compatible with the operation of a responsibility accounting system.   (8 marks)
(b)  Shadow prices (net opportunity costs or dual prices) may be used in the setting of transfer prices between divisions in a group of companies, where the intermediate products being transferred are in short supply.
     Explain why the transfer prices thus calculated are more likely to be favoured by the management of the divisions supplying the intermediate products rather than the management of the divisions receiving the intermediate products.            (9 marks)
                                  (Total 17 marks)
*ACCA Level 2 Management Accounting*

### 21.5 Advanced
Exel Division is part of the Supeer Group. It produces a basic fabric which is then converted in other divisions within the group. The fabric is also produced in other divisions within the Supeer Group and a limited quantity can be purchased from outside the group. The fabric is currently charged out by Exel Division at total actual cost plus 20% profit mark-up.
(a)  Explain why the current transfer pricing method used by Exel Division is unlikely to lead to:
     (i)   maximization of group profit and
     (ii)  effective divisional performance measurement.                          (6 marks)
(b)  If the supply of basic fabric is insufficient to meet the needs of the divisions who convert it for sale outside the group, explain a procedure

which should lead to a transfer pricing and deployment policy for the basic fabric for group profit maximization. (6 marks)

(c) Show how the procedure explained in (b) may be in conflict with other objectives of transfer pricing and suggest how this conflict may be overcome. (5 marks)

(Total 17 marks)

*ACCA Level 2 – Cost and Management Accounting II*

### 21.6 Advanced: Discussion of transfer price where there is an external market for the intermediate product

Fabri Division is part of the Multo Group. Fabri Division produces a single product for which it has an external market which utilizes 70% of its production capacity. Gini Division, which is also part of the Multo Group requires units of the product available from Fabri Division which it will then convert and sell to an external customer. Gini Division's requirements are equal to 50% of Fabri Division's production capacity. Gini Division has a potential source of supply from outside the Multo Group. It is not yet known if this source is willing to supply on the basis of (i) only supplying *all* of Gini Division's requirements or (ii) supplying any part of Gini Division's requirements as requested.

(a) Discuss the transfer pricing method by which Fabri Division should offer to transfer its product to Gini Division in order that group profit maximization is likely to follow.

You may illustrate your answer with figures of your choice. (14 marks)

(b) Explain ways in which (i) the degree of divisional autonomy allowed and (ii) the divisional performance measure in use by Multo Group may affect the transfer pricing policy of Fabri Division. (6 marks)

(Total 20 marks)

*ACCA Level 2 Cost and Management Accounting II*

### 21.7 Advanced

(a) Spiro Division is part of a vertically integrated group of divisions allocated in one country. All divisions sell externally and also transfer goods to other divisions within the group. Spiro Division performance is measured using profit before tax as a performance measure.

(i) Prepare an outline statement which shows the costs and revenue elements

which should be included in the calculation of divisional profit before tax. (4 marks)

(ii) The degree of autonomy which is allowed to divisions may affect the absolute value of profit reported.

Discuss the statement in relation to Spiro Division. (6 marks)

(b) Discuss the pricing basis on which divisions should offer to transfer goods in order that corporate profit maximising decisions should take place. (5 marks)

(Total 15 marks)

*ACCA Paper 9 Information for Control and Decision Making*

### 21.8 Advanced

(a) The transfer pricing method used for the transfer of an intermediate product between two divisions in a group has been agreed at standard cost plus 30% profit markup. The transfer price may be altered after taking into consideration the planning and operational variance analysis at the transferor division.

Discuss the acceptability of this transfer pricing method to the transferor and transferee divisions. (5 marks)

(b) Division A has an external market for product X which fully utilises its production capacity.

Explain the circumstances in which division A should be willing to transfer product X to division B of the same group at a price which is less than the existing market price. (5 marks)

(c) An intermediate product which is converted in divisions L, M and N of a group is available in limited quantities from other divisions within the group and from an external source. The total available quantity of the intermediate product is insufficient to satisfy demand.

Explain the procedure which should lead to a transfer pricing and deployment policy resulting in group profit maximisation. (5 marks)

(Total 15 marks)

*ACCA Paper 9 Information for Control and Decision Making*

### 21.9* Advanced

P plc is a multi-national conglomerate company with manufacturing divisions, trading in numerous countries across various continents. Trade takes place between a number of the divisions in different countries, with partly-completed products being transferred between them. Where a transfer takes place between divisions trading in different countries, it is the policy of the Board of P plc to determine centrally the appropriate transfer price without reference to the divisional managers concerned. The Board of plc justifies this policy to divisional managers on the grounds that its objective is to maximise the conglomerate's post-tax profits and that the global position can be monitored effectively only from the Head Office.

Requirements:

(a) Explain and critically appraise the possible reasoning behind P plc's policy of centrally determining transfer prices for goods traded between divisions operating in different countries. (10 marks)

(b) Discuss the ethical implications of P plc's policy of imposing transfer prices on its overseas divisions in order to maximise post-tax profits. (10 marks)
(Total 20 marks)
*CIMA Stage 4 Strategic Management Accounting and Marketing*

### 21.10* Advanced: Calculating the effects of a transfer pricing system on divisional and company profits

Division A of a large divisionalized organization manufactures a single standardized product. Some of the output is sold externally whilst the remainder is transferred to Division B where it is a sub-assembly in the manufacture of that division's product. The unit costs of Division A's product are as follows:

|  | (£) |
|---|---|
| Direct material | 4 |
| Direct labour | 2 |
| Direct expense | 2 |
| Variable manufacturing overheads | 2 |
| Fixed manufacturing overheads | 4 |
| Selling and packing expense – variable | 1 |
|  | 15 |

Annually 10 000 units of the product are sold externally at the standard price of £30.

In addition to the external sales, 5000 units are transferred annually to Division B at an internal transfer charge of £29 per unit. This transfer price is obtained by deducting variable selling and pack-

ing expense from the external price since this expense is not incurred for internal transfers.

Division B incorporates the transferred-in goods into a more advanced product. The unit costs of this product are as follows:

|  | (£) |
|---|---|
| Transferred-in item (from Division A) | 29 |
| Direct material and components | 23 |
| Direct labour | 3 |
| Variable overheads | 12 |
| Fixed overheads | 12 |
| Selling and packing expense – variable | 1 |
|  | 80 |

Division B's manager disagrees with the basis used to set the transfer price. He argues that the transfers should be made at variable cost plus an agreed (minimal) mark-up since he claims that his division is taking output that Division A would be unable to sell at the price of £30.

Partly because of this disagreement, a study of the relationship between selling price and demand has recently been made for each division by the company's sales director. The resulting report contains the following table:

Customer demand at various selling prices:

| Division A |  |  |  |
|---|---|---|---|
| Selling price | £20 | £30 | £40 |
| Demand | 15 000 | 10 000 | 5000 |
| Division B |  |  |  |
| Selling price | £80 | £90 | £100 |
| Demand | 7 200 | 5 000 | 2800 |

The manager of Division B claims that this study supports his case. He suggests that a transfer price of £12 would give Division A a reasonable contribution to its fixed overheads while allowing Division B to earn a reasonable profit. He also believes that it would lead to an increase of output and an improvement in the overall level of company profits.

You are required:
(a) to calculate the effect that the transfer pricing system has had on the company's profits, and (16 marks)
(b) to establish the likely effect on profits of adopting the suggestion by the manager of Division B of a transfer price of £12.
(6 marks)
(Total 22 marks)

*ACCA Level 2 Management Accounting*

## 21.11 Advanced: Resolving a transfer price conflict

Alton division (A) and Birmingham division (B) are two manufacturing divisions of Conglom plc. Both of these divisions make a single standardized product; A makes product I and B makes product J. Every unit of J requires one unit of I. The required input of I is normally purchased from division A but sometimes it is purchased from an outside source.

The following table gives details of selling price and cost for each product:

|  | Product I (£) | Product J (£) |
|---|---|---|
| Established selling price | 30 | 50 |
| Variable costs |  |  |
| Direct material | 8 | 5 |
| Transfers from A | — | 30 |
| Direct labour | 5 | 3 |
| Variable overhead | 2 | 2 |
|  | 15 | 40 |
| Divisional fixed cost (per annum) | £500 000 | £225 000 |
| Annual outside demand with current selling prices (units) | 100 000 | 25 000 |
| Capacity of plant (units) | 130 000 | 30 000 |
| Investment in division | £6 625 000 | £1 250 000 |

Division B is currently achieving a rate of return well below the target set by the central office. Its manager blames this situation on the high transfer price of product I. Division A charges division B for the transfers of I at the outside supply price of £30. The manager of division A claims that this is appropriate since this is the price 'determined by market forces'. The manager of B has consistently argued that intra group transfers should be charged at a lower price based on the costs of the producing division plus a 'reasonable' mark-up.

The board of Conglom plc is concerned about B's low rate of return and the divisional manager has been asked to submit proposals for improving the situation. The board has now received a report from B's manager in which he asks the board to intervene to reduce the transfer price charged for product I. The manager of B also informs the board that he is considering the possibility of opening a branch office in rented premises in a nearby town, which should enlarge the market for product J by 5000 units per year at the existing price. He estimates that the branch office establishment costs would be £50 000 per annum.

You have been asked to write a report advising the board on the response that it should make to the plans and proposals put forward by the manager of division B. Incorporate in your report a calculation of the rates of return currently being earned on the capital employed by each division and the changes to these that should follow from an implementation of any proposals that you would recommend.

(22 marks)

*ACCA Level 2 Management Accounting*

## 21.12* Advanced: Make or buy decision and intercompany trading

Companies RP, RR, RS and RT are members of a group. RP wishes to buy an electronic control system for its factory and, in accordance with group policy, must obtain quotations from companies inside and outside of the group.

From outside of the group the following quotations are received:

Company A quoted £33 200.
Company B quoted £35 000 but would buy a special unit from RS for £13 000. To make this unit, however, RS would need to buy parts from RR at a price of £7500.

The inside quotation was from RS whose price was £48 000. This would require RS buying parts from RR at a price of £8000 and units from RT at a price of £30 000. However, RT would need to buy parts from RR at a price of £11 000.

Additional data are as follows:

(1) RR is extremely busy with work outside the group and has quoted current market prices for all its products.

(2) RS costs for the RP contract, including purchases from RR and RT, total £42 000. For the Company B contract it expects a profit of 25% on the cost of its own work.

(3) RT prices provide for a 20% profit margin on total costs.

(4) The variable costs of the group companies in respect of the work under consideration are:
RR: 20% of selling price
RS: 70% of own cost (excluding purchases from other group companies)

RT: 65% of own cost (excluding purchases from other group companies)

You are required, from a group point of view, to:
(a) recommend, with appropriate calculations, whether the contract should be placed with RS or Company A or Company B;
(b) state briefly *two* assumptions you have made in arriving at your recommendations.

(30 marks)

*CIMA P3 Management Accounting*

## 21.13 Advanced: Apportionment of company profit to various departments

AB Limited which buys and sells machinery has three departments:

New machines (manager, Newman)
Second-hand machines (manager, Handley)
Repair workshops (manager, Walker)

In selling new machines Newman is often asked to accept an old machine in part exchange. In such cases the old machine is disposed of by Handley.

The workshops do work both for outside customers and also for the other two departments. Walker charges his outside customers for materials at cost and for labour time at £8 per hour. This £8 is made up as follows:

**Per hour**
**(£)**

| | | |
|---|---|---|
| Fixed costs | 2.00 | (10 000 budgeted |
| Variable costs | 4.50 | hours per |
| Profit | 1.50 | annum) |
| | £8.00 | |

AB Limited wishes to go over to a profit centre basis of calculations so as to be able to reward its three managers according to their results. It wishes to assess the situation in the context of the following transaction:

Newman sold to PQ Limited a new machine at list price of £16 000, the cost of which to AB Limited was £12 000.

To make the sale, however, Newman had to allow PQ Limited £5000 for its old machine in part exchange.

PQ Limited's old machine was in need of repair before it could be re-sold and Newman and Handley were agreed in their estimate of those repairs as £50 in materials and 100 hours of workshops labour

time. That estimate was proved to be correct when the workshops undertook the repair.

At the time of taking PQ Limited's machine in part exchange Handley would have been able to buy a similar machine from other dealers for £3700 without the need for any repair. When the machine had been repaired he sold it to ST Limited for £4200.

You are required to:
(a) show how you would calculate the profit contribution for each of the three departments from the above transaction.
(b) re-calculate the profit contribution for each department if there were the following alternative changes of circumstances:
   (i) When the workshops came to repair the old machine they found that they required an extra 50 hours of labour time because of a fault not previously noticed.
   (ii) Before deciding on the figure he would allow PQ Limited for their old machine, Newman asks Walker to estimate the cost of repairs. This estimate is £50 in materials and 100 hours of workshops labour time. When, however, workshops came to repair the old machine, it took them 50% longer than estimated.
(c) recommend briefly how to deal with the following situations in the context of profit centre calculation:
   (i) The manufacturer of the new machines allows AB Limited £200 per machine for which AB Limited undertakes to do all warranty repairs. Over the year the total cost of repairs under warranty exceeds the amount allowed by the supplier.
   (ii) Although 4000 hours of workshop time were budgeted to be reserved for the other two departments, their load increases over the year by 20% (at standard efficiency). The load from outside customers, however, stays as budgeted.

(25 marks)

*CIMA P3 Management Accounting*

## 21.14* Advanced: Market based transfer prices

A group has two companies –

K Ltd, which is operating at just above 50% capacity, and

L Ltd, which is operating at full capacity (7000 production hours).

L Ltd produces two products, X and Y, using the same labour force for each product. For the next year its budgeted capacity involves a commitment to the sale of 3000 kg of Y, the remainder of its capacity being used on X.

Direct costs of these two products are:

|  | X (£ per kg) | Y (£ per kg) |
|---|---|---|
| Direct materials | 18 | 14 |
| Direct wages | 15 | 10 |
|  | (1 production hour) | ($\frac{2}{3}$ production hour) |

The company's overhead is £126 000 per annum relating to X and Y in proportion to their direct wages. At full capacity, £70 000 of this overhead is variable. L Ltd prices its products with a 60% mark-up on its total costs.

For the coming year, K Ltd wishes to buy from L Ltd 2000 kg of product X which it proposes to adapt and sell, as product Z, for £100 per kg. The direct costs of adaptation are £15 per kg. K Ltd's total fixed costs will not change, but variable overhead of £2 per kg will be incurred.

You are required to recommend, as group management accountant,

(a) at what range of transfer prices, if at all, 2000 kg of product X should be sold to K Ltd;

(14 marks)

(b) what other points should be borne in mind when making any recommendations about transfer prices in the above circumstances.

(6 marks)

(Total 20 marks)

*CIMA Stage 4 Management Accounting – Decision Making*

### 21.15 Advanced: Computation of three different transfer prices and the extent to which each price encourages goal congruence

English Allied Traders plc has a wide range of manufacturing activities, principally within the UK. The company operates on the divisionalized basis with each division being responsible for its own manufacturing, sales and marketing, and working capital management. Divisional chief executives are expected to achieve a target 20% return on sales.

A disagreement has arisen between two divisions which operate on adjacent sites. The Office Products Division (OPD) has the opportunity to manufacture a printer using a new linear motor which has recently been developed by the Electric Motor Division (EMD). Currently there is no other source of supply for an equivalent motor in the required quantity of 30 000 units a year, although a foreign manufacturer has offered to supply up to 10 000 units in the coming year at a price of £9 each. EMD's current selling price for the motor is £12. Although EMD's production line for this motor is currently operating at only 50% of its capacity, sales are encouraging and EMD confidently expects to sell 100 000 units in 2001, and its maximum output of 120 000 units in 2002.

EMD has offered to supply OPD's requirements for 2001 at a transfer price equal to the normal selling price, less the variable selling and distribution costs that it would not incur on this internal order. OPD responded by offering an alternative transfer price of the standard variable manufacturing cost plus a 20% profit margin. The two divisions have been unable to agree, so the corporate operations director has suggested a third transfer price equal to the standard full manufacturing cost plus 15%. However, neither divisional chief executive regards such a price as fair.

EMD's 2001 budget for the production and sale of motors, based on its standard costs for the forecast 100 000 units sales, but excluding the possible sales to OPD, is as follows:

|  | (£000) |
|---|---|
| Sales Revenue (100 000 units at £12.00 each) | 1200 |
| Direct Manufacturing Costs |  |
| Bought-in materials | 360 |
| Labour | 230 |
| Packaging | 40 |
| Indirect Manufacturing Costs |  |
| Variable overheads | 10 |
| Line production managers | 30 |
| Depreciation |  |
| Capital equipment | 150 |
| Capitalized development costs | 60 |
| Total manufacturing costs | 880 |
| Sales and Distribution Costs |  |
| Salaries of sales force | 50 |
| Carriage | 20 |
| General Overhead | 50 |
| Total costs | 1000 |
| Profit | 200 |

Notes

(1) The costs of the sales force and indirect production staff are not expected to increase up to the current production capacity.

(2) General overhead includes allocations of divisional administrative expenses and corporate charges of £20 000 specifically related to this product.

(3) Depreciation for all assets is charged on a straight line basis using a five year life and no residual value.

(4) Carriage is provided by an outside contractor.

Requirements

(a) Calculate each of the three proposed transfer prices and comment on how each might affect the willingness of EMD's chief executive to engage in inter-divisional trade. (10 marks)

(b) Outline an alternative method of setting transfer prices which you consider to be appropriate for this situation, and explain why it is an improvement on the other proposals.

(5 marks)
(Total 15 marks)
*ICAEW P2 Management Accounting and Financial Management 2*

## 21.16* Advanced: Computation of divisional profits using market based transfer prices and a discussion of market based transfer prices where market imperfections exist

L Ltd and M Ltd are subsidiaries of the same group of companies.

L Ltd produces a branded product sold in drums at a price of £20 per drum.

Its direct product costs per drum are:

– Raw material from M Ltd: At a transfer price of £9 for 25 litres.

– Other products and services from outside the group: At a cost of £3.

L Ltd's fixed costs are £40 000 per month. These costs include process labour whose costs will not alter until L Ltd's output reaches twice its present level.

A market research study has indicated that L Ltd's market could increase by 80% in volume if it were to reduce its price by 20%.

M Ltd produces a fairly basic product which can be converted into a wide range of end products. It sells one third of its output to L Ltd and the remainder to customers outside the group.

M Ltd's production capacity is 1000 kilolitres per month, but competition is keen and it budgets to sell no more than 750 kilolitres per month for the year ending 31 December.

Its variable costs are £200 per kilolitre and its fixed costs are £60 000 per month.

The current policy of the group is to use market prices, where known, as the transfer price between its subsidiaries. This is the basis of the transfer price between M Ltd and L Ltd.

You are required

(a) to calculate the monthly profit position for each of L Ltd and M Ltd if the sales of L Ltd are
   (i) at their present level, and
   (ii) at the higher potential level indicated by the market research, subject to a cut in price of 20%;

(10 marks)

(b) (i) to explain why the use of a market price as the transfer price produces difficulties under the conditions outlined in (a) (ii) above; (3 marks)

   (ii) to explain briefly, as chief accountant of the group, what factors you would consider in arriving at a proposal to overcome these difficulties; (7 marks)

(c) to recommend, with supporting calculations, what transfer prices you would propose.

(5 marks)
(Total 25 marks)
*CIMA Stage 4 Management Accounting– Decision Making*

## 21.17* Advanced: Setting an optimal transfer price when there is an intermediate imperfect market

(a) Memphis plc is a multi-division firm operating in a wide range of activities. One of its divisions, Division A, produces a semi-finished product Alpha, which can be sold in an outside market at a price $P_S$. It can also be sold to Division B, which can use it in manufacturing its finished product Beta. The outside market in which Alpha is traded is perfect in all respects, except in so far as the buying division would have to incur transportation costs, which are included in the buying price $P_B$ if it buys Alpha in the open market. The finished product of Division B, Beta, can be sold only in another perfect external market. Assume also that the marginal cost of each division is a rising linear function of output, and that the goal for Memphis plc is to maximize its total profits.

You are required to explain how the optimal transfer price for Alpha should be derived in these circumstances, and to outline any rules which should be stipulated by the management of Memphis plc to ensure attaining its goal of profit maximization.

(15 marks)

(b) Assume that Divisions A and B as above, except (i) that Division A is a monopolist facing a downward sloping demand curve and (ii) that it can sell Alpha externally at a price higher than the price it charges internally to Division B. Relevant information about both divisions is given below.

| Output of Alpha (units) | Total cost of Alpha (£000) | Revenue from outside selling of Alpha (£000) | Net marginal revenue of Beta (£000) |
|---|---|---|---|
| 60 | 112 | 315 | 47 |
| 70 | 140 | 350 | 45 |
| 80 | 170 | 380 | 43 |
| 90 | 203 | 405 | 40 |
| 100 | 238 | 425 | 36 |
| 110 | 275 | 440 | 33 |
| 120 | 315 | 450 | 30 |
| 130 | 359 | 455 | 25 |

You are required to calculate the optimal transfer price for Alpha and the optimal activity level for each division.

(10 marks)
(Total 25 marks)
*ICAEW Management Accounting*

### 21.18 Advanced: Optimal output and transfer price where the market for the intermediate product is imperfect

Engcorp and Flotilla are UK divisions of Griffin plc, a multinational company. Both divisions have a wide range of activities. You are an accountant employed by Griffin plc and the Finance Director has asked you to investigate a transfer pricing problem.

Engcorp makes an engine, the Z80, which it has been selling to external customers at £1350 per unit. Flotilla wanted to buy Z80 engines to use in its own production of dories; each dory requires one engine. Engcorp would only sell if Flotilla paid £1350 per unit. The managing director of Engcorp commented:

'We have developed a good market for this engine and £1350 is the current market price.

Just because Flotilla is not efficient enough to make a profit is no reason for us to give a subsidy.'

Flotilla has now found that engines suitable for its purpose can be bought for £1300 per unit from another manufacturer. Flotilla is preparing to buy engines from this source.

From information supplied by the divisions you have derived the following production and revenue schedules which are applicable over the capacity range of the two divisions:

| | Engcorp's data for Z80 engines | | Flotilla's data for dories | |
|---|---|---|---|---|
| Annual number of units | Total manufacturing cost (£000) | Total revenue from outside sales (£000) | Total cost of producing dories excluding engine costs (£000) | Total revenue from sales of dories (£000) |
| 100 | 115 | 204 | 570 | 703 |
| 200 | 185 | 362 | 1120 | 1375 |
| 300 | 261 | 486 | 1670 | 2036 |
| 400 | 344 | 598 | 2220 | 2676 |
| 500 | 435 | 703 | 2770 | 3305 |
| 600 | 535 | 803 | 3320 | 3923 |
| 700 | 645 | 898 | 3870 | 4530 |
| 800 | 766 | 988 | 4420 | 5126 |

Requirements

(a) Ignoring the possibility that Flotilla could buy engines from another manufacturer, calculate to the nearest 100 units:

(i) the quantity of Z80 production that would maximize profits for Griffin plc, and

(ii) the consequent quantity of Z80 units that would be sold to external customers and the quantity that would be transferred to Flotilla.

(8 marks)

(b) Explain the issues raised by the problems of transfer pricing between Engcorp and Flotilla, and discuss the advantages and disadvantages of the courses of action which could be taken.

(10 marks)

(c) Discuss the major considerations in setting transfer prices for a profit-maximizing international group.

(7 marks)
(Total 25 marks)
*ICAEW P2 Management Accounting*

### 21.19* Advanced: Calculation of optimal selling price using calculus and the impact of using the imperfect market price as the transfer price

AB Ltd has two Divisions – A and B. Division A manufactures a product called the aye and Division B manufactures a product called the bee. Each bee uses a single aye as a component. A is the only manufacturer of the aye and supplies both B and outside customers.

Details of A's and B's operations for the coming period are as follows:

| | Division A | Division B |
|---|---|---|
| Fixed costs | £7 500 000 | £18 000 000 |
| Variable costs per unit | £280 | £590* |
| Capacity – units | 30 000 | 18 000 |

*Note*: Excludes transfer costs

Market research has indicated that demand for AB Ltd's products from outside customers will be as follows in the coming period:

- *the aye*: at unit price £1000 no ayes will be demanded but demand will increase by 25 ayes with every £1 that the unit price is reduced below £1000;
- *the bee*: at unit price £4000 no bees will be demanded, but demand will increase by 10 bees with every £1 that the unit price is reduced below £4000.

Requirements:
(a) Calculate the unit selling price of the bee (accurate to the nearest £) that will maximize AB Ltd's profit in the coming period.
(10 marks)
(b) Calculate the unit selling price of the bee (accurate to the nearest £) that is likely to emerge if the Divisional Managers of A and B both set selling prices calculated to maximize Divisional profit from sales to outside customers and the transfer price of ayes going from A to B is set at 'market selling price'.
(10 marks)
(c) Explain why your answers to parts (a) and (b) are different, and propose changes to the system of transfer pricing in order to ensure that AB Ltd is charging its customers at optimum prices.
(5 marks)
(Total 25 marks)
*CIMA Stage 3 Management Accounting Applications*

**21.20\* Advanced: Demonstration of how a badly designed transfer pricing system can distort decision-making involving the use of calculus**
AB Ltd comprises two divisions. Division A produces the aye – a component sold to outside

customers and transferred to division B. Division B produces the bee – each unit of which incorporates one aye in its construction. Divisional Managers are paid an incentive bonus linked to divisional profit.

Demand for the two products from outside customers for the next year is forecast to be as follows:

| | |
|---|---|
| Product aye | 2000 units demanded at £40 unit selling price |
| Produce bee | 1000 units demanded at £100 unit selling price |
| Produce aye | 40 units change in demand with each £1 change in unit selling price |
| Product bee | 10 units change in demand with each £1 change in unit selling price |

The marginal cost of producing 1 unit of aye is £20, and that of producing 1 unit of bee (not including the aye) is £25 – in both cases, at all levels of output.

AB Ltd's Chief Accountant comments that

Setting selling prices is simply an exercise in mathematics. Once you understand the cost and revenue structures of a business, then it is an easy matter to find the unique selling price for each product that maxmises profit.

Requirements:
(a) Calculate the unit selling price and output that divisions A and B should adopt for the next year in order to maximise the profit of AB Ltd.
(10 marks)
(b) Calculate the unit selling price and output that divisions A and B are likely to adopt in the next year if the manager of division A is instructed to transfer units of aye to division B at 'market price' and with no other constraints.
You may assume that divisional managers will always adopt unit selling prices and output levels that maximise the profit of their own division.
(10 marks)
(c) Critically evaluate the Chief Accountant's comment.
(5 marks)
(Total 25 marks)
*CIMA Stage 3 Management Accounting Applications*

**21.21 Advanced: Calculation of optimum selling price using calculus as the effect of using the imperfect market price as the transfer price**

HKI plc has an Engineering Division and a Motorcycle Division. The Engineering Division produces engines which it sells to 'outside' customers and transfers to the Motorcycle Division. The Motorcycle Division produces a powerful motorbike called the 'Beast' which incorporates an HKI engine in its design.

The Divisional Managers have full control over the commercial policy of their respective Divisions and are each paid 1% of the profit that is earned by their Divisions as an incentive bonus.

Details of the Engineering Division's production operation for the next year are expected to be as follows:

| | |
|---|---|
| Annual fixed costs | £3 000 000 |
| Variable cost per engine | £350 |

Details of the Motorcycle Division's production operation for the next year are expected to be as follows:

| | |
|---|---|
| Annual fixed costs | £50 000 |
| Variable cost per Beast | £700* |

*Note:* this figure excludes 'transfer costs'

Both Divisions have significant surplus capacity. Market research has indicated that demand from 'outside' customers for HKI plc's products is as follows:

- 9000 engines are sold at a unit selling price of £700; sales change by an average of 10 engines for each £1 change in the selling price per engine;
- 1000 Beasts are sold at a unit selling price of £2200; sales change by an average of 125 Beasts for each £100 change in the selling price per Beast.

It is established practice for the Engineering Division to transfer engines to the Motorcycle Division at 'market selling price'.

You are required

(a) to calculate the unit selling price of the Beast (accurate to the nearest penny) that should be set in order to maximize HKI plc's profit;

(7 marks)

(b) to calculate the selling price of the Beast (accurate to the nearest penny) that is likely to emerge if the Engineering Division Manager sets a market selling price for the engine which is calculated to maximize profit from engine sales to outside customers. You may assume that both Divisional Managers are aware of the information given above. Explain your reasoning and show your workings;

(8 marks)

(c) to explain why you agree or disagree with the following statement made by the Financial Director of HKI plc:

'Pricing policy is a difficult area which offers considerable scope for dysfunctional behaviour. Decisions about selling prices should be removed from the control of Divisional Managers and made the responsibility of a Head Office department.'

(12 marks)

(Total 27 marks)

*CIMA Stage 4 Management Accounting–*
*Decision Making*

**21.22\* Advanced: Calculating optimum transfer prices and profits using differential calculus**

Megacorp plc is a divisionalized enterprise. Among its divisions are Chem and Drink. Both of these divisions have a wide range of independent activities. One product, Fizz, is made by Chem for Drink. Chem does not have any external customers for the product.

The central management of Megacorp plc delegates all pricing decisions to divisional management, and the pricing of Fizz has been a contentious issue. It has been suggested that Chem should give a transfer price schedule for the supply of Fizz, based on Chem's own production costs, and that all transfers would be made at Chem's marginal cost. Drink would then order the quantity it requires each month.

Chem estimates its monthly total costs, $TC_C$, for producing Fizz are as follows:

$$TC_c = £10\,000 + £5.50Q_C + £0.002Q_C^2$$

where $Q_C$ is the quantity of Fizz manufactured.

Drink incurs costs in using Fizz. Its monthly total costs $(TC_D)$ in using Fizz, excluding the transfer price, are:

$$TC_D = £15\,000 + £11Q_D + £0.001Q_D^2$$

where $Q_D$ is the quantity of product, each unit of which incorporates one unit of Fizz.

Drink estimates that the demand function for its product incorporating Fizz is:

$$P_D = £45 - £0.0008Q_D$$

where $P_D$ is the price per unit of the product incorporating Fizz.

Neither division holds any stocks of Fizz.

Requirements

(a) (i) Calculate the quantity of Fizz production which would maximize profits for Megacorp plc;

(ii) calculate the transfer price corresponding to that production if Chem's marginal cost is adopted for transfer pricing, and show the resulting profits for each division. (6 marks)

(b) (i) Calculate the quantity of Fizz which Drink would take (at Chem's marginal cost) *if it wanted to maximize its own profits*;

(ii) calculate the transfer price corresponding to that quantity, and show the resulting profits for each division. (5 marks)

(c) Examine the implications for Megacorp plc of the transfer pricing issues involved in requirements (a) and (b). (6 marks)

(d) Briefly describe the other main methods of transfer pricing and discuss their limitations. (8 marks)

(Total 25 marks)

*ICAEW Management Accounting*

## 21.23* Advanced: Scarce capacity and the use of shadow prices

Black and Brown are two divisions in a group of companies and both require intermediate products Alpha and Beta which are available from divisions A and B respectively. Black and Brown divisions convert the intermediate products into products Blackalls and Brownalls respectively. The market demand for Blackalls and Brownalls considerably exceeds the production possible, because of the limited availability of intermediate products Alpha and Beta.

No external market exists for Alpha and Beta and no other intermediate product market is available to Black and Brown divisions.

Other data are as follows:

*Black division*

| Blackalls: | Selling price per unit £45 |
| | Processing cost per unit £12 |
| | Intermediate products required per unit: |
| | Alpha: 3 units |
| | Beta: 2 units |

*Brown division*

| Brownalls: | Selling price per unit £54 |
| | Processing cost per unit £14 |
| | Intermediate products required per unit: |
| | Alpha: 2 units |
| | Beta: 4 units |

*A division*

| Alpha: | Variable cost per unit £6 |
| | Maximum production capacity 1200 units |

*B division*

| Beta: | Variable cost per unit £4 |
| | Maximum production capacity 1600 units |

The solution to a linear programming model of the situation shows that the imputed scarcity value (shadow price) of Alpha and Beta is £0.50 and £2.75 per unit respectively and indicates that the intermediate products be transferred such that 200 units of Blackalls and 300 units of Brownalls are produced and sold.

Required:

(a) Calculate the contribution earned by the group if the sales pattern indicated by the linear programming model is implemented. (3 marks)

(b) Where the transfer prices are set on the basis of variable cost plus shadow price, show detailed calculations for

(i) the contribution per unit of intermediate product earned by divisions A and B and

(ii) the contribution per unit of final product earned by Black and Brown divisions. (4 marks)

(c) Comment on the results derived in (b) and on the possible attitude of management of the various divisions to the proposed transfer pricing and product deployment policy. (6 marks)

(d) In the following year the capacities of divisions A and B have each doubled and the following changes have taken place:

1. *Alpha:* There is still no external market for this product, but A division has a large demand for other products which could use the capacity and earn a contribution of 5% over cost. Variable cost per unit for the other products would be the same as for Alpha and such products would use the capacity at the same rate as Alpha.

2. *Beta:* An intermediate market for this product now exists and Beta can be bought and sold in unlimited amounts at £7.50 per unit. External sales of Beta would incur additional transport costs of £0.50 per unit which are not incurred in inter-divisional transfers.

The market demand for Blackalls and Brownalls will still exceed the production availability of Alpha and Beta.

(i) Calculate the transfer prices at which Alpha and Beta should now be offered to Black and Brown divisions in order that the transfer policy implemented will lead to the maximization of group profit.

(ii) Determine the production and sales pattern for Alpha, Beta, Blackalls and Brownalls which will now maximize group contribution and calculate the group contribution thus achieved. It may be assumed that divisions will make decisions consistent with the financial data available. (9 marks)

(Total 22 marks)

*ACCA Level 2 Management Accounting*

### 21.24 Advanced: Various aspects of divisional performance evaluation and transfer pricing involving the algebraic manipulation of figures to identify likely outcomes

*Scenario*

Chambers plc produces motor components and a vehicle called the *Rambler*. The company is split into three operating divisions – Engines, Transmissions and Assembly. The Rambler is produced in the Assembly division. Each Rambler incorporates an engine produced in the Engines division and a transmission system produced in the Transmissions division.

Each operating division is both a profit and an investment centre, with the performance of divisional managers assessed on return on capital employed (ROCE) achieved. In addition to their salary, each manager is paid a bonus each year linked to ROCE achieved in the current year. Chambers plc is financed by various means and has an average cost of capital of 7% per annum.

Relevant details concerning the three operating divisions in the coming year are as follows:

*Engines division:*

- The variable cost of engine production is £600 per unit.
- Annual demand from outside customers for engines varies with price: it is 5000 units at unit price £1000 and changes by 5 units with each £1 change in unit price.
- Fixed costs are £5 000 000 per year, and capital employed is £5 200 000.

*Transmissions division:*

- The variable cost of transmission unit production is £350 per unit.
- Annual demand from outside customers for transmission units varies with price: it is 2500 units at unit price £1200 and changes by 5 units with each £2 change in unit price.
- Fixed costs are £5 200 000 per year, and capital employed is £8 100 000.

*Assembly division:*

- The variable cost (excluding transfer charges) of Rambler production is £1500 per unit.
- Annual demand for ramblers varies with price: it is 4000 units at a unit price of £6000 and changes by 2 units with each £1 change in unit price.
- Fixed costs are £5 800 000 per year, and capital employed is £10 200 000.

There are no capacity constraints in any of the divisions.

Chambers plc's transfer pricing policy is that goods transferred between divisions should be at the price charged to outside customers for the relevant units. In setting selling prices to outside customers, the Engines and Transmissions divisions must ignore the effect of transfers to the Assembly division. The manager of the Assembly division treats transfer prices for units received as variable costs.

An investment in new equipment (having a life of 5 years and a residual value of nil) is being considered by the management of the Transmissions division. The equipment would cost £850 000 and would reduce the variable cost per transmission unit by £30.

*Part One*

Requirements:

(a)  Calculate for each division the output, product price, profit and ROCE that is likely to emerge, given the existing transfer pricing system and assuming that each divisional manager will act to maximise the ROCE of his/her own division.
Ignore the investment in new equipment.
(7 marks)

(b)  Determine and state the optimum output level and selling price for each division from the point of view of Chambers plc as a whole.
Prepare a statement showing the resultant profit and ROCE of each division, assuming that the existing transfer policy system remains in place.
Ignore the investment in new equipment.
(7 marks)

(c)  Prepare a financial analysis to show the impact of the investment in new equipment on the profit and ROCE of the three divisions, given the existing transfer pricing and performance appraisal systems. State whether or not the management of the Transmissions division is likely to adopt the proposed new investment.
(6 marks)

(d)  State whether or not the proposed new investment is to the advantage of Chambers plc as a whole, assuming that decisions concerning output, etc. continue to be determined by the existing transfer pricing and performance appraisal systems.
Support your answer with a discounted cash flow analysis.
(5 marks)

*Note*: The following information is given to illustrate a methodology that might be used to solve the requirements of the question:

• The demand function for sales by the Engines

division to outside customers may be represented by the following equation, where $y =$ unit selling price and $x =$ demand:

$$y = 2000 - \frac{x}{5}$$

• The corresponding marginal revenue function may be represented by:

$$y = 2000 - \frac{x}{2.5}$$

(Total 25 marks)

*Part Two*

The concept of divisional organisation is to place divisional managers in the same risk/reward position as independent entrepreneurs. In theory, this induces divisional managers to act in a manner calculated to maximise the wealth of the company's shareholders. This may or may not work in practice but you may be sure of one thing – divisional organisation creates a lot of employment for chartered management accountants.

Requirements:

Having regard to the above statement,

(a)  explain how the divisional performance appraisal and transfer pricing systems at Chambers plc might contribute to maximising the wealth of shareholders;   (7 marks)

(b)  explain the limitations of ROCE as a divisional performance indicator, and suggest alternative measures that might be more effective;   (7 marks)

(c)  explain why and how the concept behind divisional organisation might be extended into many areas of government/public service;   (5 marks)

(d)  explain why divisional organisation generates work for management accountants, and suggest actions which might be taken to make such work cost-effective.   (6 marks)
(Total 25 marks)

*Part Three*

An effective transfer pricing system in the context of a divisional organisation has to satisfy several basic criteria. The problem is that nobody has yet invented a system of transfer pricing that is capable of doing this with perfection.

Requirements:

Having regard to the above statement,

(a) explain what criteria an effective system of transfer pricing has to satisfy; (7 marks)

(b) state how far the system used by Chambers plc meets the criteria you have identified in your answer to (a); advise Chambers plc on how it might modify its transfer pricing system in order to make it more effective.

(9 marks)

(c) explain the features of transfer pricing systems based on

(i) marginal cost,

(ii) opportunity cost, and

(iii) cost plus;

state how far each of these systems meets the criteria you have identified in your answer to requirement (a).

(9 marks)

(Total 25 marks)

*CIMA Stage 3 Management Accounting Applications*

# PART FIVE

# Cost Management and Strategic Management Accounting

In Part Four the major features of traditional management accounting control systems and the mechanisms that can be used to control costs were described. The focus was on comparing actual results against a pre-set standard (typically the budget), identifying and analysing variances and taking remedial action to ensure that future outcomes conform with budgeted outcomes. Traditional cost control systems tend to be based on the preservation of the *status-quo* and the ways of performing existing activities are not reviewed. The emphasis is on cost containment rather than cost reduction. In contrast, cost management focuses on cost reduction rather than cost containment. Chapter 22 examines the various approaches that fall within the area of cost management

During the late 1980s criticisms of traditional management accounting practices were widely publicized and new approaches were advocated which are more in tune with today's competitive and business environment. In particular, strategic management accounting has been identified as a way forward. However, there is still no comprehensive framework as to what constitutes strategic management accounting. Chapter 23 examines the elements of strategic management accounting and describes the different contributions that have been made to its development. In addition, recent developments that seek to incorporate performance measurement within the strategic management process are described.

CHAPTER 22   COST MANAGEMENT
CHAPTER 23   STRATEGIC MANAGEMENT ACCOUNTING

# Cost management

In Chapters 16–19 the major features of traditional management accounting control systems and the mechanisms that can be used to control costs were described. The focus was on comparing actual results against a pre-set standard (typically the budget), identifying and analysing variances and taking remedial action to ensure that future outcomes conform with budgeted outcomes. Traditional cost control systems tend to be based on the preservation of the *status quo* and the ways of performing existing activities are not reviewed. The emphasis is on cost containment rather than cost reduction.

Cost management focuses on cost reduction rather than cost containment. Indeed, the term cost reduction could be used instead of cost management but the former is an emotive term. Therefore cost management is preferred. Whereas traditional cost control systems are routinely applied on a continuous basis, cost management tends to be applied on an *ad hoc* basis when an opportunity for cost reduction is identified. Also many of the approaches that are incorporated within the area of cost management do not involve the use of accounting techniques. In contrast, cost control relies heavily on accounting techniques.

Cost management consists of those actions that are taken by managers to reduce costs, some of which are prioritized on the basis of information extracted from the accounting system. Other actions, however, are undertaken without the use of accounting information. They involve process improvements, where an opportunity has been identified to perform processes more effectively and efficiently, and which have obvious cost reduction outcomes. It is important that accountants are aware of all the approaches that can be used to reduce costs even if these methods do not rely on accounting information. You should also note that although cost management seeks to reduce costs, it should not be at the expense of customer satisfaction. Ideally, the aim is to take actions that will both reduce costs and enhance customer satisfaction.

## Learning objectives

After studying this chapter, you should be able to:

- explain the typical pattern of cost commitment and cost incurrence during the three stages of a product's life cycle;

- describe the target costing approach to cost management;

- describe tear-down analysis, value engineering and functional analysis;

- distinguish between target costing and *kaizen* costing;

- describe activity-based cost management;

- distinguish between value added and non-value added activities;

- explain the purpose of a cost of quality report;

- describe how value chain analysis can be used to increase customer satisfaction and manage costs more effectively;

- explain the role of benchmarking within the cost management framework;

- explain how management audits can be used to facilitate cost management;

● outline the main features of a just-in-time philosophy.

# Life-cycle costing

**AR** Traditional management accounting control procedures have focused primarily on the manufacturing stage of a product's life cycle. Pre-manufacturing costs, such as research and development and design and post-manufacturing abandonment and disposal costs are treated as period costs. Therefore they are not incorporated in the product cost calculations, nor are they subject to the conventional management accounting control procedures.

Life-cycle costing estimates and accumulates costs over a product's entire life cycle in order to determine whether the profits earned during the manufacturing phase will cover the costs incurred during the pre- and post-manufacturing stages. Identifying the costs incurred during the different stages of a product's life cycle provides an insight into understanding and managing the total costs incurred throughout its life cycle. In particular, life-cycle costing helps management to understand the cost consequences of developing and making a product and to identify areas in which cost reduction efforts are likely to be most effective.

Most accounting systems report on a period-by-period basis, and product profits are not monitored over their life cycles. In contrast, product life-cycle reporting involves tracing costs and revenues on a product-by-product basis over several calendar periods throughout their life cycle. A failure to trace all costs to products over their life cycles hinders management's understanding of product profitability, because a product's actual life-cycle profit is unknown. Consequently, inadequate feedback information is available on the success or failure in developing new products.

Figure 22.1 illustrates a typical pattern of cost commitment and cost incurrence during the three stages of a product's life cycle – the planning and design stage, the manufacturing stage and the service and abandonment stage. Committed or locked-in costs are those costs that have not been incurred but that will be incurred in the future on the basis of decisions that have already been made. Costs are incurred when a resource is used or sacrificed. Costing systems record costs only when they have been incurred. It is difficult to significantly alter costs after they have been committed. For example, the product design specifications determine a product's material and labour inputs and the production process. At this stage costs become committed and broadly determine the future costs that will be incurred during the manufacturing stage.

You will see from Figure 22.1 that approximately 80% of a product's costs are *committed* during the planning and design stage. At this stage product designers determine the product's design and the production process. In contrast, the majority of costs are *incurred* at the manufacturing stage, but they have already become locked-in at the planning and design stage and are difficult to alter.

The pattern of cost commitment and incurrence will differ based on the industry and specific product introduced. For example, cost incurrence is high at the planning and development stage for manufacturing new aeroplanes or large product abandonment costs may be incurred for those products whose disposal involves harmful effects to the environment, such as nuclear waste or other toxic chemicals.

It is apparent from Figure 22.1 that cost management can be most effectively exercised during the planning and design stage and not at the manufacturing stage when the product design and processes have already been determined and costs have been

**FIGURE 22.1** *Product life-cycle phases: relationship between costs committed and costs incurred.*

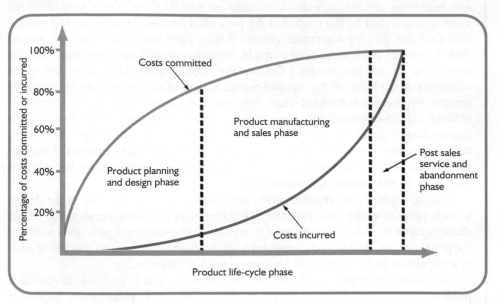

committed. At this latter stage the focus is more on cost containment than cost management. An understanding of life-cycle costs and how they are committed and incurred at different stages throughout a product's life cycle led to the emergence of target costing, a technique that focuses on managing costs during a product's planning and design phase.

# Target costing

In Chapter 11 we briefly looked at target costing as a mechanism for determining selling prices. We shall now consider how target costing can be used as a cost management tool. Target costing involves the following stages:

Stage 1: Determine the target price which customers will be prepared to pay for the product.

Stage 2: Deduct a target profit margin from the target price to determine the target cost.

Stage 3: Estimate the actual cost of the product.

Stage 4: If estimated actual cost exceeds the target cost investigate ways of driving down the actual cost to the target cost.

Target costing is a customer-oriented technique that is widely used by Japanese companies and which has recently been adopted by companies in Europe and the USA. The first stage requires market research to determine the customers' perceived value of the product based on its functions and its attributes (i.e. its functionality), its differentiation value relative to competing products and the price of competing products. The target profit margin depends on the planned return on investment for the organization as a whole and profit as a percentage of sales. This is then decomposed into a target profit for each product which is subsequently deducted from the target price to give the target cost. The target cost is compared with the predicted actual cost. If the predicted actual cost is above the target cost intensive efforts are made to close the gap so that the predicted cost equals the target cost.

A major feature of target costing is that a team approach is adopted to achieve the target cost. The team members include designers, engineers, purchasing, manufacturing, marketing and management accounting personnel. Their aim is to achieve the target cost specified for the product at the prescribed level of functionality and quality. The discipline of a team approach ensures that no particular group is able to impose their functional preferences. For example, design engineers pursuing their flair for design may design into products features that increase a product's costs but which customers do not value, or features that require the use of unique parts when alternative designs requiring standardized parts may meet customer requirements. Similarly, without a multi-functional team approach a marketing emphasis might result in the introduction of product features that customers find attractive, but not essential, and so they are not prepared to pay to have them included in the product's design. Therefore the aim during the product design process is to eliminate product functions that add cost but which do not increase the market price.

In some organizations representatives from the suppliers are included in the design team in order to obtain their expertise. They can often provide suggestions of design changes that will enable standard parts to replace custom-designed parts, thus reducing the product's cost. Alternatively, suppliers have the expertise to suggest alternative parts or components at the lowest cost for a given level of functionality.

The major advantage of adopting target costing is that it is deployed during a product's design and planning stage so that it can have a maximum impact in determining the level of the locked-in costs. It is an iterative process with the design team, which ideally should result in the design team continuing with its product and process design attempts until it finds designs that give an expected cost that is equal or less than the target cost. If the target cost cannot be attained then the product should not be launched. Design teams should not be allowed to achieve target costs by eliminating desirable product functions. Thus, the aim is to design a product with an expected cost that does not exceed target cost and that also meets the target level of functionality. Design teams use tear-down analysis and value engineering to achieve the target cost.

## TEAR-DOWN ANALYSIS

Tear-down analysis (also known as reverse engineering) involves examining a competitor's product in order to identify opportunities for product improvement and/or cost reduction. The competitor's product is dismantled to identify its functionality and design and to provide insights about the processes that are used and the cost to make the product. The aim is to benchmark provisional product designs with the designs of competitors and to incorporate any observed relative advantages of the competitor's approach to product design.

## VALUE ENGINEERING

Value engineering (also known as value analysis) is a systematic interdisciplinary examination of factors affecting the cost of a product or service in order to devise means of achieving the specified purpose at the required standard of quality and reliability at the target cost. The aim of value engineering is to achieve the assigned target cost by (i) identifying improved product designs that reduce the product's cost without sacrificing functionality and/or (ii) eliminating unnecessary functions that increase the product's costs and for which customers are not prepared to pay extra for.

Value engineering requires the use of functional analysis. This process involves decomposing the product into its many elements or attributes. For example, in the case of automobiles, functions might consist of style, comfort, operability, reliability, quality, attractiveness and many others (Kato, 1993). A price, or value, for each element is determined which reflects the amount the customer is prepared to pay. To obtain this information companies normally conduct surveys and interviews with customers. The total of the values for each function gives the estimated selling price from which the target profit is deducted to derive the target cost. The cost of each function of a product is compared with the benefits perceived by the customers. If the cost of the function exceeds the benefit to the customer, then the function should be either eliminated, modified to reduce its cost, or enhanced in terms of its perceived value so that its value exceeds the cost. Also by focusing on the product's functions, the design team will often consider components that perform the same function in other products, thus increasing the possibility of using standard components and reducing costs.

## THE NEED FOR ACCURATE COST MEASUREMENT SYSTEMS

It is important that target costing is supported by an accurate cost system. In particular, cost drivers should be established that are the significant determinants of the costs of the activities so that cause-and-effect allocations are used. Arbitrary cost allocations should be avoided. If arbitrary cost allocations are used the allocation base will not be a significant determinant of cost. Let us assume that an arbitrary allocation base, say direct labour hours, is used to allocate support costs to products. To reduce the projected cost towards the target cost the target costing team will be motivated to focus on reducing direct labour hours. Why? Because this will result in a smaller proportion of the support costs being assigned to the product. However, the support costs incurred by the organization will not be reduced because there is no cause-and-effect relationship between direct labour hours and the resulting costs. Therefore the target costing exercise will merely result in a reduction in the costs that are allocated to the product but organizational costs will not be reduced. In contrast, if cause-and-effect allocation bases (i.e. cost drivers) are established, reductions in cost driver usage should be followed by a reduction in organizational support costs.

Therefore it is very important that cost systems use cost drivers that are the determinants of costs so that they will motivate designers to take actions that will reduce organizational costs. Decisions taken at the design stage lead to the committed usage of cost drivers which can be difficult to change in the future.

## AN ILLUSTRATION OF TARGET COSTING

Example 22.1 is used to illustrate the target costing process. You will have noted from reading the information presented in this example that the projected cost of the product is £700 compared with a target cost of £560. To achieve the target cost the company establishes a project team to undertake an intense target costing exercise. Example 22.1 indicates that the end result of the target costing exercise is a projected cost of £555 which is marginally below the target cost of £560. Let us now look at how the company has achieved the target cost and also how the costs shown in Example 22.1 have been derived.

In response to the need to reduce the projected cost the project team starts by purchasing video cameras from its main competitors and undertaking a tear-down analysis. This process involves dismantling the cameras to provide insights into potential design improvements for the new camera that will be launched. Value engineering is also undertaken with the project team working closely with the design engineers. Their objective is to identify new designs that will accomplish the same

**EXAMPLE 22.1**

The Digital Electronics Company manufactures cameras and video equipment. It is in the process of introducing a new digital video camera. The company has undertaken market research to ascertain the customers' perceived value of the product based on its special features and a comparison with competitors' products. The results of the survey, and a comparison of the new camera with competitors' products and market prices, have been used to establish a target selling price and projected lifetime volume. In addition, cost estimates have been prepared based on the proposed product specification. The company has set a target profit margin of 30% on the proposed selling price and this has been deducted from the target selling price to determine the target cost. The following is a summary of the information that has been presented to management:

| | |
|---|---|
| Projected lifetime sales volume | 300 000 units |
| Target selling price | £800 |
| Target profit margin (30% of selling price) | £240 |
| Target cost (£800 − £240) | £560 |
| Projected cost | £700 |

The excess of the projected cost over the target cost results in an intensive target costing exercise. After completing the target costing exercise the projected cost is £555 which is marginally below the target cost of £560. The analysis of the projected cost before and after the target costing exercise is as follows:

| | Before (£) | (£) | After (£) | (£) |
|---|---|---|---|---|
| *Manufacturing cost* | | | | |
| Direct material (bought in parts) | 390 | | 325 | |
| Direct labour | 100 | | 80 | |
| Direct machining costs | 20 | | 20 | |
| Ordering and receiving | 8 | | 2 | |
| Quality assurance | 60 | | 50 | |
| Rework | 15 | | 6 | |
| Engineering and design | 10 | 603 | 8 | 491 |
| *Non-manufacturing costs* | | | | |
| Marketing | 40 | | 25 | |
| Distribution | 30 | | 20 | |
| After-sales service and warranty costs | 27 | 97 | 19 | 64 |
| Total cost | | 700 | | 555 |

functions at a lower cost and also to eliminate any functions that are deemed to be unnecessary. This process results in a simplified design, the reduction in the number of parts and the replacement of some customized parts with standard parts. The outcome of the tear-down analysis and value engineering activities is a significant reduction in the projected direct materials, labour and rework costs, but the revised cost estimates still indicate that the projected cost exceeds the target cost.

Next the team engages in functional analysis. They identify the different elements, functions and attributes of the camera and potential customers are interviewed to ascertain the values that they place on each of the functions. This process indicates that several functions that have been included in the prototype are not valued by customers. The team therefore decide to eliminate these functions. The functional analysis results in further cost reductions being made, principally in the areas of materials and direct labour assembly costs but the revised cost estimates still indicate that the target cost has not been attained.

The team now turn their attention to redesigning the production and support processes. They decide to redesign the ordering and receiving process by reducing the number of suppliers and working closely with a smaller number of suppliers. The suppliers are prepared to enter into contractual arrangements whereby they are periodically given a pre-determined production schedule and in return they will inspect the shipments and guarantee quality prior to delivery. In addition, the marketing, distribution and customer after-sales services relating to the product are subject to an intensive review, and process improvements are made that result in further reductions in costs that are attributable to the camera. The projected cost after undertaking all of the above activities is £555 compared with the target cost of £560 and at this point the target costing exercise is concluded.

Having described the target costing approach that the Digital Electronics Company has used let us now turn our attention to the derivation of the projected costs shown in Example 22.1. The projected cost for direct materials prior to the target costing exercise is £390 but value engineering and the functional analysis have resulted in a reduction in the number of parts that are required to manufacture the video camera. The elimination of most of the unique parts, and the use of standard parts that the company currently purchases in large volumes, also provides scope for further cost savings. The outcome of the redesign process is a direct material cost of £325.

The simplified product design enables the assembly time to be reduced thus resulting in the reduction of direct labour costs from £100 to £80. The direct machine costs relate to machinery that will be used exclusively for the production of the new product. The estimated cost of acquiring, maintaining and operating the machinery throughout the product's life cycle is £6 million. This is divided by the projected lifetime sales volume of the camera (300 000 units) giving a unit cost of £20. However, it has not been possible to reduce the unit cost because the machinery costs are committed, and fixed, and the target costing exercise has not resulted in a change in the predicted lifetime volume.

Prior to the target costing exercise 80 separate parts were included in the product specification. The estimated number of orders placed for each part throughout the product's life cycle is 150 and the predicted cost per order for the order and receiving activity is £200. Therefore the estimated lifetime costs are £2.4 million (80 parts × 150 orders × £200 per order) giving a unit cost of £8 (£2.4 million/300 000 units). The simplified design, and the parts standardization arising from the functional analysis and the value engineering activities, have enabled the number of parts to be reduced to 40. The redesign of the ordering and receiving process has also enabled the number of orders and the ordering cost to be reduced (the former from 150 to 100 and the latter from £200 to £150 per order). Thus the projected lifetime ordering and receiving costs after the target costing exercise are £600 000 (40 parts × 100 orders × £150 per order) giving a revised unit cost of £2 (£600 000/300 000 units).

Quality assurance involves inspecting and testing the cameras. Prior to the target costing exercise the projected cost was £60 (12 hours at £5 per hour) but the simplified design means that the camera will be easier to test resulting in revised cost of £50 (10 hours at £5 per hour). Rework costs of £15 represent the average rework costs per camera. Past experience with manufacturing similar products suggests that 10% of the output will require rework. Applying this rate to the estimated total lifetime volume of 300 000 cameras results in 30 000 cameras requiring rework at an estimated average cost of £150 per reworked camera. The total lifetime rework cost is therefore predicted to be £4.5 million (30 000 × £150) giving an average cost per unit of good output of £15 (£4.5 million/300 000). Because of the simplified product design the rework rate and the average rework cost will be reduced. The predicted rework rate is now 5% and the average rework cost will be reduced from £150 to £120. Thus, the revised estimate of the total lifetime cost is £1.8 million (15 000 reworked units at £120 per unit) and the projected unit cost is £6 (£1.8 million/300 000 units).

The predicted total lifetime engineering and design costs and other product sustaining costs are predicted to be £3 million giving a unit cost of £10. The simplified design and reduced number of parts enables the lifetime cost to be reduced by 20%, to £2.4 million, and the unit cost to £8. The planned process improvements have also enabled the predicted marketing, distribution and after-sales service costs to be reduced. In addition, the simplified product design and the use of fewer parts has contributed to the reduction to the after-sales warranty costs. However, to keep our example brief the derivation of the non-manufacturing costs will not be presented, other than to note that the company uses an activity-based-costing system. All costs are assigned using cost drivers that are based on established cause-and-effect relationships.

# Kaizen costing

In addition to target costing *kaizen* costing is widely used by Japanese organizations as a mechanism for reducing and managing costs. *Kaizen* is the Japanese term for making improvements to a process through small incremental amounts, rather than through large innovations. The major difference between target and *kaizen* costing is that target costing is applied during the design stage whereas *kaizen* costing is applied during the manufacturing stage of the product life cycle. With target costing the focus is on the product, and cost reductions are achieved primarily through product design. In contrast, *kaizen* costing focuses on the production processes and cost reductions are derived primarily through the increased efficiency of the production process. Therefore the potential cost reductions are smaller with *kaizen* costing because the products are already in the manufacturing stage of their life cycles and a significant proportion of the costs will have become locked-in.

The aim of *kaizen* costing is to reduce the cost of components and products by a pre-specified amount. Monden and Hamada (1991) describe the application of *kaizen* costing in a Japanese automobile plant. Each plant is assigned a target cost reduction ratio and this is applied to the previous year's actual costs to determine the target cost reduction. *Kaizen* costing relies heavily on employee empowerment. They are assumed to have superior knowledge about how to improve processes because they are closest to the manufacturing processes and customers and are likely to have greater insights into how costs can be reduced. Thus, a major feature of *kaizen* costing is that workers are given the responsibility to improve processes and reduce costs. Unlike target costing it is not accompanied by a set of techniques or procedures that are automatically applied to achieve the cost reductions.

# Activity-based management

The early adopters of activity-based costing (ABC) used it to produce more accurate product (or service) costs but it soon became apparent to the users that it could be extended beyond purely product costing to a range of cost management applications.

The terms **activity-based management (ABM)** or **activity-based cost management (ABCM)** are used to describe the cost management applications of ABC. To implement an ABM system only the first three of the four stages described in Chapter 10 for designing an activity-based product costing system are required. They are:

1. identifying the major activities that take place in an organization;
2. assigning costs to cost pools/cost centres for each activity;
3. determining the cost driver for each major activity.

Thus, firms can omit the final stage of assigning activity costs to products and adopt ABC solely for cost management without activity-based product costing. Alternatively, organizations can design an activity-based system that incorporates both ABM and activity-based product costing but note that only the first three stages are required for ABM.

ABM views the business as a set of linked activities that ultimately add value to the customer. It focuses on managing the business on the basis of the activities that make up the organization. ABM is based on the premise that activities consume costs. Therefore by managing activities costs will be managed in the long term. The goal of ABM is to enable customer needs to be satisfied while making fewer demands on organizational resources.

Traditional budget and control reports analyse costs by types of expense for each responsibility centre. In contrast, ABM analyses costs by activities and thus provides management with information on why costs are incurred and the output from the activity (in terms of cost drivers). Exhibit 22.1 illustrates the difference between the conventional analysis and the activity-based analysis. The major differences are that the ABM approach reports by activities whereas the traditional analysis is by departments. Also ABM reporting is by sub-activities but traditional reporting is by expense categories. Another distinguishing feature of ABM reporting is that it often reports information on activities that cross departmental boundaries. For example, different production departments and the distribution department might undertake customer processing activities. They may resolve customer problems by expediting late deliveries. The finance department may assess customer credit worthiness and the remaining customer processing activities might be undertaken by the customer service department. Therefore the total cost of the customer processing activity could be considerably in excess of the costs that are assigned to the customer service department. However, to simplify the presentation it is assumed in Exhibit 22.1 that the departmental and activity costs are identical but if the cost of the customer order processing activity was found to be, say, three times the amount assigned to the customer service department, this would be important information because it may change the way in which the managers view the activity. For example, the managers may give more attention to reducing the costs of the customer processing activity.

It is apparent from an examination of Exhibit 22.1 that the ABM approach provides more meaningful information. It gives more visibility to the cost of undertaking the activities that make up the organization and may raise issues for management action that are not highlighted by the traditional analysis. For example, why is £90 000 spent on resolving customer problems? Attention-directing information such as this is important for managing the cost of the activities.

Johnson (1990) suggests that knowing costs by activities is a catalyst that eventually triggers the action necessary to become competitive. Consider a situation where salespersons, as a result of costing activities, are informed that it costs £50 to process a customer's order. They therefore become aware that it is questionable to pursue orders with a low sales value. By eliminating many small orders, and concentrating on larger

**EXHIBIT 22.1**

*Customer order processing activity*

value orders, the demand for customer-processing activities should decrease, and future spending on this activity should be reduced.

Prior to the introduction of ABM most organizations have been unaware of the cost of undertaking the activities that make up the organization.

|  | (£000s) |
| --- | --- |
| *Traditional analysis* | |
| Salaries | 320 |
| Stationery | 40 |
| Travel | 140 |
| Telephone | 40 |
| Depreciation of equipment | 40 |
|  | 580 |
| *ABM analysis* | |
| Preparing quotations | 120 |
| Receiving customer orders | 190 |
| Assessing the creditworthiness of customers | 100 |
| Expediting | 80 |
| Resolving customer problems | 90 |
|  | 580 |

Knowing the cost of activities enables those activities with the highest cost to be highlighted so that they can be prioritized for detailed studies to ascertain whether they can be eliminated or performed more efficiently. To identify and prioritize the potential for cost reduction many organizations have found it useful to classify activities as either value added or non-value added. Definitions of what constitutes value added and non-value added activities vary. A common definition is that a **value added activity** is an activity that customers perceive as adding usefulness to the product or service they purchase. For example, painting a car would be a value added activity in an organization that manufactures cars. Other definitions are an activity that is being performed as efficiently as possible or an activity that supports the primary objective of producing outputs.

In contrast, a **non-value added activity** is an activity where there is an opportunity for cost reduction without reducing the product's service potential to the customer. Examples of non-value added activities include inspecting, storing and moving raw materials. The cost of these activities can be reduced without reducing the value of the products to the customers. Non-value added activities are essentially those activities that customers should not be expected to pay for. Reporting the cost of non-value added activities draws management's attention to the vast amount of waste that has been tolerated by the organization. This should prioritize those activities with the greatest potential for cost reduction by eliminating or carrying them out more effectively, such as reducing material movements, improving production flows and taking actions to reduce stock levels. Taking action to reduce or eliminate non-value added activities is given top priority because by doing so the organization permanently reduces the cost it incurs without reducing the value of the product to the customer.

Kaplan and Cooper (1998) criticize the classification of activities by simplistic value added and non-value added categories. They point out, that apart from the extreme examples similar to the ones illustrated above, people cannot consistently define what constitutes a value added or non-value added activity. To reinforce this point they discuss whether the activity of setting up a machine is value added or non-value added. One view is that customers do not perceive performing set-ups as adding usefulness to products and the activity is non-value added. However, without set-ups a plant can only produce single products. If customers value customized or diverse products, changing machine settings from the ability to produce different product varieties creates value for customers. Kaplan and Cooper also point out the demotivating impact when employees are informed that they are performing non-value added activities.

To overcome the above problems Kaplan and Cooper advocate that instead of using a value added/non-value added classification the following simple five point scale should be used to summarize an ABC project team's initial judgement about the current efficiency of an activity:

1. highly efficient, with little (less than 5%) apparent opportunity for improvement;

2. modestly efficient, some (5–15%) opportunity for improvement;

3. average efficiency, good opportunities (15–25%) for improvement;

4. inefficient, major opportunities (25–50%) for improvement;

5. highly inefficient, perhaps should not be done at all; 50–100% opportunity for improvement.

By identifying the cost of activities that make up their organization and classifying them into the above five categories, opportunities for cost reduction can be prioritized. Cost reduction can be achieved by either eliminating the activities, performing them more efficiently with fewer organizational resources or redesigning them so that they are performed in an entirely different and more cost efficient way. We shall consider how activities can be redesigned later in the chapter.

Our discussion so far has related to the application of ABM during the manufacturing or service phase of a product's life cycle. However, some organizations have used their activity-based costing systems to influence future costs at the design stage within the target costing process. In particular, they have opted for behaviourally orientated cost systems that are less accurate than costing technology allows in order to induce desired behavioural responses (Merchant and Shields, 1993). Hiromoto (1991) illustrated how a Japanese company used cost drivers to implement a policy of parts standardization as one component of a cost reduction strategy. The manufacturer identified the number of part numbers as its key cost driver, or strategic behavioural cost driver, to implement the chosen strategy of standardizing and reducing parts, simplifying the manufacturing process and decreasing manufacturing costs. Management devised a method of allocating manufacturing overhead so that product costs increased with the number of parts used and with the number of non-standard parts used. The standardization rate (number of common parts/total number of parts) increased steadily over a 12-year period, despite increasing product variety, from 20% to 68%.

A further example that is cited in the literature is the cost system operated by Tektronix Portable Instruments Division. The company assigned material support expenses using a single cost driver-number of part numbers. The company wanted to encourage design engineers to focus their attention on reducing the number of part numbers, parts and vendors in future generations of products. Product timeliness was seen as a critical success factor and this was facilitated by designs which simplified parts procurement and production processes. The cost system motivated engineers to design simpler products requiring less development time because they had fewer parts and part numbers. The cost system designers knew that most of the material support expenses were not incurred in direct proportion to the single cost driver chosen, but the simplified and imprecise cost system focused attention on factors deemed to be most critical to the division's future success.

A survey of activity-based costing applications by Innes and Mitchell (1995a) indicated that many organizations use cost driver rates as a measure of cost efficiency and performance for the activity concerned. The cost driver rate is computed by dividing the activity costs by the cost driver volume. For example, if the cost of processing 10 000 purchase orders is £100 000, the cost per purchasing order is £10. Assume now that improvements in procedures in the purchasing activity enable costs to be reduced to £80 000. If the same number of orders can be processed with fewer resources the cost of processing an order will be reduced to £8. Reporting and focusing on cost driver rates can thus be used to motivate managers to reduce the cost of performing activities.

There is a danger, however, that cost driver rates can encourage dysfunctional behaviour. An improvement in the cost driver rate can be achieved by splitting some purchase orders and increasing the orders processed to, say, 12 000. Assuming that the cost of the activity remains unchanged at £100 000 the cost per purchasing order will be reduced from £10 to £8.33 if all costs are fixed in the short term. The overall effect is that the workload will be increased and, in the long term, this could result in an increase in costs. Care should therefore be taken to avoid these dysfunctional consequences by using cost driver rates as feedback information to guide employees in improving the efficiency of performing activities. If the measures are interpreted in a recriminatory or threatening manner, there is a danger that they will lead to dysfunctional behaviour.

# Business process re-engineering

**Business process re-engineering** involves examining business processes and making substantial changes to how the organization currently operates. It involves the redesign of how work is done through activities. A business process consists of a collection of activities that are linked together in a co-ordinated manner to achieve a specific objective. For example, material handling might be classed as a business process consisting of separate activities relating to scheduling production, storing materials, processing purchase orders, inspecting materials and paying suppliers.

The aim of business process re-engineering is to improve the key business processes in an organization by focusing on simplification, cost reduction, improved quality and enhanced customer satisfaction. Consider the materials handling process outlined in the above paragraph. The process might be re-engineered by sending the production schedule direct to nominated suppliers and entering into contractual agreements to deliver the materials in accordance with the production schedule and also guaranteeing their quality by inspecting them prior to delivery. The end result might be the elimination, or a permanent reduction, of the storing, purchasing and inspection activities. These activities are non-value added activities since they represent an opportunity for cost reduction without reducing the products' service potentials to customers.

A distinguishing feature of business process re-engineering is that it involves radical and dramatic changes in processes by abandoning current practices and reinventing completely new methods of performing business processes. The focus is on major changes rather than marginal improvements. A further example of business process re-engineering is moving from a traditional functional plant layout to a just-in-time cellular product layout and adopting a just-in-time philosophy. Adopting a just-in-time (JIT) system and philosophy has important implications for cost management and performance reporting. It is therefore important that you understand the nature of such systems and how they differ from traditional systems, but rather than deviating at this point from our discussion of cost management the description of a JIT system will be deferred until the end of the chapter.

# Cost of quality

To compete successfully in today's global competitive environment companies are becoming 'customer-driven' and making customer satisfaction an overriding priority. Customers are demanding ever-improving levels of service regarding cost, quality, reliability, delivery and the choice of innovative new products. Quality has become one of the key competitive variables and this has created the need for management accountants to become more involved in the provision of information relating to the quality of products and services and activities that produce them. In the UK quality related costs have been reported to range from 5 to 15% of total company sales revenue (Plunkett *et al.*, 1985). Eliminating inferior quality can therefore result in substantial savings and higher revenues.

**Total quality management (TQM)**, a term used to describe a situation where *all* business functions are involved in a process of continuous quality improvement, has been adopted by many companies. TQM has broadened, from its early concentration on the statistical monitoring of manufacturing processes, to a customer-oriented process of continuous improvement that focuses on delivering products or services of consistent high quality in a timely fashion. In the 1980s most European and American companies considered quality to be an additional cost of manufacturing, but by the end of the decade they began to realize that quality saved money. The philosophy of emphasizing production volume over quality resulted in high levels of stocks at each production stage in order to protect against shortages caused by inferior quality at previous stages and excessive expenditure on inspection, rework, scrap and warranty repairs. Companies discovered that it was cheaper to produce the items correctly the first time rather than wasting resources by making substandard items that have to be detected, reworked, scrapped or returned by customers. In other words, the emphasis of TQM is to design and build quality in, rather than trying to inspect it in, by focusing on the causes rather than the symptoms of poor quality.

Management accounting systems can help organizations achieve their quality goals by providing a variety of reports and measures that motivate and evaluate managerial efforts to improve quality. These will include financial and non-financial measures. Many companies are currently not aware of how much they are spending on quality. A cost of quality report should be prepared to indicate the total cost to the organization of producing products or services that do not conform with quality requirements. Four categories of costs should be reported.

1. **Prevention costs** are the costs incurred in preventing the production of products that do not conform to specification. They include the costs of preventive maintenance, quality planning and training and the extra costs of acquiring higher quality raw materials.

2. **Appraisal costs** are the costs incurred to ensure that materials and products meet quality conformance standards. They include the costs of inspecting purchased parts, work in process and finished goods, quality audits and field tests.

**EXHIBIT 22.2**

*Cost of quality report*

|  | (£000s) | % of sales (£50 million) |
|---|---|---|
| *Prevention costs* |  |  |
| Quality training | 1 000 |  |
| Supplier reviews | 300 |  |
| Quality engineering | 400 |  |
| Preventive maintenance | 500 |  |
|  | 2 200 | 4.4 |
| *Appraisal costs* |  |  |
| Inspection of materials received | 500 |  |
| Inspection of WIP and completed units | 1 000 |  |
| Testing equipment | 300 |  |
| Quality audits | 800 |  |
|  | 2 600 | 5.2 |
| *Internal failure costs* |  |  |
| Scrap | 800 |  |
| Rework | 1 000 |  |
| Downtime due to quality problems | 600 |  |
| Retesting | 400 | 2 800 | 5.6 |
| *External failure costs* |  |  |
| Returns | 2 000 |  |
| Recalls | 1 000 |  |
| Warranty repairs | 800 |  |
| Handling customer complaints | 500 |  |
| Foregone contribution from lost sales | 3 000 |  |
|  | 7 300 | 14.6 |
|  | 14 900 | 29.8 |

3. **Internal failure costs** are the costs associated with materials and products that fail to meet quality standards. They include costs incurred before the product is despatched to the customer, such as the costs of scrap, repair, downtime and work stoppages caused by defects.

4. **External failure costs** are the costs incurred when inferior products are delivered to customers. They include the costs of handling customer complaints, warranty replacement, repairs of returned products and the costs arising from a damaged company reputation.

Exhibit 22.2 presents a typical cost of quality report. Note that some of the items in the report will have to be estimated. For example, the forgone contribution from lost sales arising from poor quality is extremely difficult to estimate. Nevertheless, the lost contribution can be substantial and it is preferable to include an estimate rather than omit it from the report. By expressing each category of costs as a percentage of sales revenues comparisons can be made with previous periods, other organizations and divisions within the same group. Such comparisons can highlight problem areas. For example, comparisons of external failure costs with other companies can provide an indication of the current level of customer satisfaction.

The cost of quality report can be used as an attention-directing device to make the top management of a company aware of how much is being spent on quality-related costs. The report can also draw management's attention to the possibility of reducing total quality costs by a wiser allocation of costs among the four quality categories. For example, by spending more on the prevention costs, the amount of spending in the internal and external failure categories can be substantially reduced, and therefore total spending can be lowered. Also, by designing quality into the products and processes, appraisal costs can be reduced, since far less inspection is required.

Prevention and appraisal costs are sometimes referred to as the **costs of quality conformance** or **compliance** and internal and external failure costs are also known as the **costs of non-conformance** or **non-compliance**. Costs of compliance are incurred with the intention of eliminating the costs of failure. They are discretionary in the sense that they do not have to be incurred whereas costs of non-compliance are the result of production imperfections and can only be reduced by increasing compliance expenditure. The optimal investment in compliance costs is when total costs of quality reach a minimum. This can occur when 100 per cent quality compliance has not been achieved. It is virtually impossible to measure accurately all quality costs (particularly the lost contribution from forgone sales) and determine the optimal investment in conformance costs. However, some people argue that a **zero-defects policy** is optimal. With a zero-defects policy the focus is on continuous improvement with the ultimate aim of achieving zero-defects and eliminating all internal and external failure costs.

A zero-defects policy does not use percentages as the unit of measurement because a small percentage defect rate can result in a large number of defects. For example, a 1% defect rate from an output of 1 million units results in 10 000 defective units. To overcome this problem the attainment of a zero-defects goal is measured in parts per million (PPM) so that seemingly small numbers can be transferred into large numbers. Thus, instead of reporting a 1% defect rate, a measure of 10 000 PPM is more likely to create pressure for action and highlight the trend in defect rates. Cost of quality reports provide a useful summary of quality efforts and progress to top management, but at lower management levels non-financial quality measures measures will be discussed appropriate target measures for quality improve… more timely and in the next chapter.

Besides using non-fin… …statistical quality control charts are used as a mechanism f… …trol chart is a graph of a series of successive observations operatin… …regular intervals of time to test whether a batch of produced items …set tolerance limits. Usually samples from a particular … between random and non-random variations in …at hourly or daily intervals. The mea… on the … range, of the The control limits are based on …ted and plotted …trol chart (see Figure 22.2). under control, and thus working e… …ries of past observations of a process when it is be represented by a normal distr…tion. It is assumed that the past observations can population mean and the popu…on standard deviation. …trol limits are regarded as worthy of of possible outcomes is nor…al, then, when the …on the expected distribution. Only expect …process is under control, we should …The past observations are used to estimate the …Assuming that the distribution

**FIGURE 22.2** *Statistical quality control charts.*

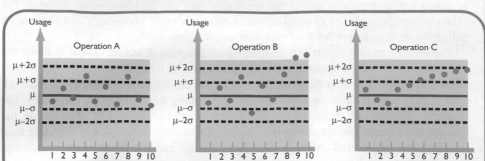

68.27% of the observation to fall within the range $+1\sigma$ from the mean;
95.45% of the observation to fall within the range $+2\sigma$ from the mean.

Control limits are now set. For example, if control limits are set based on two standard deviations from the mean then this would indicate 4.55% (100% − 95.45%) of future observations would result from pure chance when the process is under control. Therefore there is a high probability that an observation outside the $2\sigma$ control limits is out of control.

Figure 22.2 shows three control charts, with the outer horizontal lines representing a possible control limit of $2\sigma$, so that all observations outside this range are investigated. You will see that for operation A the process is deemed to be in control because all observations fall within the control limits. For operation B the last two observations suggest that the operation is out of control. Therefore both observations should be investigated. With operation C the observations would not prompt an investigation because all the observations are within the control limits. However, the last six observations show a steadily increasing usage in excess of the mean, and the process may be out of control. Statistical procedures (called casum procedures) that consider the trend in recent usage as well as daily usage can also be used.

# Cost management and the value chain

Increasing attention is now being given to value-chain analysis as a means of increasing customer satisfaction and more effectively. The value chain is illustrated in Figure 22.3. It is the linked set of value-creating activities all the way from basic raw material sources for components to the ultimate end-use product or service delivered to the customer through to the individual satisfaction, particularly in terms of cost efficiency, quality and delivery. A firm that performs the value chain together creates the conditions to outperform the competitors will gain a competitive advantage and at a lower cost, than how value chain activities are performed efficiently, and at a lower cost, than activities are not just a collection of independent activities but a system of interdependent activities in which the performance of one activity affects the cost of other activities.

It is also appropriate to view the value chain from the customer's perspective, with each link being seen as the customer of the previous link. If each link in the value chain is designed to meet the needs of its customers, then end-customer satisfaction should

**FIGURE 22.3**  *The value chain.*

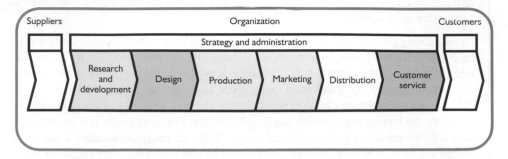

ensue. Furthermore, by viewing each link in the value chain as a supplier–customer relationship, the opinions of the customers can be used to provide useful feedback information on assessing the quality of service provided by the supplier. Opportunities are thus identified for improving activities throughout the entire value chain.

Shank and Govindarajan (1992) advocate that a company should evaluate its value chain relative to the value chains of its competitors or the industry. They suggest that the following methodology should be adopted:

1. Identify the industry's value chain and then assign costs, revenues and assets to value activities. These activities are the building blocks with which firms in the industry created a product that buyers find valuable.

2. Diagnose the cost drivers regulating each value activity.

3. Develop sustainable cost advantage, either through controlling cost drivers better than competitors or by reconfiguring the chain value. By systematically analysing costs, revenues and assets in each activity, a firm can achieve low cost. This is achieved by comparing the firm's value chain with the value chains of a few major competitors and identifying actions needed to manage the firm's value chain better than competitors manager their value chains.

Shank and Govindarajan also point out that focusing on the value chain results in the adoption of a broader strategic approach to cost management. They argue that traditional management accounting adopts an internal focus which, in terms of the value chain, starts too late and stops too soon. Starting cost analysis with purchases misses all the opportunities for exploiting linkages with the firm's suppliers and stopping cost analysis at the point of sale eliminates all opportunities for exploiting linkages with customers. Shank (1989) illustrates how an American automobile company failed to use the value chain approach to exploit links with suppliers and enhance profitability. The company had made significant internal savings from introducing JIT manufacturing techniques, but, at the same time, price increases from suppliers more than offset these internal cost savings. A value chain perspective revealed that 50% of the firm's costs related to purchases from parts suppliers. As the automobile company reduced its own need for buffer stocks, it placed major new strains on the manufacturing responsiveness of suppliers. The increase in the suppliers' manufacturing costs was greater than the decrease in the automobile company's internal costs. Shank states:

For every dollar of manufacturing cost the assembly plants saved by moving towards JIT management concepts, the suppliers' plant spent much more than one dollar extra because of schedule instability arising from the introduction of JIT. Because of its narrow value added perspective, the auto company had ignored the impact of its changes on its suppliers' costs. Management had ignored the idea that JIT involves a partnership with suppliers (Shank, 1989: 51).

By examining potential linkages with suppliers and understanding supplier costs it may be possible for the buying organization to change its activities in order to reduce the supplier's costs. For example, cost generating activities in the supplying organizations are often triggered by purchasing parameters (e.g. design specifications, lot size, delivery schedule, number of shipments, design changes and level of documentation). However, the buying organization can only be sensitive to these issues if it understands how supplier costs are generated (Seal *et al.*, 1999). In many organizations materials purchased from suppliers account for more than 60% of total manufacturing costs (Drury *et al.*, 1993) and therefore managing supply chain costs has become a critical element in overall cost management. Because of this some companies have established strategic supply partnerships. Seal *et al.* (1999) describe the attempt at a strategic supply partnership between two UK companies and how the buying company was seeking information sharing and research and development collaboration with the supplier for strategic components. In return the supplier was wishing to develop a higher level of cooperation and trust. Such developments represent an attempt to apply cost management throughout the entire value chain.

Similarly, by developing linkages with customers mutually beneficial relationships can be established. For example, Shank and Govindarajan (1992), drawing off research by Hergert and Morris (1989) point out that some container producers in the USA have constructed manufacturing facilities near beer breweries and deliver the containers through overhead conveyers directly onto the customers' assembly lines. This practice results in significant cost reductions for both the container producers and their customers by expediting the transport of empty containers, which are bulky and heavy.

# Benchmarking

In order to identify the best way of performing activities and business processes organizations are turning their attention to benchmarking, which involves comparing key activities with world-class best practices. Benchmarking attempts to identify an activity, such as customer order processing, that needs to be improved and finding a non-rival organization that is considered to represent world-class best practice for the activity and studying how it performs the activity. The objective is to find out how the activity can be improved and ensure that the improvements are implemented.

Benchmarking is cost beneficial since an organization can save time and money avoiding mistakes that other companies have made and/or the organization can avoid duplicating the efforts of other companies. The overall aim should be to find and implement best practice.

# Management audits

Management audits (also called performance audits and value for money audits) can be used to facilitate cost management in both profit and non-profit organizations. Management audits are intended to help management to do a better job by identifying waste and inefficiency and recommending corrective action. Management audits investigate the entire management control system and focus on the following aspects of an organization's performance:

1. the nature and functioning of the organization's managerial systems and procedures;
2. the economy and efficiency with which the organization's services are provided;
3. the effectiveness of the organization's performance in achieving its objectives.

There are a number of different ways in which a management audit can be carried out. However, Fielden and Robertson (1980) suggest, on the basis of their own experience of undertaking management audits in non-profit organizations in the UK, that a management audit should consist of the following:

1. *An initial analysis of financial statistics, unit costs and other performance indicators*. This analysis should involve a comparison with past statistics and other organizations of a similar character. The auditors should seek an explanation of trends and major differences from other similar organizations. The results of this initial analysis should give some guidance to those areas requiring further study.

2. *Management and systems review*. The purpose of this is to investigate the ways in which objectives are established, policies implemented and results monitored. The emphasis is on how efficiently this process is carried out rather than reviewing the objectives and policies themselves.

3. *Analysis of planning and control processes*. This involves exploring questions on the ways of comparing the objectives with the needs of the population, methods of identifying activities that are not meeting objectives, the use of investment appraisal techniques and the methods of monitoring projects against the initial appraisal. In addition, methods of reviewing operating results should be studied by analysing control and reporting systems and the extent to which they alert members and officers of the need for action.

4. *Efficiency assessment*. This is extremely difficult to assess, but suggestions include the use of checklists of good practice whereby the reviewers build up a detailed knowledge of cost effective practices, and, based on this, a checklist is developed and debated by the auditors with service managers. Another suggestion is for a small number of specific investigations to be carried out into activities with high unit costs, poor performance measures or suspected poor management in order to try and determine the reasons for adverse performance measures and identify the appropriate remedial action.

5. *... review*. This ... will involve ... determine whether or not the activities and committee members ... the details of particular services, and requires answers to such questions as to why a service is provided, the reasons for the service being organized in the way it is, what alternatives have been considered and why they have been rejected, and how performance is to be measured. The interpretation of the answers to such questions may involve some element of judgement, but all the reviewer can do is to report as factually as possible his or her conclusions.

6. *Reporting*. The draft report should be discussed in detail with members and officers before it is finalized and presented. Management audits can be performed by internal auditors as well as by independent outsiders. Some internal auditing staffs of non-profit organizations have performed management audits for many years, and have developed sophisticated procedures for conducting them. Alternatively, management audits may be undertaken by outside audit firms or management consultants. In the UK a number of large audit firms have developed audit teams that specialize in management audits in non-profit organizations.

# Just-in-time systems

Earlier in this chapter it was pointed out that re-organizing business processes and adopting a just-in-time (JIT) system was an illustration of business process engineering but so far a JIT system has not been explained. Given that implementing a JIT system is a mechanism for reducing non-value added costs and long-run costs it is important that you understand the nature of such a system and its cost management implications.

The success of Japanese firms in international markets generated interest among many Western companies as to how this success was achieved. The implementation of **just-in-time (JIT) production methods** was considered to be one of the major factors contributing to this success. The JIT approach involves a continuous commitment to the pursuit of excellence in all phases of manufacturing systems design and operations. The aims of JIT are to produce the required items, at the required quality and in the required quantities, at the precise time they are required. In particular, JIT seeks to achieve the following goals:

- elimination of non-value added activities;
- zero inventory;
- zero defects;
- batch sizes of one;
- zero breakdowns;
- a 100% on-time delivery service.

The above goals represent perfection, and are most unlikely to be achieved in practice. They do, however, offer targets, and create a climate for continuous improvement and excellence. Let us now examine the major features of a JIT manufacturing philosophy.

## ELIMINATION OF NON-VALUE ADDED ACTIVITIES

JIT manufacturing is best described as a philosophy of management dedicated to the elimination of waste. Waste is defined as anything that does not add value to a product. The lead or cycle time involved in manufacturing and selling a product consists of process time, inspection time, move time, queue time and storage time. Of these five steps, only process time adds value to the product. All the other activities add cost but no value to the product, and are deemed non-value added processes within the JIT philosophy. According to Berliner 10% of total manufacturing lead time in many companies is spent in the process time, 90% of the manufacturing lead time associated with a product adds costs, but no value, to the product. By adopting a JIT philosophy and focusing on reducing lead times, it is claimed that total costs can be significantly reduced. The ultimate goal of JIT is to convert raw materials to finished products with lead times equal to processing times, thus eliminating all non-value added activities.

## FACTORY LAYOUT

The first stage in implementing JIT manufacturing techniques is to rearrange the factory floor away from a **batch production functional layout** towards a product layout using flow lines. With a functional plant layout products pass through a number of specialist departments that normally contain a group of similar machines. Products are processed in large batches so as to minimize the set-up times when machine settings are changed between processing batches of different products. Batches move via different and complex routes through the various departments, travelling over much of the factory floor before they are completed. Each process normally involves a considerable amount of waiting time. In addition, much time is taken transporting items from one process to another. A further problem is that it is not easy at any point in time to determine what progress has been made on individual batches. Therefore detailed cost accumulation records are necessary to track work in progress. The consequences of this complex routing process are high work in progress levels and long manufacturing cycle times.

The JIT solution is to reorganize the production process by dividing the many different products that an organization makes into families of similar products or components. All of the products in a particular group will have similar production requirements and routings. Production is rearranged so that each product family is manufactured in a well-defined production cell based on flow line principles. In a **product flow line**, specialist departments containing *similar* machines no longer exist. Instead groups of *dissimilar* machines are organized into product or component family flow lines that function like an assembly line. For each product line the machines are placed close together in the order in which they are required by the group of products to be processed. Items in each product family can now move, one at a time, from process to process more easily, thereby reducing work in progress and lead times. The aim is to produce products or components from start to finish without returning to the stock room.

The ideal layout of each flow line is normally U-shaped. This layout, which is called **cellular manufacturing**, allows the operatives access to a number of machines, thus enabling each to operate several machines. Operatives are trained to operate all machines on the line and undertake routine preventive maintenance. Any worker can stop the production line if a problem arises. The emphasis is on employee empowerment, involving a high level of trust and greater responsibility for workers. It is assumed that workers will perform better when they are given greater authority to control their activities.

JIT manufacturing aims to produce the right parts at the right time, only when they are needed, and only in the quantity needed. This philosophy has resulted in a **pull manufacturing system**, which means that parts move through the production system based on end-unit demand, focusing on maintaining a constant flow of components rather than batches of WIP. With the pull system, work on components does not commence until specifically requested by the next process. JIT techniques aim to keep the materials moving in a continuous flow with no stoppages and no storage. Material movements between operations are minimized by eliminating space between work stations and grouping dissimilar machines into manufacturing cells on the basis of product groups and functioning like an assembly line.

The pull system is implemented by monitoring the consumption of parts at each operation stage and using various types of visible signalling systems (known as *Kanbans*) to authorize production and movement of the part to the using location. The producing cell cannot run the parts until authorized to do so. The signalling mechanism usually involves the use of *Kanban* containers. These containers hold materials or parts for movement from one work centre to another. The capacity of *Kanban* containers tends to vary from two to five units. They are just big enough to permit the production line to operate smoothly despite minor interruptions to individual work centres within the cell. To illustrate how the system works consider three machines forming part of a cell where the parts are first processed by machine A before being further processed on machine B and then machine C. The *Kanbans* are located between the machines. As long as the *Kanban* container is not full, the worker at machine A continues to produce parts, placing them in the *Kanban* container. When the container is full the worker stops producing and recommences when a part has been removed from the container by the worker operating machine B. A similar process applies between the operations of machines B and C. This process can result in idle time within certain locations within the cell, but the JIT philosophy considers that it is more beneficial to absorb short-run idle time rather than add to inventory during these periods. During idle time the workers perform preventive maintenance on the machines.

With a pull system problems arising in any part of the system will immediately halt the production line because work centres at the earlier stages will not receive the pull signal (because the *Kanban* container is full) if a problem arises at a later stage. Alternatively, work centres at a later stage will not have their pull signal answered (because of empty *Kanban* containers) when problems arise with work centres at the earlier stages of the production cycle. Thus attention is drawn immediately to production problems so that appropriate remedial action can be taken. This is deemed to be preferable to the approach adopted in a traditional manufacturing system where large stock levels provide a cushion for production to continue. This can lead to a situation where major problems can remain hidden, or deferred indefinitely, rather than triggering a search for immediate long-term solutions.

In contrast, the traditional manufacturing environment is based on a **push manu-facturing system**. With this system, machines are grouped into work centres based on the similarity of their functional capabilities. Each manufactured part has a designated routing, and the preceding process supplies parts to the subsequent process without any consideration being given to whether the next process is ready to work on the parts or not. Hence the use of the term 'push-through system'.

## BATCH SIZES OF ONE

Set-up time is the amount of time required to adjust equipment and to retool for a different product. Long set-up and changeover times make the production of batches with a small number of units uneconomic. However, the production of large batches leads to substantial throughput delays and the creation of high inventory levels. Throughput delays arise because several lengthy production runs are required to process larger batches through the factory. The JIT philosophy is to reduce and eventually eliminate set-up times. For example, by investing in advanced manufacturing technologies some machine settings can be adjusted automatically instead of manually. Alternatively, some set-up times can be eliminated entirely by redesigning products so that machines do not have to be reset each time a different product has to be made.

If set-up times are approaching zero, this implies that there are no advantages in producing in batches. Therefore the optimal batch size can be one. With a batch size of one, the work can flow smoothly to the next stage without the need for storage and to schedule the next machine to accept this item. In many situations set-up times will not be approaching zero, but by significantly reducing set-up times, small batch sizes will be economical. Small batch sizes, combined with short throughput times, also enable a firm to adapt more readily to short-term fluctuations in market demand and respond faster to customer requests, since production is not dependent on long planning lead times.

## JIT PURCHASING ARRANGEMENTS

The JIT philosophy also extends to adopting JIT purchasing techniques, whereby the delivery of materials immediately precedes their use. By arranging with suppliers for more frequent deliveries, stocks can be cut to a minimum. Considerable savings in material handling expenses can be obtained by requiring suppliers to inspect materials before their delivery and guaranteeing their quality. This improved service is obtained by giving more business to fewer suppliers and placing longer-term purchasing orders. Therefore the supplier has an assurance of long-term sales, and can plan to meet this demand.

Companies that have implemented JIT purchasing techniques claim to have substantially reduced their investment in raw materials and work in progress stocks. Other advantages include a substantial saving in factory space, large quantity discounts, savings in time from negotiating with fewer suppliers and a reduction in paperwork arising from issuing blanket long-term orders to a few suppliers rather than individual purchase orders to many suppliers.

## JIT AND MANAGEMENT ACCOUNTING

Management accountants in many organizations have been strongly criticized because of their failure to alter the management accounting system to reflect the move from a traditional manufacturing to a just-in-time manufacturing system. Conventional management accounting systems can encourage behaviour that is inconsistent with a just-in-time manufacturing philosophy. Management accounting must support just-in-time manufacturing by monitoring, identifying and communicating to decision-makers any delay, error and waste in the system. Modern management accounting systems are now placing greater emphasis on providing information on supplier reliability, set-up times, throughput cycle times, percentage of deliveries that are on time and defect rates. All of these measures are critical to supporting a just-in-time manufacturing philosophy.

## Summary

Traditional cost control systems emphasize cost containment whereas cost management focuses on cost reduction. Cost management consists of those actions that are taken by managers to reduce costs, some of which are prioritized using information extracted from the accounting system. Other actions, however, are undertaken without the use of accounting information. They involve process improvements, where an opportunity has been identified to perform processes more effectively and efficiently, and which have obvious cost reduction outcomes. Several approaches have been described within this chapter that fall within the cost management area.

*Life-cycle costing* estimates and accumulates costs over a product's entire life cycle in order to determine whether the profits earned during the manufacturing phase will cover the costs incurred during the pre- and post-manufacturing stages. Approximately 80% of a product's costs are committed during the planning and design stage. At this stage product designers determine the product's design and the production process. In contrast, the majority of costs are incurred at the manufacturing stage, but they have already become locked-in at the planning and design stage and are difficult to alter. Cost management can be most effectively exercised during the planning and design stage and not at the manufacturing stage when the product design and processes have already been determined and costs have been committed.

*Target costing* is a customer-oriented technique that is widely used by Japanese companies and which has recently been adopted by companies in Europe and the USA. The first stage requires market research to determine the target selling price for a product. Next a standard or desired profit margin is deducted to establish a target cost for the product. The target cost is compared with the predicted actual cost. If the predicted actual cost is above the target cost intensive efforts are made to close the gap. Value engineering and functional analysis are used to drive the predicted actual cost down to the target cost. The major advantage of adopting target costing is that it is deployed during a product's design and planning stage so that it can have a maximum impact in determining the level of the locked-in costs.

In addition to target costing *kaizen costing* is widely used by Japanese organizations as a mechanism for reducing and managing costs. The major difference between target and *kaizen* costing is that target costing is applied during the design stage whereas *kaizen* costing is applied during the manufacturing stage of the product life cycle. With target costing the focus is on the product and cost reductions are achieved primarily through product design. In contrast, *kaizen* costing focuses on the production processes and cost reductions are derived primarily through the increased efficiency of the production process. The aim of *kaizen* costing is to reduce the cost of components and products by a pre-specified amount. A major feature is that workers are given the responsibility to improve processes and reduce costs. Unlike target costing it is not accompanied by a set of techniques or procedures that are automatically applied to achieve the cost reductions.

*Activity-based management (ABM)* focuses on managing the business on the basis of the activities that make up the organization. It is based on the premise that activities consume costs. Therefore by managing activities costs will be managed in the long term. The goal of ABM is to enable customer needs to be satisfied while making fewer demands on organization resources. Prior to the introduction of ABM most organizations have been unaware of the cost of undertaking the activities that make up the organization. Knowing the cost of activities enables those activities with the highest cost to be highlighted so that they can be prioritized for detailed studies to ascertain whether they can be eliminated or performed more efficiently. To identify and prioritize the potential for cost reduction many organizations have found it useful to classify activities as either value added or non-value added. A value added activity is an activity that customers perceive as adding usefulness to the product or service they purchase whereas a non-value added activity is an activity where there is an opportunity for cost reduction without reducing the product service potential to the customer. Taking action to reduce or eliminate non-value added activities given top priority because by doing so the organization permanently reduces the cost it incurs without reducing the value of the product to the customer.

A business process consists of a collection of activities that are linked together in a coordinated manner to achieve a specific objective. *Business process re-engineering* involves examining business processes and making substantial changes to how the organization currently operates. The aim is to improve the key business processes in an organization by focusing on simplification, cost reduction, improved quality and enhanced customer satisfaction.

A *cost of quality report* indicates the total cost to the organization of producing products or services that do not conform with quality requirements. Quality costs are analysed by four categories for reporting purposes (prevention, appraisal, and internal and external failure costs). The report draws management's attention to the possibility of reducing total quality costs by a wiser allocation of costs among the four quality categories.

Increasing attention is now being given to *value-chain analysis* as a means of increasing customer satisfaction and managing costs more effectively. The value chain is the linked set of value-creating activities all the way from basic raw material

sources from component suppliers through to the ultimate end-use product or service delivered to the customer. Understanding how value-chain activities are performed and how they interact with each other creates the conditions to improve customer satisfaction, particularly in terms of cost efficiency, quality and delivery.

*Benchmarking* involves comparing key activities with world-class best practices by identifying an activity that needs to be improved, finding a non-rival organization that is considered to represent world-class best practice for the activity, and studying how it performs the activity. The objective is to establish how the activity can be improved and ensure that the improvements are implemented.

In recent years many companies have sought to eliminate and/or reduce the costs of non-value added activities by introducing *just-in-time (JIT) systems*. The aims of a JIT system are to produce the required items, at the required quality and in the required quantities, at the precise time they are required. In particular, JIT aims to eliminate waste by minimizing inventories and reducing cycle or throughput times (i.e. the time elapsed from when customers place an order until the time when they receive the desired product or service). Adopting a JIT manufacturing system involves moving from a batch production functional layout to a cellular flow line manufacturing system. ●●●

## Key Terms and Concepts

## Recommended Reading

You should refer to Kato (1993) and Tani *et al.* (1994) for a description of target costing in Japanese companies. A more detailed description of activity-based cost management can be found in chapter 8 of Kaplan and Cooper (1998). For a description of the application of value-chain analysis to cost management see Shank and Govindarajan (1992).

## Key Examination Points

Much of the content of this chapter relates to relatively new topics. Therefore fewer examination questions have been set by the professional examining bodies on the content of this chapter. The questions that follow provide an illustration of the type of questions that have been set. It is likely that most of the questions that will be set on cost management topics will be essays and will require students to demonstrate that they have read widely on the various topics covered in this chapter. Questions set are likely to be open-ended and there will be no ideal answer.

## Questions

* Indicates that a suggested solution is to be found in the *Students' Manual*.

### 22.1 Advanced
(a) Overtime premiums and shift allowances can be traced to specific batches, jobs or products and should be considered to be direct labour rather than indirect labour.

    You are required to discuss the above statement. (12 marks)
(b) Your managing director, after hearing a talk at a branch meeting on just-in-time (JIT) manufacturing would like the management to consider introducing JIT at your unit which manufactures typewriters and also keyboards for computing systems.

    You are required as the assistant management accountant, to prepare a discussion paper for circulation to the directors and senior management, describing just-in-time manufacturing, the likely benefits which would follow its introduction and the effect its introduction would probably have on the cost accounting system. (13 marks)
    (Total 25 marks)
    *CIMA Stage 2 Cost Accounting*

### 22.2* Advanced
The implementation of budgeting in a world class manufacturing environment may be affected by the impact of (i) a total quality ethos (ii) a just-in-time philosophy and (iii) an activity based focus.

Briefly describe the principles incorporated in EACH of (i) to (iii) and discuss ways in which each may result in changes in the way in which budgets are prepared as compared to a traditional incremental budgeting system. (15 marks)
*ACCA Paper 9 Information for Control and Decision Making*

### 22.3* Advanced
New techniques are often described as contributing to cost reduction, but when cost reduction is necessary it is not obvious that such new approaches are used in preference to more established approaches. Three examples are:

| new technique compared with | established approach |
|---|---|
| (a) benchmarking | interfirm comparison |
| (b) activity based budgeting | zero base budgeting |
| (c) target costing | continuous cost improvement |

You are required, for two of the three newer techniques mentioned above:

• to explain its objectives
• to explain its workings
• to differentiate it from the related approach identified
• to explain how it would contribute to a cost reduction programme. (20 marks)
*CIMA Stage 4 Management Accounting – Control and Audit*

## 22.4 Advanced

(a) Life Cycle Costing normally refers to costs incurred by the user of major capital equipment over the whole of the useful equipment life. Explain the determination and calculation of these costs and the problems in their calculation. (8 marks)

(b) In the strategy and marketing literature there is continual discussion of the product life cycle.

You are required to explain, for *each* of the *four* stages of the product life cycle,
- start-up
- growth
- maturity
- harvest,

which system of product costing would be most useful for decision making and control, and why.

Explain briefly in your answer possible alternative organizational structures at each stage in the life cycle. (12 marks)
(Total 20 marks)
*CIMA Stage 4 Management Accounting – Control and Audit*

## 22.5 Advanced

Kaplan ('Relevance Regained', *Management Accounting*, September 1988) states the view that the 'time-honoured traditions of cost accounting' are 'irrelevant, misleading and wrong'. Variance analysis, product costing and operational control are cited as examples of areas where information provided by management accountants along traditional lines could well fail to meet today's needs of management in industry.

You are required to

(a) state what you consider to be the main requirements for effective operational control and product costing in modern industry;
(10 marks)

(b) identify which 'traditional cost accounting' methods in the areas quoted in (a) *may be considered* to be failing to supply the appropriate information to management, and explain why; (9 marks)

(c) recommend changes to the 'traditional cost accounting' methods and information which would serve to meet the problems identified in (b). (6 marks)
(Total 25 marks)

*CIMA Stage 4 Management Accounting – Control and Audit*

## 22.6* Advanced

'ABC is still at a relatively early stage of its development and its implications for process control may in the final analysis be more important than its product costing implications. It is a good time for every organisation to consider whether or not ABC is appropriate to its particular circumstances.'

J Innes & F Mitchell, *Activity Based Costing, A Review with Case Studies*, CIMA, 1990.

You are required:

(a) to contrast the feature of organisations which would benefit from ABC with those which would not; (8 marks)

(b) to explain in what ways ABC may be used to manage costs, and the limitations of these approaches; (11 marks)

(c) to explain and to discuss the use of target costing to control product costs. (6 marks)
(Total 25 marks)
*CIMA Stage 4 Management Accounting – Control and Audit*

## 22.7 Advanced

A company is proposing the introduction of an activity-based costing (ABC) system as a basis for much of its management accounting information.

(a) Briefly describe how ABC is different from a traditional absorption approach to costing and explain why it was developed. (8 marks)

(b) Discuss the advantages and limitations of this 'approach based on activities' for management accounting information in the context of:
(i) preparing plans and budgets
(ii) monitoring and controlling operations
(iii) decision-making, for example, product deletion decisions. (12 marks)
(Total 20 marks)
*ACCA Paper 8 Managerial Finance*

## 22.8* Advanced

(a) You are required to:
(i) explain the basic principles on which value for money audits (VFM) in local authorities are conducted;
(ii) give *three* specific examples of methods of analysis which may be employed in practice (10 marks)

(b) Discuss the problems experienced with programme planning and budgeting systems (PPBS) and the major differences between PPBS and VFM. (10 marks)

(Total 20 marks)

*CIMA Stage 4 Management Accounting – Control and Audit*

## 22.9 Advanced

'Japanese companies that have used just-in-time (JIT) for five or more years are reporting close to a 30% increase in labour productivity, a 60% reduction in inventories, a 90% reduction in quality rejection rates, and a 15% reduction in necessary plant space. However, implementing a just-in-time system does not occur overnight. It took Toyota over twenty years to develop its system and realize significant benefits from it.' *Source*: Sumer C. Aggrawal, *Harvard Business Review* (9/85)

Requirements:

(a) Explain how the benefits claimed for JIT in the above quotation are achieved and why it takes so long to achieve those benefits.

(15 marks)

(b) Explain how management information systems in general (and management accounting systems in particular) should be developed in order to facilitate and make best use of JIT.

(10 marks)

(Total 25 marks)

*CIMA Stage 3 Management Accounting Applications*

## 22.10* Advanced

Within a diversified group, one division, which operates many similar branches in a service industry, has used internal benchmarking and regards it as very useful.

Group central management is now considering the wider use of benchmarking.

Requirement:

(a) Explain the aims, operation, and limitations of internal benchmarking, and explain how external benchmarking differs in these respects. (10 marks)

(b) A multinational group wishes to internally benchmark the production of identical components made in several plants in different countries. Investments have been made with some plants in installing new Advanced Manufacturing Technology (AMT) and supporting this with manufacturing manage-

ment systems such as Just in Time (JIT) and Total Quality Management (TQM). Preliminary comparisons suggest that the standard cost in plants using new technology is no lower than that in plants using older technology.

Requirement:

Explain possible reasons for the similar standard costs in plants with differing technology. Recommend appropriate benchmarking measures, recognising that total standard costs may not provide the most useful measurement of performance.

(10 marks)

(Total 20 marks)

*CIMA Stage 4 Management Accounting Control Systems*

## 22.11* Advanced

You are Financial Controller of a medium-sized engineering business. This business was family-owned and managed for many years but has recently been acquired by a large group to become its Engineering Division.

The first meeting of the management board with the newly appointed Divisional Managing Director has not gone well.

He commented on the results of the division:

- Sales and profits were well below budget for the month and cumulatively for the year, and the forecast for the rest of the year suggested no improvement.

- Working capital was well over budget.

- Even if budget were achieved the return on capital employed was well below group standards.

He proposed a Total Quality Management (TQM) programme to change attitudes and improve results.

The initial responses of the managers to these comments were:

- The Production Director said there was a limit to what was possible with obsolete machines and facilities and only a very short-term order book.

- The Sales Director commented that it was impossible to get volume business when deliveries and quality were unreliable and designs out of date.

- The Technical Director said that there was little point in considering product improvements when the factory could not be bothered to update designs and the sales executives were reluctant to discuss new ideas with new potential customers.

You have been asked to prepare reports for the next management board meeting to enable a more constructive discussion.

You are required:

(a) to explain the critical success factors for the implementation of a programme of Total Quality Management. Emphasize the factors that are crucial in changing attitudes from those quoted; (11 marks)

(b) to explain how you would measure quality cost, and how the establishment of a system of measuring quality costs would contribute to a TQM programme. (9 marks)

(Total 20 marks)

*CIMA Stage 4 Management Accounting – Control and Audit*

## 22.12 Advanced: Feedback control theory and product quality measurement

(a) In control theory, a 'feedback control' mechanism is one which supplies information to determine whether corrective action should be taken to re-establish control of a system.

You are required to:

(i) illustrate by means of a diagram how the feedback mechanism operates within a control system, adding a commentary describing how the system functions; (9 marks)

(ii) distinguish 'feedforward' from 'feedback' control, giving *two* examples of *each* from within management accounting. (4 marks)

(b) Achievement of a high standard of product quality has become a major issue in modern manufacturing industry.

In support of programmes aimed at achieving acceptable quality standards, some companies have introduced detailed 'quality cost' measurement schemes.

In others, the philosophy has been that no measurement procedures should be devoted especially to the measurement of quality costs: quality cost schemes designed to measure performance in this area are considered to add to administrative burdens; in reality 'quality' should be the expected achievement of the required product specification.

(i) set out a classification of quality costs which would be useful for reporting purposes. Give examples of actual costs which would be represented in each classification; (7 marks)

(ii) discuss the reality of the differences of philosophy expressed in the opening statement. Do they represent fundamental differences or may they be reconciled? (5 marks)

(Total 25 marks)

*CIMA Stage 4 Management Accounting – Control and Audit*

## 22.13* Advanced: Calculation of costs before and after introduction of a quality management programme

Calton Ltd make and sell a single product. The existing product unit specifications are as follows:

| | |
|---|---|
| Direct material X: | 8 sq. metres at £4 per sq. metre |
| Machine time: | 0.6 running hours |
| Machine cost per gross hour: | £40 |
| Selling price: | £100 |

Calton Ltd require to fulfil orders for 5000 product units per period. There are no stocks of product units at the beginning or end of the period under review. The stock level of material X remains unchanged throughout the period.

The following additional information affects the costs and revenues:

1. 5% of incoming material from suppliers is scrapped due to poor receipt and storage organization.

2. 4% of material X input to the machine process is wasted due to processing problems.

3. Inspection and storage of material X costs £0.10 pence per sq. metre purchased.

4. Inspection during the production cycle, calibration checks on inspection equipment, vendor rating and other checks cost £25 000 per period.

5. Production quantity is increased to allow for the downgrading of 12.5% of product units at the final inspection stage. Downgraded units

are sold as 'second quality' units at a discount of 30% on the standard selling price.

6.  Production quantity is increased to allow for returns from customers which are replaced free of charge. Returns are due to specification failure and account for 5% of units initially delivered to customers. Replacement units incur a delivery cost of £8 per unit. 80% of the returns from customers are rectified using 0.2 hours of machine running time per unit and are re-sold as 'third quality' products at a discount of 50% on the standard selling price. The remaining returned units are sold as scrap for £5 per unit.

7.  Product liability and other claims by customers is estimated at 3% of sales revenue from standard product sales.

8.  Machine idle time is 20% of gross machine hours used (i.e. running hours = 80% of gross hours).

9.  Sundry costs of administration, selling and distribution total £60 000 per period.

10. Calton Ltd is aware of the problem of excess costs and currently spends £20 000 per period in efforts to prevent a number of such problems from occurring.

Calton Ltd is planning a quality management programme which will increase its excess cost prevention expenditure from £20 000 to £60 000 per period. It is estimated that this will have the following impact:

1.  A reduction in stores losses of material X to 3% of incoming material.

2.  A reduction in the downgrading of product units at inspection to 7.5% of units inspected.

3.  A reduction in material X losses in process to 2.5% of input to the machine process.

4.  A reduction in returns of products from customers to 2.5% of units delivered.

5.  A reduction in machine idle time to 12.5% of gross hours used.

6.  A reduction in product liability and other claims to 1% of sales revenue from standard product sales.

7.  A reduction in inspection, calibration, vendor rating and other checks by 40% of the existing figure.

8.  A reduction in sundry administration, selling and distribution costs by 10% of the existing figure.

9.  A reduction in machine running time required per product unit to 0.5 hours.

Required:

(a) Prepare summaries showing the calculation of (i) total production units (pre-inspection), (ii) purchases of material X (sq. metres), (iii) gross machine hours. In each case the figures are required for the situation both before and after the implementation of the additional quality management programme, in order that the orders for 5000 product units may be fulfilled. (10 marks)

(b) Prepare profit and loss accounts for Calton Ltd for the period showing the profit earned both before and after the implementation of the additional quality management programme. (10 marks)

(c) Comment on the relevance of a quality management programme and explain the meaning of the terms internal failure costs, external failure costs, appraisal costs and prevention costs giving examples for each, taken where possible from the information in the question. (10 marks)

(Total 30 marks)

*ACCA Level 2 Cost and Management Accounting II*

## 22.14 Advanced: Financial evaluation of implementing a quality management programme

Bushworks Ltd convert synthetic slabs into components AX and BX for use in the car industry. Bushworks Ltd is planning a quality management programme at a cost of £250 000. The following information relates to the costs incurred by Bushworks Ltd both before and after the implementation of the quality management programme:

1.  *Synthetic slabs*

Synthetic slabs cost £40 per hundred. On average 2.5% of synthetic slabs received are returned to the supplier as scrap because of deterioration in stores. The supplier allows a credit of £1 per hundred slabs for such returns. In addition, on receipt in stores, checks to ensure that the slabs received conform to specification costs £14 000 per annum.

A move to a just-in-time purchasing system will eliminate the holding of stocks of synthetic slabs. This has been negotiated with the supplier who will deliver slabs of guaranteed design specification for £44 per hundred units, eliminating all stockholding costs.

2. *Curing/moulding process*

The synthetic slabs are issued to a curing/holding process which has variable conversion costs of £20 per hundred slabs input. This process produces sub-components A and B which have the same cost structure. Losses of 10% of input to the process because of incorrect temperature control during the process are sold as scrap at £5 per hundred units. The quality programme will rectify the temperature control problem thus reducing losses to 1% of input to the process.

3. *Finishing process*

The finishing process has a bank of machines which perform additional operations on type A and B sub-components as required and converts them into final components AX and BX respectively. The variable conversion costs in the finishing process for AX and BX are £15 and £25 per hundred units respectively. At the end of the finishing process 15% of units are found to be defective. Defective units are sold for scrap at £10 per hundred units. The quality programme will convert the finishing process into two dedicated cells, one for each of component types AX and BX. The dedicated cell variable costs per hundred sub-components A and B processed will be £12 and £20 respectively. Defective units of components AX and BX are expected to fall to 2.5% of the input to each cell. Defective components will be sold as scrap as at present.

4. *Finished goods*

A finished goods stock of components AX and BX of 15 000 and 30 000 units respectively is held throughout the year in order to allow for customer demand fluctuations and free replacement of units returned by customers due to specification faults. Customer returns are currently 2.5% of components delivered to customers. Variable stock holding costs are £15 per thousand component units.

The proposed dedicated cell layout of the finishing process will eliminate the need to hold stocks of finished components, other than sufficient to allow for the free replacement of those found to be defective in customer hands. This stock level will be set at one month's free replacement to customers which is estimated at 500 and 1000 units for types AX and BX respectively. Variable stock-holding costs will remain at £15 per thousand component units.

5. *Quantitative data*

Some preliminary work has already been carried out in calculating the number of units of synthetic slabs, sub-components A and B and components AX and BX which will be required both before and after the implementation of the quality management programme, making use of the information in the question. Table 1 summarises the relevant figures.

**Table 1**

| | Existing situation | | Amended situation | |
| --- | --- | --- | --- | --- |
| | Type A/AX (units) | Type B/BX (units) | Type A/AX (units) | Type B/BX (units) |
| Sales | 800 000 | 1 200 000 | 800 000 | 1 200 000 |
| Customer returns | 20 000 | 30 000 | 6 000 | 12 000 |
| Finished goods delivered | 820 000 | 1 230 000 | 806 000 | 1 212 000 |
| Finished process losses | 144 706 | 217 059 | 20 667 | 31 077 |
| Input to finishing process | 964 706 | 1 447 059 | 826 667 | 1 243 077 |
| | 2 411 765 | | 2 069 744 | |
| Curing/moulding losses | 267 974 | | 20 907 | |
| Input to curing/moulding | 2 679 739 | | 2 090 651 | |
| Stores losses | 68 711 | | — | |
| Purchase of synthetic slabs | 2 748 450 | | 2 090 651 | |

**Required:**

(a) Evaluate and present a statement showing the net financial benefit or loss per annum of implementing the quality management programme, using the information in the question and the data in Table 1.

(*All relevant workings must be shown*)

(27 marks)

(b) Explain the meaning of the terms internal failure costs, external failure costs, appraisal costs and prevention costs giving examples of each.

(8 marks)

**22.15\* Advanced: Traditional and activity-based budget statements and life-cycle costing**

The budget for the Production, Planning and Development Department of Obba plc, is currently prepared as part of a traditional budgetary planning and control system. The analysis of costs by expense type for the period ended 30 November 2000 where this system is in use is as follows:

| Expense type | Budget % | Actual % |
| --- | --- | --- |
| Salaries | 60 | 63 |
| Supplies | 6 | 5 |
| Travel cost | 12 | 12 |
| Technology cost | 10 | 7 |
| Occupancy cost | 12 | 13 |

The total budget and actual costs for the department for the period ended 30 November 2000 are £1 000 000 and £1 060 000 respectively.

The company now feels that an Activity Based Budgeting approach should be used. A number of activities have been identified for the Production, Planning and Development Department. An investigation has indicated that total budget and actual costs should be attributed to the activities on the following basis:

| | Budget % | Actual % |
|---|---|---|
| *Activities* | | |
| 1. Routing/scheduling – new products | 20 | 16 |
| 2. Routing/scheduling – existing products | 40 | 34 |
| 3. Remedial re-routing/scheduling | 5 | 12 |
| 4. Special studies – specific orders | 10 | 8 |
| 5. Training | 10 | 15 |
| 6. Management & administration | 15 | 15 |

Required:

(a) (i) Prepare *two* budget control statements for the Production Planning and Development Department for the period ended 30 November 2000 which compare budget with actual cost and show variances using

   1. a traditional expense based analysis and

   2. an activity based analysis. (6 marks)

   (ii) Identify and comment on *four* advantages claimed for the use of Activity Based Budgeting over traditional budgeting using the Production Planning and Development example to illustrate your answer. (12 marks)

   (iii) Comment on the use of the information provided in the activity based statement which you prepared in (i) in activity based performance measurement and suggest additional information which would assist in such performance measurement. (8 marks)

(b) Other activities have been identified and the budget quantified for the three months ended 31 March 2001 as follows:

| Activities | Cost Driver Unit basis | Units of Cost Driver | Cost (£000) |
|---|---|---|---|
| Product design | design hours | 8 000 | 2000 (see note 1) |
| Purchasing | purchase orders | 4 000 | 200 |
| Production | machine hours | 12 000 | 1500 (see note 2) |
| Packing | volume (cu.m.) | 20 000 | 400 |
| Distribution | weight (kg) | 120 000 | 600 |

*Note 1*: this includes all design costs for new products released this period.

*Note 2*: this includes a depreciation provision of £300 000 of which £8000 applies to 3 months depreciation on a straight line basis for a new product (NPD). The remainder applies to other products.

New product NPD is included in the above budget. The following additional information applies to NPD:

(i) Estimated total output over the product life cycle: 5000 units (4 years life cycle).

(ii) Product design requirement: 400 design hours

(iii) Output in quarter ended 31 March 2001: 250 units

(iv) Equivalent batch size per purchase order: 50 units

(v) Other product unit data: production time 0.75 machine hours: volume 0.4 cu. metres; weight 3 kg.

Required:

Prepare a unit overhead cost for product NPD using an activity based approach which includes an appropriate share of life cycle costs using the information provided in (b) above. (9 marks)

(Total 35 marks)

*ACCA Paper Information for Control and Decision Making*

# 23

# Strategic management accounting

During the late 1980s criticisms of traditional management accounting practices were widely publicized and new approaches were advocated which are more in tune with today's competitive and business environment. In particular, strategic management accounting has been identified as a way forward. However, there is still no comprehensive framework as to what constitutes strategic management accounting. In this chapter we shall examine the elements of strategic management accounting and describe the different contributions that have been made to its development.

One of the elements of strategic management accounting involves the provision of information for the formulation of an organization's strategy and managing strategy implementation. To encourage behaviour that is consistent with an organization's strategy, attention is now being given to developing an integrated framework of performance measurement that can be used to clarify, communicate and manage strategy. In the latter part of this chapter recent developments that seek to incorporate performance measurement within the strategic management process are described.

## Learning objectives:

After studying this chapter, you should be able to:

- describe the different elements of strategic management accounting;

- describe the balanced scorecard;

- explain each of the four perspectives of the balanced scorecard;

- provide illustrations of performance measures for each of the four perspectives;

- describe the distinguishing features of performance measurement in service organizations.

## What is strategic management accounting?

**AR** For many years strategic management accounting has been advocated as a potential area of development that would enhance the future contribution of management accounting. In the late 1980s the UK Chartered Institute of Management Accountants commissioned an investigation to review the current state of development of management accounting. The findings were published in a report entitled *Management Accounting: Evolution not Revolution*, authored by Bromwich and Bhimani (1989). In the report, and a follow-up report (*Management Accounting: Pathways to Progress*, 1994) Bromwich and Bhimani drew attention to strategic management accounting as an area for future development. Despite the publicity that strategic management accounting has received there is still no comprehensive conceptual framework of what strategic management accounting is (Tomkins and Carr, 1996).

Innes (1998) defines strategic management accounting as the provision of information to support the strategic decisions in organizations. Strategic decisions usually involve the longer-term, have a significant effect on the organization and, although they may have an internal element, they also have an external element. Adopting this definition suggests that the provision of information that supports an organization's major long-term decisions, such as the use of activity-based costing information for product profitability analysis, falls within the domain of strategic management accounting. This view is supported by Cooper and Kaplan (1988) who state that strategic accounting techniques are designed to support the overall competitive strategy of the organization, principally by the power of using information technology to develop more refined product and service costs.

Other writers, however, have adopted definitions that emphasize that strategic management accounting is externally focused. Simmonds (1981, 1982), who first coined the term strategic management accounting, views it as the provision and analysis of management accounting data about a business and its competitors which is of use in the development and monitoring of the strategy of that business. More recently, Bromwich (1990), a principal advocate of strategic management accounting, has provided the following definition:

> The provision and analysis of financial information on the firm's product markets and competitors' costs and cost structures and the monitoring of the enterprise's strategies and those of its competitors in these markets over a number of periods (Bromwich, 1990: 28).

Because of the lack of consensus on what constitutes strategic management accounting Lord (1996) reviewed the literature and identified several strands that have been used to characterize strategic management accounting. They include:

1. The extension of traditional management accounting's internal focus to include external information about competitors.
2. The relationship between the strategic position chosen by a firm and the expected emphasis on management accounting (i.e. accounting in relation to strategic positioning).
3. Gaining competitive advantage by analysing ways to decrease costs and/or enhance the differentiation of a firm's products, through exploiting linkages in the value chain and optimizing cost drivers.

Let us now examine each of the above characteristics in more detail.

## EXTERNAL INFORMATION ABOUT COMPETITORS

Much of the early work relating to strategic management accounting can be attributed to the writings of Simmonds (1981, 1982 and 1986). He argued that management accounting should be more outward looking and should help the firm evaluate its competitive position relative to the rest of the industry by collecting data on costs and prices, sales volumes and market shares, and cash flows and resources availability for it main competitors. To protect an organization's strategic position and determine strategies to improve its future competitiveness managers require information that indicates by whom, by how much and why they are gaining or being beaten. This information provides advance warning of the need for a change in competitive strategy.

Simmonds also stressed the importance of the **learning curve** (see Chapter 24) as a means of obtaining strategic advantage by forecasting cost reductions and consequently selling price reductions of competitors. He also drew attention to the importance of early experience with a new product as a means of conferring an unbeatable lead over competitors. The leading competitor should be able to reduce its selling price for the product (through the learning curve effect) which should further increase its volume and market share and eventually force some lagging competitors out of the industry.

An organization may also seek to gain strategic advantage by its pricing policy. Here the management accounting function can assist by attempting to assess each major competitor's cost structure and relate this to their prices. In particular, Simmonds suggests that it may be possible to assess the cost–volume–profit relationship of competitors in order to predict their pricing responses. He states:

> Clearly, competitor reactions can substantially influence the outcome of a price move. Moreover, likely reactions may not be self-evident when each competitor faces a different cost–volume–profit situation. Competitors may not follow a price lead nor even march in perfect step as they each act to defend or build their own positions. For an adequate assessment of the likelihood of competitor price reactions, then, some calculation is needed of the impact of possible price moves on the performance of individual competitors. Such an assessment in turn requires an accounting approach that can depict both competitor cost–volume–profit situations and their financial resources (Simmonds: 1982: 207).

Besides dealing with costs and prices Simmonds focused on volume and market share. By monitoring movements in market share for its major products, an organization can see whether it is gaining or losing position, and an examination of relative market shares will indicate the strength of different competitors. Including market-share details in management accounting reports helps to make management accounting more strategically relevant. Competitor information may be obtained through public, formal sources, such as published reports and the business press, or through informal channels, such as the firm's salesforce, its customers and its suppliers.

Simmonds (1981) also suggested some changes and additions to traditional management accounting reporting systems in order to include the above information. Market share statements could be incorporated into management accounts. In addition, budgets could be routinely presented in a strategic format with columns for Ourselves, Competitor A, Competitor B, etc. According to Ward (1992) very few firms regularly report competitor information.

## ACCOUNTING IN RELATION TO STRATEGIC POSITIONING

Various classifications of strategic positions that firms may choose have been identified in the strategic management literature. Porter (1985) suggests that a firm has a choice of three generic strategies in order to achieve sustainable competitive advantage. They are:

- *cost leadership*, whereby an enterprise aims to be the lowest-cost producer within the industry;
- *differentiation*, whereby the enterprise seeks to offer some unique dimension in its products/service that is valued by customers and which can command a premium price;
- *focus*, which involves seeking advantage in a narrow segment of the market either by way of cost leadership or by product differentiation.

Miles and Snow (1978) distinguish between *defenders* and *prospectors*. Defenders operate in relatively stable areas, have limited product lines and employ a mass production routine technology. They compete through making operations efficient through cost, quality and service leadership, and engage in little product/market research. Prospectors compete through new product innovations and market development and are constantly looking for new market opportunities. Hence, they face a more uncertain task environment.

The accounting literature suggests that firms will place more emphasis on particular accounting techniques, depending on which strategic position they adopt. For example, Simons (1987) found that business units that follow a defender strategy tend to place a greater emphasis on the use of financial measures (e.g., short-term budget targets) for compensating financial managers. Prospector firms placed a greater emphasis on forecast data and reduced importance on cost control. Ittner *et al.* (1997) also found that the use of non-financial measures for determining executive's bonuses increases with the extent to which firms follow an innovation-oriented prospector strategy. Shank (1989) stresses the need for management accounting to support a firm's competitive strategies, and illustrates how two different competitive strategies – cost leadership and product differentiation – demand different cost analysis perspectives. For example, carefully engineered product cost standards are likely to be a very important management control tool for a firm that pursues a cost leadership strategy in a mature commodity business. In contrast, carefully engineered manufacturing cost standards are likely to be less important for a firm following a product differentiation strategy in a market-driven, rapidly changing and fast-growing business. A firm pursuing a product differentiation strategy is likely to require more information than a cost leader about new product innovations, design cycle times, research and development expenditures and marketing cost analysis. Exhibit 23.1 illustrates some potential differences in cost management emphasis, depending on the primary strategic thrust of the firm.

## GAINING COMPETITIVE ADVANTAGE

Porter (1985) advocated using value-chain analysis (see Chapter 22) to gain competitive advantage. The aim of value chain analysis is to find linkages between value-creating activities which result in lower cost and/or enhanced differentiation. These linkages can be within the firm or between the firm and its suppliers, and customers. The value chain comprises five primary activities and a number of support activities. The primary activities are defined sequentially as inbound logistics, operations, outbound logistics, marketing and sales and services. The secondary activities exist to support the primary activities and include the firm's infrastructure, human resource management, technology and procurement. Costs and assets are assigned to each activity in the value chain. The cost behaviour pattern of each activity depends on a number of causal factors which Porter calls cost drivers. These cost drivers operate in an interactive way and it is management's success in coping with them which determines the cost structure.

Strategic cost analysis also involves identifying the value chain and the operation of cost drivers of competitors in order to understand relative competitiveness. Porter advocates that organizations should use this information to identify opportunities for cost reduction, either by improving control of the cost drivers or reconfiguring the value chain. The latter involves deciding on those areas of the value chain where the firm has a comparative advantage and those which it should source to suppliers. It is essential that the cost reduction performance of both the organization and its principal competitors is continually monitored if competitive advantage is to be sustained.

You may be able to remember the illustration in the previous chapter relating to how an American automobile company failed to use the value chain approach to exploit links with suppliers and enhance profitability.[1] The company had made significant internal

| EXHIBIT 23.1 |
|---|

**Relationship between strategies and cost management emphasis**

savings from introducing JIT manufacturing techniques, but, at the same time, price increases from suppliers more than offset these internal cost savings. A value chain perspective revealed that 50% of the firm's costs related to purchases from parts suppliers. As the automobile company reduced its own need for buffer stocks, it placed major new strains on the manufacturing responsiveness of suppliers.

| | Product differentiation | Cost leadership |
|---|---|---|
| Role of standard costs in assessing performance | Not very important | Very important |
| Importance of such concepts as flexible budgeting for manufacturing cost control | Moderate to low | High to very high |
| Perceived importance of meeting budgets | Moderate to low | High to very high |
| Importance of marketing cost analysis | Critical to success | Often not done at all on a formal basis |
| Importance of product cost as an input to pricing decisions | Low | High |
| Importance of competitor cost analysis | Low | High |

*Source*: Shank (1989)

The increase in the suppliers' manufacturing costs was greater than the decrease in the automobile company's internal costs. Shank (1989) states:

> For every dollar of manufacturing cost the assembly plants saved by moving towards JIT management concepts, the suppliers' plant spent much more than one dollar extra because of schedule instability arising from the introduction of JIT. Because of its narrow value added perspective, the auto company had ignored the impact of its changes on its suppliers' costs. Management had ignored the idea that JIT involves a partnership with suppliers (Shark, 1989: 51).

## OTHER CONTRIBUTIONS TO STRATEGIC MANAGEMENT ACCOUNTING

In this section we shall briefly consider further approaches to strategic management accounting which have not been included within Lord's classification of the literature. Bromwich (1990) has attempted to develop strategic management accounting to consider the benefits which products offer to customers, and how these contribute to sustainable competitive advantage. Bromwich sought to compare the relative cost of product attributes or characteristics with what the customer is willing to pay for them. Products are seen as comprising of a package of attributes which they offer to customers. It is these attributes that actually constitute commodities, and which appeal to customers so that they buy the product. The attributes might include a range of quality elements (such as operating performance variables, reliability and warranty arrangements, physical features – including the degree of finish and trim, and service factors – such as the assurance of supply and after-sales service). A firm's market share depends on the match between the attributes provided by its products and consumers' tastes and on the supply of attributes by competitors. Bromwich argues that it is the product attributes which need to be the subject of appropriate analysis. The purpose of the analysis should be to attribute those costs which are normally treated as product costs to the benefits they provide to the consumer for each of those attributes which are believed to be of strategic importance.

Bromwich concludes that information about a number of demand and cost factors appertaining to attributes possessed by a firm's products and those of its rivals is needed for optimal decision-making. Management accountants can play an important role here in costing the characteristics provided and in monitoring and reporting on these costs regularly. Similarly, they need to be involved in determining the cost of any package of attributes which is being considered for introduction to the market because deciding to provide a product with a particular configuration of attributes or characteristics requires the organization to achieve this at a competitive cost level.

Roslender (1995) has identified **target costing** as falling within the domain of strategic management accounting. The justification for this is the external focus and that it is a market driven approach to product pricing and cost management. In addition it involves the diffusion of management accounting information throughout the organization and the active involvement of staff from across a broad spectrum of management functions. Their aim is to achieve the target cost which involves identifying, valuing and costing product attributes using functional analysis and examining cost reduction opportunities throughout the entire value chain. For a detailed explanation of target costing you should refer back to Chapter 22.

More recent contributions have emphasized the role of management accounting in formulating and supporting the overall competitive strategy of an organization. To encourage behaviour that is consistent with an organization's strategy, attention is now being given to developing an integrated framework of performance measurement that can be used to clarify, communicate and manage strategy implementation. In the remainder of the chapter our focus will be on integrated approaches to performance measurement that are linked to an organization's strategy. These approaches differ from the financial performance measures that have been described in Chapters 16–20. These measures tend to be used primarily as a financial control mechanism whereas the approaches that are described in the remainder of the chapter attempt to integrate both financial and non-financial measures and incorporate performance measurement within the strategic management process.

# The balanced scorecard

Prior to the 1980s management accounting control systems tended to focus mainly on financial measures of performance. The inclusion of only those items that could be expressed in monetary terms motivated managers to focus excessively on cost reduction and ignore other important variables which were necessary to compete in the global competitive environment that emerged during the 1980s. Product quality, delivery, reliability, after-sales service and customer satisfaction became key competitive variables, but none of these were measured by the traditional management accounting performance measurement system.

During the 1980s much greater emphasis was given to incorporating into the management reporting system those non-financial performance measures that provided feedback on the key variables that are required to compete successfully in a global economic environment. However, a proliferation of performance measures emerged. This resulted in confusion when some of the measures conflicted with each other and it was possible to enhance one measure at the expense of another. It was also not clear to managers how the non-financial measures on which they were evaluated contributed to the whole picture of achieving success in financial terms.

The need to link financial and non-financial measures of performance and identify key performance measures led to the emergence of the balanced scorecard – a set of measures that gives *top* management a fast but comprehensive view of the organizational unit (i.e. a division/strategic business unit). The balanced scorecard was devised by Kaplan and Norton (1992) and refined in later publications (Kaplan and Norton, 1993, 1996a, 1996b). Therefore the following discussion is a summary of Kaplan and Noton's writings on this topic. They use a diagram similar to the one shown in Figure 23.1 to illustrate how the balanced scorecard links performance measures.

You can see that it allows managers to look at the business from four different perspectives by seeking to provide answers to the following four basic questions:

1. How do customers see us? (customer perspective)

2. What must we excel at? (internal business process perspective)

3. Can we continue to improve and create value? (learning and growth perspective)

4. How do we look to shareholders? (financial perspective)

The aim of the scorecard is to provide a comprehensive framework for translating a company's strategic objectives into a coherent set of performance measures. In order to minimize information overload the number of measures in each of the boxes in Figure 23.1 is limited. Typically each box ought to comprise three to five measures.

Kaplan and Norton recommend that organizations should articulate the major goals for each of the four perspectives and then translate these goals into specific performance measures. Each organization must decide what are its critical performance measures. The choice will vary over time and should be linked to the strategy that the organization is following.

As a result of their experiences in implementing the balanced scorecard in organizations Kaplan and Norton became aware of the importance of tying the measures in the balanced scorecard to an organization's strategies. They observed that most companies were not aligning performance measures to their strategies. Instead, they were trying to improve the performance of existing processes (through lower cost, improved quality and shorter customer response times) but they were not identifying the processes that were truly strategic (i.e. those that require exceptional performance) for an organization's strategy to succeed.

Kaplan and Norton's experiences of innovative companies implementing the balanced scorecard indicated that they were using it, not only to clarify and communicate strategy, but also to manage strategy. They conclude that the balanced scorecard has evolved from an improved performance measurement system to a core strategic management system. This strategic thrust is reflected in the titles of their later publications – 'Using the balanced scorecard as a strategic management system' (1996a) and *The Balanced Scorecard: Translating Strategy into Action* (1996b).

**FIGURE 23.1** *The balanced scorecard (source: Kaplan and Norton 1996b).*

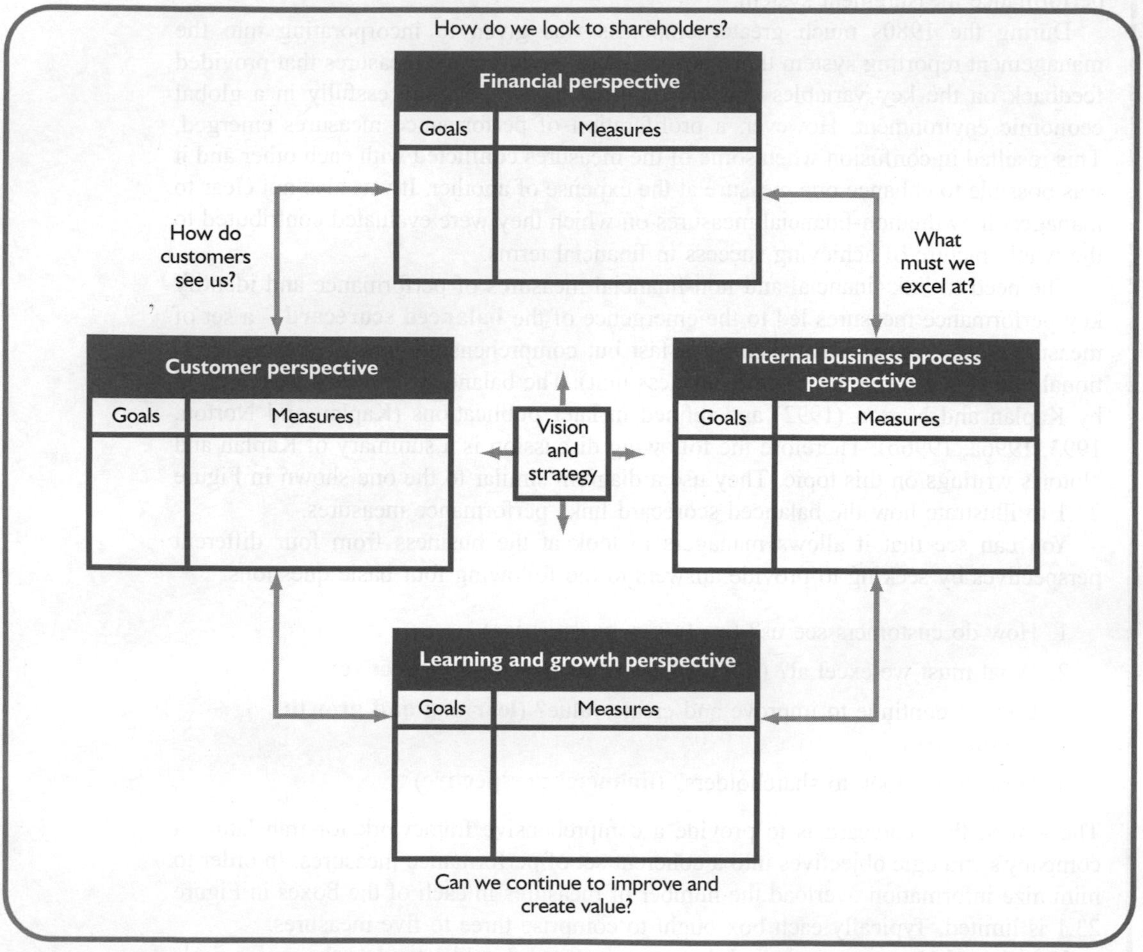

How do we look to shareholders?

**Financial perspective**

| Goals | Measures |
|-------|----------|
|       |          |

How do customers see us?

**Customer perspective**

| Goals | Measures |
|-------|----------|
|       |          |

Vision and strategy

What must we excel at?

**Internal business process perspective**

| Goals | Measures |
|-------|----------|
|       |          |

**Learning and growth perspective**

| Goals | Measures |
|-------|----------|
|       |          |

Can we continue to improve and create value?

# THE BALANCED SCORECARD AS A STRATEGIC MANAGEMENT SYSTEM

Although many companies have performance measurement systems that incorporate financial and non-financial measures they use them mainly for the feedback and control of short-term operations. According to Kaplan and Norton the objectives of the balanced scorecard are more than just an *ad hoc* collection of financial and non-financial performance measures; they are derived from a top-down process driven by the mission and strategy of the business unit. In particular, the balanced scorecard should translate a business unit's mission and strategy into a linked set of measures that define both the long-term strategic objectives, as well as the mechanisms for achieving those objectives. The measures incorporate a balance between external measures relating to customers and internal measures relating to critical business processes and innovation and learning. They also incorporate a balance between outcome measures (the results from past efforts) and the measures that drive future performance.

Kaplan and Norton (1996b) describe how innovative companies are using the measurement focus of the scorecard to accomplish the following critical management processes:

1. Clarifying and translating vision and strategy into specific strategic objectives and identifying the critical drivers of the strategic objectives.

2. Communicating and linking strategic objectives and measures. Ideally, once all the employees understand the high level objectives and measures, they should establish local objectives that support the business unit's global strategy.

3. Planning, setting targets, and aligning strategic initiatives. Such targets should be over a 3–5 year period broken down on a yearly basis so that progression targets can be set for assessing the progress that is being made towards achieving the longer-term targets.

4. Enhancing strategic feedback and learning so that managers can monitor and adjust the implementation of their strategy, and, if necessary, make fundamental changes to the strategy itself.

They approach strategy as choosing the market and customer segments the business unit intends to serve, identifying the critical internal processes that the unit must excel at to deliver value to customers in the targeted market segments, and selecting the individual and organizational capabilities required for the internal and financial objectives.

# Establishing objectives and performance measures

Having explained the general principles of the balanced scorecard we shall now consider the process of establishing objectives and performance measures in each of the four scorecard perspectives (financial, customer, internal business process, and learning and growth). Throughout this section the generic measures that have been presented by Kaplan and Norton are described. In practice, companies should customize these measures to fit their own specific needs and circumstances.

## The financial perspective

In Chapters 16–21 financial performance measures have been extensively discussed. At the strategic business unit level operating profit, return on investment, residual income and economic value added were discussed and such measures should be used for measuring the financial objective of the business unit. Other financial objectives include revenue growth, cost reduction and asset utilization. Typical financial objectives are to increase return on investment by 20% and/or to increase sales and operating income by 100% over the next five years. Because the financial measures have already been described in earlier chapters we shall concentrate mainly on the remaining three scorecard perspectives.

You should note, however, that some people have argued that by improving the non-financial measures in the scorecard improved financial measures should follow. They argue that financial measures should be de-emphasized on the grounds that by making fundamental improvements in operations the financial measures will take care of themselves. In other words, financial success should be the logical consequence of doing the fundamentals well. Kaplan and Norton reject the view that financial measures are unnecessary on the grounds that improvements in the operational measures are not automatically followed by an improvement in the financial measures. Operational improvements can create excess capacity but this excess capacity will only yield financial benefits if it is eliminated or used to generate additional revenues. The financial measures therefore provide feedback on whether improved operational performance is being translated into improved financial performance. They also summarize the economic consequences of strategy implementation.

# The customer perspective

In the customer perspective of the balanced scorecard managers should identify the customer and market segments in which the businesses unit will compete. Target segments may include both existing and potential customers. Managers should then develop performance measures that track the business unit's ability to create satisfied and loyal customers in the targeted segments. The customer perspective typically includes several core or generic measures that relate to customer loyalty and the outcomes of the strategy in the targeted segments. They include market share, customer retention, new customer acquisition, customer satisfaction and customer profitability.

## MARKET SHARE

Market share represents the proportion of sales in a particular market that a business obtains. It can be measured in terms of sales revenues, unit sales volume or number of customers. It is a measure of market penetration. Estimates of total market size can sometimes be derived from public sources such as trade associations and industry groupings. The major contribution of this measure is that it indicates whether the strategy adopted is achieving the expected results in the targeted market segment. It is possible that a company may temporarily be meeting its total sales growth objectives arising from sales in the non-targeted segments, but not increasing its share in the segment that the company has targeted for strategic reasons, such as being the dominant future market or providing a broader marketing base.

## CUSTOMER RETENTION AND LOYALTY

One method of maintaining or increasing market share in targeted customer segments is to ensure that existing customers are retained in those segments. Customer retention can be measured in terms of the average duration of a customer relationship. In addition surveying defecting customers to ascertain where they have taken their business and why they have left can provide valuable feedback on the effectiveness of the firm's strategy. Customer loyalty can be measured by the number of new customers referred by existing customers since this would suggest that a customer must be highly satisfied before recommending a company's products or services to others.

## CUSTOMER ACQUISITION

Customer acquisition can be measured by either the number of new customers or the total sales to new customers in the desired market segment. Other measures include the number of new customers expressed as a percentage of prospective inquiries or the ratio of new customers per sales call.

## CUSTOMER SATISFACTION

Measuring customer satisfaction typically involves the use of questionnaire surveys and customer response cards. Customer satisfaction can also be measured by examining letters of complaint, feedback from sales representatives and the use of 'mystery shoppers'. The latter normally involves external agencies sampling the service as customers and formally reporting back on their findings. The major limitation of customer satisfaction measures is that they measure attitudes and not actual buying behaviour.

## CUSTOMER PROFITABILITY

A company can be very successful in terms of market share, customer retention and acquisition, and customer satisfaction but this may be achieved at the expense of customer profitability. A company does not want just satisfied customers, it also wants profitable customers. The four measures described above relate to the means required to achieve customer profitability but they do not measure the outcome. Customer profitability measures meet this requirement. Profitability should be analysed by different customer segments and unprofitable segments identified. Newly acquired customers may initially be unprofitable and life-cycle profitability analysis should be used for determining whether the focus should be on retention or on abandoning them. For unprofitable existing customers, actions should be taken to try and make them profitable. Such actions might include trying to alter their buying behaviour so that they consume less resources, or price increases. If neither of these strategies is successful they should not be retained.

## MEASURING VALUE PROPOSITIONS

Besides describing the core or generic measures relating to the customer perspective Kaplan and Norton focus on the value propositions, which they define as the attributes the supplying companies provide through their products and services to create loyalty and satisfaction in targeted customer segments. The value proposition is the key concept for understanding the drivers of the core measurements of customer satisfaction, acquisition, retention and market share. Although value propositions vary across industries and across different market segments within industries, there are a common set of attributes that establish the value propositions in most industries. These attributes fall into three categories:

1. product/service attributes;
2. customer relationship;
3. image and reputation.

Product and service attributes encompass desirable product or service features, price and quality. The customer relationship dimension includes the delivery of the product or service to the customer, including the response and delivery time, and how the customer feels about the buying experience. The image and reputation dimension reflects the intangible factors that attract a customer to a company.

Although individual companies have developed their own ways of measuring attributes along the above three dimensions, Kaplan and Norton point out that in virtually all the balanced scorecards they have observed three dimensions stand out as particularly important. They are time, quality and price. Let us now consider typical generic measures that companies can use to measure these dimensions.

Many organizations seek to increase customer satisfaction by providing a speedier response to customer requests, ensuring 100% on-time delivery and reducing the time taken to develop and bring new products to market. For these reasons performance measurement systems are starting to place more emphasis on time-based measures, which are now an important competitive variable. Customer lead time, the time taken from when a customer initiates a request for a product or service until the time taken when the product or service is delivered, is a widely used measure for providing feedback on the extent to which lead times are being reduced for meeting target customers' expectations. Some customers, particularly those that operate a just-in-time system will place greater emphasis on reliable lead times which are constantly met rather than the shortest lead times. Why? Because a late delivery to a customer may disrupt the entire production process. To provide feedback on delivery reliability a measure of on-time delivery such as the number of late deliveries, or late deliveries as a percentage of total deliveries, is required. Such a measure represents a performance driver for customer satisfaction and retention.

Quality is also a key competitive variable. We shall focus on *quality measures* in some detail within the internal business perspective but for the customer perspective the emphasis is on the quality of goods or services delivered to the customer rather than the quality measures within the manufacturing process. Typical quality measures include number of defective units delivered to customers, number of customer complaints, returns by customers and warranty claims. In addition, many companies conduct surveys to measure customer satisfaction in relation to product or service quality.

Irrespective of whether a business unit is pursuing a low cost or a differentiated strategy customers will be concerned about the *price* they are paying for a product or service. To determine how competitive companies are in terms of price, business units should establish a reporting mechanism for comparing the net selling prices of their products or services with those of their competitors. Where sales are dependent on a competitive bidding process, the percentage of bids accepted provides an indication of price competitiveness.

# The internal business perspective

In the internal business perspective, managers identify the critical internal processes for which the organization must excel in implementing its strategy. The internal business process measures should focus on the internal processes that will have the greatest impact on customer satisfaction and achieving the organization's financial objectives. Kaplan and Norton identify three principal internal business processes. They are:

1. innovation processes;
2. operation processes;
3. post-service sales processes.

## INNOVATION PROCESSES

In the innovation process, managers research the needs of customers and then create the products or services that will meet those needs. In particular, companies identify new markets, new customers, and the emerging and latent needs of existing customers. They then design and develop new products and services that enable them to reach these new markets and customers.

As part of the innovation process, managers undertake market research to identify the size of the market and the nature of the customers' preferences and the price sensitivity for the targeted product or service. As organizations deploy their internal processes to meet these customer needs, accurate information on market size and customer preferences becomes essential for successful performance. In addition to surveying existing and potential customers, there is also a need for organizations to consider entirely new opportunities and markets for products and services.

Historically, because of difficult measurement problems and the over-emphasis on easily quantifiable financial measures little attention has been given to developing performance measures for product design and development processes. Companies are becoming increasingly aware that success in developing a continuous stream of innovative products and services can provide a competitive advantage. Research and development has therefore become a more important element in the value chain of most businesses and increasing attention is now being given to specifying objectives and measures for this business process.

A major problem with measuring the success of the research and development process is the long time period before the outcomes arising from the inputs occur. Kaplan and Norton point out that a typical development process in the electronics industry could have two years of product development followed by five years of sales. The first success indicator of a product's development process may not therefore appear for three years (i.e. the first year after the initial year of sales).

Kaplan and Norton highlight some of the innovation measures they have observed in organizations using balanced scorecards. They include:

1. percentage of sales from new products;
2. new product introduction versus competitors'; also new product introduction versus plan;
3. time to develop next generation of the products;
4. number of key items in which the company is first or second to the market;
5. break-even time, being the time from the beginning of product development work until the product has been introduced and has generated enough profit to pay back the investment originally made in its development.

# OPERATION PROCESSES

The operations process starts with the receipt of a customer order and finishes with the delivery of the product or service to the customer. The aim of these processes is to provide efficient, consistent and timely delivery of existing products and services to customers. Historically, the operations process has been the major focus of most of an organization's performance measurement system. The performance and control measures have traditionally relied on financial measures such as standard costs, budgets and variance analysis. The over-emphasis on financial measures, particularly price and efficiency variances sometimes motivated dysfunctional actions. For example, the pursuit of efficiency encouraged the maximum utilization of labour and machines resulting in excessive inventories that were not related to current customer orders. Also an over-emphasis on purchase price variances motivated the purchasing function to focus on obtaining the materials at the lowest possible prices even if this resulted in:

- the use of many suppliers (all of them selected on the basis of price);
- large-quantity purchases, thus resulting in higher inventories;
- delivery of lower quality goods;
- indifference to attaining on-time delivery.

The emergence of the global competitive environment and the need to make customer satisfaction an overriding priority has resulted in many companies supplementing their financial measures with measures of quality, reliability, delivery and those characteristics of product and service offerings that create value for customers. Companies that can identify the differentiating characteristics of their products and services should incorporate measures of these characteristics in the operation processes component of the balanced scorecard. These developments have created the need to focus on measures relating to achieving excellence in terms of time, quality and cost.

## Cycle time measures

Many customers place a high value on short and reliable lead times, measured from the time elapsed from when they place an order until the time when they receive the desired product or service. Traditionally companies met this requirement by holding large inventories of many different products but, as indicated in the previous chapter, this approach is not consistent with being a low-cost supplier. Because of this many companies are adopting just-in-time (JIT) production systems with the aim of achieving both the low-cost and short lead time objectives. Reducing cycle or throughput times is therefore of critical importance for JIT companies.

Delivery performance can focus on cycle time measures and supplier delivery performance. Cycle times can be measured in various ways. Total cycle time measures the length of time required from the placing of an order by a customer to the delivery of the product or service to the customer. Manufacturing cycle time measures the time it takes from starting and finishing the production process. Cycle times should be measured and monitored and trends observed.

The total manufacturing cycle time consists of the sum of processing time, inspection time, wait time and move time. Only processing time adds value, and the remaining activities are non-value added activities. The aim is to reduce the time spent on non-value added activities and thus minimize manufacturing cycle time. A measure of cycle time that has been adopted is manufacturing cycle efficiency (MCE):

$$MCE = \frac{\text{processing time}}{\text{processing time} + \text{inspection time} + \text{wait time} + \text{move time}}$$

The MCE measure is particularly important for JIT manufacturing companies. With a computerized manufacturing process, it may be possible to report the time taken on each of the above non-value-added activities. This will pinpoint those activities that are causing excessive manufacturing cycle times. At the operational level, cycle times should be measured for each product or product line, and trends reported. The emphasis should be on continuous improvements and a shortening of the cycle times.

Reducing set-up times enables manufacturing lot sizes to be reduced, thus leading to shorter manufacturing cycles and greater flexibility. Set-up times should therefore also be measured at the operational level for each process and monitored over time. Modern manufacturing techniques also advocate preventive maintenance to ensure that machines are working effectively at all times, so that quality problems and late deliveries do not occur. A useful measure of machine downtime is the number of lost machine hours in each manufacturing cell. However, downtime when a machine is not needed is not relevant. The focus should be on downtime when a machine is needed but is not ready. In addition, bottleneck operations should be monitored. The aim is to obtain 100% utilization of equipment where bottleneck occurs.

Poor quality also lengthens the cycle time. The time required to inspect parts, rework or replace parts or wait for a machine breakdown to be repaired result in lengthening throughput times. Hence there is a need to measure and reduce the incidence of these events. We shall consider appropriate performance measures later within this section when process quality measurements are discussed.

Although JIT production processes and MCE measures were initially developed for manufacturing operations, they are also applicable to service companies. For example, many customers are forced to queue to receive a service. Companies that can eliminate waiting time for a service will find it easier to attract customers. The time taken to process mortgage and loan applications by financial institutions can take a considerable time period involving a considerable amount of non-value added waiting time. Thus, reducing the time to process the applications enhances customer satisfaction and creates the potential for increasing sales revenues.

## Quality measures

Besides time, quality measures should also be included in the measures relating to operating processes. Most organizations now have established quality programmes and use all, or some of the following process quality measurements:

- process parts-per-million (PPM) defect rates
- yields (ratio of good items produced to good items entering the process)
- first-pass yields
- waste
- scrap
- rework
- returns
- percentages of processes under statistical process control.

In many companies suppliers also have a significant influence on the ability of a company to achieve its time, quality and cost objectives. Performance measures relating to suppliers' performance include the frequency of defects, the number of late deliveries and price trends.

## Cost measurement

Kaplan and Norton recommend that activity-based costing should be used to produce cost measures of the important internal business processes. These costs, together with measurements relating time and quality should be monitored over time and/or benchmarked with a view to continuous improvement or process re-engineering.

The above measures represent generic measures but aspects of quality, time and cost measurement are likely to be included as critical performance measures in any organization's internal business perspective within its balanced scorecard.

## POST-SALES SERVICE PROCESSES

This final category relating to the internal business process perspective includes warranty and repair activities, treatment of defects and returns and the process and administration of customer payments. In addition, excellent community relations is an important strategic objective for ensuring continuing community support to operate manufacturing facilities in companies where environmental factors are involved. For such companies appropriate environmental measures, such as those relating to the safe disposal of waste and by-products, should be established.

Kaplan and Norton suggest that companies attempting to meet their target customers' expectations for superior post-sales service can measure their performance by applying some of the time, quality and cost measurements that have been suggested for the operating processes. For example, cycle time from customer request to the ultimate resolution of the problem can measure the speed of response to failures. Activity-cost measurement can be used to measure the cost of the resources used for the post-sale service processes. Also first-pass yields can measure what percentage of customer requests are handled with a single service call, rather than requiring multiple calls to resolve the problem. These time, quality and cost measurements can also be applied to companies with extensive sales on credit. The aim should be to reduce the length of time between project completion and the final cash payment by the customer.

# The learning and growth perspective

The fourth and final perspective on the balanced scorecard identifies the infrastructure that the business must build to create long-term growth and improvement. This perspective stresses the importance of investing for the future in areas other than investing in assets and new product research and development (which is included in the innovation process of the internal business perspective). Organizations must also invest in their infrastructure (people, systems and organizational procedures) if they are to achieve their long-term financial objectives. Based upon their experiences of building balanced scorecards across a wide variety of organizations Kaplan and Norton have identified the following three principal categories, or enablers, for the learning and growth objectives:

1. employee capabilities;
2. information system capabilities;
3. motivation, empowerment and alignment.

They point out that although they have found that many companies have made excellent progress on specific measures for their financial, customer, innovation and operating processes virtually no effort has been devoted to measuring the outcomes relating to the above three categories. As companies implement management processes based on the balanced scorecard framework more creative and customized measures relating to the learning and growth perspective are expected to emerge.

## EMPLOYEE CAPABILITIES

Kaplan and Norton observed that most companies use three common core measurement outcomes – employee satisfaction, employee retention and employee productivity. Within this core, the employee satisfaction objective is generally considered to be the driver of the other two measures. Satisfied employees are normally a pre-condition for increasing customer satisfaction. Many companies periodically measure employee satisfaction using surveys. Typically, they are requested to specify on a scale, ranging from dissatisfied to highly satisfied, their score for a list of questions that seek to measure employee satisfaction. For example, questions may relate to involvement in decisions and active encouragement to be creative and to use one's initiative. An aggregate index is constructed which can be analysed on a departmental or divisional basis.

Employee retention can be measured by the annual percentage of key staff that leave and many different methods can be used to measure employee productivity. A generic measure of employee productivity that can be applied throughout the organization and compared with different divisions is the sales revenue per employee.

## INFORMATION SYSTEM CAPABILITIES

For employees to be effective in today's competitive environment they need excellent information on customers, internal processes and the financial consequences of their decisions. Measures of strategic information availability suggested by Kaplan and Norton include percentage of processes with real time quality, cycle time and cost feedback available and the percentage of customer-facing employees having on-line information about customers. These measures seek to provide an indication of the availability of internal process information to front-line employees.

## MOTIVATION, EMPOWERMENT AND ALIGNMENT

The number of suggested improvements per employee is proposed as a measure relating to having motivated and empowered employees. The performance drivers for individual and organizational alignment focus on whether departments and individuals have their goals aligned with the company objectives articulated in the balanced scorecard. A suggested outcome measure is the percentage of employees with personal goals aligned to the balanced scorecard and the percentage of employees who achieve personal goals.

# Performance measurement in service organizations

Although Kaplan and Norton illustrate how the balanced scorecard can be applied in both the manufacturing and service sectors most of the performance measurement literature relates to the manufacturing sector. To remedy this deficiency this section focuses on performance measurement in the service sector. Based on their research into the management accounting practices of a range of companies in several different service industries Fitzgerald *et al.* (1989) identified four unique characteristics distinguishing service companies from manufacturing organizations. First, most services are intangible. Fitzgerald *et al.* state:

> In travelling on a particular airline the customer will be influenced by the comfort of the seat, the meals served, the attitudes and confidence of the cabin staff, the boarding process and so on. This makes managing and controlling the operation complex because it is difficult to establish exactly what an individual customer is buying; is it the journey or the treatment? (Fitzgerald *et al.*, 1989: 2)

Secondly, service outputs vary from day to day, since services tend to be provided by individuals whose performance is subject to variability that significantly affects the service quality the customer receives. Thirdly, the production and consumption of many services are inseparable such as in taking a rail journey. Fourthly, services are perishable and cannot be stored. Fitzgerald *et al.* illustrate this characteristic with a hotel, which contains a fixed number of rooms. If a room is unoccupied, the sales opportunity is lost for ever and the resource is wasted.

With regard to the control of the intangible aspects, the authors found that companies used the following methods to measure performance:

1. *Measures of satisfaction after the service.* The most common method was the monitoring and analysis of letters of complaint, but some companies interviewed samples of customers or used questionnaires to ascertain the customers' perception of service quality.

2. *Measures during the service.* An approach used by some companies was for management to make unannounced visits, with the aim of observing the quality of service offered. Another mechanism was the use of 'mystery shoppers', where staff employed by external agencies were sent out to sample the service as customers and formally report back on their findings.

3. *Tangibles as surrogates for intangibles.* The researchers observed that some firms used internal measures of tangible aspects of the service as indicators of how the customers might perceive the service. Some companies measured waiting times and the conditions of the waiting environment as surrogates of customers' satisfaction with the service.

Fitzgerald *et al.* also draw attention to the importance of relating the performance measures to the corporate and marketing strategies of the organizations. For example, if the delivery of high quality service is seen to be a key strategic variable then quality measures should be the dominant performance measures. On the other hand, if a low cost of the service relative to competitors is seen as the key strategic variable then strict adherence to budgets will be a key feature of the control system. There is also a greater danger in service organizations of focusing excessively on financial performance measures, which can be easily quantified, thus placing an undue emphasis on maximizing short-term performance, even if this conflicts with maximizing long-term performance. Consequently, it is more important in service organizations that a range of non-financial performance indicators be developed providing better predictors for the attainment of long-term profitability goals.

In developing an overall framework for a performance measurement system in the service sector Moon and Fitzgerald (1996) draw off the approach advocated by Otley (1987), that is common to all performance measurement systems. Otley suggests that there is a need to answer the following three basic questions when forming the basic building blocks of a performance measurement system:

1. What are the *dimensions* of performance that the organization is seeking to encourage?

2. How are appropriate *standards* to be set?

3. What *rewards* and/or penalties are to be associated with the achievement of performance targets?

## DIMENSIONS OF PERFORMANCE MEASUREMENT

Fitzgerald *et al.* (1991) advocate the measurement of service business performance across six dimensions. They propose that managers of every service organization need to develop their own set of performance measures across the six dimensions to monitor the continued relevance of their competitive strategy. Exhibit 23.2 shows the six dimensions with examples of types of performance measures for each dimension. You

**EXHIBIT 23.2**

*Performance measures for service organizations*

should note that the dimensions fall into two conceptually different categories. Competitiveness and financial performance reflect the success of the chosen strategy (i.e. ends or results). The remaining four dimensions (quality, flexibility, resource utilization and innovation) are the drivers or determinants that determine competitive success. Fitzgerald

| | Dimensions of performance | Types of measures |
|---|---|---|
| *Results* | Competitiveness | Relative market share and position |
| | | Sales growth |
| | | Measures of the customer base |
| | Financial performance | Profitability |
| | | Liquidity |
| | | Capital structure |
| | | Market ratios |
| *Determinants* | Quality of service | Reliability |
| | | Responsiveness |
| | | Aesthetics/appearance |
| | | Cleanliness/tidiness |
| | | Comfort |
| | | Friendliness |
| | | Communication |
| | | Courtesy |
| | | Competence |
| | | Access |
| | | Availability |
| | | Security |
| | Flexibility | Volume flexibility |
| | | Delivery speed flexibility |
| | | Specification flexibility |
| | Resource utilization | Productivity |
| | | Efficiency |
| | Innovation | Performance of the innovation process |
| | | Performance of individual innovations |

*Source*: Fitzgerald *et al.*, 1991

*et al.* conclude that the design of a balanced range of performance measures should be dependent upon the company's service type, competitive environment and chosen strategy.

Moon and Fitzgerald (1996) point out the similarities between the Fitzgerald *et al.* framework and the balanced scorecard. Both frameworks emphasize the need to link performance measures to corporate strategy, include external (customer type) as well as internal measures, include non-financial as well as financial measures and make explicit the trade-offs between the various measures of performance. In addition, both frameworks distinguish between 'results' of actions taken and the 'drivers' or 'determinants' of future performance. The balanced scorecard complements 'financial measures with operational measures on customer satisfaction, internal processes, and the organization's innovation and improvement activities that are the drivers of future financial performance' (Kaplan and Norton, 1992). The Fitzgerald *et al.* framework specifies that measures of financial performance and competitiveness are the 'results' of actions previously taken and reflect the success of the chosen strategy. The remaining four dimensions (quality, flexibility, resource utilization and innovation) are the factors or drivers that determine competitive success, either now or in the future. The objective of both approaches is to ensure that a balanced set of performance measures is used so that no dimension is overly stressed to the detriment of another.

## SETTING STANDARDS OF PERFORMANCE

The second of Otley's questions relates to the setting of appropriate standards once the actual dimensions and performance measures have been established. This involves consideration of who sets the standards, at what levels the standards are set and whether the standards facilitate comparison across business units.

Determining who sets the standards requires a consideration of whether the standards should be imposed on subordinates by their superiors or whether subordinates should be able to fully participate in the setting of standards. The level of achievability influences both the aspiration level and performance. The general conclusion that emerges from the literature is that performance is maximized by setting challenging targets. Finally, relative comparisons are only likely to be appropriate where business units face similar environmental and business conditions. For a more detailed discussion of the above issues you should refer back to Chapter 16.

## LINKING REWARDS TO THE ACHIEVEMENT OF PERFORMANCE MEASURES

The reward structure is concerned with motivating individuals towards achieving the performance measures. Motivation is maximized when individuals are clear about what the organization is trying to do, what is expected of them, and exactly how and why their own contribution to the organization's performance in meeting its objectives will be appraised. In addition, there is a need to determine the types of rewards and penalties that will apply on achievement or non-achievement of the performance targets. Rewards can take many forms including monetary, promotion, recognition, praise, etc.

## COMPARISON WITH THE BALANCED SCORECARD

In determining the dimensions of performance we have noted that there are many similarities with the balanced scorecard. However, when the balanced scorecard is compared with the *overall* performance measurement system for service organizations advocated by Fitzgerald and Moon significant differences emerge. The balanced scorecard focuses on performance measurement at the strategic unit level whereas the framework suggested by Fitzgerald and Moon would appear to be aimed at both senior and lower level managers. The balanced scorecard also focuses primarily on strategy implementation rather than performance evaluation and therefore little attention is given to setting standards of performance and linking the rewards to achievement of performance targets. In particular, Kaplan and Norton stress that the balanced scorecard should be used as a communication, informing and learning system, and not as a control system. In contrast, the framework suggested by Fitzgerald and Moon would appear to be broader, being used both as a strategy implementation mechanism and a control system.

## Recommended Reading

For a more detailed discussion of the elements of strategic management accounting you should refer to the articles by Lord (1996) or Roslender (1995 and 1996). The balanced scorecard was designed by Kaplan and Norton and in their writings they describe its development and the experiences of companies that have implemented it. This chapter has summarized Kaplan and Norton's writings but for a more detailed description of their work you should refer to the book they have written on the balance scorecard – *The Balance Scorecard: Translating Strategy into Action* (1996b). For a broader description of performance measurement linked to strategy you should refer to Simons (1999).

## Key Examination Points

Strategic management accounting and the balanced scorecard are relatively new topics so they have not been extensively examined in the past. Consequently fewer past examination questions are included in this chapter. Strategic management accounting can be viewed as incorporating a wide range of topics. In addition, other approaches to performance measurement have been examined that do not adopt a balanced scorecard perspective.

Therefore some questions are included that do not relate directly to the chapter content. However, where questions are set on performance measurement you should try and adopt a balanced scorecard approach by emphasizing the need to integrate financial and non-financial measures and link performance measurement to an organization's strategies.

## Questions

### 23.1 Advanced

Management accounting practice has traditionally focused on techniques to assist organisational decision-making and cost control. In concentrating on the internal environment, the management accounting function has been criticised for not addressing the needs of senior management to enable effective strategic planning. In particular, the criticism has focused on inadequate provision of information which analyses the organisation's exposure to environmental change and its progress towards the achievement of corporate objectives.

Requirement:
Explain how Strategic Management Accounting can provide information which meets the requirements of senior managers in seeking to realise corporate objectives. (20 marks)
*CIMA Stage 4 Strategic Management Accountancy and Marketing*

### 23.2* Advanced

The concept of Generic Strategies was established by Professor Michael Porter during the 1980s. He stated that a company must choose one of these strategies in order to compete and gain sustainable competitive advantage. In addition to assessing the source of competitive advantage. Porter also explained that it was necessary to identify the target for the organisation's products or services. This involved distinguishing between whether the target was broad and covered the majority of the overall market, or narrow and concentrated on a small but profitable part of it.

Requirements:
(a) Critically appraise the value of Porter's Generic Strategy model for strategic planning purposes. (12 marks)
(b) Explain how the theoretical principles of the Experience Curve may be applied to determine a generic strategy for a company.
(8 marks)
(Total 20 marks)
*CIMA Stage 4 Strategic Management Accountancy and Marketing*

### 23.3* Advanced

The introduction of improved quality into products has been a strategy applied by many organisations to obtain competitive advantage. Some organisations believe it is necessary to improve levels of product quality if competitive advantage is to be preserved or strengthened.

Requirement:

Discuss how a management accountant can assist an organisation to achieve competitive advantage by measuring the increase in added value from improvement in its product quality.

(20 marks)

*CIMA Stage 4 Strategic Management Accounting and Marketing*

### 23.4 Advanced

The new manufacturing environment is characterised by more flexibility, a readiness to meet customers' requirements, smaller batches, continuous improvements and an emphasis on quality. In such circumstances, traditional management accounting performance measures are, at best, irrelevant and, at worst, misleading.

You are required:

(a) to discuss the above statement, citing specific examples to support or refute the views expressed; (10 marks)

(b) to explain in what ways management accountants can adapt the services they provide to the new environment. (7 marks)

(Total 17 marks)

*CIMA Stage 3 Management Accounting Techniques*

### 23.5 Advanced

Research on Performance Measurement in Service Businesses, reported in *Management Accounting*, found that 'performance measurement often focuses on easily quantifiable aspects such as cost and productivity whilst neglecting other dimensions which are important to competitive success'.

You are required:

(a) to explain what 'other dimensions' you think are important measures of performance; (8 marks)

(b) to describe what changes would be required to traditional information systems to deal with these 'other dimensions'. (9 marks)

(Total 17 marks)

*CIMA Stage 3 Management Accounting*

### 23.6* Advanced: Performance measurement in non-profit organizations

(a) The absence of the profit measure in Not for Profit (NFP) organisations causes problems for the measurement of their efficiency and effectiveness.

You are required to explain:

(i) why the absence of the profit measure should be a cause of the problems referred to; (9 marks)

(ii) how these problems extend to activities within business entities which have a profit motive. Support your answer with examples. (4 marks)

(b) A public health clinic is the subject of a scheme to measure its efficiency and effectiveness. Amongst a number of factors, the 'quality of care provided' has been included as an aspect of the clinic's service to be measured. Three features of 'quality of care provided' have been listed:

Clinic's adherence to appointment times
Patients' ability to contact the clinic and make appointments without difficulty
The provision of a comprehensive patient health monitoring programme.

You are required to:

(i) suggest a set of quantitative measures which can be used to identify the effective level of achievement of each of the features listed; (9 marks)

(ii) indicate how these measures could be combined into a single 'quality of care' measure. (3 marks)

(Total 25 marks)

*CIMA Stage 4 Management Accounting – Control and Audit*

### 23.7* Advanced

Thomas Sheridan, writing in *Management Accounting* in February 1989, pointed out that Japanese companies have a different approach to cost information with 'the emphasis – based on physical measures', and 'the use of non-financial indices, particularly at shop floor level'. He argues that their approach is much more relevant to modern conditions than traditional cost and management accounting practices.

You are required

(a) to explain what is meant by 'physical measures' and 'non-financial indices'; (3 marks)

(b) to give *three* examples of non-financial indices that might be prepared, with a brief note of what information each index would provide. (5 marks)

(c) What existing cost and management accounting practices do you consider inappropriate in modern conditions? (9 marks)

(Total 17 marks)

*CIMA Stage 3 Management Accounting Techniques*

### 23.8 Advanced

The 'Balanced Scorecard' approach aims to provide information to management to assist strategic policy formulation and achievement. It emphasises the need to provide the user with a set of information which addresses all relevant areas of performance in an objective and unbiased fashion.

Requirements

(i) Discuss in general terms the main types of information which would be required by a manager to implement this approach to measuring performance; and

(ii) comment on three specific examples of performance measures which could be used in a company in a service industry, for example a firm of consultants. (10 marks)

*CIMA Stage 4 Strategic Financial Management*

### 23.9 Advanced: Design and discussion of key performance indicators for DIY outlets and regional companies

Duit plc has recently acquired Ucando Ltd which is a regional builders' merchants/DIY company with three outlets all within a radius of 40 miles. Duit plc is building up its national coverage of outlets. Duit plc has set up regional companies each with its own board of directors responsible to the main board situated in London.

It is expected that eventually each regional company will have between 10 and 20 outlets under its control. A regional company will take over control of the three Ucando Ltd outlets. Each outlet will have its own manager, and new ones have just been appointed to the three Ucando Ltd outlets.

The outlets' managers will be allowed to hire and fire whatever staff they need and the introduction of a head count budget is being considered by Head Office. Each outlet manager is responsible for his own sales policy, pricing, store layout, advertising, the general running of the outlet and the purchasing of goods for resale, subject to the recommendations below. Duit plc's policy is that all outlet managers have to apply to the regional board for all items of capital expenditure greater than £500, while the regional board can sanction up to £100 000 per capital expenditure project.

The outlets will vary in size of operations, and this will determine the number of trade sales representatives employed per outlet. There will be a minimum of one trade sales representative per outlet under the direction of the outlet manager. Each manager and representative will be entitled to a company car.

Outlet sales are made to both retail and trade on either cash or credit terms. Debtor and cash control is the responsibility of regional office. Cash received is banked locally, and immediately credited to the Head Office account. Credit sales invoices are raised by the outlet with a copy sent to regional office. Within each outlet it is possible to identify the sales origin, e.g. timber yard, saw mill, building supplies, kitchen furniture, etc.

Timber for resale is supplied to an outlet on request from stocks held at regional office or direct from the ports where Duit (Timber Importers) Ltd has further stocks. Duit Kitchens Ltd provides kitchen furniture that the outlets sell. Duit plc also has a small factory making windows, doors and frames which are sold through the outlets. When purchasing other products for resale, the outlet is requested to use suppliers with which Head Office has negotiated discount buying arrangements. All invoices for outlet purchases and overheads are passed by the respective outlet manager before being paid by regional office. In existing Duit outlets a perpetual inventory system is used, with a complete physical check once a year.

Information concerning last year's actual results for one of Ucando Ltd's outlets situated at Birport is given below:

**Birport DIY outlet**
**Trading and profit and loss account**
**for year to 31 March**

| | (£) | (£) |
|---|---|---|
| Sales (1) | | 1 543 000 |
| Less Cost of sales | | 1 095 530 |
| Prime gross margin (29%) | | 447 470 |
| Less: | | |
| Wages (2) | 87 400 | |
| Salaries (3) | 45 000 | |
| Depreciation: | | |
| equipment (4) | 9 100 | |
| buildings | 3 500 | |
| vehicles (3 cars) | 6 500 | |
| Vehicle running expenses | 6 170 | |

## Summary

For many years strategic management accounting has been advocated as a potential area of development that would enhance the future contribution of management accounting. Despite the publicity that strategic management accounting has received there is still no comprehensive conceptual framework of what strategic management accounting is. Because of the lack of consensus on what constitutes strategic management accounting the elements that have been identified in the literature to characterize strategic management accounting have been described. Three elements were identified:

1. The extension of traditional management accounting's internal focus to include external information about competitors;

2. The relationship between the strategic position chosen by a firm and the expected emphasis on management accounting.

3. Gaining competitive advantage by analysing ways to decrease costs and/or enhance the differentiation of a firm's products, through exploiting linkages in the value chain and optimizing cost drivers.

Despite many papers on the subject Lord (1996) observes that there still seems to be a paucity of examples of strategic management accounting actually being used. In a study of a New Zealand cycle manufacturer she concluded that although some form of strategic management accounting was evident, and influential in this firm, the management accountants played little or no part in the process.

A broader view of strategic management accounting is that it is the provision of information to support senior management to achieve, and sustain, a strategic (i.e. commanding) position in the market place relative to competitors (Roslender 1996). Adopting a broader view of strategic management accounting encompasses activity-based costing, target costing and the cost management approaches described in the previous chapter.

Recent developments in performance evaluation have sought to integrate financial and non-financial measures and assist in clarifying, communicating and managing strategy. The balanced scorecard attempts to meet these requirements. It allows managers to look at the business from four different perspectives by seeking to provide answers to the following four basic questions:

1. How do customers see us? (customer perspective)

2. What must we excel at? (internal business process perspective)

3. Can we continue to improve and create value? (learning and growth perspective)

4. How do we look to shareholders? (financial perspective)

The aim of the scorecard is to provide a comprehensive framework for translating a company's strategic objectives into a coherent set of performance measures. Organizations should articulate the major goals for each of the four perspectives and then translate these goals into specific performance measures. Each organization must decide what are its critical performance measures. The choice will vary over time and should be linked to the strategy that the organization is following. ●●●

## Key Terms and Concepts

balanced scorecard (p. 929)
cost measures (p. 937)
customer perspective (p. 929)
cycle time measures (p. 936)
financial perspective (p. 929)
internal business process perspective (p. 929)
learning and growth perspective (p. 929)
learning curve (p. 924)

manufacturing cycle efficiency (MCE) (p. 936)
quality measures (p. 937)
strategic management accounting (p. 923)
target costing (p. 928)
time-based measures (p. 934)
value-chain analysis (p. 926)
value propositions (p. 933)

| | |
|---|---|
| Leasing of delivery lorry | 6 510 |
| Lorry running expenses | 3 100 |
| Energy costs | 9 350 |
| Telephone/stationery | 9 180 |
| Travel and entertaining | 3 490 |
| Commission on sales | 7 770 |
| Bad debts written off | 9 440 |
| Advertising | 25 160 |
| Repairs | 6 000 |
| Rates, insurance | 13 420 |
| Sundry expenses | 10 580 |
| Delivery expenses | 7 400 |

|  |  |
|---|---|
| | 269 070 |
| Net profit | £178 400 |
| (11.56%) | |

**Position at 31 March**

| | (£) |
|---|---|
| Debtors | 100 900 |
| Stock | 512 000 |

*Notes:*

(1) Sales can be identified by till code–cash/credit, trade/retail, timber, kitchen furniture, frames, heavy building supplies, light building supplies, sawmill etc.

(2) Workforce distributed as follows: timber yard (3), sawmill (1), sales (7), general duties (1), administration (3).

(3) Paid to sales representatives (2), assistant manager, manager.

(4) Equipment used in sales area, sawmill, yard.

Requirements:

(a) Describe a cost centre, a profit centre and an investment centre and discuss the problems of and benefits from using them for management accounting purposes. (7 marks)

(b) Suggest key performance indicators which can be used either individually or jointly by each member of the management team for the regional outlet network, i.e. those in the regional office, the outlets and their departments, in a responsibility reporting system for their evaluation purposes. (6 marks)

(c) Justify the key performance indicators that you have suggested in (b) incorporating, where appropriate, reference to whether the individuals or entities are being treated as cost, profit or investment centres. (6 marks)

(d) Design a pro forma monthly report without figures which can be used by both the outlet manager for his management and control needs and by the regional board to evaluate the outlet. The report can include two or more

sections if you wish. Provide a brief explanation for the format chosen. (6 marks)

*Note:* The manufacturing companies and the importing company report direct to the main board. (Total 25 marks)
*ICAEW Management Accounting*

### 23.10 Advanced: Financial and non-financial performance measures

Scotia Health Consultants Ltd provides advice to clients in medical, dietary and fitness matters by offering consultation with specialist staff.

The budget information for the year ended 31 May is as follows:

(i) Quantitative data as per Appendix.

(ii) Clients are charged a fee per consultation at the rate of: medical £75; dietary £50 and fitness £50.

(iii) Health foods are recommended and provided only to dietary clients at an average cost to the company of £10 per consultation. Clients are charged for such health foods at cost plus 100% mark-up.

(iv) Each customer enquiry incurs a variable cost of £3, whether or not it is converted into a consultation.

(v) Consultants are *each* paid a fixed annual salary as follows: medical £40 000; dietary £28 000; fitness £25 000.

(vi) Sundry other fixed cost: £300 000.

Actual results for the year to 31 May incorporate the following additional information:

(i) Quantitative data as per Appendix.

(ii) A reduction of 10% in health food costs to the company per consultation was achieved through a rationalisation of the range of foods made available.

(iii) Medical salary costs were altered through dispensing with the services of two full-time consultants and sub-contracting outside specialists as required. A total of 1900 consultations were sub-contracted to outside specialists who were paid £50 per consultation.

(iv) Fitness costs were increased by £80 000 through the hire of equipment to allow sophisticated cardio-vascular testing of clients.

(v) New computer software has been installed to provide detailed records and scheduling of all client enquiries and consultations. This software has an annual operating cost (including depreciation) of £50 000.

Required:

(a) Prepare a statement showing the financial results for the year to 31 May in tabular format. This should show:

  (i) the budget and actual gross margin for each type of consultation and for the company

  (ii) the actual net profit for the company

  (iii) the budget and actual margin (£) per consultation for each type of consultation.

  (Expenditure for each expense heading should be shown in (i) and (ii) as relevant.)                    (15 marks)

(b) Suggest ways in which each of the undernoted performance measures (1 to 5) could be used to supplement the financial results calculated in (a). You should include relevant quantitative analysis from the Appendix below for each performance measure:

  1. Competitiveness; 2 Flexibility; 3. Resource utilisation; 4. Quality; 5. Innovation.

  (20 marks)

  (Total 35 marks)

**Appendix**
**Statistics relating to the year ended 31 May**

| | Budget | Actual |
|---|---|---|
| Total client enquiries: | | |
| new business | 50 000 | 80 000 |
| repeat business | 30 000 | 20 000 |
| Number of client consultations: | | |
| new business | 15 000 | 20 000 |
| repeat business | 12 000 | 10 000 |
| Mix of client consultations: | | |
| medical | 6 000 | 5 500 |
| | | (note 1) |
| dietary | 12 000 | 10 000 |
| fitness | 9 000 | 14 500 |
| Number of consultants employed: | | |
| medical | 6 | 4 |
| | | (note 1) |
| dietary | 12 | 12 |
| fitness | 9 | 12 |
| Number of client complaints: | 270 | 600 |

*Note 1:* Client consultations *includes* those carried out by outside specialists. There are now 4 full-time consultants carrying out the remainder of client consultations.

*ACCA Paper 9 Information for Control and Decision Making*

## 23.11* Advanced: Financial and non-financial performance measures

BS Ltd provides consultancy services to small and medium sized businesses. Three types of consultants are employed offering administrative, data processing and marketing advice respectively. The consultants work partly on the client's premises and partly in BS Ltd premises, where chargeable development work in relation to each client contract will be undertaken. Consultants spend some time negotiating with potential clients attempting to secure contracts from them. BS Ltd has recently implemented a policy change which allows for a number of follow-up (remedial) hours at the client's premises after completion of the contract in order to eliminate any problems which have arisen in the initial stages of operation of the system. Contract negotiation and remedial work hours are not charged directly to each client. BS Ltd carries out consultancy for new systems and also to offer advice on existing systems which a client may have introduced before BS Ltd became involved. BS Ltd has a policy of retaining its consultancy staff at a level of 60 consultants on an ongoing basis.

Additional information for the year ended 30 April is as follows:

(i) BS Ltd invoices clients £75 per chargeable consultant hour.

(ii) Consultant salaries are budgeted at an average per consultant of £30 000 per annum. Actual salaries include a bonus for hours in excess of budget paid for at the budgeted average rate per hour.

(iii) Sundry operating costs (other than consultant salaries) were budgeted at £3 500 000. Actual was £4 100 000.

(iv) BS Ltd capital employed (start year) was £6 500 000.

(v) Table 1 shows an analysis of sundry budgeted and actual quantitative data.

Required:

(a) (i) Prepare an analysis of actual consultancy hours for the year ended 30 April which shows the increase or decrease from the standard/allowed non-chargeable hours. This increase or decrease should be analysed to show the extent to which it may be shown to be attributable to a change from standard in:

  1. standard chargeable hours; 2. remedial

advice hours; 3. contract negotiation hours; 4. other non-chargeable hours.

(13 marks)

(ii) Calculate the total value of each of 1 to 4 in (a) above in terms of chargeable client income per hour. (4 marks)

(b) BS Ltd measure business performance in a number of ways. For each of the undernoted measures, comment on the performance of BS Ltd using quantitative data from the question and your answer to (a) to assist in illustrating your answer:

(i) Financial performance
(ii) Competitive performance
(iii) Quality of service
(iv) Flexibility
(v) Resource utilisation
(vi) Innovation. (18 marks)

(Total 35 marks)

### Table 1: BS Ltd Sundry statistics for year ended 30 April

|  | Budget | Actual |
|---|---|---|
| Number of consultants: |  |  |
| Administration | 30 | 23 |
| Data processing | 12 | 20 |
| Marketing | 18 | 17 |
| Consultants hours analysis: |  |  |
| contract negotiation hours | 4 800 | 9 240 |
| remedial advice hours | 2 400 | 7 920 |
| other non-chargeable hours | 12 000 | 22 440 |
| general development work hours (chargeable) | 12 000 | 6 600 |
| customer premises contract hours | 88 800 | 85 800 |
| Gross hours | 120 000 | 132 000 |
| Chargeable hours analysis: |  |  |
| new systems | 70% | 60% |
| existing systems advice | 30% | 40% |
| Number of clients enquiries received: |  |  |
| new systems | 450 | 600 |
| existing systems advice | 400 | 360 |
| Number of client contracts worked on: |  |  |
| new systems | 180 | 210 |
| existing systems advice | 300 | 288 |
| Number of client complaints | 5 | 20 |
| Contracts requiring remedial advice | 48 | 75 |

*ACCA Paper 9 Information for Control and Decision Making*

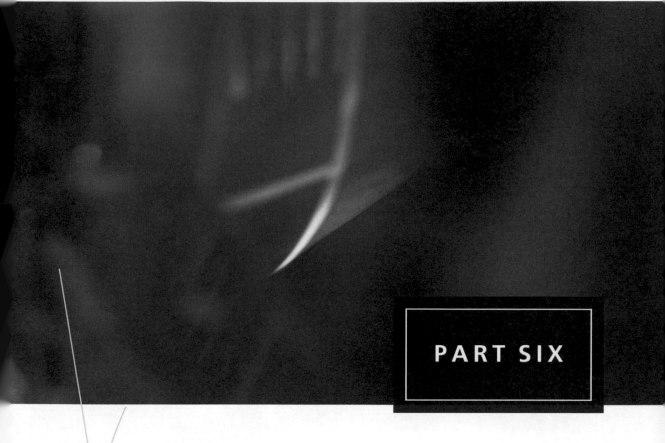

# PART SIX

# The Application of Quantitative Methods to Management Accounting

In this part we examine the application of quantitative methods to various aspects of management accounting. In Chapters 12 and 19 we considered how probability theory and normal distribution theory were applied to decision-making and the investigation of variances; Chapters 24–26 now look at the further applications of quantitative methods to management accounting.

Chapter 24 examines the contribution of mathematical and statistical techniques in determining cost behaviour patterns for cost–volume–profit analysis and the planning and control of costs and revenues. Chapter 25 concentrates on the application of quantitative models to determine the optimum investment in inventories. We also consider in this chapter how the performance evaluation system conflicts with the optimum quantitative decision models. Chapter 26 looks at the application of linear programming to decision-making and planning and control activities.

Rather than delaying the chapters on the application of quantitative techniques to management accounting until Part Six you may prefer to read

Chapter 24 immediately after reading Chapter 8 on cost–volume–profit analysis. Chapter 25 is self-contained and may be assigned to follow any of the chapters in Part Four. Chapter 26 should be read only after you have studied Chapter 9.

# 24

# Cost estimation and cost behaviour

Determining how cost will change with output or other measurable factors of activity is of vital importance for decision-making, planning and control. The preparation of budgets, the production of performance reports, the calculation of standard costs and the provision of relevant costs for pricing and other decisions all depend on reliable estimates of costs and distinguishing between fixed and variable costs, at different activity levels.

Unfortunately, costs are not easy to predict, since they behave differently under different circumstances. For example, costs may behave differently when they are tightly controlled compared with a situation where control is relaxed or removed. Direct labour, which is often presumed to be variable, may be non-variable (i.e. a fixed cost) in companies that employ a fixed number of people and maintain this number even when output declines.

Depreciation is often quoted as a non-variable cost, but it may well be variable if asset value declines in direct proportion to usage. Therefore we cannot generalize by categorizing direct labour as a variable cost and depreciation as a non-variable cost.

Whether a cost is fixed or variable with respect to a particular activity measure or cost driver is affected by the length of the time span under consideration. The longer the time span the more likely the cost will be variable. For example, maintenance staff salaries are likely to be fixed in the short run and will thus remain unchanged when the volume of maintenance hours changes. However, in the long run, maintenance salaries are likely to vary with the maintenance time required. If maintenance activity expands, extra staff will be appointed but, if activity contracts, staff will be redeployed or made redundant. It is therefore important to specify the length of the time period under consideration when predicting costs for different activity levels.

The importance of accurately estimating costs and the complexity of cost behaviour means that accountants must use increasingly sophisticated techniques. The introduction of the microcomputer, with its supporting software, has made it possible for more sophisticated techniques to be used for estimating costs, even by small businesses. These development have led to an increasing awareness of the important potential of mathematical and

## Learning objectives

After studying this chapter, you should be able to:

- discuss the strengths and weaknesses of the different methods of estimating costs;

- calculate regression equations using the high–low, scattergraph and least-squares techniques;

- calculate and interpret the coefficient of determination ($r^2$), standard error of the estimate and beta coefficient;

- describe multiple regression analysis and indicate the circumstances when this method should be used;

- explain the requirements which should be observed when using statistical regression analysis;

- explain the six steps required to estimate cost functions from past data;

- calculate average hours/cost per unit of *cumulative production* and incremental hours/cost per order using the learning curve;

- describe three situations where the management accountant can incorporate the learning curve effect.

statistical techniques for estimating costs, and it is the aim of this chapter to provide an understanding of these techniques.

Some non-mathematical techniques will also be explained so that you can assess the additional benefits that can be obtained from using the more sophisticated techniques. We shall then examine the effect of experience on cost, which is normally referred to as the learning curve. The emphasis in this chapter will be on manufacturing costs, and we shall consider various techniques for estimating how these costs change with activity; similar techniques, however, can be applied to non-manufacturing costs that change with activity.

A major objective of this chapter is to ascertain the **activity measure** or **cost driver** that exerts the major influence of the cost of a particular activity. A cost driver can be defined as any factor whose change causes a change in the total cost of an activity. Examples of cost drivers include direct labour hours, machine hours, units of output and number of production run set-ups. Throughout this chapter the terms 'cost-driver' and 'activity measure' will be used synonymously.

# General principles applying to estimating cost functions

Before we consider the various methods that are appropriate for estimating costs, we need to look at some of the terms that will be used. A **regression equation** identifies an estimated relationship between a dependent variable (cost) and one or more independent variables (i.e. an activity measure or cost driver) *based on past observations*. When the equation includes only one independent variable, it is referred to as **simple regression** and it is possible in this situation to plot the regression equation on a graph as a regression line. When the equation includes two or more independent variables, it is referred to as **multiple regression**. If there is only one independent variable and the relationship is linear, the regression line can be described by the equation for a straight line:

$$y = a + bx$$

Assuming that we wish to express the relationship between the **dependent variable** (cost) and the **independent variable** (activity), then

$y$ = total cost for the period at an activity level of $x$
$a$ = total non-variable (fixed) cost for the period
$b$ = average variable cost per unit of activity
$x$ = volume of activity levels or cost driver for the period

If non-variable (fixed) costs for a particular period are £5000, the average unit variable cost is £1, and direct labour hours represent the cost driver, then

$$\text{total cost} = £5000 + [£1 \times \text{direct labour hours } (x)]$$

or

$$y = a + bx$$

so that

$$y = £5000 + £1x$$

The term **cost function** is also used to refer to a regression equation that describes the relationship between a dependent variable and one or more independent variables. Cost functions are normally estimated from past cost data and activity levels. Cost estimation begins with measuring *past* relationships between total costs and the potential drivers of those costs. The objective is to use past cost behaviour patterns as an aid to predicting future costs. Any expected changes of circumstances in the future will require past data to be adjusted in line with future expectations.

There is a danger that cost functions derived from past data may be due to a spurious correlation in the data which can end at any time without warning. High correlation is only likely to continue if the relationship between the variables is economically plausible. Cost functions should not be derived solely on the basis of past observed statistical relationships. The nature of the observed statistical relationship should make sense and be economically plausible. If these conditions do not exist one cannot be confident that the estimated relationship will be repeated when the cost function is used to predict outcomes using a different set of data.

Economic plausibility exists when knowledge of operations or logic implies that a cause-and-effect relationship may exist. For example, the number of component parts is a potential cost driver for material handling costs since the greater the number of parts the higher the material handling costs. Logic suggests that a potential cause-and-effect relationship exists.

# Cost estimation methods

The following approaches to cost estimation will be examined:

1. engineering methods;
2. inspection of the accounts method;
3. graphical or scattergraph method;
4. high–low method;
5. least-squares method

These approaches differ in terms of the costs of undertaking the analysis and the accuracy of the estimated cost functions. They are not mutually exclusive and different methods may be used for different cost categories.

## ENGINEERING METHODS

**Engineering methods** of analysing cost behaviour are based on the use of engineering analyses of technological relationships between inputs and outputs – for example methods study, work sampling and time and motion studies. The approach is appropriate when there is a physical relationship between costs and the cost driver. The procedure when undertaking an engineering study is to make an analysis based on *direct* observations of the underlying physical quantities required for an activity and then to convert the final results into cost estimates. Engineers, who are familiar with the technical requirements, estimate the quantities of materials and the labour and machine hours required for various operations; prices and rates are then applied to the physical measures to obtain the cost estimates. The engineering method is useful for estimating costs of repetitive processes where input–output relationships are clearly defined. For example, this method is usually satisfactory for estimating costs that are usually associated with direct materials, labour and machine time, because these items can be directly observed and measured.

The engineering method is not restricted to manufacturing activities – time and motion studies can also be applied to well-structured administrative and selling activities such as typing, invoicing and purchasing. It is not generally appropriate, however, for estimating costs that are difficult to associate directly with individual units of output, such as many types of overhead costs, since these items cannot easily be directly observed and measured.

One disadvantage of engineering methods is that methods study, work sampling and time and motion study techniques can be expensive to apply in practice. The use of these is most appropriate when direct costs form a large part of the total costs and when input–output relationships are fairly stable over time. Engineering methods may also be applied in situations where there are no historical data to analyse past cost relationships. For an explanation of how engineering methods can be used to derive direct labour and material costs for specific operations you should refer back to Chapter 18 (pages 675–6).

## INSPECTION OF THE ACCOUNTS

The inspection of accounts method requires that the departmental manager and the accountant inspect each item of expenditure within the accounts for a particular period, and then classify each item of expense as a wholly fixed, wholly variable or a semi-variable cost. A single average *unit* cost figure is selected for the items that are categorized as variable, whereas a single *total* cost for the period is used for the items that are categorized as fixed. For semi-variable items the departmental manager and the accountant agree on a cost function that appears to best describe the cost behaviour. The process is illustrated in Example 24.1.

Note that repairs and maintenance have been classified as a semi-variable cost consisting of a variable element of £0.50 per unit of output plus £5000 non-variable cost. A check on the total cost calculation indicates that the estimate of a unit variable cost of £24.50 will give a total variable cost of £245 000 at an output level of 10 000 units. The non-variable costs of £50 000 are added to this to produce an estimated total cost of £295 000. The cost function is therefore $y = 50\,000 + £24.50x$. This cost function is then used for estimating costs at other output levels for each of the individual items of expense.

You will see from this example that the analysis of costs into their variable and non-variable elements is very subjective. Also, the latest cost details that are available from the accounts will normally be used, and this may not be typical of either past or future cost behaviour. Whenever possible, cost estimates should be based on a series of observations. Cost estimates based on this method involve individual and often arbitrary judgements, and they may therefore lack the precision necessary when they are to be used in making decisions that involve large sums of money and that are sensitive to measurement errors.

## GRAPHICAL OR SCATTERGRAPH METHOD

This method involves plotting on a graph the total costs for each activity level. The total cost is represented on the vertical (Y axis) and the activity levels are recorded on the horizontal (X axis). A straight line is fitted to the scatter of plotted points by visual approximation. Figure 24.1 illustrates the procedure using the data presented in Example 24.2.

**EXAMPLE 24.1**

The following cost information has been obtained from the latest monthly accounts for an output level of 10 000 units for a cost centre.

| | (£) |
|---|---|
| Direct materials | 100 000 |
| Direct labour | 140 000 |
| Indirect labour | 30 000 |
| Depreciation | 15 000 |
| Repairs and maintenance | 10 000 |
| | 295 000 |

The departmental manager and the accountant examine each item of expense and analyse the expenses into their variable and non-variable elements. The analysis might be as follows:

| | Unit variable cost (£) | Total non-variable cost (£) |
|---|---|---|
| Direct materials | 10.00 | |
| Direct labour | 14.00 | |
| Indirect labour | | 30 000 |
| Depreciation | | 15 000 |
| Repairs and maintenance | 0.50 | 5 000 |
| | 24.50 | 50 000 |

**EXAMPLE 24.2**

The total maintenance costs and the machine hours for the past ten four-weekly accounting periods were as follows:

| Period | Machine hours x | Maintenance cost y |
|---|---|---|
| 1 | 400 | 960 |
| 2 | 240 | 880 |
| 3 | 80 | 480 |
| 4 | 400 | 1200 |
| 5 | 320 | 800 |
| 6 | 240 | 640 |
| 7 | 160 | 560 |
| 8 | 480 | 1200 |
| 9 | 320 | 880 |
| 10 | 160 | 440 |

You are required to estimate the regression equation using the graphical method.

**FIGURE 24.1** *Graph of maintenance costs at different activity levels.*

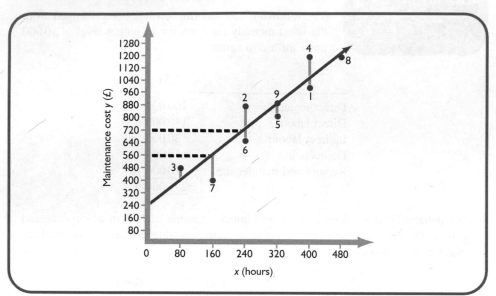

You will see by referring to Figure 24.1 that the maintenance costs are plotted for each activity level, and a straight line is drawn through the middle of the data points as closely as possible so that the distances of observations above the line are equal to the distances of observations below the line.

The point where the straight line in Figure 24.1 cuts the vertical axis (i.e. £240) represents the non-variable costs, item $a$ in the regression formula $y = a + bx$. The unit variable cost $b$ in the regression formula is found by observing the differences between any two points on the straight line (see the dashed line in Figure 24.1 for observations of 160 and 240 hours) and completing the following calculations:

$$\frac{\text{difference in cost}}{\text{difference in activity}} = \frac{£720 - £560}{240 \text{ hours} - 160 \text{ hours}} = £2 \text{ per hour}$$

This calculation is based on a comparison of the changes in costs that can be observed on the straight line between activity levels of 160 and 240 hours. This gives a regression formula.

$$y = £240 + £2x$$

If $x$ is assigned a value of 100 hours then

$$y = 240 + (2 \times 100) = £440$$

The graphical method is simple to use, and it provides a useful visual indication of any lack of correlation or erratic behaviour of costs. However, the method suffers from the disadvantage that the determination of exactly where the straight line should fall is subjective, and different people will draw different lines with different slopes, giving different cost estimates. To overcome this difficulty, it is preferable to determine the line of best fit mathematically using the least-squares method.

The monthly recordings for output and maintenance costs for the past 12 months have been examined and the following information has been extracted for the lowest and highest output levels:

| | Volume of production (units) | Maintenance costs (£) |
|---|---|---|
| Lowest activity | 5 000 | 22 000 |
| Highest activity | 10 000 | 32 000 |

The variable cost per unit is calculated as follows:

$$\frac{\text{difference in cost}}{\text{difference in activity}} = \frac{£10\ 000}{5000} = £2 \text{ variable cost per unit of output}$$

# HIGH–LOW METHOD

The high–low method consists of selecting the periods of highest and lowest activity levels and comparing the changes in costs that result from the two levels. This approach is illustrated in Example 24.3.

The non-variable (fixed) cost can be estimated at any level of activity (assuming a constant unit variable cost) by subtracting the variable cost portion from the total cost. At an activity level of 5000 units the total cost is £22 000 and the total variable cost is £10 000 (5000 units at £2 per unit). The balance of £12 000 is therefore assumed to represent the non-variable cost. The cost function is therefore:

$$y = £12\ 000 + £2x$$

The method is illustrated in Figure 24.2, with points A and B representing the lowest and highest output levels, and $TC_1$ and $TC_2$ representing the total cost for each of these levels. The other crosses represent past cost observations for other output levels. The straight (blue) line joining the observations for the lowest and highest activity levels represent the costs that would be estimated for each activity level when the high–low method is used.

You will see from this illustration that the method ignores all cost observations other than the observations for the lowest and highest activity levels. Unfortunately, cost observations at the extreme ranges of activity levels are not always typical of normal operating conditions, and therefore may reflect abnormal rather than normal cost relationships. Figure 24.2 indicates how the method can give inaccurate cost estimates when they are obtained by observing only the highest and lowest output levels. It would obviously be more appropriate to incorporate all of the available observations into the cost estimate, rather than to use only two extreme observations.

The lower straight (green) line, using the graphical or scattergraph approach described in the previous section, incorporates all of the observations. It is likely to provide a better estimate of the cost function than a method that relies on only two observations. The high–low method cannot therefore be recommended.

**FIGURE 24.2** *High–low method.*

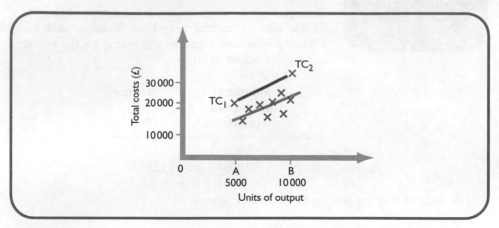

## THE LEAST-SQUARES METHOD

This method determines mathematically the regression line of best fit. It is based on the principle that the sum of the squares of the vertical deviations from the line that is established using the method is less than the sum of the squares of the vertical deviations from any other line that might be drawn. The regression equation for a straight line that meets this requirement can be found from the following two equations by solving for *a* and *b*:

$$\sum y = Na + b \sum x \qquad (24.1)$$
$$\sum xy = a \sum x + b \sum x^2 \qquad (24.2)$$

where $N$ is the number of observations.

To illustrate the **least-squares method** let us assume that past observations of maintenance costs and machine hours have been recorded and computations have been made as shown in Exhibit 24.1. We can now insert the computations into the formulae as follows:

$$19\,800 = 12a + 1260b \qquad (24.1)$$
$$2\,394\,000 = 1260a + 163\,800b \qquad (24.2)$$

To solve for *b* multiply equation (24.1) by 105 (1260/12), to give

$$2\,079\,000 = 1260a + 132\,300b \qquad (24.3)$$

Subtracting equation (24.3) from equation (24.2), the '*a*' terms will cancel out to yield $315\,000 = 31\,500b$, so that

$$b = £10$$

Substituting this value of *b* into equation (24.1) and solving for *a*, we have

$$19\,800 = 12a + 1260 \times 10$$

and so

$$a = 600$$

Substituting these values of *a* and *b* into the regression equation $y = a + bx$, we find that the regression line (i.e, cost function) can be described by

$$y = £600 + £10x$$

We can now use this formula to predict the cost incurred at different activity levels, including those for which we have no past observations. For example, at an activity level of 100 hours the cost prediction is £600 non-variable cost, plus £1000 variable cost (100

EXHIBIT   24.1

Past
observations of
maintenance
costs

hours × £10). The regression line and the actual observations (represented by the dots) are recorded in Figure 24.3. The closer the vertical distances of the plotted actual observations are to the straight line the more reliable is the estimated cost function in predicting cost behaviour. In other words, the

| Hours $x$ | Maintenance cost $y$ (£) | $x^2$ | $xy$ |
|---|---|---|---|
| 90 | 1 500 | 8 100 | 135 000 |
| 150 | 1 950 | 22 500 | 292 500 |
| 60 | 900 | 3 600 | 54 000 |
| 30 | 900 | 900 | 27 000 |
| 180 | 2 700 | 32 400 | 486 000 |
| 150 | 2 250 | 22 500 | 337 500 |
| 120 | 1 950 | 14 400 | 234 000 |
| 180 | 2 100 | 32 400 | 378 000 |
| 90 | 1 350 | 8 100 | 121 500 |
| 30 | 1 050 | 900 | 31 500 |
| 120 | 1 800 | 14 400 | 216 000 |
| 60 | 1 350 | 3 600 | 81 000 |
| $\sum x = 1\,260$ | $\sum y = 19\,800$ | $\sum x^2 = 163\,800$ | $\sum xy = 2\,394\,000$ |

closer the observations are to the line the stronger the relationship between the independent variable (machine hours in our example) and the dependent variable (i.e. total maintenance cost).

In Exhibit 24.1 the cost function was derived using machine hours as the activity measure/cost driver. However, a number of other potential cost drivers exist, such as, direct labour hours, units of output and number of production runs. Various tests of reliability can be applied to see how reliable potential cost drivers are in predicting the dependent variable. The most simplistic approach is to plot the data for each potential cost driver and examine the distances from a straight line derived either from a visual fit (using the graphical method) or the least-squares method. Alternatively, more sophisticated tests of reliability can be applied. In the appendix to this chapter three methods are described. They are the coefficient of determination, the standard error of the estimate and the standard error of the coefficient. If your curriculum requires an understanding of these methods you should read the appendix after you have completed reading the chapter. You should, however, note at this point that the coefficient of determination calculation (known as $r^2$) measures the percentage of variation in the dependent variable (i.e. the actual cost observations) that is explained by the independent variable (i.e. maintenance hours in our example). For the data given in Exhibit 24.1 the coefficient of variation is 0.89. This indicates that 89% of the variation in maintenance cost is explained by variations in machine hours and the remaining 11% is explained by random variations and/or the other omitted variables that are not included in the cost function.

The coefficient of variation is a goodness-of-fit measure. A goodness-of-fit measure indicates how well the predicted values of the dependent variable ($y$), based on the chosen cost driver (X), matches the actual cost observations (Y). Generally, an $r^2$ of 0.30 or higher passes the goodness-of-fit test but remember that the cost diver must also meet the

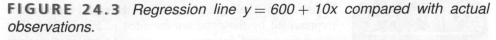

**FIGURE 24.3** *Regression line y = 600 + 10x compared with actual observations.*

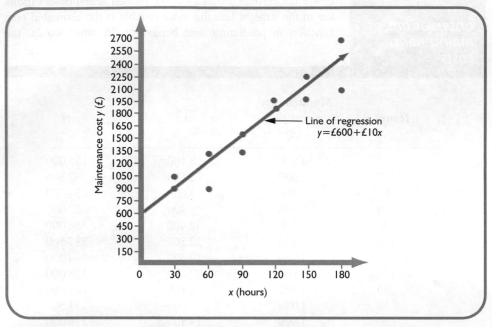

requirement of being economically plausible. Given that a relationship between hours and maintenance cost is economically plausible, and the high $r^2$ score of 0.89 we can conclude that maintenance hours would appear to be a suitable cost driver. For a more detailed discussion of tests of reliability you should refer to the appendix to this chapter.

# Multiple regression analysis

The least-squares regression equation was based on the assumption that total cost was determined by one activity-based variable only. However, other variables besides activity are likely to influence total cost. A certain cost may vary not only with changes in the hours of operation but also with the weight of the product being made, temperature changes or other factors. With simple least-squares regression, only one factor is taken into consideration; but with multiple regression, several factors are considered in combination. As far as possible, all the factors related to cost behaviour should be brought into the analysis so that costs can be predicted and controlled more effectively.

The equation for simple regression can be expanded to include more than one independent variable. If there are two independent variables and the relationship is assumed to be linear, the regression equation will be

$$y = a + b_1x_1 + b_2x_2$$

Item $a$ represents the non-variable cost item. Item $b_1$ represents the average change in $y$ resulting from a unit change in $x_1$, assuming that $x_2$ and all the unidentified items remain constant. Similarly, $b_2$ represents the average change in $y$ resulting from a unit change in $x_2$

assuming that $x_1$ remains constant. The normal equations for a regression equation with two independent variables are

$$\sum y = aN + b_1 \sum x_1 + b_2 \sum x_2$$

$$\sum x_1 y = a \sum x_1 + b_1 \sum x_1^2 + b_2 \sum x_1 x_2$$

$$\sum x_2 y = a \sum x_2 + b_1 \sum x_1 x_2 + b_2 \sum x_2^2$$

The value of $y$ can be determined by solving these equations, but the calculations are very tedious. Fortunately, standard computer programs are available that can generate the value of $y$ together with details of standard errors of the individual regression coefficients. We shall therefore now concentrate on the principles and application of multiple regression analysis and ignore the tedious arithmetical calculations.

Consider a plant that generates its own steam and uses this steam for both heating and motive power. A simple least-squares regression based on machine hours is likely to provide a poor estimate of the total cost of steam generation, and will produce a relatively low coefficient of determination. The cost of steam generation is likely to be determined by both temperature and machine hours, and a multiple regression equation is therefore likely to produce a more accurate estimate of the total costs. The equation could take the form

$$y = a + b_1 x_1 + b_2 x_2$$

where $y$ is the total cost, $a$ the total non-variable cost, $x_1$ the number of machine hours, $b_1$ the regression coefficient for machine hours, $x_2$ the number of days per month in which the temperature is less than 15°C, and $b_2$ the regression coefficient for temperature. The equations for this formula can be developed by using past monthly observations of the number of machine hours, the days on which the temperature was below 15°C and the total cost. This information is used to develop equations and the result will be an output similar to the following:

$$y = 20 + 4x_1 + 12x_2$$

Estimates of total steam cost can now be developed based on the estimated machine hours and the temperature for future periods. For example, if the number of estimated machine hours for a particular month is 1000, and past experience indicates that the temperature is likely to be below 15°C for the full month of 30 days, the estimated cost will be

$$y = 20 + (4 \times 1000) + (12 \times 30) = £4380$$

The value of the coefficients $b_1$ and $b_2$ enables us to determine the marginal cost associated with each of the determining factors. For example, the value of $b_1$ is £4, which indicates the marginal change in the total cost for each additional machine hour with the effects of temperature remaining constant.

# MULTICOLLINEARITY

**AR** Multiple regression analysis is based on the assumption that the independent variables are not correlated with each other. When the independent variables are highly correlated with each other, it is very difficult, and sometimes impossible, to separate the effects of each of these variables on the dependent variable. This occurs when there is a simultaneous movement of two or more independent variables in the same direction and at approximately the same rate. This condition is called **multicollinearity**.

An example of this is where several complementary products are manufactured and the output of each product is treated as an independent variable. If the demand for each of these products is highly correlated, the output of all the products will be similar – all being high in one period and low in another period. In this situation the regression coefficients have no meaning; they cannot estimate the likely changes in cost that will arise from a unit change in given independent variables while the other dependent variables are held constant. This is because there is a lack of independence among the independent variables, which prevents the availability of sufficient information to enable the regression coefficients to be determined. However, multicollinearity does not affect the validity of the predictions of the total cost if the past relationships between the independent variables are maintained.

Multicollinearity can be found in a variety of ways. One way is to measure the correlation between the independent variables. Generally, a coefficient of correlation between independent variables greater than 0.70 indicates multicollinearity. Kaplan (1982) makes the following comment on the effect of multicollinearity and the accounting implications:

> The collinearity problem is most severe when we are trying to obtain accurate coefficient estimates for product planning, pricing, and a cost–volume–profit analysis. If we are mainly interested in using the regression equation to predict cost behaviour in a period (i.e. as a flexible budget), then we are not concerned with the individual coefficient estimates. The standard error of the regression and of the forecasts from the regression are not affected by collinearity among subsets of the independent variables. Therefore, if the analyst feels that the correlated variables are all necessary for predicting overall costs, they can remain in the regression equation. ●●●

# Factors to be considered when using past data to estimate cost functions

Several requirements are necessary to ensure that a sound system is developed for estimating costs. If these requirements are not met, there is a danger that less accurate cost estimates will be produced, and there will be an increased probability that the quality of the information system will be impaired. Let us now consider some of these requirements.

## THE COST DATA AND ACTIVITY SHOULD BE RELATED TO THE SAME PERIOD

It is not uncommon for some costs to lag behind the associated activity. For example, wages paid in one period may be calculated by reference to the output from a previous period. Let us consider the following situation where a piecework system is in operation and where wages are paid on the basis of £1 per unit produced:

| | Activity $x$ (units) | Wages paid $y$ (£) |
|---|---|---|
| Week 10 | 5000 | 3000 (output for week 9 was 3000 units) |
| Week 11 | 2500 | 5000 |
| Week 12 | 4000 | 2500 |

In this example the firm follows a policy of paying the labour force for the output that was achieved in the previous week. It is clearly incorrect to relate costs to output for each week when calculating the cost estimation equation. It is therefore necessary to correct the bias in the data by relating the cost in period $t$ to the output in period $t-1$ before the cost equation is calculated.

## NUMBER OF OBSERVATIONS

If acceptable cost estimates are to be produced, a sufficient number of observations must be obtained. If figures are used only from recent periods, there may be insufficient observations. However, if observations other than those from previous periods are used, some adjustment of the data will be required. If insufficient observations are obtained, the standard error (see the appendix to this chapter for an explanation) is likely to be large, and the confidence intervals or ranges of costs will be quite large for each activity level. Wherever possible, many observations should be obtained over very short time periods. Weekly costs will yield considerably more observations for analysis than will monthly costs.

## ACCOUNTING POLICIES

The data must be examined to ensure that the accounting policies do not lead to distorted cost functions. For example, if *fixed* maintenance costs are allocated to production departments on the basis of the number of maintenance hours, this accounting allocation may make the fixed costs appear to be variable. There is a danger that the regression analysis will imply that these costs are variable rather than fixed. If the objective is to determine the cost of behaviour pattern in a single production department, only those costs incurred within the department should be included. Allocated costs should be excluded from the analysis.

## ADJUSTMENTS FOR PAST CHANGES

An analysis of past data will yield estimates of future costs that are based on the cost relationships of previous periods. The appropriateness of using past data depends on the extent to which the future will correspond with the past. Any changes of circumstances in the future will require past data to be adjusted in line with future data. For example, if it is estimated that future costs will increase by 10%, all past data should be adjusted by a price index to future price levels before the cost estimation equation is established.

It is also possible that technological changes in the production process may have taken place (such as changes in the type of equipment used), and past data must then be adjusted to reflect the circumstances which will apply in the future. Conversely, any observations from past periods that represent abnormal situations which are not expected to occur again in the future should be excluded from the analysis. The major problem is one of ensuring that a correct balance is maintained between obtaining sufficient observations to produce a reliable cost estimate, and keeping the time span short enough for the data to be appropriate to the circumstances in the future.

# Relevant range and non-linear cost functions

It may be very misleading to use a cost estimation equation (cost function) to estimate the total costs for ranges of activities outside the range of observations that were used to establish the cost function. This is because a cost function is normally only valid within the range of the actual observations that were used to establish the equation.

You will see from Figure 24.4 that in the past the company has operated only between activity levels $x_1$ and $x_2$ (this represents the actual observations). A cost equation developed from this information may provide satisfactory cost estimates for activity levels between $x_1$ and $x_2$, but it may not do so for activity levels outside this range of observations. For example, the dashed line that meets the vertical axis at A might represent a cost equation that has been developed from these observations; the dashed line will represent a satisfactory estimate of total cost only between activity levels $x_1$ and $x_2$. However, any extrapolation of the dashed line outside the range of observations may result in an unsatisfactory estimate of total cost.

You will remember that in Chapter 8 it was stressed that linear cost functions may only apply over the relevant production range (i.e. between activity levels $x_1$, and $x_2$ in Figure 24.4), and that over a very wide range of activity a curvilinear (non-linear) relationship may exist, similar to the curved line BC in Figure 24.4. It therefore follows that the extrapolation of the dashed line represents an unsatisfactory estimate outside the relevant range if a curvilinear relationship exists. Also, the non-variable item (i.e. $a$ in the equation $y = a + bx$) is unlikely to represent the total non-variable cost at zero activity. The cost equation in Figure 24.4 gives an estimated non-variable cost of OA compared with an actual non-variable cost of OB. Hence the value of the constant term $a$ in the cost equation is not the amount of cost that would be expected if there were zero output; it should be interpreted only as the amount of cost that does not vary with the activity level in the activity range $x_1$ to $x_2$.

In practice, the problem of extrapolation may not occur, since the majority of decisions are normally taken within the relevant operating range over which the firm has had experience of operating in the past. However, if decisions are to be based on cost information that is projected beyond the relevant range, the cost estimates must be used with care.

To determine whether a curvilinear relationship exists, the observations should be plotted on a graph, so that a simple examination of the graph may indicate whether or not such relationships exist. Indeed, it is a good idea always to prepare graphs and look carefully at the plotted data to ensure that some of the important requirements of cost estimation are not violated – blind reliance on mathematical techniques can be very dangerous.

# A summary of the steps involved in estimating cost functions

We can now summarize the stages involved in the estimation of a cost function based on the analysis of past data. They are:

1. Select the dependent variable $y$ (the cost variable) to be predicted.
2. Select the potential cost drivers.
3. Collect data on the dependent variable and cost drivers.
4. Plot the observations on a graph.

**FIGURE 24.4**  *Effect of extrapolation costs.*

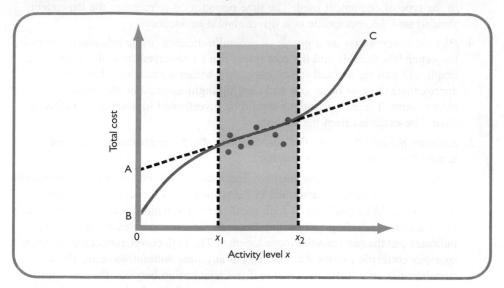

5. Estimate the cost function.

6. Test the reliability of the cost function.

It may be necessary to undertake each of these stages several times for different potential cost drivers before an acceptable cost function can be identified.

1. *Select the dependent variable y*: The choice of the cost (or costs) to be predicted will depend upon the purpose of the cost function. If the purpose is to estimate the indirect costs of a production or activity cost centre then all indirect costs associated with the production (activity) centre that are considered to have the same cause-and-effect relationship with the potential costs drivers should be grouped together. For example, if some overheads are considered to be related to performing production set-ups and others are related to machine running hours then it may be necessary to establish two cost pools: one for set-up-related costs and another for machine-related costs. A separate cost function would be established for each cost pool.

2. *Select potential cost drivers*: Examples of potential cost drivers include direct labour hours, machine hours, direct labour cost, number of units of output, number of production run set-ups, number of orders processed and weight of materials. A knowledge of operations or activities is necessary to determine the potential cost drivers. This may mean interviewing personnel involved in specific activities to ascertain what causes a particular activity to consume resources and so incur costs. Innes and Mitchell (1992) suggest the following questions might be used to determine potential cost drivers:

   - Why are $X$ number of staff needed for this activity?
   - What might cause you to need more/less staff?
   - What determines the amount of time spent on this activity?
   - Why does idle time occur?

   The end result will be a set of potential cost drivers. A potential cost driver should be plausible (i.e. make economic sense) and accurately measurable.

3. *Collect data on the dependent variable and cost drivers*: A sufficient number of past observations must be obtained to derive acceptable cost functions. The data should

be adjusted to reflect any changes of circumstance, such as price changes or changes in the type of equipment used. The time period used to measure the dependent variable and the appropriate cost driver should be identical.

4. *Plot the observations on a graph*: A general indication of the relationship between the dependent variable and the cost driver can be observed from the graph. The graph will provide a visual indication as to whether a linear cost function can approximate the cost behaviour and also highlight extreme or abnormal observations. These observations should be investigated to ascertain whether they should be excluded from the analysis.

5. *Estimate the cost function*: The cost function should be estimated using the approaches described in this chapter.

6. *Test the reliability of the cost function*: The reliability of the cost function should be tested using the methods described in the Appendix of this chapter. The cost function should be plausible. A high coefficient of variation $r^2$ does not necessarily mean a cause-and-effect relationship between the two variables exists. It merely indicates that the two variables move together. The high correlation could be due to a spurious correlation in the data and end at any time without warning. High correlation is only likely to continue if the relationship between the variables is plausible. Cost functions should not be derived solely on the basis of observed past statistical relationships. Instead, they should be used to confirm or reject beliefs that have been developed from a study of the underlying process. The nature of the statistical relationship should be understood and make economic sense.

The intelligent application of regression analysis requires an understanding of the underlying operations. Consider maintenance costs that are scheduled to be undertaken mainly in low-production periods so that production will not be disrupted. In this situation the regression analysis will indicate that the higher the level of production, the lower the maintenance costs, and vice versa. The true underlying relationship, however, is that the higher the level of production, the higher the maintenance costs. It is therefore important that maintenance costs should not be pooled with other costs, since this might result in a failure to isolate the true relationship between maintenance costs and the level of production.

# Cost estimation when the learning effect is present

Difficulties occur in estimating costs when technological changes take place in the production process: past data is not then very useful for estimating costs. For example, changes in the efficiency of the labour force may render past information unsuitable for predicting future labour costs. A situation like this may occur when workers become more familiar with the tasks that they perform, so that less labour time is required for the production of each unit. The phenomenon has been observed in a number of manufacturing situations, and is known as the learning-curve-effect. From the experience of aircraft production during World War II, aircraft manufacturers found that the rate of improvement was so regular that it could be reduced to a formula, and the labour hours required could be predicted with a high degree of accuracy from a learning curve. Based on this information, experiments have been undertaken in other industries with learning curves, and these experiments also indicate some regularity in the pattern of a worker's ability to learn a new task.

The first time a new operation is performed, both the workers and the operating procedures are untried. As the operation is repeated, the workers become more familiar with the work, labour efficiency increases and the labour cost per unit declines. This process continues for some time, and a regular rate of decline in cost per unit can be established at the outset. This rate of decline can then be used in predicting future labour costs. The learning process starts from the point when the first unit comes off the production line. From then on, each time cumulative production is doubled, the average time taken to produce each unit of cumulative production will be a certain percentage of the average time per unit of the previous cumulative production.

An application of the 80% learning curve is presented in Exhibit 24.2, which shows the labour hours required on a sequence of six orders where the cumulative number of units is doubled for each order. The first unit was completed on the first order in 2000 hours; for each subsequent order the *cumulative production* was doubled (see column 3), so that the average hours per unit were 80% of the average hours per unit of the previous *cumulative production*. For example, the *cumulative average time* shown in column 4 for each unit of output is calculated as follows:

$$
\begin{aligned}
\text{order number } 1 &= 2000 \text{ hours} \\
2 &= 1600 \text{ hours } (80\% \times 2000) \\
3 &= 1280 \text{ hours } (80\% \times 1600) \\
4 &= 1024 \text{ hours } (80\% \times 1280) \\
5 &= 819 \text{ hours } (80\% \times 1024) \\
6 &= 655 \text{ hours } (80\% \times 819)
\end{aligned}
$$

Exhibit 24.2 provides information for specific quantities only. No information is available for other quantities such as 10, 20 or 30 units, although such information could be obtained either graphically or mathematically.

## GRAPHICAL METHOD

The quantities for the average time per unit of cumulative production (column 4 of Exhibit 24.2) are presented in graphical form in Figure 24.5. The entries in column 4 are plotted on the graph for each level of cumulative production, and a line is drawn through these points. (You should note that more accurate graphs can be constructed if the observations are plotted on log-log graph paper.)

The graph shows that the average time per unit declines rapidly at first and then more slowly, until eventually the decline is so small that it can be ignored. When no further improvement is expected and the regular efficiency level is reached, the situation is referred to as the steady-state production level. The cumulative average hours per unit is 953 hours for 10 units and 762 hours for 20 units. To obtain the total number of hours, we merely multiply the average number of hours by the cumulative quantity produced, which gives 9530 total hours for 10 units and 15 240 total hours for 20 units.

## MATHEMATICAL METHOD

The learning curve can be expressed in equation form as:

$$Y_x = aX^b$$

where $Y_x$ is defined as the cumulative average time required to produce $X$ units, $a$ is the time required to produce the first unit of output and $X$ is the number of units of output under consideration. The exponent $b$ is defined as the ratio of the logarithm of the learning curve improvement rate (e.g. 0.8 for an 80% learning curve) divided by the

**EXHIBIT 24.2**

*Labour hours for 80% learning curve*

logarithm of 2. The improvement exponent can take on any value between $-1$ and zero. For example, for an 80% learning curve

$$b = \frac{\log 0.8}{\log 2} = \frac{-0.2231}{0.6931} = -0.322$$

| | Number of units | | Cumulative hours | | Hours for each order | |
|---|---|---|---|---|---|---|
| (1) | (2) | (3) | (4) | (5) | (6) | (7) |
| Order no. | Per order | Cumulative production | Per unit | Total | Total | Per unit |
| | | | | $(3) \times (4)$ | | $(6) \div (2)$ |
| 1 | 1 | 1 | 2000 | 2 000 | 2000 | 2000 |
| 2 | 1 | 2 | 1600 | 3 200 | 1200 | 1200 |
| 3 | 2 | 4 | 1280 | 5 120 | 1920 | 960 |
| 4 | 4 | 8 | 1024 | 8 192 | 3072 | 768 |
| 5 | 8 | 16 | 819 | 13 104 | 4912 | 614 |
| 6 | 16 | 32 | 655 | 20 960 | 7856 | 491 |

**FIGURE 24.5** *80% learning curve.*

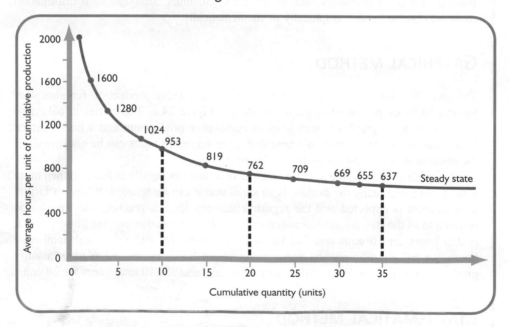

The cumulative average time taken to produce 10 and 20 units can therefore be calculated as follows:

$$Y_{10} = 2000 \times 10^{-0.322}$$
$$= 2000 \times 0.476\,431$$
$$= \underline{953}$$

and

$$Y_{20} = 2000 \times 20^{-0.322}$$
$$= 2000 \times 0.381\,126$$
$$= \underline{762}$$

A computation of the exponent values may be made by using either logarithm tables or a calculator with exponent functions.

# Estimating incremented hours and incremental cost

Incremental hours cannot be determined directly from the learning-curve graph or formula, since the results are expressed in terms of cumulative average hours. It is possible, however, to obtain incremental hours by examining the differences between total hours for various combinations of cumulative hours. For example, assume that for Exhibit 24.2 the company has completed orders such that cumulative production is 4 units and that an enquiry has been received for an order of 6 units. We can calculate the incremental hours for these 6 units as follows:

| | |
|---|---:|
| Total hours if an additional 6 units are produced ($10 \times 953$) | 9530 |
| (cumulative production will be ten units) | |
| Total hours for the first 4 units ($4 \times 1280$) | 5120 |
| Hours required for 6 units after completion of 4 units | $= 4410$ |

Note that the total hours are calculated by taking the average hours for cumulative production and multiplying by the cumulative production. The incremental hours for 6 units are obtained by taking the difference between the time required for 10 units and the time required for 4 units.

Let us assume that the company completes the order for the 6 units and then receives a new order for an additional 10 units. How many labour hours will be needed? The cumulative quantity is now 20 units (10 already completed plus 10 now on order). The estimated hours for the 10 new units are calculated as follows:

| | |
|---|---:|
| Total hours for first 20 units ($20 \times 762$) | 15\,240 |
| Total hours for first 10 units ($10 \times 953$) | 9\,530 |
| Hours required for 10 units after completion of 10 units | 5\,710 |

The learning curve can be used to estimate labour costs and those other costs which vary in direct proportion to labour costs. Note that the learning effect only applies to direct labour costs and those variable overheads that are a direct function of labour hours of input. It does not apply to material costs, non-variable costs or items that vary with output rather than input.

Let us now assume that a company has just completed the first two units of production of a new product that is subject to an 80% learning curve at a labour cost of £10\,000. Assuming that the company now receives an enquiry for the production of two further units, what is the estimated labour cost and variable overhead cost if the variable overheads amount to 20% of direct labour cost? As the cumulative production will be doubled if the two units are produced, the incremental labour and variable overhead costs for the two units can be calculated as follows:

(A)  Cumulative average labour cost for two first two units was £5000 (£10 000/2)

(B)  Cumulative average labour cost for first four units will be £4000 (80% × £5000)

(C)  The labour costs for the enquiry for the two units will be calculated as follows:

|                                      | (£)     |
| ------------------------------------ | ------- |
| Labour cost for four units (£4000×4) | 16 000  |
| Labour cost for two units            | 10 000  |
| Cost for new order of two units      | 6 000   |

(D)  The estimated labour and variable overhead costs for the two additional units are as follows:

|                                 | (£)   |
| ------------------------------- | ----- |
| Direct labour cost              | 6000  |
| Variable overheads (20% of 6000)| 1200  |

# Learning curve applications

The learning curve generally applies to those situations where the labour input for an activity is large and the activity is complex. Learning curves are not theoretical abstractions, but are based on observations of past events. When new products have been made in previous periods, the learning-curve principles can be applied from the experience that has been gained. In new situations where there are no historical data the curves for previous products or processes with known improvement factors can be used if management can identify similarities with the new situation. We have considered in this chapter an 80% learning curve, but this percentage may vary, depending on the technology. In the aircraft industry studies indicated that a learning curve of 80% was appropriate, but other industries may suggest that other percentages should be applied to take account of the learning factor. Generally, the figures vary between 70% and 90%.

Unfortunately, the true nature of the learning curve associated with a new product or process will never be known. However, a reasonable assumption of its shape is better than an assumption of no learning curve at all. The learning curve may be applied to the following situations.

## 1. PRICING DECISIONS

The main impact of the learning curve is likely to be in providing better cost predictions to enable price quotations to be prepared for potential orders. An ability to forecast cost reductions and consequent selling price reductions may make the difference between landing and losing profitable orders. Simmonds (1981) suggests that early experience with a *new* product could confer an unbeatable lead over competitors, and that the leading competitor should be able to reduce its selling price for the product (through the learning-curve effect), which would further increase their volume and market share and eventually force some lagging competitors out of the industry.

## 2. WORK SCHEDULING

Learning curves enable firms to predict their required inputs more effectively, and this enables them to produce more accurate delivery schedules. This in turn can lead to improved customer relationships and possibly result in increased future sales.

## 3. STANDARD SETTING

If budgets and standards are set without considering the learning effect, meaningless variances are likely to occur. For example, if the learning effect is ignored, inapproporiate labour standards will be set that can be easily attained. If management creates a climate where learning is encouraged and expected then improvements in efficiency are more likely to occur. ●●●

# Cost estimation techniques used in practice

The survey of Drury *et al.* (1993) reported that statistical techniques are not widely used to separate fixed and variable costs. The following results were reported:

2% used statistical regression techniques;
59% classified costs on a subjective basis based on managerial experience;
28% classified all overheads as fixed costs and direct costs were classified as variable costs;
11% did not separate fixed and variable costs.

With regard to the use of learning curves and multiple regression techniques for cost and sales estimation, the following results were reported:

| Extent of usage | Learning curves (%) | Multiple regression techniques (%) |
|---|---|---|
| Never | 35 | 64 |
| Rarely | 26 | 23 |
| Sometimes | 22 | 10 |
| Often | 14 | 2 |
| Always | 3 | 1 |

## Self-Assessment Questions

You should attempt to answer these questions yourself before looking up the suggested answers, which appear on pages 1134–5. If any part of your answer is incorrect, check back carefully to make sure you understand where you went wrong.

1. Albatross Plc, the Australian subsidiary of a British packaging company, is preparing its budget for the year to 30th June 2001. In respect of fuel oil consumption, it is desired to estimate an equation of the form $y = a + bx$, where $y$ is the total expense at an activity level $x$, $a$ is the fixed expense and $b$ is the rate of variable cost.

The following data relates to the year ending 30 June 2000:

| Month | Machine hours (000) | Fuel oil expense (£000) | Month | Machine hours (000) | Fuel oil expense (£000) |
|-------|------|------|-------|------|------|
| July | 34 | 640 | January | 26 | 500 |
| August | 30 | 620 | February | 26 | 500 |
| September | 34 | 620 | March | 31 | 530 |
| October | 39 | 590 | April | 35 | 550 |
| November | 42 | 500 | May | 43 | 580 |
| December | 32 | 530 | June | 48 | 680 |

The annual total and monthly average figures for the year ending 30 June 2000 were as follows:

| | Machine hours (000) | Fuel oil expense ($) |
|---|---|---|
| Annual total | 420 | 6840 |
| Monthly average | 35 | 570 |

You are required to:

(a) estimate fixed and variable elements of fuel oil expense from the above data by both the following methods:

    (i) high and low points                                       (4 marks)

    (ii) least-squares regression analysis                          (8 marks)

(b) compare briefly the methods used in (a) above in relation to the task of estimating fixed and variable elements of a semi-variable cost;        (7 marks)

(c) accepting that the coefficient of determination arising from the data given in the question is approximately 0.25, interpret the significance of this fact.    (6 marks)

                                         *ICAEW Management Accounting*

2. You have been asked about the application of the learning curve as a management accounting technique.

You are required to:

(a) define the learning curve;

(b) explain the theory of learning curves;

(c) indicate the areas where learning curves may assist in management accounting;

(d) illustrate the use of learning curves for calculating the expected average unit cost of making:

  (i)  4 machines

  (ii) 8 machines

using the data given below.

Data:

Direct labour needed to make the first machine: 1000 hours
Learning curve: 80%
Direct labour cost: £3 per hour
Direct materials cost £1800 per machine
Fixed cost for either size order: £8000

(20 marks)
*CIMA P3 Management Accounting*

## Summary

Total costs for a particular expense may be a function of the number of units produced, direct labour hours of input, machine hours of input, quantities of materials used and so on. The objective is to find the activity measure (cost driver) that exerts the major influence on cost. Various tests of reliability can be applied to see how reliable each of these activity measures is in predicting specific costs. Such tests include the coefficient of determination, the standard error of the estimate and the standard error of the coefficient. If a single activity measure is found to be sufficiently reliable, a regression equation should be established using the least-squares method.

If the tests of reliability suggest unreliable cost estimates and it is considered that total cost is a function of more than one variable, estimates based on multiple regression should be established for the important cost items.

A number of requirements are necessary before statistical cost estimation techniques can be used. The time period should be long enough to enable meaningful information to be collected; the cost data and activity must be related to the same period, the analysis should consist of a sufficient number of observations and past data should be adjusted to reflect future expectations. A further problem is that the cost equation is only valid within the range of actual observations that were

used to establish the equation. Incorrect cost estimates will result if the estimates are projected outside this activity level as curvilinear relationships might exist. Some of the problems can be spotted by plotting a graph and looking carefully at the data.

We concluded our discussion of cost estimation by summarizing the following procedure for estimating cost functions from past data:

1. Select the dependent variable.

2. Select potential cost drivers.

3. Collect data on the dependent variable and cost drivers.

4. Plot the observations on a graph.

5. Estimate the cost function.

6. Test the reliability of the cost function.

When technological changes occur in the production process, past costs cannot be used to predict future costs. If the labour content per unit is expected to decline as workers become more familiar with the process, learning curve principles can be applied.

Recent developments in activity-based costing theory suggest that the cost estimation techniques described in this chapter may not be appropriate for estimating some costs. In particular, where there is a considerable time lag between changes in resource consumption and adjustments for changes in the spending on the supply of resources the use of past data to establish cost functions may be questionable. For a description of alternative cost estimation approaches you should refer to the discussion relating to the sections on 'Resource consumption models' and 'Selecting the cost driver denominator level' in Chapter 10. The regression analysis techniques described in this chapter are most appropriate for those resources where changes in resource consumption are continuously matched by changes in the spending on the supply of resources.

## Key Terms and Concepts

activity measure (p. 954)
coefficient of determination, $r^2$ (p. 978)
correlation (p. 978)
cost driver (p. 954)
cost function (p. 955)
correlation coefficient, $r$ (p. 978)
dependent variable (p. 954)
engineering methods (p. 955)
goodness-of-fit (p. 961)
high–low method (p. 959)
independent variable (p. 954)
inspection of accounts method (p. 956)

learning curve (p. 968)
learning-curve effect (p. 968)
least-squares method (p. 960)
multicollinearity (p 963)
multiple regression (p. 954)
regression equation (p. 954)
simple regression (p. 954)
standard error of the $b$ coefficient, Sb (p. 981)
standard error of the estimate, Se (p. 980)
steady state production level (pp. 969)
tests of reliability (pp. 961, 977)

## Recommended Reading

This chapter has provided an introduction to the various cost estimation techniques. For a more detailed discussion of these techniques you should refer to chapter 4 of Scapens (1991) and chapters 4 and 5 of Kaplan and Atkinson (1989).

# Appendix 24.1 Tests of reliability

**AR** Various **tests of reliability** can be applied to see how reliable potential cost drivers are in predicting the dependent variable (i.e. total cost) or the beta coefficient (variable cost). Three such tests will be described. They are:

1. the coefficient of determination;
2. the standard error of the estimate;
3. the standard error of the coefficient.

Throughout this appendix we shall use the data presented in Exhibit 24.1 and Figure 24.3 to illustrate the tests of reliability.

## THE COEFFICIENT OF DETERMINATION

If the regression line ($y = £600 + £10x$) calculated by the least-squares method for the data given in Exhibit 24.1 were to fit the actual observations perfectly, all of the observed points would lie on the regression line in Figure 24.3. You will see from this diagram that reliability is based on the size of the deviations of the actual observations ($y^a$) from the estimated values on the regression line ($y^e$). The size of these deviations can be ascertained by squaring the difference between the estimated and the actual values. (The sums of the deviations will always add to zero, and it is therefore necessary to square the deviations.) The average of these squared deviations is defined as the residual variation. In statistical terms this represents the variance of the actual observations from the regression line, and is denoted by $\sigma$. The calculation of the residual variation for the information represented in Exhibit 24.1 is shown in Exhibit 24.A1.

The residual variation is calculated from the formula:

$$\sigma^2 = \frac{\sum(y_a - y_e)^2}{N} = \frac{405\,000}{12} = 33\,750$$

To determine how reliable the chosen cost driver is in predicting costs, we must determine the total dispersion of the observations and compare this with the dispersion that occurs when machine hours of activity are used in predicting costs. The total dispersion of the cost observations can be found by removing machine hours from the cost equation and working out what the dispersion would then be. Any estimate of cost would then be based on a simple calculation of the average of all the actual cost observations. In Exhibit 24.A1 there are 12 observations of actual cost, which add up to £19 800, the average being £1650 (£19 800/12). Let us now calculate the dispersion of the actual observations around the average. This calculation is shown in Exhibit 24.A2.

The dispersion from the average $\sigma^2$, is calculated from the formula

$$\sigma^2 = \frac{\sum(y_a - \bar{y}_a)^2}{N} = \frac{3\,555\,000}{12} = 296\,250$$

The total dispersion is £296 250 but, by introducing hours into the regression equation as a possible way of predicting variations in cost, we have accounted for all but £33 750 of the total variation of £296 250. In percentage terms this means that the activity base used has failed to account for 11.39% (i.e. (33 750/296 250)×100) of the variation of cost. In other words, 88.61% of the variation in total cost is explained by variations in the activity base (cost driver), and the remaining 11.39% is explained by either entirely random variation or random variation plus the combined effect that other (omitted variables) have on the dependent variable (total cost).

The term used for describing the calculation of 88.61% is the **coefficient of determination**, $r^2$. This is calculated from the formula

$$r^2 = 1 - \frac{\sum(y_a - y_e)^2/N}{\sum(y_a - \bar{y}_a)^2/N} = 1 - \frac{33\,750}{296\,250} = 0.8861$$

The degree of association between two variables such as cost and activity is normally referred to as **correlation**. The **correlation coefficient** $r$ is the square root of the coefficient of determination. If the degree of association between the two variables is very close, it will be almost possible to plot the observations on a straight line, and $r$ and $r^2$ will be very near to 1. In this situation a high correlation between costs and activity exists, as illustrated in Figure 24.A1.

At the other extreme, costs may be so randomly distributed that there is little or no correlation between costs and the activity base selected. The $r^2$ calculation will be near to zero. An illustration of the situation where no correlation exists is given in Figure 24.A2.

## STANDARD ERROR OF THE ESTIMATE

The coefficient of determination gives us an indication of the reliability of the estimate of *total cost* based on the regression equation but it does not give us an indication of the absolute size of the probable deviations from the line. This information can be obtained

## EXHIBIT 24.A1

*Calculation of residual variation*

| Hours $x$ | Actual cost $(y_a)$ | Estimated cost $(y_e)$ $(y = 600 + 10x)$ | Deviations $(y_a - y_e)$ | Deviations squared $(y_a - y_e)^2$ |
|---|---|---|---|---|
| 90 | 1 500 | 1500 | 0 | 0 |
| 150 | 1 950 | 2100 | −150 | 22 500 |
| 60 | 900 | 1200 | −300 | 90 000 |
| 30 | 900 | 900 | 0 | 0 |
| 180 | 2 700 | 2400 | 300 | 90 000 |
| 150 | 2 250 | 2100 | 150 | 22 500 |
| 120 | 1 950 | 1800 | 150 | 22 500 |
| 180 | 2 100 | 2400 | −300 | 90 000 |
| 90 | 1 350 | 1500 | −150 | 22 500 |
| 30 | 1 050 | 900 | 150 | 22 500 |
| 120 | 1 800 | 1800 | 0 | 0 |
| 60 | 1 350 | 1200 | 150 | 22 500 |
| | 19 800 | | | 405 000 |

## EXHIBIT 24.A2

*Dispersion of observations around the average*

| Actual cost $(y_a)$ | Average $(\bar{y}_a)$ | Deviation $(y_a - \bar{y}_a)$ | Deviation squared $(y_a - \bar{y}_a)^2$ |
|---|---|---|---|
| 1500 | 1650 | −150 | 22 500 |
| 1950 | 1650 | 300 | 90 000 |
| 900 | 1650 | −750 | 562 500 |
| 900 | 1650 | −750 | 562 500 |
| 2700 | 1650 | 1050 | 1 102 500 |
| 2250 | 1650 | 600 | 360 000 |
| 1950 | 1650 | 300 | 90 000 |
| 2100 | 1650 | 450 | 202 500 |
| 1350 | 1650 | −300 | 90 000 |
| 1050 | 1650 | −600 | 360 000 |
| 1800 | 1650 | 150 | 22 500 |
| 1350 | 1650 | −300 | 90 000 |
| | | | 3 555 000 |

**FIGURE 24.A1** *High correlation.*

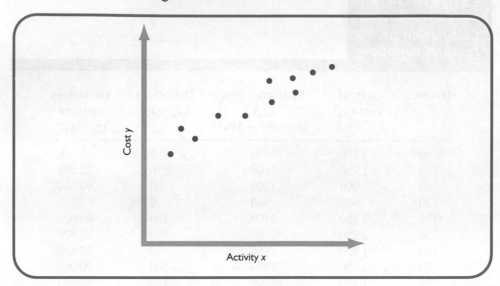

**FIGURE 24.A2** *No correlation.*

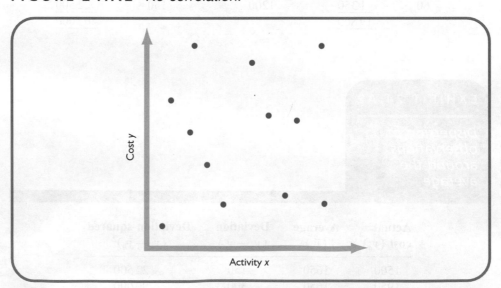

by calculating the **standard error of the estimate, Se**, based on the formula

$$\text{Se} = \sqrt{\left[\frac{\sum(y_a - y_e)^2}{N - 2}\right]} = \sqrt{\left(\frac{405\ 000}{10}\right)} = 201.25$$

The sample size $N$ is reduced by 2 because two variables ($a$ and $b$) in the regression equation had to be estimated from the sample of observations. Note that $\sum(y_a - y_e)^2$ has been obtained from Exhibit 24.A1.

The calculation of the standard error is necessary because the least-squares line was calculated from sample data. Other samples would probably result in different estimates. Obtaining the least-squares calculation over all the possible observations that might occur for the maintenance cost would result in a calculation of the true least-squares line. The question is how close does the sample estimate of the least-squares line ($y = 600 + 10x$) come to the true least-squares line. The standard error enables us to establish a range of values of the dependent variable $y$ within which we may have some degree of confidence that the true value lies. Different ranges can be calculated for different degrees of confidence. Thus the standard error of the estimate is quite similar to a standard deviation in normal probability analysis. It is a measure of variability around the regression line.

Statistical theory indicates that for least-squares analysis the points are $t$-distributed about the regression line and that the distribution becomes normal as the number of observations reaches 30. As our estimate of the regression line was based on twelve observations, we shall assume that the points are $t$-distributed about the regression line. An important characteristic of this distribution is that there is a 0.90 probability that the true cost lies within $\pm1.812$ standard errors from the estimated cost. (An explanation of this is presented later in this appendix.) If you refer back to Exhibit 24.A1, you will see that the estimated cost for 180 hours of activity is £2400. This means that there is a 0.90 probability that the true cost will fall within the range

$$£2400 \pm 1.812 \,(201.25) = £2035 \text{ to } £2765$$

If a narrower range is required, the probability that the true cost will fall within this narrower range will be less than 0.9. For example, the $t$-distribution (see page 983) indicates that there is a probability of 0.80 that the true cost will fall within 1.372 standard errors from the estimated cost. This means that there is a 0.80 probability that the true cost will fall within the following range:

$$£2400 \pm 1.372 \,(201.25) = £2124 \text{ to } £2676$$

Alternatively, if a greater degree of confidence is required, a probability higher than 0.90 can be obtained, but this will give a wider range within which the true cost lies. The tighter the observations around the regression's line, the lower the value of Se. When observations of costs and output are widely distributed around the regression line, we can expect a high Se, since we need a much larger range to describe our estimate of true costs.

These principles can usefully be applied to flexible budgeting by presenting a flexible budget that portrays a range of possible costs for each level of activity. A flexible budget based on a 0.90 probability for activity levels of 150 and 180 hours is presented in Exhibit 24.A3.

We should expect costs to fall within the given range for 90% of the time. Alternatively, we should expect costs to fall outside the range for 10% of the time when they are from the same population from which the least-squares estimate was derived. Therefore for any actual cost observations that are outside the range there is a high probability that the costs are out of control. We discussed this principle in Chapter 19 when we considered the investigation of variances.

## STANDARD ERROR OF THE COEFFICIENT

We have previously computed the standard error of the estimate to measure the reliability of the estimates of *total cost*. However, we may also be interested in the reliability of the estimate of the regression coefficient $b$ (i.e. the *variable cost*). This is because the analyst often focuses on the rate of variability rather than on the absolute level of the prediction. The formula for the standard error of the $b$ coefficient, Sb can

## EXHIBIT 24.A3

*Flexible budgets*

| Activity | 150 hours | | | 180 hours | | |
|---|---|---|---|---|---|---|
| | Lower limit | Mean | Upper limit | Lower limit | Mean | Upper limit |
| | £1735 | £2100 | £2465 | £2035 | £2400 | £2765 |

be expressed as

$$Sb = \frac{Se}{\sqrt{[\sum(x - \bar{x})^2]}}$$

This can be simplified to

$$Sb = \frac{Se}{\sqrt{(\sum x^2 - \bar{x} \sum x)}}$$

If we use the standard error that we have calculated earlier and the data that we used for calculating the regression equation in Exhibit 24.1 (see page 961), the calculation is as follows:

$$Sb = \frac{201.25}{\sqrt{[163\,800 - (1260/12)1260]}} = \frac{201.25}{\sqrt{(31\,500)}} = 1.134$$

We can now use the $t$-distribution, again noting that there is a 0.9 probability that the true variable cost lies within ±1.812 standard errors from the estimated cost. Using the regression equation $y = 600 + 10x$, we can state that we are 90% confident that the true variable cost lies within the range.

$$£10 \pm 1.812 \times 1.134 = £7.95 \text{ to } £12.05$$

We can calculate different ranges of variable costs based on different probability levels. For example, the $t$-distribution shown at the end of this appendix indicates that there is a 0.8 probability that the true variable cost lies within 1.372 standard errors from the mean. Therefore we can be 80% confident that the true variable cost lies within the range.

$$£10 \pm 1.372 \, Sb$$

## PARTIAL TABLE OF $t$-VALUES

The relevant numbers for the probabilities of 0.80 and 0.90 quoted in this chapter are 1.372 and 1.812. These items are obtained from the appropriate columns for the line representing 10 degrees of freedom. The number of degrees of freedom are obtained from the number of observations (namely 12), reduced by the number of variables in the simple regression equation which had to be estimated from the sample observations (i.e. two for regression coefficients $a$ and $b$ in the equation $y = a + bx$).

Note that the headings of *t*-tables usually identify the probabilities of values falling in one tail of the *t*-distribution. However, to simplify the situation, the normal presentation has been reversed for the sake of greater clarity, and the probabilities of the value falling in the main body of the distribution, and not the tail, are presented. For example, the

| | Probabilities of occurrence (range 0.80 to 0.99) | | | | |
|---|---|---|---|---|---|
| **Degrees of freedom** | **0.80** | **0.90** | **0.95** | **0.98** | **0.99** |
| 1 | 3.078 | 6.314 | 12.706 | 31.821 | 63.657 |
| 2 | 1.886 | 2.920 | 4.303 | 6.965 | 9.925 |
| 3 | 1.638 | 2.353 | 3.182 | 4.541 | 5.841 |
| 4 | 1.533 | 2.132 | 2.776 | 3.747 | 4.604 |
| 5 | 1.476 | 2.015 | 2.571 | 3.365 | 4.032 |
| 6 | 1.440 | 1.943 | 2.447 | 3.143 | 2.707 |
| 7 | 1.415 | 1.895 | 2.365 | 2.998 | 3.499 |
| 8 | 1.397 | 1.860 | 2.306 | 2.896 | 3.355 |
| 9 | 1.383 | 1.833 | 2.262 | 2.821 | 3.250 |
| 10 | 1.372 | 1.812 | 2.228 | 2.764 | 3.169 |
| 11 | 1.363 | 1.796 | 2.201 | 2.718 | 3.106 |
| 12 | 1.356 | 1.782 | 2.179 | 2.681 | 3.055 |
| 13 | 1.350 | 1.771 | 2.160 | 2.650 | 3.012 |
| 14 | 1.345 | 1.761 | 2.145 | 2.624 | 2.977 |
| 15 | 1.341 | 1.753 | 2.131 | 2.602 | 2.947 |
| Infinite | 1.282 | 1.645 | 1.960 | 2.326 | 2.576 |

**FIGURE 24.A3** *A t-distribution.*

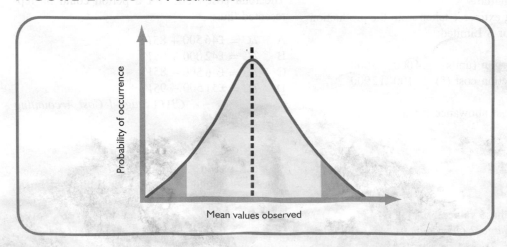

entries in Exhibit 24.A4 indicate the probability of an observation falling in the orange area of Figure 24.A3.

Assuming that the blue shaded area in each tail of the distribution represents $t = 0.025$, then 0.05 of the area under the curve falls in the tails of the distribution. Consequently, 0.95 of the area under the curve falls in the orange area. Therefore the entries in Exhibit 24.A4 are for 0.95 and not 0.025 which is the normal presentation.

●●●

## Key Examination Points

In recent years emphasis has switched from calculation to interpretation. Do make sure you can interpret regression equations and explain the meaning of the various statistical tests of reliability. Different formulae can be used to calculate regression equations, standard errors and $r^2$. You should use the formulae that you prefer; but where a formula is given, use it. The examiner will have set the question assuming you will use the formula. You will probably find that you have insufficient data or excessive calculations are required if you use an alternative formula. Do not worry if you are unfamiliar with the formula. All that is necessary is for you to enter the figures given in the question into it. (See Question 24.8 and 24.12 for an illustration.)

Remember with learning curves that only labour costs and variable overheads that vary with labour costs are subject to the learning effect. A common requirement is for you to calculate the incremental hours per order. Make sure that you understand columns 6 and 7 of Exhibit 24.2.

## Questions

*Indicates that a suggested solution is to be found in the *Students' Manual*.

Note that for Questions 24.12 and 24.13 the examination paper provided the following formulae for answering the questions:

*Linear regression analysis*: When $y = a + bx$,

$$b = \frac{\sum(x - \bar{x})(y - \bar{y})}{\sum(x - \bar{x})^2} \text{ or } \frac{n\sum xy - \sum x \sum y}{n\sum x^2 - (\sum x)^2}$$

and $a = \bar{y} - b\bar{x}$

### 24.1* Intermediate
The following extract is taken from the production cost budget for S Limited:

| Production (units) | 4 000 | 6 000 |
|---|---|---|
| Production cost (£) | 11 100 | 12 900 |

The budget cost allowance for an activity level of 8000 units is

A    £7 200.
B    £14 700.
C    £17 200.
D    £22 200.
E    none of these values.

*CIMA Stage 2 Operational Cost Accounting*

### 24.2* Intermediate
The Valuation Department of a large firm of surveyors wishes to develop a method of predicting its total costs in a period. The following past costs have been recorded at two activity levels:

| | Number of valuations (V) | Total cost (TC) (£) |
|---|---|---|
| Period 1 | 420 | 82 200 |
| Period 2 | 515 | 90 275 |

The total cost model for a period could be represented thus:

A    $TC = £46\,500 + 85V$.
B    $TC = £42\,000 + 95V$.
C    $TC = £46\,500 - 85V$.
D    $TC = £51\,500 - 95V$.

*CIMA Stage 1 Cost Accounting*

### 24.3 Advanced
Discuss the conditions that should apply if linear regression analysis is to be used to analyse cost behaviour.                    (6 marks)
*ACCA Level 2 Management Accounting*

## 24.4 Advanced

(a) Briefly discuss the problems that occur in constructing cost estimation equations for estimating costs at different output levels.
(7 marks)

(b) Describe four different cost estimation methods and for each method discuss the limitations and circumstances in which you would recommend their use. (18 marks)

## 24.5 Advanced

Explain the 'learning curve' and discuss its relevance to setting standards. (5 marks)
*ACCA Level 2 Management Accounting*

## 24.6 Advanced

(a) Comment on factors likely to affect the accuracy of the analysis of costs into fixed and variable components. (8 marks)

(b) Explain how the analysis of costs into fixed and variable components is of use in planning, control and decision-making techniques used by the management accountant. (9 marks)
(Total 17 marks)
*ACCA Level 2 Management Accounting*

## 24.7* Advanced

The theory of the experience curve is that an organisation may increase its profitability through obtaining greater familiarity with supplying its products or services to customers. This reflects the view that profitability is solely a function of market share.

Requirement:
Discuss the extent to which the application of experience curve theory can help an organisation to prolong the life cycle of its products or services.
(20 marks)
*CIMA Stage 4 Strategic Management Accounting and Marketing*

## 24.8 Advanced: Comparison of independent variables for cost estimates

Abourne Ltd manufactures a microcomputer for the home use market. The management accountant is considering using regression analysis in the annual estimate of total costs. The following information has been produced for the twelve months ended 31 December:

| Month | Total cost Y (£) | Output, $X_1$ (numbers) | Number of Direct employees, $X_2$ (numbers) | Direct labour hours, $X_3$ (hours) |
|---|---|---|---|---|
| 1 | 38 200 | 300 | 28 | 4 480 |
| 2 | 40 480 | 320 | 30 | 4 700 |
| 3 | 41 400 | 350 | 30 | 4 800 |
| 4 | 51 000 | 500 | 32 | 5 120 |
| 5 | 52 980 | 530 | 32 | 5 150 |
| 6 | 60 380 | 640 | 35 | 5 700 |
| 7 | 70 440 | 790 | 41 | 7 210 |
| 8 | 32 720 | 250 | 41 | 3 200 |
| 9 | 75 800 | 820 | 41 | 7 300 |
| 10 | 71 920 | 780 | 39 | 7 200 |
| 11 | 68 380 | 750 | 38 | 6 400 |
| 12 | 33 500 | 270 | 33 | 3 960 |
| | $\Sigma Y =$ 637 200 | $\Sigma X_1 =$ 6 300 | $\Sigma X_2 =$ 420 | $\Sigma X_3 =$ 65 220 |

Additionally:

$$\Sigma Y^2 = 36\,614.05 \times 10^6$$
$$\Sigma X_1^2 = 3.8582 \times 10^6$$
$$\Sigma X_2^2 = 14\,954$$
$$\Sigma X_3^2 = 374.423 \times 10^6$$
$$\Sigma X_1 Y = 373.537\,4 \times 10^6$$
$$\Sigma X_2 Y = 22.812\,84 \times 10^6$$
$$\Sigma X_3 Y = 3692.277\,4 \times 10^6$$

The management accountant wants to select the best independent variable ($X_1$, $X_2$ or $X_3$) to help in future forecasts of total production costs using an ordinary least-squares regression equation. He is also considering the alternatives of using the Hi-Lo and multiple regression equations as the basis for future forecasts.

You are required to:

(a) Identify which one of the three independent variables ($X_1$, $X_2$, $X_3$) given above is likely to be the least good estimator of total costs ($Y$). Give your reasons, but do not submit any calculations. (3 marks)

(b) Compute separately, for the remaining two independent variables, the values of the two parameters $\alpha$ and $\beta$ for each regression line. Calculate the coefficient of determination ($R^2$) for each relationship. (6 marks)

(c) State, with reasons, which one of these independent variables should be used to estimate total costs in the future given the results of (b) above. (3 marks)

(d) Devise the two equations which could be used, using the Hi-Lo technique, instead of the two regression lines computed in (b) above and comment on the differences found between the two sets of equations. (5 marks)

(e) Comment critically on the use of Hi-Lo and ordinary least-squares regression as forecasting and estimating aids using the above results as a basis for discussion. In addition, comment on the advantages and problems of using multiple regression for forecasting and estimating; and state whether, in your opinion, the management accountant should consider using it in the present circumstances.

(8 marks)

*Note*: The following formulae can be used to answer the above question.

$$\beta = \frac{\sum xy - n\bar{x}\bar{y}}{\sum x^2 - n\bar{x}^2}$$

$$\alpha = \bar{y} - \beta\bar{x}$$

$$R^2 = \frac{\alpha \sum y + \beta \sum xy - n\bar{y}^2}{\sum y^2 - n\bar{y}^2}$$

$$Se = \sqrt{\frac{\sum y^2 - \alpha \sum y - \beta \sum xy}{n - 2}}$$

$$S\beta = \frac{Se}{\sqrt{\sum x^2 - nx^2}}$$

*ICAEW P2 Management Accounting*

### 24.9* Advanced: Linear regression analysis with price level adjustments

Savitt Ltd manufactures a variety of products at its industrial site in Ruratania. One of the products, the LT, is produced in a specially equipped factory in which no other production takes place. For technical reasons the company keeps no stocks of either LTs or the raw material used in their manufacture. The costs of producing LTs in the special factory during the past four years have been as follows:

| | 1998 (£) | 1999 (£) | 2000 (£) | (2001) (estimated) (£) |
|---|---|---|---|---|
| Raw materials | 70 000 | 100 000 | 130 000 | 132 000 |
| Skilled labour | 40 000 | 71 000 | 96 000 | 115 000 |
| Unskilled labour | 132 000 | 173 000 | 235 000 | 230 000 |
| Power | 25 000 | 33 000 | 47 000 | 44 000 |
| Factory overheads | 168 000 | 206 000 | 246 000 | 265 000 |
| Total production costs | £435 000 | £583 000 | £754 000 | £786 000 |
| Output (units) | 160 000 | 190 000 | 220 000 | 180 000 |

The costs of raw materials and skilled and unskilled labour have increased steadily during the past four years at an annual compound rate of 20%, and the costs of factory overheads have increased at an annual compound rate of 15% during the same period. Power prices increased by 10% on 1 January 1999 and by 25% on the 1 January of each subsequent year. All costs except power are expected to increase by a further 20% during 2002. Power prices are due to rise by 25% on 1 January 2002.

The directors of Savitt Ltd are now formulating the company's production plan for 2002 and wish to estimate the costs of manufacturing the product LT. The finance director has expressed the view that 'the full relevant cost of producing LTs can be determined only if a fair share of general company overheads is allocated to them.' No such allocation is included in the table of costs above.

You are required to:

(a) use linear regression analysis to estimate the relationship of total production costs to volume for the product LT for 2002 (ignore general company overheads and do *not* undertake a separate regression calculation for each item of cost), (12 marks)

(b) discuss the advantages and limitations of linear regression analysis for the estimation of cost–volume relationships, (8 marks)

(c) comment on the view expressed by the finance director. (5 marks)

Ignore taxation.

*ICAEW Elements of Financial Decisions*

### 24.10* Advanced: Regression analysis and confidence intervals

CB p.l.c. produces a wide range of electronic components including its best selling item, the Laser Switch. The company is preparing the budgets for 2001 and knows that the key element in the Master Budget is the contribution expected from the Laser Switch. The records for this component for the past four years are summarised below, with the costs and revenues adjusted to 2001 values:

| | 1997 | 1998 | 1999 | 2000 |
|---|---|---|---|---|
| Sales (units) | 150 000 | 180 000 | 200 000 | 230 000 |
| | (£) | (£) | (£) | (£) |
| Sales revenue | 292 820 | 346 060 | 363 000 | 448 800 |
| Variable costs | 131 080 | 161 706 | 178 604 | 201 160 |
| Contribution | 161 740 | 184 354 | 184 396 | 247 640 |

It has been estimated that sales in 2001 will be 260 000 units.

You are required:

(a) as a starting point for forecasting 2001 contribution, to project the trend, using linear regression; (10 marks)

(b) to calculate the 95% confidence interval of the individual forecast for 2001 if the standard error of the forecast is £14 500 and the appropriate $t$ value is 4.303, and to interpret the value calculated; (3 marks)

(c) to comment on the advantages of using linear regression for forecasting and the limitations of the technique. (7 marks)

(Total 20 marks)

*CIMA Stage 3 Management Accounting Techniques*

## 24.11 Advanced: Calculation of co-efficient of determination

A management accountant is analysing data relating to retail sales on behalf of marketing colleagues. The marketing staff believe that the most important influence upon sales is local advertising undertaken by the retail store. The company also advertises by using regional television areas. The company owns more than 100 retail outlets, and the data below relate to a sample of 10 representative outlets.

| Outlet number | Monthly sales (£000) | Local advertising by the retail store (£000 per month) | Regional advertising by the company (£000 per month) |
|---|---|---|---|
| | $y$ | $x_1$ | $x_2$ |
| 1 | 220 | 6 | 4 |
| 2 | 230 | 8 | 6 |
| 3 | 240 | 12 | 10 |
| 4 | 340 | 12 | 16 |
| 5 | 420 | 2 | 18 |
| 6 | 460 | 8 | 20 |
| 7 | 520 | 16 | 26 |
| 8 | 600 | 15 | 30 |
| 9 | 720 | 14 | 36 |
| 10 | 800 | 20 | 46 |

The data have been partly analysed and the intermediate results are available below.

$$\sum y = 4550 \quad \sum y^2 = 2\,451\,300 \quad \sum x_1 y = 58\,040$$
$$\sum x_1 = 113 \quad \sum x_1^2 = 1\,533 \quad \sum x_2 y = 121\,100$$
$$\sum x_2 = 212 \quad \sum x_2^2 = 6\,120 \quad \sum x_1 x_2 = 2\,780$$

You are required to examine closely, using coefficients of determination, the assertion that the level of sales varies more with movements in the level of local advertising than with changes in the level of regional company advertising. (8 marks)

Note that the co-efficient of determination for $y$ and $x_1$ may be calculated from

$$r^2 = \frac{n\sum x_1 y - \sum x_1 \sum y}{\left(n\sum x_1^2 - \left(\sum x_1\right)^2\right) \times \left(n\sum y^2 - \left(\sum y\right)^2\right)}$$

*CIMA Stage 3 Management Accounting Techniques*

## 24.12* Advanced: Regression analysis and an analysis of costs where unit variable cost is not constant (See note on page 984)

Babel Ltd produces a single product. The company's directors want to explore new markets, and they require an accurate analysis of the firm's cost structure for both forecasting and pricing purposes. An attempt to provide this analysis from the aggregation of individual costs has produced a poor correspondence between actual and predicted costs. You are an accountant employed by Babel Ltd, and you have been asked to provide a statistical approach to the problem.

The financial director has given you the following data:

| Month | Output (000 units) | Average unit cost (£) |
|---|---|---|
| January | 9 | 12.8 |
| February | 14 | 13.0 |
| March | 11 | 11.4 |
| April | 8 | 12.0 |
| May | 6 | 13.0 |
| June | 12 | 11.7 |

You obtain the following further information:

(1) The costs from which the averages have been computed consist of the firm's entire costs for the relevant month.

(2) Fixed costs can be assumed to be unaffected by seasonal factors except for winter heating. In January and February a supplementary heating system was employed; this cost £10 000 per month to operate.

You are asked to transform the original data in any way which may be necessary. Work to the nearest £100 for total costs and to the nearest £0.10p for unit cost calculations.

Requirements

(a) Estimate Babel Ltd's normal fixed and variable cost of production using linear regression, showing full workings. (7 marks)

(b) Draw a graph of Babel Ltd's costs versus output to provide a better analysis of costs than the regression estimates in part (a), estimate the point at which variable costs change and estimate the linear cost relationships over the relevant ranges. (5 marks)

(c) Use your answer from part (b) to provide an analysis of costs from January to June, set out in spreadsheet format (i.e. rows and columns). Divide the rows into relevant cost categories to explain observed costs, and treat any residual amounts as unexplained differences. (6 marks)

(d) Discuss the difficulties which may be encountered in preparing and using statistical cost estimation in practice. (7 marks)

(Total 25 marks)

*ICAEW P2 Management Accounting*

## 24.13 Advanced: Estimates of sales volume and revenues using regression analysis and calculation of optimum price using differential calculus (See note on page 984)

The Crispy Biscuit Company (CBC) has developed a new variety of biscuit which it has successfully test marketed in different parts of the country. It has, therefore, decided to go ahead with full-scale production and is in the process of commissioning a production line located in a hitherto unutilized part of the main factory building. The new line will be capable of producing up to 50 000 packets of new biscuit each week.

The factory accountant has produced the following schedule of the expected unit costs of production at various levels of output:

| | Production level (packets per week) | | | | |
| | (10 000) | (20 000) | (30 000) | (40 000) | (50 000) |
| --- | --- | --- | --- | --- | --- |
| Unit costs (pence) | | | | | |
| Labour (1) | 20.0 | 15.0 | 13.3 | 12.5 | 12.0 |
| Materials | 8.0 | 8.0 | 8.0 | 8.0 | 8.0 |
| Machine costs (2) | 8.0 | 5.0 | 4.0 | 3.5 | 3.2 |
| Total direct costs | 36.0 | 28.0 | 25.3 | 24.0 | 23.2 |
| Factory overhead (3) | 9.0 | 7.0 | 6.3 | 6.0 | 5.8 |
| Total costs | 45.0 | 35.0 | 31.6 | 30.0 | 29.0 |

(1) The labour costs represent the cost of the additional labour that would require to be taken on to operate the new line.

(2) Machine costs include running costs, maintenance costs and depreciation.

(3) Factory overhead costs are fixed for the factory overall but are allocated to cost centres at 25% of total direct costs.

In addition to establishing product acceptability, the test marketing programme also examined the likely consumer response to various selling prices. It concluded that the weekly revenue likely to be generated at various prices was as follows:

| Retail price | Revenue to CBC |
| --- | --- |
| £0.62 | £15 190 |
| £0.68 | £14 960 |
| £0.78 | £11 310 |
| £0.84 | £10 500 |
| £0.90 | £10 350 |
| £0.98 | £4 900 |

The above prices represent the prices at which the product was test marketed, but any price between £0.60 and £0.99 is a possibility. The manufacturer receives 50% of the retail revenue.

Requirements

(a) Estimate the variable costs of producing the new biscuit, using any simple method (such as the high–low method). (3 marks)

(b) Using linear regression, estimate the relationship between the price charged by CBC and the expected demand. (6 marks)

(c) Using the above estimates, calculate the optimum price and evaluate how sensitive your solution is to changes in this price. (8 marks)

(d) Outline the practical problems faced in attempting to derive a unit cost for a new product. (8 marks)

(Total 25 marks)

*ICAEW P2 Management Accounting*

## 24.14 Advanced: Learning curves

Present a table of production times showing the following columns for E. Condon Ltd, which produces up to 16 units while experiencing a 90% learning curve, the first unit requiring 1000 hours of production time:

(1) units produced,

(2) total production time (hours),

(3) average production time per unit in each successive lot (hours),

(4) cumulative average production time per unit (hours), and

(5) percentage decline in (4).

(10 marks)

*ICAEW Management Accounting*

## 24.15* Advanced: Learning curve and the calculation of NPV

RS p.l.c. manufactures domestic food mixers. It is investigating whether or not to accept a three-year contract to make a new model for sale through a supermarket chain. The contract uses skilled labour which cannot be increased above that currently available and RS p.l.c. will receive a fixed price of £42 per mixer for all the mixers it can produce in the three-year period. The following estimates have been made:

| | |
|---|---|
| Capital investment | £50 000 payable now, with nil scrap value. |
| Additional overhead | £25 000 per annum. |
| Materials | £30 per mixer. |
| Labour | £6 per hour. |

The factory manager knows from experience of similar machines that there will be a learning effect for labour. He estimates that this will take the form:

$$y = ax^{-0.3}$$

where  $y$ = average labour hours per unit
 $a$ = labour hours for first unit
 $x$ = cumulative production

He estimates that the first mixer will take 10 hours to produce and that the fixed amount of labour available will enable 5000 mixers to be produced in the first year.

Apart from the capital investment, all cash flows can be assumed to arise at year ends.

The company has a cost of capital of 15%.

You are required

(a) to calculate the NPV of the proposed contract; (16 marks)

(b) to state what other factors need to be considered before a final decision is made.

(6 marks)

(Total 22 marks)

*CIMA Stage 3 Management Accounting Techniques*

## 24.16* Advanced: Estimation of costs and incremental hours using the learning curve

(a) Z p.l.c. experiences difficulty in its budgeting process because it finds it necessary to quantify the learning effect as new products are introduced. Substantial product changes occur and result in the need for retraining.

An order for 30 units of a new product has been received by Z p.l.c. So far, 14 have been completed; the first unit required 40 direct labour hours and a total of 240 direct labour hours has been recorded for the 14 units. The production manager expects an 80% learning effect for this type of work.

The company uses standard absorption costing. The direct costs attributed to the centre in which the unit is manufactured and its direct material costs are as follows:

| | |
|---|---|
| Direct material | £30.00 per unit |
| Direct labour | £6.00 per hour |
| Variable overhead | £0.50 per direct labour hour |
| Fixed overhead | £6000 per four-week operating period |

There are ten direct employees working a five-day week, eight hours per day. Personal and other downtime allowances account for 25% of the total available time.

The company usually quotes a four-week delivery period for orders.

You are required to

(i) determine whether the assumption of an 80% learning effect is a reasonable one in this case, by using the standard formula $y = ax^b$

where $y$ = the cumulative average direct labour time per unit (productivity)

$a$ = the average labour time per unit for the first batch

$x$ = the cumulative number of batches produced

$b$ = the index of learning (5 marks)

(ii) calculate the number of direct labour hours likely to be required for an expected second order of 20 units; (5 marks)

(iii) use the cost data given to produce an estimated product cost for the initial order, examining the problems which may be created for budgeting by the presence of the learning effect.

(10 marks)

(b) It is argued that in many areas of modern technology, the 'learning curve' effect is of diminishing significance. An 'experience curve' effect would still be present and possibly strengthened in importance. However, the experience curve has little to do with short-term standard setting and product costing.

You are required to discuss the validity of the above statement, in particular the assertion that the experience curve has little relevance to costing. (6 marks)

(Total 26 marks)
*CIMA Stage 4 Management Accounting – Control and Audit*

## 24.17* Advanced: Construction of cost and revenue functions when learning curve effects exist

Delroads Electronics Ltd (DEL) produces a variety of products including an electronic navigational unit for use in ships. Construction of the unit is a delicate assembly operation by a team of highly-skilled operatives. Components used in the unit are purchased from outside manufacturers. The unit is sold in relatively small numbers, and a new model is produced each year.

Costs associated with production of the new model of the unit are:

- fixed costs £35 000
- variable costs £20 wages per labour hour worked, plus £20 materials per unit

Production of the first unit of the new model will take 60 labour hours, and work of the operatives is known to be subject to an 83% learning curve effect. Learning curve effects are achieved only within a model.

Market research has forecast that annual sales of the new model are associated with unit prices as follows:

1 unit can be sold at unit price £10 000
500 units can be sold at unit price £327.80

Requirements:

(a) Explain what a learning curve effect is, and suggest reasons for the effect in this particular case. (6 marks)
(b) Draw a diagram (accurately to scale) on the graph paper supplied, demonstrating the relationship between units of output, total costs

and total revenues in respect of the new model. Set out sufficient workings to justify your diagram. (12 marks)
(c) Use your diagram and supporting workings to identify the profit-maximising units of output and unit price in respect of the new model. (7 marks)

*Notes:* In evaluating learning curve effects you should use the cumulative average time equation

$$y = a/x^{0.269} \text{ or } y = ax^{-0.269}$$

In evaluating the link between revenue and output you should use the equation

$$y = ax^n$$

(Total 25 marks)
*CIMA Stage 3
Management Accounting Applications*

## 24.18 Advanced: The application of the learning curve to determine target cash flows

Leano plc is investigating the financial viability of a new product X. Product X is a short life product for which a market has been identified at an agreed design specification. It is not yet clear whether the market life of the product will be six months or 12 months.

The following estimated information is available in respect of product X:

(i) Sales should be 10 000 units per month in batches of 100 units on a just-in-time production basis. An average selling price of £1200 per batch of 100 units is expected for a six month life cycle and £1050 per batch of 100 units for a 12 month life cycle.
(ii) An 80% learning curve will apply in months 1 to 7 (inclusive), after which a steady state production time requirement will apply, with labour time per batch stabilising at that of the final batch in month 7. Reductions in the labour requirement will be achieved through natural labour turnover. The labour requirement for the first batch in month 1 will be 500 hours at £5 per hour.
(iii) Variable overhead is estimated at £2 per labour hour.
(iv) Direct material input will be £500 per batch of product X for the first 200 batches. The next 200 batches are expected to cost 90% of the initial batch cost. All batches thereafter will cost 90% of the batch cost for each of the second 200 batches.

(v) Product X will incur directly attributable fixed costs of £15 000 per month.

(vi) The initial investment for the new product will be £75 000 with no residual value irrespective of the life of the product.

A target cash inflow required over the life of the product must be sufficient to provide for:

(a) the initial investment plus 33 1/3% thereof for a six month life cycle, or

(b) the initial investment plus 50% thereof for a 12 month life cycle.

*Note*: learning curve formula:

$$y = ax^b$$

where $y$ = average cost per batch

$a$ = cost of initial batch

$x$ = total number of batches

$b$ = learning factor $(= -0.3219$ for 80% learning rate)

Required:

(a) Prepare detailed calculations to show whether product X will provide the target cash inflow over six months and/or 12 months.

(17 marks)

(b) Calculate the initial batch labour hours at which the cash inflow achieved will be exactly equal to the target figure where a six month life cycle applies. It has been determined that the maximum labour and variable overhead cost at which the target return will be achieved is £259 000. All other variables remain as in part (a). (6 marks)

(c) Prepare a report to management which:

(i) explains why the product X proposal is an example of a target costing/pricing situation; (3 marks)

(ii) suggests specific actions which may be considered to improve the return on investment where a six month product cycle is forecast; (6 marks)

(iii) comments on possible factors which could reduce the rate of return and which must, therefore, be avoided.

(3 marks)

(Total 35 marks)

*ACCA Paper 9 Information for Control and Decision Making*

**24.19\* Advanced: Calculation of learning rate and contract completion using the learning curve**

Maxmarine plc builds boats. Earlier this year the company accepted an order for 15 specialized

'Crest' boats at a fixed price of £100 000 each. The contract allows four months for building and delivery of all the boats and stipulates a penalty of £10 000 for each boat delivery late.

The boats are built using purchased components and internally manufactured parts, all of which are readily available. However, there is only a small team of specialized technicians and boatyard space is limited, so that only one boat can be built at a time. Four boats have now been completed and as Maxmarine plc has no previous experience of this particular boat the building times have been carefully monitored as follows:

| Boat number | Completion time (days) |
|---|---|
| 1 | 10.0 |
| 2 | 8.1 |
| 3 | 7.4 |
| 4 | 7.1 |

Maxmarine plc has 23 normal working days in every month and the first four boats were completed with normal working.

Management is now concerned about completing the contract on time.

The management accountant's estimate of direct costs per boat, excluding labour costs, is as follows:

| | (£000) |
|---|---|
| Purchased components | 40 |
| Manufactured parts | 15 |
| Other direct expenses | 5 |
| | 60 |

Direct labour costs are £2500 per day for the normal 23 working days per month. Additional weekend working days at double the normal pay rates can be arranged up to a maximum of 7 days per month (making 30 possible working days per month in total).

Overheads will be allocated to the contract at a rate of £3000 per *normal* working day and no overheads will be allocated for overtime working.

Requirements:

(a) Using the completion time information provided, calculate the learning rate showing full workings. (6 marks)

(b) Discuss the limitations of the learning curve in this type of application. (6 marks)

(c) Calculate whether it would be preferable for Maxmarine plc to continue normal working or to avoid penalties by working weekends. Support your calculations with any reservations or explanations you consider appropriate. (13 marks)
(Total 25 marks)
*ICAEW Management Accounting*

**24.20 Advanced: Application of learning curve to determine the incremental costs for different production batches**

Limitation plc commenced the manufacture and sale of a new product in the fourth quarter of 2000. In order to facilitate the budgeting process for quarters 1 and 2 of 2001, the following information has been collected:

(i) Forecast production/sales (batches of product):

| | | |
|---|---|---|
| quarter 4, | 2000 | 30 batches |
| quarter 1, | 2001 | 45 batches |
| quarter 2, | 2001 | 45 batches |

(ii) It is estimated that direct labour is subject to a learning curve effect of 90%. The labour cost of batch 1 of quarter 4, 2000 was £600 (at £5 per hour). The labour output rates from the commencement of production of the product, after adjusting for learning effects, are as follows:

| Total batches produced (batches) | Overall average time per batch (hours) |
|---|---|
| 15 | 79.51 |
| 30 | 71.56 |
| 45 | 67.28 |
| 60 | 64.40 |
| 75 | 62.25 |
| 90 | 60.55 |
| 105 | 59.15 |
| 120 | 57.96 |

Labour hours worked and paid for will be adjusted to eliminate spare capacity during each quarter. All time will be paid for at £5 per hour.

(iii) Direct material is used at the rate of 200 units per batch of product for the first 20 batches of quarter 4, 2000. Units of material used per batch will fall by 2% of the original level for each 20 batches thereafter as the learning curve effect improves the efficiency with which the material is used. All material will be bought at £1.80 per unit during 2001. Delivery of the total material requirement for a quarter will be made on day one of the quarter. Stock will be held in storage capacity hired at a cost of £0.30 per quarter per unit held in stock. Material will be used at an even rate throughout each quarter.

(iv) Variable overhead is estimated at 150% of direct labour cost during 2001.

(v) All units produced will be sold in the quarter of production at £1200 per batch.

Required:
(a) Calculate the labour hours requirement for the second batch and the sum of the labour hours for the third and fourth batches produced in quarter 4, 2000. (3 marks)
(b) Prepare a budget for each of quarters 1 and 2, 2001 showing the contribution earned from the product. Show all relevant workings. (14 marks)
(c) The supplier of the raw material has offered to deliver on a 'just-in-time' basis in return for a price increase to £1.90 per unit in quarter 1, 2001 and £2 per unit thereafter.
  (i) Use information for quarters 1 and 2, 2001 to determine whether the offer should be accepted on financial grounds.
  (ii) Comment on other factors which should be considered before a final decision is reached. (8 marks)
(d) Limitation plc wish to prepare a quotation for 12 batches of the product to be produced at the start of quarter 3, 2001.
  Explain how the learning curve formula $y = ax^b$ may be used in the calculation of the labour cost of the quotation. Your answer should identify each of the variables $y$, $a$, $x$ and $b$. No calculations are required. (5 marks)
(Total 30 marks)
*ACCA Level 2 Cost and Management Accounting II*

# Quantitative models for the planning and control of stocks

Investment in stocks represents a major asset of most industrial and commercial organizations, and it is essential that stocks be managed efficiently so that such investments do not become unnecessarily large. A firm should determine its optimum level of investment in stocks – and, to do this, two conflicting requirements must be met. First, it must ensure that stocks are sufficient to meet the requirements of production and sales; and, secondly, it must avoid holding surplus stocks that are unnecessary and that increase the risk of obsolescence. The optimal stock level lies somewhere between these two extremes. Our objective in this chapter is to examine the application of quantitative models for determining the optimum investment in stocks, and describe the alternative methods of scheduling material requirements. We shall also consider the economic order quantity and the level at which stocks should be replenished. We shall concentrate here on manufacturing firms, but the same basic analysis can also be applied to merchandising companies and non-profit organizations.

## Learning objectives

After studying this chapter, you should be able to:

- justify which costs are relevant and should be included in the calculation of the economic order quantity (EOQ);

- calculate the EOQ using the formula and tabulation methods;

- determine whether or not a company should purchase larger quantities in order to take advantage of quantity discounts;

- calculate the optimal safety stock when demand is uncertain;

- describe the ABC classification method;

- describe materials requirement planning (MRP) systems;

- explain just-in-time purchasing and list the benefits arising from adopting JIT concepts.

# Why do firms hold stocks?

There are three general reasons for holding stocks; the transactions motive, the precautionary motive and the speculative motive. The transactions motive occurs whenever there is a need to hold stocks to meet production and sales requirements, and it is not possible to meet these requirements instantaneously. A firm might also decide to hold additional amounts of stocks to cover the possibility that it may have underestimated its future production and sales requirements. This represents a precautionary motive, which applies only when future demand is uncertain.

When it is expected that future input prices may change, a firm might maintain higher or lower stock levels to *speculate* on the expected increase or decrease in future prices. In general, quantitative models do not take into account the speculative motive. Nevertheless, management should be aware that optimum stock levels do depend to a certain extent on expected price movements. For example, if prices of input factors are expected to rise significantly, a firm should consider increasing its stocks to take advantage of a lower purchase price. However, this decision should be based on a comparison of future cost savings with the increased costs due to holding additional stocks.

Where a firm is able to predict the demand for its inputs and outputs with perfect certainty and where it knows with certainty that the prices of inputs will remain constant for some reasonable length of time, it will have to consider only the transactions motive for holding stocks. To simplify the introduction to the use of models for determining the optimum investment in stocks, we shall begin by considering some quantitative models which incorporate only the transactions motive for holding stocks.

# Relevant costs for quantitative models under conditions of certainty

The relevant costs that should be considered when determining optimal stock levels consist of holding costs and ordering costs. Holding costs usually consist of the following:

1. opportunity cost of investment in stocks;
2. incremental insurance costs;
3. incremental warehouse and storage costs;
4. incremental material handling costs;
5. cost of obsolescence and deterioration of stocks.

The relevant holding costs for use in quantitative models should include only those items that will vary with the levels of stocks. Costs that will not be affected by changes in stock levels are not relevant costs. For example, in the case of warehousing and storage only those costs should be included that will vary with changes in the number of units ordered. Salaries of storekeepers, depreciation of equipment and fixed rental of equipment and buildings are often irrelevant because they are unaffected by changes in stock levels. On the other hand, if storage space is owned and can be used for other productive purposes or to obtain rent income then the opportunity cost must be included in the analysis. Insurance costs should be included only when premiums are charged on the fluctuating value of stocks. A fixed annual insurance cost will not vary with different levels of stocks, and is therefore not a relevant holding cost.

To the extent that funds are invested in stocks, there is an opportunity cost of holding them. This opportunity cost is reflected by the required return that is lost from investing in stocks rather than some alternative investment. What required rate of return should we use to determine the lost return on funds invested in stocks? The answer is that the rate of return should be determined in the manner described in Chapter 14, with investments in stocks being treated as an asset to which capital is committed, as in any capital budgeting project. In particular, the cost of capital should be applied only to those costs that vary with the number of units purchased. The relevant holding costs for other items such as material handling, obsolescence and deterioration are difficult to estimate, but we shall see that these costs are unlikely to be critical to the investment decision. Normally, holding costs are expressed as a percentage rate per pound of average investment.

Ordering costs usually consist of the clerical costs of preparing a purchase order, receiving deliveries and paying invoices. Ordering costs that are common to all stock decisions are not relevant, and only the incremental costs of placing an order are used in formulating the quantitative models. In practice, it is extremely difficult to distinguish between variable and non-variable ordering costs, but this problem can be resolved by developing a cost equation as described in Chapter 24, where the number of orders placed represents the independent variable.

The costs of acquiring stocks through buying or manufacturing are not a relevant cost to be included in the quantitative models, since the acquisition costs remain unchanged, irrespective of the order size or stock levels, unless quantity discounts are available. (We shall discuss the effect of quantity discounts later in this chapter.) For example, it does not matter in terms of acquisition cost whether total annual requirements of 1000 units at £10 each are purchased in one 1000-unit batch, ten 100-unit batches or one hundred 10-unit batches; the acquisition cost of £10 000 will remain unchanged. The acquisition cost is not therefore a relevant cost, but the ordering and holding costs will change in relation to the order size, and these will be relevant for decision-making models.

# Determining the economic order quantity

If we assume certainty, the optimum order will be determined by those costs that are affected by either the quantity of stocks held or the number of orders placed. If more units are ordered at one time, fewer orders will be required per year. This will mean a reduction in the ordering costs. However, when fewer orders are placed, larger average stocks must be maintained, which leads to an increase in holding costs. The problem is therefore one of trading off the costs of carrying large stocks against the costs of placing more orders. The optimum order size is the order quantity that will result in the total amount of the ordering and holding costs being minimized. This optimum order size is known as the **economic order quantity (EOQ)**; it can be determined by tabulating the total costs for various order quantities, by a graphical presentation or by using a formula. All three methods are illustrated using the information given in Example 25.1.

## TABULATION METHOD

The annual relevant costs for various order quantities are set out in Exhibit 25.1.

You will see that the economic order quantity is 400 units. At this point the total annual relevant costs are at a minimum.

**EXAMPLE 25.1**

A company purchases a raw material from an outside supplier at a cost of £9 per unit. The total annual demand for this product is 40 000 units, and the following additional information is available.

|  | (£) | (£) |
|---|---|---|
| Required annual return on investment in stocks (10%×£9) | 0.90 | |
| Other holding costs per unit | 0.10 | |
| Holding costs per unit | | 1.00 |
| Cost per purchase order: | | |
| Clerical costs, stationery, postage, telephone etc. | | 2.00 |

You are required to determine the optimal order quantity.

**EXHIBIT 25.1**

*Relevant costs for various order quantities*

| Order quantity | 100 | 200 | 300 | 400 | 500 | 600 | 800 | 10 000 |
|---|---|---|---|---|---|---|---|---|
| Average stock in units[a] | 50 | 100 | 150 | 200 | 250 | 300 | 400 | 5000 |
| Number of purchase orders[b] | 400 | 200 | 133 | 100 | 80 | 67 | 50 | 4 |
| Annual holding costs[c] | £50 | £100 | £150 | £200 | £250 | £300 | £400 | £5000 |
| Annual ordering cost | £800 | £400 | £266 | £200 | £160 | £134 | £100 | £8 |
| Total relevant cost | £850 | £500 | £416 | £400 | £410 | £434 | £500 | £5008 |

[a]If there are no stocks when the order is received and the units received are used at a constant rate, the average stock will be one-half of the quantity ordered. Even if a minimum safety stock is held, the average stock relevant to the decision will still be one-half of the quantity order, because the minimum stock will remain unchanged for each alternative order quantity.
[b]The number of purchase orders is ascertained by dividing the total annual demand of 40 000 units by the order quantity.
[c]The annual holding cost is ascertained by multiplying the average stock by the holding cost of £1 per unit.

## GRAPHICAL METHOD

The information tabulated in Exhibit 25.1 is presented in graphical form in Figure 25.1 for every order size up to 800 units. The vertical axis represents the relevant annual costs for the investment in stocks, and the horizontal axis can be used to represent either the various order quantities or the average stock levels; two scales are actually shown on the horizontal axis so that both items can be incorporated. You will see from the graph that as the average stock level or the order quantity increases, the holding cost also increases. Alternatively, the ordering costs decline as stock levels and order quantities are increased. The total cost line represents the summation of both the holding and the ordering costs.

Note that the total cost line is at a minimum for an order quantity of 400 units and occurs at the point where the ordering cost and holding cost curves intersect. That is, the

**FIGURE 25.1**   *Economic order quantity graph.*

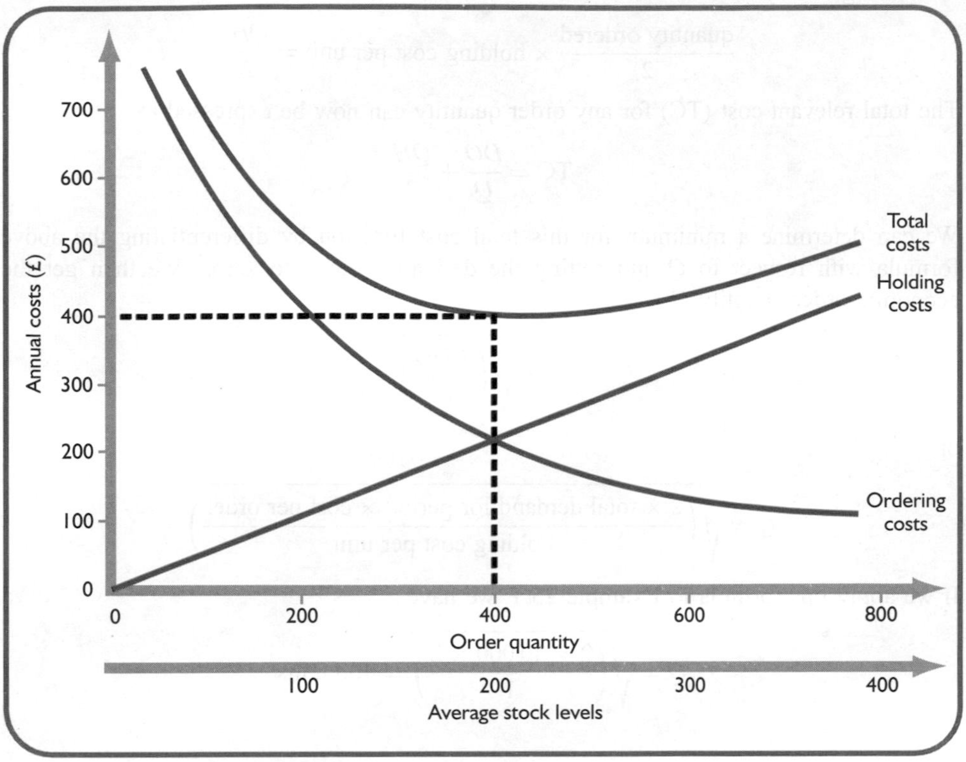

economic order quantity is found at the point where the holding costs equal the ordering costs. It is also interesting to note from the graph (see also Exhibit 25.1) that the total relevant costs are not particularly sensitive to changes in the order quantity. For example, if you refer to Exhibit 25.1 you will see that a 25% change in the order quantity from 400 units to either 300 or 500 units leads to an increase in annual costs from £400 to £410 or £416, an increase of 2.5% or 4%. Alternatively, an increase of 50% in the order quantity from 400 units to 600 units leads to an increase in annual costs from £400 to £434 or 8.5%.

## FORMULA METHOD

The economic order quantity can be found by applying a formula that incorporates the basic relationships between holding and ordering costs and order quantities. These relationships can be stated as follows: the number of orders for a period is the total demand for that item of stock for the period (denoted by $D$) divided by the quantity ordered in units (denoted by $Q$). The total ordering cost is obtained by multiplying the number of orders for a period by the ordering cost per order (denoted by $O$), and is given by the formula

$$\frac{\text{total demand for period}}{\text{quantity ordered}} \times \text{ordering cost per order} = \frac{DO}{Q}$$

Assuming that holding costs are constant per unit, the total holding cost for a period will be equal to the average stock for the period, which is represented by the quantity ordered divided by two ($Q/2$), multiplied by the holding cost per unit (denoted by $H$); it is therefore given by

$$\frac{\text{quantity ordered}}{2} \times \text{holding cost per unit} = \frac{QH}{2}$$

The total relevant cost (TC) for any order quantity can now be expressed as

$$\text{TC} = \frac{DO}{Q} + \frac{QH}{2}$$

We can determine a minimum for this total cost function by differentiating the above formula with respect to $Q$ and setting the derivative equal to zero.[1] We then get the economic order quantity $Q$:

$$Q = \sqrt{\left(\frac{2\,DO}{H}\right)}$$

or

$$Q = \sqrt{\left(\frac{2 \times \text{total demand for period} \times \text{cost per order}}{\text{holding cost per unit}}\right)}$$

If we apply this formula to Example 25.1, we have

$$Q = \sqrt{\left(\frac{2 \times 40\,000 \times 2}{1}\right)} = 400 \text{ units}$$

# Assumptions of the EOQ formula

The calculations obtained by using the EOQ model should be interpreted with care, since the model is based on a number of important assumptions. One of these is that the holding cost per unit will be constant. While this assumption might be correct for items such as the funds invested in stocks, other costs might increase on a step basis as stock levels increase. For example, additional storekeepers might be hired as stock levels reach certain levels. Alternatively, if stocks decline, it may be that casual stores labour may be released once stocks fall to a certain critical level.

Another assumption that we made in calculating the total holding cost is that the average balance in stock was equal to one-half of the order quantity. If a constant amount of stock is not used per day, this assumption will be violated; there is a distinct possibility that seasonal and cyclical factors will produce an uneven usage over time. It was also assumed that if safety stocks were maintained, they would remain the same irrespective of the order size, and they could therefore be ignored in the calculation of average stock. However, the size of safety stocks are probably not independent of order quantity, since relatively larger safety stocks are likely to be associated with smaller order quantities.

## EFFECT OF APPROXIMATIONS

Despite the fact that much of the data used in the model represents rough approximations, calculation of the EOQ is still likely to be useful. If you examine Figure 25.1, you will see that the total cost curve tends to flatten out, so that total cost may not be significantly affected if some of the underlying assumptions are violated or if there are minor variations in the cost predictions. For example, assume that the cost per order in Example 25.1 was predicted to be £4 instead of the correct cost of, say, £2. The cost of this error would be as follows:

$$\text{revised EOQ} = \sqrt{\left(\frac{2\,DO}{H}\right)} = \sqrt{\left(\frac{2 \times 40\,000 \times 4}{1}\right)} = 565$$

$$\text{TC for revised EOQ but using the correct ordering cost} = \frac{DO}{Q} + \frac{QH}{2}$$

$$= \frac{40\,000 \times 2}{565} + \frac{565 \times 1}{2} = £425$$

TC for original EOQ of 400 units based on actual ordering cost

$$= \frac{40\,000 \times 2}{400} + \frac{400 \times 1}{2} = £400$$

$$\therefore \text{ cost of prediction error} = £25$$

The cost of the prediction error of £25 represents an error of 6% from the optimal financial result. Similarly, if the holding cost was predicted to be £2 instead of the correct cost of £1, the calculations set out above could be repeated to show a cost of prediction error of approximately 6%.

# Application of the EOQ model in determining the length of a production run

The economic order quantity formula can be adapted to determine the optimum length of the production runs when a set-up cost is incurred only once for each batch produced. Set-up costs include incremental labour, material, jigs, machine down-time, and other ancillary costs of setting up facilities for production. The objective is to find the optimum number of units that should be manufactured in each production run, and this involves balancing set-up costs against stock holding costs. To apply the EOQ formula to a production run problem, we merely substitute set-up costs for the production runs in place of the purchase ordering costs.

To illustrate the formula let us assume that the annual sales demand D for a product is 9000 units. Labour and other expenditure in making adjustments in preparation for a production run require a set-up cost $S$ of £90. The holding cost is £2 per unit per year. The EOQ model can be used for determining how many units should be scheduled for each production run to secure the lowest annual cost. The EOQ formula is modified to reflect the circumstances: the symbol $O$ (ordering costs) is replaced by the symbol $S$ (set-up cost). Using the formula

$$Q = \sqrt{\left(\frac{2\,DS}{H}\right)} = \sqrt{\left(\frac{2 \times 9000 \times 90}{2}\right)} = 900$$

With an annual demand of 9000 units and an optimum production run of 900 units, 10 production runs will be required throughout the year. If we assume there are 250 working days throughout the course of the year, this will mean that production runs are undertaken at 25-day intervals. If demand is uniform throughout the year, 36 units will be demanded per working day (i.e. 9000 units annual demand divided by 250 working days). To

**FIGURE 25.2** *EOQ model and length of production run.*

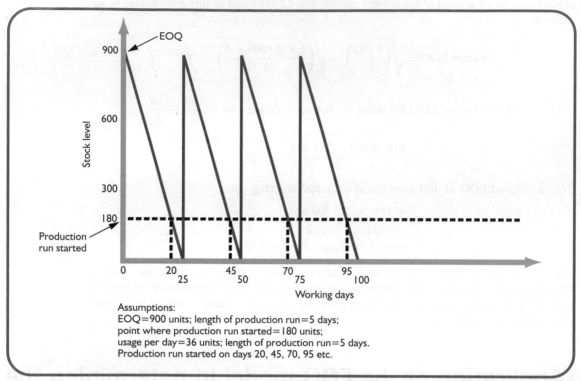

Assumptions:
EOQ=900 units; length of production run=5 days;
point where production run started=180 units;
usage per day=36 units; length of production run=5 days.
Production run started on days 20, 45, 70, 95 etc.

determine the point when the production run should be started, we need to ascertain the number of days required for a production run. Let us assume it is five. So during this period, 180 units (five days at 36 units per day) will be demanded before any of the production run is available to meet demand. If we assume that no safety stock is required, we can establish that a production run should be started when the stock level reaches 180 units. This situation should occur 25 days after the start of the previous production run. The process is illustrated in Figure 25.2.

# Quantity discounts

Circumstances frequently occur where firms are able to obtain quantity discounts for large purchase orders. Because the price paid per unit will not be the same for different order sizes, this must be taken into account when the economic order quantity is determined. However, the basic EOQ formula can still be used as a starting point for determining the optimum quantity to order. Buying in larger consignments to take advantage of quantity discounts will lead to the following savings:

1. A saving in purchase price, which consists of the total amount of discount for the period.
2. A reduction in the total ordering cost because fewer orders are placed to take advantage of the discounts.

These cost savings must, however, be balanced against the increased holding cost arising from higher stock levels when larger quantities are purchased. To determine whether or not

**EXAMPLE 25.2**

A company purchases a raw material from an outside supplier at a cost of £7 per unit. The total annual demand for this product is 9000 units. The holding cost is £4 per unit and the ordering cost is £5 per order. A quantity discount of 3% of the purchase price is available for orders in excess of 1000 units. Should the company order in batches of 1000 units and take advantage of quantity discounts?

a discount is worthwhile, the benefits must be compared with the additional holding costs. Consider the information presented in Example 25.2.

The starting point is to calculate the economic order quantity and then to decide whether the benefits exceed the costs if the company moves from the EOQ point and purchases larger quantities to obtain the discounts. The procedure is as follows:

$$\text{EOQ} = \sqrt{\left(\frac{2 \times 9000 \times 5}{4}\right)} = 150 \text{ units}$$

The savings available to the firm if it purchases in batches of 1000 units instead of batches of 150 units are as follows:

|  | (£) |
|---|---|
| 1. Saving in purchase price | 1890 |
| (3% of annual purchase cost of £63 000) | |
| 2. Saving in ordering cost | |
| $\dfrac{DO}{Q_d} - \dfrac{DO}{Q} = \dfrac{9000 \times 5}{1000} - \dfrac{9000 \times 5}{150}$ | 255 |
| ($Q_d$ represents the quantity order to obtain the discount and $Q$ represents EOQ) | |
| Total savings | $\underline{2145}$ |

The additional holding cost if the larger quantity is purchased is calculated as

$$\frac{(Q_d - Q)H}{2} = \frac{(1000 - 150) \times £4}{2} = £1700$$

The additional savings of £2145 exceed the additional costs, and the firm should adopt the order quantity of 1000 units. If larger discounts are available, for example by purchasing in batches of 2000 units, a similar analysis should be applied that compares the savings from purchasing in batches of 2000 units against purchasing in batches of 1000 units. The amount of the savings should then be compared with the additional holding costs. Note that the EOQ formula serves as a starting point for balancing the savings against the costs of a change in order size.

## Determining when to place the order

To determine the point at which the order should be placed to obtain additional stocks (i.e. the re-order point), we must ascertain the time that will elapse between placing the order and the actual delivery of the stocks. This time period is referred to as the lead time. In a world of certainty the re-order point will be the number of days/weeks lead time multiplied by the daily/weekly usage during the period. For materials, components and supplies the re-order point is the point in time when the purchase requisition is initiated and the order is sent to the supplier. For the finished goods stock of a manufacturer the re-order point is the level of finished goods stock at which the production order should be issued.

If we assume that an annual usage of a raw material is 6000 units and the weekly usage is constant then if there are 50 working weeks in a year, the weekly usage will be 120 units. If the lead time is two weeks, the order should be placed when stocks fall to 240 units. The economic order quantity can indicate how frequently the stocks should be purchased. For example, if the EOQ is 600 then, with an annual demand of 6000 units, ten orders will be placed every five weeks. However, with a lead time of two weeks, the firm will place an order three weeks after the first delivery when the stock will have fallen to 240 units (600 units EOQ less three weeks usage at 120 units per week). The order will then be repeated at five-weekly intervals. The EOQ model can therefore under certain circumstances be used to indicate when to replenish stocks and the amount to replenish. This process is illustrated in Figure 25.3(a).

# Uncertainty and safety stocks

**AR** In practice, demand or usage of stocks is not known with certainty. In addition, there is usually a degree of uncertainty associated with the placement of an order and delivery of the stocks. To protect itself from conditions of uncertainty, a firm will maintain a level of safety stocks for raw materials, work in progress and finished goods stocks. Thus safety stocks are the amount of stocks that are carried in excess of the expected use during the lead time to provide a cushion against running out of stocks. For example, a firm that sets its re-order point on the assumption that the average lead time will be two weeks with an average weekly usage of 120 units will re-order when stocks fall to 240 units. However, the firm will run out of stock if actual demand increases to 140 units per week or if the lead time is three weeks. A firm might respond to this possibility by setting a re-order point of 420 units based on a *maximum usage* of 140 units per week and a lead time of three weeks. This will consist of a re-order point based on *expected usage* and lead time of 240 units (two weeks at 120 units) plus the balance of 180 units *safety stocks* to cover the possibility that lead time and expected usage will be greater than expected. Thus when demand and lead time are uncertain the re-order point is computed by adding the safety stock to the average usage during the average lead time.

In this illustration the safety stock was calculated on the basis of maximum demand and delivery time. It may well be that the probability of both these events occurring at the same time is extremely low. Under such circumstances the managers of the company are adopting a very risk-averse approach and taking no chances of running out of stock. Maintaining high safety stocks may not be in the company's best interests if the cost of holding the excessive stocks exceeds the costs that will be incurred if the company runs out of stock. It is therefore desirable to establish a sound quantitative procedure for determining an acceptable level of safety stocks. The level should be set where the cost of a stockout plus the cost of holding the safety stocks are minimized.

Stockout costs are the opportunity cost of running out of stock. In the case of finished goods the opportunity cost will consist of a loss of contribution if customers take their business elsewhere because orders cannot be met when requested. In the case of regular customers who are permanently lost because of a failure to meet delivery, this

**FIGURE 25.3** *Behaviour of stocks under conditions of certainty and uncertainty: (a) demand known with certainty: (b) demand not known with certainty and role of safety stocks.*

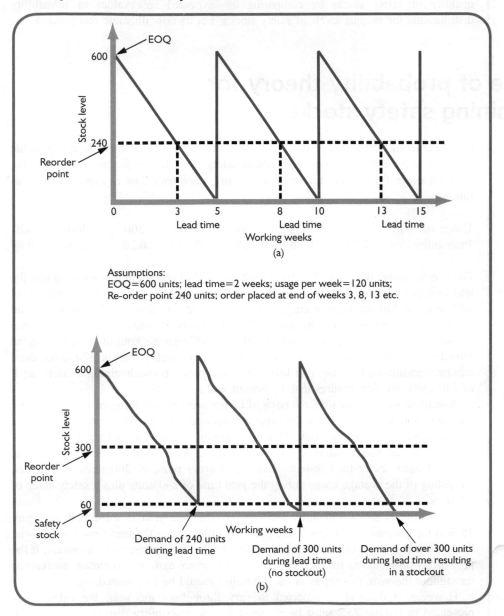

Assumptions:
EOQ=600 units; lead time=2 weeks; usage per week=120 units;
Re-order point 240 units; order placed at end of weeks 3, 8, 13 etc.

will be the discounted value of the lost contribution on future sales. When a stockout occurs for raw materials and work in progress stocks, the cost of being out of stock is the stoppage in production and the resulting inefficiencies that occur. This may be reflected by an estimate of the labour costs of idle time assuming that sales are *not* lost because of the stockout. Clearly, stockout costs are very difficult to estimate, and there are strong arguments for applying sensitivity tests to any analysis that uses estimated stockout costs. In practice, the lost contribution resulting from failure to meet demand may provide a reasonable approximation.

Once the stockout costs have been estimated, the costs of holding safety stocks should be compared for various demand levels. However, it is preferable to attach probabilities to different potential demand levels and to decide on the appropriate quantity of safety stocks by comparing the expected cost values or probability distributions for various levels of safety stocks. Let us now illustrate this process.

# The use of probability theory for determining safety stocks

By constructing probability distributions for future demand and lead time, it is possible to calculate the expected values for various safety stock levels. Suppose, for example, the total usage for an item for stock *over a two-week lead time* is expected to be as follows:

| Usage (units) | 60 | 120 | 180 | 240 | 300 | 360 | 420 |
|---|---|---|---|---|---|---|---|
| Probability | 0.07 | 0.08 | 0.20 | 0.30 | 0.20 | 0.08 | 0.07 |

The average usage during the two week lead time is 240 units, and it is assumed that the lead time is known with certainty. If the firm carries no safety stock, the re-order level will be set at 240 units (i.e. average usage during the lead time), and there will be no stockouts if actual usage is 240 units or less. However, if usage during the lead time period proves to be 300 units instead of 240 there will be a stockout of 60 units, and the probability of this occurring is 0.20. Alternatively, if usage is 360 or 420 units, there will be stockouts of 120 units and 180 units respectively. By maintaining a safety stock of 180 units, the firm ensures that a stockout will *not* occur.

Assuming we estimate stockout costs of £5 per unit and a holding cost of £1 per unit for the period, we can calculate the expected stockout cost, holding cost and total cost for various levels of safety stock. This information is presented in Exhibit 25.2.

You will see that a safety stock of 60 units represents the level at which total expected costs are at their lowest. Hence a re-order point of 300 units will be set, consisting of the average usage during the lead time of 240 units plus a safety stock of 60 units.

A re-order point of 300 units with an uncertain demand is illustrated in Figure 25.3(b) for demands of 240, 300 and over 300 units during the lead time period. Note that the declines in stock do not fall on a straight line when demand is uncertain. If the probability distributions for each two-weekly period are expected to remain unchanged throughout the year, this safety stock (60 units) should be maintained.

However, if demand is expected to vary throughout the year, the calculations presented in Exhibit 25.2 must be repeated for the probability distributions for each period in which the probability distribution changes. The safety stock should then be adjusted prior to the commencement of each period.

In Exhibit 25.2 it was assumed that the lead time was known with certainty but that demand was uncertain. In practice, both the lead time and demand are likely to be uncertain. In this situation the analysis becomes more complex, but the expected value method may still be applied. However, a decision tree will be required to determine the various combinations of delivery times and demand. A discussion of decision trees was presented in Chapter 12. The expected costs for various levels of safety stocks based on various combinations of lead time and demand can then be ascertained, and the safety stock that results in the lowest expected total cost should be adopted. When estimates of

**EXHIBIT 25.2**

*Expected costs for various safety stocks*

demand and lead times vary over a wide range and the probability distributions include a larger number of possible events, it may be extremely difficult to construct a decision tree because of the large number of possible observations. The problem can be resolved, however, by the use of Monte

| Average usage (units) | Safety stock (units) | Re-order point (units) | Stockout (units) | Stockout cost (£5 per unit) | Probability | Expected stockout cost (£) | Holding cost[a] (£) | Total expected cost (£) |
|---|---|---|---|---|---|---|---|---|
| 240 | 180 | 420 | 0 | 0 | 0 | 0 | 180 | 180 |
| 240 | 120 | 360 | 60 | 300 | 0.07 | 21 | 120 | 141 |
| 240 | 60 | 300 | 120 | 600 | 0.07 | 42 | | |
| | | | 60 | 300 | 0.08 | 24 | | |
| | | | | | | 66 | 60 | 126 |
| 240 | 0 | 240 | 180 | 900 | 0.07 | 63 | | |
| | | | 120 | 600 | 0.08 | 48 | | |
| | | | 60 | 300 | 0.20 | 60 | | |
| | | | | | | 171 | 0 | 171 |

[a]To simplify the analysis, it is assumed that a safety stock is maintained throughout the period. The average safety stock will therefore be equal to the total of the safety stock.

Carlo simulation analysis using random numbers to represent the cumulative probability distributions for demand and lead time.[2] For an illustration of simulation applied to determining stock levels see Flower (1973).

Because of the difficulty in estimating the cost of a stockout, some firms might prefer not to use quantitative methods to determine the level of safety stocks. Instead, they might specify a maximum probability of running out of stock. If the firm in our illustration does not wish the probability of a stockout to exceed 10%, it will maintain a safety stock of 120 units and a re-order point of 360 units. A stockout will then occur only if demand is in excess of 360 units; the probability of such an occurrence is 7%. ●●●

# Control of stocks through classification

In large firms it is quite possible for tens of thousands of different items to be stored. It is clearly impossible to apply the techniques outlined in this chapter to all of these. It is therefore essential that stocks be classified into categories of importance so that a firm can apply the most elaborate procedures of controlling stocks only to the most important items. The commonest procedure is known as the ABC classification method. This is illustrated in Exhibit 25.3.

The ABC method requires that an estimate be made of the total purchase cost for each item of stock for the period. The sales forecast is the basis used for estimating the quantities of each item of stock to be purchased during the period. Each item is then grouped in decreasing order of annual purchase cost. The top 10% of items in stock in

**EXHIBIT 25.3**

*ABC
Classification of
stocks*

terms of annual purchase cost are categorized as A items, the next 20% as B
items and the final 70% as C items. If we assume there are 10 000 stock items
then the top 1000 items in terms of annual purchase costs will be classified as
A items, and so on. In practice, it will be unnecessary to estimate the value of

**Stage 1.** For each item in stock multiply the estimated usage for a period by the
estimated unit price to obtain the total purchase cost:

| Item | Estimated usage | Unit price (£) | Total purchase cost (£) |
|------|-----------------|----------------|-------------------------|
| 1 | 60 000 | 1.00 | 60 000 |
| 2 | 20 000 | 0.05 | 1 000 |
| 3 | 1 000 | 0.10 | 100 |
| 4 | 10 000 | 0.02 | 200 |
| 5 | 100 000 | 0.01 | 1 000 |
| 6 | 80 000 | 2.00 | 160 000 |

(This list is continued until all items in stock are included.)

**Stage 2.** Group all the above items in descending order of purchase price and then
divide into class A (top 10%), class B (next 20%) and then class C (bottom 70%).
The analysis might be as follows:

| | Number of items in stock | | Total cost | |
|---------|------|-----|------------|-----|
| | No | % | Amount (£) | % |
| Class A | 1 000 | 10 | 730 000 | 73 |
| Class B | 2 000 | 20 | 190 000 | 19 |
| Class C | 7 000 | 70 | 80 000 | 8 |
| | 10 000 | 100 | 1 000 000 | 100 |

many of the 7000 C items, since their annual purchase cost will be so small it will be
obvious that they will fall into the C category.

You will see from Exhibit 25.3 that 10% of all stock items (i.e. the A items) represents
73% of the total cost; 20% of the items (B items) represent 19% of the total cost; and 70%
of the items (C items) represent 8% of the total cost. It follows that the greatest degree of
control should be exerted over the A items, which account for the high investment costs,
and it is the A category items that are most appropriate for the application of the
quantitative techniques discussed in this chapter. For these items an attempt should be
made to maintain low safety stocks consistent with avoiding high stockout costs. Larger
orders and safety stocks are likely to be a feature of the C-category items. Normally, re-
order points for these items will be determined on a subjective basis rather than using
quantitative methods, the objective being to minimize the expense in controlling these
items. The control of B-category items is likely to be based on quantitative methods, but
they are unlikely to be as sophisticated as for the A-category items.

The percentage value of total cost for the A, B and C categories in Exhibit 25.3 is
typical of most manufacturing companies. In practice, it is normal for between 10 and 15%
of the items in stock to account for between 70 and 80% of the total value of purchases. At
the other extreme, between 70 and 80% of the items in stock account for approximately

10% of the total value. The control of stock levels is eased considerably if it is concentrated on that small proportion of stock items that account for most of the total cost.

# Other factors influencing the choice of order quantity

## SHORTAGE OF FUTURE SUPPLIES

For various reasons, a firm may depart from quantitative models that provide estimates of the economic order quantity and the re-order point. A company may not always be able to rely on future supplies being available if the major suppliers are in danger of experiencing a strike. Alternatively, future supplies may be restricted because of import problems or transportation difficulties. In anticipation of such circumstances a firm may over-order so that stocks on hand will be sufficient to meet production while future supplies are restricted.

## FUTURE PRICE INCREASES

When a supplier announces a price increase that will be effective at some future date, it may be in a firm's interest to buy in excess of its immediate requirements before the increase becomes effective. Indeed, in times of rapid inflation firms might have an incentive to maintain larger stocks than would otherwise be necessary.

## OBSOLESCENCE

Certain types of stocks are subject to obsolescence. For example, a change in technology may make a particular component worthless. Alternatively, a change in fashion may cause a clothes retailer to sell stocks at considerably reduced prices. Where the probability of obsolescence is high or goods are of a perishable nature, frequent purchases of small quantities and the maintenance of low stocks may be appropriate, even when the EOQ formula may suggest purchasing larger quantities and maintaining higher stock levels.

## STEPS TO REDUCE SAFETY STOCKS

When demand is uncertain, higher safety stocks are likely to be maintained. However, safety stocks may be reduced if the purchasing department can find new suppliers who will promise quicker and more reliable delivery. Alternatively, pressure may be placed on existing suppliers for faster delivery. The lower the average delivery time, the lower will be the safety stock that a firm needs to hold, and the total investment in stocks will be reduced.

## PERFORMANCE REPORTING

Formal performance reports may not record all the relevant costs used in the decision models for calculating the economic order quantity or optimum stock levels. In Chapter 16 we noted that a manager is likely to concentrate only on those variables that are measured, and ignore other important variables that are not measured. Indeed, a manager is likely to take action that will improve his or her performance rating, as indicated on the performance report, even if this is not always in the best interest of the company. For example, if annual holding costs are not allocated in a performance report to each manager, a manager may be induced to obtain larger order sizes even though this may not be the correct policy for the company as a whole. This may occur when a production manager engages in longer, but less frequent production runs, since this is likely to reduce the total annual costs that are charged to him or her, although larger stocks (with large holding costs) will be required to meet demand between the production runs.

Thus, it is important that accountants be aware of the adverse motivational implications that are likely to arise when the performance reporting system conflicts with the decision-making model. This type of situation can be avoided by charging holding costs to the appropriate manager. One way of doing this is to charge an imputed interest charge on the stocks for which a manager is responsible. (See the answer to Self-Assessment Question 2 at the end of this chapter for an illustration.)

## ADVANCED QUANTITATIVE MODELS

With the increasing use of computers, it is now possible to use more advanced quantitative models for determining optimum stock levels. For example, changes in carrying costs, ordering costs and stockout costs can be simultaneously considered in the more advanced models. A review of these models is beyond the scope of this book, but the models presented in this chapter provide an appropriate framework for approximating the optimum level of stocks, indicating how much should be ordered and when. However, such models normally require some elaboration to overcome the complex stock control problems encountered in practice. For a description of the more advanced models see Samuels *et al.* (1998) and Wilkes (1989).

# Materials requirements planning

**AR** Prior to the widespread use of material requirements planning (MRP), material requirements were determined by continuously reviewing stock levels, and a predetermined quantity was ordered each time stocks fell below a predetermined level (the re-order point). This stock control approach was based on the assumption that replenishment of stocks could be planned *independently* of each other. However, the demand for materials is *dependent* upon the demand for the assemblies of which they are part. MRP originated in the early 1960s as a computerized approach for coordinating the planning of materials acquisition and production. MRP is a flow control system in the sense that it orders only what components are required to maintain the manufacturing flow. The orders can be for purchased parts or manufactured parts, and MRP thus provides the basis for production scheduling and raw materials purchasing. MRP can be defined as a computerized planning system that first determines the quantity and timing of finished goods demanded (i.e. the master production schedule) and then uses this to determine the requirements for raw materials components and sub-assemblies at each of the prior stages of production. Figure 25.4 provides an overview of the approach. You can see that the top-level items represent three finished goods items (FG1, FG2 and FG3). The MRP system breaks the requirements for each product into its primary subcomponents (SC)/sub-assemblies, and these in turn are further separated into second, third and so on levels of subcomponents, until at the lowest level in the hierarchy only purchased items (i.e.

**FIGURE 25.4** *An overview of the structure of an MRP system.*

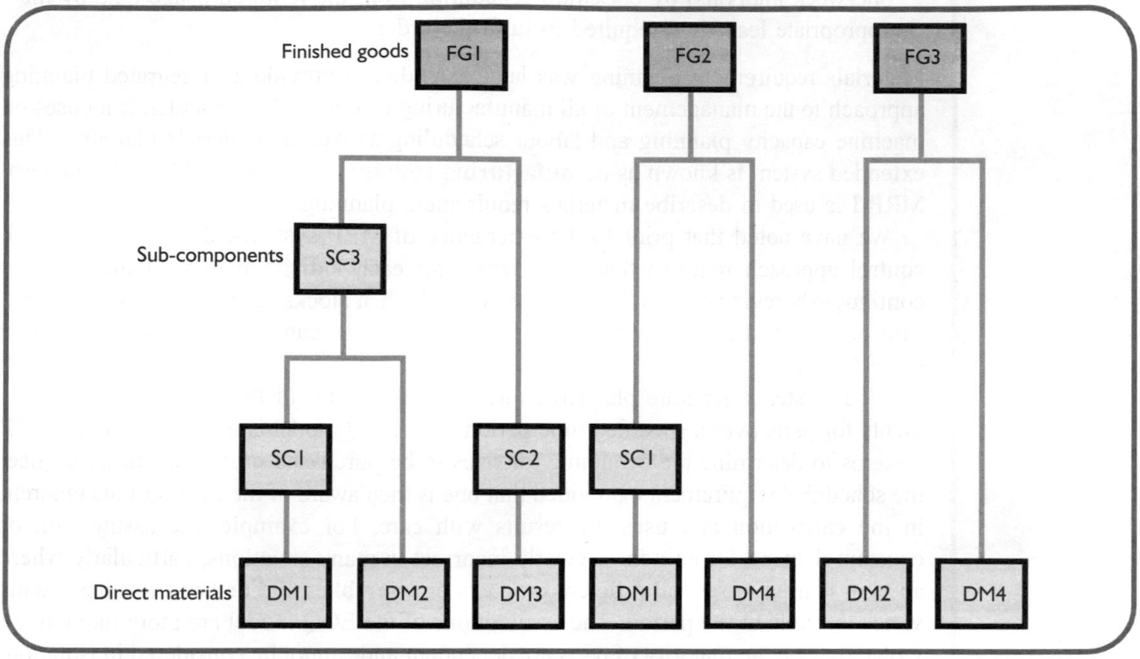

direct materials, DM) exist. For both FG1 and FG2 purchased raw materials are used to produce *components* before production of the *end product*. For FG3 no components are required in order to produce the finished product.

The prerequisites to operate an MRP system include the following:

1. A *master production schedule*, which specifies both the timing, and quantity demanded of each of the top-level finished goods items.

2. A *bills of materials file*, which specifies the sub-assemblies, components and materials required for *each* finished good.

3. An *inventory file* for *each* sub-assembly, component and part, containing details of the number of items on hand, scheduled receipts and items allocated to released orders but not yet drawn from stocks.

4. A *master parts file* containing planned lead times of all items to be purchased and sub-assemblies and components produced internally.

MRP produces a time-phased schedule of planned order releases of lower-level items for purchasing and manufacturing after taking into account items on hand and expected lead times to determine the correct requirement date. This time-phased schedule is known as the **materials requirement plan**.

A materials requirement planning system starts with the master production schedule, and then works down the bill of materials (BOM), level by level and component by component, until all parts are planned. It applies the following procedure for each item in the BOM:

- Determining the net requirements after taking into account scheduled receipts, projected target stock levels and items already allocated from the current inventory.

- Conversion of the net requirements to a planned order quantity using an appropriate lot size.

- Placing orders in appropriate periods (time is normally represented by a series of one-week intervals) by backward scheduling from the required usage date by the appropriate lead time required to fulfil the order.

Materials requirement planning was later extended to provide an integrated planning approach to the management of all manufacturing resources. In particular, it focuses on machine capacity planning and labour scheduling as well as materials planning. This extended system is known as manufacturing resource planning or MRP II. The term MRP I is used to describe materials requirement planning.

We have noted that prior to the emergence of MRP systems, the traditional stock control approach requires that stock levels for each individual item of materials be continuously reviewed and the EOQ be ordered when stocks reach their re-order point. This approach assumes that the replenishment of stocks can be planned *independently* of each other.

MRP systems generate planned coordinated schedules of the time-phased requirements for parts over a specified time period. The EOQ model can be used within MRP systems to determine the economic lot sizes to be purchased or manufactured to meet the scheduled requirements, provided that one is then aware of the assumptions inherent in the calculation and uses the results with care. For example, the assumption of constant demand for an item is clearly incorrect in many situations, particularly where an item is used in several different products or assemblies and demand for these items varies throughout the period. The assumptions of the EOQ model are more likely to be violated when the majority of parts are dependent and cannot be considered in isolation. The EOQ formulation implicitly assumes that the demand for an item is independent and that its batch size need not take account of the demand for other items. Organizations implement MRP systems because the demand for parts is dependent and cannot be considered in isolation. Therefore the assumptions of the EOQ model are more likely to be violated where MRP systems have been implemented. However, where the MRP schedule indicates that the demand for a part during a planning period is reasonably constant, the EOQ model can be used to determine the optimum lot size to be purchased or manufactured. ●●●

# Just-in-time purchasing and manufacturing

In Chapter 22 the JIT manufacturing philosophy was described. At this stage you might find it useful to refer back to Chapter 22 and read pages 907–11. You will see that the goals of JIT include eliminating non-value added activities (such as some of the activities related to purchasing), a batch size of one, and zero inventories. To achieve these goals, JIT firms have extended the JIT philosophy to the purchasing function and the management of materials requirements.

The JIT philosophy has resulted in firms giving increasing attention to reducing stock levels to a minimum by implementing JIT purchasing techniques. The objective of JIT purchasing is to purchase goods so that delivery immediately precedes their use. To achieve this, the company and the suppliers work together cooperatively. By arranging with suppliers for more frequent deliveries of smaller quantities of materials, so that each delivery is just sufficient to meet immediate production requirements, stocks can be cut to a minimum. Considerable savings in material handling expenses can also be made by requiring suppliers to inspect materials before their delivery and guaranteeing their quality.

This improved service is obtained by giving more business to fewer suppliers (who can provide high quality and reliable deliveries) and placing long-term purchasing orders. Therefore the supplier has assurance on long-term sales and can plan to meet this demand.

Companies that have implemented JIT purchasing techniques have substantially reduced their investment in raw material and work in progress stocks. Other advantages include a substantial saving in factory space, large quantity discounts and a reduction in paperwork arising from issuing blanket long-term orders to fewer suppliers instead of purchase orders.

The effect of negotiating prompt, reliable and frequent deliveries is that the need to carry raw material stocks can be virtually eliminated. Furthermore, the issue of blanket long-term purchasing orders causes the ordering costs to be substantially reduced. The effect of using the EOQ formula in this situation ties in with the JIT philosophy: namely more frequent purchases of smaller quantities.

The JIT manufacturing philosophy has also been applied to reducing the optimal number of units that should be scheduled for each production run (i.e. the batch size). The production of large batch sizes results in large stocks of work in progress and finished goods being held. Introducing advanced manufacturing technologies enables set-up times, set-up cost and the capacity lost during a set-up to be considerably reduced. Therefore the economic batch size will fall until eventually it is unnecessary to produce more than the amount needed for current consumption. The effect of reducing set-up time to a limit of zero is to produce an economic batch size of one unit. In this situation the need to maintain stocks would be eliminated.

## Self-Assessment Questions

You should attempt to answer these questions yourself before looking up the suggested answers, which appear on pages 1135–7. If any part of your answer is incorrect, check back carefully to make sure you understand where you went wrong.

(*Hint*: Prepare a schedule of costs for each order size in Question 1, since the purchasing cost is not constant per unit.)

1   A company is reviewing its stock policy, and has the following alternatives available for the evaluation of stock number 12789:

   (i)    Purchase stock twice monthly, 100 units
   (ii)   Purchase monthly, 200 units
   (iii)  Purchase every three months, 600 units
   (iv)   Purchase six monthly, 1200 units
   (v)    Purchase annually, 2400 units.

   It is ascertained that the purchase price per unit is £0.80 for deliveries up to 500 units. A 5% discount is offered by the supplier on the whole order where deliveries are 501 up to 1000, and 10% reduction on the total order for deliveries in excess of 1000.
   Each purchase order incurs administration costs of £5.
   Storage, interest on capital and other costs are £0.25 per unit of average stock quantity held.
   You are required to advise management on the optimum order size.          (9 marks)

   *AAT*

2   The annual demand for an item of raw materials is 4000 units and the purchase price is expected to be £90 per unit. The incremental cost of processing an order is £135 and the cost of storage is estimated to be £12 per unit.

   (a)  What is the optimal order quantity and the total relevant cost of this order quantity?

   (b)  Suppose that the £135 estimate of the incremental cost of processing an order is incorrect and should have been £80. Assume that all other estimates are correct. What is the cost of this prediction error, assuming that the solution to part (a) is implemented for one year?

   (c)  Assume at the start of the period that a supplier offers 4000 units at a price of £86. The materials will be delivered immediately and placed in the stores. Assume that the incremental cost of placing this order is zero and the original estimate of £135 for placing an order for the economic batch size is correct. Should the order be accepted?

   (d)  Present a performance report for the purchasing officer, assuming that the budget was based on the information presented in (a) and the purchasing officer accepted the special order outlined in (c).

## Summary

The objective of stock control models is to determine the order quantity that minimizes the cost of holding stocks. The costs of maintaining stocks consist of ordering costs and holding costs. Ordering costs decline and holding costs increase when the order quantity is increased. The economic order quantity is at the point where ordering costs are equal to holding costs. This point can be derived by the EOQ formula. This formula can also be used to determine the optimum length of a production run, and it can be used as the starting point for determining whether a firm should increase the order quantity so as to take advantage of quantity discounts.

When uncertainty of demand and lead times are incorporated into the analysis, firms must hold safety stocks to cover the possibility that demand and lead time may be different from that used in the EOQ formula. Safety stocks should be determined using probability analysis.

In practice, approximately 20% of the total quantity of stocks may account for about 80% of its value, this principle is known as **Pareto analysis** and is based on observations by Pareto (1848–1923) that a very small proportion of items usually accounts for the majority of value. By concentrating on the small proportion of stock items that jointly account for 80% of the total value, a firm may well be able to control most of its monetary investment in stocks.

Prior to the emergence of MRP systems, the traditional stock control approach required that stock levels for each individual item of material be continuously reviewed and the EOQ be ordered when stocks reach their re-order point. This approach assumes that the replenishment of stocks can be planned independently of each other. MRP is a planning system that first determines the quantity and timing of finished goods demanded, and then determines time phased requirements of the demand for materials, components and sub-assemblies over a specified planning time horizon. The major feature of MRP is that it highlights that the demand for materials is dependent upon the demand for assemblies of which they are a part.

EOQ models are most suited to situations where the demand for a specific item of material tends to be constant from period to period. These circumstances are less likely to exist when MRP systems have been implemented.

Recently, JIT purchasing and production techniques have focused on reducing the cost of placing an order, set-up time and therefore the capacity lost during the set-up time. If these costs are reduced to zero, the EOQ model implies an economic batch size of one.

## Key Terms and Concepts

ABC classification method (p. 1005)
cost of prediction error (p. 999)
economic order quantity (EOQ) (p. 995)
holding costs (p. 994)
just-in-time purchasing techniques (p. 1010)
lead time (p. 1002)
manufacturing resource planning (p. 1010)
master production schedule (p. 1008)
materials requirement plan (p. 1009)

materials requirements planning (MRP) (p. 1008)
ordering costs (p. 995)
Pareto analysis (p. 1014)
precautionary motive (p. 994)
re-order point (p. 1001)
safety stocks (p. 1002)
speculative motive (p. 994)
stockout costs (p. 1002)
transactions motive (p. 994).

## Recommended Reading

For a more detailed review of stock control models see Samuels *et al.* (1998) and Wilkes (1989).

## Key Examination Points

A common mistake is to unitize fixed ordering and holding costs and include these costs in the EOQ formula. The EOQ should be calculated using variable unit costs. The EOQ formula does not include the cost of purchasing materials, since it is assumed that the cost per unit is the same for all order quantities. If the question includes quantity discounts, you should adopt the approach illustrated in this chapter.

The EOQ formula should not be used when the purchase cost per unit varies with the quantity ordered. Instead, you should prepare a schedule of the relevant costs for different order quantities. For an illustration of this approach see the answer to Self-Assessment Question 1. You should also ensure that you can cope with problems where future demand is uncertain. Compare your answers to Questions 25.18, 25.21 and 25.22 with the answers in the *Students' Manual*.

## Questions

*Indicates that a suggested solution is to be found in the *Students' Manual*.

### 25.1* Intermediate

A domestic appliance retailer with multiple outlets stocks a popular toaster known as the Autocrisp 2000, for which the following information is available:

| | |
|---|---|
| Average sales | 75 per day |
| Maximum sales | 95 per day |
| Minimum sales | 50 per day |
| Lead time | 12–18 days |
| Re-order quantity | 1750 |

(i) Based on the data above, at what level of stocks would a replenishment order be issued?
   A 1050.    B 1330.    C 1710.
   D 1750.

(ii) Based on the data above, what is the maximum level of stocks possible?
   A 1750.    B 2860.    C 3460.
   D 5210.

*CIMA Stage 1 Cost Accounting*

### 25.2 Intermediate: Calculation of EOQ and frequency at ordering

A company is planning to purchase 90 800 units of a particular item in the year ahead. The item is purchased in boxes, each containing 10 units of the item, at a price of £200 per box. A safety stock of 250 boxes is kept.

The cost of holding an item in stock for a year (including insurance, interest and space costs) is 15% of the purchase area. The cost of placing and receiving orders is to be estimated from cost data collected relating to similar orders, where costs of £5910 were incurred on 30 orders. It should be assumed that ordering costs change in proportion to the number of orders placed. 2% should be added to the above ordering costs to allow for inflation.

Required:
Calculate the order quantity that would minimize the cost of the above item, and determine the required frequency of placing orders, assuming that usage of the item will be even over the year.

(8 marks)
*ACCA Foundation Stage Paper 3*

### 25.3* Intermediate

(a) Write short notes to explain each of the following in the context of materials control:
   (i)   Continuous stocktaking.
   (ii)  Perpetual inventory system.
   (iii) ABC inventory analysis.    (9 marks)

(b) State the factors that should influence the decision regarding economic order quantities of raw materials.    (7 marks)

(c) Calculate three normal control levels, which may be used in stock control systems, from the following information for a particular raw material:
    Economic order quantity, 12 000 kilos
    Lead time, 10 to 14 working days
    Average usage, 600 kilos per day
    Minimum usage, 400 kilos per day
    Maximum usage, 800 kilos per day

(9 marks)
(Total 25 marks)
*ACCA Level 1 Costing*

### 25.4* Intermediate: Calculation of EOQ using tabulation and formula method

A large local government authority places orders for various stationery items at quarterly intervals.

In respect of an item of stock coded A32, data are:

| | |
|---|---|
| annual usage quantity | 5000 boxes |
| minimum order quantity | 500 boxes |
| cost per box | £2 |

Usage of material is on a regular basis and on average, half of the amount purchased is held in inventory. The cost of storage is considered to be 25% of the inventory value. The average cost of placing an order is estimated at £12.5.

The chief executive of the authority has asked you to review the present situation and to consider possible ways of effecting cost savings.

You are required to:
(a) tabulate the costs of storage and ordering item A32 for each level of orders from four to twelve placed per year;
(b) ascertain from the tabulation the number of orders which should be placed in a year to minimize these costs;
(c) produce a formula to calculate the order level which would minimize these costs – your answer should explain each constituent part of the formula and their relationships;
(d) give an example of the use of the formula to confirm the calculation in (b) above;
(e) calculate the percentage saving on the annual cost which could be made by using the economic order quantity system;
(f) suggest *two* other approaches which could be introduced in order to reduce the present cost of storage and ordering of stationery.

(25 marks)
*CIMA Cost Accounting 2*

### 25.5* Intermediate: Calculation of EOQ

XYZ Ltd produces a product which has a constant monthly demand of 4000 units. The product requires a component which XYZ Ltd purchases from a supplier at £10 per unit. The component requires a three-day lead time from the date of order to the date of delivery. The ordering cost is £0.60 per order and the holding cost is 10% per annum.

(a) You are required to calculate:
(i) The economic order quantity.
(ii) The number of orders required per year.
(iii) The total cost of ordering and holding the components for the year.
(b) Assuming that there is no safety stock and that the present stock level is 400 components, when should the next order be placed? (Assume a 360-day year.)
(c) Discuss the problems which most firms would have in attempting to apply the EOQ formula.

### 25.6 Intermediate: Calculation of EOQ

Most textbooks consider that the optimal re-order quantity for materials occurs when 'the cost of storage is equated with the cost of ordering'. If one assumes that this statement is acceptable and also, in attempting to construct a simple formula for an optimal re-order quantity, that a number of basic assumptions must be made, then a recognised formula can be produced using the following symbols:

$C_o$ = cost of placing an order
$C_h$ = cost of storage per annum, expressed as a percentage of stock value
$D$ = demand in units for a material, per annum
$Q$ = re-order quantity, in units
$Q/2$ = average stock level, in units
$p$ = price per unit

You are required:
(a) to present formulae, using the symbols given above, representing:
(i) total cost of ordering,
(ii) total cost of storage,
(iii) total cost of ordering and storage,
(iv) optimal re-order quantity; (4 marks)
(b) to state the limitations experienced in practice which affect the user of the formula for optimal re-order quantity as expressed in (a) (iv) above; (4 marks)
(c) to calculate the optimal re-order quantity from the following data:
Cost of storage is 20% per annum of stock value
Cost of placing an order is £30 each
Demand for material is 2000 units per annum
Price of material is £70 per unit; (3 marks)
(d) to explain a system of stock usage which renders economic order quantity re-ordering obsolete. (4 marks)

(Total 15 marks)
*CIMA Stage 2 Cost Accounting*

### 25.7 Intermediate: Calculation of EOQ

Sandy Lands Ltd carries an item of inventory in respect of which the following data apply:

| | |
|---|---|
| fixed cost of ordering per batch | £10 |
| expected steady quarterly volume of sales | 3125 units |
| cost of holding one unit in stock for one year | £1 |

You are required to:
(i) calculate the minimum annual cost of ordering and stocking the item; (4 marks)

(ii) calculate to the nearest whole number of units the optimal batch size if the expected steady quarterly volume of sales
 *first* falls to 781 units and
 *second* rises to 6250 units
and to state the relationship between the rates of change of sales and the optimal batch size;
(4 marks)
(iii) explain the basis of the derivation of the formula for the optimal batch size which is given in the table of formulae. (4 marks)
*ICAEW Management Accounting*

### 25.8* Intermediate: Calculation of re-order and maximum stock levels

A retail company has been reviewing the adequacy of its stock control systems and has identified three products for investigation. Relevant details for the three products are set out below:

| Item code | EOQ (000 units) | Stock (warehouse and stores) (000 units) | (£/unit at cost) | Weekly sales (£000) mini-mum | nor-mal | maxi-mum | Gross* margin (% of sales) |
|---|---|---|---|---|---|---|---|
| 14/363 | 25 | 32.5 | 2.25 | 26 | 28 | 30 | 42 |
| 11/175 | 500 | 422.7 | 0.36 | 130 | 143 | 160 | 46 |
| 14/243 | 250 | 190 | 0.87 | 60 | 96 | 128 | 37 |

*Gross margin = sales – purchase cost of product.

Outstanding order: Item code 14/243 – order for 250 000 units placed 2 trading days ago.

There are 6 trading days per week.

All orders are delivered by suppliers into the retailer's central warehouse. The lead time is one week from placement of order. A further week is required by the retailer in order to transfer stock from central warehouse to stores. Both of these lead times can be relied upon.

Required:
(a) Calculate for each product:
 (i) the minimum and maximum weekly sales units
 (ii) the stock re-order level
 (iii) the maximum stock control level.
(9 marks)
(b) Comment upon the adequacy of the existing stock control of the three products. (5 marks)
(Total 14 marks)
*ACCA Foundation Stage Paper 3*

### 25.9* Intermediate: Quantity discounts

A company uses 50 000 units of material per annum to service a steady demand for its products. Order costs are £100 per order and holding costs are £0.40 per order.

(a) Determine the optimal order quantity.
(b) The supplier now offers a quantity discount of £0.02 per unit if it buys in batches of 10 000 units. Should the company take advantage of the quantity discount?

### 25.10 Intermediate: Calculation of EOQ and a make or buy decision

A company is considering the possibility of purchasing from a supplier a component it now makes. The supplier will provide the components in the necessary quantities at a unit price of £9. Transportation and storage costs would be negligible.

The company produces the component from a single raw material in economic lots of 2000 units at a cost of £2 per unit. Average annual demand is 20 000 units. The annual holding cost is £0.25 per unit and the minimum stock level is set at 400 units. Direct labour costs for the component are £6 per unit, fixed manufacturing overhead is charged at a rate of £3 per unit based on a normal activity of 20 000 units. The company also hires the machine on which the components are produced at a rate of £200 per month.

Should the company make the component?

### 25.11 Intermediate: Calculation of minimum purchase cost when cost per unit is not constant

A company is reviewing the purchasing policy for one of its raw materials as a result of a reduction in production requirement. The material, which is used evenly throughout the year, is used in only one of the company's products, the production of which is currently 12 000 units per annum. Each finished unit of the product contains 0.4 kg of the material. 20% of the material is lost in the production process. Purchases can be made in multiples of 500 kg, with a minimum purchase order quantity of 1000 kg.

The cost of the raw material depends upon the purchase order quantity as follows:

| Order quantity (kg) | Cost per kg (£) |
|---|---|
| 1000 | 1.00 |
| 1500 | 0.98 |
| 2000 | 0.965 |
| 2500 | 0.95 |
| 3000 and above | 0.94 |

Costs of placing and handling each order are £90, of which £40 is an apportionment of costs which are not expected to be affected in the short term by the number of orders placed. Annual holding costs of stock are £0.90 per unit of average stock, of which only £0.40 is expected to be affected in the short term by the amount of stock held.

The lead time for the raw materials is one month, and a safety stock of 250 kg is required.

Required:
(a) Explain, and illustrate from the situation described above, the meaning of the terms 'variable', 'semivariable' and 'fixed' costs.
(8 marks)
(b) Calculate the annual cost of pursuing alternative purchase order policies and thus advise the company regarding the purchase order quantity for the material that will minimize cost.
(14 marks)
(Total 22 marks)
*ACCA Level 1 Costing*

## 25.12 Advanced: Evaluation of an increase in order size incorporating quantity discounts

Whirlygig plc manufactures and markets automatic dishwashing machines. Among the components which it purchases each year from external suppliers for assembly into the finished article are window units, of which it uses 20 000 units per annum.

It is considering buying in larger amounts in order to claim quantity discounts. This will lower the number of orders placed but raise the administrative and other costs of placing and receiving orders. Details of actual and expected ordering and carrying costs are given in the table below:

|                                                              | **Actual** | **Proposed** |
| ------------------------------------------------------------ | ---------- | ------------ |
| O = Ordering cost per order                                  | £31.25     | £120         |
| P = Purchase price per item                                  | £6.25      | £6.00        |
| I = (annual) Inventory holding cost (as a percentage of the purchase price) | 20%        | 20%          |

To implement the new arrangements will require reorganisation costs estimated at £10 000 which can be wholly claimed as a business expense for tax purposes in the tax year before the system comes into operation. The rate of corporate tax is 33%, payable with a one-year delay.

Required:
(a) Determine the change in the economic order quantity (EOQ) caused by the new system.
(4 marks)
(b) Calculate the payback period for the proposal and comment on your results. (10 marks)
(c) Briefly discuss the suitability of the payback method for evaluating investments of this nature.
(6 marks)
(Total 20 marks)
*ACCA Paper 8 Managerial Finance*

## 25.13 Advanced: Quantity discounts and calculation of EOQ

Wagtail Ltd uses the 'optimal batch size' model (see below) to determine optimal levels of raw materials. Material B is consumed at a steady, known rate over the company's planning horizon of one year; the current usage is 4000 units per annum. The costs of ordering B are invariant with respect to order size; clerical costs of ordering have been calculated at £30 per order. Each order is checked by an employee engaged in using B in production who earns £5 per hour irrespective of his output. The employee generates a contribution of £4 per hour when not involved in materials checks and the stock check takes five hours. Holding costs amount to £15 per unit per annum.

The supplier of material B has very recently offered Wagtail a quantity discount of £0.24 a unit on the current price of £24, for all orders of 400 or more units of B.

You are required to:
(a) calculate the optimal order level of material B, ignoring the quantity discount; (3 marks)
(b) evaluate whether the quantity discount offered should be taken up by Wagtail; (5 marks)
(c) explain how uncertainties in materials usage and lead time may be incorporated into the analysis.
(8 marks)

*Note:* Ignore taxation.
*ICAEW P2 Financial Management*

## 25.14 Advanced: Calculation of EOQ and a comparison of relevant purchasing costs of different suppliers

Mr Evans is a wholesaler who buys and sells a wide range of products, one of which is the Laker. Mr Evans sells 24 000 units of the Laker each year at a unit price of £20. Sales of the Laker normally follow an even pattern throughout the year but to protect himself against possible deviations Mr

Evans keeps a minimum stock of 1000 units. Further supplies of the Laker are ordered whenever the stock falls to this minimum level and the time lag between ordering and delivery is small enough to be ignored.

At present, Mr Evans buys all his supplies of Lakers from May Ltd, and usually purchases them in batches of 5000 units. His most recent invoice from May Ltd was as follows:

|  | (£) |
| --- | --- |
| Basic price: 5000 Lakers at £15 per unit | 75 000 |
| Delivery charge: Transport at £0.50 per unit | 2 500 |
| Fixed shipment charge per order | 1 000 |
|  | 78 500 |

In addition, Mr Evans estimates that each order he places costs him £500, comprising administrative costs and the cost of sample checks. This cost does not vary with the size of the order.

Mr Evans stores Lakers in a warehouse which he rents on a long lease for £5 per square foot per annum. Warehouse space available exceeds current requirements and, as the lease cannot be cancelled, spare capacity is sublet on annual contracts at £4 per square foot per annum. Each unit of Laker in stock requires 2 square feet of space. Mr Evans estimates that other holding costs amount to £10 per Laker per annum.

Mr Evans has recently learnt that another supplier of Lakers, Richardson Ltd, is willing, unlike May Ltd, to offer discounts on large orders. Richardson Ltd sells Lakers at the following prices:

| Order size | Price per unit (£) |
| --- | --- |
| 1–2999 | 15.25 |
| 3000–4999 | 14.50 |
| 5000 and over | 14.25 |

In other respects (i.e. delivery charges and the time between ordering and delivery) Richardson Ltd's terms are identical to those of May Ltd.

You are required to:

(a) calculate the optimal re-order quantity for Lakers and the associated annual profit Mr Evans can expect from their purchase and sale, assuming that he continues to buy from May Ltd, (10 marks)

(b) prepare calculations to show whether Mr Evans should buy Lakers from Richardson Ltd rather than from May Ltd and, if so, in what batch sizes, (8 marks)

(c) explain the limitations of the methods of analysis you have used. (7 marks)

Ignore taxation.

(Total 25 marks)

*ICAEW Elements of Financial Decisions*

### 25.15* Advanced: Relevant costs and calculation of optimum batch size

Pink Ltd is experiencing some slight problems concerning two stock items sold by the company.

The first of these items is product Exe which is manufactured by Pink. The annual demand for Exe of 4000 units, which is evenly spread throughout the year, is usually met by production taking place four times per year in batches of 1000 units. One of the raw material inputs to product Exe is product Dee which is also manufactured by Pink. Product Dee is the firm's major product and is produced in large quantities throughout the year. Production capacity is sufficient to meet in full *all* demands for the production of Dees.

The standard costs of products Exe and Dee are:

**Standard costs – per unit**

|  | Product | |
| --- | --- | --- |
|  | Exe (£) | Dee (£) |
| Raw materials – purchased from external suppliers | 13 | 8 |
| – Dee standard cost | 22 | — |
| Labour – unskilled | 7 | 4 |
| – skilled | 9 | 5 |
| Variable overheads | 5 | 3 |
| Fixed overheads | 4 | 2 |
| Standard cost | £60 | £22 |

Included in the fixed overheads for Exe are the set-up costs for each production run. The costs of each set-up, which apply irrespective of the size of the production run, are:

**Costs per set-up**

|  | (£) |
| --- | --- |
| (i) Labour costs – skilled labour | 66 |
| (ii) Machine parts | 70 |
| Total | £136 |

The 'Machine parts' relate to the cost of parts required for modifications carried out to the machine on which Exe is produced. The parts can be used for only one run, irrespective of run length, and are destroyed by replacement on reinstatement of the machine. There are no set-up costs associated with Dee.

The cost of financing stocks of Exe is 15% p.a. Each unit of Exe in stock requires 0.40 square metres of storage space and units *cannot* be stacked on top of each other to reduce costs. Warehouse rent is £20 p.a. per square metre and Pink is only required to pay for storage space actually used.

Pink is not working to full capacity and idle-time payments are being made to all grades of labour except unskilled workers. Unskilled labour is not guaranteed a minimum weekly wage and is paid only for work carried out.

The second stock item causing concern is product Wye. Product Wye is purchased by Pink for resale and the 10 000 unit annual demand is again spread evenly throughout the year. Incremental ordering costs are £100 per order and the normal unit cost is £20. However the suppliers of Wye are now offering quantity discounts for large orders. The details of these are:

| Quantity ordered | Unit price (£) |
| --- | --- |
| Up to 999 | 20.00 |
| 1000 to 1999 | 19.80 |
| 2000 and over | 19.60 |

The purchasing manager feels that full advantage should be taken of discounts and purchases should be made at £19.60 per unit using orders for 2000 units or more. Holding costs for Wye are calculated at £8.00 per unit per year and this figure will not be altered by any change in the purchase price per unit.

Required:
(a) Show the optimum batch size for the production of Exes. If this differs from the present policy, calculate the annual savings to be made by Pink Ltd from pursuing the optimal policy. Briefly explain the figures incorporated in your calculations. (The time taken to carry out a production run may be ignored.) (10 marks)
(b) Advise Pink Ltd on the correct size of order for the purchase of Wyes. (6 marks)

(c) Briefly describe two major limitations, or difficulties inherent in the practical application, of the model used in (a) to determine the optimum batch size. (4 marks)
(Total 20 marks)
*ACCA P2 Management Accounting*

**25.16\* Advanced: Calculation of reduction in storage costs arising from the implementation of JIT production and purchasing**
Prodco plc has an annual turnover of £30 000 000 from a range of products. Material costs and conversion costs account for 30% and 25% of turnover respectively.

Other information relating to the company is as follows:
(i) Stock values are currently at a constant level, being:
   (a) Raw material stock: 10% of the material element of annual turnover.
   (b) Work in progress: 15% of the material element of annual turnover together with a proportionate element of conversion costs allowing for 60% completion of work in progress as to conversion costs and 100% completion as to material cost. The material cost : conversion cost ratio is constant for all products.
   (c) Finished goods stock: 12% of the material element of annual turnover together with a proportionate element of conversion cost.
(ii) Holding and acquisition costs of materials comprise fixed costs of £100 000 per annum plus variable costs of £0.10 per £ of stock held.
(iii) Movement and control costs of work in progress comprise fixed costs of £140 000 per annum plus variable costs of £0.05 per £ of material value of work in progress.
(iv) Holding and control costs of finished goods comprise fixed costs of £180 000 per annum plus variable costs of £0.02 per £ of finished goods (material cost + conversion cost).
(v) Financial charges due to the impact of stock holding on working capital requirement are incurred at 20% per annum on the value of stocks held.

Prodco plc are considering a number of changes which it is estimated will affect stock levels and costs as follows:

1. Raw material stock: Negotiate delivery from suppliers on a just-in-time basis. Stock levels will be reduced to 20% of the present level. Fixed costs of holding and acquiring stock will be reduced to 20% of the present level and variable costs to £0.07 per £ of stock held.
2. Work in progress: Convert the layout of the production area into a 'dedicated cell' format for each product type instead of the existing system which comprises groups of similar machines to which each product type must be taken. Work in progress volume will be reduced to 20% of the present level with the same stage of completion as at present. Fixed costs of movement and control will be reduced to 40% of the present level and variable costs to £0.03 per £ of material value of work in progress.
3. Finished goods stock: Improved control of the flow of each product type from the production area will enable stocks to be reduced to 25% of the present level. Fixed costs of holding and control will be reduced to 40% of the present level and variable costs to £0.01 per £ of finished goods held.

Required:
(a) Calculate the annual estimated financial savings from the proposed changes in *each* of raw material stock, work in progress and finished goods stock. (12 marks)
(b) Suggest reasons for the reductions in the costs associated with each of raw material stock, work in progress and finished goods stock which it is estimated will occur if the proposed changes are implemented. (6 marks)
(c) Discuss additional costs and benefits which may result from the proposed changes about which information should be obtained before implementation of the changes takes place. (12 marks)
(Total 30 marks)
*ACCA Level 2 Cost and Management Accounting II*

### 25.17* Advanced: Calculation of EOQ, discussion of the limitations of EOQ and a discussion of JIT

The newly-appointed managing director of a division of Bondini plc is concerned about the length of the division's cash operating cycle. Extracts from the latest budget are given below:

**Budgeted Profit and Loss Account for the year ending 30 June 2001**

| | (£000) | (£000) |
|---|---|---|
| Sales (43 200 units at £55) | | 2376 |
| Opening Stock (21 600 units at £30) | 648 | |
| Purchases (43 200 units at £30) | 1296 | |
| | 1944 | |
| Closing Stock (21 600 units at £30) | 648 | 1296 |
| Budgeted Gross Profit | | 1080 |

**Budgeted Balance Sheet as at 30 June 2001**
(£000)

*Current Assets*
Stock 648
Trade debtors 198
*Current Liabilities*
Trade creditors 216

The following information has also been gathered for the managing director:
(1) Sales were made evenly during the twelve months to 30 June 2000.
(2) The amount for trade creditors relates only to purchases of stock.
(3) The division is charged interest at the rate of 15% per annum on the average level of net assets held in a year.
(4) The company rents sufficient space in a warehouse to store the necessary stock at an annual cost of £3.25 per unit.
(5) The costs of ordering items of stock are as follows:
Insurance cost per order £900
Transport cost per order £750
(6) There will be no change in debtor and creditor payment periods.

In addition, the division maintains a purchasing department at an annual budgeted cost of £72 000.
The managing director has heard about the economic order quantity (EOQ) model and would prefer this basis to be used to calculate the order quantity. He estimates that the buffer stock level should be equal to one month's sales in order to prevent loss of revenue due to stock-outs.

Requirements:
(a) Calculate the EOQ for the division and, assuming that the division uses this as the basis for ordering goods from 1 July 2000, calculate the cash amounts which would be paid to trade creditors in each of the eight months to 28 February 2001. (12 marks)
(b) Determine the length of the cash operating cycle at 30 June 2000 and calculate the improvement that will have taken place by 30 June 2001. (4 marks)
(c) Discuss the practical limitations of using the EOQ approach to determining order quantities. (5 marks)
(d) Describe the advantages and disadvantages of the Just-In-Time approach (i.e. when minimal stocks are maintained and suppliers deliver as required). (4 marks)

(Total 25 marks)
*ICAEW P2 Financial Management*

### 25.18* Advanced: Safety stocks and probability theory
A company has determined that the EOQ for its only raw material is 2000 units every 30 days. The company knows with certainty that a four-day lead time is required for ordering. The following is the probability distribution of estimated usage of the raw material for the month:

| Usage (units) | 1800 | 1900 | 2000 | 2100 | 2200 | 2300 | 2400 | 2500 |
|---|---|---|---|---|---|---|---|---|
| Probability | 0.06 | 0.14 | 0.30 | 0.16 | 0.13 | 0.10 | 0.07 | 0.04 |

Stockouts will cost the company £10 per unit, and the average monthly holding cost is £1 per unit.
(a) Determine the optimal safety stock.
(b) What is the probability of being out of stock?

### 25.19 Advanced: Calculation of EOQ and discussion of safety stocks
A company needs to hold a stock of item X for sale to customers.

Although the item is of relatively small value per unit, the customers' quality control requirements and the need to obtain competitive supply tenders at frequent intervals result in high procurement costs.

Basic data about item X are as follows:

| | |
|---|---|
| Annual sales demand ($d$) over 52 weeks | 4095 units |
| Cost of placing and processing a purchase order (procurement costs, $C_s$) | £48.46 |

| | |
|---|---|
| Cost of holding one unit for one year ($C_h$) | £4.00 |
| Normal delay between placing purchase order and receiving goods | 3 weeks |

You are required to:
(a) calculate
(i) the economic order quantity for item X,
(ii) the frequency at which purchase orders would be placed, using that formula,
(iii) the total annual procurement costs and the total annual holding costs when the EOQ is used; (6 marks)
(b) explain why it might be unsatisfactory to procure a fixed quantity of item X at regular intervals if it were company policy to satisfy all sales demands from stock and if
(i) the rate of sales demand could vary between 250 and 350 units per four-week period or
(ii) the delivery delay on purchases might vary between 3 and 5 weeks
suggesting in each case what corrective actions might be taken; (6 marks)
(c) describe in detail a fully-developed stock control system for item X (or other fast-moving items), designed to ensure that stock holdings at all times are adequate but not excessive. Illustrate your answer with a free-hand graph, not to scale. (8 marks)

(Total 20 marks)
*CIMA Stage 4 Financial Management*

### 25.20 Advanced: Calculation of EOQ, safety stocks and stockholding costs where demand is uncertain
The financial controller of Mexet plc is reviewing the company's stock management procedures. Stock has gradually increased to 25% of the company's total assets and, with finance costs at 14% per annum, currently costs the company £4.5 million per year, including all ordering and holding costs.

Demand for the company's major product is not subject to seasonal fluctuations. The product requires £6 million of standard semi-finished goods annually which are purchased in equal quantities from three separate suppliers at a cost of £20 per unit. Three suppliers are used to prevent problems that could result from industrial disputes in a single supplier.

Stock costs £2 per unit per year to hold, including insurance costs and financing costs, and each order made costs £100 fixed cost and £0.10 per unit variable cost. There is a lead time of one month between the placing of an order and delivery of the goods. Demand fluctuation for the company's finished products results in the following probability distribution of monthly stock usage.

| Usage per month | 19 400 | 23 000 | 25 000 | 27 000 | 30 000 |
|---|---|---|---|---|---|
| Probability | 0.10 | 0.22 | 0.36 | 0.20 | 0.12 |

The cost per unit of running out of stock is estimated to be £0.4.

Required:
(a) Calculate the economic order quantity for the semi-finished goods. (3 marks)
(b) Determine what level of safety stock should be kept for these goods. (8 marks)
(c) Calculate the change in annual stock management costs that would result if the goods were bought from only one supplier. Assume that no quantity discounts are available. (5 marks)
(d) The financial controller feels that JIT (just in time) stock management might be useful for the company, but the three suppliers will only agree to this in return for an increase in unit price.
Explain the possible advantages and disadvantages of JIT, and briefly discuss whether or not Mexet should introduce it. (9 marks)
(Total 25 marks)
*ACCA Level 3 Financial Management*

## 25.21* Advanced: Safety stocks and uncertain demand

DB p.l.c. operates a conventional stock control system based on reorder levels and Economic Ordering Quantities. The various control levels were set originally based on estimates which did not allow for any uncertainty and this has caused difficulties because, in practice, lead times, demands and other factors do vary.

As part of a review of the system, a typical stock item, Part No. X206, has been studied in detail as follows:

**Data for Part No. X206**

| Lead times | Probability |
|---|---|
| 15 working days | 0.2 |
| 20 working days | 0.5 |
| 25 working days | 0.3 |

| Demand per working day | Probability |
|---|---|
| 5000 units | 0.5 |
| 7000 units | 0.5 |

*Note:* it can be assumed that the demands would apply for the whole of the appropriate lead time.

DB p.l.c. works for 240 days per year and it costs £0.15 p.a. to carry a unit of X206 in stock. The re-order level for this part is currently 150 000 units and the re-order cost is £1000.

You are required:
(a) to calculate the level of buffer stock implicit in a re-order level of 150 000 units; (4 marks)
(b) to calculate the probability of a stock-out; (2 marks)
(c) to calculate the expected annual stock-outs in units; (3 marks)
(d) to calculate the stock-out cost per unit at which it would be worthwhile raising the re-order level to 175 000 units; (3 marks)
(e) to discuss the possible alternatives to a re-order level EOQ inventory system and their advantages and disadvantages. (5 marks)
(Total 17 marks)
*CIMA Stage 3 Management Accounting Techniques*

## 25.22* Advanced: Calculation of EOQ and safety stocks assuming uncertainty

The retailing division of Josefa plc sells Hofers and its budget for the coming year is given below:

| | (£) | (£) |
|---|---|---|
| Sales (4200 units at £85 each) | | 357 000 |
| Cost of goods sold: | | |
| Opening stock (200 units at £65 per unit) | 13 000 | |
| Purchases (4200 units at £750 per unit) | 294 000 | |
| | 307 000 | |
| Closing stock (200 units at £70 per unit) | 14 000 | 293 000 |
| Gross profit | | 64 000 |
| Purchasing department cost | | |
| Variable (7 orders at £300 per order) | 2 100 | |
| Fixed | 8 400 | |
| Transportation costs for goods received (7 orders at £750 per order) | 5 250 | |

Stock insurance costs based on average stockholding (500 units at £4 per unit)  2 000

Fixed warehouse costs  43 000

60 750

Budgeted net profit  3 250

The supplier of Hofers is responsible for their transportation and charges Josefa plc accordingly. Recently the supplier has offered to reduce the cost of transportation from £750 per order to £650 per order if Josefa plc will increase the order size from the present 600 units to a minimum of 1000 units.

The management of Josefa plc is concerned about the retailing division's stock ordering policy. At present, a buffer stock of 200 units is maintained and sales occur evenly throughout the year. Josefa plc has contracted to buy 4200 Hofers and, irrespective of the order quantity, will pay for them in equal monthly instalments throughout the year. Transportation costs are to be paid at the beginning of the year. The cost of capital of Josefa plc is 20% p.a.

Requirements:

(a) Determine the quantity of Hofers which Josefa plc should order, assuming the buffer stock level of 200 units is maintained, and calculate the improvement in net profit that will result.  (11 marks)

(b) Calculate what the buffer stock level should be, assuming that:

(i) Josefa plc changes its ordering frequency to one order (of 700 units) every two months;

(ii) stockout costs are £18 per unit;

(iii) the distribution of sales within each two-month period is not even but the following two-monthly sales pattern can occur:

| 2-monthly sales | Probability |
| --- | --- |
| 500 units | 0.15 |
| 600 units | 0.20 |
| 700 units | 0.30 |
| 800 units | 0.20 |
| 900 units | 0.15 |

(7 marks)

(c) Discuss the problems which might be experienced in attempting to maintain a stock control system based upon economic order quantities and buffer stocks.  (7 marks)

(Total 25 marks)

Ignore taxation.

*ICAEW P2 Financial Management*

### 25.23 Advanced: Calculation of stockholding costs, costs of stockouts when demand is uncertain and a discussion of JIT

Rainbow Ltd is a manufacturer which uses alkahest in many of its products. At present the company has an alkahest plant on a site close to the company's main factory. A summary of the alkahest plant's budget for the next year is shown below.

| | |
| --- | --- |
| Production | 3 000 000 litres of alkahest |
| Variable manufacturing costs | £840 000 |
| Fixed manufacturing costs | £330 000 |

The budget covers costs up to and including the cost of piping finished alkahest to the main factory. At the main factory alkahest can be stored at a cost of £20 per annum per thousand litres, but additional costs arise in storage because alkahest evaporates at a rate of 5% per annum. Production of alkahest is adjusted to meet the demands of the main factory; in addition safety stocks of 60 000 litres are maintained in case of disruption of supplies.

The alkahest plant has a limited remaining life and has been fully depreciated. The management of Rainbow Ltd is considering whether the plant should be retained for the time being or should be closed immediately. On closure the equipment would be scrapped and the site sold for £400 000. Employees would be redeployed within the company and supplies of alkahest would be bought from an outside supplier.

Rainbow Ltd has found that Alchemy plc can supply all its alkahest requirements at £370 per thousand litres. Transport costs of £30 per thousand litres would be borne by Rainbow Ltd. There would be administration costs of £15 000 per year, in addition to order costs of £60 for each delivery. It has been decided that if purchases are made from Alchemy plc the safety stock will be increased to 100 000 litres.

Rainbow Ltd has 250 working days in each year and a cost of capital of 15% per annum. The company's current expectations for demand and costs apply for the foreseeable future.

Requirements:

(a) Calculate the total annual costs of the options

available to Rainbow Ltd for its supply of alkahest and interpret the results for management. (10 marks)

(b) Calculate the expected annual stock-outs in litres implied by a safety stock of 100 000 litres and calculate the stock-out cost per litre at which it would be worthwhile to increase safety stock from 100 000 litres to 120 000 litres, under the following assumptions:

(i) for any delivery there is a 0.8 probability that lead time will be 5 days and a 0.2 probability that lead time will be 10 days, and

(ii) during the lead time for any delivery there is a 0.5 probability that Rainbow Ltd will use alkahest at the rate of 10 000 litres per day and a 0.5 probability that the company will use alkahest at the rate of 14 000 litres per day. (6 marks)

(c) Explain the requirements for the successful adoption of a just-in-time inventory policy and discuss the relative costs and benefits of just-in-time policies compared with economic-order-quantity policies. (9 marks)

(Total 25 marks)

*ICAEW P2 Management Accounting*

### 25.24* Advanced: Safety stocks and uncertain demand and quantity discounts

Runswick Ltd is a company that purchases toys from abroad for resale to retail stores. The company is concerned about its stock (inventory) management operations. It is considering adopting a stock management system based upon the economic order quantity (EOQ) model.

The company's estimates of its stock management costs are shown below:

### Percentage of purchase price of toys per year

| | |
|---|---|
| Storage costs | 3 |
| Insurance | 1 |
| Handling | 1 |
| Obsolescence | 3 |
| Opportunity costs of funds invested in stock | 10 |

'Fixed' costs associated with placing each order for stock are £311.54

The purchase price of the toys to Runswick Ltd is £4.50 per unit. There is a two week delay between the time that new stock is ordered from suppliers and the time that it arrives.

The toys are sold by Runswick at a unit price of £6.30. The variable cost to Runswick of selling the toys is £0.30 per unit. Demand from Runswick's customers for the toys averages 10 000 units per week, but recently this has varied from 6000 to 14 000 units per week. On the basis of recent evidence the probability of unit sales in any two week period has been estimated as follows:

| Sales (units) | Probability |
|---|---|
| 12 000 | 0.05 |
| 16 000 | 0.20 |
| 20 000 | 0.50 |
| 24 000 | 0.20 |
| 28 000 | 0.05 |

If adequate stock is not available when demanded by Runswick's customers in any two week period approximately 25% of orders that cannot be satisfied in that period will be lost, and approximately 75% of customers will be willing to wait until new stock arrives.

Required:

(a) Ignoring taxation, calculate the optimum order level of stock over a one year planning period using the economic order quantity model. (3 marks)

(b) Estimate the level of safety stock that should be carried by Runswick Ltd. (6 marks)

(c) If Runswick Ltd were to be offered a quantity discount by its suppliers of 1% for orders of 30 000 units or more, evaluate whether it would be beneficial for the company to take advantage of the quantity discount. Assume for this calculation that no safety stock is carried. (4 marks)

(d) Estimate the expected total annual costs of stock management if the economic order quantity had been (i) 50% higher (ii) 50% lower than its actual level. Comment upon the sensitivity of total annual costs to changes in the economic order quantity. Assume for this calculation that no safety stock is carried.

(4 marks)

(e) Discuss briefly how the effect of seasonal sales variations might be incorporated within the model. (3 marks)

(f) Assess the practical value of this model in the management of stock. (5 marks)

(Total 25 marks)

*ACCA Level 3 Financial Management*

**25.25\* Advanced: Safety stocks, uncertain demand and quantity discounts**

Kattalist Ltd is a distributor of an industrial chemical in the north east of England. The chemical is supplied in drums which have to be stored at a controlled temperature.

The company's objective is to maximize profits, and it commenced business on 1 October.

The managing director's view:

The company's managing director wishes to improve stock holding policy by applying the economic order quantity model. Each drum of the chemical costs £50 from a supplier and sells for £60. Annual demand is estimated to be for 10 000 drums, which the managing director assumes to be evenly distributed over 300 working days. The cost of delivery is estimated at £25 per order and the annual variable holding cost per drum at £45 plus 10% of purchase cost. Using these data the managing director calculates the economic order quantity and proposes that this should be the basis for purchasing decisions of the industrial chemical in future periods.

The purchasing manager's view:

Written into the contract of the company's purchasing manager is a clause that he will receive a bonus (rounded to the nearest £1) of 10% of the amount by which total annual inventory holding and order costs before such remuneration are below £10 000. Using the same assumptions as the managing director, the purchasing manager points out that in making his calculations the managing director has not only ignored her bonus but also the fact that suppliers offer quantity discounts on purchase orders. In fact, if the order size is 200 drums or above, the price per drum for an entire consignment is only £49.90, compared to £50 when an order is between 100 and 199 drums; and £50.10 when an order is between 50 and 99 drums.

The finance director's view.

The company's finance director accepts the need to consider quantity discounts and pay a bonus, but he also feels the managing director's approach is too simplistic. He points out that there is a lead time for

an order of 3 days and that demand has not been entirely even over the past year. Moreover, if the company has no drums in stock, it will lose specific orders as potential customers will go to rival competitors in the region to meet their immediate needs.

To support his argument the finance director summarizes the evidence from salesmen's records over the past year, which show the number of drums demanded during the lead times were as follows:

| Drums demanded during 3 day lead time | Number of times each quantity of drums was demanded |
|---|---|
| 106 | 4 |
| 104 | 10 |
| 102 | 16 |
| 100 | 40 |
| 98 | 14 |
| 96 | 14 |
| 94 | 2 |

In the circumstances, the managing director decides he should seek further advice on what course of action he should take.

Requirements:

(a) Calculate the economic order quantity as originally determined by the company's managing director. (1 mark)

(b) Calculate the optimum economic order quantity, applying the managing director's assumptions and after allowing for the purchasing manager's bonus and for supplier quantity discounts, but without using an expected value approach. (3 marks)

(c) Adopting the financial director's assumptions and an expected value approach, and assuming that it is a condition of the supplier's contract that the order quantity is to be constant for all orders in the year, determine the expected level of safety (i.e. buffer) stock the company should maintain. For this purpose, use the figures for the economic order quantity you have derived in answering (b). Show all workings and state any assumptions you make. (5 marks)

(d) As an outside consultant, write a report to the managing director on the company's stock ordering and stock holding policies, referring where necessary to your answers to (a)–(c).

The report should *inter alia* refer to other factors he should consider when taking his final decisions on stock ordering and stock holding policies.                                      (9 marks)

*Note*: Ignore taxation.

(Total 18 marks)

*ICAEW Management Accounting and Financial Management Part Two*

# The application of linear programming to management accounting

In the previous chapters we have seen that there is an opportunity cost for scarce resources that should be included in the relevant cost calculation for decision-making and variance calculations. Our previous discussions, however, have assumed that output is limited by one scarce resource, but in practice several resources may be scarce. The opportunity costs of these scarce resources can be determined by the use of linear programming techniques. Our objective in this chapter is to examine linear programming techniques and to consider how they can be applied to some specific types of decisions that a firm may have to make.

## Learning objectives

After studying this chapter, you should be able to:

- formulate the linear programming model and calculate marginal rates of substitution and opportunity costs using the graphical approach;

- construct the initial tableau using the Simplex method;

- explain the meaning of the entries in each column of the final tableau;

- describe how linear programming can be used in decision-making, planning and control;

- formulate the linear programming model that will maximize net present value;

- identify the major deficiencies of linear programming.

## Single-resource constraints

In Chapter 9 we considered how accounting information should be used to ensure that scarce resources are efficiently allocated. We established that where a scarce resource exists, that has alternative uses, the contribution per unit should be calculated for each of

**EXHIBIT 26.1**

*A single-resource constraint problem*

these uses. The available capacity for this resource is then allocated to the alternative uses on the basis of contribution per scarce resource. A typical problem is presented in Exhibit 26.1.

If we follow the procedure suggested in Chapter 9, we can ascertain the contribution per unit of the scarce resource. Product Y yields a contribution of

The LP company currently produces two products. The standards per unit of product are as follows:

| Product Y | (£) | (£) | Product Z | (£) | (£) |
|---|---|---|---|---|---|
| Standard selling price | | 110 | Standard selling price | | 118 |
| Less standard costs: | | | Less standard costs: | | |
| Materials (8 units at £4) | 32 | | Materials (4 units at £4) | 16 | |
| Labour (6 hours at £10) | 60 | | Labour (8 hours at £10) | 80 | |
| Variable overhead | | | Variable overhead | | |
| (4 machine hours at £1) | 4 | | (6 machine hours at £1) | 6 | |
| | | 96 | | | 102 |
| Contribution | | 14 | Contribution | | 16 |

During the next accounting period, it is expected that the availability of labour hours will be restricted to 2880 hours. The remaining production inputs are not scarce, but the marketing manager estimates that the maximum sales potential for product Y is 420 units. There is no sales limitation for product Z.

£14 and uses 6 scarce labour hours. Hence the contribution is £2.33 per labour hour. Similarly, the contribution per labour hour for product Z is £2. The company should therefore allocate scarce labour hours to the manufacture of product Y. Sales of product Y, however, are limited to 420 units, which means that 2520 labour hours (420 units at 6 hours per unit) will be used. The remaining 360 hours will then be allocated to product Z. As one unit of product Z requires 8 labour hours, the total output of product Z will be 45 units.

Profits will be maximized when the firm manufactures 420 units of product Y and 45 units of product Z. This will give a total contribution of £6600, which is calculated as follows:

| | (£) |
|---|---|
| 420 units of Y at a contribution of £14 per unit | 5880 |
| 45 units of Z at a contribution of £16 per units | 720 |
| | 6600 |

## Two-resource constraints

Where more than one scarce resource exists, the optimum production programme cannot easily be established by the process previously outlined. Consider the situation in Exhibit 26.1, where there is an additional scarce resource besides labour. Let us assume that both products Y and Z use a common item of material and that the supply of this material in the next accounting period is restricted to 3440 units. There are now two scarce resources – labour and materials. If we apply the procedure outlined above, the contribution per unit of scarce resource would be as follows:

| | Product Y (£) | Product Z (£) |
|---|---|---|
| Labour | 2.33 (£14/6 hours) | 2.00 (£16/8 hours) |
| Material | 1.75 (£14/8 units) | 4.00 (£16/4 units) |

This analysis shows that product Y yields the largest contribution per labour hour, and product Z yields the largest contribution per unit of scarce materials, but there is no clear indication of how the quantity of scarce resources should be allocated to each product. In such circumstances there is a need to resort to higher-powered mathematical techniques to establish the optimal output programme.

# Linear programming

Linear programming is a powerful mathematical technique that can be applied to the problem of rationing limited facilities and resources among many alternative uses in such a way that the optimum benefits can be derived from their utilization. It seeks to find a feasible combination of output that will maximize or minimize the objective function. The objective function refers to the quantification of an objective, and usually takes the form of maximizing profits or minimizing costs. Linear programming may be used when relationships can be assumed to be linear and where an optimal solution does in fact exist.

To comply with the linearity assumption, it must be assumed that the contribution per unit for each product and the utilization of resources per unit are the same whatever quantity of output is produced and sold within the output range being considered. It must also be assumed that units produced and resources allocated are infinitely divisible. This means that an optimal plan that suggests we should produce 94.38 units is possible. However, it will be necessary to interpret the plan as a production of 94 units.

Let us now apply this technique to the problem outlined in Exhibit 26.1, where there is a labour restriction plus a limitation on the availability of materials and machine hours. The revised problem is presented in Exhibit 26.2.

The procedure that we should follow to solve this problem is, first, to formulate the problem algebraically, with $Y$ denoting the number of units of product Y and $Z$ the number of units of product Z that are manufactured by the company. Secondly, we must specify the objective function, which in this example is to maximize contribution (denoted by $C$), followed by the input constraints. We can now formulate the linear programming model as follows:

$$\text{Maximize } C = 14Y + 16Z \text{ subject to}$$
$$8Y + 4Z \leqslant 3440 \text{ (material constraint)}$$
$$6Y + 8Z \leqslant 2880 \text{ (labour constraint)}$$
$$4Y + 6Z \leqslant 2760 \text{ (machine capacity constraint)}$$
$$0 \leqslant Y \leqslant 420 \text{ (maximum and minimum sales limitation)}$$
$$Z \geqslant 0 \text{ (minimum sales limitation)}$$

In this model, 'maximize $C$' indicates that we wish to maximize contribution with an unknown number of units of $Y$ produced, each yielding a contribution of £14 per unit, and an unknown number of units of $Z$ produced, each yielding a contribution of £16. The labour constraint indicates that 6 hours of labour are required for each unit of product Y that is made, and 8 hours for each unit of product Z. Thus (6 hours × Y) + (8 hours × Z) cannot exceed 2880 hours. Similar reasoning applies to the other inputs.

Because linear programming is nothing more than a mathematical tool for solving constrained optimization problems, nothing in the technique itself ensures that an answer will 'make sense'. For example, in a production

---

The LP company currently makes two products. The standards per unit of product are as follows:

| **Product Y** | (£) | (£) | **Product Z** | (£) | (£) |
|---|---|---|---|---|---|
| Product Y | | | Product Z | | |
| Standard selling price | | 110 | Standard selling price | | 118 |
| Less standard costs: | | | Less standard costs: | | |
|   Materials (8 units at £4) | 32 | |   Materials (4 units at £4) | 16 | |
|   Labour (6 hours at £10) | 60 | |   Labour (8 hours at £10) | 80 | |
|   Variable overhead | | |   Variable overhead | | |
|   (4 machine hours at £1) | 4 | |   (6 machine hours at £1) | 6 | |
| | | 96 | | | 102 |
| Contribution | | 14 | Contribution | | 16 |

During the next accounting period, the availability of resources are expected to be subject to the following limitations:

| | |
|---|---|
| Labour | 2800 hours |
| Materials | 3440 units |
| Machine capacity | 2760 hours |

The marketing manager estimates that the maximum sales potential for product Y is limited to 420 units. There is no sales limitation for product Z. You are asked to advise how these limited facilities and resources can best be used so as to gain the optimum benefit from them.

---

problem, for some very unprofitable product, the optimal output level may be a negative quantity, which is clearly an impossible solution. To prevent such non-sensical results, we must include a non-negativity requirement, which is a statement that all variables in the problem must be equal to or greater than zero. We must therefore add to the model in our example the constraint that $Y$ and $Z$ must be greater than or equal to zero, i.e. $Z \geqslant 0$ and $0 \leqslant Y \leqslant 420$. The latter expression indicates that sales of Y cannot be less than zero or greater than 420 units. The model can be solved graphically, or by the Simplex method. When no more than two products are manufactured, the graphical method can be used, but this becomes impracticable where more than two products are involved, and it is then necessary to resort to the Simplex method.

# Graphical method

Taking the first *constraint for the materials* input $8Y + 4Z \leqslant 3440$ means that we can make a maximum of 860 units of product Z when production of product Y is zero. The 960

**FIGURE 26.1** *Constraint imposed by limitations of materials.*

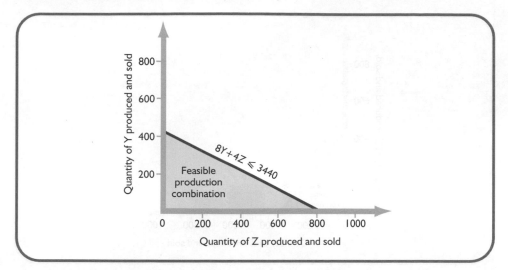

units is arrived at by dividing the 3440 units of materials by the 4 units of material required for each unit of product Z. Alternatively, a maximum of 430 units or product Y can be made (3440 units divided by 8 units of materials) if no materials are allocated to product Z. We can therefore state that

$$\text{when } Y = 0, Z = 860$$
$$\text{when } Z = 0, Y = 430$$

These items are plotted in Figure 26.1, with a straight line running from $Z = 0$, $Y = 430$ to $Y = 0$, $Z = 860$. Note that the vertical axis represents the number of units of $Y$ produced and the horizontal axis the number of units of Z produced.

The area to the left of line $8Y + 4Z \leqslant 3440$ contains all possible solutions for $Y$ and $Z$ in this particular situation, and any point along the line connecting these two outputs represents the maximum combinations of $Y$ and $Z$ that can be produced with not more than 3440 units of materials. Every point to the right of the line violates the material constraint.

The *labour constraint* $6Y + 8Z \leqslant 2880$ indicates that if production of product Z is zero, then a maximum of 480 units of product Y can be produced (2880/6), and if the output of Y is zero then 360 units of Z (2880/8) can be produced. We can now draw a second line $Y = 480$, $Z = 0$ to $Y = 0$, $Z = 360$, and this is illustrated in Figure 26.2. The area to the left of line $6Y + 8Z \leqslant 2880$ in this figure represents all the possible solutions that will satisfy the labour constraint.

The *machine input constraint* is represented by $Z = 0$, $Y = 690$ and $Y = 0$, $Z = 460$, and the line indicating this constraint is illustrated in Figure 26.3. The area to the left of the line $4Y + 6Z \leqslant 2760$ in this figure represents all the possible solutions that will satisfy the machine capacity constraint.

The final constraint is that the *sales output* of product Y cannot exceed 420 units. This is represented by the line $Y \leqslant 420$ in Figure 26.4, and all the items below this line represent all the possible solutions that will satisfy this sales limitation.

It is clear that any solution that is to fit all the constraints must occur in the shaded area ABCDE in Figure 26.5, which represents Figures 26.1–26.4 combined together. The point must now be found within the shaded area ABCDE where the contribution $C$ is the greatest. The maximum will occur at one of the corner points ABCDE. The objective function is $C = 14Y + 16Z$, and a random contribution value is chosen that will result in a line for the objective function falling within the area ABCDE.

**FIGURE 26.2** *Constraint imposed by limitations of labour.*

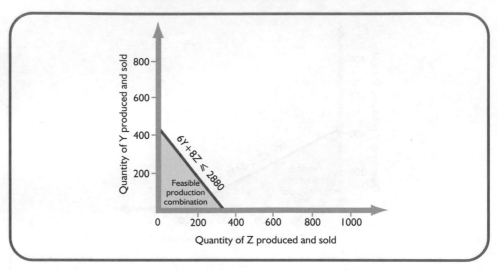

**FIGURE 26.3** *Constraint imposed by machine capacity.*

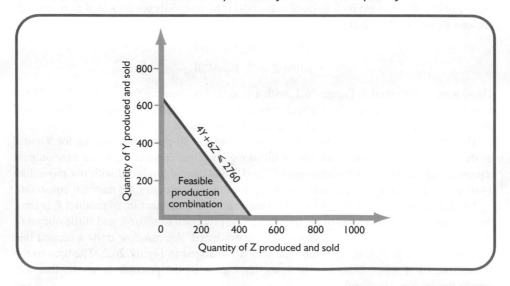

If we choose a random total contribution value equal to £2240, this could be obtained from producing 160 units of Y at £14 contribution per unit or 140 units of Z at a contribution of £16 per unit. We can therefore draw a line $Z = 0$, $Y = 160$ to $Y = 0$, $Z = 140$. This is represented by the dashed line in Figure 26.5. Each point on the dashed line represents all the output combinations of Z and Y that will yield a total contribution of £2240. The dashed line is extended to the right until it touches the last corner of the boundary ABCDE. This is the optimal solution and is at point C, which indicates an output of 400 units of Y (contribution £5600) and 60 units of Z (contribution £960), giving a total contribution of £6560.

The logic in the previous paragraph is illustrated in Figure 26.6. The shaded area represents the feasible production area ABCDE that is outlined in Figure 26.5, and parallel lines represent possible contributions, which take on higher values as we move to the right.

**FIGURE 26.4** *Constraint imposed by sales limitation of product Y.*

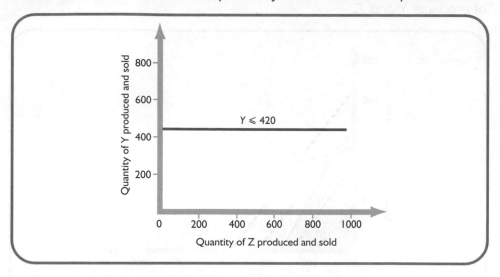

**FIGURE 26.5** *Combination of Figures 26.1–26.4.*

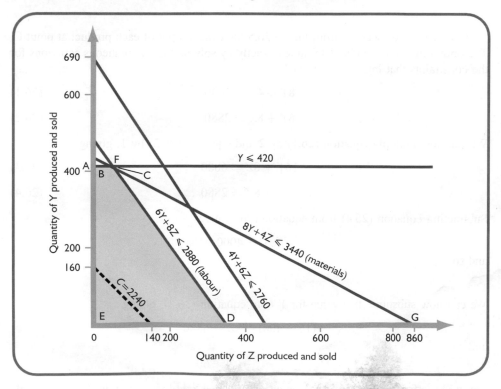

If we assume that the firm's objective is to maximize total contribution, it should operate on the highest contribution curve obtainable. At the same time, it is necessary to satisfy the production constraints, which are indicated by the shaded area in Figure 26.6. You will see that point C indicates the solution to the problem, since no other point within the feasible area touches such a high contribution line.

**FIGURE 26.6** *Contribution levels from different potential combinations of products Y and Z.*

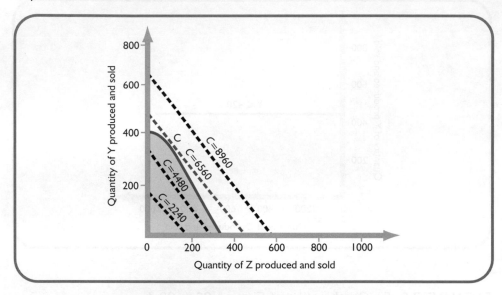

It is difficult to ascertain from Figure 26.5 the exact output of each product at point C. The optimum output can be determined exactly by solving the simultaneous equations for the constraints that intersect at point C:

$$8Y + 4Z = 3440 \tag{26.1}$$

$$6Y + 8Z = 2880 \tag{26.2}$$

We can now multiply equation (26.1) by 2 and equation (26.2) by 1, giving

$$16Y + 8Z = 6880 \tag{26.3}$$

$$6Y + 8Z = 2880 \tag{26.4}$$

Subtracting equation (26.4) from equation (26.3) gives

$$10Y = 4000$$

and so

$$Y = 400$$

We can now substitute this value for $Y$ onto equation (26.3), giving

$$(16 \times 400) + 8Z = 6880$$

and so

$$Z = 60$$

You will see from Figure 26.5 that the constraints that are binding at point C are materials and labour. It might be possible to remove these constraints and acquire additional labour and materials resources by paying a premium over and above the existing acquisition cost. How much should the company be prepared to pay? To answer this question, it is necessary to determine the optimal use from an additional unit of a scarce resource.

We shall now consider how the optimum solution would change if an additional unit of materials were obtained. You can see that if we obtain additional materials, the line

$8Y + 4Z \leqslant 3440$ in Figure 26.5 will shift upwards and the revised optimum point will fall on line CF. If one extra unit of materials is obtained, the constraints $8Y + 4Z \leqslant 3440$ and $6Y + 8Z \leqslant 2880$ will still be binding, and the new optimum plan can be determined by solving the following simultaneous equations:

$$8Y + 4Z = 3441 \text{ (revised materials constraint)}$$
$$6Y + 8Z = 2880 \text{ (unchanged labour constraint)}$$

The revised optimal output when the above equations are solved is 400.2 units of Y and 59.85 units of Z. Therefore the planned output of product Y should be increased by 0.2 units, and planned production of Z should be reduced by 0.15 units. This optimal response from an independent marginal increase in a resource is called the **marginal rate of substitution**. The change in contribution arising from obtaining one additional unit of materials is as follows:

|  | **(£)** |
| --- | --- |
| Increase in contribution from $Y$ $(0.2 \times £14)$ | 2.80 |
| Decrease in contribution of $Z$ $(0.15 \times £16)$ | (2.40) |
| Increase in contribution | 0.40 |

Therefore the value of an additional unit of materials is £0.40. The value of an independent marginal increase of scarce resource is called the **opportunity cost** or **shadow price**. We shall be considering these terms in more detail later in the chapter. You should note at this stage that for materials purchased in excess of 3440 units the company can pay up to £0.40 over and above the present acquisition cost of materials of £4 and still obtain a contribution towards fixed costs from the additional output.

From a practical point of view, it is not possible to produce 400.2 units of Y and 59.85 units of Z. Output must be expressed in single whole units. Nevertheless, the output from the model can be used to calculate the revised optimal output if additional units of materials are obtained. Assume that 100 additional units of materials can be purchased at £4.20 per unit from an overseas supplier. Because the opportunity cost (£0.40) is in excess of the additional acquisition cost of £0.20 per unit (£4.20 − £4), the company should purchase the extra materials. The marginal rates of substitution can be used to calculate the revised optimum output. The calculation is

$$\text{Increase } Y \text{ by 20 units } (100 \times 0.2 \text{ units})$$
$$\text{Decrease } Z \text{ by 15 units } (100 \times 0.15 \text{ units})$$

Therefore the revised optimal output is 420 outputs $(400 + 20)$ of Y and 35 units $(60 − 15)$ of Z. You will see later in this chapter that the substitution process outlined above is applicable only within a particular range of material usage.

We can apply the same approach to calculate the opportunity cost of labour. If an additional labour hour is obtained, the line $6Y + 8Z \leqslant 2880$ in Figure 26.5 will shift to the right, and the revised optimal point will fall on line CG. The constraints $8Y + 4Z \leqslant 3440$ and $6Y + 8Z \leqslant 2880$ will still be binding, and the new optimum plan can be determined by solving the following simultaneous equations:

$$8Y + 4Z = 3440 \text{ (unchanged materials constraint)}$$
$$6Y + 8Z = 2881 \text{ (revised labour constraint)}$$

The revised optimal output when the above equations are solved is 399.9 units of Y and 60.2 units of Z. Therefore the planned output of product Y should be decreased by 0.1

units and planned production of Z should be increased by 0.2 units. The opportunity cost of a scarce labour hour is

|  | (£) |
|---|---|
| Decrease in contribution from $Y$ (0.1 × £14) | (1.40) |
| Increase in contribution from $Z$ (0.2 × £16) | 3.20 |
| Increase in contribution (opportunity cost) | 1.80 |

# Simplex method

**AR** Where more than two products can be manufactured using the scarce resources available, the optimum solution cannot easily be established from the graphical method. An alternative is a non-graphical solution known as the **Simplex method**. This method also provides additional information on opportunity costs and marginal rates of substitution that is particularly useful for decision-making, and also for planning and control.

The Simplex method involves making many tedious calculations, but there are standard computer programs that will complete the task within a few minutes. The aim of this chapter is therefore not to delve into these tedious calculations but rather to provide an understanding of their nature and their implications for management accounting. Nevertheless, to provide a basic understanding of the method, the procedure for completing the calculations must be outlined, and we shall do this by applying the procedure to the problem set out in Exhibit 26.2.

To apply the Simplex method, we must first formulate a model that does not include any *inequalities*. This is done by introducing what are called **slack variables** to the model. Slack variables are added to a linear programming problem to account for any constraint that is unused at the point of optimality, and one slack variable is introduced for each constraint. In our example, the company is faced with constraints on materials, labour, machine capacity and maximum sales for product Y. Therefore $S_1$ is introduced to represent unused material resources, $S_2$ represents unused labour hours, $S_3$ represents unused machine capacity and $S_4$ represents unused potential sales output. We can now express the model for Exhibit 26.2 in terms of equalities rather than inequalities:

$$\text{Maximize } C = 14Y + 16Z$$

subject to

$$8Y + 4Z + S_1 = 3440 \text{ (materials constraint)}$$
$$6Y + 8Z + S_2 = 2880 \text{ (labour constraint)}$$
$$4Y + 6Z + S_3 = 2760 \text{ (machine capacity constraint)}$$
$$1Y + S_4 = 420 \text{ (sales constraint for product } Y)$$

For labour (6 hours × Y) + (8 hours × Z) plus any unused labour hours ($S_2$) will equal 2880 hours when the optimum solution is reached. Similar reasoning applies to the other production constraints. The sales limitation indicates that the number of units of Y sold plus any shortfall on maximum demand will equal 420 units.

We shall now express all the above equations in matrix form, with the slack variables on the left-hand side:

*First matrix*

| Quantity | Y | Z | |
|---|---|---|---|
| $S_1 = 3440$ | −8 | −4 | (1) (material constraint) |
| $S_2 = 2880$ | −6 | −8 | (2) (labour constraint) |
| $S_3 = 2760$ | −4 | −6 | (3) (machine hours constraint) |
| $S_4 = 420$ | −1 | 0 | (4) (sales constraint) |
| $C = 0$ | +14 | +16 | (5) contribution |

Note that the quantity column in the matrix indicates the resources available or the slack that is not taken up when production is zero. For example, the $S_1$ row of the matrix indicates that 3440 units of materials are available when production is zero. Column $Y$ indicates that 8 units of materials, 6 labour hours and 4 machine hours are required to produce 1 unit of product Y, and this will reduce the potential sales of Y by 1. You will also see from column $Y$ that the production of 1 unit of Y will yield £14 contribution. Similar reasoning applies to column $Z$. Note that the entry in the contribution row (i.e. the $C$ row) for the quantity column is zero because this first matrix is based on nil production, which gives a contribution of zero.

## CHOOSING THE PRODUCT

The next stage is to examine the matrix to determine which product we should choose. As product Z yields the highest contribution, we should choose this, but our production is limited because of the input constraints. Materials limit us to a maximum production of 860 units (3440 units/4 per unit), labour to a maximum production of 360 units (2880 hours/8 per hour) and machine capacity to a maximum production of 460 units (2760 hours/6 per hour). We are therefore restricted to a maximum production of 360 units of product Z because of a labour constraint. The procedure that we should follow is to *rearrange the equation that results in the constraint (i.e. $S_2$) in terms of the product we have chosen to make (i.e. product Z)*. Therefore equation (2), which is

becomes

$$S_2 = 2880 − 6Y − 8Z$$
$$8Z = 2880 − 6Y − S_2$$

and so

$$Z = 360 − 3/4Y − 1/8 S_2$$

We now substitute this value for $Z$ into each of the other equations appearing in the first matrix. The calculations are as follows:

$$S_1 = 3440 - 8Y - 4(360 - \tfrac{3}{4}Y - \tfrac{1}{8}S_2)$$
$$= 3440 - 8Y - 1440 + 3Y + \tfrac{1}{2}S_2 \tag{1}$$
$$= 2000 - 5Y + \tfrac{1}{2}S_2$$

$$S_3 = 2760 - 4Y - 6(360 - \tfrac{3}{4}Y - \tfrac{1}{8}S_2)$$
$$= 2760 - 4Y - 2160 + 4\tfrac{1}{2}Y + \tfrac{3}{4}S_2 \tag{3}$$
$$= 600 + \tfrac{1}{2}Y + \tfrac{3}{4}S_2$$

$$C = 0 + 14Y + 16(360 - \tfrac{3}{4}Y - \tfrac{1}{8}S_2)$$
$$= 0 + 14Y + 5760 - 12Y - 2S_2 \tag{5}$$
$$= 5760 + 2Y - 2S_2$$

Note that equation (4) in the first matrix remains unchanged because $Z$ is not included. We can now restate the revised five equations in a second matrix:

Second matrix

| Quantity | $Y$ | $S_2$ | |
|---|---|---|---|
| $S_1 = 2000$ | $-5$ | $+\tfrac{1}{2}$ | (1) (material constraint) |
| $Z = 360$ | $-\tfrac{3}{4}$ | $-\tfrac{1}{8}$ | (2) |
| $S_3 = 600$ | $+\tfrac{1}{2}$ | $+\tfrac{3}{4}$ | (3) (machine hours constraint) |
| $S_4 = 420$ | $-1$ | $0$ | (4) (sales constraint) |
| $C = 5760$ | $+2$ | $-2$ | (5) |

The substitution process outlined for the second matrix has become more complex, but the logical basis still remains. For example, the *quantity column* of the second matrix indicates that 2000 units of material are unused, 360 units of Z are to be made, 600 machine hours are still unused and sales of product Y can still be increased by another 420 units before the sales limitation is reached. The contribution row indicates that a contribution of £5760 will be obtained from the production and sale of 360 units of product Z. Column $Y$ indicates that production of 1 unit of product Y uses up 5 units of the stock of materials, but, because no labour hours are available, $\tfrac{3}{4}$ units of product Z must be released. This will release three units of materials ($\tfrac{3}{4} \times 4$), 6 labour hours ($\tfrac{3}{4} \times 8$ hours) and $4\tfrac{1}{2}$ machine hours ($\tfrac{3}{4} \times 6$). From this substitution process we now have 8 units of materials (5 units + 3 units), 6 labour hours and $4\tfrac{1}{2}$ machine hours.[1]

From the standard cost details in Exhibit 26.2 you can see that one unit of Y requires 8 units of materials, 6 labour hours and 4 machine hours. This substitution process thus provides the necessary resources for producing 1 unit of product Y, as well as providing an additional half an hour of machine capacity. This is because production of 1 unit of product Y requires that production of item Z be reduced by $\tfrac{3}{4}$ units, which releases $4\tfrac{1}{2}$ machine hours. However, product Y only requires 4 machine hours, so production of 1 unit of Y will increase the available machine capacity by half an hour. This agrees with the entry in column $Y$ of the second matrix for machine capacity. Column Y also indicates that production of 1 unit of Y reduces the potential sales of product Y ($S_4$) by 1 unit.

*The optimum solution is achieved when the contribution row contains only negative or zero values.* Because row $C$ contains a positive item, our current solution can be improved by choosing the product with the highest positive contribution. Thus we should choose to manufacture product Y, since this is the only positive item in the contribution row. The second matrix indicates that the contribution can be increased by £2 by substituting 1 unit of Y for $\frac{3}{4}$ units of Z. We therefore obtain an additional contribution of £14 from Y but lose a £12 contribution from Z ($\frac{3}{4} \times 16$) by this substitution process. The overall result is an increased contribution of £2 by adopting this substitution process.

The procedure is then repeated to formulate the third matrix. Column $Y$ of the second matrix indicates that we should use 5 units of materials and release $\frac{3}{4}$ units of Z to obtain an additional unit of Y, but there are limitations in adopting this plan. The unused materials are 2000 units, and each unit of Y will require 5 units, giving a maximum production of 400 units of Y. We have 360 units of Z allocated to production, and each unit of Y requires us to release $\frac{3}{4}$ units of Z. A maximum production of 480 units of Y ($360/\frac{3}{4}$) can therefore be obtained from this substitution process. There is no limitation on machine hours, since the second matrix indicates that the substitution process increases machine hours by half an hour for each unit of Y produced. The sales limitation of Y indicates that a maximum of 420 units of Y can be produced. The following is a summary of the limitations in producing product Y:

$S_1$ (materials) = 400 units (2000/5)
$Z$ (substitution of product Z) = 480 units ($360/\frac{3}{4}$)
$S_4$ (maximum sales of Y) = 420 units (420/1)

In other words, we merely divide the *negative* items in column $Y$ into the quantity column. The first limitation we reach is 400 units, and this indicates the maximum production of Y because of the impact of the materials constraint.

The procedure that we applied in formulating the second matrix is then repeated; that is, *we rearrange the equation that results in the constraint ($S_1$) in terms of the product we have chosen to make (i.e. product Y)*. Therefore equation (1), which is

$$S_1 = 2000 - 5Y + \tfrac{1}{2}S_2$$

becomes

$$5Y = 2000 - S_1 + \tfrac{1}{2}S_2$$

and so

$$Y = 400 - \tfrac{1}{5}S_1 + \tfrac{1}{10}S_2$$

Substituting for Y in each of the other equations in the second matrix, we get the following revised equations:

$$Z = 360 - \tfrac{3}{4}(400 - \tfrac{1}{5}S_1 + \tfrac{1}{10}S_2) - \tfrac{1}{8}S_2 \tag{2}$$
$$= 360 - 300 + \tfrac{3}{20}S_1 - \tfrac{3}{40}S_2 - \tfrac{1}{8}S_2$$
$$= 60 + \tfrac{3}{20}S_1 - \tfrac{1}{5}S_2$$
$$S_3 = 600 + \tfrac{1}{2}(400 - \tfrac{1}{5}S_1 + \tfrac{1}{10}S_2) + \tfrac{3}{4}S_2 \tag{3}$$
$$= 600 + 200 - \tfrac{1}{10}S_1 + \tfrac{1}{20}S_2 + \tfrac{3}{4}S_2$$
$$= 800 - \tfrac{1}{10}S_1 + \tfrac{4}{5}S_2$$
$$S_4 = 420 - 1(400 - \tfrac{1}{5}S_1 + \tfrac{1}{10}S_2) \tag{4}$$
$$= 20 + \tfrac{1}{5}S_1 - \tfrac{1}{10}S_2$$
$$C = 5760 + 2(400 - \tfrac{1}{5}S_1 + \tfrac{1}{10}S_2) = 2S_2 \tag{5}$$
$$= 5760 + 800 - \tfrac{2}{5}S_1 + \tfrac{1}{5}S_2 - 2S_2$$
$$= 6560 - \tfrac{2}{5}S_1 - 1\tfrac{4}{5}S_2$$

We now restate the revised five equations in a third matrix:

*Third matrix*

| Quantity | | $S_1$ | $S_2$ | |
|---|---|---|---|---|
| $Y = 400$ | | $-\frac{1}{5}$ | $+\frac{1}{10}$ | (1) |
| $Z = 60$ | | $+\frac{3}{20}$ | $-\frac{1}{5}$ | (2) |
| $S_3 = 800$ | | $-\frac{1}{10}$ | $+\frac{4}{5}$ | (3) |
| $S_4 = 20$ | | $+\frac{1}{5}$ | $-\frac{1}{10}$ | (4) |
| $C = 6560$ | | $-\frac{2}{5}$ | $-1\frac{4}{5}$ | (5) |

The contribution row (equation (5)) contains only negative items, which signifies that the optimal solution has been reached. The quantity column for any products listed on the left hand side of the matrix indicates the number of units of the product that should be manufactured when the optimum solution is reached. 400 units of Y and 60 units of Z should therefore be produced, giving a total contribution of £6560. This agrees with the results we obtained using the graphical method. *When an equation appears for a slack variable, this indicates that unused resources exist.* The third matrix therefore indicates that the optimal plan will result in 800 unused machine hours ($S_3$) and an unused sales potential of 20 units for product Y ($S_4$). The fact that there is no equation for $S_1$ and $S_2$ means that these are the inputs that are fully utilized and that limit further increases in output and profit.

# Interpreting the final matrix

The $S_1$ column (materials) of the third matrix indicates that the materials are fully utilized. (*Whenever resources appear as column headings in the final matrix, this indicates that they are fully utilized.*) So, to obtain a unit of materials, the column for $S_1$ indicates that we must alter the optimum production programme by increasing production of product Z by $\frac{3}{20}$ of a unit and decreasing production of product Y by $\frac{1}{5}$ of a unit. The effect of removing one scarce unit of material from the production process is summarized in Exhibit 26.3.

Let us focus on the machine capacity column of Exhibit 26.3. If we increase production of product Z by $\frac{3}{20}$ of a unit then more machine hours will be required, leading to the available capacity being reduced by $\frac{9}{10}$ of an hour. Each unit of product Z requires 6 machine hours, so $\frac{3}{20}$ of a unit will require $\frac{9}{10}$ of an hour ($\frac{3}{20} \times 6$). Decreasing production of product Y by $\frac{1}{5}$ unit

**EXHIBIT 26.3**

*The effect of removing 1 unit of material from the optimum production programme*

| | $S_3$ Machine capacity | $S_4$ Sales of Y | $S_1$ Materials | $S_2$ Labour | Contribution (£) |
|---|---|---|---|---|---|
| Increase product Z by $\frac{3}{20}$ of a unit | $-\frac{9}{10}(\frac{3}{20} \times 6)$ | — | $-\frac{3}{5}(\frac{3}{20} \times 4)$ | $-1\frac{1}{5}(\frac{3}{20} \times 8)$ | $+2\frac{2}{5}(\frac{3}{20} \times 16)$ |
| Decrease product Y by $\frac{1}{5}$ of a unit | $+\frac{4}{5}(\frac{1}{5} \times 4)$ | $+\frac{1}{5}$ | $+1\frac{3}{5}(\frac{1}{5} \times 8)$ | $+1\frac{1}{5}(\frac{1}{5} \times 6)$ | $-2\frac{4}{5}(\frac{1}{5} \times 14)$ |
| Net effect | $-\frac{1}{10}$ | $+\frac{1}{5}$ | $+1$ | Nil | $-\frac{2}{5}$ |

will release $\frac{4}{5}$ of a machine hour, given that 1 unit of product Y requires 4 machine hours. The overall effect of this process is to reduce the available machine capacity by $\frac{1}{10}$ of a machine hour. Similar principles apply to the other calculations presented in Exhibit 26.3.

Let us now reconcile the information set out in Exhibit 26.3 with the materials column ($S_1$) of the third matrix. The $S_1$ column indicates that to release 1 unit of materials from the optimum production programme we should increase the output of product Z by $\frac{3}{20}$, and decrease product Y by $\frac{1}{5}$ of a unit. This substitution process will lead to the unused machine capacity being reduced by $\frac{1}{10}$ of a machine hour, an increase in the unfulfilled sales demand of product Y ($S_4$) by $\frac{1}{5}$ of a unit and a reduction in contribution of £$\frac{2}{5}$. All this information is obtained from column $S_1$ of the third matrix, and Exhibit 26.3 provides the proof. Note that Exhibit 26.3 also proves that the substitution process that is required to obtain an additional unit of materials releases exactly 1 unit. In addition, Exhibit 26.3 indicates that the substitution process for labour gives a net effect of zero, and so no entries appear in the $S_1$ column of the third matrix in respect of the labour row (i.e. $S_2$).

# Opportunity cost

The contribution row of the final matrix contains some vital information for the accountant. The figures in this row represent opportunity costs (also known as shadow prices) for the scarce factors of materials and labour. For example, the reduction in contribution from the loss of 1 unit of materials is £$\frac{2}{5}$ (£0.40) and from the loss of one labour hour is £$1\frac{4}{5}$ (£1.80). Our earlier studies have indicated that this information is vital for decision-making, and we shall use this information again shortly to establish the relevant costs of the resources.

The proof of the opportunity costs can be found in Exhibit 26.3. From the contribution column we can see that the loss of one unit of materials leads to a loss of contribution of £0.40.

# Substitution process when additional resources are obtained

Management may be able to act to remove a constraint which is imposed by the shortage of a scarce resource. For example, the company might obtain substitute materials or it may purchase the materials from an overseas supplier. A situation may therefore occur where resources additional to those included in the model used to derive the optimum solution are available. In such circumstances the marginal rates of substitution specified in the final matrix can indicate the optimum use of the additional resources. However, when additional resources are available it is necessary to *reverse* the signs in the final matrix. The reason is that the removal of one unit of materials from the optimum production programme requires that product Z be increased by $\frac{3}{20}$ of a unit and product Y decreased by $\frac{1}{5}$ of a unit. If we then decide to return released materials to the optimum production programme, we must reverse this process—that is, increase product Y by $\frac{1}{5}$ of a unit and reduce product Z by $\frac{3}{20}$ of a unit. The important point to remember is that *when considering the response to obtaining additional resources over and above those specified in the initial model, the signs of all the items in the final matrix must be reversed.*

We can now establish how we should best use an additional unit of scarce materials. Inspection of the third matrix indicates that product Y should be increased by $\frac{1}{5}$ of a unit and product Z reduced by $\frac{3}{20}$, giving an additional contribution of £0.40. Note that this is identical with the solution we obtained using the graphical method.

Note that this process will lead to an increase in machine hours of $\frac{1}{10}$ hour ($S_3$) and a decrease in potential sales of product Y by $\frac{1}{5}$ ($S_4$). Similarly, if we were to obtain an additional labour hour, we should increase production of Z by $\frac{1}{5}$ of a unit and decrease production of product Y by $\frac{1}{10}$ of a unit, which would yield an additional contribution of £1.80. These are the most efficient uses that can be obtained from additional labour and material resources. From a practical point of view, decisions will not involve the use of fractions; for example, the LP company considered here might be able to obtain 200 additional labour hours; the final matrix indicates that optimal production plan should be altered by increasing production of product Z by 40 units (200 × $\frac{1}{5}$ of a unit) and decreasing production of product Y by 20 units. This process will lead to machine capacity being reduced by 160 hours and potential sales of product Y being increased by 20 units. ●●●

# Uses of linear programming

## CALCULATION OF RELEVANT COSTS

The calculation of relevant costs is essential for decision-making. When a resource is scarce, alternative uses exist that provide a contribution. An opportunity cost is therefore incurred whenever the resource is used. The relevant cost for a scarce resource is calculated as

$$\text{acquisition cost of resource} + \text{opportunity cost}$$

When more than one scarce resource exists, the opportunity cost should be established using linear programming techniques. Let us now calculate the relevant costs for the resources used by the LP company. The costs are as follows:

| | |
|---|---|
| materials | = £4.40 (£4 acquisition cost plus £0.40 opportunity cost) |
| labour | = £11.80 (£10 acquisition cost plus £1.80 opportunity cost) |
| variable overheads | = £1.00 (£1 acquisition cost plus zero opportunity cost) |
| fixed overheads | = nil |

Because variable overheads are assumed to vary in proportion to machine hours, and because machine hours are not scarce, no opportunity costs arise for variable overheads. Fixed overheads have not been included in the model, since they do not vary in the short term with changes in activity. The relevant cost for fixed overheads is therefore zero.

## SELLING DIFFERENT PRODUCTS

Let us now assume that the company is contemplating selling a modified version of product Y (called product L) in a new market. The market price is £160 and the product requires 10 units input of each resource. Should this product L be manufactured? Conventional accounting information does not provide us with the information necessary to make this decision. Product L can be made only by restricting output of Y and Z, because of the input constraints, and we need to know the opportunity costs of releasing the scarce resources to this new product. Opportunity costs were incorporated in our calculation of the relevant costs for each of the resources, and so the relevant information for the decision is as follows:

|  | (£) | (£) |
|---|---|---|
| Selling price of product L |  | 160 |
| Less relevant costs: |  |  |
|    Materials (10 × 4.40) | 44 |  |
|    Labour (10 × 11.80) | 118 |  |
|    Variable overhead (10 × 1.00) | 10 |  |
| Contribution |  | 172 |
|  |  | (−12) |

Total planned contribution will be reduced by £12 for each unit produced of product L.

## MAXIMUM PAYMENT FOR ADDITIONAL SCARCE RESOURCES

Opportunity costs provide important information in situations where a company can obtain additional scarce resources, but only at a premium. How much should the company be prepared to pay? For example, the company may be able to remove the labour constraint by paying overtime. The matrix indicates that the company can pay up to an additional £1.80 over and above the standard wage rate for each hour worked in excess of 2880 hours and still obtain a contribution from the use of this labour hour. The total contribution will therefore be improved by any additional payment below £1.80 per hour. Similarly, LP will improve the total contribution by paying up to £0.40 in excess of the standard material cost for units obtained in excess of 3440 units. Hence the company will increase short-term profits by paying up to £11.80 for each additional labour hour in excess of 2880 hours and up to £4.40 for units of material that are acquired in excess of 3440 units.

## CONTROL

Opportunity costs are also important for cost control. In Chapter 19 we noted that standard costing could be improved by incorporating opportunity costs into the variance calculations. For example, material wastage is reflected in an adverse material usage variance. The responsibility centre should therefore be identified not only with the acquisition cost of £4 per unit but also with the opportunity cost of £0.40 from the loss of one scarce unit of materials. This process highlights the true cost of the inefficient usage of scarce resources and encourages responsibility heads to pay special attention to the control of scarce factors of production. This approach is particularly appropriate where a firm has adopted an optimized production technology (OPT) strategy (see Chapter 9) because variance arising from bottleneck operations will be reported in terms of opportunity cost rather than acquisition cost.

## CAPITAL BUDGETING

Linear programming can be used to determine the optimal investment programme when capital rationing exists. This topic is dealt with in the appendix to this chapter.

## SENSITIVITY ANALYSIS

**AR** Opportunity costs are of vital importance in making management decisions, but production constraints do not exist permanently, and therefore opportunity costs cannot be regarded as permanent. There is a need to ascertain the range over which the opportunity cost applies for each input. This information can be obtained from the final matrix. For materials we merely examine the negative items for column $S_1$ in the final matrix and divide each item into the quantity column as follows:

$$Y = 400/(-\tfrac{1}{5}) = -2000$$
$$S_3 = 800/(-\tfrac{1}{10}) = -8000$$

The number closest to zero in this calculation (namely $-2000$) indicates by how much the availability of materials used in the model can be reduced. Given that the model was established using 3440 units of materials, the lower limit of the range is 1440 units $(3440 - 2000)$. The upper limit is determined in a similar way. We divide the positive items in column $S_4$ into the quantity column as follows:

$$Z = 60/\tfrac{3}{20} = 400$$
$$S_4 = 20/\tfrac{1}{5} = 100$$

The lower number in the calculation (namely 100) indicates by how much the materials can be increased. Adding this to the 3440 units of materials indicates that the upper limit of the range is 3540 units. The opportunity cost and marginal rates of substitution for materials therefore apply over the range of 1440 to 3540 units.

Let us now consider the logic on which these calculations are based. The lower limit is determined by removing materials from the optimum production programme. We have previously established from the final matrix and Exhibit 26.3 that removing one unit of material from the optimum production programme means that product Y will be reduced by $\tfrac{1}{5}$ and machine capacity will be reduced by $\tfrac{1}{10}$ of an hour. Since the final matrix indicates an output of 400 units of product Y, this reduction can only be carried out 2000 times $(400/\tfrac{1}{5})$ before the process must stop. Similarly, 800 hours of machine capacity are still unused, and the reduction process can only be carried out 8000 times $(800/\tfrac{1}{10})$ before the process must stop. Given the two constraints on reducing materials, the first constraint that is reached is the reduction of product Y. The planned usage of materials can therefore be reduced by 2000 units before the substitution process must stop. The same reasoning applies (with the signs reversed) in understanding the principles for establishing the upper limit of the range.

Similar reasoning can be applied to establish that the opportunity cost and marginal rates of substitution apply for labour hours over a range of 2680 to 3880 hours. For any decisions based on scarce inputs outside the ranges specified a revised model must be formulated and a revised final matrix produced. From this matrix revised opportunity costs and marginal rates of substitution can be established. ●●●

## Self-Assessment Questions

You should attempt to answer these questions yourself before looking up the suggested answers, which appear on pages 1137–41. If any part of your answer is incorrect, check back carefully to make sure you understand where you went wrong.

1 LP Ltd is a manufacturing company that currently produces three products. The standards per unit of product are as follows:

|  | Product X | | Product Y | | Product Z | |
|---|---|---|---|---|---|---|
|  | (£) | (£) | (£) | (£) | (£) | (£) |
| Standard selling price |  | 49 |  | 23 |  | 24 |
| Less standard costs: |  |  |  |  |  |  |
| Materials | 2 units at £3 = 6 |  | 3 units at £3 = 9 |  | 4 units at £3 = 12 |  |
| Labour | 4 hours at £10 = 40 |  | 1 hour at £10 = 10 |  | 1 hour at £10 = 10 |  |
| Machine time | 1 hour at £1 = 1 | 47 | 5 hours at £1 = 5 | 24 | 1 hour at £1 = 1 | 23 |
| Standard profit | | 2 | | (−1) | | 1 |
| per unit |  |  |  |  |  |  |

*Note:* The charge for materials and labour is based on their cost of acquisition. The charge for machine time is based on the allocation of £8000 overheads (all of which are fixed costs) over an estimated capacity of 8000 hours.

During the next cost period, the availability of resources is expected to be subject to the following limitations:

> Materials 9000 units
> Labour 9200 hours
> Machinery 8000 hours

Furthermore, the output of the products is limited because of a marketing constraint. The marketing manager estimates the maximum sales of the 3 products to be as follows:

> Product X 2100 units
> Product Y 1400 units
> Product Z 380 units

During the next period, the standard costs and selling prices are expected to remain unchanged.

The managing director is aware that a rival company uses mathematical programming to plan its production, and has asked you to apply the same technique to the above data. You have used a computer package, and the following final linear programming model has just been received from the computer.

|  |  | *L* (labour) | *M/c* (machinery) | *SZ* (sales of Z)[a] |
|---|---|---|---|---|
| *M* (Materials) | 220 | 7/19 | 10/19 | 3.2/19 |
| *SY* (Sales of Y)[a] | 260 | −1/19 | 4/19 | −3/19 |
| *X* (Product X) | 1920 | −5/19 | 1/19 | 4/19 |

| | | | | |
|---|---|---|---|---|
| $SX$ (Sales of X)[a] | 180 | 5/19 | −1/19 | −4/19 |
| $Y$ (Product Y) | 1 140 | 1/19 | −4/19 | 3/19 |
| $Z$ (Product Z) | 380 | 0 | 0 | −1 |
| | 11 080 | −11/19 | −13/19 | −14/19 |

[a] $SX$, $SY$ and $SZ$ relate to slack variables for the sales demand for each product.

Required:

(a) Prepare the first tableau of the linear programming model to which the solution is given.
(5 marks)

(b) The managing director has requested an explanation of the meaning of the final tableau. You are required to provide an explanation of the meaning of each of the items in the final tableau, and also to provide any other information that would be of use that can be derived from the final tableau.
(14 marks)

(c) Discuss briefly the possible uses of linear programming for short-term planning, and indicate whether there are any limitations in using a model of this kind.
(6 marks)

2 Brass Ltd produces two products, the Masso and the Russo. Budgeted data relating to these products on a unit basis for August are as follows:

| | Masso (£) | Russo (£) |
|---|---|---|
| Selling price | 150 | 100 |
| Materials | 80 | 30 |
| Salesmen's commission | 30 | 20 |

Each unit of product incurs costs of machining and assembly. The total capacity available in August is budgeted to be 700 hours of machining and 1000 hours of assembly, the cost of this capacity being fixed at £7000 and £10 000 respectively for the month, whatever the level of usage made of it. The number of hours required in each of these departments to complete one unit of output is as follows:

| | Masso | Russo |
|---|---|---|
| Machining | 1.0 | 2.0 |
| Assembly | 2.5 | 2.0 |

Under the terms of special controls recently introduced by the Government in accordance with EEC requirements, selling prices are fixed and the maximum permitted output of either product in August is 400 units (i.e. Brass Ltd may produce a maximum of 800 units of product). At the present controlled selling prices the demand for the products exceeds this considerably.

You are required:

(a) to calculate Brass Ltd's optimal production plan for August, and the profit earned,
(10 marks)

(b) to calculate the value to Brass Ltd of an independent marginal increase in the available capacity for each of machining and assembly, assuming that the capacity of the other department is not altered and the output maxima continue to apply,
(10 marks)

(c) to state the principal assumptions underlying your calculations in (a) above, and to assess their general significance. (5 marks)

*ICAEW Management Accounting*

## Summary

When there is more than one scarce input factor, linear programming can be used to determine the production programme that maximizes total contribution. This information can be obtained by using either a graphical approach or the Simplex method. The graphical approach, however, is inappropriate where more than two products can be produced from the scarce inputs, and in such a situation the Simplex method should be used. This method has the added advantage that the output from the model provides details of the opportunity costs and the marginal rates of substitutions for the scarce resources.

Linear programming can be applied to a variety of management accounting problems. In particular, the technique enables the relevant cost of production inputs to be computed. This information can

be used for decision-making, standard costing variance analysis and the setting of transfer prices in divisionalized companies. It can also be applied to capital budgeting in multi-period capital rationing situations.

Linear programming has a number of limitations when applied to real world situations, but some of these problems can be overcome by establishing more complex models and using integer programming techniques. Linear programming is a technique that can be applied to establish the optimum allocation of scarce resources. In the long-term resource constraints can be removed by acquiring resources. Therefore linear programming is only appropriate for short-term allocation decisions.

## Key Terms and Concepts

capital rationing (p. 1049)
integer programming (p. 1051)
linear programming (p. 1031)
marginal rate of substitution (p. 1037)
objective function (p. 1031)

opportunity cost (p. 1037)
shadow price (p. 1037)
simplex method (p. 1038)
slack variables (p. 1038).

# Appendix 26.1 The application of linear programming to capital budgeting

**AR** In Chapter 14 we discussed capital rationing and identified this as being a situation where there is a budget ceiling or constraint on the amount of funds that can be invested during a specific period of time. In such a situation we should select the combination of investment proposals that provide the highest net present value, subject to the budget constraint for the period. In Chapter 14 we assumed that investment funds were restricted to one period only, but it was suggested that in practice more than one period constraint must be considered. Where there is multi-period capital rationing, we should use linear programming techniques to maximize the net present value. Let us consider the example set out in Exhibit 26.A1 to illustrate the application of linear programming to capital rationing where there are budget constraints for three periods.[2]

We can formulate the linear programming model by representing each of the projects numbered 1, ..., 6 by $X_j$, (where $j = 1, ..., 6$); $X_1$ represents investment number 1, $X_2$

**EXHIBIT 26.A1**

*Multi-period
capital rationing*

The Flanders Company is constrained by capital rationing. Details of the projects available during the period where capital rationing applies are as follows:

| Investment project | Present value of outlay in period 1 £ million | Present value of outlay in period 2 £ million | Present value of outlay in period 3 £ million | Net present value of investment £ million |
|---|---|---|---|---|
| 1 | 12 | 3 | 5 | 14 |
| 2 | 54 | 10 | 4 | 30 |
| 3 | 6 | 6 | 6 | 17 |
| 4 | 6 | 2 | 5 | 15 |
| 5 | 30 | 35 | 10 | 40 |
| 6 | 6 | 10 | 4 | 6 |

The present value of the outlays for the budget constraints for each of periods 1–3 are as follows:

| | £ million |
|---|---|
| Period 1 | 35 |
| Period 2 | 20 |
| Period 3 | 20 |

You are required to formulate the linear programming model that will maximize net present value.

represents investment number 2, and so on. Our objective is to maximize the net present value subject to the budget constraints for each of the three periods. The model is as follows:

Maximize $14X_1 + 30X_2 + 17X_3 + 15X_4 + 40X_5 + 6X_6$
subject to:
$12X_1 + 54X_2 + 6X_3 + 6X_4 + 30X_5 + 6X_6 + S_1 = 35$ (period 1 constraint)
$3X_1 + 10X_2 + 6X_3 + 2X_4 + 35X_5 + 10X_6 + S_2 = 20$ (period 2 constraint)
$5X_1 + 4X_2 + 6X_3 + 5X_4 + 10X_5 + 4X_6 + S_3 = 20$ (period 3 constraint)
$0 \leqslant X_j \leqslant 1 \ (j = 1, \ldots, 6)$

The final term in the model indicates that $X_j$ may take any value from 0 to 1. This ensures that a project cannot be undertaken more than once, but allows for a project to be partially accepted. The terms $S_1$, $S_2$ and $S_3$ represent the slack variables (i.e. unused funds) for each of the three periods. *It is assumed that the budgeted capital constraints are absolute and cannot be removed by project generated cash inflows.* The solution to the problem is presented in Exhibit 26.A2.

**EXHIBIT 26.A2**

*Optimum values for multi-period capital rationing problem*

You can see from these figures that we should fully accept projects 1, 3 and 4, 7% of project 2, 23.5% of project 5 and zero of project 6. Substituting these values into the equations for the objective function gives a net present value of £57.5 million.

| | | | | | |
|---|---|---|---|---|---|
| $X_1 = 1.0$ | $X_2 = 0.07$ | $X_3 = 1.0$ | $X_4 = 1.0$ | $X_5 = 0.235$ | $X_6 = 0.0$ |
| $S_1 = 0.408$ | $S_2 = 0.792$ | $S_3 = 0.0$ | Objective function = £57.5 million | | |

The slack variables indicate the opportunity costs of the budget constraints for the various future periods. These variables indicate the estimated present value that can be gained if a budget constraint is relaxed by £1. For example, the slack variable of £0.408 for period 1 indicates that the present value is expected to increase by £0.408 if the budget of funds available for investment in period 1 is increased by £1, while the slack variable of £0.792 indicates that present value can be expected to increase by £0.792 if the budget is increased by £1 million in period 2. If the budget is increased by £1 million in period 1, the present value is expected to increase by £408 000. The slack variables can also indicate how much it is worth paying over and above the market price of funds that are used in the net present value calculation for additional funds in each period. A further use of the opportunity costs is to help in appraising any investment projects that might be suggested as substitutes for projects 1–6. For example, assume that a new project whose cash inflows are all received in year 3 is expected to yield a net present value of £4 million for an investment of £5 million for each of years 1 and 2; this project should be rejected because the opportunity cost of the scarce funds will be £6 million (£5 million × £0.408 + £5 million × £0.792), and this is in excess of the net present value.

So far we have assumed that capital constraints are absolute and cannot be removed by project-generated cash inflows. *Let us now assume that project-generated cash inflows are available for investment* and that the cash inflows for period 2 are £5 million, £6 million, £7 million, £8 million, £9 million and £10 million respectively for projects 1–6. The revised constraint for period 2 is

$$3X_1 + 10X_2 + 6X_3 + 2X_4 + 35X_5 + 10X_6 + S_2$$
$$= 20 + 5X_1 + 6X_2 + 7X_3 + 8X_4 + 9X_5 + 10X_6$$

You can see that the cash inflows are entered on the right-hand side of the equation, and this increases the amount of funds available for investment. The same approach should be adopted for cash inflows arising in periods 1 and 3. Note that it is assumed that any unused funds cannot be carried forward and used in future periods. For an illustration of how unused funds can be carried forward to future periods and also how project-generated cash flows are incorporated into the LP model see answers to Questions 26.15 and 26.16 in the *Students' Manual*.

Note that in formulating the model we have assumed that the investment projects were divisible in the sense that a partial acceptance of an investment proposal was possible. In the optimal solution both projects 2 and 5 were fractional. However, in practice, investment projects are unlikely to be divisible – acceptance will involve acceptance of the full amount of the investment and rejection will involve zero investment. To overcome this problem, it is possible to use an **integer programming** model by requiring that $X_j$ be an integer – either 0 or 1. This process excludes fractional investments.

The model can also be modified to take account of mutually exclusive projects. For example, if projects 1, 3 and 6 are mutually exclusive, we can simply add the constraint $X_1 + X_3 + X_6 \leqslant 1$. When this constraint is used with integer programming, we are assured that only one of these projects will appear in the final solution. Also, if project 2 is contingent upon the acceptance of project 1, the constraint $X_2 \leqslant X_1$ ensures that the contingency is recognized in the final solution of an integer programming model.

The major problem with the application of linear programming to the capital budgeting process is that it is based on the assumption that future investment opportunities are known. However, management may be aware of future investment opportunities for the earliest years only. Budget constraints for later years are likely to be utilized only as new investment proposals are generated, and they are unlikely to be binding. To overcome this problem, the selection process must be revised continually. ●●●

## Key Examination Points

A common error is to state the objective function in terms of profit per unit. This is incorrect, because the fixed cost per unit is not constant. The objective function should be expressed in terms of contribution per unit. You should note that there are several ways of formulating the tableaux for a linear programming model. The approach adopted in this chapter was to formulate the first tableau with positive contribution signs and negative signs for the slack variable equations. The optimal solution occurs when the signs in the contribution row are all negative. Sometimes examination questions are set that adopt the opposite procedure.

That is, the signs are the reverse of the approach presented in this chapter. For an illustration of how to cope with this situation you should refer to the answers to Questions 26.9 and 26.11 in the *Students' Manual*.

Most examination questions include the final tableau and require you to interpret the figures. You may also be required to formulate the initial model. It is most unlikely that you will be required to complete the calculations and prepare the final tableau. However, you may be asked to construct a graph and calculate the marginal rates of substitution and opportunity costs.

## Questions

*Indicates that a suggested solution is to be found in the *Students' Manual*.

### 26.1 Intermediate: Optimal output using the graphical approach

G Limited, manufacturers of superior garden ornaments, is preparing its production budget for the coming period. The company makes four types of ornament, the data for which are as follows:

| Product | Pixie (£ per unit) | Elf (£ per unit) | Queen (£ per unit) | King (£ per unit) |
|---|---|---|---|---|
| Direct materials | 25 | 35 | 22 | 25 |
| Variable overhead | 17 | 18 | 15 | 16 |
| Selling price | 111 | 98 | 122 | 326 |

| Direct labour hours: | Hours per unit | Hours per unit | Hours per unit | Hours per unit |
|---|---|---|---|---|
| Type 1 | 8 | 6 | — | — |
| Type 2 | — | — | 10 | 10 |
| Type 3 | — | — | 5 | 25 |

Fixed overhead amounts to £15 000 per period.

Each type of labour is paid £5 per hour but because of the skills involved, an employee of one type cannot be used for work normally done by another type.

The maximum hours available in each type are:

Type 1  8 000 hours
Type 2  20 000 hours
Type 3  25 000 hours

The marketing department judges that, at the present selling prices, the demand for the products is likely to be:

Pixie    Unlimited demand
Elf      Unlimited demand
Queen    1500 units
King     1000 units

You are required:

(a) to calculate the product mix that will maximize profit, and the amount of the profit;
(14 marks)

(b) to determine whether it would be worthwhile paying Type 1 Labour for overtime working at time and a half and, if so, to calculate the extra profit for each 1000 hours of overtime;
(2 marks)

(c) to comment on the principles used to find the optimum product mix in part (a), pointing out any possible limitations; (3 marks)

(d) to explain how a computer could assist in providing a solution for the data shown above. (3 marks)

(Total 22 marks)
*CIMA Stage 3 Management Accounting Techniques*

## 26.2* Intermediate: Optimal output using the graphical approach

MNO Ltd produces two products – W and B. Both are components that have a wide range of industrial applications. MNO Ltd's share of the market for W is insignificant but it is one of a limited number of suppliers of B. W is a long-established product and B is a new product.

The market price of W is £128 and that of B is £95. MNO Ltd is unable to influence these prices.

The resource requirements for producing one unit of each of the two products are:

| | process hours | kg of material | labour hours |
|---|---|---|---|
| W | 4 | 8 | 21.8 |
| B | 3 | 14.25 | 7.5 |

Materials cost £3 per kg and labour costs £3.20 per hour. Other costs are fixed.

During the coming period the company will have the following resources available to it:

1200 process hours
4000 kg of material
6000 labour hours

You are required, as MNO Ltd's management accountant:

(a) to advise the company of the output combination of W and B that will maximize its profit in the coming period (support your advice with a full financial analysis); (14 marks)

(b) to write a memorandum suitable for circulation to MNO Ltd's board of directors explaining the commercial limitations of the model you have used in your answer to part (a).
(6 marks)
(Total 20 marks)
*CIMA Stage 4 Management Accounting – Decision Making*

## 26.3 Advanced: Optimal output using the graphical approach and the impact of an increase in capacity

A company makes two products, X and Y. Product X has a contribution of £124 per unit and product Y £80 per unit. Both products pass through two departments for processing and the times in minutes per unit are:

| | Product X | Product Y |
|---|---|---|
| Department 1 | 150 | 90 |
| Department 2 | 100 | 120 |

Currently there is a maximum of 225 hours per week available in department 1 and 200 hours in department 2. The company can sell all it can produce of X but EEC quotas restrict the sale of Y to a maximum of 75 units per week.

The company, which wishes to maximize contribution, currently makes and sells 30 units of X and 75 units of Y per week.

The company is considering several possibilities including

(i) altering the production plan if it could be proved that there is a better plan than the current one;

(ii) increasing the availability of either department 1 or department 2 hours. The extra costs involved in increasing capacity are £0.5 per hour for each department;

(iii) transferring some of their allowed sales quota for Product Y to another company. Because of commitments the company would always retain a minimum sales level of 30 units.

You are required to

(a) calculate the optimum production plan using

the existing capacities and state the extra contribution that would be achieved compared with the existing plan; (8 marks)

(b) advise management whether they should increase the capacity of *either* department 1 *or* department 2 and, if so, by how many hours and what the resulting increase in contribution would be over that calculated in the improved production plan. (7 marks)

(c) calculate the minimum price per unit for which they could sell the rights to their quota, down to the minimum level, given the plan in (a) as a starting point. (5 marks)

(Total 20 marks)

*CIMA Stage 3 Management Accounting Techniques*

## 26.4 Advanced: Maximizing profit and sales revenue using the graphical approach

Goode, Billings and Prosper plc manufactures two products, Razzle and Dazzle. Unit selling prices and variable costs, and daily fixed costs are:

|  | Razzle (£) | Dazzle (£) |
|---|---|---|
| Selling price per unit | 20 | 30 |
| Variable costs per unit | 8 | 20 |
| Contribution margin per unit | 12 | 10 |
| Joint fixed costs per day | | £60 |

Production of the two products is restricted by limited supplies of three essential inputs: Raz, Ma, and Taz. All other inputs are available at prevailing prices without any restriction. The quantities of Raz, Ma, and Taz necessary to produce single units of Razzle and Dazzle, together with the total supplies available each day, are:

|  | kg per unit required Razzle | Dazzle | Total available (kg per day) |
|---|---|---|---|
| Raz | 5 | 12.5 | 75 |
| Ma | 8 | 10 | 80 |
| Taz | 2 | 0 | 15 |

William Billings, the sales director, advises that any combination of Razzle and/or Dazzle can be sold without affecting their market prices. He also argues very strongly that the company should seek to maximize its sales revenues subject to a minimum acceptable profit of £44 per day in total from these two products.

In contrast, the financial director, Silas Prosper, has told the managing director, Henry Goode, that he believes in a policy of profit maximization at all times.

You are required to:

(a) calculate:
   (i) the profit and total sales revenue per day, assuming a policy of profit maximization, (10 marks)
   (ii) the total sales revenue per day, assuming a policy of sales revenue maximization subject to a minimum acceptable profit of £44 per day, (10 marks)

(b) suggest why businessmen might choose to follow an objective of maximizing sales revenue subject to a minimum profit constraint. (5 marks)

(Total 25 marks)

*ICAEW Management Accounting*

## 26.5* Advanced: Optimal output, shadow prices and decision making using the graphical approach

The instruments department of Max Ltd makes two products: the XL and the YM. Standard revenues and costs per unit for these products are shown below:

|  | XL (£) | XL (£) | YM (£) | YM (£) |
|---|---|---|---|---|
| Selling price | | 200 | | 180 |
| Variable costs: | | | | |
| Material A (£10 per kg) | (40) | | (40) | |
| Direct labour (£8 per hour) | (32) | | (16) | |
| Plating (£12 per hour) | (12) | | (24) | |
| Other variable costs | (76) | | (70) | |
| | | (160) | | (150) |
| Fixed overheads (allocated at £7 per direct labour hour) | | (28) | | (14) |
| Standard profit per unit | | 12 | | 16 |

Plating is a separate automated operation and the costs of £12 per hour are for plating materials and electricity.

In any week the maximum availability of inputs is limited to the following:

| Material A | 120 kg |
|---|---|
| Direct labour | 100 hours |
| Plating time | 50 hours |

A management meeting recently considered ways of increasing the profit of the instrument department. It was decided that each of the following possible changes to the existing situation should be examined *independently* of each other.

(1) The selling price of product YM could be increased.

(2) Plating time could be sold as a separate service at £16 per hour.

(3) A new product, ZN, could be sold at £240 per unit. Each unit would require the following:

| | |
|---|---|
| Material A | 5 kg |
| Direct labour | 5 hours |
| Plating time | 1 hour |
| Other variable costs | £90 |

(4) Overtime could be introduced and would be paid at a premium of 50% above normal rates.

Requirements:

(a) Formulate a linear programme to determine the production policy which maximizes the profits of Max Ltd in the present situation (i.e. ignoring the alternative assumptions in 1 to 4 above), solve, and specify the optimal product mix and weekly profit. (6 marks)

(b) Determine the maximum selling price of YM at which the product mix calculated for requirement (a) would still remain optimal. (3 marks)

(c) Show how the linear programme might be modified to accommodate the sale of plating time at £16 per hour (i.e. formulate but do not solve). (3 marks)

(d) Using shadow prices (dual values), calculate whether product ZN would be a profitable addition to the product range. (4 marks)

(e) Ignoring the possibility of extending the product range, determine whether overtime working would be worthwhile, and if so state how many overtime hours should be worked. (3 marks)

(f) Discuss the limitations of the linear programming approach to the problems of Max Ltd. (6 marks)

(Total 25 marks)

*ICAEW P2 Management Accounting*

## 26.6* Advanced: Relevant material costs, optimal output and shadow prices using the graphical approach

The Milton Carpet Company has been manufacturing two ranges of carpet for many years, one range for commercial use, the other for private use. The main difference between the two ranges is in the mix of wool and nylon; with the commercial range having 80% wool and 20% nylon and the private range 20% wool and 80% nylon. The designs of each range are the same and each range can be made in 5 different colours. There are variations in the cost of the dyes used for the different colours in the range, but they are all within 5% of each other so the accountant takes an average cost of dyeing in her costing.

The Board has just decided to use up its remaining stocks of wool and nylon and transfer its production over to making acrylic carpets in three months' time. The company's objective is to maximize the contribution from the running down of the stocks of wool and nylon over that period subject to any operating constraints. Data concerning its present carpet range is given below. It is assumed that sufficient demand exists to ensure all production can be sold at the stated price.

| | Per roll | |
|---|---|---|
| | Private use (£) | Commercial use (£) |
| Selling price | 2400 | 3200 |
| Manufacturing costs: | | |
|   Material – Wool | 140 | 700 |
|      – Nylon | 320 | 100 |
|   Direct labour | 90 | 108 |
|   Variable production costs | 250 | 312 |
|   Fixed production overheads based on 200% direct labour | 180 | 216 |
| Standard full cost | 980 | 1436 |
| Production requirements: | | |
|   Wool (kg) | 40 | 200 |
|   Nylon (kg) | 160 | 50 |
|   Direct machine time (hours) | 30 | 36 |

There are 24 000 kg of wool and 25 000 kg of nylon in the stores to be used up. At the end of the quarter, when it changes production to the new carpet, any wool or nylon left can be sold for £1 per kg. The production manager forecasts that the machines can operate for a total of 6600 hours during the next quarter.

You are required to:

(a) Formulate the above problem in a linear programming format. Solve the problem and provide the production manager with the required output mix of rolls of private and commercial carpets. State whether any of the raw material has to be sold off as scrap at the end and thus what the total contribution for the quarter's production should be.

(10 marks)

(b) Show whether or not it will be necessary to recompute the optimum solution if due to economic difficulties, the costs of the dyes for the carpets are to be increased by £110 and £40 per roll of private and commercial carpet respectively. (4 marks)

(c) Describe what would happen in physical and financial terms if the availability of one of the fully utilized resources were to be increased by a small amount. (6 marks)

(d) Comment on the advisability of introducing the concept of opportunity costs into the budgetary control framework, by using the output from the linear programming solution to the optimum production mix. (5 marks)

(Total 25 marks)

*ICAEW P2 Management Accounting*

### 26.7 Advanced: Optimal output and shadow prices using the graphical approach

Usine Ltd is a company whose objective is to maximize profits. It manufactures two speciality chemical powders, gamma and delta, using three processes: heating, refining and blending. The powders can be produced and sold in infinitely divisible quantities.

The following are the estimated production hours for each process per kilo of output for each of the two chemical powders during the period 1 June to 31 August:

| | Gamma (hours) | Delta (hours) |
|---|---|---|
| Heating | 400 | 120 |
| Refining | 100 | 90 |
| Blending | 100 | 250 |

During the same period, revenues and costs per kilo of output are budgeted as

| | Gamma (£ per kilo) | Delta (£ per kilo) |
|---|---|---|
| Selling price | 16 000 | 25 000 |
| Variable costs | 12 000 | 17 000 |
| Contribution | 4 000 | 8 000 |

It is anticipated that the company will be able to sell all it can produce at the above prices, and that at any level of output fixed costs for the three month period will total £36 000.

The company's management accountant is under the impression that there will only be one scarce factor during the budget period, namely blending hours, which cannot exceed a total of 1050 hours during the period 1 June to 31 August. He therefore correctly draws up an optimum production plan on this basis.

However, when the factory manager sees the figures he points out that over the three month period there will not only be a restriction on blending hours, but in addition the heating and refining hours cannot exceed 1200 and 450 respectively during the three month period.

Requirements:

(a) Calculate the initial production plan for the period 1 June to 31 August as prepared by the management accountant, assuming blending hours are the only scarce factor. Indicate the budgeted profit or loss, and explain why the solution is the optimum. (4 marks)

(b) Calculate the optimum production plan for the period 1 June to 31 August, allowing for both the constraint on blending hours and the additional restrictions identified by the factory manager, and indicate the budgeted profit or loss. (8 marks)

(c) State the implications of your answer in (b) in terms of the decisions that will have to be made by Usine Ltd with respect to production during the period 1 June to 31 August after taking into account all relevant costs. (2 marks)

(d) Under the restrictions identified by the management accountant and the factory manager, the shadow (or dual) price of one extra hour of blending time on the optimum production plan is £27.50. Calculate the shadow (or dual) price of one extra hour of refining time. Explain how such information might be used by management, and in so doing indicate the limitations inherent in the figures. **(6 marks)**

*Note*: Ignore taxation.

Show all calculations clearly. **(20 marks)**

*ICAEW Management Accounting and Financial Management I Part Two*

### 26.8* Advanced: Formulation of initial tableau and interpretation of final tableau

*Hint*: Reverse signs in Final tableau.

D Electronics produces three models of satellite dishes – Alpha, Beta and Gamma – which have contributions per unit of £400, £200 and £100 respectively.

There is a two-stage production process and the number of hours per unit for each process are:

|           | Alpha | Beta | Gamma |
|-----------|-------|------|-------|
| Process 1 | 2     | 3    | 2.5   |
| Process 2 | 3     | 2    | 2     |

There is an upper limit on process hours of 1920 per period for Process 1 and 2200 for Process 2.

The Alpha dish was designed for a low-power satellite which is now fading and the sales manager thinks that sales will be no more than 200 per period.

Fixed costs are £40 000 per period.

You are required to

(a) formulate these data into a Linear Programming model using the following notation:

$x_1$: number of Alphas
$x_2$: number of Betas
$x_3$: number of Gammas **(5 marks)**

(b) formulate (but do not attempt to solve) the initial Simplex Tableau using

$x_4$: as Slack for Process 1
$x_5$: as Slack for Process 2
$x_6$: as Slack for any sales limit

and describe the meaning of Slack; **(5 marks)**

(c) interpret the final Simplex Tableau below

|       | $x_1$ | $x_2$ | $x_3$ | $x_4$ | $x_5$ | $x_6$ | Solution |
|-------|-------|-------|-------|-------|-------|-------|----------|
| $x_2$ | 0     | 1     | 0.83  | 0.33  | 0     | − 0.67 | 506.7    |
| $x_5$ | 0     | 0     | 0.33  | − 0.67 | 1    | − 1.67 | 586.7    |
| $x_1$ | 1     | 0     | 0     | 0     | 0     | 1     | 200      |
| Z     | 0     | 0     | 66.67 | 66.67 | 0     | 266.7 | 181 333.8 |

**(6 marks)**

(d) investigate the effect on the solution of each of the following:

(i) an increase of 20 hours per period in Process 1,

(ii) an increase of 10 units per period in the output of Alpha,

(iii) receiving an order, which must be met, for 10 units of Gamma. **(6 marks)**

**(Total 22 marks)**

*CIMA Stage 3 Management Accounting Techniques*

### 26.9* Advanced: Optimal output with a single limiting factor and interpretation of a final matrix

*Hint*: Reverse the signs in the final matrix.

(a) Corpach Ltd manufactures three products for which the sales maxima, for the forthcoming year, are estimated to be:

| Product 1 | Product 2 | Product 3 |
|-----------|-----------|-----------|
| £57 500   | £96 000   | £125 000  |

Summarized unit cost data are as follows:

|                          | Product 1 (£) | Product 2 (£) | Product 3 (£) |
|--------------------------|---------------|---------------|---------------|
| Direct material cost     | 10.00         | 9.00          | 7.00          |
| Variable processing costs | 8.00          | 16.00         | 10.00         |
| Fixed processing costs   | 2.50          | 5.00          | 4.00          |
|                          | £20.50        | £30.00        | £21.00        |

The allocation of fixed processing costs has been derived from last year's production levels and the figures may need revision if current output plans are different.

The established selling prices are:

| Product 1 | Product 2 | Product 3 |
|-----------|-----------|-----------|
| £23.00    | £32.00    | £25.00    |

The products are processed on machinery housed in three buildings:

Building A contains type A machines on which 9800 machine hours are estimated to be available in the forthcoming year. The fixed overheads for this building are £9800 p.a.

Building B1 contains type B machines on which 10 500 machine hours are estimated to be available in the forthcoming year.

Building B2 also contains type B machines and again 10 500 machine hours are estimated to be available in the forthcoming year.

The fixed overheads for the B1 and B2 buildings are, in total, £11 200 p.a.

The times required for one unit of output for each product on each type of machine, are as follows:

| | Product 1 | Product 2 | Product 3 |
|---|---|---|---|
| Type A machines | 1 hour | 2 hours | 3 hours |
| Type B machines | 1.5 hours | 3 hours | 1 hour |

Assuming that Corpach Ltd wishes to maximize its profits for the ensuing year, you are required to determine the optimal production plan and the profit that this should produce.

(9 marks)

(b) Assume that, before the plan that you have prepared in part (a) is implemented, Corpach Ltd suffers a major fire which completely destroys building B2. The fire thus reduces the availability of type B machine time to 10 500 hours p.a. and the estimated fixed overhead for such machines, to £8200. In all other respects the conditions set out, in part (a) to this question, continue to apply.

In his efforts to obtain a revised production plan the company's accountant makes use of a linear programming computer package. This package produces the following optimal tableau:

| Z | X1 | X2 | X3 | S1 | S2 | S3 | S4 | S5 | |
|---|---|---|---|---|---|---|---|---|---|
| 0 | 0 | 0 | 0 | 0.5 | 1 | 0 | 0.143 | −0.429 | 1 150 |
| 0 | 0 | 1 | 0 | −0.5 | 0 | 0 | −0.143 | 0.429 | 1 850 |
| 0 | 0 | 0 | 0 | 0 | 0 | 1 | −0.429 | 0.286 | 3 800 |
| 0 | 0 | 0 | 1 | 0 | 0 | 0 | 0.429 | −0.286 | 1 200 |
| 0 | 1 | 0 | 0 | 1 | 0 | 0 | 0 | 0 | 2 500 |
| 1 | 0 | 0 | 0 | 1.5 | 0 | 0 | 2.429 | 0.714 | 35 050 |

In the above: $Z$ is the total contribution,
$X1$ is the budgeted output of product 1,
$X2$ is the budgeted output of product 2,
$X3$ is the budgeted output of product 3,
$S1$ is the unsatisfied demand for product 1,
$S2$ is the unsatisfied demand for product 2,
$S3$ is the unsatisfied demand for product 3,
$S4$ is the unutilized type A machine time,
$S5$ is the unutilized type B machine time.
and

The tableau is interpreted as follows:
Optimal plan – Make 2500 units of Product 1,
1850 units of Product 2,
1200 units of Product 3,
Shadow prices – Product 1 £1.50 per unit,
Type A Machine Time £2.429 per hour,
Type B Machine Time £0.714 per hour.
Explain the meaning of the shadow prices and consider how the accountant might make use of them. Calculate the profit anticipated from the revised plan and comment on its variation from the profit that you calculated in your answer to part (a). (9 marks)

(c) Explain why linear programming was not necessary for the facts as set out in part (a) whereas it was required for part (b).

(4 marks)

(Total 22 marks)

*ACCA Level 2 Management Accounting*

## 26.10 Advanced: Formulation of initial tableau and interpretation of final tableau

The Alphab Group has five divisions A, B, C, D and E. Group management wish to increase overall group production capacity per year by up to 30 000 hours. Part of the strategy will be to require that the minimum increase at any one division must be equal to 5% of its current capacity. The maximum funds available for the expansion programme are £3 000 000.

Additional information relating to each division is as follows:

| Division | Existing capacity (hours) | Investment cost per hour (£) | Average contribution per hour (£) |
|---|---|---|---|
| A | 20 000 | 90 | 12.50 |
| B | 40 000 | 75 | 9.50 |
| C | 24 000 | 100 | 11 |
| D | 50 000 | 120 | 8 |
| E | 12 000 | 200 | 14 |

A linear programme of the plan has been prepared in order to determine the strategy which will maximise additional contribution per annum and to provide additional decision-making information. The Appendix to this question shows a print-out of the LP model of the situation.

Required:
(a) Formulate the mathematical model from which the input to the LP programme would be obtained. (6 marks)

(b) Use the linear programme solution in the Appendix in order to answer the following:

(i) State the maximum additional contribution from the expansion strategy and the distribution of the extra capacity between the divisions. (3 marks)

(ii) Explain the cost to the company of providing the minimum 5% increase in capacity at each division. (3 marks)

(iii) Explain the effect on contribution of the limits placed on capacity and investment. (2 marks)

(iv) Explain the sensitivity of the plan to changes in contribution per hour. (4 marks)

(v) Group management decide to relax the 30 000 hours capacity constraint. All other parameters of the model remain unchanged. Determine the change in strategy which will then maximise the increase in group contribution. You should calculate the increase in contribution which this change in strategy will provide. (6 marks)

(vi) Group management wish to decrease the level of investment while leaving all other parameters of the model (as per the Appendix) unchanged.
Determine and quantify the change in strategy which is required indicating the fall in contribution which will occur. (6 marks)

(c) Explain the limitations of the use of linear programming for planning purposes. (5 marks)

(Total 35 marks)

### Appendix
### Divisional investment evaluation
### Optimal solution – detailed report

| Variable | Value |
|---|---|
| 1 DIV A | 22 090.91 |
| 2 DIV B | 2 000.00 |
| 3 DIV C | 1 200.00 |
| 4 DIV D | 2 500.00 |
| 5 DIV E | 2 209.09 |

| Constraint | Type | RHS | Slack | Shadow price |
|---|---|---|---|---|
| 1 Max. Hours | < = | 30 000.00 | 0.00 | 11.2727 |
| 2 DIV A | > = | 1 000.00 | 21 090.91 | 0.0000 |
| 3 DIV B | > = | 2 000.00 | 0.00 | − 2.7955 |
| 4 DIV C | > = | 1 200.00 | 0.00 | − 1.6364 |
| 5 DIV D | > = | 2 500.00 | 0.00 | − 4.9091 |
| 6 DIV E | > = | 600.00 | 1 609.09 | 0.0000 |
| 7 Max. Funds | < = | 3 000 000.00 | 0.00 | 0.0136 |

Objective function value = 359 263.6

### Sensitivity Analysis of Objective Function Coefficients

| Variable | Current coefficient | Allowable minimum | Allowable maximum |
|---|---|---|---|
| 1 DIV A | 12.50 | 10.7000 | 14.0000 |
| 2 DIV B | 9.50 | − Infinity | 12.2955 |
| 3 DIV C | 11.00 | − Infinity | 12.6364 |
| 4 DIV D | 8.00 | − Infinity | 12.9091 |
| 5 DIV E | 14.00 | 12.5000 | 27.7778 |

### Sensitivity Analysis of Right-hand Side Values

| Constraint | Type | Current value | Allowable minimum | Allowable maximum |
|---|---|---|---|---|
| 1 Max. Hours | < = | 30 000.00 | 18 400.00 | 31 966.67 |
| 2 DIV A | > = | 1 000.00 | − Infinity | 22 090.91 |
| 3 DIV B | > = | 2 000.00 | 0.00 | 20 560.00 |
| 4 DIV C | > = | 1 200.00 | 0.00 | 18 900.00 |
| 5 DIV D | > = | 2 500.00 | 0.00 | 8 400.00 |
| 6 DIV E | > = | 600.00 | − Infinity | 2 209.09 |
| 7 Max. Funds | < = | 3 000 000.00 | 2 823 000.00 | 5 320 000.00 |

*Note*: RHS = Right-hand side

*ACCA Paper 9 Information for Control and Decision Making*

### 26.11* Advanced: Formulation of an initial tableau and interpretation of final matrix using the Simplex method

*Hint*: Reverse the signs and ignore the entries of 0 and 1. You are not required to solve the model.

A chemical manufacturer is developing three fertilizer compounds for the agricultural industry. The product codes for the three products are $X1$, $X2$ and $X3$ and the relevant information is summarized below:

### Chemical constituents: percentage make-up per tonne

| | Nitrate | Phosphate | Potash | Filler |
|---|---|---|---|---|
| $X1$ | 10 | 10 | 20 | 60 |
| $X2$ | 10 | 20 | 10 | 60 |
| $X3$ | 20 | 10 | 10 | 60 |

**Input prices per tonne**

| | |
|---|---|
| Nitrate | £150 |
| Phosphate | £ 60 |
| Potash | £120 |
| Filler | £ 10 |

**Maximum available input in tonnes per month**

| | |
|---|---|
| Nitrate | 1200 |
| Phosphate | 2000 |
| Potash | 2200 |
| Filler | No limit |

The fertilizers will be sold in bulk and managers have proposed the following prices per tonne.

$X1$ £83
$X2$ £81
$X3$ £81

The manufacturing costs of each type of fertilizer, excluding materials, are £11 per tonne.

You are required to:

(a) formulate the above data into a linear programming model so that the company may maximize contribution;　　(4 marks)

(b) construct the initial Simplex tableau and state what is meant by 'slack variables' (Define $X4$, $X5$, $X6$ as the slack variables for $X1$, $X2$, and $X3$ respectively);　　(2 marks)

(c) indicate, with explanations, which will be the 'entering variable' and 'leaving variable' in the first iteration;　　(2 marks)

(d) interpret the final matrix of the simplex solution given below:

| Basic Variable | $X_1$ | $X_2$ | $X_3$ | $X_4$ | $X_5$ | $X_6$ | Solution |
|---|---|---|---|---|---|---|---|
| X1 | 1 | 0 | 3 | 20 | −10 | 0 | 4 000 |
| X2 | 0 | 1 | −1 | −10 | 10 | 0 | 8 000 |
| X6 | 0 | 0 | −0.4 | −3 | 1 | 1 | 600 |
| Z | 0 | 0 | 22 | 170 | 40 | 0 | 284 000 |

(8 marks)

(e) use the final matrix above to investigate:
　(i) the effect of an increase in nitrate of 100 tonnes per month;
　(ii) the effect of a minimum contract from an influential customer for 200 tonnes of $X3$ per month to be supplied.　　(4 marks)
　　(Total 20 marks)
　　*CIMA Stage 3 Management Accounting Techniques*

**26.12 Advanced: Formulation of an initial tableau and interpretation of a final tableau using the simplex method**

*Hint*: Reverse the signs and ignore entries of 0 and 1.

The Kaolene Co. Ltd has six different products all made from fabricated steel. Each product passes through a combination of five production operations: cutting, forming, drilling, welding and coating.

Steel is cut to the length required, formed into the appropriate shapes, drilled if necessary, welded together if the product is made up of more than one part, and then passed through the coating machine. Each operation is separate and independent, except for the cutting and forming operations, when, if needed, forming follows continuously after cutting. Some products do not require every production operation.

The output rates from each production operations, based on a standard measure for each product, are set out in the tableau below, along with the total hours of work available for each operation. The contribution per unit of each product is also given. It is estimated that three of the products have sales ceilings and these are also given below:

| Products | $X_1$ | $X_2$ | $X_3$ | $X_4$ | $X_5$ | $X_6$ |
|---|---|---|---|---|---|---|
| Contribution per unit (£) | 5.7 | 10.1 | 12.3 | 9.8 | 17.2 | 14.0 |
| Output rate per hour: | | | | | | |
| Cutting | 650 | 700 | 370 | 450 | 300 | 420 |
| Forming | 450 | 450 | — | 520 | 180 | 380 |
| Drilling | — | 200 | 380 | — | 300 | — |
| Welding | — | — | 380 | 670 | 400 | 720 |
| Coating | 500 | — | 540 | 480 | 600 | 450 |
| Maximum sales units (000) | — | — | 150 | — | 20 | 70 |

| | Cutting | Forming | Drilling | Welding | Coating |
|---|---|---|---|---|---|
| Production hours available | 12 000 | 16 000 | 4000 | 4000 | 16 000 |

The production and sales for the year were found using a linear programming algorithm. The final tableau is given on the next page.

Variables $X_7$ to $X_{11}$ are the slack variables relating to the production constraints, expressed in the order of production. Variables $X_{12}$ to $X_{14}$ are the slack variables relating to the sales ceilings of $X_3$, $X_5$ and $X_6$ respectively.

After analysis of the above results, the production manager believes that further mechanical work

| $X_1$ | $X_2$ | $X_3$ | $X_4$ | $X_5$ | $X_6$ | $X_7$ | $X_8$ | $X_9$ | $X_{10}$ | $X_{11}$ | $X_{12}$ | $X_{13}$ | $X_{14}$ | Variable in basic solution | Value of variable in basic solution |
|---|---|---|---|---|---|---|---|---|---|---|---|---|---|---|---|
| 1 | 0 | -1.6 | -0.22 | -0.99 | 0 | 10.8 | 0 | -3.0 | -18.5 | 0 | 0 | 0 | 0 | $X_1$ | 43 287.0 units |
| 0 | 0 | -0.15 | -0.02 | 0.12 | 0 | -1.4 | 1 | -0.3 | 0.58 | 0 | 0 | 0 | 0 | $X_8$ | 15 747.81 hours |
| 0 | 1 | 0.53 | 0 | 0.67 | 0 | 0 | 0 | 3.33 | 0 | 0 | 0 | 0 | 0 | $X_2$ | 13 333.3 units |
| 0 | 0 | 1.9 | 1.08 | 1.64 | 1 | 0 | 0 | 0 | 12 | 0 | 0 | 0 | 0 | $X_6$ | 48 019.2 units |
| 0 | 0 | 0.06 | 0.01 | 0 | 0 | -1.3 | 0 | 0.37 | 0.63 | 1 | 0 | 0 | 0 | $X_{11}$ | 150 806.72 hours |
| 0 | 0 | 1 | 0 | 0 | 0 | 0 | 0 | 0 | 0 | 0 | 1 | 0 | 0 | $X_{12}$ | 150 000.0 units |
| 0 | 0 | 0 | 0 | 1 | 0 | 0 | 0 | 0 | 0 | 0 | 0 | 1 | 0 | $X_{13}$ | 20 000.0 units |
| 0 | 0 | -1.9 | -1.0 | -1.6 | 0 | 0 | 0 | 0 | -12 | 0 | 0 | 0 | 1 | $X_{14}$ | 21 980.8 units |
| 0 | 0 | 10.0 | 4 | 6.83 | 0 | 61.7 | 0 | 16.0 | 62.1 | 0 | 0 | 0 | 0 | $(Z_i - C_i)$ | £1 053 617.4 |

on the cutting and forming machines costing £200 can improve their hourly output rates as follows:

| | $X_1$ | $X_2$ | $X_3$ | $X_4$ | $X_5$ | $X_6$ |
|---|---|---|---|---|---|---|
| Cutting | 700 | 770 | 410 | 500 | 330 | 470 |
| Forming | 540 | 540 | — | 620 | 220 | 460 |

The optimal solution to the new situation indicates the shadow prices of the cutting, drilling and welding sections to be £59.3, £14.2 and £71.5 per hour respectively.

Requirements:
(a) Explain the meaning of the seven items ringed in the final tableau. (9 marks)
(b) Show the range of values within which the following variables or resources can change without changing the optimal mix indicated in the final tableau
   (i) $c_4$: contribution of $X_4$
   (ii) $b_5$: available coating time. (4 marks)
(c) Formulate the revised linear programming problem taking note of the revised output rates for cutting and forming. (5 marks)
(d) Determine whether the changes in the cutting and forming rates will increase profitability. (3 marks)
(e) Using the above information discuss the usefulness of linear programming to managers in solving this type of problem. (4 marks)
(Total 25 marks)
*ICAEW P2 Management Accounting*

## 26.13 Formulation of initial tableau and interpretation of final tableau using the simplex method

(a) The Argonaut Company makes three products, Xylos, Yo-yos and Zicons. These are assembled from two components, Agrons and Bovons, which can be produced internally at a variable cost of £5 and £8 each respectively. A limited quantity of each of these components may be available for purchase from an external supplier at a quoted price which varies from week to week.

The production of Agrons and Bovons is subject to several limitations. Both components require the same three production processes (L, M and N), the first two of which have limited availabilities of 9600 minutes per week and 7000 minutes per week respectively. The final process (N) has effectively unlimited availability but for technical reasons must produce at least one Agron for each Bovon produced. The processing times are as follows:

| Process | L | M | N |
|---|---|---|---|
| Time (mins) required to produce | | | |
| 1 Agron | 6 | 5 | 7 |
| 1 Bovon | 8 | 5 | 9 |

The component requirements of each of the three final products are:

| Product | Xylo | Yo-yo | Zicon |
|---|---|---|---|
| Number of components required | | | |
| Agrons | 1 | 1 | 3 |
| Bovons | 2 | 1 | 2 |

The ex-factory selling prices of the final products are given below, together with the standard direct labour hours involved in their assembly and details of other assembly costs incurred:

| Product | Xylo | Yo-yo | Zicon |
|---|---|---|---|
| Selling price | £70 | £60 | £150 |
| Direct labour hours used | 6 | 7 | 16 |
| Other assembly costs | £4 | £5 | £15 |

The standard direct labour rate is £5 per hour. Factory overhead costs amount to £4350 per week and are absorbed to products on the basis of the direct labour costs incurred in their assembly. The current production plan is to produce 100 units of each of the three products each week.

Requirements:
(i) Present a budgeted weekly profit and loss account, by product, for the factory. (4 marks)
(ii) Formulate the production problem facing the factory manager as a linear program:
  (1) assuming there is no external availability of Agrons and Bovons; (5 marks) and
  (2) assuming that 200 Agrons and 300 Bovons are available at prices of £10 and £12 each respectively. (4 marks)
(b) In a week when no external availability of Agrons and Bovons was expected, the optimal solution to the linear program and the shadow prices associated with each constraint were as follows:

Production of Xylos  50 units
Production of Yo-yos  0 units; shadow price £2.75
Production of Zicons  250 units

Shadow price associated with:

| Process L | £ 0.375 per minute |
|---|---|
| Process M | £ 0.450 per minute |
| Process N | £ 0.000 per minute |
| Agron availability | £ 9.50 each |
| Bovon availability | £13.25 each |

If sufficient Bovons were to become available on the external market at a price of £12 each, a revised linear programming solution indicated that only Xylos should be made.

Requirement:
Interpret this output from the linear program in a report to the factory manager. Include calculations of revised shadow prices in your report and indicate the actions the manager should take and the benefits that would accrue if the various constraints could be overcome.
(12 marks)
(Total 25 marks)
*ICAEW P2 Management Accounting*

## 26.14* Advanced: Multi-period capital rationing

Alexandra Ltd is a newly established manufacturing company. The company's only asset is £5 million in cash from the amount received on the issue of the ordinary shares. This is available for investment immediately. A call on the shares will be made exactly a year from now. This is expected to raise a further 2.5 million which will be available for investment at that time. The directors do not wish to raise finance from any other source and so next year's (year 1's) investment finance is limited to the cash to be raised from the call plus any cash generated from investments undertaken this year.

Six possible investment projects have been identified. Each of these involves making the necessary initial investment to establish a manufacturing facility for a different product. Information concerning the projects is as follows:

| Project Estimated cash flows (including tax cash flows) | A (£m) | B (£m) | C (£m) | D (£m) | E (£m) | F (£m) |
|---|---|---|---|---|---|---|
| Year 0 (immediately) | (2.0) | (0.5) | (2.2) | (4.0) | (1.4) | — |
| 1 | 0.8 | (3.2) | 0.5 | 1.1 | (0.8) | (3.0) |
| 2 | 0.9 | 2.3 | 1.2 | 2.0 | 1.5 | 1.0 |
| 3 | 0.6 | 1.9 | 1.0 | 1.8 | 1.2 | 2.0 |
| 4 | 0.6 | 1.1 | 0.9 | 1.2 | 1.0 | 1.3 |
| 5 | 0.5 | — | — | — | — | 0.7 |
| Net present value (at 15%) | 0.36 | 0.34 | 0.31 | 0.34 | 0.39 | 0.56 |

None of these projects can be brought forward, delayed or repeated. Each project is infinitely divisible.

Any funds not used to finance these projects will be invested in the ordinary shares of a rival listed company, expected to generate a 15% return.

Generally there is no shortage of labour and materials. Both Project A and Project E, however, require the use of a special component which the company will have to obtain from a far eastern supplier. Because of the relatively short notice, the supply of these will be limited during year 1 to 5000 units.

The estimates in the table (above) are based on a usage of the special component during year 1 as follows:

> Project A  3000 units
> Project E  4000 units

From year 2 onwards the company will be able to obtain as many of the components as it needs.

The finance director proposes using linear programming to reach a decision on which projects to undertake. The company has access to some Simplex linear programming software, but no one in the company knows how to use it and your advice has been sought.

Requirements:

(a) Prepare the objective function and the various constraint statements which can be used to deduce the optimum investment schedule, giving a brief narrative explanation of each statement and stating any assumptions made. The solution to the linear programming problem is not required. (7 marks)

(b) State the information (not the actual figures) which the linear programming process will produce in respect of Alexandra Ltd's allocation problem and explain how that information can be used. (4 marks)

(Total 11 marks)

*ICAEW Business Finance and Decisions – Part Two*

### 26.15* Advanced: Single and multi-period capital rationing

Schobert Ltd is a retailing company which operates a small chain of outlets. The company is currently (i.e. December 2000) finalizing its capital budgets for the years to 31 December 2001 and 31 December 2002. Budgets for existing trading operations have already been prepared and these indicate that the company will have cash available of £250 000 on 1 January 2001 and £150 000 on 1 January 2002. This cash will be available for the payment

of dividends and/or for the financing of new projects.

Seven new capital projects are currently being considered by Schobert Ltd. Each is divisible but none is repeatable. Relevant data for each of the investments for the periods to 31 December 2003 are provided below:

| | Cash Flows Year to 31 December | | | Net Present Value at 10% per annum | Internal Rate of Return |
| Project | 2001 (£000) | 2002 (£000) | 2003 (£000) | (£000) | |
| --- | --- | --- | --- | --- | --- |
| A | (80) | (30) | 50 | 39 | 36% |
| B | (70) | 20 | 50 | 35 | 38% |
| C | (55) | 40 | 20 | 5 | 20% |
| D | (60) | 30 | 30 | 15 | 28% |
| E | | (140) | 55 | 14 | 19% |
| F | | (80) | 70 | 32 | 46% |
| G | | (100) | 30 | 24 | 29% |

The financial director of Schobert Ltd predicts that no new external sources of capital will become available during the period from 1 January 2001 to 31 December 2002, but believes conditions will improve in 2003, when the company would no longer expect capital to be rationed.

The objective of the directors of Schobert Ltd is to maximize the present value of the company's ordinary shares, assuming that the value of ordinary shares is determined by the dividend growth model. The company's cost of capital is 10% per annum, and all cash surpluses can be invested elsewhere to earn 8% per annum. A dividend of at least £100 000 is to be paid to 1 January 2000, and the company's policy is to increase its annual dividend by at least 5% per annum.

Requirements:

(a) Formulate, but do not solve, the company's capital rationing problem as a linear programme. (8 marks)

(b) Assuming that the results of the linear programme show a dual price of cash in 2001 of £0.25 and 2002 of £0, and a range of cash amounts for which the dual price is relevant of £120 000 to £180 000, explain their significance to the directors of Schobert Ltd. (7 marks)

(c) Discuss the circumstances under which capital might be rationed, and the problems these present for capital budgeting decisions. (10 marks)

(Total 25 marks)

*Note*: Ignore taxation.

*ICAEW P2 Financial Management*

### 26.16* Multi-period capital rationing and minimum profit constraints

Details of projects available to Glaser Ltd, a wholly owned subsidiary of a publicly quoted company, are:

| | Cash flows at time | | | | NPV | IRR | Accounting profit in year to time | | |
|---|---|---|---|---|---|---|---|---|---|
| | **0** | **1** | **2** | **3** | | | **1** | **2** | **3** |
| Project | **(£M)** | **(£M)** | **(£M)** | **(£M)** | **(£M)** | **(%)** | **(£M)** | **(£M)** | **(£M)** |
| A | (7) | 1.5 | 2.0 | 2.0 | 1.0 | 10 | 0.6 | 0.6 | 1.4 |
| B | (6) | 2.0 | 1.0 | 1.0 | 0.8 | 21 | 0.8 | 0.3 | 0.8 |
| C | (2) | 4.0 | (0.5) | (2.0) | (0.6) | — | (0.1) | (0.2) | (0.3) |
| D | | (8.0) | (2.0) | (1.0) | 3.0 | 17 | | (0.3) | (0.2) |
| E | | | (3.0) | 1.0 | 0.7 | 25 | | | 1.5 |

Each of the projects have cash flows which extend beyond time 3 and this has been reflected in the NPV and IRR calculations. The investment shown is the maximum possible for each project but partial investment in a project is possible and this would result in strictly proportional cash flows, accounting profits and NPV figures. The timing of the start of each project cannot be altered and, if started, a project must run for its whole life.

External funds available for investment are:

Time 0      up to £12 M, of which £5 M is a loan to be repaid with interest at 10% at time 1.

Time 1      a new equity injection from Glaser's holding company of £7.5 M.

Time 2 and 3  nil.

Funds generated from investment in the five available projects will also be available for further investment by Glaser. None of the funds generated by Glaser's existing activities are available for investment in projects A to E or for the payment of interest, or principal, relating to the loan.

At time 0, Glaser's holding company will require the surrender of any cash not used for investment. With effect from time 1 confiscation of surplus cash will cease and excess funds can be put on deposit to earn the competitive risk free interest rate of 8% per year, the gross amount then being available for investment. After time 3 Glaser will be free to seek funds from the capital market.

The holding company requires Glaser to produce accounting profits from projects (i.e. ignoring interest payments or receipts) which are always at least 10% higher than those of the previous year. Existing projects will produce profits of

| Year to time | Profits (£M) |
|---|---|
| 0 | 10 |
| 1 | 10 |
| 2 | 12 |
| 3 | 11 |

Required:

(a) Provide an appropriate linear programming formulation which is capable of assisting in, or indicating the impossibility of, deriving a solution to the problem of selecting an optimum mix of projects within the constraints imposed on Glaser.

Glaser's objective is to maximize the economic well being of the shareholders of the holding company. Clearly specify how this objective is to be incorporated in the programming formulation.

Specify the meaning of each variable and describe the purpose of every constraint used. You are required to formulate the problem, you are not required to attempt a solution. Ignore tax.                   (10 marks)

(b) Briefly explain the circumstances under which it may be rational for a firm to undertake a project with a negative NPV, such as project C.                               (3 marks)

(c) Outline the main merits and deficiencies of mathematical programming and mathematical modelling in practical financial planning.
(7 marks)
(Total 20 marks)
*ACCA P3 Financial Management*

### 26.17 Advanced: Single and multi-period capital rationing

Raiders Ltd is a private limited company which is financed entirely by ordinary shares. Its effective cost of capital, net of tax, is 10% per annum. The directors of Raiders Ltd are considering the company's capital investment programme for the next two years, and have reduced their initial list of projects to four. Details of the projects are as follows:

| Cash flows (net of tax) | | | | | |
|---|---|---|---|---|---|
| Immediately (£000) | After one year (£000) | After two years (£000) | After three years (£000) | Net present value (at 10%) (£000) | Internal rate of return (to nearest 1%) |

**Project**

| | | | | | | |
|---|---|---|---|---|---|---|
| A | −400 | +50 | +300 | +350 | +157.0 | 26% |
| B | −300 | −200 | +400 | +400 | +150.0 | 25% |
| C | −300 | +150 | +150 | +150 | +73.5 | 23% |
| D | 0 | −300 | +250 | +300 | +159.5 | 50% |

None of the projects can be delayed. All projects are divisible; outlays may be reduced by any proportion and net inflows will then be reduced in the same proportion. No project can be undertaken more than once. Raiders Ltd is able to invest surplus funds in a bank deposit account yielding a return of 7% per annum, net of tax.

You are required to:

(a) prepare calculations showing which projects Raiders Ltd should undertake if capital for immediate investment is limited to £500 000, but is expected to be available without limit at a cost of 10% per annum thereafter;

(5 marks)

(b) provide a mathematical programming formulation to assist the directors of Raiders Ltd in choosing investment projects if capital available immediately is limited to £500 000, capital available after one year is limited to £300 000, and capital is available thereafter without limit at a cost of 10% per annum;

(8 marks)

(c) outline the limitations of the formulation you have provided in (b); (6 marks)

(d) comment briefly on the view that in practice capital is rarely limited absolutely, provided that the borrower is willing to pay a sufficiently high price, and in consequence a technique for selecting investment projects which assumes that capital is limited absolutely, is of no use.

(6 marks)

(Total 25 marks)

*ICAEW Financial Management*

## 26.18 Advanced: Capital rationing and beta analysis

The directors of Anhang plc are considering how best to invest in four projects, details of which are given below.

| | Project I | Project II | Project III | Project IV |
|---|---|---|---|---|
| Net present value (£000) | +80 | +40 | +120 | +110 |
| Beta factor of project | 1.0 | 1.0 | 0.8 | 1.2 |
| Initial payment (£000) | 50 | 40 | 90 | 55 |

The net present values of the projects have been calculated using specific, risk-adjusted discount rates. The director's choice is complicated because Anhang plc has only £90 000 currently available for investment in new projects. Each project must start on the same date and cannot be deferred. Acceptance of any one project would not affect acceptance of any other and all projects are divisible. The directors at a recent board meeting were unable to agree upon how best to invest the £90 000. A summary of the views expressed at the meeting follows:

(i) Wendling argued that as the presumed objective of the company was to maximize shareholder wealth, project III should be undertaken as this project produced the highest net present value.

(ii) Ramm argued that as funds were in short supply investment should be concentrated in those projects with the lowest initial outlay, that is in projects I and II.

(iii) Ritter suggested that project III should be accepted on the grounds of risk reduction. Project III has the lowest beta, and by its acceptance the risk of the company (the company's present beta is 1.0) would be reduced. Ritter also cautioned against acceptance of project IV as it was the most risky project; he pointed out that its high net present value was, in part, a reward for its higher level of associated risk.

(iv) Punto argued against accepting project III, stating that if the project were discounted at the company's cost of capital, its net present value would be greatly reduced.

Requirements:

(a) Write a report to the directors of Anhang plc advising them how best to invest the £90 000, assuming the restriction on capital to apply for one year only. Your report should address the issues raised by each of the *four* directors.

(17 marks)

(b) Explain why the criteria you have used in (a) above to determine the best allocation of capital may be inappropriate if funds are rationed for a period longer than one year.

(4 marks)

(c) Describe the procedures available to a company for the selection of projects when capital is rationed in more than one period.

(4 marks)

(Total 25 marks)

*ICAEW Financial Management*

# Notes

.......................................................................................................

## CHAPTER 1

1 The total profits over the life of a business are identical with total net cash inflows. However, the profits calculated for a particular accounting period will be different from the net cash flows for that period. The difference arises because of the accruals concept in financial accounting. For most situations in this book, decisions that will lead to changes in profits are also assumed to lead to identical changes in net cash flows.

## CHAPTER 2

1 The Statement of Standard Accounting Practice on Stocks and Work in Progress (SSAP 9) requires that all manufacturing costs be regarded as product costs. In Chapter 7 we shall consider a system of variable costing where only variable manufacturing costs are recorded as product costs and fixed manufacturing costs are regarded as period costs.

2 The Statement of Standard Accounting Practice (SSAP 9) requires that inventories be valued at the lower of cost or net realizable value. It is assumed that the closing inventory which is valued at a *cost* of £400 000 is lower than the net realizable value.

## CHAPTER 7

1 There is a limit to how long managers can continue to increase inventories, and eventually the situation will arise when it is necessary to reduce them, and the deferred fixed overheads will eventually be allocated to the periods when the inventories are reduced. Nevertheless, there remains some scope for manipulating profits in the short-term but top management can implement control measures to guard against managers engaging in such behaviour. For example, control measures that monitor changes in inventory volumes will highlight those situations where managers are manipulating profits by unnecessarily increasing inventories.

## CHAPTER 11

1 In a monopolistic competitive market there are many sellers of similar but not necessarily identical products, with no single seller having a large enough share of the market to permit competitors to identify the effect of other individual sellers' pricing decisions on their sales.

## CHAPTER 12

1 Fixed costs will remain unchanged when activity changes. Consequently the standard deviation calculated is the standard deviation of sales volume multiplied by the unit contribution.

## CHAPTER 13

1 Consider a project that costs £10 000 and has a life of four years and an estimated scrap value of £2000. The following diagram illustrates why the project's scrap value is added to the initial outlay to calculate the average capital employed. You can see that at the mid-point of the project's life the capital employed is equal to £6000 (i.e. $\frac{1}{2}(10\,000 + £2000)$).

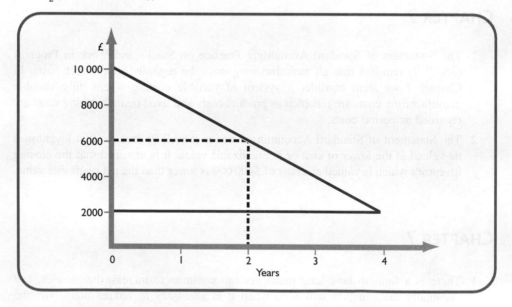

## CHAPTER 14

1 In 1999 the profits of UK companies were subject to a corporate tax rate of 30%. For small companies with annual profits of less than £300 000 the corporate tax rate was 25%.

2 Future payments of interest and the principal repayment on maturity are fixed and known with certainty. Gilt-edged securities are therefore risk-free in nominal terms. However, they are not risk-free in real terms because changes in interest rates will result in changes in the market values.

3 It is assumed that the company does not intend to change its target financing mix of debt and equity.

4 The calculation of the variance of the cash flows for year 1 is as follows:

| Cash flow | Deviation from expected value | Squared deviation | Probability | Weighted amount |
|---|---|---|---|---|
| 10 000 | −10 000 | 100 000 000 | 0.10 | 10 000 000 |
| 15 000 | −5 000 | 25 000 000 | 0.25 | 6 250 000 |
| 20 000 | 0 | 0 | 0.30 | 0 |
| 25 000 | 5 000 | 25 000 000 | 0.25 | 6 250 000 |
| 30 000 | 10 000 | 100 000 000 | 0.10 | 10 000 000 |
| | | Sum of squared deviation (variance) | | 32 500 000 |

# CHAPTER 15

1 The criteria specified are derived from Johnson and Scholes (1999), ch 9.

# CHAPTER 16

1 Managerial interdependency is the extent to which each manager perceives his or her work-related activities to require the joint or cooperative effort of other managers within the organization.

2 Task uncertainty is the extent to which managers can predict confidently the factors that have effects on their work-related activities.

# CHAPTER 19

1 The standard quantity of materials for an actual production of 1800 units is 9000 kg. The actual usage of materials is 10 000 kg, which means an excess usage of 1000 kg.

2 For an output of 1800 units 7200 labour hours should have been used, but the actual number of hours used was 8000. Consequently, 800 excess labour hours were required.

3 The probability of 0.025 is derived from a $t$-distribution with 9 degrees of freedom.

4 We have assumed that the actual observations used to establish the standard performance can be represented by a normal distribution. There is no reason, however, why the analysis could not be modified to accommodate some other probability distribution.

5 We assume here that all favourable variances are in control or do not warrant an investigation. If favourable variances 2 standard deviations from the mean is deemed to be out of control then the probability of observing a variance plus or minus 2 standard deviations from the mean is 0.0455 (0.02275 × 2). Consequently, the probability that the process is out of control is 0.9545 (1 − 0.0455). The variance should still be investigated. Bierman *et al.* (1977) advocate a similar approach by stating that the probability of an event, given that another event (in this case an unfavourable variance) has already occurred, is based on considering only one-half of the probability distribution. Therefore the probabilities derived from normal probability tables should be divided by 0.5. Thus 0.02275/0.5 = 0.0455.

# CHAPTER 20

1 This exhibit and subsequent comments were adapted from Flower, J.F. (1977). Measurement of divisional performance, *Readings in Accounting and Business Research*, *Accounting and Business Research Special Issue*, pp. 121–30.

2 Amey argues that residual income is an inappropriate measure for profit centres and investment centres, whereas for practical reasons Tomkins argues that performance should be measured by a comparison of budgeted and actual cash flows. However, for profit centres where the manager can control the amount invested in working capital Tomkins suggests that residual income is an appropriate measure. For a discussion of each writer's views see Amey (1975), Tomkins (1975), Emmanuel and Otley (1976).

3 Assuming that the actual cash flows in Exhibit 20A.5 were £15 000 for year 1, instead of £20 000, the capital outstanding will be as follows:

| Year | Cash inflow | Capital outstanding (WDV) | Interest (10%) | Depreciation | Residual income |
|---|---|---|---|---|---|
| | (1) | (2) | (3) | $(4) = (1) - (3)$ | $(5) = (1) - [(3) + (4)]$ |
| | (£) | (£) | (£) | (£) | (£) |
| 0 | | 100 000 | | | |
| 1 | 15 000 | 95 000 | 10 000 | 5000 | 0 |

You will see that the capital outstanding is £95 000 compared with £90 000 in Exhibit 20.A5. Any difference between this calculation of capital outstanding and Exhibit 20.A5 will be due entirely to the actual cash inflow (£15 000) being different from the budgeted cash inflow (£20 000).

# CHAPTER 21

1 Exhibits 21.4 and 21.6 are adapted from illustrations first presented by Solomons (1965).

2 The supplying division will obtain marginal revenue in excess of the transfer price of £27.01/£27.49 for the sale of the first five units on the external market and it will not be motivated to follow the optimal company plan for the company as a whole. Similarly, the receiving division will maximize its own profits by accepting all transfers until the net marginal revenue equals the transfer price, and it will therefore wish to sell six units of the final product.

3 The models presented in this appendix are adapted from Tomkins, C., *Financial Planning in Divisionalised Companies*, Haymarket, 1973, Ch. 3.

# CHAPTER 23

1 This illustration has been derived from Shank (1989).

## CHAPTER 25

1 The steps are as follows;

$$TC = \frac{DO}{Q} + \frac{QH}{2}$$

$$\frac{dTC}{dQ} = \frac{-DO}{Q^2} + \frac{H}{2}$$

set

$$\frac{dTC}{dQ} = 0 : \frac{H}{2} - \frac{DO}{Q^2} = 0$$

$$HQ^2 = 2DO = 0$$

$$Q^2 = \frac{2DO}{H}$$

$$\text{Therefore } Q = \sqrt{\left(\frac{2DO}{H}\right)}$$

2 This topic was discussed in Chapter 14.

## CHAPTER 26

1 The eight units of materials consist of five units from the 2000 unused units plus three units released from the reduction in production of product Z by $\frac{3}{4}$ unit.

2 This example was adapted from a problem in Salkin, G. and Kornbluth, J. (1973) *Linear Programming in Financial Planning*, Prentice-Hall, p. 59.

# Bibliography

Accounting Standards Committee (1988) Accounting for Stocks and Work in Progress (SSAP 9).

Ackoff, R.L. (1981) *Creating the Corporate Future*, Wiley.

Adelberg, A. (1986) Resolving conflicts in intracompany transfer pricing, *Accountancy*, November, 86–9.

Ahmed, M.N. and Scapens, R.W. (1991) Cost allocation theory and practice: the continuing debate, in *Issues in Management Accounting* (eds D. Ashton, T. Hopper and R.W. Scapens), Prentice-Hall, pp. 39–60.

American Accounting Association (1957) *Accounting and Reporting Standards for Corporate Financial Statements and Preceding Statements and Supplements*, p. 4.

American Accounting Association (1966) *A Statement of Basic Accounting Theory*, American Accounting Association.

Amey, L.R. (1975) Tomkins on residual income, *Journal of Business Finance and Accounting*, 2(1), Spring, 55; 68.

Ansari, S. (1979) Towards an open system approach to budgeting, *Accounting, Organisations and Society*, 4(3), 149–61.

Anthony, R.N. and Young, D.W. (1988) *Management Control in Non-Profit Organizations*, R.D. Irwin.

Armitage, H.M. and Nicholson, R. (1993) Activity based costing: a survey of Canadian practice, Issue Paper No. 3, Society of Management Accountants of Canada.

Ask, U. and Ax, C. (1992) Trends in the Development of Product Costing Practices and Techniques – A Survey of Swedish Manufacturing Industry, Paper presented at the 15th Annual Congress of the European Accounting Association, Madrid.

Ask, U., Ax, C. and Jonsson, S. (1996) Cost management in Sweden: from modern to post-modern, in Bhimani, A. (ed.) *Management Accounting: European Perspectives*, Oxford, Oxford University Press, pp. 199–217.

Ballas, A. and Venieris, G. (1996) A survey of management accounting practices in Greek firms, in Bhimani, A. (ed.) *Management Accounting: European Perspectives*, Oxford, Oxford University Press, pp. 123–39.

Banerjee, J. and Kane, W. (1996) Report on CIMA/JBA survey, *Management Accounting*, October, **30**, 37.

Barbato, M.B., Collini, P. and Quagli, (1996) Management accounting in Italy, in Bhimani, A. (ed.) *Management Accounting: European Perspectives*, Oxford, Oxford University Press, pp. 140–163.

Barrett, M.E. and Fraser, L.B. (1977), Conflicting roles in budget operations, *Harvard Business Review*, July–August, pp. 137–146.

Bastable, C.W. and Bao, B.H.H. (1988) The fiction of sales-mix and sales quantity variances, *Accounting Horizons*, June, 10–17.

Baxter, W.T. and Oxenfeldt, A.R. (1961) Costing and pricing: the cost accountant versus the economist, *Business Horizons*, Winter, 77–90; also in *Studies in Cost Analysis*, 2nd edn (ed. D. Solomons) Sweet and Maxwell (1968), pp. 293–312.

Berliner, C. and Brimson, J.A. (1988) *Cost Management for Today's Advanced Manufacturing*, Harvard Business School Press.

Bierman, H., Fouraker, I.E. and Jaedicke, R.K. (1977) A use of probability and statistics in performance evaluation, in *Contemporary Cost Accounting and Control*, (ed. G.J. Benston) Dickenson Publishing.

Bjornenak T. (1997a) Diffusion and accounting: the case of ABC in Norway, *Management Accounting Research*, **8**(1), 3–17.

Bjornenak T. (1997b) Conventional wisdom and accounting practices, *Management Accounting Research*, **8**, (4) pp 367–82.

Blayney, P. and Yokoyama, I. (1991), Comparative analysis of Japanese and Australian cost accounting and management practices, Working paper, University of Sydney, Australia.

Boer, G. (1990) Contribution margin analysis: no longer relevant/ strategic cost management: the new paradigm, *Journal of Management Accounting Research* (USA), Fall, 24–7.

Boland, R. (1979) Causality and information system requirements, *Accounting, Organisations and Society*, 4 (4), 259–72.

Boons, A., Roozen, R.A. and Weerd, R.J. de (1994), Kosteninformatie in de Nederlandse Industrie, in *Relevantie methoden en ontwikkelingen* (Rotterdam: Coopers and Lybrand).

Borkowski, S.C. (1990) Environmental and organizational factors affecting transfer pricing: a survey, *Journal of Management Accounting Research*, **2**, 78–99.

Bower, J.L. (1970) *Managing the Resource Allocation Process*, Division of Research, Graduate School of Business Administration, Harvard University.

Brealey, R.A. and Myers, S.C. (1999) *Principles of Corporate Finance*, McGraw-Hill, New York.

Bromwich, M. (1990) The case for strategic management accounting: the role of accounting information for strategy in competitive markets, *Accounting, Organisations and Society*, **1**, 27–46.

Bromwich, M. and Bhimani, A. (1989) *Management Accounting: Evolution not Revolution*, Chartered Institute of Management Accountants.

Bromwich, M. and Bhimani, A. (1994) *Management Accounting: Pathways to Progress*, Chartered Institute of Management Accountants.

Brownell, P. (1981) Participation in budgeting, locus of control and organisational effectiveness, *The Accounting Review*, October, 944–58.

Bruggeman, W., Slagmulder, R. and Waeytens, D. (1996) Management accounting changes; the Belgian experience, in Bhimani, A. (ed.) *Management Accounting: European Perspectives*, Oxford, Oxford University Press, pp. 1–30.

Burchell, S., Clubb, C., Hopwood, A.G., Hughes, J. and Jahapier, J. (1980) The roles of accounting in organizations and society, *Accounting, Organisations and Society*, 1, 5–27.

Cats-Baril, W.L. *et al.* (1986) Joint Product Costing, *Management Accounting* (USA), September, 41–5.

Chandler, A.D., Jr. (1962) *Strategy and Structure: Chapters in the History of the Industrial Enterprise*, Cambridge, MA: MIT Press.

Charles, I. (1985a) The economics approach to transfer price, *Accountancy*, June, 110–12.

Charles, I. (1985b) Transfer-price solution where market exists, *Accountancy*, July, 96.

Chartered Institute of Management Accountants (1996) *Management Accounting: Official Terminology*, CIMA.

Cheatham, C.B. and Cheatham, L.R. (1996) Redesigning cost systems: Is standard costing obsolete?, *Accounting Horizons*, December, 23–31.

Chenhall, R.H. and Langfield-Smith, K. (1998a) Adoption and benefits of management accounting practices: an Australian perspective, *Management Accounting Research*, **9**(1), 1–20.

Chenhall, R.H. and Langfield-Smith, K. (1998b) The relationship between strategic priorities, management techniques and management accounting: An empirical investigation using a systems approach, *Accounting, Organizations and Society*, **23**(3), 243–64.

Chenhall, R.H. and Morris, D. (1985) The impact of structure, environment and interdependence on the perceived usefulness of management accounting systems, *The Accounting Review*, 1, 16–35.

Chow, C.W. (1983) The effect of job standards, tightness and compensation schemes on performance: an exploration of linkages, *The Accounting Review*, October, 667–85.

Chua, W.F. (1988) Interpretive sociology and management accounting research: a critical review, *Accounting, Auditing & Accountability Journal*, **1** (1), 59–79.

Clarke, P.J. (1992) Management Accounting Practices and Techniques in Irish Manufacturing Firms, The 15th Annual Congress of the European Accounting Association, Madrid, Spain.

Clarke, P. (1995), Management accounting practices and techniques in Irish manufacturing companies, Working paper, Trinity College, Dublin.

Cohen, M.D., March, J.G. and Olsen, J.P. (1972) A garbage can model of organizational change. *Administrative Science Quarterly*, March, 1–25.

Collins, F. (1978) The interaction of budget characteristics and personality variables with budget response attitudes, *The Accounting Review*, April, 324–35.

Cooper, D.J. (1980) Discussion of 'Towards a Political Economy of Accounting', *Accounting, Organisations, and Society*, **5** (1), 161–6.

Cooper, D.J., Hayes, D. and Wolf, F. (1981) Accounting in organised anarchies: understanding and designing accounting systems in ambiguous situations, *Accounting, Organisations and Society*, **6**(3) 175–91.

Cooper, R. (1990a) Cost classifications in unit–based and activity–based manufacturing cost systems, *Journal of Cost Management*, Fall, 4–14.

Cooper, R. (1990b) Explicating the logic of ABC, *Management Accounting*, November, 58–60.

Cooper, R. (1997) Activity-Based Costing: Theory and Practice, in Brinker, B.J. (ed.), *Handbook of Cost Management*, Warren, Gorham and Lamont, pp. B1–B33.

Cooper, R. and Kaplan, R.S. (1987) How cost accounting systematically distorts product costs, in *Accounting and Management: Field Study Perspectives* (eds W.J. Bruns and R.S. Kaplan), Harvard Business School Press, Ch. 8.

Cooper, R. and Kaplan, R.S. (1988) Measure costs right: make the right decisions, *Harvard Business Review*, September/October, 96–103.

Cooper, R. and Kaplan, R.S. (1991) *The Design of Cost Management Systems: Text, Cases and Readings*, Prentice-Hall.

Cooper, R. and Kaplan, R.S. (1992) Activity based systems: measuring the costs of resource usage, *Accounting Horizons*, September, 1–13.

Cornick, M., Cooper, W. and Wilson, S. (1988) How do companies analyze overhead?, *Management Accounting*, June, 41–3.

Covaleski, M. and Dirsmith, M. (1980) Budgeting as a Means for Control and Loose Coupling in Nursing Services (unpublished), Pennsylvania State University.

Cress, W. and Pettijohn, J. (1985) A survey of budget-related planning and control policies and procedures, *Journal of Accounting Education*, 3, Fall, 61–78.

Currie, W. (1990) Strategic management of advanced manufacturing technology, *Management Accounting*, October, 50–2.

Currie, W. (1991a) Managing technology: a crisis in management accounting, *Management Accounting*, February, 24–7.

Currie, W. (1991b) Managing production technology in Japanese industry, *Management Accounting*, June, 28–9, July/August, 36–8.

Cyert, R.M. and March, J.G. (1969) *A Behavioural Theory of the Firm*, Prentice-Hall.

Dardenne, P. (1998) Capital budgeting practices – Procedures and techniques by large companies in Belgium, paper presented at the 21st Annual Congress of the European Accounting Association, Antwerp, Belgium.

Demski, J.S. (1968) Variance analysis using a constrained linear model, in *Studies in Cost Analysis*, 2nd edn (ed. D. Solomons), Sweet and Maxwell.

Demski, J.S. (1977) Analysing the effectiveness of the traditional standard costing variance model, in *Contemporary Cost Accounting and Control* (ed. G.J. Benston), Dickenson Publishing.

Dhavale, D.G. (1989) Product costing in flexible manufacturing systems, *Journal of Management Accounting Research* (USA), Fall, 66–88.

Dirsmith, M.W. and Jablonsky, S.F. (1979) MBO, political rationality and information inductance, *Accounting, Organisations and Society*, 1, 39–52.

Dittman, D.A. and Ferris, KR. (1978) Profit centre: a satisfaction generating concept, *Accounting and Business Research*, **8**(32), Autumn, 242–5.

Drucker, P.F. (1964) Controls, control and management, in *Management Controls: New Directions in Basic Research* (eds C.P. Bonini, R. Jaedicke and H. Wagner), McGraw-Hill.

Drury, C. (1998) *Costing: An Introduction*, International Thomson Business Press, Ch.3.

Drury C. and Tayles M. (1994) Product costing in UK manufacturing organisations, *The European Accounting Review*, **3**(3), 443–69.

Drury C. and Tayles M. (2000), *Cost system design and profitability analysis in UK companies*, Chartered Institute of Management Accountants.

Drury, C., Braund, S., Osborne, P. and Tayles, M. (1993) A survey of management accounting practices in UK manufacturing companies, ACCA Research Paper, Chartered Association of Certified Accountants.

Dugdale, D. (1989) Contract accounting and the SSAP, *Management Accounting*, June, 62–4.

Dugdale, D. and Jones, T.C. (1998) Throughput accounting: trans-formation practices?, *British Accounting Review*, **30**(3), 203–20.

Earl, M.J. and Hopwood, A.G. (1981) From management information to information management, in *The Information*

*Systems Environment* (ed. Lucas, H.C. Jr. *et al.*), Amsterdam, Holland.

Egginton, D. (1995) Divisional performance measurement: residual income and the asset base, *Management Accounting Research*, September, 201–22.

Elphick, C. (1983) A new approach to cost allocations, *Management Accounting*, December, 22–5.

Emmanuel, C. and Mehafdi, M. (1994) *Transfer Pricing*, Academic Press.

Emmanuel, C.R. and Otley, D. (1976) The usefulness of residual income, *Journal of Business Finance and Accounting*, 13(4), Winter, 43–52.

Emmanuel, C., Otley, D. and Merchant, K. (1990) *Accounting for Management Control*, International Thomson Business Press.

Emore, J.R. and Ness, J.A. (1991) The slow pace of meaningful changes in cost systems, *Journal of Cost Management for the Manufacturing Industry*, Winter, 36–45.

Evans, H. and Ashworth, G. (1996) Survey conclusions: wakeup to the competition, *Management Accounting* (UK), May, 16–18.

Ezzamel, M. and Hart, H. (1987) *Advanced Management Accounting: An Organisational Emphasis*. London, Cassell.

Ezzamel, M.A. and Hilton, K. (1980) Divisionalization in British industry: a preliminary study, *Accounting and Business Research*, Summer, 197–214.

Feldman, M.S. and March, J.G. (1981) Information in organizations as signal and symbol, *Administrative Science Quarterly*, **26** (2) 171–86.

Fielden, J. and Robertson, J. (1980) The content of a value for money review of performance audit, *Public Finance and Accounting*, November, 23–5.

Fisher, I. (1930) *The Theory of Interest*, Macmillan.

Fisher, J. (1995) Contingency-based research on management control systems: Categorization by level of complexity, *Journal of Accounting Literature*, 14, pp 24–53.

Fitzgerald, L., Johnston, R., Silvestro, R. and Steele, A. (1989) Management control in service industries, *Management Accounting*, April, 44–6.

Fitzgerald, L., Johnston, R., Brignall, T.J., Silvestro, R. and Voss, C. (1991) *Performance Measurement in Service Businesses*, Chartered Institute of Management Accountants.

Fitzgerald, L. and Moon, P. (1996) *Performnce Management in Service Industries*, Chartered Institute of Management Accountants.

Flower, J. (1973) *Computer Models for Accountants*, Haymarket, Chs 4, 5.

Foster, G. and Horngren, C.T. (1988) Cost accounting and cost management in a JIT environment, *Journal of Cost Management for the Manufacturing Industry*, Winter, 4–14.

Fremgen, J.M. and Liao, S.S. (1981) The Allocation of Corporate Indirect Costs, National Association of Accountants, New York.

Friedman, A.L. and Lyne, S.R. (1995) *Activity-based Techniques: The Real Life Consequences*, Chartered Institute of Management Accountants.

Galloway, D. and Waldron, D. (1988) Throughput accounting – 1: the need for a new language for manufacturing, *Management Accounting*, November, 34–5.

Gibson, B. (1990) Determining meaningful sales relational (mix) variances, *Accounting and Business Research*, Winter, 35–40.

Goetz, B. (1949) *Management Planning and Control: A Managerial Approach to Industrial Accounting*, McGraw-Hill, p. 142.

Goldratt, E.M. and Cox, J. (1984) *The Goal*, London, Gower.

Goldratt, E.M. and Cox, J. (1992) *The Goal* (2nd edn), London, Gower.

Gould, J.R. (1964) Internal pricing on firms when there are costs of using an outside market, *Journal of Business*, **37**(1), January, 61–7.

Govindarajan, V. (1984) Appropriateness of accounting data in performance evaluation: an empirical evaluation of environmental uncertainty as an intervening variable, *Accounting, Organisations and Society*, **9**(2), 125–36.

Govindarajan, V. and Gupta, A.K. (1985) Linking control systems to business unit strategy: Impact on performance, *Accounting, Organizations and Society*, **10**(1), 51–66.

Green, F.B. and Amenkhienan, F.E. (1992) Accounting innovations: A cross sectional survey of manufacturing firms, *Journal of Cost Management for the Manufacturing Industry*, Spring 58–64.

Guilding, C., Lamminmaki, D. and Drury, C. (1998) Budgeting and standard costing practices in New Zealand and the United Kingdom, *The International Journal of Accounting*, **33**(5), 41–60.

Gul, F.A. and Chia, Y.M. (1994) The effects of management accounting systems, perceived environmental uncertainty and decentralization on managerial performance: A test of three–way interaction, *Accounting, Organizations and Society*, **19**(4/5), 413–26.

Hedberg, B. and Jonsson, S. (1978) Designing semi-confusing information systems for organizations in changing environments, *Accounting, Organisations and Society*, 1, 47–64.

Hergert, M. and Morris, D. (1989) Accounting data for value chain analysis, *Strategic Management Journal*, **10**, 175–88.

Hiromoto, T. (1991) Restoring the relevance of management accounting, *Journal of Management Accounting Research*, **3**, 1–15.

Hirshleifer, J. (1956) On the economies of transfer pricing, *Journal of Business*, July, 172–84.

Hirst, M.K. (1981) Accounting information and the evaluation of subordinate performance, *The Accounting Review*, October, 771–84.

Hirst, M.K. (1987) The effects of setting budget goals and task uncertainty on performance: a theoretical analysis, *The Accounting Review*, October, 774–84.

Hofstede, G.H. (1968) *The Game of Budget Control*, Tavistock.

Holzer, H.P. and Norreklit, H. (1991) Some thoughts on the cost accounting developments in the United States, *Management Accounting Research*, March, 3–13.

Hopper, T.M., Storey, J. and Willmott, H. (1987) Accounting for accounting: towards the development of a dialectical view, *Accounting, Organisations and Society*, **12** (5) 437–56.

Hopper, T., Kirkham, L., Scapens, R.W. and Turley, S. (1992) Does financial accounting dominate management accounting – A research note, *Management Accounting Research*, 3(4), 307–11.

Hopwood, A.G. (1976) *Accountancy and Human Behaviour*, Prentice-Hall.

Hopwood, A.G. (1978) Towards an organisational perspective for the study of accounting and information systems, *Accounting, Organisations and Society*, 3(1), 3–14.

Horngren, C.T. (1967) Process costing in perspective: forget FIFO, *Accounting Review*, July.

Horngren, C.T. (1990) Contribution margin analysis: no longer relevant/strategic cost management: the new paradigm,

*Journal of Management Accounting Research* (USA), Fall, 21–4.

Horngren, G.T. and Sorter, G.H. (1962) Asset recognition and economic attributes: the relevant costing approach, *The Accounting Review*, **37**, July, 394, also in *Contemporary Cost Accounting and Control*, (ed G.J. Benston), Dickenson (1977), pp. 462–74.

Imoisili, O.A. (1989) The role of budget data in the evaluation of managerial performance, *Accounting, Organizations and Society*, **14**(4), 325–35.

Innes, J. (1998) Strategic Management Accounting, in Innes, J (ed.), *Handbook of Management Accounting*, Gee, Ch. 2.

Innes, J. and Mitchell, F. (1991) ABC: A survey of CIMA members, *Management Accounting*, October, 28–30.

Innes, J. and Mitchell, F. (1992) A review of activity based costing practice, in *Handbook in Management Accounting Practice* (ed. C. Drury), Butterworth-Heinemann, Ch. 3.

Innes, J. and Mitchell, F. (1995a) A survey of activity-based costing in the UK's largest companies, *Management Accounting Research*, June, 137–54.

Innes, J. and Mitchell, F. (1995b) Activity-based costing, in *Issues in Management Accounting* (eds D. Ashton, T. Hopper and R.W. Scapens), Prentice-Hall, pp. 115–36.

Innes, J. and Mitchell, F. (1997) The application of activity-based costing in the United Kingdom's largest financial institutions, *The Service Industries Journal*, **17**(1), 190–203.

Israelsen, P., Anderson, M., Rohde, C. and Sorensen, P.E. (1996) Management accounting in Denmark: theory and practice, in Bhimani, A. (ed.) *Management Accounting: European Perspectives*, Oxford, Oxford University Press, pp. 31–53.

Ittner, C.D., Larcker, D.F. and Rajan, M.V. (1997) The choice of performance measures in annual bonus contracts, *The Accounting Review*, **72**(2), 231–55.

Jaedicke R.K. and Robichek, A.A. (1964) Cost–volume–profit analysis under conditions of uncertainty, *The Accounting Review*, **39**(4), October, 917–26; also in *Studies in Cost Analysis* (ed. D. Solomons), Sweet and Maxwell (1968); also in *Cost Accounting, Budgeting and Control* (ed. W.E. Thomas), pp. 192–210, South Western Publishing Company.

Johnson, H.T. (1990) Professors, customers and value: bringing a global perspective to management accounting education, in *Performance Excellence in Manufacturing and Services Organizations* (ed. P. Turney), American Accounting Association.

Johnson, H.T. and Kaplan, R.S. (1987) *Relevance Lost: The Rise and Fall of Management Accounting*, Harvard Business School Press.

Johnson, G. and Scholes, K. (1999) *Exploring Corporate Strategy*, Prentice-Hall.

Jones, T.C. and Dugdale, D. (1998) Theory of constraints: transforming ideas?, *British Accounting Review*, **30**(1), 73–92.

Joseph, N., Turley, S., Burns, J., Lewis, L., Scapens, R.W. and Southworth, A. (1996) External financial reporting and management information: A survey of UK management accountants, *Management Accounting Research* **7**(1), 73–94.

Joshi, P.L. (1998) An explanatory study of activity-based costing practices and benefits in large size manufacturing companies in India, *Accounting and Business Review*, **5**(1), 65–93.

Joye, M.P. and Blayney, P.J. (1990) Cost and management accounting practice in Australian manufacturing companies: survey results, Monograph No 7, University of Sydney.

Joye, M.P. and Blayney, P.J. (1991) Strategic management accounting survey, Monograph No. 8, University of Sydney.

Kaplan, R.S. (1975) The significance and investigation of cost variances: survey and extensions, *Journal of Accounting Research*, **13**(2), Autumn, 311–37, also in *Contemporary Issues in Cost and Managerial Accounting* (eds H.R. Anton, P.A. Firmin and H.D. Grove), Houghton Mifflin (1978).

Kaplan, R.S. (1982) *Advanced Management Accounting*, Prentice-Hall.

Kaplan, R.S. (1990) Contribution margin analysis: no longer relevant/strategic cost management: the new paradigm, *Journal of Management Accounting Research* (USA), Fall, 2–15.

Kaplan, R.S. (1994a) Management accounting (1984–1994): development of new practice and theory, *Management Accounting Research*, September and December, 247–60.

Kaplan, R.S. (1994b) Flexible budgeting in an activity-based costing framework, *Accounting Horizons*, June, 104–109.

Kaplan, R.S. and Atkinson, A.A. (1989) *Advanced Management Accounting*, Prentice-Hall.

Kaplan, R.S. and Atkinson, A.A. (1998) *Advanced Management Accounting*, Prentice-Hall, Ch.3

Kaplan, R.S. and Cooper, R. (1998) *Cost and Effect: Using Integrated Systems to Drive Profitability and Performance*, Harvard Business School Press.

Kaplan, R.S. and Norton, D.P. (1992) The balanced scorecard: measures that drive performance, *Harvard Business Review*, Jan–Feb, 71–9.

Kaplan, R.S. and Norton, D.P. (1993) Putting the balanced scorecard to work, *Harvard Business Review*, September–October, 134–47.

Kaplan, R.S. and Norton, D.P. (1996a) Using the balanced scorecard as a strategic management system, *Harvard Business Review*, Jan–Feb, 75–85.

Kaplan, R.S. and Norton, D.P. (1996b) *The Balanced Scorecard: Translating strategy into action*, Harvard Business School Press.

Kato, Y. (1993) Target costing support systems: lessons from leading Japanese companies, *Management Accounting Research*, March, 33–48.

Kelly, M. and Pratt, M. (1992) Purposes and paradigms of management accounting: beyond economic reductionism, *Accounting Education*, **1**(3), 225–46.

Kenis, I. (1979) The effects of budgetary goal characteristics on managerial attitudes and performance, *The Accounting Review*, October, 707–21.

Khandwalla, P.N. (1972) The effects of different types of competition on the use of management controls, *Journal of Accounting Research*, Autumn, 275–85.

Lauderman, M. and Schaeberle, F.W. (1983) The cost accounting practices of firms using standard costs, *Cost and Management* (Canada), July/August, 21–5.

Lawrence, P.R. and Lorsch, J.W. (1986) *Organization and Environment*, Harvard Business School Press.

Lee, T.A. (1996) *Income and Value Measurement*, Thomson Business Press.

Licata, M.P., Strawser, R.H. and Welker, R.B. (1986) A note on participation in budgeting and locus of control, *The Accounting Review*, January, 112–17.

Lindblom, C.E. (1959) The science of 'Muddling Through', *Public Administration Review*, Summer, 79–88.

Lister, R. (1983) Appraising the value of post-audit procedures, *Accountancy Age*, 20 October, 40.

Lord, B.R. (1996), Strategic management accounting: the emperor's new clothes? *Management Accounting Research*, 7(3), 347–66.

Lukka, K. and Granlund, M. (1996) Cost accounting in Finland: Current practice and trends of development, *The European Accounting Review*, 5(1), 1–28.

Macintosh, N.B. (1985) *The Social Software of Accounting and Information Systems*, Wiley.

Macintosh, N.B. (1994) *Management Accounting and Control Systems: An Organisational and Behavioural Approach*, Wiley.

Mak, Y.T. and Roush, M.L. (1994) Flexible budgeting and variance analysis in an activity-based costing environment, *Accounting Horizons*, June, 93–104.

Mak, Y.T. and Roush, M.L. (1996) Managing activity costs with flexible budgets and variance analysis, *Accounting Horizons*, September, 141–6.

Manes, R.P. (1983) Demand elasticities: supplements to sales budget variance reports, *The Accounting Review*, January, 143–56.

Mauriel, J. and Anthony, R.N. (1986) Mis-evaluation of investment centre performance, *Harvard Business Review*, March/April, 98–105.

Merchant, K.A. (1989) *Rewarding Results: Motivating Profit Center Managers*, Harvard Business School Press.

Merchant, K.A. (1990) How challenging should profit budget targets be? *Management Accounting*, November, 46–8.

Merchant, K.A. (1998) *Modern Management Control Systems: Text and Cases*, Prentice-Hall, New Jersey.

Merchant, K.A. and Shields, M.D. (1993) When and why to measure costs less accurately to improve decision making, *Accounting Horizons*, June, 76–81.

Mia, L. (1989) The impact of participation in budgeting and job difficulty on managerial performance and work motivation: a research note, *Accounting, Organisations and Society*, 14(4), 347–57.

Milani, K. (1975) The relationship of participation in budget setting to industrial supervisor performance and attitudes: a field study, *The Accounting Review*, April, 274–84.

Miles, R.E. and Snow, C.C. (1978) *Organizational Strategies, Structure and Process*, New York, McGraw-Hill.

Mills, R.W. (1988) Pricing decisions in UK manufacturing and service companies, *Management Accounting*, November, 38–9.

Monden, Y. and Hamada, K. (1991) Target costing and Kaizen costing in Japanese automobile companies, *Journal of Management Accounting Research*, Autumn, 16–34.

Moon, P. and Fitzgerald, L. (1996) *Performance Measurement in Service Industries: Making it Work*, Chartered Institute of Management Accountants, London.

Moore, P.G. and Thomas, H. (1991) *The Anatomy of Decisions*, Penguin.

Neale, C.W. and Holmes, D. (1988) Post-completion audits: The costs and benefits, *Management Accounting*, 66(3), 27–31.

Neale, C.W. and Holmes, D. (1991) *Post-completion Auditing*, Pitman.

Nicholls, B. (1992) ABC in the UK – a status report, *Management Accounting*, May, 22–3.

Osni, M. (1973) Factor analysis of behavioural variables affecting budgetary stock, *The Accounting Review*, 535–48.

Otley, D.T. (1978) Budget use and managerial performance, *Journal of Accounting Research*, 16(1), Spring, 122–49.

Otley, D.T. (1980) The contingency theory of management accounting: achievement and prognosis, *Accounting, Organizations and Society*, 5(4), 413–28.

Otley, D.T. (1987) *Accounting Control and Organizational Behaviour*, Heinemann.

Ouchi, W.G. (1979) A conceptual framework for the design of organizational control mechanisms, *Management Science*, 833–48.

Pendlebury, M. (1996) Management accounting in local government, in *Handbook of Management Accounting Practice* (ed. C. Drury), Butterworth-Heinemann, London.

Pfeffer, J. and Salancik, G.R. (1974) Organisational decision making as a political process: the case of a university budget, *Administrative Science Quarterly*, June, 135–50.

Phyrr, P.A. (1976) Zero-based budgeting – where to use it and how to begin, *S.A.M. Advanced Management Journal*, Summer, 5.

Pike, R.H. (1996) A longitudinal study of capital budgeting practices, *Journal of Business Finance and Accounting*, 23(1), 79–92.

Pike, R. and Neale, B. (1999) *Corporate Finance and Investment*, Prentice-Hall Europe.

Plunkett, J.J., Dale, B.G. and Tyrrell, R.W. (1985) *Quality Costs*, London, Department of Trade and Industry.

Porter, M. (1985) *Competitive Advantage*, New York, Free Press.

Puxty, A.G. (1993) *The Social and Organisational Context of Management Accounting*, Academic Press.

Puxty, A.G. and Lyall, D. (1990) *Cost Control into the 1990s: A Survey of Standard Costing and Budgeting Practices in the UK*, Chartered Institute of Management Accountants; see also *Management Accounting*, February, 1990, 44–5.

Ramadan, S.S. (1989) The rationale for cost allocation: A study of UK companies, *Accounting and Business Research*, Winter, 31–7.

Reece, J.S. and Cool, W.R. (1978) Measuring investment centre performance, *Harvard Business Review*, May/June 29–49.

Roslender, R. (1992) *Sociological Perspectives on Modern Accountancy*, Routledge.

Roslender, R. (1995) Accounting for strategic positioning: Responding to the crisis in management accounting, *British Journal of Management*, 6, 45–57.

Roslender, R. (1996) Relevance lost and found: Critical perspectives on the promise of management accounting, *Critical Perspectives on Accounting*, 7(5), 533–61.

Saez-Torrecilla, A., Fernandez-Fernandez, A., Texeira-Quiros, J. and Vaquera-Mosquero, M. (1996) Management accounting in Spain: trends in thought and practice, in Bhimani, A. (ed.) *Management Accounting: European Perspective 3*, Oxford, Oxford University Press, pp. 180–90.

Salkin, G. and Kornbluth, J. (1973) *Linear Programming in Financial Planning*, Prentice-Hall, Ch. 7.

Samuels, J.M., Wilkes, F.M. and Brayshaw, R.E. (1998) *Management of Company Finance*, Chapman and Hall.

Scapens, R.W. (1991) *Management Accounting: A Review of Recent Developments*, Macmillan.

Scarborough, P.A., Nanni, A. and Sakurai, M. (1991) Japanese management accounting practices and the effects of assembly and process automation, *Management Accounting Research*, 2, 27–46.

Scherrer, G. (1996) Management accounting: a German perspective, in Bhimani, A. (ed.), *Management Accounting: European Perspectives*, Oxford, Oxford University Press, pp. 100–22.

Schiff, M. and Lewin, A.Y. (1970) The impact of people on budgets, *The Accounting Review*, April, 259–68.

Schwarzbach, H.R. (1985) The impact of automation on accounting for direct costs, *Management Accounting* (USA), **67**(6), 45–50.

Seal, W., Cullen, J., Dunlop, D., Berry, T., and Ahmed, M. (1999) Enacting a European supply chain: a case study on the role of management accounting, *Management Accounting Research*, **10**(3), 303–22.

Sen, P.K. (1998) Another look at cost variance investigation, *Accounting Horizons*, February, 127–37.

Shank, J.K. (1989) Strategic cost management: new wine or just new bottles?, *Journal of Management Accounting Research* (USA), Fall, 47–65.

Shank, J. and Govindarajan, V. (1992) Strategic cost management: the value chain perspective, *Journal of Management Accounting Research*, **4**, 179–97.

Shields, M.D. (1995) An empirical analysis of firms' implementation experiences with activity-based costing, *Journal of Management Accounting Research*, **7**, Fall, 148–66.

Shim, E. and Stagliano, A. (1997) A survey of US manufacturers on implementation of ABC, *Journal of Cost Management*, March/April, 39–41.

Simmonds, K. (1981) Strategic management accounting, *Management Accounting*, **59**(4), 26–9.

Simmonds, K. (1982) Strategic management accounting for pricing: a case example, *Accounting and Business Research*, **12**(47), 206–14.

Simmonds, K. (1986) The accounting assessment of competitive position, *European Journal of Marketing, Organisations and Society*, **12**(4), 357–74.

Simon, H.A. (1959) Theories of decision making in economics and behavioural science, *The American Economic Review*, June, 233–83.

Simons, R. (1987) Accounting control systems and business strategy, *Accounting, Organizations and Society*, **12**(4), 357–74.

Simons, R. (1999) *Performance Measurement and Control Systems for Implementing Strategy*, Prentice-Hall, New Jersey.

Sizer, J. (1989) *An Insight into Management Accounting*, Penguin, Chs 11, 12.

Sizer, J. and Mottram, G. (1996) Successfully evaluating and controlling investments in advanced manufacturing technology, in *Management Accounting Handbook* (ed. C. Drury), Butterworth-Heinemann.

Skinner, R.C. (1990) The role of profitability in divisional decision making and performance, *Accounting and Business Research*, Spring, 135–41.

Slater, K. and Wootton, C. (1984) *Joint and By-product Costing in the UK*, Institute of Cost and Management Accounting.

Solomons, D. (1965) *Divisional Performance: Measurement and Control*, R.D. Irwin.

Stedry, A. and Kay, E. (1966) The effects of goal difficulty on performance: a field experiment, *Behavioural Science*, November, 459–70.

Stewart, G.B. (1991) *The Quest for Value: A Guide for Senior Managers*, Harper Collins, New York.

Stewart, G.B. (1994) EVA$^{(TM)}$: Fact and Fantasy, *Journal of Applied Corporate Finance*, Summer, 71–84.

Stewart, G.B. (1995) EVA$^{(TM)}$ works – But not if you make common mistakes, *Fortune*, 1 May, 81–2.

Tang, R. (1992) Canadian transfer pricing in the 1990s, *Management Accounting* (USA), February.

Tani, T., Okano, H., Shimizu, N., Iwabuchi, Y, Fukuda, J. and Cooray, S. (1994) Target cost management in Japanese companies: current state of the art, *Management Accounting Research*, **5**(1), 67–82.

Thompson, J.D. (1967) *Organisations in Action*, McGraw-Hill.

Thompson, J.D. and Tuden, A. (1959) Strategies, structures and processes of organizational decision, in *Comparative Studies in Administration* (eds Thompson, J.D. *et al.*), University of Pittsburg Press.

Thompson, J.L. (1997) *Strategic Management*, Chapman and Hall, London.

Tomkins, C. (1973) *Financial Planning in Divisionalised Companies*, Haymarket, Chs 4 and 8.

Tomkins, C. (1975) Another look at residual income, *Journal of Business Finance and Accounting*, **2**(1), Spring 39–54.

Tomkins, C. and Carr, C. (1996) Editorial in Special Issue of Management Accounting Research: Strategic Management Accounting, *Management Accounting Research*, **7**(2), 165–7.

Tomkins, C. and McAulay, L. (1996) Modelling fair transfer prices where no market guidelines exist, in *Management Accounting Handbook* (ed. C. Drury), Butterworth-Heinemann, Ch. 16.

Trahan, E.A. and Gitman, L.J. (1995) Bridging the theory–practice gap in corporate finance: A survey of chief finance officers, *The Quarterly Review of Economics and Finance*, **35**(1), Spring, 73–87.

Turney, P. (1993) *Common Cents: The ABC Performance Breakthrough*, Cost Technology, Hillsboro, Oregon, USA.

Umapathy, S. (1987) *Current Budgeting Practices in U.S. Industry: The State of the Art*, New York, Quorum.

Virtanen, K., Malmi, T., Vaivio, J. and Kasanen, E. (1996) Drivers of management accounting in Finland, in Bhimani, A. (ed.) *Management Accounting: European Perspectives*, Oxford, Oxford University Press, pp. 218–41.

Vroom, V.H. (1960) *Some Personality Determinants of the Effects of Participation*, Prentice-Hall.

Ward, K. (1992) Accounting for marketing strategies, in *Management Accounting Handbook* (ed. C. Drury), Butterworth-Heinemann, Ch. 7.

Watson, D.H. and Baumler, J.V. (1975) Transfer pricing: a behavioural context, *Accounting Review*, **50**(3), July, 466–74.

Wetnight, R. B. (1958) Direct costing passes the future benefit test, *NAA Bulletin*, **39**, August, 84.

Weick, K.E. (1969) *The Social Psychology of Organising*, Addison Wesley.

Wildavsky, A. (1974) *The Politics of Budgetary Process*, Little Brown.

Wilkes, F.M. (1989) *Operational Research: Analysis and Applications*, McGraw-Hill.

Wilson, R.M. and Chua W.E. (1993) *Management Accounting: Method and Meaning*, International Thomson Business Press, Ch. 7.

Woodward, J. (1965) *Industrial Organization; Theory and Practice*, Oxford University Press.

Yoshikawa, T., Innes, J., Mitchell, F. and Tanaka, M. (1993) *Contemporary Cost Management*, Chapman and Hall.

Young, P. H. (1985) *Cost Allocation: Methods, Principles, Applications*, Amsterdam: North Holland.

# Appendices

# Appendix A: Present value factors

The table gives the present value of a single payment received $n$ years in the future discounted at $x\%$ per year. For example, with a discount rate of 7% a single payment of £1 in six years time has a present value of £0.6663 or 66.63p.

| Years | 1% | 2% | 3% | 4% | 5% | 6% | 7% | 8% | 9% | 10% |
|---|---|---|---|---|---|---|---|---|---|---|
| 1 | 0.9901 | 0.9804 | 0.9709 | 0.9615 | 0.9524 | 0.9434 | 0.9346 | 0.9259 | 0.9174 | 0.9091 |
| 2 | 0.9803 | 0.9612 | 0.9426 | 0.9426 | 0.9070 | 0.8900 | 0.8734 | 0.8573 | 0.8417 | 0.8264 |
| 3 | 0.9706 | 0.9423 | 0.9151 | 0.8890 | 0.8638 | 0.8396 | 0.8163 | 0.7938 | 0.7722 | 0.7513 |
| 4 | 0.9610 | 0.9238 | 0.8885 | 0.8548 | 0.8227 | 0.7921 | 0.7629 | 0.7350 | 0.7084 | 0.6830 |
| 5 | 0.9515 | 0.9057 | 0.8626 | 0.8219 | 0.7835 | 0.7473 | 0.7130 | 0.6806 | 0.6499 | 0.6209 |
| 6 | 0.9420 | 0.8880 | 0.8375 | 0.7903 | 0.7462 | 0.7050 | 0.6663 | 0.6302 | 0.5963 | 0.5645 |
| 7 | 0.9327 | 0.8706 | 0.8131 | 0.7599 | 0.7107 | 0.6651 | 0.6227 | 0.5835 | 0.5470 | 0.5132 |
| 8 | 0.9235 | 0.8535 | 0.7894 | 0.7307 | 0.6768 | 0.6274 | 0.5820 | 0.5403 | 0.5019 | 0.4665 |
| 9 | 0.9143 | 0.8368 | 0.7664 | 0.7026 | 0.6446 | 0.5919 | 0.5439 | 0.5002 | 0.4604 | 0.4241 |
| 10 | 0.9053 | 0.8203 | 0.7441 | 0.6756 | 0.6139 | 0.5584 | 0.5083 | 0.4632 | 0.4224 | 0.3855 |
| 11 | 0.8963 | 0.8043 | 0.7224 | 0.6496 | 0.5847 | 0.5268 | 0.4751 | 0.4289 | 0.3875 | 0.3505 |
| 12 | 0.8874 | 0.7885 | 0.7014 | 0.6246 | 0.5568 | 0.4970 | 0.4440 | 0.3971 | 0.3555 | 0.3186 |
| 13 | 0.8787 | 0.7730 | 0.6810 | 0.6006 | 0.5303 | 0.4688 | 0.4150 | 0.3677 | 0.3262 | 0.2897 |
| 14 | 0.8700 | 0.7579 | 0.6611 | 0.5775 | 0.5051 | 0.4423 | 0.3878 | 0.3405 | 0.2992 | 0.2633 |
| 15 | 0.8613 | 0.7430 | 0.6419 | 0.5553 | 0.4810 | 0.4173 | 0.3624 | 0.3152 | 0.2745 | 0.2394 |
| 16 | 0.8528 | 0.7284 | 0.6232 | 0.5339 | 0.4581 | 0.3936 | 0.3387 | 0.2919 | 0.2519 | 0.2176 |
| 17 | 0.8444 | 0.7142 | 0.6050 | 0.5134 | 0.4363 | 0.3714 | 0.3166 | 0.2703 | 0.2311 | 0.1978 |
| 18 | 0.8360 | 0.7002 | 0.5874 | 0.4936 | 0.4155 | 0.3503 | 0.2959 | 0.2502 | 0.2120 | 0.1799 |
| 19 | 0.8277 | 0.6864 | 0.5703 | 0.4746 | 0.3957 | 0.3305 | 0.2765 | 0.2317 | 0.1945 | 0.1635 |
| 20 | 0.8195 | 0.6730 | 0.5537 | 0.4564 | 0.3769 | 0.3118 | 0.2584 | 0.2145 | 0.1784 | 0.1486 |
| 21 | 0.8114 | 0.6598 | 0.5375 | 0.4388 | 0.3589 | 0.2942 | 0.2415 | 0.1987 | 0.1637 | 0.1351 |
| 22 | 0.8034 | 0.6468 | 0.5219 | 0.4220 | 0.3418 | 0.2775 | 0.2257 | 0.1839 | 0.1502 | 0.1228 |
| 23 | 0.7954 | 0.6342 | 0.5067 | 0.4057 | 0.3256 | 0.2618 | 0.2109 | 0.1703 | 0.1378 | 0.1117 |
| 24 | 0.7876 | 0.6217 | 0.4919 | 0.3901 | 0.3101 | 0.2470 | 0.1971 | 0.1577 | 0.1264 | 0.1015 |
| 25 | 0.7798 | 0.6095 | 0.4776 | 0.3751 | 0.2953 | 0.2330 | 0.1842 | 0.1460 | 0.1160 | 0.0923 |
| 26 | 0.7720 | 0.5976 | 0.4637 | 0.3607 | 0.2812 | 0.2198 | 0.1722 | 0.1352 | 0.1064 | 0.0839 |
| 27 | 0.7644 | 0.5859 | 0.4502 | 0.3468 | 0.2678 | 0.2074 | 0.1609 | 0.1252 | 0.0976 | 0.0763 |
| 28 | 0.7568 | 0.5744 | 0.4371 | 0.3335 | 0.2551 | 0.1956 | 0.1504 | 0.1159 | 0.0895 | 0.0693 |
| 29 | 0.7493 | 0.5631 | 0.4243 | 0.3207 | 0.2429 | 0.1846 | 0.1406 | 0.1073 | 0.0822 | 0.0630 |
| 30 | 0.7419 | 0.5521 | 0.4120 | 0.3083 | 0.2314 | 0.1741 | 0.1314 | 0.0094 | 0.0754 | 0.0573 |
| 35 | 0.7059 | 0.5000 | 0.3554 | 0.2534 | 0.1813 | 0.1301 | 0.0937 | 0.0676 | 0.0490 | 0.0356 |
| 40 | 0.6717 | 0.4529 | 0.3066 | 0.2083 | 0.1420 | 0.0972 | 0.0668 | 0.0460 | 0.0318 | 0.0221 |
| 45 | 0.6391 | 0.4102 | 0.2644 | 0.1712 | 0.1113 | 0.0727 | 0.0476 | 0.0313 | 0.0207 | 0.0137 |
| 50 | 0.6080 | 0.3715 | 0.2281 | 0.1407 | 0.0872 | 0.0543 | 0.0339 | 0.0213 | 0.0134 | 0.0085 |

| 11% | 12% | 13% | 14% | 15% | 16% | 17% | 18% | 19% | 20% | Years |
|---|---|---|---|---|---|---|---|---|---|---|
| 0.9009 | 0.8929 | 0.8850 | 0.8772 | 0.8696 | 0.8621 | 0.8547 | 0.8475 | 0.8403 | 0.8333 | 1 |
| 0.8116 | 0.7972 | 0.7831 | 0.7695 | 0.7561 | 0.7432 | 0.7305 | 0.7182 | 0.7062 | 0.6944 | 2 |
| 0.7312 | 0.7118 | 0.6931 | 0.6750 | 0.6575 | 0.6407 | 0.6244 | 0.6086 | 0.5934 | 0.5787 | 3 |
| 0.6587 | 0.6355 | 0.6133 | 0.5921 | 0.5718 | 0.5523 | 0.5337 | 0.5158 | 0.4987 | 0.4823 | 4 |
| 0.5935 | 0.5674 | 0.5428 | 0.5194 | 0.4972 | 0.4761 | 0.4561 | 0.4371 | 0.4190 | 0.4019 | 5 |
| 0.5346 | 0.5066 | 0.4803 | 0.4556 | 0.4323 | 0.4104 | 0.3898 | 0.3704 | 0.3521 | 0.3349 | 6 |
| 0.4817 | 0.4523 | 0.4251 | 0.3996 | 0.3759 | 0.3538 | 0.3332 | 0.3139 | 0.2959 | 0.2791 | 7 |
| 0.4339 | 0.4039 | 0.3762 | 0.3506 | 0.3269 | 0.3050 | 0.2848 | 0.2660 | 0.2487 | 0.2326 | 8 |
| 0.3909 | 0.3606 | 0.3329 | 0.3075 | 0.2843 | 0.2630 | 0.2434 | 0.2255 | 0.2090 | 0.1938 | 9 |
| 0.3522 | 0.3220 | 0.2946 | 0.2697 | 0.2472 | 0.2267 | 0.2080 | 0.1911 | 0.1756 | 0.1615 | 10 |
| 0.3173 | 0.2875 | 0.2607 | 0.2366 | 0.2149 | 0.1954 | 0.1778 | 0.1619 | 0.1476 | 0.1346 | 11 |
| 0.2858 | 0.2567 | 0.2307 | 0.2076 | 0.1869 | 0.1685 | 0.1520 | 0.1372 | 0.1240 | 0.1122 | 12 |
| 0.2575 | 0.2292 | 0.2042 | 0.1821 | 0.1625 | 0.1452 | 0.1299 | 0.1163 | 0.1042 | 0.0935 | 13 |
| 0.2320 | 0.2046 | 0.1807 | 0.1597 | 0.1413 | 0.1252 | 0.1110 | 0.0985 | 0.0876 | 0.0779 | 14 |
| 0.2090 | 0.1827 | 0.1599 | 0.1401 | 0.1229 | 0.1079 | 0.0949 | 0.0835 | 0.0736 | 0.0649 | 15 |
| 0.1883 | 0.1631 | 0.1415 | 0.1229 | 0.1069 | 0.0930 | 0.0811 | 0.0708 | 0.0618 | 0.0541 | 16 |
| 0.1696 | 0.1456 | 0.1252 | 0.1078 | 0.0929 | 0.0802 | 0.0693 | 0.0600 | 0.0520 | 0.0451 | 17 |
| 0.1528 | 0.1300 | 0.1108 | 0.0946 | 0.0808 | 0.0691 | 0.0592 | 0.0508 | 0.0437 | 0.0376 | 18 |
| 0.1377 | 0.1161 | 0.0981 | 0.0829 | 0.0703 | 0.0596 | 0.0506 | 0.0431 | 0.0367 | 0.0313 | 19 |
| 0.1240 | 0.1037 | 0.0868 | 0.0728 | 0.0611 | 0.0514 | 0.0433 | 0.0365 | 0.0308 | 0.0261 | 20 |
| 0.1117 | 0.0926 | 0.0768 | 0.0638 | 0.0531 | 0.0443 | 0.0370 | 0.0309 | 0.0259 | 0.0217 | 21 |
| 0.1007 | 0.0826 | 0.0680 | 0.0560 | 0.0462 | 0.0382 | 0.0316 | 0.0262 | 0.0218 | 0.0181 | 22 |
| 0.0907 | 0.0738 | 0.0601 | 0.0491 | 0.0402 | 0.0329 | 0.0270 | 0.0222 | 0.0183 | 0.0151 | 23 |
| 0.0817 | 0.0659 | 0.0532 | 0.0431 | 0.0349 | 0.0284 | 0.0231 | 0.0188 | 0.0154 | 0.0126 | 24 |
| 0.0736 | 0.0588 | 0.0471 | 0.0378 | 0.0304 | 0.0245 | 0.0197 | 0.0160 | 0.0129 | 0.0105 | 25 |
| 0.0663 | 0.0525 | 0.0417 | 0.0331 | 0.0264 | 0.0211 | 0.0169 | 0.0135 | 0.0109 | 0.0087 | 26 |
| 0.0597 | 0.0469 | 0.0369 | 0.0291 | 0.0230 | 0.0182 | 0.0144 | 0.0115 | 0.0091 | 0.0073 | 27 |
| 0.0538 | 0.0419 | 0.0326 | 0.0255 | 0.0200 | 0.0157 | 0.0123 | 0.0097 | 0.0077 | 0.0061 | 28 |
| 0.0485 | 0.0374 | 0.0289 | 0.0224 | 0.0174 | 0.0135 | 0.0105 | 0.0082 | 0.0064 | 0.0051 | 29 |
| 0.0437 | 0.0334 | 0.0256 | 0.0196 | 0.0151 | 0.0116 | 0.0090 | 0.0070 | 0.0054 | 0.0042 | 30 |
| 0.0259 | 0.0189 | 0.0139 | 0.0102 | 0.0075 | 0.0055 | 0.0041 | 0.0030 | 0.0023 | 0.0017 | 35 |
| 0.0154 | 0.0107 | 0.0075 | 0.0053 | 0.0037 | 0.0026 | 0.0019 | 0.0013 | 0.0010 | 0.0007 | 40 |
| 0.0091 | 0.0061 | 0.0041 | 0.0027 | 0.0019 | 0.0013 | 0.0009 | 0.0006 | 0.0004 | 0.0003 | 45 |
| 0.0054 | 0.0035 | 0.0022 | 0.0014 | 0.0009 | 0.0006 | 0.0004 | 0.0003 | 0.0002 | 0.0001 | 50 |

| Years | 21% | 22% | 23% | 24% | 25% | 26% | 27% | 28% | 29% | 30% |
|---|---|---|---|---|---|---|---|---|---|---|
| 1 | 0.8264 | 0.8197 | 0.8130 | 0.8065 | 0.8000 | 0.7937 | 0.7874 | 0.7813 | 0.7752 | 0.7692 |
| 2 | 0.6830 | 0.6719 | 0.6610 | 0.6504 | 0.6400 | 0.6299 | 0.6200 | 0.6104 | 0.6009 | 0.5917 |
| 3 | 0.5645 | 0.5507 | 0.5374 | 0.5245 | 0.5120 | 0.4999 | 0.4882 | 0.4768 | 0.4658 | 0.4552 |
| 4 | 0.4665 | 0.4514 | 0.4369 | 0.4230 | 0.4096 | 0.3968 | 0.3844 | 0.3725 | 0.3611 | 0.3501 |
| 5 | 0.3855 | 0.3700 | 0.3552 | 0.3411 | 0.3277 | 0.3149 | 0.3027 | 0.2910 | 0.2799 | 0.2693 |
| 6 | 0.3186 | 0.3033 | 0.2888 | 0.2751 | 0.2621 | 0.2499 | 0.2383 | 0.2274 | 0.2170 | 0.2072 |
| 7 | 0.2633 | 0.2486 | 0.2348 | 0.2218 | 0.2097 | 0.1983 | 0.1877 | 0.1776 | 0.1682 | 0.1594 |
| 8 | 0.2176 | 0.2038 | 0.1909 | 0.1789 | 0.1678 | 0.1574 | 0.1478 | 0.1388 | 0.1304 | 0.1226 |
| 9 | 0.1799 | 0.1670 | 0.1552 | 0.1443 | 0.1342 | 0.1249 | 0.1164 | 0.1084 | 0.1011 | 0.0943 |
| 10 | 0.1486 | 0.1369 | 0.1262 | 0.1164 | 0.1074 | 0.0992 | 0.0916 | 0.0847 | 0.0784 | 0.0725 |
| 11 | 0.1228 | 0.1122 | 0.1026 | 0.0938 | 0.0859 | 0.0787 | 0.0721 | 0.0662 | 0.0607 | 0.0558 |
| 12 | 0.1015 | 0.0920 | 0.0834 | 0.0757 | 0.0687 | 0.0625 | 0.0568 | 0.0517 | 0.0471 | 0.0429 |
| 13 | 0.0839 | 0.0754 | 0.0678 | 0.0610 | 0.0550 | 0.0496 | 0.0447 | 0.0404 | 0.0365 | 0.0330 |
| 14 | 0.0693 | 0.0618 | 0.0551 | 0.0492 | 0.0440 | 0.0393 | 0.0352 | 0.0316 | 0.0283 | 0.0254 |
| 15 | 0.0573 | 0.0507 | 0.0448 | 0.0397 | 0.0352 | 0.0312 | 0.0277 | 0.0247 | 0.0219 | 0.0195 |
| 16 | 0.0474 | 0.0415 | 0.0364 | 0.0320 | 0.0281 | 0.0248 | 0.0218 | 0.0193 | 0.0170 | 0.0150 |
| 17 | 0.0391 | 0.0340 | 0.0296 | 0.0258 | 0.0225 | 0.0197 | 0.0172 | 0.0150 | 0.0132 | 0.0116 |
| 18 | 0.0323 | 0.0279 | 0.0241 | 0.0208 | 0.0180 | 0.0156 | 0.0135 | 0.0118 | 0.0102 | 0.0089 |
| 19 | 0.0267 | 0.0229 | 0.0196 | 0.0168 | 0.0144 | 0.0124 | 0.0107 | 0.0092 | 0.0079 | 0.0068 |
| 20 | 0.0221 | 0.0187 | 0.0159 | 0.0135 | 0.0115 | 0.0098 | 0.0084 | 0.0072 | 0.0061 | 0.0053 |
| 21 | 0.0183 | 0.0154 | 0.0129 | 0.0109 | 0.0092 | 0.0078 | 0.0066 | 0.0056 | 0.0048 | 0.0040 |
| 22 | 0.0151 | 0.0126 | 0.0105 | 0.0088 | 0.0074 | 0.0062 | 0.0052 | 0.0044 | 0.0037 | 0.0031 |
| 23 | 0.0125 | 0.0103 | 0.0086 | 0.0071 | 0.0059 | 0.0049 | 0.0041 | 0.0034 | 0.0029 | 0.0024 |
| 24 | 0.0103 | 0.0085 | 0.0070 | 0.0057 | 0.0047 | 0.0039 | 0.0032 | 0.0027 | 0.0022 | 0.0018 |
| 25 | 0.0085 | 0.0069 | 0.0057 | 0.0046 | 0.0038 | 0.0031 | 0.0025 | 0.0021 | 0.0017 | 0.0014 |
| 26 | 0.0070 | 0.0057 | 0.0046 | 0.0037 | 0.0030 | 0.0025 | 0.0020 | 0.0016 | 0.0013 | 0.0011 |
| 27 | 0.0058 | 0.0047 | 0.0037 | 0.0030 | 0.0024 | 0.0019 | 0.0016 | 0.0013 | 0.0010 | 0.0008 |
| 28 | 0.0048 | 0.0038 | 0.0030 | 0.0024 | 0.0019 | 0.0015 | 0.0012 | 0.0010 | 0.0008 | 0.0006 |
| 29 | 0.0040 | 0.0031 | 0.0025 | 0.0020 | 0.0015 | 0.0012 | 0.0010 | 0.0008 | 0.0006 | 0.0005 |
| 30 | 0.0033 | 0.0026 | 0.0020 | 0.0016 | 0.0012 | 0.0010 | 0.0008 | 0.0006 | 0.0005 | 0.0004 |
| 35 | 0.0013 | 0.0009 | 0.0007 | 0.0005 | 0.0004 | 0.0003 | 0.0002 | 0.0002 | 0.0001 | 0.0001 |
| 40 | 0.0005 | 0.0004 | 0.0003 | 0.0002 | 0.0001 | 0.0001 | 0.0001 | 0.0001 | | |
| 45 | 0.0002 | 0.0001 | 0.0001 | 0.0001 | | | | | | |
| 50 | 0.0001 | | | | | | | | | |

| 31% | 32% | 33% | 34% | 35% | 36% | 37% | 38% | 39% | 40% | Years |
|---|---|---|---|---|---|---|---|---|---|---|
| 0.7634 | 0.7576 | 0.7519 | 0.7463 | 0.7407 | 0.7353 | 0.7299 | 0.7246 | 0.7194 | 0.7143 | 1 |
| 0.5827 | 0.5739 | 0.5653 | 0.5569 | 0.5487 | 0.5407 | 0.5328 | 0.5251 | 0.5176 | 0.5102 | 2 |
| 0.4448 | 0.4348 | 0.4251 | 0.4156 | 0.4064 | 0.3975 | 0.3889 | 0.3805 | 0.3724 | 0.3644 | 3 |
| 0.3396 | 0.3294 | 0.3196 | 0.3102 | 0.3011 | 0.2923 | 0.2839 | 0.2757 | 0.2679 | 0.2603 | 4 |
| 0.2592 | 0.2495 | 0.2403 | 0.2315 | 0.2230 | 0.2149 | 0.2072 | 0.1998 | 0.1927 | 0.1859 | 5 |
| 0.1979 | 0.1890 | 0.1807 | 0.1727 | 0.1652 | 0.1580 | 0.1512 | 0.1448 | 0.1386 | 0.1328 | 6 |
| 0.1510 | 0.1432 | 0.1358 | 0.1289 | 0.1224 | 0.1162 | 0.1104 | 0.1049 | 0.0997 | 0.0949 | 7 |
| 0.1153 | 0.1085 | 0.1021 | 0.0962 | 0.0906 | 0.0854 | 0.0806 | 0.0760 | 0.0718 | 0.0678 | 8 |
| 0.0880 | 0.0822 | 0.0768 | 0.0718 | 0.0671 | 0.0628 | 0.0588 | 0.0551 | 0.0516 | 0.0484 | 9 |
| 0.0672 | 0.0623 | 0.0577 | 0.0536 | 0.0497 | 0.0462 | 0.0429 | 0.0399 | 0.0371 | 0.0346 | 10 |
| 0.0513 | 0.0472 | 0.0434 | 0.0400 | 0.0368 | 0.0340 | 0.0313 | 0.0289 | 0.0267 | 0.0247 | 11 |
| 0.0392 | 0.0357 | 0.0326 | 0.0298 | 0.0273 | 0.0250 | 0.0229 | 0.0210 | 0.0192 | 0.0176 | 12 |
| 0.0299 | 0.0271 | 0.0245 | 0.0223 | 0.0202 | 0.0184 | 0.0167 | 0.0152 | 0.0138 | 0.0126 | 13 |
| 0.0228 | 0.0205 | 0.0185 | 0.0166 | 0.0150 | 0.0135 | 0.0122 | 0.0110 | 0.0099 | 0.0090 | 14 |
| 0.0174 | 0.0155 | 0.0139 | 0.0124 | 0.0111 | 0.0099 | 0.0089 | 0.0080 | 0.0072 | 0.0064 | 15 |
| 0.0133 | 0.0118 | 0.0104 | 0.0093 | 0.0082 | 0.0073 | 0.0065 | 0.0058 | 0.0051 | 0.0046 | 16 |
| 0.0101 | 0.0089 | 0.0078 | 0.0069 | 0.0061 | 0.0054 | 0.0047 | 0.0042 | 0.0037 | 0.0033 | 17 |
| 0.0077 | 0.0068 | 0.0059 | 0.0052 | 0.0045 | 0.0039 | 0.0035 | 0.0030 | 0.0027 | 0.0023 | 18 |
| 0.0059 | 0.0051 | 0.0044 | 0.0038 | 0.0033 | 0.0029 | 0.0025 | 0.0022 | 0.0019 | 0.0017 | 19 |
| 0.0045 | 0.0039 | 0.0033 | 0.0029 | 0.0025 | 0.0021 | 0.0018 | 0.0016 | 0.0014 | 0.0012 | 20 |
| 0.0034 | 0.0029 | 0.0025 | 0.0021 | 0.0018 | 0.0016 | 0.0013 | 0.0012 | 0.0010 | 0.0009 | 21 |
| 0.0026 | 0.0022 | 0.0019 | 0.0016 | 0.0014 | 0.0012 | 0.0010 | 0.0008 | 0.0007 | 0.0006 | 22 |
| 0.0020 | 0.0017 | 0.0014 | 0.0012 | 0.0010 | 0.0008 | 0.0007 | 0.0006 | 0.0005 | 0.0004 | 23 |
| 0.0015 | 0.0013 | 0.0011 | 0.0009 | 0.0007 | 0.0006 | 0.0005 | 0.0004 | 0.0004 | 0.0003 | 24 |
| 0.0012 | 0.0010 | 0.0008 | 0.0007 | 0.0006 | 0.0005 | 0.0004 | 0.0003 | 0.0003 | 0.0002 | 25 |
| 0.0009 | 0.0007 | 0.0006 | 0.0005 | 0.0004 | 0.0003 | 0.0003 | 0.0002 | 0.0002 | 0.0002 | 26 |
| 0.0007 | 0.0006 | 0.0005 | 0.0004 | 0.0003 | 0.0002 | 0.0002 | 0.0002 | 0.0001 | 0.0001 | 27 |
| 0.0005 | 0.0004 | 0.0003 | 0.0003 | 0.0002 | 0.0002 | 0.0001 | 0.0001 | 0.0001 | 0.0001 | 28 |
| 0.0004 | 0.0003 | 0.0003 | 0.0002 | 0.0002 | 0.0001 | 0.0001 | 0.0001 | 0.0001 | 0.0001 | 29 |
| 0.0003 | 0.0002 | 0.0002 | 0.0002 | 0.0001 | 0.0001 | 0.0001 | 0.0001 | 0.0001 | | 30 |
| 0.0001 | 0.0001 | | | | | | | | | 35 |

# Appendix B: Cumulative present value factors

The table gives the present value of $n$ annual payments of £1 received for the next $n$ years with a constant discount of $x$% per year.

For example, with a discount rate of 7% and with six annual payments of £1, the present value is £4.767.

| Years 0 to: | 1% | 2% | 3% | 4% | 5% | 6% | 7% | 8% | 9% | 10% |
|---|---|---|---|---|---|---|---|---|---|---|
| 1 | 0.990 | 0.980 | 0.971 | 0.962 | 0.952 | 0.943 | 0.935 | 0.926 | 0.917 | 0.909 |
| 2 | 1.970 | 1.942 | 1.913 | 1.886 | 1.859 | 1.833 | 1.808 | 1.783 | 1.759 | 1.736 |
| 3 | 2.941 | 2.884 | 2.829 | 2.775 | 2.723 | 2.673 | 2.624 | 2.577 | 2.531 | 2.487 |
| 4 | 3.902 | 3.808 | 3.717 | 3.630 | 3.546 | 3.465 | 3.387 | 3.312 | 3.240 | 3.170 |
| 5 | 4.853 | 4.713 | 4.580 | 4.452 | 4.329 | 4.212 | 4.100 | 3.993 | 3.890 | 3.791 |
| 6 | 5.795 | 5.601 | 5.417 | 5.242 | 5.076 | 4.917 | 4.767 | 4.623 | 4.486 | 4.355 |
| 7 | 6.728 | 6.472 | 6.230 | 6.002 | 5.786 | 5.582 | 5.389 | 5.206 | 5.033 | 4.868 |
| 8 | 7.652 | 7.325 | 7.020 | 6.733 | 6.463 | 6.210 | 5.971 | 5.747 | 5.535 | 5.335 |
| 9 | 8.566 | 8.162 | 7.786 | 7.435 | 7.108 | 6.802 | 6.515 | 6.247 | 5.995 | 5.759 |
| 10 | 9.471 | 8.983 | 8.530 | 8.111 | 7.722 | 7.360 | 7.024 | 6.710 | 6.418 | 6.145 |
| 11 | 10.368 | 9.787 | 9.253 | 8.760 | 8.306 | 7.887 | 7.499 | 7.139 | 6.805 | 6.495 |
| 12 | 11.255 | 10.575 | 9.954 | 9.385 | 8.863 | 8.384 | 7.943 | 7.536 | 7.161 | 6.814 |
| 13 | 12.134 | 11.348 | 10.635 | 9.086 | 9.394 | 8.853 | 8.358 | 7.904 | 7.487 | 7.103 |
| 14 | 13.004 | 12.106 | 11.296 | 10.563 | 9.899 | 9.295 | 8.745 | 8.244 | 7.786 | 7.367 |
| 15 | 13.865 | 12.849 | 11.938 | 11.118 | 10.380 | 9.712 | 9.108 | 8.559 | 8.061 | 7.606 |
| 16 | 14.718 | 13.578 | 12.561 | 11.652 | 10.838 | 10.106 | 9.447 | 8.851 | 8.313 | 7.824 |
| 17 | 15.562 | 14.292 | 13.166 | 12.166 | 11.274 | 10.477 | 9.763 | 9.122 | 8.544 | 8.022 |
| 18 | 16.398 | 14.992 | 13.754 | 12.659 | 11.690 | 10.828 | 10.059 | 9.372 | 8.756 | 8.201 |
| 19 | 17.226 | 15.678 | 14.324 | 13.134 | 12.085 | 11.185 | 10.336 | 9.604 | 8.950 | 8.365 |
| 20 | 18.046 | 16.351 | 14.877 | 13.590 | 12.462 | 11.470 | 10.594 | 9.818 | 9.129 | 8.514 |
| 21 | 18.857 | 17.011 | 15.415 | 14.029 | 12.821 | 11.764 | 10.836 | 10.017 | 9.292 | 8.649 |
| 22 | 19.660 | 17.658 | 15.937 | 14.451 | 13.163 | 12.042 | 11.061 | 10.201 | 9.442 | 8.772 |
| 23 | 20.456 | 18.292 | 16.444 | 14.857 | 13.489 | 12.303 | 11.272 | 10.371 | 9.580 | 8.883 |
| 24 | 21.243 | 18.914 | 16.939 | 15.247 | 13.799 | 12.550 | 11.469 | 10.529 | 9.707 | 8.985 |
| 25 | 22.023 | 19.523 | 17.413 | 15.622 | 14.094 | 12.783 | 11.654 | 10.675 | 9.823 | 9.077 |
| 26 | 22.795 | 20.121 | 17.877 | 15.983 | 13.375 | 13.003 | 11.826 | 10.810 | 9.929 | 9.161 |
| 27 | 23.560 | 20.707 | 18.327 | 16.330 | 14.643 | 13.211 | 11.987 | 10.935 | 10.027 | 9.237 |
| 28 | 24.316 | 21.281 | 18.764 | 16.663 | 13.898 | 13.406 | 12.137 | 11.051 | 10.116 | 9.307 |
| 29 | 25.066 | 21.844 | 19.188 | 16.984 | 15.141 | 13.591 | 12.278 | 11.158 | 10.198 | 9.370 |
| 30 | 25.808 | 22.396 | 19.600 | 17.292 | 15.372 | 13.765 | 12.409 | 11.258 | 10.274 | 9.427 |
| 35 | 29.409 | 24.999 | 21.487 | 18.665 | 16.374 | 14.498 | 12.948 | 11.655 | 10.567 | 9.644 |
| 40 | 32.835 | 27.355 | 23.115 | 19.793 | 17.159 | 15.046 | 13.332 | 11.925 | 10.757 | 9.779 |
| 45 | 36.095 | 29.490 | 24.519 | 20.720 | 17.774 | 15.456 | 13.606 | 12.108 | 10.881 | 9.863 |
| 50 | 39.196 | 31.424 | 25.730 | 21.482 | 18.256 | 15.762 | 13.801 | 12.233 | 10.962 | 9.915 |

| 11% | 12% | 13% | 14% | 15% | 16% | 17% | 18% | 19% | 20% | Years 0 to: |
|---|---|---|---|---|---|---|---|---|---|---|
| 0.901 | 0.893 | 0.885 | 0.877 | 0.870 | 0.862 | 0.855 | 0.847 | 0.840 | 0.833 | 1 |
| 1.713 | 1.690 | 1.668 | 1.647 | 1.626 | 1.605 | 1.585 | 1.566 | 1.547 | 1.528 | 2 |
| 2.444 | 2.402 | 2.361 | 2.322 | 2.283 | 2.246 | 2.210 | 2.174 | 2.140 | 2.106 | 3 |
| 3.102 | 3.037 | 2.974 | 2.914 | 2.855 | 2.798 | 2.743 | 2.690 | 2.639 | 2.589 | 4 |
| 3.696 | 3.605 | 3.517 | 3.433 | 3.352 | 3.274 | 3.199 | 3.127 | 3.058 | 2.991 | 5 |
| 4.231 | 4.111 | 3.998 | 3.889 | 3.784 | 3.685 | 3.589 | 3.498 | 3.410 | 3.326 | 6 |
| 4.712 | 4.564 | 4.423 | 4.288 | 4.160 | 4.039 | 3.922 | 3.812 | 3.706 | 3.605 | 7 |
| 5.146 | 4.968 | 4.799 | 4.639 | 4.487 | 4.344 | 4.207 | 4.078 | 3.954 | 3.837 | 8 |
| 5.537 | 5.328 | 5.132 | 4.946 | 4.772 | 4.607 | 4.451 | 4.303 | 4.163 | 4.031 | 9 |
| 5.889 | 5.650 | 5.426 | 5.216 | 5.019 | 4.833 | 4.659 | 4.494 | 4.339 | 4.192 | 10 |
| 6.207 | 5.938 | 5.687 | 5.453 | 5.234 | 5.029 | 4.836 | 4.656 | 4.486 | 4.327 | 11 |
| 6.492 | 6.194 | 5.918 | 5.660 | 5.421 | 5.197 | 4.988 | 4.793 | 4.611 | 4.439 | 12 |
| 6.750 | 6.424 | 6.122 | 5.842 | 5.583 | 5.342 | 5.118 | 4.910 | 4.715 | 4.533 | 13 |
| 6.982 | 6.628 | 6.302 | 6.002 | 5.724 | 5.468 | 5.229 | 5.008 | 4.802 | 4.611 | 14 |
| 7.191 | 6.811 | 6.462 | 6.142 | 5.847 | 5.575 | 5.324 | 5.092 | 4.876 | 4.675 | 15 |
| 7.379 | 6.974 | 6.604 | 6.265 | 5.954 | 5.668 | 5.405 | 5.162 | 4.938 | 4.730 | 16 |
| 7.549 | 7.120 | 6.729 | 6.373 | 6.047 | 5.749 | 5.475 | 5.222 | 4.990 | 4.775 | 17 |
| 7.702 | 7.250 | 6.840 | 6.467 | 6.128 | 5.818 | 5.534 | 5.273 | 5.033 | 4.812 | 18 |
| 7.839 | 7.366 | 6.938 | 6.550 | 6.198 | 5.877 | 5.584 | 5.316 | 5.070 | 4.843 | 19 |
| 7.963 | 7.469 | 7.025 | 6.623 | 6.259 | 5.929 | 5.628 | 5.353 | 5.101 | 4.870 | 20 |
| 8.075 | 7.562 | 7.102 | 6.687 | 6.312 | 5.973 | 5.665 | 5.384 | 5.127 | 4.891 | 21 |
| 8.176 | 7.645 | 7.170 | 6.743 | 6.359 | 6.011 | 5.696 | 5.410 | 5.149 | 4.909 | 22 |
| 8.266 | 7.718 | 7.230 | 6.792 | 6.399 | 6.044 | 5.723 | 5.432 | 5.167 | 4.925 | 23 |
| 8.348 | 7.784 | 7.283 | 6.835 | 6.434 | 6.073 | 5.746 | 5.451 | 5.182 | 4.937 | 24 |
| 8.422 | 7.843 | 7.330 | 6.873 | 6.464 | 6.097 | 5.766 | 5.467 | 5.195 | 4.948 | 25 |
| 8.488 | 7.896 | 7.372 | 6.906 | 6.491 | 6.118 | 5.783 | 5.480 | 5.206 | 4.956 | 26 |
| 8.548 | 7.943 | 7.409 | 6.935 | 6.514 | 6.136 | 5.798 | 5.492 | 5.215 | 4.964 | 27 |
| 8.602 | 7.984 | 7.441 | 6.961 | 6.534 | 6.152 | 5.810 | 5.502 | 5.223 | 4.970 | 28 |
| 8.650 | 8.022 | 7.470 | 6.983 | 6.551 | 6.166 | 5.820 | 5.510 | 5.229 | 4.975 | 29 |
| 8.694 | 8.055 | 7.496 | 7.003 | 6.566 | 6.177 | 5.829 | 5.517 | 5.235 | 4.979 | 30 |
| 8.855 | 8.176 | 7.586 | 7.070 | 6.617 | 6.215 | 5.858 | 5.539 | 5.251 | 4.992 | 35 |
| 8.951 | 8.244 | 7.634 | 7.105 | 6.642 | 6.233 | 5.871 | 5.548 | 5.258 | 4.997 | 40 |
| 9.008 | 8.283 | 7.661 | 7.123 | 6.654 | 6.242 | 5.877 | 5.552 | 5.261 | 4.999 | 45 |
| 9.042 | 8.304 | 7.675 | 7.133 | 6.661 | 6.246 | 5.880 | 5.554 | 5.262 | 4.999 | 50 |

| Years 0 to: | 21% | 22% | 23% | 24% | 25% | 26% | 27% | 28% | 29% | 30% |
|---|---|---|---|---|---|---|---|---|---|---|
| 1 | 0.826 | 0.820 | 0.813 | 0.806 | 0.800 | 0.794 | 0.787 | 0.781 | 0.775 | 0.769 |
| 2 | 1.509 | 1.492 | 1.474 | 1.457 | 1.440 | 1.424 | 1.407 | 1.392 | 1.376 | 1.361 |
| 3 | 2.074 | 2.042 | 2.011 | 1.981 | 1.952 | 1.923 | 1.896 | 1.868 | 1.842 | 1.816 |
| 4 | 2.540 | 2.494 | 2.448 | 2.404 | 2.362 | 2.320 | 2.280 | 2.241 | 2.203 | 2.166 |
| 5 | 2.926 | 2.864 | 2.803 | 2.745 | 2.689 | 2.635 | 2.583 | 2.532 | 2.483 | 2.436 |
| 6 | 3.245 | 3.167 | 3.092 | 3.020 | 2.951 | 2.885 | 2.821 | 2.759 | 2.700 | 2.643 |
| 7 | 3.508 | 3.416 | 3.327 | 3.242 | 3.161 | 3.083 | 3.009 | 2.937 | 2.868 | 2.802 |
| 8 | 3.726 | 3.619 | 3.518 | 3.421 | 3.329 | 3.241 | 3.156 | 3.076 | 2.999 | 2.925 |
| 9 | 3.905 | 3.786 | 3.673 | 3.566 | 3.463 | 3.366 | 3.273 | 3.184 | 3.100 | 3.019 |
| 10 | 4.054 | 3.923 | 3.799 | 3.682 | 3.571 | 3.465 | 3.364 | 3.269 | 3.178 | 3.092 |
| 11 | 4.177 | 4.035 | 3.902 | 3.776 | 3.656 | 3.543 | 3.437 | 3.335 | 3.239 | 3.147 |
| 12 | 5.278 | 4.127 | 3.985 | 3.851 | 3.725 | 3.606 | 3.493 | 3.387 | 3.286 | 3.190 |
| 13 | 4.362 | 4.203 | 4.053 | 3.912 | 3.780 | 3.656 | 3.538 | 3.427 | 3.322 | 3.223 |
| 14 | 4.432 | 4.265 | 4.108 | 3.962 | 3.824 | 3.695 | 3.573 | 3.459 | 3.351 | 3.249 |
| 15 | 4.489 | 4.315 | 4.153 | 4.001 | 3.859 | 3.726 | 3.601 | 3.483 | 3.373 | 3.268 |
| 16 | 4.536 | 4.357 | 4.189 | 4.033 | 3.887 | 3.751 | 3.623 | 3.503 | 3.390 | 3.283 |
| 17 | 4.576 | 4.391 | 4.219 | 4.059 | 3.910 | 3.771 | 3.640 | 3.518 | 3.403 | 3.295 |
| 18 | 4.608 | 4.419 | 4.243 | 4.080 | 3.928 | 3.786 | 3.654 | 3.529 | 3.413 | 3.304 |
| 19 | 4.635 | 4.442 | 4.263 | 4.097 | 3.942 | 3.799 | 3.664 | 3.539 | 3.421 | 3.311 |
| 20 | 4.657 | 4.460 | 4.279 | 4.110 | 3.954 | 3.808 | 3.673 | 3.546 | 3.427 | 3.316 |
| 21 | 4.675 | 4.476 | 3.292 | 4.121 | 3.963 | 3.816 | 3.679 | 3.551 | 3.432 | 3.320 |
| 22 | 4.690 | 4.488 | 4.302 | 4.130 | 3.970 | 3.822 | 3.684 | 3.556 | 3.436 | 3.323 |
| 23 | 4.703 | 4.499 | 4.311 | 4.137 | 3.976 | 3.827 | 3.689 | 3.559 | 3.438 | 3.325 |
| 24 | 4.713 | 4.507 | 4.318 | 4.143 | 3.981 | 3.831 | 3.692 | 3.562 | 3.441 | 3.327 |
| 25 | 4.721 | 4.514 | 4.323 | 4.147 | 3.985 | 3.834 | 3.694 | 3.564 | 3.442 | 3.329 |
| 26 | 4.728 | 4.520 | 4.328 | 4.151 | 3.988 | 3.837 | 3.696 | 3.566 | 3.444 | 3.330 |
| 27 | 4.734 | 4.524 | 4.332 | 4.154 | 3.990 | 3.839 | 3.698 | 3.567 | 3.445 | 3.331 |
| 28 | 4.739 | 4.528 | 4.335 | 4.157 | 3.992 | 3.840 | 3.699 | 3.568 | 3.446 | 3.331 |
| 29 | 4.743 | 4.531 | 4.337 | 4.159 | 3.994 | 3.841 | 3.700 | 3.569 | 3.446 | 3.332 |
| 30 | 4.746 | 4.534 | 4.339 | 4.160 | 3.995 | 3.842 | 3.701 | 3.569 | 3.447 | 3.332 |
| 35 | 4.756 | 4.541 | 4.345 | 4.164 | 3.998 | 3.845 | 3.703 | 3.571 | 3.448 | 3.333 |
| 40 | 4.760 | 4.544 | 4.347 | 4.166 | 3.999 | 3.846 | 3.703 | 3.571 | 3.488 | 3.333 |
| 45 | 4.761 | | | | | | | | | |
| 50 | 4.762 | 4.545 | 4.348 | 4.167 | 4.000 | 3.846 | 3.704 | 3.571 | 3.448 | 3.333 |

| 31% | 32% | 33% | 34% | 35% | 36% | 37% | 38% | 39% | 40% | Years 0 to: |
|---|---|---|---|---|---|---|---|---|---|---|
| 0.763 | 0.758 | 0.752 | 0.746 | 0.741 | 0.735 | 0.730 | 0.725 | 0.719 | 0.714 | 1 |
| 1.346 | 1.331 | 1.317 | 1.303 | 1.289 | 1.276 | 1.263 | 1.250 | 1.237 | 1.224 | 2 |
| 1.791 | 1.766 | 1.742 | 1.719 | 1.696 | 1.673 | 1.652 | 1.630 | 1.609 | 1.589 | 3 |
| 2.130 | 2.096 | 2.062 | 2.029 | 1.997 | 1.966 | 1.935 | 1.906 | 1.877 | 1.849 | 4 |
| 2.390 | 2.345 | 2.302 | 2.260 | 2.220 | 2.181 | 2.143 | 2.106 | 2.070 | 2.035 | 5 |
| 2.588 | 2.534 | 2.483 | 2.433 | 2.385 | 2.339 | 2.294 | 2.251 | 2.209 | 2.168 | 6 |
| 2.739 | 2.677 | 2.619 | 2.562 | 2.508 | 2.455 | 2.404 | 2.355 | 2.308 | 2.263 | 7 |
| 2.854 | 2.786 | 2.721 | 2.658 | 2.598 | 2.540 | 2.485 | 2.432 | 2.380 | 2.331 | 8 |
| 2.942 | 2.868 | 2.798 | 2.730 | 2.665 | 2.603 | 2.544 | 2.487 | 2.432 | 2.379 | 9 |
| 3.009 | 2.930 | 2.855 | 2.784 | 2.715 | 2.649 | 2.587 | 2.527 | 2.469 | 2.414 | 10 |
| 3.060 | 2.978 | 2.899 | 2.824 | 2.752 | 2.683 | 2.618 | 2.555 | 2.496 | 2.438 | 11 |
| 3.100 | 2.013 | 2.931 | 2.853 | 2.779 | 2.708 | 2.641 | 2.576 | 2.515 | 2.456 | 12 |
| 3.129 | 3.040 | 2.956 | 2.876 | 2.799 | 2.727 | 2.658 | 2.592 | 2.529 | 2.469 | 13 |
| 3.152 | 3.061 | 2.974 | 2.982 | 2.814 | 2.740 | 2.670 | 2.603 | 2.539 | 2.478 | 14 |
| 3.170 | 3.076 | 2.988 | 2.905 | 2.825 | 2.750 | 2.679 | 2.611 | 2.546 | 2.484 | 15 |
| 3.183 | 3.088 | 2.999 | 2.914 | 2.834 | 2.757 | 2.685 | 2.616 | 2.551 | 2.489 | 16 |
| 3.193 | 3.097 | 3.007 | 2.921 | 2.840 | 2.763 | 2.690 | 2.621 | 2.555 | 2.492 | 17 |
| 3.201 | 3.104 | 3.012 | 2.926 | 2.844 | 2.767 | 2.693 | 2.624 | 2.557 | 2.494 | 18 |
| 3.207 | 3.109 | 3.017 | 2.930 | 2.848 | 2.770 | 2.696 | 2.626 | 2.559 | 2.496 | 19 |
| 3.211 | 3.113 | 3.020 | 2.933 | 2.850 | 2.772 | 2.698 | 2.627 | 2.561 | 2.497 | 20 |
| 3.215 | 3.116 | 3.023 | 2.935 | 2.852 | 2.773 | 2.699 | 2.629 | 2.562 | 2.498 | 21 |
| 3.217 | 3.118 | 3.025 | 2.936 | 2.853 | 2.775 | 2.700 | 2.629 | 2.562 | 2.438 | 22 |
| 3.219 | 3.120 | 3.026 | 2.938 | 2.854 | 2.775 | 2.701 | 2.630 | 2.563 | 2.499 | 23 |
| 3.221 | 3.121 | 3.027 | 2.939 | 2.855 | 2.776 | 2.701 | 2.630 | 2.563 | 2.499 | 24 |
| 3.222 | 3.122 | 3.028 | 2.939 | 2.856 | 2.777 | 2.702 | 2.631 | 2.563 | 2.499 | 25 |
| 3.223 | 3.123 | 3.028 | 2.940 | 2.856 | 2.777 | 2.702 | 2.631 | 2.564 | 2.500 | 26 |
| 3.224 | 3.123 | 3.029 | 2.940 | 2.856 | 2.777 | 2.702 | 2.631 | | | 27 |
| 3.224 | 3.124 | 3.029 | 2.940 | 2.857 | 2.777 | 2.702 | 2.631 | | | 28 |
| 3.225 | 3.124 | 3.030 | 2.941 | 2.857 | 2.777 | 2.702 | 2.631 | | | 29 |
| 3.225 | 3.124 | 3.030 | 2.941 | 2.857 | 2.778 | 2.702 | 2.631 | | | 30 |
| 3.226 | 3.125 | | | | | | | | | 35 |
| 3.226 | | | | | | | | | | 40 |
| 3.226 | 3.125 | 3.030 | 2.941 | 2.857 | 2.778 | 2.703 | 2.632 | 2.564 | 2.500 | 45 |
| 3.226 | 3.125 | 3.030 | 2.941 | 2.857 | 2.778 | 2.703 | 2.632 | 2.564 | 2.500 | 50 |

# Appendix C: Areas in tail of the normal distribution

| $\dfrac{x-\mu}{\sigma}$ | 0.00 | 0.01 | 0.02 | 0.03 | 0.04 | 0.05 | 0.06 | 0.07 | 0.08 | 0.09 |
|---|---|---|---|---|---|---|---|---|---|---|
| 0.0 | 0.5000 | 0.4960 | 0.4920 | 0.4880 | 0.4840 | 0.4801 | 0.4761 | 0.4721 | 0.4681 | 0.4641 |
| 0.1 | 0.4602 | 0.4562 | 0.4522 | 0.4483 | 0.4443 | 0.4404 | 0.4364 | 0.4325 | 0.4286 | 0.4247 |
| 0.2 | 0.4207 | 0.4168 | 0.4129 | 0.4090 | 0.4052 | 0.4103 | 0.3974 | 0.3936 | 0.3897 | 0.3589 |
| 0.3 | 0.3821 | 0.3783 | 0.3745 | 0.3707 | 0.3669 | 0.3632 | 0.3594 | 0.3557 | 0.3520 | 0.3483 |
| 0.4 | 0.3446 | 0.3409 | 0.3372 | 0.3336 | 0.3300 | 0.3264 | 0.3228 | 0.3192 | 0.3156 | 0.3121 |
| 0.5 | 0.3085 | 0.3050 | 0.3015 | 0.2981 | 0.2946 | 0.2912 | 0.2877 | 0.2843 | 0.2810 | 0.2776 |
| 0.6 | 0.2743 | 0.2709 | 0.2676 | 0.2643 | 0.2611 | 0.2578 | 0.2546 | 0.2514 | 0.2483 | 0.2451 |
| 0.7 | 0.2420 | 0.2389 | 0.2358 | 0.2327 | 0.2296 | 0.2266 | 0.2236 | 0.2206 | 0.2177 | 0.2148 |
| 0.8 | 0.2119 | 0.2090 | 0.2061 | 0.2033 | 0.2005 | 0.1977 | 0.1949 | 0.1922 | 0.1894 | 0.1867 |
| 0.9 | 0.1841 | 0.1814 | 0.1788 | 0.1762 | 0.1736 | 0.1711 | 0.1685 | 0.1660 | 0.1635 | 0.1611 |
| 1.0 | 0.1587 | 0.1562 | 0.1539 | 0.1515 | 0.1492 | 0.1469 | 0.1446 | 0.1423 | 0.1401 | 0.1379 |
| 1.1 | 0.1357 | 0.1335 | 0.1314 | 0.1292 | 0.1271 | 0.1251 | 0.1230 | 0.1210 | 0.1190 | 0.1170 |
| 1.2 | 0.1151 | 0.1131 | 0.1112 | 0.1093 | 0.1075 | 0.1056 | 0.1038 | 0.1020 | 0.1103 | 0.0985 |
| 1.3 | 0.0968 | 0.0951 | 0.0934 | 0.0918 | 0.0901 | 0.0885 | 0.0869 | 0.0853 | 0.0838 | 0.0823 |
| 1.4 | 0.0808 | 0.0793 | 0.0778 | 0.0764 | 0.0749 | 0.0735 | 0.0721 | 0.0708 | 0.0694 | 0.0681 |
| 1.5 | 0.0668 | 0.0655 | 0.0643 | 0.0630 | 0.0618 | 0.0606 | 0.0594 | 0.0582 | 0.0571 | 0.0559 |
| 1.6 | 0.0548 | 0.0537 | 0.0526 | 0.0516 | 0.0505 | 0.0495 | 0.0485 | 0.0475 | 0.0465 | 0.0455 |
| 1.7 | 0.0446 | 0.0436 | 0.0427 | 0.0418 | 0.0409 | 0.0401 | 0.0392 | 0.0384 | 0.0375 | 0.0367 |
| 1.8 | 0.0359 | 0.0351 | 0.0344 | 0.0336 | 0.0329 | 0.0322 | 0.0314 | 0.0307 | 0.0301 | 0.0294 |
| 1.9 | 0.0287 | 0.0281 | 0.0274 | 0.0268 | 0.0262 | 0.0256 | 0.0250 | 0.0244 | 0.0239 | 0.0233 |
| 2.0 | 0.02275 | 0.02222 | 0.02169 | 0.02118 | 0.02068 | 0.02018 | 0.01970 | 0.01923 | 0.01876 | 0.01831 |
| 2.1 | 0.01786 | 0.01743 | 0.01700 | 0.01659 | 0.01618 | 0.01578 | 0.01539 | 0.01500 | 0.01463 | 0.01426 |
| 2.2 | 0.01390 | 0.01355 | 0.01321 | 0.01287 | 0.01255 | 0.01222 | 0.01191 | 0.01160 | 0.01130 | 0.01101 |
| 2.3 | 0.01072 | 0.01044 | 0.01017 | 0.00990 | 0.00964 | 0.00939 | 0.00914 | 0.00889 | 0.00866 | 0.00842 |
| 2.4 | 0.00820 | 0.00798 | 0.00776 | 0.00755 | 0.00734 | 0.00714 | 0.00695 | 0.00676 | 0.00657 | 0.00639 |
| 2.5 | 0.00621 | 0.00604 | 0.00587 | 0.00570 | 0.00554 | 0.00539 | 0.00523 | 0.00508 | 0.00494 | 0.00480 |
| 2.6 | 0.00466 | 0.00453 | 0.00440 | 0.00427 | 0.00415 | 0.00402 | 0.00391 | 0.00379 | 0.00368 | 0.00357 |
| 2.7 | 0.00347 | 0.00336 | 0.00326 | 0.00317 | 0.00307 | 0.00298 | 0.00289 | 0.00280 | 0.00272 | 0.00264 |
| 2.8 | 0.00256 | 0.00248 | 0.00240 | 0.00233 | 0.00226 | 0.00219 | 0.00212 | 0.00205 | 0.00199 | 0.00193 |
| 2.9 | 0.00187 | 0.00181 | 0.00175 | 0.00169 | 0.00164 | 0.00159 | 0.00154 | 0.00149 | 0.00144 | 0.00139 |
| 3.0 | 0.00135 | | | | | | | | | |
| 3.1 | 0.00097 | | | | | | | | | |
| 3.2 | 0.00069 | | | | | | | | | |
| 3.3 | 0.00048 | | | | | | | | | |
| 3.4 | 0.00034 | | | | | | | | | |
| 3.5 | 0.00023 | | | | | | | | | |
| 3.6 | 0.00016 | | | | | | | | | |
| 3.7 | 0.00011 | | | | | | | | | |
| 3.8 | 0.00007 | | | | | | | | | |
| 3.9 | 0.00005 | | | | | | | | | |
| 4.0 | 0.00003 | | | | | | | | | |

# Appendix D: Capital recovery factors equal annuity rate)

The table gives the equal annual payment to be made for $n$ years in the future to repay loan principal and interest with interest at $x$% per year.

For example, to repay £1 borrowed now at 7% in six annual payments, the value an annual payment is £0.2098 or 20.98p.

| Years | 1% | 2% | 3% | 4% | 5% | 6% | 7% | 8% | 9% | 10% |
|---|---|---|---|---|---|---|---|---|---|---|
| 1 | 1.0100 | 1.0200 | 1.0300 | 1.0400 | 1.0500 | 1.0600 | 1.0700 | 1.0800 | 1.0900 | 1.1000 |
| 2 | 0.5075 | 0.5150 | 0.5226 | 0.5302 | 0.5378 | 0.5454 | 0.5531 | 0.5608 | 0.5685 | 0.5762 |
| 3 | 0.3400 | 0.3468 | 0.3535 | 0.3603 | 0.3672 | 0.3741 | 0.3811 | 0.3880 | 0.3951 | 0.4021 |
| 4 | 0.2563 | 0.2626 | 0.2690 | 0.2755 | 0.2820 | 0.2886 | 0.2952 | 0.3019 | 0.3087 | 0.3155 |
| 5 | 0.2060 | 0.2122 | 0.2184 | 0.2246 | 0.2310 | 0.2374 | 0.2439 | 0.2505 | 0.2571 | 0.2638 |
| 6 | 0.1725 | 0.1785 | 0.1846 | 0.1908 | 0.1970 | 0.2034 | 0.2098 | 0.2163 | 0.2229 | 0.2296 |
| 7 | 0.1486 | 0.1545 | 0.1605 | 0.1666 | 0.1728 | 0.1791 | 0.1856 | 0.1921 | 0.1987 | 0.2054 |
| 8 | 0.1307 | 0.1365 | 0.1425 | 0.1485 | 0.1547 | 0.1610 | 0.1675 | 0.1740 | 0.1807 | 0.1874 |
| 9 | 0.1167 | 0.1225 | 0.1284 | 0.1345 | 0.1407 | 0.1470 | 0.1535 | 0.1601 | 0.1668 | 0.1736 |
| 10 | 0.1056 | 0.1113 | 0.1172 | 0.1233 | 0.1295 | 0.1359 | 0.1424 | 0.1490 | 0.1558 | 0.1627 |

| Years | 11% | 12% | 13% | 14% | 15% | 16% | 17% | 18% | 19% | 20% |
|---|---|---|---|---|---|---|---|---|---|---|
| 1 | 1.1100 | 1.1200 | 1.1300 | 1.1400 | 1.1500 | 1.1600 | 1.1700 | 1.1800 | 1.1900 | 1.2000 |
| 2 | 0.5839 | 0.5917 | 0.5995 | 0.6073 | 0.6151 | 0.6230 | 0.6308 | 0.6387 | 0.6466 | 0.6545 |
| 3 | 0.4092 | 0.4163 | 0.4235 | 0.4307 | 0.4380 | 0.4453 | 0.4526 | 0.4599 | 0.4673 | 0.4747 |
| 4 | 0.3223 | 0.3292 | 0.3362 | 0.3432 | 0.3503 | 0.3574 | 0.3645 | 0.3717 | 0.3790 | 0.3863 |
| 5 | 0.2706 | 0.2774 | 0.2843 | 0.2913 | 0.2983 | 0.3054 | 0.3126 | 0.3198 | 0.3271 | 0.3344 |
| 6 | 0.2364 | 0.2432 | 0.2502 | 0.2572 | 0.2642 | 0.2714 | 0.2786 | 0.2859 | 0.2933 | 0.3007 |
| 7 | 0.2122 | 0.2191 | 0.2261 | 0.2332 | 0.2404 | 0.2476 | 0.2549 | 0.2624 | 0.2699 | 0.2774 |
| 8 | 0.1943 | 0.2013 | 0.2084 | 0.2156 | 0.2229 | 0.2302 | 0.2377 | 0.2452 | 0.2529 | 0.2606 |
| 9 | 0.1806 | 0.1877 | 0.1949 | 0.2022 | 0.2096 | 0.2171 | 0.2247 | 0.2324 | 0.2402 | 0.2481 |
| 10 | 0.1698 | 0.1770 | 0.1843 | 0.1917 | 0.1993 | 0.2069 | 0.2146 | 0.2225 | 0.2305 | 0.2385 |

# Appendix E: Future value of £1 at the end of *n* periods

| Period | 1% | 2% | 3% | 4% | 5% | 6% | 7% | 8% | 9% | 10% |
|---|---|---|---|---|---|---|---|---|---|---|
| 1 | 1.0100 | 1.0200 | 1.0300 | 1.0400 | 1.0500 | 1.0600 | 1.0700 | 1.0800 | 1.0900 | 1.1000 |
| 2 | 1.0201 | 1.0404 | 1.0609 | 1.0816 | 1.1025 | 1.1236 | 1.1449 | 1.1664 | 1.1881 | 1.2100 |
| 3 | 1.0303 | 1.0612 | 1.0927 | 1.1249 | 1.1576 | 1.1910 | 1.2250 | 1.2597 | 1.2950 | 1.3310 |
| 4 | 1.0406 | 1.0824 | 1.1255 | 1.1699 | 1.2155 | 1.2625 | 1.3108 | 1.3605 | 1.4116 | 1.4641 |
| 5 | 1.0510 | 1.1041 | 1.1593 | 1.2167 | 1.2763 | 1.3382 | 1.4026 | 1.4693 | 1.5386 | 1.6105 |
| 6 | 1.0615 | 1.1262 | 1.1941 | 1.2653 | 1.3401 | 1.4185 | 1.5007 | 1.5869 | 1.6771 | 1.7716 |
| 7 | 1.0721 | 1.1487 | 1.2299 | 1.3159 | 1.4071 | 1.5036 | 1.6058 | 1.7138 | 1.8280 | 1.9487 |
| 8 | 1.0829 | 1.1717 | 1.2668 | 1.3686 | 1.4775 | 1.5938 | 1.7182 | 1.8509 | 1.9926 | 2.1436 |
| 9 | 1.0937 | 1.1951 | 1.3048 | 1.4233 | 1.5513 | 1.6895 | 1.8385 | 1.9990 | 2.1719 | 2.3579 |
| 10 | 1.1046 | 1.1290 | 1.3439 | 1.4802 | 1.6289 | 1.7908 | 1.9672 | 2.1589 | 2.3674 | 2.5937 |
| 11 | 1.1157 | 1.2434 | 1.3842 | 1.5395 | 1.7103 | 1.8983 | 2.1049 | 2.3316 | 2.5804 | 2.8531 |
| 12 | 1.1268 | 1.2682 | 1.4258 | 1.6010 | 1.7959 | 2.0122 | 2.2522 | 2.5182 | 2.8127 | 3.1384 |
| 13 | 1.1381 | 1.2936 | 1.4685 | 1.6651 | 1.8856 | 2.1329 | 2.4098 | 2.7196 | 3.0658 | 3.4523 |
| 14 | 1.1495 | 1.3195 | 1.5126 | 1.7317 | 1.9799 | 2.2609 | 2.5785 | 2.9372 | 3.3417 | 3.7975 |
| 15 | 1.1610 | 1.3459 | 1.5580 | 1.8009 | 2.0789 | 2.3966 | 2.7590 | 3.1722 | 3.6425 | 4.1772 |
| 16 | 1.1726 | 1.3728 | 1.6047 | 1.8730 | 2.1829 | 2.5404 | 2.9522 | 3.4259 | 3.9703 | 4.5950 |
| 17 | 1.1843 | 1.4002 | 1.6528 | 1.9479 | 2.2920 | 2.6928 | 3.1588 | 3.7000 | 4.3276 | 5.0545 |
| 18 | 1.1961 | 1.4282 | 1.7024 | 2.0268 | 2.4066 | 2.8543 | 3.3799 | 3.9960 | 4.7171 | 5.5599 |
| 19 | 1.2081 | 1.4568 | 1.7535 | 2.1068 | 2.5270 | 3.0256 | 3.6165 | 4.3157 | 5.1417 | 6.1159 |
| 20 | 1.2202 | 1.4859 | 1.8061 | 2.1911 | 2.6533 | 3.2071 | 3.8697 | 4.6610 | 5.6044 | 6.7275 |
| 21 | 1.2324 | 1.5157 | 1.8603 | 2.2788 | 2.7860 | 3.3996 | 4.1406 | 5.0338 | 6.1088 | 7.4002 |
| 22 | 1.2447 | 1.5460 | 1.9161 | 2.3699 | 2.9253 | 3.6035 | 4.4304 | 5.4365 | 6.6586 | 8.1403 |
| 23 | 1.2572 | 1.5769 | 1.9736 | 2.4647 | 3.0715 | 3.8197 | 4.7405 | 5.8715 | 7.2579 | 8.9543 |
| 24 | 1.2697 | 1.6084 | 2.0328 | 2.5633 | 3.2251 | 4.0489 | 5.0724 | 6.3412 | 7.9111 | 9.8497 |
| 25 | 1.2824 | 1.6406 | 2.0938 | 2.6658 | 3.3864 | 4.2919 | 5.4274 | 6.8485 | 8.6231 | 10.834 |
| 30 | 1.3478 | 1.8114 | 2.4273 | 3.2434 | 4.3219 | 5.7435 | 7.6123 | 10.062 | 13.267 | 17.449 |
| 40 | 1.4889 | 2.2080 | 3.2620 | 4.8010 | 7.0400 | 10.285 | 14.974 | 21.724 | 31.409 | 45.259 |

| Period | 12% | 14% | 15% | 16% | 18% | 20% | 24% | 28% | 32% | 36% |
|---|---|---|---|---|---|---|---|---|---|---|
| 1 | 1.1200 | 1.1400 | 1.1500 | 1.1600 | 1.1800 | 1.2000 | 1.2400 | 1.2800 | 1.3200 | 1.3600 |
| 2 | 1.2544 | 1.2996 | 1.3225 | 1.3456 | 1.3924 | 1.4400 | 1.5376 | 1.6384 | 1.7424 | 1.8496 |
| 3 | 1.4049 | 1.4815 | 1.5209 | 1.5609 | 1.6430 | 1.7280 | 1.9066 | 2.0972 | 2.3000 | 2.5155 |
| 4 | 1.5735 | 1.6890 | 1.7490 | 1.8106 | 1.9388 | 2.0736 | 2.3642 | 2.6844 | 3.0360 | 3.4210 |
| 5 | 1.7623 | 1.9254 | 2.0114 | 2.1003 | 2.2878 | 2.4883 | 2.9316 | 3.4360 | 4.0075 | 4.6526 |
| 6 | 1.9738 | 2.1950 | 2.3131 | 2.4364 | 2.6996 | 2.9860 | 3.6352 | 4.3980 | 5.2899 | 6.3275 |
| 7 | 2.2107 | 2.5023 | 2.6600 | 2.8262 | 3.1855 | 3.5832 | 4.5077 | 5.6295 | 6.9826 | 8.6054 |
| 8 | 2.4760 | 2.8526 | 3.0590 | 3.2784 | 3.7589 | 4.2998 | 5.5895 | 7.2058 | 9.2170 | 11.703 |
| 9 | 2.7731 | 3.2519 | 3.5179 | 3.8030 | 4.4355 | 5.1598 | 6.9310 | 9.2234 | 12.166 | 15.916 |
| 10 | 3.1058 | 3.7072 | 4.0456 | 4.4114 | 5.2338 | 6.1917 | 8.5944 | 11.805 | 16.059 | 21.646 |
| 11 | 3.4785 | 4.2262 | 4.6524 | 5.1173 | 6.1759 | 7.4301 | 10.657 | 15.111 | 21.198 | 29.439 |
| 12 | 3.8960 | 4.8197 | 5.3502 | 5.9360 | 7.2876 | 8.9161 | 13.214 | 19.342 | 27.982 | 40.037 |
| 13 | 4.3635 | 5.4924 | 6.1528 | 6.8858 | 8.5994 | 10.699 | 16.386 | 24.758 | 36.937 | 54.451 |
| 14 | 4.8871 | 6.2613 | 7.0757 | 7.9875 | 10.147 | 12.839 | 20.319 | 31.691 | 48.756 | 74.053 |
| 15 | 5.4736 | 7.1379 | 8.1371 | 9.2655 | 11.973 | 15.407 | 25.195 | 40.564 | 64.358 | 100.71 |
| 16 | 6.1304 | 8.1372 | 9.3576 | 10.748 | 14.129 | 18.488 | 31.242 | 51.923 | 84.953 | 136.96 |
| 17 | 6.8660 | 9.2765 | 10.761 | 12.467 | 16.672 | 22.186 | 38.740 | 66.461 | 112.13 | 186.27 |
| 18 | 7.6900 | 10.575 | 12.375 | 14.462 | 19.673 | 26.623 | 48.038 | 85.070 | 148.02 | 253.33 |
| 19 | 8.6128 | 12.055 | 14.231 | 16.776 | 23.214 | 31.948 | 59.567 | 108.89 | 195.39 | 344.53 |
| 20 | 9.6463 | 13.743 | 16.366 | 19.460 | 27.393 | 38.337 | 73.864 | 139.37 | 257.91 | 468.57 |
| 21 | 10.803 | 15.667 | 18.821 | 22.574 | 32.323 | 46.005 | 91.591 | 178.40 | 340.44 | 637.26 |
| 22 | 12.100 | 17.861 | 21.644 | 26.186 | 38.142 | 55.206 | 113.57 | 228.35 | 449.39 | 866.67 |
| 23 | 13.552 | 20.361 | 24.891 | 30.376 | 45.007 | 66.247 | 140.83 | 292.30 | 593.19 | 117.86 |
| 24 | 15.178 | 23.212 | 28.625 | 35.236 | 53.108 | 79.496 | 174.63 | 374.14 | 783.02 | 160.29 |
| 25 | 17.000 | 26.461 | 32.918 | 40.874 | 62.668 | 95.396 | 216.54 | 478.90 | 103.25 | 218.00 |
| 30 | 29.959 | 50.860 | 66.211 | 85.849 | 143.37 | 237.37 | 634.81 | 1645.5 | 414.20 | 101.43 |
| 40 | 93.050 | 188.88 | 267.86 | 378.72 | 750.37 | 1469.7 | 5455.9 | 1942.6 | 665.20 | 219.561 |

# Answers to self-assessment questions

## CHAPTER 2

1. (a) SV (or variable if direct labour can be matched exactly to output)
   (b) F
   (c) F
   (d) V
   (e) F (Advertising is a discretionary cost. See Chapter 16 for an explanation of this cost.)
   (f) SV
   (g) F
   (h) SF
   (i) V

2. Controllable c, d, f
   Non-controllable a, b, e, g, h

## CHAPTER 3

1. (a) (i) Calculation of budgeted overhead absorption rates:

### Apportionment of overheads to production departments

| | Machine shop (£) | Fitting section (£) | Canteen (£) | Machine maintenance section (£) | Total (£) |
|---|---|---|---|---|---|
| Allocated overheads | 27 660 | 19 470 | 16 600 | 26 650 | 90 380 |
| Rent, rates, heat and light[a] | 9 000 | 3 500 | 2 500 | 2 000 | 17 000 |
| Depreciation and insurance of equipment[a] | 12 500 | 6 250 | 2 500 | 3 750 | 25 000 |
| | 49 160 | 29 220 | 21 600 | 32 400 | 132 380 |
| Service department apportionment | | | | | |
| Canteen[b] | 10 800 | 8 400 | (21 600) | 2 400 | — |
| Machine maintenance section | 24 360 | 10 440 | — | (34 800) | — |
| | 84 320 | 48 060 | — | — | 132 380 |

**Calculation of absorption bases**

| | | Machine shop | | | Fitting section | |
| | | Machine | Total | Direct labour | Total |
| | Budgeted | hours per | machine | cost per | direct |
| Product | production | product | hours | product | wages |
| | | | | (£) | (£) |
|---|---|---|---|---|---|
| X | 4200 units | 6 | 25 200 | 12 | 50 400 |
| Y | 6900 units | 3 | 20 700 | 3 | 20 700 |
| Z | 1700 units | 4 | 6 800 | 21 | 35 700 |
| | | | 52 700 | | 106 800 |

**Budgeted overhead absorption rates**

| Machine shop | Fitting section |
|---|---|
| $\dfrac{\text{budgeted overheads}}{\text{budgeted machine hours}} = \dfrac{£84\,320}{£52\,700}$ | $\dfrac{\text{budgeted overheads}}{\text{budgeted direct wages}} = \dfrac{48\,060}{106\,800}$ |
| $= £1.60$ per machine hour | $= 45\%$ of direct wages |

*Notes*

[a] Rents, rates, heat and light are apportioned on the basis of floor area. Depreciation and insurance of equipment are apportioned on the basis of book value.

[b] Canteen costs are reapportioned according to the number of employees. Machine maintenance section costs are reapportioned according to the percentages given in the question.

    (ii) The budgeted manufacturing overhead cost for producing one unit of product X is as follows:

| | (£) |
|---|---|
| Machine shop: 6 hours at £1.60 per hour | 9.60 |
| Fittings section: 450 of £12 | 5.40 |
| | 15.00 |

(b) The answer should discuss the limitations of blanket overhead rates and actual overhead rates. See 'Blanket overhead rates' and 'Predetermined overhead rates' in Chapter 3 for the answer to this question.

2  (a) The calculation of the overhead absorption rates are as follows:

    Forming department machine hour rate
     = £6.15 per machine hour (£602 700/98 000 hours)

    Finishing department labour hour rate
     = £2.25 per labour hour (£346 500/154 000 hours)

    The forming department is mechanized, and it is likely that a significant proportion of overheads will be incurred as a consequence of employing and running the machines. Therefore a machine hour rate has been used. In the finishing department several grades of labour are used. Consequently the direct wages percentage method is inappropriate, and the direct labour hour method should be used.

(b) The decision should be based on a comparison of the incremental costs with the purchase price of an outside supplier if spare capacity exists. If no spare capacity exists then the lost contribution on displaced work must be considered. The calculation of incremental costs requires that the variable element of the total overhead absorption rate must be calculated. The calculation is:

Forming department variable machine hour rate
= £2.05 (£200 900/98 000 hours)
Finishing department variable direct labour hour rate
= £0.75 (£115 500/154 000 hours)

The calculation of the variable costs per unit of each component is:

|  | A (£) | B (£) | C (£) |
|---|---|---|---|
| Prime cost | 24.00 | 31.00 | 29.00 |
| Variable overheads: Forming | 8.20 | 6.15 | 4.10 |
| Finishing | 2.25 | 7.50 | 1.50 |
| Variable unit manufacturing cost | 34.45 | 44.65 | 34.60 |
| Purchase price | £30 | £65 | £60 |

On the basis of the above information, component A should be purchased and components B and C manufactured. This decision is based on the following assumptions:

(i) Variable overheads vary in proportion to machine hours (forming department) and direct labour hours (finishing department).
(ii) Fixed overheads remain unaffected by any changes in activity.
(iii) Spare capacity exists.

For a discussion of make-or-buy decisions see Chapter 9.

(c) Production overhead absorption rates are calculated in order to ascertain costs per unit of output for stock valuation and profit measurement purposes. Such costs are inappropriate for decision-making and cost control. For an explanation of this see 'Extracting relevant costs for decision making' in Chapter 3.

# CHAPTER 4

1 The company's cost accounts are not integrated with the financial accounts. For a description of a non-integrated accounting system see 'Interlocking accounts' in Chapter 4. The following accounting entries are necessary:

**Cost ledger control account**

|  | (£) |  |  | (£) |
|---|---|---|---|---|
| Sales a/c | 410 000 | 1.5.00 | Balance b/f | 302 000 |
| Capital under | 50 150 |  | Stores ledger | 42 700 |
| construction a/c |  |  | a/c – Purchases |  |
| Balance c/f | 237 500 |  | Wages control a/c | 124 000 |
|  |  |  | Production overhead a/c | 152 350 |
|  |  |  | WIP a/c – Royalty | 2 150 |
|  |  |  | Selling overhead a/c | 22 000 |
|  |  |  | Profit | 52 450 |
|  | £697 650 |  |  | £697 650 |

### Stores ledger control account

| | | (£) | | (£) |
|---|---|---|---|---|
| 1.5.00 | Balance b/f | 85 400 | WIP a/c | 63 400 |
| | Cost ledger control | 42 700 | Production overhead a/c | 1 450 |
| | a/c – Purchases | | Capital a/c | 7 650 |
| | | | 31.5.X0 Balance c/£ | 55 600 |
| | | £128 100 | | £128 100 |

### Wages control account

| | (£) | | (£) |
|---|---|---|---|
| Cost ledger control a/c | 124 000 | Capital a/c | 12 500 |
| | | Production | 35 750 |
| | | WIP a/c | 7 550 |
| | £124 000 | | £124 000 |

### Production overhead control account

| | (£) | | (£) |
|---|---|---|---|
| Stores ledger a/c | 1 450 | Capital a/c | 30 000 |
| Wages control a/c | 35 750 | WIP a/c – Absorption | 152 000 |
| Cost ledger control a/c | 152 350 | (balancing figure) | |
| | | Costing P/L a/c (under absorption) | 7 550 |
| | £189 550 | | £189 550 |

### Work in progress control account

| | | (£) | | | (£) |
|---|---|---|---|---|---|
| 1.5.00 | Balance b/f | 167 350 | Finished goods | | 281 300 |
| | Stores ledger a/c– | | control a/c | | |
| | Issues | 63 400 | (balancing figure) | | |
| | Wages control a/c | 75 750 | 31.5.X0 | Balance c/f[a] | 179 350 |
| | Production overhead absorbed | 152 000 | | | |
| | Cost ledger control a/c – Royalty | 2 150 | | | |
| | | £460 650 | | | £460 650 |

### Finished goods control account

| | | (£) | | (£) |
|---|---|---|---|---|
| 1.5.00 | Balance b/f | 49 250 | Cost sales a/c[b] | 328 000 |
| | WIP a/c | 281 300 | 31.5.X0 Balance c/f | 2 550 |
| | | £330 550 | | £330 550 |

### Capital under construction account

|  | (£) |  | (£) |
|---|---|---|---|
| Stores ledger a/c | 7 650 | Cost ledger control a/c | 50 150 |
| Wages control a/c | 12 500 |  |  |
| Production overhead |  |  |  |
| absorbed | 30 000 |  |  |
|  | £ 50 150 |  | £50 150 |

### Sales account

|  | (£) |  | (£) |
|---|---|---|---|
| Costing P/L a/c | £410 000 | Cost ledger control a/c | £410 000 |

### Cost of sales account

|  | (£) |  | (£) |
|---|---|---|---|
| Finished goods a/c[b] | £328 000 | Cost P/L a/c | £328 000 |

### Selling overhead account

|  | (£) |  | (£) |
|---|---|---|---|
| Cost ledger control a/c | £ 22 000 | Costing P/L a/c | £22 000 |

### Costing profit and loss account

|  | (£) |  | (£) |
|---|---|---|---|
| Selling overhead a/c | 22 000 | Sales A/c | 410 000 |
| Production overhead (under | 7 550 |  |  |
| absorbed) |  |  |  |
| Cost of sales a/c | 328 000 |  |  |
| Profit – Cost ledger control | 52 450 |  |  |
| a/c |  |  |  |
|  | £410 000 |  | £410 000 |

*Notes*
[a] Closing balance of work in progress = £167 350 (opening balance)

£12 000 (increase per question)

£179 350

[b] Transfer from finished goods stock to cost of sales account: £410 000 sales × (100/125) = £328 000

# CHAPTER 5

1                                   **Process 1 account**

|  | (kg) | (£) |  | (kg) | (£) |
|---|---|---|---|---|---|
| Material | 3000 | 750 | Normal loss (20%) | 600 | 120 |
| Labour |  | 120 | Transfer to process 2 | 2300 | 1150 |
| Process plant time |  | 240 | Abnormal loss | 100 | 50 |
| General overhead |  |  |  |  |  |
| (£120/£204 × £357) |  | 210 |  |  |  |
|  | 3000 | 1320 |  | 3000 | 1320 |

$$\text{cost per unit} = \frac{\text{cost of production less scrap value of normal loss}}{\text{expected output}}$$

$$= \frac{\text{£1320} - \text{£120}}{2400 \text{ kg}} = \text{£0.50}$$

**Process 2 account**

| | (kg) | (£) | | (kg) | (£) |
|---|---|---|---|---|---|
| Previous process cost | 2300 | 1150 | Normal loss | 430 | 129 |
| Materials | 2000 | 800 | Transfer to finished stock | 4000 | 2400 |
| Labour | | 84 | | | |
| General overhead (£84/£204 × £357) | | 147 | | | |
| Process plant time | | 270 | | | |
| | | 2451 | | | |
| Abnormal gain (130 kg at £0.60) | 130 | 78 | | | |
| | 4430 | 2529 | | 4430 | 2529 |

$$\text{cost per unit} = \frac{\text{£2451} - \text{£129}}{3870 \text{ kg}} = \text{£0.60}$$

**Finished stock account**

| | (£) |
|---|---|
| Process 2 | 2400 |

**Normal loss account (income due)**

| | (£) | | (£) |
|---|---|---|---|
| Process 1 normal loss | 120 | Abnormal gain account | 39 |
| Process 2 normal loss | 129 | Balance or cash received | 230 |
| Abnormal loss account | 20 | | |
| | 269 | | 269 |

**Abnormal loss account**

| | (£) | | (£) |
|---|---|---|---|
| Process 1 | 50 | Normal loss account (100 × £0.20) | 20 |
| | | Profit and loss account | 30 |
| | 50 | | 50 |

**Abnormal gain account**

| | (£) | | (£) |
|---|---|---|---|
| Normal loss account (Loss of income 130 × £0.30) | 39 | Process 2 | 78 |
| Profit and loss account | 39 | | |
| | 78 | | 78 |

2  (a)  Calculation of input for process 1

|  | (litres) | (£) |
|---|---|---|
| Opening stock | 4 000 | 10 800 |
| Receipts | 20 000 | 61 000 |
| Less closing stock | (8 000) | (24 200) |
| Process input | 16 000 | 47 600 |
| Output |  | (litres) |
| Completed units |  | 8 000 |
| Closing WIP |  | 5 600 |
| Normal loss (15% of input) |  | 2 400 |
|  |  | 16 000 |

Because input is equal to output, there are no abnormal gains or losses.

*Calculation of cost per unit (Process 1)*
It is assumed that the loss occurs at the point of inspection. Because WIP has passed the inspection point, the normal loss should be allocated to both completed units and WIP.

| (1) Element of cost | (2) (£) | (3) Completed units | (4) Normal loss | (5) Closing WIP | (6) Total equiv. units | (7) Cost per unit | (8) = (5) × (7) WIP |
|---|---|---|---|---|---|---|---|
| Materials | 47 600 | 8000 | 2400 | 5600 | 16 000 | £2.975 | £16 660 |
| Conversion cost[a] | 21 350 | 8000 | 1800 | 4200 | 14 000 | £1.525 | £6 405 |
|  | 68 950 |  |  |  |  | £4.50 | £23 065 |

*Note*
[a] Conversion cost = direct labour (£4880) + direct expenses (£4270) + overhead (250% × £4880)

| Cost of normal loss | (£) |
|---|---|
| Materials | 2400 × £2.975 = 7140 |
| Conversion cost | 1800 × £1.525 = 2745 |
|  | 9885 |

The apportionment of normal loss to completed units and WIP is as follows:

|  | (£) |
|---|---|
| Completed units | (8000/13 600 × 9885) = 5815 |
| WIP | (5600/13 600 × 9885) = 4070 |
|  | 9885 |

The cost of completed units and WIP is as follows:

|  |  | (£) | (£) |
|---|---|---|---|
| Completed units: | 8000 units × £4.50 | 36 000 |  |
|  | Share of normal loss | 5815 | 41 815 |
| WIP: | Original allocation | 23 065 |  |
|  | Share of normal loss | 4070 | 27 135 |
|  |  |  | 68 950 |

For an explanation of the above procedure see Chapter 5.
*Where the normal loss is apportioned to WIP and completed units, a simple (but less accurate) approach is to use the short-cut approach and not to include the normal loss in the unit cost statement.* The calculation is as follows:

| Element of cost | (£) | Completed units | Closing WIP | Total equiv. units | Cost per unit (£) | WIP (£) |
|---|---|---|---|---|---|---|
| Materials | 47 600 | 8000 | 5600 | 13 600 | 3.50 | 19 600 |
| Conversion cost | 21 350 | 8000 | 4200 | 12 200 | 1.75 | 7 350 |
| | | | | | £5.25 | £26 950 |

Completed units 8000 × £5.25 = £42 000

### Process 1 account – May 2000

| | (litres) | (£) | | (litres) | (£) |
|---|---|---|---|---|---|
| Materials | 16 000 | 47 600 | Transfers to process 2 | 8 000 | 42 000 |
| Labour | | 4 880 | Normal loss | 2 400 | — |
| Direct expenses | | 4 270 | Closing stock C/f | 5 600 | 26 950 |
| Overheads absorbed | | 12 200 | | | |
| | 16 000 | 68 950 | | 16 000 | 68 950 |

With process 2, there is no closing WIP. Therefore it is unnecessary to express output in equivalent units. The cost per unit is calculated as follows:

$$\frac{\text{cost of production less scrap value of normal loss}}{\text{expected output}} = \frac{£54\,000^a}{(90\% \times 8000)} = £7.50$$

*Note*
[a] Cost of production = transferred in cost from process 1 (42 000) + labour (£6000) + overhead (£6000).

### Process 2 account – May 2000

| | Litres | (£) | | Litres | (£) |
|---|---|---|---|---|---|
| Transferred from Process 1 | 8000 | 42 000 | Finished goods store[b] | 7500 | 56 250 |
| Labour | | 6 000 | Normal loss | 800 | |
| Overheads absorbed | | 6 000 | Closing stock | — | — |
| Abnormal gain[b] | 300 | 2 250 | | | |
| | 8300 | 56 250 | | 8300 | 56 250 |

### Finished goods account

| | Litres | (£) |
|---|---|---|
| Ex Process 2 | 7500 | 56 250 |

**Abnormal gain account**

| | (£) | | Litres | (£) |
|---|---|---|---|---|
| Profit and loss account | 2250 | Process 2 account | 300 | 2250 |

*Notes*
[a] Input = 8000 litres. Normal output = 90% × 8000 litres = 7200 litres.
Actual output = 7500 litres. Abnormal gain = 300 litres × £7.50 per litre = £2250.
[b] 7500 litres at £7.50 per litre.

(b) If the materials can be replaced then the loss to the company will consist of the replacement cost of materials. If the materials cannot be replaced then the loss will consist of the lost sales revenue less the costs not incurred as a result of not processing and selling 100 litres.

# CHAPTER 6

(a) Operating statement for October 2000

| (£) | | (£) |
|---|---|---|
| Sales: Product A (80 000 × £5) = | 400 000 | |
| Product B (65 000 × £4) = | 260 000 | |
| Product C (75 000 × £9) = | 675 000 | 1 335 000 |
| Operating costs | 1 300 000 | |
| Less closing stock[a] | 200 000 | |
| | | 1 100 000 |
| Profit | | 235 000 |

*Note*
[a] Production for the period (kg):

| | A | B | C | Total |
|---|---|---|---|---|
| Sales requirements | 80 000 | 65 000 | 75 000 | |
| Closing stock | 20 000 | 15 000 | 5 000 | |
| Production | 100 000 | 80 000 | 80 000 | 260 000 |

$$\text{Cost per kg} = 260\,000\,\text{kg} = \frac{£1\,300\,000}{260\,000} = £5 \text{ per kg}$$

Therefore
Closing stock = 40 000 kg at £5 per kg

(b) Evaluation of refining proposal

| | A | B | C | Total (£) |
|---|---|---|---|---|
| Incremental revenue per kg (£) | 12 | 10 | 11.50 | |
| Variable cost per kg (£) | 4 | 6 | 12.00 | |
| Contribution per kg (£) | 8 | 4 | (0.50) | |
| Monthly production (kg) | 100 000 | 80 000 | 80 000 | |
| Monthly contribution (£) | 800 000 | 320 000 | (40 000) | 1 080 000 |

| | | | |
|---|---|---|---|
| Monthly fixed overheads (specific to B) | | 360 000 | 360 000 |
| Contribution to refining general fixed costs (£) | 800 000 | (40 000) (40 000) | 720 000 |
| Refining general fixed overheads | | | 700 000 |
| Monthly profit | | | 20 000 |

1. It is more profitable to sell C in its unrefined state and product B is only profitable in its refined state if monthly sales are in excess of 90 000 kg (£360 000 fixed costs/£4 contribution per unit).

2. If both products B and C are sold in their unrefined state then the refining process will yield a profit of £100 000 per month (£800 000 product A contribution less £700 000 fixed costs).

3. The break-even point for the refining process if only product A were produced is 87 500 kg (£700 000 fixed costs/£8 contribution per unit). Consequently if sales of A declined by $12\frac{1}{2}\%$, the refining process will yield a loss. Note that 80 000 kg of A were sold in October.

# CHAPTER 7

| | £ |
|---|---|
| Calculation of product cost | |
| Materials | 10 |
| Labour | 2 |
| Variable production cost | 12 |
| Variable distribution cost | 1 |
| Total variable cost | 13 |
| Fixed overhead (£10 000/1000 units) | 10 |
| Total costs | 23 |

The product costs for stock valuation purposes are as follows:

| | |
|---|---|
| Variable costing | £12 (variable production cost) |
| Absorption costing | £22 (variable production cost + fixed manufacturing overhead) |

It is assumed that all of the fixed overhead relates to production. Note that the distribution cost is per unit *sold* and not per unit *produced*.

    (a) (i) *Variable costing*

| | $t_1$ | $t_2$ | $t_3$ |
|---|---|---|---|
| Opening stock | 1 200 | 1 200 | 1 200 |
| Production | 12 000 | 12 000 | 12 000 |
| | 13 200 | 13 200 | 13 200 |
| Closing stock | 1 200 | 1 200 | 1 200 |

| | | | |
|---|---|---|---|
| Cost of sales | 12 000 | 12 000 | 12 000 |
| Sales at £25 per unit | 25 000 | 25 000 | 25 000 |
| Gross profit | 13 000 | 13 000 | 13 000 |
| Distribution costs | 1 000 | 1 000 | 1 000 |
| Fixed labour costs | 5 000 | 5 000 | 5 000 |
| Fixed overhead costs | 5 000 | 5 000 | 5 000 |
| Net profit | £2 000 | £2 000 | £2 000 |
| Total profit £6000 | | | |

*Absorption costing*

| | $t_1$ (£) | $t_2$ (£) | $t_3$ (£) |
|---|---|---|---|
| Opening stock | 2 200 | 2 200 | 2 200 |
| Production | 22 000 | 22 000 | 22 000 |
| | 24 200 | 24 200 | 24 200 |
| Closing stock | 2 200 | 2 200 | 2 200 |
| Cost of sales | 22 000 | 22 000 | 22 000 |
| Sales at £25 per unit | 25 000 | 25 000 | 25 000 |
| Gross profit | 3 000 | 3 000 | 3 000 |
| Distribution cost | 1 000 | 1 000 | 1 000 |
| Net profit | £2 000 | £2 000 | £2 000 |
| Total profit £6000 | | | |

(ii)  *Variable costing*

| | $t_1$ (£) | $t_2$ (£) | $t_3$ (£) |
|---|---|---|---|
| Opening stock | 1 200 | 7 200 | 4 800 |
| Production | 18 000 | 9 600 | 8 400 |
| | 19 200 | 16 800 | 13 200 |
| Closing stock | 7 200 | 4 800 | 1 200 |
| Cost of sales | 12 000 | 12 000 | 12 000 |
| Sales at £25 per unit | 25 000 | 25 000 | 25 000 |
| Gross profit | 13 000 | 13 000 | 13 000 |
| Distribution costs | 1 000 | 1 000 | 1 000 |
| Fixed labour costs | 5 000 | 5 000 | 5 000 |
| Fixed overhead costs | 5 000 | 5 000 | 5 000 |
| Net profit | £2 000 | £2 000 | £2 000 |
| Total profit £6000 | | | |

*Absorption costing*

| | $t_1$ (£) | $t_2$ (£) | $t_3$ (£) |
|---|---|---|---|
| Opening stock | 2 200 | 13 200 | 8 800 |
| Production | 33 000 | 17 600 | 15 400 |
| | 35 200 | 30 800 | 24 200 |
| Under/(over) recovery | (5 000) | 2 000 | 3 000 |
| | 30 200 | 32 800 | 27 200 |
| Closing stock | 13 200 | 8 800 | 2 200 |
| Cost of sales | 17 000 | 24 000 | 25 000 |
| Sales at £25 per unit | 25 000 | 25 000 | 25 000 |
| Gross profit | 8 000 | 1 000 | — |
| Distribution cost | 1 000 | 1 000 | 1 000 |
| Net profit | £7 000 | — | £(1 000) |
| Total profit £6000 | | | |

(iii) *Variable costing*

| | $t_1$ (£) | $t_2$ (£) | $t_3$ (£) |
|---|---|---|---|
| Opening stock | 1 200 | 7 200 | 4 800 |
| Production | 12 000 | 12 000 | 12 000 |
| | 13 200 | 19 200 | 16 800 |
| Closing stock | 7 200 | 4 800 | 1 200 |
| Cost of sales | 6 000 | 14 400 | 15 600 |
| Sales at £25 per unit | 12 500 | 30 000 | 32 500 |
| Gross profit | 6 500 | 15 600 | 16 900 |
| Distribution costs | 500 | 1 200 | 1 300 |
| Fixed labour costs | 5 000 | 5 000 | 5 000 |
| Fixed overhead costs | 5 000 | 5 000 | 5 000 |
| Net profit | £(4 000) | £4 400 | £5 600 |
| Total profit £6000 | | | |

*Absorption costing*

| | $t_1$ (£) | $t_2$ (£) | $t_3$ (£) |
|---|---|---|---|
| Opening stock | 2 200 | 13 200 | 8 800 |
| Production | 22 000 | 22 000 | 22 000 |
| | 24 200 | 35 200 | 30 800 |
| Closing stock | 13 200 | 8 800 | 2 200 |
| Cost of sales | 11 000 | 26 400 | 28 600 |
| Sales at £25 per unit | 12 500 | 30 000 | 32 500 |
| Gross profit | 1 500 | 3 600 | 3 900 |
| Distribution cost | 500 | 1 200 | 1 300 |
| Net profit | £1 000 | £2 400 | £2 600 |
| Total profit £6000 | | | |

(b) For the answer to this question see Chapter 7: Note that profits are identical for both systems in (i), since production equals sales. In (ii) and (iii) profits are higher with absorption costing when production exceeds sales, whereas profits are higher with variable costing when production is less than sales. Taking the three periods as a whole there is no change in the level of opening stock in $t_1$ compared with the closing stock in $t_3$, so that the disclosed profit for the three periods is the same under both systems. Also note that the differences in profits disclosed in (a) (ii) and (a) (iii) is accounted for in the fixed overheads included in the stock valuation changes.

# CHAPTER 8

1 (a)

$$BEP = \frac{£400\,000 \text{ (fixed costs)} \times £1\,000\,000 \text{ (sales)}}{£420\,000 \text{ (contribution)}}$$

$$= \underline{£952\,380}$$

(b) (i)

|  | (£) | (£) |
|---|---|---|
| Revised selling price | | 9.00 |
| Less variable costs: | | |
|     Direct materials | 1.00 | |
|     Direct labour | 3.50 | |
| Variable overhead | 0.60 | |
| Delivery expenses | 0.50 | |
| Sales commission | 0.18 | |
|     (2% of selling price) | | 5.78 |
| Contribution per unit | | 3.22 |

| | |
|---|---|
| Number of units sold | 140 000 |
| Total contribution (140 000 × £3.22) | £450 800 |
| Fixed costs | £400 000 |
| Profit from proposal (i) | £50 800 |

(ii)

| | |
|---|---|
| Desired contribution | = £480 000 |
| Contribution per unit for present proposal | = £3.22 |
| Required units to earn large profit | = £149 068 |

(c) (i) The variable cost of selling to the mail order firm is:

| | (£) |
|---|---|
| Direct material | 1.00 |
| Direct labour | 3.50 |
| Variable overhead | 0.60 |
| Delivery expenses | nil |
| Sales commission | nil |
| Additional package cost | 0.50 |
| | 5.60 |

To break even, a contribution of £1.20 is required $\left(\dfrac{60\,000\text{ fixed cost}}{50\,000\text{ units sold}}\right)$.

Therefore selling price to break even is £6.80 (£5.60 + £1.20).

(ii) To earn £50 800 profit, a contribution of £110 800 (£60 000 + £50 800) is required.

That is, a contribution of £2.22 per unit is required. Therefore required selling price is £7.82 (£5.60 + £2.22).

(iii) To earn the target profit of £80 000, a contribution of £140 000 is required. That is, £2.80 per unit. Therefore required selling price = £8.40 (£5.60 + £2.80).

(d) Contribution per unit is £3.22 per (B)

| | |
|---|---:|
| Unit sold | 160 000 |
| Total contribution | £515 200 |
| Fixed costs | £430 000 |
| Profit | £ 85 200 |

2 (a) (i)  P    Total sales revenue

q    Total cost (fixed cost + variable cost)

r    Total variable cost

s    Fixed costs at the specific level of activity

t    Total loss at the specific level of activity

u    Total profit at that level of activity

v    Total contribution at the specific level of activity

W    Total contribution at a lower level of activity

X    Level of activity of output sales

Y    Monetary value of cost and revenue function for level of activity

(ii) At event M the selling price per *unit* decreases, but it remains constant. Note that P is a straight line, but with a lower gradient above m compared with below m.

At event n there is an increase in fixed costs equal to the dotted line. This is probably due to an increase in capital expenditure in order to expand output beyond this point. Also note that at this point the variable cost per unit declines as reflected by the gradient of the variable cost line. This might be due to more efficient production methods associated with increased investment in capital equipment.

(iii) Break-even analysis is of limited use in a multi-product company, but the analysis can be a useful aid to the management of a small single product company. The following are some of the main benefits:

(a) Break-even analysis forces management to consider the functional relationship between costs, revenue and activity, and gives an insight into how costs and revenue change with changes in the level of activity.

(b) Break-even analysis forces management to consider the fixed costs at various levels of activity and the selling price that will be required to achieve various levels of output.

For more specific uses of break-even analysis see Chapter 8. Break-even analysis can be a useful tool, but it is subject to a number of assumptions that restrict its usefulness (see 'Cost–volume–profit analysis assumptions' in Chapter 8).

(b) *Preliminary workings*

$$\text{Gudgeon unit contribution} = £4 \; (40\% \times £10)$$

$$\text{Bludgeon unit contribution} = £3 \; (60\% \times £5)$$

Let $x$ = output and sales volume of each product. Then

$$4x + 3x - 100\,000 = 14\,000 - 2000$$

$$\text{giving } 7x = 112\,000$$

$$\text{and } x = 16\,000$$

Budgeted sales of both products are 16 000 units.

*Proposal 1*

It is assumed that, because the price elasticity of demand is unity, total revenue will be unchanged.

Budgeted revenue = £80 000 (16 000 units × £5)

So revised demand volume = 12 800 units (£80 000/£6.25 selling price)

Total revised contribution = £54 400 (12 800 units at (6.25 − £2))

Existing budgeted contribution = £48 000 (16 000 units × £3)

Increase in contribution = £6400

*Proposal 2*

Revised variable costs: Gudgeons £6.60 (£6 + 10%)

Bludgeons £2.20 (£2 + 10%)

Revised budgeted profit:

| | **(£)** |
|---|---|
| Gudgeon contribution | 54 400 (16 000 × (£10 − £6.60)) |
| Bludgeon contribution | 44 800 (16 000 × (£5 − £2.20)) |
| Total contribution | 99 200 |
| Less revised fixed costs | 87 500 |
| Revised profit | 11 700 |
| Budgeted profit | 12 000 |

Therefore profits will decline by £300

*Proposal 3*

Revised budgeted profit:

| | **(£)** |
|---|---|
| Gudgeon contribution | 54 400 (As proposal 2) |
| Bludgeon contribution | 51 840 (12 800 units × £6.25 − £2.20) |
| Total contribution | 106 240 |
| Less fixed costs | 87 500 |
| Revised profit | 18 740 |
| Budgeted profit | 12 000 |

Therefore profits will increase by £6740, and the greatest improvement in profits occurs from implementing this proposal.

## CHAPTER 9

1 (a) *Preliminary calculations*

Variable costs are quoted per acre, but selling prices are quoted per tonne. Therefore, it is necessary to calculate the planned sales revenue per acre. The calculation of the selling price and contribution per acre is as follows:

|  | Potatoes | Turnips | Parsnips | Carrots |
|---|---|---|---|---|
| (a) Yield per acre in tonnes | 10 | 8 | 9 | 12 |
| (b) Selling price per tonne | £100 | £125 | £150 | £135 |
| (c) Sales revenue per acre, (a) × (b) | £1000 | £1000 | £1350 | £1620 |
| (d) Variable cost per acre | £470 | £510 | £595 | £660 |
| (e) Contribution per acre | £530 | £490 | £755 | £960 |

(a) (i)

   (i)  Profit statement for current year

|  | Potatoes | Turnips | Parsnips | Carrots | Total |
|---|---|---|---|---|---|
| (a) Acres | 25 | 20 | 30 | 25 | |
| (b) Contribution per acre | £530 | £490 | £755 | £960 | |
| (c) Total contribution (a × b) | £13 250 | £9800 | £22 650 | £24 000 | £69 700 |
| | | | | Less fixed costs | £54 000 |
| | | | | Profit | £15 700 |

   (ii)  Profit statement for recommended mix

|  | Area A (45 acres) Potatoes | Turnips | Area B (55 acres) Parsnips | Carrots | Total |
|---|---|---|---|---|---|
| (a) Contribution per acre | £530 | £490 | £755 | £960 | |
| (b) Ranking | 1 | 2 | 2 | 1 | |
| (c) Minimum sales requirements in acres[a] | | 5 | 4 | | |
| (d) Acres allocated[b] | 40 | | | 51 | |
| (e) Recommended mix (acres) | 40 | 5 | 4 | 51 | |
| (f) Total contribution, (a) × (e) | £21 200 | £2450 | £3020 | £48 960 | £75 630 |
| | | | | Less fixed costs | £54 000 |
| | | | | Profit | £21 630 |

*Notes*

[a] The minimum sales requirement for turnips is 40 tonnes, and this will require the allocation of 5 acres (40 tonnes/8 tonnes yield per acre). The minimum sales requirement for parsnips is 36 tonnes, requiring the allocation of 4 acres (36 tonnes/9 tonnes yield per acre).

[b] Allocation of available acres to products on basis of a ranking that assumes that acres are the key factor.

(b) (i)  Production should be concentrated on carrots, which have the highest contribution per acre (£960).

|  | (£) |
|---|---|
| (ii)  Contribution from 100 acres of carrots (100 × £960) | 96 000 |
| Fixed overhead | 54 000 |
| Profit from carrots | 42 000 |

(iii)  Break-even point in acres for carrots = $\dfrac{\text{fixed costs (£54 000)}}{\text{contribution per acre (£960)}}$

$= 56.25$ acres

Contribution in sales value for carrots

$= £91 125$ (56.25 acres at £1620 sales revenue per acre).

2  (a)  Relevant costs and relevant revenues from acceptance of contract

|  | (£000) | (£000) |
|---|---|---|
| Sales revenue (20 000 kg at £100) |  | 2000 |
| Relevant costs: |  |  |
| Labour[a] (20 000 × 6 hrs × £2) | 240 |  |
| Materials |  |  |
| A (20 000 × 2 units × £10 replacement cost) | 400 |  |
| B (20 000 × 1 litre × £25 NRV) | 500 |  |
| Variable overheads[b] (20 000 × 8 hrs × £3) | 480 |  |
|  |  | 1620 |
| Add increase in fixed costs[d] | 228 |  |
| Net incremental costs | 1848 |  |
| Add |  |  |
| Loss on product Y |  |  |
| Lost contribution[c] (5000 × £38) | 190 |  |
| Fixed costs avoided[d] | (58) | 132 | 1980 |
| Excess of relevant revenues over relevant costs |  | 20 |

*Notes*
[a] Grade 1 labour is not an incremental cost.
[b] Variable overheads vary with *production* labour – 8 labour hours per unit are used, causing variable overheads to increase by £3 per hour. Grade 1 labour is not an incremental cost, but it does cause variable overheads to increase.

|  | (£) |  |
|---|---|---|
| [c] Lost contribution: |  |  |
| Selling price |  | 70 |
| Less |  |  |
| Grade 2 labour (4 hrs × £2) | 8 |  |
| Materials | 12 |  |
| Variable overheads (4 hrs × £3) | 12 | 32 |
| Contribution |  | 38 |

[d] Assumed fixed costs represent incremental costs or incremental savings.

(b)  To calculate the product cost for job costing purposes it is necessary to calculate the fixed overhead rate. The calculation is as follows:

|  | Fixed overheads | Direct labour hours |
|---|---|---|
| Initial budget | £600 000 | 300 000 |
| Plus contract | £228 000 | 160 000[a] |
| Less product Y | (£ 58 000) | (20 000) |
|  | £770 000 | 440 000 |

Fixed overhead absorption rate = £1.75 (£770 000/440 000 hrs).

*Note*

[a] The fixed overhead rate is per productive labour hour. Grade 1 labour hours represent additional *productive* labour hours. If the contract is not accepted then grade 1 labour hours will be non-productive.

The job costing calculation will be as follows:

|  | (£000) | (£000) |
|---|---|---|
| Direct labour: |  |  |
| Grade 1 (20 000 × 2 hrs × £4) | 160 |  |
| Grade 2 (20 000 × 6 hrs × £2) | 240 | 400 |
| Direct materials: |  |  |
| A (20 000 × 2 units × £8) | 320 |  |
| B (20 000 × 1 litre × £30) | 600 | 920 |
| Fixed overheads |  |  |
| 20 000 × 8 hrs × £1.75 | 280 |  |
| Variable overheads |  |  |
| 20 000 × 8 hrs × £3 | 480 | 760 |
| Total cost |  | 2080 |
| Sales revenue |  | 2000 |
| Reported loss |  | 80 |

(c) The relevant cost and revenue approach in part (a) represents the *additional* costs and revenues resulting from the contract's acceptance, whereas the job costing calculation represents costs allocated to the job in accordance with the historic cost principle. The main differences are as follows:

1. Labour: Grade 1 Labour is not an incremental cost. Therefore it is not included in the relevant cost calculation.
2. Materials: Relevant costs for decision-making purposes are replacement and opportunity costs. Book values are used in the job costing calculation. For a discussion of this point see 'Pricing the issues of raw materials' in Chapter 4.
3. Fixed overhead: The relevant cost calculation only includes incremental fixed costs whereas the job costing calculation includes a share of *all* fixed overheads.
4. Loss on Y: The relevant cost calculation charges this to the contract, since the company loses this amount on product Y if the contract is accepted.

# CHAPTER 10

(a) (i)

$$\text{Direct labour overhead rate} = \frac{\text{total overheads (£1 848 000)}}{\text{total direct labour hours (88 000)}}$$

$$= \text{£21 per direct labour hour}$$

*Product costs*

| Product | X | Y | Z |
|---|---|---|---|
| | **(£)** | **(£)** | **(£)** |
| Direct labour | 8 | 12 | 6 |
| Direct materials | 25 | 20 | 11 |
| Overhead[a] | 28 | 42 | 21 |
| Total cost | 61 | 74 | 38 |

*Note*

[a] X = $1\frac{1}{3}$ hours × £21

Y = 2 hours × £21

Z = 1 hour × £21

(ii) Materials handling

$$\text{Overhead rate} = \frac{\text{receiving department overheads (£435\,000)}}{\text{direct material cost (£1\,238\,000)}} \times 100$$

$$= 35.14\% \text{ of direct material cost}$$

$$\text{Machine hour overhead rate} = \frac{\text{other overheads (£1\,413\,000)}}{76\,000 \text{ machine hours}}$$

$$= \text{£18.59 per machine hour}$$

*Product costs*

| Product | X | Y | Z |
|---|---|---|---|
| | **(£)** | **(£)** | **(£)** |
| Direct labour | 8.00 | 12.00 | 6.00 |
| Direct materials | 25.00 | 20.00 | 11.00 |
| Materials handling overhead | 8.78 | 7.03 | 3.87 |
| | (£25 × 35.14%) | (£20 × 35.14%) | (£11 × 35.14%) |
| Other overheads[a] (machine hour basis) | 24.79 | 18.59 | 37.18 |
| Total cost | 66.57 | 57.62 | 58.05 |

*Note*

[a] X = $1\frac{1}{3}$ × £18.59

Y = 1 × £18.59

Z = 2 × £18.59

(b) The cost per transaction or activity for each of the cost centres is as follows:

*Set-up cost*

$$\text{Cost per setup} = \frac{\text{setup cost (£30\,000)}}{\text{number of production runs (30)}} = \text{£1000}$$

*Receiving*

$$\text{Cost per receiving order} = \frac{\text{receiving cost (£435\,000)}}{\text{number of orders (270)}} = \text{£1611}$$

*Packing*

$$\text{Cost per packing order} = \frac{\text{packing cost (£250\,000)}}{\text{number of orders (32)}} = \text{£7812}$$

*Engineering*

$$\text{Cost per production order} = \frac{\text{engineering cost (£373\,000)}}{\text{number of production orders (50)}} = \text{£7460}$$

The total set-up cost for the period was £30 000 and the cost per transaction or activity for the period is £1000 per set-up. Product X required three production runs, and thus £3000 of the set-up cost is traced to the production of product X for the period. Thus the cost per set-up per unit produced for product X is £0.10 (£3000/30 000 units).

Similarly, product Z required 20 set-ups, and so £20 000 is traced to product Z. Hence the cost per set-up for product Z is £2.50 (£20 000/8000 units).

The share of a support department's cost that is traced to each unit of output for each product is therefore calculated as follows:

$$\text{cost per transaction} \times \frac{\text{number of transactions per product}}{\text{number of units produced}}$$

The unit standard costs for products X, Y and Z using an activity-based costing system are

|  | X | Y | Z |
|---|---|---|---|
| Direct labour | £8.00 | £12.00 | £6.00 |
| Direct materials | 25.00 | 20.00 | 11.00 |
| Machine overhead[a] | 13.33 | 10.00 | 20.00 |
| Set-up costs | 0.10 | 0.35 | 2.50 |
| Receiving[b] | 0.81 | 2.82 | 44.30 |
| Packing[c] | 2.34 | 1.17 | 19.53 |
| Engineering[d] | 3.73 | 3.73 | 23.31 |
| Total manufacturing cost | 53.31 | 50.07 | 126.64 |

*Notes*
[a] Machine hours × machine overhead rate (£760 000/76 000 hrs)
[b] X = (£1611 × 15)/30 000
   Y = (£1611 × 35)/20 000
   Z = (£1611 × 220)/8 000
[c] X = (£7812 × 9)/30 000
   Y = (£7812 × 3)/20 000
   Z = (£7812 × 20)/8 000
[d] X = (£7460 × 15)/30 000
   Y = (£7460 × 10)/20 000
   Z = (£7460 × 25)/8 000

(c) The traditional product costing system assumes that products consume resources in relation to volume measures such as direct labour, direct materials or machine hours. The activity-based system recognizes that some overheads are unrelated to production volume, and uses cost drivers that are independent of production volume. For example, the activity-based system assigns the following percentage of costs to product Z, the low volume product:

| | | |
|---|---|---|
| Set-up-related costs | 66.67% | (20 out of 30 set-ups) |
| Delivery-related costs | 62.5% | (20 out of 32 deliveries) |
| Receiving costs | 81.5% | (220 out of 270 receiving orders) |
| Engineering-related costs | 50% | (25 out of 50 production orders) |

In contrast, the current costing system assigns the cost of the above activities according to production volume, measured in machine hours. The total machine hours are

$$\text{Product X } 40\,000 \ (30\,000 \times 1\tfrac{1}{3})$$
$$\text{Product Y } 20\,000 \ (20\,000 \times 1)$$
$$\text{Product Z } \underline{16\,000} \ (8\,000 \times 2)$$
$$\underline{76\,000}$$

Therefore 21% (16 000/76 000) of the non-volume-related costs are assigned to product Z if machine hours are used as the allocation base. Hence the traditional system undercosts the low-volume product, and, on applying the above approach, it can be shown that the high-volume product (product X) is overcosted. For example, 53% of the costs (40 000/76 000) are traced to product X with the current system, whereas the activity-based system assigns a much lower proportion of non-volume-related costs to this product.

# CHAPTER 11

(a) *New machine not leased*

$$\text{Marginal cost per unit} = \text{materials } (\pounds 2) + \text{piecework rate } (\pounds 0.50)$$
$$+ \text{royalties } (\pounds 0.50)$$
$$= \pounds 3$$

So total cost function = £50 000 fixed costs + £3$x$

If the selling price is £5, sales demand will be zero. To increase demand by 1 unit, selling price must be reduced by £0.01/1000 units or £0.0 0001.

Therefore the maximum selling price attainable for an output of $x$ units is £5 − £0.0 0001$x$

Therefore

$$P = 5 - \pounds 0.0\,0001x$$
$$\text{TR} = x(5 - 0.0\,0001x)$$
$$= 5x - 0.00001x^2$$
$$\text{MR} = \frac{d\text{TR}}{dx} = 5 - 0.0\,0002x$$
$$\text{Marginal cost} = \pounds 3$$

So the optimum output is where MC = MR
i.e. $3 = 5 - 0.000\,02x$

That is,

$$0.000\,02x = 2$$

Therefore $x = 100\,000$ units (optimum output level)
Selling price at optimum level $= 5 - 0.000\,01 \times 100\,000$
$$= \underline{\pounds 4}$$

Maximum profit is TR − TC

$$\text{TR} = \pounds 400\,000 \ (100\,000 \times \pounds 4)$$
$$\text{TC} = \pounds \underline{350\,000} \ (100\,000 \times \pounds 3) + (\pounds 50\,000 \text{ FC})$$
$$\text{Profit} = \ \underline{\pounds 50\,000}$$

*New machine leased*

Revised total cost function = £165 000 + £2x

Note that fixed costs increase by £115 000

Optimal output is where MC = MR

i.e., $2 = 5 - 0.00002x$

That is,

$0.00002x = 3$

Therefore $x = 150 000$ units (optimum output level)

Selling price at optimum output level= $5 - 0.00001 \times 150 000 = £3.50$

Maximum profit is TR − TC

$$TR = £525 000 (150 000 \times £3.50)$$

$$TC = £465 000 (150 000 \times £2) + £165 000$$

$$Profit = £60 000$$

The new machine should be hired, since profit will increase by £10 000. In order to obtain the maximum profit, a price of £3.50 per unit should be charged, which will produce a demand of 150 000 units.

(b) (i)

$$P = 100 - 2Q$$

$$TR = Q(100 - 2Q)$$

$$= 100Q - 2Q^2$$

$$MR = \frac{dTR}{dQ} = 100 - 4Q$$

Total cost function = $Q^2 + 10Q + 500$

$$MC = \frac{dTC}{dQ} = 2Q + 10$$

The optimal output level is where MC = MR, i.e.

$$2Q + 10 = 100 - 4Q$$

So

$$6Q = 90$$

$$Q = 15$$

Therefore, optimal output level is 15 000 units.

Substituting into the demand function

$$P = 100 - 2Q:$$
$$P = 100 - 2 \times 15$$
$$P = £70 \text{ per unit optimum selling price}$$

$$Profit = TR - TC$$

$$TR = 1050 (15 \text{ units} \times £70)$$

$$TC = 875 (15^2 + (10 \times 15) + 500))$$

$$Profit = 175$$

So the maximum profit = £175 000

(ii) TR = $100Q - 2Q^2$

Total revenue will be maximized when MR = 0

MR = $100 - 4Q$ (see b(i))

So the total revenue is maximized where $100 - 4Q = 0$

$$Q = 25 \text{ (i.e. 25 000 units)}$$

Substituting into the demand function:

$$P = 100 - 2Q$$
$$= 100 - 2 \times 25$$
$$= £50 \text{ per unit}$$

Total sales revenue will be £1 250 000 (25 000 units × £50)

$$\text{Loss} = TR - TC$$
$$TR = £1\,250\,000$$
$$TC = \underline{£1\,375\,000}\ (25^2 + (10 \times 25) + 500))$$
$$\text{Loss} = \underline{(£125\,000)}$$

*Summary of results*

|  | Output level (units) | Selling price | Total revenue | Total profit (loss) |
|---|---|---|---|---|
| (i)  Profit maximization | 15 000 | £70 | £1 050 000 | £175 000 |
| (ii) Sales maximization | 25 000 | £50 | £1 125 000 | (£125 000) |

# Chapter 12

(a) There are two possible selling prices and three possible direct material costs for each selling price. The calculation of unit contributions are as follows:

|  | £15 sales price | | | £24 sales price | | |
|---|---|---|---|---|---|---|
|  | No purchasing contract | Contract (40 000 kg) | Contract (60 000 kg) | No purchasing contract | Contract (40 000 kg) | Contract (60 000 kg) |
| Selling price | 15 | 15 | 15 | 24 | 24 | 24 |
| Material cost | (8) | (7.50) | (7) | (8) | (7.50) | (7) |
| Other variable cost | (5) | (5) | (5) | (5) | (5) | (5) |
| Unit contribution | £2 | 2.5 | 3 | £11 | 11.50 | 12 |

The realizable value from the sale of excess materials is as follows:

|  | 16 000 kg and over | Less than 16 000 kg |
|---|---|---|
| Sales price | 2.90 | 2.40 |
| Less selling, delivery and insurance costs | 0.90 | 0.90 |
| Realizable value per kg | £2.00 | £1.50 |

**Statement of outcomes**

| Sales quantities (000) | Total contribution (£000) | Fixed costs (£000) | Profit/(loss) on sale of materials (£000) | Profit (£000) | Probability | Expected value (£000) |
|---|---|---|---|---|---|---|
| Sales price of £15 (no contract) | | | | | | |
| 20 | 40 | 50 | — | −10 | 0.1 | −1 |
| 30 | 60 | 50 | — | 10 | 0.6 | 6 |
| 40 | 80 | 50 | — | 30 | 0.3 | 9 |
| | | | | | | 14 |
| Sales price of £15 (40 000 kg contract) | | | | | | |
| 20 | 50 | 50 | — | — | 0.1 | — |
| 30 | 75 | 50 | — | 25 | 0.6 | 15 |
| 40 | 100 | 50 | — | 50 | 0.3 | 15 |
| | | | | | | 30 |
| Sales price of £15 (60 000 kg contract) | | | | | | |
| 20 | 60 | 50 | −30[a] | −20 | 0.1 | −2 |
| 30 | 90 | 50 | — | 40 | 0.6 | 24 |
| 40 | 120 | 50 | — | 70 | 0.3 | 21 |
| | | | | | | 43 |
| Sales price of £24 (no contract) | | | | | | |
| 8 | 88 | 160 | — | −72 | 0.1 | −7.2 |
| 16 | 176 | 160 | — | 16 | 0.3 | 4.8 |
| 20 | 220 | 160 | — | 60 | 0.3 | 18.0 |
| 24 | 264 | 160 | — | 104 | 0.3 | 31.2 |
| | | | | | | 46.8 |
| Sales price of £24 (40 000 kg contract) | | | | | | |
| 8 | 92 | 160 | −42[b] | −110 | 0.1 | −11.0 |
| 16 | 184 | 160 | −18[b] | 6 | 0.3 | 1.8 |
| 20 | 230 | 160 | — | 70 | 0.3 | 21.0 |
| 24 | 276 | 160 | — | 116 | 0.3 | 34.8 |
| | | | | | | 46.6 |
| Sales price of £24 (60 000 kg contract) | | | | | | |
| 8 | 96 | 160 | −66 | −130 | 0.1 | −13 |
| 16 | 192 | 160 | −42 | −10 | 0.3 | −3 |
| 20 | 240 | 160 | −30 | 50 | 0.3 | 15 |
| 24 | 288 | 160 | −24 | 104 | 0.3 | 31.2 |
| | | | | | | 30.2 |

*Notes*

[a] Sales quantity of 20 000 units results in 40 000 kg being used. Therefore 20 000 kg of the raw material are sold at a realizable value of £2 per kg. The cost of acquiring the raw materials is £3.50 per kg. Consequently 20 000 kg are sold at a loss of £1.50 per kg.

[b] 24 000 kg sold at a loss of £1.75 per kg.

(b) (i) The highest expected value of profits occurs when the sales price is £24 with no contract for the supply of raw materials.

(ii) In order to minimize the effect of the worst outcome then the sales price should be £15 and a contract to purchase 40 000 kg entered into.

(iii) Applying Central's own 'Desirability' measure, the best choice is a sales price of £15 combined with entering into a contract of 60 000 kg. The 'Desirability' measure is calculated as follows:

| Strategy Price per unit | Contract | Expected monetary value (£000) | Worst outcome (£000) | 'Desirability' $L + 3E$ |
|---|---|---|---|---|
| £15 | none | 14 | −10 | 32 |
| £15 | 40 000 kg | 30 | 0 | 90 |
| £15 | 60 000 kg | 43 | −20 | 109 |
| £24 | none | 46.8 | −72 | 68.4 |
| £24 | 40 000 kg | 46.6 | −110 | 29.8 |
| £24 | 60 000 kg | 30.2 | −130 | −39.4 |

(c) (i) Other factors to be considered are:
   (A) The reliability of future supplies of raw materials might be subject to uncertainty. In this situation it may be preferable to operate at a lower production volume and sales.
   (B) If there is spare production capacity then the labour cost might not be a relevant cost. More information is required regarding the alternative use of the labour if a lower production volume is selected.
   (ii) For a discussion of the expected value approach see Chapter 12. The criteria of pessimism in (b) (ii) focuses on the least desirable outcome. The 'desirability' measure is an attempt to formalize the importance of the two relevant measures to a particular decision-maker by attaching a weighting to the expected value and the worst possible outcome. It may be better to compare the probability distributions rather than using summary measures of the distributions.

# CHAPTER 13

(a)

$$\text{Project A} = 3 \text{ years} + \frac{350 - 314}{112} = 3.32 \text{ years}$$

Project B = 3.0 years

Project C = 2.00 years

(b) Accounting rate of return = average profit/average investment

Project A = 79/175 = 45%

Project B = 84/175 = 48%

Project C = 70/175 = 40%

Note that average profit = (sum of cash flows − investment cost)/project's life.

(c) The report should include:
   (i) NPVs of each project (project A = £83 200 (W1), project B = £64 000 (W2), project C = £79 000 (W3). A simple description of NPV should also be provided. For example, the NPV is the amount over and above the cost of the project which could be borrowed, secure in the knowledge that the cash flows from the project will repay the loan.

(ii)   The following rankings are based on the different evaluation procedures:

| Project | IRR | Payback | ARR | NPV |
|---------|-----|---------|-----|-----|
| A | 2 | 3 | 2 | 1 |
| B | 3 | 2 | 1 | 3 |
| C | 1 | 1 | 3 | 2 |

(iii)  A discussion of each of the above evaluation procedures.

(iv)   IRR is subject to the following criticisms:
1.  Multiple rates of return can occur when a project has unconventional cash flows.
2.  It is assumed that the cash flows received from a project are re-invested at the IRR and not the cost of capital.
3.  Inability to rank mutually exclusive projects.
4.  It cannot deal with different sized projects. For example, it is better to earn a return of 35% on £100 000 than 40% on £10 000.

Note that the above points are explained in detail in Chapter 13.

(v)    Payback ignores cash flows outside the payback period, and it also ignores the timing of cash flows within the payback period. For example, the large cash flows for project A are ignored after the payback period. This method may be appropriate for companies experiencing liquidity problems who wish to recover their initial investment quickly.

(vi)   Accounting rate of return ignores the timing of cash flows, but it is considered an important measure by those who believe reported profits have a significant impact on share prices.

(vii)  NPV is generally believed to be the theoretically correct evaluation procedure. A positive NPV from an investment is supposed to indicate the increase in the market value of the shareholders' funds, but this claim depends upon the belief that the share price is the discounted present value of the future dividend stream. If the market uses some other method of valuing shares then a positive NPV may not represent the increase in market value of shareholders' funds. Note that the cash flows have been discounted at the company's cost of capital. It is only suitable to use the company's cost of capital as the discount rate if projects A, B and C are equivalent to the average risk of all the company's existing projects. If they are not of average risk then project risk-adjusted discount rates should be used.

(viii) The projects have unequal lives. It is assumed that the equipment will not be replaced. If the equipment is to be replaced, it will be necessary to consider the projects over a common time horizon using the techniques described for projects with unequal lives in Chapter 14.

(ix)   It is recommended that NPV method is used and project A should be selected.

(d) Stadler prefers project C because it produces the highest accounting profit in year 3. Stadler is assuming that share prices are influenced by short-run reported profits. This is in contrast with theory, which assumes that the share price is the discounted present value of the future dividend stream. Stadler is also assuming that the market only has access to reported historical profits and is not aware of the future benefits arising from the projects. The stock market also obtains company information on future prospects from sources other than reported profits. For example, press releases, chairman's report and signals of future prosperity via increased dividend payments.

*Workings*

(W1) Project A $= (100 \times 0.8333) + (110 \times 0.6944) + (104 \times 0.5787)$
$+ (112 \times 0.4823) + (138 \times 0.4019) + (160 \times 0.3349)$
$+ (180 \times 0.2791) - £350$

(W2) Project B $= (40 \times 0.8333) + (100 \times 0.6944) + (210 \times 0.5787)$
$+ (260 \times 0.4823) + (160 \times 0.4019) - £350$

(W3) Project C $= (200 \times 0.8333) + (150 \times 0.6944) + (240 \times 0.5787)$
$+ (40 \times 0.4823) - £350$

# CHAPTER 14

1 (a) The NPV calculations can be adjusted in two basic ways to account for inflation. Real cash flows can be discounted at the real discount rate or inflation adjusted cash flows can be discounted at a discount rate which incorporates a premium for inflation. It is only appropriate to leave the cash flows in terms of present-day prices and discount these cash flows at the real cost of capital when all the cash flows are expected to increase at the general level of inflation. The cash flows in the question are subject to different levels of inflation. In particular, capital allowances are based on the original cost and do not change in line with changing prices. Therefore the cash flows should be adjusted for inflation and discounted at a cost of capital which incorporates a premium for inflation. The inflation adjusted revenues, expenses and taxation liabilities are:

| Year | 1 | 2 | 3 | 4 | 5 |
|---|---|---|---|---|---|
| Sales at 5% inflation (W1) | 3675 | 5402 | 6159 | 6977 | 6790 |
| Materials at 10% inflation | (588) | (907) | (1198) | (1537) | (1449) |
| Labour at 10% inflation | (1177) | (1815) | (2396) | (3075) | (2899) |
| Overheads at 5% inflation | (52) | (110) | (116) | (122) | (128) |
| Capital allowances (W2) | (1125) | (844) | (633) | (475) | (1423) |
| Taxable profits | 733 | 1726 | 1816 | 1768 | 891 |
| Taxation at 35% | 256 | 604 | 636 | 619 | 312 |

The interest payments are not included because they are taken into account when the cash flows are discounted.

*Workings*

(W1) Year 1 $= £3500 \, (1.05)$, year 2 $= £4900 \, (1.05)^2$, year 3 $= £5320 \, (1.05)^3$, year 4 $= £5740 \, (1.05)^4$, year 5 $= £5320 \, (1.05)^5$. The same approach is used to calculate the inflation adjusted cash flows for the remaining items.

(W2) 25% writing down allowances on £4500 with a balancing allowance in year 5.

The cash flow estimates and NPV calculation are as follows:

| Year | 0 | 1 | 2 | 3 | 4 | 5 | 6 |
|------|---|---|---|---|---|---|---|
| Inflows | | | | | | | |
| Sales | — | 3675 | 5402 | 6159 | 6977 | 6790 | — |
| Outflows | | | | | | | |
| Materials | — | 588 | 907 | 1198 | 1537 | 1449 | — |
| Labour | — | 1177 | 1815 | 2396 | 3075 | 2899 | — |
| Overheads | — | 52 | 110 | 116 | 122 | 128 | — |
| Fixed assets | 4500 | | | | | | |
| Working capital (W1) | 300 | 120 | 131 | 144 | 156 | (851) | — |
| Taxation | | | 256 | 604 | 636 | 619 | 312 |
| | 4800 | 1937 | 3219 | 4458 | 5526 | 4244 | 312 |
| Net cash flows | (4800) | 1738 | 2183 | 1701 | 1451 | 2546 | (312) |
| Discount factors at 15% | | 0.870 | 0.756 | 0.658 | 0.572 | 0.497 | 0.432 |
| Present values | (4800) | 1512 | 1650 | 1119 | 830 | 1265 | (135) |

The NPV is £1 441 000 and it is therefore recommended that the project should be undertaken. Note that the interest cost is already incorporated in the DCF calculation and should not be included in the cash flows when calculating present values.

*Workings*

(W1) It is assumed that the working capital is released at the end of the project.
Year 1 = 400 (1.05) − 300, year 2 = 500 (1.05)$^2$ − 420, and so on.

(b) Calculating the IRR will produce an NPV of zero. NPV is £1 441 000 at a 15% discount rate. In order to use the interpolation method to calculate the IRR, it is necessary to ascertain a negative NPV. At a discount rate of 30% the NPV is

| Year | Cash flow (£000) | Discount factor | PV (£000) |
|------|-----------------|-----------------|-----------|
| 0 | (4800) | 1.0000 | (4800) |
| 1 | 1738 | 0.7692 | 1337 |
| 2 | 2183 | 0.5917 | 1292 |
| 3 | 1701 | 0.4552 | 774 |
| 4 | 1451 | 0.3501 | 508 |
| 5 | 2546 | 0.2693 | 686 |
| 6 | (312) | 0.2071 | (65) |
| | | | (268) |

Using the interpolation method, the IRR is

$$15\% + \frac{1441}{1441 - (-205)} \times 15\% = 28\%$$

(c) See 'Sensitivity analysis' in Chapter 14 for a description and discussion of the weaknesses of sensitivity analysis. Other traditional techniques include the use of probability distributions to calculate expected net present value and standard deviation, simulation and certainty equivalents. More recent techniques include portfolio theory and the capital asset pricing model. Theorists would suggest that risk should be incorporated into the analysis by discounting the expected value of a project's cash flows at a risk-adjusted discount rate using the capital asset pricing model.

2 (a) The tax liability calculations are

### Standard (£)

| Year | 1 | 2 | 3 | 4 | |
|---|---|---|---|---|---|
| Operating cash flows | 20 500 | 22 860 | 24 210 | 23 410 | |
| Capital allowance | 12 500 | 9 375 | 7 031 | 21 094 | (W1) |
| | 8 000 | 13 485 | 17 179 | 2 316 | |
| Taxation (35%) | 2 800 | 4 720 | 6 013 | 811 | |

### De-luxe (£)

| Year | 1 | 2 | 3 | 4 | 5 | 6 | |
|---|---|---|---|---|---|---|---|
| Operating cash flows | 32 030 | 26 110 | 25 380 | 25 940 | 38 560 | 35 100 | |
| Capital allowance | 22 000 | 16 500 | 12 375 | 9 281 | 6 961 | 20 883 | (W1) |
| | 10 030 | 9 610 | 13 005 | 16 659 | 31 599 | 14 217 | |
| Taxation (35%) | 3 511 | 3 363 | 4 552 | 5 831 | 11 060 | 4 976 | |

The NPV calculations are

### Standard (£)

| Year | 0 | 1 | 2 | 3 | 4 | 5 |
|---|---|---|---|---|---|---|
| Fixed assets | (50 000) | | | | | |
| Working capital | (10 000) | | | | 10 000 (W3) | |
| Operating cash flows | | 20 500 | 22 860 | 24 210 | 23 410 | |
| Taxation (W2) | — | — | (2800) | (4720) | (6013) | (811) |
| | (60 000) | 20 500 | 20 060 | 19 490 | 27 397 | (811) |
| Discount factor (12%) | | 0.893 | 0.797 | 0.712 | 0.636 | 0.567 |
| Present values | (60 000) | 18 307 | 15 988 | 13 877 | 17 424 | (460) |

Payback period is approximately 3 years
Net present value is £5136

### De-luxe (£)

| Year | 0 | 1 | 2 | 3 | 4 | 5 | 6 | 7 |
|---|---|---|---|---|---|---|---|---|
| Fixed assets | (88 000) | | | | | | | |
| Working capital | (10 000) | | | | | | 10 000 (W3) | |
| Operating cash flows | | 32 030 | 26 110 | 25 380 | 25 940 | 38 560 | 35 100 | |
| Taxation (W2) | | | (3 511) | (3 363) | (4 552) | (5 831) | (11 060) | (4 976) |
| | (98 000) | 32 030 | 22 599 | 22 017 | 21 388 | 32 729 | 34 040 | (4976) |
| Discount factor (14%) | | 0.877 | 0.769 | 0.675 | 0.592 | 0.519 | 0.456 | 0.400 |
| Present values | (98 000) | 28 090 | 17 379 | 14 861 | 12 662 | 16 986 | 15 522 | (1990) |

Payback period is approximately 4 years
Net present value is £5510

*Workings*

(W1) Final-year balancing allowance.

(W2) It is assumed that the capital allowance for the purchase of the asset is included in $t_1$ accounts, which are submitted to the Inland Revenue, and the cash flow effect arises in $t_2$.

(W3) It is assumed that the working capital is realized immediately the project ends.

The de-luxe model has the largest NPV, but the projects have unequal lives and this factor needs to be taken into account. One method of doing this is to convert the cash flows into an equivalent annual cash flow with NPVs of £5136 for the standard machines and £5510 for the de-luxe machines. The following formula is used to calculate the equivalent annual cash flow:

$$\frac{\text{NPV}}{\text{annuity factor for N years at R\%}}$$

$$\text{Standard} = \frac{5136}{3.605} = £1425$$

$$\text{De-luxe} = \frac{5510}{4.288} = £1285$$

The cash flow effects are for 5 years for the standard machine and 7 years for the de-luxe machine. Therefore the annuity factors are for 5 years at 12% and 7 years at 14% respectively. The equivalent annual cash flow for the standard machine indicates that a sequence of cash flows from this machine is exactly like a sequence of cash flows of £1425 per year. Note that the equivalent annual cash flow method is based on the assumption that reinvestment takes place over a period of 12 years (the common denominator of 4 years and 6 years) or infinity.

As the standard machine has the higher equivalent annual cash flow, it is recommended that this machine be purchased.

(b) Possible reasons for the widespread use of accounting rate of return and payback include:

1. Simple to calculate and widely understood.
2. Appropriate for small projects which do not warrant detailed appraisal.
3. They are often used as initial screening tools and supplementary to a DCF analysis.
4. Return on capital employed (ROCE) is a widely used measure by outsiders to judge company performance and ROCE is also a popular measure for evaluating a divisional manager's performance. Managers might also consider it appropriate to judge individual projects on the same well-known criterion.
5. Payback might be appropriate for companies experiencing liquidity problems who wish to recover their investment quickly.
6. Lack of understanding of more sophisticated techniques.

# CHAPTER **15**

(a)  (i)

**Sales quantity and value budget**

| | **Products** | | | |
|---|---|---|---|---|
| | **A** | **B** | **C** | **Total** |
| Sales quantities | 1 000 | 2 000 | 1 500 | |
| Selling prices | £100 | £120 | £140 | |
| Sales value | £100 000 | £250 000 | £210 000 | £550 000 |

(ii)

**Production quantities budget**

| | **Products** | | |
|---|---|---|---|
| Sales quantities | 1000 | 2000 | 1500 |
| Add closing stock | 1100 | 1650 | 550 |
| | 2100 | 3650 | 2050 |
| Deduct opening stock | 1000 | 1500 | 500 |
| Units to be produced | 1100 | 2150 | 1550 |

(iii)

**Material usage budget (quantities)**

| Production quantities | **Materials** | | | | | |
|---|---|---|---|---|---|---|
| | **M1** | | **M2** | | **M3** | |
| | Units per product | Total | Units per product | Total | Units per product | Total |
| A   1100 | 4 | 4 400 | 2 | 2 200 | — | — |
| B   2150 | 3 | 6 450 | 3 | 6 450 | 2 | 4 300 |
| C   1550 | 2 | 3 100 | 1 | 1 550 | 1 | 1 550 |
| Usage in quantities | | 13 950 | | 10 200 | | 5 850 |

(iv)

**Material purchases budget (quantities and value)**

| | **M1** | **M2** | **M3** | **Total** |
|---|---|---|---|---|
| Materials usage budget | 13 950 | 10 200 | 5 850 | |
| Add closing stock | 31 200 | 24 000 | 14 400 | |
| | 45 150 | 34 200 | 20 250 | |
| Deduct opening stock | 26 000 | 20 000 | 12 000 | |
| Purchases in quantities | 19 150 | 14 200 | 8 250 | |
| Price per unit | £4 | £6 | £9 | |
| Value of purchases | £76 600 | £85 200 | £74 250 | £236 050 |

(b) The principal budget factor is also known as the limiting factor or key factor. The CIMA Terminology describes the principal budget factor as follows: 'The factor which, at a particular time, or over a period, will limit the activities of an undertaking. The limiting factor is usually the level of demand for the products or services of the undertaking but it could be a shortage of one of the productive resources, e.g. skilled labour, raw material, or machine capacity. In order to ensure that the functional budgets are reasonably capable of fulfillment, the extent of the influence of this factor must first be assessed.'

In the absence of any information to the contrary in the question, it is assumed that the principal budget factor is sales demand. See 'Determining factor that restricts performance' in Chapter 15 for a discussion of the importance of the principal budget factor in the budgeting process.

# CHAPTER 16

1 (a) (i) Activity varies from month to month, but quarterly budgets are set by dividing total annual expenditure by 4.
   (ii) The budget ought to be analysed by shorter intervals (e.g. monthly) and costs estimated in relation to monthly activity.
   (iii) For control purposes monthly comparisons and cumulative monthly comparisons of planned and actual expenditure to date should be made.
   (iv) The budget holder does not participate in the setting of budgets.
   (v) An incremental budget approach is adopted. A zero-based approach would be more appropriate.
   (vi) The budget should distinguish between controllable and uncontrollable expenditure.

(b) The information that should flow from a comparison of the actual and budgeted expenditure would consist of the variances for the month and year to date analysed into the following categories:
   (i) controllable and uncontrollable items;
   (ii) price and quantity variances with price variance analysed by inflationary and non-inflationary effects.

(c) (i) Flexible budgets should be prepared on a monthly basis. Possible measures of activity are number of patient days or expected laundry weight.
   (ii) The laundry manager should participate in the budgetary process.
   (iii) Costs should be classified into controllable and non-controllable items.
   (iv) Variances should be reported and analysed by price and quantity on a monthly and cumulative basis.
   (v) Comments should be added explaining possible reasons for the variances.

2 (a) *Budget statement*

|  | Budget Fixed (£) | Budget Variable (£) | Total (£) | Actual (£) | Variance Adverse (£) | Variance Favourable (£) |
|---|---|---|---|---|---|---|
| Overhead: |  |  |  |  |  |  |
| Management | 30 000 | — | 30 000 | 30 000 | — | — |
| Shift premium | — | 3 600 | 3 600 | 4 000 | 400 |  |
| National Insurance | 6 000 | 7 920 | 13 920 | 15 000 | 1080 |  |
| Inspection | 20 000 | 9 000 | 29 000 | 28 000 |  | 1000 |

| | | | | | | |
|---|---|---|---|---|---|---|
| Supplies | 6 000 | 6 480 | 12 480 | 12 700 | 220 | |
| Power | — | 7 200 | 7 200 | 7 800 | 600 | |
| Light and heat | 4 000 | — | 4 000 | 4 200 | 200 | |
| Rates | 9 000 | — | 9 000 | 9 000 | | |
| Repairs | 8 000 | 5 400 | 13 400 | 15 100 | 1700 | |
| Materials handling | 10 000 | 10 800 | 20 800 | 21 400 | 600 | |
| Depreciation | 15 000 | — | 15 000 | 15 000 | | |
| Administration | 12 000 | — | 12 000 | 11 500 | | 500 |
| Idle time | — | — | — | 1 600 | 1600 | |
| | 120 000 | 50 400 | 170 400 | 175 300 | 6400 | 1500 |

4900A

(b) *National Insurance*: It appears that National Insurance rates have increased. If this assumption is correct then the variance will be beyond the control of management. Note that actual activity is less than budgeted activity. It is therefore unlikely that total wages will have increased because of an increase in the number of labour hours worked. It is possible that wage rates might have increased, thus increasing the National Insurance payments. (Note that the latter are a fixed percentage of wages.)

*Inspection*: It is possible that the standard inspection has been lowered, thus resulting in a saving in costs. If this has not been a policy decision taken by management then the variance should be investigated. Another possibility is that a member of staff has resigned. Consequently the actual labour cost will be less than the budget.

*Repairs and maintenance*: This variance may be due to unexpected repairs which were not envisaged when the budget was set. It is likely that variances for repairs and maintenance will fluctuate considerably from month to month. It is therefore appropriate to compare budgeted and actual expenditure for several months rather than focus on a single month.

*Idle time*: No allowance for normal idle time is included in the budget. Consequently the idle time must be of an abnormal nature. Possible uncontrollable causes include a power failure or machine breakdowns. Controllable causes include bottlenecks arising from poor production scheduling or a lack of materials.

(c) (i) Commenting on variances in excess of a specific figure may not be satisfactory for control purposes. Variances should only be investigated if the investigation is likely to yield benefits in terms of identifying ineffi- ciencies and remedying them. It may be preferable to use statistical tests to establish the probability that the variance is out of control.

(ii) The statement could be improved by analysing the expense items into their controllable and non-controllable elements. Where possible, variances should be analysed according to whether they are due to price and quantity changes. The statement should also include non-financial measures such as a comparison of actual hours worked with standard hours produced.

(d) (i) Overhead absorbed = £158 400 (£4.40 × 36 000 hours).

(ii) Overspending = £4900 (see part (a) of answer).

(iii) Actual production was 4000 standard hours less than budgeted production, and this decline in output has resulted in a failure to recover £12 000 fixed overheads. This under recovery of £12 000 is also known as the volume variance.

# CHAPTER 18

1. *Preliminary calculations*

The standard product cost and selling price are calculated as follows:

|  | (£) |
|---|---|
| Direct materials | |
| X (10 kg at £1) | 10 |
| Y (5 kg at £5) | 25 |
| Direct wages (5 hours × £3) | 15 |
| Fixed overhead (5 hours × 200% of £3) | 30 |
| Standard cost | 80 |
| Profit (20/(100 − 20)) × £80 | 20 |
| Selling price | 100 |

The actual profit for the period is calculated as follows:

|  | (£) | (£) |
|---|---|---|
| Sales (9500 at £110) | | 1 045 000 |
| Direct materials: X | 115 200 | |
| Y | 225 600 | |
| Direct wages (46 000 × £3.20) | 147 200 | |
| Fixed overhead | 290 000 | 778 000 |
| Actual profit | | 267 000 |

It is assumed that the term 'using a fixed budget' refers to the requirement to reconcile the budget with the original fixed budget.

|  | (£) | (£) |
|---|---|---|
| Material price variance: | | |
| (standard price − actual price) | | |
| × actual quantity | | |
| X: (£1 − £1.20) × 96 000 | 19 200 A | |
| Y: (£5 − £4.70) × 48 000 | 14 400 F | 4800 A |
| Material usage variance: | | |
| (standard quantity − actual quantity) | | |
| × standard price | | |
| X: (9500 × 10 = 95 000 − 96 000) × £1 | 1000 A | |
| Y: (9500 × 5 = 47 500 − 48 000) × £5 | 2500 A | 3500 A |

The actual materials used are in standard proportions. Therefore there is no mix variance.

|  | (£) | (£) |
|---|---|---|
| Wage rate variance: | | |
| (standard rate − actual rate) × actual hours | | |
| (£3 − £3.20) × 46 000 | 9200 A | |
| Labour efficiency variance: | | |
| (standard hours − actual hours) × standard rate | | |
| (9500 × 5 = 47 500 − 46 000) × £3 | 4500 F | 4700 A |

Fixed overhead expenditure:
 budgeted fixed overheads − actual fixed overheads
 (10 000 × £30 = £300 000 − £290 000)       10 000 F
Volume efficiency variance:
 (standard hours − actual hours) × fixed overhead rate
 (47 500 − 46 000) × £6         9 000 F
Volume capacity variance:
 (actual hours − budgeted hours) × fixed overhead rate
 (46 000 − 50 000) × £6       24 000 A  15 000 A
Sales margin price variance:
 (actual margin − standard margin) × actual sales volume
 (£30 − £20) × 9500        95 000 F
Sales margin volume variance;
 (actual sales volume − budgeted sales volume)
 × Standard margin
 (9500 − 10 000) × £20       10 000 A  85 000 F
       Total variance        67 000 F

|  | (£) |
|---|---|
| Budgeted profit (10 000 units at £20) | 200 000 |
| Add favourable variances (see above) | 67 000 |
| Actual profit | 267 000 |

2 (a) *Standard product cost for one unit of product XY*

|  | (£) |
|---|---|
| Direct materials (8 kg (W2) at £1.50 (W1) per kg) | 12.00 |
| Direct wages (2 hours (W4) at £4 (W3) per hour) | 8.00 |
| Variable overhead (2 hours (W4) at £1 (W5) per hour) | 2.00 |
|  | 22.00 |

*Workings*

(W1) Actual quantity of materials purchased at standard price is £225 000
   (actual cost plus favourable material price variance).
   Therefore standard price = £1.50 (£225 000/150 000 kg).

(W2) Material usage variance = 6000 kg (£9000/£1.50 standard price).
   Therefore standard quantity for actual production = 144 000 kg
   (150 000 − 6000 kg).
   Therefore standard quantity per unit = 8 kg (144 000 kg/18 000 units).

(W3) Actual hours worked at standard rate = £128 000 (£136 000 − £8000).
   Therefore standard rate per hour = £ 4 (£128 000/32 000 hours).

(W4) Labour efficiency variance = 4000 hours (£16 000/£4).
   Therefore standard hours for actual production = 36 000 hours
   (32 000 + 4000).
   Therefore standard hours per unit = 2 hours (36 000 hours/18 000 units).

(W5) Actual hours worked at the standard variable overhead rate is £32 000
   (£38 000 actual variable overheads less £6000 favourable expenditure
   variance).
   Therefore, standard variable overhead rate = £1 (£32 000/32 000 hours).

(b) See 'Types of cost standards' in Chapter 18 for the answer to this question.

## CHAPTER 19

(a) Material price:

(standard price − actual price) × actual quantity (£3 − £4) × 22 000 = £22 000 A

Material usage:

(standard quantity − actual quantity) × standard price

$((1400 \times 15 = 21\,000) - 22\,000) \times £3$ = £3000 A

Wage rate:

(standard rate − actual rate) × actual hours (£4 − £5) × 6800 = £6800 A

Labour efficiency:

$((1400 \times 5 = 7000) - 6800) \times £4$ = £800 F

Fixed overhead expenditure:

(budgeted fixed overheads − actual fixed overheads)

$(1000 \times £5 = £5000 - £6000)$ = £1000 A

Volume efficiency:

(standard hrs − actual hrs) × FOAR

$(1400 \times 5 = 7000 - 6800) \times £1$ = £200 F

Volume capacity:

(actual hrs − budgeted hrs) × FOAR (6800 − 5000) × £1 = £1800 F

Variable overhead efficiency:

(standard hrs − actual hrs) × VOAR (7000 − 6800) × £2 = £400 F

Variable overhead expenditure:

(flexed budgeted variable overheads − actual variable overheads)

$(6800 \times £2 - £11\,000)$ = £2600 F

Sales margin price:

(actual margin − standard margin) × actual sales volume

$(£102 - £80 = £22 - £20) \times 1200$ = £2400 F

Sales margin volume:

(actual sales − budgeted sales) × standard margin

$(1200 - 1000) \times £20$ = £4000 F

### Reconciliation of budgeted and actual profit

|  | Adverse (£) | Favourable (£) | (£) |
|---|---|---|---|
| Budgeted profit |  |  | 20 000 |
| Sales margin price |  | 2 400 |  |
| Sales margin volume |  | 4 000 |  |
| Material price | 22 000 |  |  |
| Material usage | 3 000 |  |  |
| Wage rate | 6 800 |  |  |
| Labour efficiency |  | 800 |  |
| Fixed overhead expenditure | 1 000 |  |  |
| Fixed overhead efficiency |  | 200 |  |
| Fixed overhead capacity |  | 1 800 |  |
| Variable overhead expenditure |  | 2 600 |  |
| Variable overhead efficiency |  | 400 |  |
|  | 32 800 | 12 200 |  |
| Net adverse variance |  |  | 20 600 |
| Actual profit/(loss) |  |  | (600) |

(b)

### Stores ledger control account

| | | | |
|---|---|---|---|
| Creditors | 66 000 | WIP | 63 000 |
| | | Material usage variance | 3 000 |
| | 66 000 | | 66 000 |

### Variance accounts

| | | | |
|---|---|---|---|
| Creditors | 22 000 | Wages control | |
| Stores ledger | | (labour efficiency) | 800 |
| (material usage) | 3 000 | Fixed overhead (volume) | 2 000 |
| Wages control (wage rate) | 6 800 | Variable overhead | |
| Fixed overhead | | (expenditure) | 2 600 |
| (expenditure) | 1 000 | Variable overhead | |
| | | (efficiency) | 400 |
| | | Costing P + L a/c (balance) | 27 000 |
| | 32 800 | | 32 800 |

### Costing P + L account

| | | | |
|---|---|---|---|
| Cost of sales | 96 000 | Sales | 122 400 |
| Variance account | | Loss for period | 600 |
| (net variances) | 27 000 | | |
| | 123 000 | | 123 000 |

### WIP control account

| | | | |
|---|---|---|---|
| Stores ledger | 63 000 | Finished goods stock | 112 000 |
| Wages control | 28 000 | | |
| Fixed factory overhead | 7 000 | | |
| Variable factory overhead | 14 000 | | |
| | 112 000 | | 112 000 |

### Wages control account

| | | | |
|---|---|---|---|
| Wages accrued account | 34 000 | WIP | 28 000 |
| Labour efficiency variance | 800 | Wage rate variance | 6 800 |
| | 34 800 | | 34 800 |

### Fixed factory overhead account

| | | | |
|---|---|---|---|
| Expense creditors | 6 000 | WIP | 7 000 |
| Volume variance | 2 000 | Expenditure variance | 1 000 |
| | 8 000 | | 8 000 |

### Variable factory overhead account

| | | | |
|---|---|---|---|
| Expense creditors | 11 000 | WIP | 14 000 |
| Expenditure variance | 2 600 | | |
| Efficiency variance | 400 | | |
| | 14 000 | | 14 000 |

**Finished goods stock**

| WIP | 112 000 | Cost of sales | 96 000 |
|---|---|---|---|
| | | Closing stock c/fwd | 16 000 |
| | 112 000 | | 112 000 |

**Cost of sales account**

| Finished goods stock | 96 000 | Cost P + L a/c | 96 000 |
|---|---|---|---|

# CHAPTER 20

*Assumptions*

It is assumed in this question that additional capital is introduced to finance the capital expenditure in transaction A. (All calculations are in £000.)

(a) *Alpha basis*

(i)
$$\frac{\text{profit for the year}}{\text{capital employed } (1000 + 250)} = 18\%$$

(ii)
$$\frac{\text{profit } (225 + (35 - 20))}{\text{capital employed } (1250 + 120)}$$

(iii) It is assumed that depreciation (50) and contribution to profit (30) from the equipment are already included in the profit for the year of £225. If the profit is adjusted by writing back these items, the equipment will have a book value of £50, and a loss on sale of £30 will arise:

$$\frac{\text{profit } 225 + (50 \text{ depn} - 30 \text{ loss on sales} - 30 \text{ profit contrib.})}{\text{capital employed } (1250 - 200 + 20)}$$

Therefore ROCE = 20.1%

(iv)
$$\frac{\text{profit } (225 + 4)}{\text{capital employed } (1250)} = 18.3\%$$

The overdraft will increase and creditors will fall. Therefore net current assets will remain unchanged.

(v)
$$\frac{\text{profit } (225 - 6)}{\text{capital employed } (1250)} = 17.5\%$$

It is assumed that net current assets remain unchanged, with stock declining by 25 and cash increasing by 25. The additional contribution is assumed to be paid out as dividends and not to increase capital employed.

(b) *Theta basis*

(i)
$$\frac{225}{525 + 250} = 29\%$$

(ii)
$$\frac{225 + (35 - 20)}{775 + (120 - 20)} = 27.4\%$$

(iii)
$$\frac{215 \text{ (as Alpha basis)}}{775 + 20} = 27.0\%$$

The WDV of the fixed assets of £525 will exclude the equipment, since it has a WDV of zero at the end of the year.

(iv) $$\frac{225 + 4}{775} = 29.5\%$$

(v) $$\frac{225 - 6}{775} = 28.2\%$$

(c) (i) The correct approach is to evaluate transaction A on the basis of the NPV rule. The NPV calculation is as follows:

|  | **(£)** |
| --- | --- |
| Cash flow savings (35 000 × 3.8887) | 136 105 |
| Less investment cost | 120 000 |
| NPV | 16 105 |

The correct decision is to purchase the equipment, but a manager will be motivated to reject the purchase using both the Alpha and Beta basis of performance evaluation. Therefore there will be a lack of goal congruence. This is because the equipment yields a lower accounting rate of return in 2000 than the present return. Consequently ROCE will decline if the project is accepted. With the Theta basis, the manager's performance will be improved in the long run as the asset base of £120 000 will decline (through depreciation) but profit will remain unchanged. Therefore the ROCE of the equipment will increase over time, and it is likely that the overall return will also increase in later years.

ROCE is a weak method of measuring performance because it focuses on a percentage return rather than the magnitude of earnings. For a discussion of the weaknesses of ROCE and a comparison with the residual income method see 'Return on investment' and 'Residual Income' in Chapter 20.

(ii) Transaction B involves a proposal to sell a machine for £20 000 that produces a cash flow of £30 000. This will result in a negative present value. The proposal can only be justified if the £20 000 received can be invested to yield a cash inflow in excess of £30 000. This is most unlikely.

The Theta measure shows a decline in ROCE, whereas the Alpha measure shows an increase in ROCE. Therefore it is likely that a manager evaluated on the Theta measure will reject the proposal, whereas a manager evaluated on the Alpha measure will accept the proposal. Consequently, the Theta measure will encourage goal congruence whereas the Alpha measure will not.

# CHAPTER 21

(a) The effects on each division and the company as a whole of selling the motor unit at each possible selling price are presented in the following schedules:

(i)  *EM division*

| Output level (units) | Total revenues (£) | Variable costs (£) | Total contribution (£) |
|---|---|---|---|
| 1000 | 16 000 | 6 000 | 10 000 |
| 2000 | 32 000 | 12 000 | 20 000 |
| 3000 | 48 000 | 18 000 | 30 000 |
| 4000 | 64 000 | 24 000 | 40 000 |
| 6000 | 96 000 | 36 000 | 60 000 |
| 8000 | 128 000 | 48 000 | **80 000** |

(ii)  *IP division*

| Output level (units) | Total revenues (£) | Variable costs (£) | Total cost of transfers (£) | Total contribution (£) |
|---|---|---|---|---|
| 1000 | 50 000 | 4 000 | 16 000 | 30 000 |
| 2000 | 80 000 | 8 000 | 32 000 | 40 000 |
| 3000 | 105 000 | 12 000 | 48 000 | **45 000** |
| 4000 | 120 000 | 16 000 | 64 000 | 40 000 |
| 6000 | 150 000 | 24 000 | 96 000 | 30 000 |
| 8000 | 160 000 | 32 000 | 128 000 | nil |

(iii)  *Enormous Engineering plc*

| Output level (units) | Total revenues (£) | Variable costs (EMD) (£) | Variable costs (IPD) (£) | Total contribution (£) |
|---|---|---|---|---|
| 1000 | 50 000 | 6 000 | 4 000 | 40 000 |
| 2000 | 80 000 | 12 000 | 8 000 | 60 000 |
| 3000 | 105 000 | 18 000 | 12 000 | 75 000 |
| 4000 | 120 000 | 24 000 | 16 000 | 80 000 |
| 6000 | 150 000 | 36 000 | 24 000 | **90 000** |
| 8000 | 160 000 | 48 000 | 32 000 | 80 000 |

The above schedules indicate that EM division maximizes profits at an output of 8000 units, whereas IP division maximizes profits at an output level of 3000 units. Profits are maximized for the company as a whole at an output level of 6000 units.

(b) (i)  Based on the tabulation in (a), IPD should select a selling price of £35 per unit. This selling price produces a maximum divisional contribution of £45 000.

(ii)  The company as a whole should select a selling price of £25 per unit. This selling price produces a maximum company contribution of £90 000.

(iii)  If IPD selected a selling price of £25 per unit instead of £35 per unit, its overall marginal revenue would increase by £45 000 but its marginal cost would increase by £60 000. Consequently it is not in IPD's interest to lower the price from £35 to £25 when the transfer price of the intermediate product is set at £16.

(c) (i) Presumably profit centres have been established so as to provide a profit incentive for each division and to enable divisional managers to exercise a high degree of divisional autonomy. The maintenance of divisional autonomy and the profitability incentive can lead to sub-optimal decisions. The costs of sub-optimization may be acceptable to a certain extent in order to preserve the motivational advantages which arise with divisional autonomy.

Within the EE group, EMD has decision-making autonomy with respect to the setting of transfer prices. EMD sets transfer prices on a full cost-plus basis in order to earn a target profit. The resulting transfer price causes IPD to restrict output to 3000 units, which is less than the group optimum. The cost of this sub-optimal decision is £15 000 (£90 000 − £75 000). A solution to the problem is to set the transfer price at the variable cost per unit of the supplying division. This transfer price will result in IPD selecting the optimum output level, but will destroy the profit incentive for the EM division. Note that fixed costs will not be covered and there is no external market for the intermediate product.

Possible solutions to achieving the motivational and optimality objectives include:
1. operating a dual transfer pricing system;
2. lump sum payments.

See 'Proposals for resolving transfer pricing conflicts' in Chapter 21 for an explanation of the above items.

(ii) Where there is no market for the intermediate product and the supplying division has no capacity constraints, the correct transfer price is the marginal cost of the supplying division for that output at which marginal cost equals the receiving division's net marginal revenue from converting the intermediate product. When unit variable cost is constant and fixed costs remain unchanged, this rule will result in a transfer price which is equal to the supplying division's unit variable cost. Therefore the transfer price will be set at £6 per unit when the variable cost transfer pricing rule is applied. IPD will then be faced with the following marginal cost and net marginal revenue schedule:

| Output level (units) | Marginal cost of transfers (£) | Net marginal revenue of IPD (£) |
|---|---|---|
| 1000 | | |
| 2000 | 6 000 | 26 000 |
| 3000 | 6 000 | 21 000 |
| 4000 | 6 000 | 11 000 |
| 6000 | 12 000 | 22 000 |
| 8000 | 12 000 | 2 000 |

IPD will select an output level of 6000 units and will not go beyond this because NMR < marginal cost. This is the optimal output for the group, but the profits from the sale of the motor unit will accrue entirely to the IP division, and the EM division will make a loss equal to the fixed costs.

## CHAPTER 24

1 (a) (i) *High- and low-point method*

| | Machine hours 000s | Fuel oil expenses (£000's) |
|---|---|---|
| High point (June 2000) | 48 | 680 |
| Low point (January 2000) | 26 | 500 |
| Difference | 22 | 180 |

Variable cost per machine hour £8.182 (£180/22)
Substituting for January 2000

| | (£000's) |
|---|---|
| Variable cost (26 × £8.182) = | 212.73 |
| Fixed Cost (difference) | 287.27 |
| Total cost | 500.00 |

The total cost equation is $y = 287.27 + 8.182x$

(ii) *Least-squares regression method*

| | Hours $x$ | Fuel oil $y$ | $x^2$ | $xy$ |
|---|---|---|---|---|
| July | 34 | 640 | 1 156 | 21 760 |
| August | 30 | 620 | 900 | 18 600 |
| September | 34 | 620 | 1 156 | 21 080 |
| October | 39 | 590 | 1 521 | 23 010 |
| November | 42 | 500 | 1 764 | 21 000 |
| December | 32 | 530 | 1 024 | 16 960 |
| January | 26 | 500 | 676 | 13 000 |
| February | 26 | 500 | 676 | 13 000 |
| March | 31 | 530 | 961 | 16 430 |
| April | 35 | 550 | 1 225 | 19 250 |
| May | 43 | 580 | 1 849 | 24 940 |
| June | 48 | 680 | 2 304 | 32 640 |
| | $\Sigma x = 420$ | $\Sigma x = 6840$ | $\Sigma x^2 = 15 212$ | $\Sigma xy = 241 670$ |
| | $\bar{x} = 35$ | $\bar{y} = 570$ | | |

$$\Sigma y = Na + bx \qquad (1)$$
$$\Sigma xy = \Sigma xa + b\Sigma x^2 \qquad (2)$$

Substituting from the above table:

$$6840 = 12a + 420b \qquad (1)$$
$$241 670 = 420a + 15 212b \qquad (2)$$

Multiply equation (1) by 35 (= 420/12):

$$239 400 = 420a + 14 700 \qquad (3)$$

Subtract equation (3) from equation (2):

$$2270 = 512b, \text{ and so } b = 2270/512 = 4.4336$$

Substitute in equation (1), giving

$$6840 = 12a + 420 \times 4.4336, \text{ so } a = \frac{6840 - 1862.112}{12}$$

$$= 414.824$$

$$y = 414.82 + 4.43x$$

(b) For the answer to this question see Chapter 24.

(c) An $r^2$ calculation of 0.25 means that 75% of the total variation of $y$ from its mean is not caused by variations in $x$ (machine hours). This means that a large proportion of changes in fuel oil expenses do not result from changes in machine hours. The cost must depend on factors other than machine hours. Other measures of activity might be examined in order to test whether they are closely related to changes in costs. If other measures do not yield a close approximation then this might indicate that cost is dependent on several variables. In these circumstances multiple regression techniques should be used.

2 (a/b) See 'Cost estimation when the learning effect is present' in Chapter 24 for the answer to this question.

(c) See 'Learning-curve applications' in Chapter 24 for the answer to this question.

(d)

| Cumulative production | Hours per unit of cumulative production |
|---|---|
| 1 | 1000 |
| 2 | 800 |
| 4 | 640 |
| 8 | 512 |
| 4 machines | 8 machines |

| | (£) | | (£) |
|---|---|---|---|
| Labour (640 × £3) | 1920 | Labour (512 × £3) | 1536 |
| Direct materials | 1800 | Direct materials | 1800 |
| Fixed costs (£8000/4) | 2000 | Fixed costs (£8000/8) | 1000 |
| | 5720 | | 4336 |

# CHAPTER 25

1 The purchase cost is not constant per unit. It is therefore not possible to use the EOQ formula. Instead the following schedule of costs should be prepared:

**Evaluation of optimum order size**

| Size of order | No. of orders | Annual purchase cost (WI) (£) | Storage cost (£) | Admin. cost (£) | Total cost (£) |
|---|---|---|---|---|---|
| 2400 | 1 | 1728 (£0.72) | 300 | 5 | 2033 |
| 1200 | 2 | 1728 (£0.72) | 150 | 10 | 1888 |
| 600 | 4 | 1824 (£0.76) | 75 | 20 | 1919 |
| 200 | 12 | 1920 (£0.80) | 25 | 60 | 2005 |
| 100 | 24 | 1920 (£0.80) | 12.50 | 120 | 2052.50 |

It is recommended that two orders be placed per year for 1200 units.

|  | | **(£)** |
|---|---|---|
| Calculation of cost 2(1200 × £0.80 − 10%) | = | £1728 |
| Add: Storage, average quantity held 600 × £0.25 | = | 150 |
| Add two orders placed per annum × £5 | = | 10 |
|  | | £1888 |

*Workings* (W1) Annual demand of 2400 units × unit purchase cost

2 (a)

$$EOQ = \sqrt{\left(\frac{2DO}{H}\right)} = \sqrt{\frac{2 \times 4000 \times 135}{12}} = 300$$

The relevant cost is

$$\text{holding cost} + \text{ordering cost} = \frac{300 \times 12}{2} + \frac{4000 \times 135}{300} = \underline{3600}$$

(b) Revised EOQ$= \sqrt{\left(\frac{2 \times 4000 \times 80}{12}\right)} = 231$

The relevant cost is

$$\text{holding cost} + \text{ordering cost} = \frac{231 \times 12}{2} + \frac{4000 \times 80}{231} = 2772$$

The relevant cost using the original EOQ of 300 units but with an incremental ordering cost of £80 is

$$\frac{300 \times 12}{2} + \frac{4000 \times 80}{300} = 2867$$

Cost of prediction error = £95 (£2867 − £2772)

(c) The annual costs of purchasing, ordering and holding the materials consist of:
Special offer at £86:

holding cost + ordering cost + purchase cost

$$\frac{4000 \times 12}{2} + 0 = 4000 \times 86 = £368\,000$$

Normal price of £90:

$$\frac{300 \times 12}{2} + \frac{4000 \times 135}{300} + 4000 \times 90 = \underline{£363\,600}$$

Additional cost of special offer £4 400

Therefore the purchase of 4000 units at £86 is not recommended.

(d)

| | **Budget (£)** | **Actual (£)** | **Variance (£)** |
|---|---|---|---|
| Material cost | 360 000 | 344 000 | 16 000F |
| | (4000 × £90) | (4000 × £86) | |
| Ordering cost | 1 800 | 0 | 1 800F |
| $\left(\frac{D}{Q} \times O\right)$ | | | |
| | | | 17 800F |

It can be seen that favourable variances would appear on the performance report, and goal congruence would not exist. The performance evaluation system conflicts with the EOQ decision model. This is because the purchasing officer is not charged for the use of capital but the EOQ model includes a charge for the use of capital. Therefore if an imputed capital charge is not included in the performance report, there is a danger that goal congruence will not exist. The revised performance report including a capital charge is shown below:

|  | Budget (£) | Actual (£) | Variance (£) |
|---|---|---|---|
| Material cost | 360 000 | 344 000 | 16 000F |
| Ordering cost | 1 800 | 0 | 1 800F |
| Holding cost | 1 800 | 24 000 | 22 200A |
|  |  |  | 4 400A |

# CHAPTER 26

1  (a)  Maximize C = 3X + 4Y + 2Z
subject to:

$$2X + 3Y + 4Z \le 9\,000 \text{ (materials constraint)}$$
$$4X + Y + Z \le 9200 \text{ (labour constraint)}$$
$$X + 5Y + Z \le 8\,000 \text{ (machine hours constraint)}$$
$$X \le 2100 \text{ (sales of product X constraint)}$$
$$Y \le 1400 \text{ (sales of product Y constraint)}$$
$$Z \le 380 \text{ (sales of product Z constraint)}$$

Let $S_m$ = unused materials
$S_L$ = unused labour hours
$S_{mH}$ = unused machine hours
$S_x$ = unfulfilled sales demand of X
$S_y$ = unfulfilled sales demand of Y
$S_z$ = unfulfilled sales demand of Z

First tableau

|  |  | X | Y | Z |
|---|---|---|---|---|
| $S_m$ | = 9000 | −2 | −3 | −4 |
| $S_L$ | = 9200 | −4 | −1 | −1 |
| $S_{mH}$ | = 8000 | −1 | −5 | −1 |
| $S_x$ | = 2100 | −1 | 0 | 0 |
| $S_y$ | = 1400 | 0 | −1 | 0 |
| $S_z$ | = 380 | 0 | 0 | −1 |
| C | = 0 | 3 | 4 | 2 |

(b) The optimum output is

| | | | (£) |
|---|---|---|---|
| 1920 units of X at a contribution of £3 per unit | = | | 5 760 |
| 1140 units of Y at a contribution of £4 per unit | = | | 4 560 |
| 380 units of Z at a contribution of £2 per unit | = | | 760 |
| | Total contribution | | 11 080 |

The slacks on the left side of the final matrix indicate the unused resources, which consist of materials (220 units) unfulfilled sales demand of 260 units for product Y and 180 units for product X. Labour and machine hours appear as columns in the final matrix. This means that these resources are fully used. The unfulfilled sales demand for product Z is also fully used. The opportunity costs of the scarce items are:

Labour = $£\frac{11}{19}$ per labour hour
Machine hours = $£\frac{13}{19}$ per machine hour
Sales of an additional unit of Z = $£\frac{14}{19}$ per unit sold

If we can obtain additional labour hours then each labour hour should be used as follows:

Increase X by $\frac{5}{19}$ of a unit
Decrease Y by $\frac{1}{19}$ of a unit

Note that we reverse the signs when additional resources are obtained. The effect of this substitution process of each of the resources and contribution is as follows:

| | Labour hours | Materials | Machine hours | Contribution |
|---|---|---|---|---|
| Increase X by $\frac{5}{19}$ | $-1\frac{1}{19}(\frac{5}{19} \times 4)$ | $-\frac{10}{19}(\frac{5}{19} \times 2)$ | $-\frac{5}{19}(\frac{5}{19} \times 1)$ | $+\frac{15}{19}(\frac{5}{19} \times 3)$ |
| Decrease Y by $\frac{1}{19}$ | $+\frac{1}{19}(\frac{1}{19} \times 1)$ | $+\frac{3}{19}(\frac{1}{19} \times 3)$ | $+\frac{5}{19}(\frac{1}{19} \times 5)$ | $-\frac{4}{19}(\frac{1}{19} \times 4)$ |
| Net effect | $-1$ | $-\frac{7}{19}$ | $0$ | $\frac{11}{19}$ |

The net effect agrees with the labour column of the final matrix. Note that increasing sales of X by $\frac{5}{19}$ of a unit reduces the unused sales potential of X ($S_x$) by $\frac{5}{19}$, and decreasing sales of Y by $\frac{1}{19}$ increases unused sales potential of Y ($S_y$) by $\frac{1}{19}$. Similar reasoning can be applied to the remaining columns in the final matrix.

The column headed $S_z$ indicates that if demand for product Z can be increased then each additional unit sold will increase contribution by $£\frac{14}{19}$. To obtain the necessary resources to produce additional units of Z, it is necessary to reduce production of X by $\frac{4}{19}$ and of Y by $\frac{3}{19}$. The opportunity costs and marginal rates of substitution for the scarce resources apply over the following range:

Labour    4260 hours (9200 − 4940) to 9797 hours (9200 + 597)
Machinery  4580 hours (8000 − 3420) to 8418 hours (8000 + 418)
Sales demand of Z 0 units (380 − 380) to 451 units (380 + 71)

(c) See 'Uses of linear programming' in Chapter 26 for the answer to this question.

2 (a) Let $M$ = number of units of Masso produced and sold.
Let $R$ = number of units of Russo produced and sold.
The linear programming model is as follows:

Maximize $Z = 40M + 50R$ (production contributions)

subject to

$$M + 2R \leq 700 \text{ (machining capacity)}$$
$$2.5M + 2R \leq 1000 \text{ (assembly capacity)}$$
$$M \leq 400 \text{ (maximum output of Masso constraint)}$$
$$R \leq 400 \text{ (maximum output of Russo constraint)}$$
$$M \geq 0$$
$$R \geq 0$$

The constraints are plotted on the graph as follows:

Machining constraint: line from ($M = 700$, $R = 0$) to ($R = 350$, $M = 0$)
Assembly constraint: line from ($M = 400$, $R = 0$) to ($R = 500$, $M = 0$)
Output of Masso constraint: line from $M = 400$
Output of Russo constraint: line from $R = 400$

At the optimum point (B in the graph) the output mix is as follows:

|  | (£) |
|---|---|
| 200 units of Masso at a contribution of £40 per unit = | 8 000 |
| 250 units of Russo at a contribution of £50 per unit = | 12 500 |
| Total contribution | 20 500 |
| Less fixed costs (£7000 + £10 000) | 17 000 |
| Profit | 3 500 |

The optimum output can be determined exactly by solving the simultaneous equations for the constraints that intersect at point B:

$$2.5M + 2R = 1000 \qquad\qquad (1)$$

$$M + 2R = 700 \qquad\qquad (2)$$

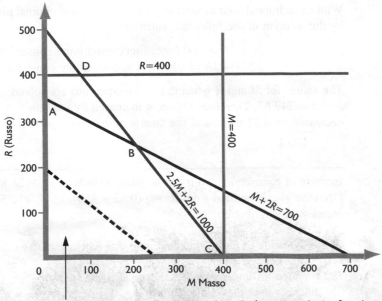

Objective function line $Z = 10\,000$ (arbitrarily chosen contribution figure)
Feasible region = OABC

Subtract equation (2) from equation (1):

$$1.5M = 300$$
$$M = 200$$

Substituting in equation (1):

$$2.5 \times 200 + 2R = 1000$$
$$R = 250$$

(b) *Machining capacity*

If we obtain additional machine hours, the line $M + 2R = 700$ will shift upward. Therefore the revised optimum point will fall on the line BD. If one extra machine hour is obtained, the constraints $M + 2R = 700$ and $2.5M + 2R$ will still be binding and the new optimal plan can be determined by solving the following equations:

$$M + 2R = 701 \text{ (revised machining constraint)}$$
$$2.5M + 2R = 1000 \text{ (unchanged assembly constraint)}$$

The values for $M$ and $R$ when the above equations are solved are $M = 199.33$ and $R = 250.83$.

Therefore Russo is increased by 0.83 units and Masso is reduced by 0.67 units and the change in contribution will be as follows:

|  | (£) |
|---|---|
| Increase in contribution from Russo (0.83 × £50) = | 41.50 |
| Decrease in contribution from Masso (0.67 × 40) = | (26.80) |
| Increase in contribution | 14.70 |

Hence the value of an independent marginal increase in machine capacity is £14.70 per hour.

*Assembly capacity*

With an additional hour of assembly capacity, the new optimal plan will be given by the solution of the following equations:

$$M + 2R = 700 \text{ (unchanged machining constraint)}$$
$$2.5M + 2R = 1001 \text{ (revised assembly constraint)}$$

The values for $M$ and $R$ when the above equations are solved are $M = 200.67$ and $R = 249.67$. Therefore Masso is increased by 0.67 units and Russo is decreased by 0.33 units, and the change in contribution will be as follows:

|  | (£) |
|---|---|
| Increase in contribution from Masso (0.67 × £40) = | 26.80 |
| Decrease in contribution from Russo (0.33 × £50) | (16.50) |
| Increase in contribution | 10.30 |

Hence the value of an independent marginal increase in assembly capacity is £10.30 per hour.

(c) The assumptions underlying the above calculations are:
  (i) linearity over the whole output range for costs, revenues and quantity of resources used;

(ii) divisibility of products (it is assumed that products can be produced in fractions of units);

(iii) divisibility of resources (supplies of resources may only be available in specified multiples);

(iv) the objectives of the firm (it is assumed that the single objective of a firm is to maximize short-term contribution);

(v) all of the available opportunities for the use of the resources have been included in the linear programming model.

# Case study problems

Additional cases, together with teaching notes, are available from the dedicated website
for this book (see Preface for details relating to how they can be accessed).

# CASE 1
# HARDHAT LTD

## Stan Brignall, Aston Business School, Aston University

Hardhat Limited's Budget Committee, which has members drawn from all the major functions in the business, is meeting to consider the projected income statement for 2000/2001, which is composed of the ten months' actuals to the end of January 2001 and estimates for the last two months of the financial year:

### Hardhat Ltd: Projected Income Statement 2000/2001

|  | (£000s) | (£000s) |
| --- | --- | --- |
| Sales (100 000 units) | 10 000 | |
| Cost of goods sold | 6 000 | |
| Gross profit | | 4 000 |
| Selling expenses | 1 500 | |
| Administrative expenses | 1 000 | |
| | | 2 500 |
| Net profit before tax | | £1 500 |

After some discussion of information principally supplied by the Finance Director, John Perks, the Committee agrees the following changes for the 2001/2002 budget:

30% increase in number of units sold
20% increase in unit cost of materials
5% increase in direct labour cost per unit
10% increase in variable indirect cost per unit
5% increase in indirect fixed costs
8% increase in selling expenses, arising solely from increased volume
6% increase in administrative expenses, reflecting anticipated higher salary and other costs rather than any effects of the expected increased sales volume.

The increase in sales volume is meant to be a significant step towards an ambitious target market share which was included in the latest review of Hardhat's strategic plan at the insistence of the marketing manager, Keith Boskin. Despite the change in volume, inventory quantities are expected to change little next year because of planned efficiency gains in the supply and handling of materials and despatch of finished goods.

The composition of the production cost of a unit of finished product in 2000/2001 for materials, direct labour and production overhead was in the ratio of 3 : 2 : 1 respectively. In 2000/2001 £40 000 of the production overhead was fixed. No changes in production methods or credit policies are anticipated for 2001/2002.

The managing director, Steve Hartley, has set a target profit before tax for 2001/2002 of £2 000 000, and the Budget Committee are now debating what this might imply for the unit selling price, on the basis of the information they have assembled so far. The consensus appears to be that the profit target is very tough, but that presumably this is what Steve and the Chairman, Lord Haretop, believe the City expects.

Keith Boskin is worried that the imposition of the short-term target profit will jeopardize the staged attainment of his long-run market share. 'I'm concerned that, in order to meet the profit (target imposed by Steve Hartley) we'll have to drastically put up our price. If that happens we *might* hit the profit, but it'll ruin my plans for damaging the prospects of Farfetched Co., who have been trying to take market share from us for some while now via heavy marketing expenditure – I think they're getting desperate because our cost structure and product quality are better than theirs! If we can just keep squeezing them for another year or two we might force them out of the market, or get them to agree to a takeover on reasonable terms. Then we'd effectively have the market to ourselves.' Dick Whittington, Keith's deputy, asked 'rather than putting up the price, could we work out how many units we'd have to sell at the old price to meet the profit target? Then we could check to see whether it would be within the plant's capacity.'

Mark Catchall, the production manager, intervened at this point, saying 'we can make up to 150 000 units a year with the present plant, but could we sustain that capacity output for long? I doubt it. We might have to invest in extra capacity, which is a whole new ball game. Besides, I don't really believe we can sell an extra 30 000 units next year, never mind 50 000 units, especially at an enhanced price. I suspect we will only manage to sell an extra 20 000 units *at best*, and perhaps only 10 000: what would that do for our profits, John?' John replied that he didn't know, but would investigate the various suggestions and come back to the next meeting in a week's time with some figures.

As he walked back to his office, John privately mused that perhaps the MD and Chairman wanted to boost short-term profits to make it easier to raise the finance to take over Farfetched Co., in which case it wouldn't hurt to give some thought as to the best source of finance for such a deal.

## Required

Write a report to the Board of Hardhat Ltd setting-out the financial effects of the various proposals and make recommendations as to what price Hardhat should charge next year and in the longer run.

Your report and presentation should cover:

(a) the sales price needed to earn the target profit, using the information compiled by the budget committee;

(b) the number of units that would have to be sold at the old price to meet the target profit, and whether this seems feasible;

(c) what the profit would be if the sales price calculated in (a) were adopted, but sales volume only rose by 10%, or at best 20%;

(d) any other factors you think should be taken into account when making decisions about the price to be charged next year, such as any change in risk involved in the cost–volume–profit structure you propose; the link between short- and long-run prices; and the interactions between acquisitions policy, financing decisions and pricing decisions.

# CASE 2
# LYNCH PRINTERS

## © *Peter Clarke, University College Dublin*

Dermot Lynch is the owner and managing director of a small printing business which carries his name. The company undertakes each printing job according to special instructions received from the customer. The type of printing orders include cards, invitations, small books and even occasional trade magazines. The nature of the printing business virtually ensures that there is no closing stock of finished goods on hand at the end of any accounting period. Work is done according to customer orders received or not at all. Sales and purchase invoices were paid on delivery so that the working capital investment in the company was virtually negligible.

According to the financial results for 20x1, the accounting year just ended, Lynch Printers had returned a net loss for the first time in its history. The loss was not of alarming proportions but Lynch wondered what had gone wrong and what he could do about it. Logic suggested that his problems were due to either low prices or excessive costs but this puzzled Lynch since each job was priced to include all costs to which a satisfactory profit margin was added. Moreover costs did not appear to have increased compared with previous years.

Lynch Printers has developed over the years a good reputation in the trade for quality work and reliability of delivery. Lynch passionately believed that these two factors were crucial in determining the success of his business. Quotation price was very much of secondary importance. Over the years his customers had continually insisted on good quality work and adherence to agreed delivery dates. For guarantees on these two issues the customer was willing to pay any price within reasonable bounds.

Lynch Printers use a system recommended by his trade association to quote a price for each printing job. When the customer specifies the type of work required, Lynch establishes an estimated cost for the job which includes direct and indirect expenses. A fixed percentage (10%) is added to total cost for profit and the final figure is given to the customer as a quotation. The quotation price as far as Lynch is concerned, is 'not negotiable'. Thus there are no special prices for any jobs. It's a take it or leave it situation as far as Lynch is concerned. If accepted by the customer it becomes a fixed price so that any cost overruns are absorbed by the printers and are not passed on to customers. This quotation system has been in operation for several years and Lynch prided himself on his estimating ability. Moreover it was a rare occurrence for a customer not to accept the quoted price. Admittedly, the absence of other printing firms in the locality meant that potential customers were placed at a slight disadvantage when dealing with Lynch.

The production process in Lynch Printers was relatively simple. Initially Lynch consulted his production manager about the feasibility of the order including the size and styles of type to be used. Once agreement was reached and the order confirmed by the customer Lynch issued a production order, which included printing instructions, and the material was sent to the composing room, where it was set in type. A galley proof was printed and sent to the copy editor who checked it against the original material. Any errors were marked on the proof which was then sent to the customer for approval. When returned by the customer the appropriate corrections were made and the order was then sent to the pressroom for production. Copies were then printed, bound and packaged for delivery to the customer.

The direct expenses of the business consisted of the cost of paper used and actual labour hours worked on each printing job. All other expenses were classified as overhead. Lynch Printers currently employ six individuals in the production process. They work a maximum of 35 hours per week, 48 weeks per year with four weeks holiday entitlements. The annual average cost of this typesetting and printing labour is €18,200 inclusive of employer's pension and social welfare contributions. Because of space limitations no more than six typesetters may be employed at any one time. The company has recently introduced the practice of 'flexitime' which has improved work practices enormously and has eliminated the necessity for overtime. For example if an employee takes Monday morning off he will work late some other evening, at no additional cost, to make up lost time.

For quotation purposes the total number of labour hours required in typesetting and printing for each job is estimated by Lynch and is priced at actual cost of labour work to be performed. To this computed labour cost a predetermined percentage is added to cover

---

**EXHIBIT 1**

**Profit and Loss Account for year ended 31 December, 20x1**

|  | € | € |
|---|---:|---:|
| Sales |  | 226 900 |
| Direct costs: |  |  |
| Cost of paper consumed | 22 000 |  |
| Wages (directly charged out) | 90 720 |  |
| Overheads: |  |  |
| Consumables (not directly chargeable) | 4 400 |  |
| Wages (not directly chargeable) | 18 480 |  |
| General production overheads, administration and delivery | 72 240 | 207 840 |
| Net Profit |  | 19 060 |

---

production overhead costs, including non-chargeable labour hours and also administration and delivery costs.

The other direct cost is that of paper. It is fairly easy to estimate the amount of paper required for each job since the customer specifies the size of the paper required, e.g. A4 size. In addition the quality of paper to be used is agreed in advance with the customer. Lynch personally discusses such requirements with each customer and offers advice. They normally accept his recommendation and are ultimately more than pleased with the completed product. To the estimated cost of paper used is added a predetermined percentage to cover 'consumables' such as ink and other minor costs incidental to the production process.

The predetermined percentages to recover both production overhead and consumables are always set equivalent to the actual percentage relationships between corresponding costs incurred during the previous financial year. In effect last year's actual cost performance becomes the budget for the following year. While this basis may compound any inefficiencies within the production process it has the advantage of considerably simplifying the accounting calculations. A summary of the actual results for 20x1 which formed the basis for 20x2 estimates is provided in Exhibit 1.

Comparing the 20x1 profit performance with the loss incurred in 20x2, Lynch was even more puzzled especially since there were no cost increases over the two years. He knew, however, that in 20x2 business had fallen – measured in terms of chargeable labour hours. In 20x1, 90% of the labour hours worked were charged to specific jobs. However, in 20x2 only 75% of hours worked represented chargeable hours. Even though the volume of trade had dropped no one had been laid off since good typesetters and printers were difficult to recruit and volume might improve in following years.

The actual general production overheads including administration and delivery costs amounted to €72 240 in 20x2. Lynch was not surprised that they were the same as the previous year since they were predominantly fixed in nature. The cost of paper consumed during 20x2 amounted to €19 000. At least it was less than last year, Lynch consoled himself, as was the €3500 incurred on consumables.

As always it was necessary to obtain reliable data on what had actually happened during the year in order to analyse the situation, Lynch thought to himself. Once obtained, he could begin to draw conclusions and implications. Even at this preliminary stage Lynch anticipated that this whole basis of pricing policy might be in need of revision for 20x3.

### Requirement

(1) What were the recovery rates used in 20x2 for both consumables and production overhead? Use these rates and other actual data to calculate actual sales for 20x2.

(2) What was the amount of the loss for 20x2? Explain how the loss has arisen. Comment critically on Lynch's pricing system.

(3) Prepare a statement comparing actual performance in 20x2 from budget. What information content do these variances have? Justify your choice of budget figures.

## CASE 3
## HIGH STREET REPRODUCTION FURNITURE LTD

### *Jayne Ducker, Antony Head, Rona O'Brien (Sheffield Hallam University) and Sue Richardson (University of Bradford Management Centre)*

This is an extract from Ducker, H., Head, A., McDonnell, B., O'Brien, R. and Richardson, S. (1998), *A Creative Approach to Management Accounting: Case Studies in Management Accounting and Control*, Sheffield Hallam University Press, ISBN 0 86339 791 3.

### Introduction

High Street Reproduction Furniture is a small, but rather exclusive, producer of reproduction bedroom furniture. Turnover last year was just over £1 million and the business continues to provide a steady profit margin. It is a private limited company owned by John Carpenter and his wife Eleanor and it has been trading for 25 years. John, who is a fully qualified cabinet maker, started in the trade immediately after leaving school. He has little formal training in management, but has much hands-on experience gained from running his business.

### Past and recent history of the company

The company originally operated from small, cold and draughty premises in the back streets of Sheffield and in the early years its only employee was Fred. Because of the cold working conditions, John always wore a 'flat' cap (a woven cap with a peak, traditionally worn by the men of Yorkshire) whilst he worked alongside Fred, a habit that seems to have stuck and has become somewhat of a trademark for John. According to John, 'In those days I had to think on my feet and we tended to exist from one job to the next, on a wing and a prayer you might say?' As a consequence of this, whenever John has a major problem at work which needs resolving, he tends to put his cap on to help him think things through. The employees always know the 'chips are down' when they see John walking about in his cap.

The business grew steadily in the early years and about ten years ago John was able to move from the original site to a high street location in Sheffield, which provides a small showroom area, a workshop, staff room and storage. However, the product range has remained fairly constant and consists of three pieces of bedroom furniture, namely, a wardrobe, a chest of drawers and a dressing table. These are sold directly to customers either as separate items or as a bedroom suite.

The furniture is hand-made to a very high standard, authentically reproducing the Baxendale style which was popular in the late nineteenth century. This requires a high degree of skill in the construction and finishing stages of the production process. Although most of John's time these days is spent in managing the business, he still keeps a watchful eye on activities and likes to help out if the men are over-stretched.

The furniture is made from mahogany supplied by Sheffield Timber Company, which imports high quality seasoned timber from South America. Although John could buy mahogany more cheaply elsewhere, he has dealt with this company for a long time and has confidence that the quality will be consistently good. The grain and colour of the wood is extremely important and, because the fronts of the furniture must match in grain and colour for each piece or suite of furniture, the company expects to have a high level of off-cuts and waste.

The unique finish to the furniture is produced through a highly-skilled hand-waxing process, using beeswax mixed to a special recipe created especially for High Street Reproduction Furniture by Charlesworth Specialist Waxes, who make and supply this recipe exclusively to the company. Mahogany and beeswax are the two main materials used to make the finished products.

Twelve people are now employed full time in the production process: ten are highly skilled cabinet makers and two are young apprentices. All the cabinet makers have been with the company for a long time and Fred is now the workshop supervisor. Fred is a bit set in his ways but, according to John, 'He does a damned good job and he is a very good craftsman.'

Careful delivery of the furniture to the customer is very important and John is proud of the fact that the company receives very few complaints of furniture damaged in transit. The company sub-contracts this part of its activities to a well established company in the city of Sheffield. This company has always been reliable and has provided a high class service to customers carefully protecting the furniture in transit, setting the piece in its position for the customer and asking them to check it over. If the customer is not satisfied with the furniture, then it is returned to the workshop immediately. Of course, High Street Reproduction Furniture pay a premium price for this service, but it has proved of benefit to both the company and the customer, since problems can be resolved immediately.

The specialised nature of the production process and the specialised delivery service results in high product costs. However, John has found that the company's products attract the type of customer who is willing to pay a premium price.

In the past year the company has invested £100 000 in the refurbishment of the offices and showroom and in the extension of the workshop and storage area to meet increasing demand for the company's products. This was funded by a five year loan from the company's bank. John believes that the increase in demand is mainly due to the showing of a television documentary of Sheffield which featured High Street Reproduction Furniture. The company appeared in a very favourable light as part of the new face of Sheffield emerging from the aftermath of the shrinking steel industry and the programme was given prime-time national coverage. In order to capitalise upon this free publicity, John also launched a national advertising campaign, using the documentary as a marketing ploy. However, the increased demand is putting pressure on the workforce and the lead time (the time between the customer ordering the furniture and the expected delivery date) is increasing.

Iris has been responsible for the paperwork ever since John started the business. Initially she worked part time whilst her children were young but has worked full time for the last five years. She has had the help of Cecil, who is a qualified accountant, for the last twelve months. Cecil spends two days each month on the company premises, assisting with costings and accounts.

Although, according to John, 'Iris has always done a great job of sorting us out', John feels that the company is getting too busy for her to cope. He has asked Cecil's advice and Cecil has suggested that it is probably time to employ a full time management accountant, even though this will mean a reduction in his own services for the company.

## Two months ago

John took Cecil's advice and contacted Sheffield Hallam University to advertise the post on the undergraduate careers board. He felt that the post would suit a new graduate and that he could offer a fair salary whilst not placing too large a burden on the company's overheads. A number of students expressed an interest and John interviewed three of these. He selected Mary, who is due to start with the company as soon as her final exams are completed.

## Last week

Mary arrived at High Street Reproduction Furniture and settled in nicely. Wisely, John involved Iris in the selection process and the two seem to be getting on well together.

John received a profit statement from Cecil for the previous six months' trading which itemised the performance of the company's three products. This is attached as Exhibit 1. John was appalled to see that the dressing tables had made a loss. He has called a meeting for next week with Mary, Iris and Fred to discuss the situation. It could not be before then, as John had important appointments for the rest of the week. First, he had to visit the beeswax suppliers who are located in the Scottish Highlands, in order to renegotiate a contract for beeswax for the coming year; second, Sheffield Timber had telephoned and asked for an urgent meeting.

John warned Mary, Iris and Fred that at next week's meeting he also wishes to discuss another matter with them. This concerns a potential new venture for the company. Much to his amazement, knowledge of the company has reached the American market through the screening of the television programme. One particular company has approached John with an enquiry for fifty chests for export to America. High Street Reproduction Furniture has never supplied bulk orders before and this customer is only willing to pay 70 per cent of the normal selling price.

He has briefly discussed the problems with Mary who, being keen and enthusiastic in her first job, wishes to anticipate John's information needs before the meeting takes place. She has been working overtime (after Iris has left for the

**EXHIBIT 1**

*Cecils Profit Statement for the last six months' trading*

|  | Wardrobes (£000) | Dressing Tables (£000) | Chests (£000) | Total |
|---|---|---|---|---|
| Sales revenue | 340 | 200 | 300 | 840 |
| Direct materials | 100 | 96 | 90 | 286 |
| Direct labour | 63 | 48 | 53 | 164 |
| Variable workshop overheads | 17 | 16 | 15 | 48 |
| Apportioned fixed workshop overheads | 60 | 70 | 68 | 198 |
| Total manufacturing costs | 240 | 230 | 226 | 696 |
| Gross profit (loss) | 100 | (30) | 74 | 144 |
| Selling & distribution costs |  |  |  | 80 |
| Net profit |  |  |  | 64 |

EXHIBIT 2

*Mary's Initial
Information
Gathering*

*Profit statement:*
Numbers of each product sold in the period covered by the statement:

| | |
|---|---|
| Wardrobes | 200 |
| Dressing tables | 160 |
| Chests of drawers | 200 |

Selling and distribution costs includes delivery costs to the customer

| | |
|---|---|
| Amount paid to delivery contractor for last six months | £19 600 |
| Average delivery cost per product | £35 each |

*Dressing tables:*
Six months ago John made the decision to buy in the mirror section of the dressing
tables from a local firm at a cost of £200 each. Mary has found the original estimate
of the cost if the company were to continue making the mirror section in house,
which was used for comparison with the sub-contract price. This is shown below:

| | (£) |
|---|---|
| Direct materials | 120 |
| Direct labour | 40 |
| Variable overheads | 20 |
| Fixed overheads | 40 |
| Total | 220 |

In order to ensure that the timber used to frame the mirror section matched the main
body of the dressing table, it was agreed that the supplying firm would buy their
timber from the same supplier, i.e. Sheffield Timber Company. The mirror sections
were delivered to High Street Reproduction Furniture in an unfinished state and were
hand-waxed by the company's own craftsmen. Control over the quality of the mirror
sections has been problematic.

**The American Enquiry**

Mary has obtained the following information:

| | |
|---|---|
| Delivery charges | |
| (50 chests to the dockside) | 3 vans @ £300 each |
| Average lead time: | |
| for the last six months | 12 weeks |
| for the six months prior to that | 8 weeks |
| Average overtime: | |
| last week | 6 hours per man |
| for the last six months | 1 hour per man per week |
| Stocks of mahogany | 3250 square metres |

| Average usage of mahogany per product: | |
|---|---|
| Wardrobes | 10 square metres |
| Dressing tables (excluding mirror) | 4 square metres |
| Mirror section | 1 square metre |
| Chests of drawers | 5 square metres |

day) to produce the information which is attached in Exhibit 2. She hopes to impress John at the meeting by being well prepared, but has only managed to obtain the raw data by the date of the meeting.

## The meeting

It is obvious to everyone (except Mary) that John is worried. He makes a strange sight in his cleanly cut business suit and his flat cap! Mary is puzzled but she dares not to comment.

The first item on the agenda is the loss-making situation of the dressing tables. John comments, 'I am appalled to find that the dressing tables are making a loss of £30 000. I can't understand it as it has never happened before. It looks as though we shall have to stop making them and concentrate on the other products, unless any of you can offer an alternative solution'.

Iris says that, given Cecil's figures, she has to agree with John about the dressing tables. Fred comments that he hasn't had time to look at the figures as he has been 'snowed under' with work. Mary decides to keep her data to herself at this stage and offers to go away and 'work on some numbers'.

The second item is the potential new venture. John passes copies of the American enquiry to all those present. 'I intimated to you all last week that we might discuss this today. Do you have any views on whether we should accept it or not?'

Iris and Fred have discussed this item before the meeting. Fred tells John that the order is totally impossible, given that the workshop is getting very overstretched, and Iris agrees with him, adding, 'How on earth do they expect us to make a profit at only 70 per cent of the normal selling price?' Mary interrupts at this stage, having gained a little more confidence, and suggests to John that the enquiry might be worth looking into. She promises to provide further information by the end of the week. John decides that they should meet again on Friday, when Mary will have more information for them and hopefully Fred will have had time to give the issues greater consideration.

As they leave the meeting, Fred comments to Iris, 'There's something else worrying him besides what he's telling us. I wonder what it can be?'

## Question 1

Mary has decided to restate Cecil's original profit statement by using the additional information she has collected and by employing a marginal costing approach.

Required:

(a) Prepare a new profit statement for Mary which clearly identifies both the contribution made by each product over the last six months and the overall profit.

(b) Prepare a profit statement which shows the potential situation if John stops production of the dressing tables and demand for the other products remains the same as that of the past six months. Assume that supplies of mahogany are unlimited.

(c) What other issues should John consider before making the decision to stop producing dressing tables?

(d) Prepare a statement which identifies the contribution which the dressing tables would have made in the last six months, had the mirror section not been sub-contracted out. Suggest other issues which might affect John's decision to make the mirror sections in house once again.

## Question 2

Utilising theoretical models and illustrating your answer with reference to the case study materials, discuss the decision situation regarding the American enquiry. Your discussion should also be supported by financial information which Mary would be likely to produce.

## Question 3

Mary has suggested to John that the company would benefit from a management information system to aid him in planning and controlling the activities of the business and to assist in organisational decision making. Join is not sure what Mary means.

Required:

(a) Illustrate the types of planning and controlling activities that are likely to take place at High Street Reproduction Furniture Limited.

(b) Describe the types of information which might be useful.

(c) Suggest the likely sources of this information.

## Question 4

At the urgent meeting last week, the Sheffield Timber Company informed John that supplies of mahogany from South America were in jeopardy. There had been a serious forest fire and much of the seasoned stock ready for export at the premises of the South American exporter had been wiped out. Sheffield Timber envisaged that there would be no more supplies of the type used by High Street Reproduction Furniture for the next six months. After that date, it seems that supplies can be restored to normal.

Required:

(a) Provide a production schedule which would maximise profits on the stocks of mahogany held by High Street Reproduction Furniture Limited and identify the forecast profit figure based on this production schedule.

   You should assume that forecast demand from the normal customer base will be 10 per cent higher than the last six months' figures and that the decision on the American enquiry is still unresolved. You should also assume that the mirror section of the dressing table will have to be produced by High Street Reproduction Furniture, since the current supplier does not hold any stock of the mahogany.

(b) Identify other issues which John would need to take account of, if this production schedule is undertaken.

(c) Compare the predicted profit in (a) above with the profit which John might have expected in the second half of the year, if the predicted demand for all three products had been met, the American contract had not been taken on and the mirror section of the dressing table had been produced by High Street Reproduction Furniture Limited. Comment on your findings.

## CASE 4
## FLEET LTD

### Lin Fitzgerald, University of Warwick Business School
### Background

Fleet operates a chain of high street retail outlets selling clothing and household items. In 1995 this company was heading for a financial loss and was deemed to have lost strategic direction. The business formula that had proved successful in the 1980s and early 1990s was no longer proving effective. A new chief executive was appointed to turn the company around. He put into effect a threefold strategy. Firstly he removed levels in the hierarchy, secondly he decentralized the organization and thirdly he focused on the core competencies or skills of the business. These core skills were identified as essentially buying and selling, and from this analysis the philosophy of outsourcing was developed. The argument put forward was that the core activities have to be world class and that the organization must strive to achieve this. You also need world class support, i.e. non-core activities, but this is difficult, if not impossible to achieve in-house. This is because you need to use people who are working in the forefront, or the core, of that industry, and by definition your people are not in the forefront because it is a non-core activity.

The corporate philosophy and its outsourcing implication was thus evolved in this organization with anything that was not buying and selling becoming a potential candidate for outsourcing. For example distribution has been outsourced and has been reduced in size from 250 staff to three; quality control, packaging, and design activities have followed a similar pattern. Security and cleaning are currently in the process of being outsourced.

### Detail

Outsourcing was thus the overall philosophy of the company but they would not do it just for the sake of it, they still needed to be shown that, if a particular activity was outsourced, improvements would result. In relation to IT the feeling of senior management was that IT was performing reasonably well in an operational sense but not really delivering its potential for the business. The IT department are based miles away from the business, off-site and are hard to manage. They had been fully centralized and told by the previous chief executive that they were going to be the hub and key to the smooth running of the company. Arrangements for the setting up of projects with the IT department were fairly informal and projects were tending to overrun budgets.

Fleet decided to explore the possibility of outsourcing all of its IT needs. The process involved the selection of a shortlist of vendors which the company felt to be capable of handling such a contract. The company provided a brief to these four who were invited to provide an initial response. The selected vendor, Results Ltd., was the one that was felt to best understand the philosophy and objectives of the company, especially in the area of development. Further detailed negotiations were carried out with Results Ltd. Most of the details of the company's performance requirements in IT had been defined in detail over the past three years, especially the key requirements of their stores and for buying and merchandising.

The proposal from Results is for a three year initial contract at a fixed price of £250 000 per year. The initial response of the IT department to the possibility of outsourcing was negative. They expressed concern over the recent large investment the company had made in replacing all its computer systems, £100 million had been spent only last year, they expected this equipment would service the company for another three years. Obviously there was deep concern over job security. Currently the IT department has ten staff earning, on average, £30 000 per year. The vendor had agreed to take on eight of these staff maintaining the terms and conditions they held with Fleet. Of the remaining two staff one, Charles Smith, was eager to take early retirement and the other was to be retained within Fleet, at a salary of £30 000 to assist with management of the contract. A contract manager would have to be appointed by Fleet – this would be a new appointment, the company did not currently have anyone with those skills in-house – at an estimated salary of £50 000.

## Additional information provided by the finance director

- If Charles Smith retired two years early the company would have to pay an extra £20 000 lump sum into the pension scheme.
- The building housing the IT department was on a three year lease and the company was committed to an annual rental of £10 000 per year for that period. This building could be sublet if IT were outsourced generating £4 000 in the first year, £8 000 in the second and £10 000 in the final year of the lease.
- Current forecasts of consumables in the IT department are £5000, £6000 and £7000 over the next three years.
- The resale value of the IT equipment bought last year is £30 000.
- Annual overheads for the IT department are £27 000 per year. 60% of the overhead varies with staff numbers, the remaining 40% is a share of central overhead charges.

## Required

You have been appointed as a consultant to prepare a report analysing the outsourcing proposal, including both the financial and non-financial effects, and give your recommendations.

## Your report should include the following:

1. an incremental costing analysis;
2. the effects on reported profits;
3. discussion of other factors that need to be taken into account before a decision is made;
4. recommendations with reasons;
5. an executive summary.

# CASE 5
# AIRPORT COMPLEX[1]

## Peter Nordgaard and Carsten Rohde, Copenhagen Business School

## Background

Airport Complex was founded in Northern Europe in the late 1940s, and at the time it primarily served as a domestic airport. During the 1970s, flights to foreign destinations became an ever more vital activity for the airport. Today, the airport functions as a hub for

---

[1] This case is written by Peter Nordgaart, part-time lecturer, and Carsten Rohde, associate professor, Copenhagen Business School. Airport Complex is a fictitious case, and the information in the case is thus constructed on the basis of the authors' knowledge about and interest in European airports. The case has been simplified for teaching purposes, and thus it cannot serve as a basis for comparison with specific airports.

a large portion of Nordic air traffic. The fact that the airport is a hub means that a great deal (approximately 35–40 per cent) of the airport's passengers only touch down at the airport to catch another plane to a new destination. The airport remained state property until the mid-1990s when the airport was transformed into a private company, though the state held on to a substantial ownership share.

| (All amounts in 1000 Euro) | (budget) 1995 | 1996 | 1997 | 1998 | 1999 |
|---|---|---|---|---|---|
| Turnover | 203 800 | 207 876 | 214 112 | 222 677 | 218 223 |
| Pre-tax profit | 61 140 | 61 751 | 61 751 | 62 492 | 60 118 |
| Assets | 680 000 | 748 000 | 782 000 | 802 400 | 816 000 |
| Profit margin | 30% | 30% | 29% | 28% | 28% |
| Return on investments (ROI) | 9% | 8% | 8% | 8% | 7% |

Naturally, this generated an increased focus on the airport's financial performance, which, however, boosted healthy profit margins. This also constituted the background for the continued extension of the airport, which today has placed itself as an airport entering the medium-size class of Nordic airports. The profit margins of the airport (see Exhibit 1) have suffered a decline over the past few years due to a combination of deteriorating income as a result of a fall in domestic traffic and costs that have not decreased correspondingly. At the same time, tax-free sales were abolished in 1999. This has contributed heavily to the decline in revenue.

Investors have consequently requested that the airport commit itself more to a focus on the overall profitability measured against the invested capital. Accordingly, the management has now decided that the efficiency of the airport should be subject to assessment. An airport is characterized by the fact that almost all costs are capacity costs. This is partly due to significant investment in buildings, runways and technology, but also to the large staff which handles the administration, operation and maintenance of the airport. The management suspects that the costs are not sufficiently adjusted to the income. In particular, the management finds it difficult to get an overview of how the various business areas utilize the airport's resources and services and thus contribute to the bottomline of the airport.

## Business areas

The revenue of Airport Complex derives from five different areas; take-off duties from air traffic, passenger fees, rental income from property, licensing income from the airport's shopping centre and sundry income related to provision of services in the airport. Each of the five business areas is briefly outlined in the following discussion.

### Take-off duties

Every time an aircraft departs from the airport, the airline pays a take-off duty. The duty is calculated on the basis of the type and weight of the aircraft. The income is related to the airline's use of the airport's control of the air space, runways, technical equipment such as runway lights, meteorological equipment, facilities on the gate for cleaning the aircraft, changing the air in the aircraft, fuelling, de-icing, etc. After the aircraft has landed, it is guided to a gate. If the pilot does not know the airport, airport personnel will guide the aircraft to its gate. There are two types of gates: gates served by a building, i.e. the gate is connected to one of the airport's terminals allowing passengers to leave the aircraft and enter the terminal directly, and remote gates where the aircraft is parked somewhere else in the airport area from where passengers are subsequently transported by buses to one of the airport terminals. Airlines are in broad consent that building-served gates service passengers far better than remote gates. Still, prices for building-served and remote gates are currently not differentiated, though the management has discussed this question. In addition to the take-off duties, a stopover duty is also payable depending on how long the aircraft stays in the gate. The first hour, however, is free.

### Passenger fees

Take-off and stopover duties are complemented by a passenger fee per passenger on the aircraft. These three sources of income are collectively referred to as traffic income. Passenger fees depend solely on the number of passengers. The passengers' points of departure and final destination are thus not relevant to the calculation of the fee. In principle, passenger fees relate to the passengers' use of the airport area and services. This covers for instance buildings, transport to the terminal, service information, luggage handling and passenger areas in the airport. A differentiation on the prices for domestic passengers and those travelling to destinations abroad was previously in force, but EU competition rules have now put an end to this differentiation. It has been discussed whether there should be different passenger fees for passengers who merely touch down at the airport, but never leave the aircraft (transit passengers) as opposed to passengers who only land at the airport in order to get on a new plane (transfer passengers), as these passengers do not use the airport's landside areas. Every year, the relation between take-off duties and passenger duties is also discussed, as there are occasional imbalances in the case of small aircraft with many passengers and large aircraft with few passengers.

### Rental income

Parts of the airport buildings are let out to airlines, travel agencies and shops. This revenue is collectively referred to as rental income. Prices are fixed as per square metre and vary with the use of the rented premises and its location within the airport area. Besides yielding a reasonable profit margin, rental income must in principle cover wear and tear, maintenance, use of common facilities such as toilets, lifts, etc.

### Services

In connection with renting of buildings, supplementary services such as cleaning, security guard surveillance of rooms and shops, access to canteens and to the airport's computer network are also offered. This income is collectively referred to as income from provision of services and is of course related to the airport's costs in connection with these services. In recent years, this income has seen a rapid increase as a result of the airport seizing ever more opportunities for expanding the range of its services offered to the airport's customers.

## Licensing income

Finally, the airport generates income from licensing agreements entered into with shops and agencies that rent premises in the airport. In addition to rent for the premises, a duty is payable for running a shop within the airport's area. The licensing agreements are based on the payment of a certain share of the turnover of shops and agencies to the airport. This income is collectively referred to as licensing income. In return, the airport takes on costs for decoration and marketing of the shopping centre such as signs, brochures, campaigns and information staff Campaigns are budgeted separately, though there is no connection between the budgeting of campaigns and that of licensing agreements. The revenue of Airport Complex is shown in Exhibit 2.

## Organization

The organization of Airport Complex is a result of a continuous development of the company. Originally, everything was collected under the traffic department, as there were no other business activities. As other commercial activities and letting

| All amount in 1000 Euro | (budget) 1995 | 1996 | 1997 | 1998 | 1999 |
|---|---|---|---|---|---|
| Aeronautical revenue | 73 368 | 78 993 | 83 504 | 89 071 | 93 836 |
| Non-aeronautical revenue | 38 722 | 41 575 | 44 964 | 46 762 | 52 374 |
| Revenue from provision of services | 4 076 | 8 315 | 8 564 | 11 134 | 17 458 |
| Licensing revenue | 87 634 | 78 993 | 77 080 | 75 710 | 54 556 |
| Total revenue | 203 800 | 207 876 | 214 112 | 222 677 | 218 223 |

**FIGURE 1** *Organization of Airport Complex A/S.*

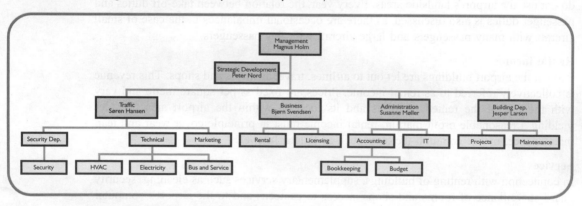

out of premises were developed, the business area was isolated. Immediately after this separation, the need for a distinct building department was recognized, and the new department was established. In connection with the transfer from a state enterprise to a private undertaking, the administrative activities were collected under their own organizational area. Figure 1 shows the organization plan of Airport Complex.

## Financial management

The accounting department handles the company's financial control. The bookkeeping department takes care of the day-to-day invoicing and bookkeeping of the company's transactions and of the company's financial accounting and tax accounting. The budget department is in charge of the co-ordination of budgets, whereas part budgets are prepared in the individual departments, which subsequently report their budget to the budget department. The budgets are entered into the airport's financial control system, which at the same time ensures that the individual department is only able to view its own budgets.

Subsequently, the total budget is subject to approval first by the management and then by the board. The exact budgeting is of course very different from one department to the other, depending on the functions of each department and the people responsible for the budget of the department. Nevertheless, some general comments can be made on the airport's budget procedure. Staff budgets are normally prepared on the basis of a combination of price and amount per staff category. The remaining costs are predominantly provided for in the budget as a fixed amount. Depreciation is not allocated to the individual departments, but is estimated as a total amount by the budget department. The budget for traffic income is based on a forecast of the number of different types of aircraft. For each type of plane, the average weight and the average number of passengers are calculated and subsequently multiplied by the current take-off and passenger fees and the number of planes of that type. Rental income is estimated on the basis of the number of square metres relative to the average rent per square metre. Different prices per square metre are used depending on the type of building, use and location. The buildings may typically be divided into terminal buildings, office buildings, workshops, hangars, and warehouses. The income from provision of services is estimated on the basis of expected sales measured as an amount, and finally, the licensing income is estimated as expected turnover per shop type multiplied by the licence percentage.

## Outline of departments

### Strategic development
The department is situated in the administrative office building. It was established three years ago with the task of supporting the management and the board in their work with strategic development of the airport. The department employs 4–5 people who make analyses of the operation of the airport and perform benchmarking analysis of the company compared to other airports. The department typically works on 3–4 projects at a time. Examples of projects are:

- the profitability of future extension projects;
- analyses of traffic statistics and forecasts of future traffic development;
- strategies for the information structure in the airport, including the future extension of the network and the number of services implemented in the network.

### Traffic department
The traffic department has the overall responsibility for the development of the airport's traffic activities. The department handles traffic-related security and co-ordination with the aviation authorities, which are in charge of the actual control of the airspace, i.e. permission to take off and land. The traffic department is also the most wage consuming department since a major part of the airport staff is employed here.

### Technical departments
The complicated technical structure of the airport such as traffic and passenger co-ordination systems, bridges from airport buildings to the aircraft, runway lights, etc. is handled by the technical department. The department has three sub-departments: electricity, HVAC, and buses and service. The department takes care of these same functions for the rest of the airport.

#### Electricity department
The electricity department employs 125 employees on an annual basis. The department is divided between five area managers, each responsible for specific parts of the airport. However, the department seeks to maintain a certain degree of job rotation to ensure that

the employees acquire a high level of knowledge within all job functions in the department. Apart from vehicles, the department is responsible for a great deal of technical equipment, cranes, lifts, etc. The tasks in the department vary from mounting and repairing of control and marking equipment in connection with the runways, to maintenance of the airport's technical equipment and more ordinary electricity work in connection with the airport buildings. Work in connection with the airport buildings is co-ordinated by the building department, apart from work in connection with the airport's rented property, which is co-ordinated by the rental department. The electricity department is naturally also involved in the implementation of the airport's network, which is performed on the basis of requirements from the IT department.

### HVAC department

The HVAC department employs approximately 150 people annually, and the department is divided on the basis of geographical areas in the airport. The division is as follows: airside undeveloped areas, airside developed areas, terminals, and finally, other landside buildings. Each area has its own head of department. Like the electricity department, the HVAC department has at its disposal a large amount of technical equipment used in its daily work. The major part of the tasks of the department is co-ordinated with the building department.

### Bus and service department

The bus and service department is responsible for transporting the passengers to the terminals and for servicing the runways and other outdoor areas. The service primarily consists of maintenance of the green areas of the airport and of snow removal, and the service department employs 25 people. The bus department employs approximately 50 chauffeurs who are responsible mainly for transporting the passengers to and from the aircraft, but who sometimes also function as guides for aircraft whose pilots do not know the airport.

## Marketing department

The marketing department is in charge of conducting negotiations with both airlines that already use the airport and airlines that wish to use the airport in the future. This applies to passenger traffic as well as freight traffic. The department employs six people on average.

## Security department

Traditionally, airports are always associated with large security risks. Therefore, security is an important work area. The security department is thus responsible for monitoring the security in the airport. The main tasks of the security department are outdoor area surveillance, indoor security check of passengers and screening of luggage, and security service in connection with the airport's own premises and rented premises. This includes security checking of all passengers and screening of luggage. If the airport uses external artisans in connection with the activities of the building department or the technical department, these will be constantly monitored by a security guard. Furthermore, the security personnel are responsible for security surveillance of rented premises.

On an annual basis, the area surveillance function employs 30 people who always work together in teams of two. Each team has at its disposal a cross-country vehicle, which enables them to turn out quickly to any place in the airport. They communicate with the central security function on a current basis via the internal communication system, which also includes GPS surveillance of all vehicles. The system has just recently been fully implemented and is controlled by the IT department. Apart from a meeting room in the terminal building, the department has at its disposal three smaller buildings located in opposite parts of the airport. There are always three teams working at the same time and their activities are co-ordinated by the central security service, which is manned by the security manager in charge and an assistant. The indoor security check function is manned in relation to the expected number of passengers during the day and employs approximately 70 people on an annual basis. The airport is divided into a landside and an airside area. The airside area can only be accessed through the security lock with a valid ticket and after screening of hand luggage and scanning of the passenger. The landside area, on the other hand, is accessible to everybody. There are three security locks in the airport that are manned according to the expected passenger flow during the day. Each lock is manned by three security employees who are in constant radio contact with the security manager in charge. Apart from this, two to three security employees are constantly patrolling the airside of the airport as well as the landside terminal areas. Moreover, both the indoor and the outdoor security personnel also function as security service in connection with the rented premises in the airport. The most cost-intensive item in the security department is therefore staff costs and staff-related costs such as uniforms and security courses. Furthermore, the department has at its disposal considerable assets such as cars, and security equipment such as scanners, X-ray equipment, etc.

### Business department

The main activities in the business department are renting of areas as well as buildings and licensing agreements with retailers, restaurants, car hire firms, etc. The eight employees in the rental department administer the rental agreements and are responsible for finding suitable premises for this purpose. Extensions, renovation and maintenance of the rented premises are co-ordinated with the technical department and the building department.

The 12 employees in the licensing department draw up agreements on how to carry on business in the airport areas, including agreements on the turnover-related fees to be paid for this. The promotion of the shopping centre is planned and carried out by the business department. The extension of the shopping centre is co-ordinated with the project department.

### Administrative department

This department handles the overall day-to-day administration in connection with in-voicing, bookkeeping and cash. Furthermore, the IT department, which is part of the administrative department, is responsible for the airport's network which is used by the airport's own departments as well as other users of the airport. This applies to both networks for administrative use, for traffic monitoring and for signboards in the airport. Moreover, access to the airport's network and support in this connection are let out. The administrative department employs 120 people on an annual basis of which approximately half are employed in the IT department.

### Building department

The project department is responsible for the continuous extension of the airport, i.e. the strategic planning in collaboration with the management as well as the actual project management. Approximately 20 people are employed on an annual basis to perform these tasks. The operative part is placed with the maintenance department, which is responsible for the continuous maintenance of both the airport area and the buildings, and which employs approximately 80 people. Exemptions are HVAC and technical appliances, which are the responsibility of the technical department under the traffic unit.

## Requirements

1. Comment on the financial management of Airport Complex.
2. Discuss the problems and opportunities connected with assessing the profitability of the different services offered by the airport to the airlines and their customers. You are, among other things, asked to consider whether you would recommend the use of Full Cost, Activity Based Costing or Contribution Margin Concept to the company and state the reasons for your recommendation.

3. Draw up a reasoned suggestion for how an assessment of the productivity of selected departments can be organized, including an indication of the financial and non-financial measures that can be used.

4. Discuss the methods used by Airport Complex for budgeting revenue and costs and give reasoned suggestions for improvements.

# CASE 6
# FOSTERS CONSTRUCTION LTD

## Deryl Northcott, University of Manchester

Permission to reprint this case study has been granted by Captus Press Inc. and the Accounting Education Resource Centre of the University of Lethbridge.

### Foster's Construction Ltd: Organizational background

Fosters Construction Ltd (FCL) is a privately owned company with revenue of £20 million per annum, and 200 employees. The company has been operating for 24 years and is well established in the market-place. However, despite a national inflation rate of 4 per cent per annum over the last few years (which is expected to continue), a general economic downturn has seen FCL's nominal revenue reduce at a rate of about 3 per cent per annum.

The company's main activity is the construction of large industrial buildings. It also provides maintenance services, mainly for those buildings which it has constructed. FCL has a large investment in construction machinery, and has always kept up with the latest technology in the industry. The company has concentrated on developing a corporate image as an innovative, technologically advanced construction firm, and many of the managers of FCL consider that this corporate image has been a major factor in securing large, competitive contracts in the past.

FCL is subject to corporation tax at 35 per cent, payable twelve months after year end, and a system of 25 per cent writing down allowance on capital assets.

### FCL's formal capital investment system

As investment in construction equipment is central to the operations of FCL, the organization has, over many years, developed a detailed system by which capital investment proposals are considered. The summary sheet in Exhibit 1 is taken from the firm's capital investment procedures manual, and outlines the formal process for capital investment decision-making within FCL.

### The current CI decision: purchase of a replacement crane

The construction site manager (CSM) has recently submitted a CI/12 application for the purchase of a new crane. This new asset would replace an existing crane which is ten years old, and which requires major maintenance in order to meet required safety standards. The CSM had indicated in the January budget-setting round that the firm would need to spend money on maintaining the old crane, but had not at that stage been aware of any replacement options. It had previously been expected that the existing crane would see out its remaining useful life, to be replaced by a more modern crane in five years' time.

The CSM's proposal is to purchase a modern crane (the Auto-Lift II, or 'AL II'). The AL II is technologically more advanced than the firm's existing crane, and is able to lift

**EXHIBIT 1**

*Fosters
Construction
Ltd. Capital
investment
procedures –
summary*

much larger loads. The new crane would cost £345 000, which is considerably more than the original £195 000 cost of the existing crane.

The CSM consulted with the site accountants, and put forward the following information in the CI/12 application:

1. Description: purchase of an AL II crane to replace an existing crane which is in need of major maintenance.

Capital investment (CI) is defined as 'any major expenditure on purchasing, constructing or upgrading capital assets, the benefits from which will accrue over several years'.

1. In early January of each year the CI budget is determined. The total amount of available funds for CI expenditure is determined by the directors, based on what they consider the company can afford.

2. Later that month, divisional managers meet to discuss forthcoming CI requirements, and the budget is allocated across divisions. Managers must present their proposed CI requirements under the following three headings:

    (i) essential replacement of existing assets (Class 1);

    (ii) strategic expansion (Class 2);

    (iii) safety and regulatory expenditure (Class 3).

    The final allocation across divisions is a decision taken jointly by the CEO and the director of CI.

3. Throughout the year, access to funds for investment requires the submission of a standard form CI/12 – Capital Expenditure Application. The information normally required with such a submission includes:

    (i) a description of the proposed investment;

    (ii) motivation for the investment, i.e. what will the investment achieve for the company;

    (iii) financial projections of the cost of the investment;

    (iv) projected future financial benefits of the investment;

    (v) key success indicators for the investment (used for assessing the riskiness of the project and for subsequent post audit);

    (vi) a projected time-scale for completion of the investment.
    However, proposed Class 3 projects may dispense with items (iv) and (v), and those in Class 1 may dispense with items (ii), (iv) and (v).

4. The CI/12 form is assessed by the director of CI, who has the following options:

    (i) accept the proposal and forward it to the CEO for financing approval;

    (ii) refer the proposal back for further refinement;

    (iii) reject the proposal.
    CI proposals will be assessed with regard as the net present value (NPV) and payback period (PP) of the proposed project, although Class I projects will be considered as 'cost minimization exercises', since there

is already an accepted need to continue with current operations and assets, and Class 3 projects are not required to meet financial criteria.

5.  All CI projects are assessed within a ten-year planning horizon, i.e. investment effects beyond this ten-year horizon are considered uncertain, and are ignored.

6.  If approved, a CI proposal is then allocated funds from the annual budget. A project supervisor is then assigned, and this person is responsible for the implementation and reporting of the CI project.

7.  In due course, some selected CI projects will be subject to post audit by the director of CI.

2.  Cost projections: purchase price = £345 000; annual running costs = £60 000. It is expected that the AL II crane would have a £30 000 scrap value at the end of its useful life in ten years' time.

3.  Projected time-scale: available for purchase from Allied Importers Ltd in one month's time. Purchase price payable on 31 March – the last day of FCL's financial year for taxation purposes.

The site accountants and the CSM had agreed that no further information was necessary, as the CI proposal qualified as a 'replacement of existing asset' Class I investment.

The CSM's CI/12 application has now been considered by the director of CI, who feels uneasy about recommending the AL II crane purchase for funding approval. The director of CI has called a meeting of concerned parties to discuss the CI application.

## The meeting participants

The following people are present at the meeting to discuss the AL II purchase proposal:

- *Sonya Carson (SC)* Director of CI. Sonya is new to this position, and is familiarizing herself with the technical nature of the firm's operations. She has an undergraduate economics degree and is considered competent, if perhaps a little over-ambitious. However, many longer-serving organizational members doubt Sonya's ability to make good decisions regarding investment in an industry about which she currently knows little. For this reason, her appointment to the position of director of CI was controversial.

- *Julian Done (JD)* Construction site manager. Julian has worked in the construction industry for 15 years, progressing through the ranks to become CSM two years ago. He is considered to be competent in his job, but is perceived as uncompromising and confrontational. Julian has no time for 'the head office bosses', and his outspoken manner at meetings has often met with disapproval from the CEO.

- *Franc Silvero (FS)* CEO of Foster's Construction Ltd. Franc came to FCL seven years ago when the construction industry was in a boom period. He received much accolade for record sales levels when he first joined the firm as contracts director, and so has continued to implement the policies which had met with success in the past. Franc is now perceived as conservative, and often resists movement towards new areas of business operations. He has a construction background, and sometimes feels uncomfortable with his new managerial role as CEO.

- *Henry Morton (HM)* Engineering manager. Henry has an engineering degree and has worked in the trade for eight years, joining FCL three years ago. Henry is often called on to give advice on the technical and operating implications of capital asset purchases, as well as their probable maintenance costs. Henry keeps up-to-date on innovation and new technology in the construction industry, and his opinion is well respected. However, Henry has in the past been frustrated in several attempts to introduce advanced technology into FCL's construction equipment, and blames this on the conservative approach of Franc Silvero.

## The meeting

The meeting called by Sonya turned out to be lengthy and lively. There was considerable debate, and the following excerpt reflects the main comments raised by the participants.

**SC:** Look Julian, there just isn't enough information here. I have to be able to work out the new crane's NPV and payback period. In the past, if projects haven't had a positive NPV at a required rate of return of 26 per cent, and paid back within five years. then they haven't been approved. Do we know anything about the financial benefits which the AL II might produce? What advantage is there in buying this thing now? Couldn't we just let our old crane run its course and consider our options once it reaches the end of its useful life in a few years' time?

**FS:** Yes, I think we need to look more closely at the details here. Julian, what do you think the outlook is if we stay with the old crane?

**JD:** The old crane really needs some maintenance work done on it, to bring it up to safety standards, If we spent about £40 000 on maintenance straight away it should be OK until it goes out of commission in five years' time.

**FS:** What does it cost us to run the old crane?

**JD:** Running costs are around £40 000 per annum. Plus, the crane's getting unreliable. I reckon there's about a 50 per cent chance that it will break down at some time during the year. If it does we lose three days' productivity on a job at a cost of around £15 000, not to mention the cost of fixing it, which was £10 000 last time. Even once it's fixed there's still a 50 per cent chance it could break down again within the next twelve months.

**FS**: OK. What if we go for the AL II?

**JD:** The running costs would be a bit higher, as it's a finely tuned machine and needs regular maintenance. I reckon we're looking at about £60 000 a year, judging by the recommended service programme. But, at least it's not likely to break down. Also, I'm sure the AL II would improve our chances of winning contracts – it's faster and it will help keep costs down. Take for example that Storex contract we missed out on last month. The kind of cost savings we could get with the AL II could have won us that bid, and jobs like that are worth around £40 000 in pre-tax profit to FCL. We could pick up a couple more like that one each year – maybe more.

**FS:** How would you rate the chances of picking up more work with the AL II?

**JD:** Well, probably about a 60 per cent chance that we'd get another two like the Storex job each year, and perhaps about a 20 per cent chance of doubling that. It's hard to say really, but the customers out there are feeling the pinch – we've got to watch our cost competitiveness if we want to stay in the game.

**HM:** That's a key point here, I think. We've got to take a long-term view. The way I read it, these AL II cranes will take over the market in the next two years, and by the time we came to replace our old crane five years from now, we'd be looking at buying an AL II anyway. The question is, do we get in on the new technology now, or in five years' time?

We really can't assume that the status quo will continue if we don't go for the AL II now. We're looking at a fall in price competitiveness, company image and profits if we don't move with the times. If we *do* go with the AL II now, we've got an edge over our competitors. Even then, we wouldn't want to hang on to the AL II for more than ten years – we need to keep upgrading to keep ahead of the game.

**JD:**  I can't see what the problem is with these numbers Sonya has to crunch. It's only an asset replacement, and I've given you all of the information the manual says you need. Besides, I told everyone in January that we'd need to spend some money on the crane, so we all knew this was coming.

**FS:**  That's true, Julian, but we're talking £345 000 now, whereas we only expected to spend £40 000 on maintenance. I'm not at all sure that we want to get into experimental technology anyway, it seems pretty risky. What's wrong with maintaining the old crane, as planned? It's still got five years left in it, and they're pretty hard to sell second-hand. It's in our books at £10 981 after accumulated WDAs. We'd probably only get about £20 000 for it if we went to sell it, which isn't much more than the £5000 scrap value we'd get for it in five years' time.

**SC:**  Julian, perhaps you, Henry and I can sit down and draw up the figures, including the cost and benefit information you've mentioned today. Then I can run the numbers and see if it meets our investment criteria.

There's just a couple of things that bother me, though. It doesn't seem right to use the same required rate of return for every project. We should be using different rates for different types of projects. I've been playing around with a few numbers, and it seems to me that 26 per cent is too high. It might be OK for risky projects that are something new to us, but here we're talking about a crane. That's run-of-the-mill stuff for FCL, and it seems to me that a 21 per cent nominal required return would be more appropriate.

Also, looking at past records of CI analyses, it looks like the 26 per cent rate has been used as a *real* discount rate, when it is actually calculated to represent a nominal rate. We really need to do some inflation adjustments to the rates we're using.

**JD:**  This is all gobbledegook to me. Perhaps *that's* the problem here – we're so tied up in the numbers that we can't see a good investment when it hits us in the face!

**FS:**  We have to be sure that any investment is financially viable, Julian. Sonya, why don't you run the numbers both ways: the way we have in the past, and again using a rate you think is appropriate. I'd be interested in seeing what difference it makes, although there's never been a shortage of projects in the past that have made the 26 per cent grade. I hope you wouldn't be cutting it too fine using a rate like 21 per cent. It doesn't seem to leave much margin for error if our project estimates turn out to be wrong.

**SC:**  I'll run the numbers, but the best way of dealing with margins for error is by getting things right in the first place. There's still a lot of uncertainty an this project. All we've got so far are 'feelings' and estimates – do you think we can firm up those figures at all?

**JD:**  No. There just isn't any other information. Look, I've been in this industry since before you finished school – I've learnt enough to know what's what. I can tell you now that sooner or later we'll need a new crane to be able to do our jobs, and doing our jobs is what makes money for this company!

**FS:** OK, Julian, no one's doubting your judgement. Sonya, how about doing what you suggested, and sitting down with Henry and Julian They should be able to give you the technical information, and you can work through the numbers. I'd like to see the IRR too – I've never been able to understand why we don't calculate IRR. I know a lot of other firms that do.

**HM:** Maybe we could think about changing the CI procedures manual too. That way, the technical people will know exactly what information the director of CI needs, and things can be settled faster.

**SC:** Fine, that's a good idea. Look, I know we haven't resolved this, but thanks for coming to this meeting. Perhaps we can all get together again in a week's time to make a decision.

## Discussion questions

1. Present the financial analyses required by FCL's CI procedures manual, as they have traditionally been calculated. Explain any assumptions you make. According to FCL's usual decision criteria, would the AL II be purchased now?

2. Explain to JD the difference between real and nominal RRRs, as mentioned by SC. What adjustment to SC's suggested RRR would be needed in order to match the discount rate with the cashflows used?

3. Re-calculate the NPV of the AL II purchase proposal, using what Sonya Carson would consider to be an appropriate RRR. Do these revised NPV results suggest that the AL II should be purchased?

4. In the light of your calculations for the AL II purchase proposal, what would be your response to FS's comment that the IRR of projects should be calculated?

5. What do you think might be the key variables in the AL II investment which will affect its viability? How might you consider these uncertain variables in better assessing the proposal?

6. What further information would be useful in analysing the AL II proposal?

7. Identify any problems that you see regarding the following:

   (a) the current CI procedures manual (as outlined in the summary)

   (b) communication and consultation between the people involved in, and affected by, the CI decision.

8. Do you consider that it would be wise to conduct a post audit if this asset were purchased, to see if it is achieving the expected benefits? If so, how might you use the findings of such a post audit?

9. Suggest changes to FCL's CI procedures which might improve future CI decision-making.

# CASE 7
## SHERIDAN CARPET COMPANY

### Professor James S. Reece (University of Michigan)

This case is reprinted from *Accounting: Text and Cases*, Anthony and Reece, 7th edition, 1983 and *Cases in Cost Management*, Shank J.K., 1996, South Western Publishing

<table>
<tr><td>

**EXHIBIT 1**

*Carpet 104: Prices and production, 1998–2000*

</td><td>

Company, by permission of Professor James S. Reece. The case was originally set in the 1980's.

Sheridan Carpet Company produced high-grade carpeting materials for use in automobiles and recreational vans. Sheridan's products were sold to finishers, who cut and bound the material so as to fit perfectly in the passenger compartment or cargo area (e.g. automobile trunk) of a specific model of automobile or van. Some

</td></tr>
</table>

| Selling Season* | Production volume (square yards) | | Price (per square yard) | |
| --- | --- | --- | --- | --- |
| | Industry total | Sheridan Carpet | Most competitors | Sheridan carpet |
| 1998-1 | 549 000 | 192 000 | $5.20 | $5.20 |
| 1998-2 | 517 500 | 181 000 | 5.20 | 5.20 |
| 1999-1 | 387 000 | 135 500 | 3.90 | 3.90 |
| 1999-2 | 427 500 | 149 500 | 3.90 | 3.90 |
| 2000-1 | 450 000 | 135 000 | 3.90 | 5.20 |
| 2000-2 | 562 500 | 112 500 | 3.90 | 5.20 |

*199x-1 means the first 6 months of 199x; 199x-2 means the second six months of 199x.

of these finishers were captive operations of major automobile assembly divisions, particularly those that assembled the 'top of the line' cars that included high-grade carpeting. Other finishers concentrated on the replacement and van customizing markets.

Late in 2000, the marketing manager and chief accountant of Sheridan met to decide on the list price for carpet number 104. It was industry practice to announce prices just prior to the January–June and July–December 'seasons'. Over the years, companies in the industry had adhered to their announced prices throughout a six-month season unless significant unexpected changes in costs occurred. Sales of carpet 104 were not affected by seasonal factors during the two six-month seasons.

Sheridan was the largest company in its segment of the automobile carpet industry. Its 1999 sales had been over $40 million. Sheridan's salespersons were on a salary basis, and each one sold the entire product line. Most of Sheridan's competitors were smaller than Sheridan. Accordingly, they usually awaited Sheridan's price announcement before setting their own selling prices.

Carpet 104 had an especially dense nap. As a result, making it required a special machine, and it was produced in a department whose equipment could not be used to produce Sheridan's other carpets. Effective 1 January 2000, Sheridan had raised its price on this carpet from $3.90 to $5.20 per square yard. This had been done in order to bring 104's margin up to that of the other carpets in the line. Although Sheridan was financially sound, it expected a large funds need in the next few years for equipment replacement and plant expansion. The 2000 price increase was one of several decisions made in order to provide funds for these plans.

Sheridan's competitors, however, had held their 2000 prices at $3.90 on carpets competitive with 104. As shown in Exhibit 1, which includes estimates of industry volume on these carpets, Sheridan's price increase had apparently resulted in a loss of market share. The marketing manager, Mel Walters, estimated that the industry would sell about 630 000 square yards of these carpets in the first half of 2001. Walters was sure Sheridan could sell 150 000 yards if it dropped the price of 104 back to $3.90. But if Sheridan held its price at $5.20, Walters feared a further erosion in Sheridan's share.

**EXHIBIT 2**

*Estimated cost of carpet 104 at various production volumes. First six months of 2001*

However, because some customers felt that 104 was superior to competitive products, Walters felt that Sheridan could sell at least 65 000 yards at the $5.20

During their discussion, Walters and the chief accountant, Terry Rosen, identified two other aspects of the pricing decision. Rosen wondered whether competitors would announce a further price decrease if Sheridan dropped back to $3.90. Walters felt it was unlikely that competitors would price below $3.90, because none of them was more efficient than Sheridan, and there were rumours that several of them were in poor financial condition. Rosen's other concern was whether a decision relating to carpet 104 would

| | Volume (square yards) | | | | | |
|---|---|---|---|---|---|---|
| Costs/sq. yd. | 65 000 | 87 500 | 110 000 | 150 000 | 185 000 | 220000 |
| Raw materials | $0.520 | $0.520 | $0.520 | $0.520 | $0.520 | $0.520 |
| Materials spoilage | 0.052 | 0.051 | 0.049 | 0.049 | 0.051 | 0.052 |
| Direct labour | 1.026 | 0.989 | 0.979 | 0.962 | 0.975 | 0.997 |
| | | | | | | |
| Department overhead: | | | | | | |
|   Direct* | 0.142 | 0.136 | 0.131 | 0.130 | 0.130 | 0.130 |
|   Indirect (A) | 1.200 | 0.891 | 0.709 | 0.520 | 0.422 | 0.355 |
| General overhead (B) | 0.308 | 0.297 | 0.294 | 0.289 | 0.293 | 0.299 |
| | | | | | | |
| Factory cost | 3.248 | 2.884 | 2.682 | 2.470 | 2.391 | 2.353 |
| Selling and administrative (C) | 2.111 | 1.875 | 1.743 | 1.606 | 1.554 | 1.529 |
| | | | | | | |
| Total cost | $5.359 | $4.759 | $4.425 | $4.076 | $3.945 | $3.882 |

\* Materiais handlers, supplies, repairs, power, fringe benefits.
(A) Supervision, equipment depreciation, heat and light.
(B) 30 per cent of direct labour.
(C) 65 per cent of factory cost.

have any impact on the sales of Sheridan's other carpets. Walters was convinced that since 104 was a specialized item, there was no interdependence between its sales and those of other carpets in the line.

Exhibit 2 contains cost estimates that Rosen has prepared for various volumes of 104. These estimates represented Rosen's best guesses as to costs during the first six months of 2001, based on past cost experience and anticipated inflation.

## Questions

1. Assuming no intermediate prices are to be considered, should Sheridan price 104 at $3.90 or $5.20?

2. If Sheridan's competitors hold their prices at $3.90, how many square yards of 104 would Sheridan need to sell at a price of $5.20 in order to earn the same profit as selling 150 000 square yards at a price of $3.90?

3. What additional information would you wish to have before making this pricing decision? (Despite the absence of this information, still answer Question 1!)

4. With hindsight, was the decision to raise the price in January of 2000 a good one?

# CASE 8
# MESTRAL

## Robin Roslender, University of Stirling

## The company

Mestral is a highly successful company manufacturing a range of quality bathroom fittings. For the past 15 years production has been carried out at three locations: at Northern town in the North East of England; at Western town on the Severn estuary; and at Newtown, thirty miles outside of London. Each plant is of more or less equal size, and equipped with the same technology. The similarity between Mestral's three operations does not end here. As a result of a policy decision made many years ago, each plant also produces the same range of products. As well as providing a measure of cost savings in terms of supplying different UK markets, this arrangement has provided a basis for a measure of healthy interplant competition, to the benefit of both customers and company.

A hybrid organization structure has evolved in the company. Each of the three plants is managed by a General Manager who is a member of the Mestral board, and who reports to the Managing Director. At each plant there is a Human Resources Manager, a Plant Manager, an Operations Manager and, more recently a Quality Manager. All four report to their respective General Managers. The company's head office is located at the Western site. A further three management functions are based here: finance; marketing; and information and communications, each headed by a director to whom the relevant plant level heads report. The Director of Corporate Affairs is also based here, and holds the position of Assistant Managing Director. There are three non-executive directors on Mestral's board, one of whom acts as the company Chairman, while a second is the Director of Western Business School.

For many years Mestral has sought, with some success, to create a flexible management team. Management trainees have a wide range of academic backgrounds. Their training is structured in order to allow them to gain experience across the whole range of functions and in all three plants. In most cases trainees identify in which particular function they wish to pursue the next stage of their management development. The company is very supportive of studying for professional qualifications, and in due course pursuing an MBA or similar management qualification. In exchange, the company expects that managers will remain geographically mobile into their mid-30s. Consequently, most of the company's senior managers have a wide-ranging experience of Mestral's activities. For example, the General Manager at Newtown was previously Human Resources Manager at the Northern town site whilst his counterpart at Northern town had served as both the company's Director of Information and Communications at headquarters, and as an Operations Manager at the Newtown plant.

The company is non-unionized. A strong staff association has evolved in the past decade, receiving both significant organizational and financial support from the company. Industrial relations have been excellent for the past fifteen years, during which time earnings have been relatively high partly as a consequence of the operation of a company-wide annual profit related bonus system. There has never been any history of lay-offs, short-time working or redundancies, nor has the size of the workforce increased since the mid-1980s. Such is the reputation of the company that a growing proportion of the current workforce has secured employment with the assistance of longer serving family and friends. Despite this, a section of Mestral's management is concerned that recent improvements in the labour market in some parts of the country may eventually be to the detriment of the company.

## *The problem*

Mestral is currently in need of a major refurbishment of its manufacturing equipment for two reasons. First, its existing machinery is now coming to the end of its useful economic life in each of its plants and requires replacement. Second, a new generation of technology, one capable of delivering a much higher level of quality across the industry, is imminently available. One of the reasons why the company has not invested in new technology earlier has been that, like most of its competitors, it has been awaiting this new generation of machinery. Funds for purchasing the new equipment are readily available within the company. Indeed Mestral has been rather too cash rich in the past couple of years, and the board has been increasingly concerned that its healthy balance sheet might attract unwanted attention from predators.

As well as promising a significantly increased quality of product, the new technology also promises to increase productivity by almost 50 per cent. This is not welcome news for the company because it means that one of its plants will inevitably have to close to take the maximum benefit from the proposed refurbishment programme. Because Mestral has been so successful in its market place, there seems little or no opportunity to grow the business to match the increased capacity that three refurbished plants would provide. It is possible that competitors who buy the new technology might soon be able to match the impressive product quality levels that Mestral has achieved in recent years. While price may not be of paramount importance in the case of the company's product range, it would be commercially naive to contemplate operating the three plants at reduced capacity in the short to medium term while searching for an alternative long-term use of the excess capacity. At best it might be possible to identify which of the three plants will be the least profitable after introducing the new machinery, then explore the case for producing a different product range at this location.

## *Board meetings*

It is usual for Mestral's board to meet on the third Wednesday of each month to discuss the previous month's performance, and how this impacts current and future operations. Strategic matters are considered in the second half of the meeting, following a short break for tea and biscuits. Custom and practice is that the latter matters and associated papers are not provided to board members in advance of the meeting, necessitating a measure of brain-storming among those in attendance. The opportunity to contribute more reasoned thoughts is afforded by means of a restricted access website, an arrangement that also has the benefit of promoting strategy formulation by communication, cooperation and consent.

At the November board meeting the Finance Director is to present the findings of an analysis of the relative profitability of the company's three plants, both currently and following the introduction of the new technology. In the light of this, he will also outline the options that appear to be available to the company.

## *The meeting*

Following the customary break for tea and biscuits, the Chair called the meeting to order. He indicated that there was only one item for discussion on this occasion, the future pattern of operations following the imminent investment in manufacturing technology by the company. The Finance Director was then invited to make an opening presentation.

The Finance Director began with the announcement that the company had finally identified the supplier of its much-needed new equipment. He thanked colleagues for their participation in what had been a lengthy process of evaluation, and expressed confidence in the company's choice of supplier. Funding the new investment remained unproblematic. In truth, he added, it has been more of a problem to have concealed the fact that we are able to contemplate such a massive outlay of funds from competitors and potential predators.

After a brief pause the Finance Director continued by revealing that there was a serious downside to the proposed refurbishment. Because the company had been largely concerned with identifying a supplier that would offer machinery capable of improving the quality of its product range, and to do so in a cost effective way, very little attention had been paid to the question of productivity. The new technology promises to increase productivity by almost 50 per cent. Normally this would be regarded as a positive situation but not in this case. The Marketing Director has identified that it is unlikely that the company can increase its market share in the short to medium term. While prices might hold up, there is a reasonable chance that those competitors who might also make similar investments in technology may be successful in challenging the company's market share. On this basis it would be commercial suicide to re-equip all three plants with the new technology. One plant has to close.

In order to identify which plant is to be closed, the finance group at headquarters has found itself involved in a novel set of investigations: determining the relative profitability of the three plants before and after the introduction of the new machinery. All three plants have been profitable for many years, generating healthy cash flows. Market share has been rising, aided partly by the flexibility afforded by the decision to continue a policy of undifferentiated production at three locations. The investment in a quality programme has added significantly to the health of the business. Taken together, all of these indicators of commercial health have obscured the possibility that old-fashioned profitability might have become a problem of late.

There was now an increasing sense of unease around the table, particularly among the three General Managers.

The Financial Director continued. All three plants remain profitable. Two continue to produce almost identical results, but there is clear blue water between them and the third site.

At this point the Managing Director, in a well-rehearsed manoeuvre, intervened to name the unfortunate location. The least profitable plant was that at Northern town. On all the evidence currently available to those who had been involved in these investigations, the long awaited move to the new technology seemed likely to see an end of company operations at Northern town. The Managing Director invited Northern's General Manager for his reaction to this shock revelation.

He began by observing that he had only returned to Northern town 18 months previously. As a local, this was the place at which he started his career with Mestral, a career that had seen him spending time in the other two plants, as well as at a fourth plant some 20 years ago. Most recently he had been the Director of Information and Communications at headquarters, a post he had occupied for a number of years following his return from his MBA studies at Harvard Business School. He had hoped to end his time with Mestral at the Northern town plant, but not like this. It was ironic that in its attempts to keep abreast of contemporary developments in management accounting, sight had been lost of the need to monitor profit levels. He felt particularly for his workforce. It had consistently demonstrated its loyalty to the company. Of course the great majority would cope with the closure, if that was the reality for them. People in this region have had to get used to coping with such shocks.

At this point Newtown's General Manager intervened. He began by suggesting that his colleague was painting a rather romantic picture of commitment at the plant. Equally, things weren't so bad job-wise nowadays. There was plenty of investment funding available, which possibly had something to do with the number of local MPs who now found themselves sitting round the Cabinet table. He and his family had certainly enjoyed themselves there. They know how to have a good time, and don't let very much get in the way of this. He felt that it was important that members recalled what they had all learned in their various accounting courses, namely that you can't argue with hard accounting numbers. Indeed they come no harder than profit measures, and it was unhelpful to suddenly begin to worry about the hard outcomes that might ensue.

Western town's General Manager was then invited to offer his thoughts. He began by saying that he felt a little uncomfortable. He too had greatly enjoyed his time in Northern town but wondered whether his colleague from Newtown had actually worked with the same people as he himself had. He continued by observing that the numbers look compelling enough, and that he was sure that colleagues in finance and marketing had worked them every way possible. Reluctantly he had to conclude that they conveyed a truth that must be faced. This said, were there any other possibilities, had the accounting people looked at alternative scenarios?

The Director of Corporate Affairs responded first. One solution was to try to dispose of the Northern town operation. It was a profitable venture, although there was clearly a problem of over capacity across this segment of the market given the potential afforded by the newly available technology. This was not the ideal time to try to sell even a profitable business unit with a loyal workforce and an enviable commitment to customer satisfaction.

One the other hand, interjected the Managing Director, there is always the option of trying something new at the Northern town site. If we are able to continue to satisfy demand from two plants, and if we can successfully segment our markets, then the company might be able to switch its production to a different product range. He continued by observing that this might prove to be an expensive venture. There would still need to be significant investment in machinery, as well as in marketing. Additionally it was difficult to estimate how much it might cost to move down market given that forgetting, like learning, could never be a costless process. In his view, pursuing such a diversification strategy could prove disastrous. If it was unsuccessful, it would inevitably mean that the company as a whole would have to bear significant losses, and then, in the last analysis, still be in a position of having to make redundancy payments.

Northern's General Manager replied that he was confident that his workforce would readily respond to such an opportunity, and that it would quickly become a profitable operation. He added that nobody could deny that they had earned the chance to show what they could do for the company in the coming years. His final observation had a certain logic to it. It was not as if Northern town's plant had contributed a succession of losses to the company, so why should it begin to now?

Newtown's General Manager was not persuaded. His case was simple. First, Mestral had not considered diversifying for the past decade. Second, the company was now entering a period of uncertainty, which was not a time for contemplating change on many fronts. Third, while agreeing that the Northern town plant had contributed a stream of profits, this could be wiped out very quickly if the proposed diversification venture failed. Finally, it was unreasonable to expect the other two General Managers to feel fully motivated knowing that there was a reasonable chance that their profits were to be used to shore up an already less profitable operation. In other words: hard numbers, hard choices, hard outcomes.

While all of this was happening, the Managing Director's secretary knocked and entered the room. She approached the Chairman and discreetly placed a short note in front of him. When the Newtown General Manager ended his contribution, the Chairman brought the proceedings to an abrupt halt. He asked the three General Managers to leave the room, together with the Marketing and Information and Communications Directors. After a brief discussion involving the six remaining directors, they were invited back only to be informed that the meeting was now adjourned, and that they would receive further information tomorrow morning.

Somewhat perplexed, they left to make their ways home.

## The message

At ten o'clock promptly, every board member received a short message from the Chairman. For whatever reason, the information on relative profitability provided to members was incorrect. It was the Newtown plant that was less profitable than the Western and Northern town plants. The figures were correct, it was the files that had been mixed up. Consequently, members were now requested to attend a continuation of the previous meeting on Wednesday next at 1.30 pm.

The Newtown General Manager was devastated by this news. Having convinced himself that the Finance Director's people couldn't possibly have got it wrong again, he summoned his most senior managers to an emergency meeting. Now that it was their plant that was to be the focus of attention, it was vital that they were able to construct a business plan that would be sufficiently convincing for the board to allocate the necessary funds to pursue it. Everyone with any accounting knowledge was drafted in to this working party. When they got down to it, it soon became apparent that there were plenty of opportunities to make savings in operating the plant. This didn't unduly encourage the General Manager as he was sure that much the same was probably likely across the company, an issue for the future. The immediate problem was to assemble a watertight case for supporting what he had only recently identified as an unnecessary set of financial risks. And by 9.00 pm the following Tuesday evening, he was convinced that his operation had a viable future.

## The settlement

As he entered the head office building, the Newtown General Manager noticed that there was a small group of people sitting quietly in one of the meeting rooms. He thought he recognized one of them as a financial journalist, but couldn't be sure. When he got to the boardroom he found that he was the first member to arrive. He had slept well the previous night, the drive down from Newtown had gone well, and he now had plenty of time to look through his papers. A positive outcome was surely on the cards!

At 1.30 pm the Chairman opened the meeting, thanking colleagues for their understanding and patience since their last meeting. He had two announcements to make before members continued their unfinished discussions of Wednesday last. First, he was delighted to be able to tell members that John Fotherglen, the General Manager at Northern town plant had accepted the post of Director of the Northern University Business School. Second, a firm offer had been received to purchase the Northern plant from the company. The buyer had assured the Managing Director and himself that all jobs at Northern were safe, and that in fact it was the plant's workforce that was the principal attraction to them. Consequently there was now no necessity to discuss closures or diversification any further. The difficulties in installing an effective system of cost management at the Newtown plant, in the first instance, was their new priority.

The meeting didn't last too long. The Chairman closed the meeting by tabling a press release. He indicated that it contained no reference to their recent administrative blunder. Nevertheless, he warned members to be careful when talking to the press after the meeting. In times of rapid change, the market situation of even the strongest players can easily be undermined. It is important to put the most positive spin possible on the disposal of the Northern plant.

On leaving the meeting, the Newtown General Manager was cornered by the familiar face he had noticed before the meeting. He was asked about the substance of rumours that the sale of the Northern town business had extracted him from a very difficult situation. He couldn't resist offering the following response: nobody could surely believe that it was a realistic option to close down an operation in his part of the world ...

## Questions

1.  Identify and discuss the various ways in which accounting information is enrolled by the members of Mestral's board.

2.  Outline the way in which the Newtown General Manager might have presented his case to the board, in the event that no buyer had emerged for the Northern plant. In terms of the theory introduced in the chapter, how might his modified stance be described?

3.  Consider the value of a continuum approach in understanding the various roles or purposes that accounting can have for different organizational participants.

4.  Burchell *et al.* (1980) observe that: 'Accounting, it would appear, is made to be purposive rather than being inherently purposeful.' (p. 13). In what ways is this borne out in the Mestral case?

# CASE 9
# DANFOSS DRIVES

## Dan Otzen, Copenhagen Business School

This case was prepared as the basis for discussion rather then to illustrate either effective or ineffective handling of an administrative situation.

Danfoss Drives A/S is a Danish producer of frequency converters located in Graasten in the southern part of the country. The company belongs to the Danfoss Group, one of the largest Danish industrial groups, but since the production of frequency converters is quite distinct from the activities of the other divisions in the group, Danfoss Drives operates as an individual company in all respects, apart from matters of financing.

The financial backing has, however, played an important role in the development of Danfoss Drives. The production of frequency converters was initiated 25 years ago, and since then Danfoss Drives has managed to achieve a position as one of the key players in the market. Today the company has an annual turnover in excess of 1 billion Danish Kroner, and more than 750 employees. As a symbol of its key position in the market, the Danfoss Drives frequency converter trademark; a VLT® has become the standard term for frequency converters used within the industry. Achieving this market position has been possible due to the commitment and financial ability of the group to support a growth strategy based on a high level of investment.

## Products and customers

A VLT® can, basically, be described as an instrument that converts electrical power in standard frequency and voltage to the frequency and voltage required by electrical motors for solving specific tasks. To illustrate, VLT® are used in brewery assembly lines to control the speed of the conveyor belts. Based on signals from the workers controlling the production process or transmitted automatically from the production system, the VLT® will adjust the speed and torque of the electrical motor accordingly. Consequently, a constant speed of the conveyor belts can be achieved at varying levels of production volume.

The VLT®s produced by Danfoss Drives can be differentiated according to the kW-range, the range of possible signals and responses, and the language and display options of the product. The largest VLT®s are capable of controlling electrical motors of up to 500 kW, i.e. as used to drive pumps in water utilities, the smallest products can handle motors with power output down to 0.37 kW. A result of the wide range of possible product specifications, has been a correspondingly large number of different VLT®s offered and produced for the market. At present, the product catalogue consists of five product families: AL, AS, B, C and D,[1] with a total of more than 5000 different product numbers. The Danfoss Drives homepage at www.danfossdrives.com provides a more comprehensive description of the VLT®-products and their range of application.

Corresponding with the range of possible applications, the VLT®s are sold to a large and diverse group of customers within the industrial market. The customers are either companies, who use the VLT® as a part of their own production system, or production system manufacturers, who integrate the VLT® as part of a total production system offered in the market. Usually, the industrial market is attributed with a set of distinct character-istics with regards to buyer behaviour. Buyers are assumed to be informed and display a relatively more rational behaviour than buyers in the consumer market. The experience of Danfoss Drives serves to moderate this view. Often, the buyers are not aware of the whole range of possible solutions, that the VLT®s offer to the problems in the production process. Further, the decision to purchase a VLT® is an integral element in an elaborate and time consuming decision related to the construction of a new production system. This is, however, not reflected in the required time for delivery. Danfoss Drives are 'the last to know', and the decision to execute the procurement of the VLT® is made in close connection with the time it is to be used. Consequently, a short delivery time is a critical success factor. This also applies to the replacement market, since the VLT® is often a critical component in a combined production system, a factor, which also makes quality a key product characteristic.

## Suppliers and competitors

The key components used in the production of a VLT® can be divided into mechanical and electrical parts. The mechanical parts are primarily cooling fans, connectors, LED-displays, keyboards and a cabinet, providing the protection of the VLT® from the often quite 'hostile' production environment in terms of, for example, temperature, humidity and dust, in which it is to be used. When in use, the VLT will develop a substantial amount of heat, and for this reason the cooling properties of the cabinet are also an important part of the product design related to the mechanical components. The electrical parts are printed circuit boards and electrical components such as resistors, capacitors and CPUs. The electrical components may be further divided into low- and high-voltage components. The key element in a VLT® is the power card, a printed circuit board mounted with high-voltage components, through which the frequency and voltage conversion process takes place. The interaction between the VLT® and the environment (through the controlling signals received) and the surveillance and programming of the VLT® (through the display and keyboards on the product) are handled by control cards and display cards respectively, consisting of low-voltage components.

The distinction between high- and low-voltage components is reflected in the markets for supplies faced by Danfoss Drives. The number of customers for high-voltage components worldwide is fairly limited. Apart from the VLT® producers, high-voltage components are used in the production of, for example, control systems in power utilities, televisions and computer monitors. Given the dominant position within the VLT® market, this provides Danfoss Drives with a strong bargaining position *vis-à-vis* its suppliers – had it not been for the fact that the suppliers of high-voltage components belong to industrial groups to whom the main competitors within the VLT® market also belong. Although the

---

[1] The real product names as mentioned on the Danfoss Drives homepage are different from the ones used in this presentation. The use of these five product names serves only as means of simplifying the presentation.

Danfoss Group is large by Danish standards, it is dwarfed by industrial groups such as Siemens, ABB and Mitsubishi.

The market for low-voltage components is quite distinct from the high-voltage market. Low-voltage components can, to a large extent, be considered to be a standardized product, almost a commodity in today's market, with a large number of suppliers worldwide. This provides Danfoss Drives with a strong bargaining position *vis-à-vis* these suppliers – had it been a major customer, which it unfortunately is not compared to such buyers as Phillips, Sony, IBM, etc. For both types of electronic components it is important to note, that the delivery time can be quite long, in some cases between six and twelve months.

## JIT production in Danfoss Drives

The original initiative to implement Just In Time (JIT) production in Danfoss Drives was taken by the present Production Manager about 15 years ago. The motive behind the adoption of the zero inventory ideal of the JIT philosophy, was a perceived, and real, need to do something about the growth in inventory at all levels in production, that was taking place. Until then, the group had provided the financial support required to pursue the growth strategy, but pressure was rising for Danfoss Drives to generate positive cash flows in return for the funds invested. The continued growth in inventory was essentially a threat to the sustained support from group management.

The main reasons for the growth in inventory were the combined effect of growth in sales and in the range of products offered. The expansion in the product range is a result of a strategic decision to focus on close relations with customers, as a means of differentiating Danfoss Drives in the VLT® market. The customers' lack of awareness with regard to the possible solutions provided by the VLT®s, is seen as a potentially important means of establishing a strong relationship with customers. Close co-operation with customers, combined with products adjusted to their specific needs, is therefore a central element in the Danfoss Drives market strategy.

The experience from Danfoss Drives confirms the point made by researchers and managers alike, that implementing JIT is an ever-continuing process. Consequently, Danfoss Drives is characterized as a JIT producer in relative terms, because it pursues the ideals of JIT production – not because it has achieved them in absolute terms. The consequence of an absolute definition will be a situation, where not even the classical example, Toyota, can be classified as a JIT producer.

The most fundamental effect of the implementation of JIT has been that Danfoss Drives only produces to order, and therefore does not hold any inventory of finished goods in the factory at all. To do this and still honour the short delivery time required by the customers, has required a dedicated effort by employees across all the functions of the organization. The focus of this effort has been on a reduction of set-up time, reconfiguration and increased flexibility of the production process, and the pursuit of a strategy of modularization in product development. Trying to understand the financial effect of the JIT-effort, it is interesting to consider the dramatic development displayed in Figure 1. The finished goods in Figure 1 refer to a limited amount of inventory held at local Danfoss sales companies across the world. The implementation of JIT has been a significant contribution to the achievement of a situation, where Danfoss Drives today is considered to be one of the financially most successful and promising divisions within the Danfoss Group.

## Product and production design

The implementation of a strategy focusing on products consisting of modules, is strongly related with the design of the production process, where a flow strategy has played a

**FIGURE 1.** *Development in turnover and inventories.*

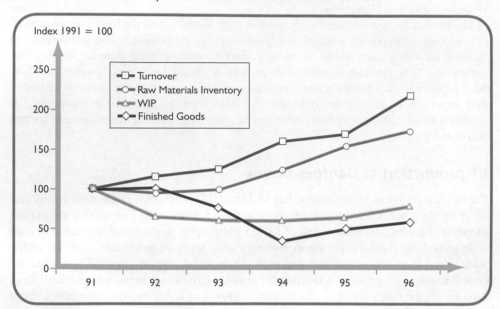

prominent role. Modularization permits Danfoss Drives to carry out a production process, with an increasing degree of product individualization to the requirements of the customer through the production process. A limited number of different power cards are combined with a range of standardized display and control cards, and finally the customer-specific software is included. The overall design of the production process to support this progressive degree of individualization is illustrated in Figure 2.

The initial stage represents the assembly of the printed circuit boards, both low- and high-voltage. At this stage, the production process is carried out in a machine centre, i.e. consisting of identical SMD-machines, with a high degree of automation. For use in this type of machine, the electrical components are kept on large tapes containing several thousand identical components. The tapes are mounted in the machine, which then automatically picks and inserts the individual components according to a programme specific to the individual type of circuit board being produced. The number of tapes which can be mounted in the machines are limited. This has in turn motivated Danfoss Drives to use preferred parts lists in the product design department, to ensure that a full assembly programme can be executed within the same set-up, and to reduce the number of set-ups required between production series.

The assembled circuit boards from the first stage in the production process are kept in racks as work in process. Upon receipt of an actual and confirmed customer order, the appropriate power card will be picked from the rack and mounted on a frame together with additional parts such as fans, coils, etc. The completed frame, a power unit, is the backbone of the product and will be subject to an extensive automated testing programme. As illustrated in Figure 2, the assembly and testing of the power units in the testing racks, represent a significant shift from machine centres to production lines. Production lines and testing racks at this stage are shared by the AL and AS product families and by the C and D families.

The main capacity constraint in this part of the production process is the number of positions in the testing racks. However, this constraint, as with all other possible capacity constraint, has not yet been effective in any systematic way, due to an aggressive investment programme in Danfoss Drives. Based on a philosophy of anticipated continued

**FIGURE 2.** *Overview of the production design in Danfoss Drives.*

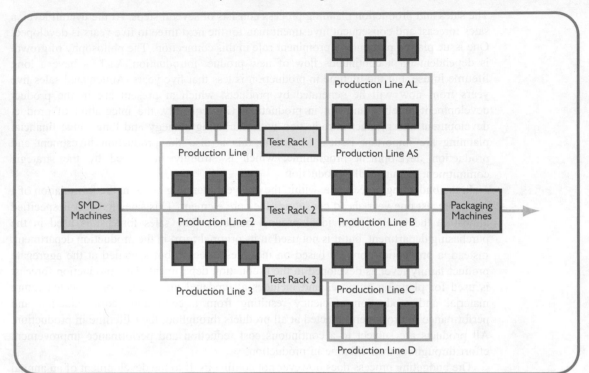

growth, the company has followed an investment programme insuring a consistent level of excess capacity in production. The ability to expand capacity is to a limited extent possible by increasing the number of employees on the production lines. Significant changes in capacity however, can, only be achieved by working extra shifts. The time required for training new employees is, on average, estimated to be three months.

A minor and time-restricted increase in capacity achieved by increasing the number of employees on one production line, does not lead to an increase in the total workforce, because employees are simply shifted from a production line with excess capacity to one with constrained capacity. For this purpose Danfoss Drives has implemented a plant-wide programme of multi-process training of employees. The effort to increase the flexibility of the workforce is further supported by a deliberate effort to include standardized processes with minimum training requirements in all production lines. The company does not distinguish between 'first class' and 'second class' processes. This makes no sense from a remuneration point of view, since all employees participate in a routine programme of process rotation. Using standardized processes is, however, of significant importance in the holiday season, since it enables Danfoss Drives to use seasonal labour, typically students on vacation, with a limited need for training. During this period, the pool of employees not on vacation will be responsible for the complicated processes.

Once the power unit is fully tested and approved, it is transferred to the specific production line of the product family, where the display and control cards are inserted, followed by the inclusion of the specific software, final test, final assembly and packaging. The throughput time of the entire production process is between 8 and 24 hours, which in turn enables Danfoss Drives to fulfil any customer orders within a period of three days.

## Sales and production planning

The sales and production planning process consists of several steps. At the overall level, a sales forecast and consequent investment plan for the next three to five years is developed. One issue plays a particularly prominent role in this connection. The philosophy of growth is dependent on a continuous flow of new product introduction. VLT®s have a long lifetime in use, but the lifetime in production is less that five years. Anticipated sales five years from now will be generated by products, which at present are in the product development pipeline and not in production. Consequently, the integration of product development and product introduction with marketing strategy and long range financial planning are important issues. Linked to this is also the production investment and production development programme, which is strongly influenced by the strategic commitment to pursue JIT production.

In the budgeting process, i.e. within the one year planning horizon, the formulation of a sales forecast one year ahead constitutes the core element. This sales forecast is specified almost to the level of individual product numbers. The sales forecast is used in the purchasing department, but it is not used in its original form in the production department. Instead, a production forecast based on the sales forecast, but specified at the aggregate product family level, is developed in the production department. This production forecast is used for planning purposes and includes all updated information on expected future material and production efficiency resulting from a continuous cost reduction and performance improvement directed at all products throughout their lifetime in production. All products are subject to a continuous cost reduction and performance improvement effort throughout their lifetime in production.

The budgeting process does however not confine itself to the development of an annual budget. Every quarter, the sales and production forecasts one year ahead are updated and subject to elaboration, in the form of a production forecast per day in the next quarter, which is communicated to the individual production sub-departments. Additional updating of the forecasts are carried out if required, at both monthly and even weekly intervals. Every Monday morning a production meeting takes place, to follow up on last week's production and decide on adjustments to the production and manning plans of the week just started.

Even though Danfoss Drives has chosen to carry out a wide range of forecasting and planning activities, it is important to keep in mind, that actual production is only initiated on the basis of actual customer orders. Consequently, the sequence in the determination of the production programme for the day, is to compare the updated pool of actual orders with the production capacity available. If the production capacity and stock of power cards, or raw materials for the production of the power cards, are sufficient to fulfil the order, a note of confirmation is sent to the customer, stating the time of delivery. This planning routine is carried out automatically in two systems. The shop-floor system contains the production capacity and production plan data. The SAP-system contains all data on materials. SAP-systems are integrated information systems, consisting of a range of standard planning and recording modules, which can be integrated and customized to cover a wide range of tasks within large companies. The logistics system used by Danfoss Drives to handle the data on materials is thus only a small part of the company wide SAP-system. Further information on SAP- systems can be found at www.SAP.com

Once the customer order has been confirmed, all materials, not just the power cards required for the order, are reserved in the SAP-system and the inventory figures are updated. Simultaneously, the shop-floor system is also updated to include the new order on the production plan. On the factory floor, monitors are placed at all workstations with direct links to the shop-floor system. The customer order directly initiates production of a new VLT® at the workstation placed just after the power card rack. Physically, this is done by automatically updating the production plan on the monitor placed at this workstation.

## Questions

1. What are the possible reasons behind the difference in the development of the raw materials inventory, as compared with the WIP and finished goods inventory?

2. Discuss the possible reasons for Danfoss Drives choosing to implement such an elaborate planning structure, considering that production is only executed on the basis of actual orders?

3. What are the driving factors behind the need to update forecasts at quarterly, monthly and even weekly intervals?

4. What are the possible consequences for sales planning given the aggressive investment strategy?

5. Discuss whether standard costing is reconcilable with the *kaizen* ideal of continuous improvement?

# CASE 10
# BRUNSWICK PLASTICS

### Professor Anthony Atkinson (University of Waterloo) and adapted by Professor John Shank (The Amos Tuck School of Business Administration Dartmouth College)

This case is reprinted from *Cases in Cost Management*, Shank, J.K, 1996, South Western Publishing Company. The case was adapted by Professor John Shank, with permission from the author from an earlier case written by Professor Anthony Atkinson under a grant from the Society of Management Accountants of Canada. The case was originally set in the mid-1980's.

In September of 2000 Michael Smith, Division Manager of Brunswick Plastics, faced an important pricing decision on a major new bid opportunity. Michael knew that pricing too high meant losing a bid that would employ currently unused capacity. On the other hand, pricing too low meant losses on the job. In the first two months after Michael arrived in November of 1998, the presses were running only about 40 per cent of available machine hours. The division had recently lost two large contracts and was struggling to find a solid market position. Michael had instituted a policy of 'contribution margin pricing' to restore profitability. He reasoned that the fixed costs were already in place and there was heavy excess capacity. Any orders that generated positive contribution would enhance bottom line profits. In two years, machine running time was up to almost 50 per cent of available machine hours and the number of different products manufactured was up from 30 to 50.

### The company

In addition to the 50 different products BP was selling, it was also typically experimenting in the factory with a few others at any given time. New product introductions seemed to Michael to be a key step in filling up the factory. Smith's best estimate of sales for 2000 was $1 200 000 and he thought BP would again be just above the break even level on profits. An estimated income statement for 2000 is shown in Exhibit 1. The division had 20 full-time employees. Since the factory was not unionized, factory employment fluctuated monthly, based on demand. Factory employment had ranged between 13 and 31 people in the past $2\frac{1}{2}$ years. Through strict attention to quality control, and by aggressively promoting its products, BP had developed a reputation as a reliable supplier of high quality products. In several markets, BP products were specified by major customers and had become the industry standard for quality.

BP sold its products in both domestic and US markets and faced a highly competitive environment. There were many injection moulding companies in eastern Canada and the northeastern part of the USA. As a result, pricing was a key to success, both from the point of view of securing contracts, and from the point of view of profitability.

Manufacturing at EP was done in two different modes. Some of the high volume products were manufactured to stock in long runs to minimize set-up costs and to maintain required inventory levels. However, for most products, production was in response to a specific order.

## The costing environment

There were five major injection moulding presses in use at BP. The machines were of varying ages and all experienced frequent down-time because of set-ups, raw material problems, regular repairs, and special repairs related to complex products or new product problems. The factory typically operated 2 shifts a day, 5 days a week, but volume fluctuations also led sometimes to one shift or three shift operations. There were four common stages involved in manufacturing a product: (1) set up of the production machine, (2) the production operation, (3) the assembly operation, and (4) the testing operation. The set up, assembly, and testing operations were labour-intensive. The labour content of the production operation varied widely from product to product.

In injection moulding, molten plastic is forced into a mould where it is 'cured'. The curing process requires cooling the mould, usually with water. Once the product has cured, the mould is opened and the product removed.

Some products were produced in stationary moulds that required little manual intervention. Water was passed through these moulds during the curing cycle. At the completion of the curing cycle, the moulds were opened and the products were ejected automatically. For these products, the direct labour content was minimal and the operation was machine-paced.

Other products were produced in removable moulds that required manual intervention. After the plastic was injected, these moulds were removed from the moulding machine and placed into a vat of water for the curing cycle. At the completion of the curing cycle, the moulds were opened manually and the product removed. For these products, the direct labour content could be significant since the operation was labour-paced.

The products also varied widely in terms of the assembly and testing time required. On the one hand, the company manufactured pediatric syringes used in the care of premature infants. These syringes required extensive attention to quality control and a considerable amount of manual assembly in a 'clean room'. On the other hand, the company also manufactured wheel chocks that required only a cursory inspection and no assembly. The other products produced by BP varied between these two extremes.

In addition to the product costing complications caused by the wide mix of manufacturing, assembly/and testing requirements, there were difficulties caused by the machines. Typical of the industry, the machines used at BP differed widely in terms of their reliability and their performance when producing different products. A machine problem meant that the machine would have to be stopped and reset. Because the machine stoppages were highly unpredictable, incorporating a normal or average machine failure cost into the product cost was difficult.

On the other hand, the materials, assembly, and testing costs of most products were well understood since each of these costs could be measured with reasonable accuracy. Materials costs could be estimated by the weight of the final product since the material in most defective products could be reused. The assembly and testing operations involved the use of machines that were both highly reliable and labour-paced.

These difficulties and the costing issues were all on Michael's mind as he considered the milk crate contract.

## The milk crate contract

Dairies in eastern Canada used plastic crates to ship milk cartons from the dairies to the stores. The annual sales volume of milk crates in the local region was about 300 000 units. Dairies merged their orders for crates through the Dairy Council in order to take maximum advantage of possible quantity discounts. Michael had been asked to submit a bid on an initial order of 150 000 units. It was clear in Michael's mind that a successful initial bid would give BP a competitive advantage in future orders.

Michael felt that the successful bid price for these crates would be '$3.00 plus or minus ten cents'. Michael had been approached by the customer several times and felt that BP's reputation for quality would ensure that a $3.00 bid would be successful. As a result, estimating the bid price was not the major issue. The question to be resolved was whether or not, given its cost structure, $3.00 could cover BP's costs of producing this product.

Discussions with Walt Roberts and Larry Bobbit, BP's technical and production supervisors, suggested that the machine cycle time to produce this product would be 50 seconds per unit. The product would be produced in a stationary mould and would be automatically ejected at the rate of one every 50 seconds. As a result, Michael calculated that it would require 2083[1] hours of machine *running* time to fill the order. On the basis of his discussion with Walt Roberts, Michael expected that the rate of defective crates produced by this process would be negligible.

Following discussions with Larry Bobbit, Michael felt that during the machine cycle time the machine operator would have sufficient time to trim the excess plastic (flash) off the previous crate that had been made and stamp that crate with the particular dairy's name.

Based on BP's experience, which was comparable to the industry average, Michael calculated that the moulding machine would run for only 60 per cent of the time that it was scheduled for operation. The rest of the time that it was scheduled for operation the machine would be down for repair, set-up or maintenance.

Consequently, Michael estimated that it would require 3472[2] hours of scheduled machine time to achieve the required 2083 hours of machine operating time. Since the operator would be required for most of the repair time, all the set-up time, and all the maintenance time, an operator would have to be scheduled for each hour of scheduled machine time.

Michael decided that the production of the milk crates could be undertaken on BP's 750 ton injection moulder. This would require that some of the production scheduled for that machine be rescheduled to other machines. Because BP currently had excess capacity available on other machines, Michael felt that the new order would not require sacrificing any production of any other products.

The cost of a production mould used to manufacture the milk crates would normally be $90 000. However, the Dairy Council already owned a suitable mould which they had agreed to lend to the successful bidder on the contract.

Each milk crate weighed 1.6 kilograms. Polyethylene would be used to produce the milk crate. The cost of polyethylene was $1.07 per kilogram. Michael felt that plastic

---

[1] $(150\,000 \times 50)/3600$

[2] $(2083/0.6)$

trimmed off crates, or plastic in defective crates, could be reprocessed at a minimal cost. Consequently, the cost of raw material per crate was estimated as $1.71.[3]

Since the machine operators were paid $6.00 per hour (including benefits), the labour cost per crate was computed as $0.14.[4]

The materials cost to stamp the crates was estimated as $0.01 per side, yielding a total cost of $0.04 per crate. In addition, a stamping machine costing $5000 would have to be acquired. The life of this simple stamping machine was estimated as 10 years, at least.

The crates did not require packaging for shipping and the Dairy Council paid for shipment. Michael estimated that the labour costs to load the crates on a truck at the factory door would be $0.02 per crate.

As a result of these calculations, Michael believed that the direct variable cost of producing the milk crates would be $1.91 (1.71 + .14 + .04 + .02).

This still left the matter of the overhead associated with producing each milk crate. This issue had been a source of continuing concern to Michael on almost every contract he negotiated. Michael knew that a common 'rule of thumb' in his plant was to apply variable overhead to products at a rate of $13 for each machine hour (running time). An industry rule of thumb was to estimate total variable cost as being 1.3 times the direct material and direct labour costs.[5]

Some analysts also advocated looking at fixed, as well as variable, manufacturing overhead. Based on a recent study of BP's costs, the corporate controller estimated that, on average, selling price must equal at least 2.33 times the sum of direct material and direct labour costs in order to earn average industry margins of 6 per cent (pre-tax) when operating at the industry average 90 per cent capacity utilization ratio (scheduled hours). Some comparative data on industry economics is summarized in Exhibit 2.

Michael wondered about the accuracy of any of these approaches in general and, in particular, he wondered if any one was suitable in this situation. Michael looked at the ratio of market price to the sum of direct material and direct labour cost for some of his more popular products and found that this ratio varied from two to seven. As a result, he wondered what, if anything, was the implication of the 2.33 factor.

As a guide to understanding the relationship between direct costs (material and labour) and fixed manufacturing overhead Michael developed the data that appears in Exhibit 3. The plant accountant advised Michael that plant fixed manufacturing overhead did not include direct materials, direct labour, variable overhead or plant supervision (about $50 000 per year).

In addition to manufacturing costs, BP was incurring about $220 000 per year in Selling, General and Administrative (S, G & A) expenses.

Michael was not sure how to use Exhibit 3 to help him assign overhead cost to the milk crate order. The results did seem to indicate that overhead was virtually unrelated to the level of output in the factory. The results thus did seem to support his 'contribution margin pricing' policy. Michael was still unsure, however, as to how he should approach this large incremental order. He observed to the case writer: 'If I only knew my cost structure better, I would feel more confident about what I am doing. Right know I feel that I am shooting in the dark'.

---

[3] 1.6 × $1.07

[4] (50/0.6) × (1/3600) × $6.00

[5] One source of this data was the publication *Financial and Operating Ratios*, published by The Society of the Plastics Industry, Inc. This survey indicated that the total of variable costs was, on average, about 74% of sales for injection moulders. Since the sum of direct materials and direct labour costs was, on average, 57% of sales, this implied that total variable costs were, on average, 1.3 times the sum of direct material and direct labour costs (74% = 1.3 × 57%).

## EXHIBIT 1

*Estimated income statement (2000)*

| | | |
|---|---|---|
| (Given) | Sales | $1200 |
| (1/2.33 = 43% of Sales) | Direct material plus direct labour | (515) |
| (15 000 × $13) | Variable overhead | (195) (16% of Sales) |
| | Contribution margin (CM) | 490 |
| (205 + 220 + 50) | Fixed overhead | (475) |
| (Just above break even) | Profit before taxes | $15 |

## EXHIBIT 2

*Industry economics*

| | At 'normal' capacity (90% Utilization) | | At full capacity | |
|---|---|---|---|---|
| | **Average** | **BP** | **Average** | **BP** |
| Sales | 100% | 100% | 100% | 100% |
| DM + DL | 57 | 43 | 57 | 43 |
| Variable overhead | 17 | 16 | 17 | 16 |
| Fixed overhead | 20 | 35 | 18 | 31.5 |
| Profit before taxes | 6% | 6% | 8% | 9.5% |

When operating *near* capacity, BP shows up as the High CM/High fixed cost/high profit player. *But note* that the profit impact (Profit % of Sales) of BP's apparent strategy only shows up near full capacity. High volume is a key to high profit for BP.

**EXHIBIT 3**

*Cost and activity data*

| Year | Month | Direct labour hours (production, assembly, testing) | Indirect labour hours (set-up, repair, and maintenance) | Total machine hours (running time) | Plant fixed manufacturing overhead (PFMOH) |
|------|-------|-------|-------|-------|-------|
| | January | 1 679 | 1 305 | 1 885 | 3 536 |
| | February | 2 298 | 863 | 1 775 | 17 196 |
| | March | 3 785 | 991 | 1 800 | 13 462 |
| | April | 2 646 | 1 287 | 1 643 | 4 194 |
| | May | 2 606 | 1 686 | 1 848 | 15 958 |
| 1998 | June | 2 661 | 1 505 | 1 274 | 7 644 |
| | July | 1 670 | 938 | 1 182 | 3 530 |
| | August | 1 844 | 1 337 | 1 003 | 7 073 |
| | September | 1 839 | 1 343 | 1 351 | 6 094 |
| | October | 2 088 | 1 295 | 1 837 | 10 072 |
| | November | 2 330 | 1 743 | 1 533 | 4 173 |
| | December | 1 434 | 1 416 | 601 | 6 078 |
| | Total | 26 880 | 15 709 | 18 321 | 99 010 |
| | January | 1 694 | 1 019 | 1 104 | 3 811 |
| | February | 1 701 | 933 | 1 128 | 4 712 |
| | March | 2 103 | 1 532 | 917 | 11 325 |
| | April | 1 756 | 1 192 | 1 211 | 1 161 |
| | May | 2 184 | 1 276 | 1 249 | 6 572 |
| 1999 | June | 1 625 | 890 | 829 | 10 063 |
| | July | 1 775 | 1 256 | 1 278 | 7 621 |
| | August | 2 007 | 1 728 | 1 095 | 11 028 |
| | September | 2 094 | 1 337 | 1 824 | 15 198 |
| | October | 2 178 | 1 503 | 1 788 | 4 690 |
| | November | 2 992 | 1 868 | 1 471 | 9 484 |
| | December | 2 079 | 1 751 | 1 313 | 5 615 |
| | Total | 24 188 | 16 290 | 15 207 | 91 280 |
| | January | 2 714 | 1 922 | 1 899 | 18 293 |
| | February | 2 240 | 1 328 | 1 567 | 15 733 |
| | March | 2 275 | 1 663 | 1 723 | 39 988 |
| | April | 1 737 | 1 157 | 954 | 3 033 |
| | May | 1 547 | 1 443 | 654 | 9 358 |
| 2000 | June | 1 389 | 1 434 | 634 | 20 166 |
| | July | 2 394 | 1 948 | 1 735 | 16 308 |
| | August | 990 | 856 | 1 005 | 14 267 |
| | Subtotal* | 15 286 | 11 751 | 10 171 | 137 146 |
| | | ~ 23 000 | ~ 17 500 | ~ 15 000 | ~ 205 000 |

* annualized for 2000 (12/8)

To explore the causal relationships reflected here, Michael developed the following four linear regressions:

|  | $R^2$ | $t$-Statistic |
|---|---|---|

1.  (PFMOH) versus Machine Hours (MH):
    PFMOH $= \$3681 + (\$4.86 \times MH)$       0.07      1.48

2.  PFMOH versus Direct Labour Hours (DLH):
    PFMOH $= \$4321 + (\$2.85 \times DLH)$      0.04      1.15

3.  PFMOH versus Indirect Labour Hours (ILH):
    PFMOH $= \$1684 + \$6.25 \times ILH)$      0.07      1.49

4.  PFMOH versus MH and DLH:
    PFMOH $= -\$79 + (\$2.89 \times MH) + (\$1.87 \times DLH)$    0.09    0.70/0.81

## *Questions*

1.  Based on your interpretation of Exhibit 3, what is your estimate of the change in 'PFMOH' cost if the factory were to run one extra batch of 150 000 milk crates?

2.  What is your estimate of the incremental cost per unit for one batch of 150 000 milk crates?

3.  What does Exhibit 2 suggest would be a 'normal' price for milk crates for an 'average' job shop? What does this suggest about the $3.00 price which seems to prevail at the time of the case?

4.  What is the 'strategically relevant' cost per unit for milk crates (for purposes of deciding whether or not the $3.00 'market price' is profitable, on an ongoing basis)?

5.  What is your advice to Mr. Smith regarding the milk crate opportunity? Be specific and show the calculations supporting your advice.

6.  What overall strategic advice do you have for Mr. Smith? Why isn't the business doing better, given the new 'specialities strategy' and good business conditions? Support your answer with relevant cost analysis.

# Index

........................................................................................................................................................